THE LETTERS OF
CHARLES DICKENS

GENERAL EDITORS

Madeline House and Graham Storey

Dickens reading *The Chimes* at 58 Lincoln's Inn Fields, 3 December 1844
From the drawing by Daniel Maclise

THE PILGRIM EDITION
The Letters of Charles Dickens

Volume Four
1844–1846

EDITED BY
Kathleen Tillotson

ASSOCIATE EDITOR
Nina Burgis

CLARENDON PRESS · OXFORD
1977

Oxford University Press, Walton Street, Oxford OX2 6DP

OXFORD LONDON GLASGOW NEW YORK
TORONTO MELBOURNE WELLINGTON CAPE TOWN
IBADAN NAIROBI DAR ES SALAAM LUSAKA ADDIS ABABA
KUALA LUMPUR SINGAPORE JAKARTA HONG KONG TOKYO
DELHI BOMBAY CALCUTTA MADRAS KARACHI

British Library Cataloguing in Publication Data

Dickens, Charles
    The letters of Charles Dickens.
    Vol. 4: 1844–1846.—Pilgrim ed.
    1. Dickens, Charles   2. Novelists, English
    —19th Century—Correspondence
    I. Tillotson, Kathleen
    823'.8   PR4581.A3

    ISBN 0-19-812475-9

PRINTED IN GREAT BRITAIN
BY BUTLER & TANNER LTD, FROME AND LONDON

CONTENTS

ILLUSTRATIONS

PREFACE

Since the publication of our third volume in 1974, the total of letters known to us has risen by 170 from 13,074 to 13,244. The present volume contains 1087 letters,[1] including extracts and mentions. Of these, 284 are published for the first time; 54 more have not previously been published complete, and many others have not hitherto been collected. The texts of 602 have been transcribed from originals or photographs of originals. The proportion from printed sources is higher than usual, owing to the large number of letters to Forster.

For more than half of the period covered in this volume, Dickens was out of England. The incidence of letters varies accordingly; there are, for example, over three times as many letters for the first half of 1844 as for the second half, and a similar disparity in 1845 and 1846. The implications suggest one reason for Dickens's decision to live abroad for a year: in England, he was constantly beset by requests of many kinds—social invitations, letters asking him to make speeches or donations or to help unknown authors, and begging letters. Many were almost like Martin Chuzzlewit's 'letters from strangers: half of them about nothing: half about borrowing money: and all requiring an instantaneous reply'.[2] (Such letters were not allowed to follow Dickens to Italy, but were evidently dealt with by Thomas Mitton.)[3] No wonder he wrote to D'Orsay from Albaro in August 1844 'I never knew what it was to be lazy, before', and was content, for the time, to 'lie down on the rocks in the evening, staring the blue water out of countenance, and watch the lizards running up and down the walls'.[4]

But it was not only for the sake of a restful holiday nor in order to live more economically, nor even to acquire 'a store of recollections and improvement',[5] that Dickens went abroad. It was a much more serious and far-reaching decision —no less than the determination to desist, for a year or two, from the writing of novels. The two years between the end of *Martin Chuzzlewit* and the beginning of *Dombey and Son* form an unprecedented pause in his writing life. Forster calls the decision 'the turning-point in his career'. He does not elaborate on the remark, except to say 'the issue, though not immediately, ultimately justified him'.[6] He knew, and Dickens knew, that the risk in this venture was great: they had no assurance, in 1844, with the disappointing sales of *Chuzzlewit*, that

---

[1] This is the total when each extract from Forster's *Life* is counted separately as in previous volumes; if not, the total is 948.

[2] Ch. 22; cf. Vol. III, p. 87; recalled also in *David Copperfield*, ch. 61 ('Letters from people of whom I had no knowledge—chiefly about nothing, and extremely difficult to answer').

[3] *To* Mitton, 12 Aug 44 (p. 178). Mitton also dealt with general money matters, while Forster was in charge of arrangements with publishers.

[4] 7 Aug 44 (pp. 169–70).

[5] *To* Maclise, 22 July 44 (p. 162).

[6] F, IV, ii, 307.

Dickens would return to novel-writing two years later with increased powers and a greatly strengthened hold on his public. As late as 1 November 1845 he spoke of his fear of 'failing health or fading popularity'.[1]

The plan had been first broached to Forster at the beginning of November 1843; but Dickens claimed to have formed it 'MONTHS AGO', and this may be confirmed by his mention in June, to two French journalists who interviewed him at Devonshire Terrace, of his intention to visit France. In November, the planned destination for the family in the following June was still France, as a base for his own travels in Switzerland and Italy; and he already thought of writing a travel-book based on letters to Forster 'exactly as I did in America'. The detail he gives, domestic and financial, and his growing conviction that the move was 'a matter of policy and duty', helped to harden him into what Forster calls 'a fixed resolve'. By 20 November 1843 the continued demands of his 'blood-petitioners' (especially his father) had exasperated him to the point of thinking of 'keeping my whole menagerie in Italy, three years'.[2]

The decision for Italy did not change, and although in January 1844 the project was still 'a secret I have hardly breathed to any one',[3] by mid-February Devonshire Terrace was in the agent's hands[4] and soon Dickens was studying Murray's Handbooks,[5] and building 'Italian Castles ... in the air'.[6] In the foreword to *Pictures from Italy*, called 'The Reader's Passport', he says his imagination had dwelt on Italy 'for years'. What aspects of Italy most appealed to his imagination must be largely matter of conjecture; no doubt his expectations were based on his reading—of Shakespeare, of the fourth canto of *Childe Harold*, Rogers's *Italy* and Bulwer's novels; on the paintings of Stanfield[7] and Turner and the banditti and contadinas of popular academicians such as Eastlake; on Italian opera and melodrama, from *Fra Diavolo* to *Masaniello*.

It was the Italy we know from the steel-engravings in old keepsakes and annuals, from the vignettes on music-sheets and the drop-curtains at theatres; an Italy we can never confess ourselves ... to have ceased to need and believe in.[8]

Dickens must often have heard accounts of Italy from his friends, especially Lady Blessington, Count D'Orsay, Rogers and Landor; possibly also from Leigh Hunt, Longfellow and most recently from Angus Fletcher, the sculptor, who was living there. To some of these he turned, late in March, for advice on a choice of residence; his own first thought of Nice soon yielded to Pisa, the favourite resort of those seeking economical living and a mild winter climate.

---

[1] p. 423.

[2] Vol. III, pp. 587–8, 590–1, 600.

[3] *To* Felton, 2 Jan 44 (p. 3). Dickens did not mention it in *To* Macready, 3 Jan.

[4] For the inventory of the contents, including Dickens's library, see Appx C.

[5] Including the *Handbook for Travellers to Northern Italy*, 1842, written by Sir Francis Palgrave.

[6] *To* T. J. Thompson, 11 Mar (p. 70).

[7] Besides the many pictures of Italian scenes which he exhibited, Stanfield had published a set of engravings in *Heath's Picturesque Annual*, 1832, illustrating Leitch Ritchie's *Travelling Sketches*.

[8] Henry James, *Roderick Hudson*, 1875, ch. 23.

(Florence, still cheaper, seems not to have been thought of, perhaps because of its distance from the sea and its large English colony.) But Dickens's impressions on his visit to Pisa in *Pictures*[1] suggest that (like the Brownings in 1846) he would have found it sleepy and dull; the final choice of Genoa was more fortunate. In May, Fletcher engaged the Villa Bagnerello from the local butcher at Albaro, an unsuitable house at an exorbitant rent, as Dickens was quickly to discover,[2] but in 'one of the most splendid situations imaginable',[3] two miles outside the city and close to the sea-shore. On 2 July the 'caravan' of twelve (including the five children, the domestics and the 'Brave Courier') departed on its fortnight's journey.

From Bradbury & Evans, his new publishers, Dickens had an advance of £2800, without conditions; he was committed only to his second Christmas book. The 'travel-book' which had figured in his earliest plans was not mentioned; 'he had not actually decided', says Forster, 'until the very last, to publish his . . . experiences at all'.[4] He and Dickens were evidently discussing the question in the spring of 1845, agreeing that 'in some form' the letters might be used, while the form itself was still left doubtful.[5] Throughout the year, Forster had shown or read the letters to selected friends, as Dickens wished; their views were probably sought, and perhaps those of Rogers, Lady Blessington, and Count D'Orsay, who received their own letters. (The series of letters to Count D'Orsay especially, here presented for the first time, are among the most vivid and racy in this volume.) By 20 May 1845 Dickens had committed himself further, when he told Mitton that he had now 'elaborately *painted* at least three-fourths' of his travels to the south, so that if he should 'determine to use these experiences, they are almost ready'.[6] He was apparently still uncertain as late as 20 October;[7] what settled the question was the *Daily News*.[8] Eight 'Travelling Letters' (as far as Bologna) were published there in January–March 1846;[9] these were then revised and twice as much added, for the book published in May.

Because of the use of the letters in *Pictures from Italy*, Forster said he must strictly observe the rule of giving 'nothing resembling his printed book, however distantly'.[10] There was much other material in the letters, including, in October 1844, a close running commentary on the writing of *The Chimes*. But in fact he did not observe his rule invariably. He included several passages, usually brief,

---

[1] p. 155 (page-references here and subsequently are to the 1st edn of 1846). William Brockedon says 'some complain of its unendurable *tristesse*, others speak favourably of its quiet' (*Italy, classical, historical, and picturesque*, 1842–3, p. 21).

[2] *To* Mitton, ?12 Aug 44 (p. 177).

[3] *Pictures*, p. 39.   [4] F, IV, iv, 333.

[5] F, IV, vii, 372.   [6] p. 313.

[7] *To* de la Rue (p. 409).   [8] *To* Bradbury & Evans, 3 Nov 45 (p. 424).

[9] Part of the MS of 'Travelling Letters' as sent to the *Daily News* is in the Forster Collection: it consists of disconnected pieces from No. VII and the whole of No. VIII, roughly corresponding to *Pictures*, pp. 72–5, 84–6, 88–97, and including a passage not given in the book. The copy for both 'Letters' is composite, about two-thirds being in Dickens's hand (with many revisions) combined with fragments of what appears to be a clerk's transcript of some of the original letters of Oct–Nov 44, with Dickens's alterations and deletions. We quote two sentences in *To* Forster, 10 Nov 44 (p. 216), and refer to the MS occasionally in the notes. It is mentioned in David Paroissien's edn of *Pictures*, 1973, pp. 31, 244 (this is the only modern edition with introduction and notes).

[10] Forster, IV, iv, 333.

which duplicate *Pictures*, as our notes show. Sometimes, no doubt, this was inadvertent; he overlooked sentences which Dickens had transferred from their expected place. But more deliberately, to preserve narrative continuity, Forster frequently summarized or paraphrased parts of the letters which appear in *Pictures*; and these are used as introductory and linking passages (in italics) where it is clear that they must be based on Dickens's own words. And he certainly included letters which resemble the book 'distantly', such as the moving account of Dickens's first impressions of Venice, which 'prefigured' the section called 'An Italian Dream'. But the letters written from Rome and Naples are reduced, in the *Life*, to one long paragraph and a single detached extract, which suggests that there, *Pictures* represents the letters closely, probably combining the original 'outlines'[1] and their later 'rich filling in'. This would come near to justifying Dickens's claim in the foreword that 'the greater part of these descriptions were written on the spot, and sent home, from time to time, in private letters';[2] and from letters sent to Lady Blessington and Count D'Orsay, he reproduced passages almost verbatim.

However complicated the process of revision, the book conveys the freshness and immediacy of a sequence of impressions. Dickens is frank about his disappointments; Genoa 'grows upon' him every day, and we share the transition from the first 'perpetual state of forlorn surprise' to 'a perfect dream of happiness'. What persisted throughout his months in Italy was the sense of contrast between splendour and squalor: 'things that are picturesque, ugly, mean, magnificent, delightful and offensive, break upon the view at every turn'.[3] This impression sank deep into his mind, to emerge a decade later as the pervading tone of the Italian chapters of *Little Dorrit*: 'misery wrestling with magnificence ... and misery throwing magnificence with the strength of fate'.[4]

At Rome, he was most nearly the typical English traveller of his period; like Clive Newcome, he 'did at Rome as the English do', and joined the crowd

> that flocks to the Vatican to behold the statues by moonlight, that bustles into the churches on public festivals ... and stares, and talks and uses opera-glasses while the pontiffs of the Roman Church are performing its ancient rites, and the crowds of the faithful are kneeling at its altars.[5]

What distinguishes him is his wry observance of other tourists; his energetic pedestrianism (walking the 14 miles to Albano, and going 'almost every day' to the Appian Way beyond the tomb of Cecilia Metella); and occasionally, his evocative feeling for landscape, as in the noble passage describing the Campagna,[6] matched only by Browning and Henry James.

Dickens's attitude to the religious ceremonies of Holy Week resembles that of most English travellers,[7] and is surprising only in his failure to imagine how it

---

[1] Dickens also kept a diary (at least in Rome), as in America; this has apparently not survived.

[2] *Pictures*, p. 2.   [3] *Pictures*, pp. 38, 49, 73.

[4] Book II, ch. 3.   [5] Thackeray, *The Newcomes*, 1855, ch. 35.

[6] *Pictures*, pp. 213–15.

[7] J. C. Eustace, author of the *Classical Tour*, is one of the few exceptions, announcing in his Preface that he 'affects not to conceal ... however unpopular it may be', that he writes as a Roman Catholic.

might strike those, like Stanfield, who did not share it. (But the omission of the account of a convent party when a nun took the black veil, which appeared in the seventh 'Travelling Letter', may suggest that he had met with some criticism.)[1] His prejudices affected his judgment of art only slightly; he found too many heads 'of the convent stamp', but forgave much 'priestly infatuation' for the sake of the great paintings which moved him most, the 'silent speaking faces of Titian and Tintoretto' and the 'transcendent sweetness and beauty' of Guido's supposed portrait of Beatrice de Cenci.[2] In his comments on pictures and architecture his prejudice lies rather in his determination to resist the 'cant' of conventional connoisseurship and his confidence in his own untutored response to what is 'natural and true'.[3]

With Italian society he had deliberately little contact, delivering 'scarcely any' of his letters of introduction;[4] he kept clear of social and political questions both in his letters (except for the inevitable complaints about censorship and customs officials) and in *Pictures*, where he touches only at the close on Italy's 'years of neglect, oppression and misrule'. But such questions are likely to have arisen in his intercourse with Emile de la Rue, the friend of Cavour; and later letters show that de la Rue and Dickens had more in common than their concern for the health and nervous stability of de la Rue's wife. The many letters on this subject (most of them now published for the first time) might be open to misinterpretation by sensation-seekers; but it is clear that while Dickens was sincerely concerned with her 'recovery and happiness',[5] and both the de la Rues became his confidants and lasting friends, what fascinated him most was the successful exertion of his own powers as an amateur mesmerist.[6] As he recognized later, it was an instance of what was common with him, 'the intense personal pursuit of any one idea that takes complete possession of me';[7] its object is an 'idea', more than a person. The intensity itself, and the sheer amount of time devoted to the correspondence and the magnetic sessions, might seem excessive to others; but it may be seen as an overflow of creative energy at a time when this had no other outlet.

Apart from the travel-letters Dickens wrote hardly anything in the twelve months between his two Christmas books of 1844 and 1845. He says himself 'I wrote nothing in Italy except The Chimes'; after his return, a single magazine article is all we can be certain of. But some time before September 1845 he must have been occupied with one fairly considerable task to which the letters do not

---

[1] The omission may have been a last-minute decision; the foreword refers to his 'dislike of nunneries for young girls' as if this appeared in the book.

[2] See pp. 218, 221, 277 and *Pictures*, pp. 211–212.

[3] *Pictures*, p. 208. Hence the high value he sets on Simond's *Tour in Italy*, a little-known book to which he was perhaps introduced by Jeffrey (see *To* Forster, 3 Aug 44, *fn*, p. 164); he was probably more influenced by its tone than he was aware of.

[4] See p. 161 and *fn*.

[5] *To* de la Rue, 20 Oct 45 (p. 410).

[6] The subject is treated fully, with much useful information about mesmerism, in Fred Kaplan, *Dickens and Mesmerism*, Princeton, 1975; this book reached us too late to be referred to in notes to the letters.

[7] *To* Mrs CD, 5 Dec 53 (*Mr and Mrs CD*, ed. W. Dexter, 1935, p. 227). The letter refers to the 'painful declaration' of her 'state of mind' which Catherine constrained him to make to de la Rue when they met again at Lausanne in 1846.

refer: the detailed revision of *Oliver Twist* for its publication in monthly parts.[1]
The changes were substantial and careful, and included the introduction of a new
and individual system of punctuation which may also be noticed in the letters
of these years, as well as in the Christmas books, and is related to oral delivery,
possibly influenced by his increasing interest in reading his work aloud. The
readings of *The Chimes* in London in December 1844, of *A Christmas Carol* at
Genoa in June 1845, and of *The Battle of Life* and the early numbers of *Dombey
and Son* at Lausanne in 1846 are the prelude to his public readings of the 1850s;
his proposal in September 1846 that a theatre might be engaged for the purpose
was, as Forster suspected, even then only partly a jest.

During these relatively leisurely years, other projects were forming in his mind,
some not destined to take shape; for example, he was 'all eagerness to write a
story about the length of . . . the *Vicar of Wakefield*'.[2] Others long lay dormant,
like 'the idea of a man imprisoned for ten or fifteen years'.[3] One piece of 'private'
writing completed in 1846, the children's New Testament, was obviously
connected (like the 'Child's History of England', begun in 1843) with his growing
concern over his own children's education; and this in turn may be associated
with his reflections on his own childhood. 'We should be devilish sharp in what
we do to children', he says when writing to Forster about Paul Dombey at
Mrs Pipchin's;[4] and this is linked with what is probably the first of his reminiscent confidences, the seed from which grew the 'autobiography' and the childhood chapters of *David Copperfield*. Earlier, in 1844, the first plans for 'our
play' had already stimulated memories of his own youthful theatrical ambitions;
the play itself, in 1845, launched him on a second, spare-time career as an amateur
actor and stage-manager which lasted until 1852.

Meanwhile he never lost sight of his concern, so clearly manifested in 1843,
with 'the condition-of-England question', especially in the related fields of
education for the poor and the prevention and treatment of crime.[5] In his
Italian palazzo, he wrote *The Chimes*, his 'great blow for the poor' and the most
powerful of his fictions on topics of the day, though not an experiment which he
chose to repeat.[6] He read the *Examiner* regularly at Genoa (evidently his copy
was not 'stopped at the frontier'); on his return, he was quick to renew his
promise of writing for the *Edinburgh*, this time on the controversial question of
Capital Punishment.[7] In 1846, a series of letters to Miss Coutts develops their
joint design for an 'Asylum' for reclaiming prostitutes, which took shape in
1847 as the 'home for "homeless women" '.

The main project that recurred throughout the 1840s was the establishing of
a periodical under his own control. Almost immediately on his return from

---

[1] See *Oliver Twist*, ed. Kathleen Tillotson, 1966, p. xxvii.
[2] *To* Forster, ?6 Oct 44 (p. 199).
[3] *To* Forster, ?25–26 July 46 (p. 590).
[4] ?4 Nov 46 (p. 653).
[5] See Vol. III, Preface, p. xviii. The newly published application to Lord Morpeth
(p. 566) shows that as late as June 1846 he was still ambitious for some public employment
connected with these subjects.
[6] Its design and reception are sufficiently apparent in the letters and footnotes of Oct–
Dec 44.
[7] *To* Napier, 28 July 45 (p. 340).

America, where he had seen the evils of the American press, he sought the influence of Lady Holland over a proposal for a new liberal evening paper to take the place of the *Courier*; but no funds were forthcoming.[1] No more is heard of such a scheme until November 1843, when in the course of discussions with Bradbury & Evans they 'offered to invest to any desired amount in . . . a magazine or other periodical to be edited by him'.[2] This time it was Dickens who was reluctant, chiefly because he was already set on going abroad. But the matter was discussed again in March 1844 and was mentioned in the negotiations of June; views were also exchanged with Forster 'from time to time during his absence',[3] and on Dickens's return, he sketched out a plan for a popular weekly called *The Cricket*. Despite its too determined chirpiness this hints at something not unlike *Household Words*. But within a few weeks it was abandoned, 'swept away by a larger scheme',[4] and by 25 July Dickens knew that £50,000 was promised for the starting of a daily newspaper.

Unknown to him, other more powerful forces had been in motion. Bradbury's friend Joseph Paxton, who had had thoughts of a newspaper as early as 1840, but was then discouraged by the Duke of Devonshire,[5] had been discussing it again in the spring of 1845; it is probable that, though Dickens's name as editor was an obvious asset, the paper would have been undertaken independently of him. 1845 seemed a propitious year for such a venture: railway money supplied most of the capital for the *Daily News*, and railway advertising part of its revenue. In Paxton's frequent letters to his wife about the paper (whenever he was away he wrote to her daily) Dickens is never mentioned, and only after the scheme was settled (on 14 October) was he summoned to Chatsworth to hear the financial details. A suspicion of his own relative unimportance may underlie his uneasy mood in the winter of 1845–6; in the setback to the scheme from a failure in the City early in November his advice was not taken, and these early troubles foreshadow the problems of divided counsels which eventually helped to cut short his editorial career. At the outset his hopes were reasonable; he expected to benefit from his share in the profits of the paper,[6] to have the security of a regular (and generous) salary, and the opportunity of promoting worthy causes which he had at heart. There were good grounds for his confidence in his abilities, from his past experience on a daily paper. What he had not foreseen was the routine grind of regular attendance, six nights a week, when the first excitement had worn off; the difficulties of dealing with a team of colleagues not all of whom were also friends; and most of all, what has bedevilled many newspapers, the uncertain line of demarcation between editorial and managerial responsibility. Finding that he could not impose his will on Bradbury & Evans, he became perhaps unduly sensitive to supposed slights and ready to find occasion

[1] See Vol. III, pp. 262, 265–7.
[2] F, IV, ii, 304.
[3] F, IV, iii, 325; cf. IV, ii, 316.
[4] F, V, i, 378–9; *To* Mitton, 25 July (p. 336).
[5] MS Devonshire Collections (Paxton group).
[6] About this there must have been some agreement which cannot now be traced. Dickens refers to himself as one of the 'proprietors', and had 'an interest' in the paper (*To* Poe, 19 Mar 46; p. 523) but was never a subscribing party 'to the value of one farthing' (pp. 701–2).

for disputes.[1] All these reasons contributed to his early resignation, after three months' involvement with the paper and less than three weeks as editor. But his connection with the *Daily News* should not be seen as a failure: there is much on the other side of the scale. He reinstated John Dickens successfully in a post of responsibility. He helped to establish a newspaper which, after its first chequered years, had a long and honourable history, and at its jubilee and centenary was proud to be associated with his name. And he found the right vehicle for his long-promised and postponed articles on Ragged Schools and Capital Punishment. By these, even more than by *The Chimes*, Dickens left his 'hand upon the time'.[2]

A few months after he gave up the editorship Dickens, unusually for him, admitted his error of judgment, publicly as well as privately,[3] referring in the foreword to *Pictures* to 'a brief mistake I made, not long ago, in disturbing the old relations between myself and my readers, and departing for a moment from my old pursuits'. He did so the more readily because he could now couple the admission with the assurance that he was 'about to resume' those pursuits 'joyfully, in Switzerland'. The volume carried the announcement of 'A NEW ENGLISH STORY . . . *in Twenty Monthly Parts* . . . *now in preparation. No. I will be published on the First of October*'. The real object and justification of the long pause in publication was now clearly in view, and the board was to be 'made quite clear and clean for the playing out of a very great stake'.[4]

Forster entitled his next chapter 'A Home in Switzerland', altering this in later editions to 'Retreat to Switzerland'. Both titles are apt. Dickens found more of a 'home' at Rosemont in Lausanne than in Genoa, entering a congenial and stimulating circle of new friends; and the move was also a 'retreat'—he assured Forster that he could not 'shut out' the *Daily News* sufficiently to write his book in London. Not all the writing was 'joyful'; he had made another mistake in the over-confidence of thinking that he could start the new novel and write his Christmas book in the same months, and for a few weeks was under considerable stress. But the novel at least did not suffer.

> Invention, thank God, seems the easiest thing in the world [he writes, while at work on the second number of *Dombey*] and I seem to have such a preposterous sense of the ridiculous, after this long rest, as to be constantly requiring to restrain myself from launching into extravagances in the height of my enjoyment.[5]

Owing to Dickens's separation from Forster and the more careful and premeditated design of the whole, the writing of the early chapters is more fully documented in letters than that of any previous novel;[6] Forster, in 1872, was at pains to emphasize Dickens's forethought (both here and for *The Chimes*) in order to rebut later criticisms. News of the 'brilliant' sale, of the first number, reaching

---

[1] *To* Bradbury & Evans, 30 Jan 46 (p. 484); *To* Evans, 26 Feb 46 (p. 505).
[2] F, IV, v, 348.
[3] *To* Miss Coutts, 22 Apr 46 (p. 539).
[4] *To* Forster, 25 June 46 (p. 571).
[5] *To* Forster, ?3 Aug 46 (p. 612).
[6] *Dombey and Son*, ed. A. Horsman, 1975, pp. xiv ff.

him in October, was an added stimulus. And in 1847 when the accounts arrived
these were

> so much in excess of what had been expected ... that from this date all
> embarrassments connected with money were brought to a close.[1]

The 'turning-point' was safely rounded.

What Dickens had seen of Switzerland on his way back from Italy had much
attracted him, and the country fulfilled expectations, not only as scenery; this,
unlike America (to which he often reverts), was a republic he could approve:
and unlike Italy it had the advantage of no priests or monks in the streets.

> They are a genuine people, these Swiss. There is better metal in them than
> in all the stars and stripes of all the fustian banners of the so-called, and falsely
> called, U-nited States. They are a thorn in the sides of European despot-
> ism, and a good wholesome people to live near Jesuit-ridden Kings on the
> brighter side of the mountains.[2]

He intended, he said, 'to get up some Mountain knowledge ... for purposes of
fiction';[3] but in fact he made no use of a specific Swiss setting (David Copperfield's travels there are left vague) until he wrote *Little Dorrit* and *No Thorough-
fare*. In any case he did not again envisage the writing of a travel-book: Switzerland (as a summer resort) was far too well known. Forster was therefore free to
print as much as he wished from Dickens's letters to him, and he was liberal
with his extracts. But he distributed these through six chapters, grouping
them approximately by their subjects rather than by chronology as in the four
'Italian' chapters. The reassembling of them under their probable dates has
been a major editorial problem for this volume. For some of Forster's undated
extracts, letters to other correspondents and the diaries kept by Richard Watson
and by Christiana Thompson[4] supply a check, but others cannot be placed
precisely.

Apart from this and some undated office-notes in the *Daily News* period we
have not many dating problems in this volume. The evidence of handwriting
is helpful for undated MS letters, if less so than in earlier volumes since changes
are slighter.

In two letters to Thomas Mitton from abroad where part of the MS (the outer
flap of a folded single sheet written on both sides) has been considerably damaged
by wear and tear,[5] we have been freer than usual with conjectural readings where
only four or five words are affected, in order to preserve a readable sequence.
The precise length of the lacunae and faint indications of missing letters, as well
as our knowledge of the circumstances, have been taken into account.

In the text of letters from abroad, we preserve Dickens's spelling of place-
names, sometimes inconsistent; and we reproduce without comment his omission
and misplacing of French accents.

[1] F, VI, i, 464.
[2] *To* Forster, ?9 Aug 46 (p. 601); cf. *To* Jerrold, 24 Oct 46 (p. 644).
[3] *To* Miss Coutts, 22 Apr 46 (p. 539).
[4] In Italy she kept a journal, in Switzerland (as in England) a diary.
[5] 14 Apr 45 (p. 295) and 20 May 45 (p. 312).

Texts of letters to Forster follow the first edition of the *Life*, 1872–4, unless otherwise stated,[9] and thus correct some later errors; a few variant readings of interest from later editions are included in the footnotes. There is a little evidence that Forster's dots (. . .) do not necessarily signify omission, but paragraph-breaks in the original.

KATHLEEN TILLOTSON

---

[9] References are to J. W. T. Ley's edition of 1928: see Preface to Vol. II, p. xiv.

By an oversight which we regret, two letters, *To* Felton, 2 Jan 44 (p. 2) and *To* Mitton, 10 Feb 44 (p. 41) have been marked with † as if not previously published complete, and the earlier omissions noted. In fact they appeared in full in *Charles Dickens 1812–1870, an Anthology*, chosen and edited by Lola L. Szladits from materials in the Berg Collection . . . New York Public Library, 1970.

ACKNOWLEDGMENTS

We are again deeply grateful to Mr Christopher Dickens, owner of the copyright in Dickens's letters, for giving us permission to use unpublished material; and to the Pilgrim Trustees for their generous initial grant which made this edition possible.

For this volume, we owe special thanks to the Leverhulme Trust for the award of a Research Fellowship made to Kathleen Tillotson in 1972.

In the last volume, our grateful tribute to the late Mr. W. J. Carlton made it clear that all future volumes would continue to draw on the wealth of detailed information he had sent us, and we wish now to emphasize the value of his contribution to the present volume. This year we have to record with great sadness the deaths of the Comtesse de Suzannet, who with great personal kindness made many letters available to us, and Mr Eric Hawksley, whose help and interest in our work we greatly appreciated; also of Mr Philip Wright who compiled the index to Volume III and became a good friend to the edition. We are fortunate in having Mr Frank T. Dunn as his successor for Volume IV.

For generously providing access to manuscript material especially valuable for the annotation of this volume, we are indebted to the Duke of Devonshire and the Trustees of the Chatsworth Settlement for permission to draw upon letters in the Paxton Group of the Devonshire Collections, and to Mr T. S. Wragg and Mr Peter Day for personal assistance; also to Commander Michael Saunders Watson for many facilities, including permission to quote from the diary of the Hon. Richard Watson in Switzerland and other related family diaries; and to Mrs Murray Sowerby for the use of letters, diaries, and much other Weller–Thompson material which she kindly made available for both this and the preceding volume. Work on the letters from abroad was valuably assisted by searches in local newspapers and records undertaken by Professor G. Singh and Signorina Anna Postiglione in Italy, and in Lausanne by Dr Michael Slater and the late Professor René Rapin.

For their generous permission to use their important Dickens collections and their continuing help when it is asked for, we are again greatly indebted to libraries in the United States mentioned in our earlier volumes and especially to the following: the Pierpont Morgan Library, New York, and Mr Herbert Cahoon; the Free Library of Philadelphia (with its Benoliel Collection) in which we owe special thanks to Mr Howell J. Heaney for the kindness with which all new letters acquired are speedily photographed for our use; the Berg Collection in the New York Public Library and Mrs Lola L. Szladits; the Robert H. Taylor Collection, Princeton University Library, its curator Mr Thomas W. Blanding and his predecessor Mr Thomas Lange; Yale University Library and Miss Marjorie Wynne; the Henry E. Huntington Library, California, and Miss Jean F. Preston; the Humanities Research Centre, University of Texas, at Austin, and Mr F. W. Roberts.

Among English libraries, our greatest debt, continuing and repeated, is to the Victoria & Albert Museum for access to manuscripts, letters, cuttings and sketches in the Forster Collection, and to the Accounts of Dickens's publishers; and to Dickens House, where the collection has been further enriched by recent gifts and bequests. For early information about these and much help in other ways, we thank the Curator, Miss Marjorie Pillers; also Dr Michael Slater for his special assistance over the Noel C. Peyrouton bequest.

To the authorities of the following institutions we express our gratitude for permission to publish the letters they have recently made available to us:

Bishopsgate Foundation; Bibliothèque Publique et Universitaire de Genève; Gordon College, Wenham, Mass.; County Council of Hereford and Worcester and Miss M. Henderson; King's College, London; Bibliothèque Cantonale et Universitaire de Lausanne; Post Office Record Room, London; the Press Club, London; Stanford University Libraries; the Times Newspapers Ltd and Mr Gordon Phillips; Watt Monument Library, Greenock.

We are also most grateful to the following owners who have kindly allowed us to see letters in their possession or have sent us photographs of them:

Mr and Mrs Robert A. Baxter; Mr and Mrs Carl Bequist; Mrs E. M. Biden; Mr Leonard Bloom; Henry Bristow of Ringwood Ltd; Mr J. Challenor Smith; the Rt Hon. Viscount Cobham, KG, PC; Major S. F. B. Codrington; Mrs C. M. Cohen; the Hon. Sir David Croom-Johnson, QC; Lt.-Col. J. R. Danson; Mrs Pauline Dower; Mrs Roger Dutnall; Dr Angus Easson; Mrs Z. O. Elliott; Eton College; Mr D. Farringdon; Dr Robert Fellman; John F. Fleming Inc. and Mr Brett E. Langstaff; Mr Richard Garnett; Mr Neville Gibbs; Mr Alan Gill; Mrs Seton Gordon; J. & S. Graphics Inc. and Mr Thomas J. Joyce; Mr L. E. S. Gutteridge; Jarndyce Books; Mr George H. E. Layton; Dr S. Lehming; Charles Letts & Co.; Mr J. D. K. Lloyd; Dr and Mrs Gordon F. Madding; Mrs Margaret B. Marshall; Mr Richard Moore; Mrs Mary Moorman; Dr Robert Newsom; Mrs Hilda Nieuhoff; Mr Frank North; Mr Maurice I. Packington; Mr C. D. Pagan; Mrs M. E. Parkinson; Mr Walter L. Pforzheimer; Professor P. M. Pittman; the Rev. W. L. W. Randall; Mr and Mrs Melville N. Rothschild, Jnr; Lady Russell of Swallowfield; Mr G. S. B. Sayer; Mrs H. A. H. and Mr David Selbourne; Mr Robert W. Stilwell; Subunso Book Store, Japan; Mr Alan G. Thomas; Mr Romer Topham; Mr E. H. Van Maurik; the Rev. Father Daniel M. Venglarik; the Executors of Mrs Henrietta Walton; Mr C. E. Wrangham; Mr G. A. Yablon; Dr Young.

For help too varied to be specified we wish to record our grateful thanks to the following:

Professor Arthur A. Adrian; Bedford College Library; Mr Alan Bell; Birkbeck College, University of London, and Mr George Caraffi; Birmingham Public Library and Mr W. A. Taylor; Birmingham University Library and Mr B. S. Bendikz; Bow Windows Bookshop and Mr C. J. F. Lucas; Mr Gyles Brandreth; the British Library and Mr D. L. Paisey; Mr Anthony Burton; Miss M. St Clare Byrne; Cambridge University Library; Charterhouse Hospital and Mr J. C. Moss, Registrar; Mr Brahma Chaudhuri; Professor P. A. W. Collins; Commander Sir Michael Culme-Seymour; Mr John R. deBruyn; Professor Carlo Dionisotti; Professor K. J. Fielding; Mr Robert A. Furtado; Mr Joseph

H. Gardner; Mr T. F. Garnham; Mr E. C. Gaye; Mr S. W. Grose; Professor Gordon Haight; Mr Theodore Hofmann; Mr Christopher Johnson; Mr W. H. Kelliher of the British Library; Dr Jessie Kocmanová; Lady Pansy Lamb; Sir George Leeds; Leeds City Libraries and Mr John Collinson; Mr Raymond Lister; the London and South Eastern Trustee Savings Bank; Miss Katharine Longley; Mr W. J. McCormack; Professor R. D. McMaster; Professor Jerome Meckier; the Mercers' Company; Sir Francis Meynell; Mr Frank Miles; Mr Charles Moore; New York Public Library; Mr Ronald Paulson; Sir Everard Radcliffe; Mr Frederick Richardson; Mr David A. Roos; the Royal Alexandra and Albert School; the Shakespeare Birthday Trust and Miss Marion J. Horn; Dr Joanne Shattock; Mr E. F. Skottowe; Professor Roger L. Slakey; Miss Sheila Smith; Mr Leslie Staples; Dr Peter W. Stine; Mr Michael Symes; Mr Miles W. Thimbleby; Mr John Thorp; Mr Pieter van der Merwe; Professor P. H. Waddington; Mr E. H. Ward; Mr Alan S. Watts; Mrs Yeats-Brown.

We are very grateful to Mrs Margaret Brown, whose continued help and co-operation have constantly contributed to this volume, especially through her regular assistance to Madeline House.

We welcome Miss Nina Burgis, a valued assistant for many years, in her capacity as Associate Editor. She has helped at all stages of the work for this volume, from the collection of material for annotation to the final preparation for press.

∗   ∗   ∗   ∗   ∗

With the foregoing acknowledgments, the editor of this volume and its general editors are equally associated. But it is fitting that the editor alone should here record, if all too briefly, her gratitude to them for guidance and help in matters both general and minute. The foundations of the volume were laid by the provision of texts and continued contacts with libraries and other owners. In addition, Madeline House has answered countless queries and made valuable comments on both texts and notes while the editing was in progress; and both she and Graham Storey gave much time and care to the reading of the proofs.

BIOGRAPHICAL TABLE

1844–1846

1844	9 Jan	Begins action against printers and publishers of *Parley's Illuminated Library*, No. 16, containing piracy of *A Christmas Carol*. Action dropped May.
	15 Jan	Francis Jeffrey Dickens born.
	30 Jan	To Bath to dine with Landor.
	31 Jan	*Martin Chuzzlewit* No. XIII published.
	25–28 Feb	At Liverpool for the Soiree of the Mechanics' Institution on 26 Feb.
	28–29 Feb	At Birmingham for the Soiree of the Polytechnic on 28 Feb.
	9 Mar	'The Agricultural Interest' published in the *Morning Chronicle*.
	5–11 Apr	In Yorkshire, at Malton Abbey and Mulgrave Castle.
	May	'Threatening Letter to Thomas Hood from an Ancient Gentleman' published in *Hood's Magazine*.
	28 May	Lets Devonshire Terrace for a year and move to Osnaburgh Terrace.
	17 June	Visits Landor at Bath.
	30 June	Final No. of *Martin Chuzzlewit* published.
	2 July	Leaves for Italy with family, travelling by Paris and Marseilles.
	6 July	John Overs's *Evenings of a Working Man*, with Preface by CD, published.
	16 July	Arrives at Genoa (Villa Bagnerello, Albaro).
	6–12 Sep	To Marseilles to bring Frederick Dickens back to Albaro.
	?23 Sep	Moves to Palazzo Peschiere, Genoa.
	6–21 Nov	Travelling in Italy (Venice, 12–13 Nov, Milan, 18–21 Nov).
	21 Nov	Leaves for London by the Simplon Pass and Paris.
	30 Nov–8 Dec	In London: reads *The Chimes* to groups of friends on 3 and 5 Dec.
	?9–13 Dec	In Paris with Macready.
	16 Dec	*The Chimes* published.

	20 Dec	Return to Peschiere.
1845	19–30 Jan	Travelling with Catherine.
	30 Jan–6 Feb	Both in Rome for the Carnival.
	9–26 Feb	In Naples (Georgina joins them).
	26 Feb–2 Mar	Travelling to Rome.
	2–25 Mar	Rome (de la Rues join them).
	25 Mar–9 Apr	Travelling (Florence, 31 Mar–24 Apr).
	9 Apr	Return to Peschiere.
	9 June	The family leaves Genoa, by the St Gothard.
	27 June	Joined in Brussels by Forster, Jerrold and Maclise.
	3 July	Return to Devonshire Terrace.
	Aug	'The Spirit of Chivalry in Westminster Hall' published in *Douglas Jerrold's Shilling Magazine*.
	15–20 Aug	At Broadstairs with family.
	30 Aug–1 Sep	At Broadstairs visiting the children, with Maclise.
	20 Sep	First performance by the amateurs (*Every Man in his Humour*).
	5–6 Oct	At Brighton with Forster.
	18–19 Oct	At Chatsworth to see Paxton about plans for the *Daily News* (undertakes editorship, 3 Nov).
	28 Oct	Alfred D'Orsay Tennyson Dickens born.
	13–17 Dec	At Liverpool for the *Daily News*.
	20 Dec	*The Cricket on the Hearth* published.
	31 Dec	No. I of *Oliver Twist* (revised edn in monthly parts) published; continued to 30 Sep 46.
1846	3 Jan	Performance of *The Elder Brother* with CD's Prologue.
	21 Jan	First number of the *Daily News*: CD's leader and first 'Travelling Letter' (continued 24, 31 Jan, 9, 16, 26 Feb, 2 and 11 Mar).
	24 Jan	'The British Lion' (verses signed 'Catnach') published in the *Daily News*.
	4 Feb	'Crime and Education' published in the *Daily News*.
	7–9 Feb	At Rochester with Catherine, Georgina, Forster and Jerrold.
	9 Feb	Resigns editorship of the *Daily News*.
	14 Feb	'Hymn of the Wiltshire Labourers' published in the *Daily News*.
	23 Feb	First in series of 'Letters on Social Questions: Capital Punishment' published in the *Daily News* (continued 28 Feb, 9, 13 and 16 Mar).

18 May	*Pictures from Italy* published.
31 May	Leaves for Switzerland with his family, travelling by the Rhine.
11 June	Arrives at Lausanne (moving into Rosemont, 15 June).
28 July–2 Aug	Expedition to Chamonix with Catherine and Georgina.
1–4 Sep	Expedition to the St Bernard with Catherine, Georgina and friends from Lausanne.
26 Sep–3 Oct	At Geneva with Catherine and Georgina.
30 Sep	*Dombey and Son* No. I published; continued monthly to 31 Mar 1848.
19–28 Oct	At Geneva with Catherine and Georgina.
16 Nov	Leaves for Paris with family.
20 Nov	Arrives at Paris and takes 48 Rue de Courcelles.
15–23 Dec	Visit to London.
19 Dec	*The Battle of Life* published.

ABBREVIATIONS AND SYMBOLS

CD	Used throughout this edition in all references to Charles Dickens and for his name in titles of books and articles.
D	*The Dickensian; a Magazine for Dickens Lovers*, The Dickens Fellowship, 1905–.
DAB	*Dictionary of American Biography*.
DNB	*Dictionary of National Biography*.
F, 1872–4	John Forster, *The Life of Charles Dickens*, 3 vols, 1872–4.
F	John Forster, *The Life of Charles Dickens*, edited by J. W. T. Ley, 1928. Our references are to this edition unless otherwise stated.
FC	The Forster Collection, Victoria & Albert Museum, London.
Macready, *Diaries*	*The Diaries of William Charles Macready 1833–51*, edited by William Toynbee, 2 vols, 1912.
MDGH	*The Letters of Charles Dickens*, edited by his Sister-in-law and his Eldest Daughter. Vols I & II, 1880. Vol. III, 1882.
MDGH, 1882	*The Letters of Charles Dickens*, edited by his Sister-in-law and his Eldest Daughter, 2 vols, 1882.
MDGH, 1893	*The Letters of Charles Dickens*, edited by his Sister-in-law and his Eldest Daughter, 1 vol., 1893.
N	*The Letters of Charles Dickens*, edited by Walter Dexter, 3 vols, Nonesuch Press, 1938.
OED	*Oxford English Dictionary*.
To	"*To*" before a correspondent's name denotes a letter from Dickens.
[ ]	Square brackets in letter-headings enclose conjectural dates. In the text they denote words conjecturally supplied and breaks caused by damage to the MS. In footnotes they indicate editorial interpolations.
*	Asterisks in letter-headings denote letters which we believe to be hitherto unpublished. (Extracts from some of these have, however, appeared in Edgar Johnson, *Charles Dickens, his Tragedy & Triumph*, 2 vols, 1953, and in sale-catalogues.)
†	Daggers in letter-headings denote letters of which we believe part to be hitherto unpublished.

THE LETTERS

1844–1846

To THOMAS HOOD,[1] [?1 JANUARY 1844]

*Extract in Sotheby's catalogue, Dec 1892. Date: answering Hood to CD (see fn),
probably written Sun 31 Dec as copies of Hood's Magazine were available 30 Dec.*

A thousand thanks for your kind and charming notice of the Carol.[2] Take my
advice, be energetic the right way, and I'll carol again when your magazine is a
twelvemonth old.

To JAMES CLEPHAN,[3] 2 JANUARY 1844

Text from N, I, 554.

> 1 Devonshire Terrace, York Gate, Regents Park
> January the Second, 1844

Dear Sir,

Pray assure the lady who has asked me through you for the enclosed autographs in furtherance of a benevolent object, that she is heartily welcome to
them;[4] and that I wish they were a far more valuable commodity.

I quite agree with you in your admiration of the forbearance and long-
suffering of the poor—everyone who knows them must. Their outbreaks,
whenever they recur, can surprise few, I think, but Governments and Parlia-
ments, who are always disposed to virtuous wonder.

> Faithfully yours
> [CHARLES DICKENS]

---

[1] Thomas Hood (1799–1845; *DNB*),
poet and humorist: see Vol. II, p. 220n.
He had just launched *Hood's Magazine*
(see Vol. III, p. 607 and n), and had moved,
at the end of Dec 43, to a new house in St
John's Wood, which he called Devonshire
Lodge after the Duke of Devonshire. In
Mar 44 he was taken ill and never really
recovered.

[2] The 6-page review of the *Carol* (reprinted in *Works*, IX, 93–103) consisted
largely of quotation, with laudatory comment. Hood had sent a copy of the magazine, saying: "There is a dead set against
it I suspect in the trade for not a showboard
is to be seen nor will they put it in their
windows. It was ready on Saturday

morning but there was a story got up &
told at all the shops we asked at that it
would not be ready till Saturday Night or
Monday" (*Letters of Thomas Hood*, ed.
Peter Morgan, Toronto, 1973, p. 585).
Despite the booksellers' obstructiveness,
the first No. sold well (1500 copies) and
received good notices—including one in
the *Observer*, 31 Dec.

[3] James Clephan (1805–88), journalist
and antiquary: see Vol. II, p. 355n.

[4] The *Gateshead Observer*, which
Clephan edited, reported on 6 Jan 44 that
"Charles Dickens, Esq., (Boz,) has made a
donation in aid of the British School
Bazaar, Gateshead". Presumably he sent
autographs for sale.

To C. C. FELTON,[1] 2 JANUARY 1844†

MS Berg Collection. *Address:* By The January Cunard Steamer | Professor
Felton | Cambridge | Massachusetts | United States.

Devonshire Terrace London | Second January 1844

My very dear Felton.

You are a Prophet, and had best retire from business straightway. Yesterday
Morning, New Year's Day, when I had walked into my little work room after
breakfast, and was looking out of window at the Snow in the Garden—not seeing
it particularly well in consequence of some staggering suggestions of last night's
Punch and Turkey[2] whereby I was beset—the Postman came to the door with
a knock for which I damned him from my heart. Seeing your hand upon the
cover of a letter which he brought, I immediately blessed him—presented him
with a Glass of Whisky—inquired after his family (they are all well)—and opened
the despatch, with a moist and oystery[3] twinkle in my eye. And on the very
day from which the new year dates, I read your New Year congratulations, as
punctually as if you lived in the next house.—Why don't you!

Now, if instantly on the receipt of this, you will send a free and independent
citizen down to the Cunard Wharf at Boston, you will find that Captain Hewett[4]
of the Britannia Steam Ship (*my* ship) has a small parcel for Professor Felton of
Cambridge; and in that parcel you will find a Christmas Carol in Prose. Being
a Ghost Story of Christmas by Charles Dickens.[5]   Over which Christmas Carol,
Charles Dickens wept, and laughed, and wept again, and excited himself in a
most extraordinary manner, in the composition; and thinking whereof, he
walked about the black streets of London, fifteen and twenty miles, many a
night when all the sober folks had gone to bed. ªHe don't like America, I am
told, but he has some friends there, as dear to him as any in England; so you
may read it safely.ª Its success is most prodigious. And by every post, all
manner of strangers write all manner of letters to him about their homes and
hearths, and how this same Carol is read aloud there, and kept on a very little
shelf by itself. Indeed it is the greatest success as I am told, that this Ruffian and
Rascal has ever achieved.

Forster[6] is out again—and if he don't go in again after the manner in which
we have been keeping Christmas, he must be very strong indeed.[7] Such dinings,

---

[1] Cornelius Conway Felton (1807–62;
DAB), Professor of Greek at Harvard: see
Vol. III, p. 28*n*.

[2] Earlier printed texts, deriving from
J. T. Fields in *Atlantic Monthly*, XXVIII,
113–14, substitute "last night" for "last
night's Punch and Turkey".

[3] See Vol. III, p. 131 and *n*.

[4] John Hewitt (born *c.* 1812), master of
the *Britannia*: see Vol. III, p. 7*n*.

[5] Felton's copy, now in the Berg collection, is inscribed "1 Jan". Fanny Longfellow wrote to her brother, Thomas
Appleton, saying CD had sent it to Felton
"in its English garb, with capital woodcuts

and a nice clear type"; she thought it "a
most admirable production" and said it
had had "great success in England, com-
forting people for the tediousness of
Chuzzlewit. It is evidently written at a
heat and from the *heart*" (*Mrs. Longfellow:
Selected Letters and Journals of Fanny
Appleton Longfellow*, ed. E. Wagenknecht,
1956, p. 105).

aa; bb; cc; dd Not previously published.

[6] John Forster (1812–76; *DNB*): see
Vol. I, p. 239*n*.

[7] He had recently recovered from an illness which confined him to the house: see
Vol. III, p. 582*n*.

such dancings, such conjurings, such blindmans-buffiings, such theatre-goings, such kissings-out of old years and kissings-in of new ones, never took place in these parts before. To keep the Chuzzlewit going, and do this little book, the Carol, in the odd times between two parts of it, was, as you may suppose, pretty tight work. But when it was done, I broke out like a Madman. And if you could have seen me at a children's party at Macreadys[1] the other night, going down a Country dance *b*something longer than the Library at Cambridge*b* with Mrs. M. you would have thought I was a country Gentleman of independent property, residing on a tip-top farm, with the wind blowing straight in my face every day.

*c*We have not yet achieved that family performance I told you of; which I expect will come off in the course of next week. Kate is not quite as well as usual: being nervous and dull. But her health is perfectly good, and I am sure she might rally, if she would. I shall be much relieved when it is well over. In the mean time total abstinence from oysters seems to be the best thing for me; and good spirits for all of us. She is much rejoiced to hear that Mrs. Felton continues to improve; and sends her cordial love. In which I, no less cordially, join.*c*

Your friend, Mr. Parker[2] dined with us one day (I don't know whether I told you this before?), and pleased us very much. Mr. Coleman[3] has dined here once, and spent an evening here. I have not seen him lately, though he has called twice or thrice; for Kate being unwell, and I busy, we have not been visible at our accustomed seasons. I wonder whether Hamlet[4] has ever fallen in your way. Poor Hamlet![4] He was a good fellow, and has the most grateful heart, I ever met with. Our journeyings with Hamlet seem to be a dream, now. Talking of dreams, strange thoughts of Italy and France—and maybe Germany[5]— are springing up within me, as the Chuzzlewit clears off. It's a secret I have hardly breathed to any one, but I "think" of leaving England for a year, next midsummer—bag and baggage, little ones and all—then coming out with *such* a story, Felton—all at once—no parts—sledge hammer blow.

I send you a Manchester paper,[6] as you desire. The report is not exactly done, but very well done, notwithstanding. It was a very splendid sight, I assure you, and an awful-looking audience. I am going to preside at a similar Meeting

---

[1] See Vol. III, pp. 613–14 and *n.*

[2] Earlier printed texts read "P——". Theodore Parker (1810–60; *DAB*), author and Unitarian minister of West Roxbury, Mass. (until 1845); a friend of Emerson and Channing and a leader of the anti-slavery movement. In Jan 43 was asked to resign because of his unorthodox writings, but was reconciled; exhausted by work, was advised to travel in Europe, and reached England Oct 43. Carlyle, whom he visited in Oct, found him "a most hardy, compact, clever little fellow, full of decisive utterance, with humour and good-humour" (*Correspondence of Emerson and Carlyle*, ed. Joseph Slater, 1964, p. 350). Parker's journal contains the note "ask Dickens about the writer on American newspapers in 'Foreign Quarterly Review'" (O. B. Frothingham, *Theodore Parker*, Boston, 1874, p. 183).

[3] Earlier printed texts read "C——". Henry Colman (1785–1849; *DAB*), Unitarian minister: see Vol. III, p. 490*n*.

[4] "H——" in Fields and MDGH, 1882; "Putnam" in MDGH, 1893 and later edns. George Washington Putnam (1812–96), CD's secretary in America: see Vol. III, p. 27*n*.

[5] See Vol. III, p. 588; Germany as a possibility is not mentioned elsewhere.

[6] The *Manchester Guardian*, 7 Oct 43, reporting the Athenaeum Soirée: see Vol. III, pp. 580*n*, 583.

at Liverpool on the 26th. of next month; and on my way home, I may be obliged to preside at another at Birmingham. I will send you papers, if the reports be at all like the real thing.

*a*Forster thought I should be very much surprised by what you told him of Lardner;[1] but I was not. I don't know much of the man—but I know the country he is in, and think he acted with great sagacity.*a* [2]

I wrote to Prescott[3] about his book, with which I was perfectly charmed. I think his descriptions, Masterly; his style, brilliant; his purpose, manly and gallant always. The introductory account of Aztec civilisation impressed me, exactly as it impressed you. From beginning to end, the whole History is enchanting and full of Genius. I only wonder that having such an opportunity of illustrating the Doctrine of Visible Judgments, he never remarks when Cortes and his men tumble the Idols down the Temple Steps and call upon the people to take notice that their Gods are powerless to help themselves[4]—that possibly if some intelligent Native had tumbled down the Image of the Virgin or patron saint after them, nothing very remarkable might have ensued, in consequence.

Of course you like Macready.[5] Your name's Felton. I wish you could [see][6]

---

[1] Dionysius Lardner, FRS (1793–1859; *DNB*), popular scientific writer: see Vol. I, p. 359*n*. Lectured in North America 1840–5, after eloping with the wife of Captain Richard Heaviside by whom he had a child; in autumn 1843 was lecturing first in New York and then in Boston. According to the *Observer*, 17 Dec 43 (quoting *New York Herald*), he had "been heard by 50,000 persons ... has been attacked by 110 newspapers, but has at length got into smooth water, with plenty of cash, a great reputation". Macready (who had known Lardner well in the 30s) recorded a different impression when he called on the family in New York on 7 Oct: he found Lardner "no longer dandy in his dress and appointments, but old and almost slovenly"; he deplored "their blind, absurd infatuation", but called again 20 Oct "lest he might think I shirked him" (*Diaries*, II, 225–6, 228).

[2] Perhaps a reference to the anti-British line taken by Lardner in his lectures: Macready heard him in Boston on 11 Nov, lecturing "on Washington, Napoleon, Wellington, etc! with transparent illustrations—miserable daubs of pictures and plans! ... What I listened to was amusing, but leaning very much to American prejudice, which is not right" (II, 234).

[3] William Hickling Prescott (1796–1859; *DAB*), historian; though almost blind

from an accident in youth, devoted himself with heroic self-discipline to historical studies, and won widespread fame with his *History of the Reign of Ferdinand and Isabella*, published after ten years' preparation in 1837 (London, 1838; translated into Spanish, French, and German). His greatest work, *The Conquest of Mexico*, 1843, was read by CD with "delight": see Vol. III, pp. 596–7. Contributed many articles to the *North American Review*; a friend of Irving, George Ticknor (his biographer), Felton and Sumner; signed the petition for International Copyright. CD met him in Boston 27 Jan 42 and dined at his house 28 Jan; their last meeting was on 3 June at Lebanon Springs (also with Prescott's parents) and several friendly letters were exchanged after CD's return: see Vol. III, pp. 294–6, 347–8, 417, 456–7. Though no further correspondence survives, no reason to suppose their friendship cooled; they met again on Prescott's visit to England in 1850.

[4] *Conquest of Mexico*, Book II, Ch. 4.

[5] William Charles Macready (1793–1873; *DNB*): see Vol. I, p. 279*n*. He had met Felton at Longfellow's, 14 Nov 43, and had dined at Felton's 18 Nov (Macready, *Diaries*, II, 235, 237). Felton could have seen him in *Macbeth* and *Hamlet* in Boston.

[6] MS reads "say".

him play Lear. It is stupendously terrible. But I suppose he would be slow to act it, with the Boston Company.[1]

Hearty remembrances to Sumner,[2] Longfellow,[3] Prescott, and all whom you know I love to remember. Countless happy years to you and yours, my dear Felton, and some instalment of them, however slight, in England, in the loving company of

The Proscribed One.

Oh breathe not his name[4]

To RICHARD LANE,[5] 2 JANUARY 1844

Composite text, from MS[6] Sir John Nicholson (*aa*) and facsimile of complete letter (without subscription) in *Autographic Mirror*, 20 Feb 64, p. 7.[7]

Devonshire Terrace | Second January 1844.

My Dear Sir

That is a very terrible case you tell me of. I would to God I could get at the parental heart of —— ——,[8] in which event I would so scarify it, that he should writhe again. But if I were to put such a father as he into a book, all the fathers going (and especially the *a*bad ones) would hold up their hands and protest against the unnatural caricature. I find that a great many people (particularly those who might have sat for the character) consider, even Mr. Pecksniff,[9] a grotesque impossibility.[10] And Mrs. Nickleby herself,[11] sitting bodily before me in a solid chair, once asked me whether I really believed there ever was such a woman.*a* [12]

So ——[13] reviewing his own case, would not believe in Jonas Chuzzlewit. "I

[1] Macready rehearsed *Lear*, but saw that "its performance would be discreditable and do *me* thereby injury in my last engagement" (11 Dec 43; II, 242).

[2] Charles Sumner (1811–74; *DAB*), statesman: see Vol. III, p. 20*n*. The present letter was doubtless shown to Sumner and by him to Prescott, who wrote: "Thank you, dear Sumner, for the letter of Boz. What a fellow he is! Champagne—the moment the cork is let off!" (Prescott *to* Sumner, Jan 44; MS Houghton Library).

[3] Henry Wadsworth Longfellow (1807–82; *DAB*): see Vol. III, p. 39*n*.

[4] "Oh! breathe not his name, let it sleep in the shade", in Moore's *Irish Melodies*. A joking reference to American criticisms of *Chuzzlewit*, including Felton's: see Vol. III, pp. 541, 547.

[5] Richard James Lane (1800–1872; *DNB*), line-engraver and lithographer: see Vol. III, p. 433*n*.

[6] Fragment mounted in album; single page with writing on both sides, from which a strip has been cut out.

[7] A collection of facsimile autographs published serially 1864–6; some from named owners, but this letter from the collection of the unnamed editor. A note on p. 6 emphasizing the interest of the letter concludes "Will Mr. Dickens forgive us for giving *him* a surprise?" (see Vol. I, p. xxx*n*).

[8] Other letters in the *Autographic Mirror* show that it was the editor's frequent practice to substitute dashes for names. The space here represents about 12 letters—probably a single surname.

[9] Based on Samuel Carter Hall: see Vol. I, p. 483*n*, and *To* Forster, 29 Jan 45 and *fn*.

[10] CD made the same point in the Preface to *Chuzzlewit*, June 44, and more specifically in the Cheap edn 1850: "All the Pecksniff family upon earth are quite agreed, I believe, that no such character as Mr. Pecksniff ever existed".

[11] Elizabeth Dickens: see Vol. I, p. 15*n*. The identification is traditional, and clearly implied by Forster (F, VI, vii, 551).

[12] The word "character" is deleted before "woman".

[13] Short spaces, suggesting that CD used imaginary names.

like Oliver Twist," says ——[1] "for I am fond of children. But the book is unnatural. For who would think of being cruel to poor little Oliver Twist!"

Nevertheless I will bear the Dog in my mind. And if I can hit him between the eyes so that he shall stagger more than you or I have done this Christmas under the combined effects of Punch and Turkey—I will.

*a*Thank you cordially for your note. Excuse this scrap of paper. I thought it was a whole sheet, until I turned over.

My Dear Sir | Faithfully Yours

R. J. Lane Esquire.*a*   CHARLES DICKENS

To THOMAS MITTON,[2] 2 JANUARY 1844*

MS Berg Collection.

Devonshire Terrace | Second January 1844.

My Dear Mitton

So long ago, as the Second of last month, I made an appointment with the Elton Treasurer[3] pro tem, to go through his accounts tonight and discharge him, before transferring the Banker's account to the Trustees. I have only just now (5 o'Clock) been reminded of it; and as I don't know how long it may take (all other Prosers in the World are chickens to this man) I think it best to postpone coming to you until Thursday at the usual time.

The subscription in the City (*exclusive* of the West End) for the Second Edition of the Carol,[4] was 1500. They have consequently printed 3000 additional, instead of 2, making in all 9000, and not 8.

Hurrah, say I! As to the letters about it, there's no saying what *they* are.

Faithfully Ever

Thomas Mitton Esquire   CD.

To WILLIAM SCHOLEFIELD,[5] 2 JANUARY 1844*

MS Authors' Club.

London. 1 Devonshire Terrace
York Gate Regents Park. | Second January 1844.

Sir.

I beg to acknowledge the receipt of your letter, inviting me to attend a public Meeting at Birmingham in behalf of the Polytechnic Institution of that town.[6]

---

[1] See last note on p. 5.
[2] Thomas Mitton (1812–78): see Vol. I, p. 35*n*.
[3] R. B. Perry: see Vol. III, p. 527*n*.
[4] The 2nd edn was advertised 6 Jan, the 3rd edn 20 Jan; by 9 Mar it had reached a 6th edn.
[5] William Scholefield (1809–67), treasurer of the Birmingham Polytechnic Institution, 102, Steelhouse Lane; Mayor 1838, and radical MP for Birmingham 1846–67. The family was known to Macready (see *Diaries*, II, 16, 269).
[6] The Institution had been formed in Apr 43 and acquired premises in Sep. When the amount raised by donations and subscriptions fell short of what was required, the Committee, "in the hope of awakening a warmer interest in the Society, determined upon holding a public meeting

I have read the Prospectus of the Institution with great interest. For I *know* that on the wise regulation and success of such Establishments, in such places, the future happiness and character of the people mainly depend; and that they are the most important and salutary influence at work for their improvement.

But honored as I feel by your communication, and gratified as I should be, to witness such a festival as you describe, in such a place as Birmingham, I regret to say that I cannot leave home at the time you mention. I have been requested, within this fortnight, to preside at a similar meeting at Liverpool, which was originally intended to have taken place early in the present month, but has been postponed until the 26th. of February, in consequence of my inability to leave town on an earlier day.

If your meeting had been fixed for the 27th. of February, or for the 28th. I should have been truly glad to take Birmingham in my way home. As it is, I can only thank you for your Invitation—assure you of my hearty and cordial sympathy with the Great object to which it relates—and hope for the pleasure of visiting Birmingham at some future time.[1]

I am Sir | Faithfully Yours

William Scholefield Esquire

CHARLES DICKENS

To T. J. SERLE,[2] 2 JANUARY [1844]

MS Mr Peter Brandt. *Date:* "1843" clearly CD's error for 1844.

Devonshire Terrace | Second January 1843.

My Dear Serle.

If I can come to you before you separate tonight—I will. But an engagement which I could not anticipate, renders it exceedingly improbable.

Will you therefore formally pass Mr. Perry's accounts, and discharge him of the same? If my signature should be necessary, I will attach it afterwards, of course. Perhaps if Mr. Perry signs an order to Coutts & Co. to the effect that the account is now to be transferred to the Three Trustees, subject to the drafts of any two of them,—and sends it to me for my signature and subsequent proceeding on—it will be the shortest course.

The Lady[3] with whom the Ali Baba Miss Elton[4] resides, has sent me the enclosed note. I answered it by saying that the Committee met tonight, and I had no doubt would readily comply with her request. We may make the sum a

---

of so popular a character as to insure the attendance of the friends to education, without distinction of party or opinion", and for this purpose to secure the attendance of CD (*Birmingham Polytechnic Institution. Report of the Proceedings at the Conversazione ... With an Address from the Committee*, Birmingham, [1844], pp. 4–6).

[1] The date was changed to 28 Feb.

[2] Thomas James Serle (1798–1889): see Vol. I, p. 355*n*, and Vol. II, p. 151*n*.

[3] Unidentified, but probably in Brompton: see *To* Mrs Hall, 29 Jan and *fn*.

[4] Rosalind, the third daughter of E. W. Elton: see Vol. III, p. 527*n*. Known to have been learning wood engraving at the Female School of Design with Mrs M'Ian a few years later (T. Marshall, *Lives of the Most Celebrated Actors and Actresses*, [1848], p. 155). Ali Baba was a woodcutter.

part of Mr. Perry's accounts perhaps. I therefore enclose a blank cheque, with my signature.

I have received ten shillings additional, the amount of sundry Subscriptions, from Mr. John Reddish of the York and London Assurance Office.[1] I have paid fifteen shillings for Three Insertions of the "Companion" advertisement in The Times.[2] Whereby the Estate owes the Inimitable B. five shillings.

The advertisement will be inserted tomorrow, Friday, and Saturday. I have delayed it at Miss Elton's request, as the young lady was absent on a little recreation.

Dr. Elliotson[3] reports his patient,[4] getting on famously.

I don't know that I have anything else to say, except to send my remembrances and seasonable congratulations to our friends. Always My Dear Serle Yours and Theirs

CHARLES DICKENS

No room for the flourish. We must "suppose that"—as you say at Rehearsals.

To ALBERT SMITH,[5] 2 JANUARY 1844*

MS Huntington Library.

Devonshire Terrace | Second January 1844.

Dear Sir

I hasten to thank you for your Three Volumes[6] received last night, and for the courteous note accompanying them.

---

[1] Reddish was the Secretary.

[2] *The Times* of 3, 5, 6 Jan 44 carried the Committee's advertisement for "one of their charges, who has already acted in that capacity" for "a SITUATION as COMPANION to, and attendant upon, an elderly lady or an invalid". Elton had six daughters, Esther (the eldest daughter of his second marriage), Rosa, Rosalind, Mary Ann, Lucy and Caroline; the companion was presumably one of the last three of whom nothing is known, and probably one of the daughters of the first marriage.

[3] John Elliotson, MD (1791–1868; *DNB*): see Vol. I, p. 416*n*, and Vol. II, p. 109*n*.

[4] Catherine Dickens.

[5] Albert Richard Smith (1816–60; *DNB*), author and entertainer; studied medicine—along with Leech—at the Middlesex Hospital 1835–8; first expedition to Mont Blanc 1838, the basis of his popular entertainments. On return, began career in journalism, establishing a reputation with his contributions to *Bentley's*

from Mar 41 and to *Punch* 1841–3—but (according to his own later account) "withdrew" being "unable to agree" with Lemon; in 1843 became dramatic critic for the *Illustrated London News*. His career as playwright began with *Blanche Heriot* at the Surrey Sep 42; later, wrote successful extravaganzas for the Princess's, and for the Lyceum with the Keeleys, whose elder daughter he married 1859. Wrote prologue for the Lyceum dramatization of *Chuzzlewit*, June 44, and himself dramatized the *Cricket on the Hearth* and *Battle of Life*. He may have met CD through the *Punch* circle, or through Ainsworth; though disliked by Jerrold (MS Silver Diary) he was generally popular.

[6] *The Adventures of Mr. Ledbury*, published by 1 Jan 44 after appearing as a serial with Leech's illustrations in *Bentley's* Sep 42–Dec 43. It contains a warm tribute to CD and his fame (II, 208): he had "made those read who never read before ... not only in perceptive London, but in many quiet and sequestered nooks and corners of the country, and even in distant

I read a specimen of a certain Miniature Magazine the other day (I believe you know something of it?) which entertained me very much indeed.[1] It is full of a pleasant humour and capital observation.

That sounds so like the Evening Paper, that I am half disposed to write another note of Thanks. But I will defer it, on second thoughts, until you send me another Book.

Dear Sir | Faithfully Yours

Albert Smith Esquire   CHARLES DICKENS

To JOHN FORSTER, [3 JANUARY 1844]

Extract in F, IV, ii, 314. *Date:* 3 Jan according to Forster.

Saying about sales of the Carol *that* two thousand of the three printed for second and third editions are already taken by the trade.[2]

To W. C. MACREADY, 3 JANUARY 1844†

MS Morgan Library. *Address:* By the Cunard Steam Packet for January | W. C. Macready Esqre. | To the Care of David Colden Esqre. | Laight Street | Hudson Square | New York | United States.[3]

Devonshire Terrace | Third January 1844.

My very dear Macready.

You know all the news, and you know I love you; so I no more know why I write, than I do why I "come round" after the play to shake hands with you in your dressing-room. I say, *Come,* as if you were at this present moment the lessee of Drury Lane, and had Jones[4] with a long face on one hand—Smith,[5] elaborately explaining that everything in creation is a joint stock Company, on the other—the Inimitable B by the fire, in conversation with *ª*Serle—and Forster confidential with everybody about nothing particular.*ª* Well a day!—I see it all, and smell that extraordinary compound of odd scents peculiar to a theatre, which bursts upon me when I swing open the little door in the hall; accompanies me, as I meet perspiring supers in the narrow passage; goes with me, up the two

---

lands"—including Italy, where in 1838 handkerchiefs imprinted with characters from *Pickwick* were on sale on stalls in Milan and in 1840 the translation of *Oliver Twist* was placarded against the walls of the Ducal Palace in Venice.

[1] CD is almost certainly referring to *Young England's Little Library,* recently published; described by the *Morning Post,* 12 Jan, as "thirteen little *brochures,* on a variety of subjects, grave, gay, lively, and severe, some of which are very cleverly illustrated"; one of the volumes was by Smith, whose "clever contribution" plunged from prose to verse and was illustrated by himself "in the broadest vein of burlesque exaggeration". Other contributors included Mrs S. C. Hall, Mary Howitt, F. W. N. Bayley, and T. Gaspey.

[2] This was the number printed for the 2nd edn: see *To Mitton, 2 Jan.*

[3] Re-addressed to "New Orleans".

[4] Name omitted in MDGH and later edns; C. Jones, Macready's treasurer at Drury Lane.

[5] Name omitted in MDGH and later edns; Henry Porter Smith (1797–1880), actuary: see Vol. II, p. 251*n.*

aa; bb; cc; dd; ee; ff; gg Not previously published.

steps; crosses the stage; winds round the third entrance P.S.[1] as I wind; and escorts me safely into your presence, where I find you *unwinding* something slowly round and round your chest, which is so long that no man ever saw the end of it.[2]

Oh that you had been in Clarence Terrace on Nina's birthday! Good God how we missed you, talked of you, drank your health, and wondered what you were doing! Perhaps you are Falkland enough (I swear I suspect you of it) to feel rather sore—just a little bit you know; the merest trifle in the world—on hearing that Mrs. Macready looked brilliant—blooming, young, and handsome; and that she danced a country dance with the writer hereof (Acres to your Falkland) in a thorough spirit of beaming good humour and enjoyment.[3] Now you don't like to be told that? Nor do you quite like to hear that Forster and I conjured bravely—that a hot plum pudding was produced from an empty saucepan, held over a blazing fire, kindled in Stanfield's[4] hat, without damage to the lining—that a box of bran was changed into a live Guinea Pig, which ran between my God child's[5] feet, and was the cause of such a shrill uproar and clapping of hands that you might have heard it (and I daresay did) in America— that three half crowns being taken from Major Burns[6] and put into a tumbler-glass before his eyes did then and there give jingling answers unto questions asked of them by me, and knew where you were, and what you were doing; to the unspeakable admiration of the whole assembly.[7] Neither do you quite like to be told that we are going to do it again, next Saturday, with the addition of Demoniacal dresses from a Masquerade Shop.[8] Nor, that Mrs. Macready, for her gallant bearing always, and her best sort of best affection, is the best creature I know. Never mind. No man shall gag me; and those are my opinions.

My dear Macready, the lecturing proposition[9] is not to be thought of. I have not the slightest doubt or hesitation in giving you my most strenuous and decided advice, against it. ᵇI am not at all clear, even of its success in America, for as it is invariably the characteristic of low, coarse, and mean minds in the circle of one's own acquaintance to delight in new faces and change of friends, so it is one of the most striking features in that low, coarse, and mean Nation to be perpetually playing skittles with different sets of Idols. And I am by no

---

[1] Prompt Side.

[2] Probably after a performance of *Virginius*.

[3] An allusion to the jealous disposition of Falkland, in Sheridan's *The Rivals*.

[4] Clarkson Stanfield (1793–1867; *DNB*): see Vol. I, p. 553*n*.

[5] Henry Macready, *b*. 21 Dec 1838, was CD's godson: he "gave him a silver cup" (*Diaries*, II, 21).

[6] James Glencairn Burns (1794–1865), youngest son of the poet; a friend of Macready and of Carlyle.

[7] For the conjuring, see Vol. III, p. 613 and *n*.

[8] See *To* Frederick Dickens, 4 Jan.

[9] *The Times*, 7 Dec 43, reported an invitation to Macready "by the Bostonians'. to deliver a course of lectures on elocution Macready's diary, 21 and 23 Nov, mentions only Ticknor's proposal, supported by Sumner, that he should give "Readings of Shakespeare"; "lecturing" in the latter entry seems also to refer to this (*Diaries*, II, 238, 240). The idea was seriously considered, but nothing came of it—except a farewell entertainment of readings and a supper party, with Macready as host, given at Papanti's, New York, 15 Oct 44 (see Longfellow *to* Macready, 13 Oct 44; *Letters of Henry Wadsworth Longfellow*, ed. A. Hilen, Cambridge, Mass., III, 1972, 45–6).

means sure, that *any* second visit of yours to any place for any purpose will be the success it ought to be, and would, with people of a higher standard, most indubitably prove. But setting aside this, *and looking only to its effect at home,*[b] I am immoveable in my conviction that the impression it would produce would be one of failure, and a reduction of yourself to the level of those who do the like here. To us who know the Boston names and honor them, and who know Boston and like it (Boston is what I would have the whole United States to be) the Boston requisition would be a valuable document of which you and your friends might well be proud. But these names are perfectly unknown to the public here, and would produce not the least effect. The only thing known to the public here, is, that they ask (when I say "they", I mean the people) every-body to lecture. It is one of the things I have ridiculed in Chuzzlewit.[1] Lecture, you, and you fall into the roll of Lardners, Vandenhoffs,[2] Eltons,[3] Knowleses,[4] Buckinghams.[5]—You are off your pedestal, have flung away your glass slipper, and changed your triumphal coach into a seedy old pumpkin. I am quite sure of it, and cannot express my strong conviction, in language of sufficient force.

"Puff-ridden"! Why to be sure they are. The Nation is a miserable Sindbad, and its boasted press (the braggarts!) the loathsome, foul old man upon his back. And yet [c]with that extraordinary disregard of Truth, that monstrous audacity of assertion, which makes a Gentleman in heart so rare a man among the people,[c] they will tell you, and proclaim to the four winds, for repetition here, that they don't heed their ignorant and brutal papers. As if the papers could exist if they didn't heed them! [d]As if a man could live in the United States a month, and not see the whole country is led and driven by a herd of rascals, who are the human lice of God's creation![d] [6] Let any two of these vagabonds in any town you go to, take it into their heads to make you an object of attack, or to direct the general attention elsewhere, and what avail those wonderful images of passion which you have been all your life perfecting, [e]and which I no more believe the rotten heart of that false land is capable of feeling, otherwise than as a fashion, a fancy, than I believe, or ever did believe, it made a distinction between me and Fanny Elssler,[7] or between her and La Fayette. Pah! I never knew what it was to feel disgust and contempt, 'till I travelled in America.[e]

---

[1] In Ch. 17, on the lectures attended by Mrs Jefferson Brick. See also Vol. III, p. 53.

[2] John Vandenhoff the actor was in America 1837–8, and again in 1844.

[3] Edward William Elton (1794–1843; *DNB*), actor: see Vol. III, p. 527*n*. He was never in America, but occasionally lectured on the drama in London.

[4] James Sheridan Knowles (1784–1862; *DNB*), dramatist and actor: see Vol. II, p. 71*n*.

[5] James Silk Buckingham (1786–1855; *DNB*), author, traveller and lecturer: see Vol. III, p. 239*n*.

[6] This attack on the American Press is even more violent than anything in CD's letters of 1842–3—perhaps partly because of their attempts at defence after Forster's article in the *Foreign Quarterly Review* (see Vol. III, p. 363*n*), and doubtless influenced by American reactions to the July and Sep Nos of *Chuzzlewit*: see Vol. III, p. 541*n*. Macready suffered considerably from press attacks: on 1 Nov 43 he was "much harassed, occupied, irritated and annoyed by the assaults in certain newspapers", and N. P. Willis continued to abuse him and to praise his rivals for some months (*Diaries*, II, 231–3, 249, 262).

[7] Fanny Elssler (1810–84), dancer; in America 1840–2, where she was so success-ful that Congress avoided sitting on the days when she was dancing in Washington

I have sent you, to the charge of our trusty and well-beloved Colden,[1] a little book I published on the 17th.[2] of December, and which has been a most prodigious success—the greatest, I think, I have ever achieved. It pleases me to think that it will bring you Home for an hour or two. And I long to hear you have read it, on some quiet morning. Do they allow you to be quiet, by the way? "Some of our most fash'nable people Sir", denounced me awfully, for liking to be alone sometimes.

Now that we have turned Christmas, I feel as if your face were directed homewards, Macready. The downhill part of the road is before us now, and we shall travel on to midsummer at a dashing pace. ʃDamn them, I can't damage you by coming with open arms to Liverpool[3] (for you won't be going back again in a hurry, much as you relish them);ʃ and please Heaven I will be there, when you come steaming up the Mersey, with that red funnel smoking out unutterable things, and your heart much fuller than your trunks, though something lighter! If I be not the first Englishman to shake hands with you on English Ground, the man who gets before me will be a brisk and active fellow, and even then need put his best leg foremost. So I warn Forster to keep in the rear, or he'll be blown.

If you should have any leisure to project, and put on paper, the outline of a scheme for opening any Theatre on your return, upon a certain List Subscribed, and on certain understandings with the actors, it strikes me that it would be well to break ground, while you are still away. Of course I need not say that I will see anybody or do anything—even to the calling together of the actors—if you should ever deem it desirable. My opinion is, that our respected and valued friend Mr. Bunn, will stagger through another season, if he don't rot first. I understand he is in a partial state of decomposition at this minute. He was very ill, but got better.[4] How is it that Bunns always *do* get better, and strong hearts are so easy to die!

ᵍBurn this letter, lest it should be abstracted from your desk (as Jeffrey's pocket book was) and published in a newspaper.[5] Being confidentially addressed to yourself, it would be very extensively read. I hope you saw Mr. Park Benjamin[6] in New York—a literary gentleman, and "smart", oh very smart. Also Mr. James Gordon Bennet[7] (think of his proposing to Chapman and Hall

Cyril W. Beaumont, *Fanny Elssler*, [1931], p. 25). Had a London season 1843; Macready thought her "exceedingly vulgar" (*Diaries*, II, 217).

[1] David Cadwallader Colden (1797–1850), lawyer and philanthropist: see Vol. III, p. 30n.

[2] The *Carol* was in fact published 19 Dec, but CD sent copies to friends on 17 Dec.

[3] For CD's decision not to see Macready off, see Vol. III, pp. 551–3 and *ns*.

[4] Alfred Bunn (1796–1860; *DNB*), lessee of Drury Lane: see Vol. I, p. 317n; his

name was omitted in MDGH and later edns. No reports of this illness have been traced; the Drury Lane season continued to be successful, especially with Balfe's *The Bohemian Girl*.

[5] In 1815 Jeffrey's private journal was published in a Philadelphia paper: see Lord Cockburn, *Life of Lord Jeffrey*, 1852, I, 149–50.

[6] Park Benjamin (1809–64; *DAB*), journalist: see Vol. III, p. 312n.

[7] James Gordon Bennett (1795–1872; *DAB*), editor of the *New York Herald*: see Vol. III, p. 84n.

to publish his travels in England!)[1] and Colonel Webb,[2] and all that holy brotherhood.*g* Kate sends her tender love. So does Georgy. So does Charley, so does Mamy, so does Katey, so does Walter, so does the other one who is to be born next week. Look homeward always, as we look abroad to you. God bless you my dear Macready. Ever your affectionate friend

C.D.

To LAMAN BLANCHARD,[3] 4 JANUARY 1844

MS Mr Douglas Jerrold.

Devonshire Terrace | Fourth January 1844.

My Dear Blanchard

I cannot thank you enough for the beautiful manner, and the true spirit of friendship, in which you have noticed my Carol.[4] But I *must* thank you, because you have filled my heart up to the brim, and it is running over.

You meant to give me great pleasure, my dear fellow, and you have done it. The tone of your elegant and fervent praise has touched me in the tenderest place. I cannot write about it; and as to talking of it, I could no more do that, than a dumb man. I have derived inexpressible gratification from what I know and feel was a labour of love on your part. And I can never forget it.

When I think it likely that I may meet you (perhaps at Ainsworth's[5] on Friday?) I shall slip a Carol into my pocket, and ask you to put it among your books for my sake.[6] You will never like it the less for having made it the means of so much happiness to me.

Always My Dear Blanchard | Faithfully Your friend

Laman Blanchard Esquire   CHARLES DICKENS

[1] Bennett landed in England 18 July 43 and left 24 Sep, after also visiting Ireland, Scotland, and Paris. The chief incident of his tour was his controversy with O'Connell, who declined to receive him: see Bennett's letter to *The Times*, 30 Aug 43. After further attacks by O'Connell's supporters he wrote, "I shall repay them all when I get home—for I have collected materials on the state of England that will be interesting and amusing" (*Memoirs of James Gordon Bennett and his Times. By a Journalist*, New York, 1855, p. 339). There is no evidence that his projected book was written, but he sent "lies and scandal" to the *New York Herald* during his travels (*Diary of Philip Hone*, ed. Bayard Tuckerman, New York, 1889, II, 192).

[2] Colonel James Watson Webb (1802–84; *DAB*), editor of the "mammoth" *Morning Courier and New-York Enquirer*; often involved in duels and in 1842 nar-

rowly escaped prison—perhaps recalled in Colonel Diver (*Chuzzlewit*, Ch. 16).

[3] Samuel Laman Blanchard (1804–45; *DNB*): see Vol. I, p. 290*n*.

[4] In the long essay, "Charles Dickens", in *Ainsworth's Magazine*, Jan 1844 (pp. 84–8); it covered *Chuzzlewit* as well as the *Carol* and in its warmth of enthusiasm and perceptiveness over detail fully justifies CD's description. Blanchard was writing regularly for *Ainsworth's* and his authorship of the essay is confirmed by a note to Ainsworth (dated "Thursday" and clearly of 4 Jan 44), referring to the current issue, which says, "I find Dickens is particularly pleased" (*New Monthly Magazine*, Feb 1846, p. 135).

[5] William Harrison Ainsworth (1805–82; *DNB*): see Vol. I, p. 115*n*, and Vol. II, p. 14*n*.

[6] See *To* Blanchard, 29 Jan 44. This copy has not been traced.

To FREDERICK DICKENS,[1] 4 JANUARY 1844*

MS L. & H. Nathan Ltd.

Devonshire Terrace. | Fourth January 1844.

My Dear Fred

Will you, and can you, make it convenient to go to the Lowther Rooms[2] for me, after the receipt of this; upon the following errand.

I want to hire for twelfth night, a Magician's Dress—that is to say a black cloak with hieroglyphics on it—some kind of doublet to wear underneath—a grave black beard—and a high black sugar-loaf hat—and a wand with a snake on it, or some such thing. Forster wants a similar set of garments in fiery red. Anything between these and the dress of Mephistopheles will suit him, but it must be blazing red, or have a good deal of red in it. Also he wants a jolly mask—such as Wieland[3] would have if he were a grinning spirit. He must be able to see well out of it. Our legs we don't care for.

I have been to Nathan's myself, but they have not such things. The production of my card will materially assist you with the Lowther Vagabond,[4] I dare say. But I want to know the cost, and must have the things sent up for inspection, that I may be quite sure they are of the right sort.

If you can effect this wonderful work, fifty people are expected to fall into fits.

Affectionately Always
CHARLES DICKENS

P.S. Don't *leave* my card if you can't get the dresses. For they'll stick it up in the chimney glass of some [se.][5]

To THOMAS MITTON, 4 JANUARY 1844*

MS Private. *Address:* Thomas Mitton Esquire | 23 Southampton Buildings | Chancery Lane.

Devonshire Terrace | Thursday Fourth January 1844

My Dear Mitton.

I must come down to you this *morning*, some time before dinner, and between 3 and 4. For I have a cold upon me, which makes me afraid to go out at night. My chest is raw, my head dizzy, and my nose incomprehensible. I tried hot

---

[1] Frederick William Dickens (1820–68): see Vol. I, p. 47*n*.

[2] In King William Street, Strand.

[3] George Wieland, actor and dancer, chiefly in pantomime; known as a brilliant mime (mentioned by CD in his notes to *Memoirs of Joseph Grimaldi*, 1838). His finest achievement was the "droll imp" in the ballet of *The Daughter of the Danube*, at Drury Lane 1837, for which he wore a mask. Played Harlequin in the Adelphi pantomime of 1843, but retired 1844, and died before Feb 1856: see F, VIII, i, 629*n*.

[4] "Mr Blake" ran the masquerades at the Lowther Rooms until Feb 44 and was connected with Nathan's, the masquerade and fancy-dress warehouse.

[5] About 9 letters inked out, of which a final "l" or "e" can be seen. Possibly "whorehouse".

water to my feet last night, but I could not sleep. And this morning I can hardly hold up my watery old eyes. I must see what a Warm Bath will do tonight.

Thomas Mitton Esquire

Faithfully Always
CD

To SIR GEORGE HAYTER,[1] 5 JANUARY 1844

Text from N, I, 558.

1 Devonshire Terrace, York Gate, Regent's Park
Fifth January 1844

Dear Sir,

However kindly and well you understand my little work, believe me that you have a most imperfect understanding of its author, if you suppose that he can ever, in public or in private, derive anything but satisfaction from the receipt of your earnest note. I am happy to say that I have received very many letters to the same effect; but not one among them has given me greater pleasure than that to which your name is appended.

I thank you *sincerely* and am always

Faithfully yours
[CHARLES DICKENS]

To R. R. M'IAN,[2] 5 JANUARY 1844*

MS Walter T. Spencer.

Devonshire Terrace. | Fifth January 1844.

My Dear McIan.

Pray tell the fair authoress of the Quadrupeds' Pic Nic,[3] that I am greatly obliged to her for sending me that pretty little book. I have put it into the very small hands of my Son and Heir, who is delighted with it—which I take to be a kind of bud of good taste in the Young Plant.

Faithfully Yours always
CHARLES DICKENS

R. R. McIan

---

[1] Sir George Hayter (1792–1871; *DNB*), artist; Principal Painter in Ordinary to the Queen in succession to Wilkie 1841; painted the coronation and official portrait of the Queen; knighted 1842. Not RA, owing to his private life (he was living with a lady not his wife)—but "these difficulties . . . did not debar him from royal favour and in fact seem to have intrigued the Queen in her early, light-hearted days" (T. S. R. Boase, *English Art 1800–1870*. 1959, p. 209).

[2] Robert Ronald M'Ian (1803–56; *DNB*), actor and painter: see Vol. II, p. 309*n* and Vol. III, p. 425*n*.

[3] Published by Pickering in 1840; prefatory advertisement signed "F. B. C." An imitation of the early 19th century William Roscoe's *The Butterfly's Ball*, Mrs Dorset's *The Peacock at Home*, and many others.

To THOMAS MITTON, 7 JANUARY 1844

MS Huntington Library.

Devonshire Terrace. | Seventh January 1844
Sunday Night.

My Dear Mitton.

I received the enclosed letter from Bradburys, *and* the enclosed yellow book[1] on Saturday afternoon at about Four o'Clock.[2]

I have not the least doubt that if these Vagabonds[3] can be stopped, they must be. So let us go to work in such terrible earnest that everything must tumble down before it.

First, register the copyright as mine.[4]

Secondly, will you get an *immediate* opinion from some man, learned in Injunction matters?[5] If he be a man who has a taste for Literature besides, so much the better. Should it be favorable, let us instantly apply for an injunction[6] or their second number will be out.[7] If we could have a conversation with the Counsel, it would be well that I, who know the original book, should be present. And I certainly would be in court too, as I know the V.C.[8] and would wish to shew that I have a strong feeling in the matter.

I shall not leave home all the morning: expecting a summons from you. I have written on a piece of paper, and slipped into the yellow book, a few remarks that occur to me. Let us be *sledge-hammer*[9] in this, or I shall be beset by hundreds of the same crew, when I come out with a long story.

Faithfully Always
CD

[1] A piracy of the *Carol* of which no copy is now known, though one was formerly in the collection of William Miller, and a page is reproduced in *D*, xxxiv (1938), 41. According to CD's affidavit of 9 Jan (see Appx B, from E. T. Jaques, *CD in Chancery*, 1914) it bore on the wrapper: "This week is commenced and will be continued until complete, 'A Christmas Ghost Story Re-originated from the original by Charles Dickens Esquire and analytically condensed expressly for this work'", and was No. 16 of *Parley's Illuminated Library*, published 6 Jan. The series was the successor of *Parley's Penny Library*, a weekly periodical of 1841–2, which had included abridged and "re-originated" versions of the *Old Curiosity Shop* and *Barnaby Rudge*, and long extracts from *American Notes*—the "yellow pamphlets" referred to in *To* Talfourd, 30 Dec 42: see Vol. III, pp. 410–11 and *ns*. The author was Henry Hewitt, of 101 White Lion St, Islington.

[2] "about the hour of three of the clock" in CD's affidavit (see Appx B). No doubt he postponed writing to Mitton because of the Twelfth Night party, which would also give him an opportunity of consulting Forster.

[3] The booksellers named on the wrapper: see *To* Mitton, 11 Jan, *fn*.

[4] This was done by Mitton on 8 Jan: for the "Form of Enquiring Entry of Proprietorship" see Parke-Bernet Galleries catalogue No. 1468.

[5] The counsel was James Bacon (1798–1895; *DNB*); see Vol. II, p. 35*n*; he had advised on the prevention of piracy of *Chuzzlewit* in the colonies (see Vol. III, p. 426*n*).

[6] See *To* Mitton, 11 Jan.

[7] This would have completed the *Carol*, of which "about one half", according to CD's affidavit (Appx B), and "two-thirds" according to Talfourd's address in moving for the injunction (Jaques, p. 69), had already appeared.

[8] The senior of the two additional Vice-Chancellors, and one of the five Chancery Judges, was Sir James Lewis Knight Bruce (1791–1866; *DNB*). It is not known when CD had met him.

[9] Underlined three times.

First.[1] To observe the title on the first page of the story under the wood cut, and Secondly the Advertisement on the bottom of the wrapper at the back.

[That the story] is precisely the same and the characters the same and the names the same with the exception of the name Fezziwig, which is printed Fuzziwig. That the incidents are the same, and follow in the same order.

That very frequently indeed (I have marked some of the instances) the language is the same. That where it is not, it is weakened, degraded; made tame, vile, ignorant, and mawkish.

[And] I particularly wish it to be put to the [Judge] and to the Counsel, that this is a [material] part of my damage and complaint. That with the idea (though not, as I think, with the effect) of evading the letter of the law in such matters, my book is made to appear a wretched, meagre, miserable thing; and is still hawked about with my title and my name—with my characters, my incidents, and whole design.[2]

To DR GEORGE SHRENBURGH,[3] 9 JANUARY 1844

Extract in N, 1, 560 and Sotheby's catalogue, July 1912; MS 1 p.; dated Devonshire Terrace, 9 Jan 44.

I believe my publishers facilitate the German translations[4] of my writings, by sending early sheets to certain German booksellers.[5] But this is a matter of arrangement between them. The books are translated in Germany, and the enterprise is not mine, or my publishers', but originates with German houses of business.

[1] These notes are on a separate piece of paper, although paged consecutively with the letter, and must be the "few remarks" referred to by CD. The paper is damaged so that some words on the left-hand margin cannot be read, and these have been supplied in square brackets; conjectural readings take account of space, traces of letters still visible, and the context.

[2] CD's first three points are made in his affidavit (see Appx B) and in that of Mitton's clerk, as well as in Talfourd's address (see Jaques, *op. cit.*, pp. 64–7, 69–70); in support of them, he also appears to have made, at some stage, an exhaustive list of the parallel passages for use by his counsel in preparation of the case (legal fair copy, undated, headed "Observations by Mr. Charles Dickens"; MS Mr Shuckburgh).

[3] Unidentified.

[4] For translators up to 1841, see Vol. II, p. 43*n*.

[5] Publishers of translations included Weber and Wigand of Leipzig, Franckh and Krabbe of Stuttgart, and Vieweg of Brunswick; all published translations of *Chuzzlewit*, and Weber, Wigand and Franckh of the *Carol* (see E. N. Gummer, *Dickens' Works in Germany*, Oxford, 1940, p. 8, and lists of publications in *Leipziger Repertorium*, 1843–4).

To CLARKSON STANFIELD, 9 JANUARY 1844

MS Mr Philo Calhoun.

Devonshire Terrace | Ninth January 1844.

My Dear Stanfield

Is your Leg really bad, or did you merely want to keep at home, when our friend W.H.A.[1] asked you to dine with him?

I was coming up to you today to make this enquiry, but was detained abroad until dinner time, swearing affidavits against a Gang of Robbers who have been printing the Carol; and against whom the most energetic vengeance of the Inimitable B, is solemnly (and lawfully) denounced.

Send me a line—literally, a line or word—in answer.

With best regards to all. | Faithfully Yours Ever
My Dear Stanfield
Philo Forecastle.[2]

P.S. I think of going back to the Garrick; having received earnest invitations from the Committee.[3] What do you say? Umph?

P.P.S. We expect, every hour, to have a Baby born here.[4] If anything happens while I am putting this in the envelope, I'll write the Sex in large text, outside.

To THOMAS MITTON, 11 JANUARY 1844

Facsimile in *Black & White*, 21 Dec 1901.

Devonshire Terrace.
Thursday Evening Eleventh January | 1844.

My Dear Mitton

It has been most brilliantly and promptly done. I am glad to find that the Publishers are frightened.[5]

[1] Ainsworth; for the dinner on 5 Jan, see *To* Blanchard, 4 Jan.

[2] Name invented on a common pattern—the first of CD's nautical jokes in letters to Stanfield.

[3] CD had become a member Dec 36 and resigned Nov 38: see Vol. I, pp. 211*n* and 468*n*. He did re-join: see *To* Frederick Dickens, 19 Feb.

[4] A false alarm: for the birth on 15 Jan, see *To* Forster, 17 Jan.

[5] Affidavits had been filed on 9 Jan by CD (see Appx B) and by Robert Bach, Mitton's clerk, describing how he had bought a copy of the work at the printing-office in Craven Yard, Drury Lane, and confirming CD's statement about it (E. T. Jaques, *CD in Chancery*, pp. 66–7). On 10 Jan Bacon's application for an interim injunction against Richard Egan Lee and John Haddock (the printers and probably the proprietors of *Parley's Illuminated Library*) was heard in private before Knight Bruce and the injunction granted (Jaques, *op. cit.*, pp. 67–8). On 11 Jan Talfourd's successful motion for an interim injunction against the publishers was heard in the Vice-Chancellor's Court; the *Times* report of 12 Jan is headed "Dickens v. Berger—Same v. Clark—Same v. Strange—Same v. Cleave". These were George Berger, of 19 Holywell St, William Mark Clark, 17 Warwick Lane, John Cleave, 1 Shoe Lane, and William Strange, 21 Paternoster Row, and were probably merely the distributors of *Parley's*; as Bacon said, "There was no regular publisher . . . but there were several names on the wrapper, of whom it was announced the same could be purchased".

Meet Mr. Cross[1] of Surrey Street, with doubled fists, and peg away at him Right and Left. I think it very likely the printers are in earnest. At all events let us seem to suppose so, and hold out no appearance of an idea of anything but War to the Knife.

I am planning and scheming my No tonight, and shall begin (I hope) in good earnest tomorrow Morning.[2] I shall expect to hear from you when anything occurs.

Faithfully Ever
CHARLES DICKENS

To MISS HANNAH MEREDITH,[3] 13 JANUARY 1844

MS Morgan Library.

Devonshire Terrace | Saturday Morning
Thirteenth January 1844.

My Dear Miss Meredith.

I am truly grieved (though not surprised) to hear of Lady Burdett's death.[4] I have very often thought of Miss Coutts[5] in her long and arduous attendance upon her poor Mother; and but that I know how such hearts as hers are sustained in such duties, should have feared for her health. For her peace of mind in this and every trial, and for her gentle fortitude always, no one who knows her truly, can be anxious in the least. If she has not the materials of comfort and consolation within herself, there are no such things in any creature's nature.

I am much concerned for Sir Francis;[6] but he has a strong mind and a young spirit; and I hope will rally soon.

Let me thank you for your kind remembrance of me at such a time. I value it very much, and am exceedingly grateful to you.

Mrs. Dickens sends her best regards. She is in hourly expectation of her confinement, but I trust is pretty well. Charley and his sisters are in rude health, and beg to add their loves.

Believe me Dear Miss Meredith

Faithfully Your friend
CHARLES DICKENS

Miss Meredith.

[1] William Henry Cross, Lee & Haddock's solicitor.

[2] *Chuzzlewit*, No. XIV (Chs 36–8).

[3] Hannah Meredith (*d.* 1878), later Mrs. William Brown: see Vol. II, p. 168*n.*

[4] Sophia, daughter of Thomas Coutts (1775–1844): see Vol. II, p. 261*n.* She died 12 Jan.

[5] Angela Georgina Burdett Coutts (1814–1906; *DNB*), later Baroness Burdett-Coutts: see Vol. I, p. 559*n.*

[6] Sir Francis Burdett, Bart (1770–1844; *DNB*): see Vol. I, p. 472*n.* He died 23 Jan.

To THOMAS MITTON, 13 JANUARY 1844*

MS Free Library of Philadelphia.

Devonshire Terrace | Saturday Thirteenth January | 1844.

My Dear Mitton

They are the damndest rascals in the World, one and all.[1] If we do not trounce them, all I can say, is, that the English Law in these matters is even worse than I take it to be. And it does not need to be that.

We had a corresponding case—corresponding I mean to that of the Liverpool Albion[2]—with a Birmingham paper[3] once. I do not remember the exact circumstances, but I know they made submission. I will go carefully over the Piracy,[4] and let you have it on Monday. Sometime on that day, I will certainly come down. The parcel shall be sent on to you, the first thing on Monday Morning. You may perhaps think it worth while to ask Chapman and Hall to tell you exactly what occurred.

The passages you have marked, don't seem to me as important as they do to you. If the Carol don't fix them, nothing will.[5]

Faithfully Ever
CD.

To THOMAS MITTON, [15 JANUARY 1844]*

MS University of Texas. *Date:* the Monday after the appearance of No. 18 of *Parley's*, presumably on 13 Jan when No. 17 would have been published but for the injunction.

Devonshire T. | Monday afternoon

My Dear Mitton

No. 18 of Parley's is out with this Inscription on the front "that for reasons stated on the back, No. 17 will not be published until next week."[6] If you have not seen this, will you let one of your people buy a Copy. The wording of the notice *may* serve our end.

Faithfully Ever
CD

[1] Mitton would have heard from Cross of Lee & Haddock's intention to move for the dissolution of the injunction.

[2] The issue of 25 Dec 43 had over five columns of summary and extensive quotation from the *Carol*—virtually an abridgement of the story. The suggestion may have been that this was no worse than Lee and Haddock's piracy.

[3] Unidentified; clearly concerning one of CD's earlier works published by Chapman & Hall.

[4] A legal fair copy of "Observations by Mr. Charles Dickens", undated (MS Mr Shuckburgh), probably embodies the notes CD then made. It includes notes on the few minor differences between the original and the piracy, as well as a list of 32 parallel passages, given as "fair specimens". The notes do not appear to have been used in the hearing of 18 Jan.

[5] Mitton may have been looking at the long extracts from *American Notes* in *Parley's Penny Library*, Oct–Dec 42; or, if "them" means pirates in general, the passages in some other piracy.

[6] No. 16 broke off in Stave III at the introduction of the goose (Talfourd's address at the hearing of 11 Jan: Jaques, *CD in Chancery*, p. 69); No. 17 would have contained the rest of the work. Lee's affidavit of 16 Jan shows that it had already been printed for publication on 13 Jan (Jaques, p. 74).

To GEORGE BERGER, [16 JANUARY 1844]

Mention in *To* Mitton, 17 Jan 44.

To JOHN FORSTER, 17 JANUARY 1844

Text from F, IV, i, 300.

DEVONSHIRE LODGE,[1] *Seventeenth of January*, 1844. FELLOW COUNTRY-MEN![2] The appeal with which you have honoured me, awakens within my breast emotions that are more easily to be imagined than described. Heaven bless you. I shall indeed be proud, my friends, to respond to such a requisition. I had withdrawn from Public Life—I fondly thought for ever—to pass the evening of my days in hydropathical pursuits, and the contemplation of virtue. For which latter purpose, I had bought a looking-glass.—But, my friends, private feeling must ever yield to a stern sense of public duty. The Man is lost in the Invited Guest, and I comply. Nurses, wet and dry; apothecaries; mothers-in-law; babbies;[3] with all the sweet (and chaste) delights of private life; these, my countrymen, are hard to leave. But you have called me forth, and I will come. Fellow countrymen, your friend and faithful servant, CHARLES DICKENS.

To THOMAS MITTON, 17 JANUARY 1844*

MS Berg Collection.

Devonshire Terrace | Seventeenth January 1844.

My Dear Mitton

First and foremost, I enclose a letter from "the Defendant Berger"[4] marked "Gammon", and an answer thereunto, marked "Spinach", which was posted before 8 this morning.

The Boston Dinner was on the 1st. of February 1842. The name of the gentleman who produced the Piracy, is Doctor Palfrey.[5]

I made the enquiry of Forster as I came home last night whether I had ever mentioned the receipt of such a book as Hewitt's to him. Without making it matter of recollection, at all, he distinctly says as a point of fact that he is certain I never did, and that he never saw or heard of any such thing. Considering that I never mentioned it to you either, and that you were both so much here, immediately before my going to America, I believe said Hewitt lies.[6]

---

[1] The name "Lodge" for a house was regarded as slightly pretentious; a reference to Hood's new house is unlikely. Compare "Gammon Lodge" in *To* Forster, 23 June 38 (Vol. I, p. 406).

[2] Maclise, Stanfield and Forster, who had invited him to dine with them at Richmond (F, *ibid*).

[3] Francis Jeffrey, born 15 Jan.

[4] The publishers made no further move after the interim injunction; Berger's letter was probably irrelevant personal abuse.

[5] John Gorham Palfrey, editor of the *North American Review*; the matter is not referred to in CD's 1842 letters.

[6] The printer, Richard Lee, had moved to dissolve the injunction on 16 Jan and in

But I should be uneasy if I swore that too strongly. To say nothing of its having occurred to me as being just barely and wildly possible that I *might* have written even, acknowledging the receipt of some book called Parley's Something or other—really without knowing what it contained—and that a Vagabond like this, may actually have such a letter to produce. I should therefore like you to alter the affidavit to this effect—"But this Deponent has *Great Doubts* of the correctness of that part" &c—"and founds his doubts upon the following circumstances &c". And then after they are all stated, and after the words "before or since", Insert this. "At the same time this Deponent is bound to admit that he is at all times in the constant receipt of very strange communications and that it is possible though not as he considers probable that the said book may have been sent to him as aforesaid and may have reached his hands and may have been by him immediately laid aside or hastily thrown into the fire as an impertinence. But he again saith that although he has a good memory he has no recollection whatever of any such circumstance as that deposed to by the said Hewitt and certainly never possessed himself of the contents of any such book otherwise than as aforesaid at Boston in America."[1]

This will reserve the distinct charge of falsehood for his other Lie,[2] & will be better every way.

At what time?

Affecy. always
CD.

To DR F. H. F. QUIN,[3] [?17 JANUARY 1844]

Text from Edward Hamilton, *A Memoir of Frederick Hervey Foster Quin M.D.*, privately printed, 1879, p. 50. *Date:* soon after 15 Jan ("new babby") and before CD had progressed far with Feb No., still in progress Sat 20 Jan: see *To* Lady Holland, that day. Not 18 or 19 Jan as "Friday" mentioned.

Devonshire Terrace.

My dear Quin,

You know as I am of a convivial turn, and should be delighted to dine with

his affidavit (Jaques, *CD in Chancery*, pp. 71–4) it was claimed that a copy of the first volume of *Parley's Penny Library*, containing abridgments of *The Old Curiosity Shop* and *Barnaby Rudge* and with a printed dedication to CD (see Vol. III, p. 410*n*), had been sent to CD before Christmas 1841, with "an autograph inscription of his this Deponent's respectful compliments to the plaintiff". This was confirmed by Hewitt's affidavit (Jaques, *op. cit.*, p. 76) where the copy was said to have been delivered by Hewitt's son. In his affidavit of 17 Jan (Jaques, pp. 82–4) CD said that in Feb 42 Dr Palfrey of Boston showed him a copy of a piracy of *The Old Curiosity Shop*, but that he looked at it only cursorily and did not know whether it was a copy of *Parley's*. But CD is disingenuous; whether or not Hewitt sent him a copy, he had procured one by 30 Dec 42 and consulted Talfourd about whether action could be taken on it: see *To* Talfourd, of that date, Vol. III, p. 410 and *n*.

[1] These alterations were not made.

[2] Lee's contention that the piracy showed so many differences from the *Carol* that it could not be, as charged, a "colourable imitation".

[3] Frederic Hervey Foster Quin, MD (1799–1878; *DNB*), homoeopathic physician: see Vol. I, p. 489*n*.

you on Friday, but I have a cold in my head, a new babby in the house, six chancery suits on my hands, and my next number unborn and unbegotten.

Distractedly yours,

Rebecca.[1]

To WILLIAM SCHOLEFIELD, 17 JANUARY 1844*

MS Cornell University Library.

Devonshire Terrace | Seventeenth January 1844.

Dear Sir

I shall be happy to preside at the Birmingham Meeting, or to do anything (in an honest way) that the Committee desire.

Faithfully Yours

William Scholefield Esquire

CHARLES DICKENS

To THOMAS MITTON, 18 JANUARY 1844

MS Chas J. Sawyer Ltd.

Devonshire Terrace | Eighteenth January 1844.

My Dear Mitton.

I am not at all clear about that: being naturally averse to putting any one over Talfourd's head.[2] If I retained Wilde[3] (after consultation with Talfourd to prevent his being against us, if T thinks right, and *without any kind of suggestion from me*) I would retain the next best Queen's Counsel junior to Talfourd, also, and have three of them. The extra fee makes very little difference.

Why can't it be in the Queen's Bench.[4] Lord Denman[5] really likes me, and has an interest in me. He is a man of the world, and would be better up to their "Literary" witnesses than Tindal,[6] I think.

I wish to God you would come *here*, from Westminster, and take what you can get, in the Study, for dinner. You and Kate must join hands when she is

---

[1] The "Rebecca riots" were again in the news.

[2] After the hearing, CD had evidently left Mitton at the court, and received from him the news that the defendants had chosen to exercise their right. CD determined to bring a common law action against them (Jaques, *CD in Chancery*, pp. 46–7); with this in mind, he and Mitton were considering retaining extra counsel.

[3] Thomas Wilde, Lord Truro (1782–1855; *DNB*), Attorney General under Melbourne in 1841; became Lord Chancellor 1850.

[4] Reports of similar cases show that such a choice was possible.

[5] Thomas, Lord Denman (1779–1854; *DNB*), Lord Chief Justice since 1832: see Vol. II, p. 259*n*. He was connected by marriage with Joanna Baillie and with Macaulay, and had many literary friends, including Rogers and Talfourd; was among the distinguished guests whom CD was anxious not to disappoint by cancelling the large dinner-party of 1 June 44: see *To* Forster, 28 May.

[6] Sir Nicholas Conyngham Tindal (1776–1846; *DNB*), Chief Justice of the Common Pleas; had tried Norton *v.* Melbourne in 1836, and was admired for his impartiality, good sense, and accurate knowledge.

about again, and I see no reason why we should make any further difficulty of a bad business from beginning to end.[1]

Affecy. always
CD.

To JOHN FORSTER, [18 JANUARY 1844]

Extract in F, IV, iii, 321. *Date:* 18 Jan, "after leaving the court", according to Forster.

The pirates are beaten flat. They are bruised, bloody, battered, smashed, squelched, and utterly undone. Knight Bruce would not hear Talfourd, but instantly gave judgment. He had interrupted Anderdon constantly by asking him to produce a passage which was not an expanded or contracted idea from my book. And at every successive passage he cried out, "That is Mr. Dickens's case. Find another!" He said that there was not a shadow of doubt upon the matter. That there was no authority which would bear a construction in their favour; the piracy going beyond all previous instances. They might mention it again in a week, he said, if they liked, and might have an issue if they pleased; but they would probably consider it unnecessary after that strong expression of his opinion.[2] Of course I will stand by what we have agreed as to the only terms of compromise with the printers. I am determined that I will have an apology for their affidavits.[3] The other men may pay their costs and get out of it, but I will stick to my friend the author.[4]

[1] There is no other evidence of this estrangement between Mitton and Catherine.

[2] Lee's motion to dissolve the injunction came before Knight Bruce on 18 Jan. Thomas Oliver Anderdon (1786–1856), QC and bencher of Lincoln's Inn, and Charles John Shebbeare were Lee's counsel. After their speeches Knight Bruce gave judgment dismissing the motion without hearing Talfourd. It was still open to the defendant to force the plaintiff to submit his case to a jury if he acted within a week, but the injunction must be continued pending the common law action.

[3] Besides those of Lee and Henry Hewitt, there were affidavits from George Stiff, the artist (1807–74), who supplied three plates (described as "a very bad wood engraver, earning little more than a pound a week", until in 1844 he succeeded in launching the *London Journal* without any capital or credit but with the aid of "a specious tongue": Henry Vizetelly, *Glances back through Seventy Years*, 1893, II, 10–12); George Mudie, one-time editor of the *Sun*, and Edward Litt (Leman) Blanchard (see *To* Blanchard, 29 Jan); the two latter giving evidence as literary men. Mudie claimed that the piracy could not be mistaken for the original, would appeal to quite a different class of purchaser, and would benefit the author—as he said the *Parley's* version of *The Old Curiosity Shop* had done—by "enhancing the demand" for his works; Blanchard took the same line (Jaques, *CD in Chancery*, pp. 77–82).

[4] Henry Hewitt. In his affidavit he claimed that besides the "defects and inconsistencies" in CD's *Carol* pointed out to him by Lee, he himself had "detected so many others as to induce him in numerous instances to abandon the plot" and substitute "a more artistical style of expression and of incident". Moreover he believed that CD had "however unconsciously been indebted to the critical remarks" made on his writings by Hewitt in *Parley's Library* "for the germ of more than one of his productions", and that for "the material of his 'Christmas Carol'" CD was heavily indebted to the works of Washington Irving (Jaques, *op. cit.*, pp. 75–7).

To T. J. SERLE, [18] JANUARY 1844

MS Mr Peter Brandt. *Date:* Thurs was 18 Jan; presumably the day rather than the date is correct.

Devonshire Terrace | Thursday January Nineteen | 1844.

My Dear Serle.

My individual opinion is distinctly opposed to the settlement of Miss Angell's claim.[1] No such thing was contemplated by the donors of the Money. And if we have run a risk in respect of Fifty Pounds, that is no reason, to me, for making it Seventy.

The family seems to be of an odd kind, and especially liable to odd influences. I shall take an opinion about the possibility of any one among them who may have less of the Fund than another, putting me into chancery one of these fine days, before I formally accept my Trustee Ship.

I don't value M'Ian's idea that nobody else would come forward if we paid Miss Angell—one peppercorn. He is a very good fellow, and I like him much. But if there be two commodities with which he is especially unfurnished, I should say they were judgment and discretion.

We must formally debate Miss A, and vote pro and con, when we meet. At Forsters let it be.

Yours up to his eyes in work

CD

To THOMAS MITTON, [19 JANUARY 1844]*

MS Huntington Library. *Date:* clearly the day before the publication of Mitton's letter to the press: see *fn*; handwriting supports.

Devonshire Terrace | Friday Morng

My Dear Mitton

Turn over leaf. If you should think it right to send that letter, will you do so? If the mistakes be repeated in any other paper, it should go to that paper too.[2]

---

[1] Miss Angell, an actress from Edinburgh, was acting at the Lyceum at about this time; presumably she claimed that Elton had borrowed money from her. Marshall (*Lives of the Most Celebrated Actors and Actresses*, p. 153n) called her "this would-be actress" and hinted at other objections ("we could add much more, but . . . no particle can possibly redound to her credit").

[2] The following letter was evidently sent to the *Morning Herald*, *Morning Post*, *Morning Chronicle*, *The Times*, and probably to other papers: "Sir,—In your report of the proceedings in the court of his Honour Vice-Chancellor Knight Bruce, yesterday, the 18th inst., one or two errors are to be found, which, as the solicitor of the plaintiff, I am desirous of correcting. | In the first place, the cause in which a motion to dissolve the injunction was yesterday made was that of 'Dickens v. Lee and Haddock' (the printers and proprietors of the publication in which the alleged piracy of my client's work is contained), not in the suit against 'Berger', who is one of the publishers thereof. Secondly, acquiescence on the part of Mr. Dickens in previous piracies of any of his works, was distinctly denied by Mr. Dickens on affidavit, and that denial was expressly referred to by the Court on giving judgment, in terms which could leave no doubt but that such alleged acquiescence was

The brief and Short Hand Writer's Notes,[1] deliver to Topping,[2] separate from your note to me. I want him to leave them at Forster's, that he may read them.

Faithfully Ever

CD.

Any time between this and 8 at night, will do for the Newspapers.

To JOHN FORSTER, [20 JANUARY 1844]

Extract in F, IV, iii, 321–2. *Date:* "two days later" than letter of ?18 Jan according to Forster.

The farther affidavits put in by way of extenuation by the printing rascals *are* rather strong, and give one a pretty correct idea of what the men must be who hold on by the heels of literature.[3] Oh! the agony of Talfourd at Knight Bruce's not hearing him! He had sat up till three in the morning, he says, preparing his speech; and would have done all kinds of things with the affidavits. It certainly was a splendid subject. We have heard nothing from the vagabonds yet.[4] I once thought of printing the affidavits without a word of comment, and sewing them up with *Chuzzlewit*. Talfourd is strongly disinclined to compromise with the printers[5] on any terms. In which case it would be referred to the master[6] to ascertain what profits had been made by the piracy, and to order the same to be paid to me. But wear and tear of law is my consideration.

disbelieved by the Court. And, lastly, so far from his Honour *directing* an action to be brought—as your reporter has it—a week's time was given the defendants to make up their minds 'as to whether they would risk the result of an action after the strong expression they had heard of his Honour's opinion.' | I am, Sir, your obedient servant, | THOMAS MITTON | 23, Southampton-buildings, Chancery-lane, | January 19, 1844." The *Herald* and *Post* published the letter on Sat 20 Jan; the *Chronicle* had a note "To Correspondents. *The letter of* Mr. Mitton *has been referred to the Reporter*", and on 24 Jan merely corrected the name from Berger to Lee; *The Times* waited until Mon 22 Jan and then had the following paragraph in its Law Report: "DICKENS v. BERGER | The motion reported in The Times . . . as having been made in this cause should have been headed as in 'Dickens v. Lee.' In the judgment given by his Honour, he said that acquiescence on the part of the plaintiff, as attempted by the defendants,

had failed. The Court gave the defendants a week's time to determine whether they would elect to bring an action". The original report in *The Times* (19 Jan; reproduced by Jaques, pp. 84–8) was much the fullest, and in spite of the "mistakes", made it clear that Knight Bruce's judgment was strongly against the pirates' case, whereas all other reports (several of them identical in wording) omitted his interruptions of Anderdon's speech and even left the outcome ambiguous; none suggested the crushing defeat of the pirates as reflected in CD's account to Forster.

[1] i.e. the brief of the Bill in Chancery and the notes of the hearing on 18 Jan.

[2] William Topping, CD's groom: see Vol. II, p. 42*n.*

[3] The affidavits supporting Lee's sworn on 16 and 17 Jan: see *To* Forster, ?18 Jan, *fns.*

[4] The four publishers.

[5] Lee & Haddock.

[6] The Master of the Rolls, one of the five Chancery Judges.

To LADY HOLLAND,[1] 20 JANUARY 1844*

MS The Earl of Ilchester.

Devonshire Terrace. | Twentieth January 1844

Dear Lady Holland.

Pray do not think me neglectful, in not having answered your kind note before now. Certain vagabonds have recently produced a flagrant and most audacious piracy of the Carol; and being resolved to put it down, I plunged immediately into *Six* Chancery Suits.[2] One is usually considered very good measure, in respect of irritation and anxiety; but half a dozen at a time have quite a powerful effect, I assure you.

I have come off victorious in all points yet decided, but have been busying myself so much in getting up the case that I have delayed my Monthly Work beyond all precedent, and am now, and have been since the receipt of your note, in the full tide of it. This is the real occasion of my not having seen you; and this prevents me from having the pleasure of accepting your kind Invitation to Dinner on Sunday.[3] I shall not fail to call upon you as soon as I have finished; and I hope to be at large again, on Wednesday.

Mrs. Dickens begs me to say, that she is much gratified by your enquiries; and that she is as well as it is possible to be. We had some apprehensions beforehand, as she was exceedingly depressed and frightened; but thank God that all passed off before the reality.

I took Serjeant Talfourd out of his own Court,[4] to lead my Chancery cases. Knight Bruce, who was the Judge, understood the matter so perfectly, and appreciated the Piracy so well, that he did not require to hear Talfourd at all. Which I think was a prodigious disappointment to the Serjeant who had made up his mind for a great speech.

I am always Dear Lady Holland | Yours faithfully and obliged

The Lady Holland.
CHARLES DICKENS

To MRS PROCTER,[5] 22 JANUARY 1844*

MS Benoliel Collection.

Devonshire Terrace
Monday Twenty Second January | 1844.

My Dear Mrs. Procter

Your kind note coming in, met, or might have met, a man in spectacles[6] going

[1] Elizabeth Vassall Fox (1770–1845; *DNB*), wife of the 3rd Baron Holland: see Vol. I, p. 412*n* and Vol. II, p. 63*n*.

[2] There were five suits, but six defendants.

[3] The nine guests listed in the Dinner Book (MS BM) included Hallam, Edwin Landseer, and Rogers, who were regular guests.

[4] The Court of Common Pleas.

[5] Anne Procter (1799–1888), daughter of Captain Thomas Skepper and Anne Dorothea (afterwards the third wife of Basil Montagu); married Bryan Waller Procter 1824; well known as the witty hostess of a wide literary circle. Had known Charles Lamb, and is "the pretty A.S." of his "Oxford in the Vacation"; an early friend of Carlyle, also of Thackeray, Forster, Milnes—indeed "everybody of

out. And *to* the man in spectacles, the unhappy writer hereof had said "Dine with me on Sunday next at 6."—to which the man in spectacles made answer, "Yes! I will!" Moreover the man in spectacles said he would bring his sister. For which, may my curse—a father's curse—!

At this crisis the five children are borne in. They twine themselves about my legs; the nurse seizes my outstretched arm; I relax—look upon my offspring —become penitent—burst into tears. At the same moment the man with the spectacles, happening to come back for his gloves (which he left behind him) looks in at the cottage window. He raises his arm and eyes, as invoking a blessing upon the family. I am heard to sob "My Love to Procter",[1] and the Curtain comes down very slowly.

Faithfully Yours always
CHARLES DICKENS

Mrs. Procter.

To DOUGLAS JERROLD,[2] 23 JANUARY 1844

Extract in Parke-Bernet Galleries catalogue, Feb 1963; *MS* 3 pp.; dated Devonshire Terrace, 23 Jan 44.

Enclosing something unidentified[3] *which he had intended to send to Jerrold out of town; because of delays, he is now sending it to him on his return.* Forster tells me that Bradbury told him that you are "discharged cured".[4] Is it true? I have faith in Hydropathy[5] myself—drink cold water night and morning—and pour it down my back besides . . . I can't tell you how often I read, Brown, Jones, and Robin-

any literary pretension whatever seemed to flow in and out of the house" (Bessie Rayner Belloc, *In a Walled Garden*, 1895, p. 162). A. W. Kinglake, who had studied law with Procter, dedicated *Eothen* to her in 1844 as "Our Lady of Bitterness". According to Fanny Kemble, she and Procter were "an incomparable compound"; "she was like a fresh lemon,— golden, fragrant, firm, and wholesome,— and he was like the honey of Hymettus" (*Records of a Girlhood*, 1878, II, 277). CD had known them since at least 1837: see Vol. I, p. 314*n*.

6 Unidentified.

1 Bryan Waller Procter (1787–1874; *DNB*), writer and lawyer: see Vol. I, p. 314*n* and Vol. III, p. 531*n*.

2 Douglas William Jerrold (1803–57; *DNB*), writer and wit: see Vol. I, p. 192*n*.

3 Doubtless a copy of the *Carol*; Jerrold's copy was a 3rd edn, published by 20 Jan.

4 Jerrold was ill again with rheumatism in Nov 43 and according to Blanchard Jerrold, went to Malvern to take the watercure with beneficial results: "The bent, immovable figure that left us, to submit to the water cure, came back happily into Park Village with a light, easy step" (*Life of Douglas Jerrold*, 1859, p. 304). He was there again in 1846 and wrote "Life at the Cold Brandy-and-Water Cure" for *Punch*, 19 Dec.

5 This method of treatment was introduced from Grafenberg in Austria; centres were set up at Malvern by Dr James Wilson and Dr James Manby Gully in 1842, and flourished for some 30 years. Other well-known patients were Bulwer Lytton (in 1844), Darwin, and Carlyle. Tennyson visited a hydropathic establishment at Cheltenham in the winter of 1843, and another at Malvern in 1848.

son,[1] whereunto I solemnly called Horne's[2] attention[3] t'other day. It is full of melancholy and pain to me, but its truth and wisdom are prodigious.[4]

To MISS HANNAH MEREDITH, 24 JANUARY 1844*

MS Morgan Library.

Devonshire Terrace. | Twenty Fourth January 1844.

My Dear Miss Meredith

Will you kindly let me know, by a brief verbal message, how Miss Coutts really is.[5] I need not offer an apology to you, for wishing to hear as an anxious friend, and not as a formal caller.

Always Believe me | Faithfully Yours

Miss Meredith   CHARLES DICKENS

To ARTHUR RYLAND,[6] 24 JANUARY 1844*

MS Benoliel Collection. *Address:* Arthur Ryland Esquire | Birmingham.

London. 1 Devonshire Terrace | York Gate Regents Park
Twenty Fourth January | 1844.

Sir.

Let me thank you cordially, for your earnest and welcome communication in reference to my little Christmas Carol. It has given me real pleasure, I assure you.

Faithfully Yours

Arthur Ryland Esquire   CHARLES DICKENS

To SIR EDWARD BULWER LYTTON,[7] 25 JANUARY 1844

MS Lytton Papers.

Athenaeum.
Thursday afternoon | Twenty Fifth January 1844.

My Dear Sir Edward.

I received your kind cheque yesterday, in behalf of the Elton Family; and am much indebted to you on their behalf.

---

[1] Jerrold's story appeared in the *New Monthly*, Sep–Nov 37, and in *Cakes and Ale*, 1842, of which he gave CD a copy in May 43 (see Vol. III, p. 481 and *n*).

[2] Richard Henry ("Hengist") Horne (1803–84; *DNB*), poet and journalist: see Vol. III, p. 578*n*.

[3] It is mentioned at the end of the passage on Jerrold in *A New Spirit of the Age*, 1844, I, 303–4, as illustrating "the deep importance of national education".

[4] Brown, Jones, and Robinson, three schoolfellows, all come to a bad end through applying the precepts of a harsh schoolmaster who himself ends in the workhouse. CD's response testifies more to his concern with the subject of education than the quality of the story.

[5] After the death of Sir Francis Burdett on 23 Jan. This had come as a shock, his condition having worsened rapidly. There were rumours that hydropathic treatment, not approved of by Miss Coutts, was partly responsible; this was denied in a letter to *The Times* from Dr Edward Johnson (27 Jan).

[6] Arthur Ryland (1807–77), solicitor in Birmingham; Mayor 1860; founded 1853

Pray do not believe that the least intentional neglect has prevented me from calling on you, or that I am not sincerely desirous to avail myself of any opportunity of cultivating your friendship. I venture to say this to you in an unaffected and earnest spirit, and I hope it will not be displeasing to you.

At the time when you called[1] and for many weeks afterwards, I was so closely occupied with my little Carol (the idea of which had just occurred to me) that I never left home before the owls went out; and led quite a solitary life. When I began to have a little time, and to go abroad again, I knew that you were in affliction, and I then thought it better to wait, even before I left a card at your door, until the pressure of your distress had passed.[2]

I fancy a reproachful spirit in your note—possibly because I know that I may appear to deserve it. But *do* let me say to you that it would give me real pain to retain the idea that there was any coldness between us, and that it would give me heartfelt satisfaction to know the reverse.

I shall make a personal descent[3] upon you before Sunday, in the hope of telling you this myself. But I cannot rest easy without writing it also. And if this should lead to a better knowledge in each of us, of the other, believe me that I shall always look upon it as something I have long wished for.

Always Faithfully Yours
CHARLES DICKENS

Sir Edward Bulwer.

To THEODORE COMPTON,[4] 26 JANUARY 1844

Text from N, I, 563.

1 Devonshire Terrace, York Gate, Regents Park
Twenty-Sixth January 1844

Sir,

I beg to acknowledge the receipt of your letter together with a copy of the address of the National Temperance Society.

Believe me that I honour and esteem the efforts of the honest advocates of

the Birmingham and Midland Institute, with which was amalgamated the Polytechnic (founded 1843: see *To* Thompson, 28 Feb 44). CD gave readings of the *Carol* and the *Cricket* in Dec 53 in aid of its funds: see *To* Ryland, 16 Jan 54 (N, II, 536).

[7] Edward George Earle Lytton Bulwer Lytton (1803–73; *DNB*), writer and politician: see Vol. I, p. 337*n*. On succeeding to the Knebworth estates under his mother's will Bulwer took the surname of Lytton. In May 46 Forster became one of his trustees in place of Henry Arthur Hoare who had withdrawn.

[1] Presumably in Oct 43.

[2] His mother Elizabeth Barbara Bulwer Lytton died 19 Dec 43; anxiety and "the crushing grief, for the loss of my nearest & dearest friend", added to overwork, had affected his health, which by Jan was thoroughly shattered. In June he went to Malvern to take the water-cure, which was successful (Bulwer *to* Macready, 29 June 44: *Bulwer and Macready*, ed. C. H. Shattuck, University of Illinois Press, 1958, p. 224, and Lytton's "Confessions and Observations of a Water Patient", *New Monthly Magazine*, LXXV, Sep 45).

[3] At his town residence, 36A Hertford St.

[4] Theodore Compton, a Quaker, and Secretary of the National Temperance Society; the second Anniversary Meeting of the Society was held 21 May 44.

Temperance, and am convinced that they have been productive of inestimable benefits to society. But in restraining Drunkards, I do not see the wisdom or the justice of depriving sober men of that which *moderately used*, is undoubtedly a cheerful, social, harmless, pleasant thing—often tending to kindness of feeling and openness of heart. If I were a Drunkard, I would take the pledge. If I had a drunkard in my family or service I would urge him by all means to do the like. But I can no more concur in the philosophy of reducing all mankind to one total abstainment level, than I can yield to that monstrous doctrine which sets down as the *consequences* of Drunkenness, fifty thousand miseries which are, as all reflective persons know, and daily see, the wretched *causes* of it.

Those who insist upon total abstinence shut me out from the possibility of helping them. I will gladly add my small subscription to your funds if I could do so, consistently with the principle I maintain, that all sober men should be left in possession of their sober enjoyments—of which there are not so many in this world of six working days to one day's rest, that we can afford to diminish them lightly. But you won't have that. You require me to bind myself to an unreasonable adaptation to all sorts and conditions of men, of one sweeping measure. And I am quite serious in saying that I cannot get it into my mind, that this is just or wise.[1]

The position that Beer, Spirits, and Wine are not natural to man, is poor and unfair. Shew me any Total Abstainer at his dinner and I will shew you fifty things making their way into his digestive organs, which are as foreign to his natural condition as the clothes he wears.

The certificate of the medical Gentleman bearing testimony to the injurious effects of even the most temperate use of liquor, might be applied with equal truth to scores of eatables in which I see my total abstaining friends continually revelling.

I am, Sir, | Yours faithfully, and obliged

[CHARLES DICKENS]

To W. B. HODGSON,[2] 26 JANUARY 1844*

MS B. H. Blackwell Ltd.

Devonshire Terrace | Twenty Sixth January 1844.

Dear Sir.

Let me thank you for your valuable addition to the kind letter of Mr. Yates.[3] I have answered it by this day's post.

Faithfully Yours

CHARLES DICKENS

W. B. Hodgson Esquire

[1] CD expressed similar views on the Temperance movement in *To* Mrs Child, 28 Dec 42: see Vol. III, p. 403.

[2] William Ballantyne Hodgson (1815–80; *DNB*), educationist and writer; secretary of the Liverpool Mechanics' Institute 1844, and Principal 1844–7.

[3] Almost certainly Richard Vaughan Yates (1785–1856), younger brother of Joseph Brooks Yates and of John Ashton Yates MP (see *To* Mrs CD, 26 Feb 44, *fn*), one of the founders of the Institute (*Memorials of the Family of the Rev. John Yates*, collected by Samuel Ashton Thompson Yates, privately printed, 1890).

To [R. V.] YATES, 26 JANUARY 1844

Mention in last.

To MRS CARLYLE,[1] 27 JANUARY 1844

MS National Library of Scotland.

Devonshire Terrace
Twenty Seventh January 1844.

My Dear Mrs. Carlyle.

Your note has no date; but if it had, I fear the figures would look reproach-fully upon a man of modest merit like myself. So I am very glad it has not. I should have written to you long ago, but have been so much engaged in another kind of Penmanship, that I have not answered a letter this fortnight. Yours is the thirty eighth in the batch. Forgive me!

I don't know how it was, but I certainly did most strongly suspect the ex-pediency of taking that story about our friend,[2] quite literally, when you and I were audience to the same. And consequently I did not back a vague suggestion thrown out by Titmarsh, touching a Subscription List in behalf of its unfor-tunate subject.[3] Perhaps it arose from my knowledge of the man (meaning Robertson) the tendency of whose manner certainly is to impress one with the idea that he is in the last stage of fasting, and exists upon the very smallest independence that can be stated in figures. I had picked him up one day in Bond Street, not long before; and such a watery, washed-out, vapid old rag of

[1] Jane Welsh Carlyle, *née* Welsh (1801–66; *DNB*), married Thomas Carlyle 1826: see Vol. II, p. 141*n*. From 1834 they lived at 5 Cheyne Row, Chelsea; Hunt, Forster, the Macreadys, Tennyson, and Thackeray were among their friends. Masson, meeting her first in 1843, remembered her as "fragile . . . very dark" with "large, soft, and lustrous eyes"; "one of the most brilliant of witty talkers . . . her most characteristic vein was . . . the satirical narrative . . . She could make a pic-turesque and witty story out of anything whatever" (David Masson, *Memories of London in the 'Forties*, 1908, pp. 36–9). CD, though always on good terms with the Carlyles, was not intimate; Jane Carlyle dined at the Dickenses' for the first time in 1849. But they had met at several parties, such as Nina Macready's on 26 Dec 43.

[2] John Robertson (?1811–75), journalist; educated at Aberdeen and Glasgow Uni-versities; called to the bar at Lincoln's Inn; reporter on the *Morning Chronicle*, and assisted J. S. Mill on the *Westminster*

Review 1837–40. He had been honorary secretary of the Society of British Authors in 1843: see Vol. III, p. 477*n*.

[3] Thackeray's story of how he had (as Jane Carlyle told her cousin) "put five shillings into Robertson's hand one night in the idea that he was reduced to the last 'extremity of fate'!! and then (what was much more inexcusable) told Dickens and myself of the transaction before witnesses in Mrs. Macready's drawing room!"— presumably on 26 Dec when all three were guests at Nina Macready's birthday party. Jane Carlyle had later heard Robertson's own account of his "total bewilderment as to what Thackeray designed him *to do* with the said shillings!" and how he called twice "to return them and ask the mean-ing", but in vain, as Thackeray had gone to Paris (which he did on 1 Jan). Having learnt the facts, Jane Carlyle "thought it but fair" to Robertson "to set his case in the right light to Dickens" (Jane Carlyle *to* Jeannie Welsh, 15 Feb 44: *Letters to her Family 1839–1863*, ed. Leonard Huxley, 1924, p. 189).

humanity, never presented itself before my mental vision. A bottle of wine left without a cork for twelve months—a vat full of Ginger Beer without the effervescing quality—an Atlantic of the feeblest milk and water, lukewarm—are figures of speech, perfectly inadequate to the expression of my feelings concerning the Projector of the Great Literary Association. I fancy that if I met him in the street within five minutes after his receiving an announcement of somebody having left him twenty thousand pounds, I should feel disposed (looking upon that meek face, and observing the gasp and struggle, which precedes all his codfish-like attempts at speech), to press half a crown into his hand, wring it, burst into tears, and run away.

I really, therefore, am not surprised at Thackeray's having, in perfect good feeling, mistaken him. But I quite agree with you that he ought to have been very sure indeed, before mentioning such a circumstance even to yourself and me.

Your countrywoman is going on very favorably—though with Northern caution and slowness. She sends her love, and hopes to come and see you as soon as she is well.

Remember me affectionately to Carlyle. I am glad he saw that American General.[1] I am quite serious when I say that it is *impossible*, following them in their own direction, to caricature that people. I lay down my pen in despair sometimes when I read what I have done, and find how it halts behind my own recollection.[2]

The Guinea Pig is dead! He left it in his will that he believed conjuring had done it; but that he forgave his enemies, and died (he was a very small Pig you know) believing in the whole Bench of Bishops.—Always Faithfully Yours

CHARLES DICKENS

To MACVEY NAPIER,[3] 27 JANUARY 1844

MS British Museum.

Athenaeum | Twenty Seventh January 1844

My Dear Sir

A very intimate and valued friend of mine—Mr. Forster, the author of the Lives of the Statesmen of The Commonwealth: who does the literary portion of Fonblanque's[4] paper, the Examiner—is desirous of propounding to you a subject

[1] General Baird. He had been brought to the Carlyles by Henry Colman, Henry James, senior, being also of the party. Jane Carlyle thought the General "the very image of Mr. Pecksniff . . . His ample breast was covered with a white waistcoat—open very far down to shew the *brooch* in his shirt—hair set round with pearls—the whole thing about the size of a five-shilling piece! He seemed . . . a living confirmation of Dickens's satires on the American *great men*" (Jane Carlyle *to* Jeannie Welsh, Jan 44, *op. cit.*, p. 177).

[2] No. XII of *Chuzzlewit*, including the last "American" chapters (Chs 33–4), had appeared on 1 Jan.

[3] Macvey Napier, FRS (1776–1847; *DNB*), editor of the *Edinburgh Review*: see Vol. II, p. 315*n*.

[4] Albany Fonblanque (1793–1872; *DNB*), editor of the *Examiner* 1830–47: see Vol. I, p. 205*n*.

on which he wishes to write an article for the Edinburgh;[1] and has asked me to make him known to you. What is the best mode of doing so? Shall I ask you whether his notion is agreeable? or shall I tell him that he may consider himself introduced?

A word in reply, will oblige me.

I am thinking of my little paper,[2] and shall not fail to be punctual.

Always My Dear Sir | Faithfully Yours

Professor Napier.   CHARLES DICKENS

To LORD JEFFREY,[3] [?LATE JANUARY 1844]

Mention in Jeffrey *to* CD, 1 Feb 44; Lord Cockburn, *Life of Lord Jeffrey*, II, 382. *Date:* probably shortly before 1 Feb since Jeffrey is unlikely to have delayed in replying.

Asking Jeffrey to be godfather to his newly-born son and telling him that Catherine wished it.[4]

To LAMAN BLANCHARD, 29 JANUARY 1844

MS Benoliel Collection.

Devonshire Terrace
Monday Morning | January Twenty Nine 1844.

My Dear Blanchard

It was a joke of Forster's. He wanted me to play it off upon you, but I hadn't the heart.

When I went down to my Solicitor's, the first thing said, was, '*Who*[5] do you think has made an affidavit?'—'God knows. Bunn?'—'Your friend Mr. Blanchard'—'D——d nonsense'—'Oh but he has. And there an't two Laman

---

[1] Forster wrote to Napier on 12 Feb specifying the subject: "You may be aware that there have been some Chancery Proceedings lately in the matter of the *Christmas Carol*: and some affidavits in the case of a most extraordinary character (sworn by the opposite party) happening to come before me, I spoke to Mr. Dickens of the materials they offered for an article on the subject of Copyright and the strange class of low pirates, and so-called literary people, who here in London hang on the skirts of literature" (MS BM). Nothing

came of this project; but as a result of the introduction, Forster in Sep wrote an article on William Tooke's edition of Charles Churchill for the *Edinburgh*, published Jan 45; and also a review of *The Chimes* (see *To* Forster, ?3–4 Nov 44, *fn*).

[2] See Vol. III, pp. 565, 585.

[3] Francis Jeffrey, Lord Jeffrey (1773–1850; *DNB*): see Vol. I, p. 479*n*.

[4] Jeffrey accepted warmly, referring to the "most flattering wish . . . of that dear Kate of yours" (*ibid*).

[5] Underlined four times.

Blanchards, for I went down to Serjeant Talfourd's directly, and his clerk says there's only one, and it's your friend'.!!![1]

But you can't see the cream of the thing, without seeing the affidavit itself. Oh my stars!

I am in for it now; and I dare say (through the villainy of the Law, which after declaring me robbed, obliges me to bring an action against men from whom it demands no security for the expences to which I shall be put) am in a fair way to lose Three Hundred Pounds or so. Never mind. I declare War against the Black Flag; and down it shall come, if strong and constant hauling will do it.[2]

Here is the little book[3] my dear Blanchard, which pray put upon your shelves for the love of Yours always

Laman Blanchard Esquire

CHARLES DICKENS

To MRS S. C. HALL,[4] 29 JANUARY 1844*

MS Free Library of Philadelphia.

Devonshire Terrace
Monday Twenty Ninth January | 1844.

My Dear Mrs. Hall

I heartily wish you success in your new Undertaking.[5] There can be no doubt that if its high end be not too much insisted on, or held too prominently before the readers' eyes, it will do great good. And I think, myself, that the opening is a wide one with rich promise about it.

But I am sorry to add that journeying towards the same goal, I have different

---

[1] The Blanchard who had sworn the affidavit was Edward Litt (Leman) Blanchard (1820–89; *DNB*), of Clement's Inn, Strand, younger son of William Blanchard the actor; writer of farces, burlesques, pantomimes and penny-number novels. His *Life and Reminiscences*, based on his diaries, makes no mention of the *Carol* case, but shows that he was employed by Richard Lee to abridge three-volume novels for *Parley's Penny Library* and "used to get about 10s for 'potting' down these famous works" (*Life and Reminiscences*, 1891, I, 31*n*). He had added Leman to his name, probably to encourage confusion with Laman Blanchard; this had previously occurred over a *Bentley's* contribution (see Vol. I, p. 290), and again in 1842 when Laman Blanchard disclaimed authorship of one of his pieces at the Olympic (*The Times*, 28 Dec).

[2] At the further hearing of 25 Jan, Knight Bruce varied the injunction; it still restrained Lee & Haddock from "publishing, selling, or otherwise disposing of the Number containing the Commence-ment", but altered the clause, "from copying or imitating, in the whole or in part, the complainant's book", by removing the words "or imitating". Talfourd and Bacon then offered a settlement if the defendants would pay the costs and apologize; this was refused by Anderdon, who said that CD "must take his remedy at law". Knight Bruce ruled that the plaintiff must now bring a common law action within ten days for the invasion of his alleged copyright (Jaques, *CD in Chancery*, pp. 88–9). CD acted at once: his writ against Lee & Haddock is dated 29 Jan (see *To Mitton*, 10 Feb).

[3] The *Carol*, evidently forgotten on 6 Jan (see *To Blanchard*, 4 Jan).

[4] Anna Maria Hall, *née* Fielding (1800–81; *DNB*), writer, wife of S. C. Hall: see Vol. I, p. 481*n*.

[5] Mrs Hall had projected a new ladies' magazine and was soliciting contributions; Elizabeth Barrett and Tennyson were also approached. Nothing came of the plan, but in 1845 she began editing *Sharpe's London Magazine*.

paths before me, and cannot bear you company. The occupation I have at this
time on my hands, will keep me in employment until June; and after that, I have
a hope of working out some cherished projects which are almost as old as myself,
and which, if entered on, will be a twelvemonth's task.[1]

Kate desires her best regards to you, and Mr. Hall, and Mrs. Fielding.[2]
She has been going on slowly, but always well; and I hope has now begun to
stride in good seven-league earnest.[3]

I must come out one day, and see the little Elton's.[4] You promised to introduce me to Miss Rogers,[5] so I shall ring your bell, in the hope of not disturbing
you.

Dear Mrs. Hall. | Faithfully Yours
CHARLES DICKENS

To T. J. SERLE, 29 JANUARY 1844

MS Mr Peter Brandt.

Devonshire Terrace
Monday Morning January Twenty Nine | 1844.

My Dear Serle.

Have you done with my Maurice Morgann on Falstaff?[6] I want to lend it to
Charles Kemble.[7]

Is it not *one* Elton we wish to advertize for? I will do it at once, and head the
advertizement P R E M I U M[8]—which, in the critical language of the day,
looks rather "soul-stirring", I think?

Faithfully Always
CD.

T. J. Serle Esquire

[1] Presumably including "the story I
have in my mind" (*To* Forster, ?1 Nov 43:
see Vol. III, p. 588), which he designed to
write while abroad.

[2] Mrs Hall's mother, Sarah Elizabeth
Fielding (*c.* 1773–1856), who had lived
with her since 1826.

[3] "She is in the drawing room, and both
she and Baby . . . are getting on capitally",
Georgina told Beard next day; she expected Catherine to be dining downstairs
by CD's birthday, for which she was inviting Beard to dine with them and Forster.
Georgina wrote at CD's request, as he had
just gone to Bath "to dine with Mr.
Landor on his birthday" (*Dickens to his
Oldest Friend*, ed. W. Dexter, 1932, p.
272). Presumably Forster went to Bath
with CD; an additional reason would be
to discuss the publication of Landor's
collected works by Moxon. Landor's
assignment of the copyright of *Imaginary
Conversations* to Forster (Forster Collection, V & A) is dated 24 Jan 44.

[4] In Brompton, where the Halls lived.

[5] Unidentified.

[6] *Essay on the Dramatic Character of Sir
John Falstaff*; CD's copy was not in the
Gad's Hill library at his death.

[7] Charles Kemble (1775–1854; *DNB*),
actor; brother of Mrs Siddons; manager of
Covent Garden 1822–32; officially retired
1836 and made his last appearance on the
stage 1840; Examiner of plays 1836–40.
He began a very successful series of
Shakespeare readings in May 44. Forster
mentions "dear old Charles Kemble and
one or other of his daughters"—Fanny
Kemble and Adelaide Sartoris—as occasional visitors to Devonshire Terrace (F,
VI, vi, 529).

[8] Written large, in ornate capitals. The
advertisement was evidently of an unidentified Elton girl who was to be appren-
ticed; it has not been traced.

To MRS S. C. HALL, 1 FEBRUARY 1844†

MS Colonel Richard Gimbel.

Devonshire Terrace | First February 1844

My Dear Mrs. Hall.

I fear it is not possible for me to comply with your request. I quite understood it in the first instance as an expression of your wish that I would write some little paper for the first number only; and if my compliance merely involved the expenditure of so much time and thought as would be required for such a purpose, I would gladly do so. But similar entreaties have been at different times strongly urged upon me by other friends; and my reply, where I have any feeling of personal regard has always been "I do not wish to write in any Magazine, or think of doing so, but if I should, I will write something for you." Departing from my total abstinence in this respect, at all, *a*I should hold myself bound to assist Hood for instance in his hazardous enterprises:[1] inclining towards him with the interest of a private friend, and with the highest admiration of his powers. For scattered scraps of writing, here and there, I really have no leisure,*a* however; and the publication of one would, in honor and good faith, involve the necessity of publishing several.

*b*The lines I wrote for Lady Blessington, I gave her in redemption of a promise *four years old.b*[2] It is two years, since I pledged myself to write a paper for the Edinburgh;[3] and I have not yet done it; although it is not open to the same objection in anything like the same degree, as it would not bear my name.

I did not mention these things when I wrote to you last, because I was unwilling to parade them as reasons for my not doing what I really should like to do, and feel disposed to do. But this is the plain truth of my situation, and I see no way out of it, except to keep my strait waistcoat on—unless you can show me another.

My Dear Mrs. Hall | Always Faithfully Yours

Mrs. S. C. Hall.

CHARLES DICKENS

To S. R. STAREY,[4] 1 FEBRUARY 1844

MS Shaftesbury Society.

Devonshire Terrace | First February 1844.

Dear Sir

Will you have the goodness to turn over in your mind, and to note down for me as briefly as you please, any little facts or details connected with the Ragged School, which you think it would benefit the design to have publicly known?

---

aa; bb Given in N, I, 566 from catalogue source; letter otherwise unpublished.

[1] For Hood's difficulties with the first three Nos of his *Magazine*, see *To* Hood, ?1 Jan and *fn*, and *To* Ward, 26 Mar and *fn*.

[2] For *The Keepsake*: see Vol. III, p. 520 and *n*.

[3] During his visit in 1841: see Vol. II, pp. 373-4.

[4] Samuel Roberts Starey (*d.* 1904), Treasurer of Field Lane Ragged School: see Vol. III, p. 554*n*.

If you could make it convenient to favor me with a call any evening next week, or on Sunday Week, and will let me hear from you to that effect, I shall be glad to make an appointment with you. But pray do not hesitate to let me know what time suits you best, as I can easily accommodate myself to your engagements.

The kind of thing I wish to know is—your average number of scholars— whether it increases or falls off—whether any boys are pretty constant in their attendance—whether, after absenting themselves, they return again—whether the ignorance of their parents be one of your rocks ahead—and the like. In short, I think I can turn any result of your experience and observation of these unfortunate creatures, to the account you would desire.[1]

Pray, mention to me the discouraging as well as the encouraging circumstances, for they are equally a part of the sad case; and without a knowledge of them, it is impossible to state it forcibly.

You are at perfect liberty to mention this to the Masters in the School. But beyond this, or such other limits as you may consider necessary, I could wish our correspondence to be confidential.

Faithfully Yours
Mr. R. Starey.   CHARLES DICKENS

To LAMAN BLANCHARD, 2 FEBRUARY 1844

MS Walter T. Spencer.

Devonshire Terrace | Friday February Second 1844

My Dear Blanchard

Jerrold and Leech[2] are coming to dine with me on Sunday, at half past five sharp. No party. Can you, and will you, join us?

Faithfully Always
Laman Blanchard Esquire.   CHARLES DICKENS

To MRS DAVID LAING,[3] 2 FEBRUARY 1844*

MS Dickens House. *Address:* Mrs. Laing | 1 Cambridge Terrace | Regents Park.

1 Devonshire Terrace. | Second February 1844.

Dear Madam.

I have found it necessary—sorely against my will—to decline attending many projected dinners in behalf of charitable Institutions. But I will most certainly make an exception in favor of the Governesses. Their cause has my warmest sympathy; and I should perform Lord Castlereagh's remarkable feat of turning my back upon myself,[4] if I hesitated for an Instant.

---

[1] CD was obviously planning his promised article for the *Edinburgh Review*.

[2] John Leech (1817–64; *DNB*): see Vol. III, p. 358*n*.

[3] Wife of the Rev. David Laing (1800–60; *DNB*), chaplain to the Middlesex Hospital and founder of the Governesses' Benevolent Institution 1843.

[4] Castlereagh was notorious for his mixed metaphors; Brougham, *Historical Sketches of Statesmen*, 2nd Series, 1845, I, 151, gives "men turning their backs upon themselves" as an example.

Allow me to thank you, cordially, for your letter; and to beg that you will do me the favor to assure Mr. Laing of my high and respectful sense of the good he is doing, and of the value which attaches to his benevolent services.

I have made a memorandum that I am engaged for Saturday the Twentieth of April. I would rather avoid being a steward; but in any other respect, the Institution may command me.[1]

Dear Madam | Yours faithfully and obliged

Mrs. Laing CHARLES DICKENS

To JOHN DILLON,[2] 3 FEBRUARY 1844

Text from *Autograph Prices Current*, I (1914–16); dated I, Devonshire Terrace, 3 Feb 44; salutation from N, I, 566.

My Dear Sir,

No, indeed. Trust me you were not wrong in believing—in feeling well assured, I hope—that the testimony you bear to the success of my little book, would sink deep into my heart, and fill it with a sad delight. Nothing could touch me half so nearly. No roar of approbation that human voices could set up would affect me like the faintest whisper from a home such as yours. . . . I shall ever prize your letter. I thank God for the high privilege of speaking to the secret hearts of those who are in grief like yours;[3] and I thank you earnestly, for the courage you have given me.

To MR WHEELER,[4] 3 FEBRUARY 1844

Mention in Sotheby's catalogue, June 1929; *MS* 1½ pp.; dated Devonshire Terrace, 3 Feb 44.

A grateful letter for a basket of game.

To SAMUEL RADLEY,[5] 6 FEBRUARY 1844

Mention in Sotheby's catalogue, Feb 1930; *MS* 1½ pp.; dated Devonshire Terrace, 6 Feb 44.

Asking him to take special care of his friend, Harrison Ainsworth, who is staying at the Adelphi, Liverpool, for a fancy ball.

[1] CD spoke at the first Anniversary Festival (see *To* Mrs Hall, 23 Apr 44 and *fn*), and sent £5 to Laing on 27 Apr (Account-book, MS Messrs Coutts).

[2] John Dillon, of Morrison, Dillon & Co., merchants, Fore St, Cripplegate; like his partner James Morrison (see *To* Stanfield, 24 Aug 44, *fn*) he was extremely rich, and was a well-known philanthropist. He spoke at the Sanatorium dinner 29 June 43, and was at the farewell dinner to Macready on 26 Aug 43: see Vol. III, pp. 500*n*, 544*n*.

[3] Dillon's second son, Edward, aged 22, died 10 Sep 43 (*The Times*, 11 Sep 43).

[4] Unidentified.

[5] Samuel Radley, proprietor of the Adelphi Hotel, Liverpool, where CD stayed in Jan 42.

To G. H. RODWELL,[1] 6 FEBRUARY 1844*

MS Free Library of Philadelphia.

Devonshire Terrace. | Sixth February 1844.

Dear Sir.

I beg to acknowledge the receipt of your note, requesting permission to have one of the Carol Designs copied, as a frontispiece to your song—and to assure you that you are at perfect liberty to have it copied for that purpose, and to consider this as your license to do so.[2]

                                        Faithfully Yours
G. H. Rodwell Esquire   CHARLES DICKENS

To THOMAS CHAPMAN,[3] 8 FEBRUARY 1844*

MS Free Library of Philadelphia. *Address:* Thomas Chapman Esquire | 14 Montague Place | Bryanstone Square.

Devonshire Terrace | Eighth February 1844.

My Dear Sir

Pray excuse my troubling you with a petition. But my City friends are not numerous; and casting about how to strive after an object I have very much at heart just now, it occurred to me as just coming within the bounds of possibility that you might be able to assist me.

I have a young brother (about Seventeen) recently come up from a Good School at Exeter,[4] and now living, with his father, at Greenwich.[5] I am extremely anxious to get employment for him in the office of some respectable house, where he would carry (in his pockets) such metal as is usually bestowed on such small craft. He is quick and clever; has never given any trouble to anybody; and has been well brought up. Above all, I have no reason to suppose that he is addicted to authorship, or any bad habits of that nature.

If any such thing should present itself before you at any time, and you will kindly think of the Committee-Man who never comes to the Sanatorium (in consequence, chiefly, of living close to it: which is a terrible drawback) you will confer a very great obligation on him.

I beg my compliments to Mrs. Chapman.[6] To whom I am happy to report that Mrs. Dickens is doing extremely well.

                            My Dear Sir | Faithfully Yours
Thomas Chapman Esquire   CHARLES DICKENS

---

[1] George Herbert Rodwell (1800–52; *DNB*), author, musical director and composer; he was responsible for the songs in Stirling's dramatic version of the *Carol*, which opened 5 Feb: see *To* Forster, 21 Feb. In 1845 published *Memoirs of an Umbrella*, a novel in weekly nos illustrated by Phiz.

[2] "The Song of Christmas" was published by D'Almaine & Co.; a copy of Leech's illustration, "Scrooge's Third Visitor", is on the cover, with the following note: "Copied from the original etching in the Christmas Carol by express permission of the Author, Charles Dickens Esqe.".

[3] Thomas Chapman, FRS (1798–1885), merchant: see Vol. III, p. 384*n*.

[4] Augustus Newnham Dickens (1827–1866): see Vol. I, p. 485*n*.

[5] At 5 Egerton Rd, Greenwich; by 10 May John Dickens was at Sandwell Place, Lewisham.

[6] Maria Louisa, *née* Hanson (*d.* 1879); married 1825.

To JOHN MORTIMER,[1] 8 FEBRUARY 1844*

MS Mr David Borowitz.

1 Devonshire Terrace | York Gate Regents Park
Eighth February 1844.

Dear Sir.

I thank you very much for your kind attention in sending me the Story Teller;[2] and beg you to believe me

Faithfully Yours
CHARLES DICKENS

John Mortimer Esquire.

To THOMAS MITTON, 10 FEBRUARY 1844†

MS Berg Collection. *Address:* Thomas Mitton Esquire | 23 Southampton Buildings | Chancery Lane.

Devonshire Terrace. | Tenth February 1844

My Dear Mitton.

Fred was telling me last night about the impudence of the Pirates—which I think I had much better not know, unless they should give us an opportunity of being down upon them in some new fashion. *For I can easily conceive the possibility of its being an advantage to us, and certainly a position of dignity, to be able to declare that I have never seen their effusions.* ᵃEven in the event of your thinking it desirable at any time that I *should* be acquainted with their doings,ᵃ I should like to receive the book, sealed up, that I might even then pause before I looked into it.[3]

ᵇHave you served the second man, and has the first appeared?[4] It seems to me that we have no course but to go on with the action pell mell.ᵇ[5] It is of no use to falter with such Rascals.

Mr. Blanchard's name is not Laman at all.[6] He was christened *Edward Lyt*, and is a desperate bad character. ᶜI can get the Certificate of his christening. Jerrold knows all about him.[7]

---

[1] John Mortimer, publisher, of Cunningham & Mortimer, Adelaide St, Trafalgar Square.

[2] *The Story-Teller; or, Table-Book of Periodical Literature*, edited by Robert Bell, May–Sep 43; published in parts (at first weekly, price 6d, later monthly) and then in 2 vols. Included comments on *American Notes*.

[3] No further publication of Lee & Haddock has been traced; the reference may be to a reprint of *Parley's Penny Library*, or possibly a volume of the *Illuminated Library* in which observations on the case had appeared.

aa; bb; cc Not previously published.

[4] Haddock was served with the writ by Mitton's clerk on 29 Jan, but Lee not until 7 Feb (Mitton's sworn statement of 10 Feb; MS Dickens House).

[5] Draft notes of instruction from Mitton to H. H. Dodgson (special pleader) to prepare a Declaration are in Dickens House. They accompanied various documents, including CD's "Observations" (see *To* Mitton, 13 Jan).

[6] See *To* Blanchard, 29 Jan.

[7] The "Mulberries", a club to which Jerrold belonged, met at the Wrekin Tavern in Broad Court where Blanchard's uncle was host (Clement Scott, *The Drama of Yesterday and To-day*, 1899, I, 311–12).

Mr. Cleave,[1] I also find, is active in the business. I have set the real Blanchard to get news of him, and think I shall be able to nail the "gent."

On we must go. Depend upon that.[c]

C and H promise the Carol accounts, today!

Faithfully Always
CD.

To JOHN FORSTER, [11 FEBRUARY 1844]

Extract in F, IV, ii, 314. Date: "Saturday morning 10 February", according to Forster; but *To Mitton, 10 Feb,* shows CD received the accounts that day, so the disturbed night must have been Sat, and the date of the letter 11 Feb.

Such a night as I have passed! I really believed I should never get up again, until I had passed through all the horrors of a fever. I found the *Carol* accounts awaiting me, and they were the cause of it. The first six thousand copies show a profit of £230![2] And the last four will yield as much more. I had set my heart and soul upon a Thousand, clear. What a wonderful thing it is, that such a great success should occasion me such intolerable anxiety and disappointment! My year's bills, unpaid, are so terrific,[3] that all the energy and determination I can possibly exert will be required to clear me before I go abroad; which, if next June come and find me alive, I shall do. Good Heaven, if I had only taken heart a year ago![4] Do come soon, as I am very anxious to talk with you. We can send round to Mac[5] after you arrive, and tell him to join us at Hampstead or elsewhere. I was so utterly knocked down last night, that I came up to the contemplation of all these things quite bold this morning. If I can let the house for this season, I will be off to some seaside place as soon as a tenant offers. I am not afraid, if I reduce my expenses; but if I do not, I shall be ruined past all mortal hope of redemption.

To MESSRS CHAPMAN & HALL, 12 FEBRUARY 1844

Mention in next.

To THOMAS MITTON, 12 FEBRUARY 1844†

MS Huntington Library.

Devonshire Terrace
Monday Morning | Twelfth February 1844.

[My][6] Dear Mitton

Prepare yourself for a shock. I never was so knocked over in my life, as when

[1] John Cleave, a radical journalist, editor and proprietor of the very successful *Weekly Gazette* (1835–41), and of *Cleave's London Satirist* and various series of popular fiction, such as the later *Penny Novelist* (1845–) for which E. L. Blanchard worked.

[2] The accounts are given by Forster (F, IV, ii, 315), who attributes CD's low profit

to "want of judgment . . . in not adjusting the expenses of production" (£1525 for the first seven editions) "with a more equable regard to the selling price". The largest items were for colouring plates, binding, "incidents and advertising".

[3] CD's accounts show this to be an exaggeration; his outgoings in Feb and Mar (which included the mysterious £40

I opened this Carol account on Saturday Night. And though I had got over it by yesterday and could look the thing good-humouredly in the face, I have slept as badly as Macbeth ever since—which is, thank God, almost a Miracle with me.

I have not the least doubt that they have run the expences up, anyhow, purposely to bring me back,[1] and disgust me with charges. If you add up the different charges for the plates, you will find that they cost more than I get.[2] I had £200 for the Young Couples[3]—a poor thing of little worth, published without my name.

You will see my letter to them in reply. I have adhered to the strict business percentage; seeing the Shadow of War before me. The Vouchers I shall inspect before I sign their books. But of course they have got *them*.

Observe little Hall's note, with the allusion to the American book.[4] Oh Heaven!

If you can send me these papers back, in the course of the day,—do. Pray do not talk of this to anyone. I shall not tell Bradbury and Evans; as I think it highly important not to dash the triumph of the book.

Faithfully Yours
CHARLES DICKENS

*a*The half years profits of Chuzzlewit are £750.*a* [5]

To THOMAS MITTON, 12 FEBRUARY [1844]

MS Huntington Library.

Devonshire Terrace. | Monday Twelfth February.

My Dear Mitton

I am afraid I cannot possibly get round to you before dinner, as I want to finish a chapter; and after that, am obliged to attend a ballot at the Athenæum, which will most likely keep me until Ten o'Clock. If you will call there and ask for me at that time, we can go over to the Parthenon, and discuss matters.— As to Chapman and Hall's, that is past and over. Nothing can remedy that.

I am, as you may suppose—not only on *my* beam ends, but tilted over on the

---

to Roper: see Vol. III, p. 486*n*) left him some margin.
⁴ In *To* Forster, 2 Nov 43 (Vol. III, p. 590), CD says he had formed the project "months ago".
⁵ Daniel Maclise (?1806–70; *DNB*): see Vol. I, p. 201*n*.
⁶ Removed by hole at the fold of the paper.
¹ i.e. to discourage him from publishing on his own account.
² About £190.
³ Published by Chapman & Hall, 10 Feb 40: see Vol. II, pp. 1–2*n*.

⁴ Perhaps saying that the 4th edn was not yet exhausted; but the book had sold well, and according to Arthur Waugh (*A Hundred Years of Publishing*, 1930, p. 57) the author's share of the profits by the end of the year was "not less than a thousand pounds".
⁵ CD's three-quarter share of these would go to the repayment of the original debt: see Vol. III, p. 516*n*.
^{aa} Not previously published.

other side. Nothing so unexpected and utterly disappointing, has ever befallen me. That you know.

The bill for £200 *must* be provided for.[1] To that, I mean to devote this precious balance.[2] The rest must be worked round somehow. I wish I could say that I see how (I am thunder-stricken by the amount) but I have been on the other side with you often, and you must do your best for me.

Nothing upholds me under this, but the very circumstance that makes it so tremendous—the wonderful success of the book.

I expect that Chapman and Hall's answer will be impertinent. Forster thinks otherwise. If you should be engaged tonight, you will find me at home, *and alone*, between this and half past Four. Faithfully Ever

                                                                                    CD

To DR SOUTHWOOD SMITH,[3] [12 FEBRUARY 1844]

Envelope only, MS Mr W. A. Foyle. *Date:* PM 12 [Feb] 44—only the "e" of the month clearly visible, but must be Feb as CD was in Italy Sep 44. *Address:* Dr. Southwood Smith | 38 Finsbury Square.

To THOMAS BEARD,[4] 14 FEBRUARY 1844

MS Dickens House. *Address:* Thomas Beard Esquire | Morning Herald Office | Shoe Lane | Fleet Street.

Devonshire Terrace | Fourteenth February 1844.

My Dear Beard

I need not tell you how truly glad I am at any time to comply with any wish of yours. And although that disposition cannot be strengthened by *any* circumstance, I should be really glad to oblige Mr. Mc Cabe[5] in so small a matter; for I entertain (I think I do, at least?) a very pleasant recollection of him as an especially cheerful and good natured old colleague. But I am in this difficulty—that I have recently stood in relations towards Chapman and Hall, which are not perfectly agreeable, and which have limited our correspondence to affairs of

---

[1] His debt to Mitton: see Vol. III, p. 604 and *n*. CD's account-book (MS Messrs Coutts) shows that he paid Mitton £45 on 23 May, £100 on 28 June and £40 on 4 July.

[2] The receipts from the *Carol* for Dec 43; CD received £137.4.4 from Chapman & Hall on 12 Feb, and another £49.12.3 on 14 Feb (Account-book, MS Messrs Coutts). By the end of 1844 he had received £726 in all from the *Carol* (F, IV, ii, 315).

[3] Thomas Southwood Smith, MD (1788–

1861; *DNB*), sanitary reformer: see Vol. II, p. 164*n*. Encouraged by Lord Normanby, he helped to found the Health of Towns Association in 1844; many public meetings were held and thousands of pamphlets circulated.

[4] Thomas Beard (1807–91): see Vol. I, p. 3*n*.

[5] William Bernard MacCabe (1801–91; *DNB*), journalist and historian; on the *Morning Chronicle* from about 1833, and on the *Morning Herald* from 1835.

business. I have had no distinct quarrel with them; but this vague kind of barrier has arisen between us; and I do not entertain the least desire to throw it down.

To the best of my recollection it is more than a year since I introduced anybody to them. And my doing so now, would consequently seem an unusual proceeding—rather out of my way, and against my ordinary course.

I leave it to you to tell Mr. Mc Cabe as little or as much of this, as you think proper; merely bearing in mind that I mention the plain Truth in confidence, because I do not wish him to suppose that I evade or slight his wish.

I have every reason to believe—I may add—that they are surrounded by translators. There is the whole Corps of the Foreign Quarterly;[1] and there are other linguists who do not write in it, to my personal knowledge.

My Dear Beard | Always Faithfully Yours

Thomas Beard Esquire

CHARLES DICKENS

To THOMAS MITTON, 14 FEBRUARY 1844*

MS Huntington Library.

Devonshire Terrace | Wednesday 14 Feby. 44

My Dear Mitton

What do you think of the enclosed????[2] If you can manage to give me a call at any time, I wish you would.

I really think I shall begin to give in, one of these days. For anything like the damnable Shadow which this father[3] of mine casts upon my face, there never was—except in a nightmare.

Faithfully Always

CHARLES DICKENS

To SIR JOHN EASTHOPE,[4] 15 FEBRUARY 1844

MS Comtesse de Suzannet.

1 Devonshire Terrace. | Fifteenth February 1844

Dear Sir John

I am exceedingly sorry not to have been able to answer your note[5] when your servant was here. But I was much engaged with visitors two deep; and lived in hopes of their business being brief—which it was not.

---

[1] Published by Chapman & Hall. N, I, 569 misreads as "Foreign quarters".

[2] No enclosure now accompanies this letter; clearly there had been some fresh demand from John Dickens.

[3] John Dickens (?1785–1851): see Vol. I, p. 43*n*.

[4] Sir John Easthope (1784–1865; *DNB*), Liberal politician and chief proprietor of the *Morning Chronicle*: see Vol. I, p. 123*n*. He had remarried 19 Sep 43, his second wife being Elizabeth, daughter of the late Col. Skyring of the Royal Artillery, and widow of Major Longley of the same regiment.

[5] Easthope probably wished to see CD about contributing to the *Chronicle*: see *To* Doyle, 5 Mar.

I am obliged to wait at home this Morning until Four; and if you could call, as you kindly propose, I should be happy to see you. I very much regret to say that I have an engagement to dine out, or I should have been truly glad to dine with you.

Faithfully Yours
CHARLES DICKENS

Sir John Easthope.

To SIR JOHN EASTHOPE, [15 FEBRUARY 1844]

MS Comtesse de Suzannet. *Date:* endorsed 15 Feb 44 in a contemporary hand.

Devonshire Terrace | Thursday afternoon

Dear Sir John

I find (which I had forgotten when I wrote to you) that in all probability, I shall have to be at my Printers' tomorrow Morning, and *may* be detained there, after the time I named in my note.[1] Allow me to say then, that I will take the chance of finding you at home on Sunday between two and three. And pray do not take the trouble to write, in the event of your being engaged as I shall be calling in your neighbourhood[2] in any case, and shall not be in the least degree inconvenienced though you be not at home.

After Tuesday next, I shall be quite free in the Morning; and should I not find you at home on Sunday, I will repeat my visit at a quarter before Eleven on Wednesday.

Faithfully Yours
CHARLES DICKENS

Sir John Easthope.

To T. J. THOMPSON,[3] 15 FEBRUARY 1844†

MS Rosenbach Foundation.

Devonshire Terrace | Fifteenth February 1844

My Dear Thompson

Yes. For my sins, I am going to Liverpool—and to Birmingham, for a similar purpose, on my way home. [a]I shall be at the Adelphi on Sunday Evening, the 25th.; and shall write to Radley the day previous. I shall order a sitting room, and shall hope to find you in it.

I need not say that if you would like to behold *my* steeple run[4] (and be d——d to it)[a] I shall be happy to mount you in a post of honor.

I don't think you quite consider the number of commissions Stanfield always has—and you certainly have not considered (for you don't know) that he has been laid up for many weeks, with a cruel old leg,[5] which appears to be emulous of raspberry Jam, and to break out into a concatenation accordingly. He is

---

[1] Easthope must have replied proposing to call next morning.

[2] Easthope lived at 19 Grafton St.

[3] Thomas James Thompson (1812–81): see Vol. I, p. 416*n.*

[4] Thompson was probably going to the Liverpool Great National Steeplechase (already occasionally known as the "Grand National") at Aintree on 28 Feb.

[aa] Not previously published.

[5] As a young sailor on the *Namur* Stanfield had severely injured his leg by a fall from the masthead and suffered from the effects intermittently for the rest of his life.

greatly better, and was *much hurt* when I told him of your note: calling me to witness that he had several times said "Now I *will* do your friend's little picture" &c &c.[1] The which I solemnly affirm to be true in all respects.

My love to Smif,[2] and all the rest. Kate is all right again; and so, they tell me, is the Baby. But I decline (on principle) to look at the latter object.

Faithfully Yours Always | In Great Haste

T. J. Thompson Esquire CHARLES DICKENS

To JOHN FORSTER, [MID-FEBRUARY 1844]

Extract in F, IV, iii, 323. *Date:* 16 Jan according to Forster (in a passage containing other dating errors); but Jonas and Mrs Gamp both appear in the Mar No., not Feb; "distractingly late" suggests mid-Feb as the No. had to be completed before CD left for Liverpool.

I had written you a line pleading Jonas and Mrs. Gamp, but this frosty day tempts me sorely. I am distractingly late; but I look at the sky, think of Hampstead, and feel hideously tempted. Don't come with Mac, and fetch me. I couldn't resist if you did.

To THOMAS MITTON, 17 FEBRUARY 1844*

Text from typescript, Huntington Library.

Devonshire Terrace, | Seventeenth February 1844.

My Dear Mitton,

Dropping the £500[3] (which we may certainly do,) what is the *exact* amount you will want for the Premium?[4] I don't remember.

Faithfully yours,

Thomas Mitton Esquire. C.D.

To J. P. HARLEY,[5] 18 FEBRUARY 1844*

MS Morgan Library. *Address:* J. P. Harley Esquire | 14 Upper Gower Street.

Sunday afternoon | Eighteenth February 1844

My Dear Harley.

I am so much depressed and worried by an intolerable cold, that I am obliged,

---

[1] See Vol. III, p. 496 and *n*.

[2] Charles Smithson (?1804–44), Thompson's brother-in-law: see Vol. I, p. 427*n*.

[3] i.e. an insurance policy for this amount; therefore not one of the first two Britannia policies, which were larger (see Vol. I, p. 352 and *n*, Vol. II, p. 346 and *n*), but presumably the third—of which only the number, 524, is known, from the rough draft of ?Dec 1841 for a document transferring all three to Chapman & Hall: see Vol. III, p. 2 and *n*.

[4] Perhaps for the Sun Fire Office insurance on the contents of Devonshire Terrace, which fell due in Feb; or for the largest Britannia policy, overdue since Nov 43—not improbable, as both CD and Mitton were short of funds this winter. Neither payment (nor any sum to Mitton) appears in CD's accounts for Feb 44, and Mitton *to* CD, 30 May 44 (MS Mr H. C. Dickens), though confused and partly illegible, does make it clear that Mitton made some payment on CD's behalf on 19 Feb.

[5] John Pritt Harley (1786–1858; *DNB*), actor and singer: see Vol. I, p. 167*n*.

with a view to tomorrow's work,[1] to deny myself the pleasure of dining with you. I have not seen you for ages; and shall hope to reverse the medal—or in other words to get you to dine with me—before we are many weeks older.

To day I am neither useful nor ornamental—simply stupid, drowsy, snivelling, ugly, red-nosed, watery-eyed, and gasping.

Kate sends her love to your sisters. She is doing brawly.—I ought to say has done, for she is off the Invalid List, Thank God.

Theatricals are looking up—AN'T THEY?[2]

Always Heartily Yours

J. P. Harley Esquire   CHARLES DICKENS

To FREDERICK DICKENS,[3] 19 FEBRUARY 1844

Text from George D. Smith catalogue, n.d. (?1910). *Date:* extract in American Art Association and Anderson Gallery catalogue, Mar 1914, dated Devonshire Terrace, 19 Feb 44.

My dear Fred.

You will find me at the Adelphi[4] tomorrow night, with Mitton, if you like to come, or at the Garrick at any time after a quarter before 6, and before the play if you will enquire there for me.

Affectly and Always

C.D.

To JOHN FOWLER,[5] 19 FEBRUARY 1844*

MS Free Library of Philadelphia. *Address:* John Fowler Esquire | Mechanics' Institution | Sheffield.

1 Devonshire Terrace, York Gate | Regents Park, London.
Nineteenth February 1844.

Sir.

I am honored and flattered by your request to preside at a Public Meeting, in behalf of the Building Fund of the Sheffield Mechanics' Institution.

Believe me, that I have too earnest and staunch an interest in such an Establishment in such a town, to decline acceding to a proposal so congenial to my feelings, if I could—with any kind of regard to my own convenience, and previous engagements—give it my reasonable acquiescence. But I regret to say, that I see no probability of being enabled to comply with your request, at any time between this and June. And in July, I have engaged to leave London for quite another Quarter.

---

[1] His No. was not finished until shortly before he left for Liverpool on 25 Feb (see *To* Mrs Burnett, 1 Mar).

[2] Probably an ironical reference to Bunn's future programme at Drury Lane, just announced (*Theatrical Journal*, 17 Feb), and confined to opera and ballet. Harley was in the company.

[3] CD's accounts show a payment to "Mr. Frederick" of £10 on 19 Feb.

[4] See *To* Forster, 21 Feb.

[5] John Fowler, steel refiner; Hon. Secretary of the Sheffield Mechanics' Institution, established 1832.

Under these circumstances, I am reluctantly compelled to say, that I cannot accept your welcome proposal.

Allow me to thank you, very cordially, for the kind terms in which you have addressed me. I am Dear Sir

Yours faithfully and obliged

Mr. John Fowler.   CHARLES DICKENS

To JOHN FORSTER, [21 FEBRUARY 1844]

Extracts in F, IV, iii, 319–20, 320. *Date:* first extract 21 Feb according to Forster; second extract said to be on his return from Liverpool and Birmingham, but clearly 21 Feb, the day after his visit to the Adelphi: see *To* Fred Dickens, 19 Feb.

Advise me on the following point. And as I must write to-night, having already lost a post, advise me by bearer. This Liverpool Institution, which is wealthy and has a high grammar-school[1] the masters of which receive in salaries upwards of £2000 a year (indeed its extent horrifies me; I am struggling through its papers this morning), writes me yesterday by its secretary a business letter about the order of the proceedings on Monday; and it begins thus. "I beg to send you prefixed, with the best respects of our committee, a bank order for twenty pounds in payment of the expenses contingent on your visit to Liverpool."—And there, sure enough, it is. Now my impulse was, *and is*, decidedly to return it. Twenty pounds is not of moment to me; and any sacrifice of independence is worth it twenty times' twenty times told. But haggling in my mind is a doubt whether that would be proper, and not boastful (in an inexplicable way); and whether as an author, I have a right to put myself on a basis which the professors of literature in other forms *connected with the Institution* cannot afford to occupy. Don't you see? But of course you do. The case stands thus. The Manchester Institution, being in debt, appeals to me as it were *in formâ pauperis*, and makes no such provision as I have named. The Birmingham Institution, just struggling into life with great difficulty, applies to me on the same grounds. But the Leeds people (thriving) write to me, making the expenses a distinct matter of business;[2] and the Liverpool, as a point of delicacy, say nothing about it to the last minute, and then send the money. Now, what in the name of goodness ought I to do?—I am as much puzzled with the cheque as Colonel Jack was with his gold.[3] If it would have settled the matter to put it in the fire

---

[1] Few Mechanics' Institutions had schools. The Liverpool school opened in 1838, offering a six-year course beginning at the age of 8–10. There were four principal masters, in charge of the departments of classics, English, mathematics and commercial subjects; in 1845 W. B. Hodgson became headmaster as well as Principal of the Institution. This and the girls' school (referred to by CD in his speech, and opened later in 1844) were eventually handed over to the City.

[2] The Leeds Mechanics' Institution and Literary Society must have asked CD to speak at the Soirée held on 14 Feb. In 1843 one of the subjects discussed at the Soirée was "The Influence of the Writings of Boz".

[3] In Defoe's *Colonel Jack*, 1722, early in the narrative, when the hero as a boy is being trained in pickpocketing, his "Instructor" steals a "Goldsmith's bill" for £12.10 which is changed into gold and shared between them; Jack, in rags and homeless, is greatly perplexed about where to hide the money.

yesterday, I should certainly have done it. Your opinion is requested.[1] I think I shall have grounds for a very good speech at Brummagem; but I am not sure about Liverpool; having misgivings of over-gentility.

I saw the *Carol*[2] last night. Better than usual, and Wright[3] seems to enjoy Bob Cratchit, but *heart-breaking* to me. Oh Heaven! if any forecast of *this* was ever in my mind! Yet O. Smith[4] was drearily better than I expected. It is a great comfort to have that kind of meat underdone; and his face is quite perfect.

To THOMAS POWELL,[5] 24 FEBRUARY 1844*

MS Free Library of Philadelphia.

Devonshire Terrace.
Saturday Twenty Fourth February | 1844.

My Dear Powell.

I enclose the brother,[6] concerning whom Mr. Chapman has been so kind as to talk with you. I need not commend him I know (being a Spirit,[7] and I hope a good one) to your favorable regard.

Faithfully Yours always
CHARLES DICKENS

Thomas Powell Esquire

---

[1] "My opinion was clearly for sending the money back, which accordingly was done" (F, IV, iii, 320).

[2] This was Edward Stirling's dramatization at the Adelphi (5 Feb–29 Mar 44), *A Christmas Carol* "in three staves", with added songs by G. H. Rodwell; O. Smith played Scrooge. Stirling announced the piece as "the only dramatic version sanctioned by C. Dickens, Esqre.", and according to his reminiscences CD attended several rehearsals and made "valuable suggestions" (*Old Drury Lane*, 1881, I, 186–7; quoted by Ley in F, IV, iii, 328n). It was reviewed favourably in the *Examiner*, 10 Feb: the musical arrangement was "excellent", and "there never was a scene better put upon the stage, in the best days of this theatre, than the Clare Market on Christmas Eve". Two other dramatic versions were also produced on 5 Feb: C. Z. Barnett's (*A Christmas Carol; or, The Miser's Warning*) at the Surrey Theatre, and Charles Webb's (*Scrooge, the Miser's Dream*) at Sadler's Wells; variants of Webb's version were also played at the Strand, Britannia, and Victoria, and anonymous versions at the City of London, and the Queen's (Malcolm Morley, "Curtain up on *A Christmas Carol*", D, XLVII [1951], 159–64).

[3] Edward Richard Wright (1813–59; *DNB*); the *Examiner* said he played the part with "humorous indulgence" but "occasional exaggeration".

[4] Richard John Smith (1786–1855; *DNB*), actor, called "O" since 1829 when he played Obi in a melodrama; generally played villains, but also Newman Noggs in the Adelphi's *Nickleby*. Probably also known to CD as a member of the Shakespeare Society.

[5] Thomas Powell (1809–87), miscellaneous writer, embezzler and forger: see Vol. III, p. 577n.

[6] Augustus: see *To* Chapman, 8 Feb.

[7] The joke, which recurs, is somehow related to *A New Spirit of the Age*: see Vol. III, p. 578n.

To MRS CHARLES DICKENS, 26 FEBRUARY 1844

MS British Museum. *Address:* Mrs. Charles Dickens | 1 Devonshire Terrace | York Gate Regents Park | London.

> Liverpool Radley's Hotel.
> Monday Twenty Sixth February 1844.

My Dear Kate.

I got down here last night (after a most intolerably wet journey) before Seven; and found Thompson sitting by my fire. He had ordered dinner; and we ate it pleasantly enough, and went to bed in good time. This morning Mr. Yates,[1] the great man connected with the Institution (and a brother of Ashton Yates's)[2] called. I went to look at it with him. It is an enormous place, and the tickets have been selling at two and even three guineas apiece. The lecture room, in which the celebration is held, will accommodate over thirteen hundred people.[3] It was being fitted with Gas—after the manner of the Ring at Astleys —I should think is an easy place to speak in: being a semi-circle, with seats rising one above another to the ceiling—and will have eight hundred ladies tonight, in full dress. I am rayther shakey just now, but shall pull up, I have no doubt. At dinner time tomorrow you will receive, I hope, a facetious document, hastily penned after I return tonight, telling you how it all went off.

When I came back here, I found Fanny.[4] And Hewitt had picked me up just before. We all went off straight to the Britannia, which lay where she did, when we went on board. We went into the old little Cabin, and the Ladies Cabin, but Mrs. Bean[5] had gone to Scotland, as the ship does not sail again before May. In the Saloon we had some champagne and biscuits; and Hewitt had set out upon the table a block of Boston Ice weighing fifty Pounds.[6] Lott of the Caledonia lunched with us—a very nice fellow. He saw Macready play Macbeth in Boston, and gave me a tremendous account of the effect.[7] Poor Burroughs of the George Washington[8] died *on board*, on his last passage home. His little wife was with him.

Hewitt dines with us today, and I have procured him admission tonight. I am very sorry indeed (and so was he) that you didn't see the old Ship. It was the strangest thing in the world to go on board again.

There is no more news that I can remember. I am lying on the sofa and keeping myself quiet. It is pouring of rain: and has been all day. Fanny and Thompson are playing back-gammon—Hewitt has gone to dress himself and

---

[1] Richard Vaughan Yates: see *To* Hodgson, 26 Feb 44, *fn.*

[2] John Ashton Yates (1781–1863; *DNB*), MP for Carlow; member of the Sanatorium Committee.

[3] According to the *Liverpool Albion*, the Institution's hall held 1250; all seats were filled and the original price raised from 2/- to 3/6. The platform no doubt accounts for CD's total of 1300; presumably the prices he mentions were charged by ticket touts.

[4] CD's sister, Fanny Burnett (1810–48): see Vol. I, p. 4n.

[5] The stewardess: see Vol. III, p. 7n.

[6] Ice was first brought from the USA in June 43.

[7] In Nov 43: see Vol. III, p. 614n. Macready had travelled on the *Caledonia*.

[8] CD had made the homeward journey in her: see Vol. III, p. 250n. Ambrose Hilliard Burrows (?1813–43) was the Master: see Vol. III, p. 252n.

order some wonderful piece of finery—and the great Burnett[1] has not yet shewn. Give my best love to Georgy, and kisses to the Darlings. Also affectionate regards to Mac and Forster.

You had better write to me by Wednesdays Post, and address me at Dee's Royal Hotel, Birmingham. I had Bacon with me as far as Watford yesterday— and very pleasant. Sheil[2] was also in the Train, on his way to Ireland.

Ever affectionately
CHARLES DICKENS

Love from Fanny, and best regards from T. and Hewitt.

Out of The Common.—Please.[3]

Dickens against The World.

Charles Dickens of No 1 Devonshire Terrace York Gate Regents Park in the County of Middlesex, Gentleman, the successful Plaintiff in the above cause, maketh oath and saith: That on the day and date hereof, to wit at seven o'clock in the evening, he this Deponent took the chair at a large assembly of The Mechanics Institution at Liverpool, and that having been received with tremendous and enthusiastic plaudits, he this Deponent did immediately dash into a vigorous, brilliant, humourous, pathetic, eloquent, fervid, and impassioned speech. That the said speech was received by Thirteen Hundred Persons with frequent, vehement, uproarious, and deafening cheers; and that to the best of this Deponent's knowledge and belief he this Deponent did speak up like a man and did to the best of his knowledge and belief, considerably distinguish himself. That after the proceedings of the Evening were over, and a Vote of Thanks was proposed to this Deponent, he this Deponent did again distinguish himself; and that the cheering at that time, accompanied with clapping of hands and stamping of feet, was in this Deponents ears Thundering and awful. And this Deponent further saith that his white and black or magpie waistcoat did create a strong sensation, and that during the hours of promenading, this Deponent heard from persons surrounding him, such exclamations as "What is it! *Is* it a waistcoat? No, its a shirt," and the like, all of which this Deponent believes to have been complimentary and gratifying. And this Deponent further saith that he is now going to supper, and wishes he may have an appetite to eat it.[4]

CHARLES DICKENS

Sworn before me at the⎫
Adelphi Hotel Liverpool,⎪
on the 26th of February⎬
1844   ⎭
　　　　　S. Radley.

[1] Henry Burnett (1811–93), CD's brother-in-law: see Vol. I, p. 342*n*.

[2] Richard Lalor Sheil (1791–1851; *DNB*), dramatist and MP: see Vol. III, p. 491*n*.

[3] In the "facetious document" CD evidently had the *Carol* case in mind. He used a scratchy pen, and wrote the words "Charles" and "Sworn" in rough imitation of a legal hand.

[4] CD was greeted by "See the Conquering Hero Comes" on the organ. Among those on the platform were the President, William Fawcett, Sir Joshua Walmsley and Joseph and Richard Yates. In his speech CD recalled the history of the Institution,

To THE REV. WILLIAM GILES,[1] 27 FEBRUARY 1844

MS Liverpool Public Library.

Adelphi Hotel Liverpool | Twenty Seventh February 1844.

My Dear Sir

I am exceedingly sorry to say, that I shall not be able to get over to your house, during my very brief stay in Liverpool. I am engaged during the whole of this day—pledged indeed to more appointments than I am likely to have it in my power to fulfil[2]—and tomorrow morning early, I start for Birmingham, where I have arranged to preside at a meeting in Behalf of a Mechanics Institution in the Evening.

I need not tell you that if I *had* time, I would most cheerfully and joyfully dispose of some of it, in seeing my old Master. Remember me with sincere kindness to Mrs. Giles and all your family, and ever believe me.

Faithfully Yours My Dear Sir

The Reverend William Giles.   CHARLES DICKENS

To MISS CHRISTIANA WELLER,[3] 27 FEBRUARY [1844]

Text from *A Dickens Friendship*, ed. W[ilfrid] M[eynell], privately printed, 1931, p. 3.

Adelphi Hotel, Liverpool. Tuesday Twentyseventh February.

My Dear Miss Weller,

Riding out to see you to-day[4]—the horse's name is *not* Pegasus—I conceived

opened 1837 and afterwards enlarged, and its triumphant success, with a membership of 3200 and a library of 11,000 volumes; he complimented Edward Stanley, Bishop of Norwich, as a "good and liberal man"; and the recent foundation of a girls' school in connexion with the Institution led him to give especial emphasis to "our fairer members". He ended by quoting Tennyson's "Kind hearts are more than coronets". After some musical entertainment—"The Ivy Green", sung by Mr Ryalls and a piano solo by Christiana Weller—there were speeches by John Smith (see *To* Thompson, 28 Feb), Dr Thorburn and W. B. Hodgson, the Secretary, further musical entertainment, refreshments, and promenading. In replying to the Secretary's vote of thanks, in "such a scene of enthusiasm as had never been seen in the walls of that institution before", CD ended by quoting Tiny Tim, "God bless us Every One!" (see *Speeches*, ed. K. J. Fielding, pp. 52–8; the *Liverpool Albion* and *Liverpool Mercury* give further details, and the *Illustrated London News*, 2 Mar, reproduces the scene in the hall; see also

D, XII [1916], 8–13). Copies of "Lines addressed to Charles Dickens Esq." by J. Stonehouse were presented to the company as they retired; the verses (*Liverpool Mercury*) referred to CD's works up to *Old Curiosity Shop*, complimented him on his lack of "ribald wit" or "scornful jest . . . at things the good revere", and referred to the present occasion: "For while proud halls like these arise, where youth is taught to think | The wretched race of '*Squeers*' must starve, and in oblivion sink". During the evening shilling copies of an "emblematic portrait" of CD were on sale: see *To* Isaacs, 2 Mar.

[1] The Rev. William Giles, FRGS (1798–1856), Baptist minister and CD's first schoolmaster: see Vol. I, p. 429*n*.

[2] For his lunch-time engagement, see next; in the evening CD was entertained by R. V. Yates at his "magnificent residence", with a "fancy dress ball" attended by 160 people, 50 of them in costume. CD danced with "Ceres" and with "his own Dolly Varden" (*Liverpool Mercury*; John Smith, the editor, was present).

[3] Christiana Jane Weller (1825–1910),

the idea of putting this bit of doggerel in your album. But you do nothing like anybody else, and therefore did not produce one. So I send it to you.[1]

Faithfully yours ever

Miss Christiana Weller.   CHARLES DICKENS

P.S. I shall not forget Tennyson.[2]

To [SIR JOHN EASTHOPE], [24–27 FEBRUARY 1844]

MS (fragment) Dr De Coursey Fales. Date: The reference to "Meetings" suggests Feb 44; handwriting confirms; either 24 Feb, the day before leaving for Liverpool, or during his absence. *Address:* as with other Easthope papers, probably to him: see *To* Easthope, 15 Feb—but just possibly to Andrew Doyle.

Preside at some Meetings in behalf of Educational Institutions. But I hope to be at home by Thursday, or at latest by Friday; and I shall be happy to find a note from you.

Believe me | Faithfully Yours Always

CHARLES DICKENS

To T. J. THOMPSON, 28 FEBRUARY [1844]

Text from A Dickens Friendship, ed. W[ilfrid] M[eynell], privately printed, 1931, p. 7.

Brummagem. Wednesday night, twentyeighth February.

Half-past-ten at night

My dear Thompson,

There never were such considerate people as there are here. After offering me

T. E. Weller's second daughter: see Vol. III, p. 446n. During the past twelve months she had continued her career as a concert pianist with engagements in Liverpool, Manchester and North Wales, all enthusiastically noticed in the provincial press; in her recent concert, at the Manchester Athenaeum 24 Feb, she had played a piece of her own composition. At the Liverpool Soirée CD introduced her as "the 'god-child of whom he was proud,' and said that he had some difficulty and tenderness in announcing her name"; he had felt a progressive loss of heart to his welcoming audience during the evening "but the last remnant he had left went out of him into the piano on which Miss Weller had been playing" (*Liverpool Journal*, 2 Mar 44).

4 According to the *Liverpool Mercury*, 1 Mar 44, CD and his "immediate friends" accepted an invitation to lunch from the Wellers. But in the *Liverpool Journal*, 2 Mar, T. E. Weller gave the true version: "the fact was that he *invited himself*. Captain Hewitt of the *Britannia*, called on

me on Tuesday morning, and said, 'Mr. Dickens had been so pleased with my daughter that he intended to pay us a visit.' The reason why I am anxious this unintentional mistake of the *Mercury* should be set right, is, to avoid being misjudged by the world on the score of presumption. I had not the most remote idea of asking so great a man to visit one so little as myself". Weller's letter also made it clear that the lunch was held at the residence of James Shaw, Weller's son-in-law (see Vol. III, p. 446n), at Walton Breck.

1 "I put in a book once, by hook or by crook, | The whole race (as I thought) of a 'feller', | Who happily pleas'd the town's taste, (much diseas'd) | —And the name of this person was Weller. | I find to my cost, that *One Weller* I lost. | Cruel Destiny so to arrange it! | I love her dear name which has won me some fame, | But Great Heaven how gladly I'd change it! | At Liverpool. | Twenty Seventh February" (Facsimile in *D*, XII [1916], 2).

2 See *To* T. E. Weller, 1 Mar.

unbounded hospitality and my declining it, they leave me to myself like gentle-men. They saved me from all sorts of intrusion at the Town Hall—brought me back and left me to my quiet supper (now upon the table) as they had left me to my quiet dinner.

I wish you had come. It was really a splendid sight. The Town Hall was crammed to the roof—by, I suppose, two thousand persons. The ladies were in full dress and immense numbers; and when Dick showed himself the whole company stood up; rustling like the leaves of a wood. *Tar-nation grand, it was, and rather unbalancing (especially after Sir Rogers[1] and brandys-and-waters), but* Dick with the heart of a lion dashed in bravely *and made decidedly the best speech I ever heard him achieve. Sir, he was jocular, pathetic, eloquent, conversational, illustrative, and wise—always wise.* He introduced that about the Genie in the casket with marvellous effect;[2] and was applauded to the echo which did applaud again.[3] He was horribly nervous when he arrived in Birming-ham, but when he stood upon the platform I don't believe his pulse increased[4] ten degrees. A better or a quicker audience never listened to man.[5]

The ladies had hung the hall (do you know what an immense place it is?) with artificial flowers, all round. And on the front of the great gallery, immediately fronting this *highly-gifted* young gentleman were the words (still in artificial flowers you'll observe) "Welcome Boz", in letters about six feet high. Behind his head, and about the great organ, were immense transparencies, representing several Fames in the act of crowning a corresponding number of Dicks—at which Victoria (taking out a poetic licence) was highly delighted. *Being positively the first time of her appearance in that character.[6]

I cannot joke about Miss Weller; for she is too good; and interest in her (spiri-tual young creature that she is, and destined to an early death, I fear) has become a sentiment with me. Good God what a madman I should seem, if the incredible feeling I have conceived for that girl could be made plain to anyone!

Well, well! There must be things of this kind in heaven; and some of us are going there, faster than we think perhaps. I shall never be a wise man (except oratorically) as long as I live on earth, unless I get Hewett to bring some Boston blocks over and ice me.

When the train moved off today I put my head out, gasping with chuckles, to ask you whether you didn't think Smith[7] looked more like an ancient Roman than

aa; bb; cc; dd Omitted in MDGH, 1882.

[1] The ball at Yates's had ended with "Sir Roger de Coverley" at 3 a.m.

[2] CD illustrated the idea that education must be extended before it was too late, by comparing the "Spirit of Ignorance" to the genie in the *Arabian Nights* who would have brought blessing instead of destruc-tion had he been released from his casket in time (*Speeches*, ed. K. J. Fielding, pp. 60–1).

[3] *Macbeth*, v, iii, 53.

[4] The reading of MDGH, 1882, III, 64; Meynell reads "measured", in error.

[5] CD's speech (*Speeches*, pp. 58–65), though rather inferior to the Liverpool address, was received with great en-thusiasm; the anecdotes of his journey by railway from Liverpool gave particular delight.

[6] The published *Report of ... the Conversazione* described the decorations in detail, confirming CD's account and add-ing that the word "Polytechnic" was in-scribed in laurel leaves and flowers over the platform.

[7] John Smith, editor of the *Liverpool Mercury*, was on the platform at the soirée

a Dane[1] last night—and whether that wouldn't be a good description of the amount of his classicality. But you were too far off, and I was alone. I continued so all the way.[d]

I am going to bed. The landlady is not literary, and calls me Mr. Digzon. In other respects it is a good house.

My dear Thompson, always yours,

CHARLES DICKENS

To MRS HENRY BURNETT, 1 MARCH 1844

MS Miss Gladys Storey.

Athenaeum | Friday First March 1844

My Dear Fanny.

I left Liverpool at half past ten on Wednesday Morning, and reached Birmingham at about half past Three; where I was received by some most excellent fellows,[2] and straightway conducted to the Town Hall, which positively took away my breath. A committee of ladies had decorated that immense building with artificial flowers,[3] to such an extent that it looked like a vast garden; and on the front of the Gallery facing the platform (which was erected below the organ) were the words "Welcome Dick", in gigantic letters of the same material. There were also transparencies representing divers Fames in the act of crowning divers Dicks: to the unspeakable admiration and delight of the queen, who looked on, approvingly. Having danced a Sir Roger of forty couple until Three o'Clock in the morning, I was rendered rather nervous by these splendid preparations—especially as I was vexed to have nobody with me to see them. But I dined by myself at the Inn—took a pint of Champagne and a pint of Sherry—dressed in the Magpie waistcoat—and was as hard as iron and as cool as a cucumber again. At ten minutes before eight, they fetched me; and immediately on my arrival, I ascended the Scaffold. The hall was crammed to the roof, with all the first-rate tories, whigs, and radicals in the town; and ladies in full-dress were standing, for want of seats, in all parts of the crowd. The moment Dick appeared the whole assembly stood up, with a noise like the rustling of leaves in a wood; and then began to cheer in the most terrific manner I ever heard; beginning again and again and again. When they at last left off, Dick dashed in—and I must say that he delivered the best speech I ever heard him make: to the great disconcertment of the Reporters, who fairly laid down their pens; sometimes to laugh, and sometimes to stare at him. On he went, right and left, hammer and tongs, until the audience (and oh such a good audience! [   ][4] London by the train at a quarter past one yesterday.

and made one of the speeches, concluding with the Latin motto of the Institution: "Non nobis solum sed toti mundi nati", which he translated as: "We must not be Ralph Nicklebys and Scrooges, but we must be Cheeryble brothers" (*Liverpool Mercury*, 1 Mar).

[1] Cf. *Hamlet*, v, ii, 355.

[2] The officials were James James,

Francis Clark, William Scholefield, Arthur Matthews, and George B. Haynes.

[3] Also natural ones "from the Botanical and other gardens in the neighbourhood of Edgbaston" (*Birmingham Journal*, 2 Mar 44).

[4] The cutting out of ending and signature has removed seven lines here.

The Newspaper with the best Report[1] will be out tomorrow. I will not fail to send you one by Monday's Post. Now that the excitement is all over, I am perfectly exhausted, dead, worn-out, and Spiritless. The wear and tear since Sunday last—to say nothing of that of the number, which I finished shortly before—has rendered me quite prostrate. And but for the recollection of Miss Weller (which has its tortures too), I don't know but I would as soon be comfortably suffocated, as continue to live in this wearing, tearing, mad, unhinged, and Most extraordinary world[2]

[   ]

[CHARLES DICKENS]

To [?WILLIAM SCHOLEFIELD], 1 MARCH 1844*

MS University of California Los Angeles. *Address:* ending of letter with subscription cut away: probably William Scholefield (see *To* Scholefield, 19 Jan).

Athenaeum. | Friday First March 1844.

My Dear Sir

I cannot resist the impulse I feel, to write and beg you not to believe that in expressing a desire for our better acquaintance yesterday, I used (as I might have done in any ordinary case) mere words of course, having no deeper root than such words strike in common politeness. I am anxious to assure you that our brief intercourse has afforded me real pleasure; and that it will gratify [   ]³ more [   ]⁴ and I do [   ]⁵ much in this plain manner, because if I were not well-assured of your receiving it in the same spirit, I should have no desire to say it at all.

I have been asked for Papers by so many people, that if you will kindly send me a dozen Journals, I shall be saved some importunity. For the cost and charge thereof, I am your Debtor.

And when you tell me how the Polytechnic is going on, let me know whether my books are in its Library.⁶ If they be not, I shall be glad to present the Members with a set.

[   ]

[CHARLES DICKENS]

---

¹ The *Birmingham Journal*, a weekly appearing on Saturdays.

² Ending and signature removed.

³ The cutting away of ending and signature has removed the whole of one line and parts of three other lines; about 13 words missing here.

⁴ About four words missing.

⁵ About four words missing.

⁶ No annual reports of the Polytechnic Institution before 1847 survive. By that year, the library had all CD's works except *Oliver Twist*, mostly in more than one copy.

To T. E. WELLER,[1] 1 MARCH 1844

Text from *A Dickens Friendship*, ed. W[ilfrid] M[eynell], privately printed, 1931, pp. 13–15.

1 Devonshire Terrace, York Gate, Regents Park.
First March, 1844

My dear Sir,

Finding that your daughter had not read the volumes[2] which I send her in the enclosed parcel (from one of which I quoted a few words last night)[3] and, knowing that they could not but prove most acceptable to a mind such as hers, I obtained her permission to send them—and made a promise which it gives me real pleasure and delight to fulfil.

Will you tell her that I have marked with a pencil in the Index to each, those pieces which I should like her to read first—as being calculated to give her a good impression of the Poet's Genius?[4] And will you say that I have sent her a copy which is not quite new, in preference to a new one; hoping she might like it none the worse for having been my companion often, and for having been given to me by Tennyson himself?[5]

I scarcely know whether I do right or wrong in not closing my note to you here. But I cannot help saying to you that your daughter's great gifts and uncommon character have inspired me with an interest which I should labour in vain to express to you, though I set myself to it as to a task. I see many people as you may suppose; and many whom Nature has endowed with talents of one kind or another. The figures which come and go before me are so numerous, and change so constantly, that, however bright they may be, I am not accustomed to care much for them, or to feel any great degree of concern in their proceedings. But I read such high and such unusual matter in every look and gesture of the spiritual creature who is naturally the delight of your heart and very dear to you, that she started out alone from the whole crowd the instant I saw her, and will remain there always in my sight.

Your affection will not be displeased to hear this, I know, and therefore I disregard the singularity of the impression—or lose it in the singularity of the cause—and tell you the honest truth.

With cordial remembrance to Mrs. Weller and all your family,

Believe me always, Faithfully yours,
CHARLES DICKENS

---

[1] Thomas Edmund Weller (1799–1884): see Vol. III, p. 446n. Text reads "T. J. Weller" in error.

[2] Tennyson's *Poems*, 1842, in 2 vols.

[3] Not in the report of his Birmingham speech; but on Monday, 26 Feb at Liverpool he had quoted "Lady Clara Vere de Vere" (*Speeches*, ed. K. J. Fielding, p. 56).

[4] See Vol. III, pp. 306–7 and *n*.

[5] Alfred Tennyson (1809–92; *DNB*): see Vol. III, p. 460n. It is not known when this gift was made. Christiana Weller's copy survived until a few years before her death; its whereabouts is not now known.

CD is confused by the date of his promise to Miss Weller (27 Feb).

To F. C. BEARD,[1] 2 MARCH 1844

Extract in *Autograph Prices Current*, V, 1919–21; *MS* 2 pp.; dated 2 Mar 44.

Having just returned from a trip to Liverpool and Birmingham and received a present of turtle soup and venison, CD invites Beard to dine with him. The notice is short, because the turtle *won't keep*, and its not a thing to be trifled with.

To J. R. ISAAC,[2] 2 MARCH 1844*

MS Mr Cedric Dickens.

London. 1 Devonshire Terrace | York Gate Regents Park
Second March 1844.

Dear Sir

Permit me from my own house (I had not leisure in Liverpool) to thank you for the presentation copies of my lithographed likeness,[3] and for your very modest letter. The first needed no apology; and the second was *exceedingly acceptable to me.*

John. R. Isaac Esquire.

Faithfully Yours
CHARLES DICKENS

To DANIEL MACLISE, 2 MARCH 1844

MS Comtesse de Suzannet.

Devonshire Terrace | Second March 1844

My Dear Mac

We dine together at the Piazza before going to Paganini's[4] tonight. I will call for you at about 10 minutes to 6.

I send you a Liverpool paper, and will add the munificent gift of a Birmingham paper when I get one. In the course of the day they will come I have no doubt.

On the other side[5] is a copy of the Graceful Impromptu penned by Dick in the album of that most wonderful girl Miss Weller. You had better have it copied in letters of gold—framed—glazed—and hung—by Green.[6]

Ever Faithfully
CD.

---

[1] Francis Carr Beard (1814–93), Thomas Beard's youngest brother: see Vol. I, p. 40*n*.

[2] Described on the lithograph as draughtsman, lithographer, and engraver of 62 Castle St, Liverpool.

[3] Now mounted in a large frame, beside the letter and a "description of the allegorical border" which surrounds the lithograph. This includes "emblems" of CD's published works ("Guilt and Innocence" represents *Oliver Twist*), and two figures, holding in one hand Comedy and Tragedy, the other supporting a pen attached to a globe; also wreaths of "Honor–Love–and Immortal Fame". Below the lithograph

is a Dedication "to the Directors and Members of the 'Liverpool Mechanics' Institution' | In commemoration of his presiding at the Annual soirée February 26th. 1844". Advertisements of the Soirée announced that copies were sold in aid of the Institution's Girls' School.

[4] Probably a joking variant for Pagliano's, i.e. the Sablonnière Hotel in Leicester Square, where they had perhaps taken a private room for carousing.

[5] The verses (see *To* Christiana Weller, 27 Feb, *fn*) are on p. 3 of the letter.

[6] Joseph Green, carver and gilder, 14 Charles St.

To CORNELIUS MATHEWS,[1] 2 MARCH 1844*

MS Robert H. Taylor Collection, Princeton. *Address:* By The Cunard Steamer. Cornelius Mathews Esquire | New York | United States of America.

London 1 Devonshire Terrace | York Gate Regents Park.
Second March 1844.

My Dear Sir.

Pray do not suppose for a moment that your letter was suggestive of any-thing but pleasure and gratification to me. I am in fault not to have replied to it, though even by a brief acknowledgement of its receipt; but my correspondence at home is something so tremendous, that I fall into arrear with my friends abroad, in spite of myself and my desire to retain their good opinion.

I am very glad you like the Christmas Carol. It has been an astonishing success here; and affected me so much in the composition, that if it had been otherwise, I verily think I should have broken my heart.

I do not remember having received the address you speak of, on the subject of Copyright.[2] But I may have done so without being able, now, to call it to mind. For the subject has long since passed from my thoughts. It only dwelt there, when I viewed the influences that make up an American government, through the mist of my own hopes and fancies. When that cleared away, I ceased to have any interest in the question.

Should you ever be in doubt again, relative to the expediency of sending me a Book, pray give me the benefit of it; and believe that I shall, at all times, be glad to hear from you.

My Dear Sir | Faithfully Yours
CHARLES DICKENS

Cornelius Mathews Esquire.

To MRS CLARKSON OSLER,[3] 2 MARCH 1844*

MS Mr Howard Smith.[4]

London. 1 Devonshire Terrace | York Gate Regents Park.
Saturday Second March 1844

Mr. Charles Dickens presents his compliments to Mrs. Clarkson Osler, and the Ladies; and begs to return them his warmest thanks for the little token of

[1] Cornelius Mathews (1817–89; *DAB*), journalist: see Vol. III, p. 405*n*.

[2] A copy of Mathews's pamphlet on International Copyright, based on his speech at the New York dinner (see Vol. III, p. 84*n*), inscribed "Charles Dickens Esq, with the respects of the Author", was in CD's library at his death (*Catalogue of the Library of CD*, ed. J. H. Stonehouse, p. 87). Mathews also signed a letter "To the People of the United States" in favour of International Copyright, 18 Oct 43 (*Morning Herald*, 22 Dec 43).

[3] Anne Lewis Osler, *née* Hornblower (1820–51), wife of Thomas Clarkson Osler, glass manufacturer, Birmingham; a member of the committee of ladies who decorated the Town Hall.

[4] A forgery of this letter was sold at Sotheby's, 28 July 1915, passed through the hands of various American dealers, and is now in the Benoliel Collection, FLP: see Vol. I, p. xxix, and reproduction, opposite.

Mr Charles Dickens sends to Mrs
Clarkson Osler his compliments to Mrs Clarkson Osler,
and the ladies, and begs to
return them his warmest thanks
for the little token of their colour
in the Town Hall, which they have
so kindly sent him. He does not
believe, and never will believe, that
the flower is an artificial one; for
that sends it will always to in
full bloom and fragrance.

London. 1 Devonshire Terrace,
Yorkgate Regents Park.
Saturday Second March 1844

164

Original and forgery of letter to Mrs Clarkson Osler

their labours in the Town Hall, which they have so kindly sent him. He does not believe, and never will believe, that the flower is an artificial one; for to his senses it will always be in full bloom and fragrance.

To THOMAS POWELL, 2 MARCH 1844*

MS Dickens House.

Devonshire Terrace. | Second March 1844.

My Dear Powell.

I really am more indebted and obliged to you than I can express, for your great interest and kindness in the matter of my small "bit of blood"[1]—to use a sporting phrase. And though there be five hundred thousand gallons of water to every scruple of Spirit in the Total abstinence Volume,[2] yet will I read it through and through, and never Wink.

Audiences of twos of thousands have been driving me mad at Liverpool and Birmingham, with their loving cheers. Ah! It is a brave thing, by Heaven it is, to walk out of the room where one is shut up for so many hours of such a short life, into a sea of agitated faces, and think that they are always looking on—

Woa, Spirit Number one. Woho my boy. Gently, gently. Don't be maudlin, Spirit. Think of your ethereal essence,[3] my buck. Steady, steady.

Come and take a little Ambrosia here, next Sunday (I mean tomorrow week) at 6 exactly, will you? I have a trifle of bottled Dawn—the old Aurora particular —the real crusted Rosy—if you can make your dinner off that, and a Zephyr or two. I shall be delighted to see you.

Ever Faithfully Yours
Ariel.

P.S. You don't happen to know anybody who wants a blossom (furnished)— do you? I think of letting my harebell.[4]

To G. H. RODWELL, 2 MARCH 1844

Mention in Sotheby's catalogue, Dec 1906; *MS* 1 p., dated 2 Mar 44.

---

[1] Augustus.

[2] A joking reference to Horne's *New Spirit of the Age*, elaborated later in the letter.

[3] Thus in MS.

[4] Endorsed by Powell: "To Sophia Iselin, I give this Autograph of Charles Dickens | Given at my palace 41 Trinity Square, On the fifteenth of January I swear." (A cancellation after "Iselin" reads: "sweetest of love's chickens Or the Doves of Venus".) Sophia Iselin, possibly the daughter of John James Iselin, merchant, 4 Austin Friars, published *My Dream Book* in Aug or Sep 1847, with a dedication to "her own friends and her father's friends . . . *Croydon*, 1847"—a mysterious volume, as a number of the poems had previously appeared in Powell's collections of 1842 and 1845. Some poems bear dates from 1826 to 1846; and for some, places are mentioned: e.g. "Dunach" (near Oban), "Egglestone", "Wimborne", "the Righi", "Croydon", and "Marshall's Wich" (i.e. Wick, near St Albans, seat of George Robert Martin). Powell was in hiding at Croydon after his exposure (see *To* Chapman, 3 July 46, *fn*).

To FREDERICK DICKENS, 4 MARCH 1844

MS Benoliel Collection. *Address:* Frederick Dickens Esquire | Commissariat | Treasury | Whitehall.

Devonshire Terrace | Monday Fourth March 1844.

My Dear Fred.

I forgot yesterday to give you the enclosed letter, addressed to yourself. Will you see the writer of the other one (who is close in your neighbourhood) and explain that I have been out of town—that I have no means whatever of giving the gentleman employment—receive scores of similar applications every day—&c &c.

If it seem a real case, I will give him my mite; but I have no knowledge whatever, so far as I know, of this Mr. Walker;[1] and you cannot watch him too sharply.

Let me know the result.

Affectionately Always
CD

To ANDREW DOYLE,[2] 5 MARCH 1844*

MS Dr De Coursey Fales. *Address:* Andrew Doyle Esquire | Morning Chronicle Office | Strand.

Devonshire Terrace | Fifth March 1844.

My Dear Sir.

Many thanks for your letter. I would rather leave the matter as I left it with you yesterday. For I should not desire to enter upon any other terms—I mean on any lower terms.[3]

I send you a short leader[4] agreeably to my promise. For tomorrow if you have room. May I ask you to give directions that the proofs are well read? Or to send them, by a boy, to me? A point is so easily spoiled.

Faithfully Yours

Andrew Doyle Esquire
CHARLES DICKENS

To JOHN FORSTER, [5 MARCH 1844]

Extract in F, IV, iii, 323. *Date:* 5 Mar according to Forster.

Sir, I will—he—he—he—he—he—he—will NOT eat with you, either at your own house or the club. But the morning looks bright, and a walk at Hampstead

---

[1] See *To* Forster, ?22 May 44.

[2] Andrew Doyle (1809–88), editor of *Morning Chronicle* 1843–8: see Vol. III, p. 514*n*.

[3] For the payment proposed by Easthope, see *To* Forster, 7 Mar.

[4] "The Agricultural Interest", not published till Sat 9 Mar (reprinted in *Miscel-laneous Papers*, ed. B. W. Matz, 1914, pp. 5–7). No other article written by CD for the *Chronicle* is known, and no leader of this period looks like his work, although Forster speaks as if several appeared (see F, IV, iii, 324–5)—clearly confusing CD's intentions with what happened.

would suit me marvellously. If you should present yourself at my gate (bringing the R. A.'s[1] along with you) I shall not be sapparized.[2] So no more at this writing from Poor MR. DICKENS.[3]

To COLONEL W. L. MABERLY,[4] 5 MARCH 1844*

MS Post Office Records.

> 1 Devonshire Terrace | York Gate Regents Park
> Fifth March 1844.

Sir.

In reply to your letter of yesterday's date, in which you do me the honor to enquire on behalf of The Postmaster General whether the representation made by the Proprietor of the Albion Newspaper, published in New York,[5] relative to his having purchased of me the Right of publishing "Martin Chuzzlewit", in Canada,[6] be correct or otherwise; I beg to say that it is perfectly accurate.[7]

Allow me to thank you for your care and attention in this regard; and to remain

> Sir | Your most obedient | Faithful Servant
Colonel Maberly CHARLES DICKENS

To JOHN MURRAY,[8] 5 MARCH 1844

Mention in *Autograph Prices Current*, V, 1919–21; MS 1 p.; dated 5 Mar 44.

Ordering books.[9]

To THE REV. R. H. BARHAM,[10] 6 MARCH 1844†

MS Benoliel Collection.

> Devonshire Terrace | Sixth March 1844.

My Dear Barham.

The Garrickers and the Aldermen are wonderful temptations; so are the

---

[1] Stanfield and Maclise.

[2] Cf. *Pickwick Papers*, Ch. 37, in the speech of the coachman at the Bath "swarry".

[3] Placed by Forster among "a few notes of besetting temptations during his busiest days at *Chuzzlewit*".

[4] William Leader Maberly (1798–1885; *DNB*), joint secretary of the General Post Office 1836–54.

[5] *The Albion, or British, Colonial, and Foreign Gazette*, edited by an Englishman, John Sherren Bartlett (see Vol. II, p. 421*n*); it had supported CD on international copyright.

[6] By the Customs and Excise Act of 9 July 42, American piracies of English works were prohibited from entering Canada and would be liable to seizure.

[7] There is no other record of the transaction; it clearly did not include the transmission of early proofs, proposed by the proprietors in 1842: see Vol. III, p. 321.

[8] John Murray III (1808–92; *DNB*), publisher: see Vol. II, p. 422*n*.

[9] No doubt some of Murray's Handbooks, for his journey abroad.

[10] The Rev. Richard Harris Barham (1788–1845; *DNB*): see Vol. I, p. 279*n*.

Vintages, if not the Vintners.[1] But I fear I must not go out to dinner next week. It is the week in every month in which I never go out to dinner, except on some tremendous provocation—such as a twin brother's coming home from China, and having appointed to return next Morning. Which does not often happen.

On one side I perceive a clear head, looking forward to the end of Chuzzlewit. On the other, a blear-eyed (but amiable and prepossessing) Youth, drinking Soda Water and incapable of any greater mental exertion than ordering it. On the one side, a solitary chop. On the other a Gregarious and Aldermanic spread.

[a]I strike myself on the breast—beat the stage doubtfully with my right russet boot—shake the feathers in my slouched hat—look darkly at you—suddenly cry "Tempter! No More!"—cross—defy you by tapping the hilt of my sword—and go off through a very little door, which has previously been shoved on sideways, by a man in scarlet plush.[a]

Faithfully Yours ever
CHARLES DICKENS

The Reverend R. H. Barham

To H. J. MORTON,[2] 6 MARCH 1844

MS Mr W. A. Foyle.

London. 1 Devonshire Terrace | York Gate Regents Park
Sixth March 1844.

Sir.

I am truly indebted to the Committee of the Wakefield Mechanics' Institution, for the Invitation with which they have honored me, through you. But I regret to add that the pressure of other engagements will render it impossible for me to attend their Anniversary Meeting on the Twenty Eighth.

I am Sir Yours faithfully and obliged
CHARLES DICKENS

H. J. Morton Esquire

To HENRY AUSTIN,[3] 7 MARCH 1844*

MS Morgan Library.

Devonshire Terrace | Seventh March 1844.

My Dear Henry.

I was coming to you yesterday, and brought Kate to walk half the way. She walked so impossibly slowly, that I was benighted at Covent Garden Market, and came back again.

---

[1] Barham had evidently invited CD to a dinner of the Vintners' Company; he had been elected their chaplain in 1834, and one of his duties was to "say grace over their turtle" (W. G. Lane, *Richard Harris Barham*, Columbia, Missouri, 1967, pp. 35, 69).

[a][a] Not previously published.

[2] H. J. Morton, Secretary of the Wakefield Mechanics' Institution and of the West Riding Union of Mechanics' Institutions.

[3] Henry Austin (?1812–61), CD's brother-in-law; architect, civil engineer, and Hon. Secretary of the Metropolitan Improvements Association: see Vol. I, p. 21n. In Apr 44 he gave evidence before the Commission for inquiring into the state of Large Towns and Populous Districts, about his experience of building for the poor.

I was coming to you to day at One. A false man[1] who was to have been here at 11 on business, took it into his head to write that he would come at 3 instead. Having disappointed him once myself, I was obliged to wait for him. And now your pavement is coming up Cheapside in a waggon, I *know*.[2]

If you lay down half as large a piece in Parliament as I have laid down in a still lower place, in right of these unfulfilled intentions, your fortune's made. I hope to Heaven you may floor both houses. *I* would if I could. I have no respect for them.

I wish you would come and see me sometimes. I have hardly set eyes on you, since we bearded an obdurate old Dragon who keeps watch and ward over Rochester Castle.[3] A question arises in my mind whether you would come and dine with me next Sunday, at 6. But God knows (as Maclise would say)—I dare say you wouldn't.

Longfellow is married—"him as got over the Wall"—(See principles of English Composition by T. Mitton).[4]

Henry Austin Esquire

Affy. Always
CHARLES DICKENS

To JOHN FORSTER, [7 MARCH 1844]

Extract in F, IV, iii, 325. Date: 7 Mar according to Forster.

Then[5] said the editor—and this I particularly want you to turn over in your

---

[1] Possibly Andrew Doyle, whom CD must have seen again before writing to Forster on 7 Mar.

[2] 7 Mar was the original closing date for submitting entries for the decoration of the Palace of Westminster, invited by the Commissioners for the Fine Arts in July 43. Austin & Rammell, of 10 Walbrook, sent in a design and specimen for an ornamental pavement; this was included in the exhibition held at Crockford's Bazaar, King St, St James's. In a letter to the *Athenæum*, 4 May, Austin corrected the description in the issue of 27 Apr: it was "inlaid veneering with the vertical fibre". Their entry was praised by the *Spectator*, 27 Apr, as "the most novel and beautiful", as well as durable and economical; it obtained an award, but was not selected for the Palace. However, the *Civil Engineer and Architect's Journal*, Sep 44, p. 363, reported that it was to be laid down in the library of the new Royal Exchange, opened in Oct; the *Morning Herald*, 24 Oct, described the floor as "inlaid woods, varied in colours so as to resemble mosaic work, the different shades and colours . . . brought out in all their brilliancy". The floor no longer

survives. Austin's partner was Thomas Webster Rammell, later Inspector to the Board of Health.

[3] During Longfellow's visit in Oct 42: see Vol. III, p. 343*n*.

[4] Forster recalls a day at Rochester during Longfellow's visit "when, met by one of those prohibitions which are the wonder of visitors and the shame of Englishmen, we overleapt gates and barriers, and, setting at defiance repeated threats of all the terrors of law coarsely expressed to us by the custodian of the place, explored minutely the castle ruins" (F, III, viii, 278). Mitton and Austin were clearly present. For Longfellow's marriage in 1843, see Vol. III, p. 550 and *n*.

[5] Immediately before the extract, Forster notes that "the proprietors of the paper rather eagerly mooted the question what payment he would ask for contributing regularly; and ten guineas an article was named". The editor, Andrew Doyle, however, pointed out that "so much would hardly be paid continuously; and thereupon an understanding was come to, that he would write as a volunteer and leave his payment to be adjusted to the results".

mind, at leisure—supposing me to go abroad, could I contemplate such a thing as the writing of a letter a week under any signature I chose, with such scraps of descriptions and impressions as suggested themselves to my mind? If so, would I do it for the *Chronicle*? And if so again, what would I do it for? He thought for such contributions Easthope would pay anything. I told him that the idea had never occurred to me; but that I was afraid he did not know what the value of such contributions would be. He repeated what he had said before; and I promised to consider whether I could reconcile it to myself to write such letters at all. The pros and cons need to be very carefully weighed. I will not tell you to which side I incline, but if we should disagree, or waver on the same points, we will call Bradbury and Evans to the council. I think it more than probable that we shall be of exactly the same mind, but I want you to be in possession of the facts and therefore send you this rigmarole.[1]

To CHARLES MACKAY,[2] 7 MARCH 1844

Text from Charles Mackay, *Forty Years' Recollections*, 1877, I, 191.

Devonshire Terrace | Seventh March, 1844.

My Dear Mackay,
I find (so far as I can judge from the few friends I have talked with) that there is an idea abroad that the Edinburgh people, or Scotch people, at all events, should finish their own monument,[3] and that some prejudice is created by the incompleteness of the testimonials to their two great men, Scott and Burns. I would, therefore, prefer to leave men to their own opinions in reference to joining the Committee, and have sent Brougham's[4] letter by post to him, without making any addition to it.

Faithfully yours,
Charles Mackay, Esq.   CHARLES DICKENS.

To H. J. [MORTON], 7 MARCH 1844

Summary in Sotheby's catalogue, June 1929; *MS* 2 pp.; dated 7 Mar 44. *Address:* "H. J. Merton" according to catalogue—clearly an error for "Morton".

Regretting that he cannot be present at a dinner on behalf of an institution; he would not in any case have entertained the idea of displacing their President.

---

[1] Forster says the "council" was held, and "in it lay the germ of another newspaper enterprise" (i.e. the *Daily News*).

[2] Charles Mackay (1814–89; *DNB*), poet and journalist: see Vol. I, p. 485*n* and Vol. III, p. 287*n*.

[3] £3000 was needed to complete the monument to Sir Walter Scott in Edinburgh, and Mackay had been applied to by Sir Thomas Dick Lauder to form a London Committee to raise money. CD, Ainsworth, Cruikshank, Jerdan and Lever were among those who joined the Committee; others, such as Bulwer Lytton, declined to serve. Subscriptions amounted only to £269 and a grand Waverley Ball was held at Willis's Rooms on 8 July which raised £1100. The monument was still incomplete in 1878 (see C. Mackay, *Forty Years' Recollections*, I, 175ff., and *Through the Long Day*, 1887, I, 143ff.).

[4] Henry Peter, Baron Brougham and Vaux (1778–1868; *DNB*): see Vol. II, p. 373*n*. Brougham did not answer Mackay's letter.

To HENRY HERSEE,[1] 9 MARCH 1844

Mention in Sotheby's catalogue, Feb 1970; *MS* 1 p.; dated Devonshire Terrace, Saturday Evening, 9 Mar 44.

Saying how much he appreciates the request by the Elocution Class of the City of London Institution[2] conveyed to him by Hersee; but he regrets that he must decline owing to his numerous engagements.

To MR PARKIN,[3] 9 MARCH 1844*

MS Benoliel Collection.

1 Devonshire Terrace | York Gate Regents Park
Ninth March 1844.

Mr. Charles Dickens presents his compliments to Mr. Parkin, and begs to thank him for his note. The dreadful thought that there was no Suet in the pudding, had already suggested itself to Miss Pinch's mind. Mr. Dickens will be careful that the Public shall not be deluded on the subject, and that the indispensability of Suet shall be distinctly recognized.[4]

To HENRY AUSTIN, 10 MARCH 1844*

MS Morgan Library.

Devonshire Terrace | Sunday Tenth March 1844.
My Dear Henry.

I cannot possibly be offended by your being mysterious, or pleasing yourself in any other harmless way. I feel much too cordially towards you for that.

I will give you a call in the city, sometime between this and June. I am bound for a long journey in July; when I turn my face towards Rome.

My hearty good wishes are with the Pavement. You must have had many anxieties and disappointments, and procrastinations of hope, I am very sure.

Affectionately Yours always
Henry Austin Esquire   CHARLES DICKENS

---

[1] Henry Hersee (1820–96), later a teacher of singing, music critic, and author of English adaptations of Bizet and Verdi. Lectured on CD in 1842.

[2] The City of London Literary and Scientific Institution in Aldersgate St. The Elocution class invited guest speakers to their public quarterly meetings; among those mentioned in the Institution's *City of London Magazine* (published 1842–3 only) are Westland Marston and Charles Cowden Clarke.

[3] Unidentified.

[4] No suet is mentioned in Ch. 39 in the March No.; but it is recognized as indispensable in Ch. 45 (May No.).

To THE COUNTESS OF BLESSINGTON,[1] 10 MARCH 1844

MS Benoliel Collection.

Devonshire Terrace | Sunday Tenth March 1844.

Dear Lady Blessington

I have made up my mind to "see the world"; and mean to decamp, bag and baggage, next midsummer, for a twelvemonth. I purpose establishing my family in some convenient place, from whence I can make personal ravages on the neighbouring country—and somehow or other have got it into my head that Nice would be a favorable spot for Headquarters.[2]

You are so well acquainted with these matters, that I am anxious to have the benefit of your kind advice.[3] I do not doubt that you can tell me whether this same Nice be a healthy place the year through—whether it be reasonably cheap—pleasant to look at and to live in—and the like. If you will tell me when you have ten minutes to spare for such a client, I shall be delighted to come to you, and guide myself by your opinion. I will not ask you to forgive me for troubling you, because I am sure beforehand that you will do so.

I beg to be kindly remembered to Count D'Orsay and to your nieces.—I was going to say "the Misses Power",[4] but it looks so like the blue Board at a Ladies' School,[5] that I stopped short.

Always Believe me | Dear Lady Blessington
Faithfully Yours

The | Countess of Blessington.   CHARLES DICKENS

To THOMAS MITTON, 10 MARCH 1844

MS Huntington Library.

Devonshire Terrace | Sunday Tenth March 1844.
On Greasy Paper.

My Dear Mitton.

Easthope is such a damned screw, and it is so impossible to fix him to anything, that I thought it best not to dally, but to do something—or the good men of the party, if they heard I was standing out on a question of Guineas (which they would be sure to do from him) might think I had rather forgotten Fred's quick appointment and rapid removal.[6] So I said to Doyle, "I won't make any bargain with him at all, or haggle like a pedlar, but I'll write a leader now and then, and leave him, in June, to send me a cheque for the whole. He shall set his own value on them; and if he sets too little, the shame is his, and not mine."

[1] Marguerite, Countess of Blessington (1789–1849; *DNB*): see Vol. II, p. 58*n*.

[2] Perhaps from studying Murray's *Handbook for . . . North Italy*.

[3] Lady Blessington had been at Nice for about a month in 1823, but settled at Genoa.

[4] Marguerite Power (1815–67; *DNB*): see Vol. III, p. 340*n*; and her sister Ellen.

[5] CD had made the same joke in writing to D'Orsay on 26 Dec 42: see Vol. III, p. 402 and *n*.

[6] Possibly referring to Whig influence in Fred's Treasury appointment and promotion.

He would pay *anything*[1] he says for letters from Italy. But that wouldn't do. I have no doubt he would pay 20 Guineas a week. But it wouldn't do.[2]

I send you a paper with my first article in it—the second leader.[3] When you have read it, send it me back, as I have no other.

The half year's account is *good*.[4] Deducting £50 a month from Chuzzlewit up to the end, the Debt is reduced to Nineteen Hundred Pounds. There will then be the half years profits to deduct and the whole Subscription.[5] So, please God, it will have come down bravely by the time I start.

This looks well, I think?

Faithfully Always

Thomas Mitton Esquire

CD

To T. J. THOMPSON, 11 MARCH 1844

Text from *A Dickens Friendship*, ed. W[ilfrid] M[eynell], privately printed, 1931, p. 18.

Devonshire Terrace. Monday, Eleventh March, 1844

My dear Thompson,

I swear to you that when I opened and read your letter this morning (I laid down my pen to break the seal, being just shut up in my room) I felt the blood go from my face to I don't know where, and my very lips turn white. I never in my life was so surprised, or had the whole current of my life so stopped, for the instant, as when I felt, at a glance, what your letter said. Which I did, correctly. For when I came to read it attentively, and several times over, I found nothing new in it.

This was not because it contained a word to astonish *me*, but because I never had imagined you remaining in Liverpool, or seriously admiring her.[6] Forgive me when I say that I did not think it lay in your temper or habit to do so unless it had become a thing of pretty long custom. I supposed you had returned to Yorkshire—I expected you in town any day—and have often wondered within myself whether you would still have an interest in recalling with me her uncommon character and wonderful endowments. I know that in many points I am an excitable and headstrong man, and ride O God what prancing hobbies!—and although I knew that the impression she had made on me was a true, deep, honest, pure-spirited thing, I thought my nature might have been prepared to receive it, and to exaggerate it unconsciously, and to keep it green long after

---

[1] Underlined twice.

[2] An additional reason against it must have been the negotiations with Bradbury & Evans: see *To* Forster, 7 Mar, *fn*.

[3] The *Morning Chronicle* of 9 Mar.

[4] Thickly underlined three times. The accounts showed the sales of *Chuzzlewit* from July to Dec. 43.

[5] To recoup the advance made to CD before he went to America, Chapman & Hall received the profits from *Chuzzlewit* and from July 43 deducted £50 from each of his monthly payments (see Vol. III, p. 516*n*); in July 44 they would receive that half-year's profits and the subscription for *Chuzzlewit* in volume form.

[6] Christiana Weller.

such a fancy as I deemed it probable you might have conceived had withered. So much for my injustice, which I *must* release myself of in the first instance.

You asked me to write, and I think you want me to write freely. I will tell you what I would do myself, if I were in your case and I will tell you without the least reserve.

If I had all your independent means, and twenty times my own reputation and fame, and felt as irresistibly impelled towards her as I should if I were in your place and as you do, I would not hesitate, or do that slight to the resolution of my own heart which hesitation would imply. But would win her if I could, by God. I would answer it to myself, if my world's breath whispered me that I had known her but a few days, that hours of hers are years in the lives of common women. That it is in such a face and such a spirit, as part of its high nature, to do at once what less etherial creatures must be long in doing.[1] That as no man ever saw a soul or caught it in its flight, no man can measure it by rule and rod. And that it has a right in such lofty development to pitch all forms laid down by bodies to the devil—the only thing, as far as I know, who was never in love himself, or inspired it in others.

And to the father I *would* point out, in very tenderness and sorrow for this gentle creature, who otherwise is lost to this sad world which needs another, Heaven knows, to set it right—lost in her youth as surely as she lives—that the course to which he is devoting her, should not be called her life but Death; for its speedy end is certain. I saw an angel's message in her face that day that smote me to the heart. He may not know this, being always with her; it is very likely he does not; and I would tell it him. Repose, change, a mind at rest, a foreign climate would be, in a springtime like hers, the dawning of a new existence. I believe, I do believe and hope, that this would save her; and that many happy years hence, she would be strong and hardy. But at the worst, contemplating the chance, the distant chance in such a case, of what is so dreadful, I could say in solemn and religious earnestness that I could bear better her passing from my arms to Heaven than I could endure the thought of coldly turning off into the World again to see her no more; to have my very name forgotten in her ears; to lose the recollection of her myself but at odd times and in remorseful glances backwards; and only to have the old thoughts stirred up at last by some indifferent person saying "You recollect her? Ah! She's dead."

As I live, I write the Truth and feel it.

So many ideas spring up within me, of the quiet happiness we might enjoy abroad, all of us together, in some delicious nook, where we should make merry over all this, that I don't know whether to be glad or sorry at my own hopefulness —Such Italian Castles, bright in sunny days, and pale in moonlight nights, as I am building in the air!—

But time is precious, and Dick is (to a certain extent) a prosing Donkey, if you

---

[1] Wilfrid Meynell notes (*A Dickens Friendship*, p. 16) that one of the first books given to Christiana by Thompson was a translation, published 1844, of De La Motte Fouqué's "The White Lady" and "Undine", inscribed in pencil: "To Her who in these lovely fictions may see her own character reflected—good and gentle as the White Phantom, spiritual as Undine —I offer this little volume. T. J. Thompson".

give him the rein. So as it is pouring very hard, and John will probably contract an asthma in running at the rate of seven miles an hour to the post-office to save the post, I will go on with my building after I have dispatched this.

I never was more in earnest, my dear Thompson, in my life.

Always faithfully your friend

CHARLES DICKENS

P.S. I am truly sorry to hear about Smithson[1] but I have been afraid of it for a long time. Write, if you remain.

P.P.S. I don't seem to have said half enough.

To W. M. THACKERAY,[2] [1–11 MARCH 1844]

Mention in Thackeray *to* his wife, 11 Mar 44 (*Letters and Private Papers*, ed. G. N. Ray, 1945–6, II, 165). *Date:* news included in Thackeray's first letter to his wife in Paris after his own return to London, 3 Mar.

Saying that Thackeray's notice[3] of him had touched him to the quick, encouraged him and done him good.

To F. W. POWELL,[4] 13 MARCH 1844

MS Columbia University Libraries.

I wish I had given this book[5] to Frank Powell; but I didn't, and couldn't How could I, you know Frank, when I was not acquainted with you? Don't you see? If you had come to my house, and had knocked at my door, and had said to my servant "Is Mr. Dickens at home?" my servant would have said "What name Sir?" Then you would have said, "Powell". Then he would have said "Powell of Peckham Sir?" Then you would have said, "The same". Then he would have said, "Walk in Sir". When you came in, I should have shewn you an Eagle (a real Eagle, you know, no nonsense or make belief), a Raven,[6] and a very small white dog;[7] curling all over; and barking, as the vulgar expression is,

---

[1] The first mention of Smithson's illness; he died 30 Mar.

[2] William Makepeace Thackeray (1811–63; *DNB*): see Vol. III, p. 432*n*.

[3] In "A Box of Novels", *Fraser's*, Feb 44, Thackeray concluded his notice with "the best [book] of all", referring to CD as "master of all the English humourists now alive" and "this delightful genius"; the *Carol*, he wrote, was "so spread over England by this time that no sceptic . . . could review it down"; it was "a national benefit, and to every man or woman who reads it a personal kindness"; Tiny Tim would be "a bond of union" between every reader and the author.

[4] Francis William Powell, second son of Thomas Powell, born 1838. Went to the USA with his parents in 1849; killed in the American Civil War.

[5] The *Carol*; the letter is written on the fly-leaf of a 1st edn.

[6] The eagle had been given to CD by M'Ian; CD's daughter Kate remembered it as "a most embarrassing gift" ("CD as a Lover of Art and Artists", *Magazine of Art*, 1903, p. 168). The raven was CD's third: see Vol. II, p. 412.

[7] Timber: see Vol. III, p. 162*n*.

like Bricks. And when you asked me to write my name in this book, I should have taken up a pen and done it so—

CHARLES DICKENS

But don't you flourish when you grow up, because its a bad habit, and don't leave room for the day of the month: which is the Thirteenth of March 1844.

To T. J. THOMPSON, 13 MARCH 1844

Text from *A Dickens Friendship*, ed. W[ilfrid] M[eynell], privately printed, 1931, pp. 25-7.

Devonshire Terrace. Thirteenth March, 1844

My dear Thompson,

"Think of Italy!" Don't give that up! Why, my house is entered, at Philipps's[1] and at Gillow's,[2] to be let for twelve months; my letter of credit lies ready at Coutts's; my last number of *Chuzzlewit* comes out in June; and the first week, (if not the first day) in July, sees me, God willing, steaming off towards the Sun.

Yes. We must have a few books, and everything that is idle, sauntering, and enjoyable. We must lie down in the bottom of those boats, and devise all kinds of engines for improving on that gallant holiday. I see myself in a striped shirt, moustache, blouse, red sash, straw hat, and white trousers, sitting astride a mule, and not caring for the clock, the day of the month, or the day of the week. Tinkling bells upon the mule, I hope? I look forward to it, day and night; and wish the time were come. Don't *you* give it up. That's all.

[a]I feel what you say in respect of your old suffering, and quite understood it as being expressed in your former letter. No man can enter on such lists with one who has trodden them, if he only knew them in imagination.

At the father, I snap my fingers. I would leap over the head of the tallest father in Europe, if his daughter's heart lay on the other side, and were worth having.

As to my chance of having it—well, I think I could make a guess about that

---

[1] William Phillips, estate and house agents, of 73 New Bond St, who let the house: see *To* Landseer, 27 May 44, *fn*. CD's description of the house, headed in a contemporary hand (presumably Phillips's clerk) "*No. 1 Devonshire Terrace* | 14 Feby. 1844", is as follows: "*On the Ground Floor.* Square Entrance-Hall, Library, Dining room, Breakfast room—now fitted as a bedroom, but carpeted and curtained as a sitting room. | *First Floor.* Drawing room, best bedroom, Second bedroom. Water closet. | *Second Floor.* Day Nursery, or large common Sitting room. Night Nursery, or bedroom with two beds. Female Servants' bedroom. | *Attic.* Mans room. | *Basement.* Large kitchen, Butler's pantry, Second kitchen, Cellars &c. | Good Garden and lawn; with two Water closets. Coach-house and two stall stable wholly detached, with Grooms Dwelling-room and Loft above. The house enclosed, and not overlooked | For any term, from 3 months to 12. To be seen from 2 to 4, every day." At the end a third hand has added "from 12 to 1"; an endorsement on the other side "*Dickens Esq* | *June 46*" suggests that the description was used again in that year, Sir James Duke's tenancy dating from 1 June (MS Dickens House).

[2] Gillow & Co., merchants and upholsterers, 176-7 Oxford St.

aa; bb Omitted in MDGH, 1882.

(tesselating a great many little things together) which should not be very wide of the mark.

But I could not tarry where I could not resolve. For aught you know, you may deal a heavier wound than you realize; and you certainly will not salve your own by keeping it open. You will crucify nothing but yourself upon that Diamond Cross unless it be *her*self too.

If you come to town I shall look to see you immediately. If you remain there, to hear from you. In either case to go abroad with you, stay there with you, and come back with you.*a*

Always, my dear Thompson, Faithfully your Friend,
CHARLES DICKENS

*b*I'll send him those verses[1] to-morrow.*b*

To MISS ISABEL BOOTH,[2] 14 MARCH 1844

Mention in Sotheby's catalogue, Dec 1911; *MS* 1 p.; dated 14 Mar 44.

To CHARLES FOWLER,[3] 14 MARCH 1844

Text from N, I, 581.

Devonshire Terrace | Fourteenth March 1844

Mr. Charles Dickens presents his compliments to Mr. Fowler and with many thanks to the President and Council of the Artists' General Benevolent Institution for the invitation with which they have honoured him, regrets that it will not be in his power to attend the dinner on Saturday the Thirtieth.

To JOHN FORSTER, [?15 MARCH 1844]

Extract in F, IV, iii, 324. *Date:* soon after 13 Mar when the *Hibernia* reached Liverpool.

I heard from Macready by the *Hibernia*. I have been slaving away regularly, but the weather is against rapid progress. I altered the verbal error, and substituted for the action you didn't like some words expressive of the hurry of the scene.[4] Macready sums up slavery in New Orleans[5] in the way of a gentle

---

[1] Not identified: presumably sent with *To* Weller, 15 Mar.

[2] Unidentified.

[3] Charles Fowler (1792–1867), architect; one of the original members of the Institute of British Architects, of which he became successively Hon. Secretary and Vice-President; Hon. Secretary of the Artists' General Benevolent Institution 1838–44. CD was refusing an invitation to the Institution's Anniversary Meeting at which Sir Martin Archer Shee presided.

[4] Forster says that CD wrote "from amidst his famous chapter in which the tables are turned on Pecksniff"; but Ch. 52 was not written until May. Perhaps Forster confused a reference to Ch. 43 (in the Mar No.), also about Pecksniff; alternatively these two sentences, which interrupt the account of Macready, may have been taken from a later letter.

[5] Macready stayed in New Orleans 3 Feb–2 Mar; according to his diary, he wrote to CD on 9 Feb. Before leaving

doubting on the subject, by a "but" and a dash. I believe it is in New Orleans that the man is lying under sentence of death, who, not having the fear of God before his eyes, did not deliver up a captive slave to the torture?[1] The largest gun in that country has not burst yet—*but it will*. Heaven help us, too, from explosions nearer home! I declare I never go into what is called "society" that I am not aweary of it, despise it, hate it, and reject it. The more I see of its extraordinary conceit, and its stupendous ignorance of what is passing out of doors, the more certain I am that it is approaching the period when, being incapable of reforming itself, it will have to submit to be reformed by others off the face of the earth.

To EDWIN LANDSEER,[2] 15 MARCH 1844*

MS Mr W. D. Varnals.

Devonshire Terrace | Fifteenth March 1844.

My Dear Landseer.

I am delighted to book myself for Sunday the Twenty Fourth. You don't say at what hour. Let me know in the meanwhile.

All well, and loving | Faithfully Yours always

Edwin Landseer Esquire.   CHARLES DICKENS

To T. E. WELLER, 15 MARCH [1844]*

MS Dr. LaFayette Butler. *Date:* CD wrote "1845" in error (impossible as he was then abroad).

1 Devonshire Terrace | York Gate Regents Park.
Fifteenth March 1845.

My Dear Sir

I return you the letter you were so kind as to send me;[3] and also the critiques, which you may naturally desire to preserve.[4] I will not fail to interest Mr. Hogarth[5] in one who needs no favor from any man, woman, or child;—though Heaven has shewn her, much.

Mobile he had witnessed a sale of slaves, and while he blamed the Abolitionists for their "indiscreet zeal", he said he would "neither wonder nor blame if I saw these black and dusky men strike their knives into the brutal bosoms of those who assert the right of might over them" (*Diaries*, II, 260, 262).

[1] *The Times*, 9 Mar, quotes from a New Orleans paper the report of the sentence of death passed by Judge O'Neall on J. L. Brown, for aiding a slave to escape, and comments on "this judicial outrage" which "must reduce the State of Louisiana to the lowest pitch of public infamy".

[2] Edwin Henry Landseer (1802–73; *DNB*), animal painter: see Vol. III, p. 298*n*.

[3] Probably Thalberg's letter to Weller of 10 Dec 42, congratulating him on Christiana's playing of the *Norma* duet with him; printed in *Liverpool Mercury*, 24 Mar 43.

[4] Probably notices of Christiana's performances from provincial papers, many of which Weller preserved.

[5] George Hogarth (1783–1870; *DNB*), CD's father-in-law; lawyer, musician and music critic: see Vol. I, p. 54*n*.

Before the Month is out, I shall take an opportunity of acknowledging the receipt of a letter from Miss Weller, which it gave me *very great pleasure* to receive. In the mean time, do me the favor to convey to her my best wishes and truest regard, and to commend me cordially to all your house.[1]

[   ]

[CHARLES DICKENS]

To THOMAS MITTON, 18 MARCH 1844

MS Huntington Library.

Devonshire Terrace | Monday Eighteenth March 1844.

My Dear Mitton

Kate heard from Mrs. Smithson yesterday. I was therefore prepared for your account of Mr. Smithson's health.

A man giving his name Smith,[2] and declining to leave his business, called here twice (thrice, I think) on Friday, and once on Saturday: giving each time a thundering double knock, and sort of fire-bell ring. On Saturday, he left a Card of *Strange's*;[3] and you being out of town, I thought it best to see him if he came again; and as he called early this morning, and said he would call again at One, I had him shewn up.

As I *must* use the Interview in a book,[4] I can't weaken it by writing it down. He was a literary gentleman—not a friend of Mr. Strange's, but acquainted with him—called out of a regard for my character—Mr. Strange had shewn him an advertizement he intended to print, which would have a dreadful effect on any man—Mr. Strange had spoken of applying to Sir Peter Laurie (!)[5] representing that the Solicitor had been going round, taking different sums of money from different people—he (Smith) would suggest to me that there was no Equity in punishing the innocent utterers of a Piracy, like the Pirates—&c &c &c &c. "Sir", said I, with my hand upon the bellrope, "I know nothing of Mr. Strange except what you tell me, which enlightens me curiously; touching that Gentleman. I regard my character as quite beyond the reach of Mr. Strange's assailment. There does not seem to me to be any particular Equity in my being one or two hundred Pounds out of pocket, even if Mr. Strange paid his full costs. Tell Mr. Strange from me that I am determined to stop this Piracy and to put it down[6]—and that if he Sent Everybody in London to me, I would not interfere

---

[1] Endorsement by "TEW" says the signature was cut off.

[2] Unidentified.

[3] William Strange, one of the booksellers proceeded against in the *Carol* case. Publisher of the first penny magazine, *The Penny Story-Teller*, 1832, *Figaro in London*, and *Chambers's London Journal* (with Clements and Berger). He was in trouble in 1848–9 over the attempt to exhibit some stolen royal etchings: see *Prince Albert v. Strange* (Jaques, *CD in Chancery*, p. 56).

[4] No such interview can be identified in any of CD's writings.

[5] Sir Peter Laurie (1779–1861; *DNB*), a Middlesex magistrate and former Lord Mayor; constantly attacked in *Punch*, and the original of Alderman Cute in *The Chimes*.

[6] Written large, perhaps because it was a phrase of Peter Laurie's.

between him and my Solicitors." So—he saying the same thing over and over again, and I doing the like—the Interview terminated.

Now, I think Mr. Strange must imperatively be looked to, forthwith.

I have been writing all day, and I have only just time to save the Post. Barely that.

Faithfully Ever
CD.

Thomas Mitton Esquire.

To COUNT D'ORSAY,[1] 19 MARCH 1844*

MS Comte de Gramont.

Devonshire Terrace | Nineteenth March 1844.

My Dear Count D'Orsay.

I am heartily obliged to you for your kind letter, and thank you, most sincerely, for the interest you take in my proceedings.

I swear by Pisa.[2] It's[3] accessibility, position, climate, recommendation, and everything else (to say nothing of the Kid;[4] upon whose grave I will shed a tear if I can find one) beckon me thither. Pisa is the Devonshire Terrace of my adoption.

I am on the look-out for some bilious colonel or dark West Indian, who will take my house for a twelvemonth. He shall have a Raven and an Eagle *in*, if he wish it. Together with a litter of little bulldogs, with very large blunt heads,

---

[1] Alfred, Count D'Orsay (1801–52; *DNB*): see Vol. II, p. 291*n*.

[2] D'Orsay had written (in French) on 16 Mar, advising CD to "go straight to Pisa"; he spoke of its central position, convenient for visiting other Italian cities, and advised strongly against "that hideous Nice . . . a kind of walking Père-Lachaise" (Maurice Lecomte, *Le Prince des Dandys: Le Comte D'Orsay (1801–1852)*, Paris, 1928, p. 226). He and the Blessingtons had lived at Pisa for six months in 1827, in Casa Chiesa on Lung'Arno; the surroundings were described in Lady Blessington's *Idler in Italy*, 1839–40, II, 296, 307–8.

[3] Thus in MS.

[4] D'Orsay had written: "You will be able to go to Leghorn to see the spot where Lady H— buried the kid". This curious incident occurred during the first marriage of Lady Holland to Sir Godfrey Webster. Several variants of it are found, but that given by her son Colonel Henry Webster in a letter to the *Literary Gazette*, 6 Jan 38 (quoted in *The Times*, 8 Jan), must be regarded as authentic. He wrote to correct the version given without a name in Lady Charlotte Bury's *Diary Illustrative of the* *Times of George IV*, recently published anonymously by Colburn—who cancelled the page accordingly. In 1796 Lady Webster, as a result of "unfortunate differences" with her husband, was left at Florence with her children and formed another attachment; when the children were "about to be torn from her by an order from England", she feigned the death of her youngest child, a daughter, and caused a kid to be buried at Leghorn in its place in order not to be deprived of the infant. The *Diary* had stated that news of the child's death drove the husband to madness and suicide; this Colonel Webster denied, saying that the effect, when the ruse was discovered, was to make Sir Godfrey "allow the child to see its mother oftener than the rest"; his death did not occur until 1800. In Colonel Webster's view, the incident threw a charm over his mother's character, and he rejoiced at the opportunity "to establish the simple facts". Most readers, however, continued to think it a rather disreputable story. The daughter whose death was faked was Harriet, afterwards Lady Pellew: see *To* Forster, 24 May 45, *fn*.

who, when they are brought into my room, think the flowers in the pattern of the carpet are milestones or some such thing, and try to get over them.

Always Dear Count D'Orsay
Yours faithfully and obliged

Le Comte D'Orsay.   CHARLES DICKENS

To T. N. TALFOURD,[1] 19 MARCH 1844

Text in N, I, 582, checked from MS Sotheby's, Dec 1964.

London 1 Devonshire Terrace York Gate Regents Park.
Nineteenth March 1844.

My Dear Talfourd.

The writer of the enclosed is Mr. Charles Mackay—"poet"; and Sub Editorial, paste-and-scissorsorial Craftsman of the Morning Chronicle. He called on me, and asked me for my name: which I gave him, chiefly because while Statues are erected to fighting men by sea and land, I like one to be put up now and then, in honor of that amiable Dragon, Intellect, which Saint George (in his court-dress) is rather fond of riding over. But in principle, I quite agree with you.

He asked me to speak to you; and my reply was, that you were on circuit, but in writing to you, he was free to say he had been with me. I have no feeling whatever on the subject, which is worthy of the name. Indeed I especially told him that there would be a prejudice abroad in reference to the Edinburgh people requiring external assistance to finish Monuments in honor of their two great men, Scott and Burns; and that unless he could get a very good Committee indeed, starting with bright prospects of success, he had better leave the thing alone. In which he entirely agreed—or so professed.

Mr. Berger[2] has paid his costs. At least, his bill was £42, and we let him off for £30. If you could have seen a man whom Mr. Strange sent to me yesterday! He had called, he said, (he was a Literary Gentleman) entirely from a regard to my reputation. Mr. Strange, indignant at Injunctions being obtained against four publishers, had drawn up an advertizement which must have an immense effect upon the reputation of any man. Mr. Strange had hinted darkly at making application to Sir Peter Laurie (!!) on the subject of costs being got from several parties; and he recommended me, for my own sake, to let Mr. Strange off, scot free. I told him, with my hand upon the bell rope, (but with a comfortable coolness which threw him out of his saddle instantly) that I had not the pleasure of knowing Mr. Strange, except as a Pirate; and that what he had mentioned of that gentleman did not dispose me to form a very high estimate of his character. That he might give my compliments to Mr. Strange, and inform him that I was determined to put the Piracy down, and Mr. Strange with it, as far as his invasion of my property was concerned; and that if Mr. Strange sent all London to me, I would not interfere between him and the attornies, who had already treated him with infinitely more consideration than he deserved. My gentleman, coming

---

[1] Thomas Noon Talfourd (1795–1854; *DNB*): see Vol. I, p. 290n.

[2] See *To* Mitton, 11 Jan, *fn*. The others had paid by 5 May.

down a peg or so, then said, that there were sentiments expressed in my books which—which Mr. Strange (I suggested) had construed into a disposition on my part to allow myself to be plundered in all directions. I would endeavour to shew Mr. Strange that he was mistaken in his reading.

So it ended. And this Strange having been in contempt for some days, I would have had him taken this morning, for his Audacity, but that Mr. Mitton is unfortunately out of town. The Action against the Assignees of the Bankrupts, we will pursue to the Death.[1]

I had a great notion myself, of making them drink something with that pudding —or rather of stating what they *did* drink (it was Punch; you are quite right) but on reconsideration I thought it best to let the Pudding stand by itself.[2] I have a little idea for the last two or three pages of the book, which I hope will please you. So far as I know, it is quite a new thought; and if I can work it out as I have it in my head, I think it will be very gentle and pretty.[3]

Horne's book[4] is Syncretic.[5] Shadows of Martinuzzi, Gregory the Seventh,[6] and Co. darken its pages, and make the leaves hideous. Don't you feel that,

[1] Lee & Haddock had taken refuge in bankruptcy, their names appearing in the Gazette of 24 Feb; CD therefore took action against their assignees (one only is named, as "Whitmore", in the list of Bankrupts in the *Jurist*, 24 Feb 44), and a declaration claiming damages of £1000 was drawn up by H. H. Dodgson on instructions by Mitton (the opening of an undated draft is in Dickens House). Talfourd (then on circuit) wrote to Mitton 28 Feb [44] suggesting amendments, including the addition of a description of the piracy; his letter ends: "I hope . . . that some means may be found to deliver our friend from the penalty which will await on success— the payment of his own costs of an action against Bankrupt Robbers" (MS Dickens House; and see S. J. Rust, "At the Dickens House. Legal Documents relating to the Piracy of *A Christmas Carol*", D, xxxiv [1938], 41ff.).

[2] Ruth Pinch's beefsteak pudding, in Ch. 39 (No. xv, published 1 Mar).

[3] Tom Pinch at the organ, in Ch. 54.

[4] *A New Spirit of the Age*, edited by R. H. Horne, was published after some delays on 9 Mar; Horne had been apprehensive about its reception, and with reason—as Elizabeth Barrett said, he was "leaping into a gulph . . . putting [his] foot into a hornet's nest", but she thought he had been "infamously used" (*Letters of Robert Browning and Elizabeth Barrett*, 1899, I, 69). Most reviews were unfavourable, objections being made to the pretentiousness of adopting Hazlitt's title and passing judgment on the work of living contemporaries, to the attacks on Barham, Ainsworth, Macready, and Mrs Trollope, and to the many omissions—for instance, of Mill, Fox, Maria Edgeworth. Several reviewers suggested that the work was the product of a clique, "the peculiar view of a peculiar set of minds" (*Athenæum*, 23 Mar); Blanchard, reviewing it in *Ainsworth's Magazine*, Apr 44, under the title "The New Gull's Horne-book", accused the contributors of "bandying personal compliment". Thackeray, in the *Morning Chronicle*, 4 Apr, complained particularly of Horne's verbosity and banality: a "cornucopia" of words, "but the thoughts are scarce . . . the opinions for the most part perfectly irreproachable, and the *ennui* caused by their utterance profound".

[5] A "Syncretic Society"—the word implying emphasis on common beliefs underlying differences—had been formed in 1839 by the philosopher James Pierrepont Greaves; Horne, J. A. Heraud, Westland Marston, George Stephens, and Frederick G. Tomlins were among the members, one of their common concerns being the authorship of various unacted dramas, rejected by managers, and their wish to break the monopoly of the patent theatres. Accordingly in Aug 41 the group hired the Lyceum Theatre in order to produce Stephens's play *Martinuzzi* (songs were added to evade the law and make it a musical drama, Horne being the musical director); they ran it for some weeks but lost money and attracted a good deal of

rather? I am a disinterested objector[1] Heaven knows—except in the regard of my portrait, which looks in my eyes a leetle like the Iron Mask,[2] without The Man in it.

I hope my dear Talfourd that when you come back, I shall see you often. For on the first of July, please God, I turn my face towards Italy—most likely for a whole year's absence. D'Orsay recommends Pisa for headquarters; and other judgments back him.

Ever My Dear Talfourd | Faithfully Your friend

Mr. Serjeant Talfourd   CHARLES DICKENS

To UNKNOWN CORRESPONDENT, 19 MARCH 1844

Mention in Sotheby's catalogue, Apr 1923; *MS* 2 pp.; 3rd person; dated 19 Mar 44.

To SAMUEL ROGERS,[3] 20 MARCH 1844*

MS Colonel Richard Gimbel.

Devonshire Terrace | Wednesday March Twentieth | 1844.

My Dear Mr. Rogers.

I am greatly vexed to say, that I have a friend from Italy[4] (you have heard of Italy?) coming to breakfast here tomorrow,[5] and most likely to sleep here tonight. As he will only be a single day in town, I cannot put him off. And I am therefore most reluctantly obliged to deny myself—or rather to be denied—the pleasure you so kindly propose.

I am sorry to hear you are confined to the house; but I take it for granted it is only Influenza. I have a very red nose myself, and wheeze incessantly.

mockery—"the spectators laughed where they ought to have cried" and the "authors' theatre . . . floundered to a bad end" (*Elizabeth Barrett to Miss Mitford*, ed. Betty Miller, 1954, p. 90). The "Syncretic" element in the *New Spirit* was the defence of the unacted drama in the essay on Knowles and Macready, and perhaps the mention of Thomas Powell's verse-plays in the essay on Marston and Browning.

[6] Horne's play, never performed but published 1840, with an "Essay on Tragic Influence"; attacked by Henry Chorley in the *Athenæum*.

[1] The essay on CD which opened the first volume was the longest in the collection and contained an elaborate comparison with Hogarth. By June 44 Horne had heard that CD was discontented with it, but Elizabeth Barrett thought this must be a mistake (*Letters . . . to R. H. Horne*, ed. S. R. Townshend Mayer, 1877, I, 261).

[2] The portrait engraved from Margaret Gillies's miniature: see Vol. III, p. 525*n*. Elizabeth Barrett thought he had "the dust and mud of humanity about him, notwithstanding those eagle eyes" (*ibid*, I, 255).

[3] Samuel Rogers (1763–1855; *DNB*), the banker-poet: see Vol. I, p. 602*n*.

[4] Angus Fletcher, who failed to turn up: see *To* Fletcher, 24 Mar.

[5] D'Orsay was also invited (D'Orsay *to* CD, 16 Mar: see *To* D'Orsay, 19 Mar).

Kate and her sister send their best loves to you. Will you give my kind remembrances to Moore?[1]

Always My Dear Mr. Rogers | Faithfully Yours

Samuel Rogers Esquire   CHARLES DICKENS

To JOHN OVERS,[2] 21 MARCH 1844

MS Harvard College Library.

Devonshire Terrace. | Thursday Twenty First March | 1844

Dear Mr. Overs.

I am very sorry to hear you are so unwell. If you have ever any particular reason for desiring to see me, let me know; and I will come out to you with pleasure.

You are quite right to *try*, in the regard of the Blue Coat School.[3] Faint heart never won anything, but has always stood towards every object in the World, in the same relative position as towards the fair lady. I must tell you, however, that these presentations are very eagerly sought after[4]—that immense influence is exerted to obtain them—and that the Institution is very much abused.

There are only two names on the list (of which I have any knowledge)[5] that appear promising. I have marked them. I know some of the other gentlemen; but I know also, that their influence has been long engaged. I do not take them into account, therefore.

Faithfully Yours

Mr. Overs.   CHARLES DICKENS

To ANGUS FLETCHER,[6] 24 MARCH 1844

MS Berg Collection. *Address:* Angus Fletcher Esqre. | Poste Restante | Carrara.

London. 1 Devonshire Terrace, York Gate
Sunday Twenty Fourth March 1844.

My Dear Fletcher

You have (unconsciously) covered me with shame; and degraded me to an ignominious and deplorable level.

In an evil hour, I invited Fred, the McIans, and Maclise, to dine here last Wednesday the Twentieth—I repeat it in capitals, THE TWENTIETH. Said

---

[1] Thomas Moore (1779–1852; *DNB*), poet: see Vol. III, p. 506*n*. He was staying in Sackville St, and on 21 Mar dined with Rogers at his sister's, "a large party" (*Memoirs, Journals, and Correspondence of Thomas Moore*, ed. Lord John Russell, 1853–6, VII, 367).

[2] John A. Overs (1808–44), a London cabinet-maker: see Vol. I, p. 504*n*.

[3] Overs was evidently trying to get a presentation to Christ's Hospital for one of his sons: see *To* Miss Coutts, 8 Dec 44.

[4] 185 were admitted in the current year.

[5] Edward Marjoribanks was a Governor.

[6] Angus Fletcher (1799–1862): see Vol. I, p. 514*n* and Vol. II, p. 57*n*.

I, "Fletcher—a punctual man—is coming from Italy, and will turn up at half past five, sharp." I made use of the expression "sharp". They jeered; they sneered; they taunted me. "He will not appear",—said they. "I know him better", said I. "We will dine", said they, "with pleasure. But Fletcher will not appear." Confiding in the rectitude and punctuality of my own heart, I ordered your knife and fork to be laid. John laid it. The guests arrived. At five and twenty minutes to six, *they became restless. At twenty minutes to six, they remonstrated formally. At a quarter to six, they grew mutinous and insolent. At ten minutes to six,* they proposed to leave me in a body, and dine together at the Star and Garter, Richmond. At five minutes to six, they rang the bell, and ordered John, on pain of death, to serve the Banquet. That wretched Innocent complied. Over my mortification and anguish, let me draw a decent veil.

* * * * * * * * * * * * *

Seventhly—I think it was seventhly I left off at, in my last—seventhly—
I find it necessary for the sake of effect to turn over. Seventhly, I am coming to Italy.[1] Bag and baggage, children and servants, I am coming to Italy for twelve months. We start, please God, on the first of next July! Take breath, and I will proceed.

I purpose establishing my head quarters in some one place, from which I can, at such intervals as suit me, harass and ravage the neighbouring countries. Lady Blessington and Count D'Orsay, who are well acquainted with the locale, assure me that I cannot do better than set up my rest at Pisa. And *to* Pisa, therefore, we shall proceed straight. Unless I hear any special reason (which does not seem likely) for giving the preference to any other place.

Now, my modern Canova, I don't know where Carrara[2] is. I dont know where anywhere is, indeed, exactly. But if you can come to Pisa, and meet us, we shall be truly delighted to see you. And the benefit of your advice in taking quarters, would be very great. *Of course I don't mean to live at an hotel: but in private apartments.* There is a Palazza[3] di Something, commanding a southern view of somewhere, in which I am told[4] we could be agreeably lodged. I want[5] to do the thing comfortably, but I don't want to fling my money away, for the benefit of the olive visaged sons of the balmy South—especially, as I have none to spare. Here is a list of the Caravan.

1. The Inimitable Boz
2. The other half of Do.
3. The sister of Do.—Do.—
4. Four babbies, ranging from two years and a half old, to seven and a half.
5. Three women servants, commanded by Anne of Broadstairs.[6]

---

aa Not previously published.
[1] These five words written very large.
[2] See *To* de la Rue, 18 Jan 45.
bb Added at end of letter, with asterisks indicating its position.
[3] Thus in MS.

[4] Presumably by D'Orsay, when they met on 21 Mar.
[5] MS reads "went".
[6] Anne Brown, Catherine's maid: see Vol. II, p. 392*n*.

Do you think a genteel stranger (No. 1) extensively *un*acquainted with the language, manners and customs, of Italy, could penetrate to Pisa (with Nos. 2, 3, 4, and 5) without engaging a sort of courier to attend him thither? If he could, do you or do you not consider that he would be most infernally done, by the way? Your reply on these points will be highly esteemed.

I have some idea of writing to the Astronomer Royal at Greenwich, to let me have a couple of solitary rooms in the observatory for Three months, that I may grow a reasonable moustache. London Society in the season, is not favorable to the cultivation of that Vegetable.

Tell me your opinion about the best way of coming, with such a train—whether we shall meet, and where—together with all other mattters and things that occur to you. I look forward to these new and brilliant scenes impatiently, as you may suppose.

Kate sends her best regards. We are all well. Fred's boots are still rather tight,[1] and he suffers in his feet. But in all other respects he is reasonably healthy.

If I have not astonished you, I am disappointed. I received your note, announcing the prolongation of your stay for six months, last Friday.

Always My Dear Fletcher | Faithfully Yours

Angus Fletcher Esquire   CHARLES DICKENS

To WALTER SAVAGE LANDOR,[2] 24 MARCH 1844*

MS New York University Library.

Devonshire Terrace | Sunday Twenty Fourth March 1844

A hundred thousand thanks my dear Landor for your note. Alas! No Bath for me, until the Chuzzlewit is done. And I am not much more advanced in it, at this present writing (I hope) than you are.[3] D'Orsay and Lady Blessington strongly insist that there is no such place for the Family Head Quarters, as Pisa; and they back this opinion by divers weighty arguments. What do *you* say?

Carry that same commodity up the Hill again, for me.[4] My mind misgives me that you play tricks with it, Landor. I see you at this instant coming out of your bedroom with that strawberry stock on. And no man knows (nor woman neither) how my blood boils at the sight.

Kate and her sister send their best loves to you. You see how fairly *I* deliver

[1] Characteristic of Fred: see Vol. II, p. 348.

[2] Walter Savage Landor (1775–1864; *DNB*), author of *Imaginary Conversations*: see Vol. II, p. 23*n*.

[3] In the reading of the monthly Nos; CD was not getting ahead.

[4] i.e. his love to the Paynters at 7 Great Bedford St, Bath: see Vol. II, p. 107 and *n*; and for the "inaccessible hill", where Paynters lived, Vol. III, p. 372.

the goods entrusted to my charge! Take care I am not down upon you, in an old Bailey point of view, for Embezzlement.

Ever Faithfully Yours
CHARLES DICKENS

To T. J. SERLE, 24 MARCH 1844

MS Mr Peter Brandt.

Devonshire Terrace | Twenty Fourth March 1844.

My Dear Serle.

I confess I have a strong personal desire to "pull"[1] Mr. Lancaster,[2] the hero of the enclosed letter; and make a Bow-street application in regard of his swindling in Charity's name. I would as soon do it, in my own person, as eat my breakfast.

I shall be glad to hear what you think of it, and also to confer with you, about Rosa's[3] passage out (which should be secured) &c &c. By the way, she is coming to you tomorrow morning for some money.

Can you come to me any Evening in this next week; or, better still, can you come and dine with me, *quite alone*, any day but Friday, at half past five? Make your own appointment, and it will be sure to be acceptable and convenient to me.

Always My Dear Serle | Faithfully Yours
CHARLES DICKENS

T. J. Serle Esquire

To T. J. THOMPSON, 24 MARCH 1844

Text from *A Dickens Friendship*, ed. W[ilfrid] M[eynell], privately printed, 1931, pp. 29–31.

Devonshire Terrace. Sunday, March Twenty-fourth, 1844

My dear Thompson,

My study fireplace having been suddenly seized with symptoms of insanity, I have been in great affliction. The brick-layer[4] was called in, and considered it necessary to perform an extensive[5] operation without delay. I don't know whether you are aware of a peculiar bricky raggedness (not unaccompanied by pendant stalactites of mortar) which is exposed to view on the removal of a

---

[1] Slang for to apprehend, to take into custody (*OED*).

[2] Possibly Edward Lancaster, theatrical agent of 3 Falcon Court, Fleet St.

[3] Rosa Elton, probably the second daughter, went to Nova Scotia in May: see *To* Serle, 2 May. She was accompanied by a friend of her father's, Mr Paine, and gave lessons in music. In 1846 she returned to England and is possibly the "Miss Elton" whom Mrs Gaskell and Mrs Cowden Clarke (the latter "representing Miss Elton's guardians") were helping to become a public singer, with assistance from Samuel Dukinfield Darbishire (T. Marshall, *Lives of the Most Celebrated Actors and Actresses*, p. 158; *Letters of Mrs. Gaskell*, ed. J. Chapple and A. Pollard, 1966, pp. 191–2; Charles and Mary Cowden Clarke, *Recollections of Writers*, 1878, p. 93).

[4] Probably J. & G. James, 11 Little York Place; CD paid "Jno James" £7.4.0 on 12 June (Account-book, MS Messrs Coutts).

[5] The reading of MDGH, 1882, III, 67–8; Meynell reads "expensive", in error.

stove, or are acquainted with the suffocating properties of a kind[1] of accidental snuff which flies out of the same cavernous region in great abundance. It is very distressing. I have been walking about the house,—after the manner of the Dove before the waters subsided—for some days, and have had no pens or ink or paper. Hence this gap in our correspondence, which I now repair.

What are you doing??? When are you coming away???? Why are you stopping there????? Do enlighten me, for I think of you constantly, and have a true and real interest in your proceedings.

D'Orsay, who knows Italy very well indeed, strenuously insists that there is no such place for Headquarters, as Pisa. Lady Blessington says so also. What do *you* say? On the first of July—the first of July!—Dick turns his head towards the orange groves.

*a*Do you eat at all yet? Are you still drinking? *What* do you drink? Thin potations that make your liver white; or generous fluids that inflame your heart to deeds of valour? At what time do you rise; at what time go to bed; where ride, and when, with whom and how; where sup and spend the evenings; what do you dream about? Give me something to guess by. Shake up the grouts[2] of that Liverpool life of yours, and let me read your fortune in the cup.*a*

Daniel not having yet come to judgment,[3] there is no news stirring. Every morning, I proclaim: "At home to Mr Thompson." Every evening I ejaculate with Monsieur Jacques: "But he *weel* come. I know he *weel*!"[4] After which I look vacantly at the boxes; put my hands to my grey wig, as if to make quite sure that it is still on my head, all safe; and go off, 1st. entrance O.P. to soft music.

*b*Give her my love. And don't appropriate it by the way.*b*

Always Faithfully your friend,
CHARLES DICKENS

To THE REV. P. GALE,[5] 25 MARCH 1844†

MS Morgan Library.

1 Devonshire Terrace | York Gate Regents Park
Twenty Fifth March 1844.

Sir.

*c*I beg to thank you for your courteous and good-humoured communication.*c* I was perfectly aware of Steevens's note in reference to the door-nail.[6] My

[1] The reading of MDGH, 1882; Meynell reads "pinch", in error.

aa; bb Omitted in MDGH, 1882.

[2] In the description of Mrs Clennam's house in *Little Dorrit*, Ch. 5, "the ceilings were so fantastically clouded by smoke and dust, that old women might have told fortunes in them, better than in grouts of tea".

[3] Possibly in reference to the *Carol* case.

[4] In Morris Barnett's musical piece, *Monsieur Jacques*, adapted from the French, and first performed at the St James's 12 Jan 36, Jacques constantly says of Mariana,

"I know it, she will come!" The part was played by Barnett (1800–56), who specialized in playing elderly Jews and foreigners (Barry Duncan, *The St. James's Theatre*, 1964, pp. 8, 20–1).

[5] There is no "P. Gale" in the *Clergy List*; possibly CD's misreading of signature of Thomas Gale (1789–1864), vicar of Milton Lilburne, Wilts, or Philip Serle (1784–1857), rector of Oddington, Oxfordshire.

cc Not previously published.

[6] George Steevens, the Shakespearean commentator, explained "door-nail" as the

meaning in observing gaily, in the Carol, that I don't know what there is particularly dead about a door-nail, is, that I don't know why a door-nail is more
dead (if I may use the expression) than anything else that never had life.

Faithfully Yours

The Reverend P. GaleCHARLES DICKENS

To RICHARD MONCKTON MILNES,[1] 25 MARCH 1844†

MS Trinity College, Cambridge.

Devonshire Terrace. | Twenty Fifth March 1844.

My Dear Milnes

 [a]I am very sorry to say, that having been out every day this last week, I have
been obliged to take a solemn vow, and make strict compact with myself, that I
will not go out to any meal, or other enjoyment this week, saving on Friday:
when I shall hope to meet you.[a]

 I have not acknowledged the receipt of your highly-esteemed present, because
I think it a poor compliment to thank an author for his book, without having
first read it. I am now in a condition to thank you; and honestly to assure you
that the elegance, tenderness, and thoughtful fancy of the Palm Leaves,[2] have
greatly charmed me, and have made an impression on me, such as I believe
you would yourself desire to produce, and would be satisfied with—fully.[3]

Believe me | With Many Thanks
Faithfully Yours

Richard Monckton Milnes EsquireCHARLES DICKENS

To MR PUNSHON,[4] 25 MARCH 1844*

MS Duke University.

1 Devonshire Terrace | York Gate Regents Park
Twenty Fifth March 1844.

Mr. Charles Dickens presents his compliments to Mr. Punshon, (if the name

nail on which the knocker strikes—dead from repeated blows on the head (Vol. V II, p. 225 of the Boswell–Malone edn of 1821 bought by CD at the Hill sale: see Vol. II, p. 229*n*).

[1] Richard Monckton Milnes, first Baron Houghton (1809–85; *DNB*): see Vol. I, p. 16*n*.

[aa] Not previously published.

[2] Milnes's latest volume of verses, published 16 Mar; a copy was in the Gad's Hill Library, inscribed "With the author's kind regards" (*Catalogue of the Library of CD*, ed. J. H. Stonehouse, p. 80).

[3] He had spent several months in the Levant and Egypt in 1842–3, and the poems, on such subjects as "The Hareem", "The Mosque", and "The Greek at Con-stantinople", show a serious interest in eastern civilization, emphasized in the long Preface. Carlyle wrote to him 17 Mar: "I find a real voice of song in it, breathings of genuine mild wisdom" and "a visible increase of earnestness"; he welcomed the sympathetic treatment of Mahometanism, which shocked some readers (T. Wemyss Reid, *Life, Letters and Friendships of Richard Monckton Milnes*, 1890–2, I, 323). Some interpreted Milnes's experiences more facetiously; a copy survives with comic illustrations by Thackeray showing him as an Eastern Pasha, and Kinglake's review in the *Quarterly*, Dec. 1844, under the title "The Rights of Women", is bantering in tone.

[4] Unidentified.

be incorrectly spelt, he begs to apologize: not being able to decypher his correspondent's signature satisfactorily), and begs to say that there is *not*, at present, any uniform Edition of his books.

To THOMAS MITTON, 26 MARCH 1844*

MS Huntington Library.

Devonshire Terrace | Twenty Sixth March 1844.

My Dear Mitton

I am afraid he[1] is in a bad way. It presented itself to me, when I came to think of it, as exceedingly probable that you would not have an opportunity of speaking to him on such a subject[2] at such a time.

I will call on you at *about* 3. There is no news of the house. All well.

Faithfully Ever

CD.

To F. O. WARD,[3] 26 MARCH 1844

MS Comtesse de Suzannet.

Devonshire Terrace. | Tuesday Twenty Sixth March 1844.

Dear Sir

It is quite unnecessary for me to say that I have a great regard for Hood; and hold his genius in the highest estimation.

I cannot promise to render any but the slightest assistance to his Magazine, in case it should recover the consequences of its late appearance this month.[4] But if it should, and if it should be in the hands of Mr. Spottiswoode,[5] I will certainly write *something* for the next Number.[6] It will necessarily be very short, and will most probably refer to its starting under new and favorable circumstances.

[1] Smithson.

[2] Probably the bond: see *To* Mitton, 30 May.

[3] Frederick Oldfield Ward, writer on sanitary subjects; educated as a surgeon, he was clerk to Joseph Hume and later worked for Edwin Chadwick, and wrote for *The Times*. A friend of Hood's since 1842, he kept the magazine going during Hood's illness in Apr–Sep 44, and also worked to obtain him a Government pension; on both matters Hood later quarrelled with him, but was reconciled on his deathbed in May 45. Browning described Ward as "a capital fellow, full of talent and congeniality" (Browning *to* Kenyon, July 1850; *Letters of Robert Browning*, ed. T. L. Hood, 1933, p. 30).

[4] The promised financial support of Edward Gill Flight for *Hood's Magazine* had proved to be fraudulent; bills were unpaid, Hood was owed £100, and both the Feb and Mar Nos had appeared late. Ward sought contributions from many authors; Tennyson and Ruskin were asked and declined, but Landor, Procter, Milnes and Mackay all responded favourably, and Browning sent poems, published in June–Aug 44 and Mar–Apr 45, including "Garden Fancies" and "The Tomb at St. Praxed's".

[5] Andrew Spottiswoode (1787–1866), head of Eyre and Spottiswoode, the Queen's Printers, agreed late in Mar to finance the magazine for 12 months (*Letters of Thomas Hood*, ed. Peter Morgan, p. 598).

[6] On hearing from Ward of CD's promise, Hood wrote on ?1 Apr to thank him, complaining of Flight's defection and

But in the case I have put, I will do that much with sincere pleasure—and would do much more, if my engagements permitted.

Faithfully Yours
CHARLES DICKENS

F. O. Ward Esquire

To THOMAS MITTON, [?27 MARCH 1844]*

MS Morgan Library. *Date:* clearly the last Wednesday before Smithson's death.
Address: Thomas Mitton Esquire | 23 Southampton Buildings | Chancery Lane.

Wednesday Morning

My Dear Mitton

I don't send you the enclosed,[1] because I think you can do anything, but because I think you would desire to know it. I have also heard from Thompson this morning: who says "I have no hopes of his getting over this Illness".

Faithfully Always
CD.

To H. J. MORTON, 27 MARCH 1844*

MS Yale University Library.

London—1 Devonshire Terrace | York Gate Regents Park.
Twenty Seventh March 1844.

Sir.

I beg to assure you, in reply to your letter, that it would have given me sincere gratification to attend the Meeting of the Delegates from the Associated Mechanics' Institutions of the West Riding of Yorkshire,[2] if I could, by any reasonable alteration of my Engagements, have done so. Nor would I allow my own

---

"Pecksniffian" behaviour, and asking how much space should be allowed for CD's contribution; he added: "I hear that you are going to learn on the spot to eat Italian macaroni" (*Letters*, pp. 599–600). CD's article was advertised at the end of the Apr No. as "a short communication from Mr. Charles Dickens", and "Threatening Letter to Thomas Hood from an Ancient Gentleman" appeared in May, with the date 23 April. It is a lively satirical piece, written in the character of a conservative who deplores the present age and the downfall of the constitution; among CD's targets are the Court's neglect of literature and the popularity of Tom Thumb. More seriously, he refers (without name) to the trial for attempted suicide of Mary Furley on 17 Apr, later recalled in *The Chimes*. Hood wrote to CD in May, thanking him for his "great kindness,

which I feel the more from knowing by experience how many obstacles there must have been in the way of it. Thanks to that & similar backing I shall now, I think turn the corner ... Your paper is capital—I had been revolted myself by the royal running after the american mite"; he longed to "have a gossip on things in general" but was unfit to go out. He still had some idea of reviewing *Chuzzlewit* for the *Edinburgh Review*, as "*the Athenæum is closed against me*" (see Vol. III, p. 559*n*), but nothing came of this. As far as is known, this is Hood's last letter to CD (*Letters*, pp. 613–15).

[1] Possibly from Alfred Dickens, from whom CD also heard on 28 and 29 Mar: see *To* Thompson, 29 Mar.

[2] The Soirée held at Wakefield on 1 May, at which Lord Morpeth presided.

personal convenience to stand in the way. But I regret exceedingly, that I could not leave town for such a purpose at the time you mention, without entailing serious inconvenience on others, whom I have no right to disappoint; and that I cannot, therefore, have the pleasure you propose to me.

The terms of your letter, sufficiently assure me, that I need not convey to you the expression of my hearty and cordial sympathy in the objects you have in view.

I am Sir | Faithfully Yours

CHARLES DICKENS

H. J. Morton Esquire

To THE COMMITTEE OF THE METROPOLITAN DRAPERS' ASSOCIATION,[1] 28 MARCH 1844

Text from *The Student . . . a Magazine of Literature, Science, and Art,* New Series, No. 1, Jan 1845, p. 19.

Devonshire Terrace, 28th March, 1844

Gentlemen,

I beg to assure you, that it gives me great satisfaction to have the honour of enrolling my name among the Vice-Presidents of your Association.

My engagements will not permit, I regret to say, of my attending your Meeting at the Hanover Square Rooms on Monday Evening.[2] But though absent in the body, I am with you in the spirit there and always. I believe that the objects you have in view, are not of greater importance to yourselves than to the welfare and happiness of society in general; to whom the comfort, happiness, and intelligence of that large class of industrious persons whose claims you advocate, is, if rightly understood, a matter of the highest moment and loftiest concern.

I understand the late-hour system to be a means of depriving very many young men of all reasonable opportunities of self-culture and improvement, and of making their labour irksome, weary, and oppressive. I understand the early-hour system to be a means of lightening their labour without disadvantage to any body or any thing, and of enabling them to improve themselves, as all rational creatures are intended to do, and have a right to do; and, therefore I hold that there is no more room for choice or doubt between the two, than there is between good and bad, or right and wrong.

I am, Gentlemen, | Your faithful Servant,

CHARLES DICKENS.

The Committee of the | Metropolitan Drapers' Association.

---

[1] Established 1842. Its President was James Emerson Tennent, MP. *The Student* was published "under the superintendence" of the Association. An editorial note to CD's "short, but most satisfactory Letter", says that "that highly gifted gentleman" had been invited to take part in the meeting and to accept the office of Vice-President.

[2] The meeting of 1 Apr was reported in *The Times* and *Morning Chronicle* of 2 Apr, with no mention of CD, though his letter was designed to be read at the meeting. CD's name was among the Vice-Presidents in 1845; others included Elliotson, Southwood Smith and S. C. Hall, who had been in the chair at the Feb 44 meeting.

To THE REV. HENRY HART MILMAN,[1] 28 MARCH 1844

Mention in unidentified catalogue.

An amusing letter, regretting the impossibility of getting to a meeting of the Geographical Association,[2] owing to prior engagements.

To T. J. THOMPSON, 29 MARCH 1844

MS Mrs Sowerby.

Devonshire Terrace | Friday Twenty Ninth March 1844

My Dear Thompson.

I congratulate you, with all my heart and soul, a million of times. It is a noble prize you have won. And I am sure you have won it, in a noble Spirit. A hearty God Bless you!

Good Heaven what a Dream it appears! Shall we ever forget that night when she came up to THE Piano—that morning when Dick, the energetic Dick, devised the visit! Shall we ever cease to have a huge and infinite delight in talking about the whole Romance from end to end—in dwelling upon it, exaggerating it; recalling it in every possible way, form, shape, and kaleidoscopic variety!

Ask her to save the dress—the dress with the fur upon it. Let it be laid up in Lavender. Let it never grow old, fade, shrink, or undergo millinerial alteration, but be a household God, Immortally Young and Perpetually Green. *Wasn't* it Green? I think so.

The father seems to have acted like a man. I had my fears of that, I confess; for the greater part of my observation of Parents and children, has shewn selfishness in the first, almost invariably.

I swear, my dear Thompson, that I am as well pleased as yourself. I send you all manner of cordiality, in this.

Of course I shall see you, as soon as you arrive here. I rather expect to hear that you have been called to Yorkshire, for I received dreary accounts of poor Smithson, this morning and yesterday, through Alfred.[3]

Always Faithfully Your friend,

T. J. Thompson Esquire

CHARLES DICKENS

[1] Henry Hart Milman (1791–1868; *DNB*), poet and historian, Dean of St Paul's from 1849; canon of Westminster and rector of St Margaret's Westminster since 1835. Nothing is known of his acquaintance with CD, but he was interested in the Metropolitan Improvements Association and in popular education, and Tothill Fields prison was close to his church.

[2] Perhaps CD was apologizing for his absence from the last soirée, on 27 Mar, at which "the élite of the literary and scientific world were assembled" (*Literary Gazette*, 30 Mar).

[3] Alfred Lamert Dickens (1822–60): see Vol. I, p. 44*n*.

To UNKNOWN CORRESPONDENT,
[JANUARY–MARCH 1844]*

MS (fragment) Mr W. J. Carlton. *Date:* Jan–Mar 44 on handwriting.

first note. But my answer must still have been, in effect, what you have already received from me.

I have not been unmindful of Mrs. and Miss Barrow's[1] condition as it is stated to me, but have made it known to Mrs. Barrow's nearest, and wealthiest relation.[2] If I decline to mention to you what kind of assurance from myself I coupled[3]

To MESSRS LEA AND BLANCHARD, 2 APRIL 1844

MS Historical Society of Pennsylvania. *Address:* By Post Office Steamer. | Messrs. Lea and Blanchard | Philadelphia | United States.

London. 1 Devonshire Terrace | York Gate Regents Park.
Second April 1844.

My Dear Sirs

Many thanks to you for your kind recollection of me, in the matter of the Indian Biography.[4] I had just given up the rest; and had my numbers bound—not doubting you, but thinking (I am sure I don't know why) that the rest were not going to be published.

It is needless for me, I hope, to say, that personal regard would lead me to break my determination in your favor, if I could possibly contemplate the breaking of it upon any consideration. But I cannot. I have made a covenant with myself, which admits of no violation.[5]

How came you to address your letter to me at my publisher's, when Mr. Willis[6] has given you (as I understand) my address so elaborately in print?[7] Surely you

[1] Possibly Mrs Charles Barrow (*née* Mary Culliford), *d.* 1851, CD's grandmother, and her unmarried daughter Mary Caroline; Mrs Barrow had left the Isle of Man after her husband's death in 1826: see W. J. Carlton, "The Barrows of Bristol", *D*, XLVI (1949), 33–6.

[2] The prosperous branch of the family were the sons of John Barrow of Bristol (1787–1841); the eldest, Robert Gay Barrow (*d.* 1880), became an alderman in 1850. CD visited him in 1851 and found him "a gentleman of condition and a very agreeable man" (*Mr and Mrs CD*, ed. W. Dexter, 1935, p. 161).

[3] The rest of the letter is lacking.

[4] Thomas L. McKenney and James Hall, *The History of the Indian Tribes of North America,* published in three vols with coloured illustrations, Philadelphia, 1836–44: see Vol. III, pp. 222–3 and *n.*

In CD's library at his death (*Catalogue of the Library of CD*, ed. J. H. Stonehouse, p. 76).

[5] His decision to send no advance sheets to any American publishers: see Vol. III, pp. 404–5.

[6] Nathaniel Parker Willis (1806–67; *DAB*), journalist: see Vol. III, p. 25*n.*

[7] A sardonic reference to Willis's report in the *National Intelligencer*, Washington, 30 Jan 44 (also in the *New Mirror*, 10 Feb 44) that CD was "within the rules of the Queen's Bench", i.e. confined for debt. The report continued: "realizing the prophecy of pecuniary ruin which has for some time been whispered about for him. His splendid genius did not need the melancholy proof of improvidence, and he has had wealth so completely within his grasp that there seems a particular and unhappy needlessness in his ruin". Willis

don't doubt the Mouthpiece of the Greatest Country in the World—do you! I will swear that neither of you will ever get into Congress if you do.

Messrs. Lea and Blanchard.

Faithfully Yours

CHARLES DICKENS

To C. C. FELTON, 2 APRIL 1844*

MS The Carl H. Pforzheimer Library.

London. 1 Devonshire Terrace | York Gate Regents Park.
Second April 1844. Tuesday

My very dear Felton.

The boat sails a day earlier than I expected;[1] and I have time for but a line. We are all well, and quite happy. Kate recovered. Babby thriving. I have been writing all the morning (it is now two) and am not dressed. At a quarter to three, we always proceed to Richmond, eleven miles off, and hold a solemn dinner on this day—our wedding day, and Forster's birthday. Party composed of the three interesting Individuals concerned; Maclise; and Kate's sister. Dinner, Forsters. Your health shall be drunk with all the honors.

My dear Felton, if I *do* go in at Willis (and I am sorely tempted),[2] I will put that mark upon him, which he shall carry red, to his grave.

Best loves from Kate and myself to Mrs. Felton, *your*self, and all your house.

Ever Your Affectionate friend

Professor Felton

The Insolvent One.

purported to have learnt this from "the English papers", but no such report has been found, and it is probable that he had simply invented it. He had hinted at the prospect in the *New Mirror*, 8 July 43: see Vol. III, p. xvii. The report of 30 Jan was copied into many American papers, and read, for example, by Macready on 14 Feb in the *Tropic* (*Diaries*, II, 262). In his letter to the *National Intelligencer* dated 5 Mar (*New Mirror*, 23 Mar 44) Willis said that CD had now "contradicted the report touching his durance for debt", but excused himself, having no reason to doubt a report which he now said was "published in the London papers", and claiming that it was supported by rumours of "the *decrease* of the prices paid for his books by publishers", coupled with "the *increase* in his pledges, with no corresponding reduction in his style of living". In the issue of 30 Jan Willis had further related how he first saw CD in Nov 35 on a visit to Newgate with Macrone (see Vol. I, p. 88*n*), and later visited him at Furnival's

Inn, in "an uncarpeted and bleak-looking room", describing his appearance as shabby but jaunty, "the very personification . . . of a close sailer to the wind". Forster, who quotes part of the passage (F, I, v, 73*n*), recalls how he and CD laughed at the description: "I give it now as no unfair specimen of the kind of garbage that since his death has also been served up too plentifully by some of his own, as well as by some of Mr. Willis's countrymen".

[1] The *Acadia*, Royal Mail steam-packet for Boston via Halifax, left on 4 Apr.

[2] There is no evidence that he did; but he or Forster may have encouraged the contemptuous comments in the Oct *Foreign Quarterly Review* (p. 106), where the revival of Willis's story in the [April] *United States Democratic Review* is called "trifling though malignant"; to say that CD was "in the King's Bench . . . at a time when he was really on his road to Italy, is not much, compared with the thunder they sometimes roll over the Atlantic".

To THOMAS MITTON, 2 APRIL 1844

MS Huntington Library.

Devonshire Terrace | Tuesday Second April 1844.

My Dear Mitton

Your second letter has thrown me upon the immediate but careful consideration of the adviseability of my complying with your suggestion and that of Mr. Jackson:[1] and coming down straightway. I am quite sure that I could not do so, with any propriety, *unless I were 'specially asked by Mrs. Smithson or Thompson.* I have not the least doubt of that. It is needless for me to say, that I would allow no consideration of personal convenience to influence my decision, in that case, or in any other. But it would not do. There would be an indelicacy—a positive impropriety—in it, which, in the after recollection of it by others, would more than outweigh any service I could possibly render. And it is quite in the nature of things that you and Jackson, who are on the spot, should not see this; while I, who am at a distance, should be fully possessed with it.

I have always thought it *possible* that, being there, I might be a check upon the Opposition of Allen[2] & Co. For this reason, if I had had such an excuse as Thompson's coming here, I think I should have seized it, and gone down with him. But without a special reason arising *in* the family, and presented to me *by* the family, I could not reconcile it to myself.

It does not strike me, that your being invited to Allen's, looks bad. I have not the least doubt of his being a Rascal—not the smallest; he is much too turfy to be anything else—but I should hardly think, if he meant mischief in that, he would think you such a confounded Jackass as to be taken in by it.

Pray communicate all this to Jackson. I have not heard from Thompson since he left Liverpool. He wrote to tell me that he was summoned away, and did not expect to find poor Smithson alive.

I am much grieved by his death; and little thought when we parted at Easthorpe, that I should never see him again. There are old fairy-tales about men being changed into stones; but the men *I* know are changed into Gravestones, with terrible rapidity and reality.

Do not fail to tell me news of Mrs. Smithson.[3] I feel for her, deeply.

Always Faithfully

CHARLES DICKENS

Thomas Mitton Esquire.

To ALFRED DICKENS, 3 APRIL 1844

Text from N, I, 590-1.

Devonshire Terrace | Wednesday April Third 1844

My Dear Alfred,

Fred sent me up your account of poor Smithson's death, last night. I had

---

[1] Henry Jackson (1811–64), solicitor: see Vol. I, p. 469n. He was practising at Malton in partnership with Alfred Smithson, and Mitton & Nealor were their London agents.

[2] Probably William Allen, solicitor at Malton.

[3] Elizabeth Dorothy Smithson (?1811–60), *née* Thompson: see Vol. II, p. 74n.

been anxious to know the particulars, having felt very much for all the house, and thought about them constantly.

It is a comfort to know, poor fellow, that his end was so peaceful. He was a kind-hearted creature; and I regret him most truly.

I need not say to you that if I were *sure* of being of the least comfort to Mrs. Smithson, or of affording her the slightest grain of consolation by my attendance at the Funeral, I should have started off to the railway immediately upon the receipt of your note of yesterday's date. But she has so many people about her, and it is so doubtful whether what one means for sympathy and kindness, be really so at such a time, or be but an aggravation of the mourner's distress; that I could not resolve to come, unless I were assured by Thompson that she actually and actively wished it. God knows that if she did, I would cheerfully and zealously render—not such a trifling attention as that—but services of patient attention and fatigue, and think myself happy in their performance. When I think, however, of the number of friends about her, I am not (as I have already said) at all confident that I am not much better and kinder, away.

I deem it best therefore, to stay where I am. But in case Thompson should happen to write to me to the same effect by to-day's post, I will order my portmanteau to be packed, and if I should hear from him (as in that case I should) by a quarter past 9 tomorrow morning, I shall be all ready for repairing to the railway which I will then do immediately, and come down by the first train after my arrival at the terminus in Euston Square which I suppose would be the Day Mail.

Affectionately always
[CHARLES DICKENS]

To MISS OSBORNE,[1] 3 APRIL 1844*

MS Text from copy, Mrs John Silcock.

1 Devonshire Terrace | April 3, 1844

Dear Miss Osborne

Let me thank you, very earnestly, for your kind remembrance of me. I shall not fail to read the little books[2] you have sent me as soon as possible; and though they were the dullest little books in the world instead of being what I expect them to be, yet would I read them with an unwearying mind for the givers sake.

---

[1] Catherine Isabella Osborne (*d.* 1880), daughter and heiress of Sir Thomas Osborne, 9th Bart (1752–1821), of New-town Anmer, Clonmel. She and Ralph Bernal, MP (1808–82; *DNB*) met frequently at Lady Morgan's during the London season of 1844, and were married 20 Aug; he took her name and arms (see P. H. Bagenal, *The Life of Ralph Bernal Osborne, M.P.*, privately printed, 1884, p. 61).

[2] Identified, in a note added 1864 by

Catherine Osborne, as books by the Rev· George Brittaine, rector of Kilcormack (*d.* 1847). He wrote several novels and tales about the Irish peasantry, most of them, like *Hyacinth O'Gara* and *Honor Delaney* (both first published anonymously about 1830 and often reprinted), frankly proselytizing attacks on priestcraft, of which the *Athenæum* (14 Dec 39) said: "the intended effect of the libel is lost in its absurdity" (see Stephen J. Brown, *Ireland in Fiction*, 1916, p. 35).

Mrs. Dickens begs me to say that we both respond to Lady Osborne's[1] desire for our better acquaintance.

Believe me | Faithfully Yours
CHARLES DICKENS

To WILLIAM PICKERSGILL,[2] 3 APRIL 1844

MS Huntington Library.

Private

1 Devonshire Terrace | York Gate Regents Park
Third April 1844.

Sir.

I fear the best reply I can give you, in acknowledging the receipt of your letter, will be rather unsatisfactory; but if it be so, it is not from any lack of interest on my part. It is in the nature of all literary beginnings to be surrounded by unsatisfactory circumstances.

You know the general character of your composition; and can tell, by looking over the Magazines for any single Month, to which Periodical it seems to be the best adapted by its resemblance to the prevailing tone. You send it addressed to the Editor, with a brief note, intimating that you wish it to be inserted at the usual rate of remuneration. If you send it at the end of one month, you will most likely know its fate at the end of the next.

A Magazine Sheet is sixteen pages. If you count the words in any one page of the Magazine you select, and then count the words in any one page of your own writing, you can easily calculate what quantity of your MS will go to a sheet. When I say that a Magazine Sheet is sixteen pages, I mean sixteen pages *of* the Magazine, of course.

The rate of remuneration to unknown writers, is six or eight Guineas a sheet, usually. Many unknown Writers, write for nothing. I wrote for the next thing to it myself, when I was one and twenty.[3]

The only additional piece of advice I can give you, is to concentrate on this pursuit all the patience that would be required in all the other pursuits of this world, put together; and to lay your account with having it tried. I have no great private knowledge of any Magazine, but I should say that Ainsworth's, Hood's and Bentley's[4] were the least likely to be already oppressed by a great accumula-

---

[1] Catherine Rebecca Osborne (1796–1856), married Sir Thomas Osborne 1816; her wide circle of friends included Bulwer Lytton. After the death of her son in 1824 she became a strict Evangelical. Devoted to her daughter, with whom she continued to live after her marriage (*Memorials of the Life and Character of Lady Osborne and Some of her Friends*, ed. Catherine Isabella Osborne, Dublin, 1870).

[2] Possibly the William Pickersgill who later published *Washington Grange*, 1859, and *The Belle of the Ball*, 1863.

[3] In the *Monthly Magazine*: see Vol. I, p. 32*n*.

[4] Pickersgill is not known to have contributed to any of these magazines.

tion of accepted contributions. So far as I know, your offering is pretty certain to be read, and to receive courteous attention.

William Pickersgill Esquire

Your obedient Servant
CHARLES DICKENS

To J. V. STAPLES,[1] 3 APRIL 1844

Text from F, IV, ii, 317*n*.

Third of April, 1844. I have been very much gratified by the receipt of your interesting letter, and I assure you that it would have given me heartfelt satisfaction to have been in your place when you read my little *Carol* to the Poor in your neighbourhood.[2] I have great faith in the poor; to the best of my ability I always endeavour to present them in a favourable light to the rich; and I shall never cease, I hope, until I die, to advocate their being made as happy and as wise as the circumstances of their condition, in its utmost improvement, will admit of their becoming. I mention this to assure you of two things. Firstly, that I try to deserve their attention; and secondly, that any such marks of their approval and confidence as you relate to me are most acceptable to my feelings, and go at once to my heart.

To GEORGE HODDER,[3] [?1–4 APRIL 1844]

Mention in George Hodder, *Memories of my Time*, 1870, p. 147. *Date:* not earlier than 1 Apr since the advertisement for a secretary to the Art-Union appeared 30 Mar (*Literary Gazette*), and before the closing date of 5 Apr.

Recommending Hodder for the post of Secretary to the Art-Union of London.[4]

[1] James Verry Staples, of Clifton, Bristol; friend of Mrs Evans of Bristol, mother of Frederick Mullet Evans.

[2] Staples described the circumstances in a letter to Forster of 19 Mar 72 (MS University of California, Los Angeles). He spent Christmas 1843 with Mrs Evans, who received a copy of the *Carol* from her son; Staples wished it might reach "a class amongst whom such literature never circulated", and decided to give a public reading to a Bristol Domestic Mission Institution, "with a running comment of explanation, if needed". Although many of his friends "pugh-pughed" the idea, as "throwing pearls before swine", the result was "a room full of the very poor, who gave undivided attention". The reading was spread over two evenings, and the numbers wishing to attend were so great that he had to give it a second time; one very old man said he had not passed so happy an evening for thirty years. Staples later decided to

tell CD of the reading and some of the "graphic" and "heartfelt" remarks of the audience—thus eliciting this letter, a copy of which he enclosed for Forster. Staples commented: "I imagine I was among the first, if not the first, to read the Carol in public, Penny readings had not become an institution in those days. Other letters than the enclosed have passed between Mr. Dickens and myself, chiefly in reference to the 'Child's History of England', being then published in 'Household Words'".

[3] George Hodder (1819–70), journalist; on the *Morning Herald* 1834–45. A friend of Henry Mayhew and Douglas Jerrold, and one of the *Punch* circle from its initiation when he helped Mayhew to find contributors; he was Jerrold's sub-editor on the *Illuminated Magazine* 1843–5. His *Sketches of Life and Character taken at Bow Street*, 1845, was illustrated by Leech. CD first met Hodder in 1843 when he acted as secretary to the committee of the

To JOHN OVERS, 4 APRIL 1844*

Text from typescript, Huntington Library.

Devonshire Terrace, | Fourth April 1844.

My Dear Mr Overs,

I am suddenly called away into Yorkshire to attend a Funeral;[1] but I have found time this morning to read your Poem.

Doing so with a pencil in my hand, I have marked here and there such slight observations as occurred to me. I think it very good all things considered, though here and there a little obscured and forced.

I fear that with Gray's Ode on the books, it is not likely to find a ready market. I would counsel you to try Tait[2] with it again. I am not hopeful in regard to it; but let me know what you determine,

In great haste, | Faithfully yours always

Mr J. A. Overs.   CHARLES DICKENS

To MRS CHARLES DICKENS, 6 APRIL 1844

MS British Museum. *Address:* Mrs. Charles Dickens | 1 Devonshire Terrace | York Gate Regents Park | London. On mourning paper.

Malton Abbey.[3] | Saturday Sixth April 1844.

My Dearest Kate. I found Alfred waiting for me at York yesterday; but one of the horses having gone lame, we had nothing to come over here in, but a Post chaise. And as we did not leave York until 7, and poor Smithson was to be buried at ½ past 9 you may suppose it was pretty sharp work to get here, and get dressed, in time. We managed it, however. When we drove in to the Gannock[4] (as that green place which you recollect, outside the house is called) it was filled with

Elton Fund (see Vol. III, p. 527*n*), and obtained for him the post of secretary to the Sanatorium after the failure of his application to the Art-Union.

[4] Hodder records (*Memories of my Time*, p. 147) that CD answered his request for a testimonial "in a letter so generous and so cordial in all his expressions towards me, that I cannot but wish it concerned some one else rather than myself, in order that I might record it *verbatim*, to exemplify the noble impulses by which the writer could be actuated"; the letter was read aloud by those responsible for appointing the secretary and Hodder afterwards received a letter from the council of the Art-Union regretting that one so highly recommended had not been successful. According to the *Art-Union Journal* of 1 May, announcing the appointment of

Thomas Simons Watson (1813–91), there had been applications from "no fewer than 100 gentlemen—among whom were many of high abilities and even conspicuous rank".

[1] *To* Catherine, 6 Apr, shows that he travelled on 5 Apr and returned 11 Apr.

[2] *Tait's Edinburgh Magazine* for 1843 had five poems signed "J.A.O.", but none in 1844.

[3] The Smithsons' home since leaving Easthorpe in Autumn 43: see Vol. III, p. 519. Built on part of the site of the Priory, it has traces of monastic buildings in the grounds, and beneath a section of the house is a Norman crypt from which leads a secret passage, now blocked up.

[4] An open space between the river and Old Malton road, still known by this name.

country-people hurrying away to the abbey churchyard; and with Malton trades-people, dressed in mourning. The sight was very affecting indeed; and so was the funeral, which was very solemnly performed in the old abbey church; the rector[1] walking there, before the Hearse. Poor Smithson is buried immediately outside his own Garden Wall—in a piece of ground which was lately taken from his garden by the abbey Property, and consecrated.[2] A tree is to be planted over his Grave.

Mrs. Smithson had been upstairs by herself ever since, but I saw her yesterday afternoon. She cried a good deal at first, and looked very lonely and miserable: her face a good deal altered by crying and anxiety: and not improved by the widow's cap. She was quite sensible about it though, and made no show of sentiment. Thompson, Fanny,[3] and I, sat with her in the Evening. She was comfortable enough, then, and came down to breakfast this morning, and was in her old place, before anybody was up. Everything goes on now again much as ever.

There appears to be no doubt whatever, that he died without a will. Every place has been searched that could be thought of: and nothing has been found.[4] He had even dropped a certain Life Insurance for £3000, which in a man of business is extremely strange. Mitton tells me that on the best calculation Jackson can make after looking over the papers in the office, the estate will not yield more than two or three thousand pounds, after everything is got in, and everything is paid.[5] But this, for the present, is mere talk. She has £330 a year, of her own. Milly[6] has the same. And this, with what Thompson pays for the two children,[7] would of course maintain them genteelly anywhere. She has not yet mentioned to Thompson what her wishes are in respect of leaving this place—But Thompson talks of Devonshire. He is going to remain with them until everything is finally arranged. It will take a long time; and all his foreign projects are of necessity broken up.

I think, being so near, I shall go over to Mulgrave[8] by the coach on Monday

[1] The Rev. William Carter (1804–82), rector 1843–55.

[2] The entry in the church register, "Charles Smithson, Old Malton Abbey, buried April 5, age 39", adds that it was the first interment in the new burial ground at the west end of the church (T. P. Cooper, *With Dickens in Yorkshire*, York, 1923, pp. 105ff.).

[3] Clearly Fanny Burnett, not Thompson's daughter.

[4] CD perhaps recalled this in *David Copperfield*, Ch. 38, where a lengthy search reveals that Mr Spenlow, the proctor, has made no will and "had never so much as thought of making one, as far as his papers offered any evidence ... What was scarcely less astonishing to me, was, that his affairs were in a most disordered state".

[5] Letters of administration in the Pre-rogative Courts of York and Canterbury were granted to Elizabeth Dorothy Smithson in June 44: the necessary bond was executed by her and "Henry Jackson of New Malton ... Gentleman and Alfred Dickens of the City of York, Esquire" on 26 Apr. The estate in the Province of York was "under £4000", and in the Province of Canterbury "under £6000".

[6] Amelia Thompson (b. ?1809), sister of Thompson and Mrs Smithson, who lived with the Smithsons: see Vol. II, p. 120n.

[7] Thomas Melville and Matilda (known as Fanny) Thompson: see Vol. II, p. 222n.

[8] Mulgrave Castle, near Whitby: see Vol. III, p. 522n. According to T. P. Cooper (*op. cit.*, p. 120) Lord Normanby took CD to see the Abbey ruins at Whitby, and the *Yorkshire Gazette*, 13 Apr, recorded their visit on 9 Apr to the fishing village of Staithes and CD's delight with

Afternoon, and return here either on Tuesday or Wednesday: coming to town most probably on Thursday *Night*, but sometime on Thursday at latest. Write to me by Tuesday's Post; and if there be any letters that you think *particular*, send them—not otherwise.[1] Pray write to Mrs. Smithson at the same time. I blushed to think yesterday, that I had come down at such a time, without bringing a line from you.

Fanny goes home again today—Alfred to York tomorrow. Mitton somewhere else on Monday, I believe. I grieve to report that Wallace was almost too drunk to wait at table yesterday; which is horribly discouraging, in reference to one's treatment of servants. I am sure no man ever had a kinder master than he had in poor Smithson.

Love to the Darlings, and to Georgy. I shall look for your letter. Of course you will open any that may come from Jeffrey.[2] Always affectionately

CHARLES DICKENS

P.S. Sunday Morning

The state of the Miss Weller business is exactly what I predicted to you. A prior attachment—kept secret by her—and *the parents with* Thompson. You have the key of my round Study Table. If you open the drawer in which I keep my cheque-book, you will see two latch keys. They both belong to the street door. Send me one of them in your letter, that I may admit myself on Thursday night.

To MISS CHRISTIANA WELLER, 8 APRIL 1844

Text from *A Dickens Friendship*, ed. W[ilfrid] M[eynell], privately printed, 1931, pp. 37–43.

Malton Abbey, Yorkshire, Monday Eighth April, 1844

My dear Miss Weller,

I was exceedingly glad to receive your letter some weeks since; and should have written to thank you for it if I had anything to say. Not being one of those remorseless persons who look upon the Penny Postage as a General Licence to let fly with a paper pellet at all sorts of game, however, I waited in the hope that I might have something to say in course of time. In which expectation I have been disappointed. Nobody's house, in whom I have recently supposed you interested, has taken fire; nothing has changed for good or evil which is likely to concern you at all; and unless the modest creature who sang about the Ugly Man[3] at Liverpool has grown bold since I was there (which is not probable:

the "picturesque scenery of Whitby, Mulgrave, and the neighbourhood".

[1] An envelope addressed to Thomas Powell in Catherine's hand (MS Dickens House), post-marked 4 Apr 44, suggests that she informed correspondents of CD's departure for Yorkshire.

[2] See *To* Jeffrey, ?12 Apr.

[3] According to the *Liverpool Mercury*, 1 Mar, at a late stage in the proceedings at Liverpool CD rose and said that Mr H. Wilkins, who was at that time delivering lectures at the Institution on perspective, was now "so much moved by the harmony of the evening that he comes out as a singer, and contemplates a song called 'The Ugly Man'", which Wilkins gave. No such song has been traced.

considering his remarkable bashfulness at that time) no man or woman whom we both know is one bit the better or the worse since we parted, that *I* know.

Yet that is not so, either. For to my amazement, I have found one friend of mine very much the worse for a visit to your town. Something comes over the paper like the light of a blush from you; I don't know what is the cause of the effect, but it is very red. I mention it on account of its singularity; and, losing the thread of my discourse in doing so—(it is so very slight that it is hard to find)—I must turn overleaf, and look back.

O, my friend! I recollect. Yes. He went to Liverpool, and fell desperately, madly, irretrieveably in Love there. Which was so perfectly natural (the circumstances of his case being quite uncommon and his provocation enormous) that I could not find it in my heart to remonstrate with him for his folly. Indeed I rather encouraged him in it than otherwise; for I had that amount of sympathy with his condition, which, but that I am beyond the reach—the lawful reach—of the Wings that fanned *his* fire, would have rendered it the greatest happiness and pleasure of my life to have run him through the body. In no poetical or tender sense, I assure you, but with good sharp Steel. He fell in love, this man; and, after divers misgivings and hesitations and deliberations and all that, mentioned the fact—first to the winds, and to the gentle airs that blow in Mr. Radley's bed-chambers; and afterwards to—to Her. Well. He thought he was getting on Hopefully, gently, reasonably, smoothly; and wrote as much to me, in London. I immediately threw up a small cap (sky-blue) which I keep on a peg in my study for such joyful occasions as very seldom happen; and remained for some days perpetually casting it into the air and catching it again, in a transport of delight.

In the midst of this enthusiasm I was summoned down here (he visits hereabouts) to attend a funeral; and at this funeral I found him, to my great amazement, acting as chief mourner to his own hopes, and attending them to an early grave with the longest hat-band and the usefullest pocket handkerchief I ever saw in my life.

At this I was very much surprised and very sorry, as you will believe; and the sky-blue cap (still in the air) fell down upon my head with the weight and velocity of a Cannon-ball.

For I found out, when I came to talk to him, that one wretchedness coming on the head of another—they always make a pyramid, God knows why—he had heard, in the very height of another distress, from Her; and She had told him that he had been a little premature, and that there were other footprints in the field—and so forth.

But, by little and little, I got the cap up again—not very high, but *up*—and there it is now, over my head as I write. For I told him that, as to other footmarks being in that course, there might be a host, and yet the best flowers might grow up at last in the steps of the last man, if he were True, Unselfish, Manly, Honourable, Patient, and Persevering. I told him that I had a Faith in such strong qualities never being inspired in a man's breast for failing purposes; that I had a Faith in his possessing them, and carrying them gallantly with his attachment; and that I had as high and confident a Faith (O Heaven what a boundless Faith it is!) in Her, and that whatever she worked out would be for

Good. I know, I *do* know it, as well as if I had known her from her cradle. As, in the spirit, I have.

In short, I went on as if I had a white head, a staff, a patriarchal beard, and a bent back—saving that I threw the sky-blue cap a *little* higher than an old man would have done perhaps, and kept it up as gaily as I could. Which I mean to do, unless you hold my hands; and that you won't do, I believe. Whatever happens in this case, of this I am quite sure—that it will all happen Wrong, and cannot happen otherwise but Wrong; the undersigned being excluded from all chance of competition, and only throwing up his cap for other men, instead of cutting it up into Favors for himself. Not last among your faithful and admiring friends, my dear Miss Weller, nor yet a cold spectator of the slightest thing that can concern your happiness,

Faithfully your friend,
CHARLES DICKENS

To LORD JEFFREY, [12 APRIL 1844]*

MS Professor Harry Stone. *Date:* the day after CD's return from Yorkshire.

Devonshire Terrace | Friday Morning

My Dear Lord Jeffrey.

I have just returned from Yorkshire, and shall wait at home today until I see or hear from you.[1] I am yours tomorrow, if that will suit you better.

Always | Affectionately Yours
CHARLES DICKENS

To THOMAS MITTON, [12 APRIL 1844]

Extract in John Waller catalogue No. 141 (1884); signed initials; undated, but clearly same letter as *To* Mitton, 12 Apr 44, mentioned in catalogue of Quabbin Book House, Ware, Mass (Jan 1942), *MS* 1 p., from Devonshire Terrace, since CD had arranged to see Jeffrey on this date (see last).

I forgot the very thing I came to town for—to see Lord Jeffrey, who is our boy's Godfather—I breakfast with him to-morrow at 10.

To [MRS. GORE],[2] 13 APRIL 1844*

MS The Carl H. Pforzheimer Library.

1 Devonshire Terrace York Gate | Saturday Thirteenth April 1844.

Mr. Charles Dickens presents his compliments to the author of Agathonia,[3]

[1] Jeffrey was in London on his usual summer visit.

[2] Catherine Grace Frances Gore (1799–1861; *DNB*), novelist and dramatist: see Vol. II, p. 200*n*.

[3] *Agathonia, a Romance*, a historical sketch in "poetic" prose, published anonymously by Moxon by 2 Apr. The *Athenæum* (11 May 44), in an unfavourable review, refers to "a sort of minikin mystery

and begs to acknowledge, with very many thanks, the receipt of that book. He is much indebted to the author for his courteous and flattering attention; and anticipates great pleasure from its perusal.

Mr. Dickens loses no time in acknowledging its receipt: having lost some days already, he fears, through being in Yorkshire, whence he only returned home yesterday.

To CHARLES KNIGHT,[1] [?13 APRIL 1844]

Text from MDGH, I, 152. *Date:* "Saturday, April 13th, 1846" according to MDGH's text; but Sat was 11 Apr in 1846, 13 Apr in 1844. Knight's book was published July 1843, and it seems very unlikely that he would have delayed sending CD a copy of so important a work for two years.

Devonshire Terrace, Saturday, April 13th, 184[4].

My Dear Sir,

Do you recollect sending me your biography of Shakespeare[2] last autumn, and my not acknowledging its receipt? I do, with remorse.

The truth is, that I took it out of town with me, read it with great pleasure as a charming piece of honest enthusiasm and perseverance,[3] kept it by me, came home, meant to say all manner of things to you, suffered the time to go by, got ashamed, thought of speaking to you,[4] never saw you, felt it heavy on my mind, and now fling off the load by thanking you heartily, and hoping you will not think it too late.

Always believe me, | Faithfully yours.
[CHARLES DICKENS]

about the authorship of this book, which has been given to very nearly as many persons as 'Cecil' ", and Mrs Gore's name was given in the advertisement of the edn published July 44. According to a letter of Forster to Bulwer Lytton (MS Lytton Papers), Mrs Gore was obliged to avow herself, as the story was found among Beckford's papers after his death on 2 May: "He put the incidents together—and wrote all the notes—and from his manuscript she recomposed the story". Beckford and Mrs Gore are known to have been friends, and Forster's account, though unconfirmed, seems not unlikely.

[1] Charles Knight (1791–1873; *DNB*), author and publisher: see Vol. II, p. 231*n*.

[2] *William Shakespeare. A Biography,—* the 8th and final volume of Knight's *Pictorial Shakespeare*; widely reviewed in Autumn 1843.

[3] Knight's book, based on his own researches in Stratford and at the Bodleian Library, was remarkable in its time for relating Shakespeare's life and works to contemporary life and manners (with hundreds of illustrations); marred only by diffuseness (544 pp.) and by the acceptance, natural at that time, of some of Collier's forged documents, it was a landmark in Shakespearean biography (S. Schoenbaum, *Shakespeare's Lives*, Oxford, 1970, pp. 387–96).

[4] Probably at the Shakespeare Society; Knight was one of its four founders in 1840, and CD was on the Council: see Vol. III, p. 455*n*.

To DR SOUTHWOOD SMITH, 13 APRIL 1844*

MS Mr W. A. Foyle. *Address:* Dr. Southwood Smith | 38 Finsbury Square.

Devonshire Terrace | Thirteenth April 1844.

My Dear Sir

I feel, on second thoughts, the delicacy of Chairmanship[1] so strong upon me, that I would rather leave Lords Normanby[2] and Seymour[3] to be written to, by the man of business.[4] All the other people we spoke of this morning, I have faithfully written to, already.[5]

Ever Yours

Dr. Southwood Smith.   CHARLES DICKENS

To EBENEZER JONES,[6] 15 APRIL 1844†

MS Private.

1 Devonshire Terrace | York Gate Regents Park
Monday Fifteenth April 1844

Dear Sir

I don't know how it has happened that I have been so long in acknowledging the receipt of your kind present of your Poems,[7] but I *do* know that I have often thought of writing to you, and have very often reproached myself for not carrying that thought into execution. *It is not my habit or intention to be dilatory in such cases; and I hope in all plain sincerity that you will excuse me.*

I have not been neglectful of the Poems themselves, I assure you, but have

---

[1] Of the Sanatorium dinner on 4 June 44, at which CD took the chair: see *To* Beard, 10 June. For the Sanatorium, see Vol. II, p. 165n.

[2] Constantine Henry Phipps, 1st Marquis of Normanby (1797–1863; *DNB*), father of Lord Mulgrave.

[3] Edward Adolphus Seymour, later 12th Duke of Somerset (1804–85; *DNB*). May have known CD through Mrs Norton, his sister-in-law.

[4] Dr Hitchman was the resident surgeon and secretary.

[5] Probably guests rather than stewards: see *To* Stanfield, 30 Apr.

[6] Ebenezer Jones (1820–60; *DNB*), poet; became a clerk in a tea office; influenced by Shelley and Carlyle; contributed verse to magazines, and in 1843 published his one collection, *Studies of Sensation and Event*, from which he hoped much, but reviews were slighting or hostile. Wrote occasionally for radical publishers, becoming a friend of W. J. Linton. According to the memoir by his brother (see below), applied for work on the *Daily News* in

1846, when there was an exchange of letters with CD, but without result. Died of consumption.

[7] Jones sent copies of *Studies of Sensation and Event* to several authors, and received favourable replies from Procter, Horne, and Carlyle—who sent a long letter of encouragement and advice, finding "great fervour of temper; a genius hopeful, though as yet in all senses *young*", and sympathizing over the *Literary Gazette*'s review, "ill-natured, ill-bred, and very unjust" (R. H. Shepherd, *Memoir of . . . Carlyle*, 1881, I, 291–3); Milnes and Ainsworth were also encouraging. Later, Rossetti was struck by the "vivid disorderly power" of his poems and thought him "a striking instance of neglected genius"; his note in *Notes and Queries*, Feb 1870, helped to revive interest in Jones, and in 1879, after Theodore Watts (-Dunton)'s articles in the *Athenæum* Sep-Oct 1878, the *Studies* were republished with other poems and a memoir by Sumner Jones, Ebenezer's brother.

aa Not previously published.

read them with very great pleasure. They struck me at the first glance as being remarkably nervous, picturesque, imaginative, and original. I have frequently recurred to them since; and never with the slightest abatement of that impression. I am much flattered and gratified by your recollection of me; I beg you to believe in my unaffected sympathy with, and appreciation of, your powers; and I entreat you to accept my best wishes, and genuine though tardy thanks.

Dear Sir | Faithfully Yours

Ebenezer Jones Esquire

CHARLES DICKENS

To MRS CHARLES SEDGWICK,[1] 15 APRIL 1844*

MS Massachusetts Historical Society. *Address:* By the Hibernia Post Office Packet. | Mrs. Sedgwick | Lenox | Massachusetts | United States | Private.

London. 1 Devonshire Terrace, York Gate, Regents Park.

Fifteenth April 1844.

Dear Madam. I am too glad to have heard from you (remembering in what earth, our correspondence first took root) to be disposed to contest the points you set forth in your letter, at any length. But I cannot help remarking, with the very best feeling and temper in the world, that the Popular Instructor of America —its gallant and veracious press—has left you uninstructed on one or two points of fact, which it was rather essential for you to have known, before you formed such very strong opinions in reference to the Pennsylvanian Penitentiary.[2] You seem to regard my opinion of the system, as something so extraordinary and unaccountable that it can only be understood or comprehended in any degree as consistent with honesty, by the supposition that I was under some strange influence—some wonderful and unparalleled perversion of judgment, unknown to all other men—when I wrote about that Prison. I have no doubt this has been very often represented to you, and very seldom so politely; but this cannot change the fact that it is no peculiar crotchet of mine—that many most excellent, amiable, virtuous, thoughtful, and enlightened men have arrived at exactly the same conclusions from exactly the same premises—that the introduction of this discipline is strongly opposed in England, and has already been attended with lamentable results—that it has lately been distinctly and decidedly reported against, in Paris, where its introduction was contemplated[3]—and that it has

[1] Mrs Charles Sedgwick, *née* Elizabeth Buckminster Dwight (1801–64), teacher and writer of educational books: see Vol. III, p. 218n.

[2] Cherry Hill, the Eastern Penitentiary in Philadelphia, run on the Separate System: see *American Notes*, Ch. 7, and *To* Colden, 10 Mar and *To* Forster, 13 Mar 42 (Vol. III, pp. 110, 123–4 and ns).

[3] In England the extension of the Pentonville experiment in the Separate System to the County Gaols had been under consideration, while the introduction of such a system into France, following De Tocque-

ville's favourable reports on its working in America, was being debated in the Chamber of Deputies. The death in Nov 43 of several political prisoners in Mont St Michel, a French prison where solitary confinement was in force, was made much of by opponents of the system in England and France; it was referred to in leaders and reports in *The Times* from Nov onwards, as was CD's description of the Eastern Penitentiary from *American Notes* (*The Times*, 29 Nov 43). By Apr 44, in England, magistrates in many counties had decided against solitary confinement; in

unquestionably, more opponents than defenders among those who are best acquainted with the subject of Prison regulations, and have most attentively studied the operations of the human mind. Of myself, and my own means of arriving at a right conclusion, I will only say that I have paid great attention to the first of these themes for several years; and that if I have no natural aptitude for the second, I have entirely mistaken my vocation, and some few readers of books have done so, likewise.

And in reference to my expressed opinion at the time, by word of mouth, I will merely remind you that not even the Governor of an American Prison can alter the Truth, or change an iota of it; the Truth being even a higher thing than such Governor, and far beyond his reach, assailment, or controul. And the Truth is, upon my honor as a Gentleman and as I must see God as a mortal creature, that after a dinner in the Prison, I, being called upon, did say in so many words to the party then assembled that the Punishment was an awful and tremendous one; and that if it were inflicted at all, it should only be inflicted for very short terms; and that I believed very few men knew what a Punishment it was. All of which sentiments, I, *of course*, separated however, from the cleanliness, order, and humanity of intention observable throughout the establishment; to which I awarded the Praise such arrangements deserved. I recollect, as distinctly as if it had been yesterday, an awkward and blank pause succeeding upon these remarks; and I have no doubt that a gentleman in Philadelphia named Ingersoll,[1] an officer in the United States Navy, remembers these circumstances as well as I; and our reference to them in a coach as we rode back together.

If you recollect a few details on this same subject—I mean the Prison generally —in your letter, and look back to my book, you will find that you have not read it quite correctly. Unless you have an American Edition with a few forged passages in it. Which is exceedingly probable. Having seen my own hand to a letter I never wrote,[2] and Mr. O'Connell's hand to a letter *he* never wrote;[3] and being possessed of some information in reference to the concoction and dispersion of those magnanimous documents by tens of thousands, through America, I can easily compass this likelihood.

The case of the interesting lady who stabbed the gentleman,[4] is exactly the

France the debate continued, and the prison system had not been reorganized when legislation was interrupted by the Revolution of 1848 (see Joseph Adshead, *Prisons and Prisoners*, 1845, a defence of Pentonville, giving details of the controversy, and George Wilson Pierson, *Tocqueville and Beaumont in America*, New York, 1938).

[1] Harry Ingersoll (1809–86): see Vol. III, p. 106*n*.

[2] See Vol. III, Appx B.

[3] A letter published in the *Hibernian Advocate*, Baltimore, and attacking CD, an extract from which was reprinted in the *Pilot* (Dublin), 22 Mar 43; O'Connell emphatically denied writing it in a letter of 23 Mar to Richard Barrett of the *Pilot*, adding "few people admire more the writings of Dickens, or read them with deeper interest than I do. I am greatly pleased with his 'American Notes'" (*Pilot*, 24 Mar 43, reprinted in W. J. Fitzpatrick, *Correspondence of Daniel O'Connell*, 1888, II, 296–7).

[4] Amelia Norman was tried in New York on 17–18 Jan 44 for stabbing her seducer, Henry S. Ballard; her guilt was not in doubt, but on 19 Jan she was acquitted by a sympathetic jury. The case caused much excitement, and Mrs Child took Amelia Norman under her protection (*National Intelligencer*, letter from New York Correspondent [N. P. Willis] dated 26 Jan); later,

illustration I should have invented, if I were putting a supposititious case, of one of the many phases in which America differs from other Countries, and does such stupendous and grievous injury to the progress of Free Institutions elsewhere. I mean the readiness of her people to take the Law into their own hands; and their manifest want of confidence in, and want of real respect for, the Institutions which they parade so noisily. In the ordinary course of events in any other civilized country, the Jury in that case *must* have found the lady guilty— inasmuch as they were upon their oaths, and she *did* unquestionably stab the gentleman. So they would have found her guilty, and would have recommended her, in their confidence in the Powers that be, to the Mercy of the authorities, with a perfect reliance on their recommendation being carefully, and honorably, and favorably considered. And as to the Constables applauding, they would have appeared in that character for positively the first and last time: and would very likely (and deservedly) have been clapped into prison to boot, for so far forgetting the dignity and decency of a solemn Court of Justice. In America, the course is what you describe—and in the absence of that respect and confidence of which I have just treated, quite naturally so. But not the less dangerously.

Of Mrs. Childe's[1] appearance as a Comforter at the Bar, I will only say (the same being a question of taste) that I am very glad I am not *Mr.* Childe.

I have marked this letter Private—not, of course, with any distrust of your delicacy, but because I wish you expressly to understand my dear Madam, that my desire is, NOT to be set right upon any subject of slander or falsehood whatever; as I have resolved not to compromise the respect which I owe to myself by rebutting, refuting, explaining, or denying, any accusation whatever which is brought against me on your side of the Atlantic; the character of such accusations and such unimpeachable Gentlemen as they originate with, being not of that kind which any person claiming the least superiority to a Scavenger, could possibly notice, without a compromise of his degree. You wrote to me first, in the confidence of grief and a full heart;[2] and for this reason I have written in a spirit of confidence to you. This being the first, as it will be the last time, of my replying to anything like a reproach from any correspondent in America.

I write to you, and no one else. And I beg you (beyond your own house) to consider this letter, as strictly private and confidential, as if it treated of none but private topics.

Mrs. Dickens sends her best regards. We are all very well, thank God, and very happy. I hope your daughter[3] is so, likewise. If I could draw (which I

---

she went to live with the Sedgwicks, where, during her "paroxysms of insane anguish", Elizabeth Sedgwick used to "sit by her and watch her, and comfort her and sing to her" (Fanny Kemble, *Records of Later Life*, 1882, III, 403).

[1] Lydia Maria Child (1802–80; *DAB*), author of *Letters from New York*, 1843, and other works; well-known opponent of slavery and of capital punishment: see Vol. III, p. 403*n*.

[2] Perhaps in 1842, about the death of her son Charles (mentioned in *Life and Letters of Catharine M. Sedgwick*, ed. Mary E. Dewey, New York, 1872, p. 283: no date given but clearly during that year).

[3] Katharine Sedgwick, her eldest child; she married William Minot, Jr, of Boston, in 1842.

can't), I could make a portrait of her engaging face at this moment: I remember
it so well.

Always Faithfully Yours

Mrs. Sedgwick.   CHARLES DICKENS

To THOMAS POWELL, 16 APRIL 1844

MS Colonel Richard Gimbel. *Address:* Thomas Powell Esquire | 2 Leadenhall
Street.

Devonshire Terrace. | Sixteenth April 1844.

My Dear Powell.

Lord bless you! Thursday or Friday!!! Why, I composed (though I say it,
as shouldn't) the best little party you can imagine; comprehending everybody
I had room for, whom I thought Mr. Chapman would like to know.[1] Let me see.
Rogers for Poetry, Sydney Smith[2] for Orthodoxy, Charles Kemble and Young[3]
for Theatricality, Lord Denman for Benchity, Lord Dudley Stuart[4] for Polarity,
Mr. and Mrs. Milner Gibson[5] for Anti Corn Law Leaguality, Mrs. Norton[6] for
beauty, and divers others for variety. Lord love you! Why, at this time of the
year it couldn't be done again under three weeks. Not to mention the Dwarf—
General Tom Thumb[7]—whom on the word of a Spiritiwal creetur, I had
summoned, and have summoned, for the Evening in question. No. We won't
come down with the run. We'll have a long notice, and see what can be done
with the second wentur. When we doos go in, we plays to win Sir.

Says Shrimp to me (I allude to the humble individual who has the honor to be
my brother) "Mr. Powell is coming up one evening".—"Shrimp", said I. "Why
evening? We dine at half past 5. Cannot said Powell, with a day's notice (to
ensure my not being out) come up to dinner?" I saw that I had touched him; and
had a modest confidence in my Message reaching you safely. Whether Shrimp
broke down, or Prawn (otherwise Powell) I don't know. But until this point is

---

[1] Evidently a message to Powell through
"Shrimp" (Augustus) had been misunderstood; CD pretends that this throws
out all his plans for a dinner-party of
notables to meet Thomas Chapman. Such
a party may actually have been under consideration (there is a letter from Denman
to CD declining an invitation for 27 Apr:
MS Morgan), and several of the guests
named were invited to a dinner-party on
Sat 1 June; but the tone and the inclusion
of General Tom Thumb show that the
present list of guests is not serious.

[2] Sydney Smith (1771–1845; *DNB*),
Canon of St Paul's: see Vol. I, p. 431*n*.

[3] Charles Mayne Young (1777–1856;
DNB), actor: see Vol. I, p. 592*n*.

[4] See next.

[5] Thomas Milner Gibson (1808–84;

DNB), MP for Manchester and an ally of
Cobden; he was on the platform at the
Manchester Athenaeum Soirée Oct 43
(see Vol. III, p. 581*n*), but may have
known CD earlier. He married 1832
Susanna Arethusa Cullum (1814–85), who
became a well-known hostess, something
of a lion-hunter, befriender of exiles, and
advocate of mesmerism.

[6] Caroline Elizabeth Sarah Sheridan
(1808–77; *DNB*), poet and novelist: see
Vol. I, p. 302*n*.

[7] Charles Sherwood Stratton (1838–83;
DAB), the dwarf (25 inches tall); arrived
from America Jan 44 with P. T. Barnum
as manager; he opened at the Royal
Adelaide Gallery of Practical Science in
March and appeared before the Court
1 Apr.

cleared up, I decline to acknowledge the receipt of *"*potted chair.¹ If indeed that *be* chair in a black bag; which I don't believe.*ᵃ* Faithfully Ever

CD.

To LORD DUDLEY COUTTS STUART,² 16 APRIL 1844

Extract in Sotheby's catalogue, Oct 1970; *MS* 1 p.; dated Devonshire Terrace, 16 Apr 44.

Saying he and the whole party *will be delighted to see him and that* I am not acquainted with the other Governesses and believe these are the genuine un-adulterated and original G's.

To THOMAS MITTON, 17 APRIL 1844

MS Huntington Library.

Devonshire Terrace | Wednesday Seventeenth April | 1844.

My Dear Mitton. I am engaged to dine tomorrow with Rodwell the Music man] at Brompton. I was coming do[wn ye]³sterday Morning to tell you [that I was, detained by my last [chapter] of the next No which I have not yet finished, as it requires great⁴ discretion.⁵

The No. will be a teazer,⁶ I think.

I am very much and pressingly in want of a hundred pounds until June. Though the time is short, my father's debts, two quarters income tax⁷ &c, coming all at once, drive me, sailing so near the wind by not drawing any profits from C and H, into a most [un]comfortable corner.⁸ Ca[n you oblige] me with

---

ᵃᵃ A later hand (probably Powell's) has added quotation marks here.

¹ Potted char, the fish. One of Powell's edible presents: see Vol. III, p. 578*n*.

² Lord Dudley Coutts Stuart (1803–54; *DNB*), philanthropist; only son of 1st Marquis of Bute by his second wife Frances Coutts; MP 1830–5 and (for Marylebone) 1847–54. From 1831 devoted himself to the cause of Polish independence; founded the Literary Association of the Friends of Poland 1833, and continued as its President. CD had met him by May 43, and no doubt much earlier through Miss Coutts (his cousin); he found a great charm, says Forster, "in Lord Dudley Stuart's gentle yet noble character, his refined intelligence and generous public life, expressed so perfectly in his chivalrous face" (F, VI, vi, 529).

³ A hole in the middle of the MS has removed letters in several places; con-jectural readings are supplied in square brackets.

⁴ MS reads "geat".

⁵ Ch. 47, the last of the May No., containing the murder of Montague Tigg.

⁶ i.e. to its readers—presumably because of the hinted disclosures of old Chuffey and Jonas's alarm; old Antony Chuzzlewit's death had been accepted as natural, and the reader is still in doubt.

⁷ CD did not pay it at this time: see *To* Mitton, 12 Aug 44.

⁸ CD's accounts show that he received two sums of £100 (source unspecified) on 19 Apr. He made four payments to "Lewisham" and one to Mrs Dickens in Apr, totalling £24.10, which was above his regular payments (Account-book, MS Messrs Coutts).

this, or devise any [means] of doing so? Send me a line, and say how the land lies in your view, and at what time you will be in the Way on[1] Friday.

Faithfully Ever

Thomas Mitton Esquire   CD.

To MRS CHARLES SMITHSON, 18 APRIL 1844*

MS Benoliel Collection.

Devonshire Terrace | Eighteenth April 1844.

My Dear Mrs. Smithson.

I send you the long-promised Carol.[2] Better now, I hope, than never.

I think it best, on consideration, *not* to send you the other books we spoke of. You will have enough to occupy your thoughts just now, I do not doubt, without them. And when you come to town, you will be better able to judge of what you wish to know, by going with us (as I hope you will) on Sunday Mornings,[3] twice, or thrice, than if you read a Library. I cannot reconcile it to myself to influence anybody's mind on such a subject. There would be happier lives and happier Deaths, perhaps, if we read our Saviour's preaching a little more, and let each other alone. If men invest the Deity with their own passions, so much the worse for them. He remains the same; and if there be any Truth in anything about us, and it be not all one vast deceit, he is full of Mercy and Compassion, and looks to what his creatures do, and not to what they think.

I was in hopes our house would have suited you for a twelvemonth; and thought it would be like a kind of Home to you. Since you were here, we have made a pretty bedchamber of the Breakfast Room.

Thompson wrote me, however, a few days since, that there were not bedrooms enough for you;[4] and that he was coming up house-hunting.[5] I am on the look-out for him.

I shrewdly suspect there was a Concert at Manchester last night—and that *she* played there[6]—and that *he* went.

Here I put my finger at the side of my nose, and pull up; with love to beauteous Bill,[7] and my Glorious Godchild whom I have proclaimed in the highways as being in all respects a Brilliant Baby.[8]

---

[1] N reads "Wagon".

[2] The copy is inscribed "Mrs. Smithson | From | Charles Dickens | Eighteenth April 1844" (F. G. Kitton, *CD by Pen and Pencil*, 1890–2, I, 51).

[3] Obviously to the Unitarian service at Little Portland St Chapel: see Vol. III, p. 455*n*.

[4] Presumably for visitors; the family was smaller than CD's, consisting only of Mrs Smithson, her sister Amelia, the two Thompson children, and the baby.

[5] By 1845 Mrs Smithson had what Christiana Weller in her diary (MS Mrs Sowerby) described as "a splendid house", evidently in Kensington; she writes as though Thompson were sharing the house, which may have been 35 Gloucester Rd, Hyde Park Gardens: see *To Head*, 13 Aug 45. He also had rooms at 63 Pall Mall.

[6] Christiana Weller and her sister Anna played at the Athenaeum Soirée on 17 Apr (*Manchester Guardian*, 10, 13 and 20 Apr).

[7] Amelia Thompson.

[8] Mary, born 16 Mar 43 at Easthorpe: see Vol. III, p. 486.

Let us have another to match, and we'll get on happily yet.

Mrs. Smithson.

Always Your faithful friend
CHARLES DICKENS

To EDWARD CHAPMAN,[1] 20 APRIL 1844*

MS John F. Fleming, Inc.

Devonshire Terrace | Saturday Twentieth April 1844

Dear Sir. The lettering is on the other side. I wondered what on earth had become of the plates.[2]

E. Chapman Esquire

Faithfully Yours
CHARLES DICKENS

Mrs. Gamp makes tea[3]
Mr. Moddle is led to the contemplation of his destiny.[4]

To DR SOUTHWOOD SMITH, 20 APRIL 1844*

MS Dr William A. Whittaker.

Devonshire Terrace | Saturday Twentieth April 1844

My Dear Dr. Smith. On Monday Morning at Ten—or a quarter before Ten if that will suit you better—I shall be delighted to see you.

Dr. Southwood Smith.

Faithfully Yours
CHARLES DICKENS

To T. J. SERLE, 22 APRIL 1844

MS Mr Peter Brandt. *Address:* T. J. Serle Esquire | 9 Southampton Row | Russell Square.

Devonshire Terrace
Monday Evening April Twenty Second 1844

My Dear Serle.

The Captain of the Britannia has written me, that unless the berth be taken straightway, she can't go by that ship,[5] as it is filling fast. Will you draw me a cheque for the passage-money (leaving the sum blank, as I don't at this moment know what it is—I will put it in when I find out) & send the same to me forthwith.

In haste Ever Yours
CD

---

[1] Edward Chapman (1804–80): see Vol. I, p. 128*n.*

[2] For the May No. of *Chuzzlewit.*

[3] CD first wrote "*Mrs. Gamp makes tea for a small party*" and then cancelled the last four words.

[4] Above this title CD wrote "*Mr. Moddle and Miss Pecksniff contemplate their destiny*" and then cancelled it.

[5] Rosa Elton's passage on the *Britannia,* which sailed 4 May: see *To Serle, 2 May.*

To JOHN FORSTER, [23 APRIL 1844]

Extract in F, IV, iii, 323. *Date:* 23 April according to Forster.

November blasts! Why it's the warmest, most genial, most intensely bland, delicious, growing, springy, songster-of-the grovy, bursting-forth-of-the-buddy, day as ever was.[1] At half-past four I shall expect you.[2] Ever, Moddle.[3]

To MRS S. C. HALL, 23 APRIL 1844

MS Brotherton Library, Leeds.

Devonshire Terrace | Twenty Third April 1844.

My Dear Mrs. Hall.

Many thanks for Chambers's Journal.[4] Your Governess[5] is an immense relief to that somewhat cast-iron and utilitarian publication (as congenial to me, generally, as the brown paper packages in which Ironmongers keep Nails); and I have read it with very great pleasure. It is delicately and beautifully done; with a womanly touch that cannot be mistaken.

When I saw you among the Ladies at the Dinner t'other night,[6] I made a valorous resolve to come out with a reference to this very tale; thinking and hoping it would not displease you. I was very much vexed when I sat down

---

[1] The temperature at noon was 67, and there had been ten days' fine weather (Meteorological Diary, *Gentleman's Magazine*).

[2] Shakespeare's birthday was "kept always as a festival" by Forster and CD (F, IV, iii, 323).

[3] Augustus Moddle appears in Ch. 46 of the May No. Forster says this letter was "signed in character expressive of his then present unfitness for any of the practical affairs of life, including the very pressing business which at the moment ought to have occupied him, namely, attention to the long-deferred nuptials of Miss Charity Pecksniff". Forster may have confused their actual wedding-day (Ch. 54, which closes the final July No.) with Ch. 46, where they are buying furniture.

[4] *Chambers's Journal*, founded 1832; published in Edinburgh and London; edited by William and Robert Chambers, assisted in 1842–5 by W. H. Wills. A popular and instructive weekly magazine, price three-halfpence, it had a circulation estimated at 50,000, sharing the market with Charles Knight's *Penny Magazine*.

[5] Mrs Hall had probably sent CD *Chambers's Journal*, 14–28 May 42, containing her tale, "The Governess", which

showed the heroine undertaking heavy responsibilities without the support and respect of her employers; it also brought out the disgracefully low wages often paid, and the governess's poor prospects in old age and ill-health. Mrs Hall collected her writings on this subject, including "The Governess", in *Tales of Woman's Trials*, 1847, and *Stories of the Governess*, printed for the benefit of the Governesses' Benevolent Institution 1852.

[6] CD had spoken at the first Anniversary Festival of the Governesses' Benevolent Institution at the London Tavern with the Duke of Cambridge in the chair, on 20 Apr (*Speeches*, ed. K. J. Fielding, pp. 65–7). Fielding points out that the choice of CD as a speaker was particularly appropriate after *Chuzzlewit*, Ch. 36 (in the Feb No.) where Tom Pinch visits Ruth at the brass-and-copper founder's in Camberwell where she is governess and removes her. A letter of Mary Carpenter to Lucy Sanford in May 1844 refers to CD's sister having been the latter's governess; perhaps this was Letitia (*Speeches*, p. 67 and *n*). The troubles of governesses were also referred to at some length in CD's Sanatorium speech on 4 June 44 (pp. 69–70).

again, to have forgotten it. And they have been laughing at me here, ever since, for swearing I would tell you what I meant to have done. "As if *that* were of any use!" they say.

Remember me to Mr. Hall and your Good Mother. And believe me always

Faithfully Yours

Mrs. S. C. Hall.   CHARLES DICKENS

To JAMES THOMSON,[1] 23 APRIL 1844

Extracts in N, I, 595, and James F. Drake catalogue No. 196 (1928); *MS* 2 pp.; dated 23 Apr 44.

[a]I am greatly indebted to you for your kind attention and Mrs. Dickens begs me to present her compliments and thanks.[a] In the execution of a peculiar faculty for which I am distinguished in an eminent degree, I quite forgot when we spoke about those tickets, that Mrs. Dickens had invited some friends at home for the very day to which they refer. In the modesty of my mind, I should not have mentioned this circumstance, but for her special desire that you should know why she is unable to avail herself of your kindness.

To THOMAS CHAPMAN, 25 APRIL 1844

MS Professor Robert D. Horn. *Address* (envelope, MS Myers & Co.): Thomas Chapman Esquire | 2 Leadenhall Street.

Devonshire Terrace. | Thursday Twenty Fifth April | 1844

My Dear Sir. Lord Lansdowne[2] has been out of town; and I only received the enclosed last night. I have written to Doctor Smith, and made him acquainted with its contents.[3]

Faithfully Yours always

Thomas Chapman Esquire   CHARLES DICKENS

To MESSRS CHAPMAN & HALL, [?25 APRIL 1844]

Mention in next.

[1] Possibly James, brother of Richard Thomson (1794–1865; *DNB*): see Vol. I, p. 218*n*.

[aa] Not in N.

[2] Henry Petty Fitz-Maurice, 3rd Marquess of Lansdowne (1780–1863; *DNB*): see Vol. III, p. 263*ns*.

[3] Evidently in connexion with arrangements for the Sanatorium Anniversary Festival on 4 June; Lord Lansdowne had been a steward at the dinner on 29 June 43, but is not named as present this year.

To THOMAS MITTON, 25 APRIL 1844

MS Huntington Library.

Devonshire Terrace. | Twenty Fifth April 1844.

My Dear Mitton.

Bradbury and Evans[1] are dead[2] and decided on my paying C and H's balance before I go, and settling the whole question of the Stock on hand of the books in which I have an interest: considering it would be leaving a power in their hands which under circumstances of separation would be full of danger and embarrassment otherwise. I think this is right; especially as C and H have never taken the slightest steps towards informing me of the state of Pickwick.

I have therefore written to them for the necessary statements, and informed them that I wish to pay them before I go, if I can. They have replied that the Statements shall be made out with all despatch.

It will now be necessary for me to discuss with Bradbury and Evans, the terms on which we are to proceed; and in doing this, I must of course give them an Interest in throwing every possible kind of briskness and alacrity into the business working of books old, and books new.

Before I enter on this, I want to look over the papers I have, in connexion with C and H, and perfectly understand the different Agreements. Will you send me up all the documents connected with my Books, that are now in your possession?

Thompson was here yesterday, and is in treaty for another house[3] (£250 for the half year, if I remember right) which will be settled today.

Faithfully Ever
CD

Thomas Mitton Esquire

Any news of the "Gent" upstairs??[4]

To CHARLES WATSON,[5] 25 APRIL 1844*

MS Free Library of Philadelphia.

1 Devonshire Terrace | York Gate Regents Park
Twenty Fifth April 1844.

Sir.

I beg to acknowledge the receipt of your obliging letter of the Twenty Third Instant.

I am perfectly aware that there are several passages in my books which, with very little alteration—sometimes with none at all—will fall into blank verse,[6] if

---

[1] This letter marks a stage in the "deliberations and discussions, many and grave" (F, IV, ii, 315) with Bradbury & Evans after CD's decision to leave Chapman & Hall on the conclusion of *Chuzzlewit* (see Vol. III, p. 587*n*): for further details of the arrangements, see *To* Bradbury & Evans, 8 May.

[2] N, I, 595 reads "here", in error.
[3] See *To* Mrs Smithson, 18 Apr and *fn*.
[4] Unidentified.
[5] Unidentified.
[6] R. H. Horne in *A New Spirit of the Age*, I, 65–8, had commented on this feature of CD's style, with illustrations from *Old Curiosity Shop* and *Nickleby*.

divided off into Lines. It is not an affectation in me, nor have I the least desire to write them in that metre; but I run into it, involuntarily and unconsciously, when I am very much in earnest. I even do so, in speaking.

I am not prepared to say that this may not be a defect in prose composition; but I attach less importance to it than I do to earnestness. And considering that it is a very melodious and agreeable march of words, usually; and may be perfectly plain and free; I cannot agree with you that it is likely to be considered by discreet readers as turgid or bombastic, unless the sentiments expressed in it, be of that character. Then indeed it matters very little how they are attired, as they cannot fail to be disagreeable in any garb.

Upon the whole I am inclined to think that if I had altered the passages which give you offence, you would not have liked my books so well as you are kind enough to say you do; and would not have given me that credit for being in earnest which has procured for me the pleasure of receiving your good-humoured and agreeable letter.

Charles Watson Esquire

Faithfully Yours
CHARLES DICKENS

To THOMAS CHAPMAN, 26 APRIL 1844

Mention in S. V. Henkels catalogue No. 1249 (1920); *MS* 4 pp.; dated Devonshire Terrace, Friday, twenty-sixth April, 1844.[1]

Referring to the Sanatorium dinner: making suggestions as to whom to invite and the manner of holding the same; very emphatic in declaring ladies should be invited.[2]

To LUDWIG DÖBLER,[3] 26 APRIL 1844

Text from N, I, 596.

1 Devonshire Terrace, York Gate, Regents Park | Twenty-sixth April 1844

Mr. Charles Dickens presents his compliments to M. Döbler, and very much regrets that being already engaged for tomorrow, he cannot avail himself of the box which M. Döbler has so kindly sent him through Mr. Schloss.[4] But if M. Döbler should have another opportunity of conferring a similar favor on Mr. Dickens, it will give Mr. D. great pleasure to accept it.

Mr. Dickens begs to add, that he had the pleasure of seeing M. Döbler at the

---

[1] Presumably the same letter as the one "To Mr. Chapman" dated "Devonshire Terrace, 1844", mentioned in undated Pickering & Chatto catalogue, also described as *MS* 4 pp., with a similar but shorter summary.

[2] See *To* Stanfield, 30 Apr.
[3] Ludwig Döbler (1801–64), conjurer: see Vol. III, p. 277*n*. His 1844 season at the St James's had begun 23 Apr.
[4] Presumably Döbler's manager.

Saint James's Theatre on the last occasion[1] of M. Döbler's being in London; and that he was much astonished and delighted by his magical performances.

To MRS TALFOURD,[2] 27 APRIL 1844

Text from N, I, 596.

Devonshire Terrace | Twenty-Seventh April 1844

My Dear Mrs. Talfourd,

I will not fail to give my best attention to the subject of the Home Mission,[3] and its report. And if its Christian aid be extended to all classes of Believers, and its Christian instruction be such as all poor creatures may receive, I will drop my mite into its treasury—not when I grow rich, like the bells of Shoreditch[4] (for that will never be), but when I have recovered my last half-dozen subscriptions, which have been rather quick—even for subscriptions—on each other's heels.[5]

Poor Fanny Chandler![6] God knows she is better where she is! Pray tell me, when I next see you, how her good nurse is, and where.

Isms ! Oh Heaven for a world without an ism. The wickedness of us moles to each other in our isms is enough to have brought a comet on the head of this, a thousand years ago.

Always My Dear Mrs. Talfourd | Faithfully yours
[CHARLES DICKENS]

To MESSRS WILLIAMS & CLAPHAM,[7] 27 APRIL 1844*

MS Messrs B. F. Stevens & Brown.

Devonshire Terrace | Twenty Seventh April 1844.

Mr Charles Dickens sends his compliments to Messrs. Williams and Clapham, and hopes the latter end of next Month (May) may suit their convenience for the settlement of their account. But if they should have any pressing occasion for the money before that time, and will let Mr. Dickens know, he will not fail to do what they require.

---

[1] In 1843.

[2] Rachel Talfourd: see Vol. I, p. 315*n*.

[3] Probably the London Domestic Mission Society, which held day schools and Sunday schools for the poor; its Anniversary Meeting took place 24 Apr, with the Rev. H. H. Piper in the chair; among those present were Bowring, Tagart (the retiring Secretary), and Travers Madge. The Home Missionary Society, with similar objects but with Congregational clergy as its officers, was appealing for funds in the Apr No. of their magazine; neither the Talfourds nor CD appears in their lists of subscribers.

[4] From "Oranges and Lemons".

[5] CD paid his £5 subscription to the Governesses' Benevolent Institution on 27 Apr; no other known subscription appears in his account-book (MS Messrs Coutts) during Apr and May.

[6] The death of Frances Mary Chandler, aged 15, was announced in the *Gentleman's Magazine*, 5 Apr.

[7] Goldsmiths and jewellers, Strand; probably the "Williams & Co" to whom CD paid £52.7.6 on 3 June (Account-book, MS Messrs Coutts).

To THE REV. EDWARD TAGART,[1] 29 APRIL 1844

MS Mr Justin Turner.

Devonshire Terrace | Monday Twenty Ninth April 1844

My Dear Sir

Many thanks for Mr. Piper's[2] letter. Will you kindly charge yourself with the enclosed for him? Also with the other enclosed for Mrs. Tagart?[3]

Dr. Dewey[4] sent me his pamphlet,[5] which, in the exercise of a stern resolve, I immediately put in the fire, without glancing at, beyond the title page. When I determined to tell the Truth about America, I determined also that I would not, from that time, read any American Paper, Pamphlet, Book, or Review, in which I had reason to suppose (from the very fact of its being sent to me) there might be the least allusion to myself.

I do not mean to say that it requires a Roman fortitude to exercise this Self-Denial. But I have beaten, by these means, every free and independent Citizen who has written to annoy me (judging from the number of packets I return to the Post Office unopened, I should think their name is Legion); and I do not think I am less wise or less honest, and I know I am more good-tempered, in consequence.

Always My Dear Sir | Faithfully Yours

The Reverend Edward Tagart.   CHARLES DICKENS

To THE REV. H. H. PIPER, [?29 APRIL 1844]

Mention in Sotheby's catalogue, July 1937; *MS* 1 p.; dated Devonshire Terrace, 1844—probably the enclosure referred to in last.

Thanking him for a generous allusion to him in a sermon.[6]

---

[1] Edward Tagart (1804–58; *DNB*), Unitarian minister: see Vol. III, p. 449n.

[2] Rev. Henry Hunt Piper (1781–1864), Unitarian minister, writer, and education-ist; his school at Norton, Derbyshire (till 1843, when he settled in Banbury) was well known in nonconformist circles, and he had been one of the founders of the Sheffield Literary and Philosophical Society. His wife (*née* Alicia Lewin) was Mrs Bowring's sister (*Transactions of the Unitarian Historical Society*, I [1918], 139–50).

[3] Helen Tagart: see Vol. III, p. 449n. CD was probably enclosing a letter from Catherine, who also wrote to her on 1 June (MS Mr Leslie C. Staples).

[4] Orville Dewey, DD (1794–1882; *DAB*), Unitarian minister of Berkshire, Mass.

Friend of Emerson and Miss Sedgwick; in Europe 1841–3.

[5] *On American Morals and Manners*, reprinted from the *Christian Examiner and Religious Miscellany*, Boston, 1844; it referred to CD's "bitterness towards America", "pictures of a vulgarity which nobody ever saw or heard or conceived of in America" and his "strain of almost insane vituperation"; believed he was "doing himself more hurt at home, even than abroad" (pp. 23–4).

[6] The allusion may have been made in Piper's sermon of 20 Apr 44 on behalf of the London Domestic Mission Society, in Dr Hutton's chapel, Little Carter Lane, Doctors' Commons (*Christian Reformer*, XI [1844], 491).

To CLARKSON STANFIELD, 30 APRIL 1844

MS Carl H. Pforzheimer Library.

Devonshire Terrace | Thirtieth April 1844.

My Dear Stanfield

The Sanatorium, or Sick House for Students, Governesses, Clerks, Young Artists, and so forth, who are above Hospitals, and not rich enough to be well attended in illness in their own Lodgings (you know its objects) is going to have a Dinner at the London Tavern on Tuesday the Fifth[1] of June.

The Committee are very anxious to have you for a Steward, as one of the heads of a large class; and I have told them that I have no doubt you will act. There is no Stewards' Fee, or Collection, whatever.[2]

They are particularly anxious also, to have Mr. Etty[3] and Edwin Landseer.[4] As you see them daily at the Academy, will you ask them, or shew them this note. Sir Martin[5] became one of the Committee some few years ago, at my solicitation, as recommending young Artists, struggling alone in London, to the better knowledge of this Establishment.

The dinner is to comprize the new feature of Ladies dining at the tables with the Gentlemen—not looking down upon them from the Gallery.[6] I hope in your reply you will not only book yourself, but Mrs. Stanfield[7] and Mary.[8] It will be very brilliant and cheerful, I hope. Dick in the cheer. Gentlemens'[9] dinner-tickets a guinea as usual. Ladies' Twelve Shillings.

I think this is all I have to say, except (which is nonsensical and needless) that I am always affectionately Yours

Clarkson Stanfield Esquire   CHARLES DICKENS

---

[1] CD's error for "Fourth".

[2] Stanfield was one of the speakers, representing Art.

[3] William Etty, RA (1787–1849; *DNB*); greatest as a figure painter, but achieved fame and fortune only in the 1840s, when his health and powers were beginning to fail. He was for many years a friend of Macready (who bought his *Bridge of Sighs*, 1840), at whose house CD met him in 1839; also a friend of Maclise and Stanfield. Was on the Council of the School of Design, and one of the judges for the cartoon competition. Exhibited at RA 1844 two pictures based on his unsuccessful fresco paintings for the Buckingham Palace pavilion (see Vol. III, p. 519*n*). In 1846 Macready found him "very thin, very asthmatic" but still "*revelling* in colour and in form" (*Diaries*, II, 335).

[4] Neither is named as a steward in press reports.

[5] Sir Martin Archer Shee (1769–1850; *DNB*), portrait painter; RA 1800, PRA 1830–50: see Vol. II, p. 262*n*.

[6] In a letter of 3 May inviting Daniel Gaskell to act as a steward, Southwood Smith told him that "we have decided to invite our lady friends to join us. Mr. Dickens was very earnest that we should do this" (MS Dr Harry Stone).

[7] Rebecca Stanfield, *née* Adcock (1808–75), Stanfield's second wife, formerly a dancer at the Surrey Theatre, married at 16.

[8] Mary Stanfield (*b.* 1821), the second of Stanfield's children by his first wife, who died at Mary's birth.

[9] Thus in MS.

To J. ASHTON YATES, 30 APRIL 1844*

MS Mrs Pauline Dower.

Devonshire Terrace | Thirtieth April 1844.

My Dear Sir

They may book you as a Sanatorium Steward. May they not? There is no Stewards' Fee whatever.

Tuesday the fifth of June is the day.

Faithfully Yours Always

J. Ashton Yates Esquire CHARLES DICKENS

To T. J. SERLE, 1 MAY 1844*

MS Dr F. H. Fuller.

My Dear Serle. I think this will be the best form of cheque. If you will send it to me, I will arrange the matter with Coutts's. Miss Elton will have, I suppose to take a Letter of Credit.

Faithfully Ever

1st May 1844. CD

Pay to your Correspondent at Halifax Nova Scotia, payable to the drafts of Miss Rosa Elton

To CHARLES EVANS,[1] 2 MAY 1844*

MS Liverpool Public Libraries.

Devonshire Terrace | Second May 1844

Dear Sir

I am much obliged to you for so promptly forwarding the letter addressed, by an unknown correspondent, to me at Birmingham. What on Earth, or above it, or under it, put it into his head to direct his communication there I cannot in the faintest degree imagine.

Faithfully Yours

Charles. M. Evans Esquire CHARLES DICKENS

To T. J. SERLE, 2 MAY 1844

MS Mr Peter Brandt.

Devonshire Terrace | Second May 1844

My Dear Serle

As Rosa will most probably have to take a letter of credit, I have thought it best to make a round Sum, and fill up the cheque for five and twenty pounds. May some Nova-Scotian bedlamite fall in love with her, and marry her!

[1] Member of the Committee of the Birmingham Polytechnic and succeeded A. Matthews as Hon. Secretary.

The passage cheque was £39..18..0. She will have to give the Steward a Guinea besides, and the Steward*ess* summut for herself.

Always Faithfully Yours

T. J. Serle Esquire   CD

To THOMAS MITTON, 3 MAY 1844*

MS Columbia University Libraries.

Devonshire Terrace. | Third May 1844

My Dear Mitton. I am just reminded that Burnett dines here today. Come and dine with us at half past 5 exactly. Will you? Kate is ill—abed—but she would have been delighted to see you.

I have a most hideous cold—and am obliged to dine with the Prince and the Academicians[1] tomorrow, nevertheless.

Faithfully Yours always

CD

To JOHN WALKER, [3 MAY 1844]

Mention in *The Times*, 23 May 44. *Date:* answering a letter from Walker of 3 May: see *To* Forster, ?22 May.

Saying that he could not aid the writer further.

To WILLIAM SANDYS,[2] 5 MAY 1844

Extract in Maggs's catalogue No. 104 (1896).

Very many thanks for the accompanying dialogues.[3]

To T. N. TALFOURD, 5 MAY 1844

Text in N, I, 598, checked from MS Sotheby's, Dec 1964.

Devonshire Terrace | Sunday Fifth May 1844.

My Dear Talfourd.

Very many thanks for the newspaper,[4] and your friendliest of eloquent memories.

---

[1] The Annual Dinner of the Royal Academy on 4 May, to which those eminent in various other fields were invited; this is the earliest reference to CD's attendance. The Prince's speech included praise of Etty's *Comus* subject (W. Ames, *Prince Albert and Victorian Taste*, 1967, p. 54); this tribute may be seen as some acknowledgment of the time and labour Etty had spent on the fresco before his withdrawal.

[2] William Sandys (1792–1874; *DNB*), FSA: see Vol. III, p. 512*n*.

[3] In the Cornish dialect; for CD's interest, and Sandys's publication of dialogues and other material, see Vol. III, pp. 394*n*, 512*n*.

[4] Not identified; evidently a provincial newspaper reporting a speech of Talfourd's while on circuit.

I have dropped—dropped!—the action and the Chancery Suit[1] against the Bankrupt Pirates. We have had communication with the assignees, and found their case quite desperate. The four booksellers have come in and compounded. So that I lose nothing by them. By Lee and Haddock[2] (the vagabonds) I *do* lose, of course, all my expences, costs and charges in those suits.[3] But it is something to know the worst of it and to be rid of Knight Bruce, whom I should call (if he were not a friend of yours) rather a pragmatical donkey—judicially speaking.

I think it is high time we invested the Elton money. When would it suit you best, to bear me company to Coutts's, and settle it in five minutes with Mr. Marjoribanks?

Always Faithfully Yours | My Dear Talfourd
CHARLES DICKENS

To HENRY and JAMES EDWARDS,[4] 6 MAY 1844

Extract in Anderson Auction Co. catalogue No. 1098 (1914); *MS* 2 pp.; dated London, 6 May 44.

I do not quite understand from your letter what it is that you want of me. If it is a contribution to your little storehouse[5] that, I regret to say I cannot give; as my acquiescence in one such request would involve me in too many sources of similar engagements to be contemplated for a moment.

To OCTAVIAN BLEWITT,[6] 6 MAY 1844

MS Royal Literary Fund.

Devonshire Terrace | Sixth May 1844 | Monday Evening
My Dear Sir

I have delayed acknowledging the courtesy of the Committee, not because I

---

[1] See *To* Talfourd, 19 Mar. Forster (F, IV, iii, 322) summarizes the conclusion: "that upon ample public apology, and payment of all costs, the offenders should be let go" (presumably by agreement between the solicitors); "but the real result was that, after infinite vexation and trouble, he had himself to pay all the costs incurred on his own behalf" (i.e. in the suits against Lee & Haddock).

[2] Nothing is known of Richard Lee's later history. John Haddock's name appears as the printer (at 126 Drury Lane) of No. III (9 Mar 44) of "The New Parley Library" and of several issues between 23 Mar and 14 Sep; and again as the printer of the first three Nos of *The Astrologer*, Feb–Mar 45. Edward Blanchard was the editor, but one day found that Haddock had disappeared, leaving the office locked; "it was whispered that years later he was seen in Jamaica" (E. L. Blanchard, *Life and Reminiscences*, I, 29).

[3] CD's accounts show the payment of £207 on 11 June as "Legal Charges" (Account-book, MS Messrs Coutts), but this can hardly have been the total; Jaques's estimate for the Chancery suits alone is £500 (*CD in Chancery*, p. 57). Perhaps the rest was paid by Bradbury & Evans: see *To* Bradbury & Evans, 8 May and *fn*.

[4] Henry is possibly Henry Edwards, Ll.D., author of *Elementary Education, its Extension in our own Country*, [its] *State on the Continent*, 1844, and works on the Corn Laws; or a brother of James Edwards of Manchester (see *To* James Edwards, 12 Oct 45) of whom nothing is known.

[5] Unidentified.

[6] Octavian Blewitt (1810–84; *DNB*), Secretary of the Literary Fund: see Vol. I, p. 602*n*.

was in the least degree insensible to it, but because I deemed it probable that I might be leaving town (to write peacefully), before the Dinner of the Literary Fund;[1] and in case I should not do so I wished to accept the Invitation with which I have been honored. But although I am not going away just now, and am not therefore prevented from attending by that course, I regret that I *am* prevented by a no less potent one; and that is, a most intolerable cold or taste of influenza, which keeps me sneezing and wheezing from morning until night, and would render the sharpening of a saw an infinitely more agreeable sound to the Literary Fund Diners than any observations from me.

Pray assure the Committee of my obligation to them, and believe me

Faithfully Yours always

Octavian Blewitt Esquire   CHARLES DICKENS

To JOHN OVERS, 6 MAY 1844*

MS Mrs Jessie Reed. *Address:* Mr. Overs | 8 John's Place | Camberwell New Road.

Devonshire Terrace | Sixth May 1844

Dear Mr. Overs.

Don't on any account come out, unless you are in a proper condition to do so; but write to me when you have any news.[2] I did not intend to imply in my note that you ought to have come, or were in any way bound to do so, but that I had, without any particular reason, expected you.[3]

[   ]

Mr. Overs.   [CHARLES DICKENS]

To DOUGLAS JERROLD, [MAY 1844]

Text from W. Blanchard Jerrold, *The Life and Remains of Douglas Jerrold*, 1859, pp. 217–18. *Date:* soon after the publication of *The Story of a Feather* on 4 May.

I am truly proud of your remembrance, and have put the 'Story of a Feather'[4] on a shelf (not an obscure one) where some other feathers are, which it shall help to show mankind which way the wind blows, long after *we* know where the wind comes from. I am quite delighted to find that you have touched the latter part again, and touched it with such a delicate and tender hand.[5] It is a wise and beautiful book. I am sure I may venture to say so to you, for nobody consulted it more regularly and earnestly than I did, as it came out in *Punch*.

[1] The Anniversary Festival held 8 May (*Times*, 9 May). CD had attended in 1837 and 1841, but declined in all years after 1843, when he accepted but was unable to go: see Vol. II, p. 264*n* and Vol. III, p. 485*n*.

[2] Doubtless of the MS he was submitting to publishers: see *To* Overs, 10 May.

[3] Ending and signature cut away.

[4] Published in volume form by the Punch Office, 4 May, following its serialization in *Punch* Jan–Dec 43: see Vol. III, p. 591 and *n*.

[5] In a prefatory note, dated "May, 1844", Jerrold said: "In the present reprint several of the latter chapters are, it is hoped, rendered less imperfect than when they originally appeared, written, as they then were, under severe illness".

To MESSRS BRADBURY & EVANS, 8 MAY 1844

MS Brotherton Library, Leeds.

Devonshire Terrace | Wednesday Evening Eighth May 1844.
My Dear Sirs.

I will begin with a statement of the amount in which I must desire to become indebted to you. The balance payable to C and H will be £1,500. The sum I shall require for my anticipated expenses will be £1,500. I owe you already £500;[1] and against this entire sum of £3,500, I propose to place to your credit, when the account for the subscription to the completed Chuzzlewit is rendered, £500. I apprehend there is little doubt of its realizing that much.[2]

But in addition to this sum of £3,000 which will then be left, I *may* require, for anything I know, in the spring of next year, or about that time, £500 more. I do not know that this will be so; but I think it right to mention it.[3]

Now, for the repayment of these advances, we must look, of course, to the following heads.

First. The New Carol,[4] and the new next Christmas issue of the old one.

Secondly. The Magazine or Journal, and the mutual relations we may agree upon, respecting it. I would suggest that it should be commenced within six months, certainly, after the expiration of my year's retirement.[5] There is also the question of other new books by me.

Thirdly. The best working of the copyrights in existence.[6]

Oliver Twist, which has not yet been published in a single volume or a cheap form, is absolutely mine; free from any conditions whatever. The stock on hand is 27 copies in cloth—583 in quires.[7]

The Christmas Carol is also mine, unconditionally. The Stock on hand is 227 copies in cloth—337 in quires.

My interest in *Pickwick* is at present one third of the copyright. They cannot

---

[1] No such sum is credited to CD in his accounts; instead, Bradbury & Evans may have paid his legal fees on his behalf.

[2] The result of the subscription must have been disappointing; CD's accounts show no payment from Chapman & Hall between 1 June 44 and 24 May 45. Presumably the subscription did not exceed the £500 required, and payment was made direct to Bradbury & Evans.

[3] The amount advanced was £2800 (F, IV, ii, 316, and Appx A, p. 691).

[4] "There was an understanding, at the time this agreement was signed, that a successor to the *Carol* would be ready for the Christmas of 1844" (F, IV, ii, 316).

[5] Forster mentions "the only farther stipulation having reference to the event of a periodical being undertaken whereof Dickens might be only partially editor or author, in which case his proprietorship of

copyright and profits was to be two thirds instead of three fourths" (*ibid*). This plan eventually developed into the *Daily News*: see *To* Mitton, 25 July 45.

[6] In *To* Mitton, 25 Apr 44, CD asked for "all the documents connected with my Books". The present letter shows that these included the agreements over *Sketches* between Chapman & Hall and Macrone, the assignment of *Pickwick*, the agreement for *Nickleby*, the agreement for *Master Humphrey's Clock*, the final agreement with Bentley over *Oliver* and *Barnaby* of 2 July 40, and the agreement for *Chuzzlewit* of 7 Sep 41. See Vol. I, Appx C, Vol. II, Appx B. The agreement for the *Carol*, presumably in Oct 43, does not survive.

[7] Of the 3-vol. edn of 1841. CD received £1000 for a half-share of the copyright: see Appx A, p. 692.

alter the form or price without my consent. If I wish to sell my third, I must offer to them. If they wish to sell their shares or any part of them, they must offer to me. If we disagree about the price in either case, two arbitrators are to be called in; one by them and one by me. If *they* disagree, they elect an umpire who decides. I may now, if I please, buy a third of the Stock on hand, but this would not give me the power of appointing any other publishers, as long as C and H hold their two thirds. I have not yet received their account of the stock (which is preparing), but as they were moving me not long ago towards a new issue of this book, I suppose it is not very large.

Nickleby. In the November of this year, the whole copyright of Nickleby becomes mine, but I cannot sell it without the offer to C and H as before. There is, however, no clause in the agreement, confirming them as the perpetual publishers. In November I may buy the Stock at Cost Price; and until November I have no right to ask what it is.

Humphrey's Clock, or, in other words, The Old Curiosity Shop, and Barnaby Rudge. In these books, I have half the copyright. The same provisions as to sale, and offers are in the agreement as in the others. I cannot exactly give you the Stock, but you can calculate it easily. It is 208,753 *numbers*. This of course has to be divided by the *number of numbers* in the two stories. The miscellaneous papers were reserved for wasting; and of them, there are on hand 99,250. There is no distinct clause as to their being always the Publishers, but I apprehend the stipulation that they shall not alter the form or price without my consent, implies that.

American Notes. I have three fourths of this book. There is no agreement whatever, respecting it. I wrote them a letter, giving them their share.[1] The Stock is, 61 copies in cloth—168 in quires.

Chuzzlewit. I have three fourths of the profits of this book (Subscription included) up to the last no., and for six months afterwards. At Christmas in this year, C and H on payment to me of a fourth of the cost price of the stock then on hand, come into half the copyright. This agreement contains the same stipulations as to disposal of the interest on either side. Same as Humphrey's Clock, with respect to their publishing.

The Sketches they bought of Macrone, with his stock, for £2,250; and hold the copyright in trust for five years from March 1840, to assign half of it to me, if it have paid the advance and expences on it at that time, or before. If it have not paid that money, and I still wish to buy, I get half the copyright and stock, if I choose to pay half the balance. All the same clauses as to offers of sale, &c.

You will see at once that the only *immediately* available books, apart from C and H, are the Oliver Twist, and the American Notes. And what I particularly wish you to consider is, whether you think it would be more advisable to publish each of them with a new publisher, in a cheap form (in which neither has appeared) or to break ground with Chapman and Hall, for a general serial Edition of *all* the books in Volumes, under your auspices. This Edition I should propose to embrace new prefaces, and here and there a note, by me; and in short anything I could think of, to increase its interest.

---

[1] See Vol. III, p. I and *n*.

The money I should want, upon the first of June,[1] or as soon afterwards as may suit your convenience. When you have considered these various heads, and got them into some shape in your minds, I shall hold myself ready for any appointment you may make with Mr. Forster.

I have confined myself entirely to the business details of the matter; not wishing to give you the trouble of having to separate them from a crowd of remarks.

My Dear Sirs | Always Faithfully Yours

Messrs. Bradbury and Evans. CHARLES DICKENS

To THOMAS [POWELL], 9 MAY 1844

Extract in Parke-Bernet catalogue, Jan 1947; *MS* 1 p.; dated 9 May 44. *Address:* "Thomas Ponele" in catalogue.

About the Sanatorium dinner.[2] I do not like to ask men to act as stewards at a dinner over which I preside, otherwise I could have had no possible objection to the bagging of Talfourd and Richard Monckton [Milnes].

To JOHN OVERS, 10 MAY 1844

MS University of Texas.

Devonshire Terrace | Tenth May 1844 | Friday

My Dear Mr. Overs. I have thought it best, for divers reasons, not to put any publisher's name in the letter; but I have slightly altered it, as you will see. Try Newby.[3] If he won't, try Mortimer. If *he* won't, let me know.

Faithfully Yours always

CD

To ANGUS FLETCHER, 13 MAY 1844†

MS Mrs R. E. Yeats-Brown. *Address:* Angus Fletcher Esq. | Poste Restante | Genoa.

Devonshire Terrace | Monday Thirteenth May 1844

My dear Fletcher.

Ten thousand thanks. Take the illustrious abiding place of the illustrious man *for three Months*[4] (I do not like to bind myself to a place I have not seen and

---

[1] The agreement (which does not survive) was clearly signed, like the others of that date (see Appx A), on 1 June: see F, IV, ii, 316 and *To* Mitton, 14 Apr 45. The precision of Forster's summary suggests that he had a copy or draft in front of him.

[2] See *To* Southwood Smith, 13 Apr.

[3] T. C. Newby, of 72 Mortimer St, Cavendish Square; published Overs's *Evenings of a Working Man.*

[4] The Villa di Bagnerello, or Villa di Bella Vista, at Albaro near Genoa. Fletcher had probably urged CD to settle on Genoa rather than Pisa in correspondence following *To* Fletcher, 24 Mar. Forster says that CD wished to take Byron's villa at Albaro (F, IV, iv, 330), and this may, as Edgar Johnson suggests (*CD, his Tragedy and Triumph*, 1953, p. 504), have been Landor's recommendation.

tried, for longer): stipulating in the agreement that if I, at the expiration of that time continue it for 12 months, I shall pay so and so. Of course you will get it as cheap as you can. But I do not wish to bind the butcher very tight for the three months, so that what I overpay, as it were, in that term, is afterwards allowed me if I hold it for twelve. You understand, bright Dugald?[1]

*a*Likewise let the butcher make a water closet. If I should leave at the end of the three months, *I* will pay for it. If I hold the house for 12 months, *he* shall pay for it. If you employ a—(what's a lawyer in Italian? Solicito I suppose?) hold me your debtor, like a good Canova, 'till I come.*a*

Hadn't your bedroom better be on the Ground floor, lest those enormous blocks of marble you will work upon, should fall through, and damage the family? I feel myself on the roof with a telescope at my Eye. You stand beside me with a blouse and chisel. But little of me is visible behind my moustache, but that is of a swarthy and Bandit hue. I look towards my Native Land, and scowl. I also drink—a little. Do I smoke at all?

A duplicate of this, has gone to the other address.[2] You are a nice man to hope I am working at Italian, when I am working my very head off at Martin Chuzzlewit! *b*How is Clara?*b* [3]

Best regards and many thanks from Kate. *c*Mrs. Wilson's[4] letter has not yet arrived. I will write again soon. Start on the 1st. of July, please God.*c*

Ever faithfully yours
Angus Fletcher Esquire   CHARLES DICKENS

To MACVEY NAPIER, 13 MAY 1844

MS British Museum.

Devonshire Terrace | Monday Thirteenth May 1844.
My Dear Sir.
I have altered all my plans, (or I should rather say so unexpectedly carried out very old plans) since our compact was made, that I must throw myself upon your merciful consideration, even with reference to next October. I am going abroad on the first of next July—to Italy—where I shall remain some time —six or eight months, I dare say. Do anything but finish Chuzzlewit before I go, I cannot. And what I may do there, it is impossible for me to say, until I know by experience what manner of life I lead in sunny places, and whether I am stupendously idle, or moderately active.

I will report to you from some Vineyard, in August or thereabouts. But do not count upon a John Doe[5] so far out of your bailiwick. It is likely, I think, that

---

[1] This nickname evidently arose in 1841, when CD wrote to Fletcher: "You shall be our 'Dougal' to the Highlands, and I your bailie"; an allusion to the turnkey in *Rob Roy*: see Vol. II, p. 256*n*.

[2] At Carrara.

[3] These three words written very large and deleted in another hand.

aa; bb; cc Not previously published.

[4] Unidentified.

[5] Here used for an anonymous person.

I might hit upon something fresh (in your way) under such new circumstances; and if I do, I shall be delighted to let you have it, to be used at your convenience.

I have just heard from Lord Jeffrey, whom I am going to see tomorrow. It gives me great concern to learn from him that he has been very ill again:[1] and has a consultation of Doctors just now, at his Hotel. He talks of returning to Scotland on Wednesday, if they will allow him.

Always My Dear Sir | Faithfully Yours

Professor Napier. CHARLES DICKENS

To H. P. SMITH, 13 MAY 1844

MS Huntington Library.

Devonshire Terrace | Monday Thirteenth May 1844

My Dear Smith

Quite Papist[2] enough, but by no means man of leisure enough. Dinners,[3] meetings, and the like, are already the Death of me—nearly. Add a Pope festival to the rest, and my Eagle Policies will fall in, prematurely.

Chapman and Hall have expressed a desire to see the Volcanic MS, and have written me to that effect. I have duly apprized the Milanese[4] thereof. I clearly foresee that he will smash some bookseller by assault and battery; and as Hall is small, perhaps he may answer his purpose better than another.

Cordial regards | Always Faithfully Yours

H. P. Smith Esquire CHARLES DICKENS

To T. E. WELLER, 13 MAY 1844

Text from *A Dickens Friendship*, ed. W[ilfrid] M[eynell], privately printed, 1931, pp. 45–9.

Private

Devonshire Terrace, Monday, Thirteenth May, 1844

My dear Sir,

It will afford me real pleasure and gratification to see your family in London, and to promote your views in reference to Miss Weller (in whom, I need not say, I have the truest and most lively interest) to the utmost of my power. That

---

[1] Jeffrey, whose health had begun to fail in 1841, had been in bed with bronchial trouble during his usual London visit, in late Apr and early May, but by 9 May was recovering (Lord Cockburn, *Life of Lord Jeffrey*, II, 386).

[2] i.e. admirer of Pope, the centenary of whose death fell on 30 May. No "festival" is reported in the contemporary press.

[3] CD had attended the Annual Dinner of the Artists' Benevolent Fund on 11 May, with Lord Palmerston in the chair, and responded to the toast of the Authors: see *Speeches*, ed. K. J. Fielding, pp. 67–8. The Rev. W. H. Brookfield was present and described the speech in a letter to his wife as "rather pompous and shapely in its construction and delivered in a rather sonorous deep voice. Not a jot of humour in it" (Charles and Frances Brookfield, *Mrs. Brookfield and her Circle*, 1905, I, 137).

[4] Unidentified.

power is not, I fear, as great as you suppose. It certainly is not with reference to the Press; from which the circumstances of my position keep me very much aloof. But, as I told you, the *Chronicle* is the most looked to, as scientifically musical in that department of its criticism; which is written by Mrs. Dickens's father, to whom I shall be delighted to present Miss Weller, immediately on her arrival. To Moscheles[1] and some of the best musical Professors we can also make her known (if she is not already so) without a moment's loss of time. And everything, or I should rather say anything, that the unreserved expression of my personal regard for, and warmest interest in, Miss Weller, can effect, shall be effected vigorously. Rely on that!

I presume you know that you will be very late in the season,[2] and that the concerts are all made up. There is a concert and Ball to come off, early in June, for the benefit of the Poles.[3] These festivals are usually attended by a great array of fashionable people, and by the opera singers. Mrs. Dickens was suggesting to me, yesterday, that it might be a very good place for Miss Weller's first appearance; and, in case you should think so, I would immediately speak to Lord Dudley Stuart who manages the whole affair, and is a friend of mine. And I have no doubt that he would gladly do anything I might suggest to him. It would be difficult to decide upon the subject without your being in town, but I will open it at a venture. Mrs. Dickens will also see her father, and ascertain whether he can suggest any other opening which it would be desirable to seize. I would strongly impress upon you that every day you lose at this time of the year (if you be bent on bringing Miss Weller out) is a very serious loss indeed.

In reference to the Press (where I think you are a little mistaken) take my word that the quieter you keep in London on that score the better. The provincial criticisms on Miss Weller are not so remarkable for their good-taste that they are likely to do any good here.[4] Indeed I am sure their injudicious obtrusion would do her serious dis-service, and prejudice her very much. I do not scruple to mention this to you, because I deem it very natural that you should be disposed to sound those provincial trumpets lustily. But let them be dumb.[5] After Mrs. Dickens's father has heard Miss Weller play, she can be very easily heralded in print,[6] with a general reference to her previous reputation, and to the times and places of its acquisition.

One can only judge of these things by their personal effect. Shall I candidly

---

[1] Ignaz Moscheles (1794–1870), composer and pianist; friend and former pupil of Thalberg; director and regular conductor for the Philharmonic Society. Fanny Burnett had studied the piano under him 1823–4.

[2] The concert season ended in mid-July and the first half of June was "the heaviest fortnight" (*Athenæum*, 15 June).

[3] Held at Willis's Rooms 10 June, in aid of the Distressed Polish Refugees (*The Times*, 11 June).

[4] Both the reports and the preliminary notices in Liverpool papers in Jan and Feb and in Manchester papers in Apr were very enthusiastic, and CD may have thought their praise excessive. His change of tone since *To* Weller, 15 Mar, may suggest that he had already discussed the project with George Hogarth.

[5] The *Musical World* of 16 May nevertheless had a fulsome paragraph reprinted from the *Liverpool Journal*.

[6] The *Morning Chronicle* had nothing until after her first concert: see *To* Beard, 10 June.

tell you that when you first wrote[1] to me sending me some provincial notices of Miss Weller, I instantly got it into my head that she *needed* every kind of puff? You cannot be too careful on this head. You may catch tittlebats by spreading such nets, but the large fish won't come near them.

I *fear* that one charge of your double-barrelled gun will hang fire; and that the difficulties in Miss Weller's way are stupendous. Faint heart never won anything, and the trial is worth making, but the number of Professors of her art and mystery in London,[2] and the immense time it takes to establish a connexion, dishearten me, I confess to you.

Let me know at your convenience on what morning you and Mrs. Weller will call here with Miss Weller, in order that Mrs. Dickens may lose no time in knowing her, as well and lovingly as I desire her to, and as I am sure she will. Make my best regards at home and believe me faithfully yours,

CHARLES DICKENS

P.S. We are going abroad in the first week in July.

To JOHN FORSTER, [MAY 1844]

Extracts in F, IV, iii, 325. *Date:* In Forster's account of CD's preparations for departure, the carriage precedes the courier (see *To* Roche, 15 May) and the tenant (see *To* Landseer, 27 May).

It occurred to him that he might perhaps get for little money some good old shabby devil of a coach—one of those vast phantoms that hide themselves in a corner of the Pantechnicon[3] *and exactly such a one he found there; sitting himself inside it, a perfect Sentimental Traveller, while the managing man told him its history.* As for comfort—let me see—it is about the size of your library; with night-lamps and day-lamps and pockets and imperials[4] and leathern cellars, and the most extraordinary contrivances.[5] Joking apart, it is a wonderful machine. And when you see it (if you *do* see it) you will roar at it first, and will then proclaim it to be "perfectly brilliant, my dear fellow."

To MESSRS BRADBURY & EVANS, 14 MAY 1844

Mention in next.

---

[1] See *To* Weller, 15 Mar.

[2] The *Athenæum*, 15 June, referred to Miss Weller and Miss Burfield as "two among the hundreds of pianoforte players".

[3] Near Belgrave Square. Forster gives the price of CD's carriage as £45. According to Mrs Cattermole, the carriage he bought had belonged to her sister Kate and her husband Charles Black, who used it for their "grand tour" some time before Aug 39 (F. G. Kitton, *CD by Pen and Pencil*, I, 181–2).

[4] Cases or trunks for luggage on a carriage roof.

[5] Ruskin described the travelling carriage bought by his parents for their first Swiss tour in 1833, with "design and distribution of store-cellars under the seats, secret drawers under front windows, invisible pockets under padded lining" in "the little apartment which was to be virtually one's home" (*Praeterita*, VI, 123–4). CD recalls similar details, including "a net for books overhead" and "a reading lamp fixed on the back", in the German travelling chariot at the London Pantechnicon: described in "Travelling Abroad", *All the Year Round*, 7 Apr 1860 (collected in *The Uncommercial Traveller*).

To MESSRS BRADBURY & EVANS, 15 MAY 1844*

MS Colonel Richard Gimbel.

Devonshire Terrace | Fifteenth May 1844.

My Dear Sirs.

The Stock on hand of the Christmas Carol, in which, as well as in the copyright of that book, you have one fourth share,[1] agreeably to my letter of yesterday, is, I find by Chapman and Hall's account,

337 copies in quires

227 in cloth: on hand, and with agents. Their account is dated 30th. April last; and from that time your interest dates.

Faithfully Yours

Messrs. Bradbury and Evans.   CHARLES DICKENS

To D. M. CORKINDALE,[2] 15 MAY 1844

Extract in Walter M. Hill catalogue No. 173; *MS* 1 p.; dated London, 15 May 44.

I am much beholden to yourself and to those other gentlemen whose sentiments you represent, for the flattering request preferred in it. But I do not desire to offer myself as a candidate for the honor of sitting in Parliament, at this time.[3]

To LOUIS ROCHE,[4] 15 MAY 1844

MS John Rylands Library.

Devonshire Terrace | Wednesday Fifteenth May 1844

Louis Roche.

If you will call upon the gentleman with whom you travelled last; or, if he should not be in town, upon the other gentleman whom you mentioned to me as being able to speak to your character; and will ask him when it will be most convenient for me to call upon him, and will let me know, I shall be happy to make the needful enquiries. In case they are quite satisfactory, I shall be glad to engage you, if we can agree upon terms.

CHARLES DICKENS

P.S. I send you one of my cards, that you may arrange with your old employer for my calling on him.

---

[1] For the draft Agreement assigning them one-quarter of the copyright for the sum of £200, see Appx A, p. 695.

[2] D. M. Corkindale of 7 Kinning Place, Glasgow, wrote to Leigh Hunt 17 July 47 (MS BM), on behalf of "a Number of Gentlemen . . . Electors of Glasgow", inviting him to stand for Parliament; CD is obviously answering a similar request.

[3] CD had declined to stand at Reading in 1841: see Vol. II, pp. 288, 300–1.

[4] Louis Roche (*d.* 1849), courier; according to Forster (F, IV, vi, 361) a native of Avignon; accompanied CD to Italy, and again to Switzerland 1846. He became ill in 1848 (see N, II, 127) and died of heart trouble 1849 (MDGH, II, 95).

To GEORGE B. WEBB,[1] 15 MAY 1844

Extract in Anderson Galleries catalogue No. 623; *MS* 2 pp.; dated Devonshire Terrace, 15 May 44.

I am much obliged to you for sending me the enclosed . . . Any sense I might otherwise have of the oddity of the letter is quenched in my pity for the poor "chance child" who wrote it. He certainly is not the son mentioned in Grimaldi's Life, for he is described as dying under very terrible circumstances.[2] Nor should I think it likely that his name is, of right, Grimaldi at all. For it is the custom in such unhappy cases to be poetic and fanciful in the choice of names; and if the Beadle is a man of fertile imagination to leave it pretty much to him.[3] Perhaps the Beadle in your Correspondent's case was fond of Pantomimes.

To FREDERICK DICKENS, 18 MAY 1844*

MS Benoliel Collection.

Devonshire Terrace | Eighteenth May 1844 | Saturday

My Dear Fred. I wish you would see this man,[4] today, or this evening. You will observe he has moved.

If he be really in the distress he states, I shod. be sorry to refuse him another Sovereign. If you have one in your pocket give it him (being thoroughly satisfied); if not, I will send it to him after I have spoken with you at breakfast tomorrow.

But I have some doubts of him. Do not be taken in. If I could establish it for a fact that he has imposed upon me, I would have him up to Queen Square[5] forthwith.

I hope you are not going behindhand in money matters. Besides my ten pounds, I am told there are five pounds due upon the Lewisham account.[6]

Affectionately Always
CD

To JOHN FORSTER, [?22 MAY 1844]

Extract in F, IV, iii, 326. *Date:* CD almost certainly sent Forster his account of the Walker case on the day of the hearing, 22 May.

When the Mendicity officers[7] themselves told me the man was in distress, I desired them to suppress what they knew about him, and slipped out of the

---

[1] Possibly George B. Webb, architect.

[2] Joseph Grimaldi the younger died of delirium tremens in a public-house in 1832 (*Memoirs of Joseph Grimaldi*, edited by "Boz", 1838, Ch. 25); his death is possibly recalled in the Stroller's Tale in *Pickwick*, Ch. 3.

[3] Cf. *Oliver Twist*, Ch. 11.

[4] John Walker: see *To* Forster, ?22 May.

[5] The police court in Westminster nearest to Walker's lodgings in Upper Crown St. Walker was in fact charged at Marylebone.

[6] i.e. to CD's parents.

[7] The case of John Walker appears, as "No. 78239.—J.W.", in the Appendix to the *Twenty-seventh Report of the Society for the Suppression of Mendicity*, 1845, pp. 39–40, without mention of CD's name. The Society had assisted him in 1842, but

bundle (in the police office) his first letter, which was the greatest lie of all.[1] For he looked wretched, and his wife had been waiting about the street to see me, all the morning. It was an exceedingly bad case however, and the imposition, all through, very great indeed. Insomuch that I could not *say* anything in his favour, even when I saw him. Yet I was not sorry that the creature found the loophole for escape.[2] The officers had taken him illegally without any warrant; and really they messed it all through, quite facetiously.

To T. J. THOMPSON, 22 MAY 1844

MS Chas. J. Sawyer Ltd.

Devonshire Terrace | Twenty Second May 1844

My Dear Thompson

I will bring that treasure[3] with me.

I have been at the Police Office. The man really was in distress tho' he had lied damnably—The Mendicity people had taken him illegally —and he got off. Thank God!

Faithfully Ever

CD.

P.S. If Hogarth isn't ecstatic,[4] I shall go into fits.

ater, finding he had become "a systematic begging letter writer", had discouraged him. *The Times*, 23 May, reported that on 22 May, as a result of representations from CD, the officers of the Society brought him before the magistrates at Marylebone Police Court; the case against him was proved, but finding that he was in genuine need, the Society's Assistant Manager, T. L. Knevitt, asked for his discharge, which was granted with an admonition. The charge was "having attempted to obtain money from Mr. Charles Dickens, No. 1 Devonshire-terrace, New-road, by means of false and fraudulent representation"; Walker, a man of about 45, was "in great distress of mind and ... frequently shed tears". CD deposed that after his "first" letter from Walker he had sent his brother to make inquiries (see *To* Frederick Dickens, 4 Mar), and accordingly assisted him on two occasions. Four further letters followed (all in May) to which CD did not respond, and finally, on 17 May, a letter saying Walker's wife was dead and begging "a few crumbs from your table" to help the children; when CD's inquiries showed that Mrs Walker was alive and well, he passed the case to the Society. The *Examiner*, 25 May, commented on Walker's discharge: "Here is fraud rewarded. As for Mr.

Dickens, he is, after all his bounty, treated as a very hard-hearted man". However, George Mogridge, the author, on reading *The Times* report, sent CD a letter complimenting him on his liberality (Rev. C. Williams, *George Mogridge*, 1856, p. 354).

[1] CD included an account of Walker's case, without his name, along with others from his own experience (see Vol. I, p. 162*n*), in "The Begging-Letter Writer", *Household Words*, I, 18 May 50 (collected in *Reprinted Pieces*). There it appears that Walker's first letter, which CD suppressed, claimed that he had had a play accepted but postponed owing to the "indisposition of a leading actor", and so was "in a state of absolute starvation"; this CD had evidently believed, and he may have wished to conceal his own credulity as well as Walker's "greatest lie".

[2] But according to the *Household Words* article, CD was told "next day" by a friend, "the governor of a large prison", that he knew all about Walker and his friends; and the Mendicity Society later discovered that he had robbed his last employer.

[3] Probably Christiana Weller, whom he was taking to Hogarth's.

[4] See *To* Lumley, 27 May.

To LEIGH HUNT,[1] 24 MAY 1844

MS Iowa University Library.

Devonshire Terrace | Twenty Fourth May 1844.

My Dear Hunt.

Very many thanks for your companionable, and welcome, and valued book.[2] I can cordially send back to you, your own words in the Inscription.

Talfourd punctually told me the news[3] you write of. No one who knows and cherishes you, can be better pleased by it than I am.

Always My Dear Hunt | Faithfully Yours

Leigh Hunt Esquire CHARLES DICKENS

To EDWIN LANDSEER, 27 MAY 1844

Text from MDGH, I, 103.

Athenæum, Monday Morning, May 27th, 1844.

My dear Landseer,

I have let my house with such delicious promptitude, or, as the Americans would say, "with sich everlass'in slickness and al-mity sprydom," that we turn out to-night! in favour of a widow lady, who keeps it all the time we are away![4]

Wherefore if you, looking up into the sky this evening between five and six (as possibly you may be, in search of the spring), should see a speck in the air— a mere dot—which, growing larger and larger by degrees, appears in course of time to be an eagle (chain and all) in a light cart, accompanied by a raven of uncommon sagacity, curse that good-nature which prompted you to say it— that you would give them house-room.[5] And do it for the love of

Boz.

P.S.—The writer hereof may be heerd on by personal enquiry at No. 9, Osnaburgh Terrace,[6] New Road.

[1] James Henry Leigh Hunt (1784–1859; *DNB*): see Vol. I, p. 341*n*.

[2] *Poetical Works*, published by Moxon, 1844. The copy, inscribed "To Charles Dickens, from his constant admirer and obliged friend, Leigh Hunt", was in the Gad's Hill library at CD's death (*Catalogue of the Library of CD*, ed. J. H. Stonehouse, p. 60).

[3] An allowance of £120 was settled on Hunt by Mary Shelley and Sir Percy Florence Shelley; Talfourd had heard the news from Hunt by 18 May (*Correspondence of Leigh Hunt*, ed. Thornton Leigh Hunt, 1862, II, 10–12).

[4] CD let 1 Devonshire Terrace, through William Phillips, to Mrs Sophia Onslow, for one year from 28 May 44 for £300 (Memorandum of Agreement dated 27 May 44, signed by CD, Sophia Onslow and Arthur Onslow; MS Mr H. C. Dickens).

Forster says the arrangement was "apparently very promising, but in the result less satisfactory. His house was let to not very careful people" (F, IV, iii, 326).

[5] Landseer kept many animals and birds in his garden at 1 St John's Wood Road. D'Orsay wrote to CD on 17 Aug that he had found Landseer "breakfasting with your raven who allowed me to stroke his back; he is looking very beautiful" (M. Lecomte, *Le Prince des Dandys*, p. 229). At some time, probably from Italy, CD wrote "a letter to the Raven" which Landseer later gave to Thomas Hood Jr, "thinking it may amuse you" (Dexter Collection, BM).

[6] Off Albany St, and only a few minutes' walk from Devonshire Terrace; photograph in Matz's edn of Forster's *Life*, 1902, I, 328.

To BENJAMIN LUMLEY,[1] 27 MAY 1844*

MS Mrs Violet Martham Jones.

Athenæum | Twenty Seventh May 1844 | Monday Morning

Dear Sir

I will not apologize for troubling you with this note; hoping that when you have read it, you may consider that unnecessary.

I have a great interest in a young Lady from Liverpool and Manchester who has just come to London, partly at my instance; and not on account of her name (which is Weller) but because she is eighteen—very handsome—accomplished in many ways—and (this is the point) a brilliant and extraordinary Piano Forte player. Mr. Hogarth has heard her; and Count D'Orsay, and Mr. Ayrton,[2] came to my house yesterday for that purpose. The latter is decidedly of opinion that she will be a great hit, and will take the town by storm. He considers her equal to Thalberg.[3]

Coming so late in the Musical Season, it became a question with us how she could be brought out, to reasonable advantage, before it draws to a close. Count D'Orsay suggested—and begged me to say as much to you—that as you had Hoffenbach,[4] and some French Singer whose name I forget,[5] to whom you desired to afford an opportunity; it might suit your views to have a Musical Act one Opera night, including those Professors and this young lady—of whom he will not fail to report beforehand as she deserves, to the best-known among the audience. Mr. Ayrton considering this a good idea, and one which might not be unacceptable to you, I engaged to write to you this morning. Hence this note.[6]

I do not know that I can add anything to this plain statement of the case, unless I say that I shall be delighted to give you an opportunity of hearing Miss Weller, if you will allow me: and that it would be an unspeakable pleasure to me, if I could be instrumental, through your means, in making her known.

I am going abroad in July, and have already let my own house, from which I remove today. But I encamp this evening, and henceforth until I leave England, at No. 9 Osnaburgh Terrace New Road, where it will be a great satisfaction to me to receive your answer, at your convenience.

I am Dear Sir | Faithfully Yours

B. Lumley Esquire   CHARLES DICKENS

---

[1] Benjamin Lumley (1811–75; *DNB*), manager of Her Majesty's Theatre since 1842: see Vol. III, p. 530*n*. Had introduced several new operas by Donizetti and others in 1842–3; his regular company still included Grisi, Mario, and Lablache.

[2] William Ayrton (1777–1858; *DNB*), writer on music: see Vol. I, p. 205*n*.

[3] Sigismond Thalberg (1812–71), Austrian pianist and composer of world-wide reputation; first appeared in London 1836, and was there this season. Christiana

Weller had played with him in Dublin 1842: see Vol. III, p. 446*n*.

[4] Jacques Offenbach (1819–80), cellist and, later, composer; he had first appeared in London on 17 May and played at several concerts during the season, mostly in Her Majesty's concert room, including one on 14 June.

[5] Possibly M. de Revial, a tenor who first appeared this season.

[6] Neither of Christiana's concerts was at Her Majesty's.

To UNKNOWN CORRESPONDENT, [?JANUARY–27 MAY 1844]

Extract in S. V. Henkels catalogue No. 1328 (1923); dated Devonshire Terrace, 5 June 44—impossible, as CD left Devonshire Terrace 27 May (see next).

I would to Heaven your letter were not one of many scores of scores, that I might give you a better proof of my sympathy with your distresses than I now enclose.

To JOHN FORSTER, [28 MAY 1844]

Extract in F, IV, iii, 326–7. *Date:* 28 May according to Forster. *From* 9 Osnaburgh Terrace.

Advise, advise, advise with a distracted man. Investigation below stairs renders it, as my father would say, 'manifest to any person of ordinary intelligence, if the term may be considered allowable,' that the Saturday's dinner cannot come off here with safety. It would be a toss-up, and might come down heads, but it would put us into an agony with that kind of people. . . . Now, I feel a difficulty in dropping it altogether, and really fear that this might have an indefinably suspicious and odd appearance. Then said I at breakfast this morning, I'll send down to the Clarendon.[1] Then says Kate, have it at Richmond. Then I say, that might be inconvenient to the people. Then she says, how could it be if we dine late enough? Then I am very much offended without exactly knowing why; and come up here, in a state of hopeless mystification. . . . What do you think? Ellis[2] would be quite as dear as anybody else; and unless the weather changes, the place is objectionable. I must make up my mind to do one thing or other, for we shall meet Lord Denman at dinner to-day. Could it be dropped decently? That, I think very doubtful. Could it be done for a couple of guineas apiece at the Clarendon? . . . In a matter of more importance I could make up my mind. But in a matter of this kind I bother and bewilder myself, and come to no conclusion whatever. Advise! Advise![3] . . . List of the invited. There's Lord Normanby. And there's Lord Denman. There's Easthope, wife, and sister. There's Sydney Smith.[4] There's you and Mac. There's Babbage. There's a Lady Osborne and her daughter. There's Southwood Smith. And there's Quin. And there are Thomas Chapman and his wife. So many of these people have never dined with us, that the fix is particularly tight. Advise! Advise!

---

[1] See Vol. III, p. 36*n*.

[2] Joseph Ellis, of the Star and Garter, Richmond.

[3] Forster advised giving it up and CD evidently wrote to the guests (see *To* Babbage and *To* Southwood Smith, 28 May); but according to Forster "addi-

tional help was obtained and the dinner went off very pleasantly" (F, IV, iii, 327).

[4] Sydney Smith accepted CD's invitation on 14 May (letter wrongly dated 1842 in *Letters of Sydney Smith*, ed. Nowell C. Smith, 1953, II, 756).

To CHARLES BABBAGE,[1] 28 MAY 1844†

MS British Museum.

9, Osnaburgh Terrace, New Road | Twenty Eighth May 1844

My Dear Sir.

I regret to say that we are placed in the preposterous situation of being obliged to postpone our little dinner party on Saturday, by reason of having no house to dine in. We have not been burnt out; but a desirable widow (as a tenant, I mean) proposed, only last Saturday, to take our own house for the whole term of our intended absence abroad—on condition that she had possession of it today. We fled, and were driven into this place, which has no convenience for the production of any other Banquet than a cold collation of Plate and Linen—the only comforts we have not left behind us.

My consolation lies in knowing what sort of dinner you would have had if you had come *here*; and in looking forward to claiming the fulfilment of your kind promise when we are again at home. *ᵃI cannot tell you how much obliged both Mrs. Dickens and I feel to you, for your very friendly interest in procuring the enclosed information for us. It is an unspeakable encouragement and relief (I had taken precisely the course which your son suggests);[2] and I assure you that we are truly indebted to you.ᵃ*

Always Believe Me | My Dear Sir
Faithfully Yours
CHARLES DICKENS

Charles Babbage Esquire

To DR SOUTHWOOD SMITH, 28 MAY 1844*

MS Mr W. A. Foyle. *Address:* Dr. Southwood Smith | 38 Finsbury Square.

9 Osnaburgh Terrace, New Road | Twenty Eighth May 1844

My Dear Dr. Smith

I regret to say that we are placed in the preposterous situation of being obliged to postpone our little dinner party on Saturday, by reason of having no house to dine in. A most desirable Widow (as a tenant, I mean) proposed, only last Saturday, to take our own house for the whole term of our intended absence abroad—on condition that she had possession of it today. We fled, and were driven into this place, which has no convenience for the production of any other banquet than a cold collation of Plate and Linen—the only comforts we have not left behind us.

I pledge myself to try and be the better man at the Sanatorium Dinner, and to make you as happy and contented as I can.

Always Faithfully Yours
CHARLES DICKENS

Dr. Southwood Smith.

[1] Charles Babbage (1792–1871; *DNB*), mathematician and inventor: see Vol. II, p. 307n.

[2] Probably Babbage's eldest son, Benjamin Herschel (1815–78), who had gone to Italy in 1840 with Brunel, surveying for the projected railway from Genoa to Turin; his second son, Dugald, followed as a pupil 1842 (H. P. Babbage, *Memoirs and Correspondence*, privately printed, [1910], p. 9).

ᵃᵃ Not previously published.

To RICHARD MONCKTON MILNES, 30 MAY 1844*

MS Trinity College, Cambridge.

> 9 Osnaburgh Terrace, New Road
> (for I have let my own house
> for the term of my absence)
> Thirtieth May 1844

My Dear Milnes

I want for a Maniac from the Agricultural Districts,[1] two Commons Gallery Orders for tomorrow night. Have you parted with yours? And if you have, will you kindly undertake to ask any mutual friend whom you may see in the house tonight, for his?

> Faithfully Yours
> CHARLES DICKENS

R. M. Milnes Esquire   over
I will send to you at 12 tomorrow.

To RICHARD MONCKTON MILNES, 31 MAY 1844*

MS Trinity College, Cambridge.

> 9 Osnaburgh Terrace | Thirty First May 1844.

My Dear Milnes.

Any day after the nineteenth, I shall be delighted to breakfast with you.[2] But for one of your days (next Wednesday) I was obliged to refuse Sydney Smith yesterday. For I am finishing Chuzzlewit—at such times I work slowly—and the break up of a morning would ruin me.

Many thanks for the orders. Much good may they do the unhappy person who is going to use them!

> Faithfully Yours always
> CHARLES DICKENS

R. M. Milnes Esquire

P.S. I am not going to live (or die, I hope) at Pisa. My head quarters are at Albaro—close to Genoa.

To THOMAS MITTON, 31 MAY 1844

MS Huntington Library.

> Osnaburgh Terrace | Thirty First May 1844.

My Dear Mitton

If Jackson[3] seeks to influence me, falsely, against you, he is a fool. And if he be only a fool, I care very little about him.

---

[1] Unidentified.

[2] See *To* Milnes, 4 June. Milnes also appears to have dined with CD on 13 June: Milnes *to* his father (dated by *The Times*, 14 June) says he was prevented from voting by being "very late at Dickens's dinner" (T. Wemyss Reid, *Life, Letters, and Friendships of ... Milnes*, I, 332).

[3] See *To* Mitton, 2 Apr 44 and *fn*.

The number of years during which I have kept the advice I felt it strongly and imperatively necessary to give you this morning, to myself, is a sufficient demonstration of two things. Firstly, that any words but words of kindness between such old friends as you and me, occasion me unaffected pain. Secondly that I had such strong reliance on you as to believe from day to day that you would see, without my shewing, what you have not seen yet.

If you know anything in which my heart has changed for the colder or the worse with the change in my fortunes, I do not. I could say that with perfect truth, or belief of perfect truth, if I were dying. And I do not think that anyone who knows me as I really am, would quarrel with me for doing so, or say I wanted cause.

I will not dash the spirit which animates me in writing to you, or which animated you in writing to me the manly letter which you left upon my desk today;[1] by making any remark in reference to this Insurance Policy—save one. It is not the Policy[2] in reference to which some passages passed between us a year or two ago,[3] that *did* endanger (for the only time) the old feeling between us. You recollect that I was to hold a policy on your life[4] for the amount of my liability under Smithson's bond.[5] The continuance of it, and the punctual

[1] Mitton wrote on 30 May a letter surviving only in a "pressed copy" so faint as to be partly illegible; it suggests that in their talk that day CD had said that he wished to have certain documents in his own possession, and Mitton, preoccupied with the negotiations with Bradbury & Evans (completed 1 June; see Appx A), had wrongly identified them: "Dear Charley, | It was not until I had got half way here that it occurred to me that I did not possess any document which would throw much light on the Insurance business, all the receipts for the premiums having been handed over to C & H. However I referred to all the papers in my possession, and amongst them I found the enclosed letter which is a Copy of that which was signed by you concurrently with the Bond in July 1841 from which you will see that the Insurance there spoken of is one of £2000 [*one word illegible*] must [*one word illegible*] from the part of the payment made by me on the 19th February. It did also occur to me as a strict matter of business I should not sanction your executing the documents the Drafts of which [? I obtained] this morning whilst matters remain in the same state that they do now with C & H, I mean with reference to your covenanting that the whole of the property assigned by you to Bradbury & Evans is *unincumbered*—here it is that you intend to settle with them immediately you

have completed with B & E [? so that] should any difficulties arise with C & H whereby you are prevented from attaing. your object you would be exposing yourself to consequences that I should like to see you steer clear of. You will therefore [*three words illegible*] intention before you actually execute [*words illegible*]" (MS formerly in the possession of Mr H. C. Dickens).

[2] i.e. not (as Mitton clearly supposed) the Britannia policy for £2000 (No. 2251) which CD had handed over to Chapman & Hall "as further security" in 1841 (see Vol. II, p. 346 and n, Vol. III, p. 2 and n), and which he was about to deposit with Bradbury & Evans as security for their advance (see Appx A).

[3] The Britannia policy had not been an issue in any surviving letters between them, but might be indirectly connected with Mitton's letter to Forster of 6 July 42: see Vol. III, p. 267n. Mitton there accused Forster of trying "to injure" him with CD.

[4] The Argus policy of 1841: see Vol. II, p. 414.

[5] The bond undertaken by CD in 1841 (to assist Mitton when he was buying the partnership) and apparently renewed in Sep 43: see Vol. III, p. 566n, 569. Legally, the amount assured by this bond would now be due to Smithson's estate, unless he had left other instructions; and he had died intestate.

payment of the premiums, is a matter of such common honor, that I will not do you the injustice of hinting at it. I know it is enough for me to say that I want that understanding acted on, and wish to have the policy in my own charge.

Faithfully Yours as always

Thomas Mitton Esquire   CHARLES DICKENS

To DOUGLAS JERROLD, [LATE MAY 1844]

Text from W. Blanchard Jerrold, *A Day with CD*, 1871, p. 6. *Date:* after CD had taken the villa at Albaro (*To* Fletcher, 13 May), and before 3 June when he knew Jerrold would not be present at the Sanatorium dinner.

Come and see me in Italy. Let us smoke a pipe among the vines. I have taken a little house surrounded by them, and no man in the world should be more welcome to it than you.

Is your modesty really a confirmed habit, or could you prevail upon yourself, if you are moderately well, to let me call you up for a word or two at the Sanatorium dinner?[1] There are some men—excellent men—connected with that institution who would take the very strongest interest in your doing so, and *do* advise me one of these days, that if I can do it well and unaffectedly, I may.

To THOMAS CHAPMAN, 3 JUNE 1844

MS Brotherton Library, Leeds.

Osnaburgh Terrace | Monday Third June 1844

My Dear Sir

I send you the name[2] of my Printers' Party. I observe that two among them (the first two) are men of great ability, whom I know; and foremost in *Punch*. They would not like to leave their party, to join the horseshoe, I dare say; but I would begin the middle table down the room with them, so that they may have very good places. Mr. Lemon (the third name) is the Editor of Punch, moreover. The names are

Mr. A'Beckett[3]
Mr. Leech
Mr. and Mrs. Lemon[4]
Mr. and Mrs. Bradbury
Mr. and Mrs. Evans
   Mrs. Hicks[5]
   Miss Chambers[6]

---

[1] Jerrold was not among the speakers, and evidently did not attend as he is not named in *To* Chapman, 3 June.

[2] Thus in MS.

[3] Gilbert Abbott à Beckett (1811–56; *DNB*), journalist, humorous writer and playwright: see Vol. I, p. 208*n*.

[4] Mark Lemon (1809–70; *DNB*), playwright and editor of *Punch*, and his wife Nelly, *née* Romer: see Vol. III, p. 469*n*.

[5] See Vol. I, p. 215*n*.

[6] Unidentified.

My own private little party, for a good place, not at the chief table, are:

Mr. Austin & Mrs. Austin[1]

Mrs. John Dickens[2]

And (I believe) Augustus and a third lady.

Mr. Thompson, of whom I spoke to you, as having an eye on Miss Weller, is coming. So I must trust to your miraculous arrangement-power (in which I have great faith) to insinuate him into that region of the horseshoe.

I find that Mr. Forster *is* coming; and I have given him the toast "The Medical Profession, but especially" &c.—thinking it would be well to have a new speaker in that place, as I shall just have been proposing The Ladies.

Always Believe me | My Dear Sir

Faithfully Yours

Thomas Chapman Esq.
CHARLES DICKENS
(Over)

I have forgotten to mention that Doctor Hitchman[3] came to me today, saying that Mr. Laing had sent for two Ladies tickets for the Gallery (!);[4] and what should he do? I advised him to reply that there was no such thing, but he could have ladies tickets for the dinner, with all the pleasure in life. Could you send to the Tavern in the morning, to tell them to lock up the Gallery, and on no account to let a single person in?

To T. J. THOMPSON, 3 JUNE 1844*

MS Morgan Library.

Osnaburgh Encampment | Third June 1844

My Dear Thompson

Will you bring your Bruffam tomorrow. Otherwise we shall be short of conveyance.

Faithfully Ever

The Cheer

[1] Letitia Mary (1816–93), CD's younger sister: see Vol. I, p. 34*n*.

[2] Elizabeth Dickens (1789–1863): see Vol. I, p. 15*n*. John Dickens was away visiting the Burnetts at Manchester, and then at Douglas, Isle of Man, from which he wrote to Chapman & Hall on 28 June, asking for the final No. of *Chuzzlewit*, "deprived of all extraneous matter" in order to save postage (MS Evergreen House Foundation, Baltimore).

[3] N, I, 605 reads "Hetelman".

[4] See *To* Stanfield, 30 Apr.

To CHARLES KNIGHT, 4 JUNE 1844

Text from MDGH, I, 104.

Devonshire Terrace, June 4th, 1844.

My dear Sir,

Many thanks for your proof, and for your truly gratifying mention of my name. I think the subject excellently chosen, the introduction exactly what it should be, the allusion to the International Copyright question most honourable and manly, and the whole scheme full of the highest interest.[1] I had already seen your prospectus,[2] and if I can be of the feeblest use in advancing a project so intimately connected with an end on which my heart is set—the liberal education of the people—I shall be sincerely glad. All good wishes and success attend you![3]

Believe me always, | Faithfully yours
[CHARLES DICKENS]

To RICHARD MONCKTON MILNES, 4 JUNE 1844*

MS Trinity College, Cambridge.

9 Osnaburgh Terrace | Fourth June 1844

My Dear Milnes

If Friday the Twenty First will do as well—at what hour? I am going away with Fonblanque on the Saturday, a sailing.

Ever Yours
W. Ferrand[4]

Sell this for two and eight,[5] if you can.

---

[1] The "proof" was evidently that of the second of Knight's "Weekly Volumes", *Mind Amongst the Spindles: a Selection from the Lowell Offering*, published Sat 6 July 44. Knight's Introduction, dated 15 June, referred to "the judgment pronounced upon the same book by a writer whose original and brilliant genius is always under the direction of kindly feeling towards his fellow-creatures, and especially towards the poor and lowly of his human brethren", and gave a quotation from *American Notes*. The conclusion of the Introduction referred to International Copyright and the writer's intention, in the absence of legislation, to set a voluntary example by sending part of the profit to the editor of the *Lowell Offering*.

[2] Knight's proposal for a "Library for the People in weekly shilling volumes" was mentioned in the *Athenæum*, 25 May; the series was advertised on 22 June to begin appearing on 29 June. Harriet Martineau

was involved in the scheme, which she described to Crabb Robinson, 6 June, as "a glorious one", telling him that *Mind Amongst the Spindles* would "make a vast sensation", and on 24 Aug she reported to him that the sales were "enormous and still weekly increasing" (MSS Dr Williams's Library).

[3] In *Passages of a Working Life*, 1864–5, II, 311–12, Knight mentions the encouragement he had received from CD, "a distinguished writer with whom I had not then the happiness of that intimate acquaintance which I have subsequently enjoyed".

[4] William Busfeild Ferrand (1809–89), son of Currer Fothergill Busfeild (1777–1832), of Cottingley Bridge, near Keighley; assumed surname of Ferrand 1839; known to the Brontë family; MP for Knaresborough 1841–7. A belligerent and eccentric controversialist in the cause of Factory Reform and against the New Poor Law (he was attacked by the *Chronicle* and

To T. PHILLIPS,[1] 4 JUNE 1844*

MS Private.

9 Osnaburgh Terrace | Fourth June 1844

Dear Sir

I beg to send you a cheque[2] for the amount of your account and to thank you for the great interest and attention with which you transacted my business.

                                                                     Faithfully Yours

T. Phillips Esquire.   CHARLES DICKENS

To H. K. BROWNE,[3] [?JUNE 1844]

MS Huntington Library. *Date:* early June, to leave Browne enough time; CD was still writing 13 June, but could have foreseen all he describes.

FRONTISPIECE

I have a notion of finishing the book, with an apostrophe to Tom Pinch, playing the organ. I shall break off the last Chapter suddenly, and find Tom at his organ, a few years afterwards.[4] And instead of saying what became of the people, as usual, I shall suppose it to be all expressed in the sounds; making the last swell of the Instrument a kind of expression of Tom's heart. Tom has remained a single man, and lives with his sister and John Westlock who are married—Martin and Mary are married—Tom is a godfather of course—Old Martin is dead, and has left him some money—Tom has had an organ fitted in his chamber, and often sits alone, playing it; when of course the old times rise up before him. So the Frontispiece is Tom at his organ with a pensive face; and any little indications of his history rising out of it, and floating about it, that you please; Tom as interesting and amiable as possible.[5]

VIGNETTE FOR TITLE PAGE.

The finger post at the end of the lane, which has been so often mentioned. You can either have Tom Pinch waiting with John Westlock and his boxes, as

by *Punch*), he became an adherent of "Young England" in 1844, and was well known to Milnes. During Apr he charged Sir James Graham in the House of Commons with accepting false evidence from Mott, an Assistant Poor Law Commissioner, and followed this up on 30 May with a pamphlet: "*The Great Mott Question;*" *or, The Mystery Unravelled, in a letter from W. B. Ferrand, Esq., to the Right Hon. Sir James Graham, Bart., M.P.* CD's reference is evidently to this letter.

[5] Unexplained.

[1] A member of the firm of estate agents who found CD his tenant.

[2] For £13.17.0 (Account-book, MS Messrs Coutts).

[3] Hablot Knight Browne, "Phiz" (1815–82; *DNB*): see Vol. I, p. 163n.

[4] The narrative proper breaks off on p. 623 of the final No. of *Chuzzlewit*—"Miss Pecksniff had fainted away in earnest",—and a short rule divides this from the apostrophe to Tom at his organ, pp. 623–4.

[5] Browne is at his best in the fanciful frontispiece.

at the opening of the book; or Mr. Pecksniff blandly receiving a new pupil from the coach (perhaps this will be better);[1] and by no means forgetting the premium in his welcome of the Young Gentleman.

Will you let me see the Designs for these two? (Over)

1st. Subject.[2]

The Room in the Temple. Mrs. Lupin, with Mary in her charge, stands a little way behind old Martin's chair. Young Martin is on the other side. Tom Pinch and his sister are there too. Mr. Pecksniff hastens in to rescue his venerable friend from this horde of plunderers and deceivers. The old man in a transport of burning indignation, rises from his chair, and uplifting his stick, knocks the good Pecksniff down; before John Westlock and Mark who gently interpose (though they are very much delighted) can possibly prevent him. Mr. Pecksniff on the ground. The old man full of fire, energy and resolution.

Lettering.

Warm Reception of Mr. Pecksniff by his Venerable friend.

2nd. SUBJECT.[3]

Represents Miss Charity Pecksniff on the bridal morning. The bridal breakfast is set out in Todgers's drawing-room. Miss Pecksniff has invited the strong-minded woman, and all that party who were present in Mr. Pecksniff's parlor, in the second number, to behold her triumph. She is not proud, but forgiving. Jinkins is also present and wears a white favor in his button hole. Merry is *not* there. Mrs. Todgers is decorated for the occasion. So are the rest of the company. The bride wears a bonnet with an orange flower. They have waited a long time for Moddle. Moddle has not appeared. The strong-minded woman has expressed a hope that nothing has happened to him; the daughters of the strong-minded woman (who are bridesmaids) have offered consolation of an aggravating nature. A knock is heard at the door. It is not Moddle but a letter from him. The bride opens it, reads it, shrieks, and swoons. Some of the company catch it up crowd about each other, and read it over one another's shoulders. Moddle writes that he can't help it—that he loves another—that he is wretched for life—and has that morning sailed from Gravesend for Van Diemen's Land.

Lettering. *The Nuptials of Miss Pecksniff receive a temporary check.*

---

[1] This second alternative was chosen.

[2] In Ch. 52 the text is fuller and suggests that Pecksniff was knocked flat and "stunned" ("he did not offer to get up again; but lay there"), but Browne's interpretation of the instructions shows him in a half-sitting position. At the bottom of the page Browne added notes on the positions of the chief characters.

[3] The instructions are very close to the description in the text (p. 622, two pages from end of No.), except that no knock is heard at the door, and that Miss Pecksniff merely "glanced at" the letter. The plate follows the instructions closely.

To JOHN KENYON,[1] 5 JUNE 1844*

MS Mrs Sheila Sokolov-Grant.

9 Osnaburgh Terrace | Fifth June 1844

My Dear Kenyon.

I am rather late this morning, or I would have answered your friendly note sooner.

First, let me thank you for your kind and liberal donation to the Sanatorium. When they send you, as they will, a little report,[2] do give it a perusal one morning at breakfast. It will shew you what an excellent Institution it is, and how well it merits your voluntary support.

On Saturday next, we dine with the Milner Gibsons. And I verily believe that we have at least one engagement for every day between this and the first of July, when we leave England. In this list I don't include the slight engagement of having to finish Chuzzlewit, which I shall be very glad to dispose of, notwithstanding.

We shall come and shake hands with you before we go; and we shall meet you one night, I hope, at Mrs. Macreadys. Let us take a vow to be better neighbours[3] in time to come. As the boys say, "I will, if you will".

Mrs. Dickens sends her best regards. And I am always

Faithfully Yours

John Kenyon Esquire.   CHARLES DICKENS

To MR HOWELL,[4] [?7 JUNE 1844]

Mention in report of meeting of Charterhouse Square Infirmary, 8 June (*Morning Herald*, 10 June 44).

Regretting his inability to attend the meeting of the Charterhouse Square Infirmary on 8 June to decide on a testimonial for Frederick Salmon.[5]

To DUDLEY COSTELLO,[6] 7 JUNE 1844

Text from MDGH, I, 104.

June 7th, 1844.

Dear Sir,

Mrs. Harris, being in that delicate state (just confined, and "made comfortable," in fact), hears some sounds below, which she fancies may be the owls (or

---

[1] John Kenyon (1784–1856; *DNB*), poet and philanthropist: see Vol. I, p. 554*n*.

[2] CD's speech at the dinner on 4 June referred to "this little record which has been laid before you to-day", giving particulars of cases assisted. No copy appears to have survived.

[3] Kenyon's London house was 39 Devonshire Place, a few minutes' walk from Devonshire Terrace.

[4] Secretary of the Charterhouse Square Infirmary.

[5] Frederick Salmon (1796–1868), the surgeon who operated on CD in 1841: see Vol. II, p. 404*n*.

[6] Dudley Costello (1803–65; *DNB*), author and journalist: see Vol. I, p. 442*n*. He had married Mary Frances, widow of J. D. Tweedy, 23 Sep 43.

howls) of the husband to whom she is devoted. They ease her mind by informing her that these sounds are only organs. By "they" I mean the gossips and attendants. By "organs" I mean instrumental boxes with barrels in them, which are commonly played by foreigners under the windows of people of sedentary pursuits, on a speculation of being bribed to leave the street. Mrs. Harris, being of a confiding nature, believed in this pious fraud, and was fully satisfied "that his owls was organs."[1]

Faithfully yours
[CHARLES DICKENS]

To THOMAS BEARD, 10 JUNE 1844

MS Dickens House. *Address:* Thomas Beard Esquire | Morning Herald Office | Shoe Lane | Fleet Street.

9 Osnaburgh Terrace. | Tenth June 1844

My Dear Beard. Many many thanks for your interest and recollection. The Sanatorium was exceedingly well done in the Herald[2]—to the great delight of its Committee—and I have no doubt the Institution will derive great benefit from that account.

Miss Weller plays tomorrow, at the Hanover Square Rooms, at one Maras's Morning Concert.[3] And she plays on Thursday, at the same place, at a Concert of her own—evening.

Will you book yourself to come and dine with us on the last Sunday in the month, at half after five? It will be the day before our departure. Kate begs her love to your sister,[4] and desires me to say how happy she will be, if she will join you.

---

[1] *Chuzzlewit*, Ch. 49, in the June No.

[2] *Speeches*, ed. K. J. Fielding, pp. 68–72, follows the report in the *Morning Herald*. CD described vividly both imaginary and actual cases of those who had been helped, and those who might benefit from the Sanatorium, contrasting its ministrations with those of the usual sick-nurse (with obvious reference to Mrs Gamp). He proposed both the toast of the evening, "Prosperity to the Sanatorium", and "the Ladies"—no longer banished to the gallery. Other speakers included Stanfield for Art, Ainsworth for Literature, Harley for the Theatre, and Travers for Medical Science.

[3] Hogarth's report in the *Morning Chronicle*, 12 June, said "the lightness, rapidity, and brilliance of her fingers are wonderful"; she was "exceedingly handsome, elegant, and lady-like" and would become "one of the greatest stars of our concerts". The *Examiner*, 15 June, called her appearance a "considerable sensation" and praised her playing of Liszt and Thalberg; this notice was probably by Ayrton, to whom Forster wrote on 10 June apprising him of the concert next day (Anderson Galleries catalogue, Mar 1916). She also played Weber's *Grand Concert-stück* with the orchestra. Almost all the press notices were equally favourable; the audience (attracted chiefly by the tenor, Maras) was "numerous and fashionable" and included the Duchess of Cambridge.

[4] See Vol. I, p. 47*n*.

Come about an hour before dinner. We will then go over to the stable at Devonshire Terrace, to see the wonderful Carriage. The price whereof shall on that tremendous occasion be made known.

Ever My Dear Beard | Heartily Yours

Thomas Beard Esquire   CHARLES DICKENS

To JOHN FOWLER, 10 JUNE 1844*

MS Free Library of Philadelphia. *Address:* John Fowler Esquire | 50 Occupation Road | Sheffield.

London Tenth June 1844

Sir.

It would afford me pleasure to comply with your request, if it were one of rare occurrence. But I am so frequently asked to do the same thing for others, and have so strong an objection to obtruding my individual opinion through the medium of the public announcement,[1] that I must beg to decline in this case, as in all others.

Faithfully Yours

John Fowler Esquire   CHARLES DICKENS

To LADY HOLLAND, 10 JUNE 1844†

MS The Earl of Ilchester.

9 Osnaburgh Terrace, New Road | Monday Tenth June 1844

Dear Lady Holland

I write from a new address, as we have happily been able to let our own house for the whole term of our absence abroad. We leave England on the First of July.[2]

I assure you that it appears a very long time to me, since I had the pleasure of seeing you. And although it has not been my fault (for I have been almost incessantly occupied, at your hours, for months past, in present and prospective engagements of all kinds) it has bred such misgivings in me, that I was on the very point of writing to you to say that if you hadn't rated me in your blackest of books, I would come and see you this week. Your kind note relieves me very much, and does not render me the less desirous of executing this intention.

*a*But not on Wednesday,[3] I grieve to say; for I am finishing Chuzzlewit; and

---

[1] Probably of one of the exhibitions or entertainments put on in aid of the Building Fund.

[2] They left on 2 July.

aa Quoted in Lord Ilchester, *Chronicles of Holland House*, 1937, pp. 243–4.

[3] Lady Holland's dinner-party on that day included the Bishop of St David's (Thirlwall), Sir Benjamin Brodie, and Charles Barry (Dinner Book, MS BM).

am this day upon the very last touches (I have not room, or story, for many more) of Tom and his sister. I do not expect to finish the book until Friday; and in the meantime I am obliged to walk about the fields and streets every evening, and to avoid all dinners; otherwise I should not be steadily enough set upon the dismissal of two of the greatest favorites[1] I have ever had. I think halfpast twelve at noon is a good time to see you? And unless I hear from you to the contrary, I will come at that time on *Saturday* next.

I am delighted to find that Chuzzlewit has risen so highly in your estimation— and I hope you perceive, now, why the undertakers[2] appeared; and how the selfishness of the book is the setting for these little sparklers; and how their influence is intended to refine and improve the rest. It is the great misery of such a form of publication that conclusions are necessarily arrived at, in reference to the design of the story, before the design becomes apparent or complete.

I mean to send over, please God, from Italy, a small successor to the little Carol, to appear next Christmas. I wish you may like it as well. That book has been a most extraordinary success; and still sells, quite rapidly. It has been reprinted eight times.[a 3]

Fonblanque called the other day—I have no doubt as the bearer of your kind message—but I was not at home. The children are all well and blooming; and Mrs. Dickens begs me to present her grateful regards.

Believe me always, Dear Lady Holland
Yours faithfully and obliged
CHARLES DICKENS

The Lady Holland

To DR SOUTHWOOD SMITH, [?11 JUNE 1844]*

MS Mr W. A. Foyle. *Date:* the Tuesday after the publication of CD's speech in the *Herald*, 5 June. *Address:* Dr. Southwood Smith | 38 Finsbury Square. PM 1844 (day and month illegible).

Osnaburgh Terrace | Tuesday Morning

My Dear Dr. Smith

Here is the Speech.[4] Word for word, and letter by letter.

I wish I could be the Patron of your scheme in better essentials than in name. Use that, as you will.

Faithfully Always
CD[5]

---

[1] Tom and Ruth Pinch, who are also clearly the "little sparklers" of the next paragraph.

[2] Mr and Mrs Mould.

[3] No eighth edn appears to be advertised. The *Carol* reached its sixth edn in Mar 44 and its tenth by 14 Dec.

[4] Clearly the report of the Sanatorium speech in the *Herald*, 5 June.

[5] At the top of the scrap of paper on which the letter is written CD had cancelled the heading "Preface | relative to the Author" (for Overs's *Evenings of a Working Man*): see *To* Forster, 28 June.

To H. G. ROGERS,[1] 11 JUNE 1844

MS Boston Public Library.

Devonshire Terrace. | Eleventh June 1844

Sir

I am exceedingly sorry to say that I am prevented from attending the dinner of the United Law Clerks' Society today,[2] and personally expressing (as it would have afforded me great gratification to do) my interest in the welfare of so excellent an Establishment.[3]

I beg to enclose you a small subscription towards its funds.[4] And am Sir

Your faithful Servant

Harry G. Rogers Esquire   CHARLES DICKENS

To MRS GORE, [11] JUNE 1844*

MS Robert H. Taylor Collection, Princeton. *Date:* Tuesday was 11 June.

9 Osnaburgh Terrace New Road
Tuesday Evening Tenth June 1844

Dear Mrs. Gore.

The Marble Halls[5] having fallen into the temporary possession of an ancient Princess (sent by a kind Fairy to take them for the term of my intended absence abroad) I am to be found in a temporary encampment as above. The which is proclaimed to all comers through the medium of a tin plate something larger than the largest sized teatray, boldly affixed to the right hand side of the Marble Porch of my vacated Castle.

I would gladly—cheerfully—heartily—help you with a Prologue,[6] if I could. But it will require my utmost exertions to finish Chuzzlewit this week; and on Monday I am going down, in pursuance of an old engagement, to see Walter Landor at Bath,[7] whence I shall only return in time for the dinner at which you

---

[1] Harry G. Rogers, a clerk in the Law Courts; Secretary of the United Law Clerks' Society 1842–82.

[2] *The Times* announcement of the Dinner, 22 May, named CD as one of the Honorary Stewards.

[3] Founded 1832; Rogers was its second Secretary. CD was a good friend to the Society and subscribed for some years; he attended the Annual Festival on 19 June 49 (*United Law Clerks' Society Centenary Souvenir, 1832–1932,* 1932; *Speeches,* ed. K. J. Fielding, pp. 97–8).

[4] Not in CD's account-book (MS Messrs Coutts).

[5] From the song "I dream'd that I dwelt in marble halls", in Act II, scene iii of *The Bohemian Girl* (Drury Lane, Nov 43) by Alfred Bunn; sung by Miss Rainforth.

[6] For *Quid Pro Quo; or, The Day of the Dupes,* the comedy awarded the prize in Webster's competition: see Vol. III, p. 509n. The award was announced on 18 May 44, and Mrs Gore's authorship was soon known. The play was put on at the Haymarket 18 June but was not a success: according to G. H. Lewes, "its very badness . . . recommended it to the committee . . . as the most resembling the stage-ideal of a comedy" (*Westminster Review,* XLII [1844], 116). The Prologue (no author given) was spoken by Webster.

[7] This farewell visit is not otherwise mentioned by Landor or CD.

will *not* be present.[1] If it ever were, at any time, an utter impossibility with me to do such a thing, it is now.

But believe that the last line of the Song you quote, is, at least, as true as the first; and that "I love you, still the same".[2] The same being very truly and admiringly, always,

My Dear Mrs. Gore | Faithfully Yours

Mrs. Gore   **CHARLES DICKENS**

P.S. I'll warrant you safe. And I write to you before going to bed, that I may not delay the answer.

To [CAPTAIN DI VILLA], 11 JUNE 1844

Extract in Anderson Galleries catalogue No. 1179 (1915); *MS* 3 pp.; dated Tuesday night, eleventh June, 1844. *Address:* name of recipient removed, but clearly Captain Di Villa: see *To* Di Villa, 15 June.

I am exceedingly sorry to say that I cannot comply with your request, in the matter of the novel and Mr [Newby].[3] You may recollect my telling you that I had the strongest objection to communicating, even with my own Publishers, on

---

[1] The farewell dinner to CD, held at the Trafalgar Tavern, Greenwich, 19 June; invitations had been sent out in May, Stanfield writing to Babbage 29 May (MS BM), and Forster sending the invitation to Milnes 29 May (MS Trinity College, Cambridge) and to Jerdan (W. Jerdan, *Autobiography*, 1853, IV, 367). Carlyle, Tennyson and Lytton were invited but declined: Tennyson was taking the water-cure at Cheltenham, and Lytton at Malvern; the latter wrote to Forster that an interruption at that stage would be dangerous "when accompanied with the excitement necessary to so convivial a meeting", and sent a message of "sincere regret at not being able to join the friends and admirers he has so worthily rallied round him ... May he find Italy as I did—a literal Bath to the mind" (MS Lytton Papers). Carlyle's letter to Forster of 6 June said: "I truly love Dickens; and discern in the inner man of him a tone of real Music, which struggles to express itself as it may, in these bewildered stupified, and indeed very empty and distracted days,—better or worse! This, which makes him in my estimation one of a thousand, I could with great joy and freedom testify to all persons, to himself first of all, in any good way. But by dinner,—at Greenwich,—in the dog-days,—under Lord Mahogany,—by leg-of-mutton eloquence: alas, my soul dies away at the idea, exclaims, *Quae nunc abibis in loco!* [*from Hadrian's epitaph*] I pray you have me excused" (MS Forster Collection; facsimile in Kitton, *CD by Pen and Pencil*, Supplement, opp. p. 32). Lord Normanby presided, and the guests (over 40 in number) included Lord Morpeth, Lord Mulgrave, Monckton Milnes, R. H. Barham, Alexander Dyce, Rev. W. H. Harness, Charles Young, Harley, Maclise, Stanfield, Turner, Edwin and Charles Landseer, Frank Stone, Cruikshank, Browne, Robert Liston, Dr Quin, Ainsworth, Robert Bell, Fonblanque, Jerdan, Jerrold, Procter, Thackeray, and Forster—who remembered sitting next to Turner, "who ... had enveloped his throat, that sultry summer day, in a huge red belcher-handkerchief which nothing would induce him to remove" (F, IV, iii, 328). The *Literary Gazette* (22 June), the source of all other reports, mentions "many speeches", but gives no details.

[2] The last lines are: "But I also dream'd, which charm'd me most, | That you lov'd me still the same".

[3] Catalogue reads "Newt".

such a subject. But I have an objection to communicating with anyone else. Even if I had read the book, or had time to read it in Manuscript, my feelings on this point would be equally strong and decided,

To MISS CHRISTIANA WELLER, 14 JUNE 1844

MS Mrs Sowerby.

Friday Morning | Fourteenth June 1844.

My Dear Miss Weller

Let me congratulate you with my whole heart, on your brilliant achievements last night.[1] You rose with the occasion, nobly. Nothing could have been more successful, graceful, charming—triumphant, in every particular.

I felt a pride in you which I cannot express. I do not write to you, therefore, with the view of expressing it, or giving language to my great delight; but merely to say that I can't do either.

Always Believe me | Faithfully Your friend

Miss Christiana Weller.   CHARLES DICKENS

P.S. Anna[2] was *great*. I adored her. I refused all comfort afterwards, because I hadn't sent her a bouquet. But writing all day put it out of my head. It *was* there, several times. Tell her it was Mr. Chuzzlewit's omission. Not mine.

To CAPTAIN DI VILLA,[3] 15 JUNE 1844

MS Mr Alan Moore. *Address:* Captain Di Villa | 1 Old Cavendish Street.

Osnaburgh Terrace | Fifteenth June 1844

My Dear Sir

I tried very hard to come to you today; but every previous engagement (I had three) turned out at least half an hour longer than I had expected, and I did not get home again: thoroughly tired: until four o'Clock.

I thank you for the privilege of reading the enclosed. The writer seems to have become my friend. I know her, perfectly well.

Do not suppose that I attach the least idea of impropriety to your request in the matter of Mr. Newby; or that I ever confounded the fair authoress of the Misjudged[4] with it; or that I ever supposed you intended it to be a public

---

[1] At the "Soirée Musicale" in the Hanover Square Rooms, advertised as her first selection of pianoforte recitals. *The Times*, 14 June, praised her "brilliancy of execution" and said her "mastery over the difficulties of the more modern composers, as exhibited for example in Thalberg's 'Dal tuo stellato toglio', elicited loud applause".

[2] Anna DeLancey Weller, *b.* 1830: see Vol. III, p. 446*n*. She and Christiana had first appeared professionally together at concerts in Wales in July 43. At the Soirée,

she was introduced for the "final surprise" to play Thalberg's grand duet for two pianofortes from *Norma*; "a pretty little girl, with a profusion of black hair", nervous, but "there was much reason for the applause that followed" (*Morning Herald*, 14 June, reproduced in *Musical World*, 20 June).

[3] Unidentified. The address to which the letter was sent was a branch post-office.

[4] Not traced; presumably never published.

recommendation; or that I ever had the least reference to the merits or demerits of the book, in declining to give it. My objection is, to addressing myself to any Publisher on such a subject. I have found my own negociations with that class of gentlemen quite sufficient to keep me in genially warm water, from my toes to the crown of my head.

Captain Di Villa.

Faithfully Yours
CHARLES DICKENS

To MISS ELIZABETH HORNE,[1] 15 JUNE 1844

MS Berg Collection. *Address:* Miss Elizabeth Horne | 124 Edgeware Road.

Fifteenth June 1844.

Dear Madam.

I believe you wrote to me for an autograph. Here it is. I do not know whether you are married, or single; but you will see that in the superscription of this note, I have given Mankind the benefit of the doubt.

Pray do not suppose that I attribute the least impropriety of motive to you, in addressing me anonymously. But I object to correspond in the slightest degree, with any one, on such terms.[2]

Miss Elizabeth Horne.

Faithfully Yours
CHARLES DICKENS

To DANIEL MACLISE, 17 JUNE 1844*

MS Mrs A. M. Stern.

Osnaburgh Terrace | Monday Seventeenth June 1844

My Dear Mac

I don't know whether you are aware (for I don't know when you went away last night, or what previous communication you had with Forster) that we meet here, to day, at half past one.[3] If you feel dispoged for a morsel of warm lunch at one exactly, you will find it on the table.

Daniel Maclise Esquire

Faithfully Ever
CD

---

[1] Although unknown to CD, she was evidently a member of the congregation at Little Portland St, since she had a copy of Tagart's Address on the presentation to him of plate (see *To* Tagart, 7 Aug 44), and noted that the inscription "was written at the time by one of the Congregation | The Illustrious Honored Charles Dickens Beloved by us all" (Catalogue of the G. B.

McCutcheon sale). She must have been one of the family of "Thomas Horne, Grocer" shown in the Post Office Directory at 124 Edgware Rd.

[2] Cf. *To* Mr Lucy, 13 June 43: Vol. III, p. 511 and *n*.

[3] Probably before going to Bath: see *To* Mrs Gore, 11 June.

To ROBERT KEELEY,[1] 24 JUNE 1844

MS J. W. Garrett Library, Johns Hopkins University.

9 Osnaburgh Terrace.
Monday Evening | Twenty Fourth June 1844.

My Dear Sir.

I have been out Yachting[2] for two or three days; and consequently could not answer your letter in due course.

I cannot, consistently with the opinion I hold, and have always held, in reference to the *principle* of adapting novels for the Stage, give you a Prologue to Chuzzlewit.[3] But believe me to be quite sincere in saying that if I felt I could reasonably do such a thing for anyone, I would do it for *you*.

I start for Italy on Monday next; but if you have the piece on the Stage, and rehearse on Friday, I will gladly come down at any time you may appoint, on that morning: and go through it with you all. If you be not in a sufficiently forward state to render this proposal convenient to you, or likely to assist your preparations, do not take the trouble to answer this note.

I presume Mrs. Keeley[4] will do Ruth Pinch. If so, I feel secure about her. And of Mrs. Gamp I am certain. But a queer sensation begins in my legs, and comes upward to my forehead, when I think of Tom.[5]

Faithfully Yours always

Robert Keeley Esquire   CHARLES DICKENS

[1] Robert Keeley (1793–1869; *DNB*), comic actor: see Vol. III, p. 247*n*. The Keeleys were managers of the Lyceum 1844–7.

[2] With Fonblanque: see *To* Milnes, 4 June.

[3] The dramatic version by Edward Stirling, played at the Lyceum on 8 July. When Stirling first approached the Keeleys, they were doubtful: "Mary and I have read carefully Dickens' work; we cannot see our way to a piece from it. But if you like to go on, do. You have done so much with Dickens' works, try again" (Robert Keeley *to* Stirling, quoted in the latter's *Old Drury Lane*, 1881, I, 180). The Prologue, written by Albert Smith, and spoken by Keeley, emphasized "the powerful romance of common life" (Albert Smith, *Wild Oats and Dead Leaves*, 1860, pp. 246–7).

[4] Mary Ann Keeley, *née* Goward (1805–99; *DNB*): see Vol. I, p. 459*n*.

[5] Ruth Pinch was played by Miss Groves and Tom by Drinkwater Meadows, of whom the *Pictorial Times* said: "no fitter actor could have been found . . . his acting was positively Shakespearian", although *The Times*, 9 July, thought Tom's "delicate organization, one of the most beautiful characters created by Mr. Dickens" impossible to represent on the stage without his "lapsing into insignificance". Miss Fortescue played Mary Graham, Frank Matthews Pecksniff; Mrs Keeley played Bailey and Keeley Mrs Gamp—they were the great attractions. *The Times* called it "a triumphant success" though much of the novel was unrepresented; Stirling claimed that it ran for 280 performances: there were in fact less than 90 at the Lyceum. Rival dramatic versions were those of Charles Webb at the Strand and the Victoria on 15 July, Thomas Higgie and T. H. Lacy's at the Queen's 29 July, and anonymous versions at the Garrick and the Pavilion 13 Aug (Malcolm Morley, "*Martin Chuzzlewit* in the Theatre", *D*, XLVII [1951], 98–102). In Oct 44, at Fryston, during the Disraelis' visit to Monckton Milnes, there were amateur theatricals with characters from *Chuzzlewit*; Milnes acted Mrs Gamp (T. Wemyss Reid, *Life, Letters and Friendships of Richard Monckton Milnes*, I, 336), and the following note in CD's hand (MS Mr Archie Nathan) may have been given or sent to him: "(Mrs. Gamp) | A rusty black

To G. CARR GLYN,[1] 25 JUNE 1844

Extract and summary in Chicago Book & Art Auction catalogue No. 2; summary in John Anderson catalogue No. 2298; mention in Sotheby's catalogue, Mar 1904; *MS* 1 p.; dated London, 25 June 44. *Address:* "G. Carr Glyn" in Sotheby's is clearly correct (see *fn*); John Anderson catalogue gives as "Seymour Glyn".

I am going abroad on Monday next. *If a proxy vote is possible he will leave one for the lady in whom the recipient is interested.*[2]

To THOMAS BEARD, 28 JUNE 1844

MS Dickens House. *Date:* PM 28 June 44. *Address:* Thomas Beard Esquire | 42 Portman Place | Edgeware Road. On the flap of the envelope above the seal is written: "It is particularly requested that if Sir James Graham should open this, he will not trouble himself to seal it [agai]n."[3]

Osnaburgh Terrace | Friday

My Dear Beard

You will see from the enclosed, that Sunday's dinner[4] is transferred to Forster's.

---

gown, the worse for snuff. A black bonnet and shawl, to correspond. She is a fat old monthly nurse with a husky voice and a short neck."

[1] George Carr Glyn (1797–1873), banker and railway director, to whom CD had written about Alfred in 1843: see Vol. III, p. 573*n*.

[2] Probably a candidate for assistance from the Governesses' Benevolent Institution.

[3] The same superscription was on *To* Forster, 28 June (F, IV, iii, 327). CD was among those who demonstrated in this way their indignation at the revelation in the House of Commons, 14 June, that Mazzini's letters had been opened on Graham's authority and sent to the Foreign Office. Mazzini, after ascertaining with the help of W. J. Linton that his correspondence was being opened, had put the matter in the hands of Thomas Duncombe, MP, who raised it in the House on 14 and 24 June and 2 July. His motions for an enquiry were defeated, but on 2 July Graham himself demanded a full enquiry by a secret committee, whose findings (published 2 Aug) were that Graham had rarely exercised his prerogative and that on this occasion he and Aberdeen, the Foreign Secretary, had not exceeded their legal rights (the Report was denounced as whitewashing by Panizzi in the *North British Review*, Nov 44; II, 257–95).

Graham wanted the enquiry because public feeling, stimulated by the press (especially the *Chronicle* and *Punch*) was running high, and it was believed—wrongly—that information obtained in this way and passed on to the Austrian Govt had resulted in the deaths of two Italian revolutionaries. An editorial comment in *The Times*, 17 June, "[Mazzini] may be the most worthless and most vicious creature in the world. But this is no reason of itself why his letters should be detained and opened", stirred Carlyle to write a letter defending Mazzini's integrity, published in *The Times* of 19 June. To Mazzini the letter-opening scandal gave publicity for himself and the cause of Young Italy which he made the most of during the next twelve months (for example, by his unsigned article, "Mazzini and the Ethics of Politicians", in the *Westminster Review*, Sep 44); to Graham it brought all the odium that should have been borne by the Govt as a whole: even after fuller explanations in 1845 had completely satisfied the House of Commons, he knew that he would "go down to posterity as the man who made the Post Office open Mazzini's letters". The best accounts of the episode are in Arvel B. Erickson, *The Public Career of Sir James Graham*, Oxford, 1952, pp. 268–73, and Harry W. Rudman, *Italian Nationalism and English Letters*, 1940, pp. 58–67.

[4] See *To* Beard, 10 June.

To which, I hope, you will not object. Will you come here, at about half past 4, that we may leisurely inspect the Magnificent Carriage?

Faithfully Ever

Thomas Beard Esquire   CHARLES DICKENS

To MESSRS CHAPMAN & HALL, 28 JUNE 1844*

MS Morgan Library.

9 Osnaburgh Terrace | Friday Twenty Eighth June | 1844

Dear Sirs.

Please to deliver to Messrs. Bradbury and Evans on my behalf; at any time when they may produce this letter as their authority; the stock on hand and plates of Oliver Twist, or The Christmas Carol, or both, as they may require.

Faithfully Yours

Messrs. Chapman and Hall.   CHARLES DICKENS[1]

To MESSRS D'ALMAINE,[2] 28 JUNE 1844

Mention in John Anderson Jr. catalogue No. 455; *MS* (3rd person) 1 p.; dated 28 Jun 44.

Granting some request.

To FREDERICK DICKENS, 28 JUNE 1844

MS John Rylands Library.

Osnaburgh Terrace. | Twenty Eighth June 1844

My Dear Frederick.

Forster tells me he has asked you to dine with him on Sunday; so I presume we shall meet there.

I wish you would get me a bottle of dye for my unprecedented Moustache at the Baron's[3] in Regent Street, or some such good place. We shall be passing the Treasury about 3 or 4 today, on our way from calling at Tracey's.[4] I will send up to you on the chance of your having received this.

We do not go until Tuesday Morning, as there is no boat on Monday.

Affecy. always

CD.

[1] Endorsed in pencil: "delivered June 25 1845", which suggests that nothing was done until *Oliver Twist* in monthly parts (1846) was being prepared.

[2] Music publishers of 20 Soho Square; publishers of the songs from *The Village Coquettes*, and of "The Ivy Green". Their only known publication relating to CD about this time is "The Christmas Carol Quadrilles", composed by Edwin Marriott and dedicated to CD (W. Miller, *The Dickens Student and Collector*, 1946).

[3] None of the several hairdressers in Regent St called himself a Baron; perhaps "Antoine Ferrer, artiste en cheveux" or "Louis Rossi".

[4] Lieut. Augustus Frederick Tracey, RN (1798–1878), Governor of the Westminster House of Correction, Tothill Fields: see Vol. II, p. 270*n*.

To JOHN FORSTER, [28 JUNE 1844]

Extract in F, IV, iii, 327. *Date:* 28 June according to Forster.

I wish you would read this,[1] and give it me again when we meet at Stanfield's to-day. Newby has written to me to say that he hopes to be able to give Overs more money than was agreed on.

To T. C. NEWBY, 29 JUNE 1844*

MS Mrs A. M. Stern.

Osnaburgh Terrace | Twenty Ninth June 1844.

Mr. Charles Dickens sends his compliments to Mr. Newby, and begs to forward him the proofs of Mr. Overs' book:[2] corrected. Mr. Dickens will be glad if Mr. Newby will send a complete revise of the whole book, title page, dedication,[3] and introduction[4] to Mr. Overs, for his attentive perusal. Mr. Overs will certainly not detain them beyond one day.[5]

Mr. Dickens will feel still further obliged to Mr. Newby, if, on the publication of the book, he will pay the five and twenty pounds agreed upon, to his account with Messrs. Coutts & Co., bankers. He begs to enclose Mr. Overs' receipt for the amount.[6]

Mr. Dickens would prefer to leave all arrangements connected with presentation copies of the work, to Mr. Newby's business discretion. He cannot terminate this correspondence, however, without expressing his very high sense of Mr. Newby's honorable and manly note, in reference to the possibility of his extending some further remuneration to Mr. Overs.

[1] The proof-sheet of his Preface to Overs's book: see *To* Newby, 29 June. The set of final page-proofs which CD gave to Forster is in the Dexter Collection, British Museum.

[2] *Evenings of a Working Man, being the occupation of his scanty leisure.* With a Preface Relative to the Author, by Charles Dickens. Its contents were several prose sketches and some verses.

[3] "This Little Book | is affectionately dedicated | to | Doctor Elliotson, | by one | who has felt his kindness | to those | who have no other claim upon him | (and on such a man can have no higher claim) | than | sickness and obscure condition".

[4] CD's Preface (pp. v–xiii; see *Miscellaneous Papers*, ed. B. W. Matz, pp. 13–17), is dated "*London, June, 1844*". It described his first correspondence with Overs in 1839 (see Vol. I, p. 622*n*); how he had helped him with counsel and by reading his compositions, but "never altered them, otherwise than by recommending con-

densation now and then"; for the present volume he had supplied only "the ordinary corrections of the press; desiring them to be his genuine work, as they have been his sober and rational amusement". He had found him always "a simple, frugal, steady, upright, honourable man" who had "risen superior to the mere prejudices of [his] class . . . without losing his sympathy for all their real wrongs and grievances"; and since he was now very ill with an affection of the lungs, he was publishing this collection in order to make "some temporary provision for his sick wife and very young family". CD concluded by recommending the cause he had at heart, "the Universal Education of the people".

[5] Newby had first advertised the volume on 1 June; it was ready for publication 6 July, and on 27 July he announced a 2nd edn.

[6] CD's account-book (MS Messrs Coutts) shows the payment of £25 to Overs on 4 July.

To LADY HOLLAND, 30 JUNE 1844*

MS The Earl of Ilchester.

Osnaburgh Terrace
Sunday Morning Thirtieth June | 1844.

My Dear Lady Holland

Let me thank you, earnestly, for the letters which you have, with so much kindness, remembered to procure for me.

I have an engagement, I am sorry to say, to a parting dinner with some very old friends today[1]—and on Tuesday Morning I leave England.[2] But I will call to say Good B'ye, before you go out tomorrow.

I was in the country yesterday; and coming home very late last night; and going out early this morning to breakfast with Rogers; could not answer your kind note until now, when I blush to hear it striking Two.

Always Dear Lady Holland
Yours faithfully and obliged

The Lady Holland   CHARLES DICKENS

To LUIGI MARIOTTI,[3] 1 JULY 1844*

MS Morgan Library.

Osnaburgh Terrace. | First July 1844

Dear Sir

I beg to send you on the other side, a cheque for the amount in which I am indebted to you;[4] and I feel greatly obliged, I assure you, by the interest you have taken in your two pupils.

They desire to be remembered to you, very kindly. And I am

Always | My Dear Sir | Faithfully Yours

M. Mariotti   CHARLES DICKENS

---

[1] The dinner at Forster's: see *To* Beard and *To* Frederick Dickens, 28 June. Forster (IV, iii, 328) and others following him seem to confuse this with the official farewell dinner at Greenwich, 19 June (see *To* Mrs Gore, 11 June). Lady Holland's dinner-party included Lord and Lady Palmerston, Lord Melbourne, and Macaulay (Dinner Book, MS BM).

[2] They would travel by the Dover road, through Rochester and Canterbury, spending the night at Dover and boarding the steam-packet in the early morning, as described by CD in "Travelling Abroad". Their departure, presumably from Osnaburgh Terrace, was witnessed by the

London correspondent of the *Revue Britannique* (Aug 44, pp. 241–2), who thought it a fine thing that nowadays a novelist could afford to play "le grand seigneur" in Italy; however, he added, "although his popularity is no longer on the decline, Charles Dickens has as yet made only sixty thousand francs from *Martin Chuzzlewit*". CD, he wrote, was "taking thirteen people away with him, fourteen counting himself. He needed two enormous carriages to accommodate his party"; but one carriage was in fact the phaeton, which was sent back from Dover (see *To* Fred Dickens, 22 July 44). In France, the single vast "travelling chariot" carried the whole

To JOHN FORSTER, [?14–15 JULY 1844]

Extract in F, IV, iv, 329. *Date:* They arrived in Marseilles 14 July, according to Forster, and left by sea the following afternoon (*Pictures from Italy*, 1846, p. 35). *From* Marseilles.

Describing the journey, he says that not being able to get vetturino horses in Paris, they had come on, post—paying for nine horses but bringing only four, and thereby saving a shilling a mile out of what the four would have cost in England. But what with distance, caravan, sight-seeing, and everything, *two hundred pounds would be nearly swallowed up before they were at their destination.*[1]
The children had not cried in their worst troubles, the carriage had gone lightly over abominable roads, and the courier had proved himself a perfect gem.

Surrounded by strange and perfectly novel circumstances, I feel as if I had a new head on side by side with my old one.[2]

---

party, "inside and out", as is clear from *Pictures from Italy*, 1846, pp. 6, 12–13. The total was 12 (including the baby), not 14; probably Forster and perhaps Fred went with them from London to Dover or some intermediate point in Kent and returned by rail.

[3] The name assumed in 1833 by Antonio Carlo Napoleone Gallenga (1810–95; *DNB*), author and Italian refugee: see Vol. III, p. 472*n*.

[4] CD's account-book (MS Messrs Coutts) shows a payment of £7.10.0 to Mariotti on 10 July; no earlier payment appears, though he is mentioned as "my Italian master" in *To* Forster, 1 Nov 43 (Vol. III, p. 588). Italian exiles teaching their language were paid only about six shillings an hour, so this represents a good many hours of tuition. Notes from Catherine to Mariotti cancelling single lessons (?3 Apr 44, MS Free Library of Philadelphia, and ?26 May 44, MS Historical Society of Pennsylvania), show that in early April and late May they were normally having two lessons a week; but CD can have made little progress, as in Aug he was finding the language "difficult": see *To* Mitton, 12 Aug.

[1] The journey from Dover to Marseilles took twelve days, including two days in Paris where they stayed at the Hotel Meurice: see *To* D'Orsay, 7 Aug 44, and *Pictures*, pp. 5–6 (page references to 1st edn). According to Murray's *Handbook for ... France*, 1843 (which CD had with him), travellers usually broke the journey

from Boulogne to Paris at Abbeville and Beauvais. Forster describes two incidents of the crossing and arrival at Boulogne which CD told him "afterwards", almost certainly by word of mouth: a conversation with the captain of the steamer, who had been suspected of having stolen specie, and the incident in a Boulogne bank where he addressed the clerk at length in French, to be answered, "How would you like to take it, sir?" (F, IV, iv, 329–30). After Paris the route is clear from *Pictures*: by road to Chalons, staying at Sens and Avallon, and then by steamboat down the Rhone to Lyons (the carriage going by barge) and on by road again to Aix and Marseilles. At Marseilles they were "pretty well accommodated" at the Hotel du Paradis: CD evidently explored the streets, the "common madhouse", and the harbour; the "novel circumstances" are described in *Pictures*, pp. 34–5.

[2] This first letter about his travels must have been a long one. Forster says he received from week to week "the first sprightly runnings" of every description in his *Pictures from Italy*, but must observe his rule as to the American letters "yet more strictly; and nothing resembling his printed book, however distantly, can be admitted into these pages" (F, IV, iv, 333; and see Vol. III, pp. vii–viii). He adds that as CD did not, "until the very last", decide to publish his experiences (but see *To* Forster, 7 Mar 44), many letters were "left unrifled".

To JOHN FORSTER, [?20 JULY 1844]

Extracts in F, IV, iv, 330, and F, 1872–4, II, v, 91n. *Date:* second extract 20 July according to Forster; first extract clearly a few days after arrival at Albaro on 16 July, therefore same letter. CD soon established a pattern of weekly letters to Forster,[1] normally writing at weekends.

The villa at once impressed him with its likeness to a pink jail. It is the most perfectly lonely, rusty, stagnant old staggerer of a domain that you can possibly imagine.[2] What would I give if you could only look round the courtyard! *I* look down into it, whenever I am near that side of the house, for the stable is so full of "vermin and swarmers"[3] (pardon the quotation from my inimitable friend) that I always expect to see the carriage going out bodily, with legions of industrious fleas[4] harnessed to and drawing it off, on their own account.[5] We have a couple

---

[1] Forster uses such phrases as "from week to week", "after seven days", "after a week's interval", "he continued to write to me every week"; most of the dates he gives confirm this, and by 14 Sep Landor knew that "Dickens has written eight letters to Forster" (Landor *to* Rose Paynter, *Letters of W. S. Landor, Private and Public,* ed. S. Wheeler, 1899, p. 136). Letters to London took seven days.

[2] The Villa Bagnerello still stands, within its high walls and courtyard, in the Via San Nazaro in Albaro, and is now called the Villa Barabino; in 1950 it was owned by Signor Petracchi, whose wife inherited it from her grandfather who bought it from Bagnerello the butcher. A plaque was put up over the door in 1894, reading: "In questa villa | dal primo prisco rosso delle sue mura | Pink Jail | ebbe gradita dimora | Carlo Dickens | geniale e profondo rivelatore | del sentimento moderno | 1844 1894" (*D*, X [1914], 246, and XLVI [1950], 84–9). The villa is called a "pink jail" and described in detail in *Pictures,* pp. 37–42.

[3] *Martin Chuzzlewit,* Ch. 52.

[4] Exhibitions of "The Industrious Fleas" were frequently held (e.g. at the Somerset Gallery, Strand, in Apr 44). CD's "Full Report of the First Meeting of the Mudfog Association for the Advancement of Everything", included a paper entitled "Some Remarks on the industrious fleas . . .", in which the supposed author described the "various pursuits and avocations" of the fleas exhibited and recommended measures to employ their labour "as part and parcel of the productive power of the country" and also to provide for the support of "superannuated and dis-abled fleas" (*Bentley's Miscellany,* Oct 1837, II, 404–5).

[5] Verbally close to *Pictures,* p. 42: "I daily expect to see the carriage going off bodily, drawn by myriads of industrious fleas in harness". Henry Burnett reported to F. G. Kitton CD's description of the fleas—perhaps recollecting some oral account after his return (he says that CD "could . . . talk playfully of a great inconvenience"), but evidently also paraphrasing or perhaps quoting a letter or letters, presumably to Fanny. CD, he says, found "tenants" already in the house, but made the best of it, encouraging his family to treat as an amusement "catching a legion or two daily"; but the fleas still made "feasts of blood". "Whenever I sat down and stretched my legs out after a walk, my white trowsers, in ten minutes, had almost changed colour up to my knees—a sort of brown-red, with little specks of white showing between. As for Kate, she employed her maid half-an-hour every night in slaughtering whole families. But our poor little silky long-haired dog was the greatest martyr. At first he could not understand what it all meant, and got up as if quite offended; then a time came when he would rise quickly, take a jump or two, growl angrily, and return to his sleeping-place. After that he became, in a few days, resigned, and, when lying, would remain fairly still, with only twitches, groans, or the breath of a smothered sigh. At last, when there had assembled so many families, and the feast was very jovial, he became so angry, that in making a start towards the door it seemed as if the two hind legs and the tail of the dog were

of Italian work-people in our establishment; and to hear one or other of them talking away to our servants with the utmost violence and volubility in Genoese, and our servants answering with great fluency in English (very loud: as if the others were only deaf, not Italian), is one of the most ridiculous things possible. The effect is greatly enhanced by the Genoese manner, which is exceedingly animated and pantomimic; so that two friends of the lower class conversing pleasantly in the street, always seem on the eve of stabbing each other forthwith. And a stranger is immensely astonished at their not doing it.

We have had a London sky until to-day, grey and cloudy as you please:[1] but I am most disappointed, I think, in the evenings, which are as commonplace as need be; for there is no twilight, and as to the stars giving more light here than elsewhere, that is humbug.

To THOMAS MITTON, [?22 JULY 1844]

Mention in next. *Date:* probably same day as next.

To FREDERICK DICKENS, 22 JULY 1844

MS Berg Collection. *Address:* Frederick Dickens Esqre. | Commissariat | Treasury | London.

Villa di Bagnerello. Albaro. Monday Twenty Second July 1844.
My Dear Fred.

I have written a rather long letter to Mitton, with a few wandering Notes of this place, which I have begged him to put you in possession of, forthwith. And as I dare say you will have heard from Forster besides, I will confine myself at this moment, to what immediately concerns you—namely, the notion you had of coming here, in your holidays. I am assured that the journey, straight through, can be very well done in something less than a week, for £15 each way. If you should decide to come, I will very gladly stand £10 of this Thirty. And I can answer for your seeing all manner of novelties, and being very much entertained in this New World. I *believe* (but I will enquire further into this, if you decide to come) that you would cross the Alps, and not steam it. In that case; or indeed in any, most probably; I would come on to some point to meet you. Such french phrases as you would want, I could give you in a letter; but you can book yourself to Paris, in London; and very nearly to this place, in Paris. And one word "combien"—how much?—would carry you further than you are ever likely to go, in Foreign Parts.

lifted off the ground by the muscular power of these thirsty vampires. I immediately had him shaved from the tip of his nose to the end of his tail" (F. G. Kitton, *CD by Pen and Pencil*, II, 8).

[1] In *Pictures*, p. 51, CD says he first saw the Strada Nuova under "the brightest and most intensely blue of summer skies", but that this brightness was not common; "even in July and August ... there were not eight blue skies in as many midsummer weeks, saving, sometimes early in the morning ... At other times, there were clouds and haze enough to make an Englishman grumble in his own climate".

Let me know what you really intend in this respect, and [I][1] can make all that part of it, easy enough, if you decide to come.

We are all very well, Thank God; and living in the queerest [sort][2] of place that ever was anywhere. We expect a Piano up from Genoa to day. I trea[ted][3] the Pigs[4] with a carriage yesterday, wherein they went to that City, with Roche, Cook, and the Nurses; and seeing a very magnificent religious Procession in the streets, came back with a decided leaning towards the Roman Catholic faith. The Genoese Ladies wear Veils[5] instead of bonnets; and we had no rest here, until the Dolls were similarly attired.

Fletcher is living with us, and desires to be heartily remembered. He says "Boots" are cheap here; and you can't do better than come and buy 'em. But I don't know what you would do on the pavements; which are very trying. It is like walking on marbles, with here and there a peg-top—all red hot, and smoking.

Kate, Georgy, and the darlings, send their loves. Give mine to everybody who comes in your way, who is worth receiving it. Address still to the Poste Restante, Genoa, as that is the shortest mode. If Mitton gives you the MS of the last 2 Nos. of Chuzzlewit, will you give it to Forster.

Always My Dear Fred | Your affectionate Brother

Frederick Dickens Esquire   CHARLES DICKENS

P.S. Will you see Topping one evening, and ascertain that the Phaeton has come home, safely?

To DANIEL MACLISE,[6] 22 JULY 1844

MS New Brunswick University Library. *Address:* Inghilterra. | Daniel Maclise Esqre. R.A. | 14 Russell Place | Fitzroy Square | London.

Villa di Bagnerello, Albaro. Monday Twenty Second July 1844.

My very dear Mac.

I address you[7] with something of the lofty spirit of an exile—a banished

---

[1] A piece torn away has removed letters at the ends of three lines. What looks like the hook of an "I" remains here.

[2] Four letters missing, the first probably "s".

[3] Three letters missing.

[4] The same pet name, used here for the children, appears in letters to Catherine in 1835: see Vol. I, pp. 110, 112.

[5] The "mezzero"; cf. *Pictures*, p. 44, where CD notices the "grace and elegance" displayed in "the management of their veils".

[6] Forster describes this as "his second letter from Albaro", implying that it was addressed to himself, but contained "an outbreak of whimsical enthusiasm ... especially for Maclise, ... followed by some capital description" (see Vol. I, p. xv). He then quotes (with minor omissions and additions, noted below) the first four paragraphs, with dots between them, and the fifth paragraph down to "retreat"; he adds, incorrectly of course, "That letter sketched for me the story of his travel through France" (F, IV, iv, 331–2). MDGH, I, 105–10 gives the whole letter (with a few errors and one omission) addressed to Maclise.

[7] Forster has "I address you, my friend".

commoner—a sort of Anglo Pole.[1] I don't exactly know what I have done for my country in coming away from it, but I feel it is something, something great—something virtuous and heroic. Lofty emotions rise within me, when I see the sun set on the blue Mediterranean. I am the limpet on the rock. My father's name is Turner, and my boots are green.[2]

Apropos of blue. In a certain picture, called the Serenade,[3] you[4] painted a sky. If you ever have occasion to paint the Mediterranean, let it be of exactly that colour. It lies before me now, as deeply and intensely blue. But no such color is above me. Nothing like it. In the South of France; at Avignon, at Aix, at Marseilles; I saw deep blue skies (not *so* deep though—oh Lord no!);[5] and also in America; but the sky above me is familiar to my sight. Is it heresy to say that I have seen its twin brother shining through the window of Jack Straw's—that down in Devonshire I have seen a better sky? I dare say it is; but like a great many other heresies, it is true.

But such green—green—green—as flutters in the vineyard down below the windows, *that* I never saw; nor yet such lilac and such purple as float between me, and the distant hills; nor yet—in anything—picture, book, or verbal[6] boredom[7]—such awful, solemn, impenetrable blue, as in that same Sea. It has such an absorbing, silent, deep, profound effect; that I can't help thinking it suggested the idea of Styx. It looks as if a draught of it—only so much as you could scoop up, on the beach, in the hollow of your hand—would wash out everything else, and make a great blue blank of your intellect.

When the Sun sets clearly, then, by Heaven, it is Majestic! From any one of eleven windows here; or from a terrace, overgrown with grapes; you may behold

---

[1] i.e. a typical refugee; the Poles were the best known group of exiles in London, partly owing to Lord Dudley Coutts Stuart's activities on their behalf over the past 12 years: see *To* Coutts Stuart, 16 Apr 44 and *fn.* English sympathy was first aroused by the visit to London in 1831 of Prince Adam Czartoryski, the leader of the army, exiled to Paris after the Warsaw rising.

[2] Forster added a brief note of explanation in "Corrections in the Second Volume", 1872–4, III, 519, but misdated Turner's picture. *War: The Exile and the Rock Limpet* (now in the Tate Gallery), exhibited RA 1842, showed Napoleon meditating beside a rock-pool, presumably over the futility of war, with a quotation from Turner's poem *The Fallacies of Hope*: "Ah! thy tent-formed shell is like | A soldier's mighty bivouac, alone | Amidst a sea of blood— | But *you* can join your comrades". It had been the object of much ridicule by contemporary critics, and recently in *Punch* ("The Duke of Wellington and the Shrimp", 11 May 44).

[3] Forster adds "for which Browning wrote that verse in Lincoln's-inn-fields".

According to Browning, Forster pressed him into writing it impromptu, on the basis of his description of the picture; but when Browning later saw it, he said, "I thought the Serenader too jolly somewhat for the notion I got from Forster" (*Letters*, ed. T. L. Hood, pp. 7, 196; letters of 30 Dec 41, 15 Sep 81). The picture was a Venetian scene, exhibited at the British Institution for promoting the Fine Arts in Mar 42, with Browning's verse quoted in the catalogue (Forster gives it in a footnote). The *Art-Union Journal*, Apr 42, praised the verse more highly than the picture. Browning made it the first stanza of "In a Gondola", published in "Dramatic Lyrics" (*Bells and Pomegranates*, No. III, 1842).

[4] Forster adds "O Mac".

[5] Forster omits this parenthesis.

[6] Forster reads "vestal".

[7] Continuous talk; cf. Maclise *to* Forster, ?23 Sep 44: "we ... received splendid impressions of the French character in every variety there but I shall reserve all these things for your own private boredom" (MS V & A).

the broad sea; villas, houses, mountains, forts; strewn with rose leaves—strewn with them? Steeped in them! Dyed, through and through and through. For a moment. No more. The Sun is impatient and fierce; like anything else in these parts; and goes down headlong. Run to fetch your hat—and it's night. Wink at the right time of black night—and it's morning. Everything is in extremes. There is an insect here (I forget its name; and Fletcher and Roche are both out)[1] that chirps all day. There is one outside the window now. The chirp is very loud: something like a Brobdignagian Grasshopper. The creature is born to chirp—to progress in chirping—to chirp louder, louder, louder—till it gives one tremendous chirp, and bursts itself. That is its life and death. Everything "is in a concatenation accordingly". The day gets brighter, brighter, brighter, 'till its night. The summer gets hotter, hotter, hotter, 'till it bursts.[2] The fruit gets riper, riper, riper, 'till it tumbles down and rots.

Ask me a question or two about fresco,[3] will you be so good? All the houses are painted in fresco, hereabout—the outside walls I mean; the fronts, and backs, and sides—and all the colour has run into damp and green seediness, and the very design has straggled away, into the component atoms of the plaster.[4] Sometimes (but not often) I can make out a Virgin with a mildewed Glory round her head; holding nothing, in **an** undiscernible lap, with invisible arms; and occasionally the leg, or arm, or what Marryat would call the arthe[5] of a cherub. But it is very melancholy and dim. There are two old fresco-painted Vases outside my own gate—one on either hand—which are so faint, that I never saw them 'till last night; and only then, because I was looking over the wall after a Lizard, who had come upon me while I was smoking a cigar above; and crawled over one of these embellishments in his retreat. There is a Church here—the Church of the Annunciation—which they are now (by "they", I mean certain noble families) restoring at a vast expence, as a work of piety. It is a large Church, with a great many little chapels in it; and a very high dome. Every Inch of this edifice is painted; and every Design is set in a great gold frame or border, elaborately wrought.[6] You can imagine nothing so splendid. It is worth coming the whole distance to see. But all sorts of splendour is in perpetual enactment through the means of these churches. Gorgeous processions in the streets, illuminations of windows on Festa nights; lightings up of Lamps, and clusterings of flowers before the shrines of Saints; all manner of show and display. The doors of the churches stand wide open; and in this hot weather great red curtains flutter and wave in their places; and if you go and sit in one of them, to get out of the Sun, you see the queerest figures kneeling against pillars, and the strangest

---

[1] Forster omits this parenthesis. The insect was clearly the cicada.

[2] Forster reads "explodes".

[3] CD would have seen Maclise's most recent fresco, "The Knight", then being exhibited at Westminster Hall for the proposed decoration of the new House of Lords (the private view was on Saturday, 29 June). *The Times*, 1 July, praised it for its triumph over the difficulties of fresco painting and the gorgeous contrasts of colour. His "Scene from Comus", exhibited RA 1844, was based on his fresco for the Garden Pavilion at Buckingham Palace: see Vol. III, p. 519*n*.

[4] Forster adds: "Beware of fresco!"

[5] Marryat evidently lisped. These seven words omitted by Forster and MDGH.

[6] Described in *Pictures*, p. 64, as "in slow progress of repair ... elaborately painted and set in gold".

people passing in and out, and such streams of women in veils (they don't wear bonnets) with great fans in their hands coming and going, that you are never tired of looking on. Except in the churches, you would suppose the City (at this time of year) to be deserted; the people keep so close within doors. Indeed it is next to impossible to go out into the heat. I have only been into Genoa twice, myself. We are deliciously cool here, by comparison; being high, and having the sea breeze. There is always some shade in the Vineyard too; and underneath the rocks on the sea shore. So if I choose to saunter, I can do it easily: even in the hot time of the day. I am as lazy, however, as—as you are; and do little but eat, and drink, and read.

As I am going to transmit regular accounts of all sight-seeings and journeyings to Forster, who will shew them to you, I will not bore you with Descriptions, however. I hardly think you allow enough, for the great brightness and brilliancy of colour which is commonly achieved on the continent, in that same fresco painting. I saw some—by a French artist and his pupil—in progress at the Cathedral at Avignon[1] which was as bright and airy as anything can be; nothing dull or dead about it. And I have observed quite fierce and glaring colours, elsewhere.

We have a Piano now (there was none in the house) and have fallen into a pretty settled, easy, track. We breakfast about half past nine or ten—dine about four—and go to bed about eleven. We are much courted by the visiting people of course; and I very much resort to my old habit of bolting from callers, and leaving their reception to Kate.[2] Green figs I have already learnt to like. Green almonds (we have them at dessert every day) are the most delicious fruit in the world. And green lemons, combined with some rare Hollands that is to be got here, make prodigious Punch, I assure you.

You ought to come over, Mac;[3] but I don't expect you, though I am sure it would be a very great move for you. I have not the smallest doubt of that. Fletcher has made a sketch of the house,[4] and will copy it in pen and ink, for transmission to you in my next letter. I shall look out for a place in Genoa between this and the winter time. In the meantime, the people who come out here, breathe delightedly, as if they had got into another climate. Landing in the City, you would hardly suppose it possible that there could be such an air within Two Miles.

---

[1] Mentioned in *Pictures*, p. 22.

[2] Forster says, "The attentions received from English residents were unremitting", and refers to their help "in moments of need at the outset", but adds that CD used hardly any of his numerous letters of introduction (F, IV, iv, 335; and see *To* Miss Coutts, 18 Mar 45).

[3] Macready had already suggested this, or assumed its probability: "I fancy that in Dickens's projected tour in Italy I see the shadow of a great man, with a palette in his hand, at Milan and Venice, Florence, Genoa, Naples, and Rome" (Macready *to*

Maclise, 14 May 44; W. Justin O'Driscoll, *A Memoir of Daniel Maclise*, R.A., 1871, p. 84), and CD enlisted D'Orsay's support: see *To* D'Orsay, 7 Aug 44. Maclise did not visit Italy until 1855 (when he "found out the Peschiere, and an old man who knew Dickens"); but in Sep 44 he was in Paris for just over three weeks, "hunting after dim old frescoes" and having "a perfect surfeit of Art"—his first visit to the continent since 1830 (Maclise *to* Forster, 29 July 55 and ?23 Sep 44; O'Driscoll, pp. 118, 88).

[4] See *To* Forster, ?3 Aug 44.

Write to me as often as you can, like a dear good fellow; and rely upon the punctuality of my correspondence. Losing you and Forster is like losing my arms and legs; and dull and lame I am without you. But at Broadstairs next year, please God, when it is all over, I shall be very glad to have laid up such a store of recollections and improvement.

I don't know what to do with Timber. He is as ill adapted to the climate at this time of year, as a suit of Fur. I have had him made a Lion Dog; but the fleas flock in such crowds into the hair he has left, that they drive him nearly frantic, and render it absolutely necessary that he should be kept by himself. Of all the miserable, hideous little frights you ever saw, you never beheld such a Devil. Apropos, as we were crossing the Seine, within two stages of Paris, Roche suddenly said to me: sitting beside me on the box: "the littel dog ave got a great lip!" I was thinking of things remote and very different, and couldn't comprehend why any peculiarity in this feature on the part of the dog, should excite a man so much. As I was musing upon it, my ears were attracted by shouts of "Helo! Hola! Hi hi hi! Le Voila! Regardez!" and the like. And looking down among the oxen—we were in the centre of a numerous drove—I saw him, Timber, lying in the road, curled up—you know his way—like a lobster, only not so stiff; yelping dismally in the pain of his "lip" from the roof of the carriage; and between the aching of his bones, his horror of the oxen, and his dread of me (whom he evidently took to be the immediate agent in, and cause of the damage) singing out to an extent which I believe to be perfectly unprecedented: while every French Man and French Boy within sight, roared for company. He wasn't hurt, but I think the fall must have affected his bowels which were very open, all through the journey.

Kate and Georgina send their best loves; and the children add theirs. Katey in particular desires to be commended to "Mr. Teese". She has a sore throat; from sitting in constant draughts I suppose; but with that exception, we are all quite well. Ever believe me, my dear Mac

Your Affectionate friend
CHARLES DICKENS

Daniel Maclise Esquire

To JOHN FORSTER, [?27 JULY 1844]

Extracts in F, IV, iv, 335, 336, 330. *Date:* These extracts, undated by Forster, suggest early but not initial impressions: Forster introduces the second extract with "I soon heard of", and follows the third by saying there had been "a whole week" of the sirocco "soon after his arrival". He says "the second letter" also "sketched the story of his travel through France", but attaches this comment to *To* Maclise, 22 July.

Sharp as the tradespeople at Albaro were after money, their idleness quenched even that propensity. Order for immediate delivery two or three pounds of tea, and the tea-dealer would be wretched. "Won't it do to-morrow?" "I want it now," *you would reply; and he would say,* "No, no, there can be no hurry!" *But everywhere there was deference, courtesy, more than civility.* In a café a little tumbler of ice costs something less than threepence, and if you give the waiter in addition what you would not offer to an English beggar, say, the third of a halfpenny, he is profoundly grateful.

Describing the Strada Nuova and Strada Balbi—the former narrower than Albany-street, the latter less wide than Drury-lane or Wych-street; but both filled with palaces of noble architecture and of such vast dimensions that as many windows as there are days in the year might be counted in one of them, and this not covering by any means the largest plot of ground. Other streets had no footways, and all varying in degrees of narrowness, but for the most part like Field-lane in Holborn, with little breathing-places like St. Martin's-court; and the widest only in parts wide enough to enable a carriage and pair to turn. Imagine yourself looking down a street of Reform Clubs[1] cramped after this odd fashion, the lofty roofs almost seeming to meet in the perspective. *He was struck by the profusion of trash and tinsel[2] in the churches; but that of the Capucin friars blazed every inch of it with gold, precious stones, and paintings of priceless art; the principal contrast to its radiance being the dirt of its masters, whose bare legs, corded waists, and coarse brown serge never changed by night or day, proclaimed amid their corporate wealth their personal vows of poverty. He preferred the country people of their suburb on festa-days, with the Indulgences that gave them the right to make merry stuck in their hats like turn-pike tickets. He did not think the peasant girls in general good-looking, though they carried themselves daintily and walked remarkably well: but the ugliness of the old women, begotten of hard work and a burning sun, with porters' knots of coarse grey hair grubbed up over wrinkled and cadaverous faces, he thought quite stupendous. He was never in a street a hundred yards long without getting up perfectly the witch part of* Macbeth.

The heat tried him less than he expected, excepting always the sirocco,[3] which, near the sea as they were and right in the course of the wind as it blew against the house, made everything hotter than if there had been no wind. One feels it most, on first getting up. Then, it is really so oppressive that a strong determination is necessary to enable one to go on dressing; one's tendency being to tumble down anywhere and lie there. *It seemed to hit him behind the knee, and made his legs so shake that he could not walk or stand.*

To SIR JAMES MURRAY,[4] 28 JULY 1844

Text from Horace G. Commins Catalogue No. 132 (1948).

Albaro, | Sunday Morning July Twenty-eighth, 1844

Dear Sir James,

Little Kate appears to be pretty well in health this morning: but the swelling

---

[1] The building, designed by Barry in the style of an Italian Renaissance palazzo, was completed in 1841.

[2] Cf. *Pictures*, p. 64.

[3] In *Pictures*, p. 43, CD says it often blew for days together "like a gigantic oven out for a holiday".

[4] Sir James Murray, MD (1785–1871; *DNB*), discoverer of fluid magnesia; had a distinguished official career as well as an extensive private practice in Dublin; resident physician to successive Lords Lieutenant of Ireland (in 1835–9, Lord Normanby), and knighted for his services

in her neck hardly seems to have subsided or softened, so far as I can judge. It will be a great satisfaction to Mrs. Dickens if you can kindly make it convenient to see our pet to-day—and certainly to myself also.

With best regards, Believe me,
Faithfully Yours,
CHARLES DICKENS.

Sir James Murray

To JOHN FORSTER, [3 AUGUST 1844]

Extracts in F, IV, iv, 331; F, 1872-4, II, v, 91*n* (*aa*), 95*n*; F, IV, iv, 333-4. *Date:* first extract 3 Aug according to Forster, and *aa* probably same letter; others, part of "that August letter".

He opened his letter by saying that there was a thick November fog, that rain was pouring incessantly, and that he did not remember to have seen in his life, at that time of year, such cloudy weather as he had seen beneath Italian skies. The story goes that it is in autumn and winter, when other countries are dark and foggy, that the beauty and clearness of this are most observable. I hope it may prove so; for I have postponed going round the hills which encircle the city, or seeing any of the sights, until the weather is more favourable. *a*My faith on that point is decidedly shaken, which reminds me to ask you whether you ever read Simond's Tour in Italy.[1] It is a most charming book, and eminently remarkable for its excellent sense, and determination not to give in to conventional lies.*a* I have never yet seen it so clear, for any long time of the day together, as on a bright, lark-singing, coast-of-France-discerning day at Broadstairs; nor have I ever seen so fine a sunset, *throughout*, as is very common there. But the scenery is exquisite, and at certain periods of the evening and the morning the blue of the Mediterranean surpasses all conception or description. It is the most intense and wonderful colour, I do believe, in all nature.

He described his first call from the French consul-general.[2] Their house is next to ours on the right, with vineyards between; but the place is so oddly contrived

in 1833. A Catholic, of liberal sympathies, admired for his generosity, vigour and tact. Father of John Fisher Murray (contributor to *Blackwood's* and author of *The World of London*, 1843). Sir James's most recent publication, on cholera, 1844, was translated into Italian—but he had no other known connection with Italy and was probably on holiday in Genoa.

[1] The *Tour in Italy and Sicily*, 1828, was in the Gad's Hill library at CD's death. Louis Simond (1767-1831) left France early in the Revolution for America and there married a sister of Charles Wilkes, whose daughter—introduced by Simond in Edinburgh in 1810—became Jeffrey's second wife. His anonymous *Journal of a Residence and Tour in Great Britain*

1810-11 was published in London 1815. The *Tour in Italy*, the journal of a year's travel in 1817-18, includes all the places visited by CD, with racy observations on men and manners as well as art and architecture. CD refers to it in *Pictures* as a "charming book" when adapting the comparison of the elaborately gilded Church of the Annunciation to a snuff-box (p. 64) and cites the "happy simile" of the Tower at Pisa and pictures of the tower of Babel (p. 153—with the misprint SISMONDI in edns up to 1867). Simond's unconventional judgments on Italian paintings especially appealed to him: see *To* Forster, 9 Mar 45.

[2] Pierre-Edouard Alletz (1798-1850), writer on literature and politics; French

that one has to go a full mile round to get to their door. *He made the visit his excuse for breaking off from a facetious description of French inns to introduce a sketch[1] from a pencil outline by Fletcher, of what bore the imposing name of the Villa di Bella Vista, but which he called by the homelier one of its proprietor, Bagnerello.* This, my friend, is quite accurate. Allow me to explain it. You are standing, sir, in our vineyard, among the grapes and figs. The Mediterranean is at your back as you look at the house: of which two sides, out of four, are here depicted. The lower story (nearly concealed by the vines) consists of the hall, a wine-cellar, and some storerooms. The three windows on the left of the first floor belong to

the sala, lofty and whitewashed, which has two more windows round the corner. The fourth window *did* belong to the dining-room, but I have changed one of the nurseries for better air; and it now appertains to that branch of the establishment. The fifth and sixth, or two right-hand windows, sir, admit the light to the Inimitable's (and uxor's) chamber; to which the first window round the right-hand corner, which you perceive in shadow, also belongs. The next window in shadow, young sir, is the bower of Miss H. The next, a nursery window; the same having two more round the corner again. The bowery-looking place stretching out upon the left of the house is the terrace, which opens out from a French window in the drawing-room on the same floor, of which you see nothing: and forms one side of the courtyard. The upper windows belong to some of those uncounted chambers upstairs; the fourth one, longer than the rest, being in F.'s[2] bedroom. There is a kitchen or two up there besides, and my dressing-room;

consul-general at Genoa, 1843–6. CD's "most valued acquaintance at Albaro . . . a student of our literature who had written on his books in one of the French reviews, and who with his English wife lived in the very next villa" (F, IV, iii, 333); no article by Alletz on CD has been traced. CD gave him a copy of *The Chimes* "with the regards of Charles Dickens, Genoa, Sixth June 1845" (Jerome Kern Sale, 1929).

[1] In *To* Maclise, 22 July, CD promised the sketch in his "next letter". This and the joking reference to "Miss H." (Georgina Hogarth) may suggest that Forster is again using a letter to Maclise. For photographs of the villa in 1949, see L. C. Staples, "Pictures from Genoa", *D*, XLV (1950), 84–9.

[2] "Fletcher's" in later edns.

which you can't see from this point of view. The kitchens and other offices in use are down below, under that part of the house where the roof is longest. On your left, beyond the Bay of Genoa, about two miles off, the Alps stretch off into the far horizon; on your right, at three or four miles distance, are mountains crowned with forts. The intervening space on both sides is dotted with villas, some green, some red, some yellow, some blue, some (and ours among the number) pink. At your back, as I have said, sir, is the ocean; with the slim Italian tower of the ruined church of St John the Baptist[1] rising up before it, on the top of a pile of savage rocks. You go through the courtyard, and out at the gate, and down a narrow lane to the sea. Note. The sala goes sheer up to the top of the house; the ceiling being conical, and the little bedrooms built round the spring of its arch. You will observe that we make no pretension to architectural magnificence, but that we have abundance of room. And here I am, beholding only vines and the sea for days together. . . . Good Heavens! How I wish you'd come for a week or two, and taste the white wine at a penny farthing the pint. It is excellent.

To COUNT D'ORSAY, 7 AUGUST 1844*

MS Comte de Gramont. *Address:* Inghilterra. | Le Comte D'Orsay | Kensington Gore. | *near* | London.

Albaro, Near Genoa. Wednesday August Seventh 1844

My Dear Count D'Orsay.

I hope you will not think me tardy in commencing that correspondence— with yourself and Lady Blessington alternately—from which I am o derive so much interest and happiness during my stay in these latitudes. I should have flung my loving glove into Gore House before now; but that the restlessness of a perfectly new life, and the illness of my pet little daughter (the smaller of the two Kensington lunchers)[2] have sadly interfered with my good resolutions. Once off, however, I think I can back myself to keep going. I am a bad starter —nothing more.

We had a charming journey here. I cannot tell you what an immense impression Paris made upon me. It is the most extraordinary place in the World. I was not prepared for, and really could not have believed in, its perfectly distinct and separate character. My eyes ached and my head grew giddy, as novelty, novelty, novelty; nothing but strange and striking things; came swarming before me. I cannot conceive any place so perfectly and wonderfully expressive of its own character; its secret character no less than that which is on its surface; as Paris is. I walked about the streets—in and out, up and down, backwards and forwards —during the two days we were there; and almost every house, and every person

---

[1] The church no longer exists, having been swept away by the sea. It is described in *Pictures*, pp. 42–3, where CD notes how many of the common people were christened Giovanni Baptista, pronouncing the name "Batcheetcha", like a sneeze.

[2] Clearly CD had taken Mamie and Katey to Gore House, perhaps on his farewell visit.

I passed, seemed to be another leaf in the enormous book that stands wide open there. I was perpetually turning over, and never coming any nearer the end. There never was such a place for a description.[1] If I had only a larger sheet of paper (I have ordered some for next time) I am afraid I should plunge, wildly, into such a lengthened account of those two days as would startle you. This is the sole and solitary sheet in the house this morning (except those on the beds)— which looks providential, and seems to be an interposition in your favor.

Let me explain to you where I am. Do you recollect Byron's old house?[2] Yes? Well. It isn't that—as they always say on the stage, when the two comic men are sitting in chairs before the lamps—but keeping on, up the hill past Byron's house, you come to another large house at the corner of a lane, with a little tumble-down blackguard old green-grocer's shop at the other corner, on which is painted, if I recollect right, Croce di San Lorenzo. The Governor lives in the large house opposite the Green Grocer's now; and turning down between the Governor's *and* the Green Grocer's, you go down a long, straggling, very narrow lane until you come to mine: which is on the left hand, with the open Sea before it—a fort close by, on the left—a vineyard sloping down towards the shore—and an old ruined church dedicated to St. John the Baptist (which I dare say Lady Blessington will remember) blotting out just so much of the sea as its walls and tower can hide. It is properly called The Villa di Bella Vista; but *I* call it the Villa di Bagnerello—that being the name of an amiable but drunken butcher[3] into whose hands it has fallen, and who, being universally known (in consequence of being carried home from some wine shop or other every night), is a famous address: which the dullest errandboy recognizes immediately.

There is a delicious air here—almost always a sea breeze—and very good bathing. The house is bare of furniture, but especially clean. The Sala is very large, and the bedrooms excellent. As it would never do for a winter residence, however, I have been looking about me, and have concluded an arrangement, I hope, for the Peschiere: entering on the possession of that Palazzo, on the first of October. I have the whole Palace except the Ground Piano. I don't know whether you ever saw the rooms. They are very splendid indeed; and every inch of the walls is painted in fresco. The Gardens also, are beautiful.[4] The last

[1] A single paragraph in *Pictures* (pp. 6–7) is all that survives elsewhere of CD's first impressions of Paris.

[2] The Villa Saluzzo at Albaro, situated on the hill of the Grand Paradise; Byron occupied the villa from the autumn of 1822 until his departure for Greece in July 1823, and at his suggestion the Blessingtons took the neighbouring Il Paradiso.

[3] D'Orsay remembered him, and wrote in his reply that the narrow roads were "providential for your landlord, who used to be able, in consequence, to hold himself up on the right and on the left" (D'Orsay *to* CD, 17 Aug 44; M. Lecomte, *Prince des Dandys*, p. 227).

[4] The Palace of the Marchese Pallavicini,

within the walls of Genoa; known as the Peschiere from the fishponds which were a feature of its gardens; built by the architect Galeazzo Alessi in about 1560. Guide-books and travel-writers noted its position on the hill of S. Bartolomeo, commanding views over the sea and surrounding mountains, the beauty of the terraced gardens with their grottoes, flowering shrubs and orange and lemon trees, and the remarkable 16th-century frescoes by the Semini brothers which decorated the lofty rooms (see, for example, H. J. Bunnett, *A Description Historical and Topographical of Genoa*, 1844, p. 52, and *Descrizione di Genova e del Genovesato*, Genoa, 1846, III, 330–1).

English resident paid Eight hundred francs a month; but I take the unexpired term of the present occupier (an English Colonel)[1] who has had it for a year and a half, and got it much cheaper in consequence. My rent will be five hundred, which, as rent goes in Genoa, will be very cheap. I had thought of a Piano in the Solicetti[2] on the Acqua Sola; but I am doubtful whether it might not be a thought too breezy in the windy weather; to say nothing of an intolerable bell which is always clashing and clanging hard by; or of the hospital,[3] which is close to the windows.

I have been turning my plans over in my mind; and I think I shall remain quiet until I have done my little Christmas Book—that will be, perhaps, about the middle of October. In November, I think I shall start, with my servant (I have a most admirable and useful fellow—a frenchman) for Verona, Mantua, Milan, Turin, Venice, Florence, Pisa, Leghorn &c. I shall come back here for Christmas, and remain here through January. In February, I think I shall start off again (attended as before) and taking the Steamboat to Civita Vecchia, go to Rome—from Rome to Naples—and from Naples to Mount Ætna, which I very much desire to see. Then I purpose returning to Naples, and coming back here, direct, by Steamer. For Easter Week, I design returning to Rome again; taking Mrs. Dickens and her sister with me, that time; then coming back here, picking up my caravan, starting off to Paris, and remaining there a month or so, before I return to England. What do you think of that?[4]

Now is it not a pity that Maclise don't come here straightway, and see all this along with me? I feel that it would be of immense service to him; and the delight to me would be, of course, unspeakable. I believe that in his heart he thinks so too; but there never lived a man who had such extraordinary difficulty in making up his mind *to anything*, as he has. I have observed indecision in many and divers men; but never in any one to one hundredth part of the extent to which it exists in him. Do pour a broadside into him, dear Count D'Orsay. You have great influence with him. Stir him up with a pole as long as that dress cane you once gave me; and let us see if one of the eighteen spare beds in the Peschiere cannot be tenanted by an R.A.[5]

I am disgusted with the Fine Arts Commission—by the way, the frescoes in the Peschiere were reported to them as among the finest in Italy. I think their

[1] Unidentified; his tenancy probably dated from July 43, when the American consul, C. E. Lester, put down a deposit on this "gorgeous palace"—only to have it returned when the agent found a tenant to pay an extra $25 a year. Lester considered the rent "very high for Italy" at $550, and the palace he took in Strada Balbi cost only $240 (C. E. Lester, *My Consulship*, New York, 1853, I, 98).

[2] CD's error for the Salicetti, in the Acqua Sola. Bunnett (*op. cit.*, p. 36) named it, after "the beautiful Peschiera", as one of several palaces "accustomed to be let for the accommodation of strangers".

[3] Possibly the Royal Institution for Education of the Deaf and Dumb near the Acqua Sola.

[4] D'Orsay approved, and these plans were carried out with modifications, and the omission of Sicily and the month in Paris.

[5] In his reply D'Orsay wrote that he had tried to persuade Maclise; "he very much wishes to, but he has begun his work and wants to finish it"; he enclosed Maclise's letter of the previous day and said he intended attacking him again.

putting Maclise anywhere but at the very head and front of the Competitors, abominable. And I think the terms on which their designs are to be sent in, are disgraceful to the Commissioners as gentlemen—disgraceful to the selected artists, as men of talent—and disgraceful to the country in which the paltry, huckstering piece of power is exercised. If I were one of the exhibitors, I would see the New Houses of Parliament blown up higher than ever the old ones were like to have been, before I would coin the smallest corner of my brain for their service.[1] A word in your ear, my dear Count D'Orsay. Do you think that when they were placing the artists, Rogers had any recollection of—the faintest and dimmest pleasure of memory in—a certain little pen and ink likeness of himself, once published in Frazer's Magazine?[2] God forgive me. But I shrewdly suspect that too smooth head of his, I swear!

What a sad place Italy is! a country gone to sleep, and without a prospect of waking again! I never shall forget, as long as I live, my first impressions of it, as I drove through the streets of Genoa, after contemplating the splendid View of the town, for a full hour, through a telescope, from the deck of the steamboat. I thought that of all the mouldy, dreary, sleepy, dirty, lagging, halting, God-forgotten towns in the wide world, it surely must be the very uttermost super-lative. It seemed as if one had reached the end of all things—as if there were no more progress, motion, advancement, or improvement of any kind beyond; but here the whole scheme had stopped centuries ago, never to move on any more, but just lying down in the sun to bask there, 'till the Day of Judgment.[3]

I have [a gre]at[4] interest in it now; and walk about, or ride about, the [town] when I go there, in a dreamy sort of way, which is very comfortable. I seem [to be] thinking, but I don't know what about—I haven't the least idea. I can sit down in a church, or stand at the end of a narrow Vico, zig-zagging uphill like a dirty snake: and not feel the least desire for any further entertainment. Just in the same way, I lie down on the rocks in the evening, staring the blue water out of countenance; or stroll up the narrow lanes, and watch the lizards running up

---

[1] In their *Third Report*, published 15 July 44, the Fine Arts Commissioners had prescribed subjects for frescoes in six arched compartments in the new House of Lords: to exemplify the functions of the Lords, three were to be allegorical repre-sentations of Religion, Chivalry, and Justice, and three, historical illustrations. Six artists were chosen to submit, for exhibition in 1845, cartoons, coloured sketches, and specimens of fresco (Richard Redgrave, W. C. Thomas, C. W. Cope, J. C. Horsley, William Dyce and Maclise—named in that order); but the Commis-sioners did not bind themselves to employ these artists, and announced that the sub-jects were also open to general competition. In his reply, D'Orsay said that studying the Peschiere frescoes would be more profit-able to Maclise than "making cartoons like a mere student; it is an insult to a man of his talent to be put in competition with such wretched daubers".

[2] Rogers was the subject of No. IV of Maclise's famous series of caricatures, "The Gallery of Illustrious Literary Char-acters", in *Fraser's* (Sep 1830, II, 237), under the pseudonym of "Alfred Croquis".

[3] In *Pictures*, pp. 36–7, CD contrasts the beauty of the city as seen from the sea, with "the disheartening dirt, discomfort, and decay" of the streets; but most of the com-ments in his letter are transferred, in almost the same words, to the description of Piacenza (p. 89). (Ruskin in 1845 noted the "vice . . . idleness . . . filth, and misery, and desecration" in this part of Italy; *Ruskin in Italy, Letters to his Parents 1845*, ed. H. Shapiro, Oxford, 1972, p. 51.)

[4] Damage to the paper has removed a few letters, here and below.

and down the walls (so slight and fast, that they always look like the shadows of something else, passing over the stones)[1] and diving into their holes so suddenly that they leave bits of their tails hanging out, and don't know it. I never knew what it was to be lazy, before.—I should think a dormouse was in very much the same condition before he goes under the wool in his cage—or a tortoise before he buries himself. I feel that I am getting rusty.—I should creak when I tried to think,[2] if it were not for some feeble efforts I am making to acquire the language: each one a tiny drop of oil upon my hinges: and the only oil they ever get.

Were you ever at Lyons? *That's* the place. It's a great Nightmare—a bad conscience—a fit of indigestion—the recollection of having done a murder. An awful place! I made a good mistake there, at which I used to laugh afterwards; before I had lost the strength of mind which laughing requires. There is a curious clock in the cathedral—I dare say you have seen it. At all events, it is covered at the top with little doors, and when the Sacristan gets inside and sets the works a going, the doors fly open, one after another, and little scriptural images bolt out suddenly, and retire again; while some shrill little bells exert themselves to the utmost. One of these doors flying open, disclosed the Virgin Mary—with a very blunt nose, like the hangman in Punch's Show. She hadn't sat there long when another little door, after trying to open itself a great many times (you know the queer, jerking manner of clockwork) flew wide open all at once, and disclosed a little doll with Wings, who dived out with surpassing suddenness, and at sight of the Virgin instantly dived in again, while its little street-door shut up of itself, with a bang. "Aha!" said I. "Yes, Yes—The Devil, of course. We have very soon settled *his* business".—"The Devil!" said the Sacristan, looking out of the clock, pale with horror. "The Angel Gabriel Monsieur! The Annunciation Monsieur!" Which it seemed (to my great confusion) had actually been represented.[3]

My dear Count D'Orsay, I am afraid this is the rustiest of letters, but blame Italy for it. Not me. I shall look to hear from you, or Lady Blessington, most eagerly. My most cordial and sincere regards to her. She cannot think how sorry she made me, by her heartiness and interest at parting—and yet how very glad, at the same time. Remember me, very cordially, to Miss Power and her sister. And believe me with the sincerest regard

Always Faithfully Your friend
CHARLES DICKENS

Le Comte D'Orsay.

What Portraits are you painting? What figures are you modelling?[4] Has that

---

[1] CD is recalling "The lizard, with his shadow on the stone, | Rests like a shadow" in Tennyson's "Oenone", *Poems*, 1842.

[2] This and the three preceding sentences reappear slightly adapted in *Pictures*, p. 89.

[3] CD devotes three long paragraphs to Lyons at the beginning of the second section of *Pictures*, pp. 17–19; he gives the incident of the clock in similar detail, with a less effective climax—" 'Pardon, Monsieur,' said the Sacristan, with a polite motion of his hand towards the little door, as if introducing somebody—'The Angel Gabriel!' " In his reply, D'Orsay said Lyons was the most wretched town he knew, and warned CD that he would see the angel Gabriel put to all sorts of work in Italy.

[4] D'Orsay produced many portrait-drawings and busts in the latter half of 1844, including drawings of Charles Sheridan (17 July) and of Ainsworth (21 Nov), and a bust and a statuette of himself in bronze; his equestrian statue of

libellous artist[1]—I am still strong on that point: feeble as I have become—finished his slander on Miss Power?

P.S. Address to the Poste Restante. The Albaro postman gets drunk—loses letters—and goes down on his knees in sober repentance. Poste Restante, Genoa.

To PIERRE-EDOUARD ALLETZ, 9 AUGUST 1844

Extract in Goodspeeds Book Shop catalogue No. 237; *MS* 2 pp.; dated Albaro, 9 Aug 44.

I shall be most happy in meeting a writer of such distinguished and eminent genius as M. Lamartine[2]—though it is for only a few moments,[3] and under the unfavorable circumstance of my not being able to speak his language with any degree of correctness or fluency. But I hold myself more than repaid in being able to read it well, since that accomplishment is a source of great delight to me and inspires me with an interest in M. Lamartine which nothing but himself, in his own beautiful productions, could have awakened.[4]

To T. C. CURRY,[5] 9 AUGUST 1844†

MS Free Library of Philadelphia. *Address:* Thomas Curry Esquire. Albaro. | Ninth August 1844.

My Dear Sir

As I find none of my unfortunate books in the chest which you so kindly forwarded to me yesterday, I write to enquire whether there is anything for me

Napoleon was exhibited at Howell & James's from the end of June. William Behnes may have assisted him with his sculptures: see Vol. III, p. 612*n*.

[1] Unidentified. She was painted several times by D'Orsay himself, and drawn by Maclise (two of the drawings dated: 22 Dec 44 and 5 Feb 45) and Landseer (*Sale Catalogues of the Libraries of Eminent Persons*, ed. A. N. L. Munby, 1971, II, 359ff.).

[2] Alphonse-Marie-Louis de Prat de Lamartine (1791–1869), poet and politician. His reputation as a poet dated from the phenomenal success of his *Méditations Poétiques*, 1820, to which he added in each of the many new editions; there were several English translations. His liberal outlook in domestic and foreign affairs would have been congenial to CD: among the causes he espoused were non-sectarian education, prison reform (he spoke against solitary confinement in the debates of

1844), the abolition of slavery, and the introduction of a copyright bill in France.

[3] Lamartine was on his way from Marseilles to Naples by sea, accompanied by his English wife (Marianne, *née* Birch, *m.* 1820) and one of his nieces. They disembarked for a few hours in Genoa to visit Marianne's cousin, Harriet Churchill, who was resident there (Laura M. Ragg, *The Lamartine Ladies*, 1954, p. 217; R. Mattlé, *Lamartine Voyageur*, Paris, 1936, pp. 124–5). According to Forster (F, IV, iv, 339), the two men met at Alletz's house; he was known to Lamartine, who accepted the dedication of his *Lettre à M. de Lamartine*, 1835 (Lamartine, *Correspondance Générale de 1830 à 1848*, ed. M. Levaillant, Paris, 1948, II, 132). There is no reference to this meeting in Lamartine's published correspondence, but he is known to have met CD in Paris in 1847 and again in 1855 (R. Mattlé, *op. cit.*, p. 274*n*).

[4] The 1849 edn of Lamartine's *Médita-*

to do in the matter—any application for me to prefer—any promise and vow for me to make—any pledge that I have no intention of reading them aloud to the Friars in the Streets, whether they will or no—or of converting the Genevese, from the true faith, to the Arabian Nights.

*a*And my stationery—my inkstand—the tools of my trade—I won't write against the Cathedral, or the King, or the Governor, or the Town Gates even; I swear—if I get 'em. But Woe to the Custom House, and the Jesuits who examine the books, if I don't.*a*

Mrs. Dickens says she will take it as a great favor, if you will buy her, at your leisure and in the course of your own marketings, three pounds of black tea, and a Ham. If blushes could be forwarded in a note, this paper would be red with a consciousness of the trouble it gives you, by the time it comes to hand.

Always My Dear Sir | Faithfully Yours

Thomas Curry Esquire   CHARLES DICKENS

To THE REV. EDWARD TAGART, 9 AUGUST 1844

Text from N, I, 614–16 (from text supplied by Comte de Suzannet).

Albaro Near Genoa Friday August Ninth 1844

My Dear Sir,

I find that if I wait to write you a long letter (which has been the cause of my procrastination in fulfilling my part of our agreement), I am likely to wait some time longer. And as I am very anxious to hear from you; not the less so because I hear *of* you through my brother, who usually sees you once a week in my absence; I take pen in hand, and stop a messenger who is going to Genoa. For my main object being to qualify myself for the receipt of a letter from you, I don't see why a ten line qualification is not as good as one of a hundred lines.

You told me it was possible that you and Mrs. Tagart might wander into these Latitudes in the autumn. I wish you would carry out that infant intention to the utmost. It would afford us the truest delight and pleasure to receive you. If you come in October, you will find us in the Palazzo Peschiere, in Genoa; which is surrounded by a delicious garden, and is a most charming habitation in all respects. If you come in September, you will find us less splendidly lodged, but on the margin of the sea, and in the midst of vineyards. The climate is delightful even now; the heat being not at all oppressive, except in the actual city, which is what the Americans would call considerable fiery, in the middle of the day.

tions was in the Gad's Hill library at CD's death. No doubt he had already read and admired their elegiac treatment of the poet's past and romantic feeling for nature; and perhaps also Lamartine's tribute to Byron, *Le Dernier Chant du Pélérinage d'Harold*, 1825.

5 Thomas C. Curry, merchant, and possibly agent for a steamship company; one of the English residents in Genoa ("large merchants and grave men"), "whose untiring kindness", according to Forster, "was long remembered" (F, IV, iii, 336); CD sent messages to his wife and children, 29 June 47 (N, II, 36), and revisited the family in Oct 53 (*Mr. and Mrs. CD*, ed. Walter Dexter, 1935, p. 204).

aa Given in N, I, 614, from catalogue source; letter otherwise unpublished.

But the sea breezes out here are refreshing and cool, every day; and the bathing in the early morning is something more agreeable than you can easily imagine. The orange trees of the Peschiere shall give you their most fragrant salutation if you come to us at that time; and we have a dozen spare beds in that house that I know of; to say nothing of some vast chambers here and there, with ancient *iron* chests in them, where Mrs. Tagart might enact Ginevra[1] *to perfection,* and never be found out. To prevent which, I will engage to watch her closely if she will only come and see us.

The flies are incredibly numerous just now. The unsightly blot, a little higher up, was occasioned by a very fine one who fell into the inkstand, and came out unexpectedly, on the nib of my pen.

We are all quite well, thank Heaven, and had a very interesting journey here. Of which, as well as of this place, I will not write a word, lest I should take the edge off those agreeable conversations with which we will beguile our walks.

Pray tell me all about the presentation of the plate,[2] and whether Ashton Yates[3] was very slow, or trotted at all, and if so, when. He is an excellent creature, and I respect him very much,[4] so I don't mind smiling when I think of him as he appeared when addressing you, and pointing mildly to the plate, with his head a little on one side, and one of his eyes turned up languidly.

Also, let me know exactly how you are travelling, and when, and all about it: that I may meet you with open arms on the threshold of the city, if, happily, you bend your steps this way. You had better address me, Poste Restante, Genoa, as the Albaro postman gets drunk; and when he has lost letters, and is sober, sheds tears—which is affecting, but hardly satisfactory.

Kate and her sister send their best regards to yourself and Mrs. and Miss Tagart, and all your family. I heartily join them in all kind remembrances and good wishes. As the messenger has just looked in at the door, and shedding on

aa Omitted in N; supplied from MDGH, I, 112.

[1] According to Samuel Rogers, *Italy*, 1826, Ginevra, one of the Orsini, the bride of Francesco Doria, disappeared on her wedding day, and her skeleton was discovered in an iron chest fifty years later. CD quoted Rogers's "charming tale" in his Preface to *Master Humphrey's Clock:* see Vol. II, p. 125*n*.

[2] A silver tea-service was presented to Tagart by the congregation of Little Portland St on 9 July; on the large salver was engraved the following inscription composed by CD: "It is not presumptuous to hope that the precepts and example of a Christian minister, wise in the spirit of his sacred trust, will awaken better testimonies to the fidelity of his stewardship, in the daily lives of those whom he instructs, than any that can be wrought in silver or gold. The Congregation of Little Portland Street Chapel, with sentiments of warm affection and respect, gratefully present this slight memorial to the Reverend Edward Tagart, not as an acquittance of the debt they owe him for his labours in the cause of that religion which has sympathy for men of every creed and ventures to pass judgment on none, but merely as an assurance that his learning, eloquence, and lessons of divine truth have sunk into their hearts, and shall not be forgotten in their practice." The *Inquirer*, 20 July 44, which has a full account of the proceedings, says that copies were made for each member of the congregation.

[3] Name omitted in all three edns of MDGH.

[4] That they were on friendly terms is suggested by the existence of a long letter from Yates to CD, dated 21 Sep 44, which included suggestions for places he might visit in Switzerland (Bodley Book Shop catalogue, New York, No. 130). His wife published a travel book, *A Winter in Italy*, in 1844.

me a balmy gale of onions, has protested against being detained any longer, I will only say (which is not at all necessary) that I am ever faithfully yours

[CHARLES DICKENS]

P.S. There is a little to see here, in the church way, I assure you.

To JOHN FORSTER, [?10–11 AUGUST 1844]

Extracts in F, IV, iv, 334; F, 1872–4, II, v, 113n; F, IV, iv, 343, 334–5, 341n, 337. *Date:* first two extracts "seven days" after 3 Aug according to Forster; next three probably same letter, as similar items of news in *To* Mitton, 12 Aug; final extract not before 11 Aug, since season at Teatro Carlo Felice opened 10 Aug, and presumably same letter.

I have got my paper and inkstand and figures now (the box from Osnaburgh-terrace only came last Thursday), and can think—I have begun to do so every morning—with a business-like air, of the Christmas book.[1] My paper is arranged, and my pens are spread out, in the usual form. I think you know the form—Don't you? My books have not passed the custom-house yet, and I tremble for some volumes of Voltaire.[2] . . . I write in the best bedroom. The sun is off the corner window at the side of the house by a very little after twelve; and I can then throw the blinds open, and look up from my paper, at the sea, the mountains, the washed-out villas, the vineyards, at the blistering white-hot fort with a sentry on the drawbridge standing in a bit of shadow no broader than his own musket, and at the sky, as often as I like. It is a very peaceful view, and yet a very cheerful one. Quiet as quiet can be.

A monk was drowned here on Saturday evening.[3] He was bathing with two other monks, who bolted when he cried out that he was sinking—in consequence, I suppose, of his certainty of going to Heaven.

Everybody wears a dress. Mine extremely theatrical: Masaniello to the life: shall be preserved for your inspection in Devonshire-terrace.[4] . . . The moustaches are glorious, glorious. I have cut them shorter, and trimmed them a little at the ends to improve the shape. They are charming, charming. Without them, life would be a blank.

He described the blank impossibility of getting native meanings conveyed to his English servants; the spell was first broken by the cook, being really a clever woman,

[1] CD did not start writing *The Chimes* until Oct: see *To* Forster, ?8 Oct.

[2] CD possessed the *Œuvres Complètes de Voltaire* in 70 vols (Kehl, 1785–9); the inventory (see Appx C, p. 717) shows that he took two of these with him to Italy. He was reading "all the minor tales as well as the plays" on a seaside holiday some years later (F, VI, iii, 505). None were in the Gad's Hill library at his death.

[3] Presumably 3 Aug; incident not traced.

[4] CD's bathing was "from the rock, and . . . of the most primitive kind. He went in whenever he pleased, broke his head against sharp stones if he went in with that end foremost, floundered about till he was all over bruises, and then climbed and staggered out again" (F, IV, iv, 343). *Masaniello* was James Kenney's adaptation of Auber's opera, first performed at Drury Lane, 4 May 29, with scenery by Stanfield, and Braham in the main part; constantly revived. Included in the private theatricals in "Mrs. Joseph Porter over the way" (*Monthly Magazine*, Jan 1834, and *Sketches by Boz*). For the dress, see *To* Stanfield, 24 Aug, *fn*.

and not entrenching herself in that astonishing pride of ignorance which induces the rest to oppose themselves to the receipt of any information through any channel, and which made A.[1] careless of looking out of window, in America, even to see the Falls of Niagara. *She had so primed herself with the names of all sorts of vegetables, meats, soups, fruits, and kitchen necessaries, that she was able to order whatever was needful of the peasantry that were trotting in and out all day, basketed and barefooted.*

Timber has had every hair upon his body cut off because of the fleas, and he looks like the ghost of a drowned dog come out of a pond after a week or so. It is very awful to see him slide into a room. He knows the change upon him, and is always turning round and round to look for himself. I think he'll die of grief.

The first play he saw at the principal theatre[2] *was a version of Balzac's* Père Goriot. The domestic Lear I thought at first was going to be very clever. But he was too pitiful—perhaps the Italian reality would be. He was immensely applauded, though. *The house was larger than Drury Lane and the arrangements were excellent. Instead of a ticket for the private box he had taken on the first tier, he received the usual key for admission which let him in as if he lived there; and for the whole set-out,* quite as comfortable and private as a box at our opera, *paid only eight and fourpence English.*

To THOMAS MITTON, [12] AUGUST 1844*

MS Morgan Library. *Date:* 12 Aug was a Monday in 1844; PM 13 Aug 44 confirms. *Address:* Inghilterra. | Thomas Mitton Esquire | 23 Southampton Buildings | Chancery Lane | London.

Albaro, Monday afternoon Eleventh August 1844.

My Dear Mitton. As you will desire to know about the taxes, I sit down to answer your letter (received to day) at once. But this will not be posted until tomorrow, as the office would be closed[3] before I could write and send it into Genoa to day.

The Income Tax, I remember, is *not* paid. I have no doubt the collector's application is correct, and may be discharged.[4] I have not my cheque-book here, to make quite sure; but he is an exceedingly respectable man, and I feel quite satisfied it is all right. I am rejoiced to learn that the partnership[5] proceeds

[1] Anne Brown, the maid who had also accompanied them to America; CD had remarked her lack of interest: see Vol. III, p. 231.

[2] The Teatro Carlo Felice, where the Da Rizzo Company opened their season on Saturday 10 Aug (Ambrogio Brocca, *Il Teatro Carlo Felice*, Genoa, 1898). According to *Pictures*, p. 66, "a very splendid, commodious and beautiful theatre".

[3] Letters for England had to be posted before 2 o'clock.

[4] Mitton appealed against the assessment for the current year, received under the hand of F. J. Burgoyne, clerk, in a letter (dated 15 Oct 44) to the Commissioner of Taxes, at 8 Foley St, Portland Place. The grounds of appeal were that as a resident abroad, CD might earn less from his writings (MS Mr H. C. Dickens).

[5] The *Law List* shows that Mitton was in partnership with William Nealor, as "Mitton & Nealor", in 1844; they were London agents for a firm of Derby solicitors, Dunnicliff & Severne.

so well; and the success of the two causes at Derby,[1] I hail as a glorious omen.

We are now in the height of the heat: which is supposed to decline after St. Lorenzo's day—which was on Saturday last.[2] Walking is wholly out of the question. I feel that deprivation very much; but I have many resources wherever I am; and get on quite happily. The Christmas Book already occupies me, in the preliminary shutting myself up and thinking all the morning; and I shall soon be in full swing with it, I hope. There are so many contrivances for coolness, that within doors it is really much less distressing than on a very hot day in London. It is out of doors—in the Sun—that one feels it; and there it really is, just now, *blazing*. I turn out before 7 every morning, and plunge into the sea instantly. It is inexpressibly delicious— though the bottom is rocky; and I cut my knees to pieces when the waves are rough. I am learning Italian, which is more difficult than I expected: partly because my book-thoughts interfere with it: and partly because of a preposterous custom the gentry have, of addressing each other—men, observe!—as *she*, and in the third person. So that instead of saying "how are you?" to a great fellow with a black moustache; you say "Is she quite well?" Charley is learning French of the same gentleman;[3] and I hope will get on nobly. The cook has picked up more Italian than any of them. She is really a clever woman. The laundress happens to speak good Italian—the Genevese speak nothing Earthly, but a Gibberish of their own—and from her, she has learnt the names of all sorts of meats and vegetables and household articles; so that she can order what is wanted for the house, quite freely. She is the most contented of all the servants too; and although this house is diabolically supplied, in even such small essentials as the commonest saucepans; she gets on just as she would in Devonshire Terrace, somehow or other; and never makes the least complaint. Roche is my right hand still, in all things. And he remains with me, gladly.

I have taken the unexpired term of an English colonel who is going away, in the Palazzo Peschiere (pronounced Peskeeairy): which I enter on the possession of, on the 1st. of October, and hold until the sixteenth of March, at 5 Guineas a week—one more than this place. To remain here in the winter would have been impossible, for there are no fire-places; and the coach-hire into Genoa is very expensive, besides being very damnable, and jolting one to death. The Peschiere is greatly esteemed as being perfectly healthy—in the midst of the most splendid prospects—within the walls of Genoa—in the heart of all the Mountain walks— and surrounded by the most delicious gardens (filled with fountains, orange

---

[1] At the Derbyshire Summer Assizes. One of the cases, Mercer *v.* Whall, an action for breach of covenant heard before Lord Denman, 31 July, excited so much interest that it was reported at length in the *Derby and Chesterfield Reporter*. Mitton was solicitor for Mercer, the plaintiff, who gained the verdict and was awarded damages of £300 for wrongful dismissal. Mitton, who had been the London agent of the late Mr Richard Gratton, Mercer's former employer, had tried to reach a compromise settlement and much of the correspondence was read out in court, Denman remarking that it "was creditable to both parties".

[2] In *Pictures*, p. 60, CD describes a visit to the Cathedral on San Lorenzo's day at sunset.

[3] See *To* Rogers, 1 Sep 44.

trees, and all sorts of lovely things) you can conceive: which are *not* maintained at the expence of the tenant. Within, it is painted: walls and ceilings, every inch: in the most gorgeous manner. There are ten rooms on one floor: few smaller than the largest habitable rooms in Hampton Court Palace: and one quite as long and wide as the Saloon of Drury Lane Theatre; with a great vaulted roof higher than that of the Waterloo Gallery in Windsor Castle—I think again, and can safely add very much higher. It is always let for the winter at £32 per month; but this colonel having taken it for a year and a half certain, got it cheap; and being a great Bozonian, he came to me privately—shewed me the offers he had for it—and said "But if you like to take it, you shall have it before anybody." I caught at it gladly; to the great discomfiture of the other competitors. And the competition for any good place here—there are not four in the whole town—is quite extraordinary.

You will have heard from Fred, I dare say, that poor little Katey has been very ill. She is now recovering, thank Heaven, and goes out every night upon a Donkey. But you would scarcely know her; she is so extremely thin. She would let nobody touch her; in the way of dressing her neck or giving her physic; when she was ill; but her Papa. So I had a pretty tough time of it. But her sweet temper was wonderful to see. I shall be very glad when they can go out for long walks. The time will very soon be here, I trust.

My plans are, to go to Marseilles again, to meet Fred; and to come back by the Cornice Road across the Alps: which I must see, and which will not fit into my other plans. I shall then remain quiet, until I have done my Christmas Book: which will be (I hope) at the end of October, or pretty early in November. I shall then go: taking Roche with me: to Milan, Bologna, Turin, Mantua, Verona, Venice, Florence, and intermediate places. I shall return here, for Christmas, and remain here through January when it is usually very bad weather, and intensely cold. In February, I purpose starting off to Rome—from Rome to Naples—and after seeing Mount Vesuvius, and Herculaneum and Pompeii, away into Sicily, to Mount Etna. Returning to Naples then, I shall come back here by a Steamboat, and remain until the week before Easter, when I shall start off again on a second visit to Rome; that being the time when all sorts of displays take place. Returning here at the End of Easter week, I shall pick up the Caravan, and go straight to Paris: arranging so as to be there, if I can, by the end of April: and remain there, in a lodging, until about the Second week in June. There is no such place for material in my way, as Paris.

These are my present designs, and they seem to be the best; as I shall go into France by the pass of the Great Saint Gotherd (which is the most tremendous pass in the Alps) and by Strasburgh—an entirely new line. Something may occur to change them; but I shall hold to them, if possible.

The novelty having worn off, I think we all like Italian life very well. Fletcher was *bit*, in this place, beyond all kind of question. But the sea breeze blows away all objections to it. He is known in Genoa (so Roche tells me) as the mad gentleman, and is renowned for believing whatever he is told. You are quite right in your conclusions touching the probable effects of heat upon his addled head. He horrified us the other night, by saying he felt as if it were going to burst; and that he had taken a walk with a lady once, who complained of being similarly affected, and who was escorted to a Madhouse next day. I had some notion of knocking him down with a chair; but he got better.

He always gives a horrible yell, when he first puts his foot in the sea. And to see him; with his very bald head & his very fat body; limping over the sharp rocks in a small, short, tight pair of striped drawers—such as they wear in Masaniello on the stage; which is the dress you are expected to wear here, in bathing—is one of the most ridiculous sights I ever beheld in my life. He is always taken faint, immediately after coming out; and so remains until breakfast is ready: when he goes in, to win, at half a dozen breakfast cups of tea: which he drinks (like Quilp) boiling hot,[1] and with his eyes standing out, like a lobster's.

The box arrived here, only last Thursday. I have not got my books yet. They are taken out at the Custom House and examined by Priests, before they are allowed to pass. As some Volumes of a French author, Voltaire, are among them, who always wrote against Priests, I fully expect them to be stopped. Though I am not likely to read them to the Genevese, and woo them to their damnation, I am sure.

The other children are all quite well; and they send their loves. The baby is a brilliant fellow. Charley is rather hove down, at times, for want of somebody to play with him. We are too far out of the world here, to get him companions. But wh[en][2] we move, there is an English Merchant[3] close by our Palazzo, (who buys all sorts of impossible [things][4] for us, at wholesale prices) who has a son very like him, and about his own age, with whom he will be able to keep it up.

Give my love to Fred, and ask him to bring—A French Grammar for Charley (we can't get one here in French and English, for Love or Money)—a copy of Overs's book[5]—and a Unitarian Prayer-Book; which he can buy at one Green's, a bookseller in Newgate Street.[6] If he can cram two or three packs of playing cards into his trunk, so much the better. Ask him to beg Forster, too, to give him some good little book of general knowledge, out of which the aforesaid Charley may prepare himself to floor his schoolfellows on his return to Ould England. And a copy of Tennyson's Poems, for me.[7]

I have some difficulty in my mind, about the best way of giving that Guinea to Overs. Let it be, for the present. Many thanks for your rigid discharge of the other commissions—poor dear Mary's[8] first, and before all. "Private and Confidential" should be at the top of all the acknowledgements of letters received, which you write: to imply that you opened them on those terms.

---

[1] In *Old Curiosity Shop*, Ch. 5, Quilp drinks "scalding tea without winking".

[2] Tear at the edge of the paper has removed last two letters.

[3] Probably Thomas Curry.

[4] About six letters missing.

[5] See *To* Newby, 29 June 44, *fn.*

[6] Green advertised a long list of devotional works in the *Inquirer*, including a number of collections of prayers; there was no standard Unitarian prayerbook.

[7] This sentence was written in as an afterthought. Forster ordered a copy on 31 Aug from Frederick Griffiths, to be charged to CD's account (Dobell's catalogue, Autumn 1953); the inventory (see Appx C, p. 717) shows that CD had left a Tennyson at Devonshire Terrace, probably bought to replace the one he gave Christiana (see *To* T. E. Weller, 1 Mar 44). A copy of the 2nd edn, 1843, with "numerous pencil marks" was in the Gad's Hill library at CD's death (*Catalogue of the Library of CD*, ed. J. H. Stonehouse, p. 109).

[8] CD may have asked Mitton to look after her grave.

The fleas here, surpass the bounds of human credulity. They don't touch *me*. I have had every atom of Timber's hair cut off. But he is so full of them, still, that it is impossible to allow him to come up stairs. I am afraid they will go before Fred comes; but tell him I will keep them for him if I can. Insects of divers sorts abound. The great Sunday amusement, is for whole families to sit outside their doors, on the pavement: picking the lice out of each other's heads.[1] As we rode through Genoa to church[2] yesterday, we saw innumerable little pleasure parties, of this description.

Fletcher is so infernally lazy, that he hasn't copied his sketch. I mean to tell him that if he don't, I'll have the tea reduced in strength. After which terrible threat, I dare say I shall get it to send you in my next. Kate and her sister desire to be heartily remembered. Ever faithfully CD.

Tuesday Morning. The books arrived last night—all complete. They never pass Voltaire; but with great politeness, passed it for me. Englishmen and other foreigners are obliged to apply to the Police for a Permission to reside here: renewable every three months; but they exempt me from these forms, and are exceedingly considerate. I had a private box at the Theatre (which is larger than Drury Lane or Covent Garden) on Saturday Night. It was comfortably fitted up with sofas and a mirror: and cost eight and fourpence English. The opera is open there, in the winter. The banker (Coutts's Correspondent) whom we visit,[3] has a box. He is a bachelor, and never goes: so he means to place it at our disposal. There is another Theatre,[4] where the performances are in the open air and in the day time—very cool and pleasant. Katey is still improving, rapidly.

To JOHN FORSTER, [?20 AUGUST 1844]

Extracts in F, IV, iv, 338, 337, 336–7, 338–9. *Date:* first extract 20 Aug according to Forster; second extract after 11 Aug (see *fn*), so probably part of same letter; third extract also, since clearly after first visit to marionettes; dinner-party in fourth extract "in the middle of August" according to Forster.

A Spanish duke[5] has taken the room under me in the Peschiere. The duchess was his mistress many years, and bore him (I think) six daughters. He always

[1] Cf. "hunting in each other's heads", *Pictures*, p. 61.

[2] The English Church in the Strada del Diavolo; the resident clergyman, the Rev. John Irvine, held services at 11.30 and 3 o'clock on Sundays.

[3] Charles Gibbs of Gibbs & Co.; one of the firm's main sources of profit was the commission charged to English travellers who presented letters of credit and circular notes from London bankers, the most important of which was Coutts's. F. A. Y. Brown, son of the English consul, recalled that Gibbs "did not trouble himself much about business; so that when his relations Mess. Antony Gibbs and Sons of London . . . wanted an agent in Genoa, they passed him over" (*Family Notes*, privately printed, Genoa, 1917, pp. 29–30). He is referred to in *Pictures*, pp. 52–3, as "the English Banker, my excellent and hospitable friend", with a detailed description of the Palazzo in the Strada Nuova, on the first floor of which were both his office and residence; he also rented a villa by the sea at Quinto, near Albaro.

[4] The Teatro Sant'Agostino or Teatro Diurno, described in *Pictures*, p. 67, as "a covered stage in the open air . . . in the cool of the afternoon".

[5] Unidentified.

promised her that if she gave birth to a son, he would marry her; and when at last the boy arrived, he went into her bedroom, saying—"Duchess, I am charmed to salute you!" And he married her in good earnest, and legitimatized (as by the Spanish law he could) all the other children.

He had seen a version of Dumas' preposterous play of Kean,[1] *in which most of the representatives of English actors wore red hats with steeple crowns, and very loose blouses with broad belts and buckles round their waists.* There was a mysterious person called the Prince of Var-lees, the youngest and slimmest man in the company, whose badinage in Kean's dressing-room was irresistible; and the dresser wore top-boots, a Greek skull-cap, a black velvet jacket, and leather breeches. One or two of the actors looked very hard at me to see how I was touched by these English peculiarities—especially when Kean kissed his male friends on both cheeks.

He wrote of the puppets. There are other things,[2] too solemnly surprising to dwell upon. They must be seen. They must be seen. The enchanter carrying off the bride is not greater than his men brandishing fiery torches and dropping their lighted spirits of wine at every shake. Also the enchanter himself, when, hunted down and overcome, he leaps into the rolling sea, and finds a watery grave. Also the second comic man, aged about 55 and like George the Third in the face, when he gives out the play for the next night. They must all be seen. They can't be told about. Quite impossible.

He had dined with the French consul-general. There was present, among other Genoese, the Marquis di Negri:[3] a very fat and much older Jerdan,[4] with the

[1] *Kean, ou Désordre et Génie,* by the elder Dumas, 1836; a performance at the Teatro Carlo Felice after that of *Père Goriot,* but before 16 Aug, when the company left. Also described in similar terms in "Foreigners' Portraits of Englishmen", by CD, W. H. Wills and E. C. Grenville Murray in *Household Words,* 21 Sep 50; the corrected proof (Forster Collection, V & A) indicates that the description was written by CD, and possibly based on this letter (see *The Uncollected Writings of Charles Dickens: Household Words 1850–1859,* ed. Harry Stone, 1969, I, 146, and II, Appendix A).

[2] According to Forster this part of the letter came after the account in *Pictures,* pp. 68–72, describing the ballet performed by "a famous company from Milan . . . one summer night"; the passage belongs to p. 69. There was more about the puppets in a passage deleted from an October letter used for *Pictures* (see Preface, including a reference to a coming "new ballet at the Puppets . . . I see by the bills that it is preceded by a serious and classical

Roman piece with a (puppet) lion in it. This promises well, I should say. There are also an army and a battle" (MS Forster Collection, V & A). C. E. Lester (*My Consulship,* I, 278) described the Marionetti as a mixture of Punchinello and the opera, held in "neat, pretty, and respectable theatres; and the boxes are filled with the children, and often the whole families of the nobility". For the performance of *St. Helena,* see *To* Robertson, 20 Apr 45.

[3] The Marchese Giovanni Carlo di Negro (c. 1770–c.1852), author and dilettante, was known as a genial host and improvisatore to most travellers to Genoa; he held soirées at his villetta on the Acqua Sola for "persons of taste, particularly foreigners, on Friday evenings" (C. E. Lester, *My Consulship,* I, 74). Had visited England in 1802 when, according to Mrs Stisted, his improvisations " astonished even our universities"; in 1835 he entertained the Stisteds "with his own translations of . . . Moore's Irish Melodies" (*Letters from the Bye-ways of Italy,* 1845, pp. 263–66). Lester, on his first meeting

same thickness of speech and size of tongue. He was Byron's friend,[1] keeps open house here, writes poetry, improvises, and is a very good old Blunderbore;[2] just the sort of instrument to make an artesian well with, anywhere. Well, sir, after dinner, the consul proposed my health, with a little French conceit to the effect that I had come to Italy to have personal experience of its lovely climate, and that there was this similarity between the Italian sun and its visitor, that the sun shone into the darkest places and made them bright and happy with its benignant influence, and that my books had done the like with the breasts of men, and so forth. Upon which Blunderbore gives his bright-buttoned blue coat a great rap on the breast, turns up his fishy eye, stretches out his arm like the living statue defying the lightning at Astley's, and delivers four impromptu verses in my honour, at which everybody is enchanted, and I more than anybody—perhaps with the best reason, for I didn't understand a word of them. The consul then takes from his breast a roll of paper, and says, "I shall read them!" Blunderbore then says, "Don't!" But the consul does, and Blunderbore beats time to the music of the verse with his knuckles on the table; and perpetually ducks forward to look round the cap of a lady sitting between himself and me, to see what I think of them. I exhibit lively emotion. The verses are in French—short line— on the taking of Tangiers by the Prince de Joinville;[3] and are received with great applause; especially by a nobleman present who is reported to be unable to read and write. They end in my mind (rapidly translating them into prose) thus,—

The cannon of France	Rendering thanks
Shake the foundation	To Heaven.
Of the wondering sea,	The King
The artillery on the shore	And all the Royal Family
Is put to silence,	Are bathed
Honour to Joinville[4]	In tears.

with di Negro in 1842, called him "the most conspicuous literary character of Genoa", described his "patriarchal style" of living, and said that he had calculated his income when he was 20, and resolved to spend his whole fortune of a hundred thousand dollars by the time he was 80 years old (Lester, *ibid*). CD describes him even more fully in "New Year's Day" (*Household Words*, 1 Jan 59; *Miscellaneous Papers*, ed. B. W. Matz, pp. 651–62), as the "rare old Italian Cavaliere, who improvises, writes poetry, plays harps, composes music, paints pictures, and is always inaugurating somebody's bust in his little garden". At the party on 1 Jan 45, he took part in charades and country dances, assuming that both were widespread English customs, and crying "Dear England, merry England, the young and joyous, home of the Fancy, free as the air, playful as the child!" At 3 a.m. he improvised "an enormous poem on the sports of England", then went home

and played the harp, next day wrote out his poem and inscribed it to CD, placing it "at the disposal of any English publisher whom it may please to undertake a translation".

[4] William Jerdan (1782–1869; *DNB*), editor of the *Literary Gazette:* see Vol. I, p. 207n.

[1] Cf. J. T. Headley, *Letters from Italy*, 1845, p. 53: "The Marquis knew Byron well, admired his genius, but shook his head when he spoke of his heart". Byron was in Albaro 1822–3, but does not mention the Marchese in his letters or journals.

[2] In *Jack the Giant-killer*.

[3] Joinville bombarded the weakly defended Tangiers on 6 Aug 44, but delayed his despatch until 13 Aug; the news was reported in *Galignani's Messenger*, 16 Aug, and the reactions of the French and British press were given in the issues of 17 and 19 Aug.

[4] Continued on p. 182.

And the Brave!	They call upon the name
The Great Intelligence	Of Joinville!
Is borne	France also
Upon the wings of Fame	Weeps, and echoes it.
To Paris.	Joinville is crowned
Her national citizens	With Immortality;
Exchange caresses	And Peace and Joinville,
In the streets!	And the Glory of France,
The temples are crowded	Diffuse themselves
With religious patriots	Conjointly.

If you can figure to yourself the choice absurdity of receiving anything into one's mind in this way, you can imagine the labour I underwent in my attempts to keep the lower part of my face square, and to lift up one eye gently, as with admiring attention. But I am bound to add that this is really pretty literal; for I read them afterwards.

To JOHN FORSTER, [24 AUGUST 1844]

Extracts in F, IV, iv, 338, 334. *Date:* 24 Aug according to Forster.

He described the great public tanks in an archway beneath the Acqua Sola, where, at all ordinary times, washerwomen were washing away, thirty or forty together.[1] *Matters were worse at Albaro: the clothes there being washed in a pond, beaten with gourds, and whitened with a preparation of lime* so that what between the beating and the burning they fall into holes unexpectedly, and my white trowsers, after six weeks' washing, would make very good fishing-nets. It is such a serious damage that when we get into the Peschiere we mean to wash at home.

He could ask in Italian for whatever he wanted in any shop or coffee-house, and could read it pretty well.

To CLARKSON STANFIELD, 24 AUGUST 1844†

MS Colonel Richard Gimbel. *Address:* Inghilterra. | Clarkson Stanfield Esquire. R.A. | Mornington Place | Hampstead Road | London.

Albaro Saturday Night Twenty Fourth August 1844

My Dear Stanfield. I love you so truly, and have such pride and joy of heart in your friendship, that I don't know how to begin writing to you. When I think how you are walking up and down London in that portly surtout, and can't receive proposals from Dick to go to the theatre, I fall into a state between laughing and crying, and want some friendly back to smite.—"Je-im! Aye aye your honor",—is in my ears every time I walk upon the seashore here; and the

---

[1] In *Pictures*, p. 62, CD describes how the women beat the linen with a flat wooden mallet "as furiously as if they were avenging themselves on dress in general for being connected with the Fall of Mankind".

number of expeditions I make into Cornwall,[1] in my sleep—the springs of flys I break, the songs I sing, and the bowls of punch I drink—would soften a heart of stone.

We have had weather here since five o'Clock this morning, after your own heart. Suppose yourself the admiral in Black Eyed Susan—after the acquittal of William, and when it was feasible to be on friendly terms with him.—I am T.P.[2] My trousers are very full at the ankles—my black neck kerchief is tied in the regular style—the name of my ship is painted round my glazed hat.—I have a red waistcoat on—and the seams of my blue jacket are "paid"[3]—permit me to dig you in the ribs, when I make use of this nautical expression—with white. In my left hand I hold the baccy box, connected with the Story of Sandominger-billy.[4] I lift up my eyebrows as far as I can (on the T.P. model) take a quid from the box—screw the lid on again (chewing at the same time, and looking pleasantly at the pit)—brush it with my right elbow—cock up my right leg—scrape my right foot on the ground—hitch up my trousers—and in reply to a question of yours: namely "Indeed! What weather, William?" deliver myself as follows:

Lord love your honor! Weather!! Such weather as would set all hands to the pumps aboard one of your fresh water cockboats, and set the purser to his wits' ends to stow away for the use of the Ship's company, the casks and casks full of blue water as would come powering in over the gunnel! The dirtiest night, your honor, as ever you see 'atween Spithead at Gunfire[5] and the Bay of Biscay! The wind Sou West, and your Honor dead in the wind's eye; the breakers running high upon the rocky beach—the light 'us no more looming through the fog, than Davey Jones's sarser eye through the blue sky of Heaven in a calm, or the blue toplights of your Honor's lady, cast down in a modest overhauling of her catheads,[6]—avast!" (whistling) "my dear eyes here am I a goin, head-on, to the breakers!" (bowing)

Admiral (smiling)—"No William! I admire plain-speaking as you know. And so does old England William, and old England's Queen. But you were saying—"

William. "Aye aye your Honor—I", (scratching his head) "I've lost my reckoning. Damme!—I ast pardon—but won't your honor throw a hencoop, or any ould end of towline to a man as is overboard?"

Admiral. (smiling still) "You were saying, William, that the wind—"

William. (again cocking up his leg and slapping the thigh very hard) "Avast heaving your honor! I see your honor's signal fluttering in the breeze, without a glass! As I was a saying, your honor, the wind a blowin from the Sou West—due Sou West your honor: not a pint to Larboard nor a pint to Starboard—the clouds a gatherin in the distance, for all the world like Beachey Head in a fog—

---

[1] See Vol. III, pp. 414–15 and *ns.*

[2] Thomas Potter ("Tippy") Cooke (1786–1864; *DNB*), actor; his most famous part was William in Jerrold's *Black-eyed Susan*: see Vol. III, p. 534n. The reference is to the closing scene of the play.

[3] Smeared with pitch or tar to make waterproof.

[4] St Domingo Billy, the shark who swallowed tobacco-boxes in *Black-eyed Susan*, II, iii. Many phrases in the following dialogue recall this play.

[5] The time at which the morning or evening gun is fired (*OED*).

[6] Beams projecting from the bows of a ship for raising the anchor.

the sea a rowling in, in heaps of foam, and running higher than the mainyard arm—the craft a scuddin by, all taught and under storms'els, for the harbor—not a blessed star a twinklin out aloft—aloft, your honor, in the little Cherub's[1] Native Country—and the spray a flying like the white foam from Jolly's lips, when Poll of Portsea[2] took him for a tailor!" (laughs)

Admiral (laughing also) "You have described it well, William, and I thank you. But who are these!"

[Enter Supers—in calico jackets to look like cloth—some in brown holland petticoat trousers and big boots, all in belts with very large buckles. Last Super rolls on a cask and pretends to tap it. Other supers apply tin mugs to the bunghole, and drink—previously holding them upside down.][3]

William (after shaking hands with everybody) "Who are these your Honor! Mess mates as staunch and true as ever broke biscuit. An't you my lads!"

All. "Aye aye William. That we are. That we are!"

Admiral. (much affected) "Oh England! What wonder that—! But I will no longer detain you from your sports my humble friends" [Admiral speaks very loud, and looks hard at the orchestra this being the cue for the dance]—"from your sports my humble friends. Farewell!"

All. Hurrah! Hurrah! [Exit Admiral]

[*Voice behind*] Suppose the dance, Mr. Stanfield. Are you all ready? Go—then!

My dear Stanfield, how I wish you would come this way, and see me in the Palazzo Peschiere! Was ever man so welcome as I would make you! What a truly gentlemanly action it would be, to bring Mrs. Stanfield—and the baby! and how Kate and her sister would wave pocket handkerchiefs from the Wharf, in joyful welcome! Ah, what a glorious proceeding!

Do you know this place? Of course you do.[4] I won't bore you with anything about it, for I know Forster reads my letters to you; but *what* a place it is! The views from the hills here, and the immense variety of prospects of the sea, are as striking, I think, as such Scenery can be. Above all, the approach to Genoa, by sea from Marseilles, constitutes a Picture which you ought to paint; for nobody else can ever do it! Villain! You made that bridge at Avignon, better than it is. Beautiful as it undoubtedly is,[5] you made it fifty times better. And if I were Morrison,[6] or one of that school (bless the dear fellows one and all!) I wouldn't stand it, but would insist on having another picture gratis, to atone for the imposition.

The night is like a seaside night in England, towards the end of September.

[1] "There's a sweet little cherub that sits up aloft", from Charles Dibdin's song, "Poor Jack".

[2] Apparently not a reference to a specific play or song, but generally typical of the nautical drama.

[3] CD's square brackets, here and below.

[4] Stanfield several times visited Italy, but it is not known when he was in Genoa and no picture of his can be certainly related to it.

[5] Stanfield exhibited *Avignon on the Rhone* in 1840 and *The Bridge at Avignon* in 1848.

[6] James Morrison (1790–1857; *DNB*), merchant and politician; partner of John Dillon in Morrison, Dillon & Co. (see *To Dillon*, 3 Feb 44), and a friend of John Black of the *Chronicle*. A man of immense fortune, he collected books and pictures and bought Fonthill 1837.

They say it is the prelude to clear weather. But the wind is roaring now, and the sea is raving, and the rain is driving down, as if they had all set in for a real hearty pic nic, and each had brought its own contribution[1] to the general festivity. I don't know whether you are acquainted with the Coast Guard men in these parts? They are extremely civil fellows, of a very amiable manner and appearance, but the most innocent men, in matters you would suppose them to be well acquainted with, in virtue of their office: that I ever encountered. One of them asked me, only yesterday, if it would take a Year to get to England in a ship. Which I thought for a Coast Guard man was rather a tidy question.—It would take a long time to catch a ship going there, if he were on board a pursuing cutter though. I think he would scarcely do it in twelve months, indeed.

[a]Forster told me, in a letter I received from him yesterday, of your mistake at the Parthenon, in respect of that marvellous likeness of Liston.[2] I laughed immoderately. He gave me an admirable description of the scene; and when I recollected the laborious manner in which I had impressed the fact of the strong resemblance upon you, in that very room—and the courteous, Academical sympathy for my uneducated eye, with which you had conceded—"Well! he *is* like him Dick"—I grinned from ear to ear.[a] So you were at Astley's[3] t'other night! "Now Mr. Stickney Sir! what can I come for to go for to do, for to bring, for to fetch, for to carry for you Sir?"—"He he he! Oh! I say Sir!"—"Well Sir?"—"Miss Woolford knows me Sir. She laughed at me!"—I see him run away after this;—not on his feet, but on his knees and the calves of his legs alternately—and that smell of sawdusty horses, which was never in any other place in the world, salutes my nose with painful distinctness.

What do you think of my suddenly finding myself a Swimmer? But I have really made the discovery; and skim about a little blue bay just below the house here, like a fish in high spirits. I hope to preserve my bathing dress for your inspection and approval—or possibly to enrich your collection of Italian Costumes—on my return. Do you recollect Yarnold[4] in Massaniello?[5] I find that I unintentionally "dress at him", before plunging into the sea. I enhanced the likeness very much last Friday Morning, by singing a barcarole on the rocks. I was a trifle too flesh-coloured (the stage knowing no medium between bright salmon, and dirty yellow); but apart from that defect, not badly made up, by any means.

[b]I see in Galignani, that a Public dinner is to be given to Mr. Bunn.[6] It is a

[1] N, I, 621 misreads as "relations".

[2] Lord Morpeth is recorded as humorously owning his remarkable likeness to Liston at a dinner to Southwood Smith in 1837 at which CD was present (J. Westland Marston, *Our Recent Actors*, 1888, I, 282n).

[a][a] Not previously published.

[3] Astley's Amphitheatre: see Vol. II, p. 6on. The clown's catch-phrases are quoted in "Astley's" in *Sketches by Boz*: "Miss Woolford knows me" and "go for to do" etc. Barry was the clown, Stickney the ring-master, and Miss Woolford the chief equestrienne.

[4] In Macready's company at Covent Garden 1838, and at the Lyceum 1845. He had played Masaniello's friend Moreno in the first production in 1829. Masaniello and the other fishermen wore doublet, striped shirt and loose breeches, of various colours, with the arms bare; the hero's first song was a barcarole.

[5] Thus in MS.

[b][b] Not previously published.

[6] *Galignani's Messenger* reported on 10 Aug that Bunn was to be entertained "with a grand dinner" by the committee of Drury Lane and his personal friends; but the

great mortification to me, not to be in England; that I might have the honor and gratification of enrolling my name in the list of stewards, and humbly testifying by that action and by my poor presence at the Festival, my sympathy with, and admiration for, a public servant, who, as a gentleman, a manager, a man: and considered either as a public or a private Individual; has no parallel in the country which claims him for her son. When I see such honors paid to this distinguished gentleman, whose speech, whose life, and whose every proceeding in every capacity, so justly entitle him to that meed of public approbation which he has so well earned, I feel, indeed that the regeneration of the Drama is at hand; and that its golden age (or it may be, brazen; at this distance the metals resemble each other, very nearly) has not departed from our happy shores. If you think Lord Glengall likely to buy this, for his speech, I will take five guineas for it, and subscribe the Sum to the Society for the Propagation of the Gospel in Foreign Parts.*b*

*c*When you write to me, my dear Stanny; as I hope you will soon; address, Poste Restante Genoa.*c* I remain out here until the end of September, and send in for my letters daily. There *is* a Postman for this place, but he gets drunk and loses the letters; after which he calls to say so, and to fall upon his knees— *d*which is affecting, but not satisfactory.*d* About three weeks ago, I caught him at a Wine shop near here; playing bowls in the garden. It was then about five o'Clock in the afternoon; and he had been airing a newspaper addressed to me, since 9 o'Clock in the Morning.

Kate and Georgina unite with me in most cordial remembrances to Mrs. and Miss Stanfield,[1] and to all the children;[2] *e*who I hope are well and thriving.*e* They particularize all sorts of messages, but I tell them they had better write themselves if they want to send any. Though I don't know that their writing would end in the safe deliverance of those commodities after all; for when I began this letter, I meant to give utterance to all kinds of heartiness, my dear Stanfield; and I come to the end of it without having said anything more than that I am— which is new to you—under every circumstance and everywhere

Your most affectionate friend

Clarkson Stanfield Esquire   CHARLES DICKENS

To T. C. CURRY, 31 AUGUST 1844*

MS University of Texas.

Albaro. | Saturday Thirty First | August 1844

My Dear Sir

I should have written to you yesterday, but was not quite sure that I should

report was probably incorrect, since such a dinner, with Lord Glengall in the chair, had already taken place on 6 Aug (*The Times*, 8 Aug 44).

cc Omitted in MDGH, 1893, and in N. *dd; ee* Not previously published.

[1] Probably Stanfield's devoted sister Mary, at one time an actress.

[2] Stanfield had in all twelve children, two by his first marriage (Clarkson and Mary) and ten (five sons and five daughters) by his second: the names of six are known —George (*b.* 1828), Francesco, John, Field, Harriet Theresa (married 1861), and Edward Herbert (see *To* Stanfield, 28 Mar 46).

get so far round the corner as to be myself again,[1] by tomorrow. In which case, I should have had nothing to say.

What I have now to ask, is, whether you will do the friendly deed of coming to dine with us tomorrow at four, along with your, and Fletcher's, friend?[2] Mrs. Dickens reports after a careful examination of the kitchen (which is very easily made, as there is hardly anything in it) that there are *plates enough* for two guests. So will you come, and say Grace before the more hospitable meat of the Peschiere.

With best Regards, in which my ladies join, to all your house

Believe me | Faithfully Yours

Thomas Currie[3] Esquire   CHARLES DICKENS

To JOHN FORSTER, [?31 AUGUST 1844]

Extracts in F, IV, iv, 341*n*, 340, 340–1; 335. *Date:* first extract "three weeks later" than letter of ?10 Aug; second and third extracts clearly after *To* Stanfield, 24 Aug —and *To* Curry, 31 Aug, shows that CD had recovered from his attack of illness; fourth extract in a letter which Forster received "before the end of the second week of September".

Timber's hair is growing again, so that you can dimly perceive him to be a dog. The fleas only keep three of his legs off the ground now, and he sometimes moves of his own accord towards some place where they don't want to go.

After the French consul's dinner-party he was invited to a great reception at the Marquis di Negro's on his daughter's birthday.[4] *The grottoes and fanciful walks in the grounds reminded him of old White-conduit-house, except that he would have been well-pleased, on the present occasion, to have discovered a waiter crying, "Give your orders, gents!" it being not easy to him at any time to keep up, the whole night through, on ices and variegated lamps merely. He was amused by the old Marquis himself,* who was constantly diving out into dark corners and then among the lattice-work and flower pots, rubbing his hands and going round and round with explosive chuckles in his huge satisfaction with the entertainment. *It occurred to him, however, with horror, that four more hours of this kind of entertainment would be too much; that the Genoa gates closed at twelve; and that as the carriage had not been ordered till the dancing was expected to be over and the gates to reopen, he must make a sudden bolt if he would himself get back to Albaro.* I had barely time to reach the gate before midnight; and was running as hard as I could go, downhill, over uneven ground, along a new street called the strada Sevra, when I came to a pole fastened straight across the street, nearly breast high, without any light or watchman—quite in the Italian style. I went over it, headlong, with such force that I rolled myself completely white in the dust; but although I tore my clothes to shreds, I hardly scratched myself except in one

---

[1] See *To* Forster, ?31 Aug.

[2] Possibly "Knowles", an artist who had been four years in Italy, mentioned as a friend of Fletcher's in Fred Dickens *to* Maclise, 8 Nov 44 (MS Benoliel).

[3] Thus in MS.

[4] Mrs Stisted speaks of meeting "his interesting daughter, Madame Balbi" (*Letters from the Bye-ways of Italy*, p. 263).

place on the knee. I had no time to think of it then, for I was up directly and off again to save the gate: but when I got outside the wall, and saw the state I was in, I wondered I had not broken my neck. I "took it easy" after this, and walked home, by lonely ways enough, without meeting a single soul. But there is nothing to be feared, I believe, from midnight walks in this part of Italy. In other places you incur the danger of being stabbed by mistake; whereas the people here are quiet and good-tempered, and very rarely commit any outrage.

*There followed a short but sharp attack of illness. It came on with the old un-*speakable and agonizing pain in the side *and yielded quickly to powerful remedies. But for a few days he had to content himself with the minor sights of Albaro. He sat daily in the shade of the ruined chapel[1] on the seashore. He looked in at the festa in the small country church,[2] consisting mainly of a tenor singer, a seraphine, and four priests sitting gaping in a row on one side of the altar,* in flowered satin dresses and little cloth caps, looking exactly like the band at a wild-beast-caravan. *He was interested in the wine-making, and in seeing the country tenants preparing their annual presents for their landlords, of baskets of grapes and other fruit prettily dressed with flowers. This brought out after dusk strong parties of rats to eat them as they ripened, and so many shooting parties of peasants to get rid of these despoilers, that as he first listened to the uproar of the firing and the echoes he half fancied it a siege of Albaro. The flies mustered strong, too, and the mosquitoes; so that at night he had to lie covered up with gauze, like cold meat in a safe.*

The servants are beginning to pick up scraps of Italian; some of them go to a weekly conversazione of servants at the Governor's[3] every Sunday night, having got over their consternation at the frequent introduction of quadrilles on these occasions; and I think they begin to like their foreigneering life.

To SAMUEL ROGERS, 1 SEPTEMBER 1844

MS Professor E. S. Pearson. *Address:* Inghilterra. | Samuel Rogers Esquire | Saint James's Place | London.

Albaro near Genoa. Sunday First September|1844.

My Dear Mr. Rogers. We have been greatly concerned to hear, through Mr. Forster, of your having been unwell,[4] and seriously so. But hearing from the same source that you had recovered, we were, like the town ladies in the Vicar of Wakefield (with a small difference in respect of sincerity) extremely glad again.[5] And to the end that we may not be made sorry once more, by any flying

[1] See To Forster, ?3 Aug.

[2] Probably San Martino, where CD watched a baptism one Sunday soon after his arrival: *Pictures*, p. 62.

[3] See *To* Forster, ?18 Oct; the Governor himself was not yet in residence.

[4] No reference to this in P. W. Clayden, *Rogers and his Contemporaries*, 1889, which prints the letter (II, 248–52), or elsewhere.

[5] In Ch. 13 the supposed Lady Blarney

and Miss Skeggs have heard of the misfortunes of the Vicar's family when riding the plough-horses to church: "at which account the ladies were greatly concerned; but being told the family received no hurt, they were extremely glad: but being informed that we were almost killed by the fright, they were very sorry; but hearing that we had a very good night, they were extremely glad again".

rumours that may shape their course this way, we entreat you to let us know, under your own hand, that you are in as good health, heart, and spirits, as we would have you. Believe me, dear friend, you need not desire to be in better condition than that.

We are living very quietly out here, close to the Seashore. I have taken a very commodious and spacious apartment in the Palazzo Peschiere for the next six months. Do you know that Palace? It is splendidly situated, in the midst of beautiful gardens, and on the side of a steep hill. The grounds being open to the Public for their recreation, I may say of it: altering three words of yours

> 'Tis in the heart of Genoa (he who comes,
> Should come on foot) and in a place of stir;
> Men on their daily pleasure, early and late,
> Thronging its very threshold.[1]

I wish you would come, and pluck an Orange from the Tree at Christmas Time. You should walk on the Terrace as early in the morning as you pleased; and there are brave breezy places in the neighbourhood to which you could transfer those stalwart Broadstairs walks of yours, and hear the Sea, too, roaring in your ears. I could shew you an old chest, in a disused room upstairs, where Ginevra's sister[2] may have hidden—alas she was an only child! But where she *might* have hidden had she ever lived and died, and left her Memory to you. Come and see it.

A little, patient, revolutionary officer;[3] exiled in England during many years; comes to and fro three times a week, to read and speak Italian with me. A poor little lame butterfly of a man, fluttering a little bit at one time, and hopping a little bit at another, and getting through life at some disadvantage or other, always. If I question him closely on some idiom which he is not in a condition to explain, he usually shakes his head dolefully, and begins to cry. But this is not what I meant to say just now, when I began to allude to him. He has initiated me in the Promessi Sposi[4]—the book which Violetta read, that night.[5] And what a clever book it is! I have not proceeded far into the story,[6] but I am quite charmed with it. The interviews between the Bridegroom and the Priest, on the

---

[1] From "Genoa" in Rogers's *Italy*, 1830, really describing the Piazza Doria; CD has altered "must come" to "should come", "business" to "pleasure" and "thy" to "its".

[2] Referring to the story in *Italy:* see *To Tagart*, 9 Aug and *fn*.

[3] Unidentified.

[4] *I Promessi Sposi*, by Alessandro Manzoni (1785–1873), published in Milan 1827, and in its finally revised version 1840–2; the first Italian historical novel, it had at once been acclaimed as a masterpiece. When visiting Genoa with his family for a month in 1827 Manzoni had been a star of literary society, and attended the Marchese di Negro's "improvisations". His fame had attracted visitors from America—Longfellow in 1828, George Ticknor in 1838, and Catherine Sedgwick in 1839. But the novel, though translated, had only recently begun to be known and appreciated in England.

[5] In the romantic prose tale of "Montorio", added in the 1839 edn of Rogers's *Italy*, Violetta reads *I Promessi Sposi* alone in a tower at night, as one "under the wand of an enchanter".

[6] He had read Chs 1–4 and part of Ch. 5.

Morning of the disappointment[1]—and between the Bridegroom and the Bride, and her Mother—and the description of poor Renzo's walk to the house of the learned doctor; with the fowls—and the scene between them[2]—and the whole idea of the character and story of Padre Christoforo are touched, I think, by a most delicate and charming hand. I have just left the good father in Don Rodrigo's boisterous Eating Hall; and am in no little anxiety, I assure you.[3]

You recollect the Church of the Cappuccini—l'Annunciata?[4] It is being entirely re-painted and regilded; and a marble portico is building, over the Great Entrance. That part of the interior—some two thirds—the redecoration of which is finished, is the most gorgeous work imaginable. Standing on a bright day before the Great Altar, and looking up into the three Domes, one is made giddy by the flash and glory of the place. The contrast between this Temple and its Ministers is the most singular and complete that the whole World could furnish, surely. But it is a land of contradictions, in everything, this Italy.

Do you know of *the Marriage Brokers*, among the Genevese? Sometimes they are old women—queer old women who are always presenting themselves mysteriously at unexpected times, like their sisterhood in the Arabian Nights.[5] But there are men brokers: shrewd, hard, thorough-paced men of business. They keep formal registers of marriageable young gentlemen and marriageable young ladies; and when they find a very good match on their books—or rather when one of these gentry does—he goes to the Young Lady's father, and says, "Signore, you have a daughter to dispose of?"—"I have," says the father. "And you will give her," says the broker, "fifty thousand francs?" "On fair terms," replies the father. "Signore," says the broker, "I know a young gentleman, with fifty thousand francs embarked in business, who will take fifty thousand francs, *and the clothes*."—"Clothes to what value?" asks the father. "Clothes to the value of five hundred francs," says the broker:—"And a gold watch. She must have a gold watch."—"His terms are too high," says the father. "My daughter hasn't got a gold watch."—"But Signore, she has a cast in her eye," says the broker; "And a cast in the eye is cheap at a gold watch."—"Say clothes worth two hundred and fifty francs," retorts the father, "and a silver bracelet. I admit the cast in the eye, and will throw in the bracelet: though its too much."—"We couldn't do it Signore," says the broker, "under a gold watch. The young gentleman might have done better in his last negociation; but he stood out for a watch. Besides, Signore, as a fair-dealing man, you must make some allowance for the ankles: which," says the broker, referring to his books, "are thick. If I did rigid justice to my employer, Signore, and hadn't a personal

---

[1] In Ch. 2, on the wedding-day of Lucia to Renzo, the silk-weaver, the ceremony is postponed by the timid village priest under threats from a mysterious emissary of the nobleman, Don Rodrigo.

[2] In Ch. 3, on the advice of Agnese, Lucia's mother, Renzo vainly consults the lawyer, carrying four capons as a gift.

[3] In Ch. 5, Fra Cristoforo, the Capuchin friar, visits Don Rodrigo's mansion, hoping to frustrate his designs on Lucia. CD must surely have finished the story, but he does not refer to it again, and there was no copy in the Gad's Hill library at his death.

[4] See *To* Maclise, 22 July 44 and *fn*.

[5] No reference to the marriage-brokers of Genoa has been found in contemporary guides or travel-books, and there are only scattered references in the *Arabian Nights*.

regard for you, I should require a hundred and fifty francs, at least, for each leg." On such terms the bargain is discussed and the balance struck; and the young people don't see each other, until it is all settled.

In short it's very like the system of our own dear Dowagers at home; except that the Broker boldly calls himself a Marriage Broker, and has his regular percentage on the fortune.—Which some of our own revered Merchants in such wares wouldn't object to, I dare say. I should like to start somebody I know at Fulham,[1] in business, on those terms.

My dear Mr. Rogers, if you ever get to the end of this letter, without leaping over the middle, forgive me. If you get to the end by a short cut, remember me not the less kindly; and however you get to the end, believe me that although it is all True, the truest part of the whole is, the assurance that I am always, with great regard, Your affectionate friend

CHARLES DICKENS

P.S. Kate and her sister, rebel, at not being mentioned by name. I am pretending to write long messages—which would take another sheet, at least.

To CHARLES KEMBLE, 3 SEPTEMBER 1844*

MS Historical Society of Pennsylvania. *Address:* Inghilterra | Charles Kemble Esquire | Garrick Club | King Street | Covent Garden | London | To be forwarded.

Albaro, Near Genoa. Tuesday Third September 1844.
My Dear Mr. Kemble.

You recollect our covenant and agreement; made and entered into, on the blank day of blank, in the Year of our Lord One Thousand Eight Hundred and Forty Four; whereby I covenanted and agreed to put you in possession of my plans as soon as I had formed them?

Here they are, then. I shall go away from here, for about Three Weeks, towards the middle of November—certainly not before, being now engaged upon a task: I shall go, then, to Milan, Turin, Mantua, Verona, Florence, Pisa, and Venice. I shall return here for Christmas and January; and burn coal fires and take long walks. Sometime in February, most likely, I shall start for Rome, and remain there, during the Carnival—then go to Naples—Herculaneum—Pompeii—and away to Mount Etna—returning to Rome for the Holy Week; coming back here afterwards; picking up bag and baggage; and going for six weeks or a couple of months to Paris.

My address is, Genoa. On the first of October, we move into the Palazzo Peschiere, within the walls. I have taken a charming apartment there, for six months. There are more beds in it than you could sleep in, if you changed once a week. There will be a welcome there, such as you have long been used to in many places and from many lips; but such, in its cordiality, as cannot be surpassed. I should be unfeignedly and heartily glad to see you. To have and to hold you, until you were tired of me.

[1] Lonsdale House, Fulham, was the home of Frances Lady Shelley: see Vol. II, p. 89*n*.

Mrs. Dickens says the same, and means it. We beg to be remembered to Mr. and Mrs. Sartoris;[1] and I shall look to hear from you at your pleasure and convenience.

Always Believe me | Faithfully Your friend

Charles Kemble Esquire.   CHARLES DICKENS

To MRS CHARLES DICKENS, 7 SEPTEMBER 1844

MS British Museum. *Address:* A Madame | Madame Charles Dickens | Poste Restante | Genes.

Hotel Du Paradis Marseilles[2] | September Seventh 1844

My dearest Kate. We arrived here this morning, about 9; after a very pleasant, though rather rough, passage.[3] I was perfectly well, and slept in a cool little cabin on deck. The Masters and I kept it up pretty gaily—dined luxuriously—and breakfasted on the same model. A person came from the hotel to the boat, as soon as we entered the Harbor, to announce that Fred[4] had arrived at 5 o'Clock and was then in bed. By the time of my arrival here, he was just sitting down to breakfast. He does not appear to be at all tired.

He has a Moustache. I have not touched on that delicate subject yet, as I desire it to be seen in the Villa di Bagnerello. But I feel (as the Stage Villains say) that Either he or I must fall. Earth will not hold us both.

I purpose leaving here for Toulon (Roche implores me to see it, on his bended knees) by coach tomorrow night at 9 o'Clock.[5] This will bring us home, most likely in the course of Friday—it may be, Thursday, but I *think* not. Do not alter any of the arrangements in the Whitest of Willys[6] on our account; beyond having something to eat, in the house, in case we should want it.

The Colonel forgot to leave the key[7] of the press in the drawing room, with Bennett.[8] He has given it to me; and I have it safe.

Fred sends his best love to you and Georgy and the darlings. In which I join. Likewise his best regards to Fletcher. In which I also unite.[9]

[   ]

[CHARLES DICKENS]

---

[1] Adelaide Sartoris (?1814–79; *DNB*), younger daughter of Charles Kemble, and her husband Edward John Sartoris: see Vol. II, p. 431*n*.

[2] The hotel where they had stayed in July: see *To* Forster, ?14 July.

[3] In *Pictures*, p. 75, he says the steamer came from Genoa in "a delicious run of eighteen hours".

[4] CD went to meet him and bring him back to spend a fortnight's holiday in Genoa (F, IV, iv, 342).

[5] Some account of the return journey, not via Toulon but by boat to Nice and on by the Corniche road, is in *Pictures*, pp.

75–83: they appear to have left Marseilles at 8 p.m. the same day on a smaller and slower boat than the one from Genoa, and he and Fred are described as sleeping in "a crowded, but cool little cabin". See also next.

[6] i.e. villas; either (facetiously) the "pink jail", or some friend's villa to which Catherine had been invited on the Thursday —possibly Charles Gibbs's at Quinto.

[7] Of the Peschiere: see *To* D'Orsay, 7 Aug.

[8] Evidently the Colonel's servant.

[9] Letter cut off here; clearly only lacks ending and signature.

To JOHN FORSTER, [?10 SEPTEMBER 1844]

Extract in F, IV, iv, 342. *Date:* Forster gives 9 Sep, but clearly the night of 8 Sep had been spent at Nice: see *fn.*

We lay last night[1] at the first halting-place[2] on this journey, in an inn which is not entitled, as it ought to be, The house of call for fleas and vermin in general, but is entitled The grand hotel of the Post! I hardly know what to compare it to. It seemed something like a house in Somers-town originally built for a wine-vaults and never finished, but grown very old. There was nothing to eat in it and nothing to drink. They had lost the teapot; and when they found it, they couldn't make out what had become of the lid, which, turning up at last and being fixed on to the teapot, couldn't be got off again for the pouring in of more water. Fleas of elephantine dimensions were gambolling boldly in the dirty beds; and the mosquitoes!—But here let me draw a curtain (as I would have done if there had been any). We had scarcely any sleep, and rose up with hands and arms hardly human.[3]

To JOHN FORSTER, [?15–16 SEPTEMBER 1844]

Extracts in F, IV, iv, 342–3, 341, 334. *Date:* third extract 16 Sep according to Forster; first extract clearly part of same letter, and possibly written on previous day; second extract more likely to belong to this letter than to 23 Sep, as reports of O'Connell would certainly have reached CD.

The morning after their arrival at Albaro, Fred very nearly drowned in the bay. He swam out into too strong a current, and was only narrowly saved by the accident of a fishing-boat preparing to leave harbour at the time. It was a world of horror and anguish, crowded into four or five minutes of dreadful agitation; and, to complete the terror of it, Georgy, Charlotte[4], and the children were on a rock in full view of it all, crying, as you may suppose, like mad creatures.[5]

I have no faith in O'Connell taking the great position he might upon this:

---

[1] Monday, 9 Sep; it is clear from *Pictures* that Sunday night was spent at Nice. The account there, doubtless taken from this letter, tells how the Genoa boat was quarantined at Nice owing to its cargo of wool; Roche, however, "telegraphed somebody", and a festive lunch was brought to the ship and "the whole party . . . were made merry", especially a Capuchin Friar (pp. 76–9). At 4 p.m. they were released in time to join a religious procession. They started for Genoa in a vettura next afternoon (9 Sep), a journey of three days on the Corniche road, described in some detail (pp. 81–3); but the only town named is San Remo, "a most extraordinary place, built on gloomy open arches" with "pretty terrace gardens"—the second or third night was perhaps spent there.

[2] Possibly Oneglia, where Murray men-

tions an inn "La Posta", to which "the postillions try to take you"; or Albenga, with a single unnamed inn, "kept by an uncivil and extortionate landlord, and affording very indifferent accommodation".

[3] Some of the details are recalled in CD's reverie on inns in "The Holly Tree" (*Household Words*, Christmas No., 1855; collected in *Christmas Stories*), where "the mosquitoes make a raisin pudding of your face" and the tea is boiled "in a pocket-handkerchief dumpling, for want of a teapot".

[4] The nurse (as Forster says).

[5] Mamie, in *CD by his Eldest Daughter*, 1885, p. 67, says: "the youngest little girl thought that it was her father who was drowning, and her shrieks of despair and fear were something terrible".

being beleaguered by vanity always. Denman delights me.[1] I am glad to think I have always liked him so well. I am sure that whenever he makes a mistake, it *is* a mistake; and that no man lives who has a grander and nobler scorn of every mean and dastard action. I would to Heaven it were decorous to pay him some public tribute of respect. . . . O'Connell's speeches are the old thing: fretty, boastful, frothy, waspish at the voices in the crowd, and all that: but with no true greatness. . . . What a relief to turn to that noble letter of Carlyle's,[2] which I think above all praise. My love to him.

I wish you could see me without my knowing it, walking about alone here. I am now as bold as a lion in the streets. The audacity with which one begins to speak when there is no help for it, is quite astonishing.

To JOHN FORSTER, [?23 SEPTEMBER 1844]

Extract in F, IV, v, 344; mention in F, IV, v, 348. *Date:* Forster mentions a "first letter" from the Peschiere (about the commissions) and puts the move in "the last week of September"; probably 23 Sep, the Monday of the dream described in CD's "second letter" dated 30 Sep by Forster. Account of storm during the move and first impression clearly from same letter.

They moved from Albaro into Genoa, with great guns blowing, *the lightning incessant, and the rain driving down in a dense thick cloud. But the worst of the storm was over when they reached the Peschiere. As they passed into it along the stately old terraces, flanked on either side with antique sculptured figures, all the seven fountains were playing in its gardens, and the sun was shining brightly on its groves of camelias and orange-trees.*

Sending commissions in regard to his wife's family.[3]

To T. C. CURRY, 30 SEPTEMBER 1844

MS Berg Collection.

Peschiere | Monday Thirtieth September | 1844

My Dear Sir

I send you the Chuzzlewit.

My Brother Frederick will be happy to avail himself of your hospitality,

[1] Daniel O'Connell had been tried for sedition early in 1844 and judgment given on 30 May; he was fined £2000 and imprisoned for a year, but under easy conditions. On appeal to the House of Lords, four of the five Law Lords were evenly divided by party; Denman had the casting voice, and used it to reverse the decision, basing his verdict on the fact that the jury had been improperly selected. CD would be "delighted" by his emphasis on the principle of trial by jury. O'Connell was released on 4 Sep and returned to Ireland where he made triumphal speeches in

Dublin on 8 Sep, abusing everyone concerned with the trial and calling for the impeachment of judges and ministers (*The Times*, 12 Sep 44).

[2] Forster adds "in which a timely testimony had been borne to the truthfulness and honour of Mazzini"; this was the letter published in *The Times* of 19 June 44, of which CD had doubtless been reminded by Mazzini's article in the Sep issue of the *Westminster Review* (see *To* Beard, 28 June 44, *fn*) which quoted the letter.

[3] See *To* Forster, ?30 Sep: "the main subject of my last letter".

whenever you like between this and Friday. I should be truly glad to do so also, but I find that I cannot very well leave home for that purpose just now.[1] I shall soon be alone here, with my own household; and then I hope we shall see each other often.

Believe me | Faithfully Yours

Thomas C. Curry Esquire   CHARLES DICKENS

To JOHN FORSTER, [?30 SEPTEMBER 1844]

Extracts in F, IV, v, 344–5, 348–9; VI, vii, 552. *Date:* first extract almost certainly his second letter from the Peschiere; second extract specified as such and dated 30 Sep by Forster; third extract "September from the Peschiere" according to Forster and therefore either 23 or 30 Sep.

Describing the rooms in the Peschiere:[2] *in the centre was the grand sala, fifty feet high,*[3] *of an area larger than* the dining-room of the Academy, *and painted, walls and ceiling, with frescoes three hundred years old,* as fresh as if the colours had been laid on yesterday. *On the same floor were a drawing-room, and a dining-room,* into which we might put your large room—I wish we could!—away in one corner, and dine without knowing it. *Out of these opened three other chambers that were turned into sleeping-rooms and nurseries. Adjoining the sala, right and left, were the two best bed-rooms;* in size and shape like those at Windsor-castle but greatly higher; *both having altars, a range of three windows with stone balconies, floors tesselated in patterns of black and white stone, and walls painted every inch: on the left, nymphs pursued by satyrs* as large as life and as wicked; *on the right,* Phaeton larger than life, with horses bigger than Meux and Co.'s, tumbling headlong down into the best bed. *The right-hand room he occupied with his wife, and of the left took possession as a study; writing behind a big screen he had lugged into it, and placed by one of the windows, from which he could see over the city, as he wrote, as far as the lighthouse in its harbour. Distant little over a mile as the crow flew, flashing five times in four minutes, and on dark nights, as if by magic, illuminating brightly the whole palace-front every time it shone, this lighthouse was one of the wonders of Genoa.*

[1] The Rev. Edward Tagart with his wife visited them on their way from Milan where they had been attending a scientific congress (F, IV, iv, 341) which ended 27 Sep (*Athenæum*, 19 Oct 44), and stayed some days; *To* Tagart, 28 Jan 47 (N, II, 9), recalls "those bright mornings at the Peschiere".

[2] Forster introduces this passage with "I soon became familiar with the several rooms" of the Peschiere, which suggests second letter, 30 Sep rather than 6 Oct, the date he attaches to the extract in his footnote (see *fn* below), and it seems very unlikely that CD would defer the main description of the rooms for a fortnight.

The account in *Pictures*, pp. 72–4, mentions "the wild fancies on the walls and ceilings, as bright in their fresh colouring as if they had been painted yesterday" and the "corridors and bed-chambers above, which we never use and rarely visit". "A score of mysterious old bedrooms" is also referred to in the description of the "old Italian palace" where CD once lived, in "The Haunted House" (*All the Year Round*, Christmas No., 1859; collected in *Christmas Stories*).

[3] This seems to be confirmed by the photograph of the sala in L. C. Staples, "Pictures from Genoa", D, XLV (1950), 88.

Let me tell you of a curious dream I had, last Monday night; and of the fragments of reality I can collect, which helped to make it up. I have had a return of rheumatism in my back, and knotted round my waist like a girdle of pain; and had laid awake nearly all that night under the infliction, when I fell asleep and dreamed this dream. Observe that throughout I was as real, animated, and full of passion as Macready (God bless him!) in the last scene of *Macbeth*. In an indistinct place, which was quite sublime in its indistinctness, I was visited by a Spirit. I could not make out the face, nor do I recollect that I desired to do so. It wore a blue drapery, as the Madonna might in a picture by Raphael; and bore no resemblance to any one I have known except in stature. I think (but I am not sure) that I recognized the voice. Anyway, I knew it was poor Mary's spirit. I was not at all afraid, but in a great delight, so that I wept very much, and stretching out my arms to it called it "Dear." At this, I thought it recoiled; and I felt immediately, that not being of my gross nature, I ought not to have addressed it so familiarly. "Forgive me!" I said. "We poor living creatures are only able to express ourselves by looks and words. I have used the word most natural to *our* affections; and you know my heart." It was so full of compassion and sorrow for me—which I knew spiritually, for, as I have said, I didn't perceive its emotions by its face—that it cut me to the heart; and I said, sobbing, "Oh! give me some token that you have really visited me!" "Form a wish," it said. I thought, reasoning with myself: "If I form a selfish wish, it will vanish." So I hastily discarded such hopes and anxieties of my own as came into my mind, and said, "Mrs. Hogarth is surrounded with great distresses"— observe, I never thought of saying "your mother" as to a mortal creature—"will you extricate her?" "Yes." "And her extrication is to be a certainty to me, that this has really happened?" "Yes." "But answer me one other question!" I said, in an agony of entreaty lest it should leave me. "What is the True religion?" As it paused a moment without replying, I said—Good God, in such an agony of haste, lest it should go away!—"You think, as I do, that the Form of religion does not so greatly matter, if we try to do good?—or," I said, observing that it still hesitated, and was moved with the greatest compassion for me, "perhaps the Roman Catholic is the best? perhaps it makes one think of God oftener, and believe in him more steadily?" "For *you*," said the Spirit, full of such heavenly tenderness for me, that I felt as if my heart would break; "for *you*, it is the best!" Then I awoke, with the tears running down my face, and myself in exactly the condition of the dream. It was just dawn. I called up Kate, and repeated it three or four times over, that I might not unconsciously make it plainer or stronger afterwards. It was exactly this. Free from all hurry, nonsense, or confusion, whatever. Now, the strings I can gather up, leading to this, were three. The first you know, from the main subject of my last letter. The second was, that there is a great altar in our bedroom, at which some family who once inhabited this palace had mass performed in old time: and I had observed within myself, before going to bed, that there was a mark in the wall, above the sanctuary, where a religious picture used to be; and I had wondered within myself what the subject might have been, *and what the face was like*. Thirdly, I had been listening to the convent bells (which ring at intervals in the night), and so had thought, no doubt, of Roman Catholic services. And yet, for all this, put the case of that wish being fulfilled by any agency in which I had no hand; and I wonder whether I should regard it as a dream, or an actual Vision![1]

There has arrived a characteristic letter for Kate from my father. He dates it Manchester, and says he has reason to believe that he will be in town with the pheasants, on or about the first of October. He has been with Fanny in the Isle of Man[2] for nearly two months: finding there, as he goes on to observe, troops of friends, and every description of continental luxury at a cheap rate.

To JOHN FORSTER, [?6 OCTOBER 1844]

Extracts in F, IV, v, 344*n*; IV, iv, 341–2 (*aa* only F, 1872–4, II, v, 111); IV, v, 345–6. *Date:* first extract 6 Oct according to Forster; second extract almost certainly same letter, as the nearest in date to Robertson's visit (see *fn*); third extract "only two days" before next, which is more likely to be 8 Oct than 7 Oct (see *hn*).

Describing the drawing-room and dining-room: Very vast you will say, and very dreary; but it is not so really. The paintings are so fresh, and the proportions so agreeable to the eye, that the effect is not only cheerful but snug. . . . We are a little incommoded by applications from strangers to go over the interior. The paintings were designed by Michael Angelo, and have a great reputation . . . Certain of these frescoes were reported officially to the Fine Arts Commissioners by Wilson[3] as the best in Italy[4] . . . I allowed a party of priests to be shown the great hall yesterday . . . It is in perfect repair, and the doors almost shut—which is quite a miraculous circumstance. I wish you could see it, my dear F. Gracious

---

[1] This was the first time CD had dreamed of Mary since Feb 38 (see Vol. I, p. 366*n*, Vol. III, pp. 483–4). In noting the fact in a long letter of 2 Feb 51 to Dr Stone who had submitted a paper, "Dreams", for *Household Words*, CD said, "it was All Souls' Night, and people were going about with Bells, calling on the Inhabitants to pray for the dead" (N, II, 269); in the paper as published, 8 Mar 51 (*Household Words*, II, 567), this was also referred to as "a very remarkable dream . . . on All Souls' Night". When CD again recalled it in "The Holly Tree Inn" (*Household Words*, Christmas No., 1855; collected in *Christmas Stories*) he placed it on "All Souls' Eve". But it is very unlikely that Forster's dating is incorrect: the letter refers to "last Monday night", and neither All Souls' Eve nor All Souls' Night fell on a Monday in 1844.

[2] They stayed at Kirkconchan (near Douglas), a "beautiful and picturesque" village, with a fine view: "the Castles and Villas which have been built around the Bay within the last few years tend much to increase the general effect" (John Dickens

to Chapman & Hall, 28 June 44: see *To Chapman*, 3 June 44, *fn*).

[3] CD may be referring to Charles Heath Wilson (1809–82; *DNB*), Director and Secretary of the School of Art at Somerset House until 1848; or to his father Andrew Wilson (1780–1848; *DNB*), landscape painter, who was in Italy from 1826 and at this date was in Genoa.

[4] Charles Heath Wilson submitted evidence on fresco-painting to the Commissioners on the Fine Arts which was published in their Report of 1842; this evidence included recent letters from his father, stressing the good condition of the frescoes in Genoa. But for the Second Report of 1843 Charles Wilson was sent to the continent to collect information; he did not include any Genoa frescoes in his examples of work by masters of the art, and concluded by dismissing them as having "no claim" to be called frescoes. The Peschiere is not mentioned in either Report. CD had evidently been misled by what he heard in Genoa; he cannot have read the Second Report.

Heavens! if you could only *come back* with me, wouldn't I soon flash on your astonished sight.

He had a visit from Lord Robertson,[1] *who had received letters about the Burns Festival*[2] *giving an* awful *narrative of Wilson's*[3] *speech and of the whole business.*[4] There was one man who spoke a quarter of an hour or so, to the toast of the navy; and could say nothing more than "the—British—navy—always appreciates—" which remarkable sentiment he repeated over and over again for that space of time; and then sat down.[5] Robertson told me also that Wilson's allusion to, or I should rather say expatiation upon, the "vices" of Burns, excited but one sentiment *of indignation and disgust:* and added, very sensibly, "By God!—I want to know *what Burns did*! I never heard of his doing anything that need be strange or unaccountable to the Professor's mind. *I think he must have mistaken the name, and fancied it a dinner to the sons of Burke"*—meaning of course the murderer.* In short he fully confirmed Jerrold in all respects.[6] *He had been reading the* Story of a Feather. Gauntwolf's sickness and the career of that snuffbox, masterly.[7] I have been deep in Voyages and

---

[1] Patrick Robertson, Lord Robertson (1794–1855; *DNB*): see Vol. II, p. 308. His *Leaves from a Journal*, 1845, shows that he was in the Apennines on 2 Oct and in Domo D'Ossola on 5 Oct; 3 or 4 Oct is therefore the likeliest date for his visit to CD, referred to in his Preface as "another friend of literary celebrity at Genoa". CD recalls their day together, including a visit to the Puppets, in *To* Robertson, 28 Apr 45 and 17 Jan 46.

[2] Held on 6 Aug 44 near Ayr; the festival was suggested by the presence in Scotland of the three surviving sons of Burns, Colonel Burns having returned from India after nearly 30 years. The Earl of Eglintoun was Chairman and Professor Wilson croupier. Many English writers were invited but declined; apologies were read from Moore, Wordsworth, Lytton, Carlyle, and Talfourd among others (*Athenæum*, 10 Aug 44), and "not a single Englishman of any note was present, except Mr. Douglas Jerrold and Mr. S. C. Hall, who attended on professional business for the press" (Charles Mackay, *Forty Years' Recollections*, I, 251). Mackay says that CD was invited "not for an English but for a Scottish reason"—because Catherine Dickens was George Thomson's granddaughter (see Vol. I, p. 134*n*).

[3] John Wilson (1785–1854; *DNB*), "Christopher North" of *Blackwood's*: see Vol. II, p. 304*n*.

[4] Wilson's speech to welcome the sons of Burns was very long (pp. 212–29 in *Works*, 1857, Vol. VII), and over half of it was devoted to moral judgments on Burns's character. Mackay, on reading Forster's *Life*, found Robertson's account to CD unfair to Wilson: his error had been to write a speech "too like a literary essay", which the impatient and indignant crowd would not allow him to finish, so that his vindication of the poet was unheard (C. Mackay, *op. cit.*, pp. 260–1).

[5] Not referred to in press accounts.

[6] In *Punch*, 17 Aug 44, Jerrold wrote an ironical account of the festival, mocking at the meanness of the organizers (a fifteen-shilling dinner in a pavilion was provided for a small proportion of the company), and at Wilson's speech, which "had one fault—it was too short;—'brief as the lightning in the collied night;' and the hearers could not repress the expression of their disappointment at this: for they now and then scraped the floor with their feet, and rattled their knives and forks"; his main and justified conclusion was: "The Professor did not, before the sons of BURNS, exhume their father to read a lecture on his moral diseases; certainly not".

[7] In the conclusion added to Jerrold's *Story of a Feather* for the publication in book form, of which he had given CD a copy: see *To* Jerrold, ?early May 44 and *fn*.

Travels,[1] and in De Foe.[2] Tennyson I have also been reading, again and again. What a great creature he is! . . . What about the *Goldsmith*?[3] Apropos, I am all eagerness to write a story about the length of that most delightful of all stories,[4] the *Vicar of Wakefield*.[5]

About the Christmas Book: Never did I stagger so upon a threshold before. I seem as if I had plucked myself out of my proper soil when I left Devonshire-terrace; and could take root no more until I return to it. . . . Did I tell you how many fountains[6] we have here? No matter. If they played nectar, they wouldn't please me half so well as the West Middlesex water-works at Devonshire-terrace. *Sitting down on the previous morning resolute for work,[7] though against the grain, his hand being out and everything inviting to idleness, such a peal of chimes[8] arose from the city as he found to be* maddening. *All Genoa lay beneath him, and up from it, with some sudden set of the wind, came in one fell sound the clang and clash of all its steeples, pouring into his ears again and again, in a tuneless, grating, discordant, jerking, hideous vibration that made his ideas* spin round and round till they lost themselves in a whirl of vexation and giddiness, and dropped down dead.[9]

To JOHN FORSTER, [?8 OCTOBER 1844]

Text from F, IV, v, 346. *Date:* "Only two days later" than last, according to Forster, and almost certainly same day as next, in which "it's a great thing to have my title".

A letter in which not a syllable was written but "We have heard THE CHIMES at midnight, Master Shallow!"[10]

To JOHN FORSTER, [8 OCTOBER 1844]

Extract in F, IV, v, 346. *Date:* 8 Oct according to Forster.

He so missed his long night-walks before beginning that he seemed dumbfounded

[1] *Voyages and Travels from the Discovery of America to the Nineteenth Century*, ed. Dr Mavor, 1820, was in the Gad's Hill library at CD's death.

[2] Presumably single vols which he had long possessed: the inventory shows that vols 4–12 of the 1831 edn with Scott's Prefaces (bought at the Hill sale in 1841: see Vol. II, p. 229*n*) were left at Devonshire Terrace (see Appx C, p. 718). The 20-vol. edn of 1840–1 was in the Gad's Hill library at his death.

[3] Forster had first begun work on the *Life and Times of Oliver Goldsmith* in 1830, and returned to it about 1840; it was published in 1848 with dedicatory sonnet to CD.

[4] This wish was not fulfilled. The *Vicar of Wakefield* is longer than any of the Christmas Books; but CD felt this length would have been right for the *Battle of Life* (see *To* Forster, 26 Sep 46).

[5] In later edns this reads "his most delightful of all stories".

[6] Described in *Pictures*, p. 72.

[7] "The subject for his new Christmas story he had chosen, but he had not found a title for it, or the machinery to work it with" (F, IV. v, 346).

[8] This suggests a festa-day, as in *Pictures*, p. 59, with the description, "in a horrible, irregular, jerking, dingle, dingle, dingle: with a sudden stop at every fifteenth dingle or so, which is maddening".

[9] Forster says "this was his description to me next day, and his excuse for having failed in a promise to send me his title" (F, *ibid*).

[10] *2 Henry IV*, III, i, 231.

without them. I can't help thinking of the boy in the school-class whose button was cut off by Walter Scott and his friends.[1] Put me down on Waterloo-bridge at eight o'clock in the evening, with leave to roam about as long as I like, and I would come home, as you know, panting to go on. I am sadly strange as it is, and can't settle. You will have lots of hasty notes from me while I am at work: but you know your man; and whatever strikes me, I shall let off upon you as if I were in Devonshire-terrace. It's a great thing to have my title, and see my way how to work the bells. Let them clash upon me now from all the churches and convents in Genoa, I see nothing but the old London belfry[2] I have set them in. In my mind's eye, Horatio. I like more and more my notion of making, in this little book, a great blow for the poor. Something powerful, I think I can do, but I want to be tender too, and cheerful; as like the *Carol* in that respect as may be, and as unlike it as such a thing can be. The duration of the action will resemble it a little, but I trust to the novelty of the machinery to carry that off; and if my design be anything at all, it has a grip upon the very throat of the time.

To T. YEATS BROWN,[3] [?OCTOBER 1844]

Mention in *To* Forster, ?18 Oct. *Date:* shortly after the Governor's arrival on 5 Oct (see *To* Forster, 18 Oct and *fns*).

Excusing himself from the Governor's levee.

To JOHN FORSTER, [?MID-OCTOBER 1844]

Extract in F, IV, v, 350. *Date:* one of the "frequent letters while he was fairly in his work".

With my steam very much up, I find it a great trial to be so far off from you, and consequently to have no one (always excepting Kate and Georgy) to whom to expatiate on my day's work. And I want a crowded street to plunge into at night. And I want to be "on the spot" as it were. But apart from such things, he life I lead is favourable to work.

[1] The story was related by Scott to Samuel Rogers; see J. G. Lockhart, *Memoirs of the Life of Sir Walter Scott, Bart*, Edinburgh, 1837–8, I, 94.

[2] Described at the opening of *The Chimes* (with heavy revision in MS; Forster Collection, V & A) as an obviously ancient belfry "high up in the steeple of an old church", its bells "baptized centuries ago"; but the illustrations by Doyle and Stanfield depict the neo-Gothic octagonal tower of the new St Dunstan's-in-the-West, Fleet St, completed by John Shaw in 1833. The old church (well known for its famous clock with the giants) which it replaced had no steeple or tower; clearly the description in the text is mainly imaginary, and the illustration was presumably accepted by CD because of the new church's general style and its situation in a street suitable for a ticket-porter, though not for the neighbouring mansion of Mr Filer.

[3] The British consul: see *To* Forster, ?17 Nov 44, *fn*.

To JOHN FORSTER, [?MID-OCTOBER 1844]

Extract in F, IV, v, 350. *Date:* "his next letter" after preceding one according to Forster; "fierce to finish" does not necessarily suggest that he was close to the end, but merely foreseeing it.

I am in regular, ferocious excitement with the *Chimes*; get up at seven; have a cold bath before breakfast; and blaze away, wrathful and red-hot, until three o'clock or so: when I usually knock off (unless it rains) for the day. . . . I am fierce to finish in a spirit bearing some affinity to those of truth and mercy, and to shame the cruel and the canting. I have not forgotten my catechism. "Yes verily, and with God's help, so I will!"[1]

To JOHN FORSTER, [?13–14 OCTOBER 1844]

Extracts in F, IV, v, 350, 354–5. *Date:* first extract "in the middle of October" according to Forster, and "in reply to my mention of what had most attracted myself" in the *Life of Dr. Arnold*—reviewed by Forster in *Examiner*, 12 Oct; second extract not later than Mon 14 Oct—*To* Macready, that day, refers to CD's visit to London, and he had received Forster's reply by the beginning of Nov (see *To* Forster, ?1–2 Nov).

I respect and reverence his memory, beyond all expression. I must have that book.[2] Every sentence that you quote from it is the text-book of my faith.[3]

He planned to come to London.[4] If I come, I shall put up at Cuttris's,[5] that I may be close to you. Don't say to anybody, except our immediate friends, that I am coming. Then I shall not be bothered. If I should preserve my present fierce writing humour, in any pass I may run to Venice, Bologna, and Florence, before I turn my face towards Lincoln's-inn-fields; and come to England by Milan and Turin. But this of course depends in a great measure on your reply.

[1] The answer to the fourth question in the Catechism, "Dost thou not think that thou art bound to believe, and to do, as they have promised for thee?"

[2] In introducing this extract, Forster says that CD's dream of Mary Hogarth (see *To* Forster, 30 Sep 44) was evidence of his troubled reflections on religion, and that, "In such disturbing fancies during the next year or two . . . the book which helped him most" was Arthur Stanley's *Life of Dr Arnold* (published June 44, 3rd edn by Sep). There was no copy in the Gad's Hill library at CD's death.

[3] Forster's long review in the *Examiner* (see *hn*) shows him deeply moved (he laid down the book "with a feeling of reverence" and "desire however humbly to imitate him"), and especially struck by Arnold's sincerity, independence, and "freedom from party spirit". Writing to Bulwer Lytton, 15 Mar 45, Forster was still "affected . . . to a painful degree", and grieved to think that Arnold "seemed to have rejected the good there is in Dickens' books" (MS Lytton Papers).

[4] Forster was surprised, but felt that "all remonstrance would be idle"; there were practical advantages, in that CD could then see his own final proofs and illustrations, and also satisfy "the stronger and more eager wish . . . to have a vivider sense than letters could give him of the effect of what he had been doing" (F, IV, v, 354).

[5] George Cuttriss's Piazza Coffee House and Hotel in Covent Garden.

To W. C. MACREADY, 14 OCTOBER 1844

MS Morgan Library.

Palazzo Peschiere. Genoa.
Fourteenth October 1844.

My Very Dear Macready.

My whole heart is with you *at home*. I have not yet felt so far off, as I do now—when I think of you there[1]—and cannot fold you in my arms. This is only a shake of the hand. I couldn't *say* much to you, if I were one to greet you. Nor can I write much, when I think of you, safe and sound, and happy, after all your wanderings.

My dear fellow, God bless you twenty thousand times. [All][2] happiness and joy be with you! I hope to see you soon. If I should be so unfortunate, as to miss you in London, I will fall upon you, with a swoop of Love, in Paris.[3] Kate says all kind things in the Language; and means more than are in the Dictionary-Capacity of all the descendants of all the Stone Masons that worked at Babel. Again and again and again, my own true friend, God bless you!

Ever yours affectionately
CHARLES DICKENS

To T. C. CURRY, 17 OCTOBER 1844*

MS New York University Library.

Peschiere | Thursday Evening | October Seventeenth | 1844.

My Dear Sir

I earnestly congratulate you on the happy termination of your anxieties in behalf of Mrs. Curry. May your new child be a new comfort and blessing to you both!

I have to thank you for something that stands on my desk at this moment, and will hold its place there (I hope) for many years.[4] You could have given me nothing so likely to be my very constant companion. And I shall never look at it, I am sure, in my working hours, without associating it with the grateful recollection of your most considerate kindness and hearty good will.

Believe me always | Faithfully Yours
CHARLES DICKENS

Thomas C. Curry Esquire

[1] Macready had originally intended to leave America in Sep (*Examiner*, 13 July 44), but in fact sailed from Boston on 16 Oct and was in London by 6 Nov (*Diaries*, II, 276).

[2] A tear has removed about three letters; "All" seems the most likely word, but "May" is possible.

[3] John Mitchell of the St James's Theatre, an impresario well known in London and Paris, had proposed that Macready's American tour should be followed by a season in Paris, with a company including

Helen Faucit as leading lady; T. J. Serle, acting on Macready's behalf, concluded the arrangements in May 44 (Alan Downer, *The Eminent Tragedian*, 1966, p. 265), and CD would have known of the project before his departure from London. The date of the Paris opening had not yet been fixed—the first report in *Galignani's Messenger* (9 Sep 44) said that Mitchell had just visited Paris and arranged for the season to commence in Dec.

[4] There is no other record of Curry's gift.

To JOHN FORSTER, [18 OCTOBER 1844]

Extract in F, IV, v, 350–3. *Date:* 18 Oct according to Forster; accompanied the MS of the First Quarter of *The Chimes*.

I send you to-day by mail, the first and longest of the four divisions. This is great for the first week,[1] which is usually up-hill. I have kept a copy in shorthand in case of accidents. I hope to send you a parcel every Monday until the whole is done. I do not wish to influence you, but it has a great hold upon me, and has affected me, in the doing, in divers strong ways, deeply, forcibly. To give you better means of judgment I will sketch for you the general idea, but pray don't read it until you have read this first part of the MS.

The general notion is this. That what happens to poor Trotty in the first part, and what will happen to him in the second (when he takes the letter to a punctual and a great man of business,[2] who is balancing his books and making up his accounts, and complacently expatiating on the necessity of clearing off every liability and obligation, and turning over a new leaf and starting fresh with the new year), so dispirits him, who can't do this, that he comes to the conclusion that his class and order have no business with a new year, and really are "intruding." And though he will pluck up for an hour or so, at the christening (I think) of a neighbour's child,[3] that evening: still, when he goes home, Mr. Filer's precepts will come into his mind, and he will say to himself, "we are a long way past the proper average of children, and it has no business to be born:" and will be wretched again. And going home, and sitting there alone, he will take that newspaper out of his pocket, and reading of the crimes and offences of the poor, especially of those whom Alderman Cute is going to put down, will be quite confirmed in his misgiving that they are bad; irredeemably bad.[4] In this state of mind, he will fancy that the Chimes are calling to him; and saying to himself "God help me. Let me go up to 'em. I feel as if I were going to die in despair—of a broken heart; let me die among the bells that have been a comfort to me!"—will grope his way up into the tower; and fall down in a kind of swoon among them.[5] Then the third quarter, or in other words the beginning of the second half of the book, will open with the Goblin part of the thing: the bells ringing, and innumerable spirits (the sound or vibration of them) flitting and tearing in and out of the church-steeple, and bearing all sorts of missions and commissions and reminders and reproaches, and comfortable recollections and

---

[1] The First Quarter was probably the work of 9 Oct–16 Oct; the Second Quarter, partly planned, may have been begun, but not more than $4\frac{1}{2}$ MS pages can have been written as Will Fern had not been introduced (see next *fn*).

[2] Sir Joseph Bowley, MP, the "Poor Man's Friend," who is introduced early in the Second Quarter. But CD had evidently not yet thought of Will Fern, who is in fact the subject of the letter carried by Trotty (or Toby) Veck.

[3] Trotty's meeting with Will Fern and

the child Lilian takes the place of the christening incident.

[4] The words from "the crimes" were adopted by Forster in his review of *The Chimes* in the *Edinburgh Review* (see *To* Forster, ?3–4 Nov 44), along with several other passages noted below, and single words or phrases (not in the text of the book) such as "mudworms".

[5] The conclusion of the Second Quarter is much as CD anticipated, though without Trotty's actual words.

what not, to all sorts of people and places. Some bearing scourges; and others flowers, and birds, and music; and others pleasant faces in mirrors, and others ugly ones: the bells haunting people in the night (especially the last of the old year) according to their deeds. And the bells themselves, who have a goblin likeness to humanity in the midst of their proper shapes, and who shine in a light of their own, will say (the Great Bell being the chief spokesman)[1] Who is he that being of the poor doubts the right of poor men to the inheritance which Time reserves for them, and echoes an unmeaning cry against his fellows? Toby, all aghast, will tell him it is he, and why it is.[2] Then the spirits of the bells will bear him through the air to various scenes, charged with this trust: That they show him how the poor and wretched, at the worst—yes, even in the crimes that aldermen put down, and he has thought so horrible—have some deformed and hunchbacked goodness clinging to them; and how they have their right and share in Time.[3] Following out the history of Meg the Bells will show her, that marriage broken off and all friends dead, with an infant child; reduced so low, and made so miserable, as to be brought at last to wander out at night. And in Toby's sight, her father's, she will resolve to drown herself and the child together. But before she goes down to the water, Toby will see how she covers it with a part of her own wretched dress, and adjusts its rags so as to make it pretty in its sleep, and hangs over it, and smooths its little limbs, and loves it with the dearest love that God ever gave to mortal creatures;[4] and when she runs down to the water, Toby will cry "Oh spare her! Chimes, have mercy on her! Stop her!"—and the bells will say, "Why stop her? She is bad at heart—let the bad die." And Toby on his knees will beg and pray for mercy: and in the end the bells will stop her, by their voices, just in time. Toby will see, too, what great things the punctual man has left undone on the close of the old year, and what accounts he has left unsettled: punctual as he is. And he will see a great many things about Richard, once so near being his son-in-law, and about a great many people. And the moral of it all will be, that he has his port on in the new year no less than any other man, and that the poor require a deal of beating out of shape before their human shape is gone; that even in their frantic wickedness there may be good in their hearts triumphantly asserting itself, though all the aldermen alive say "No," as he has learnt from the agony of his own child; and that the truth is Trustfulness in them, not doubt, nor putting down, nor filing them away.[5] And when at last a great sea rises, and this sea of Time comes sweeping down, bearing the alderman and such mudworms of the earth away to nothing, dashing them to fragments in its fury—Toby will climb a rock and hear the bells (now faded from his sight) pealing out upon the waters. And as he hears them, and looks round for help, he will wake up and find himself with the newspaper

---

[1] The three preceding sentences were followed by Forster with minor changes.

[2] In the first ten pages of the Third Quarter (pp. 92–101) Trotty's vision of the goblin spirits of the bells and the dialogue between him and the spirit of the Great Bell follows these general lines, with some of the same details ("knotted whips", "music", "birds" and "flowers"), but the Great Bell's speeches are much elaborated.

[3] This sentence was taken word for word by Forster.

[4] From "But before" taken almost word for word by Forster.

[5] The whole sentence was taken by Forster.

lying at his foot; and Meg sitting opposite to him at the table, making up the ribbons for her wedding to-morrow; and the window open, that the sound of the bells ringing the old year out and the new year in may enter. They will just have broken out, joyfully; and Richard will dash in to kiss Meg before Toby, and have the first kiss of the new year (he'll get it too); and the neighbours will crowd round with good wishes; and a band will strike up gaily (Toby knows a Drum in private); and the altered circumstances, and the ringing of the bells, and the jolly musick, will so transport the old fellow that he will lead off a country dance forthwith in an entirely new step, consisting of his old familiar trot. Then quoth the inimitable—Was it a dream of Toby's after all? Or is Toby but a dream? and Meg a dream? and all a dream![1] In reference to which, and the realities of which dreams are born, the inimitable will be wiser than he can be now, writing for dear life, with the post just going, and the brave C booted. . . . Ah how I hate myself, my dear fellow, for this lame and halting outline of the Vision I have in my mind. But it must go to you. . . . You will say what is best for the frontis-piece.[2]

To JOHN FORSTER, [18 OCTOBER 1844]

Extract in F, IV, v, 346–7. *Date:* 18 Oct according to Forster, but clearly a distinct letter from preceding one, which concludes at post-time; unlikely that CD would begin that letter with the present extract.

He described how, bent upon his work, he had been disturbed by hearing that he must attend the levee of the Governor[3] *who had unexpectedly arrived in the city, and who, Fletcher told him, would be affronted if he did not go.* It was the morning on which I was going to begin, so I wrote round to our consul *praying that excuse should be made. Don't bother yourself, he replied, for all the consuls and governors alive; but shut yourself up by all means.* So he went next morning in

---

[1] Much of what is here indicated is contained in the Third and Fourth Quarters, but is both modified and enlarged by the parts played by Will Fern and Lilian. The vision of Meg resolving to drown the child is placed later than CD evidently first intended in the Fourth Quarter; the words of the chimes are not used; and less is made of the exposure of Bowley, the "punctual man". The vision of the Sea of Time and Trotty on the rock is not presented, but the Third Quarter begins with the "Sea of Thought", and the idea of time is referred to, both in the Great Bell's speech and the last of Trotty's "visionary" speeches in the Fourth Quarter (p. 166). As in the outline, this is immediately followed by his waking with Meg preparing for her wedding. The details about the first kiss, the Drum's being a private friend of Trotty's, and the new step, all appear, and the concluding

paragraph beginning "Had Toby dreamed?" is on the lines that CD had proposed. For further discussion of the composition, see Michael Slater, "Dickens (and Forster) at work on *The Chimes*", *Dickens Studies*, II, (1966), 106–40.

[2] A fanciful picture of the bells and their spirits, by Maclise.

[3] The arrival of the Governor, the Marchese Paulucci, was announced in the daily *Gazzetta di Genova* of 5 Oct; the levee was not reported, but probably took place within a few days of his arrival. This is consistent with CD's saying it was the morning that he was going to begin *The Chimes*. It may seem surprising that he did not give this account in an earlier letter; on the other hand, it is quite natural that having finished the First Quarter he should look back to the difficulties attending its beginning.

great state and full costume, to present two English gentlemen. "Where's the great poet?" said the Governor. "I want to see the great poet." "The great poet, your excellency," said the consul, "is at work, writing a book, and begged me to make his excuses." "Excuses!" said the Governor, "I wouldn't interfere with such an occupation for all the world. Pray tell him that my house is open to the honour of his presence when it is perfectly convenient for him; but not otherwise. And let no gentleman," said the Governor, a surweyin' of his suite with a majestic eye, "call upon Signor Dickens till he is understood to be disengaged." And he sent somebody with his own cards next day. Now I *do* seriously call this, real politeness and pleasant consideration—not positively American, but still gentlemanly and polished.[1] The same spirit pervades the inferior departments; and I have not been required to observe the usual police regulations, or to put myself to the slightest trouble about anything.

To JOHN FORSTER, [?21 OCTOBER 1844]

Extract in F, ɪv, v, 353; mention in F, 1872–4, ɪɪ, v, 91*n*; extract in F, ɪv, v, 354. *Date:* first extract "after a week's interval" (from 18 Oct) according to Forster; but 25 Oct hardly possible in view of "eight more days" interval before next letter, and CD intended to send "a parcel every Monday" (see *To* Forster, 18 Oct); probably same date as letter mentioned by Forster as 21 Oct (a Monday). Final extract "after three Mondays" according to Forster—i.e. the first three Mondays in Oct, and clearly before Sat 26 Oct when the weather changed, and so probably part of same letter, written late on third Monday.

Sending the Second Quarter, and explaining some changes in the plan.[2] I am still in stout heart with the tale. I think it well-timed and a good thought; and as you know I wouldn't say so to anybody else, I don't mind saying freely thus much. It has great possession of me every moment in the day; and drags me where it will. . . . If you only could have read it all at once!—But you never would have done that, anyway, for I never should have been able to keep it to myself; so that's nonsense. I hope you'll like it. I would give a hundred pounds (and think it cheap) to see you read it. . . . Never mind.

They had had, so far, only four really clear days since they came to Italy.

Weather worse than any November English weather I have ever beheld, or any weather I have had experience of anywhere. So horrible to-day that all power has been rained and gloomed out of me. Yesterday, in pure determination to get the better of it, I walked twelve miles in mountain rain. You never saw it rain. Scotland and America are nothing to it.

---

[1] Paulucci is described by Lester (*My Consulship,* ɪ, 155ff.), at about this time, as "a burly rough, imperious soldier", who had "made a rupture with every foreign representative"; but he was probably more concerned to have good relations with the English than with the Americans.

[2] An "enlargement . . . by which he hoped better to carry out the scheme of the story, and to get, for its following part, an effect for his heroine that would increase the tragic interest": see *To* Forster, ?29 Oct 44, *fn.*

To JOHN FORSTER, [?29 OCTOBER 1844]

Extract in F, IV, v, 353. *Date:* with the Third Quarter, "after eight more days" according to Forster. The Fourth Quarter was finished on 3 Nov, and four to five days spent on it seems likely.

This book (whether in the Hajji Baba sense or not I can't say, but certainly in the literal one) has made my face white in a foreign land.[1] My cheeks, which were beginning to fill out, have sunk again; my eyes have grown immensely large; my hair is very lank; and the head inside the hair is hot and giddy. Read the scene at the end of the third part, twice.[2] I wouldn't write it twice, for something. . . . You will see that I have substituted the name of Lilian for Jessie. It is prettier in sound, and suits my music better.[3] I mention this, lest you should wonder who and what I mean by that name. To-morrow I shall begin afresh (starting the next part with a broad grin,[4] and ending it with the very soul of jollity and happiness); and I hope to finish by next Monday at latest. Perhaps on Saturday. I hope you will like the little book. Since I conceived, at the beginning of the second part, what must happen in the third, I have undergone as much sorrow and agitation as if the thing were real; and have wakened up with it at night. I was obliged to lock myself in when I finished it yesterday, for my face was swollen for the time to twice its proper size, and was hugely ridiculous.[5] . . . I am going for a long walk, to clear my head. I feel that I am very shakey from work, and throw down my pen for the day. There! (That's where it fell.)[6]

To JOHN FORSTER, [?31 OCTOBER 1844]

Extract in F, IV, v, 354. *Date:* "two days later" than last according to Forster (353).

The weather changed on Saturday night,[7] and has been glorious ever since. I am afraid to say more in its favour, lest it should change again.

---

[1] A recurrent expression, meaning "to glorify" someone, in James J. Morier's *Hajji Baba in England*, 1828; Mirza Firouz the ambassador says he is "ordered to make the Shah's face white in this foreign land" (I, 195).

[2] The vision of Meg and Richard in poverty, Richard's pathetic narrative of Lilian, and her scene with Meg.

[3] The name of the child is "Jess" or "Jessie" throughout the MS of the Second Quarter. On her reappearance as a woman in the Third Quarter (p. 107) CD first wrote "Jessie" again, but a few lines below "Lilian", and went back and altered the

"Jessie". The context suggests an additional reason; "Jessy" was the name of the repentant prostitute who visited the heroine, in a scene resembling Lilian's visit to Meg, in Jerrold's *Story of a Feather*: see Michael Slater, *Dickens Studies*, II (1966), p. 118.

[4] The second paragraph of the Fourth Quarter introduces the rosy-cheeked couple, who turn out to be Tugby and the former Mrs Chickenstalker, now his wife.

[5] Forster adds that "His letter ended abruptly" (F, *ibid*).

[6] "A huge blot" (F, *ibid*).

[7] 26 Oct.

To JOHN FORSTER, [?27 OCTOBER–2 NOVEMBER 1844]

Extracts in F, IV, v, 354. *Date:* The several expeditions and outings which Forster combines in a single paragraph must have followed the change in the weather (see last) and preceded the return of the sirocco (see next).

Describing his walks in the mountain wind, lovely, enjoyable, exquisite past expression; mountain walks behind the Peschiere, most beautiful and fresh, among which, and along the beds of dry rivers and torrents, he could pelt away *in any dress, without encountering a soul but the contadini. One day he started off after finishing work* fifteen miles to dinner—oh my stars! at such an inn!!! *Another day there was a dinner-party at their pleasant little banker's at Quinto six miles off, to which, while the ladies drove, he was able* to walk in the sun of the middle of the day and to walk home again at night. *Another day, an expedition up the mountain on mules. Another day, a memorable tavern-dinner with their merchant friend Mr. Curry, in which there were such successions of surprising dishes of genuine native cookery that they took two hours in the serving, but of the component parts of not one of which was he able to form the remotest conception: the site of the tavern being on the city wall,[1] its name in Italian sounding very romantic and meaning "the Whistle", and its bill of fare kept for an experiment to which, before another month should be over, he would challenge Forster's cookery in Lincoln's-inn.*

To JOHN FORSTER, [?1–2 NOVEMBER 1844]

Extracts in F, IV, v, 355, 354. *Date:* first extract before 3 Nov as CD had not yet finished *The Chimes*, but not earlier than 1 Nov to allow for the arrival of Forster's comments on the First Quarter, despatched by CD 18 Oct; confirmed by Fred Dickens *to* Maclise, 8 Nov (MS Benoliel), which assumes that Maclise had heard from Forster that "Charles is expected over ... very shortly". Second extract "just before he sent his last manuscript" according to Forster, therefore clearly same letter.

Notwithstanding what you say, I am still in the same mind about coming to London.[2] Not because the proofs concern me at all[3] (I should be an ass as well as a thankless vagabond if they did), but because of that unspeakable restless something which would render it almost as impossible for me to remain here and not see the thing complete, as it would be for a full balloon, left to itself, not to go

---

[1] No doubt the first of many such dinners; CD later identified the dishes. The typical "good entertainment" at a "real Genoese tavern" on the city walls, described in *Pictures*, p. 49, includes "Tagliarini; Ravioli; German sausages, strong of garlic, sliced and eaten with fresh green figs; cocks' combs and sheep-kidneys, chopped up with mutton-chops and liver; small pieces of some unknown part of a calf, twisted into small shreds, fried, and served up in a great dish like white-bait; and other curiosities of that kind".

[2] Forster had replied to CD's letter of ?13–14 Oct, by "dwelling on the fatigue and cost" of a visit to London (F, IV, v, 355).

[3] The proof copies in the Forster Collection (V & A) and the Dexter Collection (BM) are the final set, evidently representing the text as emended in the first proof by Forster. The copy in the Forster Collection has MS emendations and additions by CD, made after his return to London.

up. I do not intend coming from *here*, but by way of Milan and Turin (previously going to Venice), and so, across the wildest pass of the Alps that may be open, to Strasburg. . . . As you dislike the Young England gentleman[1] I shall knock him out, and replace him by a man (I can dash him in at your rooms in an hour) who recognizes no virtue in anything but the good old times, and talks of them, parrot-like, whatever the matter is. A real good old city tory, in a blue coat and bright buttons and a white cravat, and with a tendency of blood to the head.[2] File away at Filer, as you please;[3] but bear in mind that the *Westminster Review*[4] considered Scrooge's presentation of the turkey to Bob Cratchit as grossly incompatible with political economy. I don't care at all for the skittle-playing.[5]

At the close of his letter:

Shall I confess to you, I particularly want Carlyle[6] above all to see it before the rest of the world, when it is done; and I should like to inflict the little story on him and on dear old gallant Macready with my own lips, and to have Stanny and the other Mac sitting by. Now, if you was a real gent, you'd get up a little circle for me, one wet evening, when I come to town: and would say, "My boy (SIR, will you have the goodness to leave those books alone and to go downstairs— WHAT the Devil are you doing! And mind, sir, I can see nobody—do you hear? Nobody. I am particularly engaged with a gentleman from Asia)—My boy, would you give us that little Christmas book (a little Christmas book of Dickens's Macready, which I'm anxious you should hear); and don't slur it, now, or be too fast, Dickens, please!"—I say, if you was a real gent, something to this effect might happen. I shall be under sailing orders the moment I have finished. And

---

[1] The character appearing in the MS of the First and Third Quarters, through whom CD satirized the Young England movement of Disraeli and Lord John Manners. Disraeli's *Coningsby*, expressing the principles of the movement, had been published in May 1844.

[2] Forster made the substitution before the printing of the final proof, basing his description of the "old city tory" on this letter, and leaving a page and a half blank for CD to "dash in" a suitable speech. The consequent alterations made by Forster and CD's additions and revisions are discussed by M. Slater (*Dickens Studies*, II, 125–34), and the cancelled passages from the MS are given in his edn of *Christmas Books*, 1971, I, Appendix A.

[3] Forster removed only Filer's remark in the Third Quarter (p. 118) that Will Fern, "by going to prison oftener than his turn, . . . kept twenty seven deserving people out".

[4] In Nassau Senior's review of Horne's *New Spirit of the Age*, June 1844: "The process whereby poor men are to be enabled to earn good wages, wherewith to buy turkeys for themselves, does not enter into the account; indeed, it would quite spoil the *dénouement* and all the generosity. Who went without turkey and punch in order that Bob Cratchit might get them—for, unless there were turkey and punch in surplus, some one must go without—is a disagreeable reflection kept wholly out of sight". CD has this in mind in Filer's comment on the tripe (p. 35): "You snatch your tripe, my friend, out of the mouths of widows and orphans".

[5] In the Third Quarter (pp. 111, 116), not despatched until ?29 Oct; CD is therefore anticipating a possible criticism, and Forster is wrong in including the skittle-playing "among things I had objected to". It was not altered, and is the only surviving hit at "Young England".

[6] Forster (F, IV, v, 347) notes that "several months before he left England . . . the hopelessness of any true solution of either political or social problems by the ordinary Downing-street methods had been startlingly impressed on him in Carlyle's writings". CD was especially influenced by *Past and Present*, 1843.

I shall produce myself (please God) in London on the very day you name. For one week: to the hour.

Wind, hail, rain, thunder and lightning. To-day has been November slack-baked,[1] the sirocco having come back; and to-night it blows great guns with a raging storm.

To JOHN FORSTER, 3 and [4] NOVEMBER 1844

Extract in F, IV, v, 356.

Third of November, 1844. Half-past two, afternoon. Thank God! I have finished the *Chimes*. This moment. I take up my pen again to-day, to say only that much; and to add that I have had what women call "a real good cry!" *Resuming his letter on* 4 *November.* Here is the brave courier measuring bits of maps with a carving-fork, and going up mountains on a tea-spoon. He and I start on Wednesday for Parma, Modena, Bologna, Venice, Verona, Brescia, and Milan.[2] Milan being within a reasonable journey from here, Kate and Georgy will come to meet me when I arrive there on my way towards England; and will bring me all letters from you. I shall be there on the 18th. . . . Now, you know my punctiwality. Frost, ice, flooded rivers, steamers, horses, passports, and custom-houses may damage it. But my design is, to walk into Cuttris's coffee-room on Sunday the 1st of December, in good time for dinner. I shall look for you at the farther table by the fire—where we generally go. . . . But the party[3] for the night following? I know you have consented to the party. Let me see. Don't have any one, this particular night, to dinner, but let it be a summons for the special purpose at half-past 6. Carlyle, indispensable, and I should like his wife of all things: *her* judgment would be invaluable. You will ask Mac, and why not his sister? Stanny and Jerrold I should particularly wish; Edwin Landseer; Blanchard; perhaps Harness;[4] and what say you to Fonblanque and Fox? I leave it to you. You know the effect I want to try. . . . Think the *Chimes* a letter,[5]

---

[1] Used of loaves insufficiently baked; a favourite word of CD's (see quotations in *OED*). Here, damp but partly warmed up by the sirocco.

[2] The tour went as planned (*Pictures*, pp. 84–141), except that from Verona CD went to Mantua and not Brescia.

[3] See *To* Mrs CD, 2 Dec 44 and *fn*.

[4] The Rev. William Harness (1790–1869; *DNB*): see Vol. II, p. 178*n*.

[5] Some days after finishing the MS, Forster, writing to Macvey Napier (to return the proofs of his article on William Tooke's *Charles Churchill* for the Jan *Edinburgh Review*), added a "P. S. *Very Private*" with the tentative suggestion that if Napier had eight or ten pages to spare, he might himself supply "an agreeable and not uninteresting little paper on Mr.

Dickens's new Christmas Tale . . . in some essential points the best of his writings'. and certain "to make a strong impression'" CD, he said, knew nothing of the proposal: "And whether you reject or accept it—I shall make no communication to him". He explained that it "would not serve" for any later number than Jan, and therefore the decision could not wait until after publication in mid-Dec: "It is on this account only I offer myself as the writer—on other grounds not so well fitted for the task perhaps, as a stranger to Mr. Dickens would be". If Napier's reply were a negative, "*I am well aware that you will have had the best reasons for returning such an answer.* Remember only that it is not for the sake of Mr. D I submit the matter to you—though of course it would be idle to

my dear fellow, and forgive this. I will not fail to write to you on my travels. Most probably from Venice. And when I meet you (in sound health I hope) oh Heaven! what a week we will have.

To THOMAS MITTON, 5 NOVEMBER 1844

MS Huntington Library.

Peschiere, Genoa. Tuesday November Fifth 1844.

My Dear Mitton.

The cause of my not having written to you, is too obvious to need any explanation. I have worn myself to Death, in the Month I have been at Work. None of my usual reliefs have been at hand; I have not been able to divest myself of the story—have suffered very much in my sleep, in consequence—and am so shaken by such work in this trying climate that I am nervous as a man who is dying of Drink: and as haggard as a Murderer.

I believe I have written a tremendous Book; and knocked the Carol out of the field. It will make a great uproar,[1] I have no doubt.

say that a sense of the pleasure and pride it would be to him does not in some degree mix itself up in it. | Again faithfully yrs. J. F." (MS BM). This cautious and diplomatic offer was accepted, and a 9-page review appeared. The fullest and most penetrating review that the book received, and not obviously partisan, it clearly reflects the effect of CD's letters (see *To* Forster, 18 Oct 44, *fns*) and of the reading of 3 Dec—and no doubt of the hearers' response. Forster did not finish writing it until more than a week after the reading. He was still writing "for dear life" when he sent Leigh Hunt a copy of *The Chimes* with CD's "most hearty and kind remembrance", and he accompanied this with a "boring request": because of the *Edinburgh*, he would be "left quite dry for the Examiner", and he asked Hunt to send him "any little thing by way of note or suggestion that may occur to you about the story, and its treatment. Not a formal notice—nothing of the kind"—"a new hint, a fresh and new impression from you, looking at it doubtless in other points of view—will be really most precious to me" (Forster *to* Hunt, Maggs catalogue No. 443; n.d., but probably 15–16 Dec as Hunt's copy was required on "Thursday *morning*", 19 Dec). Hunt evidently sent an extended notice: Forster wrote apologizing for the "great liberties" he had taken—it was "of inexpressible value", but "there was a particular reason that I should in some points, manner it in my own way . . . And the extracts used had already been set, so that I could not use yours also". He would, however, preserve Hunt's notice for CD (Forster *to* Hunt, n.d.; L. A. Brewer, *My Leigh Hunt Library. The Holograph Letters*, Iowa, 1938, p. 249).

[1] Because of its radical tendency—seen especially in the satire on Filer, the "facts and figures" economist, Alderman Cute the callous magistrate (aimed at Sir Peter Laurie), and Sir Joseph Bowley the landowner. CD's expectations were fulfilled: a fortnight after publication the book had been "attacked and defended with a degree of ardour which scarcely any other subject is capable of inspiring" (*Globe*, 31 Dec). Reviews were fairly evenly divided, mainly on class and party lines; CD was charged, for example, with sentimentalizing "the ruffian and the wanton, the rickburner and the felon" (*Morning Post*, 19 Dec), with setting class against class, fomenting discontent and mob violence, and encouraging the poor to early marriage. Private objectors on similar lines included Lord Monteagle ("His Pol. Econy. is up in arms", Empson *to* Napier, 14 Jan 45; MS BM), Bulwer Lytton, who told Forster the moral was "untrue and dangerous" and "the fierce tone of menace to the rich . . . unreasonable and ignorant" (Lytton *to* Forster, 25 Dec 44; MS Lytton Papers),

I leave here tomorrow, for Venice and many other places; and I shall certainly come to London to see my proofs—coming by new ground all the way: cutting through the Snow in the Valleys of Switzerland: and plunging through the Mountains in the Dead of Winter. I would accept your hearty offer with right good-will; but my visit being one of business and consultation, I see impediments in the way, and insurmountable reasons for not doing so. Therefore I shall go to an Hotel in Covent Garden where they know me very well, and with the landlord of which, I have already communicated. My orders are not upon a mighty scale—extending no further than a Good bedroom and a cold Shower Bath.

*a*Bradbury and Evans are going at it, Ding Dong,[1] and are wild with excitement. All news on that subject (and on every other) I must defer 'till I see you. That will be immediately after I arrive, of course. Most likely on Monday 2nd. Dec.*a*

*b*I am very anxious to hear *your* News too. And indeed I have been constantly expecting some long Narrative from you.*b*

*c*Kate and her sister (who send their best regards) and all the children, are as well as possible.*c* The house is *perfect*; the servants are as quiet and well-behaved as at home—which very rarely happens here—and Roche is my right hand. There never was such a fellow.

We have now got carpets down—burn fires at night—draw the Curtains—and are quite wintry. We have a box at the opera which is close by (for Nothing) and sit there when we please, as in our own Drawing Room. There have been three fine days in four weeks. On every other, the Water has b[een][2] falling down in one continued sheet: and it has been [thun]dering and lightening every day and night.

My hand shakes in that feverish and horrible manner, that I can hardly hold a pen. And I have so bad a cold that I can't see.

> In haste to save the Post
> Ever Faithfully
> CHARLES DICKENS

Thomas Mitton Esquire

Charley has a Writing Master every day—and a French Master. He and his sisters are to be waited on, by a Professor of the noble art of Dancing, next Week.

---

and Lockhart, who thought the *Edinburgh*'s review "a most sonorous puff"—"ascribed to old Jeffrey", and did not wish to have a review in the *Quarterly* since there seemed to be "a general conspiracy am[on]g novelists to inflame low passions against the most humane & charitable aristocracy that ever existed, and the vast popularity of Boz has on various occasions of late been enlisted in this most mischievous cause" (Lockhart *to* Croker, 13 Feb 45; *Notes & Queries*, CLXXXIX, [1945], 11).

[1] *The Chimes* was first advertised on 26 Oct, with the full title but without the names of the illustrators.

aa; cc Passages published in MDGH 1880, but omitted in later editions, including N.

bb Not previously published.

[2] A piece missing from edge of paper has removed three or four letters in two places.

To JOHN FORSTER, [?JULY–NOVEMBER 1844]

Extract in F, IV, vii, 366*n*. *Date:* a letter from Genoa, "previous" to 22 Dec according to Forster—therefore before 6 Nov.

Apropos of servants, I must tell you of a child-bearing handmaiden of some friends of ours, a thorough out and outer, who, by way of expiating her sins, caused herself, the other day, to be received into the bosom of the infallible church. She had two marchionesses for her sponsors; and she is heralded in the Genoa newspapers[1] as Miss B——, an English lady, who has repented of her errors and saved her soul alive.

To MRS CHARLES DICKENS, 8 NOVEMBER 1844

MS British Museum. *Address:* Alla Signa. | Signa. Dickens | Palazzo Peschiere | Genova.

Parma. Albergo Della Posta.[2] Friday November Eighth 1844.

My Dearest Kate. "If Missis could see us to-night, what would she say!"—That was the brave C's remark last night at Midnight; and he had reason. We left Genoa, as you know, soon after 5 on the evening of my departure; and in company with the lady whom you saw, and the Dog whom I don't think you did see—travelled all night *at the rate of Four Miles an Hour*, over bad roads, without the least refreshment, until Daybreak, when the Brave and myself escaped into a miserable Caffe while they were changing horses, and got a cup of that drink, hot. That same day a few hours afterwards—between 10 and 11, we came to (I hope) the damndest Inn in the world,[3] where, in a vast chamber, rendered still more desolate by the presence of a most offensive specimen of what D'Israeli calls The Mosaic Arab[4] (who had a beautiful girl with him) I regaled upon a breakfast, almost as cold and damp and cheerless as myself. Then, in another coach, much smaller than a small fly, I was packed up with an old Padre, a Young Jesuit, a provincial avvocato, a private gentleman with a very red nose and a very wet brown umbrella, and the Brave C; and so went on again, at the same pace through the same Mud and Rain, until Four in the afternoon, when there was a place in the coupee (two indeed) which I took: holding that select compartment in company with a very ugly, but very agreeable Tuscan "Gent", who said "Gia" instead of "Si" and rung some other changes on this changing language, but with whom I got on very well: being extremely conversational. We were bound, as you know,—perhaps,—for Piacenza, but it was discovered that we couldn't get to Piacenza; and about 10 o'Clock at night we halted at a place called Stradella, where the Inn was a series of queer Galleries open to the

---

[1] No such report has been traced.

[2] Named first in Murray and described as "decent" (*Handbook for ... Northern Italy*).

[3] At Alessandria (*Pictures*, p. 84); two good hotels are mentioned in Murray.

[4] In *Coningsby*, Book IV, Ch. 10, Sidonia's history and his descent from the "Mosaic Arabs"—a race of "ancient ... unmixed blood ... the aristocracy of Nature"—are described; CD is amused by Disraeli's idealization of the Jews (also mocked at by Thackeray in his *Morning Chronicle* review, 13 May).

night, with a great courtyard full of Waggons, and horses, and Veloceferi and what not, in the centre.[1] It was bitter cold and very wet; and we all walked into a bare room (Mine!) with two immensely broad beds on two deal dining tables— a third great empty table—the usual washing-stand tripod with a slop basin on it—and two chairs. And here we walked up and down for three quarters of an hour or so, while dinner, or supper, or whatever it was, was getting ready. This was set forth (by way of variety) in the old Priest's bedroom, which had two more immensely broad beds on two more deal dining-tables in it. The first dish was a cabbage boiled in a great quantity of rice and hot water: the whole flavored with cheese. I was so cold that I thought it comfortable: and so hungry that a bit of cabbage, when I found such a thing floating my way, charmed me. After that, we had a dish of very little pieces of Pork, fried: with pigs kidneys. After that, a fowl. After that, something very red and stringy, which I think was veal; and after that two tiny little new-born-baby-looking turkeys. Very red and very swollen. Fruit, of course, to wind up. And Garlic in one shape or another with every course. I made three Jokes at supper (to the immense delight of the company) and retired early. The brave brought in a bush or two, and made a fire: and after that, a glass of screeching[2] hot brandy and water; that bottle of his, being full of brandy. I drank it at my leisure—undressed before the fire—and went into one of the beds. The brave reappeared about an hour afterwards, and went into the other; previously tying a pocket-handkerchief round and round his head in a strange fashion: and giving utterance to the sentiment with which this letter begins. At 5 this morning, we resumed our journey—still through mud and rain—and at about 11, arrived at Piacenza; where we fellow passengers took leave of one another in the most affectionate manner. As there was no coach on, 'till six at night—and as it was a very grim, despondent sort of place—and as I had had enough of Diligences for one while—I posted forward here, in the strangest carriages ever beheld, which we changed, when we changed horses. We arrived here before 6. The hotel is quite French. I have dined, very well, in my own room on the second floor; and it has two beds in it, screened off from the room by drapery. I only use one tonight; and that is already made.[3]

I purpose posting on to Bologna, if I can arrange it, at 12 tomorrow: seeing the sights here, first. *If there be a Mail from Bologna to Venice, and it serves my time, I will write you again on my arrival at the latter place. You *may* not have that letter before you leave for Milan. But we will take our chance of it.*

My dear Kate, be very careful if no opportunity occur for Susan's[4] leaving Genoa before you come to Milan, that you set aside every little consideration, and bring her with you. Remember how much we owe to Macready, and to Mrs. Macready too, for their constancy to us when we were in such great

---

[1] No inns are mentioned in Murray.

[2] *Mr & Mrs CD*, ed. Walter Dexter, p. 10, reads "scorching" in error.

[3] Many of these details of the first two days' journey occur also in *Pictures*, pp. 84–90, for which CD may have used this letter as well as *To* Forster, 10 Nov.

a a Omitted in MDGH, I, 125.

[4] Susan Atkins, Mrs Macready's sister; their parents were a scene-painter and an actress: see Vol. II, p. 149*n*. Susan is only twice mentioned in Macready's *Diaries* (II, 99, 179). It is not known why she came to Genoa; CD does not refer to her in *To* Macready, 14 Oct or 28 Nov 44.

anxiety about the Darlings;[1] and do not let any natural dislike to her inanities, interfere in the slightest degree with an obligation so sacred. You are too easily run away with—and Georgy is too—by the irritation and displeasure of the moment, in such a case. Far[2] too easily, for the lasting honorable and just remembrance of such a bond; and I was pained to see (as I should have told Georgy before I left if I had had an opportunity) that in such a case as the Messages to Forster (she will know what I mean) she does a glaringly foolish and unnecessary silliness, and places huge means of misrepresentation in very willing hands. I should never forgive myself or you, if the smallest drop of coldness or misunderstanding were created between me and Macready, by means so monstrously absurd. And mind what I say. It will be created—I see it very clearly—unless you are as careful with that girl as if you were treading on hot ploughshares; and unless you are something more tender too. I am sure her presence at the Peschiere during the past month, has worried nobody more than me. I am sure her presence at our short reunion at Milan would be a positive grievance to me. But I do hold hospitality, even when there is no other tie upon it, to be so high a thing, that I spare even Fletcher, when I am tempted to "put him down." And do, for God's sake, look beyond the hour into six or twelve months hence. Say I beg to be remembered kindly to her; and whether she leaves you, or not, have it understood that you intended to bring her to Milan. And observe. *I positively object, and say No, to her going to Rome under the protection of any entire stranger. I cannot allow it to be, until I have seen Macready.*[3] I have thought of this, very much.[a]

It is dull work, this travelling alone. My only comfort is, in Motion. I look forward with a sort of shudder to Sunday, when I shall have a day to myself in Bologna; and I think I must deliver my letters in Venice, in sheer desperation. Never did anybody want a companion after dinner (to say nothing of after supper) so much as I do.

There has been Music on the landing outside my door to night. Two violins and a violincello. One of the violins played a Solo; and the others, struck in, as an orchestra does now and then—very well. Then he came in, with a small tin platter. "Bella Musica!" said I. "Bellissima Musica Signore. Mi piace Multissimo." "Sono Felici Signore!" said he. I gave him a franc. "E multissimo generoso. Tanto generoso Signore!"

It was a joke to laugh at, when I was learning, but I swear that unless I could stagger on, Zoppa-wise,[4] with the people, I verily believe I sh[ould turn][5] back, this morning.

In all other respects, I think the entire change has done me ser[vice—] undoubted service, already. I am free of the Book: and am red-faced; [;] and feel marvellously disposed to sleep.

---

[1] In 1842: see Vol. III, p. 8*n*.

[2] MS reads "For".

[3] A suitable escort must have been found; Susan was in Rome, staying with Mrs Reid (see *To Mrs Reid, 25 Mar 45, fn*), by 2 Jan 45 when Thackeray wrote to her apologizing for his lateness in answering Mrs Reid's invitation for that evening (Thackeray *to*

Susan Atkins, MS Bedford College). CD underlined the second sentence twice.

[4] Haltingly, from the Italian *zoppo, zoppa,* a cripple.

[5] A tear on the right-hand side has removed words at the end of this and the next few lines.

So for all the straggling qualities of this straggling letter, want [of sleep] must be responsible. Give my best love to Georgy, and my paternal blessing to

> Mamey
> Katey
> Charley
> Walley
> and
> Chickenstalker.[1]

Ever My Dearest | Yours with true affection
CHARLES DICKENS

P.S. Keep things in their places. I can't bear to picture them otherwise.
P.P.S. I *think* I saw Roche sleeping with his head on the lady's shoulder—in the coach. I couldn't swear it, and the light was deceptive. But I think I did.

To JOHN FORSTER, [10 NOVEMBER 1844]

Extracts from fragments of MS of *Pictures*, Forster Collection, V & A (see Preface, pp. xv–xvi); also in F, IV, vi, 357 and n.[2] *Date:* 10 Nov according to Forster. *From* Ferrara.[3]

I left my disconsolate wife (who is now living shut up in her palace like a Baron's lady in the time of the Crusades) on Wednesday afternoon last, at 5 o'clock.

If you want an antidote to this[4] I may observe that I got up this moment, to fasten the window; and the street looked as like some byeway in Whitechapel— or—I look again—like Wych-street, down by the little barber's shop on the same side of the way as Holywell Street[5]—or—I look again—as like Holywell Street itself—as ever street was like to street, or ever will be, in this world.

To JOHN FORSTER, [12 NOVEMBER 1844]

Extracts in F, IV, vi, 357–8 and n. *Date:* "Tuesday night the 12th of November" according to Forster. *From* Venice.

I began this letter, my dear friend, with the intention of describing my travels as I went on.[6] But I have seen so much, and travelled so hard (seldom dining,

---

[1] The baby, Francis Jeffrey, nicknamed after Mrs Chickenstalker in *The Chimes*.

[2] Forster draws on the first extract in the opening of his chapter, and quotes the second (accurately except for punctuation). The MS fragment shows that the intervening part included CD's arrival at Parma at 8 p.m., followed by a description of the vineyards.

[3] CD describes this "dreary" but "picturesque" town in *Pictures*, pp. 102–4.

[4] i.e. "the very pretty description of the vineyards between Piacenza and Parma" (F, *ibid*), only part of which survives in the MS fragment; see *Pictures*, p. 90.

[5] Wych St ran from Drury Lane to Pickett St near Temple Bar, Holywell St joining it from Catherine St; "Oliver Davoren, hairdresser", was at 39 Wych St.

[6] CD left Ferrara for Venice on 11 Nov, visiting Padua on the way.

and being almost always up by candle light), that I must reserve my crayons for the greater leisure of the Peschiere after we have met, and I have again returned to it. As soon as I have fixed a place in my mind, I bolt—at such strange seasons and at such unexpected angles, that the brave C stares again. But in this way, and by insisting on having everything shewn to me whether or no, and against all precedents and orders of proceeding, I get on wonderfully.

I must not anticipate myself. But, my dear fellow, nothing in the world that ever you have heard of Venice,[1] is equal to the magnificent and stupendous reality. The wildest visions of the Arabian Nights are nothing to the piazza of Saint Mark, and the first impression of the inside of the church. The gorgeous and wonderful reality of Venice is beyond the fancy of the wildest dreamer. Opium couldn't build such a place, and enchantment couldn't shadow it forth in a vision. All that I have heard of it, read of it in truth or fiction, fancied of it, is left thousands of miles behind. You know that I am liable to disappointment in such things from over-expectation, but Venice is above, beyond, out of all reach of coming near, the imagination of a man. It has never been rated high enough. It is a thing you would shed tears to see. When I came *on board* here last night (after a five miles' row in a gondola; which somehow or other, I wasn't at all prepared for); when, from seeing the city lying, one light, upon the distant water, like a ship, I came plashing through the silent and deserted streets; I felt as if the houses were reality—the water, fever-madness. But when, in the bright, cold, bracing day, I stood upon the piazza this morning, by Heaven the glory of the place was insupportable! And diving down from that into its wickedness and gloom—its awful prisons, deep below the water; its judgment chambers, secret doors, deadly nooks, where the torches you carry with you blink as if they couldn't bear the air in which the frightful scenes were acted; and coming out again into the radiant, unsubstantial Magic of the town; and diving in again, into vast churches, and old tombs—a new sensation, a new memory, a new mind came upon me. Venice is a bit of my brain from this time. My dear Forster, if you could share my transports (as you would if you were here) what would I not give! I feel cruel not to have brought Kate and Georgy; positively cruel and base. Canaletti[2] and Stanny,[3] miraculous in their truth. Turner,[4] very noble. But the reality itself, beyond all pen or pencil. I never saw the thing before that I should be afraid to describe. But to tell what Venice is, I feel to be an impossibility. And here I sit alone, writing it: with nothing to urge me on, or goad me to that estimate, which, speaking of it to anyone I loved, and being spoken to in return, would lead me to form. In the sober solitude of a famous inn; with the great bell of Saint Mark ringing twelve at my elbow; with three arched windows in my room (two stories high) looking down upon the Grand Canal and away, beyond, to where the sun went down to-night in a blaze;

[1] Described in *Pictures*, pp. 107–19, "An Italian Dream"; written, says Forster, "after his London visit" (F, *ibid*), and clearly not based on a letter.

[2] Ruskin also used this form up to 1843 (1st edn of *Modern Painters*, I).

[3] Besides nine pictures of Venice ex-hibited at the RA between 1831 and 1843, Stanfield painted a series of ten for Lord Lansdowne, begun in 1830, and another set for the Duke of Sutherland in 1834.

[4] Of Turner's many paintings of Venice, three were exhibited at the RA in 1843 and three in 1844.

and thinking over again those silent speaking faces of Titian and Tintoretto; I swear (uncooled by any humbug I have seen) that Venice is *the* wonder and the new sensation of the world! If you could be set down in it, never having heard of it, it would still be so. With your foot upon its stones, its pictures before you, and its history in your mind, it is something past all writing of or speaking of— almost past all thinking of. You couldn't talk to me in this room, nor I to you, without shaking hands and saying "Good God my dear fellow, have we lived to see this!"

To DOUGLAS JERROLD, 16 NOVEMBER 1844†

MS Mr Douglas Jerrold. *Address:* Inghilterra. | Douglas Jerrold Esqre. | Care of | Messrs. Bradbury and Evans | Printers | Whitefriars | London.

Cremona | Saturday Night Sixteenth November 1844.

My Dear Jerrold. As half a loaf is better than no bread, so I hope that half a sheet of paper may be better than none at all coming from one who is sincerely anxious to live in your memory and friendship. I should have redeemed the pledge I gave you in this regard, long since; but occupation at one time, and absence from pen and ink at another, have prevented me.

Forster has told you, or will tell you, that I very much wish you to hear my little Christmas Book; and I hope you will meet me, at his bidding, in Lincolns Inn Fields. I have tried to strike a blow upon that part of the brass countenance of Wicked Cant, where such a compliment is sorely needed at this time. And I trust that the result of my training is at least the exhibition of a strong desire to make it a staggerer. If *you* should think at the end of the four rounds (there are no more) that the said Cant, in the language of Bell's Life, "comes up piping",[1] I shall be very much the better for it.

I am now on my way to Milan; and from thence (after a day or two's rest) I mean to come to England by the grandest Alpine Pass that the Snow may leave open. You know this place as famous, of yore, for fiddles. I don't see any, here, now. But there is a whole street of coppersmiths not far from this Inn; and they throb so damnably and fitfully, that I thought I had a palpitation of the heart, after dinner just now—and have seldom been more relieved than when I found the noise to be none of mine.[2]

I was rather shocked, yesterday (I am not strong in geographical details) to find that Romeo was only banished twenty five miles. That is the distance between Mantua and Verona.[3] The latter is a quaint old place, with great houses in it that are now solitary and shut up—exactly the place it ought to be. The former has a great many apothecaries in it at this moment, who could play that part to the life. For of all the stagnant little ponds I ever beheld, it is the

---

[1] Boxing slang for "panting with exhaustion" (*OED*): the Game Chicken (*Dombey*, Ch. 44) had "come up piping".

[2] Cremona is mentioned briefly in *Pictures*, p. 132; for the coppersmiths, see p. 102, where CD wonders "why the head coppersmith in an Italian town, always

lives next door to the Hotel, or opposite: making the visitor feel as if the beating hammers were his own heart, palpitating with a deadly energy!"

[3] See *Pictures*, pp. 120–31 and *To* Lady Blessington, 20 Nov 44.

greenest and weediest. I went to see the old Palace of the Capulets, which is still distinguished by their cognizance (a hat) carved in stone on the Courtyard Wall. It is a miserable Inn.[1] The court was full of crazy coaches, carts, geese, and pigs: and was ankle-deep in mud and dung. The Garden is walled off and built out. There was nothing to connect it with its old inhabitants but a very unsentimental lady at the kitchen-door, who resembled old Capulet in the one particular of being very great indeed, in the "Family" way.[2] The Montagues used to live, some two or three miles off, in the country. It does not appear quite clear whether they ever inhabited Verona itself. But there is a Village bearing their name to this day, and traditions of the quarrels between the two families are still as nearly alive as anything can be, in [this][3] drowsy neighbourhood.

It was very hearty and good of you, Jerrold, to make that affectionate mention of the Carol, in Punch;[4] and I assure you it was not lost upon the distant object of your manly regard, but touched him as you wished and meant it should. I wish we had not lost so much time in improving our personal knowledge of each other. But I have so steadily read you, and so selfishly gratified myself in always expressing the admiration with which your gallant truths inspired me,[5] that I must not call it lost time, either.

You rather entertained the notion once, of coming to see me at Genoa. I shall return, straight, on the 9th. of December—limiting my stay in town to one week. Now, couldn't you come back with me? The journey, that way, is very cheap: costing little more than Twelve Pounds; and I am sure the gratification to you, would be high. I am lodged in quite a wonderful place, and would put you in a painted room, as big as a church and much more comfortable. There are pens and ink upon the premises; orange trees, gardens, battledores and shuttlecocks, rousing wood-fires for evenings; and a welcome worth having. *a*If you were disposed to give Mrs. Jerrold[6] a Christmas Holiday, I will warrant my Wife to be as gentle a little woman, and as free from affectation or formality of any kind, as ever breathed. And it would delight her very much to have an opportunity of confirming my judgment.*a*

Come! Letter from a Gentleman in Italy, to Bradbury and Evans in London. Letter from a gentleman in a country gone to sleep, to a gentleman in a country that would go to sleep too, and never wake again, if some people had their way. You can work in Genoa—the house is used to it—it is exactly a week's Post— Have that portmanteau looked to: and when we meet, say "I am coming".

I have never in my life been so struck by any place as by Venice. It is *the*

---

[1] According to Murray, the Casa de' Capelletti, "now an inn for the vetturini, may possibly have been the dwelling of the family".

[2] This joke appears in the same words in *Pictures*, but is omitted by MDGH, followed by all other published versions.

[3] A small part of the letter was torn by the seal.

[4] In the No. for 6 July 44 there had been a reference to the "worldly wisdom of the excellent Mr. Scrooge", in a piece on governesses with Jerrold's signature of "Q".

[5] He had recently been reading the *Story of a Feather* (see *To* Forster, ?6 Oct 44), and continued to follow Jerrold's work in the *Illuminated Magazine* as well as *Punch* (see *To* Jerrold, 26 May 46).

[6] *Née* Mary Swann, of Wetherby, Yorks, m. 1824.

aa Omitted in all editions of MDGH.

wonder of the world. Dreamy, beautiful, inconsistent, impossible, wicked, shadowy, damnable old place. I entered it by night, and the sensation of that night, and the bright morning that followed, is a part of me for the rest of my existence. And oh God the cells below the water, underneath the Bridge of Sighs—the nook where the Monk came at midnight to confess the political offender—the bench where he was strangled—the deadly little vault in which they tied him in a sack—and the stealthy crouching little door through which they hurried him into a boat, and bore him away to sink him where no fisherman dare cast his net—all shewn by torches that blink and wink as if they were ashamed to look upon the gloomy theatre of such horrors: past and gone as they are—these things stir a man's blood, like a great Wrong or Passion of the Instant. And with them in their minds; and with a Museum there, having a chamber full of such frightful instruments of torture, as the Devil in a brain Fever could scarcely invent, there are hundreds of parrots who will declaim to you in speech and print by the hour together, on the degeneracy of the times in which a Railroad is building across the Water to Venice![1] Instead of going down upon their knees, the drivellers, and thanking Heaven that they live in a time when Iron makes Roads instead of Prison Bars, and engines for driving screws into the skulls of innocent men. Before God!—I could almost turn bloody-minded, and shoot the Parrots[2] of our Island, with as little compunction as Robinson Crusoe shot the parrots in his!—

I have not been in bed, these ten days, after five in the morning; and have been travelling many hours every day. If this be the cause of my inflicting a very stupid and sleepy letter on you, my dear Jerrold, I hope it will be a kind of signal at the same time, of my wish to hail you lovingly, even from this sleepy and unpromising station. And believe me, as I am, always Your friend and admirer.

CHARLES DICKENS

To JOHN FORSTER, [17 and 18 NOVEMBER 1844]

Extracts in F, IV, vi, 359, 359–63. *Date:* all extracts 17 Nov according to Forster, except the last, "next day". *From* Lodi (17 Nov) *and from* Milan (18 Nov).

Saying he had been, like Leigh Hunt's pig, up all manner of streets[3] *since he left his palazzo; that with one exception he had not on any night given up more than five hours to rest; that all the days except two had been bad,* the last two foggy as Blackfriars Bridge on Lord Mayor's Day; *and that the cold had been dismal.*

I am already brim-full of cant about pictures,[4] and shall be happy to enlighten

[1] Opened before the end of 1845. In *Douglas Jerrold's Weekly Newspaper*, 25 July 46, Jerrold supported Mrs Jameson in refusing "to join the outcry, to echo sentimental denunciations, quoted out of Murray's Handbook" against the railroad.

[2] See Vol. III, p. 481 and *n*.

[3] In "The Anxieties of Pig-Driving" (*The Companion*, 26 Mar 1828). The pig bolts when his driver has almost reached Smithfield: " 'Oh, Ch—st!' exclaimed the

man . . . with all the weight of a prophecy which the spectators felt to be too true,— '*he'll go up all manner of streets!*' ": at this point in Hunt's own reading of the essay, he "raised his tone of voice to the highest pitch, hurling himself forward the while upon air, as if in wild desire to retrieve the bolting pig" (Charles and Mary Cowden Clarke, *Recollections of Writers*, 1878, p. 46).

[4] See *To* Forster, ?9 Mar 45 and *fns*.

you on the subject of the different schools, at any length you please. It seems to me that the preposterous exaggeration in which our countrymen delight in reference to this Italy, hardly extends to the really good things. Perhaps it is in its nature, that there it should fall short. I have never seen any praise of Titian's great picture of the Assumption of the Virgin[1] at Venice, which soared half as high as the beautiful and amazing reality. It is perfection.Tintoretto's picture too, of the Assembly of the Blest, at Venice also,[2] with all the lines in it (it is of immense size and the figures are countless) tending majestically and dutifully to Almighty God in the centre, is grand and noble in the extreme. There are some wonderful portraits there, besides; and some confused, and hurried, and slaughterous battle pieces, in which the surprising art that presents the generals to your eye, so that it is almost impossible you can miss them in a crowd though they are in the thick of it, is very pleasant to dwell upon. I have seen some delightful pictures; and some (at Verona and Mantua) really too absurd and ridiculous even to laugh at. Hampton Court is a fool to 'em[3]—and oh there are some rum 'uns there, my friend. Some werry rum 'uns. . . . Two things are clear to me already. One is, that the rules of art are much too slavishly followed; making it a pain to you, when you go into galleries day after day, to be so very precisely sure where this figure will be turning round, and that figure will be lying down, and that other will have a great lot of drapery twined about him, and so forth.[4] This becomes a perfect nightmare. The second is, that these great men, who were of necessity very much in the hands of the monks and priests, painted monks and priests a vast deal too often. I constantly see, in pictures of tremendous power, heads quite below the story and the painter; and I invariably observe that those heads are of the convent stamp, and have their counterparts, exactly, in the convent inmates of this hour. I see the portraits of monks I know at Genoa, in all the lame parts of strong paintings: so I have settled with myself that in such cases the lameness was not with the painter, but with the vanity and ignorance of his employers, who *would* be apostles on canvas at all events.

It is a great thing—quite a matter of course—with English travellers, to decry

---

[1] F, 1872–4, II, 143, reads "Transfiguration of the Virgin"; the correction is made in III, 519. Presumably Forster's error, as *Pictures*, p. 209, reads "Assumption".

[2] Titian's *Assumption* (then in the Accademia, but returned to Santa Maria dei Frari in 1919) was generally recognized as a masterpiece, but CD's admiration for the *Assembly of the Blest* (usually known as the *Paradise*, in the Sala del Gran Consiglio) was uncommon at this date. Ruskin's overwhelming discovery of the genius of Tintoretto, especially the *Paradise*, occurred in 1845: he was "crushed to the earth"— "he's at the top, top, top of everything, with a great big black line underneath" (*Ruskin in Italy. Letters to his Parents, 1845*, ed. H. Shapiro, pp. 211–12).

[3] In Felix Summerly's *Handbook to Hampton Court*, 1843, Henry Cole says: "Since William and Mary's time . . . Hampton Court may be considered to have been the great storehouse, or receptacle . . . for all the pictures—the rejected of the other palaces—until at last above 1000 pictures, not counting others still in the lumber rooms, have been collected together" (p. 83). The pictures are satirized, and one of them described as a "stagnant pool of blacking in a frame", in "Please to leave your Umbrella", *Household Words*, 1 May 58.

[4] This sentence is verbally close to *Pictures*, p. 209 (under "Rome").

the Italian inns. Of course you have no comforts that you are used to in England; and travelling alone, you dine in your bedroom always. Which is opposed to our habits. But they are immeasurably better than you would suppose. The attendants are very quick; very punctual; and so obliging, if you speak to them politely, that you would be a beast not to look cheerful, and take everything pleasantly. I am writing this in a room like a room on the two-pair front of an unfinished house in Eaton-square: the very walls make me feel as if I were a bricklayer distinguished by Mr. Cubitt[1] with the favour of having it to take care of. The windows won't open, and the doors won't shut; and these latter (a cat could get in, between them and the floor) have a windy command of a colonnade which is open to the night, so that my slippers positively blow off my feet, and make little circuits in the room—like leaves. There is a very ashy wood-fire, burning on an immense hearth which has no fender (there is no such thing in Italy); and it only knows two extremes—an agony of heat when wood is put on, and an agony of cold when it has been on two minutes. There is also an uncomfortable stain in the wall, where the fifth door (not being strictly indispensable) was walled up a year or two ago, and never painted over. But the bed is clean; and I have had an excellent dinner; and without being obsequious or servile, which is not at all the characteristic of the people in the North of Italy, the waiters are so amiably disposed to invent little attentions which they suppose to be English, and are so lighthearted and goodnatured, that it is a pleasure to have to do with them. But so it is with all the people. Vetturino-travelling involves a stoppage of two hours in the middle of the day, to bait the horses. At that time I always walk on. If there are many turns in the road, I necessarily have to ask my way, very often: and the men are such gentlemen, and the women such ladies, that it is quite an interchange of courtesies.

The brave C continues to be a prodigy. He puts out my clothes at every inn as if I were going to stay there twelve months; calls me to the instant every morning; lights the fire before I get up; gets hold of roast fowls and produces them in coaches at a distance from all other help, in hungry moments; and is invaluable to me. He is such a good fellow, too, that little rewards don't spoil him. I always give him, after I have dined, a tumbler of Sauterne or Hermitage or whatever I may have; sometimes (as yesterday) when we have come to a public-house at about eleven o'clock, very cold, having started before day-break and had nothing, I make him take his breakfast with me; and this renders him only more anxious than ever, by redoubling attentions, to show me that he thinks he has got a good master. . . . I didn't tell you that the day before I left Genoa, we had a dinner-party—our English consul and his wife;[2] the banker;[3]

<hr/>

[1] Thomas Cubitt (1788–1855; *DNB*), builder. Eaton Square was begun in 1827 but not completed till 1853.

[2] Timothy Yeats Brown (1789–1858), British consul at Genoa from 1840 till his death. During the lifetime of his father (Timothy Brown, 1751–1810, banker), he enjoyed a large income and was a collector of books and pictures (most of which he later sold to feed and educate his children),

but he inherited less than he expected. From 1825 to 1832 he was travelling on the continent, and in Munich in 1829 he met and married his 2nd wife, Stuarta (1810–93), daughter of the 2nd Lord Erskine. They settled on the island of Palmaria 1832, where they remained until the influence of his wife's family obtained for him the appointment at Genoa. As a young man he had been intimate with many of the Italian

Sir George Crawford and his wife;[1] the De la Rues;[2] Mr. Curry; and some others, fourteen in all. At about nine in the morning, two men in immense paper caps enquired at the door for the brave C, who presently introduced them in triumph as the Governor's cooks, his private friends, who had come to dress the dinner! Jane wouldn't stand this, however; so we were obliged to decline. Then there came, at half-hourly intervals, six gentlemen having the appearance of English clergymen; other private friends who had come to wait. . . . We accepted *their* services; and you never saw anything so nicely and quietly done. He had asked, as a special distinction, to be allowed the supreme control of the dessert; and he had ices made like fruit, had pieces of crockery turned upside down so as to look like other pieces of crockery non-existent in this part of Europe, and carried a case of tooth-picks in his pocket. Then his delight was, to get behind Kate at one end of the table, to look at me at the other, and to say to Georgy in a low voice whenever he handed her anything, "What does master think of datter 'range-ment? Is he cŏntĕnt?" . . . If you could see what these fellows of couriers are when their families are not upon the move, you would feel what a prize he is. I can't make out whether he was ever a smuggler, but nothing will induce him to give the custom-house-officers anything: in consequence of which that port-manteau of mine has been unnecessarily opened twenty times. Two of them will

---

refugees in England, with whose aspira-itons he sympathized. The Browns occupied the Palazzo Cambiaso on Salita Sta Maria della Sanita, and one of his sons recalled their life there as "very pleasant. We children had a good deal of liberty, my mother being chiefly taken up with my father, and many friends amongst the foreign colonies and the Genoese. They did not go out much, my father not being inclined that way, but people came to dinner etc. very often". (Information from F. A. Y. Brown, *Family Notes*, privately printed, Genoa, 1917, and John Evelyn Wrench, *Francis Yeats-Brown, 1866–1944*, 1948.)

[3] Charles Gibbs.

[1] Sir George William Gregan Craufurd, 3rd Bart (1797–1881). Divinity lecturer at Cambridge 1831–8, Vicar of Burgh with Winthorpe, Lincs 1838–45; succeeded to the baronetcy 1839; author of several books. He married 1843 Hester (*d.* before 1849), daughter of Peter, Baron King, sister of Lord Lovelace. According to Forster (VI, vi, 527), it was through the Craufurds, "so friendly in Genoa", that CD met the Love-laces.

[2] Emile de la Rue (*d.* 1870), Swiss banker resident in Genoa; director until his death of the important and highly respected banking-house founded by his grandfather, André de la Rue of Geneva. Camillo

Cavour (whose family had known the de la Rues in Geneva) became an intimate friend of his contemporary, Emile, when he was stationed in Genoa in 1830–1; during the next thirty years he relied greatly on de la Rue's services and advice, as friend and banker, consulting him about finance, commercial legislation and politics. De la Rue married before 1830 Augusta Granet (*d.* 1887), member of an English family resident in Genoa; Cavour found her a charming and lively woman, although something of an invalid during the 1830s and 40s. The de la Rues lived on a floor of the Palazzo Brignole Rosso where they entertained the society of Genoa, including many foreign visitors. Christiana Thompson (*née* Weller) and her husband were frequent guests during their stay in Genoa in 1845–6 (see *To* Thompson, 17 Oct 45, *fn*), and in her Journal (MS Mrs Sowerby) she approved the "absence of restraint and ceremony" in their hospitality, and discovered in Mme de la Rue a likeness to Fanny Burnett. (Information about the de la Rues and their friendship with Cavour from Camillo Cavour, *Epistolario*, ed. D. Zanichelli, Bologna, 1962, I, which includes a genea-logical table of the de la Rues; Cavour, *Nouvelles Lettres Inédites*, ed. Amédée Bert, Turin, 1889; and D. Berti, *Il Conte di Cavour avanti il 1848*, Rome, 1856.)

come to the coach-door, at the gate of a town. "Is there anything contraband in this carriage, signore?"—"No, no. There's nothing here. I am an Englishman, and this is my servant." "A buono mano signore?" "Roche" (in English), "give him something, and get rid of him." He sits unmoved. "A buono mano signore?" "Go along with you!" says the brave C. "Signore, I am a custom-house-officer!" "Well, then, more shame for you!"—he always makes the same answer. And then he turns to me and says in English: while the custom-house-officer's face is a portrait of anguish framed in the coach-window,[1] from his intense desire to know what is being told to his disparagement: "Datter chip," shaking his fist at him, "is greatest tief—and you know it you rascal—as never did en-razh me so, that I cannot bear myself!" I suppose chip to mean chap, but it may include the custom-house-officer's father and have some reference to the old block, for anything I distinctly know.

Catherine and Georgina met him next day at Milan, having travelled 80 *miles from Genoa.* We shall go our several ways on Thursday morning, and I am still bent on appearing at Cuttris's on Sunday the first, as if I had walked thither from Devonshire-terrace. In the meantime I shall not write to you again . . . to enhance the pleasure (if anything *can* enhance the pleasure) of our meeting. . . . I am opening my arms so wide!

To THE COUNTESS OF BLESSINGTON, 20 NOVEMBER 1844†

MS Benoliel Collection. *Address:* Inghilterra | The | Countess of Blessington | Gore House | Kensington | London.

Milan. Wednesday November Twentieth 1844.

My Dear Lady Blessington. Appearances are against me. Don't believe them. I have written you, in intention, fifty letters. And I can claim no credit for any one of them (though they were the best letters you ever read), for they all originated in my true desire to live in your memory and regard.

Since I heard from Count D'Orsay, I have been beset in I don't know how many ways. First of all, I went to Marseilles, and came back to Genoa by the Cornice Road. Then I moved to the Peschiere. Then some people who had been present at the Scientific Congress here, made a sudden inroad on that Establishment and over-ran it. Then they went away, and I shut myself up for one month, close and tight, over my Christmas Book. All my affections and passions got twined and knotted up in it, and I became as haggard as a Murderer, long before I wrote "The End". When I had done that; like *the* Man of Thessaly[2] who having scratched his eyes out in a quickset hedge, plunged into a Bramble-bush to scratch them in again, I fled off to Venice, to recover the composure I

---

[1] See the account of the passport officers in *Pictures*, p. 105 ("Ferrara"), when Roche was "stone deaf to my entreaties that the man might have a trifle given him, and . . . was wont to sit reviling the functionary in broken English"; the description of the man's "mental agony framed in the coach window" is verbally close.

[2] Quotation from nursery-rhyme; *Oxford Dictionary of Nursery Rhymes*, No. 498.

had disturbed. From thence, I went to Verona and to Mantua. And now I am here. Just come up from underground; and earthy all over, from seeing that extraordinary Tomb[1] in which the Dead Saint lies in an Alabaster Case, with sparkling Jewels all about him to mock his dusty eyes: and robes of gold and fine linen dressing out his miserable old mummied carcase. Not to mention the Twenty Franc pieces which devout votaries were ringing down upon a sort of skylight in the Cathedral pavement above, as if it were the Counter of his Heavenly Shop.

You know Verona? You know everything in Italy, *I* know.[2] *a*I am not learned in Geography, and it was a great blow to me to find that Romeo was only banished five and twenty miles. It was a greater blow to me, to see the old house of the Capulets, with their cognizance still carved in stone, over the Gateway of the Court Yard. It is a most miserable little Inn, at this time; ankle-deep in dirt; and noisy Vetturini and muddy market carts were disputing possession of the Yard, with a brood of geese—all splashed and bespattered, as if they had their yesterday's white trousers on. There was nothing to connect it with the beautiful story, but a very unsentimental middle-aged lady—the Padrona, I suppose—in the doorway, who resembled old Capulet in the one particular of being very great indeed, in the "Family" way.*a*

The Roman amphitheatre[3] there, delighted me beyond expression. I never saw anything so full of such a solemn interest. There are the Four and forty rows of seats, as fresh and perfect as if their Roman occupants had vacated them but yesterday—the entrances, passages, dens, rooms, corridors; the very numbers over some of the arches. An equestrian troop had been there a few days before, and had scooped out a little ring at one end of the arena, and had their performances on that spot. I should like to have seen it, of all things, for its very dreariness. Fancy a handfull of people sprinkled over one corner of the great place (the whole population of Verona wouldn't fill it now) and a clown being funny[4] to the echoes, and the grass-grown walls! I climbed to the topmost seat, and looked away at the beautiful view for some minutes; and turning round, and looking down into the Theatre again, it had exactly the appearance of an immense straw hat, to which the helmet in the Castle of Otranto was a Baby: the rows of seats representing the different plaits of straw: and the arena, the inside of the crown. *b*Do shut your eyes and think of it, a moment.

I came through Modena[5] (I am reminded of it by the mention of the strollers), on a brilliant day. One of those days when the sky is so blue that it hardly seems

---

[1] The Chapel of San Carlo Borromeo; *Pictures*, pp. 132–3. Here and elsewhere the letter has clearly been used for *Pictures*: see *To* Lady Blessington, 1 Mar 46.

[2] See *To* Lady Blessington, 9 May 45 and *fn*.

aa Omitted in MDGH, 1882, although included in R. R. Madden, *The Literary Life and Correspondence of the Countess of Blessington*, III, 101–3, which is MDGH's source. Madden's text has numerous omissions (the longer ones indicated below), a large number of errors and some gratuitous additions (not enumerated), in which he is followed by all later printings of the letter.

[3] *Pictures*, pp. 123–4.

[4] These words crowded in at foot of page and difficult to read; "funny" seems clear, and the preceding word ends in "ing".

bb Not previously published.

[5] The passage that follows is incorporated almost word for word in *Pictures*, p. 93.

blue at all, but some other colour.—Lord Castlereagh[1] might have said it, but it's true. I passed from all this glory into a dark mysterious church, where high mass was performing, feeble tapers were burning, and people were kneeling about in all directions, and before all manner of shrines. Thinking how strange it was to find in every stagnant town, this same heart beating with the same monotonous pulsations; the centre of the same languid, torpid, listless circulation; I came out again by another door, and was scared to Death by the blast of the shrillest trumpet that ever was blown. Forthwith, there came tearing round the corner, an equestrian Company from Paris, marshalling themselves under the very walls of the church: flouting with their horses' heels, the very Griffins and Tigers supporting its pillars. First of all, there came an Austrian Prince without a hat: bearing an enormous banner on which was inscribed "Mazeppa.[2] Oggi Sera!" Then a Mexican chief, with a great club upon his shoulder, like Hercules. Then six or eight Roman Chariots: each with a beautiful lady in extremely short petticoats, and unnaturally pink silks, erect within: shedding beaming looks upon the crowd, in which there was an unaccountable expression of discomposure and anxiety, until the open back of each chariot presented itself, and one saw the immense difficulty with which the Pink Legs maintained their perpendicular over the uneven stones of the town—which was the drollest thing I ever beheld, and gave me quite a new idea of the ancient Romans and ancient Britons. The procession was brought to a close by some dozen warriors of different Nations, riding two and two; and when it passed on, the people who had come out of the church to look at it, went in again to *that* spectacle. One old lady kneeling on the pavement near the door, had seen it all, and had been immensely interested— without getting up. Catching my eye when it was all over, she crossed herself devoutly, and went down at full length on her face before a figure in a blue silk petticoat and a gilt crown; which was so like one of the other figures, that I thought her interest in the Circus quite excusable and appropriate.[b]

I had great expectations of Venice, but they fell immeasurably short of the wonderful reality. The short time I passed there, went by me in a dream. I hardly think it possible to exaggerate its beauties, its sources of interest, its uncommon novelty and freshness. A Thousand and One realizations of the Thousand and One Nights could scarcely captivate and enchant me, more than Venice.

[c]Pray tell Count D'Orsay, dear Lady Blessington, with my heartiest remembrances, that the receipt of his letter, was a long and deep notch in my then very wooden Calendar at Albaro. He did me but justice in supposing me able to read it without difficulty, as I have long been accustomed to read French almost as easily as English. But its sound is rather strange in my ears. I know it, as I know some men, perfectly well by sight—and therefore I design, Please God, to spend

[1] Cf. *To* Mrs Laing, 2 Feb 44 and *fn.*

[2] The first "hippodramatic spectacle" based on Byron's *Mazeppa* was produced at the Royal Coburg 3 Nov 23, and the first French adaptation at the Cirque Olympique, Paris, 1825; but its real popularity dates from the version staged at Astley's in 1831, and repeatedly revived over the next fifty years, becoming a staple in the repertory of circuses in England and abroad (see A. H. Saxon, *Enter Foot and Horse. A History of Hippodrama*, 1968, Ch. 7).

[cc] Not previously published.

next May and June in Paris,[1] that I may enlarge my acquaintance with it, and encounter it upon easy terms. I have applied very little to the Italian: being lazy at first, and otherwise busy since. But I have great pleasure in what I know of it; and can understand, and be understood, without difficulty.

We like Italy more and more, every day. We are splendidly lodged—have a noble Sala—fifty feet high, and splendidly painted—and beautiful gardens. Mrs. Dickens and the children are as well as possible; our servants (contrary to all predictions) as contented and orderly as at home; and everything else "in a concatination accordingly".[c]

Your old house Il Paradiso, is spoken of as yours to this day. What a gallant place it is! I don't know the present Inmate, but I hear that he bought and furnished it not long since, with great splendour, in the French style—and that he wishes to sell it. I wish I were rich, and could buy it. There is a third rate Wine Shop below Byron's house; and the place looks dull and miserable and ruinous enough. Old De Negro[2] is a trifle uglier than when I first arrived. He has periodical parties at the Villetta; at which there are a great many flowerpots and a few ices—no other refreshments. He goes about, constantly charged with extemporaneous poetry, and is always ready, like Tavern Dinners, on the shortest notice and the most reasonable terms. He keeps a Gigantic Harp in his bedroom, together with pen and paper for fixing his ideas as they flow—a kind of profane King David, but very harmless. Very.

[d]I am in great hopes that I shall make you cry, bitterly, with my little Book; and that Miss Power and her sister will take it, also, to heart. I dare say you have forgotten that when we parted, I promised myself the pleasure of sending you an early proof to read, but *I* have not. So in the course of the first week of December, "about this time"—as Moore's almanack says—"a packet may be looked for"—It will be a great pleasure to me to think that you have bestowed an hour upon it.[d]

Pray say to Count D'Orsay, everything that is cordial and loving from me. His purse has been of immense service. It has been constantly opened. All Italy seems to yearn to put its hand in it. When I come back to England I shall have it hung up, on a nail, as a trophy. And I think of gashing the brim like the blade of an old sword, and saying to my son and heir, as they do upon the stage—"You see this notch boy? Five hundred francs were laid low on that day, for post horses. Where this gap is, a waiter charged me treble the correct amount—and got it. This end, worn into teeth like a file, is sacred to the Custom Houses, boy—the passports—and the shabby soldiers at town-gates who put an open hand and a coat-cuff into the coach-windows of all Forestieri. Take it, boy. Thy father has nothing else to give."

My desk is cooling itself in a Mail coach, somewhere down at the back of the Cathedral. And the pens and ink in this house (where the Great Mr. Lumley tarries, by the way) are so detestable, that I have no hope of your ever getting to this portion of my letter. But I have the less misery in this state of mind, from knowing that it has nothing in it to repay you for the trouble of perusal, [e]and

---

[1] CD changed his plans in Apr 45; for his reasons see *To* Mitton, 20 May 45.

[2] Name omitted in previously published texts.

dd; ee Not previously published.

that you do not require its formal close to assure you (or you would not have parted from me with such unaffected and genuine kindness) that I am ever, My Dear Lady Blessington, Faithfully and truly Yours,

CHARLES DICKENS

P.S. I beg to be remembered to your Nieces. I saw a picture very like Miss Power, at Venice—and again denounced that Frankenstein of an Artist, who had his Easel at Gore House when I left.*e*

To MRS CHARLES DICKENS, 23 NOVEMBER 1844

MS British Museum. *Address:* Italia | A Madame | Madame Dickens | Palazzo Peschiere | Genova | Italia.

Fribourg. Saturday Night November Twenty Third 1844.

My Dearest Kate. For the first time since I left you, I am sitting in a room of my own hiring, with a fire and a bed, in it. And I am happy to say that I have the best and fullest intentions of sleeping in the bed; having arrived here at half past four this afternoon, without any cessation of travelling, night or day, since I parted from Mrs. Bairr's[1] cheap firewood.

The Alps appeared in sight, very soon after we left Milan—by 8 or 9 o'Clock in the morning; and the Brave C was so far wrong in his calculations, that we began the ascent of the Simplon that same night, while you were travelling (as I would I were) towards the Peschiere. Most favourable state of circumstances for journeying up that tremendous Pass! The brightest moon I ever saw, all night; and daybreak on the summit. The Glory of which: making great wastes of snow, a rosy red: exceeds all telling. We *sledged* through the snow on the summit, for two hours or so. The weather was perfectly fair and bright; and there was neither difficulty nor danger—except the danger that there always must be in such a place, of a horse stumbling on the brink of an immeasurable precipice. In which case, no piece of the unfortunate traveller would be left, large enough, to tell his story in dumb-show. You may imagine something of the rugged grandeur of such a scene as this great passage of these great mountains; and indeed Glencoe, well-sprinkled with Snow, would be very like the ascent. But the top itself, so wild, and bleak, and lonely, is a thing *by* itself, and not to be likened to any other sight. The cold was piercing; the north-wind, high and boisterous; and when it came driving in our faces, bringing a sharp shower of little points of snow and piercing it into our very blood, it really was, what it is often said to be, "cutting" —with a very sharp edge too. There are houses of refuge here—bleak, solitary places—for travellers overtaken by the snow, to hurry to, as an escape from death; and one great house, called the Hospital, kept by monks, where wayfarers get supper and bed for nothing. We saw some coming out and pursuing their journey. If all Monks devoted themselves to such uses, I should have little fault to find with them.[2]

---

[1] Of the Hotel de la Ville, Milan.

[2] There is a fuller account of the journey over the Simplon Pass, in *Pictures*, pp. 136–40; the Hospital is referred to as "the Hospice founded by Napoleon". CD and Roche left Milan on 21 Nov and travelled through two days and nights.

The cold in Switzerland, since, has been something quite indescribable. My eyes are tingling tonight, as one may suppose cymbals to tingle when they have been lustily played.—It is positive purgatory to me to write. The Great Organ[1] which I was to have had "pleasure in hearing" don't play on a Saturday at which the Brave is inconsolable. But the town is picturesque and quaint, and worth seeing. And the Inn (with a German bedstead in it, about the size and shape of a baby's linen-basket) is perfectly clean and comfortable. Butter is so cheap hereabouts, that they bring you a great mass, like the squab of a sofa, for tea. And of honey, which is most delicious, they set before you a proportionate allowance. We start tomorrow morning at 6, for Strasburgh; and from that town, or the next halting-place on the Rhine; I will report progress; if it be only in half a dozen words.

I am anxious to hear that you reached Genoa quite comfortably—and shall look forward with impatience to that letter, which you are to indite, with so much care and pains, next Monday. My best love to Georgy. And to Charley, and Mamey, and Katey,[2] and Walley, and Chickenstalker. I have treated myself to a new travelling-cap tonight (my old one being too thin), and it is rather a prodigious affair I flatter myself.

Swiss towns, and mountains, and the Lake of Geneva, and the famous suspension-Bridge[3] at this place, and a great many other objects (with a very low thermometer conspicuous among them) are dancing up and down me, strangely. But I am quite collected enough, notwithstanding, to have still a very distinct idea that this Hornpipe travelling is uncomfortable, and that I would gladly start for my Palazzo out of hand, without any previous rest. Stupid as I am, and much as I want it!

Ever my Dear Love Affectionately Yours

Mrs. Charles Dickens.

CHARLES DICKENS

P.S. I hope the Dancing Lessons will be a success. Don't fail to let me know.

To JOHN FORSTER, [25 NOVEMBER 1844]

Extract in F, IV, vi, 363. *Date:* "Monday night the 25th" according to Forster. *From* Strasburg.[4]

Saying that Forster might look for him one day earlier, so rapid had been his progress. He had been in bed only once, at Friburg for two or three hours, since he left Milan, and he had sledged through the snow on the top of the Simplon in the midst of prodigious cold. I am sitting here *in* a wood-fire, and drinking brandy and water scalding hot, with a faint idea of coming warm in time. My face is at present tingling with the frost and wind, as I suppose the cymbals may, when that turbaned Turk attached to the Life Guards' band has been newly clashing at

---

[1] In Fribourg Cathedral.

[2] Written large.

[3] The longest of a single curve in the world; completed 1834.

[4] CD passed through Basle on 24 Nov and evidently dined at the Hotel of the Three Kings ("below [its] windows . . . the swollen Rhine ran fast and green"; *Pictures*, p. 141).

them in St. James's-park. I am in hopes it may be the preliminary agony of returning animation.

To W. C. MACREADY, 28 NOVEMBER 1844*

MS Missouri Historical Society. *Date:* clearly 28 Nov; it is the "Exhibit Marked A" referred to in *To* Macready, written later the same night.

Hotel Bristol. Place Vendomme[1] | Thursday Nigh

My Dearest Macready.

I have been travelling for weeks, and have not been five minutes in Paris, on my way to London—after a 50 hours' spell in a horrible coach. Are you at Meurice's? If you are, I shall come and rush into your arms—as soon as I am clean enough—unless you anticipate me by coming here and rushing into mine. I go on to London at 8 tomorrow morning.

Affecy. Ever & Ever
CD.

To MRS CHARLES DICKENS, 28 NOVEMBER 1844

MS British Museum. *Address:* Italie | A Madame | Madame Dickens | Palazzo Peschiere | Genes | Italie.

Hotel Bristol, Paris. | Thursday Night November 28th. 1844

My Dearest Kate. With an intolerable pen, and no ink, I am going to write a few lines to you, to report progress.

I got to Strasburgh on Monday Night: intending to go down the Rhine. But the weather being foggy, and the Season quite over: they could not insure out getting on, for certain, beyond Mayence: or our not being detained by unpropitious weather. Therefore I resolved (the Malle Poste being full) to take the Diligence hither—next day in the afternoon. I arrived here at halfpast five tonight, after 50 hours of it, in a French coach. I was so beastly dirty when I got to this house, that I had quite lost all sense of my identity, and if anybody had said 'Are you Charles Dickens?' I should have unblushingly answered 'No. I never heard of him.' A good wash, and a good dress, and a good dinner, have revived me, however: and I can report of this house concerning which the Brave was so anxious when we were here before, that it is the best I ever was in. My little apartment—consisting of three rooms, and other conveniences—is a perfect curiosity of completeness. You never saw such a charming little baby-house. It is infinitely smaller than those first rooms we had at Meurice's, but for elegance, compactness, comfort, and quietude, exceeds anything I ever met with at an Inn.[2]

The moment I arrived here, I enquired, of course, after Macready. They said

---

[1] Thus in MS.
[2] The Hotel Bristol was described by

Galignani's Paris *Guide* as "the Mivart's or Clarendon of Paris, expensive but good".

the English Theatre had not begun yet, but they thought he was at Meurice's, where they knew some members of the company to be. I instantly dispatched the Porter with a note, to say that if he were there, I would come round and hug him, as soon as I was clean. They referred the Porter to the Hotel Brighton. He came back and told me, that the answer, there, was, 'M. Macready's rooms *(I feel that I am writing rather like him)*[a] were engaged, but he had not arrived. He was expected *tonight*.' If we meet tonight, I will add a Postscript. Wouldn't it be odd if we met upon the road between this and Boulonge,[1] tomorrow?

I mean, as a recompense for my late sufferings, to get a Hackney carriage if I can—and post that journey—starting from here, at 8 tomorrow morning—getting to Boulonge sufficiently early next morning to cross at once, and dining with Forster that same day: to wit, Saturday. I have notions of taking you with me on my next journey (if you would like to go!) and arranging for Georgy to come to us by Steamer—under the protection of the English captain, for instance —to Naples—where I would top and cap all our walks, by taking her up to the crater of Vesuvius with me. But this is dependent on her ability to be perfectly happy for a fortnight or so, in our stately palace, with the children, and such foreign aid as the Simpsons.[2] For I love her too dearly, to think of any project, which would involveher being uncomfortable for that space of time.

You can think this over, and talk it over—and I will join you in doing so, Please God, when I return to our Italian Bowers, which I shall be heartily glad to do. I will write to you again, by Monday's Post, from London. They tell us here, that the Landlord of this house, going to London some week or so ago, was detained at Boulonge two days by a high sea in which the Packets could not put out. So I hope there is the greater chance of no such bedevilment happening to me.

Paris is better than ever. Oh dear how grand it was, when I came through it in that Caravan tonight! I hope we shall be very hearty here—and able to say with Walley "Han't it plassant!"

*Apropos of nothing. The Babbages. My mind sorely misgives me, that the Babbages ought to be at the Reading. I hardly think we have taken as much notice of them as we should have done, or as they have shewn they desired.[b3]

Love to Charley, Mamey, Katey,[4] Walley, and Chickenstalker. The last-named, I take it for granted, is indeed Prodigious.

Best love to Georgy.
Ever my dearest Kate | Affectionately Yours

Mrs. Charles Dickens CHARLES DICKENS

P.S. I have been round to Macreadys hotel—it is now past 10—and he has not arrived, nor does it seem at all certain that he seriously intended to arrive tonight. So I shall not see him, I take it for granted until my return.

---

[1] Thus in MS and throughout this letter, though correctly elsewhere.

[2] Unidentified.

aa; bb Omitted in MDGH.

[3] Not Charles Babbage, a widower, but Benjamin Herschel Babbage and his wife Laura.

[4] Written large.

To W. C. MACREADY, 28 NOVEMBER 1844†

MS Morgan Library.

Hotel Bristol, Paris.
Thursday Night November 28th. 1844. | Half Past Ten.

My Dearest Macready.

Since I wrote to you, what would be called in Law Proceedings the Exhibit Marked A, I have been round to the Hotel Brighton, and personally examined, and cross-examined, the attendants. It is painfully clear to me, that I shall not hug you tonight.[1] Nor until Tuesday the 10th: of December; when, Please God, I shall re-arrive here, on my way to my Italian Bowers. I mean to stay, all the Wednesday, and all the Thursday, in Paris. One night to see you act (my old delight when you little thought of such a Being in existence), and one night to read to you[2] and Mrs. Macready (if that Scamp of Lincolns Inn Fields have not anticipated me) my little Christmas Book. In which I have endeavoured to plant an indignant right-hander on the eye of certain Wicked Cant that makes my blood boil, which I hope will not only cloud that eye with black and blue, but many a gentler one with chrystal of the purest sort. God forgive me,—but I think there are good things in the little Story!

*a*I want you, meanwhile, to execute a little commission for me here; and to advertize me in one line, addressed to the Piazza Coffee House Covent Garden London (did you ever dine there?) that you have done so, successfully. Will you, *as soon after your arrival as convenient*; for the conveyance is in great request; take me Two Places in the Malle Poste to Marseilles, for Friday afternoon the Thirteenth of December—paying the money, or as much as may be necessary, and holding me your Debtor until we meet.

The Malle Poste, observe. And nothing but the Malle Poste. Should it be unfortunately engaged for that day (which, with so long a notice, is not likely) then the day before or the day after. But *that* is the day I want.*a*

I took it for granted you were, as your American friends say, "in full blast" here—and meant to have sent a card into your dressing-room with "Mr. G. S. Hancock Muggridge. United States"—upon it. But Paris looks coldly on me, without your eye in its head; and not being able to shake your hand, I shake my own head dolefully. Which is but poor satisfaction.

My love to Mrs. Macready. I will swear to the Death that it is truly hers for her Gallantry in your absence if for nothing else. And to you my Dear Macready I am ever a devoted friend   CHARLES DICKENS

---

[1] When CD left Genoa Macready was expected to open his Paris season at the Théâtre des Italiens on 25 Nov (*Galignani's Messenger*, 3 Nov); postponements to 2 Dec (*ibid*; 15 Nov) and 4 Dec (advertisement, 27 Nov) followed; in order to be ready by 4 Dec Macready planned to leave London 26 Nov, but on 25 Nov he had a serious fall which delayed his arrival in Paris until 7 Dec and caused two further postponements—to 9 Dec and, finally, to 16 Dec (*Galignani's Messenger*, 15 Nov–16 Dec, *Examiner*, 20 Nov, 30 Nov, 21 Dec).

[2] CD read *The Chimes* to Macready in London on Sunday, 1 Dec: see *To* Mrs CD, 2 Dec 44.

aa Not previously published.

To JOHN LEECH, 1 DECEMBER 1844

MS Comtesse de Suzannet. *Address:* John Leech [Esquire][1] | 9 Powis Place | Great Ormond Street.

Piazza Coffee House | Covent Garden
Sunday December First 1844.

My Dear Leech.

You have done gallantly, for my little book.[2] And I am greatly pleased with this new token of your talent and interest, believe me.

Will you come and breakfast with me here, tomorrow, at Ten? There is a slight alteration in one of your blocks[3] (explainable in half a minute) which I want to tell you of.

Always | Faithfully Yours
CHARLES DICKENS

I beg my compliments to Mrs. Leech.[4] Mrs. Dickens and her sister, charged me with many kind messages to you both.

To JOHN LEECH, 3 DECEMBER 1844

MS Comtesse de Suzannet. *Address:* John Leech Esquire | Powis Place | Great Ormond Street.

Piazza Coffee House Covent Garden | Tuesday Morning

My Dear Leech.

On coming *home* here, late last night, I found your note. The alteration in respect of the figure of Richard will be quite sufficient; and I assure you that your cheerful readiness to give yourself trouble on my account gratifies me exceedingly. It is a real pleasure to me to say so, and to work with you. I have the greatest diffidence in suggesting any change, however slight, in what you do—you are so ready to make it.

Always Believe me | Faithfully Yours
John Leech Esquire   CHARLES DICKENS

To THE GOVERNORS OF THE ORPHAN WORKING SCHOOL, [?DECEMBER 1844]

Mention in *To* Miss Coutts, 8 Dec 44. *Date:* shortly before 8 Dec when CD told Miss Coutts that he had heard from the Governors.

Nominating John Richard Overs, eldest son of John Overs, for a place in the Orphan Working School.[5]

[1] Envelope torn.
[2] Leech supplied five of the thirteen illustrations.
[3] Of the figure of Richard in the Third Quarter, p. 125. The original version, showing Richard with a battered hat and looking more dissipated, is in the proof copies in the Forster Collection and the

J. F. Dexter Collection; reproduced in F. G. Kitton, *CD by Pen & Pencil*, 1, 52.
[4] Ann, *née* Eaton: see Vol. III, p. 358*n*.
[5] See *To* Soul, 26 May 43: Vol. III, p. 497 and *n*. CD had become a Life Governor in 1844 by subscribing five guineas, which entitled him to nominate children for admission and to vote at each election.

To MRS CHARLES DICKENS, 2 DECEMBER 1844

MS British Museum. *Address:* Mrs. Charles Dickens | Palazzo Peschiere | Genoa |
North Italy.

Piazza Coffee House, Covent Garden.
December Second 1844. Monday.

My Dearest Kate. I received, with great delight, your *excellent* letter of this
morning. Do not regard this, as my answer to it. It is merely to say that I have
been at Bradbury and Evans's all day, and have barely time to write more, than
that I *will* write tomorrow. I arrived about 7 on Saturday Evening, and rushed
into the arms of Mac and Forster[1]—Both of whom, send their best loves to you
and Georgy. With a heartiness, not to be described.

The little book, is now, so far as I am concerned, all ready. One cut of Doyle's,[2]
and one of Leech's, I found so unlike my idea, that I had them both to breakfast
with me this morning, and with that winning manner which you know of, got
them with the highest good humour, to do both afresh. They are now hard at it.
[Stan]field's[3] readiness—delight—wonder at my being pleased—in what *he* has
done[4] is delicious. Mac's frontispiece is charming. The book is quite splendid,
—the expences will be very great, I have no doubt.

Anybody who has heard it, has been moved in the most extraordinary manner.
Forster read it (for dramatic purposes) to A Beckett[5]—not a man of very quiet
feeling. He cried so much, and so painfully, that Forster didn't know whether
to go on or stop; and he called next day to say that any expression of his feeling
was beyond his power. But that he believed it, and felt it, to be—I won't say
what.

As the reading comes off tomorrow night,[6] I had better not despatch my letter

---

[1] Forster recalls "the eager face and
figure, as they flashed upon me so suddenly
this wintry Saturday night that almost
before I could be conscious of his presence
I felt the grasp of his hand" (F, IV, vi, 363).

[2] Richard Doyle supplied designs for the
opening of each Quarter; the first appears
in the proof copies (exactly as in the 1st
edn) but none of the others: "Trotty at
Home", "Trotty and the Bells", "Margaret
and her Child".

[3] A small tear has removed a few letters.

[4] "The Old Church" and "Will Fern's
Cottage".

[5] CD apparently authorized the dramatization of *The Chimes* by Gilbert
A'Beckett and Mark Lemon and allowed
them to have advance sheets of the work.
Their version was put on at the Adelphi on
Wednesday, 18 Dec, two days after publication of the book. There were several
other dramatizations, including Edward
Stirling's which opened at the Lyceum on
26 Dec, with Keeley as Trotty Veck,

Samuel Atkyns's at the Albert Saloon and
Edward Edwards's at the Apollo Saloon
on 28 Dec (Malcolm Morley, "Ring up
The Chimes", D, XLVII [1951], 202–61).

[6] Forster's note of invitation to W. J. Fox
says: "It is a *tea party*—D. objecting to
anything more jovial—we assemble *punctually* [*doubly underlined*] *at* ½ *past* 6. Tomorrow—Tuesday" (MS Suzannet); he
wrote in similar terms to William Harness
(extract in Anderson Galleries catalogue
No. 1659, May 1922). Forster describes
the reading, at his rooms in Lincoln's Inn
Fields, in F, IV, vi, 363 (misdating it Monday
2 Dec), naming as present Carlyle, Maclise,
Stanfield, Laman Blanchard, Jerrold, Fox,
Harness and Alexander Dyce, and reproducing Maclise's sketch, which shows that
Frederick Dickens was also there. All those
CD had wished for (see *To* Forster, 3 and
4 Nov 44) were present except Jane Carlyle,
Miss Maclise and Edwin Landseer. A
second reading was given on 5 Dec after
dinner at Forster's, at Barham's request,

to you, until *Wednesday's* Post. I must close to save this (heartily tired I am; and I dine at Gore House today!) so with love to Georgy, Mamey, Katey, Charley, Walley, and Chickenstalker, Ever believe me Yours with true [affec]tion. CD.

P.S. If you had seen Macready last night—undisguisedly sobbing, and crying on the sofa, as I read—you would have felt (as I did) what a thing it is to have Power.
P.P.S. "In[".][1]

To THE COUNTESS OF BLESSINGTON, 6 DECEMBER 1844

MS Carl H. Pforzheimer Library.

Piazza Coffee House.
Friday Sixth December 1844. | In the greatest haste.

My Dear Lady Blessington.

My proofs have been delayed. I send them to you the moment I receive them. As the book is not published until the Sixteenth,[2] I need not ask you to keep them "close".

I purpose coming to you on Sunday to say good bye. Meanwhile remember me most cordially to Count D'Orsay, and to the young ladies, and believe me, with earnest regard.

Ever Faithfully Yours
The Countess of Blessington.   CHARLES DICKENS

To THE COUNTESS OF BLESSINGTON, [8 DECEMBER 1844]

MS Carl H. Pforzheimer Library. *Date:* Sunday was 8 Dec and the day of CD's departure (see next).

Covent Garden Sunday Noon
My Dear Lady Blessington.

Business for other people (and by no means of a pleasant kind)[3] has held me prisoner during two whole days, and will so detain me today, in the very agony of departure, that I shall not even be able to reach Gore House, on which I had

he and Fonblanque being present with Stanfield and Maclise again (F, 1872–4, IV, vii, 150n). The only known contemporary account of the first reading is in Maclise's letter of 8 Dec, sent with the sketch, to Catherine: "there was not a dry eye in the house ... We should borrow the high language of the minor theatre and even then not do the effect justice—shrieks of laughter—there were indeed—and floods of tears as a relief to them—I do not think

that there ever was such a triumphant hour for Charles—" (K. J. Fielding, "Two Sketches by Maclise", *Dickens Studies*, II [1966], 13).

[1] A tear has removed several letters; possibly CD wrote "Inimitable!"
[2] The *Athenæum* first gives this date in an advertisement of 7 Dec. The copyright was registered on 16 Dec (MS of certified copy, Mr H. C. Dickens).
[3] Mrs Overs's troubles: see next.

set my heart. I cannot bear the thought of going away without some sort of reference to the happy day you gave me last Monday, and the pleasure and delight I had in your earnest greeting. I shall never forget it, believe me. It would be worth going to China—it would be worth going even to America—to come home again and feel as I feel in the friendship of yourself and Count D'Orsay.[1]

To whom my love—and something as near it to Miss Power and her sister, as it is lawful to send. It will be an unspeakable satisfaction to me, though I am not maliciously disposed, to know under your own hand at Genoa, that my little book made you cry.[2] I hope to prove a better correspondent on my return to those shores. But better or worse or anyhow, I am ever my Dear Lady Blessington, in no common degree and not with an every-day regard,

Yours

The Countess of Blessington.   CHARLES DICKENS

To MISS BURDETT COUTTS, 8 DECEMBER 1844

MS Morgan Library. *Address:* Miss Burdett Coutts | Bolton Street | Piccadilly.

Piazza Coffee House, Covent Garden | Sunday December Eighth 1844.

Dear Miss Coutts. I have been in town a very few days; and leave it again, and start for Italy, tonight. I hoped to have seen you as a matter of course; but when I had disposed of the business part of my Christmas Book (which mainly brought me here, and imprisoned me at the Printer's two days) I had some arrangements to make for the extrication of some unhappy people from circumstances of great distress and perplexity, which have occupied my whole time. So that I have seen no one, and gone nowhere.

I had the greatest pleasure some months ago, in the receipt of your interesting letter from Germany. I was going to answer it with some account of my Italian adventures; but as soon as I had any to narrate, the time had come for my sitting down to my little book; and when I got up again, it was to come here. I hope you will like those Chimes, which will be published on the 16th. and though I am not malicious, I am bent on making you cry, or being most horribly disappointed.

The Sanatorium Committee have informed me of your munificent donation[3] to that Establishment. There is not in England an Institution whose design is more noble, useful, and excellent. I know some little histories connected with that place, and the blessing it has proved in sickness and Death, which are among the most affecting incidents that have ever come within my observation.

[1] Earlier printed texts, following Madden, read "for the pleasure of such a meeting with you and Count D'Orsay".

[2] Lady Blessington wrote to Forster, 10 Dec, "'The Chimes' delighted me, although it beguiled me of many tears", and thought it would do "great good . . . melt hearts and open purse strings"; and again, 1 Jan 45, after reading it a third time, saying she found it "as impossible to repress [her] tears when perusing the last scene between Meg and Lilian as at the first" (R. R. Madden, *Literary Life and Correspondence of the Countess of Blessington,* II, 400–1). For Jeffrey's similar response, see *To* Forster, 22 Dec 44, *fn.*

[3] £50 (*Galignani's Messenger,* 29 Nov).

You may possibly have seen a Preface I wrote, before leaving England, to a little book by a Working Man; and may have learned from the Newspapers that he is dead:[1] leaving a destitute wife and six children, of whom one is a Cripple.[2] I have addressed a letter to the Governors of the Orphan Working School in behalf of the eldest boy: and they tell me he has a good chance of being elected into that Institution in April next.[3] It has occurred to me that at some time or other you might have an opportunity of presenting one of the Girls to some other School or Charity.[4] And as I know full well that in such an event you would rather thank than blame me for making a real and strong case known to you, I send you the children's names and ages.

> Amelia Overs — 11 years old
> John Richard — 9
> Harriett ——— 7
> Geraldine ——— 6
> Editha ——— 4
> John ——————— 4 months

They live, at present, at 55 Vauxhall Street Lambeth.

My head quarters in Italy, are at Genoa: where we live in a Palace (the Palazzo Peschiere) something larger than Whitehall multiplied by four; and where Charley and his Giant sisters play among Orange Trees and Fountains all day long. They were particularly anxious when I came away, that I should give their loves to you, and they entrusted me with the Private commission that I should ascertain whether "That Lady" was still in bed upstairs. In pursuing my enquiries on this head, I have received information in reference to that lady, which has quite delighted me, and not at all surprised me.[5] I hope I may still live in her memory; and that I may venture to send her my regards and congratulations.

I have been to Modena, Parma, Bologna, Ferrara, Cremona, Venice, and a hundred other places. Florence, Rome, Naples, and Palermo lie before me. I never could have believed, and never did imagine, the full splendour and glory of Venice. That wonderful dream! The three days that I passed there, were like a Thousand and One Arabian Nights, wildly exaggerated a thousand and one

---

[1] John Overs, who had been in poor health for the past year, died suddenly on 28 Sep; his death was widely reported in the press (with references to his book and CD's Preface), and there was an obituary in the *Gentleman's Magazine*, Nov 44.

[2] Newby wrote to the press 19 Oct 44, referring to CD's "able and eloquent preface" to *Evenings of a Working Man*, and deeply regretting his absence from England; "and I still regret that he is not at hand to advocate the cause of his distressed family; but although I cannot urge their claims so eloquently and forcibly as he would have done, yet I can and do earnestly appeal to the benevolent". He gave some details of the family and a first list of subscriptions including £20 from himself.

[3] John Richard Overs was not finally elected until Nov 45, according to an early report in the School's records (see *To Miss Coutts*, 1 Dec 45).

[4] See *To Forster*, ?10–11 Apr 45.

[5] Miss Hannah Meredith's engagement to Dr William Brown (see Vol. III, p. 589 and *n*); he was junior partner in the medical firm of Tupper, Chilvers and Brown. They were married 19 Dec 44, and lived at 80 Piccadilly, next door to Miss Coutts.

times. I read Romeo and Juliet in Verona too, and bought some tooth-ache mixture of an Apothecary in Mantua, lean enough and poor enough to "go on" in the Tragedy.[1] I came to England by the Simplon—sledging through the Snow upon the top—and through Switzerland, which was cool. But beautiful and grand, beyond expression. I shall remain in Paris—at the Hotel Brighton—until Friday Evening next; and if at that place or at any other, you could give me any commission to execute for you, I need not say how happy it would make me.

Mrs. Dickens begged me to present her best regards, if I saw you. I do so with a very ill will, in this miserable substitute for the pleasure I had anticipated in doing so, after so long an interval.

I am Ever Dear Miss Coutts
Yours most faithfully

Miss Coutts.   CHARLES DICKENS

To T. C. NEWBY, 8 DECEMBER 1844*

MS Mrs A. M. Stern. *Address:* Paid. | T.C. Newby Esquire | Publisher | Mortimer Street | Cavendish Square | Private.

Piazza Coffee House, Covent Garden | Sunday Eighth December 1844.

Mr. Charles Dickens presents his compliments to Mr. Newby, and begs to say that he thinks it will be best for Mrs. Overs, if Mr. Newby will have the goodness to pay into Messrs. Coutts's Bank, to the account of Mr. Dickens in trust for Mrs. Overs; all the money he has collected. Mr. Dickens (who leaves town again to day) has arranged for its immediate Investment in a Savings Bank in the name of Dr. Elliotson;[2] as it will then bear some interest, instead of lying idle.

To JOHN FORSTER, [?13 DECEMBER 1844]

Extracts in F, IV, vi, 364. *Date:* Forster clearly implies that CD wrote on the day he left Paris: confirmed by Macready's reference to performance of *Christine* (see *fn*).

I would not recall an inch of the way to or from you, if it had been twenty times as long and twenty thousand times as wintry.[3] It was worth any travel—anything! With the soil of the road in the very grain of my cheeks, I swear I wouldn't have missed that week, that first night of our meeting, that one evening

---

[1] According to the account in *Pictures* (pp. 125–6), CD, after reading the play in his inn at night ("of course, no Englishman had ever read it there, before"), repeated to himself Romeo's words, and imagined his impressions, in the omnibus on his way to Mantua—to which he thought "the lean Apothecary" well fitted.

[2] Elliotson later advised Mrs Overs as to the expenditure of the fund, after consulting CD on her behalf (Elliotson *to* Mrs Overs, 13 Feb 45, MS Morgan): see *To* Mrs Overs, 10 Apr 45 and *fn*.

[3] In Paris there had been "no such frost and snow since 1829, and he gave dismal report of the city" (F, *ibid*).

of the reading at your rooms, aye, and the second reading too, for any easily stated or conceived consideration.

With Macready he had gone two nights before to the Odéon to see Dumas' Christine *played by Madame St. George*[1] once Napoleon's mistress; now of an immense size, from dropsy I suppose; and with little weak legs which she can't stand upon. Her age, withal, somewhere about 80 or 90. I never in my life beheld such a sight. Every stage-conventionality she ever picked up (and she has them all) has got the dropsy too, and is swollen and bloated hideously. The other actors never looked at one another, but delivered all their dialogues to the pit, in a manner so egregiously unnatural and preposterous that I couldn't make up my mind whether to take it as a joke or an outrage. You and I, sir, will reform this altogether.[2] *The next night he went to the Italian Opera, where Grisi was singing in* Il Pirata[3] *and* the passion and fire of a scene between her, Mario, and Fornasari,[4] was as good and great as it is possible for anything operatic to be. They drew on one another, the two men—not like stage-players, but like Macready himself: and she, rushing in between them; now clinging to this one, now to that, now making a sheath for their naked swords with her arms, now tearing her hair in distraction as they broke away from her and plunged again at each other; was prodigious. *Next day*[5] *he saw Macready rehearse the scene before the Doge and council in* Othello,[6] not as usual facing the float but arranged on one side, *with an effect that seemed to him to heighten the reality of the scene.*

[1] Mlle Marguerite-Joséphine Weyma George (1787–1867) played in the first production of *Christine* in 1829. CD's visit was on 11 Dec (Macready, *Diaries*, II, 277–8).

[2] Forster calls this an "allusion to a project we had started on the night of the reading, that a private play should be got up by us on his return from Italy". The implication clearly is that he and CD alone originated the plan; but Stanfield and Jerrold, also present at the reading, may have joined in at the outset with the more enthusiasm because of their long-past joint experience. W. Blanchard Jerrold, in one of several passages added to the 2nd edn of his *Life of Douglas Jerrold*, 1869, even attributes the idea to them: apparently, "some years" after their reunion in 1832, they were "sauntering in Richmond Park" with other friends when Jerrold said, " 'Let's have a play, Stanfield, like we had on board the Namur' ... Hence those many merry evenings [of rehearsal] ... curious evenings spent upon the stage of Miss Kelly's little theatre". He goes on to describe a typical incident with Jerrold, clearly authentic (pp. 109–10). But the main impetus obviously came from CD's stimulating experience in the Montreal theatricals in 1842: see *To* Forster, ?30 Dec 44–1 Jan 45.

[3] Bellini's *Il Pirata*, 1827; the performance was at the Théâtre-Italien, where Macready's season was to open.

[4] Giulia Grisi (1811–69), soprano opera singer, then at the height of her fame; Mario, the stage-name of Giovanni Matteo di Candia (1810–83), tenor (later became Grisi's second husband); Luciano Fornasari, bass.

[5] "Dickens dined with us, and left us at half-past five, taking with him the last pleasant day that I expect to pass in Paris" (*Diaries*, II, 278).

[6] Macready opened with *Othello* on 16 Dec; the season, which included *Hamlet*, *Virginius*, *Werner* and *Macbeth*, continued until 15 Jan 45. The authorities, after representations by the director of the Opéra, limited the number of performances to the three a week normally allowed at the Théâtre-Italien, which meant that Mitchell, the impresario, could not hope for any profit. Louis-Philippe, recognizing this, sent him 3000 francs, and the company gave a Command performance of *Hamlet* on 16 Jan to inaugurate the Théâtre des Tuileries (B. Juden and J. Richer, "L'-Entente cordiale au théâtre. Macready et Hamlet à Paris en 1844", *Revue des Lettres Modernes*, No. 74, 1963).

To JOHN FORSTER, [17 DECEMBER 1844]

Extract in F, IV, iii, 327n. Date: 17 Dec according to Forster. *From* Marseilles.[1]

When poor Overs was dying he suddenly asked for a pen and ink and some paper, and made up a little parcel for me which it was his last conscious act to direct. She[2] told me this and gave it me. I opened it last night. It was a copy of his little book in which he had written my name, "With his devotion." I thought it simple and affecting of the poor fellow.

To W. S. LANDOR, [?13–19 DECEMBER 1844]

Mention in Landor to Rose Paynter, ?26 Dec 44 (letter clearly written just after Christmas), in *Letters of Walter Savage Landor, Private and Public,* ed. Stephen Wheeler, 1899, pp. 138–9. *Date:* evidently sent so as to reach Landor for Christmas, but after leaving England.

A delightful letter, saying he had been in England[3] *for a week, and describing his plans for visiting Rome, Naples, and Sicily.*

To T. YEATS BROWN, 20 DECEMBER 1844*

MS Free Library of Philadelphia. *Address:* Subito Subito | T. Yeates[4] Brown Esqre | Console Inglese.

Steamer Charlemagne | Genoa Harbor
Friday Morning December Twentieth 1844.

My Dear Sir.
   I write to you in great haste and by the first opportunity. I arrived last night. Through my passport having fallen into the hands of a rival boat at Marseilles, which promised to sail, and didn't,[5] and still wanted to keep it and me, waiting at that delightful town until Heaven knows when—and through my having only rescued it from those Sharks by main force, in time to leap on board this Vessel— *it has not the visa of the Sardinian Minister at Marseilles upon it:* which ought to have been obtained. Our Captain advises me (he is now going ashore, with the

---

[1] CD was four nights on the way (not three as Forster says) because the malle poste from Paris, which normally took 66 hours, was 15 hours late (F, IV, vi, 364). He arrived 17 Dec and left 19 Dec: see *To* Mrs Macready, 10 Mar 45, referring to two or three days "of waking nightmare" at Marseilles.

[2] Mrs Overs.

[3] CD had probably not written to Landor before, knowing that Forster would keep him informed. Landor's verses "To Charles Dickens" in the *Examiner*, 21 Sep 44, conclude: "Write me few letters: I'm content | With what for all the world is

meant; | Write then for all: but, since my breast | Is far more faithful than the rest, | Never shall any other share | With little Nelly nestling there". In writing to Forster about the proof, he said "Yes, I *am* more fond of Nelly than you are, and only just as fond of Dickens" (MS Huntington).

[4] Thus in MS.

[5] "In a confusion between the two rival packets for Genoa, he unwillingly detained one of them more than an hour from sailing; and only managed at last to get to her just as she was moving out of harbour" (F, IV, vi, 364–5).

passports[1] of the passengers) that I had best write to you, to ask you to send down to the Police to explain the omission—state that I am an undoubted gentleman, resident here without evil intentions—and release me from this scene of sickness and suffering.

I needn't tell you how anxious I am to get home; and I am sure I need not apologize to you for this early and pressing importunity. Ever believe me

Faithfully Yours

T. Yeats Brown Esquire. CHARLES DICKENS

To JOHN FORSTER, [22 DECEMBER 1844]

Extracts in F, IV, vi, 365, IV, vii, 366. *Date:* second extract 22 Dec according to Forster; first extract clearly same letter, the first on his return to Genoa.

He described his departure from Marseilles. As he went up the side of the packet, he saw a strange sensation among the angry travellers whom he had detained so long[2], *heard a voice exclaim* "I am blarmed if it ain't DICKENS!" *and stood in the centre of a group of* Five Americans![3] *But they were all glad to see him; their chief man, who had met him in New York, introduced them all round with the remark,* "Personally our countrymen, and you, can fix it friendly sir, I do expectuate",[4] *and through the stormy passage to Genoa they were excellent friends. He had to keep to his cabin, but contrived to get enjoyment out of them. The member of the party who had the travelling dictionary wouldn't part with it, though he was dead sick in the next cabin, and every now and then CD was conscious of his fellow-travellers coming down to him, crying out in varied tones of anxious bewilderment* "I say, what's French for a pillow?" "Is there any Italian phrase for a lump of sugar? Just look, will you?" "What the devil does echo mean? The garsong says echo to everything!"[5] *They were excessively curious to know the population of every little town on the Cornice, and all its statistics;* perhaps the very last subjects within the capacity of the human intellect that would ever present themselves to an Italian steward's mind. He was a very willing fellow, our steward; and, having some vague idea that they would like a large number, said at hazard fifty thousand, ninety thousand, four hundred thousand, when they asked about the population of a place not larger than Lincoln's-inn-fields. And when they said *Non Possible !*

---

[1] Travellers leaving any part of Italy except the Austrian states had to obtain a new visa from the Sardinian minister before re-entering the country.

[2] On 1 Aug 45, CD presented to one of his fellow passengers (of whom nothing further is known) a copy of *The Chimes*, with the following inscription: "This is my part of a bargain made with Mr. Davis, on board the Charlemagne Steamer, between Marseilles and Genoa, on the Nineteenth of December 1845 [*thus*]. Charles Dickens | London. First August | 1845" (Free Library of Philadelphia).

[3] These two words quoted from the letter printed in italics in F.

[4] The *Atlantic Monthly*, Feb 1873, XXXI, 237, reviewing Forster's *Life of Dickens*, thought this remark was CD's invention. "Honest Mr. Forster sets down this frantic rubbish, and seems to believe that it reports the parlance of the American people."

[5] The return journey is briefly described in *Pictures*, pp. 142–3, including the story of the dictionary.

(which was the leader's invariable reply), he doubled or trebled the amount; to meet what he supposed to be their views, and make it quite satisfactory.

A letter from Jeffrey[1] *about* The Chimes *was* most energetic and enthusiastic.[2] Filer sticks in his throat rather, but all the rest is quivering in his heart. He is very much struck by the management of Lilian's story, and cannot help speaking of that; writing of it all indeed with the freshness and ardour of youth, and not like a man whose blue and yellow[3] has turned grey.

Miss Coutts has sent Charley, with the best of letters to me, a Twelfth Cake[4] weighing ninety pounds, magnificently decorated;[5] and only think of the characters, Fairburn's Twelfth Night characters,[6] being detained at the custom-house for Jesuitical surveillance! But these fellows are—— Well! never mind. Perhaps you have seen the history of the Dutch minister at Turin,[7] and of the spiriting away of his daughter by the Jesuits? It is all true; though, like the history of our friend's servant, almost incredible. But their devilry is such that I am assured by our consul that if, while we are in the south, we were to let our

[1] Forster adds, wrongly, that the *Chimes* was dedicated to him, confusing it with the *Cricket*, the first Christmas book to carry a dedication.

[2] CD had clearly sent Jeffrey a proof copy, probably on 6 Dec (see *To* Lady Blessington, that day), as his reply is dated 12 Dec. He wrote at length, commending CD for his "kind and courageous advocacy of the rights of the poor"; the "opening chorus of the church-going wind" was "full of poetry and painting". He was particularly touched by "the thrilling pathos" of Lilian's dialogues with Meg—"beyond the reach of any pen but your own, and *it* never did anything better". He could not "*reserve* [his] tears" for the Third Quarter: "From the meeting with Will, they flowed and ebbed at your bidding . . . I do not care about your Alderman and his twaddling friends". The pathos was even "painfully oppressive . . . making us despise and loathe ourselves for passing our days in luxury". He predicted "a great run" but "more objections this time than last" (Lord Cockburn, *Life of Lord Jeffrey*, II, 390–3; another extract is quoted in F, IV, v, 356).

[3] The old Whig colours, used for the *Edinburgh Review*.

[4] Described in the reminiscent essay, "New Year's Day": it came "as a present all the way from Signor Gunter's della Piazza Berkeley, Londra", and was cracked and went to the "street of Happy Charles" to be mended, but was ready to be put on show on New Year's Day (*Miscellaneous Papers*, p. 658).

[5] The fullest contemporary description of Twelfth cakes is in R. H. Horne's *Memoirs of a London Doll*, 1846, Chs 2 and 3: "immense cakes, the round white sugar island of each being covered with its extraordinary inhabitants"; he instances scenes with "negro people and tigers" and polar bears, "Kings and Queens . . . Jem Crow . . . girls with tambourines . . . and all these standing or walking, or dancing upon white sugar." There were also "cakes of a smaller sort, and all covered with Twelfth-Night characters, in coloured sugar."

[6] Coloured sheets of "characters", published by J. Fairburn of the Minories; surviving examples of this period show the Royal family (with an enormous "Twelfth cake"), and humorous invented characters, some from fiction, including *Pickwick*; the latter are accompanied by riddles, and intended to be cut out and distributed at parties.

[7] This was an old story probably recalled to CD by Yeats Brown. Forster had long known of the incident, as the *Examiner*, 6 July 44 (after CD's departure), reported it from the *Journal des Débats*, as "a symptom of the dangerous pretensions of the Jesuits". The minister's daughter fell in love with a young Catholic barrister; her father disapproved, and she took refuge in the convent of St Croix, from which he was unable to reclaim her although he appealed to the king and the Prussian and English ministers.

children go out with servants on whom we could not implicitly rely, these holy men would trot even their small feet into churches with a view to their ultimate conversion! It is tremendous even to see them in the streets, or slinking about this garden.[1]

To EMILE DE LA RUE, 26 DECEMBER 1844*

MS Berg Collection. *Address:* A Monsieur | M. Emile De La Rue.

Peschiere December Twenty Sixth 1844.

My Dear Sir

I am truly distressed to hear that Madame De La Rue has had so severe an attack of her sad disorder; but if it has been more than usually trying, I am not without hope that the Mesmerism may have increased it for the moment.[2]

At Eleven tomorrow, I shall be ready and happy to come to you—equally so, at any other time or season when I can entertain the smallest expectation of rendering Mad. De La Rue the lightest service.

I have the truest interest in her, and her sufferings; and if I could lessen them in any degree, I should derive great happiness from being the fortunate instrument of her relief.

Believe that I reciprocate all your friendly feeling with genuine cordiality, and that I am, with great regard

Faithfully Yours
CHARLES DICKENS

P.S. I am going out to Quinto at twelve. Do not take the trouble of calling *formally*. We may eschew all that, I hope.

To JOHN FORSTER, [?AUGUST–DECEMBER 1844]

Extract in F, VI, vii, 552. *Date:* from Genoa in 1844 according to Forster; after 28 July if reference is to Sir James Murray.

We are very sorry to lose the benefit of his advice[3]—or, as my father would

---

[1] "The Jesuits ... go slinking noiselessly about, in pairs, like black cats" (*Pictures*, p. 57).

[2] According to de la Rue, CD began to mesmerize her on 23 Dec 44 (see *To* de la Rue, 8 June 45, *fn*) which the tone of this letter confirms; but for the next few weeks the "treatment" was probably frequent— see *To* de la Rue, 27 Jan 45. CD had long been interested in the subject, attending Dr Elliotson's experiments in 1838 and 1840 (see Vol. I, p. 461*n*, Vol. II, pp. 109, 148 and *ns*), and first tried it himself at Pittsburgh in 1842, when he successfully induced "the magnetic sleep" in Catherine,

later exhibiting his powers over her and Georgina at an evening party in London: see Vol. III, pp. 180, 409*n*. Mesmerism was widely discussed in 1844: the mesmeric "treatment" of Harriet Martineau's supposedly incurable illness and her recovery were much talked of, and her "Letters on Mesmerism" first appeared in the *Athenæum* 23 Nov–28 Dec 44 (with sceptical concluding comments by the editor, Charles Dilke). The movement was becoming more respectable: Elliotson, whose practice had been vetoed by the council of University College, London, in 1838, was in 1846 invited to give the Harveian oration at the

say, to be deprived, to a certain extent, of the concomitant advantages, whatever they may be, resulting from his medical skill, such as it is, and his professional attendance, in so far as it may be so considered.

To JOHN FORSTER, [?30–31 DECEMBER 1844 and 1 JANUARY 1845]

Extracts in F, v, i, 380; F, 1872–4, II, ix, 179–81;[1] F, IV, vii, 366. *Date:* last extract a postscript, dated 1 Jan 45, to a letter written after Christmas and in the week "following" CD's first letter according to Forster's summary; preceding extracts probably 30–31 Dec, since comments on play are in answer to Forster's first letter to Genoa (the second being about his brother's death: see *To* Forster, 8 Jan 45).

ARE we to have that play????[2] Have I spoken of it, ever since I came home from London, as a settled thing! I do not know if I have ever told you seriously, but I have often thought, that I should certainly have been as successful on the boards as I have been between them. I assure you, when I was on the stage at Montreal[3] (not having played for years) I was as much astonished at the reality and ease, to myself, of what I did as if I had been another man. See how oddly things come about! When I was about twenty, and knew three or four successive years of Mathews's At Homes from sitting in the pit to hear them, I wrote to Bartley[4] who was stage manager at Covent-garden, and told him how young I was, and exactly what I thought I could do; and that I believed I had a strong perception of character and oddity, and a natural power of reproducing in my own person what I observed in others. There must have been something in the letter that struck the authorities, for Bartley wrote to me, almost immediately, to say that they were busy getting up the *Hunchback* (so they were!) but that they

Royal College of Physicians. (The best account of "one of the most curious and revealing byways of early Victorian intellectual history" is in R. K. Webb, *Harriet Martineau, a Radical Victorian*, 1960, Ch. 8.)

[3] "Describing . . . the departure from Genoa of an English physician and acquaintance" (F, *ibid*); almost certainly Sir James Murray. It is not known when he left.

[1] In the 1st edn of the *Life* Forster used the whole of this extract to introduce his account of the amateur theatricals in 1845. He explained that he had overlooked the "passage of autobiography" it contained when writing the chapter to which that passage belonged, and commented: "It will startle and interest the reader, and I must confess that it took myself by surprise; for I did not thus early know the story of his boyish years, and I thought it strange that he could have concealed from me so much". But for the 2nd edn he removed to the narrative of CD's early

years (F, I, iv, 59–60) the part of the letter telling of CD's application to Bartley and its result ("I wrote to Bartley . . . where the answer came also"), altering the order slightly and introducing it with a summary of CD's account of his preparations for a stage career ("It wasn't very good . . . a great number"). When he came to the theatricals (F, v, i, 380), he referred readers back, and gave two further extracts ("ARE . . . come about!" and "This was at the time . . . how little they suspect me!"), the second including the material summarized at I, iv, 59–60.

[2] Forster "had asked him, after his return to Genoa, whether he continued to think that we should have the play; and this was his reply" (F, 1872–4, II, ix, 179).

[3] On 25 May 42; see Vol. III, p. 237 and *n.*

[4] George Bartley (?1782–1858; *DNB*), stage-manager at Covent Garden 1829–43: see Vol. I, p. 3*n.*

would communicate with me again, in a fortnight. Punctual to the time, another letter came: with an appointment to do anything of Mathews's I pleased, before him and Charles Kemble, on a certain day at the theatre. My sister Fanny was in the secret, and was to go with me to play the songs. I was laid up, when the day came, with a terrible bad cold and an inflammation of the face; the beginning, by the bye, of that annoyance in one ear to which I am subject at this day. I wrote to say so, and added that I would resume my application next season. I made a great splash in the gallery soon afterwards; the *Chronicle* opened to me; I had a distinction in the little world of the newspaper, which made me like it; began to write; didn't want money; had never thought of the stage, but as a means of getting it; gradually left off turning my thoughts that way; and never resumed the idea. I never told you this, did I? See how near I may have been, to another sort of life.

This was at the time when I was at Doctors' Commons as a shorthand writer for the proctors. And I recollect I wrote the letter from a little office I had there, where the answer came also.[1] It wasn't a very good living (though not a *very* bad one), and was wearily uncertain; which made me think of the Theatre in quite a business-like way. I went to some theatre every night, with a very few exceptions, for at least three years: really studying the bills first, and going to where there was the best acting: and always to see Mathews whenever he played. I practised immensely (even such things as walking in and out, and sitting down in a chair): often four, five, six hours a day: shut up in my own room, or walking about in the fields. I prescribed to myself, too, a sort of Hamiltonian system for learning parts;[2] and learnt a great number. I haven't even lost the habit now, for I knew my Canadian parts immediately, though they were new to me. I must have done a good deal: for, just as Macready found me out,[3] they used to challenge me at Braham's:[4] and Yates,[5] who was knowing enough in those things, wasn't to be parried at all. It was just the same, that day at Keeley's, when they were getting up the *Chuzzlewit* last June.[6]

If you think Macready would be interested in this Strange news from the South, tell it him. Fancy Bartley or Charles Kemble *now!* And how little they suspect me!

He wrote that he and Catherine intended to start for the south of Italy in the middle of January; he dwelt on all he had missed, in that first Italian Christmas, of their old enjoyments of the season in England; and closed with a postscript at midnight:

[1] The correspondence with Bartley can be dated Mar–Apr 1832: see Vol. I, pp. 3–4 and *ns*.

[2] James Hamilton (1769–1831; *DNB*) published his system for teaching languages, "by observation, not by rules", *The History, Principles, Practice and Results of the Hamiltonian System*, in 1829.

[3] CD read *The Lamplighter* to Macready 4 Dec 37: see Vol. I, p. 465*n*.

[4] John Braham (?1774–1856; *DNB*), singer; opened the St James's Theatre 14 Dec 35: see Vol. I, p. 118*n*. Braham pro-

duced *The Strange Gentleman* and *The Village Coquettes* at the St James's in 1836 (see Vol. I); CD was closely associated with the production as well as the writing, telling Bentley when the farce was in rehearsal: "I have been superintending its preparation morning, noon, and night" (Vol. I, pp. 177–8).

[5] Frederick Henry Yates (1797–1842; *DNB*), actor and manager of the Adelphi Theatre from 1825: see Vol. II, p. 10*n*.

[6] See *To* Keeley, 24 June 44 and *fn*.

First of January, 1845. Many many many happy returns of the day! A life of happy years! The Baby is dressed in thunder, lightning, rain, and wind. His birth is most portentous here.[1]

To JOHN FORSTER, 7 JANUARY [1845]

Extract in Sotheby's catalogue, July 1929; *MS* 2 pp.; dated Genoa, 7 Jan 44— clearly CD's error for 1845.

Introducing a friend and asking him to open the doors of some of the Theatres and suchlike places for him.

To MESSRS BRADBURY & EVANS, 8 JANUARY 1845

Extract in Anderson Auction Co. catalogue, June 1914; *MS* 1 p.; dated Genoa, 8 Jan 45; marked "Private".

Mentioning Forster and the death of his brother, and asking for the balance of £500;[2] the estimated expenses of the journey in Carnival and Holy Time,[3] and among all sorts of damnable Potentates in frogged coats with stars upon them have made my hair stand on end to that extent that I can't get my hat on. Never mind. We will turn it to good account.[4] *Saying they drank healths on the first.* Punch's Almanac[5] is brilliant, but don't your Woodcutters require a leetle remonstrance? . . . Has George Cruikshank[6] been fined since? Don't mention it to anybody. It's quite in confidence.

To JOHN FORSTER, [8 JANUARY 1845]

Extract in F, IV, vii, 367n. *Date:* 8 Jan according to Forster.

I feel the distance between us now, indeed. I would to Heaven, my dearest friend, that I could remind you in a manner more lively and affectionate than this dull sheet of paper can put on, that you have a Brother left.[7] One bound to you by ties as strong as ever Nature forged. By ties never to be broken, weakened,

---

[1] The party at the Palazzo Peschiere is described in "New Year's Day": see *To* Forster, ?20 Aug 44, *fn.*

[2] See *To* Bradbury & Evans, 8 May 44; £500 was paid to him on 17 Jan (Accountbook, MS Messrs Coutts).

[3] In Rome.

[4] The catalogue summary includes the words "alluding to his proposed *Pictures from Italy*", and the two closing sentences probably also refer to this.

[5] Published Christmas 1844. Many of the woodcuts were by Leech, and the social criticism conveyed was on the lines of *The Chimes*. The remonstrance may have been

because there was some imitation of Cruikshank's *Comic Almanac.*

[6] George Cruikshank (1792–1878; *DNB*): see Vol. I, p. 82n.

[7] Forster's elder brother Christopher, broker, of the firm of Slack & Forster, Quarryside, died suddenly, aged 37, at Wilkinson's Buildings, Newcastle-upon-Tyne, 24 Dec 44 (*Newcastle Chronicle*, 4 Jan 45, and a note by J. T. Gilmore, a relation of the Forsters, quoted in *Monthly Chronicle of North-country Lore and Legend*, Feb 1888, p. 54). *DNB* wrongly calls him Forster's younger brother.

changed in any way—but to be knotted tighter up, if that be possible, until the same end comes to them as has come to these. That end but the bright beginning of a happier union, I believe; and have never more strongly and religiously believed (and oh! Forster, with what a sore heart I have thanked God for it) than when that shadow has fallen on my own hearth, and made it cold and dark as suddenly as in the home of that poor girl[1] you tell me of. . . . When you write to me again, the pain of this will have passed. No consolation can be so certain and so lasting to you as that softened and manly sorrow which springs up from the memory of the Dead. I read your heart as easily as if I held it in my hand, this moment. And I know—I *know*, my dear friend—that before the ground is green above him, you will be content that what was capable of death in him, should lie there. . . . I am glad to think it was so easy, and full of peace. What can we hope for more, when our own time comes!—The day when he visited us in our old house is as fresh to me as if it had been yesterday. I remember him as well as I remember you. . . . I have many things to say, but cannot say them now. Your attached and loving friend for life, and far, I hope, beyond it. C. D.

To [EMILE DE LA RUE], 15 JANUARY [1845]*

MS Berg Collection. *Address:* clearly to Emile de la Rue:[2] see *fn.*

Wednesday January Fifteenth. Having been asleep some twenty minutes, I drew her into a conversation, as follows—occasionally with some little difficulty, and by dint of repeating the same question three or four times. "Well! where are you today? On the Hillside as usual?"—"Yes."—"Quite alone?"—"No."—"Are there many people there?"—"Yes. A good many." "Men, or women?"—"Both." "How they are[3] dressed?"—"I can't see. I have too many things to look at."—"But you can tell me what they are doing. Can't you?"—"Yes. They are walking about, and talking."—"To you?"—"No. To each other."—"What are they saying?"—"I don't know."—"Try and find out"—"I am too busy."—"But not so busy that you can't listen to them, surely?"—"Yes I am. I have so many things to attend to."—"Are they a crowd?"—"Yes; quite a crowd."

Suddenly, she cried out, in great agitation. "Here's my brother! Here's my brother!"— and she breathed very quickly, and her figure became stiff. "Where?

---

[1] Jane Forster; Elizabeth, the other sister, was away as a governess. Jane, with Forster's mother and his uncle John, moved after Christopher's death to "a little house in Shieldfield" (according to Gilmore). Forster had evidently gone north for the funeral and probably did not write to CD until his return. Lady Blessington and Count D'Orsay were concerned about Forster, who was "miserable at the loss", and himself fell ill again (R. R. Madden, *The Literary Life and Correspondence of the Countess of Blessington*, II, 409; J. F. Molloy,

The Most Gorgeous Lady Blessington, 1896, I, 237).

[2] These are notes of one of the many sessions during which CD was mesmerizing Mme de la Rue; evidently made on the spot, perhaps in "the accustomed literary station in your drawing room" (see *To* de la Rue, 27 Jan 45), and given to de la Rue; endorsed "15 Jan. 1845. Gênes Notes de Dickens sur une Vision de A. pendant le magnétism de 11. h à 1.3 [?] de l'après midi".

[3] Thus in MS.

In the crowd?"—"No. In a room."—"Who is with him?"—"Nobody."—
"What is he doing?"—"Leaning against a window: looking out. Oh he is so
sad! He is so sad!"—shedding tears as she spoke, and shewing the greatest
sympathy. "What Brother? The Brother I know?"[1]—"No no. Not the
Brother you know. Another."—"What is his name?"—"Charles.[2] Oh how
sad he is!"—"What makes him so?"—"I don't know, I don't know. I must try
to find out."—"Watch the door, and perhaps somebody will come in"—"Yes
yes, I will. I am very busy, looking. I am trying to see."

After a pause, I said:
"Well! Has anybody come in?"—"No. He is still alone."—"Leaning against
the window?"—"No. Walking up and down the room."—"Still sad?"—"Oh!
Very sad! What *can* make him so sad!"—"Tell me what you see through the
window."—"No. I can't, I can't. I am looking at him."—"Yes. But look at the
window too. I'm sure you will if I ask you. What do you see through the
window? Fields?"—"No no. The sea."—"How is your brother dressed?"—
"In his uniform."—"With a sword?"—"No."—"With a hat?"—"No."—"You
will be sure to tell me, if anyone comes in?"—"Yes yes. But I am trying to
find out what makes him so sad, poor fellow!"—still crying, and in great distress.
After a time, she said, with increased agitation. "He is thinking of me!"—and
after another interval, she cried that she had found out the reason of his despond-
ency. That he thought himself forgotten. That the letters had miscarried,
and he had not received them. Then she fell back in the chair, like one whose
mind was relieved; and said it was gone and she saw him no more.

She said all this, with as much earnestness as if the scene had been actually
present to her view; and spoke in the peculiar tone of voice which is natural to a
person who watches intently, and is afraid of losing any glimpse of what is
passing. She several times brushed her closed eyes with her hands, as if to wipe
away her tears, and see him more distinctly.

I do not make any note of the other visions of today, on this paper; as they are
incomplete. And I am very curious to see whether she resumes them tomorrow.
It is sufficient to remark just now, that she always imagines herself lying on a
hill-side with a very blue sky above, green grass about her, and a pleasant air
stirring. That the sensation of pain, suggests to her the rolling of stones down
this hill, by some unseen people: which she is much distressed in her en-
deavours to avoid: and which occasionally strike her. There is a man haunting
this place—dimly seen, but heard talking sometimes—whom she is afraid of,
and "dare not" look at. I connect it with the figure whom she calls her bad
spirit; in consequence of her trembling very much, when I once asked her,
lying on this imaginary hill, if that phantom were to be seen: when she implored
me not to speak of him. She said today that this creature was talking of me; and
at my request, she tried hard to overhear what he said. But "she couldn't make
it all out", she complained, and suddenly added, "Don't go away upon a Monday.

---

[1] William Granet, resident in Genoa: see
To de la Rue, 28 July 45 and *fn*.

[2] Charles Granet was evidently in the
army; he may have been the Captain
Granet, 12th Regiment of Foot, eldest son
of Augustus Granet (*d*. 4 Aug 53), Com-
missary-General to the Forces, who married Rose Staveley at Mauritius, 20 Nov 44
(*Galignani's Messenger*, 10 Mar 45).

Be sure not to go away upon a Monday. It's not he who says that. *I* say it."
Immediately afterwards, she complained of being tired, and begged me to
awaken her.[1]

To [EMILE DE LA RUE], [18 JANUARY 1845]*

MS Berg Collection. *Date:* endorsed by de la Rue: "Plan du Voiage de Dickens
18 Jan. 1845. Gênes".

Leave Genoa on Sunday 19th. January. Arrive at Carrara on Tuesday
Evening January 21st. Stop at Carrara on Wednesday 22nd. Leave Carrara on
Thursday 23rd. Arrive at Pisa, the same night. To Leghorn on Friday 24th.
and sleep there, that night. Leave Leghorn on Saturday 25th. Arrive in Rome
on the morning of Thursday 30th.—Leave Rome on Wednesday 5th. February.
Arrive in Naples on Friday 7th.

My proceedings in Naples, and the length of my stay there, I shall regulate
entirely, by what I hear from you and Madame De La Rue. My present idea is,
to return to Rome ten days or a fortnight before the beginning of the Holy Week.
But I have no fixed plan upon the subject; and shall be guided *solely* by your
letters. Of course I shall write and let you know my intentions and movements,
in any case, from Naples.

To EMILE DE LA RUE, 25 JANUARY 1845*

MS Berg Collection. *Address:* A Monsieur | Monsr. Emile De la Rue | Genova.

Leghorn. Saturday Morning Twenty Fifth January 1845.
My Dear De la Rue.

Your most interesting Journal is exactly what I wished to have. Nothing could
be more clearly or plainly stated. Having her at a distance from me at all, I
think it hardly possible that her state of mind could be more favorable to the
preservation of the influence; for the more she accustoms herself to rely on the
idea of her anxious Physician, the more prepared she will necessarily be to
confide in, and to yield to, the Reality, when it is at hand.

I have read her letter many times since its receipt last night. It is full of
interest, patience, the most winning confidence, strong hope, and the best side
of the best nature that belongs to a woman.

The impression made on the disorder, generally, is beyond all question very
great. But the extent to which her thoughts are directed to, and clustered round,
that bad phantom—and the manner in which she watches the effect upon it, and
trusts to my influence over it, and refers all her suffering to it—is most remarkable. So remarkable, and so needing to be helped, and tenderly and carefully
directed, that if anything should occur (which Heaven forbi[d)][2] to prevent your
coming to Rome together, I cannot too strongly urge you to think of [the] easiest

---

[1] Followed by a flourish, such as CD
uses to indicate "finis" of a chapter.

[2] A small tear has removed the final "d"
and a few letters in other places.

and most expedient way of inducing her to come, in any case. I see, af[ar] off, how *essential it is that this Phantom should not regain its power* for an instant. And we can hardly expect, yet, that she will very long be able to combat it, successfully, alone.

I have but a few moments this morning, and am forced to be very brief. I will write you at greater length from Rome, where I anxiously expect to hear from you again.[1] I fear that before that time she may have had a bad attack. It keeps off wonderfully.

We have every reason for Hope, Courage, Confidence, Resolution, and Perseverance. And we will entertain them all, my dear De La Rue, and with God's leave to a right good end, or my name is not

CHARLES DICKENS

P.S. Don't consider this, a letter—for it's no such thing. Mrs. Dickens sends her best regards. It seems quite unnatural and strange to me, to write to you in *anything but Pencil.*[2]

To JOHN FORSTER, [25 JANUARY 1845]

Extracts in F, IV, vii, 367 and *n*. *Date:* first and third extracts "five days later" than 20 Jan according to Forster; second extract 25 Jan according to Forster. *From La Scala.*

Describing the little inn at La Scala, supported on low brick arches like a British haystack, *the bed in their room* like a mangle, *the ceiling without lath or plaster, nothing to speak of available for comfort or decency, and nothing particular to eat or drink.* But for all this I have become attached to the country and I don't care who knows it.

They had left Pisa that morning and the day before, Carrara, where Fletcher was staying with an English marble-merchant: A Yorkshireman, who talks Yorkshire Italian with the drollest and pleasantest effect; a jolly, hospitable, excellent fellow; as odd yet kindly a mixture of shrewdness and simplicity as I have ever seen. He is the only Englishman in these parts who has been able to erect an English household out of Italian servants, but he has done it to admiration. It would be a capital country-house at home; and for staying in "first-rate." (I find myself inadvertently quoting *Tom Thumb*.)[3] Mr. Walton[4] is a man of an extraordinarily kind heart, and has a compassionate regard for Fletcher, to whom his

---

[1] De la Rue's endorsement shows that he wrote to CD at Rome on 27 Jan "with two enclosed from England".

[2] None of these pencil reports appear to survive.

[3] Not the play, as italics suggest, but General Tom Thumb: see *To* Powell, 16 Apr 44. Barnum, the showman, encouraged him to use American slang: the colloquial use of "first-rate" was commoner in American English. CD included it in a list

of "pure Americanisms of the first water": see *To* Forster, 25 Feb 42; Vol. III, pp. 89–90.

[4] W. Walton, marble-merchant; described by CD as a "good plain workaday bachelor" (*To* H. P. Smith, 9 July 46). He visited CD in London in July 45 (*To* de la Rue, 28 July), and CD gave him a portrait of himself in a gilt frame (Chapman & Hall's Accounts, 9 Jan 46, Forster Collection, V & A).

house is open as a home, which is half affecting and half ludicrous. He paid the other day a hundred pounds for him, which he knows he will never see a penny of again.[1]

At Carrara: There is a beautiful little theatre there, built of marble; and they had it illuminated that night, in my honour.[2] There was really a very fair opera: but it is curious that the chorus has been always, time out of mind, made up of labourers in the quarries, who don't know a note of music, and sing entirely by ear.[3] It was crammed to excess, and I had a great reception; a deputation waiting upon us in the box, and the orchestra turning out in a body afterwards and serenading us at Mr. Walton's.

To EMILE DE LA RUE, 26 JANUARY 1845*

MS Berg Collection. *Address:* A Monsieur | Monsr. Emile De la Rue. | Genova.

Siena.[4] Sunday Night. | Twenty Sixth January 1845.

My Dear De la Rue.

When I halt tomorrow night, I will write you a letter—a real letter—and despatch it by post immediately afterwards. I am anxious to answer your journal day by day; and intended to have sat down for that purpose this evening, when it came into my head to write her a cheerful note instead.[5]

And the reason was, that I have had a strange and uncommon anxiety upon me, all day, which has amounted to a positively great distress. I cannot help fearing that she must be ill; and silence, with such an apprehension on me, seems to double distance.

I am looking, with the greatest impatience and interest, for your next. The debt I owe you for your last, I will not fail to pay tomorrow. In the meantime, and ever,

Believe me | Faithfully Your friend

CHARLES DICKENS

I write in great haste; with the last candle going out, and the Lamp gone.

---

[1] In F, 1872–4, II, viii, 168n, two stories told to CD by Walton (evidently on this occasion) are given: the first, which CD made "wonderfully amusing", "related the introduction by Fletcher of an unknown Englishman to the marble-merchant's house; the stay there of the Englishman, unasked, for ten days; and finally the walking off of the Englishman in a shirt, pair of stockings, neckcloth, pocket-handkerchief, and other etceteras belonging to Mr. Walton, which never reappeared after that hour." The second was an occasion when Fletcher confessed to having "given a bill to a man in Carrara for £30; the marble-merchant having asked, 'And pray, Fletcher, have you arranged to meet it when it falls due?' Fletcher at once replied,

'Yes,' and to the marble-merchant's farther enquiry 'how?' added, in his politest manner, 'I have arranged to blow my brains out the day before!' "

[2] "the result of the zeal of our eccentric friend Fletcher" (F, IV, vii, 367). CD was greatly impressed by Carrara: see *Pictures*, pp. 147–51.

[3] *Pictures*, p. 151, with the same details of the chorus, adds that it was "a comic opera" and "an act of 'Norma' ".

[4] Briefly described in *Pictures*, p. 157.

[5] This does not survive, but the endorsement ("Siene 26 Janv. 1845 Charles Dickens [&] 3 fév. | 6 à Naples") suggests that it contained a reference to the Naples plans.

To EMILE DE LA RUE, 27 JANUARY 1845*

MS Berg Collection. *Address:* A Monsieur | Monsr. Emile De la Rue | Genova.

> La Scala, No. 2[1] (for we were in another
> place of the same name, the night
> before last.)
> Monday January 27th. 1845.

My Dear De La Rue.

Having disposed, in this very lone house, of a much better dinner than any reasonable person could have expected to find in such a place,[2] I am going to bestow a little tediousness[3] on you. And I heartily wish you were "crackling"[4] your very loudest in your own Palazzo, and I were writing it in my accustomed literary station in your drawing-room; instead of sitting (as I am) at the corner of an immense table, much larger than any table on which Billiards were ever[5] played: with one very sharp corner forcing my centre waistcoat-button into my chest, and stamping[6] a lively impression of it into my skin. Which is the only position in which I can find the least approach to warmth. In consequence of all the fire going up the chimney; and nothing of it coming into the room except the smoke.

I shall come to the subject which is nearest to my heart (and yours) last. As Hope stepped out of Pandora's box when all its stock of troubles was exhausted, so that topic shall shew itself from the depths of my letter, when other and less interesting matters are disposed of.

They are few enough. You know how gloomy it was, when we left Genoa, and you know how it rained next day. On reflection, I don't think anybody knows that, to the full extent, except myself, my wife, Roche and the Vetturino— and the four horses: I had almost forgotten the horses. Perhaps because they were under water nearly all the way. Something wet and heavy—feeling, to the touch, like the toast out of a jug of toast and water—was put into the carriage by a postilion, after it was dark on that Monday night, and when we were within some four miles from Spezzia. It appeared, on examination, to be a letter from Fletcher, who had got wet through, in crossing the Magra to meet us; and described himself as taking dinner in a blanket while his clothes were drying.

When we reached the Inn we found him in this state; very red and warm; and looking like a perfectly new-born baby, suddenly grown up. He had by that time taken two dinners; and on my ordering our own, he requested that a knife and fork might be placed for him—and so took a third. You recollect the dimensions (in round numbers) of his nose? Well! By the time he had finished this third dinner, his eyes protruded infinitely beyond the tip of that feature.

---

[1] An "osteria" a few miles beyond Poderina, referred to by Murray as "one of the resting places of the vetturini".

[2] The "perfectly lone house" with a waitress "like a dramatic brigand's wife" is described in *Pictures*, pp. 158–9, with humorous details of the meal—"a very good dinner . . . when you are used to it"—

assisted by flasks of Orvieto and Monte Pulciano.

[3] Cf. *Much Ado about Nothing*, III, v, 21–2.

[4] Probably, making the fire crackle.

[5] MS reads "every".

[6] CD first wrote "printing".

You never saw such a human Prawn as he looked, in your life. When he retired to bed in a state of insensibility, I had the faintest expectation possible, of ever seeing him again, alive.

But he got through it, somehow or other, and turned up again at breakfast. He was soft and pulpy, all over: and much swollen. This last appearance subsided in course of time, and the Magra subsiding also, we got over it (not, as I thought, without some danger) on Tuesday afternoon. We remained with Mr. Walton until Thursday Morning[1]—started for Pisa that day (taking him and Fletcher with us)—dined and slept at Pisa that night—climbed up the Leaning Tower next morning—took the Railroad to Leghorn[2] that afternoon—and dined at Mr. Gower's[3] that Evening. Next day we started from Pisa, alone— slept at the other La Scala, that night—at Siena last night; where there is a very beautiful Cathedral, a picturesque Piazza, and a very quaint old town—and arrived here this evening, at Six. That is to say, Two Hours ago. It rained rather heavily in the night, last night. But since this day week, the weather has been fine and pleasant: though generally cool, and sometimes very cold.

Before I take up your Diary and read it over for the hundredth time; let me tell you what happened today. And if you think it will interest Madame De la Rue, pray read it to her: giving her, at the same time, something as near my love as you may feel disposed to deliver. I was on the Box of the Carriage; and, as usual, at Eleven by the Genoa time, composed myself for one hour's abstraction, in rigid pursuance of our agreement. Now, it happened that I was not alone, as it is my custom to be then; but that Mrs. Dickens had been hoisted up, to get the air. As I very often sit a long time without saying anything at all—when I am thinking, or when I am thinking I am thinking—and as she is well used to it, I didn't mind her, but sat quite still and quiet. Observe.—I didn't move hand or foot. I engaged myself, in imagination, in mesmerizing our Patient; and my whole Being, for the time, was set upon it, certainly, with the greatest stedfastness. But it was impossible for anybody to know in what I was engaged, otherwise than that I was very intent on some subject. Will you believe me when I tell you that I had not remained thus, more than five or ten minutes, when I was disturbed by Mrs. Dickens' letting her muff fall. And *can* you believe me when I tell you that looking at her I found her, as I live! in the Mesmeric trance, with her eyelids quivering in a convulsive manner peculiar to some people in that state—her hands and feet suddenly cold—her senses numbed—and that on my rousing her, with some difficulty, and asking her what was the matter, she said she had been magnetized?[4] She was so discomposed that it was necessary to put her into the carriage immediately; and she had a bad fit of trembling until the influence wore off.

No word had ever passed my lips in reference to my compact with Madame De La Rue. She was as utterly ignorant of it, as she is of any business-secret in

[1] 23 Jan.

[2] The sights of Pisa, and the excursion to Leghorn, "made illustrious by SMOLLETT'S grave", are described in *Pictures*, pp. 151–5, 157.

[3] Unidentified. *To* de la Rue, 25 Jan,

written from Leghorn, is marked "Gower, Livorno", showing that they stayed the night there and returned to Pisa next morning to resume the journey to Rome.

[4] Several words heavily deleted by CD here.

your banking house. There is no possibility of any mistake or exaggeration in this. She is quite well, and has been ever since we left Genoa. Within five minutes of my shutting myself up within myself, I had been teaching her some Italian words; and I supposed her to be still engaged in conning them over, when this surprise occurred. It was really quite a fearful thing, and the strongest instance of the strange mysteries that are hidden within this power, that I have ever seen or heard of. Picture to yourself the stupendous difficulty of believing such a statement, if you read it in Print. Even imagine the difficulty of getting anybody to believe it, who knew the parties and could not doubt their veracity. Yet there can be nothing more true. For it is Truth itself. I have purposely stated it in the plainest manner, and have not presented it to you in anything like the remarkable aspect, in which it actually occurred.

Now, with reference to your Journal. Pray do not think you have put down too much, and pray do not depart from that system of writing it, as nothing could be more concise and intelligible. I cannot express to you the delight with which I read it, for with that strong trust in me on the part of Madame de la Rue—that most indubitable token of the strength of our position, and the power of the Magnetism—how can we despair of anything, or fail to hope for everything! Preserving that, and steadily increasing it (which is my desire and expectation) I do hope and believe that with God's leave the worst parts of her disorder will fall down prostrate, and be crushed the soonest, before it. If she were clairvoyant, or (to say the wildest thing I can think of) if she were omniscient, I should not value the wonder more than I do this gentle Trust of hers in my power to help her—I should not care for it, as a bright star of Hope, half so much. It is an assurance to me that the root of that Tree which shall peacefully shelter your Home for years to come, has struck deep into the Earth; and that the relief she has already experienced in her Mind is hardly to be estimated.

But this last assurance I have from herself. Set down in her own words, and not to be read with dry eyes. It is in that letter which you forwarded to me at Leghorn; and from it, I learn that her *mental* agony has been immensely beyond anything she has ever led you (on whom, she says, she could not bear to bring more sorrow than she could help: having already brought so much) to suppose. She speaks of that, as a thing past. She speaks, with confidence, of her nightly horrors as dreadful trials whose days were numbered—almost as trials already past. It is impossible to imagine the weight of the load she has begun to lay down in this respect, without the affecting knowledge of her grateful heart.

She has now no secret in connexion with the devilish figure; for that chain is utterly broken. That it bound her to the disease, and the disease to her, and that it must have linked her (she says so) in the course of time to Madness, I have no earthly doubt. I cannot yet quite make up my mind, whether the phantom originates in shattered nerves and a system broken by Pain; or whether it is the representative of some great nerve or set of nerves on which her disease has preyed —and begins to loose its hold now, because the disease of those nerves[1] is itself

---

[1] MS reads "neves". Mme de la Rue's affliction may have been *tic douloureux* (recognized before 1800); for CD's later mention of "tic in the brain" see *To* Bodenham, 24 Mar 45, *fn*. In 1848 he referred to her case when illustrating the "coincidence . . . between real effects and imaginary causes", as part of a general and

attacked by the inexplicable agency of the Magnetism. I think upon the whole, I incline to this last opinion; but I could not make up my mind without more observation of, and more conversation with, herself. I should also like to discuss it, at full length, with you.

However this may be, what I want to impress upon you; and what your affection will, I know, readily see, is this. That figure is so closely connected with the secret distresses of her very soul—and the impression made upon it is so entwined with her confidence and trust in me, and her knowledge of the power of the Magnetism—*that it must not make head again.* From what I know from her, I know there is more danger and delay in one appearance of that figure than in a dozen fits of the severest bodily pain. Believe nothing she says of her capacity of endurance, if the reappearance of that figure should become frequent. Consult that, mainly, and before all other signs. I shudder at the very thought of the precipice on which she has stood, when that Fancy has persecuted her. If you find her beset by it, induce her to be got to me by one means or other; for there the danger lies so deep, that she herself can hardly probe it, even now.

My dear De la Rue, I have written, or have meant to write, very strongly on this point, for I hold her clue now, and am acquainted with its vast importance. This letter will cross your second, which is already, I hope, on its way to Rome. I will write to you, when I have heard from her and you at that place. I have come to the end of my paper, and to bed time, at the same moment. Very many thanks for your kindness to my pet little sister in law. Best remembrances from Mrs. Dickens. All cordial assurances of friendship and regard From Yours Heartily

CHARLES DICKENS

To JOHN FORSTER, [?29 JANUARY 1845]

Extracts in F, IV, vii, 368–9, 367–8*n. Date:* second extract 29 Jan according to Forster; first extract clearly same letter, since it describes the journey up to that point. *From* Ronciglione.

Describing the journey, he said that before Radicofani[1] was reached there were disturbing rumours of bandits[2] and even uncomfortable whispers as to their night's lodging-place.[3] I really began to think we might have an adventure; and as I had

rational argument about ghosts in his review of Catherine Crowe's *The Night Side of Nature* (*Examiner*, 26 Feb 48: see next vol.); there he says that the "lady" had learnt by experience to recognize the origin of the phantoms.

[1] Twelve miles from La Scala (the intervening country was "as barren, as stony, and as wild as Cornwall in England", *Pictures,* p. 160); they passed through Radicofani 28 Jan, and its "ghostly, goblin inn" with "rambling corridors, and gaunt rooms" is described in *Pictures*. Ruskin stayed there in 1840: "Inn melancholy in appearance, but very comfortable" (*The Diaries of John Ruskin 1835–1847,* ed. Joan Evans, 1956, I. 115); Catharine Taylor (*Letters to a Younger Sister,* 1840, p. 90) thought Radicofani "a place to awaken all one's recollections of Italian romances . . . fitted for the exploits of banditti".

[2] *Pictures,* p. 158 specifies the rumours: they had stopped the mail near that very place, and "had waylaid some travellers not long before, on Mount Vesuvius".

[3] Bolsena ("celebrated for malaria"), which they reached late on 28 Jan, after crossing "the dismal dirty Papal Frontier";

brought (like an ass) a bag of napoleons with me from Genoa, I called up all the theatrical ways of letting off pistols that I could call to mind, and was the more disposed to fire them from not having any. *The inhabitants of Radicofani, being all of them beggars, had the habit of swooping down, like so many birds of prey,*[1] *upon any carriage that approached it.* Can you imagine [Samuel Carter Hall][2] in a very frowsy brown cloak concealing his whole figure, and with very white hair and a very white beard, darting out of this place with a long staff in his hand, and begging? There he was, whether you can or not; out of breath with the rapidity of his dive, and staying with his staff all the Radicofani boys, that he might fight it out with me alone. It was very wet, and so was I: for I had kept, according to custom, my box-seat. It was blowing so hard that I could scarcely stand; and there was a custom-house[3] on the spot, besides. Over and above all this, I had no small money; and the brave C never has, when I want it for a beggar. When I had excused myself several times, he suddenly drew himself up and said, with a wizard look (fancy the aggravation of [Hall] as a wizard!) "Do you know what you are doing, my lord? Do you mean to go on, to-day?" "Yes," I said, "I do." "My lord," he said, "do you know that your vetturino is unacquainted with this part of the country; that there is a wind raging on the mountain, which will sweep you away; that the courier, the coach, and all the passengers, were blown from the road last year; and that the danger is great and almost certain?" "No," I said, "I don't." "My lord, you don't understand me, I think?" "Yes I do, d——you!" nettled by this (you feel it? I confess it). "Speak to my servant. It's his business. Not mine"—for he really was too like [Hall] to be borne. If you could have seen him!—"Santa Maria, these English lords! It's not their business, if they're killed! They leave it to their servants!" He drew off the boys; whispered them to keep away from the heretic; and ran up the hill again, almost as fast as he had come down. He stopped at a little distance as we moved on; and pointing to Roche with his long staff cried loudly after me, "It's *his* business if you're killed, is it, my lord? Ha! ha! ha! whose business is it, when the English lords are born! Ha! ha! ha!" The boys taking it up in a shrill yell, I left the joke and them at this point. But I must confess that I thought he had the best of it. And he had so far reason for what he urged, that when we got on the mountain pass the wind became terrific, so that we were obliged to take Kate out of the carriage lest she should be blown over, carriage and all, and had ourselves to hang on to it, on the windy side, to prevent its going Heaven knows where![4]

Do you think, in your state room, when the fog makes your white blinds yellow, and the wind howls in the brick and mortar gulf behind that square

next day they arrived at Ronciglione, "a little town like a large pig-sty" (*Pictures*, pp. 161–2), where they spent the last night before Rome—Murray advised the traveller not to stay there as both inns were "dirty and inferior".

[1] Verbally close to *Pictures*, p. 160.

[2] Text reads "M.F.G."; Forster explains that this has been substituted for the name of "a first-rate bore". CD was again

at Radicofani on 21 Nov 53 and wrote to Catherine: "The same man whom I formerly said was like Samuel Carter Hall, told the same story" (*Mr & Mrs CD*, ed. Walter Dexter, p. 216).

[3] The Papal frontier station and custom house at Ponte Centino, where passports were examined.

[4] Verbally close to *Pictures*, p. 160, where Catherine is called "my other half".

perspective, with a middle distance of two ladder-tops and a back-ground of Drury-lane sky—when the wind howls, I say,—as if its eldest brother, born in Lincoln's-inn-fields, had gone to sea and was making a fortune on the Atlantic—at such times do you ever think of houseless Dick?[1]

To JOHN FORSTER, [?31 JANUARY 1845]

Extract in F, IV, vii, 369. *Date:* probably the day after their arrival at Rome on 30 Jan.

Describing his arrival in Rome,[2] *he said that the cloudy sky, dull cold rain and muddy footways, he was prepared for; but not for the long streets of commonplace shops and houses like Paris or any other capital, the busy people, the equipages, the ordinary walkers up and down.* It was no more my Rome, degraded and fallen and lying asleep in the sun among a heap of ruins, than Lincoln's-inn-fields is. So I really went to bed in a very indifferent humour.[3]

To EMILE DE LA RUE, 31 JANUARY 1845*

MS Miss Gladys Storey.

Hotel Meloni,[4] Rome.
Friday Night Thirty First January | 1845.

My Dear De la Rue.

We arrived here last night; and I received your packet safely, this morning. Very many thanks. I hope that before this reaches you, you will have received a couple of missives from me, over and above that sent from Leghorn.

The weather has been, and is, atrocious. We found this Hotel full to the throat —except one apartment. And what do you say to that apartment having been the very one you occupied when you were here? *I* say there is something Magnetic in it. I didn't know it until just now at dinner, when Roche, my man, came up, red hot, with the intelligence which had transpired in a conversation between himself and Meloni.

We arrived yesterday, just in time for the horse Race. It was very pretty, but uncommonly short. I sneezed as I put my head out of window to look at it; and the whole business was begun and ended during that short convulsion. It was not a strong sneeze either. Quite a mild one.

As to the Masks, of which there were many scores going round and round the Piazza, afoot and in coaches; I must confess that my present impression of their

---

[1] The passage recalls popular songs about homeless orphan boys wandering in the storm.

[2] They had arrived at about four in the afternoon of 30 Jan; in the distance Rome had "looked like—I am half afraid to write the word—like LONDON!!!" (*Pictures*, pp. 163–5).

[3] The summary and extract are almost exactly in *Pictures*, p. 166, with some expansion and the substitution of "the Place de la Concorde in Paris" for "Lincoln's-inn-fields".

[4] In the Piazza del Popolo; recommended by Coghlan's *Handbook* as "first-rate"; later the Hotel des Iles Britanniques (N, II, 513, 514).

powers is not a very high one. They were marvellously dull and stupid, so far as I could see.[1] There have been none today, and there will be none tomorrow (when there is a Festa); but I shall correct my judgment on Monday and Tuesday. I have been to St. Peters,[2] and to the Coliseum. The former struck me of course, immensely. But the latter is the great sensation. And I never *can* forget it.[3]

It is lucky for you that I am going to write forthwith to Madame De la Rue—that I may enclose the note in this—or I would have come down upon you with a blaze of description and fancy, worthy of old Di Negro, when he screws his right hand round, and looks out at the corners of those sly old leering Peepers of his, after the manner of the inspired Improvisatori. Heaven send you may never find me in that humour, with opportunity added to it! For I am much longer about it than a Carnival Horse—and am infinitely slower in my pace, I fear.

I don't know the Writings you ask me about. Not at all. I have a kind of sense that I ought to know them. But I don't.

Now to our serious subject.

Madame De la Rue writes cheerfully. But she says in her note (which is very short) "My head is certainly not as *cool* as when I was mesmerized every day,—once or twice I have had the sensation of Fire burning and raging in my head, to a painful degree."

But it is not so much that passage to which I am anxious to call your attention, as this:—

After speaking of the struggle which, she says, she feels must occur with the Bad Spirit, she adds this:

"Do not think me very foolish in again requesting you not to go to St. Trinita di Monti. Although I am so much better, I cannot yet bring myself to believe all I heard and saw there, was a fevered dream. And without, as yet, being able to explain to myself the reason, I dread your going there, without me. I trust I shall soon be able to tell you what has left so fearful an impression, but as yet I find it *impossible*. Heaven preserve me from passing another such day and night as I did then!"

I extract this, to shew you that I did not lay great stress on this creature, in my last, without strong reason. There can be no doubt that her position in reference to it is a very critical one; and that she is now in a state most favorable and advantageous to the best influence The Mesmerism could possibly exert upon her.

Therefore I am more than ever anxious for your news from Geneva.[4] I shall not fail, in writing to her tonight, to urge her again, to have no secret whatever from me, in connexion with this Fancy; and I shall try to shew her how unwise it is, and how opposed to all my earnest wishes, that she should retain one, hidden

[1] They saw only the "fag end of the masks" (*Pictures*, p. 165).

[2] The description in *Pictures*, pp. 166–7, has more reservations.

[3] He afterwards told Forster that "he had never in his life . . . been so moved or overcome by any sight as by that of the Coliseum, 'except perhaps by the first contemplation of the Falls of Niagara' " (F, IV, vii, 369).

[4] Whether they could join CD on his return to Rome depended on the return of de la Rue's partner, who was evidently visiting the family banking house in Geneva: see *To* de la Rue, 4 Feb 45.

in her breast. Do not lead in any way to the subject, lest she should think (which she would immediately) that I had given you any hint of this. But how unnecessary it is, that I should caution you who know her so well, and have studied and tended her with such delicate and loving care! My dear De la Rue, forgive me.

My agony is, lest any portion of the existing influence should be lost in prolonged separation—and lest that Devil in torturing her, should establish other secret horrors. In that case, how disheartening it would be to us (though I have no doubt of getting the better of them in time, even then) and what dreadful endurance to her!

Suppose—only suppose—it haunted her, night after night, and threatened her with revenge upon herself and upon me, of some prodigious and inconceivable kind, if she resumed the Mesmerism. And suppose *that* became a fixed idea! If it were once rooted in her unselfish and enduring nature, that I could bring the Malice of this Fancy on myself, by trying to heal her; I believe she would rather suffer, and would never tell why.

Could anything of this kind have been in her mind, when she was in that strange state we have so often spoken of, at Brown's one night—and so inconsistently and unaccountably proposed to drop the Mesmerism, of which she had then just begun to feel the Relief and Benefit? It may seem a monstrous idea of mine; but I am staggered[1] by the possibility of such a thing.

Therefore, once again, I am the more anxious for your news from Geneva. And heartily glad I shall be to hear that it is what we could desire, and what we *do* desire. And if your plans are unfolded in your next letter, and promise to lead you soon this way, it will be one of the most welcome letters I have ever read in my life.

Mrs. Dickens begs to be most cordially and Sincerely remembered to you. I wish, for your sake, I wrote a better hand. But it was a better hand once, before I wrote books. Which must be a great satisfaction to you, no doubt.

Always My Dear de la Rue | Yours most Faithfully

M. De la Rue

CHARLES DICKENS

To CHARLES BODENHAM,[2] 2 FEBRUARY 1845

Text from N, I, 657.

Hotel Meloni | Sunday Afternoon, Second February 1845

My Dear Sir,

I am much indebted to you for your kind recollection of me, this morning. I was in the act of making myself as clerical as possible,[3] when your note arrived.

Mrs. Dickens had a very good place (though we were rather late); and we saw

[1] After "I", about 16 words cancelled by CD, of which "see that this Thing has had a [?curious effect]" and "in [*or* on] her mind" are decipherable.

[2] Charles Thomas Bodenham (1783–1865), *m.* 1820 Elizabeth, d. of Thomas Weld of Dorset; both of Catholic families.

[3] CD was "attired in black (no other passport is necessary)" to attend High Mass at St Peter's on 2 Feb, the Feast of the Purification, when a great crowd was present to see the Pope bless the candles. The description in *Pictures*, pp. 169–73, hardly conveys an impression of "magnitude and bewilderment".

the sight to great advantage. I regret that we missed you, but in a scene of such magnitude and bewilderment, I scarcely hoped to find you.

Believe me | My Dear Sir | Faithfully yours

[CHARLES DICKENS]

To EMILE DE LA RUE, 4 FEBRUARY 1845*

MS Miss Gladys Storey. *Address* (envelope, MS Berg Collection): A Monsieur | Monsr. Emile De la Rue | Genova.

Rome Tuesday February Fourth 1845.

My Dear De La Rue. I have read your two notes; this morning received; with a more painful interest than usual. But not with the least surprise.

I am decidedly of opinion that the poor housekeeper's condition and all its attendant anxieties have little or nothing to do, in reality, with Madame De La Rue's gradually altering state. You know that from the first I have had a great fear that the influence so recently established, would gradually wear away—I, the cause of the influence, not being present—before the pressure and returning strength of the disorder represented by the bad figure. I believe the influence to be fading fast. She may not distinguish it, herself, from her faith in me, and may think that as long as the latter exists, the former remains with her. But it is not so. The figure is obtaining the ascendant—and will get it, until I can mesmerize her again; when I shall *not* be able to take her up, I fear, at the point where I left her, but shall have to work on to it.

It is a great point that she has conquered her horror of breaking confidence with this shadow, and that she has told me, in this last note, all it said when it broke silence in her bedroom. On the other hand, I cannot but observe that her fear of it is greater than her subservience to me. I find this exemplified in a slight incident, but one which shews it as strongly as a greater circumstance could. She had written me that she would leave the Casino Ball, exactly at One: remembering that I had appointed that hour before: and thinking it would please me. She laid great stress on this, and underlined the words. Notwithstanding this promise and her desire to keep it, her dread of the shadow becomes so great that she utterly disregards her voluntary pledge to me, and remains abroad until the morning is far advanced (as I learn from you) to escape it. I see in this, an increasing power on the part of the figure, beyond all kind of question.

As to what she says of her confidence in not requiring the Magnetism (if need were) until my return to Genoa, we can place no reliance on it whatever. It is merely a piece of that strange inconsistency which we know to be, at times, a part of her state. In the very same packet of letters in which you told me that; she expressed to me a perfect pain of Hope that nothing would prevent your bringing her to Rome.

Thank Heaven your good partner[1] comes, and you will be able to do so! For

[1] His brother, Hyppolite de la Rue (1794–1876), and his cousin, David-Jullien de la Rue (1798–1876), were partners in the bank; David retired in 1850 and Hyppolite at an unknown, perhaps earlier, date (Camillo Cavour, *Nouvelles Letters Inédites*, ed. Amédée Bert, p. iv).

on the beating down of this Phantom—worst symptom of her disorder, and most alarming evidence of its progress and strong hold upon her; mind and body— all depends. I *cannot* beat it down, or keep it down, at a distance. Pursuing that Magnetic power, and being near to her and with her, I believe that I can shiver it like Glass.

I am obliged to write to you in great haste, as this packet must go to Torlonia's[1] before Rome goes mad—which will be soon after Mid-day.[2] I shall look, with great impatience, for your letters at Naples. I am full of anxiety for her; and would to God the Holy Week were here.

Always My Dear De la Rue | Yours wholly
CHARLES DICKENS

To GEORGINA HOGARTH, 4 FEBRUARY 1845†

MS Morgan Library.

Rome. Tuesday Fourth February 1845

My Dearest Georgy.

This is a very short note, but time is still shorter. *Come by the first boat, by all means. If there be a good one a day or two before it, come by that.* [a]In case of any missing, or unforseen[3] arrival (which is not likely) we shall be at the Vittoria Hotel, Naples. Write to us (by De la Rue as usual) and let us know; if there be time; exactly on what day and by what boat you leave Genoa.[a] Don't delay on any account. I am very sorry you are not here. The Carnival is a very remarkable, and beautiful sight. I have been regretting the having left you at home, all the way here.

Kate says will you [b]bring her a box of toothpowder. Anne knows where it is. Also will you[b] take counsel with Charlotte about colour (I put in my word, as usual, for brightness) and have the darlings bonnets made at once, by the same artist as before. Kate would have written, but is gone, with Black,[4] to a day-

[1] Chief banking-house of Rome, in the Via Condotti; the envelope is stamped "de la part des Messrs. Torlonia & Cie".

[2] The postmark, however, is 6 Feb.

[3] Thus in MS.

aa; bb; cc; dd; ee; ff Not previously published.

[4] Charles Christopher Black (1809–79); his wife, Kate (*née* Elderton), was the sister of Mrs Cattermole, who lived with the Blacks in St John's Wood until her marriage in 1839 (see Vol. I, p. 576*n* and F. G. Kitton, *CD by Pen and Pencil*, I, 181). According to Forster "there was intimate intercourse both before and during the residence in Italy" between CD and the Blacks (F, VI, vi, 531). Crabb Robinson described him in June 46 as "a friend of *Dickens*" and also of Mrs Reid—"a sensible & gentlemanly man" who "talks so well that one thinks he lays himself out for talking and does not write" (MS Diary, Dr Williams's Library). The Blacks were in Naples in Nov 45 when a son was born (*Examiner*, 8 Nov 45), and in 1852 CD knew them to be in Italy but had "received no intelligence of them for I don't know how long" (*To* George Scott, 13 Aug 52; see also *To* Catherine, 14 Nov 53, *Mr and Mrs CD*, ed. W. Dexter, p. 212). Later, Black carried out special commissions for the South Kensington Museum (established 1862; now the Victoria & Albert), and from about 1864 to 1869 was first a "Provisional", then a "Supplementary" Assistant Keeper. He wrote several books on art, including *Michael Angelo Buonarotti*, 1875; Black's Preface refers to a "reverential study of his works during a lengthened residence in Florence and Rome".

Performance at the opera, to see Cerito[1] dance. At two each day, we sally forth in an open Carriage *c*(bearing dear Susan[2] with us)*c*—with a *large sack* of sugar plums and at least five hundred little Nosegays, to pelt people with. I should think we threw away yesterday, a thousand of the latter. We had the Carriage filled with flowers, three or four times. I wish you could have seen me catch a Swell Brigand *d*(Mr. Wood,[3] exactly)*d* on the nose with a handfull of very large confetti, every time we met him.[4] It was the best thing I have ever done. The Chimes are nothing to it.

*e*Best loves to Mamey, Katey, Charley, Walley, and Chickenstalker (whose name, I beg to observe, is written all in one).*e*

Anxiously expecting you, I am ever
Dear Georgy | Yours most Affectionately
CHARLES DICKENS

*f*Mrs. Charles Gibbs.[5]

Yours received this morning, of course.*f*

To EMILE DE LA RUE, 10 FEBRUARY 1845*

MS Miss Gladys Storey.

Vittoria Hotel,[6] Naples. Monday Night
February Tenth 1845.

My Dear De la Rue.

We were delayed a day longer than I had expected, in Rome; and did not get here, until yesterday Evening.[7] The Steamer which brought me your most welcome Packet arrived at breakfast-time this morning. I saw it coming; and had your letter in my hand, almost as soon as I had shut the telescope, through which I watched it into Port.

I am much concerned that you should think it possible I had the faintest

---

[1] Fanny Cerrito (1817–1909), the favourite dancer of the London public after her immensely successful season in 1843 (she and Fanny Elssler danced a *pas de deux* at the express request of the Queen). She opened her season at the Teatro di Apollo in Rome, 26 Dec 44, and included in it a new ballet, *La Vendetta d'Amore*, from 4 Jan, and *La Festa in Maschera* from 25 Jan.

[2] Susan Atkins: see *To* Mrs CD, 8 Nov 44, *fn.*

[3] Unidentified.

[4] The last two days of the Carnival were 3 and 4 Feb; there is a long account in *Pictures*, pp. 173–84, including references to "two very respectable sacks of sugarplums (each about three feet high)", the throwing of flowers, and the "light-whiskered brigand".

[5] A joke; Charles Gibbs was "a little man, and, one would have thought, a confirmed old bachelor, never having had any one to look after except himself", and a "great admirer" of Yeats Brown, whose daughter Stuarta (*b.* 1832) he married shortly before CD's return to Genoa in 1853, to the general surprise (F. A. Y. Brown, *Family Notes*; *To* Mrs CD, 8 Oct and 4 Nov 53, *Mr and Mrs CD*, pp. 195–6, 204–5—with "Stuarta" misread as "Sartoris" on p. 205).

[6] "On the Chiaja, opposite the entrance to the Villa Reale, a large and well-managed establishment" (Murray, *Handbook for . . . Southern Italy*, 1853).

[7] They left Rome Thurs 6 Feb, probably spending that night at Albano, and certainly 7 Feb at Terracina; crossed the Neapolitan frontier next day, went through Fondi, stayed the night of 8 Feb at St Agata, and rested at Capua on the way to Naples (*Pictures*, pp. 234–7).

doubt of the true depth, intensity, and earnestness, of your devotion to Madame De la Rue; or of the affectionate and zealous watch you have kept over her in all her sufferings. Believe me, I admire and feel your constancy under such a trial, scarcely less than hers; and that everything I have seen of you, in reference to her (it has been much, though in a short time) has filled me with a sorrowful pleasure, not easy of expression. When I wrote to you, strongly, on the Great and terrible symptom which is hovering about her, and over which—God be thanked for it!—we know we can exercise great power; I wrote as I felt. As I felt, do I say! Not one twentieth part as strongly as I felt, and feel. For the mystery of her mind in connexion with this Phantom, was then just opening to me. And the vast extent of the danger by which I saw she was beset, made me clench the pen as if it were an iron rod—Made me use it too, as clumsily as if it were a poker, when it became the instrument of conveying such a wrong and groundless idea to you.

My full reasons for entertaining this fervid opinion of the necessity of following up the blow that has been struck at this worst symptom of her state, I cannot give you. For she makes a condition with me that I shall not, *until*—she looks forward, you see, to being quite composed upon the subject, one day—*until* she gives me leave. Under the impression that with all your anxious care you might not know what she had kept hidden so fearfully in her breast, I wrote as I did. With no other grain of meaning or intention my dear friend, believe me.

I think it possible, even now—I think it probable, indeed—that as the time approaches for your journey to Rome, she may raise objections, and be disinclined to go. The more she shews this state of mind, the greater the danger is, and the more urgent and imperative the necessity for her being *brought*—I underline the word "brought" to express—by your determination. You feel with me, I know.

Observe, my dear De la Rue. On Sunday the Second, she confesses to you that she feels stronger against the figures, now that the journey is decided on. That night, she sees the Figure, and apparently overcomes it. But before it disappears, it says something, which she does not distinctly hear. *On the next day*, she vaguely damps the ardour of your preparations for the journey. I strongly incline, with you, to the belief that trying in the interval to put together what scattered words she heard the figure say, she joined and dovetailed them into some threat, having reference to her venturing to undertake the journey. And I think you will always find that her otherwise unaccountable indisposition to go, manifests itself, *after* an interview with this Phantom. That her own heart is set on going—that her whole being is full of the most earnest hope and expectation of relief that all her wishes tend that way— I know. In this very last letter, received to day, she speaks of it with greater Earnestness than ever. With an earnestness that seems to make her hand tremble as she writes.

In my two last letters—I mean the last of the two from Rome, and that just written from here, and to be enclosed in this—I have battled this point, with the greatest perseverance and doggedness I could use. I have told her that she must set no store whatever, by anything this creature says. That it is in its Nature a false thing—an unreal creation; a lie of her eyes and Ears—and cannot speak the Truth. That if it could speak the Truth, it couldn't *be*, at all. That if I could call it up, when she and I were together, and could represent it as letting fall the Blade of a Guillotine upon my head, I would do so, and would have her look on immoveably: triumphant in the conviction that it was a powerless shadow. That if she thinks, for a moment, it could hurt me; she cannot have faith and trust in me, and I must magnetize her, 'till I win them in reality—&c&c. Anticipating what may happen.

The Magnetism between us on that Sunday, is especially remarkable—if I can call anything so, which is a part of such a strange and mysterious whole.

The *Tuesday*, on which she was so restless, was the day on which I last wrote to you, I think. It was the last day of the Carnival in any case; and I was out, in the streets, all the afternoon. I was not very gay, certainly; but I was not unusually gloomy. I am not quite sure whether it was on that night or on Monday, that I woke up suddenly, about one or two o'Clock, in a state of indescribable horror and emotion. Not caused by any dream, for I had not dreamed. And when I say "woke up", I don't express it properly; for I was quite myself when I awoke, and the feeling came on, immediately afterwards, when I was broad awake. It was so intense that I was obliged to get up, and walk about, and light the candles. I could almost swear this happened on the Tuesday Night, but I am not quite sure, and cannot fix it, by any helping circumstance. I thought continually about her, both awake and asleep, on the nights of Monday, Tuesday, and Wednesday. And it is remarkable that I don't dream of her, in the ordinary sense; but merely have an anxiety about her, and a sense of her being somehow a part of me, as I have when I am awake.—It turns me quite cold to think, with a start, that this *may* have been on *Wednesday*! I cannot find out at this moment, but I will do so, and tell you when I am quite certain.

I quite agree with you in your construction of that extraordinary circumstance about the voices in the sick-room. It is a philosophical explanation of many Ghost Stories. Though it is hardly less chilling than a Ghost-Story itself. There is no reasonable doubt that the woman received the impression magnetically from Madame De la Rue.

I shall hope to hear from you again (and shall rely on doing so) by my little Mrs. Gibbs. I will write by the next Steamer after that; and if there be a boat in two or three days from this time, I will write a line to Madame De la Rue, without waiting for Mrs. G's arrival.

A capital apartment (though at the top of the house) secured for *us*[1] at Meloni's! I purpose returning there, on the first of March; and leaving here, four *days* beforehand, at most. The exact day of leaving here, I will tell you in my next. Besides other letters to this place, I shall hear from you, of course, at Rome, before you start, and when you start. Write as often as possible—and do not think you can write at too great length. I shall be glad to arrange with you, for catching Madame de la Rue with a joyful note, upon the road; and also for making a false appointment for meeting you, and coming on her sooner than we agree upon.

Of all the walks and talks we shall have together—and the sights we shall see together—and our merry journey home together—and our weighty conversation

---

[1] Underlined twice.

(yours and mine I mean) about our summer plans, and how we can best arrange to pursue the great end before us, steadily, to *its* end: of which I am constantly thinking—I dare say nothing, now, lest the clocks of Rome and Naples should stand still for a Month to come. But when I think of your coming to Rome, and of Madame de la Rue growing day by day and week by week, better in health, quieter in mind, happier in everything; when I picture her restored to peace and rest, with nothing lingering and cankering in her breast to make her nights hideous and her days weary; I feel such enthusiasm at work within me, that every hour's postponement is an hour of heaviness. Mrs. Clive the actress said of Garrick[1] (crying at his Lear) that she believed he could act a Gridiron. When I think of all that lies before us, I have a perfect conviction that I could magnetize a Frying-Pan.

I don't know the American Gentleman—God forgive me for putting two such words together!—whose name you mention. I never heard of him. Do you know what the population of the United States is?—I forget the figures myself, but I will answer for it, that every man and boy in the sum total knows me intimately. I never heard of an American, since I was in "our country",[2] who didn't.

Too much set upon the one subject tonight, my dear De la Rue, to tell you anything about our travels! Except that as we came South, it got colder and colder. That yesterday it was painfully and bitingly cold! That the night before last, the Fleas (at a place called Saint Agata) really overdid the thing, and sowed themselves, like self-acting mustard and cress, in my flannel dressing-gown. That I find myself perpetually stopping in public places to scratch myself, like a Dog. And that when I listen very hard outside my Portmanteau, I think I can distinctly hear them, leaping up inside the lid, and knocking their heads against it.

Ever believe me *a*though—With them or without
them (if I ever should be
again)*a*

Faithfully Yours
CHARLES DICKENS

P.S. Here is a letter for Charley, and two (English) for the Post.

To JOHN FORSTER, [11 FEBRUARY 1845]

Extracts in F, IV, vii, 369–70 and *n*. *Date:* first extract 11 February according to Forster; second extract probably same letter, since so placed by Forster. *From* Naples.

He had found the wonderful aspects of Rome before he left; for loneliness and grandeur of ruin nothing could transcend the southern side of the Campagna. But farther and

---

[1] A well-known story, recorded by John Taylor in *Records of my Life*, 1832, I, 346.

[2] Recalling the stock question, "How do you like our country?"—the first question

addressed to Martin by Colonel Diver before he has landed in New York: see *Chuzzlewit*, Ch. 16, and elsewhere.

aa Squeezed in as an afterthought.

farther south the weather had become worse; the only bright sky he had seen was just as the sun was coming up across the sea at Terracina. Of which place, a beautiful one, you can get a very good idea by imagining something as totally unlike the scenery in *Fra Diavolo*[1] as possible. *He thought the bay less striking at Naples than at Genoa, the shape of the latter being more perfect in its beauty, and the smaller size enabling you to see it all at once, and feel it more like an exquisite picture. He disliked the city.* The condition of the common people here is abject and shocking. I am afraid the conventional idea of the picturesque is associated with such misery and degradation that a new picturesque will have to be established as the world goes onward. Except Fondi,[2] there is nothing on earth that I have seen so dirty as Naples. I don't know what to liken the streets to where the mass of the lazzaroni live. You recollect that favourite pigstye of mine near Broadstairs? They are more like streets of such apartments heaped up story on story, and tumbled house on house, than anything else I can think of, at this moment.

In Naples, the burying place of the poor people is a great paved yard with three hundred and sixty-five pits in it: every one covered by a square stone which is fastened down. One of these pits is opened every night in the year; the bodies of the pauper dead are collected in the city; brought out in a cart (like that I told you of at Rome);[3] and flung in, uncoffined. Some lime is then cast down into the pit; and it is sealed up until a year is past, and its turn again comes round. Every night there is a pit opened; and every night that same pit is sealed up again, for a twelvemonth. The cart has a red lamp attached, and at about ten o'clock at night you see it glaring through the streets of Naples: stopping at the doors of hospitals and prisons, and such places, to increase its freight: and then rattling off again. Attached to the new cemetery (a very pretty one, and well kept: immeasurably better in all respects than Père-la-Chaise) there is another similar yard, but not so large.[4] . . . About Naples, the dead are borne along the street, uncovered, on an open bier; which is sometimes hoisted on a sort of palanquin, covered with a cloth of scarlet and gold.[5] This exposure of the deceased is not peculiar to that part of Italy; for about midway between Rome and Genoa we encountered a funeral procession attendant on the body of a woman, which was presented in its usual dress, to my eyes (looking from my elevated seat on the box of a travelling carriage) as if she were alive, and resting on her bed. An attendant priest was chanting lustily—and as badly as the priests invariably do. Their noise is horrible.

---

[1] They had passed "the ruins of a fort . . . traditionally called the Fort of Fra Diavolo" (*Pictures*, p. 236). *Fra Diavolo; or, the Inn of Terracina*, 1831, M. R. Lacy's adaptation from Scribe, was frequently performed.

[2] In *Pictures*, pp. 235–6, the town is called "wretched and beggarly" with "a filthy channel of mud and refuse" in the centre of the street.

[3] See *Pictures*, pp. 188–9; CD also described the common pits at Genoa (pp. 64–5).

[4] The old and new cemetery are more briefly described in *Pictures*, p. 243; Forster, in error, says the pauper burial-place is not mentioned there (F, *ibid*).

[5] This sentence is verbally close to one at the beginning of the description of Naples (*Pictures*, p. 237).

To EMILE DE LA RUE, 14 FEBRUARY 1845*

MS Berg Collection.

Naples. | Friday Morning February Fourteenth 1845.

My Dear De la Rue.

I have but a moment. The Castore[1] is going suddenly.—My little Pet,[2] just arrived, and safely.—Your journal full of interest—Madame De la Rue, sliding fast back—Good God, how glad I am, you made your arrangements in good time!

We will see everything when you come—and do everything—and talk about everything. We leave here for Rome (by the Monte Cassino road) on the 24th.[3] arriving there, on the 1st.—I was desperately mindful of my Patient yesterday and the day before. Intensely so, last night. I half expect some reason for it in your next Journal.

Ever Yours at heart
CD.

To DOUGLAS CHEAPE,[4] 15 FEBRUARY 1845*

MS Free Library of Philadelphia.

Vittoria Hotel Naples | Saturday Fifteenth February 184

My dear Sir

I am exceedingly sorry to say that we are engaged on Monday—and indeed for every day during the short remainder of our stay here—otherwise it would have afforded both Mrs. Dickens and myself the greatest pleasure to have accepted your kind Invitation.

Believe me | Faithfully Yours
Douglas Cheape Esquire.   CHARLES DICKENS

To THOMAS MITTON, 17 and 22 FEBRUARY 1845

Text from MDGH, I, 136–41, with some readings from extracts in unidentified catalogue at Eastgate House, Rochester.

Naples, Monday, February 17th, 1845.

My dear Mitton,

This will be a hasty letter, for I am as badly off in this place as in America—

---

[1] The boat from Marseilles to Naples, which called at Genoa, Leghorn, and Civita Vecchia.

[2] Georgina. A letter to her in 1853 (N, II, 511) show that she was escorted by a "little parrot-marquess".

[3] They left a day later than planned (see *To* Cotterell, 25 Feb), and had "a three

days' journey along bye-roads", in order to see Monte Cassino (described in *Pictures*, pp. 260–2), and spent one night at Valmontone.

[4] Douglas Cheape (1797–1861; *DNB*), lawyer and writer of legal squibs; Professor of Civil Law, University of Edinburgh, 1827–42.

beset by visitors at all times and seasons, and forced to dine out every day.[1] I have found, however, an excellent man for me—an Englishman, who has lived here many years, and is well acquainted with *the people*, whom he doctored in the bad time of the cholera, when the priests and everybody else fled in terror.[2]

Under his auspices, I have got to understand the low life of Naples (among the Fishermen and Idlers) almost as well as I do[3] the do. do. of my own country; always excepting the language, which is very peculiar and extremely difficult, and would require a year's constant practice at least. It is no more like Italian than English is to Welsh. And as they don't say half of what they mean, but make a wink or a kick stand for a whole sentence, it's a marvel to me how they comprehend each other. At Rome they speak beautiful Italian (I am pretty strong at that, I believe); but they are worse here than in Genoa, which I had previously thought impossible.

It is a fine place, but nothing like so beautiful as people make it out to be. The famous bay is, to my thinking, as a piece of scenery, immeasurably inferior to the Bay of Genoa, which is the most lovely thing I have ever seen. The city, in like manner, will bear no comparison with Genoa. But there is none in Italy that will, except Venice. As to houses, there is no palace like the Peschiere for architecture, situation, gardens, or rooms. It is a great triumph to me, too, to find how cheap it is. At Rome, the English people live in dirty little fourth, fifth, and sixth floors, with not one room as large as your own drawing-room, and pay, commonly, seven or eight pounds a week.

I was a week in Rome on my way here, and saw the Carnival, which is perfectly delirious, and a great scene for a description. All the ancient part of Rome is wonderful and impressive in the extreme, far beyond the possibility of exaggeration. As to the modern part, it might be anywhere or anything—Paris, Nice, Boulogne, Calais, or one of a thousand other places.

The weather is so atrocious (rain, snow, wind, darkness, hail, and cold) that I can't get over into Sicily. But I don't care very much about it, as I have planned out ten days of excursion into the neighbouring country.[4] One thing of course— the ascent of Vesuvius, Herculaneum and Pompeii, the two cities which were covered by its melted ashes, and dug out in the first instance accidentally, are more full of interest and wonder than it is possible to imagine. I have heard of some ancient tombs (quite unknown to travellers) dug in the bowels of the earth,

[1] A correspondent of *Galignani's Messenger* reported from Naples, 26 Feb, that CD had been "gloriously *fêted*" and should have stayed three months rather than three weeks; "he might then perhaps have accepted about one half the invitations he received. The last banquet offered him was on Sunday last, at the hospitable board of H.B.M.'s Minister [*William Temple: see* To *Lady Blessington*, 9 May 45, *fn*]. The Marquis and Marchioness of Clanricarde, and Lady E. De Burgh, Earl and Countess of Lichfield and Lady H. Anson, Sir Charles and Lady Napier, Lord George Quin, etc.,

were of the party" (*Galignani's Messenger*, 12 Mar 45).
[2] Possibly Mr Roskilly, said by Murray (*Handbook for . . . Southern Italy*) to have been long resident in Naples as an English surgeon.
[3] From catalogue extract; MDGH reads "understand".
[4] Three days, 18–20 Feb, were spent at Paestum; Herculaneum and Pompeii were visited on the morning of 21 Feb, the day the expedition to Vesuvius started (*Pictures*, pp. 243–7).

and extending for some miles underground. They are near a place called Viterbo,[1] on the way from Rome to Florence. I shall lay in a small stock of torches, etc., and explore them when I leave Rome. I return there on the 1st of March, and shall stay there nearly a month.

Saturday, February 22nd.—Since I left off as above, I have been away on an excursion of three days. Yesterday, leaving[2] at four o'clock, we began (a small party of six) the ascent of Mount Vesuvius, with six saddle-horses,[3] an armed soldier for a guard, and twenty-two guides. The latter rendered necessary by the severity of the weather, which is greater than has been known for twenty years, and has covered the precipitous part of the mountain with deep snow, the surface of which is glazed[4] with one smooth sheet of ice from the top of the cone to the bottom. By starting at that hour I intended to get the sunset about halfway up, and night at the top, where the fire is raging. It was an inexpressibly lovely night without a cloud; and when the day was quite gone, the moon (within a few hours of the full) came proudly up, showing the sea, and the Bay of Naples, and the whole country, in such majesty as no words can express. We rode to the beginning of the snow and then dismounted. Catherine and Georgina were put into two litters, just chairs with poles, like those in use in England on the 5th of November; and a fat Englishman, who was of the party, was hoisted into a third, borne by eight men. I was accommodated with a tough stick, and we began to plough our way up. The ascent was as steep as this line /—very nearly perpendicular.[5] We were all tumbling at every step; and looking up and seeing the people in advance tumbling over one's very head, and looking down and seeing hundreds of feet of smooth ice below, was, I must confess, anything but agreeable. However, I knew there was little chance of another clear night before I leave this, and gave the word to get up, somehow or other. So on we went, winding a little now and then, or we should not have got on at all. By prodigious exertions we passed the region of snow, and came into that of fire—desolate and awful, you may well suppose. It was like working one's way through a dry waterfall, with every mass of stone burnt and charred into enormous cinders, and smoke and sulphur bursting out of every chink and crevice, so that it was difficult to breathe. High before us, bursting out of a hill at the top of the mountain, shaped like this Λ, the fire was pouring out, reddening the night with flames, blackening it with smoke, and spotting it with red-hot stones and cinders that fell down again in showers.[6] At every step everybody fell, now into a hot

---

[1] At Castel d'Assai, 5 miles from Viterbo; Murray recommends torches.

[2] From catalogue extract; MDGH reads "Yesterday evening", but *Pictures*, p. 248, has "at four o'clock in the afternoon".

[3] CD probably wrote "saddled horses"; cf. "saddled ponies" in *Pictures, ibid.* Catalogue extract reads "horses saddled".

[4] Catalogue extract reads "glassed"; "ss" is a possible misreading of CD's "z".

[5] Ruskin ascended Vesuvius in Feb 41: "Up the cone steep enough . . . but much easier than Scawfell, and not one twentieth part so bad as it is described" (Ruskin, *Diaries*, 1, 155).

[6] *Galignani's* remarked on CD's good fortune; on the night of his ascent "a new cone burst forth, and throwing up red-hot stones and cinders, was awfully grand, the whole mountain, from the crater to its base, being white with snow, nothing like it having been seen since the eruption of January, 1839". The next eruption occurred in the following April (Murray, *Handbook for . . . Southern Italy*).

chink, now into a bed of ashes, now over a mass of cindered iron; and the confusion in the darkness (for the smoke obscured the moon in this part), and the quarrelling and shouting and roaring of the guides; and the waiting every now and then for somebody who was not to be found, and was supposed to have tumbled[1] into some pit or other, made such a scene of it as I can give you no idea of. My ladies were now on foot, of course; but we dragged them on as well as we could (they were thorough game,[2] and didn't make the least complaint), until we got to the foot of that topmost hill I have drawn so beautifully. Here we all stopped; but the head guide, an English gentleman of the name of Le Gros[3]— who has been here many years, and has been up the mountain a hundred times— and your humble servant, resolved (like jackasses) to climb that hill to the brink, and look down into the crater itself. You may form some notion of what is going on inside it, when I tell you that it is a hundred feet higher than it was six weeks ago. The sensation of struggling up it, choked with the fire and smoke, and feeling at every step as if the crust of ground between one's feet and the gulf of fire would crumble in and swallow one up (which is the real danger), I shall remember for some little time, I think. But we did it. We looked down into the flaming bowels of the mountain and came back again, alight in half-a-dozen places, and burnt from head to foot. You never saw such devils. And *I* never saw anything so awful and terrible.

Roche had been tearing his hair like a madman, and crying that we should all three be killed, which made the rest of the company very comfortable, as you may suppose. But we had some wine in a basket, and all swallowed a little of that and a great deal of sulphur before we began to descend. The usual way, after the fiery part is past—you will understand that to be all the flat top of the mountain, in the centre of which, again, rises the little hill I have drawn—is to slide down the ashes, which, slipping from under you, make a gradually increasing ledge under your feet, and prevent your going too fast. But when we came to this steep place last night, we found nothing there but one smooth solid sheet of ice. The only way to get down was for the guides to make a chain, holding by each other's hands, and beat a narrow track in it into the snow below with their sticks. My two unfortunate ladies were taken out of their litters again, with half-a-dozen men hanging on to each, to prevent their falling forward; and we began to descend this way. It was like a tremendous dream. It was impossible to stand, and the only way to prevent oneself from going sheer down the precipice, every time one fell, was to drive one's stick into one of the holes the guides had made, and hold on by that. Nobody could pick one up, or stop one, or render one the least assistance. Now, conceive my horror, when this Mr. Le Gros I have mentioned, being on one side of Georgina and I on the other, suddenly staggers away from the narrow path on to the smooth ice, gives us a jerk, lets go, and plunges headforemost down the smooth ice into the black night, five hundred

[1] From catalogue extract; MDGH reads "stumbled".

[2] A boxing term; see *OED*, Game *sb*, sense 14.

[3] W. B. Le Gros (*d.* 1850), author of *Fables and Tales, suggested by the Frescoes of Pompeii and Herculaneum*, 1835; on hearing of his death CD wrote to Lytton: "Forster told me that you knew Le Gros (who interested me a good deal) at Naples" (*To* Lytton, 9 Dec 50; N, II, 249). He is called "Mr. Pickle of Portici" in *Pictures*, p. 249.

feet below! Almost at the same instant, a man far behind, carrying a light basket on his head with some of our spare cloaks in it, misses his footing and rolls down in another place; and after him, rolling over and over like a black bundle, goes a boy, shrieking as nobody but an Italian can shriek, until the breath is tumbled out of him.

The Englishman is in bed to-day, terribly bruised but without any broken bones. He was insensible at first and a mere heap of rags; but we got him before the fire, in a little hermitage there is halfway down, and he so far recovered as to be able to take some supper, which was waiting for us there. The boy was brought in with his head tied up in a bloody cloth, about half an hour after the rest of us were assembled. And the man who had had the basket was not found when we left the mountain at midnight. What became of the cloaks (mine was among them) I know as little. My ladies' clothes were so torn off their backs that they would not have been decent, if there could have been any thought of such things at such a time. And when we got down to the guides' house, we found a French surgeon (one of another party who had been up before us) lying on a bed in a stable, with God knows what horrible breakage about him, but suffering acutely and looking like death. A pretty unusual trip for a pleasure expedition,[1] I think!

I am rather stiff to-day but am quite unhurt, except a slight scrape on my right hand. My clothes are burnt to pieces. My ladies are the wonder of Naples, and everybody is open-mouthed.

Address me as usual. All letters are forwarded. The children well and happy. Best regards.

Ever faithfully
C.D.

To JOHN FORSTER, [?22 FEBRUARY 1845]

Extracts in F, IV, vii, 370, 370*n*. *Date:* second extract "Naples, 2nd February, 1845" according to Forster—impossible, since CD did not reach Naples until 9 Feb; probably a mistake for 22 Feb, as he would certainly send Forster an account of Vesuvius, and "English letters" already written are mentioned in *To* de la Rue, 23–25 Feb; first extract "a later letter" than 11 Feb according to Forster; probably same letter as second extract.

What would I give that you should see the lazzaroni as they really are—mere squalid, abject, miserable animals for vermin to batten on; slouching, slinking, ugly, shabby, scavenging scarecrows! And of the raffish counts and more than doubtful countesses, the noodles and the blacklegs,[2] the good society! And oh the miles of miserable streets and wretched occupants, to which Saffron-hill or the Borough-mint is a kind of small gentility, which are found to be so picturesque by English lords and ladies; to whom the wretchedness left behind at home is

---

[1] Described rather more fully in *Pictures*, pp. 247–54; the head guide is named as Signor Salvatore, who also appears in Ruskin's account in 1841, and in Basil Hall's both in 1828 and 1833. He was "the person to whom the government of Naples look for a daily report of the state of the mountain" (Basil Hall, *Patchwork*, 1841, II, 135–42). Still active as a guide when CD returned in 1853 (*To* Mrs CD, 4 Nov 53, *Mr and Mrs CD*, ed. Walter Dexter, p. 213).

[2] "Swindlers" (*OED*).

lowest of the low, and vilest of the vile, and commonest of all common things.[1]
Well! well! I have often thought that one of the best chances of immortality for
a writer is in the Death of his language, when he immediately becomes good
company; and I often think here,—What *would* you say to these people, milady
and milord, if they spoke out of the homely dictionary of your own "lower
orders."

Thackeray praises the people of Italy for being kind to brutes.[2] There is
probably no country in the world where they are treated with such frightful
cruelty. It is universal.

To EMILE DE LA RUE, 23 and 25 FEBRUARY 1845*

MS Berg Collection. *Address:* M. Emile De la Rue.

Naples. Sunday Twenty Third February 1845.

My Dear De la Rue.

We have been away from here for three or four days—at Pæstum. We took
Vesuvius on our way back—in the only perfectly clear weather I have seen since
we left Genoa, and on the night before that on which the Moon was at the full.
We began the ascent at 4 o'Clock in the afternoon, and came down at Midnight.
The coming down was extremely difficult and dangerous; the ashes lying deep
under Snow and Ice, and the whole side of the Cone being like a smooth sheet of
Glass. A Guide was much hurt; and an English Gentleman fell head foremost
down the whole side of the Cone. He has been in bed ever since, greatly bruised
but in no wise dangerously hurt. A french gentleman, one of a party who were
an hour or so in advance of us, was not so fortunate. When we got down to the
Guide's house, we found him stretched on a litter in a stable, with some horrible
breakage about him, and looking like Death. He could not be moved, or I would
have brought him back to Naples in my carriage.

My ladies were perfectly "Game", and covered themselves with Glory. They
had need to cover themselves with something, for their clothes were literally
torn off their backs, and hanging in Rags about them. The Mountain is blazing
away prodigiously; the little crater at the top being one hundred feet higher than
it was, six weeks ago. I burnt my clothes off my back by climbing up to the top
of it, on the windy side (with the English Gentleman before mentioned and
Salvatore the head Guide, while the twenty five assistant Guides were roaring
and yelling that we should be killed) and looking down into the flaming Hell
below. The red hot ashes were falling in showers; and the noise and fire, and
smoke, and sulphur, made me feel as if I were dead drunk. To which effect, the
trembling crust of ground below my feet, contributed, no doubt.

It is a tremendous sight. Awful and terrible indeed. Between the stately
moon, and the fire, and the black smoke, and the white Snow, and the red going-

---

[1] The same idea is in *Pictures*, p. 240:
"It is not well to find Saint Giles's so
repulsive, and the Porta Capuana so
attractive".

[2] Not found in Thackeray's writings.

down of the Sun, there was a combination of Lights and Shadows upon it, such as I could never have imagined. It is more terrible than Niagara: the effect of which (to me at least) is peacefully and gently solemn, as the happy deaths of ten thousand people, without pain or blood, might be.[1] But the two things are as different in the impression they produce as—in short as fire and water are, which I suppose is the long and the short of it.

The weather has been bad, and very cold. But we have been here and there, and everywhere. Among other places to the Teatro San Carlino,[2] where there is the most extraordinary acting I ever beheld. As an exact copy of the life out of doors; set before one without much art—not heightened here, and kept out of view there, but presented broadly and plainly as the real thing itself is—it is quite wonderful.

Naples itself, rather—very slightly—disappoints me. I don't think the Bay so beautiful a picture as the Bay of Genoa. Its shape is not so easily made out and understood; and the effect of the hills is dissipated by its great size. Neither is the out-of-door life half so picturesque and uncommon as our travelling wiseacres are fond of making it. Herculaneum and Pompeii have impressed me beyond all description. I couldn't say how much, if I had the power of forty Gaberels[3] rolled into one.

Your Journal proceeds as I expected it would. I have no doubt the shadows will thicken more and more, until you start. But I hardly imagine they will be *very* troublesome on the journey; though I have no doubt it will be a trying time for Madame De la Rue. I have not observed the hour from eleven to twelve, for sometime—for twelve days; being curious to see whether she became at all worse at that time, after I left off. I have not told her this, in my note.

I live in the hope that you start on the third. And I take it for granted that when you write to me, on the road, you will address me at Meloni's, so that I may get the letters straight. I felt last night, between 11 and 12 o'Clock, as if Madame De la Rue were alarmed and uneasy. Very suddenly; as I was writing letters to England; this idea took possession of me. I felt so very uncomfortable, that I shut my desk and went to bed. Where was she, and how was she, I wonder!

On the day you come to Rome, you will start in the morning from Ronciglione, will you not? Let me know where you come from, and at what hour. I will leave Rome on horseback, at about the same hour; and meet you, as near as possible, *halfway*. When you have made half your distance therefore, look out for a Gallant Figure, apparently possessing an angelic Nature. All others are counterfeits.

I have always forgotten to tell you that I read French as easily as English; and that if it be pleasanter to you to write in that language (though I can hardly think it; you write English so well) it is all one to me. I am afraid I have lost a steamer in being away at Pæstum; and am in a state of irritable impatience to

---

[1] See Vol. III, p. 211.

[2] Cf. *Pictures*, p. 255. The theatre, in the Piazza del Municipio, was without a permanent company 1842–8 but later became the headquarters of the Pulcinella.

[3] Gaberel was a resident of Genoa, and evidently a clergyman: see *To* de la Rue, 20 Oct 45.

shut this packet up. As if closing it and getting it to you were one and the same thing!

Will you Post these English letters for me; and charge yourself with the small correspondence for the Peschiere?

Madame De la Rue's last letter to me was full of hope and impatience in reference to Rome; but was remarkably incoherent and unconnected. So much so, that I could scarcely make out, here and there, what she really had in her mind. I am very feverishly looking for the next Packet; and have damned it so much that I begin to fear it is going to revenge itself by not coming at all. My mind misgives me that she must have had a bad attack, after this long interval. The tenth of March, the tenth of March, the tenth of March!

Ever My dear De la Rue, Heartily Yours,

CD.

—I won't sign my name at full length, because I haven't room for the Flourish.

Tuesday 25th.—The weather is so very bad, my dear De la Rue; and the boat after 2 postponements, seems still so uncertain in its departure (as the Leopoldo is in its long expected and long-protracted arrival) that I have taken my English letters out of this Packet, and sent them by the Land Post today.

Ever Yours

CD.

To C. E. COTTERELL,[1] 25 FEBRUARY 1845*

MS Mitchell Library, Sydney. *Address:* Al Sigr. | Sigr. C. E. Cotterell.

Vittoria | Twenty Fifth February 1845

My Dear Sir

I thank you very much for your kind letter, and its enclosures.

I am horrified to find that my Servant has despatched Le Gros' book to Capua in the carriage, along with many other volumes that usually have a place there. I will not fail to return it to you, carefully, by the railroad.

Nor will I forget to make you better acquainted with the principles on which the School we spoke of (Bruce Castle,[2] Tottenham) is conducted. But I shall not be able to do so, before I reach Genoa.[3]

---

[1] Charles E. Cotterell, partner in Cotterell, Iggulden & Co., bankers, wine-merchants and general agents, Casina della Villa Reale, Naples (Coghlan, *Handbook*). In 1837 James Minet (who later married Iggulden's daughter) described Cotterell as "an extremely active little man, and I should think he must be making a good business of it here" (*The Diary of James Minet*, privately printed, 1958, p. 496). Cotterell left the firm in 1853: see *To* Mrs CD, 4 Nov 53 (*Mr and Mrs CD*, ed. Walter Dexter, p. 203). He was the brother of the consumptive Miss Cotterell, aged 18, who was the fellow-passenger of Keats and

Severn on the *Maria Crowther* in 1820; Cotterell met them on arrival at Naples in November, helped them during the quarantine period, and entertained them to a farewell dinner party on 6 or 7 Nov. According to his friend Charles MacFarlane he was "a *ci-devant* officer in the British Navy", and therefore probably the "Charles Edward Cotterell", appointed Purser in 1812 (*The Keats Circle*, ed. Hyder Rollins, 1948, I, 165 and *n*).

[2] See *To* Macready, 17 Aug 45, *fn*.

[3] He left on the morning of 26 Feb according to the Naples correspondent of *Galignani's Messenger*.

Let me assure you that I would infinitely rather be a familiar star to you, than a distantly glorious one; and that I have had sincere pleasure in our frank and unaffected intercourse.

Mrs. Dickens and Miss Hogarth unite with me in best regards to Mrs. Cotterell, and I am always My Dear Sir

Faithfully Yours

C. E. Cotterell Esquire.   CHARLES DICKENS

To JOHN FORSTER, [?2 MARCH 1845]

Extract in F, IV, vii, 370–1. *Date:* CD was back at Rome on Sunday 2 Mar (the expected date) according to Forster, who says, "Sad news from me as to a common and very dear friend[1] awaited him there"; CD would naturally write at once.

No philosophy will bear these dreadful things, or make a moment's head against them, but the practical one of doing all the good we can, in thought and deed. While we can, God help us! ourselves stray from ourselves so easily; and there are all around us such frightful calamities besetting the world in which we live; nothing else will carry us through it. . . . What a comfort to reflect on what you tell me.[2] Bulwer Lytton's conduct is that of a generous and noble-minded man,[3] as I have ever thought him. Our dear good Procter too! And Thackeray—how earnest they have all been! I am very glad to find you making special mention of Charles Lever.[4] I am glad over every name you write.[5] It says

[1] Laman Blanchard, who took his own life on 14 Feb; his wife had died on 15 Dec 44 after paralysis lasting about a year, since when he had suffered from fits of depression. On 14 Feb Ainsworth and Lytton, anxious about him, agreed to meet next day at Forster's and discuss plans to help him, only to learn of his suicide (S. M. Ellis, *W. H. Ainsworth and his Friends*, 1911, II, 130). Macready called on Forster and heard the "dreadful news"; the three men were "devising plans to keep the statement of the suicide from the papers, and to concert means for assisting his orphan children" (*Diaries*, II, 289).

[2] Their plan to start a benefit fund for the support and education of the four children, three sons and a daughter; enough was raised to support them for three years. The eldest, Sidney Laman (*d.* 1883), was soon launched on a career in journalism (see *To* Beard, 4 Sep 45), Lavinia at the Royal Academy of Music, and by 1846 the other two sons at Chapman & Hall's and in a merchant's house—according to Thackeray, reviewing Lytton's Memoir of Blanchard (*Fraser's*, Mar 46, XXXIII, 332–42).

[3] In a letter to Lytton 15 Mar 45 (MS Lytton Papers), Forster referred to CD's "feeling, affecting letter" and promise to subscribe, and quoted this phrase. He also mentioned Lytton's earlier assistance "and what a glow it sent into poor Blanchard's heart, when things were looking coldly". By this time Forster was preparing material for the Memoir which Lytton later wrote and published with a selection of Blanchard's papers (*Sketches from Life*, 1846).

[4] Charles James Lever (1806–72; *DNB*), novelist: see Vol. II, p. 399*n*. CD's irritation over the advertisements of *Harry Lorrequer* and his refusal of Lever's invitation to Brussels in Oct 41 doubtless checked the development of friendly relations, but they must have been acquainted.

[5] Forster had a circular printed (not published) presumably with these and other names, such as Jerrold's; Colburn and Ainsworth gave up their copyrights of Blanchard's essays in *Ainsworth's Magazine*. The subscription moved slowly at first, but on 12 Mar the Literary Fund voted £100.

something for our pursuit, in the midst of all its miserable disputes and jealousies, that the common impulse of its followers, in such an instance as this, is surely and certainly of the noblest.

To JOHN FORSTER, [9 MARCH 1845]

Extracts in F, 1872–4, II, v, 91–2n; F, IV, vi, 359–60n. *Date:* first extract 9 Mar according to Forster; second extract "four months later" than 17 Nov 44, clearly before CD left Rome *c.* 25 Mar, and since also concerned with pictures, likely to be same letter.

None of the books are unaffected and true but Simond's, which charms me more and more by its boldness, and its frank exhibition of that rare and admirable quality which enables a man to form opinions for himself without a miserable and slavish reference to the pretended opinions of other people.[1] His notices of the leading pictures enchant me. They are so perfectly just and faithful, and so whimsically shrewd.[2]

The most famous of the oil paintings in the Vatican[3] you know through the medium of the finest line-engravings in the world;[4] and as to some of them I much doubt, if you had seen them with me, whether you might not think you had lost little in having only known them hitherto in that translation. Where the drawing is poor and meagre, or alloyed by time,—it is so, and it must be, often; though no doubt it is a heresy to hint at such a thing,—the engraving presents the forms and the idea to you, in a simple majesty which such defects impair. Where this is not the case, and all is stately and harmonious, still it is somehow in the very grain and nature of a delicate engraving to suggest to you (I think) the utmost delicacy, finish, and refinement, as belonging to the original. Therefore, though the Picture in this latter case will greatly charm and interest you, it does not take you by surprise. You are quite prepared beforehand for the fullest

---

[1] In his Introduction Simond mentioned his attempt (which he feared was vain) "to stem the current of received opinion"; he thought that "the majority are enthusiastic upon trust", and when about to describe some of the paintings and statues in the Vatican wrote: "I shall give a faithful and plain account of what I saw, without pretending an admiration which I did not feel" (*A Tour in Italy and Sicily*, pp. 204–5). That his frankness and independence appealed to CD is evident in *Pictures*, especially pp. 207–12; both are influenced, in praise or blame, by the subject of a painting and by their ideas of what is "natural and true".

[2] Examples are his detailed and unfavourable descriptions of the *Incendia di Borgo* (one of Raphael's *Loggie*), and of Michael

Angelo's *Last Judgment*; also, his tart summary of the frescoes of Christian martyrs in S. Stefano Rondo ("every barbarous as well as every ludicrous expedient to torment the bodies of men is delineated with revolting diversity", p. 320), which probably encouraged CD's more elaborately horrific catalogue (*Pictures*, pp. 195–6).

[3] Cf. *Pictures*, pp. 207–11.

[4] CD almost certainly meant the engravings of Raphael by his pupil, the engraver Marco-Antonio Raimondi, still very highly regarded—as by Benjamin Delessert, *Notice sur la Vie de . . . Raimondi*, with "reproductions photographiques" (Paris and London, 1854), who thought his engravings, unrivalled for feeling and grace, to be works of art in themselves (p. 20).

excellence of which it is capable.[1] *He thought the paintings in private palaces[2] seen to greater advantage than those in galleries; because in numbers not so large as to distract attention or confuse the eye.* There are portraits innumerable by Titian, Rubens, Rembrandt and Vandyke; heads by Guido, and Domenichino, and Carlo Dolci; subjects by Raphael, and Correggio, and Murillo, and Paul Veronese, and Salvator; which it would be difficult indeed to praise too highly, or to praise enough.[3] It is a happiness to me to think that they cannot be felt, as they should be felt, by the profound connoisseurs who fall into fits upon the longest notice and the most unreasonable terms. Such tenderness and grace, such noble elevation, purity, and beauty, so shine upon me from some well-remembered spots in the walls of these galleries, as to relieve my tortured memory from legions of whining friars and waxy holy families. I forgive, from the bottom of my soul, whole orchestras of earthy angels, and whole groves of St. Sebastians stuck as full of arrows according to pattern as a lying-in pincushion is stuck with pins.[4] And I am in no humour to quarrel even with that priestly infatuation, or priestly doggedness of purpose, which persists in reducing every mystery of our religion to some literal development in paint and canvas, equally repugnant to the reason and the sentiment of any thinking man.

To MRS MACREADY, 10 MARCH 1845

MS Morgan Library. *Address:* Inghilterra. | Mrs. Macready. | 5 Clarence Terrace | Regents Park | London.

Rome, Monday Tenth March 1845.

My Dear Mrs. Macready

More in recollection of your two welcome notes, heartily received and blushingly unanswered, than as one labouring under the delusion of having anything to say, I append my Sign-Manual to the highly illegible letter of my worser half.[5] I was so cold after leaving you and dear Macready in Paris, that I was taken out of the coach at Marseilles (it was sixteen hours behind its time) in a perfectly torpid state, and was at first supposed to be luggage. But the Porter's not being able to find any direction upon me, led to a further examination; and what the newspapers call, "the vital spark", was finally discovered twinkling under a remote corner of the travelling-shawl, which you were pleased to approbate— love the word; it belongs to our dear and enlightened friends the Great American People—in the Hotel Brighton.

After that, I passed three days of waking nightmare at Marseilles. I think it was three. It may have been two, but I crowded into the space, the noisome

---

[1] Forster, writing in 1872, says this view had "since had eloquent reinforcement from critics of undeniable authority".

[2] e.g. the Barberini, Borghese, Braschi, Chigi, Doria-Pamfili—all containing works of some of the painters named by CD. The same point is made in almost the same words in *Pictures*, p. 211.

[3] The same painters, except for Veronese and Rubens (and with the addition of

Spagnoletto) are named in *Pictures*, p. 211, and Guido's portrait of Beatrice di Cenci in the Barberini is described in moving detail.

[4] In *Pictures*, p. 208, CD complains of the "compound multiplication" of "libellous Angels" and of "Saint Francis and Saint Sebastian".

[5] Catherine's letter does not survive, but the address is in her hand.

smells of a patriarchal life. After that, I was so horribly ill on board a steamboat that I should have made my Will if I had had anything to leave—but I had only the basin; and I couldn't leave that, for a moment. That suffering over, I rushed into the arms of my expectant family. Their happiness is more easily conceived than described. You know me; and will paint the Picture for yourself.

I was greatly distressed to hear from you that you had been so unwell in Paris. What *can* have been the matter with you? I laid down your note, and thought of all manner of possibilities[1]—My particular love to my Godson.

Sometimes I have a terrible apprehension that Macready, conscience-stricken beyond endurance by the reflection that he has never written a word to me of his triumphs and projects (I have a great desire to know his secret mind upon the latter head)[2] will play the Roman Fool,[3] and die upon the Jewelled Dagger the French King gave him.[4] Adjure him to be of good-cheer. My forgiveness and blessing are enclosed.

How anxiously I look forward to finding myself once again in the dining parlor at Clarence Terrace—just the old, snug, little party of *ourselves*—I should vainly try to say, though I wrote a quire! But Midsummer, please God, will find us all together—well and happy—and mainly so, in our mutual friendship and attachment.

In any case, as poor Power[5] used to say *I*'m mutual. And I am sure you are too—though you Do attack me sometimes.

When Willy has finished his Complete Guide to Paris and its Environs, I shall be happy to edit the Book, and to preface it with some account of the author, founded on a personal correspondence with him in that Capital.[6] With best regards to Miss Macready, and all the Pets, I am ever My Dear Mrs. Macready Faithfully Your friend CHARLES DICKENS

---

[1] Nothing is known of this indisposition, and no child was born in 1845.

[2] Macready was in the provinces (see *To Black*, 12 Apr 45 and *fn*), but the project of which CD had doubtless heard from Forster was the establishment in London of a new home for the national drama, now that the patents were abrogated (see Vol. III, p. 521*n*) and Drury Lane and Covent Garden were given up to opera and ballet. Macready had arranged the Paris season partly in order to avoid making a decision immediately on his return from America, but by this date he was considering the possibility of building a new theatre or taking over an existing one. He told John Willmott on 28 Mar that if he could obtain the ideal theatre—not too large and in a good locality—"I think there could not be a doubt on the subject". Rumours had reached *Galignani's Messenger*, which reported on 8 and 14 Mar and 1 May 45 that Macready was spoken of as the future lessee of Covent Garden. The scheme was still under active consideration when he returned to London in May; he consulted Fox and Forster, who proposed the St James's—a venture abandoned in July for financial reasons,—and the Lyceum and even Covent Garden were investigated and rejected. During the next two years Macready had a series of successful London and provincial engagements. (A. S. Downer, *The Eminent Tragedian*, 1966, pp. 273–8.)

[3] Cf. *Macbeth*, V, vii, 30.

[4] Louis Philippe presented Macready with "a poniard" or "ataghan" at the end of his Paris season in Jan 45 (*Diaries*, II, 284 and *n*, and *Athenæum*, 25 Jan 45). The jewels turned out to be sham, and Macready referred to the king as a "*shabby dog*" (*Diaries*, II, 291).

[5] Tyrone Power (1797–1841; *DNB*), actor: see Vol. II, p. 104*n*.

[6] William Macready, *b.* 1832 (for whom Browning wrote "The Pied Piper of Hamelin", May 1842), was with his parents in Paris 15 Dec (*Diaries*, II, 278).

To MISS BURDETT COUTTS, 18 MARCH 1845

MS Morgan Library. *Address:* Inghilterra. | Miss Burdett Coutts | Stratton Street | Piccadilly | London.

Rome Eighteenth March 1845.

My Dear Miss Coutts. I am very much afraid that the date of this letter will contrast, to my disadvantage, with the date of Twelfth Night, which you made a proud night for Charley in Genoa, and a happy night to me in the more secret quarter of my own breast, by your kind and generous remembrance. But I have been so constantly and incessantly on the wing since that great finale of the Christmas Holidays; and have been so cold, and so wet, and so muddy, and so everything which is currently supposed to be incompatible with Italy—and have been into such extraordinary places, and have eaten such unaccountable meals, and have slept in such incredible beds, and have led, altogether, such a wildly preposterous life—that I have not had the heart to write to you, lest my letter, partaking in some degree of the character of my existence, should be of too vagabond a nature for delivery at your door.

Before I left Genoa, I had all the knives locked up: fearing that Charley would otherwise, in the excitement of his feelings, lay hands upon a sharp one, and do himself a mischief—I don't mean with any evil design upon his life, but in the endeavour to make a pen wherewith to write a note to you. The intention was so very active within him that I should have allowed him to gratify it, but for his writing being something large for the Foreign Post, which, at his rate of penman-ship, would hardly carry more than his name. But I gave him a solemn promise that I would thank you twenty thousand times. That I would report him tolerant of Italian life and manners, but not attached to them: yielding a strong preference to those of his own country. That I would say, he never could forget his ride with you to Hampstead. That I should tell you that such a thing as a Twelfth Cake was never seen in Genoa before; and that when it went to a Swiss Pastry-Cook's in that City, to have the sugar repaired (it was a very little chipped at one corner) it was *exhibited* to the principal Inhabitants, as a wonder and marvel. That I would give his love and his sisters' loves to "that lady",[1] and would add that I had at length succeeded in impressing on their minds the great truth that she didn't always live in bed. That I would say, that he looked forward to coming with me to see and thank you, on our return to England. And that I would be sure to tell you a great deal more, which I will not inflict upon you on any account.

The weather has been atrocious, ever since I returned from England at Christmas. I do not think I ever felt it so cold as between this place and Naples, about a Month ago. Between Naples and Paestum too, three weeks ago; with a cold North wind blowing over Mountains covered with Snow; it was quite intolerable. Within the last three days, there have been glimpses of Spring. I will not say more, in the fulness of my heart; for experience has taught me that tomorrow may be deep Winter again. I have certainly seen more Sun in England, between the end of December and the middle of March, than I have seen in

---

[1] Mrs Brown.

Italy in that time. And for violent and sudden changes, there is surely no country in the world, more remarkable than this. When it *is* fine (as people say) it is very fine—so beautiful, that the really good days blot out the recollection of the bad ones. But I do honestly believe that it is not oftener fine here, than it is elsewhere; and that we are far better off at home in that respect, than anything short of the Rack, would induce most people to confess.

In the mass, I like the common people of Italy, very much—the Neapolitans least of all; the Romans next, for they are fierce and brutal. Not falling on very good specimens of the higher orders, in the beginning, I have not pursued that Enquiry. I have had no leisure to do so, if I had had the inclination, so I have avoided them as much as possible, and have kept the greater part of my letters of introduction in my own desk. Florence I have not yet seen: intending to take it, next week,[1] on my way back to Genoa. But of all the places I *have* seen, I like Venice, Genoa, and Verona, most. The Bay of Genoa has charms, in my eyes, which the Bay of Naples wants. The City of Genoa is very picturesque and beautiful. And the house we live in, is really like a Palace in a Fairy Tale.

I cannot remember, to my satisfaction, whether you were ever at Herculaneum and Pompeii. Though my impression is, that I have heard you speak of them. The interest and wonder of those ruined places, far exceeded my utmost expectations. Venice was such a splendid Dream to me, that I can never speak of it,—from sheer inability to describe its effect upon my mind. The ancient parts of Rome, and a portion of the Campagna, are *what I meant* when I came here; the rest a little below my imaginary mark, and very unlike it. The Coliseum by daylight, moonlight, torchlight, and every sort of light, most stupendous and awful. Saint Peters not so impressive within, as many Cathedrals I have seen at home. The great altar, and the state entrance to the Subterranean Church, might be Rundell and Bridge's[2] show-room. And the canopies, hangings, and carpets (of all sorts of reds and greens) now hung up, and put down, for the Holy-Week Ceremonies,[3] have the effect of an enormous Bon-bon. Before which, and round which, and in and out of which, they are perpetually carrying the poor old Pope about on men's shoulders, like a Gorgeous Guy Faux.[4]

The drollest thing I have seen, is a daily gathering of Artists' "Models" on the steps of a church near the house (Meloni's Hotel) in which we live: where they dispose themselves in conventionally picturesque attitudes, and wait to be hired as Sitters. The first time I went up there, I could *not* conceive how their faces were familiar to me—how they seemed to have bored me, for many years, in every variety of action and costume—and to come back upon my sight as perfect nightmares. At last it flashed upon me all at once that we had made acquaintance, and improved it, on the walls of the Royal Academy. So we had indeed. And there is not one among them whom you wouldn't know, at first sight, as well as the Statue at Charing Cross. The most aggravating of the party is a dismal old patriarch, with very long white hair and beard, who carries a great staff in his

---

[1] CD left on 25 Mar.
[2] Jewellers and goldsmiths of 32 Ludgate Hill up to 1843.
[3] Described in detail in *Pictures*, pp.

217–30; the comparison of the hangings to a "stupendous Bon-bon" is on p. 170.
[4] Cf. *Pictures*, p. 172.

hand: which staff has been faithfully copied at the Exhibition in all its twists and knots, at least once through the Catalogue. He is the venerable model. Another man in a sheepskin, who always lies asleep in the Sun (when there is any) is the Pastoral Model. Another man in a brown cloak who leans against a wall with his arms folded, is the assassin Model. Another man who looks over his shoulder and always seems to be going away, but never goes, is the haughty model. Several women and children form the family models. And the cream of the whole is, that they are one and all the falsest Rascals in Rome or out of it: being specially made up for their trade, and having no likeness among the whole population. It is a good illustration of the Student life as it is, that young men should go on copying these people elaborately time after time and time out of mind, and find nothing fresh or suggestive in the actual world about them.[1]

My English papers tell me of the death of Sydney Smith,[2] whom I deeply regret. I also hear, privately, that Hood, the author, is past all chance of recovery.[3] He was (I have a sad presentiment that even now I may speak of him as something past) a man of great power—of prodigious force and genius as a poet—and not generally known, perhaps, by his best credentials. Personally, he had a most noble and generous spirit. When he was under the pressure of severe misfortune and illness, and I had never seen him, he went far out of his way to praise me; and wrote (in the Athenæum) a paper on The Curiosity Shop; so full of enthusiasm and high appreciation, and so free from any taint of envy or reluctance to acknowledge me, a young man far more fortunate than himself, that I can hardly bear to think of it.[4]

I hope to be in Genoa again, before the middle of next month;[5] and have arranged to leave there and turn homeward, in the middle of June. Whether we may linger on the way in France or Switzerland, I do not yet quite know. But in that case it is probable that I may run over to London for two or three days to preside at a Public Dinner in aid of the Sanatorium.[6] I shall hope to see you then, at latest, unless (I wish there were any hope of it!) you should be coming Genoa-way, and would give me a chance of shewing you the Peschiere orange trees.

In any case, when I am among them again, I shall trouble you with at least one more of Charley's messages, and a few words of my own. For I fear that I may otherwise (not undeservedly) pass out of your remembrance; and believe me dear

[1] The whole paragraph closely resembles *Pictures*, pp. 186–7, but was further elaborated for *To* D'Orsay, same day. Most travellers made similar observations: William Collins, the painter, saw in 1837, a "burly, handsome fellow ... ready to ... assume any appearance", and painted him as a cardinal, a Roman gamekeeper, a monk and a country shepherd (*Memoirs of the Life of William Collins R.A.*, 1848, II, 93); Ruskin on 6 Dec 40 (*Diaries*, I, 120), had noted "three peasants sitting on the steps ... quite the Hurlstone cut and well got up; the most striking piece of costume I have seen since leaving Genoa".

[2] Died 22 Feb, aged 76.

[3] Hood had been confined to bed since Nov 44 (his financial situation relieved by his reluctant acceptance of a government pension of £100, paid at his request to Mrs Hood), and was now rapidly sinking, but still, up to 24 Mar, able to write an occasional letter.

[4] *Athenæum*, 7 Nov 40: see Vol. II, p. 220 and *n*.

[5] He returned 9 Apr.

[6] Its date was not yet fixed: see *To* Thomas Chapman, 10 Apr 45.

Miss Coutts there are not many memories from which it would give me so much pain to fade, as from yours. I rate its worth too highly.

Ever Yours faithfully
CHARLES DICKENS

P.S. Mrs. Dickens begs to unite in best regards to yourself, and "the lady"— who is well, I hope—and happy, I know. I hope you cried when you read the Chimes?

To COUNT ALFRED D'ORSAY, 18 MARCH 1845*

MS Comte de Gramont.

Rome. Tuesday Night. March Eighteenth 1845.

My Dear Count D'Orsay. If I didn't love you as much as I do, and hadn't given my whole heart to Lady Blessington (except the two pieces which belong to the Miss Powers) I never should have the courage to begin this letter. For have I not preserved a dismal silence for three whole Months? Did I not receive the charmingest of charming notes from Lady Blessington, within a fortnight after my return to Genoa, which note is still unanswered? And have I not been actually yearning to write, week after week and month after month; during the whole of which time I have been on the wing, and have scarcely once taken pen in hand?

I hardly know where I have not been, since we parted in that cold weather at Kensington. But I have been at Naples—and don't like it. It disappointed me greatly. The weather was not fine, certainly; was often very bad; but even if it had been better, I should not have liked the place. Its attractions seem to me to have been greatly exaggerated. Nor do the common people there, please me as well as in other parts of Italy. For the Bay—I like the Bay of Genoa better. It can be better seen in one view, and its beauty is not so diffused and wasted. Of all the picturesque abominations in the World, commend me to Fondi. It is the very pink of hideousness and squalid misery.

As to Rome, you know all about *that*. You know how one goes to see the Coliseum by daylight, moonlight, torchlight, and every sort of light. You know what an awful and tremendous place it is, and what an impression the first sight of it produces. Not that it weakens day by day, or does anything but strengthen. For it has greater claims upon me now, than ever.

The Holy Week is in full force at this time; and hundreds of English people with hundreds of Murray's Guide Books and a corresponding number of Mrs. Starkes'[1] in their hands are chattering in all the silent places, worrying the professional Ciceroni to death, and doubting the authenticity of everything on the spot—to defend it to the last gasp, when they get home again. The Pope is being perpetually carried up and down Saint Peter's like a glorious Guy Faux;

---

[1] Mariana Starke, *Travels on the Continent* (1820; 8th enlarged edn, called *Travels in Europe*, 1833); remained popular for many years after her death in 1838. She had a scale of exclamation marks to indicate pictures worth seeing.

some very long ceremony takes place every day; everybody says that everything is not worth seeing; and everybody goes to see everything else notwithstanding, by day and by night, with unabated vigour.

You know that great flight of steps, which leads from the Piazza di Spagna, to the Church of Trinita del Monte? Perhaps you don't know that it is the place of resort for the Artists' Models—their Bourse, as it were—where they wait to be hired. It has amused me more than anything I have seen in the way of drollery. The first time I went up there, I could not conceive why the faces seemed familiar to me—why they appeared to have bored me, for years, in every possible variety of action and costume—and how it was that they started up before me in the broad day, like so many saddled and bridled nightmares. I soon found that we had made acquaintance (and improved it for several years) on the walls of the Royal Academy. There is one old villain with long white hair and an immense beard, who I am convinced has gone, at least once, through the whole catalogue. This is the venerable or patriarchal model. He carries a long staff: every knot and twist in which staff I have seen faithfully depicted at innumerable exhibitions. There is another man in a blue cloak who always pretends to lie asleep in the Sun (when there is any), and who I needn't say is always very wide awake, and very attentive to the disposition of his legs. This is the dolce far niente Model. There is another man in a brown cloak who leans against a wall with his arms folded in his mantle, and looks out of the corners of his eyes, which are just visible beneath his slouched hat. This is the Assassin Model. There is another man who constantly looks over his own shoulder, and is always going away, but never goes. This is the haughty or scornful model. As to Domestic Happiness and Holy Families, they must come very cheap, for there are lumps of them all up the steps. And the grand thing is that they are all the falsest Rascals in the World; specially made up for the purpose; and having no counterparts in Rome or any other part of the habitable Globe.[1] It is a good illustration of the Student System that young men should go on, batch after batch, reproducing and reproducing these people: and finding nothing fresh or stirring in the active real world about them. Is it not?

You know all the Pictures and Statues I have seen—and how many of them are really good, and how many really bad. I am guilty of all sorts of heresies in these respects; and when I see a Jolly Young Waterman representing a cherubim, or a Barclay and Perkins's Drayman depicted as an Evangelist, am obliged to confess that it is not exactly my idea of either character. Neither am I partial to angels who play on Genuine Cremonas and brazen bassoons, for the edification of sprawling monks apparently in liquor[2]—nor to Josephs surveying Nativities, from shiny backgrounds, in a state of considerable mystification—nor to Saint Sebastians, of whom I wouldn't have a specimen on any terms, notwithstanding the extreme rarity of the subject. All this kind of High Art is out of my reach, I acknowledge. Not the less so, because I have the purest and most enduring

---

[1] This passage, from "The first time", appears almost identically in *Pictures*, pp. 186–7; CD probably borrowed and used D'Orsay's letter.

[2] These comments were clearly drawn on for *Pictures* (p. 208) where much appears word for word.

delight in those achievements of the pencil which are truly great and grand, and worthy of their theme. But there is such an extensive amount of humbug afloat on these matters; and people are so strangely disposed to take what they have heard or read for granted and not use their own intellects and senses, that whenever I go into a Gallery I hang out "No Trust" in legible white letters on a black ground—like an English Turnpike.[1]

I was enchanted by Herculaneum and Pompeii—with Paestum also, which is wonderfully solemn and dreary. Vesuvius I saw under very remarkable circumstances, with not an ash upon the surface of the cone—nothing but deep snow frozen hard; up which we climbed, with poles, as if we were toiling up an Antedeluvian Twelfth Cake.[2] There was a great deal of fire pouring out of the crater, and it was in a state of violent agitation. The Moon was at the full; the night intensely cold; the sky without a cloud. First, day; then sunset; then darkness; then the rising of the moon; then the dark night of the black smoke; then the raging of the red fire; then the coming out again into the shining of the moon upon the waste of Snow—it was the finest sight conceivable. There were some accidents, as you may have heard from poor Forster. But happily they befel neither me nor mine. The loneliness and grandeur of the scene, I never can forget.

We intend taking Florence on our way back to Genoa, for which place we start, on Wednesday the Twenty Sixth. We shall remain at the Peschiere until the middle of June, as I at present purpose; and may linger for a month or so, in France or Switzerland, on our way home. I look forward to seeing you again my dear Count D'Orsay, with the greatest impatience and delight; and project dinners in Devonshire Terrace of the most glorious description.

Will you tell Lady Blessington with my best regards and most affectionate and earnest remembrances, that I will not fail to write to her, as soon as I set foot in my Genoa Palazzo. Ten thousand thanks to her for her little piece of Fiction in the Court Journal.[3] The real subscription was *much larger* than any there has ever been to any of my books; and the Sale has gone on nobly. But all this, she knows, I dare say, better than I. It has given me great pain to read in the newspapers of the death of Sydney Smith, and of the wife of my good friend Tracey[4]—greater to hear from Forster that there are no hopes of Hood's recovery. He was a man of extraordinary power as a writer: and personally had a most generous and noble spirit. At a time when I had never set eyes upon him, and when he was sick and in circumstances of great distress, he went far out of his way to write a gallant and enthusiastic paper on my Curiosity Shop, in the

---

[1] Such a notice meant that the toll-road was not controlled by a turnpike trust, but was the responsibility of the parish—and therefore likely to be incompetently maintained. Hood made a similar joke in a letter of July 44: see *Letters*, ed. P. Morgan, p. 631.

[2] The same comparison is in *Pictures*, p. 249.

[3] In the issue of 14 Dec the subscription for the *Chimes* was said to be 30,000, an obvious exaggeration. The editor was now Baroness Calabrella, but Lady Blessington continued to supply items of gossip.

[4] Georgina Tracey died on 20 Feb.

Athenæum. Nor had he, I sincerely believe, one atom of base envy in his nature. I speak of him in the past tense, for I fear he has by this time ceased to be.

The weather has been something too preposterous to write about, ever since I returned. There are glimpses of Spring now, but I am afraid to say more lest I should find myself in winter again, before the conclusion of the sentence. The last day and evening of the Carnival quite charmed me. I returned hither from Naples by the Monte Cassino Road; where there are no Post Horses, and where there are such Inns, that travelling in that direction is quite a practical joke. It is a beautiful country. In the Convent of Monte Cassino, high up in the clouds, I found a Ra[ven][1] speaking the lingua Toscana admirably, and expressing in all his looks and gestures that the system of convents in general was perfectly understood between himself and the Friars.[2]

Poor Forster, what a Martyr he is![3] I wish to God he would marry somebody and not be ill by himself in that howling Mansion, with dear old Landor's Lion[4] looking down upon him in a state of absurd grimness which renders that Picture quite unique. I greatly lament that I am not in London to carry him up, bodily, to my own home. Which I wanted to do when he was last ill.[5]

And poor Blanchard. What a tremendous history is that! I never was more shocked and horrified. I see in the Examiner, accounts of a bad murder in one of my daily walks near Hampstead.[6] Which, as a mere matter of dirty speculation —a mercantile venture for a trifle of money—is one of the worst murders I ever read of.

When you write to me, address at the Peschiere. Tell me what you have been painting[7] since I was at Gore House—and whether you have seen Maclise's Cartoon—and what you think of it. I am particularly anxious to know. All scraps of intelligence of any kind will be thankfully received. I am truly sorry to hear that the Miss Powers have lost a near relative.[8] Remember me to them, with all sincerity and cordiality.

And think of me sometimes, for I think of you often. Being as truly attached to you as to any man alive.

Ever Faithfully Yours
CHARLES DICKENS

[1] A small tear has removed three letters.

[2] The jest is much elaborated in *Pictures*, pp. 261–2.

[3] D'Orsay had written to Forster in Jan, "We are really in despair to see what a maryr you are" (R. R. Madden, *Literary Life and Correspondence of the Countess of Blesington*, II, 413). He had been unable to vsit Landor for his 70th birthday on 30 Jan.

[4] See Vol. II, p. 37*n*. Landor must have given this picture to Forster.

[5] In 1843: see Vol. III, p. 440.

[6] Henry Hocker's murder of one Delarue on the footpath leading from Chalk Farm to Belsize Park, 21 Feb 45; he was tried 11 Apr and executed 28 Apr.

[7] D'Orsay had recently begun to paint portraits in oil; but the most interesting news of his artistic activities would be his great success in modelling an equestrian statuette of the Duke of Wellington in Feb: the Duke was so pleased that he ordered numerous copies (Willard Connely, *Count D'Orsay*, 1952, pp. 409–13).

[8] Their brother, who died of fever in India (Lady Blessington *to* Forster, 13 Feb 45: R. R. Madden, *Literary Life and Correspondence of the Countess of Blessington*, II, 402).

To CHARLES BLACK, [?21 MARCH 1845]

MS Dickens House. *Date:* a "Pilgrims' Banquet" took place on Good Friday,
21 Mar.

Hotel Meloni | Friday Evening | 10 'Clock[1]

My Dear Sir
    I am truly sorry to have missed you—the more so, as I fancy you can scarcely
have left here, ten minutes before our return from the Pilgrims' Banquet.[2] We
propose 7 sharp, tomorrow; and to come straight to the top of your street—
Ladies to start at half after 9. We also propose (not to cram too much into a
little time), "cutting" the Mountain, and strolling round the Lake.[3]
    I send this in haste, that you may not think me indifferent to a trip from which
I anticipate a great deal of pleasure.

With best Regards, | Believe me | always
Faithfully Yours
Charles Black Esquire   CHARLES DICKENS

To CHARLES BODENHAM, [24 MARCH] 1845

Text from N, I, 667. *Date:* Easter Monday was 24 Mar in 1845.

Hotel Meloni | Easter Monday 1845

My Dear Sir,
    In case I should not have the pleasure of finding you at home this morning
when I call with the accompanying books, I write this note to thank you for the
pleasure I have derived from them; and for the interest I have had in your own
notes especially.
    We have not seen the alabaster columns![4] The lady who is with us, being a
sad invalid,[5] has been ill three days and on every one of those days we had

[1] Thus in MS.

[2] Not a "banquet" but one of the "Pilgrims' Suppers: where lords and ladies waited on the Pilgrims, in token of humility, and dried their feet when they had been well washed by deputy" (*Pictures*, p. 224). These were held at the Trinita de' Pellegrini, a church near the Ponte Sisto, on Wed, Thurs and Fri in Holy Week. The "lords" included several cardinals; the "ladies", led by Princess Rospigliosi, washed the feet of the female pilgrims (Murray, *Handbook for ... Central Italy*). Newman's diary for 1847 shows that he and Ambrose St John went "to the Pellegrini to wash feet" on Good Friday (*Letters and Diaries of John Henry Newman*, ed. C. S. Dessain, 1961–, XII, 67).

[3] Almost certainly the walking expedition by "a little party of three", starting at half past seven, across the Campagna to Albano,

"with its lovely lake" (*Pictures*, pp. 213–14); de la Rue was the third of the walkers: see *To* de la Rue, 29 June 45.

[4] Possibly in the Villa Albani, beyond the Porta Salara, where the long gallery was "decorated with two columns of jasper and alabaster" (Murray, *Handbook for ... Central Italy*).

[5] See *To* Mme de la Rue, 17 Apr 46, where CD quotes his diary for 19 Mar 45: "Madame De la Rue very ill in the night, up till four". Many years later, in his retrospective account to Sheridan Le Fanu (24 Oct 69; N, III, 752), CD described what is presumably the same occasion: "Her husband called me up to her, one night at Rome, when she was rolled into an apparently impossible ball, by tic in the brain". Although such attacks had previously continued for "at least 30 hours", under his treatment she was peacefully

deliberately projected availing ourselves of your kindness. Once I had actually taken pen in hand to propose to call for you.

Believe me that I am not the less indebted to you for your good offices. I shall carry away with me from Rome tomorrow, a living recollection of the pleasant Sunday walk we had together towards the Metella Tomb:[1] and shall deem myself fortunate if I have (as I hope I may) some future opportunity of renewing our acquaintance in England.

Mrs. Dickens and her sister beg to unite in compliments to yourself and Mrs. Bodenham. And I am My Dear Sir

Faithfully Yours
[CHARLES DICKENS]

To MRS ELISABETH JESSER REID,[2] 25 MARCH 1845*

MS Bedford College, London.

Hotel Meloni, Rome.
Tuesday Morning | Twenty Fifth March 1845.

My Dear Mrs. Reid.

I was coming over to see you this morning (having at last hunted down the whole preserve of Roman Lions); but they tell me you will not be up, before we are some miles on the road. Therefore I send you this small representative to wish you health and happiness until we meet again, and then, and always afterwards; and to assure you that I am ever, with Sincerity,

Faithfully Yours
CHARLES DICKENS

Mrs. Reid.

---

sleep after half an hour. In the same etter he wrote, "every day I magnetized her; sometimes under olive trees, sometimes in vineyards, sometimes in the travelling carriage, sometimes at wayside inns during the midday halt" (evidently referring to the weeks in Rome, and to the homeward journey).

[1] The Tomb of Cecilia Metella on the Appian Way. In *Pictures*, p. 184, CD says he walked past it, "almost every day".

[2] Elisabeth Jesser Reid, *née* Sturch (1789–1866); widow, since 1822, of Dr John Reid, and lived with her sister Mary at York Terrace, Regent's Park; was active in many good causes, and in 1849 founded the Ladies' College, Bedford Square, where Katey Dickens attended classes in 1852. A fervent Unitarian, and devoted friend of Harriet Martineau (despite her "atheism"), Crabb Robinson, and the Macreadys—

through whom CD probably first met her in 1839 (*Diaries*, I, 503). In 1842 he took letters of introduction to some of her many abolitionist friends in America (see Vol. III, p. 99*n*). Warm-hearted, impulsive, but "wanting discretion in her benevolence" and "a charming subject for playful and good-humoured attacks" (Crabb Robinson, MS diary, 16 July 38, and letter to Thomas Robinson, 18 May 44; quoted from MSS in Dr Williams's Library in Margaret Tuke, *A History of Bedford College for Women, 1849-1937*, 1938, pp. 7–8). Jane Carlyle attacked her without good humour as an "old haddock" and "a humbug" (Jane Carlyle *to* Jeannie Welsh, Nov 42, *Letters to her Family*, p. 53; and cf. Vol. III, p. 641*n*). From Aug 44 to June 47 she resided in Italy with her brother and his wife, making Rome her winter headquarters.

To ANGUS FLETCHER, 26 MARCH 1845*

MS Morgan Library. *Address:* Al Sig: | Il Sig. Angelo Fletcher | Scultore | Carrara.

Narni.[1] | Wednesday Night | March Twenty Sixth 1845.

My Dear Fletcher. If I wait to write you a letter with anything in it, I shall never write at all, I clearly see. So here is one with nothing at all.

If I ever said, I should be in Carrara by the first of April, it must have been after innumerable fiaschi of Carrara Wine. For no such idea ever entered my rational head, or my rational pocket-book, wherein I find myself entered as due *to leave Florence* either on Friday the fourth or Saturday the Fifth of April. To that purpose I still hold, with a bulldog tenacity. So write me a note, addressed Poste Restante Florence, telling me whether Walton is base enough to go to England in the meantime, and where you would have us come, with a view of passing One Day in and about some quarries or other. On receipt of that letter, I will, from Florence, tell you exactly when we leave; and will furthermore charge you with an exact statement of our wants and wishes in the way of Inn-accommodation at Massa or wherever else you summon us.[2]

We are exceedingly happy, and don't fight much. If I could be supposed to express myself disinterestedly on such a theme, I should say we were facetious.[3] I should also say that the Holy Week is unmitigated hum[bug—except][4] the Benediction[5] (as a bright spectacle) and the Illumination of St. Peters[6]—which is glorious. The Coliseum[7] *enchanted* me—I went there continually, and never could see enough of it. The Open Campagna[8] also, beyond the tomb of Cecilia Metella (some two miles beyond, and thence to Albano: I have walked it all) is sublime. The first time I saw it from that spot, was when the Sun was going down; and it seemed to set on such a Ruined World, that I could have almost fancied it had done its work and would never rise again.[9, 10]

[   ]

[CHARLES DICKENS]

---

[1] Murray's *Handbook for ... Central Italy*, recommends Narni, the ancient Umbrian city, as a sleeping-place for travellers on the second day from Rome and convenient for visiting Terni.

[2] CD left Florence 4 or 5 Apr and reached Genoa 9 Apr; one night (probably 7 Apr) was spent at Carrara, recalled in *To* de la Rue, 28 July 45. When Maclise went to Carrara in July 55, their guide, Guido Merli, remembered conducting CD, with Catherine and Georgina, to the quarries (Maclise *to* Forster, in W. Justin O'Driscoll, *A Memoir of Daniel Maclise, R.A.*, p. 118).

[3] Fletcher may have expressed some doubts about the possible strains of spend-

ing a whole month, including a fortnight's travel, with the de la Rues.

[4] About 10 letters missing where the paper is rubbed away.

[5] On Easter Sunday, a day of brilliant weather; described in *Pictures*, pp. 227–8.

[6] The same night: described in *Pictures*, pp. 229–30.

[7] CD "never could get through a day without going back to it" (*Pictures*, p. 231; and cf. p. 184).

[8] There is a long description in *Pictures*, p. 214.

[9] Verbally close to *Pictures*, p. 215.

[10] Ending and signature have been removed.

To JOHN FORSTER, [?30 MARCH 1845]

Mention in F, IV, iii, 327*n*. *Date:* According to Forster, CD wrote to him from Montevarchi,[1] 30 Mar 45; but the extract he quotes cannot have been written before 10 Apr (see *To* Forster, that day).

To JOHN FORSTER, [?2–4 APRIL 1845]

Extracts in F, IV, vii, 371–2, 371*n* (two extracts), 372. *Date:* second extract 2 Apr according to Forster; first extract also from Florence, so probably same letter; third extract placed here by Forster; fourth extract "Before he left Florence (on the 4th of April)" according to Forster.

There are some places[2] here,—oh Heaven how fine! I wish you could see the tower of the Palazzo Vecchio as it lies before me at this moment, on the opposite bank of the Arno! But I will tell you more about it, and about all Florence, from my shady arm-chair up among the Peschiere oranges. I shall not be sorry to sit down in it again. . . . Poor Hood, poor Hood! I still look for his death, and he still lingers on. And Sydney Smith's brother[3] gone after poor dear Sydney himself! Maltby[4] will wither when he reads it; and poor old Rogers[5] will contradict some young man at dinner, every day for three weeks.

He drove out from Florence to see Landor's villa and asked his coachman which it was.[6] He was a dull dog, and pointed to Boccaccio's.[7] I didn't believe him. He was so deuced ready that I knew he lied. I went up to the convent, which is on a height, and was leaning over a dwarf wall basking in the noble view over a vast range of hill and valley, when a little peasant girl came up and began to point out the localities. *Ecco la villa Landora!*[8] was one of the first half-dozen sentences

[1] Between Arezzo and Florence; perhaps near "the summit of a hill" from which they first saw Florence (*Pictures*, pp. 264–5). The only places named on the route in *Pictures* are the Falls of Terni, Perugia, Castiglione, and Arezzo (pp. 263–4).

[2] Possibly Forster's error for "palaces".

[3] Robert Percy ("Bobus") Smith (1770–1845; *DNB*) died on 10 Mar.

[4] William Maltby (1763–1854; *DNB*), lifelong friend of Rogers: see Vol. I, p. 643*n*.

[5] Maltby and Rogers were among his friends, and some years older. Sydney Smith's death was "the going out of a great source of warmth and light" from Rogers's circle, and "the death of his elder brother . . . was even a more serious deprivation". Rogers visited Bobus on his deathbed (P. W. Clayden, *Rogers and his Contemporaries*, 1889, II, 267–8).

[6] Forster's extract and his comments are quoted (as he says) from his *Life of Landor*, 1869, II, 224.

[7] The Villa Gherardi. "Boccaccio's house" and "the convent" (of the Doccia) are mentioned in *Pictures*, p. 268.

[8] The Villa Gherardescha in the village of San Domenica di Fiesole where Landor lived 1829–35, and left because of his quarrel with his wife; it is shown in a vignette on the title-page of Forster's *Life of Landor*. In his review of the *Life* (*All the Year Round*, 24 July 69; reprinted in *Miscellaneous Papers*, pp. 720–7) CD recounts an embarrassing incident on the drive, which he related to Landor on his return, of the coachman "suddenly stopping his horses in a narrow lane" and presenting him "to 'La Signora Landora' ", having inferred that CD was a visitor to the villa. "I pulled off my hat . . . apologised for the coachman's mistake, and drove on. The lady was walking with a rapid and

she spoke. My heart swelled[1] as Landor's would have done when I looked down upon it, nestling among its olive-trees and vines, and with its upper windows (there are five above the door) open to the setting sun. Over the centre of these there is another story, set upon the housetop like a tower; and all Italy, except its sea, is melted down into the glowing landscape it commands. I plucked a leaf of ivy[2] from the convent-garden as I looked; and here it is. For Landor. With my love.

You know that in the streets and corners of roads, there are all sorts of crosses and similar memorials to be seen in Italy. The most curious are, I think, in Tuscany.[3] There is very seldom a figure on the cross, though there is sometimes a face; but they are remarkable for being garnished with little models in wood of every possible object that can be connected with the Saviour's death. The cock that crowed when Peter had denied his master thrice, is generally perched on the tip-top; and an ornithological phenomenon he always is. Under him is the inscription. Then, hung on to the cross-beam, are the spear, the reed with the sponge of vinegar and water at the end, the coat without seam for which the soldiers cast lots, the dice-box with which they threw for it, the hammer that drove in the nails, the pincers that pulled them out, the ladder which was set against the cross, the crown of thorns, the instrument of flagellation, the lantern with which Mary went to the tomb—I suppose; I can think of no other—and the sword with which Peter smote the high priest's servant. A perfect toyshop of little objects; repeated at every four or five miles all along the highway.

Describing a very pleasant and very merry day *at Lord Holland's.*[4]

firm step, had bright eyes, a fine fresh colour, and looked animated and agreeable". Landor "checked off each clause of the description, with a stately nod of more than ready assent, and replied, with all his tremendous energy concentrated into the sentence: 'And the Lord forbid that I should do otherwise than declare that she always WAS agreeable—to every one but *me!*' "

[1] "almost swelled" in *Life of Landor.*

[2] Forster adds that CD had asked Landor before leaving (on 16 June 44: see *To* Mrs Gore, 10 June 44 and *fn*) what he would most wish to have in remembrance of Italy, and Landor said, "An ivy-leaf from Fiesole"; and twenty years after, Forster found the ivy leaf in Landor's papers.

[3] This paragraph is almost word for word in *Pictures*, pp. 156–7, but occurs in the description of the journey to Rome in January.

[4] Henry Edward Fox (1802–59), 4th Baron Holland, succeeded his father 1840; entered diplomatic service 1831; British Minister to Tuscany 1839–46. Married, 1833, Mary Augusta, d. of 8th Earl of Coventry. Often entertained English visitors (but no record in his Dinner-book, MS BM, of CD's visit); Ruskin dined with him 12 June 45, and described him as "a little of the exquisite—but I daresay amiable enough in his way". He admired the house: "Nice cool rooms after dinner, open every way, vines and geraniums coming up through the floor and all over the ceiling—birds—fish—fountains—everything that can flutter or splash—& orange garden below" (*Ruskin in Italy. Letters to his Parents 1845*, ed. H. Shapiro, p. 112). T. A. Trollope thought Lord Holland "one of the most amusing talkers I ever knew". CD (with Catherine) also visited the Trollopes at Palazzo Berti, and T. A. Trollope recalled him as "a dandified, pretty-boy-looking sort of figure, singularly young looking, I thought, with a slight flavour of the whipper-snapper genus of humanity" (*What I Remember*, 1887, II, 93, 110).

To THOMAS CHAPMAN, [10 APRIL 1845]

MS Brotherton Library, Leeds. *Date:* 10 Apr was Thursday, and the date, not the day, is correct, since written the day after his return to Genoa on 9 Apr (see next and *To* Mitton, 14 Apr). *Address:* Inghilterra | Thomas Chapman Esquire | 14 Montague Place | Bryanstone Square | London.

Palazzo Peschiere, Genoa | Wednesday, April Tenth 1845.
My dear Sir.

As I have rather altered my arrangements in reference to my return home, I deem it best to write to you in reference to the Sanatorium dinner. And I do not delay a single day, for I returned hither from Rome and Naples and Heaven knows where else, only yesterday.[1]

The nature of my agreement for this place (I wish you could see it, by the way, for I really believe it is the most beautiful in Italy)—coupled with some other domestic considerations[2]—has determined me to remain here until about the Tenth or Twelfth of June. I could not, therefore, safely pledge myself to preside at a dinner in London, before the expiration of the First Week in July. But I would arrange to return in good time for Saturday the Fifth of that month, or Monday the Seventh, or any day afterwards. And I can warrant myself in all things, as punctual as the clock at the Horse-Guards.

Now, what I wish you and the committee to do is, to balance the possible disadvantages of dining so late in the season, against the possible advantages of your humble servant's first appearance after a Year's absence—of which you are welcome to make any use you please. And I beg you, most hear[tily][3] and un-affectedly, to consider nothing but the welfare of that excellent Institution in which we are all so warmly interested. Though I had ad[hered] to my original intention of leaving here this month, I should still have written to you to say that if any other President would have served your turn better than I, I should count on your appointing him, and using me in any other way in which I could be useful to our common object. And I should take it ill, if, in coming to a conclusion on the doubt I present to you now, you considered me in the least, or supposed me to have any feeling on the subject which could, by possibility, differ from your own.

As soon as you have decided, I shall be glad to hear from you, as I shall not settle my homeward route until I know your determination. In the event of the Committee deciding to wait until July, I hold myself bound, of course, to any of the days I have named.[4]

---

[1] Little is known of the journey from Florence to Genoa between 4 or 5 and 9 April; the latter part of the route would be over the same ground as the January journey, but *Pictures* (pp. 144–6) describes the coast-road in spring or summer.

[2] Probably the redecoration of the house: see *To* Mitton, 14 Apr.

[3] Letters covered by seal.

[4] The Sanatorium dinner did not take place in 1845, because the future of the institution was in doubt. A letter from Leigh Hunt to the Duke of Devonshire of 28 Apr 45 explained that in spite of its success the Sanatorium had never been self-supporting, "owing to the smallness of the scale, on which, for want of larger funds, it has been necessary to conduct it"; as the lease of the house in Devonshire Place had expired, the Committee had closed the institution for the present and were "en-deavouring to raise a building fund for the

Mrs. Dickens unites with me in best remembrances to yourself and Mrs. Chapman. The children are all well and rosy: and I find my waistcoat-buttons flying off occasionally, with great violence. From which I conclude that I am growing stouter.

Believe me always, and with great sincerity,
Faithfully Yours

Thomas Chapman Esquire.   CHARLES DICKENS

To MRS JOHN OVERS, 10 APRIL 1845*

MS in the Selbourne Collection, now deposited in Birmingham University Library. *Address:* Inghilterra | Mrs. Overs | 16 Carthusian Street | Charter-House Square | London.

Palazzo Peschiere, Genoa. | Thursday Tenth April 1845.

Dear Mrs. Overs.

Yours of the sixteenth of last month has just reached me. I have been travelling in many parts of Italy, and only returned here yesterday.

I really do not know what Mr. Forster has in hand for you. I think he wrote me word, but I do not remember—and I deem it best not to keep you in a state of expectation, while I search out that fragment from an extensive correspondence. But if you will send him this letter, he will take it as an authority to pay to you whatever he may have.

I trust in God you will succeed in your undertaking.[1] Your account of Miss Coutts's kindness is very gratifying to me. But it does not surprise me, for she is always kind and good to those who need her help.

Faithfully Yours

Mrs. Overs.   CHARLES DICKENS

---

erection of one of their own, capable of holding a hundred persons". Hunt hoped that the Duke might persuade the Commissioners of Woods and Forests to grant a plot of ground on favourable terms; he also suggested that he might obtain for the Sanatorium the patronage of the Queen and of foreign monarchs, in order to bring in subscriptions from the "monied part of the metropolis". But the Duke, as Hunt told Southwood Smith a month later, was unable to assist them (MSS BM). An advertisement in *The Times* of 14 June 45, signed "Henry Smyth, Secretary", promised the reopening as soon as the necessary funds and premises could be found. But the Committee could not "procure a house suited to its object", and though they formed an "Accumulating Building Fund" (*People's Journal*, 28 Feb 46), no later record has been discovered. Sampson Low (*The Charities of London*, 1850, p. 50n) says of the Sanatorium "our inquiries have failed to trace it".

[1] A paragraph in the *Examiner*, 24 May 45, stated that Mrs Overs had been established in a "small millinery and fancy stationery business" at 16 Carthusian St, Charterhouse Square; but the venture had had little success, and her husband's friends who had subscribed were appealed to for further assistance and patronage.

To AMÉDÉE PICHOT,[1] 10 APRIL 1845

Extract in *Le Neveu de ma Tante*, traduit et précédée d'une Notice Biographique et Littéraire, par Amédée Pichot, Paris, 1851, I, viii; dated Genoa, 10 Apr 45.

Après quelques observations sur la traduction des Carillons de Nöel.[2] Je suis né à Portsmouth, dans le comté de Hampshire, en Angleterre, le 7 février 1812. Ce serait un plaisir pour moi de vous donner quelques détails sur ma vie, comme vous le désirez, n'était que j'ai formé le dessein, il y a longtemps, de l'écrire moi-même[3] . . . cela vous amusera peut-être de savoir que j'ai lu maintes fois ma biographie, et que j'y ai trouvé toujours quelque nouveau et bizarre incident qui m'était révélé à moi-même;[4] mais la plus bizarre et la plus neuve peut-être de toutes ces histoires a été écrite en français.[5]

To JOHN FORSTER, [?10–11 APRIL 1845]

Extract in F, IV, iii, 327*n*. *Date:* wrongly given as 30 Mar 45 by Forster (see that day): *To* Mrs Overs, 10 Apr shows that he had only just heard the news.

Mrs. Overs tells me that Miss Coutts has sent her, at different times, sixteen pounds, has sent a doctor to her children, and has got one of the girls into the Orphan School. When I wrote her a word in the poor woman's behalf,[6] she wrote me back to the effect that it was a kindness to herself to have done so, "for what is the use of my means but to try and do some good with them?"

To CHARLES BLACK, 12 APRIL 1845†

MS Mr Robert H. Taylor. *Address:* Al Sigr. | Il Sigr Carlo Black | 13 Via Gregoriana | Roma.

Peschiere, Genoa. April Twelfth 1845.

My Dear Black.

As you were kind enough to mediate between Mr. Scott[7] and me; and further-more as I don't know Mr. Scott's address; I trouble you with a Bill on Torlonias

---

[1] Amédée Pichot (1795–1877), translator, and editor of the *Revue Britannique*: see Vol. III, p. 501*n*.

[2] See *To* Pichot, 30 Dec 46, *fn*.

[3] For this intention, see *To* Forster, ?4 Nov 46. Since CD did not give helpful detail to Pichot, he speculated, in his introduction to *Les Contes de Charles Dickens*, 1847, on how much CD had been painting himself in Oliver Twist and Nicholas Nickleby; he repeated these speculations and extended them to David Copperfield in his introduction to *Le Neveu de ma Tante*, and went on to give this extract from CD's

letter to him as showing that he intended some day to satisfy the curiosity of his readers.

[4] He had said this to the editor of the *New England Weekly Review* in Feb 42: see Vol. III, p. 61 and *n*.

[5] Not traced; presumably when he was in Paris in June or Dec 44.

[6] See *To* Miss Coutts, 8 Dec 44.

[7] George Scott, artist, a resident in Rome; CD wrote to him there on 13 Aug 52 (N, II, 409), again mentioning Mrs Scott.

for the price of the Merry Boy.[1] It will be necessary for Mr. Scott to write his name across the back, under that of our distinguished countryman, the author of A Christmas Carol in prose and other works. Pray convey to Mr. Scott my best regards and thanks; and couple Mrs. Dickens's name with mine when you call me to the recollection of his good wife.

It was my intention, as you may remember, to have sent you this from Florence; but on enquiry at that place (what a charming place it is!) I found it would be easier to make the remittance from Genoa. That last-mentioned city stands pretty much where it did. The De la Rues are very anxious that I should impress upon you how much they hope to see you, if, on your return you come this way. You will find them at the top of the Palazzo Brignole Rosso in an apartment which is a very charming one when you get up to it.

I heard last from Forster a few days ago. He is better and able to take a carriage airing now and then. But he is still very ill.[2] I have strenuously urged him to come over here, and return with us through Switzerland. Macready is making one vast Tom Tidler's[3] ground of the provinces in general, and picking up gold and silver in great quantities.[4] Mrs. Macready is full of compassion for him in consequence; and writes piously.

We found the children well and happy; and the house very comfortable after all our wanderings. Gwilt's Architecture[5] looms large and grim from a table in the Sala. I will exert myself to the utmost to find somebody coming to Rome who will take charge of it. And if my blushes for having twice left it behind, should have any effect upon the cover, you will find it neatly bound in Red, by the time it reaches you.

I hope you have seen Parke's address to the Murderous Quaker, in passing sentence. Also Fonblanque's article on the probability of that miserable culprit having imitated Belaney. [a]I thought the first quite magnificent in its stern and just indignation, after the dispassionate charge (it is vigorous English too; witness the use of the word 'tearing'); and the second quite unanswerable in all its wise positions.[a][6]

---

[1] "G. Scott" exhibited pictures at the Royal Society of British Artists from 1838 to 1847, with a Rome address (8 Via de Porta Pinciano) from 1843 to 1847. Either *A Genoese Boy*, 1841, or *A Boy at a Fountain—Rome*, 1843, might be the "Merry Boy", but neither can be traced among the pictures CD is known to have possessed.

[2] Forster postponed a visit to Marryat on account of "engagements (to say nothing of my lame leg)" (Forster *to* Marryat, 11 Apr 45; MS Mr R. M. R. Church).

[3] Thus in MS.

[4] Macready was in Newcastle, Sheffield, and Manchester in Feb–Mar; at Manchester he received £50 a night (*Diaries*, II, 289–91). During March, *Galignani's Mess-* enger carried reports of the success of his tour.

[5] Joseph Gwilt wrote various works on architecture; probably this was either *Notizia Architectoria Italiana*, 1818, or *An Encyclopaedia of Architecture*, 1842.

[a][a] Only part of this sentence appears in N, I, 669, from catalogue source.

[6] John Tawell, who murdered Sarah Hart at Salt Hill, was executed at Aylesbury 28 Mar; he had been sentenced by Baron Parke on 14 Mar. Towards the end, after a passage in which his indignation was evident, Parke said, "I will say nothing more of your heinous offence, because I do not wish to aggravate those feelings which I hope and would believe are at this moment tearing your mind" (*The Times*, 15 Mar 45).

If you can find time in the midst of the Stations,[1] to acknowledge the safe receipt of the Bill, I shall be glad to know that it has not fallen into the possession of a nefarious Roman. Kate and Georgy send their best loves to Mrs. Black and Miss Elderton.[2] I beg to forward the next thing to it. And uniting with them in all cordial regards to yourself, am always

Faithfully Yours

Charles Black Esquire.   CHARLES DICKENS

To JOHN FORSTER, [13 APRIL 1845]

Extract in F, IV, vii, 372. *Date:* 13 Apr according to Forster.

Seriously, it is a great pleasure to me to find that you are really pleased with these shadows in the water,[3] and think them worth the looking at.[4] Writing at such odd places, and in such odd seasons, I have been half savage with myself, very often, for not doing better. But d'Orsay, from whom I had a charming letter three days since, seems to think as you do of what he has read in those shown to him,[5] and says they remind him vividly of the real aspect of these scenes. . . . Well, if we should determine, after we have sat in council, that the experiences they relate are to be used, we will call B. and E. to their share and voice in the matter.

To MESSRS BRADBURY & EVANS, [?9–14 APRIL 1845]

Mention in next.

To THOMAS MITTON, 14 APRIL 1845†

MS Huntington Library.

Peschiere, Genoa. Monday April Fourteenth 1845

My Dear Mitton. I arrived here last Wednesday, well and flourishing: and found the children looking beautiful. You shall see Mamey and Charley dance

---

Belaney, charged with poisoning his wife June 44, had been acquitted on 21 Aug 44; Fonblanque (*Examiner*, 29 Mar 45) contrasted the summing-up by Sir John Gurney (*d*. Mar 1845), with its "signal omissions", with Parke's and said that had Belaney been convicted "Tawell might never have been encouraged to his crime".

[1] i.e. visits to specified churches in Rome on certain days appointed by the Pope for prayers and the obtaining of indulgences; clearly a joking reference.

[2] Presumably a sister of Mrs Black; probably Juliet Elderton, from whom CD heard in Nov 1861, when she wrote from

Cheltenham "imploring" him to visit her there and sending her love to Georgina (*To* Georgina Hogarth, 25 Nov 61).

[3] In the introductory section of *Pictures*, "The Reader's Passport", CD says, "This Book is a series of faint reflections—mere shadows in the water" (p. 2).

[4] Introducing this extract, Forster says that CD, continuing his weekly letters, was writing "with no definite purpose as yet"; see *To* Forster, 7 June 45 and *fn*.

[5] D'Orsay (replying to CD's of 18 Mar) must also have been impressed by the letters written to himself and Lady Blessington.

the Polka,[1] when we return—which you will really consider a very brilliant performance. Master Frank is a prodigious blade, and more full of queer tricks than any of his predecessors have been at his time of life. Katey has been quite lamed by chilblains, but she is now hobbling about again. They have not affected her rosy looks.

I have decided to remain here, until about the Tenth of June, and to come home by Switzerland. I hope to pass the Alps over the Great St. Gothard; and in that case shall have taken its two finest passages. This arrangement will probably shut out Paris; but I can run over there, at any time; whereas the country I propose to traverse is not so easy of access from England. This house is as faultless as it always has been. There are very few houses in Italy, I do believe, where the children could have kept their health in such an extraordinary year.

It would be easier to tell you what I haven't seen, than what I have. I have been upon the Wing, now, full six months on end; and have crowded such an immense number of objects into that time, that it makes me weary to think of them.

Bradbury and Evans have sent me an account of the Chimes.[2] They make *the Profit* on the first 20,000, from fourteen to fifteen hundred pounds. And they add that if they had charged only their own small commission, and had not been obliged to employ Chapman and Hall, the profit wod. have been from £150 to £200 more. C and H's accounts make a profit of £726 only, on a sale of 15,000 of the Carol.[3] So that supposing it had sold 20,000, the gross profit would have been about £1,000. This is a slight difference! Think of the difference too, in the appearance and production[4] of the two books—and I think you will agree with me that Bradbury and Evans are the Men for me to work with.[5]

They were very anxious to know what I thought of their management in general, under the disadvantageous circumstance of having C and H in the business at all. I wrote and told them that I was greatly pleased, and that I was quite certain it couldn't have been better done. As I am.

Chapman and Hall's account has been rendered to Forster and settled. Before I left, I settled all the profits of the different books up to April and credited

---

[1] For their dancing lessons, see *To Mitton*, 5 Nov and *To Mrs CD*, 23 Nov 44. Before CD left England the polka (introduced from Paris) was "the fashionable epidemic of the season" and "verge[d] on delirium" (*Court Journal*, 1 June 44). According to Mamie, the early dancing lessons "were very funny . . . the children's legs were pulled about, stretched, and turned in the most extraordinary manner"; their father "took an immense interest in these lessons", and Roche "liked to show the little sisters off whenever he could get an opportunity" (*Charles Dickens*, 1885, pp. 74–5).

[2] Bradbury & Evans's accounts (in the V & A) do not include the first 20,000 of the *Chimes*.

[3] See *To* Forster, ?11 Feb, *To* Mitton, 10 and 12 Feb 44, and *fns*.

[4] It is difficult to know what CD means as there is no great difference; the *Carol* is slightly more elaborate with its hand-coloured plates. The price was the same, five shillings.

[5] Forster thought the difference in the profit "undoubtedly justified him" (F, IV, ii, 314).

myself with the estimated amount of my share of the Chuzzlewit profits up to the time of the subscription, and exclusive of it. I also paid them £81..9..8 for my purchase of my share of the Stock of Pickwick.[1]

The account of my Profits with C and H from April to the close of the Year/44 stands thus:

	£ . S . D
Chuzzlewit	611..12.. 4
Humphrey's Clock	24.. 2.. 3
Pickwick	50.. 2.. 4
Carol	189..11.. 5
Oliver Twist	54.. 0..10
German Bookseller, for proofs[2]	5..10.. 0

Total £934..19.. 2—which they have

received directions from Lincoln's Inn Fields, to pay into Coutts's. This is "not so bad" either?[3]

When I thought you might have a balance in my favor, I forgot the taxes, and took the gross receipt for rent for the whole Year. You were quite right in not paying anything in. I hope the balance will turn on my side, the next time the old lady pays.

This reminds me. *The moment she turns out,* will you set your man to work to paint the outside of the house? I should like all the doors and railings in the garden to be a nice bright cheerful green, except the little staircases from the windows, which I should prefer being painted white, as they are now. I should like to have the hall and staircase painted inside, to the top of the house—a good green: not too decided, of course, to spoil the effect of the prints—The little skirting-board there is, wainscoat.[4] The ceiling, white. The outside of the street door, wainscoat—if you see no reason for any other colour—a letter box made in it, with a glass back; so that John may see when there are letters in the inside. I will pay him ready money, so please to make him produce an Estimate for all this, beforehand. I will *not* new-point the house; really not caring about it.

I know you will take care, better than anybody else could, that it is done on reasonable terms. Therefore he may go to work on all this, without your consulting me upon his Estimate.

But there is another job I should like to do, which I must know the expence of, before I decide. I should like to new-paper the drawing-room; taking away the ugly hand rail, and bringing the paper down to the skirting board. I should like the skirting board to be painted in imitation of Satin-Wood—the ceiling to have a faint pink blush in it—and a little wreath of flowers to be painted round

---

[1] See *To* Bradbury & Evans, 8 May 44 and *fn*.

[2] Bernhard Tauchnitz: see Vol. III, p. 579 and *ns*.

[3] CD's accounts (MS Messrs Coutts)

show a payment of £928.14.2 from Chapman & Hall on 24 May.

[4] Sense not in *OED*: presumably the colour of oak panelling.

the lamp. The paper must be blue and gold or purple and gold—to agree with the furniture and curtains; and I should wish it to be cheerful and gay. I can safely trust to your taste, if you will choose it. I have sd. nothing about this to Mrs. D: wishing it to be a surprise, if I do it at all.—Gold moulding round the paper.

If the old lady would allow the man to go up one morning before she is out of bed; and see the room,—he might make his Estimate: then you could send it to m[e[1] here. If I] decided on this improvement, he [could begin] on all his work at on[ce as soon as Mrs. Onslow] was out of the house. Will you [let me know] what you do in this [matter, as it will be] necessary to set him to work on [the painti]ng, as soon as she vacates [the house, as I fear the] smell would damage the children['s health. The] long travelling in the air[2] [   ].

I don't think we [shall stop] upon the way except to r[est, unless we stay at] the coast for bathing. But I d[on't think] it likely.

Write me about [your affair]s when you have leisure[2] [   ] have by this time: Elliotson ha[s probably] set your poor facto[tum[3] on his unsteady legs] again. I wonder you got over su[ch a wet sta]te, without Rheumati[sm; that is something] gained, at all events.

I begin to be anxious to get home, a [   ] with Bradbury and Evans,[4] for the Campaign which [   ].

Here is a World of trouble for you![5]—[   ] whenever you can serve me, so I will say nothing [   ].

Mrs. Dickens and Miss Hogarth as[k me to send you their kindest] remembrances. In all its travelling, the Carria[ge[6]   ] of iron the size of a toothpick. Roche says[6] [   ] with.

> Faithfully Always
> CD.

To JOHN FORSTER, [?APRIL 1845]

Extract in F, IV, v, 345. *Date:* "one Spring day" according to Forster; probably April.

Beyond the town is the wide expanse of the Mediterranean, as blue, at this moment, as the most pure and vivid prussian blue on Mac's palette[7] when it is

---

[1] The rest of the letter is previously unpublished. It becomes a fragment at this point: readings in square brackets are wholly conjectural, allowing for the approximate number of letters missing.

[2] About 23 letters missing.

[3] Perhaps Mitton's clerk, Robert Bach.

[4] About 34 letters missing after "home, a" and about 36 after "which". This may be a reference to the proposed periodical: see *To* Forster, 7 Mar and *fn*, and F, IV, ii,

316. Some rumour of it was circulating at this time; the *Critic*, 15 Apr 45, says "Boz is about to start a magazine of his own".

[5] About 36 letters missing here and again at the end of the sentence.

[6] About 36 letters missing.

[7] Cf. *To* Maclise, 22 July 44. Some critics had objected to Maclise's use of a "heavy and intense" blue: e.g. *Athenæum*, 11 May 44.

newly set; and on the horizon there is a red flush, seen nowhere as it is here. Immediately below the windows are the gardens of the house, with gold fish swimming and diving in the fountains; and below them, at the foot of a steep slope, the public garden and drive, where the walks are marked out by hedges of pink roses, which blush and shine through the green trees and vines, close up to the balconies of these windows. No custom can impair, and no description enhance, the beauty of the scene.

To JOHN FORSTER, [?MID-APRIL 1845]

Extract in F, IV, iv, 335*n*. *Date:* "a couple of months before he left the country" according to Forster.

We are living very quietly; and I am now more than ever glad that I have kept myself aloof from the "receiving" natives always, and delivered scarcely any of my letters of introduction. If I had, I should have seen nothing and known less. I have observed that the English women who have married foreigners are invariably the most audacious in the license they assume.[1] Think of one lady married to a royal chamberlain (not here) who said at dinner to the master of the house at a place where I was dining—that she had brought back his *Satirist*,[2] but didn't think there was quite so much "fun" in it as there used to be. I looked at the paper afterwards, and found it crammed with such vile obscenity as positively made one's hair stand on end.

To JOHN FORSTER, [27 APRIL 1845]

Extract in F, IV, vii, 372-3. *Date:* 27 Apr according to Forster.

Since our return we have had charming spring days.[3] The garden is one grove of roses;[4] we have left off fires; and we breakfast and dine again in the great hall, with the windows open. To-day we have rain, but rain was rather wanted I believe, so it gives offence to nobody. As far as I have had an opportunity of judging yet, the spring is the most delightful time in this country. But for all that I am looking with eagerness to the tenth of June, impatient to renew our happy old walks and old talks in dear old home.

---

[1] Hobhouse had a similar impression of the foreign women in Naples, and mentioned "a celebrated Englishwoman whose amours are as public and carried on as publicly as if they were creditable" (Diary of Lord Broughton, 1 Feb 43; MS BM).

[2] See Vol. III, p. 84*n*.

[3] Ruskin, in Genoa 26-29 Apr, spoke of the "glorious weather . . . no heat, just air that one likes to sit out in" (*Ruskin in Italy.*

Letters to his Parents, 1845, ed. H. Shapiro, p. 40).

[4] *Pictures*, p. 72, describing the Palazzo, mentions "groves of roses and camelias" and "walks of orange trees". Forster says that "from his 'shady arm-chair up among the Peschiere oranges'" CD sent him "at regular intervals what he calls his rambling talk" (F, IV, vii, 372).

To LORD ROBERTSON, 28 APRIL 1845*

MS Mr W. A. Foyle.

Peschiere, Genoa. Twenty Eighth April 1845.

My Dear Lord Robertson.

Don't think me unmindful of the pleasant day we passed together here last autumn—or of your no less pleasant letter, afterwards received—or of anything connected with your pleasant Self; because I am a Beast in appearance (correspondentially speaking), and have never wafted a half sheet of paper to Edinburgh. I have been travelling hither and thither, ever since; with the exception of one month, when I was hard at work. And this is my excuse.

I saw the friend to whom you introduced me—at Naples.[1] He was on the eve of departing for Sicily, so I only saw him once. He prepossessed me most agreeably; and I should have been well pleased to have known him better.

Your friends the Puppets gave their last performance, last Friday.[2] I attended, of course. The Piece (of a pathetic character) was entitled St. Helena, or the Death of Napoleon; and opened by a Valet coming into Napoleon's room, with this obscure announcement:

"Sir Yew ud se on Low! (the "ow" as in cow)

Sir Hudson was represented as an Ogre—and wore a suit of regimentals which I wish you could have seen. There was no mistake about his being an Englishman, for at the end of every long Italian Speech he delivered, he said "Yes"—in English—which never failed to bring down thunders of a[pplause. His] brutality to Napoleon awakened one general sentiment of execration in the breasts of [the audience]: and so affected the Emperor himself, that once he fainted away on the spot, and [was carried out by two] other Puppets. He never recovered the shock, for he was next seen in a clea[n shirt (with an i]mmense collar to it) in a bed with red and white drapery, where he made a decent [end; the last] word on his lips being "Vatterloo".

It was very ludicrous [and absurd,] Napoleon's boots being particularly unmanageable—[getting under ta]bles—and doubling up [themselves]—and quivering in the air—and sometimes skaiting [away with him,] out of all human [sight. Then][3] he had to stand at a table, reading a book. And to [see his bo]dy bent over the Volume like a [boot-jack,] with his mournful eyes (his face expressed a [sett]led melancholy) glaring o[ut into the] Pit, was the finest spectacle I ever beheld.

Kate says you have h[ad another] daughter married,[4] if Galignani tells the Truth, and that she congratulates you, and w[ishes her] joy and happiness. Do

---

[1] Possibly Douglas Cheape (see *To Cheape*, 15 Feb 45); Robertson was in Naples in Sep 44.

[2] The following passage is often verbally close to parts of the fuller account in *Pictures*, pp. 69–72; words missing from mutilation and damage to the MS have been supplied from this where possible.

Missing words elsewhere in the letter are conjecturally supplied.

[3] "knowledge", in *Pictures*, p. 71, is too long for the first word.

[4] Mary-Cameron Robertson married William Gates, at Edinburgh, 10 Mar 45 (*Gentleman's Magazine*, May 45).

you remember our Highland engagement? I fear it will not come [off this au]tumn, for a coming event, which I hadn't reckoned on, is casting its shadow before Mrs. [Dickens in] a very disconcerting manner.[1]

She sends her best regards to you, however, and so does her sister. We are dying to know what that book[2] is, to which we see your name attached in newspaper announcements. I expect to reach my English Home, at the end of June. If I don't find a copy of said book then and there, with your hand-writing on the title page, I shall run over to Edinburgh about September or so, I think, to denounce you in person. And if I *do* find it—to thank you.

Have you ever been into a church since you were at Rome? *I* haven't. I took the Valet de place by the throat on the Tenth day of churches, and on the steps of the Eighty Second church;[3] and swore I would strangle him if he shewed me another. He resigned next [mor]ning.

Ever My Dear Lord Robertson | Faithfully Yours
CHARLES DICKENS

[Remem]ber us all, cordially, to [Lady R.][4]

P.P.S. In the Holy Week[5] at Rome [while the Pope was] waiting at table on the 12 [apostles & Judas,[6] there] were two Englishmen behind me—[in an] immense crowd, and we were all struggling and standing on tiptoe to see—whose whole interest in the scene seemed to have resolved itself into a desire to see what there was to eat. "There are two decanters to the right there!" sd. one of them. "I distinctly see white wine! I think I perceive red, but I'll swear to white!"—"Mustard by G—!" cried the second gentleman in great excitement. "Will any gentleman in front be kind enough to inform me whether he sees any Pepper anywhere! I distinctly saw the Mustard Pot a moment ago!"[7]

To EMILE DE LA RUE, [2 MAY 1845]*

MS Berg Collection. *Date:* endorsed by de la Rue, "2 mai", and clearly the Friday just before the execution: see *To* Maclise, 9 May.

Peschiere | Friday Evening

My Dear De La Rue.

Many thanks for your notice. I think, however, I will leave the two wretched creatures to their fate; and take their behaviour on your report of it.[8]

---

[1] Alfred D'Orsay Tennyson was born 28 Oct 45.

[2] *Leaves from a Journal and other Fragments in Verse,* published early in Apr 1845.

[3] In *Pictures,* p. 184, CD says he "explored so many churches that I abandoned that part of the enterprise at last, before it was half over, lest I should never, of my own accord, go to church again, as long as I lived".

[4] Only 4 or 5 letters missing here.

[5] On Maundy Thursday.

[6] The ceremony is described in *Pictures,* pp. 221–3, where CD says there were thirteen men, representing the twelve apostles and Judas Iscariot; the 1st edn of Murray's *Handbook for ... Central Italy* gives the number as 12, but later edns agree with CD, and this is confirmed by other travellers (some of whom say that the thirteenth represented an angel who appeared among 12 poor guests of St Gregory the Great).

[7] The anecdote about the Englishmen is in *Pictures,* p. 223, in a slightly different form.

[8] CD had seen an execution in Rome on 8 Mar and describes it at great length in *Pictures,* pp. 200–7.

I have taken an Eight mile walk this Evening: and am all the better for it—
Slept badly last night.

Best regards to Madame. At Eleven tomorrow, I will present myself.

Faithfully Ever CD.

To JOHN FORSTER, [?4 MAY 1845]

Extract in F, IV, vii, 373. *Date:* shortly after *To* de la Rue, ?2 May, and presumably
in his usual week-end letter.

*Saying that two men had been hanged in the city, and describing how two ladies of
quality agreed to keep up for a time a prayer for the souls of these two miserable
creatures so incessant that Heaven should never for a moment be left alone, and*
they relieved each other *so that, for the whole of the stated time, one of them was
always on her knees in the cathedral church of San Lorenzo. From which he
inferred that* a morbid sympathy for criminals is not wholly peculiar to England,
though it affects more people in that country perhaps than in any other.

To THE COUNTESS OF BLESSINGTON, 9 MAY 1845†

MS Benoliel Collection. *Address:* Inghilterra. | The | Countess of Blessington |
Gore House | Kensington | London.

Palazzo Peschiere, Genoa. | Ninth May 1845.

My Dear Lady Blessington.

Once more in my old quarters; and, *ᵃunlike the Dove of the Ark,ᵃ* with
rather a tired sole to my foot, from having found such an immense number of
different resting-places for it since I went away; I write you my last Italian letter
for this bout—designing to leave here, please God, on the Ninth of next month,
and to be in London again, by the end of June. I am looking forward, with great
delight, to the pleasure of seeing you once more: and mean to come on Gore
House with such a swoop as shall astonish the Poodle, if, after being accustomed
to his own size and sense, he retain the power of being astonished at anything
in the wide world.

You know where I have been, and every inch of ground I have travelled over,
and every object I have seen.[1] It is next to impossible, surely, to exaggerate the
interest of Rome: though I think it *is* very possible to find the main source of
interest in the wrong things—*ᵇand very often done, moreover.ᵇ* Naples disappointed me, greatly. The weather was bad during a great part of my stay there,
ᶜto be sure.ᶜ But if I had not had mud, I should have had dust. And though I
had had Sun, I must still have had the Lazzaroni; and they are so ragged, so
dirty, so abject, so full of degradation, so sunk and steeped in utter hopelessness
of better things, that they would make Heaven uncomfortable, if they could ever
get there. I didn't expect to see a handsome City, but I expected something

---

aa; bb; cc Not previously published.   *The Idler in Italy,* 1839–40, described her
[1] Lady Blessington's 3-volume work,   residence and travels in 1822–30.

better than that long dull line of squalid houses which stretches from the Chiaja to the Quarter of the Porta Capuana;[1] and while I was quite prepared for a miserable populace, I had some dim belief that there were bright rags among them, and dancing legs, and shining sun-browned faces. Whereas the honest truth is, that connected with Naples itself, I have not one solitary *pleasant* recollection. The country round it, charmed me, I need not say. Who can forget Herculaneum and Pompeii? As to Vesuvius, it burns away, in my thoughts, beside the roaring waters of Niagara; and not a splash of the water extinguishes a spark of the fire; but there they go on tumbling and flaming, night and day, each in its fullest glory.

I have seen so many wonders, and each of them has such a voice of its own, that I sit all day listening to the roar they make, as if it were in a seashell; and have fallen into an idleness so complete, that I can't rouse myself sufficiently, to go to Pisa on the Twenty Fifth,[2] when the triennial illumination of the Cathedral and Leaning Tower, and Bridges, and what not, takes place. But I have already been there once; and it cannot beat St. Peters, I suppose. So I don't think I shall pluck myself up by the roots, and go aboard a Steamer for Leghorn.

[a]There were some wonderful people in Rome for the Holy week, of course; both French and English. The latter especially. There was one Mrs. Davis[3] —I know her name from her being always in great request among her party, and her party being everywhere—who was in every part of every scene of every ceremony; and who for a fortnight before, had been in every tomb, and every Church, and every Ruin, and every Picture Gallery: and who never for one instant held her tongue. Deep underground, high up in St. Peters, out on the Campagna, and in the Jews Quarter, Mrs. Davis turned up all the same. I don't think she saw anything or ever looked at anything; and she had always lost something out of a straw hand-basket, and was trying to find it with all her might and main, among an immense quantity of English halfpence which lay, like sands upon the seashore, at the bottom of it. There was a Cicerone always attached to the party (which had been brought over from London, some fifteen or twenty strong, by contract I believe);[4] and if he so much as looked at Mrs. Davis, she invariably cut him short by saying, "there! God bless the man, don't worrit me: I don't understand a word you say, and shouldn't if you was to talk 'till you was black in the face!"[5] Mr. Davis always had a snuff-colored great coat on, and an umbrella in his hand: and had a sort of slow curiosity always devouring him: which prompted him to do extraordinary things, such as taking the covers off Urns, and looking in at the ashes as if they were Pickles—and tracing out Inscriptions with his umbrella, and saying with intense thoughtfulness, "here's a B, you see—and a R—And this is the way we goes on in!" His antiquarian

---

[1] See *Pictures*, p. 240.

[2] 25 May was the feast of San Ranieri; Murray's *Handbook for ... Northern Italy* calls it "the most remarkable spectacle of Pisa ... celebrated as a species of national jubilee".

[aa] Not previously published.

[3] The whole of the following passage is almost word for word in *Pictures*, pp. 185–6, which is obviously taken from this letter.

[4] No particulars of such arrangements have been found; it was not until the 50s that Thomas Cook began to organize excursions to the continent.

[5] This sentence is not in *Pictures*.

habits occasioned his being frequently in the rear of the rest; and one of the agonies of Mrs. Davis and the party in general, was, an ever-present fear that Davis would be lost: causing them to scream for him in the strangest places and at the most improper seasons. And when he came slowly emerging out of some Sepulchre or other, like a peaceful Ghoul, saying "Here I am!"—Mrs. Davis invariably replied "You'll be buried alive in a foreign country Davis; and it's no use trying to prevent you!"

It would be idle to endeavour to thank you my dear Lady Blessington, for all your enthusiasm and friendship in behalf of the Chimes. Trust me, I am deeply and truly sensible of it; and that is far from being the least of the pleasures which that book has yielded me. Forster will have told you of its prodigious success; and how, from the time of the subscription to this hour, it has, in its results to me, left its Predecessors far behind.[a]

Let me thank you, heartily, for the Keepsake and the Book of Beauty. They reached me a week or two ago. I have been very much struck by two papers in them. One, Landor's conversation; among the most charming, profound, and delicate productions I have ever read. The other, Your lines on Byron's Room at Venice.[1] I am as sure that you wrote them from your heart, as I am that they found their way, immediately, to Mine. [e]They are as full of Strength, and Truth, and Feeling, as anything can be. I cannot say how much they moved me.

Poor Forster must have had a sad winter of it, but I hope to find him quite well, when I return. He tells me in his last letter, that you had Lord Robertson with you the other day. He is a good creature, and (out of Edinburgh where they spoil him) very humourous. We had a happy day together here, last Autumn, when he passed through Genoa on his way home.—[e]

It delights me to receive such accounts of Maclise's fresco.[2] If he will only

---

[1] The "Imaginary Conversation" of Aesop and Rhodope was in the 1845 *Book of Beauty* (most of the "Imaginary Conversations" written after the 5-vol. collection of 1826–9 appeared singly in one of Lady Blessington's annuals), and Lady Blessington's lines on Byron's room in the *Keepsake*.

[ee] Not previously published.

[2] The cartoon, coloured sketch, and specimen of fresco for *The Spirit of Chivalry*, all exhibited in Westminster Hall in May; a rather different version in oil was afterwards added (*Daniel Maclise 1806–70*: catalogue of exhibition, 1972, pp. 84–6). Maclise's work was the most popular of the exhibits, and was eventually approved by the Commissioners; but the cartoon was criticized for its overcrowded composition —later much simplified, as indeed Maclise had always intended. The "specimen" was a single figure (the poet-historian) submitted as an experiment in the medium. CD saw them on his return in July, and

wrote an article for *Douglas Jerrold's Shilling Magazine*, Aug 1845; his praise is superlative, suggesting that the picture is one of the masterpieces of all time; Maclise, on seeing the MS or proof, wrote to Forster saying "Dear Dick how good he is—he sets me in a glow when I read his warm praise". But as it had still not been announced that his work was to be chosen, he was anxious about CD's assumption of the fact and his jibes at the Commissioners: "I certainly would not print what is contained *in the last page*, nor in *any way* allude to my not being employed to execute this cartoon . . . When the matter is concluded —I should then see no harm even in the most caustic part of this article— —Pray my dear Forster exercise your dispassionate power on this and entreat D to draw his pen through some of his finest writing" (MS Forster Collection, V & A). Forster's diplomacy was successful, and the dangerous passages, including the four concluding paragraphs, were not printed in the

give his magnificent Genius fair play, there is not enough of Cant and Dulness even in Criticism—the Criticism of Art; from which Sterne prayed kind Heaven to defend him, as 'the worst of all the Cants continually canted in this Canting World'[1]—to keep the Giant down, an hour.

*f*Do you recollect a Picture by Vandyke in the Durazzo Palace here, commonly known as The Boy in White Satin?—a picture of a child standing near an old chair. It is a noble painting, and is such a curious accidental likeness of my Son and Heir that I have written to Paris (where I understand a good one is to be had) for a Copy.[2] Old Di Negro is gone to his country house. For which I am very grateful . . He wanted to improvise here, one night; but I couldn't stand it. I respect the old man for his goodness to the poor followers of the Muses here (despised of Genoa Nobles, whose Nature and cultivation you know) but I *could not* bear it.*f*

Poor Tracey[3] has lost his wife, I am sorry to hear, since you and I spoke of his pleasant face. And Blanchard—what a terrible history that was! Forster did himself enduring honor by his manly and zealous devotion to the interests of that Orphan Family, in the midst of all his pains and troubles. It was very good of him.

Do not let your Nieces forget me, if you can help it. And give my love to Count D'Orsay, with many thanks to him for his charming letter. I was greatly amused by his account of Bulwer.[3] There was a "cold shade of aristocracy"[4] about it, and a dampness of cold water; which entertained me, beyond measure.

*g*Everybody in England is mad, it seems to me, about Maynooth. And long memories are shaking off their slumbers, I see, and besetting D'Israeli: a little.[5] He has certainly done his best to be attacked—and done it well too.

Has the Sybil[6] spoken yet?

Believe me always My Dear Lady Blessington
With the truest Regard | Faithfully Yours
CHARLES DICKENS

Do you know Mr. Temple, the Minister at Naples?[7] I like him exceedingly.*g*

---

magazine; the original version from the galley proof is given in *Miscellaneous Papers*, pp. 42–7. CD had emphasized the influence of the painting on "ignorant, unlettered, drudging men" as well as experts, and in the close advised the Commissioners to give it the place of honour behind the throne, ironically contrasting the Spirit of Chivalry with their spirit of meanness and injustice. The fresco in the House of Lords, completed 1847, is in fact on the wall behind the throne with Maclise's *Spirit of Justice* (1849) as a companion-piece.

[1] *Tristram Shandy*, Book III, Ch. 12; also quoted by Lady Blessington, *Idler in Italy*, II, 313, and at the beginning of CD's article on *The Spirit of Chivalry*.

ff Not previously published.

[2] *Il Putto Bianco*, reproduced in *Archivia*

Storico dell'Arte, Serie Secunda, Rome 1897, p. 436; a boy (possibly of the Durazzo family), apparently about eight years old, standing on a footstool by a window; noted by Simond as "dressed . . . in the formal style of old times, yet so gracefully simple and natural under the awkward attire, so charmingly vacant and childish, that I could not withdraw my eyes from it" (*A Tour in Italy and Sicily*, p. 591). There is a discernible likeness of expression to the Richmond portrait of Charley of 1852.

[3] Name omitted in previously published texts.

[4] "The British soldiers conquered under the cool shade of aristocracy" (Sir William Napier, *Peninsular War*, 1810, II, xi, 3).

gg Not previously published.

[5] The protracted debates on the grant

To DANIEL MACLISE, 9 MAY 1845

MS Free Library of Philadelphia. *Address:* Inghilterra. | Daniel Maclise Esquire.
R.A. | 14 Russell Place | Fitzroy Square | London.

Palazzo Peschiere, Genoa. Ninth May 1845.

My Very Dear Mac. I should be ashamed of having observed this long silence
towards such a correspondent as *you*,[1] if I were not comforted by the belief that
you hear of all our proceedings from Forster—hear, sometimes, more than you
could desire, perhaps, of the prolix Dick—and that you have us as fully in that
astonishing eye of yours ("and Good God, my dear Mac, what an Eye you
have!")[2] as if you saw us all bodily, in No. 1 Devonshire Terrace, which please
God, old fellow, you will shortly do, again and again; for on Monday, the Ninth
of next month we turn homewards. The main object of my letter—its sole
object—is to say that I *can't* say how happy I am in the hope of speedily seeing
you again, my dear friend, and holding all manner of glorious jollifications in
your beloved company.

Would you like to know a piece of domestic news that Forster *don't* know?
Would you permit me to put you in the position of crushing him? I will do so.
Forthwith. You recollect our Cook, our nice Cook, our good-looking Cook;
the best Servant as ever trod (excuse my being nautical) 'twixt stem and stern
your Honor? Yesterday she came up to her Mistress, and announced that she
was not going to return to England, but intended to be married, and to settle
here! ! !³

The Bridegroom is the Governor's Cook: who has been visiting in the kitchen
ever since our first arrival. The Governor's servants have a weekly ball in the
Summer, and there they first met—'twas in a Crowd,⁴ I believe. He is a Frenchman by birth, but has been here a long time. They have courted in Italian,
as he knows no English, and she no French. They are to be married as soon as
her Baptism Certificate can arrive from England (at Leghorn; they must go
there, for the purpose; it is not legal here: she being a Protestant)—and intend
opening a Restaurant in Genoa. It is a great venture on her part, for she is well
brought-up: quite delicate in her ideas: full of English notions of comfort and
cleanliness and decency—and must, for some time at all events, live in some
miserable rooms in some miserable neighbourhood, of which you can form no
idea, without seeing the ordinary residences of an Italian Town. I do not

to the Catholic college at Maynooth helped
to split the Young England party. Disraeli's
speech on 11 Apr, violently attacking Peel
and the Whigs, referred to memories of
Catholic Emancipation.

⁶ Disraeli's *Sybil* was published on 17
May.

⁷ William Temple (1788–1856), younger
son of 2nd Viscount Palmerston; envoy
extraordinary and minister plenipotentiary
at Naples 1832–56. Forster remarks on
how much CD was gratified at Naples by
the attentions of Temple, "whom he des-

cribed as a man supremely agreeable, with
everything about him in perfect taste, and
with the truest gentleman-manner which
has its root in kindness and generosity of
nature" (F, IV, vii, 372). See also *To*
Mitton, 17 Feb 45, *fn*.

¹ Written large.

² Cf. Vol. III, p. 94*n*.

³ See *To* Forster, 12 May and *To* Mitton,
20 May 45.

⁴ "We met—'twas in a crowd", Thomas
Haynes Bayly's popular song (first published in *Songs of the Boudoir, c.* 1830).

remember a single English person of her own station who will be here, after we have left. But she is resolved. And [all][1] I can do, is to take care that the Marriage is lawfully and properly solemnized before we depart.

This is the second of them who has found a lover here; the Nurse, Charlotte,[2] having "provi[ded][1] herself" with that commodity the other day. I am in daily expectation of finding that Anne is secretly married to Roche and has a young family. I have interrogated Charley in private, but I believe he is still free, also his sisters. Chickenstalker (whom I think you will like—you always predicted well of him) is still heartwhole, I believe.

The greatest public news of this place, is, that Two Men were hanged here the other day. It was the first public execution for many years, and made an immense sensation. They had broken into and robbed a Priest's house (the Priest was the uncle of one of them) in broad day, in the most crowded part of the town: and had murdered the Woman Servant who had opened the door to them, by throttling her with their hands, that there might be no Weapon, and no Blood. They suffered on the Outer Mole of the Harbor—a stone wall, out in the broad blue sea—and the great crowd were gathered together in Boats. On their way to the Scaffold, they had the Sacrament given them, I am told, *no fewer than Seven times*, at the doors of seven different Churches. I was afraid to go, for I know how they manage things here: and knew I should be horrified. It was very dreadful, I understand: one man standing by, while the other was hanged: and Jack Ketch dangling with his arms on the cross beam, and dancing on the quivering body! Roche went—and could eat nothing for a long time afterwards. Ketch came from Turin, express. He used to live here. But it being accidentally discovered that he prowled about the town after nightfall, wrapped up in a great cloak, attending the poor people as a Physician (!), he was ordered off, a few years ago.

I ought to have filled this Half sheet with a little critical talk about the Farnese Hercules, and the Do. Bull, and the Venuses (all bad by the bye, and like anything but women—they may be like Goddesses: I don't know about that), and the Apollo, and Laöcoon, and other Novelties. But I can think of no Art but your Cartoon, of which Forster gives me such a tremendous and rapturous account. So we will be critical in our walks home at night. And there is no chance of our disagreeing, I know. For is not our motto Truth for ever, and cant[3] be damned?

Goodbye my dear Mac. I am looking forward, with perfect enthusiasm, to shaking you by the hand. So are Kate and Georgy (who send loves); so are all the children! Ever and Ever Yours

CHARLES DICKENS

P.S Best remembrances to your Good Sister.[4]

---

[1] Paper slightly torn at seal.

[2] She married Johnson, a servant of Sir George Craufurd's: see *To* Bradbury & Evans, 7 July 45.

[3] Written large.

[4] Isabella Maclise (*d.* 1865), the elder of Maclise's two sisters; she "loved her brother so intensely that nothing would induce her to separate from him" and never married (W. Justin O'Driscoll, *Memoir of Daniel Maclise*, p. 15).

To CLARKSON STANFIELD, 9 MAY 1845*

MS Colonel Richard Gimbel. *Address:* Inghilterra. | Clarkson Stanfield Esquire. R.A. | Mornington Place | Hampstead Road | London.

Palazzo Peschiere Genoa. Maggio 9 1845.

Carissimo Amico Mio!

Siete stato in Italia e capite ben'la lingua.[1]

Perche non vi ho scritto tre, quattro, cinqui mesi fa! Perche non ho mandato mai, una piccola lettera al pittore famosissimo; al figlio del Mare; al Meglio di camaradi; al meglio d'amici; al meglio di Uomini—in una parola, a Stanny! Non c'e che—un Stanny nel mondo. Lo se chiama, generalmente vecchio Stanny. Non importa. E un Giovane.

Amico mio, vi sono, quasi, sei mesi che son stato in cammino qua e la. Son stato a Roma, a Napoli, a Firenze,—ad ogni parte d'Italia. Non vi sono che tre settimane—circa—che son' venuto ancora, a mia casa. Ecco la mia scusa! Ma in tutti questi viaggii, caro mio, ho pensato costantamente degli amici chi lasciai in Inghilterra, in Decembre del' anno passato. E Stanny e stato sempre, nel mio cuore di cuori.

Domanderete "che si dice di nuovo in Genova?" Niente. Veramente, Niente. L'intelligenza la piu interressante a mi (e, spero, a [te][2] anche) e, che partiremo fra, li otto di Giugno, per ritornare al nos[tro][2] paese ben' amate; ed ai nostri amici.

Lesi, l'altro jeri, in Galignani, che foste partito per America, per pingere un prodigioso quadro nella Sala di Congresso.[3] Questa Intelligenza mi fece molto tristo. Ma, quando ne lesi (poi a pochi giorni) il contraddizione, scoppiai dalle risa, e fu ben' contento!

Si! Spero passare molti felici giorni con voi, e caro Forster, e Maclise, in Inghilterra! Spero che pranzeremo, molte volte, al Castello di Giovanni Straw— a Greenwich—a tutti gl'antichi luoghi. Spero che faremo (quando arrivera la stagione d'Autumno) un altro buon' viaggio come quello alle Mine di Cornwall! Bisogna avere pazienza, come se dice; ma, son' tutto pieno d'impazienza a rivedervi,[4] ed abbracciarvi!

Mia moglie, e mia cognata, e tutti i piccolini, stanno bene. Bacciano le mani della Signora vostra sposa, e della bella Maria, e di tutta la vostra famiglia.

Via Saro sempre vostro amico

Dick.

Al Sigr. | Il Sigr. Clarkson Stanfield | Membro dell Accademia Reale.

---

[1] There are several small errors of spelling, grammar, and idiom, but the letter shows a fair command of the language.

[2] Paper damaged by seal.

[3] *Galignani's Messenger* of 25 Apr carried a report (attributed to the *Morning Chronicle*) that "Chalon, Stanfield, Leslie, Christall, Stump, and Ward, have left in the packet-ship *Victoria* for New York, it is understood, to paint the hall of Congress of the United States. There were a large number of people to see them off. They left on the 20th". The issue of 29 Apr carried a denial of the story, reprinted from the *Globe*.

[4] Thus in MS.

To JOHN FORSTER, [12 MAY 1845]

Extracts in F, IV, iv, 335*n*, 342*n*. *Date:* 12 May according to Forster.

About the cook: She will have to go to Florence, I find, to be married in Lord Holland's house: and even then is only married according to the English law: having no legal rights from such a marriage, either in France or Italy. The man hasn't a penny. If there were an opening for a nice clean restaurant in Genoa—which I don't believe there is, for the Genoese have a natural enjoyment of dirt, garlic, and oil—it would still be a very hazardous venture; as the priests will certainly damage the man, if they can, for marrying a Protestant woman. However, the utmost I can do is to take care, if such a crisis should arrive, that she shall not want the means of getting home to England. As my father would observe, she has sown and must reap.

I wish you would suggest to Jerrold for me as a Caudle[1] subject (if he pursue that idea), "Mr. Caudle has incidentally remarked that the housemaid is good-looking."

To T. C. CURRY, 13 MAY 1845

Text from N, I, 676.

Peschiere, Genoa | Tuesday, Thirteenth May, 1845

My Dear Sir,

As there is some mystery in the artful packing of the smaller boxes (which contain some little ornaments that are liable to duty) I think it will be best for them *not* to pass the London Custom House until Roche arrives in town, which will be without doubt the end of June. I will immediately send him to Messrs. Pickernell Brothers.[2] The large box had better stand over too, that they may all be cleared at the same time. It contains wearing apparel and books belonging to me in England, and brought out here in the Musica.

Always faithfully yours
[CHARLES DICKENS]

To CHARLES BLACK, 14 MAY 1845*

MS Mrs E. M. Biden. *Address:* Charles Black Esquire | 13 Via Gregoriana | Roma.[3]

Genoa. | Wednesday Fourteenth May 1845.

My Dear Black

I write in great haste, to get this off by today's post, lest I should play the very

---

[1] "Mrs. Caudle's Curtain Lectures" had been appearing in *Punch* since 11 Jan, and continued until 8 Nov.

[2] Pickernell Brothers, ship and insurance brokers of 159 Fenchurch St. (N reads "Pickernele Brothers" in error). CD's account-book (MS Messrs Coutts) shows a payment to them of £6.1.0. on 5 Aug 45.

[3] Across the top CD has written "Inclosed and re-directed, for fear of Eternal-City-Postmen", and on the next line "More haste worse speed". The letter, with address on back, was then apparently enclosed in a cover, sealed and addressed: "Al Sigr. | Sigr. Carlo Black | 13 Via Gregoriana | Roma".

Capital D— with your arrangements. I have been waiting for a letter from Carrara, before I could decide on the feasibility of meeting you at Pisa on the Twenty Fifth. It has now arrived; and as I shall most probably have a gentleman from the same place staying here at that time on his way to England (from whom we received the greatest attention in our Progress:)[1] I am obliged to deny myself the pleasure—it would have been a real pleasure to me—of seeing you.

Forlorn and wretched Gwilt! If no means of conveyance present themselves before we quit this place, I will leave him at Gibbs's the English Banker's office in the Strada Nuova, under cover for you.

Kate and her sister join with me in all sorts of loves to Mrs. Black and Miss Elderton and the olive branches. Katey is cut to the heart by your son's devotion —the penknife has penetrated into her soul.

Ever Faithfully Yours

Charles Black Esquire   CHARLES DICKENS

To JOHN FORSTER, [?12–17 MAY 1845]

Extract in F, IV, vii, 373*n*. *Date:* The letter from Felton about his wife's death (clearly forwarded by Forster) would not reach CD before about 12 May.

Give my love to Colden, and tell him if he leaves London before I return[2] I will evermore address him and speak of him as *Colonel* Colden.[3] Kate sends *her* love to him also, and we both entreat him to say all the affectionate things he can spare for third parties—using so many himself—when he writes to Mrs. Colden: whom you ought to know, for she, as I have often told you, is BRILLIANT.[4] I would go five hundred miles to see her for five minutes. I am deeply grieved by poor Felton's loss.[5] His letter is manly, and of a most rare kind in the dignified composure and silence of his sorrow.

To JOHN FORSTER, [?17–18 MAY 1845]

Extract in F, IV, vii, 373. *Date:* According to Forster "his next letter" after this was 24 May.

A gentleman of Fletcher's acquaintance living four miles from Genoa had lost his wife; and no attendance on the dead beyond the city gate, nor even any decent conveyance, was practicable. Fletcher nevertheless promised him the sad satisfaction of an English funeral, which he had meanwhile taken enormous secret pains to arrange with a small Genoese upholsterer. The mourner was waited upon, on the appointed morning, by a very bright yellow hackney-coach-and-pair driven by a

---

[1] Mr Walton; see *To* Forster, ?25 Jan 45 and *fn*.

[2] Colden was in London by 14 May (*Macready's Reminiscences*, ed. F. Pollock, 1875, II, 262).

[3] Like Colonel Diver, in *Chuzzlewit*, Ch. 16. Colden's father was a colonel.

[4] Mrs Colden, *née* Frances Wilkes: see Vol. III, p. 80*n*.

[5] Mrs Felton, *née* Mary Whitney, died 12 Apr 45.

coachman in yet brighter scarlet knee-breeches and waistcoat, who wanted to put the husband and the body inside together. They were obliged to leave one of the coach-doors open for the accommodation even of the coffin; the widower walked beside the carriage to the protestant cemetery; and Fletcher followed on a big grey horse.[1]

To THOMAS BEARD, 20 MAY 1845

MS Comtesse de Suzannet. *Address:* Inghilterra. | Thomas Beard Esquire | 42 Portman Place | Edgeware Road | London.

Palazzo Peschiere, Genoa. Twentieth May 1845.

My Dear Bardolph.

This is to give you notice and require you, from and after the end of this next coming month of June, to be and hold yourself in readiness to eat and drink a Sunday Dinner at No. 1 Devonshire Terrace York Gate Regents Park London; on the receipt of a brief and hasty slip of paper, signed sealed and delivered by the Writer hereof. Said Writer purporting to leave the Sunny clime of Italy (respecting which clime, much Gammon is afloat among the subjects of her Britannic Majesty) very early in June next; and to return to his native and admiring country, by the Pass of the Great St. Gothard, and the river of the Rhine.

I take it for granted, my dear Beard, that you have occasionally declaimed, with mingled vehemence and misgiving, against the apparently oblivious memory of the humble Individual who has now the honor to &c. But the life I have led—roaming from place to place, and scene to scene—the objects I have crammed and crowded into my inimitable mind—the gentlemanly vagabond I have been, for the last six or eight months—the extraordinary beds I have slept in—and the bewildering amount of fleas, mosquitoes, bugs, and other Insects I have unwillingly bepastured—these things have hardly left me any leisure in my holiday, until within the last four or five weeks. During the whole of which time I have been employed, chiefly, in lying on my back on sofas, and leaning out of windows and over balconies, in a sort of mild intoxication.

Some of the many things I have seen, and many delights I have had (Venice at their head: and the mournful Roman Campagna shining like moonlight through them all) shall be yours over a glass of average good claret and a "light Cigar" [On reflection, I think that if I mean that for a quotation, it ought to be "Guitar," but never mind.].[2] I wish you could smoke one with me here. The house is considerably larger than Whitehall; and the great room is fifty feet high, and painted all over. It stands in the midst of Terrace Gardens—overlooks the towers and steeples of the town—and comprehends, beyond them, the whole

---

[1] The incident is much more fully described in "Medicine Men of Civilisation", *All the Year Round*, 26 Sep 63 (collected in *The Uncommercial Traveller*, 1868); Fletcher is called "Mr. Kindheart", and the description ends with a reference to Fletcher's own death which is quoted in F, IV, vii, 373*n*.

[2] CD's square brackets. The popular song, "The Light Guitar", by John Barnett: "Oh leave the gay and festive scene" is also quoted by Dick Swiveller and Silas Wegg. It had been parodied by L. Devereaux (?1840) as "The Light Cigar".

blue range of the Mediterranean. There is a perfect forest of orange trees below the windows: which are now in blossom; and the air is sleepy with their fragrance.

Moreover there is a marble bath below stairs, from which in all weathers, cold or warm, wet or dry, the heels of the Inimitable B may be beheld protruding, as the clock strikes 8 every morning.

But I don't intend to be descriptive. I reserve myself. So do Charley and his two sisters; who will rather astonish you, I *think*, with sundry Polka, Mazurka, and other fierce performances. The last one (boy, I mean) is decidedly a success —a perpetual grin is on his face; and in the spoon exercise he is amazing.

Kate and her sister send their loves to *your* sister,[1] and add that they are overjoyed with the expectation of soon seeing her again. They also send their heartiest remembrances to you. Mine wait on all your house—and I am always my Dear Beard—now as ever—in Italy or England—Palaces or postchaises—as a tourist for a twelvemonth, or a mere Pashanger Marjit—

Cordially and faithfully your friend
CHARLES DICKENS

PS You will be glad to hear that The Chimes has been a most sweeping success
PPS. I thought I saw Conway Lingham[2] in the Ruins of the Coliseum—but I couldn't swear it.

To THOMAS MITTON, 20 MAY 1845†

MS Free Library of Philadelphia. *Address:* Inghilterra | Thomas Mitton Esquire | 23 Southampton Buildings | Chancery Lane | London.

Palazzo Peschiere, Genoa. Tuesday Twentieth May | 1845

My Dear Mitton. I received your letter yesterday. I had expected to hear from you sooner; but when I found, day after day, that nothing arrived from Southampton Buildings, I felt sure you were delayed by some cause independent of yourself: and immediately booked the old lady as its head and front.

Kate thinks with you, that Green for the hall and staircase is quite out of the question. I merely mentioned the color without much reflection, as one for which I have a natural partiality. So let it be whatever you and the Decorator think best—not so cold as to be dull, and not so warm as to suffocate the prints.

The Drawing-room Estimate is what Mr. Swiveller calls, a Staggerer.[3] I had no idea it would mount so high. It really should be done; for as it is, it is very poor and mean in comparison with the house—and I have been "going" to do it these five years. But before I quite decide, will you let me know in one line, by return, *about* the cost of the other repairs in the lump. I will write to you by

[1] Catherine Charlotte, Beard's eldest sister: see Vol. III, p. 228 and *n*.
[2] Conway Lingham, actor, playing several seasons at the Theatre Royal, Margate: see *To* Beard, 27 June, 14 July and 12 Aug 47 (N, II, 35, 44, 49); CD probably saw him there in 1842, when "Lingham" was one of the company under J. D. Robins's management (Malcolm Morley, *Margate and its Theatres*, 1966, p. 58).
[3] *Old Curiosity Shop*, Ch. 34.

return again, and if I say "yes", there will be abundant time to get the job done before we arrive, and to get the smell of the paint (in that instance confined to one room) well out of the house. All the work except the drawing-room, will be in hand, I take it for granted, as soon as the old lady turns out.

I don't think you quite do justice to B and E. I don't think you quite understand that the little book is in a very expensive form—that you remember it is not sold at five shillings[1]—or that you sufficiently consider the enormous difference between its [total][2] Profit, and the Carol's.[3] I say nothing about feeling bound to give men some credit for [4] [intending to give so] much to me in the very wide confidence of their agreement.

Every day has shewn me the prudence of my alteration in my [travelling plans. I] could know no more of Paris than I do now—having its general characteristics [already clear in my] mind—unless I resided there, at least a month or two. If I went there now [I could not possibly] prevail upon myself to remain that time: as I am growing anxious to arran[5][ge   If I had] gone there straight, in April, I should have been immediately involved in a [(and] I dare say from the King downwards) of which you can hardly form an idea. [And besides this, all the] materials of my greatest trip into the South, would have been sh[uffled together and] brought home in dire confusion: for my whole time would have been a [But now I have] elaborately *painted* at least three fourths of it:[6] and all the most difficul[t part is already done.] So that if I should determine to use these experiences, they are almost rea[dy now and I shall] be hard at work tomorrow. Add to this, that going to Paris I must have tak[en the route that I] have already travelled; whereas I cross, now, the Great St. Gotherd[7]—the m[ost tremendous pass in] the Alps—and coming down the Rhine (a trip in itself) see some of [   ] curious towns in Germany.

I suppose Letitia really has had a Miscarriage?[8] She ha[d one before that] existed only in my Mother's brain, and led to the dilution of more gu[shing floods of] tears, than any failure of that kind, being real, has probably ever do[ne in the whole history of] the World.

Topping and Co. had better go into the house to take charge of it [and you had better] have Rudkin[9] the Carpenter to take up the carpets: beat them: and p[ut all of them] down in the course of the last week in June. He does this job annually [and knows all about] them and their fittings. Also will you tell him to

---

[1] *The Chimes* was sold at five shillings to the public; either CD is referring to the trade discount or the "not" is an error.

[2] Word of about 5 letters missing here with trace of final ascender: cf. "gross profit" in *To* Mitton, 14 Apr 44.

[3] The rest of the letter is not previously published.

[4] From this point most lines of the letter are damaged, a strip being torn away along the fold, removing between 18 and 24 letters on each line. All words in square brackets are conjectural.

[5] Perhaps some business arrangement with Bradbury & Evans was referred to here.

[6] In letters to Forster after his return to Genoa: "the more important scenes and cities, such as Venice, Rome, and Naples, received such rich filling-in to the first outlines sent, as fairly justified the title of *Pictures* finally chosen for them" (F, IV, vii, 372).

[7] Thus in MS.

[8] CD's sister, Mrs Henry Austin, had no children.

[9] Henry Rudkin, carpenter and builder of 8 Paddington St, Marylebone.

have "Josephine" ([who is to be heard] of at Mr. Brown's our Grocer's in Paddington Street)[1] to clean the house fro[m top to bottom including] paint and wainscoatting. This lady is also employed once a year, and also knows all about it. The process usually occupies eight or ten days. Of course she will not begin until the workmen have finished, or until our arrival is so near, as that we may find her work all fresh and bright. Further, will you tell Topping to lay on the Gardener (he knows where he lives) to come and put the garden into perfect order, and afterwards to attend once a week as usual. I think there should be a coat of gravel on the walks; and if he [wants to put any plant]s in—he may. But I should wish this head of expence, certainly not to exceed [£   including the fi]lling of the boxes for the Drawing-room windows, with the Stocks and other things [that he knows about. Sn]oxell[2] in Chancery Lane may be sent to take down all the blinds, and clean, and [put them back. He] also is acquainted with his duties, and experienced in their discharge.

[All this app]ears, on paper, to be the Devil's own quantity of trouble: and I am afraid it will [be a world of trouble of]f paper. I shall be truly pleased to see you once more; and have pretty strong [hopes that you will find the] Caravan in blooming order. I was afraid we should lose our Cook, who was going to [be married but *his* religion] is in the way of a lawful and binding performance of the Ceremony with a Protestant, [so we are still] in hopes that she will return. Not only on her own account (for she would certainly be [unhappy) but because sh]e is a most capital Servant. I have some misgivings that she speaks Italian better than [I do, or at least mo]re fluently. Ever Faithfully CD.

To EMILE DE LA RUE, [22 MAY 1845]*

MS Berg Collection. *Date:* endorsed by de la Rue "Fête Dieu Juin 1845"; Corpus Christi fell on 22 May in 1845, and "Juin" is obviously de la Rue's error.

Just out of the Bath | Thursday Morning

My Dear De la Rue

Roche will see to the carriage. We will come to the Show in good time. Many thanks for your note.

Ever Yours
CD.

To EMILE DE LA RUE, 24 MAY 1845

MS Mr S. A. Rochlin.

Saturday Twenty Fourth May | 1845

My Dear De la Rue.

Mr. Walton has glimmerings of business engagements with Mr. Curry tomorrow morning; so I think it best to send you timely notice that we will *not* walk. Unless you have other plans for yourself and tell me so at the opera[3]

---

[1] John Brown, grocer, 53 Paddington St.
[2] William Snoxell, 96 Regent's Quadrant and 131 Chancery Lane, window-blind maker: see Vol. I, p. 608 and *n*.

[3] The season at the Teatro Carlo Felice had begun 24 Mar and between then and 30 June the programme included *Bonifazio dei Geremei, I Due Foscari, La Sonnambula,*

tonight: perhaps you might as well make your magnetic start,[1] tomorrow instead of Monday. But all times are alike to me.

Ever Faithfully Yours

à Monsieur M. De la Rue   CHARLES DICKENS

To JOHN FORSTER, [24 MAY 1845]

Extract in F, IV, vii, 374. *Date:* 24 May according to Forster.

He wrote of two English travellers who had taken a portion of the ground floor of the Peschiere. They had with them a meek English footman who immediately confided to CD's servants that he was made to do everything, even cooking, in crimson breeches; which in a hot climate, he protested, was "a grinding of him down." He is a poor soft country fellow; and his master locks him up at night, in a basement room with iron bars to the window. Between which our servants poke wine in, at midnight. His master and mistress buy old boxes at the curiosity shops, and pass their lives in lining 'em with bits of parti-coloured velvet. A droll existence, is it not? We are lucky to have had the palace to ourselves until now, but it is so large that we never see or hear these people; and I should not have known even, if they had not called upon us, that another portion of the ground floor had been taken by some friends of old Lady Holland[2]—whom I seem to see again, crying about dear Sydney Smith, behind that green screen as we last saw her together.[3]

To MISS GEORGINA HOGARTH, [?11 APRIL–30 MAY 1845]*

MS Huntington Library. *Date:* endorsed by Georgina "First two letters I receive from C.D. | *Genoa 1845*" (for the first see 4 Feb 45); the latest possible Friday is 30 May. *Address:* Miss Hogarth.

Peschiere | Friday Evening

My Dear Georgy

Unless there should be some reason beyond my comprehension, for *your* staying where you are, I really think you had best come home to dinner. Do as you will.

Affecy. CD.

I Lombardi alla prima crociata, and *Adelia* (Ambrogio Brocca, *Il Teatro Carlo Felice*, Genoa, 1898, p. 46).

[1] CD was presumably teaching de la Rue to magnetize his wife in view of his own impending departure. Christiana Thompson recorded in her Journal, 1 Jan 46: "M. de la Rue mesmerised me—at least as far as to prove I should be an excellent subject for experiments"; she added that the Pope had forbidden the practice and "we must never speak of it openly here" (MS Mrs Sowerby).

[2] In fact, her daughter by her first marriage and her grand-daughter (as CD

must have said in this letter). Lady Pellew, *née* Harriet Webster (?1793–1849), married Sir Fleetwood Pellew, son of Lord Exmouth, in 1816; her only daughter Harriet Bettina Frances (1820–86) married Horatio William Walpole in 1841, but the marriage was shortly to break up; for Lord Walpole's ill-treatment of her, see *To* Mrs CD, 3 Oct 53 (*Mr & Mrs CD*, ed. W. Dexter, p. 201), and for CD's meeting with her and her mother in Geneva, see *To* Forster, ?10 Oct 46.

[3] In Dec 44, when Smith was already seriously ill; CD had of course not seen her since his death in Feb.

To JOHN FORSTER, [1 and 2 JUNE 1845]

Extracts in F, IV, vii, 374–5; F, 1872–4, II, v, 89*n*; F, IV, vii, 375. *Date:* according to Forster, first extract 1 June; second extract 2 June; third extract, ending of same letter as first extract.

He began by saying that his letter had been twice begun and twice flung into the basket, so great was his indisposition to write as the time for departure came.

He described how an English ship of war, the Fantôme, appeared in the harbour; and from her commander, Sir Frederick Nicolson,[1] *he received, among attentions very pleasant to him, an invitation to lunch on board and bring his wife, for whom, at a time appointed, a boat was to be sent to the Ponte Reale. But no boat being there at the time, CD sent off his servant in another boat to the ship to say he feared some mistake.* While we were walking up and down a neighbouring piazza in his absence, a brilliant fellow in a dark blue shirt with a white hem to it all round the collar, regular corkscrew curls, and a face as brown as a berry, comes up to me and says, "Beg your pardon sir—Mr. Dickens?" "Yes." "Beg your pardon sir, but I'm one of the ship's company of the Phantom sir, cox'en of the cap'en's gig sir, she's a lying off the pint sir—been there half an hour." "Well but my good fellow," I said, "you're at the wrong place!" "Beg your pardon sir, I was afeerd it was the wrong place sir, but I've asked them Genoese here sir, twenty times if it was Port Real; and they knows no more than a dead jackass!"—Isn't it a good thing to have made a regular Portsmouth name of it?

I saw last night an old palazzo of the Doria,[2] six miles from here, upon the sea, which De la Rue urged Fletcher to take for us, when he was bent on that detestable villa Bagnerello; which villa the Genoese have hired, time out of mind, for one fourth of what I paid, as they told him again and again before he made the agreement. This is one of the strangest old palaces in Italy, surrounded by beautiful *woods* of great trees (an immense rarity here) some miles in extent: and has upon the terrace a high tower, formerly a prison for offenders against the family, and a defence against the pirates. The present Doria lets it as it stands for £40 English—for the year ... And the grounds are no expense; being proudly maintained by the Doria, who spends this rent, when he gets it, in repairing the roof and windows. It is a wonderful house;[3] full of the most unaccountable pictures and most incredible furniture: every room in it like the most quaint and fanciful of Cattermole's pictures; and how many rooms I am afraid to say.

[1] "the Phantom", and "Sir Henry Nicholson", in F, 1872–4, II, viii, 168; corrected by Forster, III, 519. Sir Frederick William Erskine Nicolson, Bart (1815–99), commander, RN, commanded the 16-gun *Fantôme* from Dec 44 to May 46.

[2] Not the Palazzo Doria Pamfili, situated within the Porta della Lanterna, which was uninhabitable, but the Villa Doria at Pegli, on the coast road about six miles off.

[3] The Villa Doria was built by Adamo Centurione; house and surroundings are clearly recalled in "To be Read at Dusk", contributed by CD to the *Keepsake*, 1852: "on the road to Nice ... an old palace, with great gardens ... a little dark and gloomy, being close surrounded by trees; but ... spacious, ancient, grand, on the sea shore" —an appropriate setting for the eerie story related by the Genoese courier Giovanni Baptista.

The fire-flies at night now, are miraculously splendid; making another firmament among the rocks on the sea-shore, and the vines inland. They get into the bedrooms, and fly about, all night, like beautiful little lamps. . . . I have surrendered much I had fixed my heart upon, as you know, admitting you have had reason for not coming to us here: but I stand by the hope that you and Mac will come and meet us at Brussels; it being so very easy. A day or two there, and at Antwerp, would be very happy for us;[1] and we could still dine in Lincoln's-inn-fields on the day of arrival.

To T. YEATS BROWN, 3 JUNE 1845

MS Mrs R. E. Yeats Brown.

Peschiere | Tuesday Evening June Third 1845

My Dear Sir

I must beg you—with the greatest reluctance—to excuse me this Evening.[2]

It has only this moment come to my knowledge that you expect guests whom I have never seen or heard of in my life. If I knew them I have no doubt I should be as happy to read to them as I should be to read to you; but I do not know them; and I have an invincible repugnance to that kind of exhibition which an otherwise pleasant recreation becomes under such circumstances. It may be a natural and rational dislike or it may be very much beside the mark. But I have it.

I am truly sorry that I did not explain this general objection of mine more explicitly to you, some days ago. But I thought in the first instance that you would perhaps infer it from my dislike to reading out of my own house. And I felt sure you were in full possession of it, when Mrs. Browne[3] proposed to make a special exception in the case of Lady Pellew and her daughter. To which I was unfeignedly glad to assent.

It is no fault of mine, but rests solely with Mrs. Dickens, that I write to you at so late a moment. It is not ten minutes since she told me what you told her of your arrangements, last Sunday.[4]

Always My Dear Sir | Faithfully Yours

T. Yeats Brown Esquire

CHARLES DICKENS

[1] For the week spent there, see *To* de la Rue, 29 June 45 and *fn*. CD had been there with Catherine and Browne in July 37: see Vol. I, pp. 280–1.

[2] CD had agreed to read the *Carol* to a party at Yeats Brown's—at first, evidently, to a family group; Yeats Brown then proposed to invite Lady Pellew and Lady Walpole. Catherine wrote to Mrs Yeats Brown: "I have communicated the contents of your note to Charles, and in reply to it he desires me to say that as he has made up his mind to read the Christmas Carol *through*, instead of any detached pieces from his other works, he has no objection

to your inviting Lady Pellew. He feels so much, he says, the want of effect and interest in the extracts that it is in fact for that reason he has so long deferred fixing the evening for the reading, but he is sure he can make a very effective thing of the Carol. Will you tell Mr. Brown this is his *decided* conclusion" (F. Yeats-Brown, "Dickens in Genoa", *Spectator*, 22 Sep 1928). Subsequently, as the present letter shows, Yeats Brown wished to add strangers to the party, and CD protested.

[3] Thus in MS.

[4] The reading took place, "to a select circle", and was recalled by the younger

To MADAME DE LA RUE, [?16 APRIL–4 JUNE 1845]†

MS University of Texas. *Date:* 1845, after his return to Genoa—since the visitor
was someone CD had met at Naples. *Address:* Madame De la Rue.

Peschiere. | Wednesday Morning
My Dear Madame De la Rue.

I have a man from Naples—come, and going, by the Mongibello—here, to
whom I am forced to pay some attention in the way of shewing him the town.
Consequently; and with a bad grace, I assure you; I am obliged to deny myself
the pleasure of coming to you this Morning.

Kate and Georgy will leave here at a quarter before 2, and will come straight
to you.

Ever Believe me | Faithfully Yours
Madame De la Rue.   CHARLES DICKENS

*a*Since sealing this, your note has come. Mrs. D will change her time
accordingly.*a*

To CHARLES RIDGWAY,[1] 5 JUNE 1845*

MS Fales Collection, New York University Library.

Palazzo Peschiere, Genoa. | Thursday June 5th 1845.

My Dear Sir

As we cannot possibly think of invading you in our ruthless numbers, I
make up the parcel containing your books, today. We leave here on Monday next;
and you will receive this by the trustiest hands I can find, when we are passing
near to your retreat. When it reaches you, we shall be upon our road to the
Mountain.

We are all quite well. Not forgetful in any degree of your kind hospitality at
Naples: and anticipating the pleasure of seeing you in England.

Mrs. Dickens and her sister unite in kindest regards.

I am Ever | Faithfully Yours
Charles Ridgway Esquire   CHARLES DICKENS

---

son, Frederick Yeats Brown(*b.* 1837): "His
table was placed near the door leading from
the middle drawing-room, and on it stood
a reading lamp, a glass of water and a paper
bag of raisins;—this at his request. The
guests sat all round the room, which was
lighted by a large Venetian glass chandelier,
with wax candles, hanging from the ceiling".
The elder son, Monty (*b.* 1834), also recalled that CD was extremely nervous and
insisted that no one should sit behind him

(F. A. Y. Brown, *Family Notes*; John
Evelyn Wrench, *Francis Yeats-Brown,
1886–1944,* 1948, p. 5).

aa Not previously published.

[1] "A great man at Naples" with a villa
at Como: see *To* D'Orsay, 26 Sep 45;
mentioned again in *To* Mme de la Rue,
27 Sep 45, and *To* Mrs CD, 4 and 14 Nov
53 (*Mr and Mrs CD*, ed. Walter Dexter,
pp. 204, 208; misprinted "Ridgney").

To JOHN FORSTER, [7 JUNE 1845]

Extracts in F, IV, vii, 375–6, 372. *Date:* both extracts 7 June according to Forster, who calls it "his last letter from Genoa".

They are all at sixes and sevens up at the Peschiere,[1] as you may suppose; and Roche is in a condition of tremendous excitement, engaged in settling the inventory with the house-agent, who has just told me he is the devil himself. I had been appealed to, and had contented myself with this expression of opinion, "Signor Noli, you are an old impostor!"[2] "Illustrissimo," said Signor Noli in reply, "your servant is the devil himself: sent on earth to torture me." I look occasionally towards the Peschiere (it is visible from this room), expecting to see one of them flying out of a window. Another great cause of commotion is, that they have been paving the lane by which the house is approached, ever since we returned from Rome. We have not been able to get the carriage up since that time, in consequence; and unless they finish to-night, it can't be packed in the garden, but the things will have to be brought down in baskets, piecemeal, and packed in the street. To avoid this inconvenient necessity, the Brave made proposals of bribery to the paviours last night, and induced them to pledge themselves that the carriage should come up at seven this evening. The manner of doing that sort of paving work here, is to take a pick or two with an axe, and then lie down to sleep for an hour. When I came out, the Brave had issued forth to examine the ground; and was standing alone in the sun among a heap of prostrate figures: with a Great Despair depicted in his face, which it would be hard to surpass. It was like a picture—"After the Battle—Napoleon by the Brave: Bodies by the Paviours."

I am in as great doubt as you about the letters I have written you with these Italian experiences. I cannot for the life of me devise any plan of using them to my own satisfaction, and yet think entirely with you that in some form I ought to use them.[3]

To EMILE DE LA RUE, 8 JUNE 1845*

MS Miss Gladys Storey.

Sunday June Eighth 1845.

She called out to me suddenly, today, that I, being in England, must be mindful to magnetize her on the *23rd. of December*[4] at 11 in the forenoon for a quarter

[1] CD was staying with the de la Rues at the Brignole Rosso, "into which he had fled from the miseries of moving" (F, IV, vii, 375).

[2] Murray's *Handbook for ... Northern Italy* recommends "Signor Noli" as the best house-agent "and an honest man".

[3] Possibly CD was hesitating between a volume of letters presented as such, and a travel-book based on them. But within the next month, if not before, report of an intended book had spread: one of Thackeray's letters to the *Calcutta Star* (signed "Squab"), dated 7 July, said: "Talking of Satire and Italy, Boz has just come back to London with a book full of both, as report says—and those who have heard portions of his book speak in high terms of it. He doesn't meddle with art or antiquities, wisely enough, but describes what he sees before him, and who can describe so well?" ("*Letters from a Club Arm-Chair:*

of an hour; and must on no account omit or forget it! It seems so odd, that it may be worth preserving. I write it down, in order that there may be no possibility of her overhearing the least allusion to the subject.

CD

To ANGUS FLETCHER, 8 JUNE 1845

Extract in George D. Smith catalogue, 1901; mention in Carnegie Book Shop catalogue No. 84; *MS* 2 pp.; dated 8 June 45.

In all the hustle and bustle of this most momentous of moments with everybody everywhere and yet nowhere—and the Carriage packing at the Door for 8 o'clock to-morrow morning. I scratch a line to you to send the loves of my ladies and babbies and the parting regard of my inimitable self.

To JOHN FORSTER, [15 JUNE 1845]

Extracts in F, IV, vii, 376–7, 381. *Date:* For the first extract Forster gives 14 June, but the reference to reaching Altdorf "yesterday afternoon" (see below) shows that 15 June is correct; CD probably wrote "14 June" in error (see next). Second extract called "the letter from Lucerne", clearly the same. *From* Lucerne.

We came over the St. Gothard,[1] which has been open only eight days.[2] The road is cut through the snow, and the carriage winds along a narrow path between two massive snow walls, twenty feet high or more. Vast plains of snow range up the mountain-sides above the road, itself seven thousand feet above the sea; and tremendous waterfalls, hewing out arches for themselves in the vast drifts, go thundering down from precipices into deep chasms, here and there and everywhere: the blue water tearing through the white snow with an awful beauty that is most sublime. The pass itself, the mere pass over the top, is not so fine, I think, as the Simplon; and there is no plain upon the summit,[3] for the moment it is reached the descent begins. So that the loneliness and wildness of the Simplon are not equalled *there*. But being much higher, the ascent and the descent range over a much greater space of country; and on both sides there are

William Makepeace Thackeray", ed. Henry Summerfield, *Nineteenth Century Fiction*, XVIII [1963], 233). By 3 Nov CD had decided to publish his "Series of the Italian letters" in the *Daily News*: see *To* Bradbury & Evans, that day.

[4] At the foot of the page de la Rue has written: "I told him that it corresponded with the first day that she was mesmerized last year by him, of which circumstance he had not thought at first. On the 23.X. [*error for* xii] the effect took place upon her from 11 to ½ past [*two words illegible*] most uncomfortable day I don't know whether D. mesmerized her on that day in London".

[1] At one time the most frequented pass—

since it was the most direct route from Basle and Zurich to Milan and Genoa— St Gothard had lost much traffic to the Simplon and St Bernard until the new carriage-road was finally completed in 1841, when it was described by Murray as "excellent" though "not well fenced" (*Handbook for . . . Switzerland*, 1843).

[2] The higher passes were not usually clear of snow before the middle of June.

[3] Described by Murray as "a scene of the most complete sterility and desolation". It is only a hundred feet higher than the St Bernard, but the ascent and descent are steeper.

places of terrible grandeur, unsurpassable, I should imagine, in the world. The Devil's Bridge, terrific! The whole descent between Andermatt (where we slept on Friday night)[1] and Altdorf, William Tell's town,[2] which we passed through yesterday afternoon, is the highest sublimation of all you can imagine in the way of Swiss scenery.[3] Oh God! what a beautiful country it is![4] How poor and shrunken, beside it, is Italy in its brightest aspect!

I look upon the coming down from the Great St. Gothard with a carriage and four horses and only one postilion, as the most dangerous thing that a carriage and horses can do. We had two great wooden logs for drags, and snapped them both like matches. The road is like a geometrical staircase,[5] with horrible depths beneath it; and at every turn it is a toss-up, or seems to be, whether the leaders shall go round or over. The lives of the whole party may depend upon a strap in the harness; and if we broke our rotten harness once yesterday, we broke it at least a dozen times. The difficulty of keeping the horses together in the continual and steep circle, is immense. They slip and slide, and get their legs over the traces, and are dragged up against the rocks; carriage, horses, harness, all a confused heap. The Brave, and I, and the postilion, were constantly at work, in extricating the whole concern from a tangle, like a skein of thread. We broke two thick iron chains, and crushed the box of a wheel, as it was; and the carriage is now undergoing repair, under the window, on the margin of the lake: where a woman in short petticoats, a stomacher, and two immensely long tails of black hair hanging down her back very nearly to her heels, is looking on— apparently dressed for a melodrama, but in reality a waitress at this establishment.

If the Swiss villages[6] looked beautiful to me in winter, their summer aspect is most charming: most fascinating: most delicious. Shut in by high mountains capped with perpetual snow; and dotting a rich carpet of the softest turf, overshadowed by great trees; they seem so many little havens of refuge from the roubles and miseries of great towns. The cleanliness of the little baby-houses of tnns is wonderful to those who come from Italy. But the beautiful Italian imanners, the sweet language, the quick recognition of a pleasant look or cheerful

---

[1] 13 June, the fifth night of the journey. Three of the nights would be spent at Milan, Como, and Faido (*Pictures*, p. 269, and *To* Cunyngham, 21 Aug 45); the additional night was probably at Bellinzona, between Como and Faido, unless they stopped between Genoa and Milan. From Zurich (16 June) they went "to Frankfurt, and so down the Rhine to Cologne, and thence to Brussels" (see *To* Cunyngham, 21 Aug).

[2] Where Tell shot the apple, in the square.

[3] Murray speaks of "desolation and awful grandeur" and "stern but magnificent scenery", and gives the history of the old and the new Devil's Bridge, saying that the latter had deprived the scene of "much

of its terror and sublimity"; the old bridge was "a thin segment of a circle, spanning a terrific abyss", which had "an air at once of boldness and fragility."

[4] "The country was so divine that he should have wondered indeed if its sons and daughters had ever been other than a patriotic people" (F, IV, vii, 376).

[5] "A series of complicated zigzag terraces, first on one side of the Reuss and then on the other" (Murray).

[6] They would also pass through Giornico, Airolo, Hospenthal and Wasen (near the Devil's Bridge). They took the journey at a leisurely pace; Murray says that in the reverse direction, from Lucerne to Lake Maggiore, it could be done in $1\frac{1}{2}$ to 2 days.

word; the captivating expression of a desire to oblige in everything; are left behind the Alps. Remembering them, I sigh for the dirt again: the brick floors, bare walls, unplaistered ceilings, and broken windows.

Did I ever tell you the details of my theatrical idea,[1] before? Strange, that I should have quite forgotten it. I had an odd fancy, when I was reading the unfortunate little farce[2] at Covent-garden, that Bartley looked as if some struggling recollection and connection were stirring up within him—but it may only have been his doubts of that humorous composition.

To EMILE DE LA RUE, [16 JUNE 1845]*

MS Berg Collection. *Date:* Monday was 16 June in 1845; PM, 17 June 45, confirms. *Address:* A Monsieur | Monsr. Emile De la Rue | Messrs. De la Rue freres | Genes | Italie.

My Dear De la Rue. I have written as cheerfully as I can.[3] I am very anxious to hear from you, and to know exactly how she is. Therefore I am growing weary for Brussels. I hope to write you at greater length then; but from my own home, certainly. I think of you always. The best part of me is in Genoa shaking hands with you. I have only the dregs here.

Ever Faithfully
CD

Zurich | Monday Night 15th. June

Late. All well, and all asleep.

To JOHN FORSTER, [?16–21 JUNE 1845]

Extract in F, IV, vii, 375*n. Date:* "During his travel home" according to Forster; probably not before 16 June, as CD had received Forster's reply to his letter of ?1–2 June (see *fn*), and unlikely to be after 21 June since they were meeting a few days later.

Odd enough that remark of yours.[4] I had been wondering at Rome that Juvenal[5] (which I have been always lugging out of a bag, on all occasions) never used the fire-flies for an illustration. But even now, they are only partially seen; and nowhere I believe in such enormous numbers as on the Mediterranean coast-road, between Genoa and Spezzia.[6] I will ascertain for curiosity's sake, whether there are any at this time in Rome, or between it and the country-house

---

[1] See *To* Forster, 28 Dec–1 Jan 45, and *fns*.

[2] *The Lamplighter:* see Vol. I, p. 465*n*.

[3] Presumably an enclosure to Mme de la Rue, now lost.

[4] Something that Forster had said in his reply to CD's letter of ?1–2 June, referring to the fireflies at Genoa; one or both of them may also have mentioned Rogers's poem "The Fire-fly" (*Italy*, 1830) which associates them with Tivoli and Horace.

[5] The 1711 edn of *Translations of Juvenal* by Dryden and others was in the Gad's Hill library.

[6] In *Pictures*, pp. 145–6, describing the same coast road, CD says it is "famous, in the warm season . . . for fireflies".

of Mæcenas[1]—on the ground of Horace's journey.[2] I know there is a place on the French side of Genoa, where they begin at a particular boundary-line, and are never seen beyond it. . . . All wild to see you at Brussels! What a meeting we will have, please God!

To EMILE DE LA RUE, 29 JUNE 1845*

MS Miss Gladys Storey. *Address:* A Monsieur | Monsr. Emile de la Rue | Messrs. De la Rue freres, | Genes | Italie.

Hotel de l'Europe, Brussels. | Sunday June Twenty Ninth 1845.

My Dear De la Rue. I safely received your kind notes and enclosures, both at Mayence and Cologne. The last, as you surmised, was from Fletcher. Poor fellow! He seemed so heavy in his mind, that the Post Office might have charged it as a double letter. The other was from a gentleman unknown, who has written a Poem called Job—and the Reader, in the perusal, represents Job in a very lively manner.

I *am* responsible for that opinion of which you find yourself possessed, in reference to Madame De la Rue's condition. It is, on the whole, quite as favorable as I have ever expected. And I have strong reason, I think, for holding that whenever I mesmerize her again, I shall find the power of the Agency which has, God be thanked!, done her so much good—greatly increased and intensified. I have little doubt of that; if any. With a lightened spirit, I find too, from her letter, that the *moral* influence gained over the Shadows, *exceeds* even my previous knowledge of it. I compare her present feeling on that subject, with her feeling when I first went to Rome; and regard the change as only short of miraculous. I believe it impossible to exaggerate the alteration of her Mind— where incalculably the greatest torment and greatest danger used to lie. She tells me that she has seen a Shadow for an instant—the Shadow of the Bad Shadow—passing in a great hurry: escaping observation; hanging its head; and nearly worn away. I like that even better than I should have liked her not seeing anything. If it should return, we know she is to be cured, with God's leave, beyond all question.

I feel how natural it is, that you should be grieved at not being able to exert the influence. But it dwells with this person and does not dwell with that person, unaccountably; and we must forget that source of regret, in the gratification of knowing (you and I) that she *can* be affected by somebody—that she has been rescued from great suffering, and still greater danger—and that if the disease should return (I hope otherwise, however) the World may be a wide one,

---

[1] Formerly identified with a villa at Tivoli—for instance, in Simond's *Tour*, p. 367, and Eustace's *Tour in Italy* (6th edn, 1821, II, 238). But Murray, *Handbook for . . . Central Italy*, 1843, admitted that serious doubt had been cast on this identification, and it has since been entirely discredited.

[2] From Rome to Tivoli (the "Tibur" of *Epistles*, I, 7, and elsewhere); but CD may possibly have confused it with the journey to Brindisium (*Satires*, I, 5) on which Horace met Maecenas at Anxur. Horace nowhere mentions fireflies.

but is not so wide still, as to keep us hopelessly asunder. Believe me, and understand it once for all, that no occupation of any sort or kind can change or affect the intensity of my desire to do her good. And if, at any future time my Dear De la Rue, you ever say to me that you have a grain of doubt or delicacy in demanding of me such help as I can render, I will blot you out from all possibility of forgiveness or kind construction, and will say within myself that I have utterly mistaken you, and you are the most notable Humbug, Imposter,[1] and Hypocrite I have ever known or heard of. And to speak more seriously on this most serious theme, I should, in my serious breast, think ill of you, and consider that you thought all this of me, if you should ever falter, for an instant, in putting me to the proof, or in believing with fullest confidence that I should respond with Great Joy of Heart. Ours is not a common knowledge of each other. Let us always remember it; and act as if we did.[2]

It is clear to me that Miss Holdscamp[3] does not love her lover. I am slow to come to the conclusion, for I should have liked her to love him; but in such a case a woman's observation is invariably right—hardly seems to possess the faculty of being wrong; Nature having ordered it otherwise. And you may rely upon it—Madame De la Rue's suspicion in that wise, is the true one. I have no more doubt about it, than I have that I am not standing on my head at this moment—and I distinctly see my boots on the carpet, I assure you.

Mr. Forster is here, and Mr. Maclise; and another Gentleman named Jerrold,[4] who is a clever author as perhaps you know. Forster is quite well. He looks thinner, and roars out sometimes, without any notice, in consequence of rheumatic twinges in one of his knees. But I hope he is quite right, notwithstanding. He is highly complimentary (of course) to Peel. Whom we have been anathematizing with extreme good will, for two days.[5] We are going to Ghent tomorrow —to Bruges next day—to Ostend next day—and across, and home, on Thursday. I will begin to send you the Examiner on the following Monday: and will write to you again soon. They are all gone to Antwerp today. I stayed here, to write to Madame De la Rue and you, and read your letters in peace. I had no heart to go with them, for I can't forget our Italian wanderings, or dear old Genoa. I never shall.

Well! You must come to England. That's clear. And I must come back to Genoa too. I shall think of both arrangements, and try to establish myself in a gayer mood in my own room. Don't say anything about it—but if I can find anybody to make a good little sketch in water colors of that mysterious chamber,

---

[1] Thus in MS.

[2] These two sentences squeezed in at end of paragraph as an afterthought.

[3] CD's error for "Holskamp". See *To de la Rue*, 28 July 45 and *fn*.

[4] CD recalled this meeting in a letter to Blanchard Jerrold after his father's death: "He was the delight of the children all the time, and they were his delight. He was in his most brilliant spirits, and I doubt if he were ever more humorous in his life" (N, II, 75).

[5] Throughout the summer the *Examiner*, like most of the press, had been attacking Peel; on 21 June 45 the leader-writer found it particularly "presumptuous" in him to criticize Lord John Russell for supporting Villiers's anti-Corn Law motion, in view of his own inconsistency: "His whole career in office has been a series of changes jarring and revolting to the party that raised him to power".

with the Inimitable B at his usual little table, I shall have it done, when I get home, that some friends of mine in a Red Palace may know how I am lodged on working days.

I can't forget Rome—and Albano—and Florence—and Perugia—and the walks uphill—and you alone, inside the big carriage, with great books dashing out your brains[1]—and Michele and Roche swearing eternal hostility on Monday, and Eternal Friendship on Tuesday—and the queer Inns—and our happy company. I can't forget anything connected with it. I live in the Past now, in sober sadness.

> Ever My Dear De la Rue, notwithstanding, | Faithfully Yours
> CHARLES DICKENS

I take it for granted that you *did* hear from me at Zurich, after the date of your last?

To GEORGE SCOTT, [?JULY 1845]

Mention in W. T. Spencer catalogue, undated, in Fitzgerald Collection at Eastgate House, Rochester. "Date torn off" according to catalogue. *From* Devonshire Terrace; addressed to Scott at Rome. *Date:* possibly soon after return to England.

Speaks of Mr. Black and asks if he is to be made a cardinal.

To MESSRS CHAPMAN & HALL, 5 JULY 1845*

MS Free Library of Philadelphia.

Devonshire Terrace | Saturday Morning | Fifth July 1845.

My Dear Sirs

Will you have the goodness to give the Bearer a Proof of my Portrait by Mr. Maclise? I have promised to send as good a one as I could get, to a friend abroad.[2]

I don't know whether you may happen to have any impressions of that earlier head by Mr. Lawrence.[3] If you should possess any, will you also send me one of those?

> Faithfully Yours
> CHARLES DICKENS

Messrs. Chapman and Hall.

To COUNT D'ORSAY, 5 JULY 1845*

MS Comte de Gramont. *Date:* PM 5 July 45.

Devonshire Terrace. | Saturday Morning

My Dear Count D'Orsay.

Once more in my own house!—If that can be called mine, which is such a heap of hideous confusion, and chaos of boxes.

---

[1] See *To* Forster, ?May 44, *fn.*
[2] Probably de la Rue.
[3] See Vol. I, p. 395*n*; probably the second of Lawrence's portraits.

I am going into the country tomorrow,[1] but promise myself the long-expected pleasure of seeing you and Lady Blessington on Monday morning. In the meanwhile, as you have been so kind as to demand personal inspection of my gem of Couriers I will send him to Gore House tomorrow (Sunday) at Twelve o'Clock, with my card in his hand.

He can do anything; and is willing at all times and seasons to do everything. I really believe him to be one of the most honest and excellent servants in the World. His face is a good letter of recommendation, but it leaves the man himself at an immense distance behind. If I could afford to keep him, and had duties for an upper servant to discharge, I wouldn't part with him for the weight of his head (though its[2] a large one) in refined Gold.[3]

With best regards to Lady Blessington, and the Miss Powers,

Ever believe me | Most Heartily Yours

Le Comte D'Orsay.   CHARLES DICKENS

To DAVID COLDEN, 6 JULY 1845

Extract in Merwin-Clayton sales catalogue, Oct 1906; MS 2 pp.; dated Devonshire Terrace, 6 July 45.

I am unwilling[ly][4] obliged to defer our engagement until we shall have an opportunity of concerting another appointment that may suit your engagements. I am obliged to go out this morning on business, and the interval between would be hardly long enough for our purpose. What say you to Tuesday at 12? I will come to you then, if you say yes.

To MESSRS BRADBURY & EVANS, 7 JULY 1845

MS Dickens House.

Devonshire Terrace | Monday Seventh July 1845.

My Dear Bradbury and Evans.

Mr. Forster is not sure whether he has or has not spoken to you about a certain young man[5] whom I begged him (writing from Genoa) to recommend to you, in case you wanted a trustworthy person of good appearance and manners in any of the new arrangements.

He is going to marry one of our nurses, who has been with us six years. He has been servant to Sir George Crawford, whom I know, and who gives him the very best of characters. He has lived with that gentleman nine years, and quits

---

[1] Perhaps to Blackheath to see his parents.

[2] Thus in MS.

[3] D'Orsay's reply of 6 July expressed his and Lady Blessington's joy at CD's return: "Voici, thank God, Devonshire Place réssuscité. Venez luncheoner demain à 1 heure, et amenez notre brave ami Forster",

and promised help in finding a position for "la perle fine des couriers"; in a postscript he added: "J'ai vu le courier, c'est le tableau de l'honnêteté, et de la bonne humeur. Don't forget to be here at one to-morrow, with Forster" (F, v, i, 379*n*).

[4] Catalogue reads "unwilling &".

[5] Johnson: see *To* Maclise, 9 May 45.

his service, on account of this Matrimonial speculation. He comes of very respectable people—can read and write, and so forth very well—and understands Italian, and I think French, to boot, if that be any additional recommendation.

He will be in town in a few days: both his late Master and I have it very much at heart to get him some occupation which will enable the young couple to make a tolerably fair start. I can think of nothing better than writing to you; but do not take the trouble to write again, as I shall see you on Thursday.

I needn't add that I know enough both of him and his intended, to be sure of their being worthy of all trust and recommendation; and that I have the greatest interest in their well-doing.

Always Faithfully Yours

Messrs. Bradbury and Evans. CD

To MESSRS CHAPMAN & HALL, 7 JULY 1845*

MS Colonel Richard Gimbel.

Devonshire Terrace | Monday Morning Seventh July | 1845.

Dear Sirs

I am very much obliged to you for the offer of your own Impression of Mr. Lawrence's portrait. But I really do not so much care to send that particular print to my friend, that I need deprive you of it. I do not thank you the less.

We are all quite well.

Faithfully Yours

Messrs. Chapman and Hall. CHARLES DICKENS

To COUNT D'ORSAY, [7 JULY 1845]

MS Free Library of Philadelphia. *Date:* endorsed in unknown hand 7 July 1845, and clearly just after D'Orsay had seen Roche.

Devonshire Terrace | Monday Night

My Dear Count D'Orsay.

A Hundred Thousand thanks to you. I will send the Unexceptionable to 9 Grosvenor Place[1] tomorrow Morning, and will tell you the result as soon as I know it.

Ever Believe me | Cordially Your friend

Le Comte D'Orsay. CHARLES DICKENS

To JOHN FORSTER, [?EARLY JULY 1845]

Extract in F, v, i, 378–9. *Date:* "his first letter" after his return according to Forster; probably in the first week.

I really think I have an idea, and not a bad one, for the periodical.[2] I have turned it over, the last two days, very much in my mind: and think it positively good. I incline still to weekly; price three halfpence, if possible; partly original

---

[1] The residence of George Dodd, MP for Maidstone: see *To* D'Orsay, 26 July 45.

[2] Forster says this letter "revived a subject on which opinions had been from time

partly select; notices of books, notices of theatres, notices of all good things, notices of all bad ones; *Carol* philosophy, cheerful views, sharp anatomization of humbug, jolly good temper; papers always in season, pat to the time of year; and a vein of glowing, hearty, generous, mirthful, beaming reference in everything to Home, and Fireside. And I would call it, sir,—

> ## THE CRICKET
> A cheerful creature that chirrups on the Hearth.
>
> *Natural History.*

Now, don't decide hastily till you've heard what I would do. I would come out, sir, with a prospectus on the subject of the Cricket that should put everybody in a good temper, and make such a dash at people's fenders and arm-chairs as hasn't been made for many a long day. I could approach them in a different mode under this name, and in a more winning and immediate way, than under any other. I would at once sit down upon their very hobs; and take a personal and confidential position with them which should separate me, instantly, from all other periodicals periodically published, and supply a distinct and sufficient reason for my coming into existence. And I would chirp, chirp, chirp away in every number until I chirped it up to——well, you shall say how many hundred thousand! ... Seriously, I feel a capacity in this name and notion which appears to give us a tangible starting-point, and a real, defined, strong, genial drift and purpose. I seem to feel that it is an aim and name which people would readily and pleasantly connect with *me*; and that, for a good course and a clear one, instead of making circles pigeon-like at starting, here we should be safe. I think the general recognition would be likely to leap at it; and of the helpful associations that could be clustered round the idea at starting, and the pleasant tone of which the working of it is susceptible, I have not the smallest doubt. . . . But you shall determine. What do you think? And what do you say? The chances are, that it will either strike you instantly, or not strike you at all. Which is it, my dear fellow? You know I am not bigoted to the first suggestions of my own fancy; but you know also exactly how I should use such a lever, and how much power I should find in it. Which is it? What do you say?—I have not myself said half enough.[1] Indeed I have said next to nothing; but like the parrot in the negro-story, I "think a dam deal."[2]

to time interchanged during his absence, and to which there was allusion in the agreement executed before his departure" (this agreement has not survived, and there is no mention of the periodical in *To* Bradbury & Evans, 8 May 44); CD, he says, wished "to establish a periodical, that, while relieving his own pen by enabling him to receive frequent help from other writers, might yet retain always the popularity of his name".

[1] This plan, Forster says, was "modified so far, in the discussions that followed, as to involve less absolute personal identification with Dickens"—but was superseded: see *To* Mitton, 25 July 45 and *fn*.

[2] This version has not been traced, but the story was well known: see Vol. I, p. 297*n*.

To JOHN FORSTER, [?8 JULY 1845]*

MS Victoria & Albert Museum (FC). *Date:* 1845 on handwriting, and after June since from Devonshire Terrace. Reference to "cleaning" (see *To* Mitton, 20 May 45) suggests shortly after CD's return.

Devonshire Terrace | Tuesday Morning

My Dear Forster.

The "cleaning" &c &c is in that advanced stage of damnability, that I find, on consultation, it will be best to dine out today—more especially as the children are not at home to Polk. Will you let our engagement for today—having reference to *this* dining-room—stand over until tomorrow? And shall we dine together somewhere else, today? Yes, of course. Well. Where shall I meet you? Name your ground, and I will bring Mac.

Ever and Ever
CD.

To DOUGLAS JERROLD, 9 JULY 1845*

MS Mr Douglas Jerrold.

Devonshire Terrace | Ninth July 1845.

My Dear Jerrold

Here is the letter I spoke to you about.[1] I am charmed with your comedy[2] —so much so, that I do not think I shall go to see it badly played.[3] I am greatly struck by the whole idea of the piece.[4] The elopement in the beginning, and the consequences that flow from it, and their delicate and masterly exposition, are of the freshest, truest, and most vigorous kind—the characters (especially the Governess)[5] among the best I know—and the wit and the wisdom of it are never asunder. I could almost find it in my heart to sit down and write you a long letter on the subject of this Play. But I won't. I will only thank you for it, heartily; and add that I agree with you in thinking it incomparably the best of your dramatic writings.

I don't know that I could express my feeling better, even if I tried, than by saying that if you didn't read it yourself to the actors (damn 'em) I feel as if I should have liked to do it, and to have belaboured them, sledge-hammer wise, with the whole five acts, so that they should have been bruised into *some* understanding of it.

We dine at 5 on Sunday, remember.

Ever My Dear Jerrold
Faithfully Your friend

Douglas Jerrold Esquire   CHARLES DICKENS

[1] Unexplained.

[2] *Time Works Wonders*, presented at the Haymarket from 26 Apr 45; it was successful both on the stage and as a publication.

[3] W. B. Hodgson recorded that Jerrold complained of the acting, apart from Miss Fortescue's playing of the heroine (*Life and Letters of William Ballantyne Hodgson*, ed. J. M. D. Meiklejohn, Edinburgh, 1883, p.

59); the *Examiner* of 21 June had mentioned "careless acting".

[4] The play satirizes both the aristocracy and the new rich; in Jerrold's view "the most radical" of his plays, although, as he told Hodgson, this was not generally appreciated (*ibid*).

[5] Miss Tucker, the elderly governess, prevents the heroine's elopement.

To CHARLES WHITEHEAD,[1] 9 JULY 1845

Text from photograph, Mr W. G. Southwell.

1 Devonshire Terrace | Ninth July 1845.

Sir.

I have been much gratified by the receipt of your letter, which I found awaiting me on my return from Italy a few days since, after a year's absence. It is a great happiness to me (remembering the circumstances under which you wrote to me on a former occasion) to learn that you are doing so well.

I am unwilling to damp your ardor by suggesting that Poetry is a dangerous pursuit better laid aside than encouraged in the position you occupy, of all others most unlikely ever to lead you to fame, happiness, or profit. But this is a grave truth; and one, believe me, which you will do well to consider.

Regard me, nevertheless, as a Subscriber to your book,[2] but have the goodness not to insert my name in your list.

Assuring you once again, that the receipt of your letter has given me great satisfaction I am

Faithfully Yours
CHARLES DICKENS

To MISS ELIZA ACTON,[3] 11 JULY 1845

Text from N, I, 686.

1 Devonshire Terrace, York Gate, Regent's Park
Eleventh July 1845

Dear Madam,

I beg to thank you cordially for your very satisfying and welcome note of the tenth of January last; and for the book that accompanied it.[4] Believe me, I am far too sensible of the value of a communication so spontaneous and unaffected, to regard it with the least approach to indifference or neglect—I should have been proud to acknowledge it long since, but I have been abroad in Italy.

Dear Madam, | Faithfully Yours
[CHARLES DICKENS]

To T. J. THOMPSON, 12 JULY 1845*

MS Berg Collection.

Devonshire Terrace. | Saturday Morning Twelfth July | 1845.

My Dear Thompson

I had a delicacy in alluding last night—even before Fred—to the subject[5]

---

[1] Charles Whitehead (1804–62; *DNB*), novelist, dramatist and poet: see Vol. I, p. 207*n*, and Vol. III, p. 592 and *n*. His revised edn of CD's *Memoirs of Grimaldi* was published 1846.

[2] The project evidently came to nothing; Whitehead's poems were first collected in *The Solitary, and other Poems*, 1849: see *To* Bulwer Lytton, 11 May 49 (N, II, 152–3).

[3] Eliza Acton (1799–1859; *DNB*), miscellaneous writer; contributed to annuals and published volumes of verse, including one in 1847 for which CD subscribed (Bradbury & Evans's Accounts, MS V & A).

[4] Presumably her *Modern Cookery in All its Branches*, published by Longmans in Jan 45; reached its 6th edn 1855.

[5] Christiana Weller. The Wellers had

which occupies your thoughts, I know, just now: and in which I take, as *you* know, a lively and fervent interest. If you had originated it, I should have had no hesitation in pursuing the theme; but as you did not, I held my peace. I should not have done so, had we been alone. You trust Fred, I believe; and I know him worthy of all trust. But I did not feel certain that I had a right to act on that belief, without your leading.

If it be any satisfaction to you to confide in me freely, as you did in the beginning of your love, pray do so. I can scarcely hope that I shall have the good fortune to assist you; but I am unfeignedly and heartily your friend and hers; and you can tell me nothing which will not have my warm heart.

I am at home every morning, and have a ready ear and an open hand for you. Being in all sincerity

T. J. Thompson Esquire.

Faithfully Yours
CHARLES DICKENS

To F. O. WARD, 12 JULY 1845*

MS Dickens House.

Devonshire Terrace | Saturday Twelfth July 1845

Dear Sir.

In reply to your favor of Thursday last, I beg to assure you that you are at full liberty to use my name, if you should desire to do so, as a Member of the Committee of the Hood Fund.[1] May all success attend it!

F. O. Ward Esquire.

Faithfully Yours
CHARLES DICKENS

moved from Liverpool to London in Jan 45 and were living at 11 Queen Terrace, Chelsea. Mrs Weller and Christiana had opened a "pianoforte academy, at M. Faucher's Rooms, 7, Half Moon Street, Piccadilly", first advertised in the *Musical World* in Mar. Christiana continued her concert career; she had several engagements at Buckingham's British and Foreign Institute, and on 20 June she gave a concert at the Hanover Square Rooms, favourably noticed and including a *valse fantastique* of her own composition. Her 1845 Diary shows that she corresponded with Catherine while the Dickenses were abroad, and that CD agreed to be sponsor to her sister Betsy Shaw's daughter, christened Lucy Weller Dickens, 8 May 45; Frederick Dickens, often mentioned in the diary, came down to Bristol for the christening. There are also several references to the Hogarths (Mrs Hogarth on one occasion "spoke about Boz and her daughter that died and who they say is like me"). Mr Weller's opposition to her marriage had not been entirely over-come, although she was seeing Thompson almost daily, often at Mrs Smithson's. On 23 June Thompson wrote from Newcastle: "my first happy letter. No doubt, no sorrow now"; but before they met again on 4 July, the diary entries record further unhappy scenes with her father. CD may have heard something of this from Thompson, and probably heard more on 13 July, when Christiana called, and saw Catherine and Georgina (Weller Album and Christiana Weller's Diary, MSS Mrs Sowerby).

[1] After Hood's death (3 May 45) his wife's pension of £100 was the sole support of her and two children. An advertisement in the *Athenæum*, 17 May 45, had named the committee organized to raise a fund; it included Milnes (the leading spirit), Ainsworth, Lytton and Talfourd, with Ward as Secretary. *The Times*, 15 July, had the added names of Carlyle and CD. By 23 July £1028.18.0 had been raised. The Fund committee met the following April, "at the residence of Mr. David Salomon, Treasurer", when it was reported that

To COUNT D'ORSAY, 14 JULY 1845*

MS Comte de Gramont.

Devonshire Terrace | Fourteenth July 1845.

My Dear Count D'Orsay

I told you yesterday that Maclise had been offered a thousand pounds for his Cartoon. I swear Forster told me so, at Brussels. *He* swears he didn't, but that I must have misunderstood something that fell from him in the ravaging torrent of News they were all pouring out at once. However this may be, I write to prevent *your* having a wrong impression of the fact also. The patriotic ma reserved by Providence to offer that tribute to Maclise's genius, has not appeared yet. The Hour is come, but the Man is, as yet, out of town.

Ever affectionately Yours

CHARLES DICKENS

To CLARKSON STANFIELD, 15 JULY 1845†

MS Colonel Richard Gimbel.

Devonshire Terrace | Fifteenth July 1845.

My Dear Stanny.

As I write to you now, not as a Private Friend, but as a Stage Manager, I have half a mind to damn your eyes by way of beginning.

Our Play Sir. Our play—

Every Man in his Humour,[1] and the Mayor of Garratt.[2] The Prompt book is Cumberland's Edition[3] in both cases. They are both cast,[4] and really very

£1000 had been invested on behalf of the family, leaving £200 to invest; it was proposed that a monument should be erected over the grave at Kensal Green, at a cost not exceeding £50, and members of the committee had subscribed 10 guineas (*Athenæum*, 18 Apr 46); but owing to mismanagement and misunderstanding this was not done until July 1854 (see later vols).

[1] Jonson's comedy was chosen, according to Forster, "with special regard to the singleness and individuality of the 'humours' portrayed in it" (F, v, i, 382).

[2] The farce by Samuel Foote, 1764, versions of which were acted in 1810 and 1837. By 7 Aug *Two O'Clock in the Morning* was substituted: see *To* Lemon, 6 Aug 45.

[3] *Every Man in his Humour* is in Vol. IX of Cumberland's *British Drama* (14 vols, 1817); also published in a separate edn [1825]. An interleaved copy of the latter is in the Forster Collection, with Forster's notes on the Kitely scenes. (For examples,

see Anthony Burton, "Forster on the Stage," *D*, LXX [1974], 172–83). It was based on Garrick's version, which was considerably cut (omitting, for example, many of Jonson's topical references) and with some scenes rewritten. Further MS revisions show some expurgation of the language and a few added and altered lines, and occasionally the restoration of a line cut by Garrick.

[4] T. J. Thompson was asked to undertake Wellbred in the play at a later date (*To* Thompson, 23 July); but the part may originally have been given to Maclise, since Forster says, "Maclise took earnest part with us, and was to have acted, but fell away on the eve of the rehearsals" (F, v, i, 382). No details other than Stanfield's part are known for the farce; but CD probably chose the swaggering part of Major Sturgeon for himself, and Douglas Jerrold would have been well suited with Jerry Sneak, the comic henpecked husband.

well. I should say, the St. James's Theatre[1] when we are quite ready, *as there is no doubt of our being able to keep that as Private as a Drawing Room.* In the meantime, merry rehearsals innumerable. *The first, here on Wednesday the 23rd. at a quarter before 7 for 7 exactly.*

You will find Downright (your part in Every Man in his Humour) very much in the Sir Anthony Absolute line. And as your best business is with me (I am Bobadil) we will make it out brilliantly. Take also, Sir Jacob Jollop[2] in the Farce; *and I am confident that both pieces will be very well done.*

Stick to us nobly. My steam is up!

Ever affectionately

Clarkson Stanfield Esquire. CD.

To LADY HOLLAND, 16 JULY 1845*

MS British Museum.

Devonshire Terrace. | Wednesday Sixteenth July 1845.

My Dear Lady Holland

I find it quite out of the question to think of availing myself, today, of the kindness of the Duchess of Bedford.[3] I am obliged to dine, if by any reasonable exertion I can do so, with a party at Greenwich in the evening;[4] the engagement being an old one, and the dinner mainly planned for me. My throat is worse instead of better: and I have such a villainous cold, that I am continually weeping, and feel as uncomfortable and heavy as if I had done some evil deed. So I am taking your remedy, and going round and round my garden in a great coat, in desperate training for tonight.

After your kind interest on Monday Evening,[5] I could not stay away from her Grace's breakfast[6] without writing you a line. I shall of course make a point of calling there before the week is out; and I will soon report to you, as in duty bound.

Always Dear Lady Holland | Faithfully Yours

The Lady Holland. CHARLES DICKENS

To EMILE DE LA RUE, 18 JULY 1845*

MS Berg Collection. *Address:* A Monsieur | M. Emile De la Rue | Messrs. De la Rue freres | Genoa | North Italy.

Devonshire Terrace. 18th. July/45. Friday

My Dear De la Rue. Your letter received this morning as I was writing to Madame. I will write to you by Monday's Post.

Ever and Ever Yours CD

---

[1] Miss Kelly's theatre in Dean Street was soon substituted (F, v, i, 381), but the St James's was used for the Sanatorium performance on 15 Nov.

aa; bb; cc Not previously published.

[2] A secondary but quite important part.

[3] Georgiana, widow of the 6th Duke: see Vol. III, p. 298*n*.

[4] Not referred to elsewhere.

[5] On 14 July CD met the Duchess of Bedford at a dinner-party given by Lady Holland; the other guests (mostly titled) included Lord Bessborough and Lord Glenelg (Holland House Dinner Book, MS BM).

[6] Clearly a private party, as not reported in the press.

To CLARKSON STANFIELD, 18 JULY 1845*

MS Berg Collection.

Devònshire Terrace. | Friday Eighteenth July 1845.

My Dear Stanny.

Your hearty note, shews me (as I knew before) that you are the boy for Downright! The gentlemen of the company beg me to *postpone* the first Rehearsal, that they may be easier in their words before it comes off. I therefore suggest Thursday the 31st. Can you start for Chatham on Tuesday the 29th? If so, let our engagement stand on those terms; and we will come back, merrily, to the Rehearsal.

I anticipate great amusement from the Play, and am quite full of it.

Kate (who was at the opera last night,[1] and is not up yet, or she would write) begs me to give her love to Mrs. Stanfield, and to ask if she and you will come and dine with us on Sunday, at 6 sharp. We shall be quite alone, with the exception of Mac and Forster, and Mr. Colden from New York: whom you know. We earnestly hope that you have no engagement to deprive us of this pleasure.

Ever Believe me

Clarkson Stanfield Esquire

My Dear Stanfield | Affectionately Yours
CHARLES DICKENS

To RICHARD MONCKTON MILNES, 21 JULY 1845*

MS Trinity College, Cambridge.

Devonshire Terrace. | Twenty First July 1845

I would if I could, Dear Milnes. But I can't. So I won't.

Ever Yours
CHARLES DICKENS

To JOHN FORSTER, [22 or 23 JULY 1845]

Extract in F, v, i, 382. *Date:* 22 or 23 July—the only days during the run of the *Gamester* when CD could have dined with Macready: see *fns.*

Man of the House. *Gamester!* By the foot of Pharaoh,[2] I will *not* see the *Gamester.* Man shall not force, nor horses drag, this poor gentleman-like carcass[3] into the presence of the *Gamester.*[4] I have said it. . . . The player Mac

---

[1] Probably *Cosi fan Tutte* at Her Majesty's, Giulia Grisi's "Benefit and Last Appearance".

[2] An oath used by Bobadil in *Every Man in his Humour,* I, v, II, ii, admirably imitated by Stephen in III, v.

[3] "This will I venture upon my poor gentlemanlike carcass to perform" (IV, vii). The rest of the letter is in Bobadil's style,

but with no further quotation; Forster introduces it as an instance of CD's "humouring the completeness of his assumption by talking and writing Bobadil".

[4] The comedy by Edward Moore (1753), an old favourite; acted seven or eight times between 21 July and 7 Aug 45 at Sadler's Wells.

hath bidden me to eat and likewise drink with him,[1] thyself, and short-necked Fox[2] to-night. An' I go not, I am a hog, and not a soldier. But an' thou goest not—Beware citizen![3] Look to it. . . . Thine as thou meritest. BOBADIL (Captain). Unto Master Kitely. These.

To EDWIN LANDSEER, 23 JULY 1845

MS Mr Noel C. Peyrouton. *Address:* Edwin Landseer Esquire.

Devonshire Terrace | Wednesday Twenty Third July 1845.
My Dear Landseer

I would if I could—but I am tied by the heels—both heels—having engagements and occupations from which I can no more cast myself off today, than I can cast myself to the top of the Church Weathercock. Which I think I would do, if I could: to get out of the way.

Best Regards. My affectionate protection to the Eagle and Raven.[4] They sound like the sign of a Public House.

Ever Believe me | Faithfully Yours
CHARLES DICKENS

To LORD DUDLEY COUTTS STUART, 24 JULY 1845

MS Mr Wyndham Payne.

Devonshire Terrace. | Twenty Fourth July 1845.
My Dear Lord Dudley.

Behold Sanvanero's little Bottle of Wine![5] His whole heart is in it, I am certain.

Faithfully Yours always
The | Lord Dudley Stuart   CHARLES DICKENS

[1] Macready was in London 22 and possibly 23 July, and again on 30 July when he dined with Lord Lansdowne; otherwise he was at Eastbourne and then St Helier until 14 Aug (*Diaries*, II, 299).

[2] W. J. Fox: see frontispiece.

[3] In II, ii, Bobadil calls Kitely "the gentleman-citizen".

[4] Left with Landseer when CD went to Italy; he never reclaimed the eagle, as it did not get on with the children.

[5] CD tells the whole story, with some admixture of fiction, in "The Italian Prisoner" (*All the Year Round*, 13 Oct 60; collected in *The Uncommercial Traveller*), calling the ex-prisoner "Giovanni Carlavero". Apparently Lord Dudley Coutts Stuart rescued him from lifelong imprisonment in horrible conditions. He had not written to his benefactor for "some two or three years" and wished to send him a bottle of wine by CD; it was shipped to London, and collected by him from the Custom House. Though it was "mere vinegar" by the time it reached its destination, "the Englishman told me, with much emotion . . . that he had never tasted wine that seemed to him so sweet and sound". The period of CD's visit to "Carlavero" appears to be Spring 1845; the only clues to the town where the wine-shop was, are "on the Mediterranean" and "far from Naples".

To THOMAS MITTON, 25 JULY 1845*

MS Mrs Humphry House. *Address:* Thomas Mitton Esquire | 23 Southampton Buildings.

Devonshire Terrace. | Twenty Fifth July 1845.

My Dear Mitton. I suppose he[1] must have it? Am I right?—As the Wizard of the North[2] used to say.

Roche is out, and I can't find the Cigars. I will send them on Monday, and see you myself, either on that day or Tuesday.

Bradbury and Evans have perfectly amazed me with another new notion—Capital, *down and ready*, fifty Thousand Pounds![3]

Ever Yours
CD.

To COUNT D'ORSAY, 26 JULY 1845*

MS Comte de Gramont.

Devonshire Terrace. | Twenty Sixth July 1845.

My Dear Count D'Orsay.

The upshot of the business between Mr. Dods[4] and the Brave Courier is, that Mr. D engages him for Three Months from the latter end of next month: on the understanding that this is the real length of the Engagement, and tha

---

[1] Probably John Dickens. The next cheque paid to him by CD was £4 on 25 Aug (Account-book, MS Messrs Coutts).

[2] John Henry Anderson (1815–74; *DNB*), conjuror: see Vol. III, p. 439n.

[3] Forster tells how, while discussion of the weekly periodical project was still going on, "discussion, project, everything was swept away by a larger scheme, in its extent and its danger more suitable to the wild and hazardous enterprises of that prodigious year"—the setting up of a daily newspaper to be edited by CD (F, V, i, 379). For the sum mentioned, see the "Memorandum" of 17 Nov 45 (*To* Bradbury & Evans, ?14 Nov, *fn*). Bradbury & Evans must already have had a promise of capital from Joseph Paxton of Chatsworth (see *To* Mitton, 20 Oct, *fn*) who was in London 23–26 July. The plan may have been broached as early as 1840, when Paxton and William Bradbury—whose native place was Bakewell, a few miles from Chatsworth—were already on friendly terms. In Feb 45, while seeing Bradbury in London, Paxton noted that "the newspaper don't look so well now" (Paxton *to*

Mrs Paxton, MS Devonshire Collections; cf. Violet Markham, *Paxton and the Bachelor Duke*, 1935, pp. 164–5). By the summer, however, the prospects for a new daily paper were much more favourable, owing to the enormous increase in railway speculation which marked "that prodigious year". The "railway mania" of 1845–6 meant that railway directors had capital to put into such an enterprise; in addition the daily influx of long advertisements for new companies would bring in large profits to a newspaper carrying them (Baldwin's *Morning Herald*, one of the chief beneficiaries, was supposed to have cleared £3000 a week from advertisements at the height of the boom). Paxton, with his long-standing involvement in the world of railway speculation, was well placed to obtain both the capital and the advertising. The choice of CD as editor shows that the new paper was to be liberal in its sympathies, and in this respect, too, the times must have seemed propitious— since the movement for the repeal of the Corn Laws and for free trade was gaining in strength.

[4] Thus in MS; i.e. Dodd.

said D does not design to travel for any longer period. And D aforesaid adds (handsomely and properly, I think) that if said Brave C should find a better place in the interval between this and the period of the proposed commencement of his engagement, it shall be understood between them that he is at full liberty to take it.[1]

My affectionate regards to Lady Blessington, whose sister, I fear, is now in great distress.[2]

Ever My Dear Count | Wholly Yours
CHARLES DICKENS

To JOHN FORSTER, [?26 JULY 1845]

Extract in F, v, i, 379–80. *Date:* "about half way through the summer" according to Forster; reference to D'Orsay and Roche suggests 26 July.

Mentioning the success of D'Orsay's kind exertions on behalf of Roche.

What do you think of a notion that has occurred to me in connection with our abandoned little weekly? It would be a delicate and beautiful fancy for a Christmas book, making the Cricket a little household god—silent in the wrong and sorrow of the tale, and loud again when all went well and happy.[3]

To EMILE DE LA RUE, 28 JULY 1845*

MS Berg Collection. *Address:* North Italy | A Monsieur | Monsr. Emile De la Rue | Messrs. De la Rue freres | Genova.

Devonshire Terrace. Monday Twenty Eighth July 1845.

My Dear De la Rue.

My left ear has been burning a good deal since last Monday, when I *didn't* write to you; and as I sit with the right side of my face towards Genoa, I am inclined to think you must have been anathematizing me, pretty considerably, for not keeping my promise. Though it has been owing to little fault of mine, believe me.

The weather here, has been truly damnable. I have no milder word for the due expression of its merits. As somebody once said to somebody else, somewhere or other, "the Summer has set in with its usual severity."[4] It has been perfectly dark for a whole week. The sky, a dull slate color. The air, by turns intensely close, and insufferably cold. The dust, doing the strangest things: getting up in clouds without any wind to stir it; flying into the sky to meet the

---

[1] CD paid Roche £114 on 5 Aug (Account-book, MS Messrs Coutts).

[2] Lady Canterbury, *née* Ellen Power (1791–1845); her husband died 21 July, after collapsing on a train journey on 18 July.

[3] The "Cricket" contributed little more than title and the opening and close of

The Cricket on the Hearth, which CD did not begin to write until Oct.

[4] "*Summer,* as my friend Coleridge waggishly writes, has set in with its usual severity": Lamb *to* Vincent Novello, 9 May 1826, repeated in a letter to Barton of 16 May. Not original with him; sometimes attributed to Horace Walpole.

fog; dancing on an imaginary tight rope, all down the longest streets and roads. Today the sun is shining. People don't know what to make of it. One man called here, this morning, quite alarmed at the sight, and thought it attributable (he said) to the comet.[1]

There is nothing new in London. Parliament is just getting up; and everybody is hurrying out of town, as fast as Railroads will carry them. Walton was here yesterday—dined here. I thought he didn't seem quite at his ease, though we had no party: only three or four of my familiars. To be sure there was no dancing. Gracious Heaven, do you remember a mad attempt at the light fantastic toe, that took place in the Town of Carrara,[2] one Sunday night, at about the Deadest Watch of the Night! The deep dejection of that hour, will never be obliterated from my memory. The Count whats-his-name!—I see him waltzing now, with the niece of that hoary old ruffian, the Swedish Professore. On whose beard, Baldness fall for evermore, Amen!

I don't know whether Roche will come your way, in the course of a short trip of three months he is about to take with one Mr. Dods, MP. But I have exhorted him to see you, if he should: and to bring me something or other out of the drawing-room, given him by Madame De la Rue's own hand. I hope to get him a longer engagement at the end of that term; and if I succeed, you will see him *then*, certainly. I shall amuse Madame De la Rue in my next letter (tell her so, with my love) by telling her all about the Master and Mistress[3] for whom I design him. I think I told her something about them, on that memorable night when you went to Torlonia's, and she and I laughed so immoderately at Meloni's.

I hope and trust she is still going on well. I hardly dare to hope that the good effects of the Mesmerism of Three Months will be lasting on her physique, but I have great hopes indeed, that they will be so durable in respect of her morale, as to sustain it until we meet again, which, please God, shall be, at latest, within One Year of my most unhappy departure from Genoa. I shall receive every account you give me of her with unceasing interest—if possible with new and higher interest than ever.

On the very day after I wrote to her, last: Miss Holdskamp (I hope I spell her name correctly, but I'm doubtful) came. I was not at home. I think Kate was not at home either, but I am not sure. Anyhow, she left a card with her address upon it; and Kate and Georgy went soon afterwards to call upon her. They found her in Somers Town—a little house, they said—not *very* comfortable— but it didn't appear to have made any unusual impression upon them, or to have had any cause of embarrassment to either side, in it. They saw a sister,[4]

---

[1] Recorded in the *Annual Register* as first observed on 8 June, "a magnificent comet", "easily perceptible by the naked eye"; referred to in the *Athenæum*, 9 Aug, as "The Great Comet of June, 1845" which was also observed in Rome, Paris and America.

[2] On the way back from Rome to Genoa, 6 Apr 45.

[3] T. J. Thompson and Christiana: see *To* Thompson, 17 Oct 45.

[4] Miss Holskamp also had brothers (see *To* Mme de la Rue, 27 Sep 45, *fn*), one of whom was probably Francis Holskamp, a clerk in the office of the Commissioners of Lunacy.

whom they describe as very pretty, though of a different kind of beauty altogether, to Miss H. The sister said she had been rallying her, on having left her
Heart in Genoa: and there was some little cross-firing on that subject. Georgy
(you may remember a small Virgin of that name) suggested that it might have
been left with a gentleman named "Grannet"—but the sister said "Oh dear
no!" and appeared surprised: observing that she often talked of *him*.

You can put on this, whatever construction your wisdom suggests. It is just a
toss-up, I think, whether the sister, on these premises, was right or wrong.
But I tell you exactly what they told me, when they came home. I am anxious
to know what has passed, in reference to your Brother-in-law. Give my love to
him. I shall be truly sorry to hear that this, or anything else, in which he has a
real interest: looks unpromising or goes wrong.[1]

The box was gone before I received your letter about Brewster, and the
Philosophy of apparitions.[2] If the steamer repeat her voyage regularly (she is
now absent on her first trip) I will not fail to send them to you by that conveyance.
The thought occurred to me more than once, that I might have put them in the
box. But the Binder made it, and didn't like to be interfered with; for when I
suggested to him that I might have some other things for him to pack, he addressed
me in these terms. "That 'ere box, Mr. Dickens, is at present dewoted, en-tirely
to your works Sir. Them works is intended, if I understand the subject, as a
present, Mr. Dickens, toe a lady. That box and them works, Mr. Dickens, is
now a complete thing, which the lady will perceive Sir, if she is the lady that no
doubt she is, when you sends your works in a gift so far Sir. Wery good Sir.
Now Sir, the Pint is this. Wotever you orders me to pack along with them works,
Sir, I packs and willing. No man more so. But if you introdooses into that
'ere box, a single blessed work as an't your own Sir, the completeness of that
'ere box is gone, and I don't care no more for it, myself, than if it wos a Tea
Kittle."

I was so much affected by this reasoning, that I begged him to nail the lid on
instantly. Being called away, I must nail the lid on this letter much sooner than
I intended. And as there is nothing in it, my dear De la Rue, only think of it as
a squeeze of the hand forwarded by Post—just such a squeeze as I used to give
you when we parted at the corner opposite the Post Office, and were going to
take a walk again—at night.

Ah!

Monsieur Emile De la Rue.

Ever Yours sincerely
CHARLES DICKENS

---

[1] Miss Holskamp was still in London in
May 46, when Catherine, who had clearly
kept in touch with her, wrote regretting
that they could not see her again before
leaving for Switzerland, and making it
clear that they were not going to Genoa
(Catherine Dickens *to* Miss Holskamp, 28

May 46, MS New York University
Library).

[2] Sir David Brewster, *Letters on Natural
Magic*, 1832, and S. Hibbert, *Sketches of
the Philosophy of Apparitions*, 1824; both
were in the Gad's Hill library at CD's
death.

To MACVEY NAPIER, 28 JULY 1845

MS British Museum.

1 Devonshire Terrace | York Gate Regents Park
Twenty Eighth July 1845

My Dear Sir

As my note is to bear reference to business, I will make it as short and plain as I can.

You want me to write a paper for you.[1] I think I could write you a pretty-good, and a well-timed[2] article on the Punishment of Death, and sympathy with Great Criminals: instancing the gross and depraved curiosity that exists in reference to them, by some of the outrageous things that were written, done, and said, in recent cases.

But as I am not sure that my views would be yours; and as their statement would be quite inseparable from such a paper; I will briefly set down their purpose, that you may decide for yourself.

Society having arrived at that state, in which it spares bodily torture to the worst criminal: and having agreed, if criminals be put to Death at all, to kill them in the speediest way: I consider the question with reference to society, and not at all with reference to the criminal. Holding that in a case of cruel and deliberate murder, he is already mercifully and sparingly treated.

But, as a question for the deliberate consideration of all reflective persons, I put this view of the case.—With such very repulsive and odious details before us, may it not be well to enquire whether the Punishment of Death be beneficial to Society. I believe it to have a horrible fascination for many of those persons who render themselves liable to it, impelling them onward to the acquisition of a frightful notoriety; and (setting aside the strong confirmation of this idea, afforded in individual instances) I presume this to be the case in very badly regulated minds, when I observe the strange fascination which everything connected with this Punishment or the object of it, possesses for tens of thousands of decent, virtuous, well-conducted people, who are quite unable to resist the published portraits, letters, anecdotes, smilings, snuff-takings &c &c &c of the bloodiest and most unnatural scoundrel with the Gallows before him. I observe that this strange interest does not prevail to anything like the same degree, where Death is not the Penalty. Therefore I connect it with the Dread and Mystery surrounding Death in any shape, but especially in this avenging form; and am disposed to come to the conclusion that it produces crime in the criminally disposed and engenders a diseased sympathy—morbid and bad, but natural and often irresistible—among the well-conducted and gentle.

[1] This was the third time within four years that Napier had asked, and CD had promised, an article for the *Edinburgh*: see Vol. II, pp. 317, 354, Vol. III, p. 565. Once again, the promise was unfulfilled; instead, CD wrote on his proposed subject in five "Letters" to the *Daily News*, 23 and 28 Feb, 9, 13, 16 Mar 46: see *To* Macready, 27 Feb 46.

[2] The recent increase in convictions for murder and the morbid excitement raised by the executions of Tawell, Hocker, and Tapping were the subject of several leading articles in the press, and also of one of W. J. Fox's *Lectures addressed chiefly to the Working Classes*.

Regarding it as doing harm to both these classes, it may even then be right to enquire whether it has any salutary influence on those small knots and specks of people, mere bubbles in the living ocean, who actually behold its infliction with their eyes. On this head, it is scarcely possible to entertain a doubt; for we know that robbery and obscenity and callous indifference are of no commoner occurrence anywhere, than at the foot of the Scaffold. Furthermore, we know that all exhibitions of agony and Death have a tendency to brutalize and harden the feelings of men, and have always been the most rife, among the fiercest people. Again, it is a great question whether ignorant and dissolute persons (ever the great body of spectators, as few others will attend), seeing that murder done, and not having seen the other, will not, almost of necessity sympathize with the man who dies before them; especially as he is shewn, a Martyr to their fancy—tied and bound—alone among scores—with every kind of odds against him.

I should take all these threads up, at the end, by a vivid little sketch of the origin and progress of such a crime as Hocker's—stating a somewhat parallel case, but an imaginary one—pursuing its hero to his Death, and shewing what enormous harm he does, *after* the crime for which he suffers. I should state none of these positions in a positive sledge-hammer way, but tempt and lure the reader into the discussion of them in his own mind; and so we come to this at last—whether it be for the benefit of society to elevate even this crime to the awful dignity and notoriety of Death; and whether it would not be much more to its advantage to substitute a mean and shameful punishment, degrading the deed, and the committer of the deed, and leaving the general compassion to expend itself upon the only theme at present quite forgotten in the history; that is to say, the murdered person.

I do not give you this as an outline of the paper: which I think I could make attractive.[1] It is merely an exposition of the inferences to which it's[2] whole philosophy must tend.[3]

Believe me always | Faithfully Yours

Professor Napier

CHARLES DICKENS

---

[1] Napier sent CD's letter to Jeffrey, who consulted Empson, and wrote, encouraging acceptance: "You see from his letter that you are perfectly safe from any risk of *Cant*, either sentimental or religious—and may rely on having the question argued on grounds which those who are most in favour of the present system, must admit to be relevant. And as he promises not to be in any degree dogmatical or presumptuous—but suggestive only, I do not see that anything but good can come from the discussion" (Jeffrey *to* Napier, 31 July 45, MS BM).

[2] Thus in MS.

[3] All the points made by CD were included and elaborated in the *Daily News*—particularly on 9 Mar 46, where he treated of the "fascination" of the "Punishment of Death" to the murderer himself, the "diseased sympathy" which it fosters in others, and the example of Hocker, rejoicing in his notoriety; CD ended by instancing Edward Oxford (who fired at the Queen in 1840) and his imitators—checked when they were no longer in danger of hanging, but of "a mean and humiliating punishment". Other letters gave details of the demoralizing and brutalizing effect of public executions. But in the *Daily News*, writing over his own name, with much more space at his disposal and more oppor-

To CLARKSON STANFIELD, 28 JULY 1845*

Text from copy in the possession of Mrs Gladys Ahern.

Devonshire Terrace | Monday Twenty Eighth July 1845

My Dear Stanny

The Chatham Excursion is to decide on keeping themselves *to* themselves on Wednesday; and to take advantage of that day for doing work which might otherwise interfere with the ultimate carrying-out of that much postponed and Stanfield slaughtered design.

Will you come to me after Lord Lansdowne has left you? I propose your coming here, because the garden is convenient. I will read your part with you, in anticipation of Thursday, to the best of my idea of it: and I think put you out of the reach of all misgiving or discomfort. After that, there is sure to be a joint on the premises. And after that, we can walk in half-price, somewhere or other if so "dispoged."

Ever Yours affectionately

Clarkson Stanfield Esquire   CHARLES DICKENS

To T. J. THOMPSON, 28 JULY 1845

MS Huntington Library.

Devonshire Terrace. | Twenty Eighth July 1845

My Dear Thompson

I hope, if you have no decided objection, you will do Wellbred in the Comedy[1] —if for no other reason, to oblige *me*, as I should very much like you to be in it. You will find the "company" perfectly good-natured and most agreeable. I never saw men go to anything in such a hearty spirit.

Write me a word, and let it be Yes. The first Rehearsal comes off *here* on Thursday at ¼ before 7.

Faithfully Always

T. J. Thompson Esquire.   CHARLES DICKENS

unity for topical references, CD did state his position not only persuasively but in "a positive sledge-hammer way". In addition, he emphasized the irrevocability of Capital Punishment and the risk of error; he demonstrated its failure in preventing crime, and rebutted, perhaps more vigorously than he would have ventured to do in the *Edinburgh*, the arguments in its favour (including those of Macaulay in a recent speech), saying in his conclusion, "I beg to be understood as advocating the total abolition of the Punishment of Death". The series (except for 23 Feb) is discussed by P. A. W. Collins in *Dickens and Crime*, 1962, pp. 225–33.

[1] A subject perhaps broached on 26 July, when Thompson joined a party to Greenwich consisting of CD, Catherine, Georgina, Mrs Smithson, Amelia Thompson and Christiana Weller. Christiana stayed the night at Devonshire Terrace, and the next day her father and Thompson called on CD and there was a "secret tribunal"—clearly about Mr Weller's objections to the marriage (Christiana Weller's Diary, MS Mrs Sowerby).

To LEWIS GAYLORD CLARK,[1] 30 JULY 1845*

MS Columbia University Libraries.

> 1 Devonshire Terrace York Gate Regents Park.
> Thirtieth July 1845

My Dear Clarke.[2]

This may seem a tardy answer to your kind remembrance of me dated the Fourth of last November. But I have passed a happy year in Italy; and am but newly come back to my Household Gods.

Thank you for your brother's book.[3] I will read it in my most quiet hours. I am prepared, as you know, to approach it in the right spirit.

Mrs. Clarke[4] is long since out of that trouble, you tell me of: no doubt. A coming event of the same character is casting its shadow over this house. But we are not so near the substance as you appear to have been when you wrote your note.

I take it for granted that Mr. Inman[5] has come and gone again, since those remote times. The remembrance of him lives with me very pleasantly. It would have gratified me to have seen him in these parts.

Knickerbocker is looking upward, I hope? Mrs. Dickens unites with me in cordial remembrances to your other half and all your house. And I am always

> Faithfully Yours

L. Gaylord Clark Esquire   CHARLES DICKENS

To A. C. M. PARISOT,[6] 30 JULY 1845*

MS Mr H. E. Quick. *Address:* A Monsieur | Monsr. A. C. M. Parisot | 1 Rue du Pont Louis Philippe | a Paris.

> London. 1 Devonshire Terrace, York Gate, Regents Park
> Thirtieth July 1845.

Dear Sir.

In the hope that you read English, I answer your letter in my own language. And I beg to assure you that I should have answered it long ago, but that I have only very recently returned to England from Italy. On my arrival here, I found your letter among many others; within this fortnight only.

I am not quite sure (for your Journal, the "Réaction",[7] has not reached me: having been, I suppose, mislaid, on its way)—I am not quite sure that I perfectly understand the nature of your request. But if the association to which it refers,

---

[1] Lewis Gaylord Clark (1808–73; *DAB*), editor of the *Knickerbocker Magazine*: see Vol. I, p. 469*n*.

[2] Thus in MS; "Clark" in subscription only.

[3] Willis Gaylord Clark (1808–41; *DAB*): see Vol. II, p. 394*n*. His *Literary Remains* appeared 1844.

[4] See Vol. III, p. 62*n*.

[5] Henry Inman, whom CD had met at Clark's on 23 Feb 42: see Vol. III, p. 79*n*.

[6] Not identified.

[7] The journal (founded 1844) of the Société protectrice des animaux.

be "The London Association for the Prevention of Cruelty to Animals",[1] and you desire to know such points connected with its management as may assist you in the formation of a similar society, I would recommend you to address a letter to the Secretary[2] of that Society, through the Post Office. I have no doubt he will be happy to give you any information in his power.

I would willingly seek it for you, though I do not belong to the association;[3] but that I feel sure the gentlemen connected with its management would be proud to render you their direct assistance. I cannot say that I have any practical knowledge on the subject. If I saw a man grossly ill-using any animal in the streets, I could, and certainly should, summon him before a Magistrate, who would fine him according to the extent of his offence. Any citizen can do this, in England, without belonging to the Society. And as I cannot belong to *all* the excellent Societies of whose objects I approve, this would be my course in such a case as I have supposed.

Accept my thanks, dear Sir, for your courteous consideration, and believe me, with a strong sympathy in your benevolent objects,

Faithfully Yours

à | Monsieur A. C. M. Parisot.   CHARLES DICKENS

To DANIEL MACLISE, 30 JULY 1845*

MS Free Library of Philadelphia.

Devonshire Terrace | Thirtieth July 1845.

My Dear Mac. Stanny is here, and we talk of going halfprice somewhere tonight. Will you come round, at your leisure?

Ever Yours
CD.

To JOHN MITCHELL,[4] [?LATE JULY 1845]

Mention in *To* Miss Kelly, 7 Aug 45. *Date:* after 15 July (*To* Stanfield, that day) when CD suggested the St James's, and some days before 6 Aug, since by then, as he told Miss Kelly next day, he had Mitchell's reply.

Asking if the amateurs might hire the St James's Theatre.

---

[1] The Royal Society for the Prevention of Cruelty to Animals, founded 1824; at 12 Pall Mall.

[2] Henry Thomas.

[3] A prospectus dated October 1844 was in the possession of Mr Henry C. Dickens.

[4] John Mitchell (1806–74), bookseller, publisher and librarian of Old Bond St, from 1834 until his death; proprietor of the St James's Theatre since 1842, and a theatrical impresario (see *To* Macready, 14 Oct 44, *fn*). Mitchell put on French plays at the St James's 1842–8, and also hired out the theatre, often to amateurs.

To WILLIAM OLIVER,[1] 1 AUGUST 1845*

MS Free Library of Philadelphia.

Devonshire Terrace First August 1845

Mr. Charles Dickens presents his compliments to Mr. Oliver, and begs to than‚ him for the gratification he has had in looking over the contents of the accompanying Portfolio. Mr. Dickens is no stranger to the taste and elegance of Mr. Oliver's pencil: and is happy to have seen, however cursorily, so many tokens of its worthy employment.

Mr. Dickens begs to add (as a reason for his not having expected Mr. Oliver this morning, and not being able to remain at home for his second visit) that he saw Mr. Hogarth yesterday, and explained to him that he could not have the pleasure of connecting himself with the proposed work.[2] Not because (as it is scarcely necessary to say) he has the least doubt of the execution of Mr. Oliver's share in it, but because he really is not open to any offer of the kind.

To T. J. THOMPSON, 1 AUGUST 1845

MS Huntington Library.

Devonshire Terrace | First August 1845.

My Dear Thompson.

I hope you will have no more misgivings.[3] I assure you, on my word, that your ease and self-possession were the subject of general commendation last night, among the whole Dram: Pers: You could not have done better.

What do you mean to do on Sunday? Will you dine here at half past 5? No Party.

Faithfully Ever

T. J. Thompson Esquire.   CD

To THOMAS POWELL, 2 AUGUST 1845

MS Mr H. E. Quick.

Devonshire Terrace | Saturday Evening | August Second 1845.

My Dear Powell.

I intend handing this to Augustus (whom I expect to see here, tomorrow) to bring to you. But he is quite innocent of its subject or contents.

---

[1] William Oliver (?1804–1853; *DNB*), landscape painter; published *Scenery of the Pyrenees* in 1842.

[2] Unidentified.

[3] His misgivings increased—a month later he wrote: "That horrid play—that returns to my mind like some hideous dream. Never was there such a good-natured person as I am—I deserve more thanks than I am likely to get . . . sacrificing myself to the vanity of others. Upon my word it would serve them right if I did everything to spoil their 'effects' on the night" (T. J. Thompson *to* Christiana Weller, 31 Aug 45; MS Mrs Sowerby).

I have thought several times of what you said to me in Broad Street,[1] and am disposed (subject always to your corrective judgment) to leave the matter where it is. I will tell you why.

In the first place, I think any grave notice of such a thing to a youth of Augustus's years, very likely to invest it with an importance not otherwise attaching to it in his eyes. In the second, I am relieved from any oppressive anxiety touching the young Lady's[2] designs upon him, by the knowledge that he has no possessions of any sort or kind. In the third, I contemplate the great possibility of there being nothing at all in it, but a means of getting rid of spare time pleasantly. In the fourth, and at the worst, I am not at all sure but it may keep him out of other harm's way.

I broke my heart into the smallest pieces, many times between thirteen and three[3] and twenty. Twice, I was very horribly in earnest;[4] and once I really set upon the cast for six or seven long years,[5] all the energy and determination of which I am owner. But it went the way of nearly all such things at last, though I think it kept me steadier than the working of my nature was, to many good things for the time. If anyone had interfered with my very small Cupid, I don't know what absurdity I might not have committed in assertion of his proper liberty; but having plenty of rope he hanged himself, beyond all chance of restoration.

I have asked no questions of my father or mother, for though I am dutiful, I am not altogether disposed to trust to their discretion in such a case. But I have sounded my brother Fred; and he seems to think the Virgin may be "only joking". She may be a Platonic Virgin, perhaps. Who knows!

In any case, without further communication with you, I am unwilling to seem to recognize the possibility of there being any danger either of contract or contact between Augustus and the Damsel. And this is not a hasty opinion, I assure you.

Now, what do *you* say?

Thomas Powell Esquire

Ever Yours Faithfully
CHARLES DICKENS

To THOMAS BEARD, 6 AUGUST 1845

MS Dickens House.

Devonshire Terrace | Sixth August 1845.

My Dear Beard
Here is a point at issue. And I am *determined* to be right!
Will you tell me (in the strictest confidence, of course) what is the gross

[1] Probably at No. 36, where Thomas and William Chapman, merchants, had their office.

[2] Unidentified. Augustus married Harriet Lovell of Sloane St in 1848.

[3] Written over "fifteen" and "five".

[4] Georgina Ross (see Vol. I, p. 7*n*) and Maria Beadnell (see Vol. I, p. 16*n*).

[5] Actually three or four years.

expence of the Foreign Department of the Herald: Expresses, Correspondents' Salaries, and Everything included: for any given period that may be fairly taken as representing a portion of the round year. And will you tell me, over and above, how much more you may suppose it to be in amount than the similar expences of our friend the Great Baronet.[1]

It seems an odd question, but I will tell you bye and bye how it came about.[2]

Ever Cordially Yours

Thomas Beard Esquire   CHARLES DICKENS

To MARK LEMON, 6 AUGUST 1845

MS Brotherton Library, Leeds.

Devonshire Terrace | Sixth August 1845.

My Dear Lemon

Forster tells me you have some doubts about the Farce.[3] I have many, also. Now let me suggest a substitute to you; and do you think of it, before to-night.

I played twice in Canada, in a version (by Mrs. Gore) of that Two o'Clock in the Morning. I bought it somewhere in America, but I don't recollect what it was called (I gave it, in the Bills, its London name). It was a most prodigious success; and went, with a roar, all through. The characters are rather better expressed in it, as I remember, than in Charles Mathews' version.[4]

I played Keeley's part. Charles Mathews' was acted by a tall, big, English officer[5]—a kind of person who expresses the remorseless intruder into the bedroom, much better than a figure like Mathews. It is an admirable part. Now if you would play that, I would play the other.[6] And there, we have the afterpiece. You and I could get it up, splendidly, between us. We want no rehearsal with the rest; we shall have no need to prolong the already very long rehearsals of Every Man in His Humour—can choose different days and times—and without dependence on anybody whomsoever, can get it so glib and pat, that it shall go like a Firework.

If you think the others do not care to play in the Farce (*I* am inclined to think it would bother them, most ruefully), I wish you would propose this, and see what they say to it. We should only want a wait of five minutes between the

---

[1] Sir John Easthope.

[2] Calculations of the expenses of the *Daily News* were evidently progressing; Beard, as an employee of a rival newspaper, was not yet in CD's confidence: see *To* Beard, 12 Oct 45.

[3] *The Mayor of Garratt*, with two acts and nine speaking parts for men, would have been more exacting and less rewarding than *Two o'Clock in the Morning*.

[4] Mrs Gore's version was *A Good Night's*

Rest; or, Two in the Morning, 1839, Charles Mathews's, *Two in the Morning*, 1840: see Vol. III, p. 237 and *n.*

[5] Captain Granville: see Vol. III, p. 250*n*, 354 and *n.*

[6] i.e. Alfred Highflyer, the intruder, and Snobbington, the occupant of the bedroom. There are various farcical coincidences, but the main fun of the piece is the contrast between the fussy bachelor ("rayther particular") and the boisterous intruder.

comedy and the second overture; and could carry the little piece off, in a "blaze of triumph" (I know its effect) in five and thirty minutes.

I send four foils, by the Bearer.[1]

Always Faithfully Yours

Mark Lemon Esquire.   CHARLES DICKENS

To W. C. MACREADY, 7 AUGUST 1845*

MS Morgan Library.

Devonshire Terrace. | Seventh August 1845

My Dear Macready.

Will Monday the fifteenth of September (at Miss Kelly's Theatre) suit you for the conveyance of your critical eye, into the Atmosphere of Amateurs.[2]

Reply, Reply, Reply![3]

Between ourselves, I think the company "*damned* bad"—no other phrase will express the sentiment, at present. This is confidential.

We do Two o'Clock in the Morning, for the last piece.

Loves from all to all.

Ever affectionately Yours

W. C. Macready Esquire.   CHARLES DICKENS

To MISS FANNY KELLY,[4] 7 AUGUST 1845†

MS Berg Collection. *Address:* Miss Kelly | 73 Dean Street | Soho.

1 Devonshire Terrace | York Gate Regents Park
Seventh August 1845.

Dear Miss Kelly.

Mr. Stanfield and I met the other gentlemen concerned in our Play (most of them more or less known to you, I believe) last night; and we impressed upon them the ease and privacy of your little Theatre, as compared with the Saint James's: which some of them were very anxious to secure—so much so, that I had already written to Mr. Mitchell on the subject, and received the assurance of his desire to do everything for us, and to place it at our disposal. In the end, they very willingly agreed to come to Dean Street. And we purpose playing there, on Monday the fifteenth of next month—unless I should hear from Mr. Macready (who is very anxious to come, and to whom I have written this

[1] Lemon was playing Brainworm in *Every Man in his Humour*.

[2] Macready was out of London from 6 to 20 Sep, and the date of the performance was accordingly changed to 20 Sep. On 15 Sep Lady Holland reported that CD said Macready was "in a perfect agony of expectation to see him act" (*Elizabeth, Lady Holland to her Son, 1821–1845*, ed. Earl of Ilchester, 1946, p. 230).

[3] Cf. *Merchant of Venice*, III, ii, 66.

[4] Frances Maria Kelly (1790–1882; *DNB*), well-known actress, and Lamb's

"Barbara S—"; retired from Drury Lane 1835; also acting in monologues at the Strand 1833–9. Under the Duke of Devonshire's patronage, she built her own theatre, the Royalty in Dean St, Soho Square, opened 1840; it was used for plays, operas, and monologues, as well as for Miss Kelly's dramatic school, and was sometimes hired by amateurs. Forster says it was "made useless . . . by her mere whims and fancies" and that "she was not more delightful on the stage than impracticable when off" (F, v, i, 381).

morning) that he has any engagement for that night. In which case, but in no other, we shall change the day.

We purpose rehearsing on the Stage, *on Monday evening next, at a quarter before seven o'Clock*, when we wish to have the float lighted, if you will have the goodness to give directions to that effect. As my Servant knows the whole party, I will send him down beforehand, if you will allow me, to attend to the door.

*a*Believe me that I had great pleasure yesterday in becoming personally known to one whose truthful observation of nature and uncommon art in portraying it, have often afforded me the highest delight. I address you in the least ceremonious form, because I have known you in your best Spirit for some years; and I feel, somehow or other, like an old acquaintance.*a*

I am always | Faithfully Yours

Miss Kelly
CHARLES DICKENS

To MACVEY NAPIER, 7 AUGUST 1845

MS British Museum.

Devonshire Terrace | Seventh August 1845.

My Dear Sir

Pray do not have the least regard to the exclusion of my paper from the next number. I will write it at my leisure; and you shall have it in good time. Rely upon me, certainly, for the January number.

Mandeville, I know. The short report, I do not. But I will make myself master of it, before I begin.[1]

I am happy to say, that the whole of my rather formidable travelling Caravan, have returned in the best preservation. Mrs. Dickens sends her best regards to you. If you should see Lord Jeffrey, pray give him my love.

And Believe me always

Faithfully Yours

Professor Napier.
CHARLES DICKENS

To JOHN WILLMOTT,[2] 7 AUGUST 1845†

MS The Governors of the Royal Shakespeare Theatre.

1 Devonshire Terrace | York Gate Regents Park
Seventh August 1845

My Dear Willmot.[3]

Mayhap you may have heard how that some friends of yours are going to have

---

a a Extract given in N, I, 687, from catalogue source; letter otherwise unpublished.

[1] Jeffrey's letter to Napier of 31 July (see *To* Napier, 28 July, *fn*) had said: "Ask D. to look in Mandeville (the Fable of the Bees man)", i.e. Bernard de Mandeville's *Enquiry into the frequent Causes of Executions at Tyburn*, 1725; it also mentioned Empson's recommendation of "a short

return made to Parliament about two years ago", which gave evidence of the effect of partial abolition—clearly the Parliamentary Paper published Aug 43 on Executions for Murder: its statistics supported CD's argument by showing that the decrease in murders was greatest in counties where the death penalty was sometimes commuted.

[2] John Willmott, formerly Macready's stage-manager and prompter at Covent

a Private Play at Miss Kelly's Theatre—how that Clarkson Stanfield Esquire is not innocent of the fact—how that John Forster Esquire has been spoken of for Kitely—and how that Charles Dickens Esquire is connected, in whispers, with Bobadil.[1]

It will not come off until the fifteenth of next month. But I and some others want our dresses made at once, in order that we may be easy in them, as well as in the words. It has occurred to me that nobody can tell us so well as you, where we can get them well and not ruinously made. *a*Perhaps the English Opera House tailor[2] might be recommended for the Job? They are to be marvellously correct; and great councils must be holden before the Shears are used.

So I want to see you. Now, shall I come to the Theatre, or will you come here?*a* If you will take a Chop with me, either on Saturday or on Tuesday, you shall have it at your own hour.[3] What do you say to Saturday? You shall be producible behind that fat silver watch you used to hang up in your box at Drury Lane, at any minute you choose.

Faithfully Yours
CHARLES DICKENS

—Willmot Esquire.

To T. J. THOMPSON, 8 AUGUST 1845

MS Huntington Library.

Devonshire Terrace | Friday Eighth August 1845

My Dear Thompson. I went to see Miss Kelly and her Theatre, the other day. I became a convert, immediately. The Stage is much wider than I had supposed —the audience part very good—the whole perfectly genteel and private—and the space sufficient for *our* actors, or the Devil's in it. We therefore decide (on my Stage-Managerial recommendation) to play there. We rehearse on the Stage next Monday Evening, at a quarter before 7. Will you take pot-luck with me that day, at half past four?[4]

I want to speak to you about your Dress. We purpose *playing* on Monday the 15th. of next Month. The farce is altered. Two o'Clock in the Morning is now the Dodge.[5]

Old W.[6] wrote to me last night, for a personal recommendation to the committee of the Liverpool Exchange Rooms.[7] I tipped them rayther a special one.

Always heartily Yours
Bobadil

T. J. Thompson Esquire

Garden and Drury Lane; now with the Keeleys at the Lyceum.

[3] Thus in MS.

[1] Mrs Procter told Milnes on 9 Aug that "Mr. Dickens and Mr. Forster are going to act, at the St. James's Theatre, *Every Man in his Humour* . . . in about a month. Mr. Thackeray has offered to sing between the Acts, but they decline his services" (T. Wemyss Reid, *Life, Letters and Friendships of Richard Monckton Milnes*, I, 358).

aa Not previously published.

[2] Presumably Head: see *To* Head, 13 Aug 45.

[3] N misreads as "house".

[4] Thompson had gone to the Lake District on 7 Aug (Christiana Weller's Diary, MS Mrs Sowerby), and did not receive CD's letter until he returned on 11 Aug for one night: see *To* Thompson, 13 Aug.

[5] N misreads as "Order".

[6] T. E. Weller.

To G. F. BAKER,[1] 10 AUGUST 1845*

MS Mr D. E. D. Lawson. *Address:* Paid. | Frederick Baker Esquire | Church Row | Limehouse.

1 Devonshire Terrace | York Gate Regents Park.
Tenth August 1845.

My Dear Sir

I am truly indebted to you for your great kindness in sending me so correct and beautiful a reminder of a place whither my heart wanders very often.[2] I shall prize it highly, always. You could not have devised any token of good-will that would have pleased me better, or gratified me more.

Believe me | Faithfully Yours

Frederick Baker Esquire   CHARLES DICKENS

To JOHN FORSTER, [?10 AUGUST 1845]

Extract in F, v, i, 381–2. *Date:* CD visited Miss Kelly 6 and 10 Aug; this letter almost certainly refers to the second meeting (and see *To* Miss Kelly, 14 Aug, in which he reassures her). Forster's date of 22 July is clearly impossible.

Heavens! Such a scene as I have had with Miss Kelly here, this morning! She wanted us put off until the theatre should be cleaned and brushed up a bit, and she would and she would not, for she is eager to have us and alarmed when she thinks of us. By the foot of Pharaoh, it was a great scene! Especially when she choked, and had the glass of water brought. She exaggerates the importance of our occupation, dreads the least prejudice against the establishment in the minds of any of our company, says the place already has quite ruined her, and with tears in her eyes protests that any jokes at her additional expense in print would drive her mad.[3] By the body of Cæsar,[4] the scene was incredible! It's like a preposterous dream.

---

[7] Christiana's diary shows that her father was in Liverpool 2–5 July, and a testimonial addressed to the Committee of the Liverpool Exchange Rooms, dated 7 Aug 45, from Francis Close of Cheltenham, described him as suitable for a position (not specified) from the "versatility of his interests—the courtesy of his manner his knowledge of some modern languages and his acquaintance with the world" (Weller Album, MS Mrs Sowerby). Weller in fact remained in London where he had a post with the Kennet & Avon Canal Co.

[1] George Frederick Baker, artist; clearly a relation of William Baker Jr and Robert B. Baker, solicitors, of 10 Church Row. A friend of Frederick Dickens (see *To* Mme de la Rue, 27 Sep 45), and probably one of the Chris Dowson set (see Vol. III, p. 516n). He was named as groomsman at Frederick's wedding in Christiana's journal, 30 Dec 48 (MS Mrs Sowerby).

[2] A picture of the Peschiere: see *To* Mme de la Rue, 27 Sep.

[3] She was particularly sensitive to jokes at her expense because of the disasters of 1840; at the opening night of her newly built theatre the noise of the stage machinery drowned the actors, and eventually half the theatre had to be dismantled in order to remove it. The nature of the proposed play and the presence of actors known as *Punch* writers would increase her anxiety.

[4] Bobadil in *Every Man in his Humour*, III, v.

To JOHN LEECH, 10 AUGUST 1845

MS Benoliel Collection. *Address:* Paid. | John Leech Esquire | Brook Green | Hammersmith.

Devonshire Terrace | Sunday Tenth August 1845.

My Dear Leech.

Can you come here tomorrow (Monday) afternoon, by *a quarter before* 6, and not later? I have appointed the English Opera House Tailor to come at that time; and I have found a picture, I think, which is the very thing for your dress.[1]

Faithfully Yours

John Leech Esquire.   CHARLES DICKENS

To MESSRS BRADBURY & EVANS, 11 AUGUST 1845

MS Dickens House.

Devonshire Terrace | Monday August Eleventh 1845.

My Dear B and E. I have always omitted to ask you in our conversations (though I have always had it in my mind to do so) how Johnson whom you so kindly took on my recommendation, goes on. He is full of satisfaction and a sincere desire to please you, in all he tells me. I thought to have mentioned to you the other day, that if in the arrangement of the multifarious establishments; you should want a couple to keep house (having no older servant with a prior claim) I think he and his Intended would suit your purpose excellently well. She is a most respectable young woman, of a very nice appearance and good manner. As we have always other things to speak of when we meet, I write thus much, lest I should forget it again.

Rather a good notion in connexion with the Cricket,[2] has occurred to me this morning. A decided chirp!

Ever Yours

Messrs. Bradbury and Evans.   CD

To MR LAKE,[3] 11 AUGUST 1845

Summary in Quaritch catalogue, No. 541 (1937); *MS* 2 pp.; dated 1 Devonshire Terrace, 11 Aug 45.

A formal note apologizing for not being able to see Mr. Lake and at the same time stating that he could not consider the proposal that Mr. Lake had in mind.

To THE REV. DAVID LAING, [12 AUGUST 1845]

MS (envelope only) Mrs D. Harmer. *Address:* The Reverend David Laing | 1 Cambridge Terrace | Regents Park. *Date:* PM 12 Aug 45.

---

[1] Leech was playing Mathew.   [3] Unidentified.
[2] The Christmas book: see *To* Forster, ?26 July and *fn.*

To GEORGE CRUIKSHANK, 13 AUGUST 1845*

MS Dickens House.

Devonshire Terrace | Thirteenth August 1845.

My Dear George. I am very sorry to say that I see no prospect of serving your unfortunate friend:[1] whose memoranda I return. But if occasion *should* present itself, rely upon me, I will seize it promptly.

I hope to see you at Margate, on Monday or so. Meantime and always
Believe me | Faithfully Yours

George Cruikshank Esquire   CHARLES DICKENS

Kate and her sister unite in Loves to Mrs. Cruikshank.

To MR HEAD,[2] 13 AUGUST 1845

MS Colonel Richard Gimbel.

Devonshire Terrace. | Wednesday Thirteenth August | 1845.

Mr. Head. I send you, on the other side, the names of the three other gentlemen who have decided to have their dresses made by you. And against their names, I have written their addresses, and the best time for measuring them. *Be very careful that the colors are bright; and that they will shew well by Lamplight.*

I enclose you three sketches, which express the figure of Bobadil, as I wish to make up. The sword I have; and I do not want spurs. But I wish the tops of the boots, and the gauntlets, and the hat-brim, to be very large. And I want the boots, gauntlets, and hat, *first*—and as soon as convenient to you. Do not forget the sword-belt. I want that to come home at the same time as the boots and gauntlets.

I wish particularly to see the red, of which you propose to make Bobadil's breeches and hat. I want it to be a very gay, fierce, bright color.

You can send to me, either between 10 and 11 tomorrow morning, or between 6 and 8 tomorrow evening. But it must be tomorrow, as I am going out of town next day for four or five days. Send a pattern of the red, at the same time. I will give an old pair of gloves to the person whom you send, that you may know the size of my hands for the gauntlets.

If you do these dresses well, as I have no doubt you will, I think it will throw some good jobs into your way, another time. If you want your Messenger to see any of the other prints to refresh your memory, I will shew them to him.
Yours
CHARLES DICKENS

P.S. Take care of the sketches.

Over

---

[1] John Wight: see *To* Miss Coutts, 17 Sep 45.
[2] Perhaps Walter George Head, tailor, of 36 Percy St. Macready's *Diaries* frequently mention "Head" as a theatrical costumier.

Wellbred. Mr. Thompson, 35 Gloucester Road, Hyde Park Gardens. Best time for measuring this gentleman, I should think tomorrow before 12.

Cash. Mr. Augustus Dickens. This gentleman will call on you at the Theatre, between 4 and 5 on Friday afternoon, to be measured. His dress to be of cloth.

Young Knowell. Mr. Frederick Dickens. This gentleman will write you a note, on Monday, and tell you when he will call at the Theatre for the same purpose

---

Master Mathew. Mr. Leech, Brook Green Hammersmith. This gentleman can be measured at his house on Friday Morning

---

To T. J. THOMPSON, 13 AUGUST 1845

MS Huntington Library.

Devonshire Terrace | Thirteenth August 1845.

My Dear Thompson. Estimate of your dress about five guineas. Shoes from 7/6 to 10/– Boots from 20/– to 30/– Beaver hat 14/– I don't think, to be safe, you can do better than employ Head. I have written him that I believe the best time for measuring you will be before 12 tomorrow Morning.[1] I have given him your address. I enclose your proposed color, as he sends it to me. Alter it, by instruction to the Measurer, if you see fit.

Au revoir in the sequestered Glades of Margate![2]

Ever Yours
T. J. Thompson Esquire.   CD

To FREDERICK DICKENS, 14 AUGUST 1845

MS Rosenbach Foundation.

Devonshire Terrace | Fourteenth August 1845.

My Dear Fred. I wish you had written, as we arranged; for Mrs. Smithson[3] says no word of terms in her letter (which is a preposterous omission, as we are no wiser than before); neither do I know whether Ballard[4] expects us tomorrow

---

[1] But unknown to CD, on 12 Aug Thompson had gone to the Shaws at Keynsham, near Bristol, where the Wellers were staying; he returned for the rehearsal on 18 Aug.

[2] Mrs Smithson and Amelia Thompson had been staying at Muthrix Farm, near Margate, since 29 July and Thompson had intended joining them on 16 Aug. The visit was postponed until 30 Aug, and on 23 Aug Thompson wrote to Christiana

from London that he had been ordering his wedding suit and that he was to dine with CD the next day (MS Mrs Sowerby).

[3] Fred was evidently staying with Mrs Smithson (see *To* Alfred Dickens, 8 Sep 45).

[4] James Ballard (?1806–74), landlord of the Albion Hotel, Broadstairs: see Vol. I, p. 303*n*.

afternoon. I have thought it best, therefore, to arrange that the children shall come down on Saturday by the Margate Boat.[1] Kate, Georgy, and I, come down tomorrow by the Ramsgate boat from London Bridge at half past 9: trusting to our good fortune for a boat coming off from Broadstairs. Affecy. always

CD
Over

Frederick Dickens Esquire

If you have not already prepared Ballard, pray do.

To MISS FANNY KELLY, 14 AUGUST 1845†

MS Berg Collection.

Devonshire Terrace | Thursday Fourteenth August 1845.
Dear Miss Kelly.

*a*As I did not happen to see, immediately before coming away the other night, the gentleman to whom you introduced me (who was most attentive and obliging); and as I am going down to Broadstairs in the interval between this and next Wednesday;*a* I think it best to let you know that we have appointed our next Rehearsal for that evening at a quarter before 6. I will then appoint an early day with Mr. Stanfield for looking at the Scenery, and will communicate it to you before we leave the Theatre, as we shall want a carpenter or two to get it down for us.

I know you will be glad to receive my assurance that there was the very best disposition on the part of all the gentlemen concerned, the other night, to be well pleased with the little Theatre and everything belonging to it. *b*I was extremely glad (remembering our conversation on Sunday) to observe their good nature.*b*

Faithfully Yours
CHARLES DICKENS

Miss Kelly.

To F. O. WARD, 14 AUGUST 1845

Text from N, 1, 694.

Devonshire Terrace | August Fourteenth 1845
Dear Sir,

My impression decidedly is, that all that can be done has been done in the matter of Mrs. Hood's Subscription.[2] The appeal as a general claim on public sympathy is greatly weakened by the existence of the pension and I do not think that more money is to be got.

In the case of the Elton Fund we received two thousand three or four hundred pounds. But it was a very peculiar case. There were six children, all females and without a mother. It was a particularly distressing accident in which Elton lost his life, and one to which public attention was very strongly attracted. Moreover the managers of theatres and the actors in theatres, had a lively interest in the catastrophe, and the endeavour to mitigate the severity of its pressure on the

---

[1] The plan was changed: see *To* Forster, 19 Aug.

aa; bb Not previously published.

[2] See *To* Ward, 12 July and *fn*.

unfortunate children; and free benefits were held in divers parts of the kingdom, from which a good deal of the money came.

Such practical knowledge as I have of these matters leads me distinctly to the conclusion that it is not advisable to press Mrs. Hood's appeal to any greater extent. I think it would be useless to her, and would be tortured into an unpleasant association with the memory of our deceased friend. I express this merely as my own individual opinion, of course, and am not expecting you to attach any greater weight to it than as it may seem to you on consideration to be reasonable and well founded. My estimate of the great genius of poor Hood is as huge as it is possible for man to form, and always has been, consequently I set her claim on very lofty grounds indeed. But in turning the question in my mind, I separate myself, or you, from the crowd who are addressed.

Faithfully yours
[CHARLES DICKENS]

_To_ W. C. MACREADY, 17 AUGUST 1845†

MS Morgan Library.

Albion Hotel Broadstairs
Sunday August Seventeenth 1845

My Dear Macready.

^aI have been obliged to communicate with the Punch men, in reference to Saturday the 20th; as that day of the week is usually their business-dinner-day;[1] and I was not quite sure that it could be conveniently altered.

Jerrold now assures me that it can, for such a purpose—and that it shall—and therefore consider _the_ Play, as being arranged to come off, on Saturday the 20th: of next month.

I don't know whether I told you that we have changed the Farce; and now mean to act Two o'Clock in the Morning, as performed by the Inimitable B at Montreal.^a

In reference to Bruce Castle School,[2] I think the question set at rest most

---

aa; bb Not previously published.

[1] They met at the Crown Tavern, near Drury Lane, along with other members of the "Punch Club", which at one time included CD, Stanfield and Landseer (according to Walter Jerrold, _Douglas Jerrold and Punch_, 1910, p. 21).

[2] Started in 1827 by Rowland Hill, son of Thomas Wright Hill, first as a "branch" of his school at Hazelwood, Birmingham, closed in 1833; he was succeeded as headmaster by his brother Arthur Hill, father of George Birkbeck Hill. Their system is described in _Public Education ... as practised at Hazelwood School_, 1825, which was widely discussed, and in _Sketch of the System of Education, Moral and Intellectual, in Practice at the Schools of Bruce Castle,_ _Tottenham, and Hazelwood, near Birmingham_, 1833. The main features were self-government, individual attention, and a minimum of punishment; there was no fagging, and moral and social training was emphasized. Science was taught, and French by the "direct method". The school committee of elected boys was given £100 a year for the library and scientific equipment. (See P. A. W. Collins, "Bruce Castle: a School CD Admired", _D_, LI [1955], 174–81.) Forster told Hunt on 1 Dec [1845]: "Dickens has particularly asked me to go with him to the Boys' Breaking up at Bruce Castle School on Wednesday—he thinks of sending one of his boys there, and we go to form judgements thereon" (MS University of Iowa).

probably, by the fact of there being no vacancy (it is always full) until Christmas; when Howitt's two boys,[1] and Jerrold's one,[2] go in, and fill it up again. But, after going carefully through the School, a question would arise in my mind whether the system—a perfectly admirable one; the only recognition of education as a broad system of moral and intellectual philosophy, that I have ever seen in practice—do not require so much preparation and progress in the mind of the boy, as that as[3] he shall have come there, younger and less advanced than Willy: or at all events without that very different sort of school experience which he must have acquired at Brighton.[4] I have no warrant for this doubt, beyond a vague uneasiness suggesting a suspicion of its great probability. On such slight ground, I would not hint it to anyone but you; who I know will give it its due weight—and no more—and no less.

I have the paper setting forth the nature of the higher classical studies, and the books they read. It is the usual course, and includes the great books in Greek and Latin. They have a Miscellaneous Library—under the Management of the boys themselves—of some five or six thousand volumes, and every means of study and recreation, and every inducement to self-reliance and self exertion, that can easily be imagined. As there is no room just now, you can turn it over in your mind again. And if you would like to see the place yourself, when you return to town, I shall be delighted to go there with you.

I come home on Wednesday. *b*It is our rehearsal night; and of course the active and enterprising stage-manager must be at his Post.*b*

Ever My Dear Macready | Affectionately Yours

W. C. Macready Esquire CHARLES DICKENS

To T. N. TALFOURD, 18 AUGUST 1845*

MS Berg Collection.

Broadstairs, Kent. | Eighteenth August 1845

My Dear Talfourd.

I have had all sorts of communications from the Manchester people, touching your Presidency in October next;[5] of which, as is natural and right and proper, they are very proud. It happens at an awkward time for me, as I shall be anxious about that period in behalf of my other moiety, who, in the ordinary rustic phrase, is likely to be worse before she is better. Still, I cannot deny myself the gratification of sharing your triumph, and holding up your train with my poor hand, in right of my old dedication[6] and older regard.

---

[1] CD seems to have been mistaken. The Howitts' third son, Alfred Botham (*b.* 1830), went to University College School in 1844, and Charlton (*b.* 1838) was also there by 1848,

[2] Must refer to the youngest, Thomas Serle Jerrold (*b.* 1833); it is not known whether he went there.

[3] Thus in MS.

[4] On leaving Mr King's school (see *To*

Miss Coutts, 10 Sep 45) Macready's son Willy went to Westminster; he seems to have been temporarily at a Brighton school in the summer of 1845.

[5] Talfourd presided at the soirée of the Manchester Athenaeum on 24 Oct; CD's acceptance was announced (*Examiner*, 23 Aug 45) but he did not go: see *To* Berlyn, 22 Oct.

[6] Of *Pickwick Papers*, 1837.

They tell me you and Mrs. Talfourd are to stay with Mr. Atherton.[1] I want to know, have you quite made up your mind to do so, as upon that, depends my own acceptance of his invitation. I have a very great dislike, I confess, to staying in peoples' houses, unless I know them very well—as it necessarily involves some tie and restraint. And we might be prodigiously comfortable at a good Inn!—

I am coming to town on Wednesday night: leaving the children here for a month or so, but returning home then, with Kate and her sister. Will you write me a line to Devonshire Terrace; telling me, at the same time, when you will be at leisure at chambers (or at leisure for a ride, like one of our old expeditions), as I want to speak to you about that Elton Fund, in pursuance of an uneasy request from Coutts's.[2]

With best regards to Mrs. Talfourd and Miss Ely[3]—Frank[4] (if he be at home)—and all the children.

I am Ever My Dear Talfourd | affectionately Yours

Mr. Serjeant Talfourd.   CHARLES DICKENS

To JOHN FORSTER, [19 AUGUST 1845]

Extracts in F, v, i, 384–5*n. Date:* first extract 19 Aug 45 according to Forster; second extract must be same letter. *From* Broadstairs.

Perhaps it is a fair specimen of the odd adventures which befall the inimitable, that the cab in which the children and the luggage were (I and my womankind being in the other) got its shafts broken in the city, last Friday morning,[5] through the horse stumbling on the greasy pavement; *and was drawn to the wharf (about a mile) by a stout man,* amid such frightful howlings and derisive yellings on the part of an infuriated populace, as I never heard before. Conceive the man in the broken shafts with his back towards the cab; all the children looking out of the windows; and the muddy portmanteaus and so forth (which were all tumbled down when the horse fell) tottering and nodding on the box! The best of it was, that *our* cabman, being an intimate friend of the damaged cabman, insisted on keeping him company; and proceeded at a solemn walk, in front of the procession; thereby securing to me a liberal share of the popular curiosity and congratulation. . . . Everything here at Broadstairs is the same as of old. I have walked 20 miles a day since I came down, and I went to a circus at Ramsgate on Saturday night, where *Mazeppa* was played in three long acts without an H in it: as if for a wager. Evven, and edds, and orrors, and ands, were as plentiful as blackberries; but the letter H was neither whispered in

---

[1] James Atherton, President in 1844; he was in fact prevented from entertaining Talfourd and other guests, owing to a family bereavement (*Manchester Guardian,* 15 Oct 45).

[2] Probably from Edward Marjoribanks, also a trustee of the Fund.

[3] Mrs Talfourd's niece.

[4] Francis Talfourd (1828–1862; *DNB*), Talfourd's eldest son; he had just entered Christ Church, Oxford. He was a minor dramatist who produced his first piece in 1847.

[5] 15 Aug.

Evven, nor muttered in Ell,[1] nor permitted to dwell in any form on the confines of the sawdust.

Describing how he saw a Giant played by a village comedian with a quite Gargan-tuesque felicity; he had a fine manner of sitting down to a hot supper (of children), with the self-lauding exalting remark, by way of grace, "How pleasant is a quiet conscience and an approving mind!"

To JOHN THOMPSON, 19 AUGUST 1845

Text from Sotheby's catalogue, June 1930; *MS* 1 p.; dated Broadstairs, 19 Aug 45.

John,

We shall come to London tomorrow by the steamboat which leaves Margate at 10 o'clock. I think she will be at **London Bridge Wharf**, at about 4 o'clock in the afternoon. Be there waiting for us, in good time.

To MISS BURDETT COUTTS, 21 AUGUST 1845

MS Morgan Library.

Devonshire Terrace. | Twenty First August 1845

Dear Miss Coutts. It is most extraordinary. There seems to be a fatality in my not seeing you.

I was at Broadstairs, when your last kind note arrived. It was past ten before I returned home last night, and found your hand-writing on my table. Mrs. Dickens was with me. And Charley and his sisters we have left behind, on the Seashore, for a month.

Under more fortunate circumstances, we should have been delighted to have come to you last night. I cannot tell you how much I have wished to see you.

I hope you are not going so far, or intend being absent so long, that you will be out of town on Saturday the 20th. of September. I am Stage Manager of a Company of Amateurs who are going to have a Play at Miss Kelly's little Theatre that night. And I don't know what I shall do, if you are not "in front"—as we say, professionally. Mr. Stanfield makes his first appearance on any stage, that night. Mr. Stone, the artist, also. And some of the "Punch" people[2] are also to appear before an admiring and delighted audience. The Comedy is Every Man in his Humour. There will be one man very much out of humour, if you are out of town.

To ease my mind on this head, I have marked this letter to be forwarded.

---

[1] From Catherine Fanshawe's "Enigma on the Letter H", as altered by James Smith: also quoted in *To* Mrs Gore, 31 Jan 41, Vol. II, p. 200*n*.
[2] Henry Mayhew, John Leech, Mark Lemon, Douglas Jerrold, Percival Leigh, and Gilbert A'Beckett; A'Beckett, who had the small part of William, did not act: see *To* Charles Eaton, 1 Oct 45, *fn.*

If I should hear in reply that you will not be in town that night—and further that Mrs. Brown will be away likewise—I shall take to drinking, immediately.

Ever Believe me with great regard

Yours faithfully

Miss Coutts.   CHARLES DICKENS

To CAPTAIN ARTHUR CUNYNGHAM,[1] 21 AUGUST 1845*

MS Free Library of Philadelphia. *Address:* Captain Arthur Cunyngham | Messrs. Cox and Co. | Charing Cross.

1 Devonshire Terrace, York Gate, Regent's Park.
Twenty First August 1845

My Dear Sir. I have had very great pleasure in the receipt of your letter. I am a bad correspondent: writing more letters, of necessity, in a week, than all the clerks in the Home Secretary's office. But I am happy to have the opportunity of acknowledging a note from you, and assuring you of the gratification I shall have in hearing from, or seeing you, at all times.

I envy you, your Spanish Trip. I envy you, your having seen Irving,[2] for whom I have a very high regard and admiration. He is coming home, I hear; having been recalled by the New President,[3] who is what they call in America "a blue-nosed[4] Presbyterian". I have hopes that he will take London in his way; and that I shall shake hands with him, once more.[5]

We left Genoa on the Ninth of June, and went, by way of Milan to Como. I wished to make the passage of the St. Gothard: having crossed the Simplon in the winter. It was open, and quite easy. The descent on the Swiss side, after Andermatt, I thought the most wonderful and glorious thing imaginable. But the whole of Switzerland delighted me beyond expression. We came to Frankfort, and so down the Rhine to Cologne, and thence to Brussels. Being joined by some friends from England at that place (who had come across to welcome us home) we went to Bruges and Ghent at our leisure; and embarking at Ostend, got home within the month after our departure from the Peschiere. I regret that Palace

---

[1] Sir Arthur Augustus Thurlow Cunyngham (1812–84; *DNB*) held the rank of Captain in the Buffs in 1845; afterwards General. Evidently had met CD in Genoa; possibly the same as the "Major Cunyngham" whom Thompson and Christiana met in Paris, 21 Nov 45; she described him as a "little bland talkative person", and said that he and his wife "had come from Genoa—claimed an acquaintance with Dickens" (Christiana's Diary, MS Mrs Sowerby).

[2] Washington Irving (1783–1859; *DAB*): see Vol. II, p. 55*n*. Appointed Minister to the Spanish Court 1842; he had reason to

expect that Polk would recall him, left Spain for Paris Sep 45, and resigned Dec 45.

[3] James Knox Polk (1795–1849; *DAB*); inaugurated President 4 Mar 45. Brought up as a Presbyterian.

[4] The word was applied to New Englanders as a term of contempt: Craigie and Hulbert, *Dictionary of American English*, 1938, cannot explain why it was also applied to Presbyterians—but clearly, in contrast to "red-nosed".

[5] No meeting took place; for Irving's change of attitude to CD, see Vol. III, p. 70*n*.

and that City very much; and am full of hopes and plans for seeing Italy again, one day.

London is as flat as it can be. There is nothing to talk about, but Railroad shares.[1] And as I am not a Capitalist, I don't find anything very interesting in that. The Gin Punch shall be yours in the snowy time (I hope) of Christmas; and it shall be preceded by a glass of rather better wine than one can get in the City of Palaces.

I am hot in the preparation of some Private Theatricals just now, which are to come off on the Twentieth of next Month. Mrs. Dickens and her sister send you their best regards. And I am ever Very faithfully Yours

CHARLES DICKENS

To JOHN FOWLER, 21 AUGUST 1845*

MS Free Library of Philadelphia. *Address:* John Fowler Esquire | Mechanics' Institute | Sheffield.

London. 1 Devonshire Terrace | York Gate Regents Park
Twenty First August 1845.

Sir.

I have been in Kent for a few days, or I should have answered your letter sooner.

It is with great reluctance that I, for the second time, feel bound to decline the Invitation with which the Directors of the Sheffield Mechanics' Institute have honored me. But at the time you mention, it would be quite impossible for me (having regard to other Engagements) to preside at the proposed Meeting. I have just now arranged to go to Manchester for a similar purpose, as a guest, on the 23rd. of October. In the interval, I am quite unable to leave town on any new invitation: having many visits to pay, and much to do, after a year's absence from England.

I am Sir | Your faithful Servant

John Fowler Esquire.   CHARLES DICKENS

To GEORGE CRUIKSHANK, [?22 AUGUST 1845]

MS Colonel Richard Gimbel. *Date:* Friday was 22 Aug, and the day, not the date, is correct (see next). The letter was evidently not posted till the next day: see *To* Cruikshank, 27 Aug.

Devonshire Terrace | Friday Night August 23rd. 1845.

My Dear George.

You have heard of our intended Play. I want you to take a part in it—a good

---

[1] The mania for railway speculation was now approaching its height; in Sep alone, 457 new schemes were registered. Thackeray's "Diary of C. Jeames de la Pluche", satirizing the mania (with feeling, for he himself lost £500), began to appear in *Punch* on 2 Aug.

part, which would not cost you much trouble, and which you would do, admirably.

First let me tell you how it comes to be vacant.

We arranged this Play one day at a country-dinner—quite offhand—and have taken nobody in, since, but two walking gentlemen. We have often wanted, among ourselves, to get you in, but have never had a reasonably good part to offer you.

The one I propose now, is *Downright* in the enclosed Comedy. It begins in the first Scene of the Second act. Until within an hour ago, it was Stanfield's, but he is so much bothered, and has so much to do with his other duties of Stage Director and Manager of the Scenery and Carpenters that he has come to me and said he will be glad to resign it, if *you* will take it. Now, do take it; and make one in as pleasant a party as was ever got together for such a purpose.

We have Miss Kelly's little Theatre—which is strictly and perfectly private. We play on Saturday the 20th. of next month—a month hence. We rehearse, on the stage, generally once a week; and the next Rehearsal is on Tuesday Evening at a quarter before Seven. If you join us, and would come up to it,[1] I can give you a Bed. No names will be printed in our Bills, but the names of the characters. It will be done with every possible appliance in the way of arrangement, correct costume, and so forth. The admissions will be by a printed card of Invitation, addressed to the person invited by all concerned, as if it were a party. And no man can have any visitor (being obliged to make the names of his list known to the rest beforehand) to whom anyone else objects. I think it will be as brilliant an audience, and as good an amateur Play, as was ever seen. The expence to *each, exclusive of the dress,* (which every man finds for himself) will not exceed Two Guineas.

I almost rely upon you from this moment, as one of the party. Write me by Sunday nights post, *or at the latest by Mondays,* a definite answer. Every actor will have the privilege of inviting about five and thirty friends. The names of the actors, I have written below.[2] Don't mind any pen and ink marks you find in the book, as they were made for my private edification.

With best regards to Mrs. C.

Ever Yours heartily

CD.

Kitely	——————	Forster	Captain Bobadil —	Myself
Old Knowell	—————	Mayhew[3]	Cash—————	Augustus Dickens
Young Knowell	———	F. Dickens	Formal ———	Evans[4]
Wellbred	—————	Thompson	Cob ———	Leigh[5]
Master Stephen	———	Jerrold	Brainworm ———	Lemon

---

[1] From Margate.

[2] Forster's MS list in his own copy of the play still has Stanfield as Downright, and also gives A'Beckett in two servants' parts.

[3] Henry Mayhew: see *To* Jerrold, 24 Oct 46, *fn*.

[4] Frederick Mullet Evans.

[5] Percival Leigh (1813–89; *DNB*), journalist. Trained as doctor; on *Punch* staff since its beginning; known as "The Professor"; author of *The Comic Latin Grammar* and *The Comic English Grammar*, 1840, and *Portraits of Children of the Mobility*, 1841.

Master Mathew——— Leech	Mrs. Kitely ——— Miss Fortescue[1]
Justice Clement——— Stone	Bridget ——————— Miss Jackson
Downright (I hope) — You	Tib ——————— Miss M. Jackson[2]

To JOHN FORSTER, [22 AUGUST 1845]

Extract in F, v, i, 382n. Date: 22 Aug according to Forster.

Look here! Enclosed are two packets—a large one and a small one. The small one, read first. It contains Stanny's renunciation as an actor!!! After receiving it, at dinner-time to-day, I gave my brains a shake, and thought of George Cruikshank. After much shaking, I made up the big packet, wherein I have put the case in the artfullest manner. "R-r-r-r-ead it!" as a certain Captain[3] whom you know observes.

To MRS M'IAN, 23 AUGUST 1845

MS Colonel Richard Gimbel.

Devonshire Terrace | Twenty Third August 1845.
My Dear Mrs. Mc Ian.

I went to Whitelands[4] yesterday. Mrs. Field was absent in the country for her health, but I saw the Second in Command,[5] and had a long talk with her.

I pressed her closely—don't be alarmed; I am not going to say to my beating heart—I pressed her closely with the question whether the school near Canterbury was still open to Esther if she chose to take it. She said, distinctly, 'Yes'. I then asked her why the Chester School had been suggested. She replied because they thought the future patronage of Lady Westminster[6] might prove most advantageous to Esther—and because there is another Virgin in the School who is equal to the Canterbury business, whereas they have nobody at present, but Esther, who is up to the Chester Mark. I said that that was unfortunate, certainly; but that Esther had always sustained herself with the hope of having her little sisters with her in the holidays. That this would be practicable at

[1] Julia Fortescue, afterwards Lady Gardner (1817–99), actress: see Vol. II, p. 331n.

[2] Bridget and Tib were played by Miss Hinton and Miss Bew, pupils of Miss Kelly.

[3] In the acting version, but not in the original text, Bobadil says to Mathew in I, v, "What new piece ha' you there? Read it".

[4] Whitelands House, King's Road, Chelsea, where Esther Elton was being trained as a teacher. Founded 1841 by the National Society (with the help of Miss Coutts) as an "Institution for educating young Women to be Schoolmistresses"; the Society's

Annual Report for 1846 shows that the institution was expanding and had 54 pupils in Mar 46. CD used their rules for the allotment of domestic duties and their books of instruction, for Urania Cottage: see *To* Miss Coutts, 3 Nov 47 (*CD to Angela Burdett-Coutts*, ed. Edgar Johnson, 1955, p. 106). The College is now at West Hill, Putney.

[5] Miss Lowman.

[6] May refer to Eleanor (*d.* 1846), daughter of Thomas Egerton, Earl of Wilton, wife of Robert Grosvenor, 1st Marquis of Westminster (*d.* Feb 1845).

Canterbury, but would be impracticable at Chester. That she stood almost in the relation of a Mother to them. And that I could not find it in my heart to do more than place before her the comparative advantages of the two Schools, and leave her to her own selection. I said that I thought the other gentlemen interested in her, would be of the same mind.

Number Two then observed that she felt the kindness and propriety of this suggested course of proceeding but that she would like to communicate it to Mrs. Field, if I would allow her, before I spoke to Esther. She could write to Mrs. Field, she said, by that day's post; and write to me on Monday: receiving that Lady's answer in the meanwhile. In the interval, she would be glad if I would not mention my sentiments to Esther.

To this, I acceded. So I saw Esther, and told her I should like to consider for a day or two before I gave her any advice on the subject—but as she looked rather depressed and anxious, I added that it would be only advice, and I would leave her to decide for herself. At this she brightened up (a most excellent girl she is, and they greatly extol her); and I left her with the promise that I would see her again, on Monday or Tuesday.

Ever believe me | Dear Mrs. Mc Ian | Faithfully Yours
Mrs. Mc Ian.   CHARLES DICKENS

To ROBERT KEELEY, 25 AUGUST 1845

MS Berg Collection.

Devonshire Terrace | Monday Twenty Fifth August | 1845.
My Dear Sir
We are going to have a tiny pair of flats painted for that most tremendous play of ours, under our friend Stanfield's direction. As there is no very good place at Miss Kelly's for the purpose, Stanfield and I have thought of your Painting Room, at the Lyceum; and I write to beg the favor of your allowing them to be painted there.

I know you are very much engaged. Pray don't take the trouble of answering this, unless you desire to say 'No'. I shall take your silence as 'Yes'.

Faithfully Yours always
Robert Keeley Esquire   CHARLES DICKENS

To GEORGE CRUIKSHANK, 27 AUGUST 1845

MS Colonel Richard Gimbel.

At Forster's | Wednesday 27th. August
My Dear George.
Have you received a letter I wrote you, *last Saturday*, and sent by the Day Mail to Margate?[1] It contained a request to you to act in our projected play—

---

[1] Forster says Cruikshank "was not for that time procurable, having engagements away from London" (F, v, i. 382*n*).

the part of one Downright in Every Man in his Humour. So many days have
elapsed since I wrote to you (in the meantime we have asked nobody of course)
that we are fast approaching to a most intensely considerable fix. I shall be at
home by 5 o'clock. In any case, pray let me see or hear from you, *this evening*.[1]

Ever Faithfully
CHARLES DICKENS

George Cruikshank Esquire.

To GEORGE CATTERMOLE,[2] 27 AUGUST 1845

MS Berg Collection. *Date:* Forster's letter (see *fn*) is dated 27 Aug.

My Dear George. I add a line to Forster's "other side",[3] to tell you what the
project is. A little party of us have taken Miss Kelly's Theatre for the Night of
the 20th of next month; and are going to act a play there, with correct and pretty
costume—good orchestra—&c &c. The affair is strictly private. The admission
will be by cards of Invitation—every man will have from 30 to 35—nobody can
ask any person without the knowledge and sanction of the rest; any objection
being final—and the expence to each (exclusive of the dress: which every man
finds for himself) will not exceed two guineas. Forster plays. And I play. And
Stone plays. And some of the Punch people play. Stanfield, having the Scenery
and Carpenters to attend to, cannot manage his part also. It is "Downright" in
Every Man in His Humour—not at all long, but very good[4]—he wants you to
take it. And so do we. We shall have a brilliant audience. The uphill part of
the thing is already done—our next Rehearsal is next Tuesday—and if you will
come in, you will find everything ready to your hand—and all very merry and
pleasant.

Always Faithfully Yours
CHARLES DICKENS

To JOHN FOWLER, 28 AUGUST 1845*

MS Free Library of Philadelphia. *Address:* John Fowler Esquire | Mechanics'
Institute | Sheffield.

London. 1 Devonshire Terrace | York Gate Regents Park
Thursday Twenty Eighth August | 1845.

Dear Sir.

I have deliberated for a few days on the subject of your letter: most sincerely
wishing to give the Sheffield Mechanics' Institute the benefit of my poor assistance, if I could possibly arrange to visit the town at the time you propose. But

---

[1] These two words underlined twice.
[2] George Cattermole (1800–68; *DNB*):
see Vol. I, p. 277*n*.
[3] Forster's letter occupies the first and
second side, CD's the third and fourth, of
the sheet. Forster said that he would "call
back to see you in half an hour. Dickens

is with me; and we wish to celebrate our
'reunion' by a petition to you to join us in
a little project of amusement we have on
foot just now".
[4] Cattermole must have refused; the part
was eventually played at Miss Kelly's by
Dudley Costello.

though I should be so very near it on the twenty third of October, I cannot pledge myself with any degree of certainty—certainly not with the requisite degree of certainty—to come to you. Domestic reasons will oblige me to return home from Manchester with all possible dispatch; and will render my flying-visit even there, an anxious one.

Under other circumstances, I should have been truly glad of so favorable an opportunity of complying with the request of the Directors.

I am Dear Sir | Your faithful Servant

John Fowler Esquire   CHARLES DICKENS

To JAMES MONTGOMERY,[1] 28 AUGUST 1845*

MS Dickens House. *Address:* J. Montgomery Esquire | "The Mount" | near | Sheffield.

London. 1 Devonshire Terrace, | York Gate, Regents Park
Twenty Eighth August 1845.

My Dear Sir.

I have had great pleasure, I assure you, in the receipt of your letter. It would have been a greater pleasure to me, if I could have hoped it would lead to a personal acquaintance between us at the time to which it refers. But, (as I have written Mr. Fowler to day) I cannot decide to come on to Sheffield from Manchester at that particular period; having special reasons for anxiety at home; and for making a rather ill-timed absence from it, as brief as possible.

If I had been wavering in my inclination to come, your persuasion—much weightier with me than the feather of the largest bird that flies—would have brought the scale down, heavily. But I am really disposed to make the visit; and would not hesitate a moment, on any lighter grounds than those which oblige me to deny myself that pleasure.[2]

Believe me Dear Sir | Faithfully Yours

J. Montgomery Esquire.   CHARLES DICKENS

To T. J. SERLE, 29 AUGUST 1845

MS Mr Peter Brandt.

Devonshire Terrace | Friday Twenty Ninth August 1845.

My Dear Serle.

I set great store by your plain-spoken letter; which comes from the Man I know you to be: and is not addressed to an inconsiderate or regardless person, believe me.

Something seemed to lead me the other night, when I was with you, to a

---

[1] James Montgomery (1771–1854), of Sheffield, journalist and well-known hymn-writer. He helped to found the Sheffield Mechanics' Library in 1824 and was its first President; he had lectured there on English poets as recently as 1843.

[2] CD did not go to Sheffield until 1855, when he read the *Carol* for the benefit of the Mechanics' Institution (*Speeches,* ed, K. J. Fielding, pp. 208–9).

suspicion of the Truth. But having been away so long, I had no idea that any-thing of an unpleasant nature had arisen between you and Macready.[1] I purposely alluded to him, to ascertain if my misgiving were well-founded.

I am quite concerned that I should have been a party to the request,[2] under such circumstances. But your letter assures me that you absolve me from all blame. Therefore I merely state the fact of my entire ignorance to you, as a satisfaction to myself.

Ever My Dear Serle | Faithfully Yours

T. J. Serle Esquire CHARLES DICKENS

To FRANK STONE,[3] 29 AUGUST 1845*

MS Benoliel Collection.

Devonshire Terrace | Twenty Ninth August 1845 | Friday

My Dear Stone.

I don't know whether you will return to town before next Tuesday; but in case you should arrive in the interval, I deem it best to let you know that we rehearse that night, and previously dine at the Bedford[4] *at 4 o'Clock*; when everybody brings his list of proposed Invitations, to the number of 2 or 3 and thirty each; and when the bills and cards of Invitation will be given out.

We have changed the night of acting, to Saturday the 20th. as Macready plays in Liverpool on the 15th. and begged hard for that much postponement.

Ever Yours
Bobadil

To MRS CHARLES DICKENS, [31 AUGUST 1845]

MS British Museum. *Date:* PM 31 Aug 45. *Address:* Mrs. Charles Dickens | Devonshire Terrace | York Gate Regents Park | London.

Broadstairs | Sunday Afternoon

My Dear Kate.

I found the darlings all well and happy—looking very brown, and in the most robust health. Chickenstalker is beyond all question a size larger. The sea was so very rough, that the Boat couldn't come off; and we were carried on to Ramsgate. As we entered Broadstairs in a Fly, we came upon the Babbies in a cornfield, plucking wheat. They have been to Ramsgate with us today: and returned in a carriage. They are coming to dessert, immediately.

We had a most abominable passage—the boat a mass of sour sickness from

---

[1] *Diaries*, II, 282, 284, show that relations between Serle and Macready had been somewhat strained during the Paris season, after which there is no further reference. Serle had clearly contributed to Macready's continued troubles over Helen Faucit.

[2] No explanation; possibly connected with the theatricals.

[3] Frank Stone (1800–59; *DNB*): see Vol. I, p. 487*n*.

[4] The Bedford Head at 41 Maiden Lane, Covent Garden.

the head to the stern. I didn't come to that pass myself, but Maclise was extremely ill. It *was*[1] intolerable. We have taken our places by coach to Dover, tomorrow Morning. I have no doubt, at present, that we shall return to town by the train at 6 from Dover. But in case we should not, and you should not see me until Tuesday Morning, take it for granted that we have decided, for some reason or other, to pass the night there.

We have seen nothing of Frederick[2] or Thompson.[3] I suppose they have not come down. Maclise sends his love to you and Georgy; and all the children add theirs.

Ever affectionately
CHARLES DICKENS

P.S. I have my latch-key in my pocket. I have written in great haste, as I have been with the children all day, and had almost missed the Post. Best love to Georgy.

To DUDLEY COSTELLO, [LATE AUGUST 1845]

Mention in *Autograph Prices Current*, III (1917–18), 83. *Date:* presumably end of Aug, after Cattermole's refusal, and in time for the next rehearsal on 2 Sep; since accompanied "by a Note admitting him", clearly for the first rehearsal that Costello attended, when he would not yet be known at the theatre.

Inviting him to come to a rehearsal.

To W. C. MACREADY,[4] 2 SEPTEMBER 1845*

MS Morgan Library.

Devonshire Terrace | Second September 1845

My Dear Macready.

Do you think Bobadil is *humble* before the Justice,[5] or still carrying it off in his swaggering way? Forster and I can't agree about it. *I* say, swagger before the Justice. *He* says, be completely hove down before the Legal presence. Now, what do *you* say?

Between you and me, and that Post which is in everybody's confidence, I don't think its a very good part, and I think the comedy anything but a very good

---

[1] Underlined twice.

[2] He was again staying with Mrs Smithson at Muthrix Farm.

[3] Thompson travelled down in the evening, also in bad weather: "Master Charles Dickens had thought proper to start in the morning without communicating with me notwithstanding that I put off my departure from Friday to Saturday that we might all come down together. But he does curious

things now & then. These geniuses are not bound by ordinary rules; he has got a brother-genius with him—Maclise" (Thompson *to* Christiana, 31 Aug 45, MS Mrs Sowerby).

[4] Macready had returned from Norwich by 31 Aug and left for Liverpool 6 Sep.

[5] Clement, in *Every Man in his Humour*, v, ii.

play. It is such a damned thing to have all the people perpetually coming on to say their part, without any action to bring 'em in, or take 'em out, or keep 'em going.

> Affectionately Ever
> CD

To DR SOUTHWOOD SMITH, 2 SEPTEMBER 1845*

MS Mr W. A. Foyle. *Address:* With Two Books. | Dr. Southwood Smith | 38 Finsbury Square.

> Devonshire Terrace | Tuesday Second September 1845.

My Dear Dr. Smith

I have been to Broadstairs to see my children (who are staying there, a few weeks, with their nurses) or I should not have left your kind note so long unanswered.

It vexes me very much that I am engaged on Thursday. Otherwise, I need not say that it would have delighted me to come to you.

I shall send you—most likely tomorrow—an Invitation to some Private Theatricals on the 20th. I hope you will be able to accept it. They may amuse you, perhaps.

I forward you with this, two Transportation reports, at the request of our friend Mr. Chesterton.[1] Very terrible books they are.[2]

We are all quite well. Mrs. Dickens and her sister send their best regards to you. And I am Ever

> Faithfully Yours
> CHARLES DICKENS

Dr. Southwood Smith.

To THOMAS BEARD, 4 SEPTEMBER 1845

MS Dickens House. *Address:* Thomas Beard Esquire | Morning Herald Office.

> Devonshire Terrace. | Thursday Fourth September 1845.

My Dear Beard.

This will be presented to you by Mr. Sidney Blanchard—a son of poor Blanchard whom you knew; and to whose melancholy history you are no stranger.

---

[1] George Laval Chesterton (*d.* 1868), Governor of the Middlesex House of Correction: see Vol. I, p. 101*n*.

[2] Presumably the two most recent Parliamentary Papers on Convict Discipline published in Apr 43 (XLII) and July 45 (XXXVIII), which indicated the breakdown in convict administration in Van Diemen's Land, following the decision to replace assigned service by a system of gang labour. Since 1841 there had been a 40% increase in the convict population, and by 1845 almost a third of the pass-holders were unemployed, as the colony was suffering an acute economic depression, and employers could not afford the wages demanded after the ending of assigned service. CD would also have found it "terrible" that there was so little evidence of efforts to rehabilitate the convicts after Maconochie's brief experiment on Norfolk Island, which had been terminated by the Colonial Office before it was possible to assess its achievements during 1840–2.

He is anxious (as you may have already heard from Hazlitt, who is much interested in his behalf) to obtain an Engagement on the Herald, in some reporting capacity. He is not untried: having attended Railway Committees for the Globe in the course of last Session: and having given, as I am assured, every satisfaction.[1]

You know how very much interested I am, my Dear Beard, in all that relates to this family—and if you can tender them any service in this regard, it will be the very greatest satisfaction to me. I need say no more; for I am sure it would be a satisfaction to yourself also.

I sent you a prodigiously formal and unique document[2] to Portland Place this morning.

Always My Dear Beard | Cordially Yours

Thomas Beard Esquire.   CHARLES DICKENS

To WILLIAM HAZLITT,[3] 4 SEPTEMBER 1845

Extract in Anderson Galleries catalogue Feb 1922; *MS* 2 pp.; dated Devonshire Terrace, 4 Sep 45.

I have given your young friend, a note to Beard: which I will back by the strongest personal recommendation. . . . It is very kind of you to interest yourself so actively in the matter.

To FREDERICK DICKENS, 4 SEPTEMBER 1845

MS Benoliel Collection.

Devonshire Terrace | Thursday Fourth September

My Dear Fred

I will take of you—First Circle of Boxes Nos. 49, 50, 51, and 52. And I give you instead, in the same circle, Nos. 72 110, 111 and 112.

Affectionately always

CD

PS. I want, after the next Rehearsal, to go over your part with you, in your dress, *almost every day*. It strikes me you are still more at sea than you ought to be. What do you do with my names on your list? Have you sent out those cards?

---

[1] On 1 Oct Jerrold also wrote a letter of recommendation to Beard (MS Dickens House); perhaps Sidney delayed presenting CD's letter.

[2] Probably an invitation to the play.

[3] William Hazlitt (1811–93), only son of the essayist; edited his father's works and *Literary Remains*, 1836; a reporter on the *Morning Chronicle* with CD. Registrar of the Court of Bankruptcy. Married Catherine Reynell; father of William Carew Hazlitt the bibliographer, *b.* 1834. He joined the reporting staff of the *Daily News*, and was later a contributor to *Household Words*.

Or do you leave them to me to send. I want exceedingly to know this, or I shall get into all sorts of difficulties.[1]

To DANIEL MACLISE, 4 SEPTEMBER 1845*

MS Colonel Richard Gimbel.

Devonshire Terrace | Thursday Fourth September

My Dear Mac.

I wish, if you can, you would come and dine with us again tomorrow at half past 5.[2] Head the tailor is coming, and I want to have the benefit of your presence when I instruct him about the Cloak.

Ever Yours

Daniel Maclise Esquire   CD

To AUGUSTUS TRACEY, 4 SEPTEMBER 1845*

MS University of Texas.

Devonshire Terrace | Fourth September 1845.

My Dear Tracey. The Bearer of this, is my Father. He is much interested in a curious case of Mysterious Disappearance[3] which has occurred lately. So am I, from its singularity, though I don't know the party. He is anxious (I mean my father is) to have the benefit of your opinion. Will you kindly give it to him: being so competent to render valuable counsel in such a case?

Ever Cordially Yours

Frederick[4] Tracey Esquire   CHARLES DICKENS

To MISS FANNY KELLY, 6 SEPTEMBER 1845

MS Free Library of Philadelphia.

Devonshire Terrace | Sixth September 1845.

Dear Miss Kelly

I send you a bill[5] and card[6]—not because you will have any need of them, but

[1] Catherine Dickens *to* Miss Buckley, of Kensal Lodge, 9 Sep 45 (MS Private), sends "tickets" for herself and her mother, saying, "You will see that they are signed by Mr. Forster, but it is all the same thing. The theatre being divided amongst so many as it is very small, we have all had some difficulty and been obliged to accommodate each other about places. For this same reason Charles is doubtful whether Mrs. Touchet has received a ticket. Will you kindly ascertain whether that is all right and let me know?"

[2] Thompson also dined with them (Christiana's Diary, MS Mrs Sowerby).

[3] See *To* Alfred Dickens, 8 Sep 45.

[4] Tracey's second name.

[5] Reproduced in Kitton, *CD by Pen and Pencil*, I, 108, and Matz's edn of Forster's *Life*, I, 394, from the original in the Forster Collection (with sketch of Kitely and Bobadil by Maclise added). It is headed "STRICTLY PRIVATE", and does not give the names of the actors.

[6] Reproduced in Kitton, I, 109; gilt-edged with gilt and blue-green lettering; headed "STRICTLY PRIVATE". The names of the cast, and of Stanfield, follow, and "request the pleasure of |— company at an | Amateur Performance | At Miss

in order that you may see that we have set forth your Theatre in due state, on each.

We shall want the Gas on, in the dressing-rooms on Tuesday Night, if you please. Also that trap-door opened, which admits of a communication below, between both sides of the stage.

Faithfully Yours

Miss Kelly.   CD

To ALFRED DICKENS, 8 SEPTEMBER 1845*

MS Colonel Richard Gimbel.

Devonshire Terrace | Monday Eighth September 1845.

My Dear Alfred. It is some time since I received your letter dated Scarborough;[1] but I have been very much engaged, in many ways; and am indeed at the best of times but a bad correspondent: having rather more letters to write, that must be written, than the Home Secretary.

There is no news in town of any sort or kind, except that the children are at Broadstairs, and that Fred seems to find a sort of dismal fascination in a windy spot called Mutrix Farm near Margate, where Mrs. Smithson has lodgings, and where he makes himself drowsy with bottled beer and great masses of meat, by the week together. Thompson was about to be married in a great hurry, but Mrs. Weller's mother (an ancient Lady, known in the family by the name of "Gran") threatens to die; and in that case, there will be a postponement of the Nuptials.[2] With his usual odd frostiness of manner, he seems to me to be rather glad of it, than otherwise.[3]

Supernatural exertions are being made for the Great Play which is to come off on the Twentieth. We have Scene Painters at work, touching up all the Scenery; and the dresses will really be very brilliant indeed. The actors rather disappoint me, so far. But they will improve perhaps, and come out better than I expect. If you should run up to London on this great occasion, I shall be happy to give you house-room.

Nothing whatever has been heard of young Birkenshaw;[4] for whose mother I

Kelly's Theatre, 73, Dean Street, Soho | On Saturday Evening the 20th September . . ."

[1] Perhaps on holiday: by Dec 45 Alfred was one of the engineers surveying the Hull & Birmingham Railway.

[2] Mrs Sarah Southerden (?1760–1845), Mrs Weller's mother, died on 8 Sep after two weeks' illness. Thompson to Christiana, 31 Aug 45 (MS Mrs Sowerby), shows that the marriage had been fixed for 22 Sep.

[3] The warmth of Thompson's letters to Christiana whenever they were separated contradicts this impression. Thompson took her down to Margate on 12 Sep, where she stayed a few days with Mrs Smithson, meeting Fred and "the little Dickens" (Diary, MS Mrs Sowerby).

[4] Alfred's employer at York was John Cass Birkinshaw (1811–67): see Vol. III, p. 263n; the missing young man was probably a younger brother. The family would be known to John Dickens as he had stayed with Alfred at Malton, possibly this year—T. W. Robertson (b. 1829) remembered them coming "constantly to the theatre" there when he was a boy of about 15 (T. E. Pemberton, The Life and Writings of T. W. Robertson, 1893, p. 34).

am sincerely sorry. Father goes about, identifying all the Male Bodies that turn up; and bearing enormous handbills in his pocket: together with a tremendously long document called a Statement of the Facts. Which he reads to Everybody. He is a sort of Private Coroner—sitting upon all the Fatal Accidents that happen, and cross-examining his witnesses (he summons all manner of Servant-girls and Policemen) with the greatest closeness.

Kate and Georgy send their loves. Always affectionately
Alfred Dickens Esquire   CHARLES DICKENS

To MISS FANNY KELLY, 8 SEPTEMBER 1845*

MS Berg Collection.

Devonshire Terrace | Monday Evening 8th Septr. | 1845.
My Dear Miss Kelly.

No, no.—No audience tomorrow night. I am afraid my hand-writing has led you into a mistake. I do not want the Drawing-Room lighted by any means. *The Dressing-Rooms* are what I wrote about.

We will find time to speak together, tomorrow evening.

This Paper is no larger than yours.[1]

                                     Faithfully Yours
Miss Kelly.   CHARLES DICKENS

To MISS BURDETT COUTTS, 10 SEPTEMBER 1845

MS Morgan Library.

Devonshire Terrace. | Wednesday Tenth September | 1845.

My Dear Miss Coutts. I am deeply sensible, believe me, of your kind interest in my dear boy. I feel it as much as it is possible to feel anything. Far too much to thank you in written words like these. I am so painfully happy in your thoughtful remembrance of him, that I can only thank you from my inmost heart; and say that I am proud to place my trust in your considerate friendship.

I could do nothing better for him than to accept—I could do nothing half so good for him as to accept—your generous offer. My object is, to make him a good man and a wise one; and to place him in the best position I can help him to, for the exercise of his abilities and acquirements. Your help towards such an end is priceless to me, and to him. You could not (but you know it, I am sure) have done a more tender service.

He will be nine years old, next Twelfth Day. He had a Governess at home originally, and used to go to school, for half a year before we went to Italy, at a Mr. King's[2] at St. John's Wood. The gentleman is a good scholar, and has sons

---

[1] Written on a tiny sheet of paper.

[2] Joseph Charles King (?1794–1854) took a small number of pupils, both boarders and day-boys, at his house at 9 Northwick Terrace; he was an intimate friend of Macready, at whose home CD had met him by 17 Nov 40 (*Diaries*, II, 95), and a member of the Shakespeare Society. A fine scholar and collector of pictures and books (his library sold by Sotheby's, 13

of Macready[1] and some other friends of ours.[2] Charley has returned to him, as a Day Boarder, since we came home; and while we were abroad, he had lessons at home in English and French, and so forth. I should not say that in small scholarship, he is very far advanced as yet, for I have been more solicitous, in the first instance, about his health than his study. But he is a child of a very uncommon capacity indeed; and I have no doubt (neither has his present Master) of his rapidly winning his way upward, in any school whatever. His natural talent is quite remarkable.

If you will let me know at what age he is presentable at Marlborough,[3] and whether it is desirable that his attention should be directed in the meantime to any particular books or branches of learning—or if you can put me in the way of ascertaining these things from the Head Master by going down there, myself—or if you can, at your leisure, tell me anything that it is advisable or necessary to do—I need not say how vigilantly I shall set about it. But do not trouble yourself to write to me, unnecessarily. I shall be quite easy until I hear from you.

I was both surprised and grieved to find, by your preceding letter, that you were at all an Invalid; of which I had not the least idea. I hope that the repose and freshness of the Devonshire Coast, have done you good, already; and that your eyes have found many beautiful objects to refresh them.

When your letter reached me yesterday, I was on the point of writing to tell you (for I knew you would be gratified to hear) that Esther Elton, the eldest, in her training at the Normal School has uniformly conducted herself in a manner for which no praise could be too high; and has now the choice of two large schools in the Country—to one of which she will go, as Mistress, early in the Spring. I never in my life saw such gentle perserverance[4] and steady goodness as this girl has displayed, from the first. Going into the establishment, a woman grown—with her character already formed, and her habits adapted, as one would have thought, to the easy kind of life she had led, as her poor father's poor housekeeper—she settled herself at once, resolutely, to the discipline and hard-

Nov 54), he "had methods of teaching far in advance of his time", introducing his boys directly to Homer and Virgil without rote learning of grammar, and no "academic mustiness" (Edith Sichel, *Life of Alfred Ainger*, 1906, pp. 11–12; confirmed by Frederic Harrison, *Autobiographical Memoirs*, 1911, I, 28ff, who thought him "the ideal schoolmaster"). Ainger says that King's eldest daughter Louisa (later Mrs Menzies) assisted him in teaching Greek—probably the sole resemblance to Dr Blimber's establishment. (That Cornelia Blimber had an original is noted both by Forster, F, VI, ii, 485, and by Charley in his Introduction to *Dombey and Son*, 1892, p. XIX.) CD thought so well of King's teaching that he sent Charley back there (after a few weeks at King's College School) in 1847–9, followed by Walter

in 1849–51, and they were well prepared for Eton and Addiscombe respectively: see next vol.

[1] Willy (see *To* Macready, 17 Aug 45, *fn*), and Edward (*b*. 1836).

[2] The sons of Thomas Landseer, R. J. Lane, and Cattermole are mentioned by Frederic Harrison, a pupil in 1841–3 (*op. cit.*, I, 30); William Elderton, a schoolfellow of Ainger in 1849–52, was possibly a nephew of Mrs Cattermole.

[3] Founded 1842, with lower fees than the older public schools; sons of the clergy were to form two-thirds of the entrants. CD may have known that Yeats Brown intended to send Montagu there (he entered 1846). But by 1 Dec (*To* Miss Coutts, that day) he had decided against boarding school for Charley.

[4] Thus in MS.

work of the place; and has never turned from it, for one moment, though it has involved her separation from her little sisters, to whom she feels as a mother— her resignation of all her old society—her self-denial in a hundred ways, in all the ways of her previous life. I regard it really as an instance of patient womanly devotion; a little piece of quiet, unpretending, domestic heroism; of a most affecting and interesting kind. And if you could see her, with her pleasant face, and her neat, composed, agreeable manner, you would recollect that time when you gave me a commission in behalf of herself and the others, with such an emotion as very few people can ever know.[1]

My Dear Miss Coutts I will not thank you again, nor will I say for Charley's Mama, all that she wants me to say. No one can imagine it, better than you.

Believe me Ever | Yours most faithfully

CHARLES DICKENS

P.S. I beg my best regards to Miss Meredith—by which name I always call her, whether I will or no. I am quite sorry you and she are not in town to see the Play on Saturday Week; being pretty sure it would have amused you.

To JOHN LEECH, 10 SEPTEMBER 1845*

MS Benoliel Collection. *Address:* John Leech Esquire | Brook Green | Hammersmith. *Date:* PM 10 Sep 45.

REHEARSAL CALLS.

Tuesday 16th. at ¼ before 7

    Not Dress

Thursday 18th. at 6 (To allow time for dressing)

    Dress

Friday 19th. at ¼ before 7

    Not Dress

John Leech Esquire

To T. J. THOMPSON, 10 SEPTEMBER 1845

MS Huntington Library.

REHEARSAL CALLS.

Tuesday 16th. at ¼ before 7

    Not Dress

---

[1] For CD's continued personal interest in Esther and her visits to Gad's Hill, see later vols.

Thursday 18th. at 6 (To allow time for dressing)
    Dress

Friday 19th. at ¼ before 7
    Not Dress

T. J. Thompson Esqre.   (Over)

Devonshire Terrace | Tenth Septr. 1845

My Dear Thompson. I will send for your table *next Tuesday Morning*. I shall want Wallace[1] to be in attendance, if you please, *at 6 on the Friday Evening* (the night before the Play) to receive his instructions and be shewn the seats.

Ever Yours
CD

To JOHN WILLMOTT, [?10 SEPTEMBER 1845]

Text from *Birmingham Gazette and Express*, 30 Apr 1904, taken from MS Memorial Library, Stratford (since mislaid). *Date:* clearly the week before the dress-rehearsal; probably when collecting properties, as in *To* Thompson, 10 Sep.

I want a couple of stage cudgels made. I don't know the technical name for them (or I have forgotten it),[2] but you know what I mean—a sort of flexible sausage to beat a man with, that seems to hurt him very much but doesn't. I have no doubt there is some genius at your elbow who will manufacture them in no time. Will you give him the commission and tell him to let me have them this week with a note of his charge for them? So may you prosper and flourish for ever!

Some of my company say that as the night approaches they begin to feel like used-up cab horses—going perceptibly at the knees. One of them has gone on the cold water system to make himself courageous.

Faithfully yours,
CHARLES DICKENS

P.S.—Good long cudgels, as long as walking-sticks.

To DANIEL MACLISE, 11 SEPTEMBER 1845*

MS University of Texas.

Devonshire Terrace | Thursday Eleventh September | 1845.
My Dear Mac.
    Many thanks! The hat is gone to be altered; and the belt to be buckled. I fear spurs: having a great dread of their coming in my way. But I will think of them.

---

[1] Presumably Thompson's servant.   [2] They were known as "trick-sausages" or "calico trick-sausages".

I do not so clearly see how to adopt your suggestion in reference to the trousers. Which I find, on looking to the books, are perfectly correct "Spanish slops".[1] But you shall shew me practically, if you will, next Sunday.

What a man Stone is! ! ! I went through some of my books of Authority[2] last night, because I was confident that I knew at least as well as he; and that he had made preposterous objections, without a shadow of reason. He pulled up Frederick's boots, like Wellington's. They were worn so low at the exact period of this Play, that they are described in the Gull's Horn Book,[3] as often having the fringe of the part turned over, trailing on the ground. He objected to gloves with large gauntlet tops—"There was no such thing at that day. Nothing of the sort".—The tops of the gloves were made so large and wide, *that it was a common practice to carry letters and such small papers in them.* Why, isn't it a lamentable thing, Grandsire,[4] that a man should bore one so, and be wrong all the time?

I will very likely give you a call sometime this morning.

Ever Yours
CD

To LADY HOLLAND, [?10–15 SEPTEMBER 1845]*

Extract from copy[5] in Holland House Dinner Book (MS British Museum), followed by "The above is Mr Dickens's account of them, which he wrote to My Lady". *Date:* between 10 and 15 Sep, since Lady Holland gave her son many of these particulars in a letter of 15 Sep (MS BM), but did not mention the theatricals on 9 Sep.

Every Man In His Humour

Old Knowell. Mr. Mayhew. Punch Writer
Edward Knowell. Frederick Dickens
Brainworm. Mark Lemon. Punch writer
George Downright. Dudley Costello (an author)
Wellbred. Thompson (a private Gentleman)
Kitely. Forster[6]
Captain Bobadil. Charles Dickens

---

[1] Very wide breeches; a common subject of contemporary satire, as in Dekker's *Seven Deadly Sins of London*, 1606—"his huge sloppes speakes Spanish".

[2] e.g., Joseph Strutt's *Complete View of the Dress and Habits of the People of England* (2 vols, 1796–9), which shows in Plate CXLIII a figure whose hat, sword-belt and boots resemble Bobadil's, the boots having wide open tops; a copy was in the Gad's Hill library at CD's death.

[3] CD bought the Bristol, 1812, edn of Dekker's *Gull's Hornbook*, 1609, at the Hill sale: see Vol. II, p. 229*n*; it was in the Gad's Hill library at his death. In Ch. 3, writing of boots, Dekker says "have the tops of them wide as the mouth of a wallet, and those with fringed boot-hose over them to hang down to thy ankles".

[4] *Romeo and Juliet*, II, iv, 30.

[5] Entry made under date 20 Sep, when Lady Holland and four guests went to the performance.

[6] The copyist added at the foot of the page, "A Lawyer & a writer in the Examiner—Sunday Paper."

Master Stephen. Douglas Jerrold. Punch Writer of "Mrs. Caudle" Punch's Letters to his Son &c. &c. &c.
Master Mathew—Leech Punch Caricaturist   He has done all their famous things—Lord Brougham as Clown; and so forth.
Thomas Cash—Augustus Dickens
Oliver Cob. Leigh. Punch Writer
Justice Clement. Frank Stone. Artist
Roger Formal. Evans. My Printer.
William—A'Becket.[1] Punch Writer   The Comic Blackstone &c &c
James—Mr. Jerrold's son
Dame Kitely—Miss Fortescue (from the Haymarket)
The two other Ladies, two of Miss Kelly's pupils.

A Good Night's Rest.

Mr. Snobbington—Mr. C. Dickens
The Stranger—Mr. Lemon again

The Company includes all the Punch corps with the exception of one gentleman. We chose them because they are so well accustomed to act in concert good humouredly.—

To OCTAVIAN BLEWITT, 15 SEPTEMBER 1845*

MS Royal Literary Fund.

Devonshire Terrace. | Monday Fifteenth September 1845.

My Dear Sir
   I called in Great Russell Street to day, to ask, under the seal of Literary-Fund-confidence, if you know anything of Mr. Frederick Tolfrey,[2] who has published two books, the Sportsman in France and the Sportsman in Canada; and who has written in several of the Magazines.[3] I am deputed to make enquiry about this gentleman privately, if I possibly can, by one to whom he has written for some temporary assistance, and I really don't know how to do it; so I catch at the possibility of your knowing something of him.

My Dear Sir Faithfully | Yours
CHARLES DICKENS

O. Blewitt Esquire.

---

[1] The copyist added that "All of them acted except Mr. A'Becket, who at the last, failed, from nervousness".

[2] Frederic Tolfrey (*b.* 1794) had applied to the Literary Fund in Apr 42, claiming to be the son of Samuel Tolfrey, Chief Judge of the Provincial Court, Ceylon, and to have lost his inheritance in a Chancery suit; the Fund was informed that he was an "adventurer" and his application was deferred. In Dec 46 he applied from the Queen's Bench Prison (his supporters included Lord William Lennox and Henry Colburn), and was granted £25 in Jan 47.

[3] The books were published by Colburn in 1841 and 1845; in a later application to the Fund Tolfrey mentioned articles in the *Sportsman, New Monthly, Bentley's Miscellany,* and *Ainsworth's Magazine.*

To MESSRS CHAPMAN & HALL, 15 SEPTEMBER 1845

Mention in Morris Book Shop Inc. catalogue, n.d.; *MS* 1 p.; dated 15 Sep 45.

Acknowledging receipt of payments.[1]

To T. J. SERLE, 16 SEPTEMBER 1845

MS[2] Mr Peter Brandt.

1 Devonshire Terrace | Sept. 16th. 1845.

My dear Serle,

There will probably be many carriages in Dean Street on Saturday night; and the half hour mentioned in the bill as the time for sitting down is so very short, that the door will be opened at half past 6, instead of seven.[3] I think it best to tell you, that if you can manage to be there *before* seven, you will certainly enter more comfortably.

Faithfully Yours
CHARLES DICKENS

To MISS BURDETT COUTTS, 17 SEPTEMBER 1845

MS Morgan Library.

Devonshire Terrace | Seventeenth September 1845.

My Dear Miss Coutts.

Immediately on the receipt of your letter, I set about enquiring into the reputation of Mr. Tolfrey. And as I knew nothing of him myself, and was even unacquainted with his name, I went away to the office of the Literary Fund (I am one of its Managing Committee); where I knew I should hear the Truth about him, if he had ever applied for assistance there; and where I knew my enquiry, in any case, would be strictly confidential; secrecy being one of the main principles of the Establishment.

I found, to my disappointment, that it being Vacation time, the Secretary (an excellent and charitable gentleman) was out of town. But I wrote to him straightway; and here is his letter in reply. I should decidedly say, on such evidence, that Mr. Tolfrey is *not* a fit subject for your generous aid. If his story be true, his bookseller will certainly purchase a Second Edition of his book from him. If his story be untrue, a Second Edition (supposing him to apply the money, if he got it

---

[1] CD's account-book (MS Messrs Coutts) shows £219.4.1 received 16 Sep.

[2] The whole letter, including the signature, is in Catherine Dickens's hand. Probably one of many letters to those invited, altering the time for the opening of the doors. On the same day, Catherine wrote a similar letter over her own name to Mrs Cruikshank (MS Dickens House).

[3] At the foot of the bill are the words: "The Cards of Invitation are presentable at the Theatre, from Seven o'clock. The performance will commence at Half-past Seven exactly . . ."

from you, in its publication) would be mere waste paper.[1] The Second Edition being all sold, would, certainly, be much more profitable to him if he published it on his own account, than if he made a bargain with Bentley, Colburn, or any other Shark of those Waters. But I can hear nothing of the book. And I do not believe its success warrants any such presumption.

A slight thing may turn the scale when the balance is going very plainly one way. I did not like his mention of his "revered and lamented father", and his "beloved mother" in his letter to you. A man who is quite in earnest, can afford to leave his estimation of his parents, I think, to the understanding of his reader.

At the same time, if you be inclined to advance him the money, I need not say that I will give it him with the greatest caution, and in the most considerate manner. All I wish to say against it, is, that I think I would not give it him, if I were you.

With a smaller sum, my dear Miss Coutts, I think I can do, on your behalf, an infinitely greater service. George Cruikshank came to me some weeks ago, and told me the facts of the melancholy little history I am going to state to you. He asked me if I thought I could influence any rich friend in the sufferer's behalf. You were not in the way. I do not know that I should have had the courage to come to you, if you had been. And I told him No; I could not then; but if I ever could, I would. I should premise that Cruikshank is one of the best creatures in the World, in his own odd way (he is a live Caricature himself); and that to the extent of his means, he has rendered assistance here, already, from his own purse.

I don't know if you ever saw a book called "Mornings at Bow Street". It is a collection of Bow Street reports that appeared, years and years ago, in the Morning Herald; and did the paper immense service at that time. The writer is a Mr. White,[2] who from that time, until very recently, has been connected with the Herald as one of its Sub-Editors. The paper changed hands[3] within this Year and a Half, or so—he was not wanted in the new arrangements—and at 60 years of age was suddenly discharged, with a month's Salary, from the Establishment that had not only been his income but his whole prospect; for he thought himself (quite naturally) a leaf of the tree, and believed he would never be shaken off until he died. He had lived upon his salary, but had done no more—I really don't see how he could have done more—and this was a blow, as if his Bank had failed, or he had become paralyzed.

His daughter had been engaged to be married, *Fourteen Years*. Her lover was not rich—was fighting his way, very slowly, to the Bar—and they had always said they would be married, when he was 'called'. After all these many years, he was called, at last; and her wedding clothes were being made, when one night (just at the time of his discharge), after they had been to the opera together, he went home to his chambers and was seized with congestion of the Brain.

---

[1] No second edn is known.

[2] John Wight (*b.* 1778), former sub-editor or manager of the *Morning Herald*; his *Mornings in Bow Street*, 1824, *More Mornings in Bow Street*, 1827, *Sunday in London*, 1833, were all illustrated by Cruikshank. On 19 May 45, supported by

Cruikshank and T. J. Pettigrew, he applied to the Literary Fund and was awarded £30; for his applications in 1848 and 1849, see next vol.

[3] Edward Baldwin bought the *Herald* in 1844.

In a very few hours she was sent for. If she wished to see him before he died, the Message said, she must come without delay. She was taken down to the Adelphi (where the chambers were) by her mother; and they arrived in the Bedroom, just in time to see him die. Quite frantic, she ran out of the chamber; opened a window, four tall stories high; and plunged herself, head-foremost, from it! By a kind of miracle, she fell into a tank of water at the back of one of the neighbouring houses; and was taken out, insensible, but unhurt. Since that time, she has been watched, day and night. Her mother has never been told the Truth, but the father knows it. The poor girl sits all day in a sort of dream, repeating little scraps of comfort from the Bible. She has never shed a tear.

The wretched father is oppressed with some small debts. But they are very small; and if he could release his plate, which he has pawned for Thirty Pounds, I have no doubt Cruikshank could compound for every one of them with the produce of its Sale; and then he could, with an easier mind, seek some employment: or at the worst, go away to live with his son[1] who is a poor Curate[2]—I think—in Wales. My dear Miss Coutts, these are all miserable facts within my knowledge. Thirty Pounds here, will be like Help from Heaven. There is no possibility of imposition; Cruikshank has known the parties twenty years[3] at least; and the circumstances surely are peculiarly affecting and distressful.

My letter is so long already that I will tell you of the other Eltons in my next. We have never had the least trouble with them; and they are all as well, as happy, and as full of promise—thank God for it!—as we could possibly desire.

With best regards to Miss Meredith

Believe me Dear Miss Coutts Ever Yours

Miss Coutts.
CHARLES DICKENS

To CLARKSON STANFIELD, 17 SEPTEMBER 1845*

MS Yale University Library.

Devonshire Terrace
Wednesday Evening | Seventeenth September 1845.

My Dear Stanny

You will have seen Rainey[4] (as I have understood from him) before this reaches you. I have a suggestion to make, for getting out of the supper business much more simply and safely. For this purpose, I will drive to you tomorrow Morning *at half past 11*, when perhaps you can ride down with me to Lemon, and discuss it.

Ever Yours
CD.

---

[1] MS reads "soon".

[2] No "Wight" appears in the Clergy List; possibly the Rev. R. W. White, curate of Mountford, Shropshire.

[3] In fact 25 years, according to Cruikshank's statement to the Literary Fund.

[4] Unidentified.

To W. C. MACREADY, 18 SEPTEMBER 1845

MS Morgan Library.

Devonshire Terrace | Thursday Eighteenth September 1845.

My Dear Macready. We hold a little supper Sir, after the Farce, at No. 9 Powis Place Great Ormond Street, in an empty house belonging to one of the company.[1] There, I am requested by my fellows to beg the favor of thy company, and that of Mrs. Macready. The guests are limited to the actors and their ladies,—with the exception of yourselves, and D'Orsay, and George Cattermole,[2] "or so"— that sounds like Bobadil a little.[3]

I am going to adopt your reading of the Fifth Act, with the worst grace in the World.[4] It seems to me that you don't allow enough for Bobadil having been frequently beaten before—as I have no doubt he had been. The part goes down, hideously, on this construction; and the end is mere lees. But never mind Sir. I intend bringing you up with the Farce, in the most brilliant manner.

Ever Yours affectionately

CD

N.B. Observe. I think of changing my present mode of life, and am open to an engagement.
NB. No. 2. I will undertake not to play Tragedy, though Passion is my strength.

(over)

N.B. No. 3. I consider myself a chained lion.[5]

To MISS MACREADY,[6] 18 SEPTEMBER 1845*

MS Morgan Library.

Devonshire Terrace | Eighteenth September 1845.

My Dear Miss Macready.

Macready's Box will hold—let me see—Miss Kelly would say, Forty, but I should really think *Six*. It is the best, for seeing, in the house, of course. And in case any of the Six should prove to be at a disadvantage in that respect, there is

---

[1] Leech's old address: earlier in 1845 he had moved to Brook Green, but his name was still at 9 Powis Place in the 1846 Directory.

[2] Other guests were Jerdan, Maclise, and Talfourd (*Diaries*, II, 305).

[3] "You talk of *Morglay, Excalibur, Durindana,* or so?" *Every Man in his Humour,* III, i; cf. II, v.

[4] See *To* Macready, 2 Sep 45. But Forster makes it an example of CD's "quickness and keenness of insight" (F, v, i, 383). Jerdan in the *Literary Gazette* (27 Sep 45) called the "new reading" of Bobadil (as

"hang-dog" and "craven" before Justice Clement) striking, though not perhaps correct; and *The Times* (22 Sep) commended his "masterly transformation".

[5] According to MDGH, I, 144*n*, "This alludes to a theatrical story of a second-rate actor, who described himself as a 'chained lion,' in a theatre where he had to play inferior parts to Mr. Macready". Source not traced.

[6] Letitia Margaret Macready (1794–1858), Macready's sister, who lived with them.

standing-room behind the First Circle of Boxes, which is really the best place in the little Theatre.

I am half dead with Managerial work—and with actual work in shirt sleeves; with a dirty face, a hammer, and a bag of Nails. I never in my life saw a place in such a state, or had to do with such an utterly careless and unbusiness-like set of dogs (with the exception of Stanfield and Brainworm) as my fellow actors. I don't except Forster:[1] for so far as he is concerned, there is nothing in the World but Kitely[2]—there is no World at all; only a something in its place that begins with a "K" and ends with a "Y".

I enclose a note for Macready when he arrives. Ever My Dear Miss Macready

Faithfully Yours

CD.

To MISS MACREADY, [?18 SEPTEMBER 1845]

MS Auckland Public Library. *Date:* evidently later on same day as last.

Devonshire T | Thursday

My Dear Miss Macready

It is rather difficult—adjoining each other, I fear it can't be done. But anything connected with the House of Macready is quite a special thing; and if you will send me the names of the parties[3] (soon:—I am going out to the Theatre in

---

[1] CD's managerial responsibilities and Forster's sense of the importance of his own part led to at least one clash during rehearsals; Blanchard Jerrold recalled a "wordy encounter" in which CD attacked Forster for his "hectoring and self-sufficiency"—but the quarrel was over by the next day: their affection "was too deep to let it live twenty-four hours" ("John Forster", *Gentleman's Magazine*, Mar 1876, N.S. XVI, 315).

[2] Kitely had been Garrick's part, and Macready's when he revived the play at the Haymarket on 29 July 38. The *Examiner* (presumably Forster) had praised his acting, though not the production as a whole, and noted that he excluded "every particle of sympathy or pity" except for one touch at the close of Act III. Browning called him "superb from his flat cap to his shining shoes" (*Works of Ben Jonson*, ed. C. H. Herford and P. Simpson, Vol. IX, 1950, p. 181). Forster's interleaved copy of the play includes very detailed notes for his own interpretation of nearly all Kitely's speeches, as well as notes of stage position and movements: notes elsewhere in the copy show his interest in earlier revivals, of which full cast lists are given. His copy of the 1777 edn of Garrick's version is also annotated in his youthful hand with special reference to the Kitely scenes. About his costume, Forster consulted Macready, and received detailed instructions about how and when he should wear his sword (quoted by Alan Downer, from MS Forster Collection, *The Eminent Tragedian*, p. 76). Maclise, writing to Mrs Macready, ?21 Sep 45, says, "Forster looked last night exactly like Harry 8th" and adds a sketch (Harkness Collection, New York Public Library); his sketch on the playbill (see *To Miss Kelly, 6 Sep 45, fn*) gives the same impression. Procter thought he would have been better without the beard which made "the lower part of your face too large and burly. This & the fact of your hair being thin towards the crown of the head gives you too *monastic* an appearance (you understand me) ... increased by the loose sort of robe or dress" (MS Forster Collection).

[3] The Macreadys' guests were "Rolls and Searles" and Mrs Milner Gibson (*Diaries*, II, 304), which would have made eight with themselves.

an hour) I will make such prodigious efforts as become an energetic Stage Manager. And you shall hear from me, tomorrow Morning.

Always Faithfully Yours

CHARLES DICKENS

P.S. Some of the actors say that as the Night draws on, they feel themselves *going at the knees*![1]

To RICHARD LANE, 19 SEPTEMBER 1845

Mention in Sotheby's catalogue, July 1933; *MS* 1 p.; dated 19 Sep 45; probably the same as mention and summary in Sotheran's Price Current of Literature, No. 822 (1931) of letter to "N. I. Lane" from Devonshire Terrace.

Stating that he is sending him an invitation card.

To SYDNEY WILLIAMS,[2] 19 SEPTEMBER 1845

Extract in Maggs catalogue No. 451 (1924); *MS* 1 p.; dated Devonshire Terrace, 19 Sep 45.

Arranging for Williams to visit him. Mr. Dickens will not be enabled at that time to conclude any negotiations with Mr. Williams; but he will be happy to understand the nature of Mr. Williams' proposal.

To MISS FANNY KELLY, 22 SEPTEMBER 1845†

MS Colonel Richard Gimbel. *Address:* Miss Kelly | 73 Dean St.

Devonshire Terrace

Monday Twenty Second September | 1845.

My Dear Miss Kelly.

If you will have the kindness to get us a note of our expences for Carpenters and Gas &c, and to send it by post to Mr. Stanfield, we shall be happy to square accounts immediately. *ªI am desirous to settle them without delay.ª*

[1] Jerrold wrote to Mrs Cowden Clarke, probably the same day: "Never give thanks for tickets for an amateur play till the show is *over*. You don't know what may be in store for you—and for *us*!" But on seeing it she thought Jerrold particularly good (Charles and Mary Cowden Clarke, *Recollections of Writers*, 1878, p. 280).

[2] Sydney Williams of Williams & Norgate, 19 Henrietta St, Covent Garden and 2 Queen's Passage; known to be Tauchnitz's London agent by 1850, when CD sent him proofs of *Copperfield* (see later vols). Possibly the same as the Thomas Sydney Williams who, with his wife, translated books from the German.

aa; bb Not previously published.

I hope you are none the worse for your anxiety and your exertions. They were both very great, I am afraid, *b*at last.*b1*

Faithfully Yours always

Miss Kelly.   CHARLES DICKENS

To MISS BURDETT COUTTS, [24 SEPTEMBER 1845]

MS Morgan Library. Date: endorsed "24/9/1845", which is consistent with *To Miss Coutts,* 17 Sep 45.

Devonshire Terrace | Wednesday

My Dear Miss Coutts. I return you Mr. Tolfrey's letter.

A thousand thanks on behalf of Mr. White. I have rigidly observed your injunctions; and will write you fully about that poor girl, when I have settled the adjustment of the Fifty Pounds.[2] Suffice it to say at this moment that I hope to be able to make such lasting use of it, as will delight your generous Heart. She is much better.

Where shall I write to you? I shall be glad to know at your perfect leisure.

Ever believe me

With the truest regard | Faithfully Yours

Miss Burdett Coutts.   CHARLES DICKENS

To T. J. SERLE, 24 SEPTEMBER 1845

MS Mr Peter Brandt.

Devonshire Terrace | Twenty Fourth September 1845.

My Dear Serle

I was in Managerial agonies at the Theatre, all day on Saturday; and did not receive your letter until a very short time before the Curtain rose. I am extremely sorry you were not there, as I really counted on your worship's presence: setting a high value on your opinion.

I waited and waited on behalf of Mr. Novello,[3] thinking it certain that out of more than five hundred people, some would send their tickets back, at the last moment. But it never came to pass. And I was powerless.

Ever Faithfully Yours

T. J. Serle Esquire   CHARLES DICKENS

[1] For the performance, see *To* Mme de la Rue, 27 Sep and *fns.*

[2] This was not finally completed for some months. CD's accounts (Account-book, MS Messrs Coutts) show a payment of £30 to Miss White on 20 Oct, and one of £10 on 12 Feb 46: see *To* Cruikshank, that day. On 17 Oct he applied to become a Depositor in the Finsbury Savings Bank as Trustee of "Bertha Wight, of Dagwell, near Oswestry" (Declaration in possession of the Bank) without naming the amount. The deposit may have been the remaining £10 of Miss Coutts's gift—his letter to her on 1 Dec 45 shows his concern that something should be kept back for Bertha's "sole use in after life", but uncertainty about the sum that would be available in view of her father's "necessities".

[3] Mrs Serle's father, Vincent Novello, the music-publisher, or one of her brothers.

To ALEXANDER SMART,[1] 24 SEPTEMBER 1845*

MS Yale University Library.

1 Devonshire Terrace | York Gate Regents Park
Twenty Fourth September 1845.

Dear Sir

I have had the truest pleasure in the perusal of your gentle little book; so feelingly and well described by my dear friend Lord Jeffrey.[2]

I thank you cordially, for your remembrance of me—enhanced in value by the kind expressions in your note; by which I set great store.

I am Dear Sir | Yours faithfully and obliged

Alexander Smart Esquire   CHARLES DICKENS

To DR J. A. WILSON,[3] 24 SEPTEMBER 1845

MS Mrs Humphry House.

1 Devonshire Terrace | York Gate Regents Park
Twenty Fourth September 1845.

Dear Sir

I perfectly recollect your obliging communication some years ago.

If we should repeat Every Man in his Humour to a Private audience, I shall be happy to send you an Invitation. But we have no plan or idea of doing so, at this time, that I know of. And I should certainly, in my managerial capacity, have early knowledge of any such intention.

Faithfully Yours

Dr. Wilson   CHARLES DICKENS

To COUNT D'ORSAY, 26 SEPTEMBER 1845

MS Huntington Library. *Address* (envelope, MS New York Public Library): A Monsieur | M. Le Comte D'Orsay | Gore House | Kensington.

Devonshire Terrace | Twenty Sixth September 1845.

My Dear Count D'Orsay

Can you, and will you, come to dine with me on Wednesday next at 6 o'Clock? I have a Mr. Ridgway coming, who is a great man at Naples now-a-days, and is the Receiver General of all distinguished travellers, both there, and at the Lake

---

[1] Alexander Smart (1798–1866), printer; worked in the University Printing Office, Edinburgh, for many years. Author of *Rambling Rhymes*, 1834, including some dialect pieces and a sonnet to Jeffrey; one of the chief contributors to *Whistle-binkie*, 1853.

[2] The book must have been the enlarged edn of *Rambling Rhymes*, 1845. Jeffrey had presumably written to CD recommending it; on 9 Oct 45 he wrote Smart a warm letter of thanks, apologizing for his delay (MS Yale).

[3] James Arthur Wilson, FRCP (1795–1882; *DNB*): see Vol. I, p. 373*n*.

of Como, where he has a beautiful Villa. He is a bit of a Bore, but can be swamped, easily.

I am under orders for Rosherville,[1] remember, and shall be punctual to any summons you give me.[2]

Ever Faithfully Yours
Bobadil

To LORD DUDLEY COUTTS STUART,
[?26 SEPTEMBER 1845]*

MS The Earl of Harrowby. *Date:* endorsed "1845—Autumn"; handwriting supports; Oct ruled out by other engagements and Catherine's health; 26 Sep the most likely Sep date.

Devonshire Terrace | Friday Morning

My Dear Lord Dudley

It will be the greatest pleasure to Mrs. Dickens and myself, if you will come and join our Family Dinner next Sunday at Six. Will you?

If this should find you otherwise engaged or out of town, I shall retire into the Wilderness: bereft of all hope of ever setting eyes on you again.

Ever Faithfully Yours

The | Lord Dudley Stuart   CHARLES DICKENS

To MADAME DE LA RUE, 27 SEPTEMBER 1845

MS Free Library of Philadelphia. *Address:* North Italy. | A Madame: | Madame Emile De la Rue | Monsieur Emile De la Rue | Messrs. De la Rue freres | Genoa | North Italy.

Devonshire Terrace, Saturday Twenty Seventh September 1845.

My Dearest Madame De la Rue. I received your letter last Monday Morning, when I was still in a whirl from the uproar of Saturday Night. But I expected it fully—had half expected it, indeed, on Saturday—and went down to the Theatre after post-time on Saturday Morning, a little disappointed by its non-arrival. So you see that occupation only makes this difference in me—I am rather damped for the time being, if you are not, in some sort, a sharer in it.

Good Heaven how I wish you could have been there! It really was a brilliant sight. The audience so distinguished for one thing or another—every one so

---

[1] Botanical and zoological gardens near Gravesend, laid out on the site of chalk pits belonging to J. Rosher; opened by 1842. Albert Smith, *The Natural History of the Gent*, 1847, p. 76, called it "the largest ornamental chalk-pit in the world".

[2] An earlier plan to go to Knebworth with D'Orsay and Forster had had to be given up because of Lady Canterbury's dangerous illness (D'Orsay *to* Forster, 25 Sep 45, R. R. Madden, *Literary Life and Correspondence of the Countess of Blessington*, II, 417.)

elegantly dressed—all in such a state of excitement and expectation.[1] As to the acting, modesty forbids me to say more than that it has been the town talk ever since.[2] I have known nothing short of a Murder, to make such a noise before. We are overwhelmed with invitations, applications, petitions, and Memorials, for a repetition of the Performance; and on the night it was as much as we could do, with a strong body of Police, to keep the doors from being carried by force. It got into the Papers, notwithstanding all our precautions;[3] and I sent you a Times[4] the other day, with some account of the proceedings. I hope it reached you safely.

We numbered every seat in the House; and assigned each by lot. I am afraid Miss Holskamp[5] (whose brother and sister I invited also) had a bad place; for it

[1] The cards of invitation had specified "Evening Dress". *The Times* (22 Sep) said the audience was "the most select that could have been found in the English metropolis", and Jane Carlyle thought "the greatest wonder ... was how they had contrived to get together some six or seven hundred ladies and gentlemen (judging from the clothes) at this season of the year", and "among them were many of the leading aristocracy; *I was told*—but to my matter of fact eye they looked rather *a rum set*" (*Letters and Memorials*, ed. Froude, 1883, I, 341; *Letters to her Family*, ed. Leonard Huxley, p. 253). The audience included, besides those mentioned by CD, Lady Holland, Lady Blessington and Count D'Orsay, Lord Nugent, Sir Alexander and Lady Gordon, Talfourd, Dyce, Browning, Dr Quin and Joseph King.

[2] Browning thought the performance "really good, really clever or better" and particularly praised Forster, CD, Jerrold and Leech ("superb"): "All were good, indeed, and were voted good, and called on, and cheered off, and praised heartily behind their backs and before the curtain ... the dresses, which were perfect, had the advantage of Mr. Maclise's experience" (*Letters of Robert Browning and Elizabeth Barrett, 1845-1846*, I, 217). Jane Carlyle, on the other hand, thought the acting, "much praised in the newspapers", was "nothing 'to speak of'", and was chiefly struck by the expense of the production, with Stanfield's scenery, and "costumes according to the strictly historical style of Macready—*cost* 'no object'" (*Letters to her Family*, p. 253).

[3] "The amusement was meant to be private, and the guests were admitted upon that understanding; but it is not easy to keep from the press secrets entrusted to

ten or fifteen score of confidants ... we have been released from our implied pledge and may speak of the representation nearly as a public event" (*Literary Gazette*, 27 Sep). A letter to Forster from J. P. Collier of the *Morning Chronicle*, 24 Sep 45 (MS Forster Collection), regrets that there was not a notice there, but says, "I took the 'strictly private' quite literally". The performers' wishes in this matter were perhaps deliberately expressed with some ambiguity: *The Times* believed that "publicity will not be disagreeable to the persons immediately concerned"; and indeed Forster kept all the cuttings as well as a number of letters praising his performance.

[4] *The Times's* notice was reproduced in the *Examiner*, 27 Sep, with an editorial note saying that in order not to be suspected of partiality, "we have gladly availed ourselves of the critique of the *Times*, which, encomiastic as it is, does not exceed the measure of praise accorded by all who saw the play". After emphasizing that "the gentlemen did not play well for amateurs, they played well absolutely", *The Times* singled out Forster, CD, Leech, Jerrold and Lemon; Forster "adopted ... a Macreadyan view of Kitely" but gave "far more than a successful imitation", bringing out the character with energy and "elaboration" of "its most subtle turns"; CD, in "a less difficult part", swaggered "with the ease of a stage veteran"; it concluded by saying that a "better play ... could not have been selected" and hoped that they might put on another Ben Jonson, perhaps *Volpone*. The notice was copied by the *Era* and, in part, by the *Athenæum*.

[5] Catherine wrote on "Saturday evening" (?13 Sep 45): "My dear Miss Holskamp, I enclose your tickets for the play which we told you of, and as we thought you and

was in the upper boxes, and looked down, rather awkwardly, upon the stage. I have not seen her since, but I hope she either has given, or will give you, some account of the Evening. The Duke of Devonshire travelled a couple of hundred miles, in one direction, to be present; and Alfred Tennyson (our friend) travelled a couple of hundred miles in another.[1] So the attraction spread itself to all sorts and conditions of men. We newly painted all the scenery; newly-carpentered all the Machinery; had the dresses (they were bright colors you may be sure, to please my Managerial eye) made expressly, from old pictures; and worked away at it, rehearsing and rehearsing, night after night, and day after day, as if it were the whole business of our lives. But I have always had a misgiving,[2] in my inmost heart, that I was born to be the Manager of a Theatre. And now, I am quite sure of it. I send you a bill, as a little Curiosity. There are whispers of Gold snuff-boxes for the indefatigable Manager, from the Performers—Hem!

And Gaberel is going to be married at last! ! ! I am glad of it. Though I find that native obstinacy of yours, in full force on the subject, still! I don't think he is exactly the man to fall in love with—I agree with you, there. But there is a vulgar saying in England "Wot's the odds so long as you're happy!" And perhaps the Bride elect starts from that point, and adopts that line of argument. When I think of the possible consequences—of little gaspers like Papa—or apple-faced Maniacs like Grandpapa—a chill runs through my blood. It is a dreadful thought.

Ridgway came in the other night (last Thursday) with his hair still crisp with yolk of egg, and his tongue still glib on the theme of certain Counts and Countesses who have been visiting his Cook—himself I should say—at the Lake of Como. He dines here, next Wednesday; and contemplates a three weeks' stay in London. I heard from Walton the other day (do you remember an evening of intoxicating and rapturous excitement, we once passed at Carrara?) who tells me he has been nearly married, and "is not out of danger yet". Una bellissima Signora, he adds—and underlines it, a great many times.

If the Champion[3] has the benefit of my good wishes, you will never get that box; for she will certainly go down in some deep water. Confound her tardy, lagging, miserable pace! I never was so vexed as by the loss of that first Steamer; for your impatience to receive the box, is nothing to that with which I burn to know that you have got it. Tell De la Rue that I will write to him immediately after the receipt of that mysterious package, which I will open in this Study of mine, with my own careful hands. You have made me desperately anxious to know what on earth it can contain. Whatever it be, as a remembrance from him, it will be very precious to me.

As to the Examiner, I have risen into the Seventh Heaven of indignant

---

your sister could not go without a *cavoliere* [*thus*] I have sent one for one of your brothers to accompany you . . ." (MS Free Library of Philadelphia).

[1] Tennyson had come from Cheltenham. Jane Carlyle met him in the interval, in "a long dim passage . . . with his head touching the ceiling like a caryatid, to all appearance asleep, or resolutely trying it under most unfavourable circumstances" (*Letters and Memorials*, I, 341).

[2] CD first wrote and cancelled "been quite su".

[3] Nothing is known of the steamship service between London and Genoa.

wonder, since I learnt from you, that it has ever miscarried. *It has always been sent.* Do not fail to let me know, if it should ever fail again. For in that case I will bestow a little of my superfluous indignation on the General Post office. The Examiner reminds me of Forster, who is quite well, and played admirably the other night— though he imitated Macready too much. I suspect Macready thought so; and would have been better pleased, if the resemblance had been less near.[1] Talking of him, reminds me of Maclise, who is exactly in his old state; from which he has in nothing, made any departure, except in being so nervous when the Overture to the Comedy was playing, the other night, that he turned a deadly white, and had nearly fainted away. Georgy is very well, and takes long country walks with me.—She is quite happy, I think. And I have left that matter where it was; trusting to its wearing itself out, on her part, in due course.[2]

The affair at Manchester is on the Twenty Third of October. I suppose there will be an audience of some Two Thousand people. I will look into the local papers, and send you the best report I see. I have been much solicited to go to Sheffield at the same time, and to Birmingham; and have had other public receptions tendered to me, both in the Country and in London. But I have declined them; firstly, because I would rather be quiet; and secondly because I am now composing myself to write my little Christmas book. I shall be actually at work upon it, I hope, when you receive this; and for a month afterwards, most likely. Christmas turned, you will see me, in the bloom of Print again, pretty often.[3]

I have forgotten to say in its right place that I took the glass you gave me, to the Theatre, in my Portmanteau of Costumes; and drank a bottle of old Sherry from it, in my dressing-Room, at divers fatiguing periods of the Evening. And I drank to you, in a great black wig, and with a peaked beard and black moustache —all stuck on, singly, by the individual hair! I had a dresser from one of the large Theatres to do it; and I never was so much astonished in my life as at the

---

[1] Most reviewers noticed Forster's imitation of Macready, but not, apparently, Macready himself. Zouch Troughton told Forster he would have given a gold piece to see Macready's face, but he kept well back in the box (Troughton *to* Forster, MS Forster Collection). Macready said Forster "played Kitely as a *tragic* character—the grand mistake" (see *To* Miss Macready, 18 Sep 45, *fn*). His general opinion was that "several of the actors were very fine as amateurs" (including Forster, CD, and Leech, but Jerrold "very bad"), but he found the comedy "a very dull business", though the farce was "very broad and laughable". He did not enjoy the supper afterwards, having an hour to wait, "my cold torturing me", at 9 Powis Place after seeing off his guests in "torrents of rain". "I took some oysters, and consented to go up to supper, but got near the door, and before it was half over took an opportunity to escape. I was very unwell". When he read Jerdan's notice in the *Literary Gazette*, he thought it "written in a false spirit, and will do harm to the persons engaged in the play" (*Diaries*, II, 304–5). Jane Carlyle, calling on the Macreadys on 24 Sep, found Macready ill in bed with two doctors in attendance; next day Letitia wrote to her saying he was better, and also indicating that there was particular resentment of *The Times's* praise—"more kind really than ever the *Times* showed itself towards William!" (*Letters and Memorials*, I, 346).

[2] Possibly connected with the joke about Charles Gibbs: see *To* Georgina Hogarth, 4 Feb 45 and *fn*. Or just possibly with Maclise.

[3] An early hint of the *Daily News*.

time it took. After I was beaten, I had all this taken off (an idea of my own) and put on lank and straight—the moustache, which had curled up towards the eyes, turned drooping *down*—and every hair dishevelled. You never saw such a Devil. But I wore real armour on my throat and breast; and most enormous boots and spurs—and looked like an old Spanish Portrait, I assure you. Maclise is going to paint the figure, as an ideal one; and I have sat to him already, in the Dress.[1] I am constantly reverting to this Play, I find; but only because I know you will like to hear whatever I happen to remember about it. It is not unlikely we may act again—some other play—at Christmas. Mr. Lemon, the Editor of Punch, who played Brainworm in the Comedy, and acted with me in the Farce, is an excellent actor. But everybody's understanding of what he was about, and what the author meant, was truly interesting in a very high degree.

Dear Madame De la Rue, I didn't wear the slippers! I couldn't find it in my heart to drag them through the dirt and destruction of a Theatre. Here they are, every morning on the rug—giving me as great a start, sometimes, when they catch my eye, as the footprint on the sand caused Robinson Crusoe—and carrying me back to Genoa at a greater pace than ever seven-league boots went. I have a new picture of the Peschiere; painted by a friend of my brother's[2] who came to see us there; and very well done. It hangs upon the staircase, just outside my bedroom door. The last thing at night, and the first thing in the morning, I see the Peschiere—and all day long, besides; for there is another in my room here. What would I give to see you, too? I carry you about with me in the shape of a Purse; and though that pocket is in a very tender place—breast pocket—left hand side—I carry you about in tenderer places still, in your own image which will never fade or change to me, come what may. Ever Yours affecy. CD.

P.S. Children at home and thriving. All well. Kate and Georgy send their loves. Both "going" to write.

To CLARKSON STANFIELD, 27 SEPTEMBER 1845

MS University of Kentucky.

Devonshire Terrace | Twenty Seventh September 1845.
My Dear Stanny
I return you the Pipe,[3] with many thanks.
You recollect that we meet at Forster's to day, at 3, to settle the accounts. A chop afterwards, I suppose, and some illegitimate Theatricals?
Have you received the statement of the Gas? If you have not, I will send down to Miss Kelly, myself, on receiving a word from you to that effect.

Ever Faithfully
CD.

---

[1] Nothing is known of this. Maclise's portrait of Forster as Kitely (without the beard objected to by Procter: see *To* Miss Macready, 18 Sep 45, *fn*), exhibited RA 1848, is now in the Forster Collection (see *Daniel Maclise*, catalogue of exhibition, National Portrait Gallery, 1972, p. 76).

[2] See *To* G. F. Baker, 10 Aug 45; its present whereabouts is not known.

[3] Used by Bobadil in III, v, when he makes his speech in praise of tobacco.

To MESSRS BRADBURY & EVANS, 29 SEPTEMBER 1845†

MS Clark Memorial Library, University of California. *Address:* Messrs. Bradbury and Evans | Whitefriars | Fleet Street.

Devonshire Terrace | Monday Twenty Ninth September
1845.

My Dear B and E.

I think it is time we determined how the Xmas book[1] shall be illustrated. If you deem it advisable to have it done as expensively as the Chimes, it may be as well to communicate with Messrs. Leech and Doyle, and prepare them for what they will have to do. I have already given Mr. Maclise to understand that he must let me know, *this week*, whether he will do the Frontispiece.[2]

*a*As soon as you have done those Chimes accounts, I shall be glad to swell my uɐ|ɐqɔɐ with the result.[3] When we settle them, I have to credit you with a small amount in right of the Carol. I have C and H's accounts, in a great deal of red and black ink, all duly ruled and rendered.*a*[4]

I have seen George Cruikshank in reference to the Oliver Twist cover,[5] which he is more than ready to do. It is clear it would never have done to have handed it on to anybody else. *b*It may be a wholesome reminder to send him a Block in the course of the next few days.[5]

I am in the preliminary seclusion and ill-temper of the Xmas book. You will find me at home, any morning.

Ever Yours

Messrs. Bradbury and Evans   CHARLES DICKENS

To THOMAS POWELL, 29 SEPTEMBER 1845

MS Dickens House.

Devonshire Terrace | Twenty Ninth September 1845.

My Dear Powell.

I have no doubt whatever, from the botheration I daily undergo on the subject of more performances, that the Theatre could be immediately filled at a Guinea a head, for the repetition of Every Man In His Humour. But I have a great doubt whether the Company in general would like to play to that kind of audience; and I am not at all clear that I should like it myself. I acted to a General audience in Canada, once—But that is far away, and quite another thing.

[1] *The Cricket on the Hearth.*

[2] Maclise supplied the frontispiece and decorated title-page: see *To* Maclise, 4 Oct 45 and *fn.* Leech did seven illustrations and Doyle three.

aa; bb Not previously published.

[3] CD's account-book (MS Messrs Coutts) shows a payment from Bradbury & Evans of £708.11.5 on 4 Oct; this probably represents his three-quarters share of the £1400 referred to in *To* Mitton, 14 Apr 45, after deduction of the £300 already paid on

17 Mar and of his three-quarters share of the expenses of the later edition of *The Chimes*—Bradbury & Evans's Accounts (Forster Collection, V & A) show that, of the 3000 copies, not enough to cover expenses had yet been disposed of.

[4] Not traced.

[5] The new cover for the shilling parts, which began to appear 1 Jan 46; reproduced as frontispiece in *Oliver Twist*, ed. K. Tillotson, 1966.

In case you should not, in the fulness of time, hear anything more from me on this subject, you may conclude that it is not feasible. Every one concerned, however, has, I do really believe, the strongest possible interest in behalf of the Sanatorium.

Ever Yours
CHARLES DICKENS

Thomas Powell Esquire

P.S. I think a letter from Southwood Smith, or from some of the Committee addressed to me as Manager would be the best mode of bringing it before the Body of Amateurs, if you really desire that they should consider it in a business-like way.

To MR ELLIS,[1] 30 SEPTEMBER 1845†

MS Mr Alan G. Thomas.

1 Devonshire Terrace, | York Gate Regents Park
Thirtieth September 1845.

Mr. Charles Dickens presents his compliments to Mr. Ellis, and begs, on behalf of the gentlemen engaged in the Amateur Performance at Miss Kelly's Theatre, to enclose him a cheque for Eight Guineas. *He will be glad to learn that it is a sufficient remuneration to Mr. Ellis for his time and trouble.*

To W. S. LANDOR, 30 SEPTEMBER 1845

Extract in Sotheby's catalogue, 9 Feb 1901; *MS* 2 pp.; dated 30 Sep 45.

Your Godson[2] flourishes. My ladies say they don't object to receive any amount of love you may forward but they question whether you have much to send.

To GEORGE CRUIKSHANK, 1 OCTOBER 1845*

MS Morgan Library.

Devonshire Terrace | First October 1845.

My Dear George. Don't let me take away your breath with too sudden a question—but can you come and dine with me *today*[3] at 6?

I have made up a small table, suddenly, for an Englishman from Naples,[4] who keeps great state there, and shewed me extreme attention. Count D'Orsay is

---

[1] Presumably the Mr Ellis to whom CD wrote about the property lists on 6 Nov; perhaps John Ellis, painter, 7 Tavistock Row, Covent Garden (to whom CD also wrote on 30 Jan 57).

aa Not previously published.
[2] Walter Landor Dickens (1841–63): see Vol. II, pp. 209–10 and *ns*.
[3] Underlined twice.
[4] Ridgway.

coming, who wishes very much to know you better. Stanfield, Maclise, and ourselves are the rest of the party.

Ever Yours
CD.

Stretch a point if needful and say Yes.

To FRANK STONE, 1 OCTOBER 1845*

MS[1] Benoliel Collection.

1 Devonshire Terrace | October 1st. 1845

My Dear Stone

I beg to inform you that the whole of the Accounts arising out of the Play, have been got in and paid; and that your share of the gross expences (including the supper and every incidental charge) amounts to £10..4..0 which you can forward to me, if you please, at your convenience.

The cost of a repetition of the Comedy and Farce, would be about £3 to each of us.

Faithfully Yours always
Frank Stone Esquire   CHARLES DICKENS

To T. J. THOMPSON, 1 OCTOBER 1845

MS[2] Huntington Library.

1 Devonshire Terrace | October 1st. 1845

My Dear Thompson

I beg to inform you that the whole of the accounts arising out of the Play, have been got in and paid; and that your share of the gross expences (including the supper and every incidental charge) amounts to £10..4..0 which you can forward to me, if you please, at your convenience.

The cost of a repetition of the Comedy and Farce, would be about £3 to each of us.

Faithfully Yours always
T. J. Thompson Esquire.   CHARLES DICKENS

Wilson the Hair dresser[3] (nearly opposite Chapman and Hall's in the Strand) has got your great coat and cigar case.

---

[1] Except for salutation, ending, and sub-scription, this letter is in Catherine's hand.

[2] Except for salutation, ending, sub-scription, and postscript, this letter is in Catherine's hand.

[3] William Wilson, theatrical hairdresser, 277 Strand; CD paid "Mr. Wilson" £4 on 4 Oct 45 (Account-book, MS Messrs

Coutts). He appears in Mrs Gamp's 1847 account (F, VI, i, 461): "a individgle—the politest as ever I see—in a shepherd's plaid suit with a long gold watch-guard hanging round his neck"; he says "There's not a theatre in London worth mentioning that I don't attend punctually".

To CHARLES EATON,[1] 1 OCTOBER 1845

MS[2] Benoliel Collection. *Address:* Charles Eaton Esquire.

1 Devonshire Terrace | October 1st. 1845

My Dear Sir

I beg to inform you that the whole of the accounts arising out of the Play, have been got in and paid; and that your share of the gross expences (including the supper and every incidental charge) amounts to £3..14..0 which you can forward to me, if you please, at your convenience.

The cost of a repetition of the Comedy and Farce, would be about £3 to each of us.

Charles Eaton Esquire.

Faithfully Yours
CHARLES DICKENS

To JOHN LEECH, 1 and 2 OCTOBER 1845

MS[3] Comtesse de Suzannet. *Address:* John Leech Esquire | Brook Green | Hammersmith.

1 Devonshire Terrace | October 1st. 1845

My Dear Leech

I beg to inform you that the whole of the accounts arising out of the Play, have been got in and paid; and that your share of the gross expences (including the supper and every incidental charge) amounts to £10..4..0 which you can forward to me, if you please, at your convenience.

The cost of a repetition of the Comedy and Farce, would be about £3 to each of us.

John Leech Esquire

Faithfully Yours
CHARLES DICKENS

Devonshire Terrace | Second October 1845.

My Dear Leech.

To my business note to you, and enclosure for your brother in law, I add a line to say that I hope I may again count on your assistance in my little Christmas Book. I am now settling myself to work; and hope in ten days or so, to be in a condition to wind you up and set you going.

If you are in the mood, therefore, to illustrate my poor fancies, we will hold discourse together on the subject, in about that time. We intend publishing earlier than usual, this Year.[4]

Ever Yours
CD.

[1] Charles Eaton, Mrs Leech's brother; he had taken over A'Beckett's part of William at the last minute: see *To* Lady Holland, ?10–15 Sep 45, *fn.*

[2] Except for salutation, ending and subscription, this letter is in Catherine's hand.

[3] Except for salutation, ending, and subscription, the letter of 1 Oct is in Catherine's hand.

[4] They did not succeed; the *Cricket* was published 20 Dec 45, the *Chimes* 16 Dec 44, the *Carol* 19 Dec 43.

To CLARKSON STANFIELD, 2 OCTOBER 1845

Text from MDGH, I, 144–5.

Devonshire Terrace, October 2nd, 1845.

My dear Stanny,

I send you the claret jug.[1] But for a mistake, you would have received the little remembrance almost immediately after my return from abroad.

I need not say how much I should value another little sketch[2] from your extraordinary hand in this year's small volume, to which Mac again does the frontispiece. But I cannot hear of it, and will not have it (though the gratification of such aid, to me, is really beyond all expression), unless you will so far consent to make it a matter of business as to receive, without asking any questions, a cheque in return from the publishers. Do not misunderstand me—though I am not afraid there is much danger of your doing so, for between us misunderstanding is, I hope, not easy. I know perfectly well that nothing can pay you for the devotion of any portion of your time to such a use of your art. I know perfectly well that no terms would induce you to go out of your way, in such a regard, for perhaps anybody else. I cannot, nor do I desire to, vanquish the friendly obligation which help from you imposes on me. But I am not the sole proprietor of these little books; and it would be monstrous in you if you were to dream of putting a scratch into a second one without some shadowy reference to the other partners, ten thousand times more monstrous in me if any consideration on earth could induce me to permit it, which nothing will or shall.

So, see what it comes to. If you will do me a favour on my terms it will be more acceptable to me, my dear Stanfield, than I can possibly tell you. If you will not be so generous, you deprive me of the satisfaction of receiving it at your hands, and shut me out from that possibility altogether. What a stony-hearted ruffian you must be in such a case!

Ever affectionately yours
[CHARLES DICKENS]

To JOSEPH ELLIS,[3] 4 OCTOBER 1845*

MS Mr H. W. Woodward.

Devonshire Terrace. London | Saturday Fourth October | 1845.

Mr. Charles Dickens presents his compliments to Mr. Ellis, and begs to say that himself and Mr. Forster are coming down to Brighton tomorrow, to remain at the Bedford until Monday; and that they will be obliged to Mr. Ellis if he will order two comfortable bedrooms to be reserved for them.

---

[1] Bradbury & Evans included £13.15.6 "for Claret Jug" among the expenses of the *Chimes* in their accounts for 1845–6 (MS V & A).

[2] Stanfield did the illustration of "The Carrier's Cart" for the *Cricket*. On 31 Dec there is a memorandum: "Mr. Stanfield has not been paid anything for the Battle or the Cricket"; he was paid £23.3.0 for the *Battle of Life*, 30 June 47.

[3] Joseph Ellis, proprietor of the Bedford Hotel, Brighton; son of Joseph Ellis of the Star and Garter Hotel, Richmond: see Vol. III, p. 265*n*.

To DANIEL MACLISE, 4 OCTOBER 1845*

MS University of Texas. *Address:* Daniel Maclise Esquire | 14 Russell Place.

Devonshire Terrace | Fourth October 1845.

My Dear Mac.

A Thousand Thanks for your kind remembrance of that dinner-table promise.[1] Nothing could be more brilliant than the knife and fork you sent. I wouldn't change them on any account.

There is an old superstition about knives—Nothing in it, I dare say—but I send you a halfpenny in payment.

Do not think so nonsensically[2] about the value of your frontispiece.[3] I can hardly believe you to be serious, when I know so much better, and so far above all possibility of dispute, what its value is.

I have had quite a noble note from Stanny: who, also, illustrates again. I will explain my idea to you, as soon as I have shaped it quite distinctly. You will find it a good subject, I think.

Has Forster told you that he and I are going to Brighton tomorrow—returning next day? You mean to bear us company, I hope? It is only a two hours' journey, now.

Affectionately Ever

Danial Maclise Esquire.   CHARLES DICKENS

To CLARKSON STANFIELD, 4 OCTOBER 1845†

MS Berg Collection.

Devonshire Terrace | Saturday Fourth October 1845.

My Dear Stanny.

[a]I am touched to the quick by the kind heartiness of your letter. Heaven forbid that there should be any of that same dirty metal in the leaven of our friendship, ever![a] The few grains I insist upon, are really not mine. From myself, I offer you nothing but Thanks.

As to the value and importance of your help—all I say on that score is, that you are a Pernicious old Humbug.

[b]I shall hope, in a fortnight or so, to shew you something of the Tale. I am thinking still; but have not yet begun.[b]

I should have made a point of coming to Liston's[4] last night, had I not been engaged all day in some painful business of my friend Wellbred's; who, on the

---

[1] Probably on 1 Oct: see *To* Cruikshank, that day.

[2] MS has "nonsenically".

[3] The frontispiece, framed in branches of holly and ivy, shows the Peerybingles brooding by the fireside, with the baby in the cradle, surrounded by the Spirits of Home as described at the end of "Chirp the First", with smaller scenes above. Thackeray's review (see *To* Felton, 1 Jan 46, *fn*) said it had seldom been surpassed

"for grace and fancy ... one of the most brilliant specimens of the art"; but the *Illustrated London News* (27 Dec 45) thought it "not suitable to the story of an English home".

[aa; bb] Given in N, I, 707; letter otherwise unpublished.

[4] Robert Liston (1794–1847; *DNB*), surgeon and FRS; well known to Macready and others of his set. Stanfield painted his portrait.

very eve of his marriage with a very beautiful girl—the ring purchased, wedding dresses made, and so forth—finds the whole contract shattered like Glass, in an instant, under the most inexplicable circumstances that ever distracted the head of "a mutual friend".

If you could have seen me yesterday, as the Acting Manager of *this* Drama (a domestic tragedy) you would have said Miss Kelly's was nothing to it. I am still up to the eyes in the miserable affair, but with no hope of a good end.[1]

Ever Affectionately Yours | Dear Stanny
CHARLES DICKENS

Kate was very queer indeed, all night on Thursday. I thought of the Doctor several times. I was more than ever sorry to have left you so soon, when I heard from Toby[2] and Mac, that Mrs. Stanfield sang in *the most charming manner*.[3]

To [JOSEPH ELLIS], [6 OCTOBER 1845]*

MS Bodleian Library. *Date:* endorsed "6 October 1845" in unknown hand; clearly the day of their return. *Address:* from a collection of letters to Joseph Ellis.

Bedford Hotel Brighton | Monday Morning

My Dear Sir

Allow me to thank you for your note, and at the same time to express my regret that we are off and away again, at too early an hour this morning, to admit of our accepting your kind Invitation.

Mr. Forster begs me to convey his compliments to you. And I am always
Dear Sir | Faithfully Yours
CHARLES DICKENS

To MISS BURDETT COUTTS, 6 OCTOBER 1845*

MS Morgan Library.

Devonshire Terrace
Monday Night Sixth October | 1845.

My Dear Miss Coutts

I cannot but think that a letter of mine must have been overlooked at your

[1] Christiana had been staying with Mrs Smithson 22–30 Sep, when she recorded "terminated my visit the day being fixed". The next day: "Mr. Thompson came in the evening—terrible unhappiness great crisis & a revolution in affairs"—evidently Mr Weller, on hearing that the wedding day had been arranged while she was staying with Mrs Smithson, refused his consent and forbade communication. Despairing entries in the diary continue until 6 Oct when Christiana was "transformed" by a letter from Thompson, in reply to one she had secretly posted. On 11 Oct she wrote, "Matters decidedly looking up"; and on

14 Oct: "the fatal discussion at Dickens' between Pa Mr & Mrs Dickens & Mr Streeter. ... Met Papa in C. Row & some one else at the door. Everything set right" (MS Mrs Sowerby).

[2] Forster—also called "Tony" in *To Stanfield, 28 Oct 45*.

[3] Rebecca Stanfield was an excellent singer and pianist, and especially devoted to Mozart; she lined up her children (and later her grandchildren) round the piano and trained them to take parts in *Le Nozze di Figaro* and other operas (information from Mr P. F. Skottowe).

house. The impression on my mind—an impression so very strong, that it amounts to everything but a moral certainty—is, that some days ago, I wrote to Stratton Street, acknowledging the safe receipt of the money, and telling you that I would write again and gratify you (I hoped) by saying how we had disposed of it—as soon as I had quite completed the business. I said in the same letter that the poor young lady was very greatly better—composed, and mentally resigned: placing her trust in a better World, and relying on a meeting there, in God's good time, with her lover. Nothing, surely, could induce me to believe that I wrote this letter, unless I had actually done so.[1] *I feel quite sure that I dispatched it to your house in town.* The more I think of it; being usually very exact in such things; the more persuaded I am, that I wrote and sent it.

I will not fail to redeem that pledge of telling you the end of your benevolence, so far as it can now be ascertained, as soon as I know it myself.

I write in great haste, lest you should miss the second letter. Ever Dear Miss Coutts Yours most faithfully

CHARLES DICKENS

To THOMAS COOPER,[2] 7 OCTOBER 1845†

MS Carl H. Pforzheimer Library.

Devonshire Terrace | Seventh October 1845.

Dear Sir

I am sorry to say that I am not yet prepared to report to you upon your MS.[3] I have been engaged for some days, in the endeavour to arrange some affairs of a distressing nature for a friend; and this business has left me no leisure whatever.

You can have access to your papers at any time you please, for the purpose of taking out the Verses. *a*If you desire it, I can very easily send them to you. Let me know which you will prefer. I should have answered your letter without delay, but for my having been at Brighton.*a*

Faithfully Yours

Thomas Cooper Esquire   CHARLES DICKENS

[1] See *To* Miss Coutts, 24 Sep 45, which acknowledges the money; CD had doubtless forgotten that he had not given these details.

[2] Thomas Cooper (1805–92; *DNB*), journalist; became a Chartist 1840, imprisoned for two years from Mar 43; later, left the movement but lectured to Radical audiences on general subjects until suddenly converted to Christianity in 1856. Contributed two papers to *Household Words*, 1853. Best known for his epic poem *The Purgatory of Suicides* (published Aug 45), written in prison. Had sought help in finding a publisher from Disraeli, Forster, Ainsworth and Jerrold; the last-named

helped him, and CD borrowed the MS to read (*Life of Thomas Cooper, written by Himself*, 1877, 276, 281–2; Walter Jerrold, *Life of Douglas Jerrold*, II, 415–17). He was accused of flattering literary figures by the *Northern Star*, 25 July 46.

[3] Probably *The Baron's Yule-feast: a Christmas-rhyme*, 1846, several stories in verse intended as a "Christmas book", but publication (by Jeremiah How) delayed till Jan, although it was advertised 20 Dec to appear 23 Dec. In a note on "The Miller of Roche", Cooper refers to CD's "kind attention" in pointing out a similar story in the *Decameron*.

aa Not previously published.

To MISS FANNY KELLY, 7 OCTOBER 1845

Extract in Maggs catalogue No. 399 (1920); *MS* 1½ pp.; dated Devonshire Terrace, 7 Oct 45. *Address* (envelope, MS Mr L. C. Staples): Miss Kelly | 73 Dean Street | Soho.

By all means. If I do not see you here tomorrow between half past 2 and 3, I will call on you at ten minutes after the last-named hour.

To FREDERICK DICKENS, 7 OCTOBER 1845*

MS Fitzwilliam Museum.

Devonshire Terrace.
Wednesday Evening | Seventh October 1845.

My Dear Fred.

I claim no right whatever to oppose your wishes. You ask me for my counsel: and I give it you. I do not expect you to take it, nor shall I be in the least offended if you do not. But I would earnestly advise you not to be hasty in rejecting it.

So far as I know myself, I think I have some reason to suppose that I am not accustomed to take "stern" views of any subject. That it is not my nature in any case. And that if I had a tendency that way it would be very unlikely to beset me in reference to any matter nearly concerning *you.*

Marriage, with your income, is a very serious affair.[1] Something on the lady's part, would certainly be desirable. But failing that, (on which I do not lay extraordinary stress, as the affections are not commonly regulated by the pocket) I do hold it very essential that the family with which you connect yourself should seem, in what one knows of them, to give you some sort of warrant for trusting in them as good, straight-forward, agreeable persons—pleasant to associate with, when their freshness has gone off—commonly discreet and rational in ordinary life—and such good governors of themselves in their sentiments, sympathies, antipathies, and what not, as to render them reasonably likely to stand the wear and tear of Home-test; which brings all metal to the proof in a very searching manner.

I do not think the Wellers are this kind of people. I want odd phrases to express my meaning when I think of them. Perhaps I cannot express myself better than by saying they are, in my opinion, an "impracticable family." They don't seem to me to have any ballast. They are very amiable, but especially uncomfortable. They are feverish, restless, flighty, excitable, uncontrollable, wrong-headed; under no sort of wholesome self-restraint; and bred to think the absence of it a very intellectual and brilliant thing. The presence of this flutter and fever in anybody's house—but especially in a poor man's, with the world before him—is not the presence that would make it comfortable, rich, or happy.

---

[1] In Aug Thompson had feared that Fred might "turn his thoughts to Anna; although he has so entire a dread of your Papa, that I know he will struggle long against any yearning towards her. But alas! poor Fred's circumstances must condemn him for some time to come to celibacy" (Thompson *to* Christiana, 31 Aug 45, MS Mrs Sowerby).

Anna is very young—surely *very* young.[1] I grant her good looks. I grant her cleverness (I think very highly of it); but I doubt her quiet wisdom in the quiet life to which you must inevitably retreat. I doubt whether that "Soul" of which the family make such frequent mention, may not be something too expansive for a domestic parlor—a little too vague for the defined and marked-out tenor of your way. I doubt whether she be in a condition to know her own mind, or your mind, or anything else, with any sort of distinctness, or with any enduring perception. The world about her seems to be a Great Electrifying Machine, from which she gets all sorts of unaccountable shocks and knocks and starts; and it seems to me to be an open question whether she will ever be shocked and knocked and started into a reasonable woman.

You will say, very naturally and with good reason, that I may be wrong in this, and how do I know it? But I may say, at least as naturally and with no less reason, that *you* may be wrong in *your* estimate, and how do *you* know better. When I went away to Italy, she was a mere child. Consider. Have your opportunities been so very numerous or good, that you can pronounce with any sort of clearness, on the dawning character half developed in her, since. These things of which I speak, are on the surface: broadly open to all observers. Have you been able to see so far below it, as to find the quiet source of all these eddies and currents?

The change in Thompson's affairs has, very naturally, hurried you on, it seems to me. For it has disturbed you in your opportunities of intercourse with her,[2] and driven you into the devising of some new occasions. But do you believe you are so much attached to her, that you cannot withdraw now, if you will? And do you believe that your Heart is already shut up against all other comers? I have nothing in my mind but your Happiness. If I thought your Happiness would be secured by this pursuit, I would encourage you at all hazards. But the little foibles of the Wellers seem to me as dangerous to domestic peace as many graver—infinitely graver—faults would be. And I should be wanting in that affection for which you give me credit (not, I can sincerely say, without as good reason as ever a Brother had; for my love for you has always been a strong and true and tender one) if I did not entreat you to be cautious—to avoid all rash conclusion—and to look steadily along the far perspective of weary years to which one hasty moment may conduct you: shutting out retreat.

I have assumed that Anna may reciprocate your attachment—that the father may approve of it—that the weakness of the mother may happen to stagger into your side of the balance—that the commercial arithmetic of Mr. Shaw may find no flaw in your proposals—that nobody's Soul may make your probation a wretched and uncertain one—but think of all these chances my dear Fred. And

[1] Anna was 15; CD was still making her youth a ground of objection in 1847. "very" is underlined twice.

[2] Christiana's diary shows that Fred was often at the Wellers' house and joined in expeditions, besides meeting them at Mrs Smithson's in both London and Margate; he had dined with the sisters on the night of the play, and again (with CD and Catherine) at Amelia Thompson's birthday party on 29 Sep ("Boz glorious ... after *he* left we fell to dancing"). Fred is not mentioned 1–14 Oct, but on 15 Oct he and Thompson accompanied the Wellers to Hampton Court.

whatever you resolve on (for I see the resolution lies with you at last) come and tell me what it is. If I cannot dissuade you from your purpose, I may guide you in its execution.

Ever Yours affectionately

Frederick Dickens Esquire   CHARLES DICKENS

To DR SOUTHWOOD SMITH, 9 OCTOBER 1845

Text from Walter T. Spencer catalogue No. 104 (1901).

Devonshire Terrace, | Thursday, October Ninth, 1845.

My dear Dr. Smith,

I have appointed them to meet at Mr. Forster's room on Saturday, at *half after Three*. I believe Mr. Jerrold has a strong objection to playing to an audience who pay for their seats.[1]

Ever yours,

Dr. Southwood Smith.   CHARLES DICKENS

To FREDERICK DICKENS, 11 OCTOBER 1845*

MS Miss Doris Minards.

Devonshire Terrace | Saturday 11th. October 1845.

My Dear Fred.

I think you have an undoubted right to go to Weller's if you please; and that you are in no way compromised by the position of Thompson's affairs in reference to the family. But you must always remember that you are there, distinctly *on your honor*; and that you can carry no word, or letter, or communication of any kind, between the parties. This *may* become your difficulty.

Shall we see you tomorrow?

Ever affectionately

Frederick Dickens Esquire   CHARLES DICKENS

To [W. C. MACREADY], 11 OCTOBER [1845]

Text from MDGH, I, 195. *Date:* 1845 was the only year when CD was acting in *Every Man in his Humour* and Macready playing Shakespeare in London. *Address:* clearly to Macready; headed "Another 'Bobadil' note" by MDGH and placed immediately after a letter to him in May 1848 in similar style. Reference to "twenty-first" confirms: see *fn*.

At Cobb's, a water-bearer, | October 11th.

I must tell you this, sir, I am no general man; but for William Shakespeare's sake[2] (you may embrace it at what height of favour you please) I will communi-

---

[1] See *To* Powell, 29 Sep 45.   [2] Macready's season at the Princess's was about to begin.

cate with you on the twenty-first,[1] and do esteem you to be a gentleman of some parts—of a good many parts in truth. I love few words.[2]

Bobadil[3]

To UNKNOWN CORRESPONDENT, 11 OCTOBER 1845*

MS Cheltenham Ladies' College.

Devonshire Terrace | Eleventh October 1845.

My Dear Sir

I beg to acknowledge the Receipt of your kind letter. I have written an authority to the Bookseller, to receive the Copies of Eugene Aram from your Publisher;[4] and will let you know what has been done with them, as soon as the business is arranged.

Faithfully Yours   Dear Sir
CHARLES DICKENS

[   ][5]

To JAMES EDWARDS,[6] 12 OCTOBER 1845

Mention in American Art Association and Anderson Galleries catalogue No. 3854; *MS* 2 pp.; dated London, 12 Oct 45.

Concerning proposed visit to Manchester.

To THOMAS BEARD, [13] OCTOBER 1845

MS Dickens House. *Date:* Monday was 13 Oct. *Address:* Thomas Beard Esquire | 42 Portman Place.

Devonshire Terrace. | Monday Twelfth October | 1845.

My Dear Beard. I have a confidential question to ask you. One that may rather

---

[1] CD dined at Macready's on 21 Oct with Maclise, Stanfield, Jerrold, Forster, Lemon, Troughton and Leech (*Diaries*, II, 307).

[2] The letter is based on a speech of Bobadil's in III, i.

[3] MDGH gives a facsimile of this signature in a large sprawling hand.

[4] Unlikely to refer to Bulwer's novel, but very probably to Hood's poem, *The Dream of Eugene Aram*, first published in *The Gem*, 1828, and separately in an edition of 1831. In 1847 (*To* Mahony, N, II, 26) CD recalled that Moxon had asked him to " 'edit' a book of Hood's after his decease", which he declined to do; but he may well have contributed by helping to collect material for *Poems by Thomas Hood*, published by

Moxon 10 Jan 1846 (anonymous preface dated "December 1845"). Moxon ("the Bookseller"?) had not previously published any of Hood's work; the publisher of *Eugene Aram* in 1831 was Charles Tilt, 86 Fleet Street (later Tilt and Bogue, and by 1844, David Bogue of the same address).

[5] Subscription cut away; room for 8–10 letters. If the "business" is correctly identified, William Harvey, engraver (1796–1866; *DNB*) is much the likeliest recipient, as the illustrator of the poem in 1831 and a promoter of the Memorial Fund in 1845.

[6] Probably the Secretary of the Manchester Athenaeum; Talfourd's letter to him accompanying the gift of his works was printed in the *Manchester Guardian*, 5 Nov 45.

amaze you.[1] If you can come round to me tonight—do. If not—tomorrow Morning.

                                                    Ever Yours
Thomas Beard Esquire   CHARLES DICKENS

To GEORGE CRUIKSHANK, 17 OCTOBER 1845

Mention in N, I, 708; *MS* I p.; dated Devonshire Terrace, 17 Oct 45, "enclosing £40 for investment".[2] Probably belongs with envelope (MS Benoliel Collection), PM 18 Oct 45, addressed "George Cruikshank Esquire | Amwell Street | Pentonville".

To JOHN LEECH, 17 OCTOBER 1845

MS Benoliel Collection. *Address:* John Leech Esquire | Brook Green | Hammersmith.

                              Devonshire Terrace. | Seventeenth October 1845.

My Dear Leech. James Heywood[3] is a man of great consideration in Manchester, and of great attainments. You must regard his invitation (Manchesterially speaking) as a great compliment. I have refused it: simply because I am beaten almost out of heart by all manner of occupations, and wouldn't be a Provincial Lion at this time, in a private way, for I don't know how many shares in the Great Grimsby Junction. No Master Mathew! Refuse James Heywood, and repair to an honest Inn with honest Gentlemen. Jerrold and I (and you) will start on *Wednesday Morning* somewhere about 9. I will tell you the exact hour when we meet at Macreadys on Tuesday.

                                              Ever Heartily Yours
                                                        Bobadil

To THE DIRECTORS OF THE ATHENAEUM, MANCHESTER, 17 OCTOBER 1845

MS Chas J. Sawyer.

            Devonshire Terrace. | Friday Night | Seventeenth October 1845.
Dear Sirs.
   M. Eugene Sue[4] has begged me to write to you, and acknowledge with many

---

[1] The question doubtless concerned the *Daily News*; by 17 Oct Beard had been told of the scheme. On 14 Oct Bradbury was to dine with Joseph Paxton "when the paper scheme will be settled" (Paxton *to* Mrs Paxton, MS Devonshire Collections).

[2] See *To* Miss Coutts, 24 Sep 45, *fn.* Probably CD said that he would have £40 available for Miss Wight, some of it for investment.

[3] James Heywood (1810–97), FRS and FSA 1839; founder of Manchester Athenaeum, 28 Oct 35, and first President; trustee of Owens College 1845–60; MP for

North Lancs 1847–57. CD met him at Manchester in 1843.

[4] Eugène Sue (1804–57), French novelist; best known in England for his feuilletons *Les Mystères de Paris* (10 vols, 1842–3; three English versions in 1844–5, and much imitated) and *Le Juif Errant* (10 vols, 1844–5; of which nine different publishers issued versions in England in 1844–5); had recently published *Rodin*, a tale of Jesuit villainy. Macready (but not CD) met him in Paris, 13 Dec 44, and thought him "a particularly agreeable man" (*Diaries*, II, 278).

heartfelt thanks the receipt of your flattering Invitation.[1] He requests me to assure you of his high and unfeigned sense of the honor you have done him; and earnestly entreats me to add that he is gratified by your recognition of him, a French Writer, in England—certainly beyond his power of expression in a foreign language, and to an extent not at all easy of expression in his own.

His state of health, however, does not admit of his attending the soirée at Manchester. He has been very unwell; and is enjoined to seek repose; in pursuance of which advice, he has already left Paris in search of temporary change and quiet.[2]

If I could convey to you an adequate idea of M. Eugene Sue's anxiety that I should do my very best to thank you on his behalf, and to find "strong words" for that purpose, you would feel with me that your remembrance of him has met with a sincere and quick response.

I have the honor to be, Gentlemen | Your faithful Servant
The Directors of The Athenaeum | Manchester.   CHARLES DICKENS

To MACVEY NAPIER, 17 OCTOBER 1845

MS British Museum.

Devonshire Terrace. | Seventeenth October 1845.

My Dear Sir

I must ask you for as broad a licence in respect of Time, as you can possibly allow me.[3] I have been forced by a perfect multitude of unexpected distractions, both business and domestic, to postpone the beginning of my little Xmas book until within these few days; and it will occupy me (allowing for such interruptions as I cannot ward off) until late in November.

Never having written in the review, I find it difficult to speak precisely about *Length*. I should say 16 or 20 pages. Certainly not less I should imagine.

How late can you afford to let me be? I have a great desire to know.

Your opinion about Rape, coincides with Lord John Russell's, I believe.[4]

---

[1] The invitation evoked some comment, the *Athenæum* (1 Nov 45) thinking it regrettable "if the particular scope and charcater of his writings is to be presumed an expression of the philosophy of ... the institution"; and in about 1849 Carlyle remarked to Milnes: "If Beelzebub were to appear in England, he would receive a letter from the Secretary of the Manchester Athenaeum, as Eugène Sue did, requesting the honour of his interesting company, and venturing to hope for an address" (T. Wemyss Reid, *Life, Letters and Friendships of Richard Monckton Milnes*, I, 435).

[2] Sue also wrote himself to Berlyn, 7 Oct, to the same effect; his letter was printed with CD's in the *Manchester Guardian*, 22 Oct, and reprinted in *The Times*, 23 Oct.

[3] Napier must have reminded CD of his promise of 7 Aug. Early Dec would not have been too late for the Jan *Edinburgh*, and at this date CD may still have believed it possible.

[4] In 1837 Russell, then Home Secretary, had introduced the bill which drastically reduced the number of offences punishable by death; those remaining included rape, which however had ceased to be a capital crime in 1841. Recently published statistics showed that committals for rape had considerably increased since the change, and those who opposed total abolition used this as an argument. In his *Daily News* articles CD avoided the subject; but there was some controversy on the matter between the *Law Magazine* and the *Daily News* in Mar–May 46 (*Law Magazine*, XXXV, 235–50, XXXVI, 52–66, and *Daily News*, 11, 15, 16 May).

I cannot bring myself to believe that *any* crime affects the broad philosophy of the question: still less a crime so very difficult of proof; so very easy to be charged: so perplexing of disentanglement from chances of palliation in the previous conduct of the woman—in her very looks and gestures. But I espy a way, I think, of not compromising you on this head. And you may rely on my being gentle and discreet.

Dear Sir | Always Faithfully Yours

Professor Napier   CHARLES DICKENS

To W. C. MACREADY, 17 OCTOBER 1845

MS Morgan Library.

Devonshire Terrace
Friday Evening | Seventeenth October 1845.

My Dear Macready.

You once (only once) gave the World assurance of a Waistcoat. You wore it Sir—I think in "Money".[1] It was a remarkable and precious Waistcoat wherein certain broad stripes of blue or purple, disported themselves as by a combination of extraordinary circumstances, too happy to occur again. I have seen it on your Manly chest in Private Life. I saw it, Sir, (I think) the other day, in the cold light of morning—with feelings easier to be imagined than described. Mr. Macready, Sir! Are you a father?[2] If so, lend me that Waistcoat for five minutes. I am bidden to a wedding[3] (where fathers are made); and my artist cannot, I find (how should he?) imagine such a waistcoat. Let me shew it to him as a sample of my tastes and wishes; and—ha ha ha ha!—*Eclipse*[4] the Bridegroom!

---

[1] Macready played Evelyn in Bulwer's *Money* at the Haymarket, opening 8 Dec 40 and a great success; Count D'Orsay designed the costumes.

[2] Referring to Macready's famous gag in *Werner* at the Theatre Royal, Bristol, when "carried away by the passion of the scene, he rushed down to Charles Kemble Mason, who played Gabor, and demanded, 'Are you a father?' Then he whispered, 'Say "No" '; whereupon Gabor shouted 'No!' and Macready, in a burst of paternal emotion, rejoined: 'Then you cannot feel for misery like mine!' " (John Coleman, *Players and Playwrights I Have Known*, 1888, I, 47).

[3] T. J. Thompson and Christiana Weller were married at St Luke's, Chelsea, 21 Oct: according to her diary, "the sweetest most picturesque poetical wedding that ever was"; CD and 45 guests attended the wedding breakfast. Georgina was one of the eight bridesmaids, having agreed to this on the previous Thursday: she wrote, "My dear

Christie (*I* will not say *Miss Weller*,—tho' *you* are so ceremonious!) I lose no time in writing to tell you how glad I am to receive your very kind summons for Tuesday morning and what great pleasure it will give me to be among your train of maidens on the happy occasion", and regretted that Catherine had "made her last public appearance for some time", but sent a message to say "how very *very* sorry" she was (Georgina *to* Christiana, 16 Oct 45, MS Mrs Sowerby). CD made a speech at the breakfast, described (in an unidentified cutting in the Weller Papers) as "a delicious oration, the best domestic speech he ever uttered, exciting tears of joy aill round". The married pair went to Tunbridge Wells 21–29 Oct, where the family and friends, including Fred Dickens, visited them on 24 Oct (Christiana's diary, MS Mrs Sowerby).

[4] Written large, with a heavy oblique line beneath it.

I will send a trusty Messenger at halfpast 9 precisely—in the Morning—He is sworn to secrecy—He durst not for his life betray us—or Swells in ambuscade would have the Waistcoat at the cost of his Heart's blood.

Thine

The Unwaistcoated One.

To SIGNOR NOLI,[1] [?17 OCTOBER 1845]

Mention in next. *Date:* probably written same day as next.

To T. J. THOMPSON, 17 OCTOBER 1845

Text from MDGH, 1882, III, 81–2.

Devonshire Terrace, 17th October, 1845.

My dear Thompson,

Roche has not returned;[2] and from what I hear of your movements,[3] I fear I cannot answer for his being here in time for you.

I enclose you, lest I should forget it, the letter to the Peschiere agent.[4] He is the Marquis Pallavicini's[5] man of business, and speaks the most abominable Genoese ever heard. He is a rascal of course; but a more reliable villain, in his way, than the rest of his kind.

You recollect what I told you of the Swiss banker's wife, the English lady? If you would like Christiana to have a friend at Genoa in the person of a most affectionate and excellent little woman, and if you would like to have a resource in the most elegant and comfortable family there, I need not say that I shall be delighted to give you a letter to those who would die to serve me.[6]

Always yours,

[CHARLES DICKENS]

To THOMAS BEARD, [17 OCTOBER 1845]

MS Dickens House. *Date:* the day before CD went to Chatsworth (18 Oct). *Address:* Thomas Beard Esquire | 42 Portman Place.

Devonshire Terrace | Friday Night

My Dear Beard. On five minutes notice, I am obliged to go into Derbyshire,[7] on matters of great moment connected with my scheme. You know my punctu-

---

[1] House agent, of Genoa: see *To* Forster, 7 June 45 and *fn.*

[2] From his engagement with George Dodd, MP.

[3] The Thompsons sailed from Dover 1 Nov, and travelled through France to Genoa, where they stayed from 16 Dec 45 until 9 Feb 46.

[4] The Thompsons called on him immediately on arrival in Genoa but decided not to take apartments in the Peschiere

[(Christiana's journal, 17 Dec 45; MS Mrs Sowerby).

[5] Owner of the Peschiere.

[6] The Thompsons were at once welcomed into the de la Rue circle and saw them almost daily; Christiana's journal shows that they talked frequently of CD, but no details are recorded.

[7] To see Joseph Paxton at Chatsworth, almost certainly to learn more about the detailed financial arrangements for the

ality, and that nothing of light import would induce me to postpone anything—much less, a dinner with you. Forgive me, my dear fellow, for putting it off until my return. I expect to be back on Sunday night (I leave Kate in a most critical condition, so strong is my necessity)—and immediately on my return, I will write to you.

Ever Yours affecy.

Thomas Beard Esquire.   CHARLES DICKENS

To THOMAS BEARD, 20 OCTOBER 1845

MS Dickens House. *Address:* Thomas Beard Esquire | 42 Portman Place | Edgeware Road.

Devonshire Terrace. | Twentieth October 1845.

My Dear Beard. If I don't hear from you to the contrary, I shall take it for granted that you will dine with me at the Parthenon (that will be best, I think; Kate being in a state of tribulation) *on Wednesday next,*[1] *at a quarter past 6.* There is some rather choice Claret in that Establishment just now.

Ever Yours affecy.

Thomas Beard Esquire.   CD.

To EMILE DE LA RUE [?OCTOBER 1845]

Mention in *To* de la Rue, 20 Oct 45. *Date:* between 17 Oct (see *To* Thompson, that day) and 20 Oct.

A note of introduction.[2]

To EMILE DE LA RUE, 20 OCTOBER 1845*

MS Berg Collection. *Address:* A Monsieur: | Monsr. Emile De la Rue | Messrs. De la Rue freres | Genoa | North Italy.

Devonshire Terrace | Monday Twentieth October 1845.

My Dear De la Rue. I received your kind present, yesterday—not 'till yesterday, in consequence of unheard of delays on the part of the Agent, whom I have liberally anathematized for his pains. I cannot tell you how much I thank you for a remembrance so valuable and dear to me, or how sensible I am of the thoughtful kindness that turned your fancy in this direction, when we parted at

paper (Paxton being the chief backer) than Bradbury & Evans felt willing to tell him without Paxton's authority. Without a clear idea of the funds available CD could not start engaging staff. Paxton, still in London on 16 Oct, had left that day or the next and was not returning for some weeks.

[1] CD had clearly already decided not to go to Manchester on 22 Oct as arranged.

[2] Presumably for T. J. Thompson, although he is not named in *To* de la Rue, 20 Oct.

Genoa. You know you could have sent me nothing, I should have received with half the pleasure I have felt, and shall always feel, in this memorial. And what folly it is in me, therefore, to talk of it, when you know what I would say, so much better than I can say it! Here it is, in my sanctum sanctorum; and here it will remain, until the principal Figure in the said Sanctum is removed from it, and laid low in a smaller and more private one.

All the little news I have, I have told Madame De la Rue. Ask her for an exact account of a man, who will come to Genoa one of these days, laden with a note of introduction to you, from the Inimitable B. Ask her for a dark hint of a mighty scheme in which I am engaged. Ask her for some faint and shadowy allusion to a hope I have of travelling a little way in some short time. Ask her whether I am idle or busy: full of plans, or full of leisure.

So they stop the Examiner on that Frontier! Heaven and Earth, what blunder-headed dolts they must be! And here have I been complacently folding it up, and sending it off, week after week; feeling, each time, as if I had written to you, and were the most regular Correspondent in the World! I could have sworn in vexation (perhaps I did), when I pictured these same Newspapers lying, four deep, in the accursed drawer of some Humbug at Turin—you, all the time, imagining the Inimitable B oblivious of his promise and his friends! Well! If I ever *do* write about Italy, I will give the Turin people something worth the trouble of stopping, in return for this; or I'm a Dutchman!

You know that all the World is raving mad, here, about Railroad speculations. There has been a great check since Saturday; and people with faces whose length is quite out of proportion to their bodies, are walking up and down in all the streets, with their hands in apparently empty pockets.[1] As I was writing those words, Ridgway came in to take leave. He stayed five minutes, and went away, after telling me how Gibbs wouldn't wash himself, at the Lake,[2] notwithstanding the abundance of water in it—and how he wanted to sit at table in a complete suit of dirty fustian. And how it couldn't be allowed, on any terms.

Madame De la Rue says nothing in her last note, about Gaberel. I suppose it's all right, and that the young lady (poor Maniac!) has had no interval of sanity, to the destruction of the Reverend's hopes? What has become of Butler?[3] Has he returned to that weeping mother and young pledge of affection, on the Acqua Sola? Is the British Consul, green, yellow, grey, mottled, or plaid?[4] Is Noli hanged? Has Palaviccini (my Marquess) been afflicted with any gleam of

---

[1] On Sat 18 Oct, according to *The Times*, "the advance in the rate of interest caused a temporary suspension of business", and the result was "general gloom". The *Morning Herald* and other papers blamed *The Times* for creating a panic, and the market soon recovered.

[2] Presumably Charles Gibbs had visited Ridgway at his villa on Lake Como.

[3] Thomas Butler, merchant, resident in Genoa; a friend of Yeats Brown: "a thin, quiet man, who liked a good glass of wine" (F. A. Y. Brown, *Family Notes*). Christiana

Thompson met him at Mrs Granet's, 1 Jan 46, as the "beau" of Mme Persano, and again 15 Jan when he "called for a subscription to the church—bored us for an hour" (Journal, MS Mrs Sowerby). He was still in Genoa in 1853, when CD left a card on him (*To Mrs CD*, 29 Oct 53; *Mr and Mrs CD*, ed. W. Dexter, p. 198).

[4] Yeats Brown's eccentricities of dress are suggested by CD's reference to his "hideous and demoniacal nightdress" in 1853 (*Mr and Mrs CD*, p. 195).

reason, since I left?[1] Is the old Governor[2] really angry (as I hear from travellers he is) because I never forced myself upon him? Is that dear young Dragoon who drove the Dog-Cart with the red wheels, shut up in Prison by a jealous Government, because of his too great wit? Is the Peschiere full of English, who would have waylaid me, had I been there, and tortured me?

How does the Idiot? How are all my old walks? How is that wicker-work fowl—that live basket—whom we once met in the street of the Madhouse? Does what's his name the Vetturino sit upon a form all day, at his own door in the Strada Nuova, still? Is there an old man with a broom, always doing nothing on the staircase of your Palace? Was I ever an idle man in a plaid coat, basking, day after day, on the box of a travelling carriage with a happy little party? Or is it all a Dream, and did I never magnetize a little Somebody; with all my heart in her recovery and happiness?

Adieu dear De la Rue! A hundred times God bless you!

Ever Yours
CD.

To C. R. LESLIE,[3] 20 OCTOBER 1845*

MS Mr Clem D. Johnston.

Devonshire Terrace | Monday Twentieth October 1845.

My Dear Sir

Many thanks for your kind note. I will come up to you, in a fortnight or three weeks, then; (when I shall either have finished, or nearly finished, my little book) to arrange our sittings.[4]

Always Faithfully Yours

C. R. Leslie Esquire   CHARLES DICKENS

To THOMAS MITTON, 20 OCTOBER 1845

Text from Daily News, 14 Dec 1915.

Devonshire-terrace | Twentieth October 1845

My Dear Mitton. I went down to Chatsworth myself, on Saturday—left here at 12 noon—got there at ½ past 9 at night—left there again at 3 o'clock next morning —and reached home at half past one yesterday afternoon. H.[5] is with us in

[1] De la Rue gave the Thompsons "a terrible account of the eccentrically wicked nature" of the Marquis (Christiana's journal, 23 Dec 45, MS Mrs Sowerby).

[2] See *To* Forster, ?18 Oct 44 and *fn*.

[3] Charles Robert Leslie (1794–1859; *DNB, DAB*), painter: see Vol. II, p. 395*n*.

[4] For his portrait as Bobadil—but the November letters suggest that CD was too busy to arrange any sittings until Jan 46: see *To* Leslie, 15 Jan 46.

[5] Obviously George Hudson (1800–71;

DNB), "the railway King", already well known to Paxton. Son of a well-to-do farmer, and formerly a linen-draper at York; made money in business and through a rather dubious bequest. Began to invest in railways in 1833, and by 1844 over 1000 miles of railway were largely under his control. In Aug 45, elected for Sunderland as a Protectionist, defeating Colonel Perronet Thompson despite help from Cobden and Bright; bought a house in Knightsbridge and two estates, Londes-

influence though not as a proprietor.[1] Paxton[2] has command of every railway and railway influence in England and abroad except the Great Western;[3] and he is in it, heart and purse. One other large shareholder is to come in; and that is to be a house which has the power of bringing a whole volley of advertisements to bear upon the paper always. The commercial influence that will come down upon it with the whole weight of its aid and energy; not only in the City of London, but in Liverpool, Manchester, Bristol, and Yorkshire, is quite stunning. I am trying to engage the best people,[4] right and left; and mean to go abroad,

borough from the Duke of Devonshire and Newby Hall from Earl De Grey. 1845 his greatest year, but "murmurings about his methods" were beginning and his latest chairmanship, of the Eastern Counties railway, led to difficulties (A. J. Peacock and David Joy, *George Hudson of York*, 1971).

[1] Hudson's "influence" was naturally kept secret, but had leaked out by 10 Jan 46, when *Herapath's Railway and Commercial Journal* reported that Paxton and Hudson had joined a new daily paper and that Hudson was "to use his influence to send it advertisements and . . . railway information"; *Mephystopheles*, a weekly paper started in opposition to *Punch*, said on 17 Jan that he had taken "command of a forthcoming daily newspaper" and that "the penny-a-liners" were "in ecstacies". On 20 Jan Hudson contradicted the rumour that he had become a proprietor of a newspaper, and the *Daily News* (21 Jan 46) observed that he was "too nice a tactician" to do so.

[2] (Sir) Joseph Paxton (1801–65; *DNB*), gardener and architect; designed the Great Exhibition of 1851 and was knighted at its opening. He rose to eminence, as CD said in that year, "by the power of his own genius and good sense" (*Speeches*, ed. K. J. Fielding, p. 134). Of humble birth and little formal education, he started as a garden-boy, then became under-gardener for the Horticultural Society at Chiswick, where his unusual knowledge attracted the attention of William George Cavendish, 6th Duke of Devonshire. Appointed superintendent of the gardens at Chatsworth in 1826, he soon became the Duke's trusted confidant and friend. In 1827 Paxton married Sarah Bown, the housekeeper's niece and daughter of a Derbyshire mill-owner; she was an active and keen-witted sharer in her husband's many interests, which by the 1840s extended widely.

While continuing his work on the Duke's estates and organizing the reception of royal visitors to Chatsworth, he was also editing the *Magazine of Botany*, designing Upton Park, Slough, and Birkenhead Park, and promoting many railway schemes. Through Bradbury (an old friend: see *To* Mitton, 25 July 45, *fn*) he met the staff of *Punch* and joined their "Table"; but he and CD probably did not meet until Oct, and their social and friendly relationship seems hardly to have developed until 1850 (see later vols).

[3] This is hardly exaggerated. In 1845 Paxton had £35,000 invested in railways; and in Sep he visited, for railway meetings and related business, London, Derby, Gloucester, Bristol, Birmingham and York —all within five days (MS Devonshire Collections; Violet Markham, *Paxton and the Bachelor Duke*, p. 160).

[4] The staff eventually engaged by CD included Eyre Evans Crowe, Albany Fonblanque, Forster, W. J. Fox and Douglas Jerrold as leader-writers; John Hill Powell, Frederick Knight Hunt (editor 1851–4), and Thomas Hodgskin as "sub-editors" (i.e. assistant editors), and W. H. Wills as sub-editor and secretary; Dudley Costello as foreign editor, William Weir (editor from 1854) as colonial editor and leader-writer, William Scott Russell as railway editor, Alfred Mallalieu as City editor and John Towne Danson as financial leader-writer; George Hogarth was music and dramatic critic. John Dickens was in charge of the reporting staff, among whom were Sidney Laman Blanchard, William Hazlitt, George Hodder, Thomas Holcroft and Blanchard Jerrold. (The salaries offered to reporters were noticeably higher than the current rate, and several were induced to leave their posts on other papers, including the *Morning Chronicle*.) Mark Lemon, with Fox, Jerrold and Forster, was among the first to be engaged (in what

myself, to establish that system, when I shall have finished my little book. The venture is quite decided on; and I have made the Plunge.[1]

The book has proceeded slowly, of course. I have not had two unbroken days together at it yet . . .[2]

Always faithfully,
CD.

To PETER BERLYN,[3] 22 OCTOBER 1845

MS Manchester Central Library. Address: Peter Berlyn Esquire | The Athenaeum | Manchester.

1 Devonshire Terrace | York Gate Regents Park
Twenty Second October 1845.

My Dear Sir

I am obliged, most reluctantly, to excuse myself from attending the Meeting tomorrow night. The state of Mrs. Dickens'[4] health at this moment, would render my absence from home a matter of such great anxiety to me, and of such distress to her, that I have no alternative but to abandon my intention of coming to Manchester.

If it were needful for me to assure you of my interest in all that relates to the Athenaeum, or of the great pleasure I had anticipated in meeting its Members and Friends once more, I should have found it very difficult to write to you to this effect. As it is, I trust the reason that I have for being absent, and the statement of my most unfeigned disappointment, are sufficient both for text and comment.

Will you do me the favor to convey to the Directors of the Athenaeum, the assurance of my regret and my esteem?[5] And if I may venture to congratutate them on the President they have this Year, I must acknowledge the influence of

---

capacity is not known). The fullest account is in Thomas Britton's reminiscences contributed to Justin McCarthy and Sir John H. Robinson, *The "Daily News" Jubilee*, 1896; see also H. R. Fox Bourne, *English Newspapers*, 1887, and Sir Joseph Crowe, *Reminiscences of Thirty-five Years of my Life*, 1895.

[1] Macready had been told the news on the previous day, and a few hours after CD's return from Chatsworth; his diary entry for 19 Oct runs: "Forster came in to tea, and informed us that Bradbury & Evans, with Paxton, Duke of Devonshire's agent, and another capitalist, a Birmingham man, had agreed on starting a daily paper on a very large scale, and that Dickens was to be at the head of it. Forster was to have some share in it, and it was instantly to

be got into train for starting. I heard the news with a sort of dismay, not feeling myself, nor seeing in others, the want of such a thing. I fear the means and chances have not been well enough considered. I hope and pray all may go well with and for them". CD, Forster, Fox, Jerrold and Lemon were among those who dined at Macready's on 21 Oct (*Diaries*, II, 307).

[2] According to the *Daily News*, 14 Dec 1915, "there follows some reference to 'Mrs. D' and to the imminent arrival of a new member of the family".

[3] Peter Berlyn: see Vol. III, p. 576 and *n*.
[4] Thus in MS.
[5] The letter was given in full in the *Manchester Guardian*, 25 Oct, and was presumably read out at the Soirée.

some selfish feeling, as I cannot do so without congratulating myself on possessing in him one of my dearest and most valued friends.

I am Dear Sir | Faithfully Yours

Peter Berlyn Esquire CHARLES DICKENS

To T. N. TALFOURD, 22 OCTOBER 1845

Text from N, i, 709.

Devonshire Terrace | Wednesday Twenty-Second October 1845

My Dear Talfourd,

My other half remains in such a doubtful state, that I cannot win any cheerful consent from her to my being absent from home. Apart from my own anxieties, it would be cruel, therefore, to attempt the Manchester flight. And I have been most reluctantly obliged to write by this post to the Athenæum people, excusing myself. Like Tony Lumpkin I shouldn't so much have minded disappointing them, but I can't abide to disappoint myself;[1] and had set my hopes on being by your side.[2]

So much for myself. A little more for business.

Stone, the painter (whom you know) will be present, as one of the Invited guests.[3] He is a Manchester Man; and this is the first occasion on which he will have met his fellow townsmen, since he left the place an unknown student.[4] I have reason to suppose that he is desperately anxious to be called up—and I found the supposition on the slight incidents of his having implored me to write him a short speech, and on my having done so.[5]

Verbum sap:

I saw Jerrold last night; and told him that if, in alluding to you, he could establish the presence of mind to advert to your old connection with the Press when you were a younger man, I believed it would not be distasteful to you.[6]

---

[1] *She Stoops to Conquer*, Act I: "I can't abear to disappoint myself".

[2] Talfourd's presidential address recalled "the first of this series of brilliant anniversaries" when "my friend Charles Dickens . . . brought to your cause . . . the most earnest sympathy with the healthful enjoyments and steady advancement of his species", and referred to "the splendour of his fame"; he also spoke of Disraeli's address of the previous year. He congratulated the society on its prosperity, fulfilling CD's "fairest prophecies" in 1843; they now had 2500 members and an income of £4000. His address, longer and more formal and rhetorical than CD's, is given in full in the *Manchester Guardian* of 25 Oct 45 and collected in his *Critical and Miscellaneous Writings* (Philadelphia, 1848).

[3] Others included Jerrold and Lover (who also spoke); Lemon and A'Beckett were asked but unable to come. The *Manchester Guardian* referred to this as the "Punch" soirée, 1843 as the "Boz" soirée and 1844 as the "Young England" soirée.

[4] Talfourd in his address referred to the "local ties" of one of the distinguished visitors, and in introducing Stone said: "he went, I believe, almost unknown from this town to London, to seek his fortune there; and there he has obtained a high and honourable name".

[5] For the *Manchester Guardian*'s report of Stone's speech, see Appx B.

[6] No such reference appears in the *Manchester Guardian*'s report of Jerrold's speech, or in the fuller report in the *Examiner* (1 Nov); according to Walter Jerrold (*Douglas Jerrold*, II, 413–14), he lost his nerve at the outset and "rambled into unconnected sentences", but later recovered and delivered an onslaught on the enemies

He said he was no speaker (which is true) but he thought he could do that much easily and plainly. I thought it best to give him this hint: remembering a conversation I had with Forster some weeks ago.

There are two or three very good reporters in Manchester—I think the best one is on The Guardian.[1] Will you have an eye on the local papers, and tell me when you come back (when I will tell you my reason for wishing to know)[2] where your speech is best done, and whether it is anywhere *well done*?

With best remembrances to Mrs. Talfourd and Miss Ely

I am always | My Dear Talfourd affectionately yours

[CHARLES DICKENS]

To MISS LEWIS,[3] 26 OCTOBER 1845

MS Mr Robert H. Taylor.

1 Devonshire Terrace | York Gate Regents Park
Twenty Sixth October 1845.

Dear Miss Lewis.

If I had forgotten you, I must have greatly changed, and so must you. If I could come to Wiltshire, I should be an idle man, and you (I hope) would like me none the better on that account. If you lengthen out that "train of persecution" of which you tell me in your letter, I will bear it like a Christian Gentleman, believe me.

I thank your Papa very heartily for his kind and acceptable remembrance of me—It was very tender—in the eating.

Mrs. Dickens and Miss Hogarth send their best regards. And I am

Always | Faithfully Yours

Miss Lewis CHARLES DICKENS

To GEORGE CATTERMOLE, 26 OCTOBER 1845*

MS Mr Edward S. Moore III.

Devonshire Terrace | Sunday Twenty Sixth October 1845.

My Dear Kittenmoles. Wellbred is married, and gone abroad. Play Wellbred, I adjure you![4] The Comedy comes off twice—both times privately. Once on

of education, enthusiastically received by the audience.

[1] Almost certainly John Harland (1806–68; *DNB*), reporter and antiquary; joined the *Manchester Guardian* 1830 and was a partner from 1839 till his retirement in 1860.

[2] Harland may have been engaged as the Manchester correspondent of the *Daily News*.

[3] Unidentified.

[4] Cattermole did take over Thompson's part; the substitution was mentioned in the *Morning Chronicle* announcement of 3 Nov, and was noted in the *Illustrated London News* review of the St James's performance (22 Nov 45), which added that Thompson had been "united to the fair pianiste, Miss Christiana Weller".

Saturday the 15th. November, when Prince Albert has officially written to say (we got the letter only last night) he will attend, at 7 to the moment. The other time, on the last Saturday in November, for the benefit of Miss Kelly. There is no expence but your Dress, in either case. Take this vacant part, like a Pupil of Johnny Britton,[1] as you are—and come or send to me tomorrow, as I can afford to lose no time! ! !

Ever Yours
CD.

To CLARKSON STANFIELD, 26 OCTOBER 1845

MS Mr Jacob Christensen.

Devonshire Terrace | Sunday Twenty Sixth October 1845.
My Dear Stanny
Here is the Devil to pay. Prince Albert[2] has written to say that he dies to see the Amateur Performance on behalf of the Sanatorium, and can it be done on the fifteenth! Lord and Lady Lansdowne and the 'Tarnal Smash knows who, have taken Boxes. And on the fifteenth (three weeks from yesterday) it must come off.[3] Write and tell me, by Bearer, that you have no unlucky engagement that night—for it can't be done; and I'm a Dutchman if I do it; without you.

Ever Faithfully
Bob

To THOMAS BEARD, [26 OCTOBER 1845]

MS Dickens House. *Date:* PM 27 Oct 45; 26 Oct was Sunday in 1845. *Address:* Thomas Beard Esquire | 42 Portman Place | Edgeware Road.

Devonshire Terrace | Sunday Night
My Dear Muster Beard
Resolve this question.—Those small correspondents at Madras, Ceylon, and Aden—do they make separate parcels of their newspapers, addressed to the agent at Malta; or do they open the parcel on its way from Calcutta, and put them in it? If so, how is the parcel addressed when it leaves Calcutta?—To the Agent at the next place? This seems to me to be a query essential to the right working of things.

Here's a pretty kettle of Fish! Prince Albert is coming to our next performance. And it will be at the St. James's Theatre on the 15th. of next Month.

---

[1] John Britton (1777–1857; *DNB*), antiquary: see Vol. III, p. 450*n*.

[2] President of the Sanatorium Committee: see Vol. III, p. 384 and *n*.

[3] Announcements in the press early in November made it clear that the performance in aid of the Sanatorium was strictly private, with a special committee for issuing invitation cards, including the Duke of Devonshire, Count D'Orsay, Lord and Lady Lansdowne, Lord Morpeth, Mrs Norton, Lord and Lady Nugent, Lord Dudley Coutts Stuart and Southwood Smith; acceptances were to be sent to Southwood Smith before 10 Nov (*Morning Chronicle*, 3 Nov 45). According to the *Annual Register*, "the invitations were eagerly sought, and were distributed to those who added the merit of liberality to those of rank and learning".

Mrs. Dickens in statu quo. I call her Joanna Southcote.[1]

The freshness of my mental faculties on the Day after the Claret, exceeds description. That must be done again, my friend.

Ever Affectionately

CHARLES DICKENS

P.S. Forster is already getting deep dents in his nose, by reason of the workings of the coming Kitely.

To GEORGE CATTERMOLE, [?27 OCTOBER 1845]

Extract in MDGH, I, 143; given as final sentence of To Cattermole, 27 Aug 45. Date: perhaps sent as part of reminder when Cattermole did not immediately reply to letter of 26 Oct.

Let me know what you decide, like a Kittenmolian Trojan. And with love from all here to all there,

Believe me, ever, | Heartily yours

[CHARLES DICKENS]

To MISS FANNY KELLY, 27 OCTOBER 1845

Extract in Sotheby's catalogue, May 1912; MS 1½ pp.; dated Devonshire Terrace, 27 Oct 45.

I am sorry to say that for the Sanatorium representation we shall be obliged to go to the St. James's Theatre. Prince Albert is coming; and they have already exceeded your means of accommodation.

To ANDREW McKEAN,[2] 27 OCTOBER 1845*

MS The Hon. Sir David Croom-Johnson.

1 Devonshire Terrace | York Gate Regents Park

Twenty Seventh October 1845.

Mr. Charles Dickens sends his compliments to Mr. McKean, and begs to say, in reply to his letter, that the Proprietress of the Mangle is certainly *not* the original Mrs. Mantalini, or (lawfully speaking) any Mrs. Mantalini at all.[3]

---

[1] Joanna Southcott (1750–1814; *DNB*): for the same joke in 1841, see Vol. II, p. 204*n*.

[2] Andrew McKean, a Scot whose wife came from Toronto; perhaps the Andrew McKean who was living at 8 Hope Crescent, Leith, in 1844–5.

[3] This is the fourth time CD had been asked the question (see Vol. I, p. 590, Vol. II, pp. 18, 435 and *ns*), but the first time he had used the words "lawfully speaking"; compare the revised reading in the Cheap edn, 1848, Ch. 64, "not the lawful Madame Mantalini".

To FRANK STONE, 27 OCTOBER 1845*

MS Benoliel Collection.

Devonshire Terrace | Twenty Seventh October 1845.

My Dear Stone.

Prince Albert is coming to the Private Performance for the benefit of the Sanatorium, with a long list of Lords and Ladies. At his entreaty we have changed the day to Saturday the 15th. of next Month; and we play at the St. Jame's Theatre.

There will be three Rehearsals, of which I will give you ample notice.

Always Faithfully Yours
CD

I hear from Talfourd that you were *brilliant* at Manchester.

To MESSRS BRADBURY & EVANS, 28 OCTOBER 1845

MS Dickens House.

Devonshire Terrace | Twenty Eighth October 1845.

My Dear B and E. I am sorry to say that I have made appointments for this Evening, both with Mr. Stanfield and Mr. Maclise, with a view to the Christmas Book. And on such hasty notice (I have only received your note this morning), I do not like to put them off.

I think it necessary that I should see you today; for the question of the Reporters is becoming very serious. I will come down to Fleet Street[1] sometime between 12 and 2 (perhaps you will tell my father[2] so); and send round for you if I do not find you there.

Do not print any of the few white Satin Play Bills for the Prince, until I give instructions for them. It occurs to me that *those* ought to have the actors' names.

I really think it very necessary (let me say so while I think of it) that you should privately represent to Mr. Paxton the serious consequences that may come from such a loose, flurried way of proceeding as in the case of that Sir George Larpent[3] the other day. To whom the whole thing has been prematurely broached, at a disadvantage, without a point the size of a Pin's head being gained. It would be injurious to anything, but to a newspaper it is Death.

Faithfully Yours always
CD.

[1] 90 Fleet St was the office of the paper, formerly used for warehousing Bradbury & Evans's stock.

[2] John Dickens was already engaged, but not the full complement of reporters.

[3] Sir George Larpent, 1st Bart (1786– 1855; *DNB*), anti-Corn Law politician, partner in the East India House of Cockerell and Larpent. In seeking further capital, Paxton was bound to give some particulars to those he approached.

To WILLIAM CHALLENOR,[1] 28 OCTOBER 1845*

Transcript by Mr J. Challenor Smith, owner of MS in 1926. *Address:* W. Challenor Esquire | 11 Godliman Street | Doctors Commons.

Devonshire Terrace | Twenty Eighth October 1845

Mr. Charles Dickens presents his compliments to Mr. Challenor and regrets to inform him that the only two occasions on which the Performance to which he refers can be repeated are already arranged. Both repetitions are for Private Benefits.[2] Mr. Dickens is sorry to add that he is so constantly and closely engaged that he really has no leisure to devote to the consideration of Mrs. Seymour's case.[3] He had great pleasure in drawing up the little statement for that lady to which Mr. Challenor refers[4] but he fears it is not in his power to be of any further service to her.

To MRS MILNER GIBSON, 28 OCTOBER 1845*

MS Mr Robert B. Riss.

Devonshire Terrace
Twenty Eighth October 1845.

My Dear Mrs. Milner Gibson.

I did not answer your note by your own Messenger this Morning, because Kate was then in the midst of her troubles; and I knew you would rather hear of her, out of them. I am happy to tell you that she has a boy;[5] and is wonderfully well. Though she suffered very much.

I care for nothing but girls by the bye; but never mind me.

I shall be delighted to come to La Scuôla Italiana on the 10th.[6] provided it

---

[1] William Challenor, managing clerk to the Proctors Nicholl Iltid and Son of this address.

[2] i.e. for the Sanatorium and for Miss Kelly.

[3] The widow of Robert Seymour, illustrator of *Pickwick Papers* (see Vol. I, p. 136*n*), who had previously had a small business as print-seller in Catherine St (*Art-Union Journal*, Sep 1839, I, 141). CD's account-book (MS Messrs Coutts) shows £5 paid to Mrs Seymour on 26 Nov 45. In 1846 her friends were endeavouring to raise £50 to complete the education of her children (*Douglas Jerrold's Weekly Newspaper*, 21 Nov 46).

[4] Not otherwise known, and not mentioned in Mrs Seymour's privately printed *Account of the Origin of the Pickwick Papers*, c. 1854. She there described a scheme for a subscription volume in 1840 in which CD declined to assist; of the present request, she wrote that "a gentleman connected with

Doctors' Commons wrote and called upon Dickens, requesting him to form a committee or get up an amateur performance for our benefit, but he firmly refused". For her attack on him in 1849 (N, II, 163), see next vol.

[5] Alfred D'Orsay Tennyson Dickens.

[6] La Scuola Italiana, 5 Greville St, Holborn, was founded by Mazzini as an evening school providing free elementary education for the poor Italians of London, adults and children, and opened on 10 Nov 41. It was run by a director and three assistants, but Mazzini himself delivered regular Sunday evening lectures, and "was revered almost as an angel and loved as a father" by his poor pupils (W. J. Linton, *European Republicans. Recollections of Mazzini and his Friends*, 1893, pp. 55–6). He publicized the plight of the children, mostly employed as organ-boys and hawkers of images, and gained for the school the support of many English friends, including Lady Byron,

is not one of our Rehearsal Nights.[1] We are going to repeat our Play for the edification of Prince Albert; and it is possible (but not probable, I hope) that my Managerial duties may rule me with an Iron Rod.

On Thursday, I grieve to say, I am far less pleasantly engaged—but irretrievably engaged nevertheless.

May I charge you with my compliments to Mr. Mariotti, and my hopeful answer to the Committee of the school?

Always Believe me | Very Faithfully Yours

Mrs. Milner Gibson. CHARLES DICKENS

To CLARKSON STANFIELD, [28 OCTOBER 1845]

MS University of Kentucky. *Date:* Handwriting shows that the birth this refers to was Alfred's (28 Oct 45).

My Dear Stanny. Yes—at the Gray's Inn Coffee House with Mac and Tony.[2] But come *here*, about 5, or a quarter before. We can have a Cab down.—I believe you are the Gent which is partial to Cabs?

If not a ill-conwenience, bring the Scrip.

Kate confined, Thank God, at half past ten this morning with what is usually called (I don't know why) a chopping[3] Boy. I am partial to girls, and had set my heart on one—but never mind me.

She sends her love to Mrs. Stanfield.

Ever affectionately
CD.

Thomas Campbell, the Carlyles, Mrs Macready, Harriet Martineau, and George and Joseph Toynbee; Mrs Milner Gibson, whom he met in 1844, not only worked for the welfare of the school but helped with his correspondence. An Anniversary Festival was held on 10 Nov each year, at which prizes were presented, followed by speeches, music and a supper; Jane Carlyle heard about the first festival (she made a donation, but did not attend because Carlyle "looked so thundery on the whole business—as if the education of organ boys were something nearly amounting to felony"), with its supper for 250—"*forty-five* gallons of beer, *fifty* pounds of macaroni, and roast beef of unascertained quantity"—and the "improvisation" by Petrucci and Professor Rossetti, who "proceeded to deliver in horrible recitative a dramatised poem written for the occasion" (*Letters to her Family*, ed. L. Huxley, pp. 50–2). The 1845 Festival was made the occasion of a sympathetic article on the school in the *Examiner* of 6 Dec, based on information supplied by Mazzini. It described the school as flourishing and financially secure, having successfully overcome earlier opposition from agents of the Italian government, Italian priests of London chapels, and—most formidable—the Italian masters who exploited their poor countrymen.

[1] There was a rehearsal of some scenes: see *To* Cattermole, 6 Nov. CD is not mentioned in the *Examiner's* account, nor in Mazzini's letters after the Festival, although he was the only Englishman named in Mazzini's invitation to the Pepolis on 31 Oct (Mazzini, *Epistolario*, Milan, 1911, III, 59). According to Forster (F, VI, vi, 530) he and CD went to the school (implying, for the first time) after CD and Mazzini had met through the affair of the begging letter in 1846: see *To* Mazzini, ?Jan 46, *fn*.

[2] One of Maclise's nicknames for Forster.

[3] "big, vigorous, strapping" (*OED*).

To FRANK STONE, [LATE OCTOBER 1845]*

MS Benoliel Collection. *Date:* after 27 Oct, but allowing "ample notice" for 5 Nov (see *To* Stone, 27 Oct 45).

Rehearsal Calls

———

St. James's Theatre—Stage Door
Mr. Stone

———

Wednesday 5th. Novr. ¼ before 7
Wednesday 12th. Novr. Same Hour

———

Attention and punctuality, indispensable, as it is doubtful whether the Theatre can be spared on any other occasion.

To MESSRS BRADBURY & EVANS, [?29 OCTOBER 1845]

MS Dickens House. *Date:* probably about the Sanatorium performance, rather than the one at Miss Kelly's, and if so almost certainly 29 Oct, to allow time for invitations to be issued.

Devonshire Terrace | Wednesday

My Dear B and E. Don't do anything final with the Theatre ticket or Bill, without sending me Proofs first. It is hardly necessary to say so, perhaps; but as I didn't mention it to Formal,[1] I do it.

Ever Yours
CD

To THE COUNTESS OF BLESSINGTON, 30 OCTOBER 1845*

MS University of Texas.

Devonshire Terrace
Thursday Thirtieth October | 1845

My Dear Lady Blessington
    More thanks than I can pay you, or than you would care to receive, for your inestimably useful kindness!
    Will you tell me where the Baboo[2] is to be found? I will leave a card at his Hotel,[3] straightway.

[1] CD had presumably seen Frederick Evans earlier the same day.
[2] Dwarkanath Tagore (1794–1846): see Vol. III, p. 304*n*; "Baboo", a Hindu title of respect—Tagore was a Brahmin of immense wealth. Arrived on his second visit to England 24 June 45, and died there 1 Aug 46. Famous for his munificence in founding hospitals and medical schools, and interested in furthering education.
[3] The St George's Hotel, Albemarle St.

Shall I speak to Dr. Southwood Smith, who is Manager of the Sanatorium Committee arrangements, about a good box for you on the 15th. Otherwise I fear they will all be gone. For how many, do you wish it?

I am very sorry I had gone out for a walk when you called yesterday. It would have delighted me to have installed you into my Sanctum.

Mrs. Dickens, I am glad to say, is going on quite brilliantly. I wish I could say as much for myself, but in the distraction of these great Newspaper arrangements, I find the little book trots slowly—sometimes walks indeed—and sometimes stops altogether.

Dear Lady Blessington | Ever Yours Most Cordially

The Countess of Blessington   CHARLES DICKENS

To DR SOUTHWOOD SMITH, [31 OCTOBER 1845]

Mention in next.

About Lady Blessington's box for the performance in aid of the Sanatorium.

To THE COUNTESS OF BLESSINGTON,
31 OCTOBER 1845

Text from City Book Auction catalogue No. 523; *MS* 1 p.; dated Devonshire Terrace, 31 Oct 45.

My Dear Lady Blessington.

Here is Lord Auckland's[1] letter, which you wished me to return. I saw the Baboo yesterday, and thanked him heartily.[2] I have written to Dr. Southwood Smith, about your box. Enclosed is a note for Count D'Orsay, if you will have the kindness to give it him.

My dear Lady Blessington. | Yours affectionately and obliged

CHARLES DICKENS

To COUNT D'ORSAY, 31 OCTOBER 1845*

MS Comte de Gramont.

Devonshire Terrace | Thirty First October 1845.

My Dear Count D'Orsay.

I saw the Baboo yesterday, and engaged him to dine here[3] on Sunday fortnight, the 16th. November at Half past Six. Will you book yourself as Mine for

---

[1] George Eden, Earl of Auckland (1784–1849; *DNB*), Governor-General of India 1835–41, when he became a friend of Tagore and constantly consulted him on Indian affairs.

[2] He had evidently made a donation to the Sanatorium, and was among those who attended the performance in aid of it on 15 Nov.

[3] Tagore also gave parties, including one at which CD, Thackeray, Jerrold and Lemon were among the guests: "The dinner was originally intended for the contributors to *Punch*, but Count D'Orsay invited himself". The conversation "sparkled with wit", but CD was at first so silent that Jerrold "chaffed him by declaring that his reticence must be attributed to adverse

that day and hour? The B (I am afraid to write Baboo again, for I am always going to put an N after it) wants to hear all about the Paper; and I told him I would ask the Gentleman who is going to India,[1] and two of the Proprietors— my printers.

Were you ever a Godfather? I mean to call my new boy after you, whether you like it or not. But if you will let me do it with your consent, you will gratify me very much, and delight my other half most heartily.

Ever affectionately Yours

The Count D'Orsay   CHARLES DICKENS

To JOHN FORSTER, [31 OCTOBER 1845]

Extracts in F, v, i, 385. *Date:* 31 Oct according to Forster.

The older and more gifted of his ravens having indulged the same illicit taste for putty and paint which had been fatal to his predecessor,[2] died unexpectedly before the kitchen-fire. He kept his eye to the last upon the meat as it roasted, and suddenly turned over on his back with a sepulchral cry of *Cuckoo*!

He was at a dead lock in his Christmas story. Sick, bothered and depressed. Visions of Brighton come upon me; and I have a great mind to go there to finish my second part,[3] or to Hampstead. I have a desperate thought of Jack Straw's. I never was in such bad writing cue as I am this week, in all my life.[4]

To FREDERICK DICKENS, [1 NOVEMBER 1845]

MS John Rylands Library. *Date:* clearly after Cattermole had accepted the part, and before the first regular rehearsal on Wed 5 Nov; therefore Sat 1 Nov. (Wrongly dated April 1848 in N, II, 84.)

Devonshire Terrace | Saturday

My Dear Fred. I want you to dine here tomorrow. At all events you must produce yourself here somehow, by hook or by crook, for George Cattermole plays Wellbred on a short notice, and I have pledged myself to produce you for his benefit[5]—Do not fail me.

Ever affecy.
CD

criticism on some of his works"—probably therefore after the *Times* review of the *Cricket*, 27 Dec, and after Thackeray's return from Paris in Jan 46 (Kissory Chand Mittra, *Memoir of Dwarkanath Tagore*, Calcutta, 1870, pp. 113–14).

[1] See *To* Bradbury & Evans, ?14 Nov 45.

[2] See Vol. II, pp. 230–1.

[3] The *Cricket* is divided into three "Chirps" of roughly equal length.

[4] Forster attributes CD's depression to the preparations for the starting of the *Daily News*: "he was now actively assisting,

and had all but consented to the publication of his name" (v, i, 385). By 2 Nov he had written the Prospectus, which Forster showed to Macready; Macready wrote: "I feel that he is rushing headlong into an enterprise that demands the utmost foresight, skilful and secret preparation and qualities of a conductor which Dickens has not. Forster agreed in many if not all of my objections, but he did not seem to entertain much hope of moving Dickens" (*Diaries*, II, 309).

[5] See *To* Cattermole, 6 Nov and *fn*.

To JOHN FORSTER, [1 NOVEMBER 1845]

Extract in F, v, i, 385–6. *Date:* "the morning after the last" according to Forster.

I have been so very unwell this morning, with giddiness, and headache, and botheration of one sort or other, that I didn't get up till noon: and, shunning Fleet-street, am now going for a country walk, in the course of which you will find me, if you feel disposed to come away in the carriage that goes to you with this. It is to call for a pull of the first part of the *Cricket,* and will bring you, is you like, by way of Hampstead to me, and subsequently to dinner. There if much I should like to discuss, if you can manage it. It's the loss of my walks, I suppose; but I am as giddy as if I were drunk, and can hardly see.

To JOHN FORSTER, [?1 or 2 NOVEMBER 1845]

Extract in F, v, i, 386. *Date:* answering Forster's reply to his last; clearly not 3 Nov, as he called at Forster's that day.

Many thanks for your affectionate letter, which is full of generous truth. These considerations weigh with me, *heavily:* but I think I descry in these times greater stimulants to such an effort; greater chance of some fair recognition of it; greater means of persevering in it, or retiring from it unscratched by any weapon one should care for; than at any other period. And most of all I have, sometimes, that possibility of failing health or fading popularity before me, which beckons me to such a venture when it comes within my reach. At the worst, I have written to little purpose, if I cannot *write myself right* in people's minds, in such a case as this.

To MESSRS BRADBURY & EVANS, 3 NOVEMBER 1845

MS Dickens House. *Address:* Favored by John Forster Esquire. | Messrs. Bradbury and Evans.

Devonshire Terrace
—I mean, at Mr. Forster's.
Monday Third November 1845.

My Dear Bradbury and Evans.

I have given my best consideration to the subject we discussed yesterday; and in this letter, you have my conclusions in reference to the Newspaper.

I will take that Post of Editor which is marked in the little statement[2] as having a Salary of a Thousand Pounds attached to it—for double that Salary.[3]

---

[1] Forster says that he, at the time, gave too little importance to considerations of health, although these "influenced" him, as well as the danger of "the labour and responsibility of a daily paper", and "the party and political involvements incident to it" (F, *ibid*).

[2] Not traced.

[3] CD was paid at the rate he asked; according to James Grant (*The Newspaper Press,* 1871, II, 84), this was double that given to the editor of any other paper except *The Times.*

In which I include the Publication of the Series of the Italian letters, with my name—my frequently writing for the Paper, from day to day—my constantly exercising an active and vigilant superintendence over the whole Machine. When I am not there, or after I have left the office, I shall (as the custom is) have a Sub Editor[1] to whom I can, with perfect confidence, hand over the practical management for the time being. The head and leading principle of the thing, I am willing to become on these terms.

I will not disguise from you—for I am pretty sure you will feel—that I think they are far from high for one in my position. And therefore I make my share in the paper[2] an object of importance. But it is quite impossible that I can say what, in my opinion, that share should be, without your first shewing me, out of what proportion of the whole it is to come.[3]

If you feel disposed to do so, on this short statement of the compensation I aim at, you can give this information to Mr. Forster, and arrange that point, as well as every other, with him. I am fully prepared to abide by any arrangement you agree upon.

Always Faithfully Yours

Messrs. Bradbury and Evans.   CHARLES DICKENS

To THOMAS BEARD, 4 NOVEMBER 1845

MS Comtesse de Suzannet. *Address:* Thomas Beard Esquire | 42 Portman Place | Edgeware Road.

Devonshire Terrace | Tuesday Fourth November | 1845.

My Dear Beard. There was a failure of a Great Broker in the City last night,[4] which so affects two of my principal people[5] that the Paper *cannot be*, on any proper footing. You may conceive that after laying aside all my usual and dear pursuits for this object, I have been a little shaken for half an hour. But never say die is the Inimitable's motto; and I have already pumped up as much courage as will set me going on my old track, please God, in four and twenty hours.

[1] John Hill Powell seems to have been the chief of the sub-editors (see *To* Mitton, 20 Oct 45, *fn*).

[2] CD clearly expected a share in the profits of the paper: others would share in proportion to the capital they had put up, and CD because of giving his name.

[3] This could not be decided until it was known what proportion of the capital Bradbury & Evans were putting up—which was probably not finally settled until the Memorandum of Agreement drawn up on 17 Nov (see *To* Bradbury & Evans, 14 Nov, *fn*). Meanwhile CD is firmly staking his claim.

[4] The news was brought by Forster: see *To* Bradbury & Evans, 6 Nov. The wholly unexpected failure of Mr S. F. Stallard, "an old and highly respectable member of the Stock Exchange", was announced on 3 Nov; some reports said it was for £100,000 (*Morning Chronicle*, 4 Nov; *Herapath's Railway and Commercial Journal*, 5 Nov). Forster gives no particulars of this setback, but refers in vague and general terms to "interruptions to the work of preparation, at one time very grave, which threw such 'changes of vexation' on Dickens's personal relations to the venture as went far to destroy both his faith and his pleasure in it" (F, v, i, 387).

[5] Clearly, Paxton and the "Birmingham man" (see *To* Mitton, 20 Oct and *fn*).

They will have to pay some five or Six Thousands[1] Pounds for engagements made. I shall take nothing, but my leave.

Ever affectionately
CD

To GEORGE JULIAN HARNEY,[2] 4 NOVEMBER 1845

MS Mrs Renee Metivier Black.

1 Devonshire Terrace | York Gate Regents Park | Fourth November 1845

Mr. Charles Dickens presents his compliments to Mr. Harney, and begs to inform that gentleman that he has no intention of connecting himself with any Newspaper. He is not the less indebted to Mr. Harney for his obliging note.

To MISS FANNY KELLY, 4 NOVEMBER 1845

MS Free Library of Philadelphia. *Address:* Miss Kelly | 73 Dean Street | Soho.

Devonshire Terrace | Tuesday Fourth November 1845.

My Dear Miss Kelly.

I would have 500 announcements such as I have written on the other side, printed (if I were you) each on a sheet of Note Paper, and laid upon the seats all over the house, wherever our Bills are laid, on the night of the 15th. Do you come down yourself, and see to their distribution; and I will take care that they are not removed.

To the Private Boxes, I would send the same announcement, enclosed in an envelope with a short note from yourself, to the effect that you ventured to take the liberty of begging attention to it. I would seal each of these, and direct it, personally, to the occupier of the Box, by name. Our box list shall be at your disposal on the previous Monday.

Will this do for you?

Faithfully Yours
CHARLES DICKENS

MISS KELLY

Begs leave to announce that the Gentlemen who perform this evening, have kindly consented, as a mark of their regard for an old Servant of the Public, who has struggled with some difficulties,

TO REPEAT THESE PERFORMANCES
FOR THE LAST TIME
AND FOR HER BENEFIT.
AT HER THEATRE IN DEAN STREET
ON   EVENING THE

---

[1] Thus in MS.

[2] George Julian Harney (1817–97), Chartist and friend of Thomas Cooper; acting editor of the *Northern Star* from 1843, editor 1845–50. This paper had found *The Chimes* "viewed in its political character and bearings decidedly the best work Mr. Dickens has produced".

With the addition of the Farce of GRETNA GREEN[1] in which Miss Kelly will appear in her old Part of Betty Finnikin.[2] The other characters by the amateurs.

Applications for Tickets to be made to Miss Kelly 73 Dean Street Soho.

Saturday 15th. November 1845.

To H. P. SMITH, 4 NOVEMBER 1845

MS Miss Mabel Hodge.

Devonshire Terrace | Fourth November 1845

My Dear Smith

My chickens and their little aunt will be delighted to do honor to the Lord Mayor on the Ninth.[3] So should I be,—but I am hard at it: grinding my teeth.

I came down with Thompson[4] the other day, hoping to see you. You were keeping it up, however, in some holiday region; and your glass-case looked like a large pantry, out of which some Giant had stolen the Meat.

Best regards to Mrs. Smith from all of us. Kate quite hearty, and the Baby, like Goldsmith's Bear, "in a concatenation accordingly".

Always My Dear Smith | Faithfully Yours

H. P. Smith Esquire   CHARLES DICKENS

To MESSRS BRADBURY & EVANS, 6 NOVEMBER 1845.

MS Comtesse de Suzannet.

Devonshire Terrace
Thursday November Sixth 1845.

My Dear Bradbury and Evans.

Mr. Forster will have told you this morning, at what conclusion I arrived last night. Such new consideration as I have been enabled to give the subject since then, strengthens and fortifies me in that view of the case. I leave you to judge how strongly it has impressed itself upon me, when it outweighs your new desire to proceed, and all the painful considerations that arise out of my own position, as well as the disgraceful circumstances in which I have unfortunately placed my father.

So far as I am personally concerned, the heart of the enterprize is broken and dead. If I could do such violence to myself, as to resume it tomorrow, I should have no faith in it. It would always oppress me as a doomed thing; and every new engagement we might make, would fill me with new fear and wretchedness.

So far as the project, as a scheme apart from myself, is involved, I think it has

---

[1] Samuel Beazley's farce, first acted 1822; not published.

[2] One of her best known parts (mentioned for example in the opening lines of Hood's "Ode to Miss Kelly on her opening the Strand Theatre", 1833), and included in her one-woman show at the reopening of her own theatre 22 Feb 41.

[3] For the Lord Mayor's Show; the Eagle Insurance office was in New Bridge St, Blackfriars, on the route of the procession.

[4] CD's servant.

received a blow from which it cannot recover. You do not know how different the little world of newspapers is, from every other—how quickly intelligence of this sort is dispersed through it—and how lingering its effect must necessarily be. The difficulty of getting the gentlemen indispensably necessary to the carrying on of the paper, *now*,[1] I cannot, I declare to you, sufficiently estimate in my own mind. Supposing that patched up, and poorly overcome by the substitution of inferior ability in the most important departments of a Newspaper, for the ability at which we have been aiming; then, the dread of this Venture among the other papers[2] (which was very great) is still gone, past all restoration. The notion that undoubtedly existed among them of there being a powerful combination of energy, experience, and money, on the side of this new Journal is shattered to atoms by your own abandonment of it. And all the prestige, and vague impression of success which surrounded this idea while it was still in the clouds, and which would have served it immensely in its first struggles, serves it no more.

Again. The advertizing power that was to be brought to bear upon it, is no longer available. If Mr. Paxton still promised to move Heaven and Earth, and still felt really disposed to do so (which I doubt) could you, in reason, set the least store by such wild and ill-considered pledges? I have rated them at less than nothing since his introduction of you to that City-House. And I distinctly believe that he has had a foreknowledge of this break-down, for many days; and that it stared him in the face (and looked out of his face too) when we met in Fleet Street the other day.[3]

If you feel so far committed, and liable to such heavy loss,[4] that you *must* go on with this Paper (not being able to contemplate the consequences of its abandonment) I will give you every advice and assistance in my power. But I cannot connect myself with it, as I originally designed. Nor can I conceal from you that I believe in my Soul it would end in your Ruin.

On the other hand, if you can look the utmost present loss, steadily in the face; and can meet it; and pay the utmost of the money; and turn the leaf down on which the amount is written, and look at it no more; I do believe that with your advantages and opportunities, and turning our connexion to the best account, you will be able, easily, to recover the ground you have lost. That you will be much happier than you ever could be with the maimed hands of this wounded Newspaper dragging at you, night and day, I am sure.

---

[1] Underlined twice.

[2] News of the scheme had begun to spread; on 2 Nov Lord Nugent had just heard from Sir John Easthope of "Charles Dickens's intention of setting up a new morning paper". Easthope was evidently afraid of its effect on the *Morning Chronicle*; Nugent reassured him—"But neither Charles Dickens's paper nor any other will hurt the M.C., if the M.C. will but be well behaved, as it *generally* is, and if—but I will talk to you more of this when we meet" (MS Mr R. M. Dawkins).

[3] Probably on 31 Oct or a little earlier; at about that time a meeting with Bradbury & Evans would be necessary to discuss the editorship and the prospectus.

[4] Bradbury & Evans must have already purchased their machinery—including the expensive steam press needed for any paper which had or expected a circulation of over 10,000. By the summer of 1846 they were using an Applegath "four-feeder", capable of printing 6000 impressions an hour.

I told Mr. Forster when he came to me with the overwhelming news of the day before yesterday, that you could not have considered, I was certain, to what extent you were already bound. And when I heard that there were flying calculations of a Thousand Pounds as a round Sum to lose,[1] I swear it stunned me—I was so amazed.

The ever having gone on such a Gigantic forgetfulness of the condition in which these gentlemen are placed (of whom some have resigned the certain Income of a whole life, for the chances of this Paper) renders it the more difficult, I know, to meet the real Truth at once, and encounter the whole force of its shock. But I would do it, if the Money and the mistake were mine. I am so certain I would, that I give you that counsel without the least misgiving or hesitation.[2]

At the same time, I think it right to enclose you a note I received from Mr. Beard[3] last night, in acknowledgement of one I had written him, to let him know the Paper was abandoned.

I have only to entreat you to read or shew this letter of mine, both to Jerrold and to Lemon; as I have a sincere regard for them both, and should be deeply hurt if they misunderstood the part I take, in any degree. And lastly, let me say that my confidence in the Paper and my confidence in you, are as distinct and separate things as Heaven and Earth; and that while the first is gone utterly— the second is not affected by a hair's-breadth or a feather's weight.

Always My Dear Bradbury and Evans | Faithfully Yours
CHARLES DICKENS

To GEORGE CATTERMOLE, 6 NOVEMBER 1845

MS Free Library of Philadelphia.

Devonshire Terrace. | Sixth November 1845.

My Dear Kittenmowls

What a fellow you are! You couldn't have done better. Heaven!—If you had seen the other men, when *they* began!

The impression of everybody who spoke to me on the Stage last night, was, that you were as cool as a Cucumber, and safer than the Bank.—I am quite serious, believe me.

I have written to Costello at Brighton, today. Frederick I will drag to Miss Kelly's by the hair of his head. And we will go at your scenes[4] on Monday, over and over again—as often as you like. You can't tire me.

---

[1] As compensation to the staff already engaged, including Jerrold and Lemon: see *To* Beard, 4 Nov 45.

[2] On 4 Nov CD seems to have proposed to see the reporters himself; for a draft of the points he wished to make, see Appx B. Instead they were seen by Bradbury & Evans, and subsequently by Beard: see *To* Bradbury & Evans, 7 Nov.

[3] Beard evidently assessed the compensation lower than CD.

[4] Seven scenes in Acts III–V; Edward Knowell (Frederick Dickens) also appeared in most of these scenes and Downright (Costello) in some of them. One report of the performance (cutting in Forster Collection, V & A) noted that Cattermole "did not sufficiently know his part in the first scene", but "elsewhere was as perfect as need be".

What an extraordinary constitution you must have! Upon my Soul of honor, I don't understand it, and can hardly believe you serious.

Ever affectionately
CD.

To DUDLEY COSTELLO, 6 NOVEMBER 1845

Extract in Anderson Galleries catalogue No. 893; *MS* 1 p; dated 6 Nov 45. *Address:* Dudley Costello, according to Hodgson's catalogue, 2 Nov 1904.

Cattermole is so hideously nervous, and so very much behind-hand, that we have appointed a rehearsal[1] at Miss Kelly's Theatre.

To MR ELLIS, 6 NOVEMBER 1845*

MS Guildhall Library.

1 Devonshire Terrace | York Gate Regents Park
Sixth November 1845

Dear Mr. Ellis.

Will you have the goodness, when you have corrected and copied the two Property Lists, to send them to me? I wish particularly to have them tomorrow, as I promised the Property Man at the St James's to put him in possession of them immediately, in order that he may get what is wanted.

Faithfully Yours
CHARLES DICKENS.

To THE COUNTESS OF BLESSINGTON, [7 NOVEMBER 1845]*

MS Benoliel Collection. *Date:* clearly same day as next.

Devonshire Terrace | Friday Morning

My Dear Lady Blessington.

A Thousand thanks for your kind note. Fifty thousand Pounds were laid down yesterday; and I assure you Forster and I passed an anxious day in discussing the expediency of renewing the Project.[2] But I resolved last night to turn my back upon it; and as it had had a shock, to know it no more.

So I have whistled it off, and am as merry again as my own Cricket—which, by the bye, has been a good deal slighted in all these distractions. I must work away, therefore, tooth and nail.

My hearty regards to Count D'Orsay, and all kind remembrances to your fair

---

[1] On 10 Nov, additional to the two on 5 and 12 Nov at the St James's.

[2] On receiving his letter of 6 Nov, Brad-

bury & Evans evidently went at once to see CD with the further news of fresh capital: see next.

Nieces. George Cattermole is going to play Wellbred, on the 15th. the original having married and gone abroad.

Ever My Dear Lady Blessington | Most Cordially Yours

CHARLES DICKENS

To MESSRS BRADBURY & EVANS, 7 NOVEMBER 1845

MS Comtesse de Suzannet.

Devonshire Terrace

Friday Morning | November Seventh 1845.

My Dear Bradbury and Evans.

My opinion remains unchanged. It has been strongly and finally confirmed since I saw you yesterday.

When you had gone, Mr. Forster and I discussed the subject again; and then we resolved to send for Mr. Beard, and be guided by his advice. He came here in the Evening; and we saw him together. We merely stated to him how the matter stood; and asked him whether he deemed it advisable to proceed. He considered for a little time, and then replied that he believed it impossible to complete the formation of such an Establishment as we should require, after the shock the project had received—that he believed it to be utterly out of the question that we could get "*one* first-rate hand" to join the Paper: all confidence in it, having been destroyed within the last two days.

He pointed out, very plainly, that when he wrote me the letter you have read, the Reporters had not been communicated with, or the design of abandoning the Paper made known. Since that time he has seen, he thinks, all the gentlemen engaged, whom you have seen. He said that even in the first bitterness of their disappointment, they uttered no word to your disparagement or mine (even spoke of your honorable and candid manner to them in high terms) but intimated in so many words that there were evidently other parties in the background who had had the power of overthrowing a scheme full of promise, at a moment's notice: and that they never could feel themselves secure from a repetition of that proceeding. Some of them have already, with the view of releasing you, written to Easthope proposing to return. Others have made application to the Herald; others to the Times. In the little newspaper World our project is understood to have gone by the Board; and to make head against that impression, he considers hopeless.

Remember how strongly I urged this same consideration to you to day;[1] and how I laboured to shew you that you were hardly Judges of its real force.

Mr. Beard spoke very cheerfully and confidently, of your means of arranging these engagements, as some of the gentlemen fall (as he has no doubt they will) into new situations. He had believed them to be more numerous; and he *knew*, he said, that your exhibition of a liberal and manly spirit in the matter, had already met, and would meet with the most sensitive and quick response. He

---

[1] CD's slip for "yesterday".

stated the probable loss at a very small sum, compared with its apparent extent; and had no doubt of your ability to retire at no enormous sacrifice, and leave the pleasantest impression on the minds of these gentlemen. But everything brought him back to this—that to go on was desperate.

He said all this, in spite of a strong belief that the Paper had, before these circumstances, a great course open to it. Which he coupled with the certain knowledge that it had filled the Times people with dismay, and had been the cause of all sorts of councils and discussions in Printing-House Square.[1]

My Dear Bradbury and Evans, in a truly earnest and affectionate Spirit, I assure you from my heart that I esteem and honor you the more, for what I have known of you since these occurrences. I hope and believe that a long course of mutual confidence and friendship, and mutual usefulness, is open to us. And I am lighter in my mind for you—who have occupied my thoughts in all this matter, quite as much as any personal considerations—when I turn my face upon this blighted scheme, as I do now, for the last time;[2] and look to brighter plans in which we are to work together.

Ever Faithfully Yours

Messrs. Bradbury and Evans.   CHARLES DICKENS

To UNKNOWN CORRESPONDENT, 7 NOVEMBER 1845

Extracts in Quaritch's catalogues Nos 898 and 931; *MS* 2½ pp.; dated 1 Devonshire Terrace, York Gate Regents Park, 7 Nov 45.

The Performance on the Fifteenth is not gratuitous, though Private. Being for the benefit of an Institution called the Sanatorium, the tickets are a Guinea each . . . I shall be glad to receive Longfellow's book and letter,[3] when you find them. In the meantime I hope you are deriving some pleasure and amusement from the Sea change you have suffered.

---

[1] William Howard Russell, writing of this period, said: "The newspaper world of London—and not only that world—was stirred to the depths by the rumours of the extraordinary preparations made by the proprietors of the new journal, the *Daily News*, to crush competition. The secession from the established papers to Bouverie Street was large; every inducement was held out to critics, leader-writers, and reporters; and to retain their best men the *Morning Chronicle*, the *Standard*, the *Morning Herald*, the *Morning Post*, and other journals had to make a distinct advance in the rates of pay" (J. B. Atkins, *The Life of Sir William Howard Russell*, 1911, I, 57–8, drawing from Russell's MS autobiography). Russell's cousin Robert Russell had already left *The Times* to join the *Daily News* and encouraged William Russell to do the same; but he was offered a higher salary by the *Morning Chronicle*.

[2] But before 14 Nov, CD had been persuaded to withdraw his resignation: see *To* Bradbury & Evans, that day.

[3] This suggests that the correspondent may have been John Hillard, of Coates & Co., American Merchants, Cheapside; used as an intermediary with Longfellow in 1842–3: see Vol. III, pp. 360 and *n*, 455. Another possibility is Longfellow's brother-in-law Thomas Gold Appleton (see Vol. III, p. 514*n*), known to have been in England by 1846. The book was probably the new illustrated edn of Longfellow's *Poems*, published by Lea & Blanchard, Nov 45.

To THOMAS BEARD, 8 NOVEMBER 1845

MS Dickens House. *Date:* PM 8 Nov 45. *Address:* Thomas Beard Esquire | 42
Portman Place | Edgeware Road.

Devonshire Terrace | Saturday.

My Dear Beard.

I wish you would look at the enclosed letter,[1] and give me your opinion of it
when we meet tomorrow. This is the case (there are two such) of a man taken
from the Chronicle, on an engagement for Three Years at 8 Guineas pr. week.
I am curious to know what you think they expect in such instances: being able to
get another engagement—£200?

Ever affecy.
CD

P.S. Don't forget to bring the letter with you.

To GEORGE CRUIKSHANK, [8 NOVEMBER 1845]

Envelope only, MS Benoliel Collection. *Address:* George Cruikshank Esq | 23
Amwell Street | Pentonville. PM 8 Nov 45.

To MESSRS BRADBURY & EVANS, 10 NOVEMBER 1845

MS Dickens House.

Devonshire Terrace | Tenth November 1845.

My Dear B and E

It is nearly, if not quite, a fortnight ago, since I arranged with Mr. Leech for
the little design for the cover.[2]

I have sent to Mr. Forster this morning—returning him Mr. Wilson's letter
to you, and telling him what Mr. Beard communicated to me, yesterday. You
had best see him *immediately*—but I think it likely you will have done so, before
you get this note.

Faithfully Always
CD

To MACVEY NAPIER, 10 NOVEMBER 1845

MS British Museum.

Devonshire Terrace | Tenth November 1845.

My Dear Sir

I write to you in great haste. I most bitterly regret the being obliged to disappoint and inconvenience you (as I fear I shall do, greatly), but I find it will be

---

[1] Presumably from "Mr. Wilson": see
To Bradbury & Evans, 10 Nov 45.

[2] The front cover of the *Cricket* has a
picture (unsigned) of the fireside and kettle,
blocked in gold and surrounded by the
titles. The first advertisements had already
appeared (*The Times*, 6 Nov), announcing
publication "in December" and naming
Stanfield, Maclise and Leech as illustrators.

impossible[1] for me to write the Paper on Capital Punishment, properly, for your next Number. The fault is really not mine. I have been involved for the last fortnight in one maze of distractions which nothing could have enabled me to anticipate or prevent. Everything I have had to do, has been interfered with, and cast aside. I have never in my life had so many insuperable obstacles crowded into the way of my pursuits. It is as little my fault, believe me, as though I were ill and wrote to you from my bed. And pray bear as gently as you can with the vexation I occasion you, when I tell you how very heavily it falls upon myself.

Dear Sir | Faithfully Yours

Professor Napier CHARLES DICKENS

To WILLIAM BRADBURY, 12 NOVEMBER 1845

Mention in Sotheby's catalogue, Dec 1920; *MS* ¾ p.; dated Devonshire Terrace, 12 Nov 45.

To THOMAS CHAPMAN, 13 NOVEMBER 1845

MS Brotherton Library, Leeds.

Devonshire Terrace | Thirteenth November 1845.

My Dear Sir

I was going to write to you this morning, to tell you that the gentlemen in general are so incensed at the manner in which they have been treated during the whole of the arrangements for the Play—and were so especially indignant last night[2]—that I have made no mention to them of the proposed dinner: being perfectly certain that they would accept no courtesy whatever, at the hands of the committee.

When I had the pen in my hand, Augustus came to tell me of the proposal to set chairs upon the Stage. I think it right to let you know without delay, that if there is a single person introduced upon the Stage, or into the Orchestra, or behind the Scenes, there is not one of the Company who will act—not one. And in such a case I would, most certainly, as having brought them into these unpleasant circumstances, be the first to leave the Theatre, though the overture were played, and the Queen and the whole Court present.

I know you are in no way responsible for the arrangements. But I am so confident that if you do not interfere promptly, this Play will not be acted, that I feel bound to express the sentiments of the rest to you—not so strongly as they expressed them last night, but with as much plainness as I have been able to get into this hasty letter.

Believe me always, My Dear Sir | Faithfully Yours

Thomas Chapman Esquire CHARLES DICKENS

(over)

I am not at all clear that Mr. Jerrold, who is most important to the Comedy, will play as it is. I could get him to do nothing last night, and could reduce him to no terms whatever.

[1] Underlined twice.
[2] At the rehearsal at the St James's. What offence had been given by the Sanatorium Committee is not known.

To C. E. COTTERELL, 14 NOVEMBER 1845†

MS Berg Collection.

Devonshire Terrace. | Fourteenth November 1845.

My Dear Sir

*a*I hope you are not making a flying visit to England,—or at all events that you will be in London on Sunday Week the 23rd. when pray dine with me, unceremoniously, at Half Past Five o'Clock.*a* My reason for placing a week's interval between your return and my appointment, is, that I have arranged to leave town on Monday Morning to finish a little Book in peace and quietness; and I do not think it likely I shall be here again, until the day on which I hope to see you.[1]

Always Believe me | Dear Sir | Faithfully Yours

C. E. Cotterell Esquire.   CHARLES DICKENS

To MESSRS BRADBURY & EVANS, [?14 NOVEMBER 1845]

MS Dickens House. *Date:* clearly the Friday before *To* Bradbury & Evans, ?17 Nov 45.

Devonshire Terrace | Friday Night

My Dear B and E. I have got hold of Mr. Barrow[2]—the gentleman I spoke of, for India—and propounded the Journey to him; making it a condition of his going, that he shall come on the Paper when he returns, *as a Reporter* for one turn a night.—He had previously declined that, but would be quite invaluable—; and that he shall have the French and Italian Papers and so forth (he is an excellent scholar) to translate. I thought it as well, if we nailed him in one place, to nail him in another. He is to give me his reply, and suggest his terms, by letter, at 90 Fleet Street at 3 tomorrow, where I shall wish to see you. I think he will go;[3] and I know there is not in London a man who could do the business better. He was the great Times man in the Days of the Queen's Trial; and is as well acquainted with Indian affairs, as you are with Railroads.

---

aa Not previously published.

[1] No evidence that CD did leave town and unlikely that he intended to.

[2] John Henry Barrow (1796–1858), CD's maternal uncle: see Vol. I, p. 33*n*; after 1841 principal leader-writer for *Morning Herald* and *Sun*. "By the winter of 1843 he found himself unemployed with a family of eight children wholly dependent on him. A letter to the Prime Minister, Sir Robert Peel, written on 31 January, fell on deaf ears" (W. J. Carlton, "Links with Dickens in the Isle of Man", *Journal of the Manx Museum*, VI [1958]).

[3] Barrow accepted and must have set out almost immediately, since on 8 Dec John Dickens had a letter from him posted at Gibraltar 27 Nov (John Dickens *to* Thomas Lawrence, 9 Dec 45; sold Sotheby's, Feb 1963). He reached Calcutta on 7 Jan 46 and his first despatch on the Sikh War was printed in the *Daily News*, "From Our Own Correspondent", on 23 Feb. He remained in India for nearly a year (see *To* Barrow, 16 Sep 46), and continued to contribute after his return (W. J. Carlton, "Dickens's Literary Mentor", *Dickens Studies*, I [1965], 60–3).

It seems to me that Mr. Paxton's City Man has broken down dead, in the very outset,[1] if the assistance we got this morning be any criterion. Never mind. We must get our letters elsewhere, written and ready by Monday Night,[2] somehow or other.

Faithfully Ever
CD.

To BENJAMIN WEBSTER, 17 NOVEMBER 1845

MS Private.

1 Devonshire Terrace | York Gate Regents Park
Seventeenth November 1845.

Dear Sir

The Gentlemen engaged in the Amateur Performance at the Saint James's Theatre on Saturday Evening last,[3] unanimously requested me to write to you;

[1] Paxton was in London on 14 Nov and probably for the next ten days; an undated letter to his wife said that in spite of the state of the stock market he thought they would "come out all right. Bradbury & Evans are downright mad at the Newspaper office they say it is the *best* thought that ever *occurred* not a doubt of success and they are full of preparation—I have seen Mr Allcard and I think he has already found me a customer for the amount but that is uncertain at the moment . . . if I don't weedle [*thus*] the amount out of him who can" (MS Devonshire Collections).

[2] 17 Nov 45 is the date of the "Memorandum of Agreement" (MS Devonshire Collections) between Joseph Paxton, William Bradbury, Frederick Mullet Evans, and Richard Seaton Wright, who agreed to "concur in establishing a daily newspaper to be called the Daily News and the publication thereof to commence as soon as practicable . . . and forthwith to prepare a Deed of Copartnership" (not traced). Paxton guaranteed £25,000, Bradbury & Evans £22,500, and Wright £2500. Wright was a member of Wright, Smith & Shepherd, solicitors and parliamentary agents, of 15 Golden Square—Bradbury & Evans's solicitors. The Memorandum also stated that they were to be free to nominate others representing "a part of the capital agreed to be brought in by the said Joseph Paxton". One other who had evidently been so nominated by Jan 46 was Paxton's cousin, John Cottingham, and probably also his friend William Jackson, MP. By May 46 Jackson, Sir Joshua Walmsley and William

Allcard were proprietors (Violet Markham, *Paxton and the Bachelor Duke*, p. 168; *The "Daily News" Jubilee*, p. 30). Jackson later told Charles Mackay that he had "thrown away £7000 on the speculation" (C. Mackay, *Through the Long Day*, I, 342); Walmsley, according to John Chapman's diary of 7 Aug 51, was "much drained by the Daily News" (Gordon Haight, *George Eliot and John Chapman*, New Haven, 1940, p. 198). According to M. H. Spielmann (*The History of "Punch"*, 1895, p. 85) Peter Rackham (*d.* 1859) was "well understood to have given financial assistance in respect to the founding of the *Daily News*"; Rackham, a merchant, was a guest at the *Punch* table and a friend of Bradbury & Evans.

[3] The performance was well received, and was most fully reported in the *Illustrated London News* (22 and 29 Nov), with illustrations by Kenny Meadows showing Leech, Jerrold, Forster, CD, and Lemon, the actors they praised most highly. Their verdict was: "The play could not have been so *intelligently* performed by any dramatic company now in London . . . The costume was perfect. The *mise en scène* might have been improved; it was better at Miss Kelly's". Greville took a different view: he thought the play "intolerably heavy" and the audience "as cold as ice"; Henry Reeve was in a box with Lord Melbourne who, between the acts, "exclaimed in a stentorian voice, heard across the pit, 'I knew this play would be dull, but that it would be so damnably dull as this I did not suppose!'" (*Greville Memoirs*, ed. Henry Reeve, 1888, v, 308 and *n*).

and on their behalf, no less than on my own, to thank you, most earnestly, for the great assistance you have rendered them in many ways.

They have an unaffected desire to acknowledge your generous courtesy in the warmest terms; and if my form of doing so be a brief one, it is because I should find it difficult to say to you, in any words, how highly we estimate both the matter and the manner of your help.

I am Dear Sir | Faithfully Yours

Benjamin Webster Esquire   CHARLES DICKENS

To MESSRS BRADBURY & EVANS, [17 NOVEMBER 1845]*

MS The Proprietors of *Punch. Date:* the Monday before Wednesday 19 Nov when Landseer's block was sent to Leech.

Devonshire Terrace | Monday Night

My Dear B and E

I would give Mr. Barrow as little more, in the way of a Prospectus,[1] than the name of the Newspaper, as possible. I have not a pull of the last Prospectus by me. If you leave[2] of it for Indian purposes, the *business part*; the general plain description of the paper, without any of the flourishes; I do not think we can do better. This would reduce it to one half or one third of its present length; and I think that will be quite enough for this object. If you will bring it to me, so altered tomorrow, between half past 4 and half half[3] past 5 I will correct the Proof immediately, and settle any point you may have a suggestion to offer on. I am not at all sure that Mr. Barrow, having the name and his credentials, has not, already, quite enough to go upon.

Now, with reference to the Cricket. There is a Dog in the story; and I have got Mr. Edwin Landseer to draw it on the wood for us. He is not sure whether he will make a Vignette of the Dog alone, or whether he will make it a larger subject.[4] Will you, therefore, *immediately*[5] send him (his address is No. 1 St. Johns Wood Road) two blocks; one for a mere Vignette; the other as large as one of Mr. Stanfield's in the Chimes. He has promised to let me have one or other on Wednesday.

Faithfully Yours always

CHARLES DICKENS

---

[1] Forster says, "Its prospectus is before me in his handwriting" (v, i, 386), but the MS, said by Kitton to be in the Forster Collection, has not been found there. It clearly differed from the printed form (see *To* Paxton, 1 Dec, *fn*); Forster says: "The paper would be kept free, it said, from personal influence or party bias; and would be devoted to the advocacy of all rational and honest means by which wrong might be redressed, just rights maintained, and the happiness and welfare of society promoted".

[2] CD wrote "take out" and substituted "leave".

[3] Thus in MS.

[4] Landseer did a woodcut of Boxer alone in "Chirp the Second" of the *Cricket* (p. 82 of 1st edn). His name was not added to the list of illustrators in the advertisement until 20 Dec.

[5] Underlined twice.

To JOHN LEECH, 18 NOVEMBER 1845

MS Comtesse de Suzannet. *Address:* John Leech Esquire | Brook Green | Hammer-smith.

Devonshire Terrace
Tuesday Evening | Eighteenth November 1845.

My Dear Leech

Edwin Landseer pledges himself to forward Boxer[1] tomorrow. I will send him to you as soon as he comes to hand.

Always Faithfully

John Leech Esquire.
CHARLES DICKENS

To MESSRS BRADBURY & EVANS, 19 NOVEMBER 1845

MS Dickens House. *Address:* Messrs. Bradbury and Evans | Whitefriars.

Nineteenth November 1845

My Dear B & E

I expect a block from Mr. Doyle today.[2] Leech is waiting to see Edwin Landseer's dog, which I hope to send him tonight.

Ever Yours
CD

I wish you would send and see if Mr. Maclise is nearly ready.[3] Send to them all, perpetually, until we have got everything. Looking after them, delays me.
I wish you would see to the furnishing of those two rooms in Fleet Street. The moment I have finished the Book, I shall come down there, every day.[4] They are not very business-looking chambers for appointments in their present condition—and are certainly not over-comfortable.

To GEORGE HOGARTH, 19 NOVEMBER 1845

MS John Rylands Library.

Devonshire Terrace | Nineteenth November 1845.

My Dear Hogarth

I shall be delighted to put you on for Music and a general liability to Theatres, at five Guineas a week. I consider that done.

---

[1] Leech must have been still at work on the first of his two designs for "Chirp the First", in which Boxer figures prominently. He had written to Forster the same day, complaining of the lack of time and harassing conditions of work (MS Forster Collection).

[2] Probably his third illustration, at the beginning of "Chirp the Third".

[3] Maclise had had to return the blocks he was sent as they were too small, and asked Forster to get CD to insist on larger ones, knowing it was vain to write to Bradbury &

Evans (Maclise *to* Forster, n.d., but shortly after 8 Nov 45; MS Forster Collection, V & A).

[4] According to Thomas Britton, a "back room on the second floor" of 90 Fleet Street was already in use as early as Sep, and "Douglas Jerrold's visits were frequent". Britton represents himself as already acting as office boy, and was called in to assist with the final arrangements for the performance at Miss Kelly's (J. McCarthy and J. R. Robinson, *The "Daily News" Jubilee*, p. 6).

But I confess I feel a greater difficulty about the time and manner of your leaving the Chronicle (after your recent return) than *you* seem to entertain. I have a doubt whether it might not be best to leave the matter as it stands, at all events until Easthope and the Chronicle people generally, shall have seen the announcement of the New Paper—which will be out in a day or two.[1] Surely it would be more agreeable, now, if you could bring them by such means to originate the idea of your leaving them.

Faithfully Yours always

George Hogarth Esquire.   CHARLES DICKENS

To DR SOUTHWOOD SMITH, 19 NOVEMBER 1845

MS Mr A. G. Schaw Miller.

Devonshire Terrace | Nineteenth November 1845.

My Dear Mr. Smith

I enclose you a very generous note from Horace Twiss.[2] I have acknowledged its receipt, and referred him to you.

On the other side is a list of all the charges on the Stage. Which I have paid. If you will pay the amount to my account at Coutts's in the Strand, it will be the most convenient course to me.[3] Faithfully Yours always

CHARLES DICKENS

	£ .. S .. D
Drink for all the Men. ⎱ Performance and Rehearsals⎰	2.. 0..0
Hire of Furniture, Carriage ⎱ of Do. and "Property Man"—⎰	2.. 4..0
Dressing Room Women. And Candles	–..10..–
Alteration of Scenery, & Repainting	11..15..0
Carpenters & Master Carpenter——	5..10..0
Male Dresses, and Barber ———	1.. 6..0
Orchestra —————————	14.. 3..0
Stage-Door Keeper —————	–..10..6
	£37..14..6

[1] See *To* Paxton, 1 Dec 45. The re-engagement of staff caused the news of the paper to spread further; on 21 Nov Elizabeth Barrett told Miss Mitford that "Boz the universal is on the threshold of an immense undertaking ... no less a one than the editing of a newspaper, a daily newspaper, to represent ultra politics at the *right end* ... anti-corn law interests and the like. It is said that some twenty-five thousand pounds have been subscribed to the speculation by great capitalists, and that seven first rate reporters have been engaged for three years at the rate of seven guineas a week: also that the newspaper is to combine literature with politics as in the French journals. What do you think of this? Is Dickens fit for it?" (*Elizabeth Barrett to Miss Mitford*, ed. Betty Miller, 1954, p. 261; cf. her letter to Mrs Martin, ?Dec 45; "He has not, I think, *breadth* of mind enough for such work, with all his gifts", *Letters of Elizabeth Barrett Browning*, 1898, I, 275). Miss Mitford passed the news on to Boner on 12 Dec 45: "One new paper, ultra-whig, is coming forth with the name of Mr. Dickens, who is to write the 'Feuilletons', and the combined aid of all

To HORACE TWISS, [?19 NOVEMBER 1845]

Mention in *To* Southwood Smith, 19 Nov 45.

To JOHN LEECH, [19 NOVEMBER 1845]

MS Comtesse de Suzannet. *Date:* clearly the same day as *To* Bradbury & Evans, 19 Nov. *Address:* John Leech Esquire | Brook Green | Hammersmith.

Devonshire Terrace | Wednesday Night

My Dear Leech

Here is Boxer, *on* Box. Everything in a concatination accordingly.

Will you send him on to B and E, tomorrow Morning?

Ever Yours

CD

To CLARKSON STANFIELD, 21 NOVEMBER 1845

MS Mr Jacob Christensen.

Devonshire Terrace | Twenty First November | 1845.

My Dear Stanny. I am heartily indebted and bounden to you for thinking of me under such circumstances. I hadn't the heart to come near you, lest you should think I wanted to bore you for these drawings.[1] Than which, nothing in the World was more distant from my thoughts.

I have no doubt they can be easily copied on the blocks; and I will send them down to Bradbury's directly. I am delighted to hear from George[2] that you are so much better.

Ever affectionately

CD

To H. P. SMITH, 24 NOVEMBER 1845*

MS Library of the Royal College of Surgeons.

Devonshire Terrace | Twenty Fourth November 1845

My Dear Smith.

Your friend[3] is right in his Information. I have made a memorandum of the

---

the 'Punch' people. It is thought a great risk" (Mary Russell Mitford, *Correspondence with Charles Boner and John Ruskin*, 1914, p. 46).

[2] Horace Twiss (1787–1849; *DNB*), politician; author of *Life of Lord Eldon*, 1844; Vice-Chancellor of the Duchy of Lancaster since 1844; well known to Macready.

[3] Smith paid on 20 Nov (CD's Account-book, MS Messrs Coutts).

[4] "14" cancelled here; but the total requires it.

[1] CD must have hoped that Stanfield would do a second illustration, presumably for "Chirp the Third": see *To* Stanfield, 28 Nov 45.

[2] George Stanfield (b. 1828; *DNB*), Stanfield's son; pupil of his father; began exhibiting 1844.

[3] Unidentified.

name and application, and will communicate with the gentleman very shortly. But I fear there is no chance of any Vacancy in the Department he speaks of.

Ever Yours

H. P. Smith Esquire   CHARLES DICKENS

To MRS TALFOURD, 25 NOVEMBER 1845

Mention in Sotheby's catalogue, July 1975; *MS* 1 p.; dated Devonshire Terrace, 25 Nov 45.

Accepting an invitation to dine with her on Saturday.

To AMEDÉE PICHOT, 27 NOVEMBER 1845*

MS Mr George Potts. *Address:* A Monsieur. | Monsr. Amedée Pichot | Revue Britannique | 1 Rue Grange Bateliere | Paris.

London. 1 Devonshire Terrace | York Gate Regents Park
Thursday Twenty Seventh November 1845.

My Dear Sir

I write (in great haste to save the Post) to acknowledge the receipt of your letter of the Nineteenth; and to say that I should be happy to supply you with some sheets of the Cricket, in advance of the Publication, if it were compatible with our business arrangements. But as it is not, I cannot have that pleasure.

There is no reference in the Chimes to the Mug of a Bell.[1] Nothing of the kind. You must have made some mistake.

My Dear Sir | Faithfully Yours

Monsr. Amedée Pichot   CHARLES DICKENS

To WILLIAM EMPSON,[2] 28 NOVEMBER 1845

MS Dickens House.

Devonshire Terrace | Twenty Eighth November 1845.

My Dear Empson—That seems to me to be the shortest cut through your difficulty.

A thousand thanks for your warm-hearted letter, which came upon me in the pleasantest way, as I was rounding off the few last chirpings of The Cricket on the Hearth. It made me feel the Cricket a hundred times more real than ever.

We play *once more*—for the benefit of Miss Kelly; and the tickets will be a Guinea each. We have not yet decided when it shall be, what it shall be, or where it shall be. But as soon as these precious morsels of intelligence become known to me (probably next week) I will write to you again.

---

[1] CD has forgotten the reference to their "silver mugs" in the fourth paragraph of *The Chimes*: see *To* Pichot, 16 Feb 46.

[2] William Empson (1791–1852; *DNB*);

Professor at East India College, Haileybury; married Charlotte, Jeffrey's daughter, 1838; succeeded Napier as editor of *Edinburgh Review* 1847.

I had a most affectionate and delightful letter from Lord Jeffrey not long ago.[1] There are very few things that are so charming to me as the way in which he has lived through all that Blue and Yellow, and remained so tender, true, and earnest. He is the freshest of friends and readers. And God send he may continue so, for as many years as you and I desire!

Kate is quite well, and begs to be kindly remembered to Mrs. Empson and yourself and all the children. Dolly lives in my memory brightly; but she must be quite another Dolly by this time.[2]

Always Faithfully Yours

W. Empson Esquire   CHARLES DICKENS

To VISCOUNT MORPETH,[3] 28 NOVEMBER 1845†

MS Mr George Howard.

Devonshire Terrace | Twenty Eighth November 1845.

My Dear Lord Morpeth.

[a]I am greatly indebted to you for your kind recollection of the Alchemist.[a4] I have delayed writing to you until now: hoping I might have been able to tell you of our dramatic plans, and of the day on which we purpose playing. But as these matters are still in abeyance, I will give you that precious information when I come into the receipt of it myself.

And let me heartily assure you that I had at least as much pleasure in seeing you the other day,[5] as you can possibly have had in seeing me; and that I shall consider all opportunities of becoming better known to you, among the most fortunate and desirable occasions of my life.

And that I am, with your conviction about the probability of our liking each other; and as Lord Lyndhurst[6] might say, "with something more,"

Ever faithfully yours

The | Viscount Morpeth.   CHARLES DICKENS

---

[1] The letter has not survived. CD had probably asked Jeffrey's permission to dedicate the *Cricket* to him. The dedication reads: "To | Lord Jeffrey | this little story is inscribed, | with | the affection and attachment of his friend, | the Author".

[2] The Empsons had four children, who were constantly with their grandparents at Craigcrook; the eldest, Charlotte, also called "Charley", "Tarley", and "Dolly", was born in 1839 and died in 1850 a few months after Jeffrey (Lord Cockburn, *Life of Lord Jeffrey*, II, *passim*).

[3] George Howard, later 7th Earl of Carlisle (1802–64; *DNB*): see Vol. I, p. 447*n*.

[aa] Not previously published.

[4] At the close of the St James's perfor-

mance on 15 Nov Forster announced that they would perform *The Alchemist* at Christmas for Miss Kelly's benefit (unidentified cutting in the Forster Collection). Fletcher's *The Elder Brother* was in fact chosen (see *To* Miss Kelly, 7 Dec 45). CD returned to *The Alchemist* two years later (*To* Cruikshank, 28 Nov 47, N, II, 61) but gave it up in Feb 48 after two or three rehearsals. His own part was Sir Epicure Mammon (F, VI, i, 469).

[5] Morpeth was on the special committee for issuing invitations for the performance on 15 Nov, and presumably attended.

[6] John Singleton Copley, Baron Lyndhurst (1772–1863; *DNB*): see Vol. III, p. 297 and *n*.

To CLARKSON STANFIELD, 28 NOVEMBER 1845

MS Mr Jacob Christensen.

Devonshire Terrace | Twenty Eighth November 1845.

My Dear Stanny

As George told me he would let me know when you became visible, I have not called at your house: fearing to worry you.

I will answer Albert Smith.[1]

And I will also insert a full-sized Blue Bottle in the ear of the Printer for not having sent you the Third Chirp. Which shall come to you today, my Boy.[2]

Ever affectionately & heartily

CD.

To JOHN LEECH, [?29 NOVEMBER 1845]

MS Comtesse de Suzannet. *Date:* Reference to "the last block" makes 29 Nov more likely than 22 Nov. *Address:* John Leech Esquire.

Devonshire Terrace | Saturday Night

My Dear Leech. If I could urge anything against the last block, it would be, that my good friend the Carrier, is *hardly* handsome enough.[3] I have not seen the others, but have no doubt Jones[4] acted wisely, to save time.

Cordially Yours

CD

To MISS BURDETT COUTTS, 1 DECEMBER 1845

MS Morgan Library.

Devonshire Terrace. | First December 1845.

My Dear Miss Coutts.

I have delayed answering your last kind note until now, because I wished, previously, to have a long talk with Charley's Mama on the subject to which it refers; and I could not very well do that, until she was quite well and downstairs again.

We have no reason to think that Charley has anything but a vigorous constitution, and good sound health. But when he is in full school employment, there is a strange kind of *fading* comes over him sometimes: the like of which, I don't think I ever saw. Whether the child is anxious at his book, or excited at his Play, or what, I cannot make out. But I see it occasionally, in a very remarkable degree—more plainly, I think, than his mother does, although I am by no means

[1] Probably about the dramatization of the *Cricket*: see *To* Thomas Fraser, 19 Dec 45 and *fn.*

[2] It contains no illustration by Stanfield.

[3] The carrier is grotesque rather than handsome in "The Dance".

[4] The printer at Bradbury & Evans's.

open to such impressions in general, and am not at all fearful for him, except as I know him to be very quick and sensitive.

But I fear if it were to continue, and he were at school at a distance from home, I should have real cause for anxiety; and as you leave the choice to me, I would, solely on this account, prefer King's College,[1] if you think well of it too. I have taken a long time to think of this, because I feel that such a kindness as yours *should* be thought of and deliberated upon. And I have come to the conclusion that this is the best course for him.

Bertha White is quite restored. She is depressed of course, but perfectly rational, composed, and resigned. I am trying to keep back a part of your gift for her own sole use in after-life. Whether the necessities of her father will admit of this, I cannot, as yet, say. But I hope they may. She is living with him just now in Wales, and is endeavouring to obtain a situation as companion to a Lady.

I have just finished my little Christmas Book, which I hope will please you. It is very quiet and domestic. I trust it is interesting and pretty. At all events I think so. If you have any fancy for reading a book before it is published, I shall be more than delighted to send you the Proofs by post, if you will let me know in one line that you are still at the place whither I address this letter.

Mrs. Overs succeeded the other day in getting one of her children into the Orphan School.[2] It is a great thing for her.

I cannot help wondering when I shall see you again: remembering how long it is since I had that pleasure. I shall be at Liverpool for a day or two towards the end of next week; and at Paris for a week or two, immediately after Christmas Day. If there be anything I can do for you in either place (especially the last) I need not tell you how glad I shall be, to do it.

Charley sends his love, and his sisters beg to add their small remembrances. Mrs. Dickens again adds messages which I do *not* send: and I have a very touching letter from Miss White, in which she expresses her gratitude to an unknown person, with as much sincerity and earnestness as ever I saw expressed in words, in my life.

Kindly keep me in "Miss Meredith's" recollection. And ever believe me Dear Miss Coutts,

Your most obliged and faithful friend

Miss Coutts.

CHARLES DICKENS

To MR FRY,[3] 1 DECEMBER 1845

Mention in Sotheby's catalogue, Dec 1912; *MS* (3rd person) 1 p.; dated 1 Dec 45.

Concerning a vacancy on the staff of the Daily News.

---

[1] See *To* Miss Coutts, 7 Jan 46 and *fn*.

[2] John Richard Overs, *b*. 27 Nov 35, was elected Nov 45 (information from Secretary of the Royal Alexandra & Albert School).

[3] Unidentified.

To JOSEPH PAXTON, 1 DECEMBER 1845†

MS Office of the *Daily News* Ltd.

90 Fleet Street | Monday First December | 1845.

My Dear Sir.

I intend going to Liverpool myself,[1] in a week or so, to blow vague Trumpets for the Daily News. *As it will be a part of my mission to appoint the Agent,[2] I will send for the gentleman you recommend, immediately on my arrival there. We have several previous offers; but this appears to be full of promise.*

I am regularly in harness now;[3] and we are getting on, vigorously and steadily. Mr. Powell[4] comes to me today, when I hope to nail him tight. And for the second Sub-Editor I have received a proposal which is likely to drive Easthope (when he knows it) raving mad.[5]

Our man in Paris[6]—*most important to our success*—has distinguished himself already: being as familiar with the most secret moves upon the road, on the part of the other papers, as if he had done nothing else but receive their unlimited confidence, from his Cradle.

You will see that the advertisement is out today.[7]

Always Faithfully Yours

Joseph Paxton Esquire   CHARLES DICKENS

[1] Paxton had doubtless written to CD about his own visit to Liverpool on 24–25 Nov in search of further financial support. CD was there on 13 Dec, as reported in the *Liverpool Mercury*, 19 Dec, "making arrangements for his new paper the *Daily News*", and remained until 17 Dec (*To* Stone, ?17 Dec 45). A letter from John Dickens to Thomas Lawrence, 9 Dec 45 (sold Sotheby's, Feb 1963), refers to CD's "few days tour in the Manufacturing Districts", during which time John Dickens was evidently left in charge at the *Daily News* office.

aa; bb; cc Not previously published.

[2] The agent appointed was Michael James Whitty, proprietor of the *Liverpool Journal*, a liberal and free-trade paper: see *To* Felton, 1 Jan 46.

[3] This is the first known letter dated from the *Daily News* office.

[4] John Hill Powell: see Vol. I, p. 59*n*.

[5] Thomas Hodgskin, formerly on the *Morning Chronicle*: see next, *fn*.

[6] Joseph Crowe, son of Eyre Crowe, one of the leader-writers, was sent to assist the Paris correspondent early in 1846 (Joseph Crowe, *Reminiscences of Thirty-five Years of my Life*, p. 55), and speaks of him as a Frenchman. This may have been Fillon-

neau, who was the agent in Paris: see *To* de la Rue, 16 Feb 46 and *fn*.

[7] The following advertisement appeared in the *Morning Herald* and *Morning Chronicle* of 1 Dec and elsewhere (but not in *The Times*—said to have refused it): "NEW MORNING PAPER, to be commenced early in the New Year.—The DAILY NEWS. A Morning Newspaper, of Liberal Politics and thorough Independence. | The leading features of the Paper may be briefly stated under the following heads:—| Its City News and Commercial Intelligence, collected from the highest sources, will be scrupulously impartial, and always early. | In Scientific and Business Information on every topic connected with Railways, whether in actual operation, in progress, or projected, will be found to be complete. | An extensive system of Foreign Correspondence in all parts of the world has been for some time, and is now, in course of organization. | Its Parliamentary Reports, its Law Reports, and every other item of such matter, will be furnished by gentlemen of the highest qualifications. | Among the writers of its Leading Articles, its Criticisms on Books, the Drama, Music, and the Fine Arts, are some of the most distinguished names of this time. | The Literary Depart-

To THOMAS HODGSKIN,[1] 2 DECEMBER 1845*

MS Fales Collection, New York University Library.

90 Fleet Street. | Second December 1845.

My Dear Sir

I have great pleasure in concluding your engagement with the Daily News, on the terms you mentioned to me this morning. My father will be happy to receive your signature to the agreement, as soon as you can conveniently call here: and to give you a counterpart, signed on behalf of the Proprietors.

Faithfully Yours

Thomas Hodgskin Esquire   CHARLES DICKENS

To MISS FANNY KELLY, 3 DECEMBER 1845*

MS Benoliel Collection.

Devonshire Terrace | Third December 1845.

Dear Miss Kelly.

Yesterday was the first opportunity the Principals in our little Corps have had, of meeting together.

We find from the nature of our various engagements, that it would be most unsafe and inexpedient to postpone the Play for your benefit until January. We could not do so, with any reasonable prospect of fulfilling our promise. And therefore we have decided to act on *Saturday the 27th. of this Month.* You may proceed accordingly, in the full confidence of that being the Night.

In case you wish us to act at any Theatre but your own, it must not be larger than the Saint James's.

We will communicate with you again, in a very few days, and tell you what Play and afterpiece we shall then have decided on, and what we shall ask you to act. But the Night is subject to no change or discussion.

Always Faithfully Yours

Miss Kelly.   CHARLES DICKENS

ment of the Daily News will be under the direction of Mr. Charles Dickens. | The Counting-house, and Office for Advertisements intended for insertion in the Daily News, will be at No. 90, Fleet-street, London; to which place any communications for the Editor should be addressed, until the publishing offices in Whitefriars shall be completed." In advertisements at the end of the month "at the opening of Parliament" was substituted for "early in the New Year".

[1] Thomas Hodgskin (1787–1869), economist and journalist: see Vol. I, p. 53*n*. At one time on the *Illustrated London News*; had recently joined the *Economist*, founded 1843 by James Wilson, with the co-operation of Lord Radnor, to spread the principles of Free Trade. Hodgskin had ceased to be a Chartist and joined the party of Cobden and free trade (Elie Halévy, *Thomas Hodgskin*, Paris, 1903, pp. 192–3).

To J. H. STOCQUELER,[1] [?1–4 DECEMBER 1845]

MS[2] The *Daily News* Ltd. *Date:* after the appearance of the advertisement on
1 Dec, and before the leader in the *English Gentleman* on 6 Dec (see *fn*).

OFFICE OF THE DAILY NEWS
90, *Fleet Street,* and *Whitefriars.*

Dear Sir,

I really do not know that I can possess you with an idea of the designs & intentions of the paper, which will be more explicit than that which you may have
already derived from the announcement in the Daily Journals. Its politics will
be decidedly liberal and all measures tending to the improvement and happiness
of the people, their education and advancement and civil & religious liberty will
have its decided sympathy & support. It is intended to be an accurate and reliable
business paper and its reports of all kinds of proceedings will be as full and good
as possible. I have every reason to believe (knowing what pens will be at work)
that it will be extremely well written: and, besides being what a first-rate daily
newspaper now is, will be something that it is not. Great attention will be paid
to foreign matters and we are particularly anxious to shine in reference to India.

So much for the "Daily News" which I hope will speak more emphatically
for itself.

Personally I can hardly tell you how much I am indebted to you for your
obliging letter and also for those previous passages[3] to which you refer, which I
assure you did not escape my recognition at the time.

Dear Sir | Faithfully Yours

J. H. Stocqueler Esquire   CHARLES DICKENS

---

[1] Joachim Hayward Stocqueler (1800–
85; *DNB*), journalist and miscellaneous
writer. According to his autobiography,
The Memoirs of a Journalist, 1873 (copy in
India Office Library), he was enlisted at
Chatham as a gunner in the Bombay
artillery and was in India for over 20 years,
discharged from the army 1823 and then
working as a journalist. After returning to
England about 1843 he acted at the Lyceum
under the name of Melford, wrote several
plays (including *Polkamania* and *An Object
of Interest,* 1845) and a pantomime, 1846,
for the same theatre, published various
books, chiefly on India, and edited the
English Gentleman (formerly the *Age*) May
45–Feb 46. Bradbury & Evans's Accounts
(MS V & A) show a payment of £10.10 "by
Cash recd from Stocqueler for proof sheets"
of the *Cricket*—presumably for an Indian
edn. There is nothing in the present letter
to confirm Stocqueler's claim of early
acquaintance with CD as a boy at Chatham,
described by him under the pseudonym
J. H. Siddons in *Wood's Illustrated Household Magazine* (New York, July–Dec 1875;

reproduced in an article by J. A. Carter,
Jr, in *D*, LXII [1966], 147–51). This quotes
a letter from CD to Stocqueler in India
(*c*. ?1838), which may be genuine. But
many other details are inaccurate and the
story of CD's having found the "originals"
of the *Cricket* in Cheshire, where he says
George Hogarth lived, impossible.

[2] Except for salutation, ending and
signature, the letter is in the hand of W. H.
Wills; the address is printed.

[3] The "passages" referred to no doubt
included his leader of 8 Nov, "Prince
Albert and CD", on the performance of
Every Man in his Humour in aid of the Sanatorium, and the notice on 22 Nov. The
issue of 6 Dec contained a leading article,
"Mr. Charles Dickens and 'The Daily
News' ", rejoicing that "a writer at once so
eminent and so personally worthy, should
be induced to connect himself with a public
journal, and *to glory in the connection.* The
whole Press owes much to Mr. Dickens—
in addition to its long-standing debt on
other grounds,—for his practical recognition
of its respectability and importance".

To R. H. HORNE, [?EARLY DECEMBER 1845]

MS Colonel Richard Gimbel. *Date:* clearly in the period when CD was completing his establishment.

OFFICE OF THE DAILY NEWS
90, Fleet Street, and *Whitefriars*[1]

My Dear Horne

What do you think of Eight Guineas pr. week and travelling expences—as a point to start from?[2] Let me see you here one day, between 12 and 2, and I will then answer your other question.

Faithfully Yours always

R. H. Horne Esquire CHARLES DICKENS

To JOHN ALLCARD,[3] 5 DECEMBER 1845*

MS Free Library of Philadelphia.

90 Fleet Street. | Fifth December 1845.

My Dear Sir.

Thinking that while we are in search of the Money Man,[4] it might be worth while to take the enclosed note into consideration (though I have no reason to attach any weight to it) I venture to enclose it to you, and to ask whether you happen to know anything about the Writer.

Faithfully Yours

John Allcard Esquire CHARLES DICKENS

---

[1] The address is printed.

[2] Horne was engaged as "Irish Commissioner" (Irish correspondent). He later recalled that he was offered the choice of working in India or Ireland. His departure was delayed by illness, but by the end of Jan he was in offices in Lower Sackville St, Dublin, organizing his staff of reporters —some from the *Freeman's Journal*—and in Feb–Apr was investigating conditions in the west, suffering much hardship and subject to suspicion of being a Government agent; in the summer he witnessed the horrors of the famine, which he believed could have been averted. Besides his regular reports in the *Daily News*, he wrote of his experiences in *Howitt's Journal*, I, 1847, and *Fraser's*, XXXVIII, 1848 (Ann Blainey, *The Farthing Poet*, 1968, pp. 158–64—partly from MS letters to W. J. Fox).

[3] John Allcard, bill broker of 65 Lombard St—this was the address of the famous bill brokers, Overend, Gurney & Co., and All- card may have been a member of the firm. A native of Derbyshire and an old friend of Paxton, whose daughter married one of the family.

[4] Presumably one of the financial editors. According to Thomas Britton (*The "Daily News" Jubilee*, p. 9), "Mr. Mitchell (of the *Public Ledger)*" was commercial editor and "Alfred Mallileau" (i.e. Mallalieu) City editor; Mallalieu was editor of the *Courier* in 1841 and had been on the staff of the *Guardian* and the *Public Ledger*, connected with journalism for 15 years, as "proprietor of daily and weekly papers, and an editor when not a proprietor", according to his letter in the *Daily News*, 21 Feb 46. Paxton would be equally concerned in such appointments: he was in London 4–6 Dec and on 5 Dec spent all day at Whitefriars, when he and Bradbury "settled with Russell abt the Railway Department after a good deal of trouble" (MS Devonshire Collections).

To BENJAMIN HAWES,[1] 6 DECEMBER 1845*

MS Mr Colin Richardson; Benjamin Hawes Collection.

1 Devonshire Terrace | York Gate Regents Park
Sixth December 1845.

My Dear Sir

Our friend Fonblanque has made a suggestion to me in reference to the New Morning Paper with which I am (as you are perhaps aware) intimately connected; on which I should greatly like to have a few minutes conversation with you, if you will kindly inform me what time is most convenient to you for the purpose.

It relates to the engagement of a gentleman, for commercial treatises and so forth, whom Fonblanque says you know well, and who would be of great service to such a design.[2]

Dear Sir | Faithfully Yours

Benjamin Hawes Esquire. MP.   CHARLES DICKENS

To MISS FANNY KELLY, 7 DECEMBER 1845†

MS Berg Collection.

1 Devonshire Terrace | York Gate Regents Park
Seventh December 1845.

Dear Miss Kelly

*a*We have decided on acting an altered version of The Elder Brother, a very remarkable play by Beaumont and Fletcher*a*[3]—and Comfortable Lodgings;[4] in which latter piece, we hope you will do Madame Pelagie yourself, and give Antoinette to whomsoever you please.[5]

---

[1] Benjamin Hawes (1797–1862; *DNB*), radical politician. MP for Lambeth; appointed Under-Secretary of State for the Colonies July 46 when the Whigs came to power. He wrote for the *Examiner*, and was an active campaigner for the repeal of the Corn Laws.

[2] Clearly John Towne Danson (1817–98), journalist, private secretary to Hawes from 1844, and reading for the Bar. In his reminiscences (MS Lieut.-Col. J. R. Danson; given in full by K. J. Fielding, "CD as J. T. Danson knew him", D, LXVIII [1972], 151–61) he says he was "known to some of the leaders of the Whig party", by one of whom (evidently Fonblanque) he was "mentioned to Mr. Dickens", who then offered him "an engagement to write leaders . . . on financial and commercial subjects". He stayed on for a time under Forster's editorship, but left probably in May 46 (when the management changed: see *To Mitton*, 20 Apr 46, *fn*), after a dispute about rates of pay. His later career in business and as a political

economist was distinguished: after his death some of his articles were collected as *Economic and Statistical Studies, 1840–1890*, 1908, with a memoir by his daughter, Mrs Mary Norman Hill.

aa; bb Given in N, I, 724 from catalogue source; letter otherwise unpublished.

[3] Now regarded as the work of Fletcher and Massinger. It had not been played since the early 18th century, and then only in Colley Cibber's adaptation *Love Makes a Man*, 1700. The present adaptation was made by Forster: see *To Beard*, 1 Jan 46. No doubt it was his suggestion; the "remarkable" feature of the play is the rivalry between the brothers, Charles and Eustace, played by Forster and CD.

[4] The farce by Richard Brinsley Peake, first acted at Drury Lane, 1827.

[5] Mme Pelagie, the comic lodging-house keeper, the chief female part, was in fact played by Miss Bew; Miss May played the girl's part of Antoinette. CD played Hippington Miff; Lemon, Rigmarole his valet.

*b*We shall have the Parts in the Elder Brother, on *Wednesday*, and we purpose coming to your Theatre,*b* if you will have the float lighted, to compare them,[1] *at 6 precisely*. There will be a little part for Miss Hinton.[2] Will you have the goodness to ask her to be there: and also the young Lady who will play in the farce?

As the time is so short, we must be very punctual and particular in the Rehearsals.

Faithfully Yours
CHARLES DICKENS

To W[ILLIAM] CARPENTER[3] and CHARLES [R.] CARTER,[4] [8 DECEMBER 1845]*

Envelope only, MS Private. *Date:* PM 8 Dec 45. *Address:* W. Carpenter Esquire | Charles M. Carter Esquire | London Mechanics' Institution.[5]

To BENJAMIN HAWES, 8 DECEMBER 1845

Extract in Goodspeeds Book Shop catalogue No. 174; *MS* 1½ pp.; dated Devonshire Terrace, 8 Dec 45. *Address:* Catalogue has "Howes" in error.

I am sorry that I had appointments[6] at both the times you suggested to me in your kind note of Saturday. I will take the chance of catching you for a moment before you leave home tomorrow morning. But pray do not depart in the least from your usual order of proceedings on my account.

I am My Dear Sir | Faithfully yours,
CHARLES DICKENS

Benjamin Hawes Esq., Junior

Stone, Leech, Cruikshank, Forster, Wills and Augustus Dickens were also in the cast.

[1] i.e. to check copies of the separate parts, which would have to be made from Forster's adaptation.

[2] She played Sylvia in *The Elder Brother*.

[3] William Carpenter, secretary to the Elocution class at the Mechanics' Institution (Minutes, MS Birkbeck College).

[4] "Mr. C. R. Carter", apparently a leading member of the Institution, sometimes on the Committee, and an occasional lecturer. A letter from "Messrs Carpenter and Carter" about the Elocution class is reported in the Minutes of 6 Oct 45. One of its regular quarterly "recitations" in the Institution's

theatre fell on 30 Dec, and perhaps Carpenter and Carter had invited CD, or approached him with some other request.

[5] Founded in 1823 by George Birkbeck (1776–1841; *DNB*); had premises at 29 Southampton Buildings, Chancery Lane; eventually became Birkbeck College, University of London. At this time it was short of funds, members' subscriptions being almost its only source of income.

[6] His appointment for Monday evening was a dinner with Forster, Crowe and Henry Reeve, noted in Reeve's journal as "about the 'Daily News' then starting" (J. K. Laughton, *Memoirs of the Life and Correspondence of Henry Reeve*, 1898, I, 176–7).

To LORD NUGENT,[1] 10 DECEMBER 1845

Mention in Dutton's catalogue, *c.* 1931–8; *MS* 2 pp.; dated Devonshire Terrace, 10 Dec 45.

Referring to Lord Johnny.[2]

To THE EDITOR OF *THE OXFORD & CAMBRIDGE REVIEW,*[3] 10 DECEMBER 1845*

MS Benoliel Collection.

> 1 Devonshire Terrace | York Gate Regents Park
> Tenth December 1845.

Mr. Charles Dickens presents his compliments to the Editor of the Oxford and Cambridge Review, and begs to say that he would feel the greatest pleasure in complying with his request, but that he has always instructed his Publishers to shew no preference in any such case, but to send out their presentation copies to all the Magazines and Reviews *on the same day*.[4] He feels that reasonable ground of complaint might exist, if he ever departed from this rule; and he is confident that the Editor of the Oxford and Cambridge Review will take no umbrage at this reply to his note, when he assures that gentleman that no personal friendship or regard has ever, in any case, led to its infringement.

To H. G. ADAMS,[5] 11 DECEMBER 1845*

MS Walter T. Spencer.

> Devonshire Terrace | Eleventh December 1845

Dear Sir

I regret to say, that I have private reasons for declining to interfere in the Election you mention. I have great faith, however, in the good intentions and

---

[1] George Nugent Grenville, Baron Nugent of Carlanstown (1788–1850; *DNB*), Whig-radical politician and man of letters: see Vol. II, p. 60*n*. He had been defeated in the election at Aylesbury in 1843; published *Lands Classical and Sacred*, 1845–6. His letters to Forster (MSS Forster Collection, V & A) show that he was on friendly terms with CD by June 43, when he invited them both to Chalgrove.

[2] At this date it was expected that Lord John Russell would form a government and repeal the Corn Law, since Peel had resigned office after failing to unite the Conservatives on a policy of partial repeal. The Queen sent for Russell on 7 Dec, and on 10 Dec he arrived in London en route for

Osborne. In the event he could not form a government (chiefly owing to Grey's refusal to serve if Palmerston were at the Foreign Office), and had to refuse the Queen's commission on 19 Dec.

[3] A recently established monthly periodical, of High church and "Young England" sympathies; the editor is not known.

[4] Nevertheless a review of the *Cricket* did appear in the Jan No.; it was not favourable: "Mr. Dickens's reputation, some time since on the decline, will gain nothing by this little book".

[5] Henry Gardiner Adams (?1811–81), chemist and miscellaneous writer: see Vol. II, p. 11*n*.

sincerity of the Managers of the Athenaeum; and I really believe that the applications will be fairly judged on their own merits.[1]

I am much indebted to you for your notice of my book;[2] to which Captain Johns[3] had previously directed my attention. I begged him to say thus much to you, if he should ever have an opportunity of doing so.

The New Paper, I fear (having a very large and expensive Establishment already completed) does not offer any vacancy to which I could recommend you. Nor do I feel justified: knowing the extent of correspondence already arranged: in holding out a hope that there is likely to be one.

Dear Sir | Faithfully Yours
H. G. Adams Esquire   CHARLES DICKENS

To THOMAS COOPER, 11 DECEMBER 1845

MS Mrs Renee Metivier Black.

Devonshire Terrace | Eleventh December 1845.
Dear Sir

I am exceedingly sorry to say that there is no chance of my being useful to your friend in the manner you suggest; for a very large Establishment has been formed for the New Paper in every one of its working departments: and there is no Vacancy whatever, to which I could recommend him.[4]

Faithfully Yours
Thomas Cooper Esquire   CHARLES DICKENS

To FRANK STONE, [17 DECEMBER 1845]*

MS Benoliel Collection. *Date:* clearly 17 Dec 45 as CD had just returned from Liverpool.

Devonshire Terrace | Wednesday Afternoon

My Dear Stone. I write to you in great haste; having just returned from Liverpool; and having to dress and go out to dinner.

We are obliged to act for Miss Kelly on Saturday the 3rd. of January—short notice! We act Fletcher's Play (altered for the purpose) of The Elder Brother, in which there is no character for you. But send for "Comfortable Lodgings"

---

[1] Adams was perhaps interested in some candidate for office in the Manchester Athenaeum.

[2] Presumably a review of *The Chimes* in a Kent paper.

[3] Richard Johns (1805–51), Captain Royal Marines: see Vol. I, p. 263*n*; a contributor to Adams's *Kentish Coronal*, 1841 (Vol. II, p. 11*n*.)

[4] Probably G. J. Harney, as this letter was among the Harney MSS: see *The Harney Papers*, ed. F. G. Black and R. M. Black, Assen, 1969, p. 16. It appears that Cooper also asked Jerrold to support Harney's application for a post on the *Daily News*, as the letter is endorsed: "No answer from Jerrold yet: but, of course, *that* is of no importance *now*" (presumably written by Cooper when he forwarded CD's note to Harney).

(No. 215 of Cumberland's Acting Plays) and study "Mr. Bonassus"[1] at Railroad speed. That is the farce; and the part is a good one.

We rehearse both play and Farce on *Friday Evening* at Miss Kellys. We take the Play first, and begin at 6.

Ever Yours
CD.

To THOMAS FRASER,[2] 19 DECEMBER 1845*

MS Yale University Library.

90 Fleet Street | Nineteenth December 1845.

My Dear Sir

I quite concur in everything you say in your note of yesterday. We are not likely to differ on such topics, I am very sure.

I am obliged to run away this morning for an hour or two, to save myself from being more direfully slaughtered than is absolutely necessary, at the English Opera House.[3] But I shall be back again between 2 and 3, when I shall hope to see you.

Faithfully Yours
CHARLES DICKENS

To WILLIAM DAVIDGE,[4] 22 DECEMBER 1845

MS Colonel Richard Gimbel.

1 Devonshire Terrace | York Gate Regents Park
Twenty Second December 1845.

Sir.

I beg to thank you for your obliging note and its enclosure, which shall be disposed of as you desire and as it deserves.

Let me assure you that I fully appreciate the honor you do me: not only in making my books the subject of your lectures,[5] but in entering into your theme with so much warmth and earnestness.

I am Sir | Faithfully Yours
CHARLES DICKENS

William Davidge Esquire

[1] Mme Pelagie's brother; Stone took the part.

[2] Thomas Fraser (?1804–69), special correspondent of *Morning Chronicle* in Paris 1836–55: see Vol. I, p. 87*n*.

[3] For rehearsals of Albert Smith's dramatization of the *Cricket*, which opened on Saturday, 20 Dec, with Mrs Keeley as Dot. CD had supplied Smith with advance sheets so that his version was ready on the day of publication, ten days ahead of Edward Stirling's at the Adelphi. See *To* Webster, 6 Jan 46, *fn*, for other versions.

[4] William Pleater Davidge (*b*. 1824), son of Thomas Davidge, the Royal Surrey dramatist; wrote one play and various songs; joined Roxby's company at Manchester 1842.

[5] In 1842–6, during annual recesses when the theatre was closed, Davidge gave "Bozonian lectures" and readings; the "synopsis" of one in the Concert Hall, Lord Nelson St, Manchester, Sep 45, includes readings from *Sketches*, and *Pickwick* (John Suddaby, *D*, VIII [1912], 272–7). Davidge had probably sent CD a copy of the synopsis.

To THE REV. EDWARD TAGART, 22 DECEMBER 1845

MS Comtesse de Suzannet.

Devonshire Terrace | Twenty Second December 1845.

My Dear Sir

I am very much pleased by your interest in the Cricket. I had great satisfaction in the writing of it, and have an uncommonly strong belief in it.

I hadn't the courage to go to the English Opera House on Saturday, but they tell me it is very well played there.[1] I took great pains with the "getting up" of the little piece: to the end that I might be slaughtered as gently as possible. And from what I saw of the Rehearsals, I really believe it is better done than anything of the kind has yet been.

I walk to Harrow still—was nearly blown away, yesterday, on Hampstead Heath—went to Finchley the other day in the pouring rain—take a cold Shower Bath every morning—and oil the Machinery of the Daily News, 'till the afternoon.

A Merry Christmas and a Happy New Year to all your house. When shall I see the Palazzo Peschiere again, I wonder!

Faithfully Yours Always

The Reverend Edward Tagart. CHARLES DICKENS

We are going to act, for the last time, for Miss Kelly's Benefit, on Saturday the 3rd. of January. Fletcher's play of the Elder Brother, and Peake's farce of Comfortable Lodgings.

To T. J. SERLE, 23 DECEMBER 1845

MS Princeton University Library. *Address:* T. J. Serle Esquire | Uxbridge Gardens | Bayswater.

Devonshire Terrace | Twenty Third December 1845.

My Dear Serle.

We have got to play once more (for our sins) for Miss Kelly's benefit. And I am playing a harder game than that, every day, to boot. When the first of these projects has come off, I will see you about the Eltons. I fancy we shall be the committee in the end, whomsoever we summon.

Of course there is no question, and can be none, about all we have done.

---

[1] Reports were favourable, with special praise for Mrs Keeley as Dot and Mary Keeley (who was making her début) as Bertha. Keeley played Caleb Plummer and Emery, Peerybingle. The *Illustrated London News* (27 Dec 45) said that at the end the crowded house "set up a cry for Mr. Dickens and Mr. Albert Smith. The former gentleman was stated not to be in the house, but the latter bowed his acknowledgments from a private box". Crabb Robinson saw it 6 Mar 46 with Wordsworth's son Willy, and thought it "a foolish thing, only rendered endurable by the good acting of Mrs. Keeley" (*The London Theatre 1811–1866. Selections from the Diary of Henry Crabb Robinson*, ed. Eluned Brown, 1966, p. 179).

I honor Esther very much. Her conduct has been gallant and true, through-out.

Ever Yours

T. J. Serle Esquire.   CHARLES DICKENS

To GEORGE HODDER, DECEMBER 1845*

MS¹ Colonel Richard Gimbel. *Date:* probably in latter half of Dec, near in date to John Dickens's other inquiries: see *fn.*

OFFICE OF THE DAILY NEWS | 90 FLEET STREET
December 1845

Sir

Having been informed by Mr. John Dickens that you have undertaken the duty of reporting the proceedings in the Court of Common Pleas, *specially* for the Daily News at an Annual Salary of Three Guineas per Week, I shall be glad if you will do me the favor (as a matter of form) to apprize me under your own hand, of your acceptance of the office.²

Perhaps I may be permitted to point out to you the urgent necessity there will be for your Reports being supplied *at the earliest possible moment* after the rising of your Court. Any unnecessary delay on this head cannot but be productive of most serious inconvenience to the Paper, and this is therefore pressed upon you as a matter of paramount importance.

The Salary attached to the duties you are so good as to undertake will commence one week before the publication of the first number of the Paper. I shall have the pleasure of informing you, in due course, on what precise day it will begin to be payable: and on what Evening your first report will be expected at the Office.³

I have the honor to be | Sir | Your faithful Servant

George Hodder Esqr.   CHARLES DICKENS

To MISS FANNY KELLY, 25 DECEMBER 1845†

MS Dickens House. *Address:* Miss Kelly | 73 Dean Street | Soho.

Devonshire Terrace | Christmas Day 1845.

My Dear Miss Kelly.

ᵃIn addition to my other tickets, will you book (as friends of mine: for good

---

¹ In John Dickens's hand except for ending and signature; endorsed: "Written by Mr. John Dickens, the father of Charles Dickens" in an unknown hand (possibly Hodder's).

² Hodder makes no reference to employment on the *Daily News* in his *Memories of my Time.*

³ The letter is evidently of John Dickens's composition. He was responsible for engaging reporters and the terms of their engagement; in a letter of 23 Dec 45 to Beard (MS Suzannet), he inquired about the number of Parliamentary reporters and "supernumeraries" on the *Herald* for the coming session, and about their arrangements and payments for circuit reporting, since the *Daily News* "must not stand [lower] than the Herald in the Money Market . . . but at the same time we must not through ignorance, if we can help it, throw money away".

aa; bb; cc Not previously published.

places—a second row in the best boxes would do well for these two) *Mr. and Mrs. Powell.*[a][1]

Will you instruct Charles when he comes on Saturday Night, to look, between that time and the Play, to all the Grooves and so forth, that everything may run smoothly and well? [b]The Gasman, too, should see to the Border battens.[b] Will you also take care, in good time, that the orchestra does us credit? Moreover will you exert yourself about the Properties: and also about an intelligent boy to take care of them, and to act as Callboy too?

[c]The Butler in the play—who, in the fourth act says one speech as "Servant". Will you secure the man you spoke of for this—give him his part—and tell him to go to Nathan, and be measured for his dress? He should be called for Saturday.[c]

I want everything to be *well done*; and, the time being short, am getting very nervous.

Faithfully Yours Always
CHARLES DICKENS

Miss Kelly

To J. LUNN,[2] 25 DECEMBER 1845

Mention in Sotheby's catalogue n.d.; *MS* 1 p.; dated "Christmas Day" 1845.

Thanking Lunn for his kind note.

To CLARKSON STANFIELD, 25 DECEMBER 1845*

MS Free Library of Philadelphia.

Devonshire Terrace | Christmas Day 1845

A Merry Christmas and a happy New Year, and many of 'em![3]

My Dear Stanny

Do you think you will be well enough to take care of our Stage and Scenery for us, on Saturday Week? And shall I (if I don't see you next Saturday, when we rehearse all the Evening) let you know what the Rehearsal Nights are, in next week? I am in great tribulation for the want of you. They are so horribly imperfect,[4] that I have no leisure to see after the Carpentering part of it: and leaden weights are on my mind, in consequence.

---

[1] Presumably Thomas Powell and his wife.

[2] Probably Joseph Lunn (1784–1863), writer of farces; original member of the Dramatic Authors' Society: see Vol. II, p. 415*n*.

[3] This sentence written large.

[4] Fred wrote to CD from "26 Maryle-bone St. | Golden Square" (evidently his lodgings) on 23 Dec, excusing himself from that night's rehearsal, and saying, "I have however learned my part *perfectly*, and will come up to you tomorrow, or Thursday, and go over it with you, in order to attain perfection for the (I suppose) final rehearsal" (MS Yale University Library).

I met your turkey in Tottenham Court Road last night. He was looking very well,—and so was Drury.[1]

Affectionately Yours always
CD.

To MRS BALL WILSON,[2] 25 DECEMBER 1845†

MS Walter T. Spencer.

Devonshire Terrace | Christmas Day 1845.

My Dear Rebecca

*a*I would counsel your friend, by all means, to have patience with the bookseller, and wait the publication of the MS at the bookseller's time. It is easy to preach thus, you may say. But I have practised the doctrine in my young day: very much against my will.*a*

As regards any influence of mine, I am quite powerless to assist this author.[3] When I tell you that requests similar to yours are made to me, *by scores*, every week of my life, you will not be surprised at my having long ago released my Publishers from any obligation of attending to a recommendation of mine. It would be a mere form: and so recognised by them, immediately.

Kate and the children are all well, and send their loves. With divers Merry Christmases and Happy New Years; in which[4]

[   ]

Mrs. Ball Wilson.   [CHARLES DICKENS]

To J. T. DANSON, 26 DECEMBER 1845

MS Lieut.-Col. J. R. Danson.

90 Fleet Street. | Twenty Sixth December 1845

My Dear Sir

You mentioned to me once that you might probably want, in your department of the Daily News, some one to transcribe Parliamentary Papers and so forth, under your direction. The object of this note (which does not require an answer) is, to say, that in case you should not desire to recommend particularly any person with whom you are acquainted, I have an application for such a Post, to which I should be most desirous—having the opportunity—to extend a favourable consideration.[5]

I am Dear Sir | Faithfully Yours
CHARLES DICKENS

J. T. Danson Esquire

[1] Probably Stanfield's servant.

[2] Rebecca Mary (1817–77), daughter of Frederick Charles Barrow; CD's first cousin; she married Alexander Ball Wilson (*d.* before 1845), and lived at 4 Mather Place, Richmond Rd, Barnsbury Park till 1866 (*D*, XLVI [1969], 180). CD gave her three leaves of the MS of *Oliver Twist* (now in the Berg Collection).

aa Paragraph given in N, I, 725 with small omissions; letter otherwise unpublished.

[3] Unidentified.

[4] Close of the letter and signature have been cut away.

[5] Danson recalled, "I had two rooms allotted to me—one for the parliamentary Papers, & similar documents coming in daily. I asked for a Clerk to look to the due

To JOSEPH PAXTON, 27 DECEMBER 1845*

MS Mrs A. M. Stern.

90 Fleet Street. | Saturday 27th. December | 1845.

My Dear Sir.

I will send our Secretary[1] to Manchester, in due course, to complete the arrangement with the Guardian[2] People. I do not (this is between you and me) very much like their letter which is rather conceited. Mr. Tootal's[3] estimate of a Manchester Reporter too, is blissfully in the clouds. But nothing of this, affects the value of the Correspondents.[4]

We are full of activity in these regions: and bent on nothing but winning. It is war to the knife, now, with the Times.[5] And if they don't repent the day that ever we started in the field against them, my name is not

CHARLES DICKENS

Joseph Paxton Esquire.   And I rather think it is.

---

receipt, and arrangemt, and custody of these: I agreeing to act as a sort of Librarian, and general Referee. I received one, in the person of a decayed elderly gentleman, who proved to be the Father of Mr. John Leech, already a prominent member of the Staff of 'Punch'. ... He was most willing, and most anxious to earn all his salary of 30/– a week; but I must confess he was of very little use" (Danson's reminiscences; *D*, LXVIII [1972], 154).

[1] W. H. Wills.

[2] At this date a bi-weekly paper, edited by Jeremiah Garnett; John Harland may have been engaged as Manchester correspondent: see *To* Talfourd, 22 Oct 45 and *fn.*

[3] Either Edward Tootal or his brother Henry, of Manchester; both were directors of railway companies with which Paxton, George Hudson and William Jackson were also associated.

[4] One of the Manchester correspondents was evidently Samuel Bamford. Carlyle, in a letter to Forster of 7 Dec 45 (MS Forster Collection), referring to the "new Enterprise" of the *Daily News*, and wishing it "clear aim and right good speed", said he was "very glad indeed that [CD] had written to the brave Bamford"; and on 7 Mar 51, asking Forster to help Bamford, he said "I know not in the least how he acquitted himself in the *Daily News*". Bamford is known to have been a "correspondent of a London newspaper" (*Passages in the Life of a Radical* and *Early Days*, ed. Henry Dunckley, 1893, I, 16).

[5] The first blow was struck by *The Times*

on 27 Dec when Samuel Phillips reviewed the *Cricket* at length, calling it a "twaddling manifestation of silliness almost from the first page to the last" which without the illustrations would be "extravagantly purchased at a groat". Macready described the review as "a most *savage* attack ... the heavy and remorseless blow of an enemy, determined to disable his antagonist by striking to maim him or kill if he can, and so render his hostility powerless". He had discussed the matter with Forster who "now *draws in* about the paper, and seems to feel it is a wrong step, and that Dickens is not qualified for the situation of director. *His tone is quite altered now.* He told me that Dickens was so intensely fixed on his own opinions and in his admiration of his own works (who could have believed it?) that he, Forster, was useless to him as a counsel ..." (*Diaries*, II, 316). Easthope was also much disturbed by the threat to the *Morning Chronicle* ("in a state that would justify a Commission of Lunacy", W. J. Fox *to* Forster, 5 Jan 46, MS Forster Collection, V & A); Lord Nugent wrote to him on 31 Dec: "You know I cannot *quite*, with my *free trade* principles, understand your grounds of anger with Dickens, unless something more, and of a different sort, has occurred than what you complained of to me when we talked over the subject. There are of course two ways of doing everything of this sort. The one an open and manly competition in the good cause of liberal politics, which competition I think you would have no right to complain of ... nor would *you*, I *think*, have any

To MISS FANNY KELLY, 28 DECEMBER 1845*

MS Free Library of Philadelphia.

Devonshire Terrace
Sunday Night | December Twenty Eighth 1845.

My Dear Miss Kelly.

I send you, on the other side, the Prologue.[1] It has the two merits of being short and modest. I hope you may like it.

I also enclose the list of Properties for the Farce, in order that you may adapt it to the calls, in reference to those properties which are taken on.

At 6 tomorrow, I shall be at the Theatre.

Faithfully Yours always
CD

To THOMAS BEARD, [?29 DECEMBER 1845]

MS Dickens House. *Date:* CD arranged to meet Beard on 28 Dec (John Dickens *to* Beard, 27 Dec 45, MS Suzannet); reference to Overland Express also fits 29 Dec 45 (see *fn*). *Address:* Private | Thomas Beard Esquire | Morning Herald Office | Shoe Lane.

90 Fleet Street | Monday Morning

My Dear Beard

Although I mentioned A'Beckett's engagement at the Times yesterday, it didn't occur to me to mention a very distinct and unmistakeable way of putting the case to the fierce Doctor.[2] We stand, with reference to the Punch men, in exactly the same position as the Times and Chronicle. Jerrold is engaged with

right, in such a case, to make common cause with the Enemy, Tory monopolists, to keep a liberal paper out of the market. If Dickens has adopted the *other* course . . . an insidious and covert one, or under false pretences, to weaken you, of course you *have* a right to complain. But I can hardly think he has done this, unless you know it *upon good evidence*. And do remember . . . you must not here rest upon the evidence entirely of persons who *may* have an interest of their own in blowing the coals" (MS Mr R. M. Dawkins).

[1] "A Play by FLETCHER; Written in that age | When the deep-hearted and strong-worded Stage | Had life in England, and could yet rehearse | Ford's, Heywood's, Webster's, Marlowe's, Shakspeare's, verse; | Acted in rev'rence simply; with no hope | Of swelling to the Poet's ample scope, |

Or rising to his passion's noble flight; | Commends itself to you, with trust, to night. | And if a word from one: who in her day, | Has sought out Nature and made faint essay, | In homely form to bring her to like pass, | And shew her Image in this shatter'd glass: | May any license with your favor take— | Receive it kindly, for Your Servant's sake." (MS Suzannet Collection, Dickens House; in CD's hand, with his note in brackets after "glass:" "*The Theatre generally*".)

[2] Stanley Lees Giffard, LLD (1788–1858; *DNB*), editor of the *Standard*, the evening paper owned by the son of the *Herald's* proprietor; "in the obduracy of his sympathies and antipathies in politics he was a man after Dr. Johnson's own heart" (*DNB*, quoting the obituary in the *Standard*).

us—Thackeray is engaged by the Chronicle[1]—A'Beckett by the Times.[2] We have no other association with Punch of any kind of sort.—To which I may add that the interests and doings of more than one of the Proprietors of the D.N. have been, on more than one occasion, very distinctly and plainly attacked in it.

So much to use[3] as you will.

Ever Faithfully
CD

I see your Overland Express triumphant this morning.[4]

To MRS HANNAH BROWN, 29 DECEMBER [1845]*

MS Morgan Library. *Date:* 29 Dec was a Monday in 1845, and letter is endorsed "1845".

Devonshire Terrace | Monday Morning December 29th.
My Dear Mrs. Brown.

I am much indebted to you (and no less to Miss Coutts) for your kind note. I have happily been enabled to send to Paris, instead of going myself; and will take the chance of finding you or Miss Coutts in Stratton Street, tomorrow (Tuesday) about 3 o'Clock.

Always Believe me | Faithfully Yours
Mrs. Brown   CHARLES DICKENS

To MRS HANNAH BROWN, [30 DECEMBER 1845]*

MS Morgan Library. *Date:* clearly the day after last.

Devonshire Terrace | Tuesday Morning
My Dear Mrs. Brown.

I shall be more than delighted to dine with Miss Coutts today. And as I shall have that pleasure, I will *not* trouble her at 3 o'clock.

I am glad you like the Cricket. Its sale is quite enormous.[5]

Ever Faithfully Yours
Mrs. Brown   CHARLES DICKENS

---

[1] Thackeray had been engaged by the *Morning Chronicle* in Mar 44 and was soon earning £20 a month for his regular contributions, which continued, with a break while he was abroad, until Jan 47. He wrote a few political articles and many reviews and art criticisms. A selection of 31 articles is in *Contributions to the Morning Chronicle*, ed. Gordon N. Ray, University of Illinois Press, 1955, including his review of the *Cricket*: see *To* Felton, 1 Jan 46, *fn.*

[2] A'Beckett was a leader-writer on *The Times* for many years.

[3] N reads "truth" for "to use", in error.

[4] The *Herald*'s express from India reached London on 28 Dec and appeared in Monday's issue. Other newspapers congratulated them on the rare feat of beating *The Times*, which attributed their success to the partiality of the French government; for their rivalry with *The Times*, see Fox Bourne, *English Newspapers*, II, 135–8. The next Overland Mail appeared in the *Herald* on Monday 19 Jan.

[5] Forster says, "Its sale at the outset doubled that of both its predecessors" (F, v, i, 380); but this is an exaggeration.

To JOSEPH PAXTON, 30 DECEMBER 1845

Text from *Daily News*, 14 Dec 1915.

90 Fleet-street | Tuesday Thirtieth December | 1845.

My Dear Sir

I have most special and urgent reason[1] (in which participate)[2] for wishing to see you here, *with as little delay as possible*, though only for a few hours. Pray order your Carpet Bag, and get into the train INSTANTLY.

Ever Yours

Joseph Paxton Esquire.   CHARLES DICKENS

To UNKNOWN CORRESPONDENT, 31 DECEMBER 1845

Mention in *Autograph Prices Current*, VI, 51; MS (3rd person) 1 p.; dated 90 Fleet Street, 31 Dec 45.

Stating that there is no vacancy on the Daily News.

To JOHN WILLMOTT, [?31 DECEMBER 1845]*

MS The Governors of the Royal Shakespeare Theatre. *Date:* Handwriting suggests Dec 45 or early 46. The Pantomime at the Pavilion ran from 26 Dec to 31 Jan; the only likely Wed in Jan is 14 Jan, and it seems improbable that Catherine would delay so long before seeing the *Cricket*.

Devonshire Terrace | Wednesday Morning

My Dear Willmott

Mrs. Dickens will be very much obliged to you, if you can let her have a Box for *tonight*.[3]

It is really worth your while to send somebody to see the Columbine at the Pavilion. I don't even know her name;[4] but I strolled in there by chance, the other night, and never saw a performance of that sort so light-hearted, graceful, pleasant, and agreeable. She is, moreover, young and very pretty; and would do you good service, I think, at the Lyceum.

Faithfully Yours

CHARLES DICKENS

To JOHN FORSTER, [1845]

Extract in F, I, iv, 61. *Date:* 1845 according to Forster: presumably in relation to plans for the *Daily News*.

There never was anybody connected with newspapers who, in the same space of time, had so much express and post-chaise experience as I. And what gentle-

---

[1] No letter of Paxton's throws light on this, and he is not known to have been in London again until 3–6 Jan.

[2] Thus in *Daily News* text.

[3] For *The Cricket on the Hearth* at the Lyceum.

[4] Miss Cushnie, the Columbine in Frederic Neale's *Butcher, Butcher, Kill the Ox, or, Harlequin and the Magic Money Box.*

men they were to serve, in such things, at the old *Morning Chronicle*![1] Great or small it did not matter. I have had to charge for half-a-dozen break-downs in half-a-dozen times as many miles. I have had to charge for the damage of a great-coat from the drippings of a blazing wax-candle, in writing through the smallest hours of the night in a swift-flying carriage and pair. I have had to charge for all sorts of breakages fifty times in a journey without question, such being the ordinary results of the pace which we went at. I have charged for broken hats, broken luggage, broken chaises, broken harness—everything but a broken head, which is the only thing they would have grumbled to pay for.

To MRS HOOD, [?AUGUST–DECEMBER 1845]

Extract in S. F. Henkels catalogue No. 1128; *Date:* presumably after the closing of the Fund, and before the publication of Moxon's edn of Hood's *Poems* (preface dated Dec 45).

Declining to allow her to dedicate a book to him.[2] I cannot honorably encourage you in the mistaken idea that such an association of my name "with any work would be a guarantee of success".

To DANIEL MACLISE, [?JULY–DECEMBER 1845]*

MS Francis Edwards. *Date:* Handwriting suggests 1845: July–Sep or Dec most probable, as Catherine was not going out in Oct–Nov.

Devonshire Terrace | Thursday Morning

My Dear Maclise

Kate is very much obliged to you, but will not interfere with the chance of your bestowing the enclosed elsewhere.

Faithfully Always

Daniel Maclise Esquire   CHARLES DICKENS

To GEORGE BEADNELL,[3] 1 JANUARY 1846

MS Myers & Co. *Address* (envelope, MS Professor Harry Stone): Immediate | George Beadnell Esquire | Messrs. Smith Payne & Co. | 2 Lombard Street.

Devonshire Terrace | Thursday Morning | New Year's Day 1846

My Dear Sir

I apprehend you will find no difficulty whatever, in getting good places of Miss Kelly *No. 73 Dean Street Soho.* The tickets (it is for her benefit, or I should have

---

[1] In 1834–6.
[2] Possibly connected with Moxon's post-humous collection of Hood's *Poems*: see *To* Unknown Correspondent, 11 Oct 45, *fn.*

[3] George Beadnell (1773–1862), father of Maria Beadnell: see Vol. 1, p. 2*n.* CD had been in touch with him in 1839 and 1840.

been delighted to send you some) are a guinea each. I would recommend you to send to her for as many as you want, in the course of today if convenient. I shall see her this morning, and will mention your name to her beforehand.

With all earnest wishes for you and yours in the years to come—for the love and remembrance of the years that are gone,[1]

I am Ever | My Dear sir | Faithfully Yours
CHARLES DICKENS

To THOMAS BEARD, 1 JANUARY 1846

MS Dickens House. *Address:* Private | Thomas Beard Esquire | Morning Herald Office | Shoe Lane.

90 Fleet Street. | New Year's Day 1846.

My Dear Bardolph.

The same to you—many on 'em—and a long life to both of us, and our jolly old friendship!

They are printing the book:[2] and no copies are to be had until Saturday, when they will be in the Theatre. I would send you mine, *but it has only my part in it*; and the exquisite unintelligibility of such a document to all but the Initiated, would (I am afraid) drive Mr. Hastings mad.[3]

Enclosed is your private ticket. Kate will leave Devonshire Terrace at ¼ before 7. If you don't appear, they will look for you at the Theatre. She, Georgy, you, Mac, and his sister, sit together.

[1] But clearly CD can have made no inquiry about Maria. She married Henry Louis Winter of 12 Artillery Place on 25 Feb 45 (he was a manager of Crampern & Winter's saw-mills in Finsbury). For her reappearance in CD's life in 1855, see later vol.

[2] Forster's edition of *The Elder Brother*, "Adapted for Modern Representation", published by Bradbury & Evans (prefatory account signed "J. F." and dated "New Year's Day, 1846"), with Forster's Prologue and Epilogue. His proof-copy, interleaved, is in the V & A; CD's copy of his part has not survived.

[3] David Hastings was dramatic and musical critic of the *Morning Herald*. His notice and that of *The Times* praised the adaptation for its removal of objectionable passages and one entire character (Lilly, wife of Charles's servant Andrew, whom Brissac attempts to seduce). The performance appears to have been only a qualified success: *The Times* noted "difficulties . . . in the shape of short memories on the part

of the less principal actors" (the *Literary Gazette* specified Leech's "failures in remembrance"), and "the blunders of scene-shifters, who had a great propensity to sing at the wrong time"; Forster, CD, Jerrold (Andrew) and Lemon (Miramant) were commended, "but the performance of this play was not to be compared with that of *Every Man in his Humour* . . . That was an exhibition worthy of any company of professional actors; this was still an amateur performance". The farce, *Comfortable Lodgings*, on the other hand, went off very well; CD, in Liston's part of Sir Hippington Miff, "was most ludicrously dismal, and played with a humour that not only kept the audience in a roar, but upset the gravity of the other performers, and their reacting proved too much for the mournfulness of Mr. Dickens himself"; Cruikshank, as Roué, was "excessively amusing, introducing a world of wild energy, and being manifestly in doubt whether he should make Roué a Frenchman or not".

When I am bullied through those Four Acts,[1]—always regard me as being ready (in serious earnest) to stab Forster to the heart. It makes me so damned savage that I could rend him limb from limb.[2]

Ever affectionately
CD

To R. W. JELF,[3] [?1 JANUARY 1846]

Mention in next.

To MISS BURDETT COUTTS, 1 JANUARY 1846*

MS Morgan Library.

Devonshire Terrace | New Years Day 1846

My Dear Miss Coutts.

Very many happy years to you, and all who are dear to you!

I have written to Dr. Jelf (in answer to his kind note) that I will call on him next Tuesday Morning. When I have primed myself with all needful particulars, I will endeavour to find you at home, and will bring Charley with me.

Always Dear Miss Coutts | Most Faithfully Yours
CHARLES DICKENS

P.S. The Nomination Papers[4] really *are* enclosed, this time.

To C. C. FELTON, 1 JANUARY 1846†

MS Harvard College Library. *Address:* By Cunard Mail Steam Packet. | Professor Felton | Cambridge | Massachusetts.

Office of the Daily News. | First January 1846.

My Dear Felton.

I am going to write a very short answer to your generous note. Read it in its spirit, my dear fellow, and not in its length.

---

[1] The "bullying" is in fact confined to Acts III, IV and V—after Charles (Forster), formerly an unworldly scholar, who was expected to disinherit himself in favour of Eustace (CD), has declined to do so and becomes his rival for Angellina just before the wedding, saying—to the surprise of all —"Room for an elder brother! here, give place". But the brothers are finally reconciled and Eustace's honour maintained.

[2] Macready called on Forster on 2 Jan and found CD and his tailor there, "he encased in his doublet and hose; it is quite ludicrous the fuss which the actors make about this play!—but I was sorry to hear of intemperate language between them, which should neither have been given nor received, as it was" (*Diaries*, II, 318).

[3] Richard William Jelf (1798–1871; *DNB*), principal of King's College, London, since 1844; canon of Christ Church, Oxford; published sermons and Bampton Lectures.

[4] The nomination paper (MS King's College) is signed "A. G. Burdett Coutts": see next vol. Coutts & Co. had given £330 to the foundation of the College, which gave them the right of nominating three candidates a year.

Try the letters. There is a Commercial Correspondent at New York.[1] So try them. Your politics are mine. I do not think you will write the worse for not being too intimate with the party leaders, or too near the roar of Washington. So try them, my dear Felton, and see how you like it. Write your first, by the Packet which leaves Boston in the beginning of February,[2] and address it to the London Daily News, Care of Mr. Whitty Journal office, Liverpool. He will get it out of the Mail Bag (being our agent) with all speed. The American Newspapers are already provided for, on this side.

[a]A general view (such as you would naturally take if you were writing to a friend) of Politics and News, will be excellent, I am sure. And the only way of ascertaining how you relish it will be by trying it. So I shall depend upon you.

We start on the 21st. of this Month,[3] and are proceeding vigorously. The Times has done us enormous service by attacking me, in its jealousy of the Paper.[4] It has brought all sorts and conditions of men, rallying round us gallantly.[a]

The Cricket is a most tremendous success.[5] It has beaten my two other Carols out of the field, and is going still, like Wildfire. [b]Best regards from Kate. And loves from my little girls to yours. Ever My Dear Felton, Your Affectionate friend[b]

Professor Felton   CD.

To MRS MACREADY, [?2 JANUARY 1846]*

MS Morgan Library. *Date:* Handwriting suggests early 1846; possibly the Friday after *To* Paxton, ?30 Dec, asking him to come to London immediately on urgent business.

Devonshire Terrace | Friday Evening

My Dear Mrs. Macready. More thanks than I can pay, for your kind note of this morning. More blushes than my face will hold, for its still being unanswered.

[1] "Our own correspondent" in New York contributed "Commercial Intelligence" to the *Daily News* of 4 Feb 46.

[2] The first letter from "Our Boston correspondent" appeared on 16 Feb, signed "X X"; it had arrived on the *Hibernia*, which left about 31 Jan.

aa; bb Not previously published.

[3] The date was first announced in advertisements on 1 Jan.

[4] See *To* Claxton, 8 Jan 46. *The Times*'s review of the *Cricket* was generally recognized as directed against the *Daily News*: according to the *Era* (4 Jan), "the Boz critique is an evidence of the volcano, heaving as yet in embryo, but ripe for an eruption on the first appearance of the *Daily News*"; cf. the article in *Mephystopheles* (10 Jan), "Charles Dickens, the *Times*, and their Motives".

[5] CD is thinking mainly of sales, but the critics' reception also was predominantly favourable. The *Athenæum* gave it over six columns (with lavish quotation) on the day of publication, welcoming its domestic interest. Many preferred it to *The Chimes* (e.g. *Illustrated London News*, 27 Dec 45: "he has rejected the *virus* which would estrange rich and poor"). The *Morning Post*, like *The Times*, took the opportunity for a violently hostile attack, especially on CD's commercialism (not a "literary Leviathan" but "a temporary catchpenny gent"). Thackeray's long notice in the *Morning Chronicle* (24 Dec 45) emphasized its immediate and immense popularity ("you hear talk of it in every company"), and found much to praise, though treating it, justly enough, mainly as entertainment: "it is a good *Christmas* book, illuminated with extra gas, crammed with extra bonbons, French plums and sweetnesses".

I have been obliged to make an indefinite appointment with a gentleman to call here today (on the most urgent business) at his own leisure between 12 at Noon and 12 at Night. I have been looking for him all day. He has not come; and I dare not go out.

Let me claim your kind promise another time. And ever believe me

Faithfully Your friend | (Not Your Enemy and Hater)

CHARLES DICKENS

To LUIGI MARIOTTI, 2 JANUARY 1846

Mention in Catalogue of the Dreer Collection, 1890; dated 2 Jan 46.

To NICHOLAS TRÜBNER,[1] 5 JANUARY [1846]

Extract in S. F. Henkels catalogue No. 1436; *MS* 1 p.; dated Devonshire Terrace, 5 Jan 45—CD's error for 1846: see *fn.*

Thanking him for a volume. I assure you that it will afford me very great pleasure to call attention (so far as I can) to the Flemish Tales.[2]

To MRS CHARLES DICKENS, 6 JANUARY 1846

MS British Museum. *Address:* Mrs. Charles Dickens | Devonshire Terrace.

Fleet Street | Twelfth Day | 1846

My Dear Kate

The weather is so very bad, that I really think you had better send down to Edginton's in Piccadilly,[3] and see if they can't, at a reasonable charge, put up an awning from the street-door to the Curb-Stone. They do such things every day. It is really too far for Ladies to go in the wet.

Affecy. always

CD.

To BENJAMIN WEBSTER, 6 JANUARY [1846]*

MS New York University Library. *Date:* clearly 1846 since referring to *Cricket.*

Devonshire Terrace | Sixth January 1845.

My Dear Sir

I am greatly obliged to you for your attention in sending me the enclosed

[1] Nicholas Trübner (1817–84), translator and publisher, founder of Trübner and Co. 1852. Came to London 1843 to work as foreign corresponding clerk for Longman's.

[2] Trübner's translation from the Flemish of Hendrik Conscience's *Sketches from Flemish Life, in Three Tales,* was published early in 1846 (preface dated December 1845 and signed "N. Tr."). A short review appeared in the *Daily News,* 22 Jan; the preface, with its high claims for Conscience's work as a pioneer in presenting everyday Flemish life, is quoted, but its view that the tales were "masterpieces" is not accepted.

[3] Benjamin Edgington & Co, 208 Piccadilly.

Card.[1] But as we have an annual Engagement[2] for tonight, I return it, in case you should be able to make another use of it. Mrs. Dickens will be very thankful to you if you can kindly bestow another Box on her, any "Cricket" night, this week.

I am | My Dear Sir | Faithfully Yours

Benjamin Webster Esquire   CHARLES DICKENS

To MISS BURDETT COUTTS, 7 JANUARY 1846

MS Morgan Library.

Devonshire Terrace | Seventh January 1846

My Dear Miss Coutts

I am sure I need not say to you that it would give me the truest pleasure to be of the least help to anyone in whom you have an interest; and that I should esteem myself most fortunate in having the power. But the Courier rumour has not the least foundation. The man who served me in that capacity abroad (one of the best Servants in the World) I recommended to some employment only the other day. He is constantly backwards and forwards here, to play with the children: who are his most intimate friends. And if I were to want any other courier, I think it would break his heart. I cannot conceive how your man got such information—unless he derived it from a newspaper. I see almost daily, in those sources of intelligence, the most prodigious accounts of my occupations, intentions, &c. &c., which are all so new to me that they make my hair stand on end.[3]

I saw Dr. Jelf the other morning, (yesterday morning) and received the greatest courtesy and attention from him. As he thinks I had best see Dr. Major, who is the Head Master of the *School*,[4] I contemplate an inroad on that gentleman tomorrow Morning. When I have seen him, and know all that is to be done, I will bring my large Son to Stratton Street. He has been writing a Play lately. There are four acts in it; two scenes in each; and about twelve words in each

[1] For Webster's dramatization of the *Cricket*, which opened at the Haymarket 6 Jan, though originally announced for 27 Dec 45; Webster played Peerybingle, Miss Fortescue Dot, and J. B. Buckstone Tilly Slowboy. By this time no fewer than 14 theatres were running the *Cricket*, with three more to follow (see Malcolm Morley, "*The Cricket* on the Stage", *D*, XLVIII [1951], 17–24).

[2] The party for Twelfth Night and Charley's birthday. Marryat was among the guests in 1846 and described the occasion as: "very pleasant indeed—lots of fun—Wilson and Parry sung; children had then a ball and supper, and made speeches, and sung convivial songs; afterwards, ball and capital supper; everyone there: Talfourd, Macready, Cruikshank, Landor, Stanfield, Forster, and a hundred more"

(Marryat *to* Mrs S—, "Wednesday", Florence Marryat, *Life and Letters of Captain Marryat*, 1872, II, 185; misdated "February 1845"— references to public events in the letter make it certain that the date was 7 Jan 46).

[3] No accounts of this kind have been found in any of the London dailies or weeklies.

[4] King's College School, started 1831 as a junior department of the College; by 1846 had over 500 pupils and had reached the height of its success, but afterwards declined; mainly middle-class pupils; the curriculum largly classical, on public school lines, but with exceptionally low fees (£6.15.2 a term). Among the pupils in 1846 were H. P. Liddon, and Frederic Harrison. The Rev. John Richardson Major (1787–1876) was headmaster 1831–67.

scene. The Hero of the piece is a certain "Boy" (it is a nautical subject) who, by reason of his always having to introduce the other characters by asking them where they come from, and having to get them off by proposing to "come along" (which he invariably does, at the end of every scene) has a part, in proportion, longer than Hamlet.

Ever Dear Miss Coutts | Most Faithfully Yours

CHARLES DICKENS

To LEIGH HUNT, 7 JANUARY 1846

Extract in P. J. Dobell catalogue No. 24 (1923); *MS* 1 p.; dated Devonshire Terrace, 7 Jan 46.

I hardly know how it came about, but I was *not* glad to receive your letter. It affected me at first, with a sensation of pain to find that you should have so carefully remembered what I had so utterly forgotten.[1]

To C. CLAXTON,[2] 8 JANUARY [1846]*

MS Free Library of Philadelphia. *Date:* clearly 1846 since referring to *Cricket* and *Daily News*.

Devonshire Terrace, London | Eighth January 1845.

Dear Sir

I am glad to hear you have been crying over the Cricket. I hope you may come to Spectacles over the Newspaper, which will begin its career on the Twenty First.

The Times has done us a great deal of service.

I cannot forward the enclosed Paper to any of the Punch Writers, because I have taken a pledge (to myself) of Total Abstinence in all such cases; otherwise, so numerous are the MSS sent to me, it would be a misfortune and grievous calamity to any Public Writer, to know me. But, if you send it in a blank cover to the Punch office, I have no doubt it will be opened and read by the gentleman, whoever he be, whose duty it is to dispose of such communications.

Dear Sir | Faithfully Yours

C. Claxton Esquire.   CHARLES DICKENS

To WILLIAM CULLENFORD,[3] 8 JANUARY 1846

Extract in Sotheby's catalogue, 2 June 1911; *MS* 1½ pp.; dated 8 Jan 46.

I shall be happy to receive the deputation who propose doing me the honor of waiting on me.[4]

[1] Perhaps the "favor", presumably a loan, of 20 Dec 42: see Vol. III, p. 398.

[2] Just possibly Christopher Claxton, Captain, RN, of Bristol, author of *A Description of the Great Britain Steam Ship*, 1845, and other works.

[3] William Cullenford (1797–1874), actor. First appeared in London at the Adelphi 1836 as Wharton in *The Christening*; acted chiefly at the Adelphi and the Haymarket until his retirement in 1864. A founder of the General Theatrical Fund 1839 and its secretary from 1839 until his death.

[4] To ask CD to speak at the first Anniversary Festival of the General Theatrical Fund: see *To* Cullenford, 19 Feb 46.

To THOMAS BEARD, 9 JANUARY 1846

MS Dickens House. *Address:* Private | Thomas Beard Esquire.

90 Fleet Street | Ninth January 1846

My Dear Beard.

If you be at leisure to see my Secretary Mr. Wills[1] who bears this, for a minute or two, will you kindly do so? I have charged him with a business enquiry.

He is a very good fellow, and late Editor of Chambers's Journal.

About the dinner to our friend[2] (who I thought spoke very manfully and honestly, yesterday). What would you recommend? Shall I write and ask him at once: giving him a week's notice?

Ever Yours
CD

To JOHN CATTERMOLE,[3] 9 JANUARY 1846*

MS The Press Club, London.

Devonshire Terrace | Ninth January 1846.

Sir.

I beg, in reply to your note, to express my regret that the Daily News cannot avail itself of your proffered services. The arrangements of the Paper are completed, I understand, in every Department.

Faithfully Yours

John Cattermole Esquire   CHARLES DICKENS

To JAMES DAVIDSON,[4] 9 JANUARY 1846

MS Mr Noel C. Peyrouton.

Devonshire Terrace | Ninth January 1846

Dear Sir

I shall be happy to do you any service in my power at the Garrick (though I should think you would need none); but the Election rests, as perhaps you know, with the Committee, and not with the Members.

Faithfully Yours

James Davidson Esquire   CHARLES DICKENS

---

[1] William Henry Wills (1810–80; *DNB*): see Vol. I, p. 264*n*. Contributor to *Punch* since 1841; went to Edinburgh Dec 42 as assistant editor of *Chambers's Journal*, and remained till 1845; married Janet, sister of William and Robert Chambers, 23 Apr 46.

[2] Unidentified.

[3] Probably John Flowerdew Cattermole, who lived at 4 Cottage Rd, Eaton Square.

[4] "James Davidson, Esq" became a member of the Garrick Club in 1846; this was James Davidson, solicitor, of Clark, Davidson & Brown, 36 Essex St, Strand.

To MISS BURDETT COUTTS, [?12 JANUARY 1846]*

MS Morgan Library. *Date:* The "Proprietor" must have been Joseph Paxton, who returned to London in the week beginning Mon 12 Jan; reference to injured hand confirms (see next). *Address:* Miss Burdett Coutts.

Devonshire Terrace | Monday Morning

My Dear Miss Coutts. I waited until the arrival of the Post this morning, before answering your kind note, as I had a half-appointment for this evening, with a gentleman resident in the Country, who is one of the Proprietors in my new Undertaking; and there was a chance of his not coming to town.[1] I have now, however, heard that he *is* coming for this special purpose; and I am sorry to say he will deprive me of the pleasure of dining with you.

Always Dear Miss Coutts | Faithfully Yours
CHARLES DICKENS

I have hurt my right hand, and write illegibly.

To H. P. SMITH, 12 JANUARY 1846*

MS Miss Mabel Hodge.

Office of the Daily News
12 January 1846

My dear Smith

Forster having done his best towards an amputation of my right hand middle finger, I dictate this note[2] to thank you heartily for your remembrance of the Daily News & for your cordial and earnest manner of remembering it.

Faithfully Your's | My dear Smith,
H. B.[3] Smith Esquire   CHARLES DICKENS

To C. R. LESLIE, 15 JANUARY 1846*

MS Mr Thomas L. Twidell.

Devonshire Terrace
Fourteenth—I mean Fifteenth | January 1846

My Dear Sir

If *Saturday Week* will suit you for a beginning, I shall be happy to sit to you in full costume,[4] and as hirsute as I was originally, all day long. Let me know whether this will do or not.

---

[1] Paxton had left London on the morning of 6 Jan (staying an extra night "at the urgent request" of the members of the *Punch* table: MS reproduced in V. Markham, *Paxton and the Bachelor Duke*, p. 166), but was in London again this week "to stir up the deities about Whitefriars—and the devils too" (John Cottingham *to* Sarah Paxton, MS Devonshire Collections).

[2] The whole letter, including signature, is in the hand of W. H. Wills.

[3] Thus in MS.

[4] For the portrait of CD as Bobadil, exhibited RA 1846, engraved by Edward Stodart and reproduced in lithography by T. H. Maguire; Mamie told Kitton it struck her as "an excellent likeness" (see Kitton, *CD by Pen and Pencil*, 1, 100, 108).

I am very glad you passed so pleasant an Evening on Twelfth Night. It gave us the greatest pleasure I assure you to have your family among our guests.[1]

Always My Dear Sir | Faithfully Yours

CHARLES DICKENS

To THOMAS BEARD, 16 JANUARY 1846

MS Dickens House. *Address:* Thomas Beard Esquire | Morning Herald Office.

OFFICES OF THE DAILY NEWS | WHITEFRIARS[2]

Sixteenth January 1846

My Dear Beard.

—Two points for you to mention to Mr. Baldwin;[3] who I hope is better of that accursed rheumatism.

There is a Meeting at Norwich on Tuesday Night—a free trade Meeting—which has this novelty that Wodehouse[4] (I think that's the way to spell his name; it looks like a Saxon God's) has challenged Cobden[5] to a discussion, and they will go at it like a couple of Crichtons.[6] We are all powerful on that Railway, and mean, if possible to have a special train in which our man or men can come up long before the Mail—write out, on the way—and give us his or their couple of Columns or so, in time for the first Edition. I don't think we should do this, but for a preliminary splash;[7] and it is possible, therefore, that you may not think it worth while to join.[8] But in the Spirit of the Alliance, I think it right to tell you exactly what we mean to do.

[1] Leslie's son, G. D. Leslie, remembered the Twelfth Night parties at Devonshire Terrace; at one of them CD and Lemon danced a country-dance in their shirt-sleeves and CD had one of the Miss Keeleys for his partner (Kitton, I, 164–5).

[2] This and next are the earliest known letters on embossed paper from the new building; all later letters with the same form of address are on this paper. The editor's room at Whitefriars was described by Thomas Britton, then the office boy: "There were no indications of lavish expenditure in the furnishing of the apartment as has been absurdly asserted. It simply comprised an ordinary office table and armchair, a stained-wood reading desk, six leather-bottomed chairs, a small bookcase, and a black horsehair sofa, the floor being carpeted. The library was not an extensive one, and was 'made up' principally of 'Hansard's Debates,' up to date, the 'Annual Register,' 'Howell's State Trials,' the 'Mirror of Parliament,' a com-

plete set of the Classics, Shakespeare and the Bible, and a fair supply of dictionaries and small works of reference. Letters for the Editor were conveyed (not on a 'silver salver' as the absurd legend has it) and placed in a kind of deed-box, a similar one being provided for the heads of every department for the reception of all 'copy' and correspondence referring thereto" (*The "Daily News" Jubilee*, p. 8).

[3] Edward Baldwin, proprietor of the *Morning Herald*.

[4] Edmond Wodehouse, MP for East Norfolk.

[5] Richard Cobden (1804–65; *DNB*), MP 1841–7, leader of the Anti-Corn Law League.

[6] Swordsmen, like "the Admirable Crichton".

[7] A report in $4\frac{1}{2}$ columns, "From our own reporters. By special express", appeared 21 Jan, dated "Norwich 10 p.m."

[8] The *Morning Herald* did not join and had no report of the meeting.

About the Queen's Speech.[1]—Can you help us to any outline? I merely ask the question, as your information may be *uncommunicable*. The Times will have it, I hear; and there are prophets who foretell its imparting the same to the drowsy but comparatively virtuous old Chronicle.

Ever My Dear Beard | Faithfully Yours

Thomas Beard Esquire   CHARLES DICKENS

To THE COUNTESS OF BLESSINGTON, 16 JANUARY 1846*

MS Berg Collection.

OFFICES OF THE DAILY NEWS | WHITEFRIARS
Sixteenth January 1846.

My Dear Lady Blessington.

I have been wanting to write to you every day since I last saw you, but have had no hand to do it with until now.

We know each other so well, and you have shown me your nature so frankly and generously, that I have no hesitation in asking you to consider whether you can reconcile it with your other engagements to let me have for the Daily News (in the strictest confidence) any sort of intelligence you may like to communicate of the sayings, doings, rumours, and movements, in that World which you know all about. Such communications from you, would be of inestimable service to the Paper; and if you will tell me how many Hundreds a Year the Paper may pay you in return, I will answer for its being as delighted as a Paper *can* be, to have the opportunity.[2]

I feel, my dear Lady Blessington, that I should be but a poor fellow if I had any delicacy in approaching that part of the subject; and that I should pay you but a slight compliment if I avoided it in the least. My personal recognition of your assistance, as my dear friend, it is idle to speak of; for that is far removed from any such considerations. But in my very different capacity as the representative of a body of Proprietors, I hold myself as much bound to recognize it plainly, as I feel pretty sure you will.—Just as I have a very distinct recognition indeed, of my own remuneration.

I shall be very glad to hear a few words from you. Meantime with love to Count D'Orsay, I am Ever

My Dear Lady Blessington | Faithfully Yours

The | Countess of Blessington   CHARLES DICKENS

[1] Summaries in anticipation of the Queen's speech were given in a leading article of 22 Jan in both the *Daily News* and the *Herald* as well as *The Times*. The "drowsy" *Chronicle* had no preliminary outline, but brought out a 2nd edn giving the speech.

[2] Lady Blessington contributed "exclusive intelligence" to the *Daily News* until May 46: see R. R. Madden, *Literary Life and Correspondence of the Countess of Blessington*, I, 275–6.

To R. S. HOBBES,[1] 16 JANUARY 1846

MS Brotherton Library, Leeds.

1 Devonshire Terrace | Sixteenth January 1846

Sir

I am extremely sorry to say that it is not in my power to be of any service to you. The Establishment of the Daily News is quite completed, as I understand, in all its Departments; and I know of at least a score of gentlemen who are candidates for the first vacant post in connexion with it, that may offer.

Nor have I the least idea who is the Editor of Bentley's Miscellany.[2] My knowledge of that Magazine ceased with my own Editorship, seven or eight years ago.

I write to you in great haste, being much pressed for time. But I beg you to believe that I am not indifferent to your note, and that I wish I could return a more encouraging reply to it.

I am Sir | Faithfully Yours

R. S. Hobbes Esquire   CHARLES DICKENS

To JOSEPH PAXTON, 16 JANUARY 1846*

MS Mrs A. M. Stern.

OFFICES OF THE DAILY NEWS | WHITEFRIARS
Sixteenth January 1846

My Dear Sir

By all means let us have the order from Mr. Hudson,[3] for a Special Engine, if it can possibly be managed. It will enable us to make a hit in our very first Number.

I should like to know when and where we can get it from you in town here (if you get it) on Monday Night, as a Reporter will be in waiting to start off immediately on its receipt.

Captain Taylor[4] writes from Paris this Morning, that his Petition was received with the greatest interest by the Count St. Aulaire,[5] and that the idea excited him

---

[1] Unidentified.

[2] After Ainsworth's departure in Dec 41 Bentley had edited it himself (Royal Gettmann, *A Victorian Publisher*, Cambridge, 1960, p. 143), but named "Mr. Wilde" as editor to Hood in Oct 43 (Hood, *Letters*, ed. Peter Morgan, p. 573); and according to Bentley's *List* the editor was now Albert Smith, though the name was not announced.

[3] George Hudson had recently become chairman of the Eastern Counties Railway. The special train was provided, and brought reports of the Anti-Corn Law meeting at Norwich (*Daily News*, 21 Jan).

[4] Captain Joseph Needham Tayler, RN (1785–1864; *DNB*), inventor and writer on coastal defences; in 1843 took out patents for improvements in steamships, breakwaters, and sound-alarms, and in 1844 exhibited at the Admiralty a so-called "telephone instrument" to convey signals in foggy weather, audible for several miles.

[5] Comte Louis de Sainte-Aulaire (1778–1849), French Ambassador in London 1841–47.

extremely, as one of most uncommon importance. The Lords of the Admiralty have granted the permission on this side of the Water.

I hope we shall derive great reputation from the trial.[1]

Everything looks well for our Start. I can't sleep; and if I fall into a doze I dream of first numbers till my head swims.

Always Faithfully Yours

Joseph Paxton Esquire CHARLES DICKENS

To THE COUNTESS OF BLESSINGTON, 17 JANUARY 1846*

MS Benoliel Collection.

OFFICES OF THE DAILY NEWS | WHITEFRIARS
Seventeenth January 1846

My Dear Lady Blessington

I am quite delighted with your letter. It occurs to me that you must have *some* figures in your mind, as what you would think fair. *Will you tell me what they are?* Without committing you at all, I will then sound the Money-Managers without the least delay, and write to you again before the Evening.

The agreement will be decidedly, for a year; and it could be stated on the face of it, that if renewed at the expiration of that time, it should be at a higher rate. I would propose for your satisfaction that you and the Money-Managers aforesaid, should interchange the form of agreement which is entered into with the Leader-Writers, who are all treated with in strict confidence.

Ever My Dear Lady Blessington | Faithfully Yours

The | Countess of Blessington CHARLES DICKENS

To DR EPPS,[2] 17 JANUARY 1846

Mention in Hodgson's catalogue, Dec 1921; dated 17 Jan 46.

To LORD ROBERTSON, 17 JANUARY 1846*

MS Yale University Library.

Devonshire Terrace | Seventeenth January 1846

My Dear Lord Robertson.

The quotation is an admirable one. But you will be glad to hear that there

---

[1] No report appeared, and no correspondence between Tayler and the Admiralty in Jan 46 is recorded. His new project may have had some connection with the 'electric telegraph" referred to in Sarah Paxton *to* Joseph Paxton, 22 Jan—"we sincerely hope that it will meet with no *mishap*" (MS Devonshire Collections; V. Markham, *Paxton and the Bachelor Duke*, p. 171).

[2] Probably John Epps (1805–69; *DNB*), homoeopathic physician, of liberal views; campaigned for repeal of Corn Laws and the abolition of capital punishment; friend Mazzini. His half-brother George Napoleon (1815–74; *DNB*) was also a homoeopathic physician, whose daughter married Edmund Gosse.

have been some fifteen or twenty Editions[1] of the Cricket, already printed. It has done more than either of its predecessors: and has been a most prodigious success.

The new calling shall not long supersede the old one. I should be glad to establish the Paper well, if I could. My share of it would then be a fine property.

Do not charge me with not thinking of you. I do so, very often. I go to the Puppets with you, never less than once a week: and see you, perpetually, in that Lemonade Shop perplexed with a handful of tin riches, bestowed upon you by the Landlord.

Also your travelling-hat is enshrined in my dearest recollection.

So are you, and always shall be.

Faithfully Yours
CHARLES DICKENS

Lord Robertson.

To THOMAS BEARD, [?MID-JANUARY 1846]

MS Dickens House. *Date:* after 9 Jan, when CD was still writing from 90 Fleet St, and probably shortly before the first number. *Address:* Wait | Thomas Beard Esquire | Morning Herald Office.

OFFICES OF THE DAILY NEWS | WHITEFRIARS
Saturday Evening

My Dear Beard

I have altered the plan[2] very much, and made it one that is more likely, I think, to suit you—I can't come over, but *before* you see your Governor[3] tonight, will you give me a call in Devonshire Terrace? It's important.

Ever
CD.

To T. N. TALFOURD, [?MID-JANUARY 1846]†

MS Mr Arnold Ziegler. *Date:* possibly connected with last.

Whitefriars | Saturday Night

My Dear Talfourd.

We of the Daily News Proprietorship, wish, in a case of sudden emergency (only Bradbury and Evans & I) to see you *tomorrow*[4] (Sunday). *a*Will you kindly make an appointment for the Afternoon by Bearer.*a* It is a most pressing case,

---

[1] Advertisements in late 1846 are inconsistent; in the *Battle of Life* it is said to be in its 22nd edn, in *Dombey and Son* in its 14th.

[2] Probably refers to the agreement to divide the cost of foreign expenses, including the services of special messengers costing not less than £10,000 a year, with the *Morning Herald*; it was to their benefit, since *The Times* had excluded the *Herald* from this service, shared with the *Chronicle* and *Post* (Fox Bourne, pp. 143–4). See *To* Beard, ?29 Dec 45.

[3] Edward Baldwin.

[4] Heavily doubly underlined.

aa; bb Not previously published.

*b*or I would not trouble you. We shall not detain you more than a quarter of an hour.*b*

Affecy. Always

Mr. Serjeant Talfourd.   CHARLES DICKENS

To THE COUNTESS OF BLESSINGTON,
[20 JANUARY 1846]*

MS Benoliel Collection. *Date:* clearly 20 Jan, the Tuesday after *To* Lady Blessington, 17 Jan; her first contribution appeared 22 Jan.

OFFICES OF THE DAILY NEWS | WHITEFRIARS
Tuesday Noon

My Dear Lady Blessington.

I have been involved in such an overwhelming pressure of business, and we are all so torn to pieces here,[1] that I have not been able to see the Money Men until today. They were with me, for the first time, when your Messenger arrived.

I should frankly tell you that Eight Hundred Pounds is certainly too much for them. Not as being too much for you, but as being more than I think it likely any Newspaper—but certainly a new one—could afford to devote to that branch of Intelligence; which is one, as you know, of very many, and forms but one item in a sum of more than a Thousand Pounds per week. I have not compromised you in any way, but I have ascertained this, beyond a doubt.

If you think you could reconcile it to your views of the subject (the justice of which I perfectly comprehend) to begin on a decidedly lower scale, and to leave the adjustment of it, for a very few weeks, to me, rely on my bringing them to the highest point to which they think they can reasonably go.[2] If that should not please you, then let Forster and I arbitrate for the Past (the then past, I mean, of course) and release you handsomely and without offence on either side.

I shall be very anxious to know what you think of this. I should have written to you by this time, though I had not heard from you.

Ever My Dear Lady Blessington | Faithfully Yours

The | Countess of Blessington   CHARLES DICKENS

---

[1] "On Saturday night, January 17th ... every one was at his post, and a trial or 'dummy' paper was produced and printed, bearing the date Monday, January 19, 1846" (Thomas Britton, in *The "Daily News" Jubilee*, 1896, p. 8). Britton preserved what is one of the only two copies known, now at the *Daily News* office with a letter of 1912 in which he gives the date of the trial run as Sunday. (The other copy is at Dickens House.) The issue consists of eight pages, its contents mainly drawn from other papers; many of the advertisements were used for the issue of 21 Jan. The first of Dickens's "Travelling Letters" appears, headed "Foreign Letters No. I", and two leading articles, one on the execu-

tion of Tapping on Easter Monday, 1845, and the other a humorous account of a supposed trial of Mr Jones (the printer) for causing the death of various workmen in the preparing of the offices in Whitefriars. The latter bears all the marks of CD's hand, and is given in Appx B.

[2] According to R. R. Madden, *Literary Life and Correspondence of the Countess of Blessington*, I, 275–6, the *Daily News* "proposed an arrangement at the rate of £500 a-year for the term of half a year, but at the rate of £400 a-year for a year certain; and the arrangement was carried into effect". On giving notice that she did not wish to renew her engagement in May 1846 she was paid £250.

To J. J. HARRISON,[1] 20 JANUARY 1846*

MS[2] New York Public Library.

OFFICES OF THE DAILY NEWS | WHITEFRIARS
Private   20 January 1846

Sir,

I beg to acknowledge the receipt of your obliging letter and to say that if you can do me the favour to call upon Mr. Wills (my secretary, a gentleman who can be treated with in entire Confidence and who perfectly represents myself) here, to morrow Wednesday evening at Nine o'clock, I shall be happy to pursue the subject you open to me.

I am Sir | Faithfully Yours
J. J. Harrison Esquire   CHARLES DICKENS

To THE UNITED TRADES ASSOCIATION, [?20 JANUARY 1846]

Mention in *The Times*, 22 Jan 46. *Date:* shortly before 21 Jan.

Regretting his inability to take part in the soirée for Thomas Duncombe.[3]

To JOHN FORSTER, [21 JANUARY 1846]

Extract in F, v, i, 387. *Date:* 21 Jan according to Forster.

A little note written before going home *at six o'clock in the morning saying they had* been at press three quarters of an hour, and were out before the *Times*.

To MRS COWDEN CLARKE,[4] [21 JANUARY 1846]

Envelope only, MS Eastgate House, Rochester. *Address:* Mrs. Cowden Clarke | 9 Craven Hill | Bayswater. PM 21 Jan 46.

[1] Possibly the J. J. Harrison who contributed weather predictions to Joseph Harrison's *Gardeners' Almanack* in 1852–5, and (with E. Harrison) succeeded him as editor of the monthly *Floricultural Cabinet*. Joseph (*d.* 1858; *DNB*) was closely associated with Paxton as joint editor of the *Horticultural Register* in 1831–6, and also through Thomas Brassey the railway contractor who married Harrison's daughter Maria in 1831.

[2] The letter is in the hand of W. H. Wills, except for ending and signature.

[3] Thomas Duncombe, MP (1796–1861; *DNB*): see Vol. III, p. 538*n*; the soirée, at the Crown & Anchor on 21 Jan, was held in his honour "for his services to the people's cause". Thomas Wakley, MP, presiding,

read letters from CD, Jerrold and Mazzini, excusing themselves, he said, from an occasion in which they took great interest, on the ground of important engagements; but in fact CD may well have felt his presence in any case inadvisable. A toast to "the people" preceded the royal toast, and one to "the Charter" followed. Thomas Cooper responded to the toast to writers such as CD, Jerrold, Eugène Sue and himself, thanks to whom "there was now a literature that made the people think for themselves . . . Despised Chartist as he was when he came from prison, Douglas Jerrold and Charles Dickens were the first to take him by the hand". CD was also mentioned by Mr J. Skelton (in proposing the toast to "our Parliamentary guests"), who expressed

To THE EDITOR OF THE *DAILY NEWS*, 21 JANUARY 1846

Text from the *Daily News*, 22 Jan 1846.

21st January, 1846

SIR,

Will you excuse my calling your attention to a variety of typographical errors in your first number? Several letters are standing on their heads, and several others seem to have gone out of town; while others, like people who are drawn for the militia, appear by deputy, and are sometimes very oddly represented. I have an interest in the subject, as I intend to be, | If you will allow me, |

YOUR CONSTANT READER.[1]

** We can assure our good-humoured correspondent, that we are quite conscious of the errors he does us the favour to point out so leniently. The very many inaccuracies and omissions in our first impression are attributable to the disadvantageous circumstances attending the production of a first number. They will not occur, we trust, in any other.—ED. DAILY NEWS.[2]

To THE REV. W. J. FOX, 21 JANUARY 1846

MS New York Public Library.

OFFICES OF THE DAILY NEWS | WHITEFRIARS
Twenty First January 1846

My Dear Fox

The boy is in waiting. I need not tell you how our Printer failed us,[3] last

---

heartfelt satisfaction in his "taking up the cudgels for the labouring classes" and "raising an interest for working people in circles where their cause had hitherto met with no advocates" (*The Times*, 22 Jan, and *Daily News*, 22 Jan—the latter a noticeably briefer report, with much less from Cooper's speech).

[4] Mary Victoria Cowden Clarke (1809–98; *DNB*), daughter of Vincent Novello, and a friend of the Lambs and Leigh Hunt; her complete *Concordance to Shakespeare* appeared in parts 1844–5, and in one volume in 1845, reviewed by Jerrold in *Punch* and by Forster in the *Examiner*. She wrote to Forster, 1 Dec 45, thanking him, and adding her congratulations on his playing of "the arduous character of Kitely" on 20 Sep; she had no idea when reading his "acute and just" dramatic criticisms that the writer could "so perfectly embody his own ideal of true Art" (MS Forster

Collection, V & A). According to her *Recollections of Writers*, 1878, and *My Long Life*, 1896, she did not meet CD until 1848: see next vol.

[1] "The letter is interesting since it is known that Mr. Charles Dickens wrote it, as well as the editorial rejoinder by which it was accentuated" (Joseph Hatton, *Journalistic London*, 1882, p. 50).

[2] The letter appeared in a prominent position above the leading articles.

[3] Paxton wrote to his wife on 21 Jan: "They had engaged an incompetent printer and all our efforts was nearly being floored at four O clock this morning and it was only by exertion almost superhuman that it was got out at all. I never passed four hours in such a state of suspence in my life." He had been "up all night and all day as busy as the best of them" (MS Devonshire Collections, quoted V. Markham, *Paxton and the Bachelor Duke*, p.

night. I hope for better things tonight; and am bent on a fight for it. If we can get a good paper tomorrow,[1] I believe we are as safe as such a thing can be.

Your leader, most excellent.[2] I made bold to take out Bright's[3] name, for reasons that I hinted at the other day,[4] and which I think have validity in them. He is unscrupulous and indiscreet. Cobden never so.

It didn't offend you?

Ever Faithfully
CHARLES DICKENS

W. J. Fox Esquire

---

173). Sir William Howard Russell recalled the general relief in the newspaper world: "At the sight of the outer sheet, hope at once lighted up the gloom of Printing House Square, the Strand, and Shoe Lane. The *Daily News*, No. 1, was ill-printed on bad paper, and 'badly made up,' and despite the brilliant picture from Italy by Dickens, was a fiasco. There were reports that there had been a Saturnalia among the printers. I am not sure that there were not social rejoicings that night in the editorial chambers which had been so long beset by dread" (J. B. Atkins, *The Life of Sir William Howard Russell*, 1911, I, 58). CD's friends were disappointed. Elizabeth Barrett thought the leading article weak, and "no broad principles laid down. A mere newspaper-support of the 'League'", but "enough advertisements to promise a long future" (*Letters of Robert Browning and Elizabeth Barrett*, I, 424–5). Macready found nothing "to stimulate curiosity or excite expectation" and "did not fancy" the "Travelling Letter", but sent CD "a few words by way of a starting cheer" (*Diaries*, II, 320). The paper cost 5*d*. and consisted of 8pp., including over 3pp. of advertisements, 1p. of railway advertisements. Accounts of Free Trade meetings and railway news were prominent, and three of the leading articles were on Free Trade—one by Fox and two by Danson. The first leading article was a statement of policy by CD (reprinted by Gerald Grubb, "Dickens and the 'Daily News': The Early Issues", *Nineteenth Century Fiction*, VI [1952], 239–41); the first of his "Travelling Letters. Written on the Road" ("Going through France" in *Pictures from Italy*) is his only other known contribution. Charles Mackay contributed an unsigned poem, "The Wants of the People", and George

Hogarth a general article on music. According to Paxton the first day's sales were "above 10,000 across the counter".

[1] Fox found "a very striking improvement" on 22 Jan, but still had many criticisms, both of the arrangement and the reporting—e.g. "*the one interesting thing* in the Duncombe meeting diluted and obscured". The "*Reading*" (i.e. press-correction) was "not so atrocious—still bad". The advertisements he thought "half sorted, half helter-skelter, in three places—etc. Does nobody *die, marry*, or *be born* in the *Daily News*" (Fox *to* Forster, 22 Jan; R. Garnett, *Life of W. J. Fox*, 1910, p. 281).

[2] According to a MS account of Fox's connection with the paper by Mrs Bridell Fox (R. Garnett, *Life of W. J. Fox*, pp. 278–82), he and Forster were the chief leader-writers, supplying four leaders a week; "Dickens' enlightened and enthusiastic views as to elevating the character of the press, as to the crying need of popular education, and for generally raising the status of the poor; and for reform of various social anomalies, were completely in sympathy with those long advocated by Mr. Fox". Fox's fame as a speaker for the Anti-Corn Law League—John Bright called him "*the* orator of the League"—and his considerable experience as a journalist, including work on the *Morning Chronicle*, made him an obvious and particularly fortunate choice. He continued as a leader-writer until 31 Oct 46.

[3] John Bright, MP (1811–89; *DNB*), orator and radical politician. MDGH omits the name.

[4] Fox's article immediately followed the statement of policy; Bright's name did not appear.

To THOMAS BEARD, [22 JANUARY 1846]

MS Dickens House. *Date:* endorsed by Beard "The Daily News just started";
clearly 22 Jan, the day of the second number.

Devonshire Terrace | Thursday

My Dear Beard

Tomorrow at 4.

I am delighted to say we have a Capital paper today. I sat at the Stone,[1] and
made it up with my own hands.

Ever Faithfully

CD.

To THE REV. W. J. FOX, [23 JANUARY 1846]

MS Office of the *Daily News* Ltd. *Date:* clearly refers to the leader of 23 Jan: see *fn.*

OFFICES OF THE DAILY NEWS | WHITEFRIARS
Friday Morning | 1 o'clock

My Dear Fox

So well as I can make out, (and you know how difficult it *is* to make anything
out at a Newspaper Office) Peel is decidedly playing false, and will creep into
small holes, & compensate, and be quite true to himself. Which I need not say is
being false to everybody else. I have therefore written in, at the point you mention, what one is pretty safe in writing about such a Customer; at the same time
reserving (like the good Vicar of Wakefield)[2] a means of coming out creditably in
any case.[3]

Ever Yours

CD

To JOHN LEECH, 23 JANUARY 1846

MS Benoliel Collection. *Date:* PM 23 Jan 46. *Address:* John Leech Esquire |
Brook Green | Hammersmith.

Devonshire Terrace | Friday

My Dear Leech

I am going (on account of not having enough to do!) to sit to Leslie as Bobadil.
Can you send me my legs—my red legs[4] I mean—in the course of tomorrow?

Ever Yours

CD.

[1] The slab on which pages of type were
imposed.

[2] In *The Vicar of Wakefield*, Ch. 12, the
Vicar says: " 'heaven grant they may both
be the better for it this day three months!'
... if the girls succeeded, then it was a
pious wish fulfilled; but if any thing unfortunate ensued, then it might be looked
upon as a prophecy".

[3] A leader of 23 Jan feared that Peel's
policy might be "vacillating, hesitating,

and weak; with here a bold suggestion of
advance, and there a timid provision for
retreat", but hoped for "a brighter future".
On 26 Jan Macready did not like "the
leading article in its abuse of Peel. I cannot
understand the sense of men who wish
persons to think and act in a certain way,
and when they do so abuse them for it"
(*Diaries*, II, 320).

[4] Perhaps borrowed by Leech for *The
Elder Brother*, in which he played Brissac

To THOMAS BEARD, [24 JANUARY 1846]

MS Dickens House. *Date:* clearly the Sat before Peel's speech on 27 Jan 46.
Address: Immediate | Thomas Beard Esquire | Morning Herald.

OFFICES OF THE DAILY NEWS | WHITEFRIARS
Saturday Afternoon

My Dear Beard

We intend—sub rosâ—having Peel's speech[1] taken in short turns[2] on Tuesday
night; published in a Second Edition of that Morning's Paper as soon as he is
down; and sent by Special Engines, to every town on every line in England.[3] I
suppose it would not be worth your while, as an old-Established Paper, to join in
this? But if there be anything our men and Engines can do for you, apart from
sharing, we shall be delighted to have them do it.

I want to express it also, to Paris. Would you feel disposed to do anything on
this score?

Faithfully Ever
CD.

To THE COUNTESS OF BLESSINGTON,
[?25 JANUARY 1846]*

MS Rosenbach Foundation. *Date:* almost certainly the Sunday before Peel's
speech on 27 Jan 46. *Address:* The | Countess of Blessington | Gore House |
Kensington.

OFFICES OF THE DAILY NEWS | WHITEFRIARS
Sunday Night

My Dear Lady Blessington

Have you heard anything tonight of an intention on the part of Peel to post-

---

[1] The eagerly awaited opening speech on
27 Jan, explaining the Government's
intention of altering the tariffs on grain so
as to produce a total repeal at the end of
three years.

[2] i.e. in relays; a common practice. No
doubt John Dickens organized this; he also
wrote to Peel asking if he would supply
copies of the documents used in his speech
(W. J. Carlton, "John Dickens, Journalist",
D, LIII [1957], 9).

[3] The speed of the *Daily News* in reporting Peel's speech was long remembered.
Charles J. Gratton, *The Gallery*, 1860, p.
102, recalls how Peel "only finished speaking between two and three o'clock in the
morning; and at five the 'Daily News' was
for sale in Bouverie Street, containing 'in
extenso' the prime-minister's speech ...
At eight o'clock it had reached Bristol and
Liverpool by special train, and at midday

it was in Scotland, and at ten the following
morning in Paris". John and Augustus
Dickens took copies of the edition to
Exeter in person, delivering them to
Thomas Latimer of the *Western Times*;
Latimer wrote in his paper on 31 Jan, "On
Wednesday morning, an express edition,
containing the whole of the speech of Sir
Robert Peel, arrived at our office soon after
seven o'clock. The express was conveyed
by Mr. Dickens, sen., the father of Boz,
who came down the line because he knows
the pace, and can go it. Mr. Dickens is a
gentleman of most enviable stamina. Time
seems to have made no impression on him
whatever. He had left London in the morning, travelled here by rail, thence to Plymouth
by chaise, and back again, and favouring
us with a call, announced his intention to
go back to London that night—and kept his
word. That is Boz's father" (*D*, LIII, 10).

pone his statement, or of any split with Graham?[1] I *cannot* find it. Forgive me
for troubling you at so late an hour (I have just come up from Richmond); and
if you have not gone to bed, send me one line.

Ever Dear Lady Blessington | Faithfully Yours

The Countess of Blessington   CHARLES DICKENS[2]

To EMILE DE LA RUE, 28 JANUARY 1846*

MS Berg Collection. *Address:* A Monsieur | Monsr. Emile De la Rue | Messrs.
De la Rue freres | Genoa | North Italy.

Devonshire Terrace | Twenty Eighth January 1846.

My Dear De la Rue. Don't consider this a letter. I am going to bespeak your
services in behalf of The Daily News. I will write to you, as the Inimitable Dick,
shortly.

The matter is simply this:—in case you should ever receive from our correspondent at Rome,[3] or in any part of Italy, a parcel addressed thus

Monsr. Emile De la Rue
Messrs. De la Rue freres
Genova.

Y. Z.

Will you, immediately address it Monsr. Mitchell[4] 18 Boulevard de Musée
Marseille (*preserving the Y. Z. in the corner*) and send it to him by the earliest
Steamboat? In case it should be a *Red*[5] parcel, it would be worth paying a handsome Sum of money to get the Steamer from Genoa to start before its proper
time, or to go to any expence (which would be immediately repaid of course), to
get it on instantly, as in that case the Pope would be dead, or something extraordinary would have happened. The Red cover announcing something of great
importance, always. You see I don't mind troubling you. For I know you don't
mind it yourself. Ever Yours CD.

P.S. I had a letter from Madame De la Rue this morning.[6] Give her my love, and
tell her it was *most welcome* to me, and that I shall write to her, very soon. I find,

---

[1] There were no grounds for such a
rumour; but if there had been any confirmation, CD would have been anxious to
hint at it in Monday's leading article.

[2] The writing of the letter is big and bold,
blotchy and untidy.

[3] Francis Sylvester Mahony, "Father
Prout" (1804–66; *DNB*): see Vol. I, p.
192n. He collected his letters as *Facts and
Figures from Italy. By Don Jeremy Savon-
arola, Benedictine Monk, Addressed during
the last two winters to Charles Dickens, Esq.*,
in 1847; CD supplied a brief note saying
that he had "engaged" him "to enter on
this correspondence". In his letter of 26

May 47 (N, II, 25) he speaks of how readily
he "fell in with" Mahony's "project of
writing these letters".

[4] Presumably the agent in Marseilles,
who would send the packet to Paris; de la
Rue thought of a more expeditious method,
and in the endorsement summarizing his
reply of 6 Feb proposed a special courier
to Paris in 96 hours for "red parcels" and
a courier to Marseilles in 40 hours for
others, at a cost of 1000 and 300 francs
respectively. For CD's reply, see *To* de la
Rue, 16 Feb.

[5] Underlined twice.

[6] Mme de la Rue evidently did not men-

after all this cramping, that I must put this paper into another half sheet. Your Newspapers will begin, tonight, to be dispatched regularly to Marseilles.[1] The Daily News is doing extremely well.[2] My regards to Thompson and his wife.[3] Tell Thompson I will write to him very shortly.

To EYRE EVANS CROWE,[4] [29 JANUARY 1846]*

MS Private. *Date:* PM 29 Jan 46. *Address:* E. E. Crowe Esquire | 5 Devonshire Place | Haverstock Hill | Hampstead.

OFFICES OF THE DAILY NEWS | WHITEFRIARS

My Dear Crowe

Welcome back! I hope you will nurse yourself at home, until you are all right and well.

It is easy to say to Lardner (if you desire to say so), that there is no vacancy on the Paper,[5] and so get rid of him pleasantly. I would not myself, have anything to do with him on any consideration whatever.

Always Faithfully Yours

E. E. Crowe Esquire   CD

To MISS FANNY KELLY, 29 JANUARY 1846

Text from N, I, 734.

Devonshire Terrace | Twenty-Ninth January 1846

My dear Miss Kelly,

I owe you Ten Guineas. Five for my own places—two for Mr. and Mrs. Powell—two for Sir Archer Croft[6]—and one for Mr. Leslie, who would not

tion that they had been expecting CD early in the month; but when the Thompsons dined with them on 6 Jan, "There was a place at the table for Dickens whom the de la Rues have been expecting with the greatest anxiety for some time—his favourite dish was prepared, his room got ready—but alas! for all their hopes and fears and tremblings!—20 passengers landed from the late boat but they numbered not the great man among them . . . he came not neither did he write" (Christiana's journal, MS Mrs Sowerby). Next day Christiana heard from Frederick Dickens "some facts connected with" CD —perhaps that his intended visit to the continent (see *To* Miss Coutts, 1 Dec 45) had not been necessary. Clearly the de la Rues had also had a December letter from CD which they had misunderstood.

[1] By 2 Feb Christiana had seen and enjoyed CD's "two graphic [Travelling] letters" in the de la Rue file of the *Daily News*: the second appeared 24 Jan.

[2] The initial sales had fallen to 5000 a day by 24 Jan, but rose to nearly 10,000 on 28 Jan.

[3] Christiana recorded in her journal that she "wrote to Mrs. Dickens" 21 Jan.

[4] Eyre Evans Crowe (1799–1868; *DNB*), historian; an old friend of Thackeray's. He was Paris correspondent of the *Morning Chronicle* until 1843, then leader-writer until his engagement by CD as foreign leader-writer in 1845; in Oct 46 he succeeded Forster as editor, continuing until 1851.

[5] Lardner must have applied for a post as a foreign correspondent; he and Mrs Heaviside had returned from America to London in June 1845, but were now living in Paris.

[6] Sir Archer Denman Croft (1801–65), 8th Bart; master of the Court of Queen's Bench from 1838.

receive his ticket free; owing you, he said, so much already for your splendid acting in old times.

I enclose you a cheque[1] for the amount, and return your "Jewels" with many thanks.

Always Faithfully Yours
[CHARLES DICKENS]

To EDWARD MOXON,[2] 29 JANUARY 1846*

Text from typescript, Huntington Library.

Devonshire Terrace, | Twenty-ninth January, 1846.

My Dear Sir,

Taking it for granted that you wished me to send the enclosed[3] to Mr Dilke,[4] I did so. He returned it with the letter I now send you.

Faithfully Yours,

Edward Moxon Esquire.   CHARLES DICKENS

To THE COUNTESS OF BLESSINGTON, [?30 JANUARY 1846]*

MS Benoliel Collection. *Date:* The only Saturday on which her paragraphs did not appear was 31 Jan. *Address:* The | Countess of Blessington | Gore House | Kensington.

Friday Night

My Dear Lady Blessington.

An unexpected botheration at the last moment, has occasioned the postponement of your Paragraphs tonight.

They are *very good indeed*,[5] I think. I wonder how you make so much of such a dull time.

It seems some man or other projected a paper under the title of The Daily News (an Evening paper) some Nine years ago; and asked Jerrold to write for it, which he agreed to do. The design was never pursued, or known, but he got a few Stamps, and he has a notion, I conceive, that he may use them to advantage now, by getting us to buy him off.[6] He reckons, however, without his host—as

---

[1] CD paid 10 guineas (for himself and his guests at *The Elder Brother*) on 31 Jan (Account-book, MS Messrs Coutts). The total sum raised for Miss Kelly was enough to pay off her most pressing creditors (Basil Francis, *Fanny Kelly of Drury Lane*, 1950, p. 183).

[2] Edward Moxon (1801–58; *DNB*), publisher: see Vol. II, p. 64*n*.

[3] Not identified; possibly connected with the Hood Fund.

[4] Charles Wentworth Dilke (1789–1864;

DNB), editor of the *Athenæum* 1830–46: see Vol. I, p. 127*n*.

[5] Among the "On Dits" appearing on Mon 2 Feb were rumours of impending resignations in the royal household, and a denial of the report of Lord Arthur Lennox's resignation, since he could not afford it.

[6] Frederick Marriott, 335 Strand, editor of cheap periodicals, advertised his *Daily News* to appear "in a few days" at 2½d, "conducted by Mr. Douglas Jerrold", in the *Morning Chronicle*, 23 Jan–4 Feb.

we shall certainly put him to some small expence instead, & into Chancery besides.

I write with one eye open, and the other quivering. But with all my Eyes and heart, I am ever My Dear Lady Blessington

Faithfully Yours

CHARLES DICKENS

I have not forgotten your agreement. I will bring it to you myself. It is drawn, & the Counterpart also.

To MESSRS BRADBURY & EVANS, 30 JANUARY 1846

MS Comtesse de Suzannet.

Devonshire Terrace

Friday Morning | Thirtieth January 1846.

My Dear Bradbury and Evans.

I cut the main subject of our conversation last night as short as possible, because I always desire to restrain myself from acting on impulse in any such case.

I quite agree with you in the necessity of the Paper being made perfect, if possible, and in the expediency of finding out where it can be improved.[1] On the other hand, I doubt your counsellors in general, very much indeed. I examine and test anyone who counsels me, very closely; and when it is such a man as Mr. Tooke[2] (of whom I spoke to you last night), I discard *his* advice altogether. But I have already told Mr. Paxton, and I have already warned you, that very sensible and far-seeing gentlemen well accustomed to newspapers regard the Railway policy of the D.N. as being too one-sided, and as threatening to taint it. And I think if you could get beyond deposit men, and provisional directors, and committee men, and the like, you would find this out. I have very little doubt if you do not, that the Times[3] will discover it for you.

This, however, is not the point of my letter.

---

[1] On 27 Jan Fox thought "the getting up, and general appearance and arrangement of the paper" was "a triumph of Forster's power" and took some credit for his own criticisms of 22 Jan (R. Garnett, *Life of W.J. Fox*, p. 282; note undated, but clearly Tues in the second week of the paper's appearance).

[2] Of the two brothers, Thomas and William Tooke, Thomas (1774–1858; *DNB*), the economist, free-trader, and writer on the currency, seems the more likely "counsellor" for Bradbury & Evans. But CD's animus might suggest William (1777–1863; *DNB*), solicitor and treasurer of the Royal Literary Fund: according to Forster he was "remarkable and distinguished for nothing that I am aware of", and he justified the severity of his review of Tooke's *Charles Churchill* (*Edinburgh Review*, Jan 45) by its introduction, into a literary work, of political attacks on Whigs, dissenters, and the spread of useful knowledge (Forster *to* Napier, 18 Sep 44, MS BM).

[3] In 1845–6 *The Times* "waged battle against railway monopolists and sharepushers" (*History of the Times, 1841–1884*, p. 14). *Mephystopheles*, 31 Jan, had a caricature indicating the attitude of other papers: "The Jackdaw Disguised, and the Peacocks. Dedicated to Charles Dickens, Esq.", showing "Great Demand for the Daily News—ance". Macready in his diary for 30 Jan said he found *The Times* manifestly so superior that he was "*in despair* for the result of the *Daily News*". (*Diaries*, II, 320)

You know that I recommended Mr. Powell to you, as the man, of all others in London, best qualified to act as one of the Sub Editors of an enterprising Paper. You know that I was very anxious to secure him, and considered it a very great point when he was engaged, and have always spoken of him with great confidence.

One week after the starting of the Paper, you come to me, and give me to understand, on certain nameless authority (which you call "gatherings") that he is quite unfit for the place he holds![1] I wish to know from whom you learn this: and I consider myself justified in putting you upon your honor to withhold from me the name of no person with whom you have taken counsel on this subject.

When I tell you, distinctly, that I shall leave the Paper immediately, if you do not give me this information, I think it but fair to add that it is extremely probable I shall leave it when you have done so. For it would be natural in any man, and is especially so in one in my position, to consider this, disrespectful, and quite unendurable. I am thoroughly disgusted, and shall act accordingly.

Faithfully Yours

Messrs. Bradbury & Evans   CHARLES DICKENS

To JOHN FORSTER, [30 JANUARY 1846]

Extract in *F*, v, i, 387. *Date:* 30 Jan according to Forster. *From* Office of the *Daily News*.

I want a long talk with you. I was obliged to come down here in a hurry to give out a travelling letter[2] I meant to have given out last night, and could not call upon you. Will you dine with us to-morrow at six sharp?[3] I have been revolving plans in my mind this morning for quitting the paper and going abroad again to write a new book in shilling numbers. Shall we go to Rochester to-morrow week (my birthday) if the weather be, as it surely must be, better?

To GIUSEPPE MAZZINI,[4] [?LATE JANUARY 1846]

Mention in *Daily News*, 16 Feb 46. *Date:* some days before Mazzini's account of 3 Feb: see *fn*.

A letter in Italian enclosing two sovereigns.[5]

---

[1] John Hill Powell did not leave the *Daily News* until after CD's resignation.

[2] The third "Travelling Letter" appeared on 31 Jan.

[3] Forster is not named among the guests at CD's dinner party on 31 Jan for the Hutchinsons: see *To* Lady Blessington, 2 Mar 46, *fn*.

[4] Giuseppe Mazzini (1805–72), Italian patriot and revolutionary; in 1831 founded the association of Young Italy to promote a united republic; lived in London 1836–48, in constant correspondence with his supporters on the continent. Living in poverty with other political exiles, he was much helped by his friendship with the Carlyles. Carlyle wrote in his journal in 1849, "Mazzini came much about us here for many years, patronised by my wife; to me very wearisome, with his incoherent Jacobinisms ... in spite of all my love and regard for him; a beautiful little man, full

To THOMAS BEARD, [1 FEBRUARY 1846]

MS Dickens House. *Date:* clearly the Sunday before *To* Walter, 3 Feb. *Address:*
Delivery | Thomas Beard Esquire | Morning Herald Office | Shoe Lane.

D.N. Office | Sunday Night

My Dear Beard.

I send you back Mr. Walter's letter, and have ordered £100 to be forwarded
to him immediately. The Calcutta letters[1] I have retained for the edification of
Crowe and Costello.[2]

Powell will come over to you, and arrange for the West Riding Election[3]
tomorrow.

He insists on my telling you that the Express[4] was never once stopped for the
D.N.; and that the only stoppages were when they took in water, & changed
engines. I may as well say to you and Mr. Baldwin (but I didn't mention the
probability to Mr. Walter that night) that by our influence at Birkenhead we
detained the Irish Mail *one hour*.

The Express has done us a World of Good. We are going ahead famously.

Ever Faithfully & truly

CD

---

of sensibilities . . . clear intelligence, and
noble virtues" (J. A. Froude, *Carlyle's Life
in London*, 1884, I, 454).

[5] CD was one of the victims of an Italian
impostor who had been begging in Mazzini's
name. Mazzini wrote a full account of the
incident to his mother on 3 Feb: a man had
called at Devonshire Terrace with a copy
of Mazzini's pamphlet, *Italy, Austria and
the Pope*, and a letter signed with his name
saying that he had been reduced to poverty
by his struggle for the emancipation of his
country and appealing for money; CD was
amazed but sent £2. He told the story to
his friends and one of them, a lady who
knew Mazzini well (probably Mrs Milner
Gibson), was able to demonstrate the im-
posture by showing CD a sample of his
hand—there had been no attempt to forge
it in the begging letter (*Edizione Nazionale
degli Scritti di Giuseppe Mazzini*, XXVIII,
284–5). A letter from Mazzini disowning
the man and his application was published
in the *Daily News*, 12 Feb, and on 13 Feb
he was arrested while trying to get money
from Joseph Hume, MP, and brought up
that day at Marylebone Police Court, when
his name was given as Dominic Scurione;
it was said in court that several persons had
succeeded in getting money in Mazzini's

name since the notoriety he had acquired
by his "exposure of the letter-opening practice". The case continued on 14 Feb when
CD, Hume and Mazzini gave evidence;
Scurione was remanded for a further week
and then committed for trial (*Daily News*,
14 Feb, 16 Feb). Mazzini told his mother
in a letter of 18 Feb (*op. cit.*, p. 295) that he
recognized Scurione as a man who had
previously tried to get from him a letter of
introduction to an English acquaintance—
fortunately refused—and that he suspected
him to be merely the tool of a so-called
"Count Bertola"; he hoped this might be
proved during the remand, but in the event
Scurione alone was charged.

[1] Walter's Calcutta letters were not used.

[2] Foreign   leader-writer   and   foreign
editor.

[3] The by-election, on 4 Feb, was reported
on Thurs 5 Feb, "by express"; Lord Morpeth was returned.

[4] See *To* Beard, 24 Jan 46 and *fn*. The
emphasis on the special express seemed to
Macready excessive: "*three columns* of
citations from country papers about the
Special Express; yesterday two and a half
columns!! How can this interest its readers?
The persons employed do not understand
their business" (3 Feb; *Diaries*, II, 321).

To [THOMAS HODGSKIN], [2 FEBRUARY 1846]†

MS Walter T. Spencer. *Date:* the day of the leader on Cobden's letter: see *fn.* *Address:* the subscription "— Hodgkin Esquire"[1] must be an error for Thomas Hodgskin.

Devonshire Terrace | Monday Morning

My Dear Sir

I am extremely sorry to hear from Mr. Danson that you appeared hurt by his coming to you last night on the subject of the leader you were kind enough to offer me.[2]

The manner of his coming is simply this—[a]I found he had written a Leader[3] on a main passage in Mr. Cobden's letter to the Tenant Farmers, and that it seemed to run counter to yours.[a][4] As I am not learned in the minute details of such a question, [b]I begged him to read your leader—compare it with his own— and talk the matter over with you.[b] Surely it is essential before writing on such subjects that you should be fully possessed of this gentleman's views; and as I have suggested some other occupation for him during the whole of this week, I considered it still more desirable that you should have this discussion—knowing that the field would be immediately open to you, if you thought fit to enter on it.

Your experience of me has been very brief, but I have been unfortunate if I have not been able generally to express to you the sincere desire I have to render an occupation which is sufficiently irksome in itself, as pleasant and agreeable as possible to every gentleman concerned; and to shew to each the delicate respect and consideration which I truly feel. I am not without a hope that on a review of this incident, you will feel that you acted—naturally, I have no doubt, but hastily, and without quite understanding what was intended on my part.

I am Dear Sir | Faithfully Yours

— Hodgkin Esquire.

CHARLES DICKENS

To THOMAS BEARD, 2 FEBRUARY 1846

MS Dickens House. *Address:* Thomas Beard Esquire | "Morning Herald".

OFFICES OF THE DAILY NEWS | WHITEFRIARS
Monday Afternoon | Second February | 1846

My Dear Beard

We contemplate expressing the whole Corn Law Debate down the Great

---

[1] CD's error in spelling Hodgskin's surname an easy one under stress; his forgetting the first name perhaps surprising.

[2] Hodgskin, as an experienced journalist, might well resent Danson's interference, and perhaps shared Fox's low opinion of him, as "a stupid man of figures and statistics" (R. Garnett, *Life of W. J. Fox,* p. 283).

[3] Danson wrote "about 4 articles a week" (*D,* LXVIII, p. 156).

aa; bb Given in N, I, 733; letter otherwise unpublished.

[4] Cobden's letter appeared in the *Daily News* of 31 Jan; it was commented on in a leader on Mon 2 Feb.

Northern Railways—and publishing that Edition at 4 every morning.[1] This is, of course, a Dead Secret. Would you like to join?

Thomas Beard Esquire

Ever Heartily Yours
CHARLES DICKENS

To THE COUNTESS OF BLESSINGTON, 3 FEBRUARY [1846]*

MS National Library of Scotland. *Date:* Tues was 3 Feb in 1846; reference to "the Paper" confirms.

Devonshire Terrace | Tuesday Third February

My Dear Lady Blessington

I shall be delighted to dine with you tomorrow, and to wish Count D'Orsay many happy returns of his Birthday.

The Market Prices are always in the Paper, you will find, I think. One day they were omitted by accident; but only once.[2]

Ever My Dear Lady Blessington | Faithfully Yours

The | Countess of Blessington.   CHARLES DICKENS

To J. WALTER,[3] 3 FEBRUARY 1846

Extract in American Art Association catalogue, Nov 1923; *MS* 1 p.; dated Office of the Daily News, Whitefriars, 3 Feb 46.

The cash you require was remitted yesterday. £200. The proprietors of the "Daily News" had already contemplated remunerating you in the way you suggest; the amount shall be arranged with Mr. Baldwin, which shall be done as soon as he is well enough to entertain the matter.

To W. H. WILLS, [3 FEBRUARY 1846]

MS New York Public Library. *Date:* Tues 3 Feb 46, since endorsed by Wills "4/2/46".

Tuesday Night

My Dear Mr. Wills.

I dine out tomorrow (Wednesday) and next day (Thursday)[4] and shall not be here, either evening, until rather late. Will you have the goodness to let the Sub Editors know this; and as I shall not wish to be detained here unnecessarily, to ask them to have ready for me anything (*if* anything) requiring my attention.

---

[1] The early edition was sent by express during the next fortnight, and numerous tributes to this expeditiousness were quoted in the *Daily News* of 16 Feb.

[2] The market prices were not omitted on any date before 3 Feb in any edn we have seen.

[3] Unidentified; probably a freelance journalist paid by both the *Daily News* and the *Morning Herald*.

[4] CD went to Macready's for the reading of White's play (see *To* White, 24 Feb 46, *fn*) and stayed on for dinner (*Diaries*, II, 321).

You may tell them at the same time, if you please, that I shall not be here, generally, on Sunday Nights; and that I shall always wish to let them know of the general arrangements for Sunday Nights, on Fridays before I go away.

Faithfully Yours always

W. H. Wills Esquire   CHARLES DICKENS

To OCTAVIAN BLEWITT, 4 FEBRUARY 1846*

MS Professor K. J. Fielding.

Devonshire Terrace | February Fourth 1846

My Dear Sir

I am much obliged to you for reminding me of the necessity of attending the next meeting.[1] I had made a memorandum of it, in pursuance of your former kind reminder.

Always My Dear Sir | Faithfully Yours

Octavian Blewitt Esquire   CHARLES DICKENS

To J. B. BUCKSTONE,[2] [?EARLY FEBRUARY 1846]

Mention in *To* Macready, ?10 Feb 46. *Date:* in time for Buckstone to receive and reply by 10 Feb.

Acknowledging his note.

To LORD JOHN RUSSELL, 5 FEBRUARY 1846

Mention in James Tregaskis catalogue No. 558 (1904); *MS* 1 p.; dated Devonshire Terrace, 5 Feb 46.

Making an appointment to call in Chesham Place.[3]

---

[1] The Annual General Meeting of the Literary Fund was held on 11 Mar 46; CD was a member of the General Committee 1845–50.

[2] John Baldwin Buckstone (1802–79; *DNB*): see Vol. I, p. 42*n*. Probably the outstanding comic actor of his generation, and later a famous actor-manager at the Haymarket. CD in 1855 spoke of having been "enchanted" by his "comicalities" for 25 years (*Speeches*, ed. K. J. Fielding, pp. 186–7). In early 46 he was playing Tilly Slowboy in the *Cricket* at the Haymarket. Was Chairman and Treasurer of the General Theatrical Fund, of which CD

was one of the Trustees (see Vol. III, p. 467 and *n*); re-elected at a meeting of subscribers on 25 Feb when arrangements were also made for the first Anniversary Festival on 6 Apr: see *To* Wills, 22 Apr 46, *fn*.

[3] Perhaps Russell had shown interest in CD's article on Ragged Schools in the *Daily News* of 4 Feb: see *To* Young, 12 Feb, *fn*, and *To* Kay-Shuttleworth, 28 Mar and *fn*. Or (if CD was proposing an appointment for the following week) he might have wished to tell Russell in advance of his intended resignation as editor.

To THOMAS BEARD, [5 FEBRUARY 1846]

MS Dickens House. *Date:* clearly 5 Feb: see *fn. Address: Deliver* | Thomas Beard
Esquire | Morning Herald Office | Shoe Lane.

OFFICES OF THE DAILY NEWS | WHITEFRIARS
Thursday Night

My Dear Beard

Cheer up the Governor! Who cares!—I don't.

Think of OUR[1] having a Bombay Times from our Alexandrian agent[2]—
posted at Kennington Cross too! (Something wrong. Black work Sir!) And *we*
have lent it to *you* tonight.

Ha ha ha! Ha ha ha!

Faithfully Ever
CD.

To THOMAS BEARD, [?12 JANUARY–6 FEBRUARY 1846]

MS Dickens House. *Date:* after the move to Whitefriars, and probably not later
than Friday 6 Feb (the last working day before CD resigned). *Address: Wait* |
Thomas Beard Esquire | Morning Herald Office.

Whitefriars

My Dear Beard

I am very sorry to find you gone. I had the Leader-Writing Men here, and
cod. not get rid of them. Shall I come round to you?

Faithfully Ever
CD

To MESSRS BRADBURY & EVANS, 6 FEBRUARY 1846*

MS The Proprietors of *Punch.*

Devonshire Terrace | Sixth February 1846

Dear Sirs

Mr. Beard has been with me this morning, to make an appointment for Mr.
Baldwin to come here on Monday at One. When I think it most desirable that
Mr. Forster should meet him; you taking counsel with Mr. Forster in the mean-
time.

Mr. Baldwin will desire to be put in communication, with whomsoever manages the accounts (I would certainly suggest Mr. Evans) that they may be examined and settled once a month. He also suggests that the Herald and Daily News
should support each other in all possible *retrenchments*,[3] and in conducting their

---

[1] Large ornate capitals.
[2] The *Daily News* of 6 Feb refers to a
summary of Bombay news in the previous
day's issue as having been taken from *The
Times,* because the copy of the *Bombay*

Times Extraordinary of 2 Jan sent by the
Daily News's Alexandrian correspondent
had failed to arrive till the afternoon.
[3] Underlined twice.

papers with less expence and greater chance of profits.[1] From what he says, there would appear to be no doubt that the Chronicle will go altogether, if the Daily News can wear out this bad time, and improve its mechanism. It is certain that they are playing a fast-losing game—that there will be a great loss (instead of gain) on the year's accounts—and that Easthope neither can nor will support it for six months as a losing paper.[2]

I am confidentially informed that the Herald is also losing at this time.

I think Mr. Baldwin's idea of the two papers supporting each other in all possible retrenchment, a very sound and sensible one, and fraught with much advantage.

Please to send this letter on to Mr. Forster when you have read it. I shall see him today, but I should like him to know exactly what it contains.

Faithfully Yours
CHARLES DICKENS

P.S. I have looked over your letter a second time, since writing the above. I do not understand what you mean by "when you are to date from", or what it refers to.[3]

To THE REV. W. J. FOX, [6 FEBRUARY 1846]

Text from typescript, Huntington Library. *Date:* clearly Fri 6 Feb, since the sonnet and Fox's leader appeared in the *Daily News* 7 Feb. Typescript reads "Friday 1850", clearly in error.

Devonshire Terrace, | Friday
My Dear Fox.

I have given out the Sonnet,[4] for insertion.

If you *can*, in your tonight's leader, introduce any reference to Lord Morpeth's Election, I think it may be desirable.[5] Don't you?

We will meet on Monday as usual. May I book you beforehand, for Monday night? It falls out that we shall have especial need of you then.

I am saving your postponed Leader for Monday morning.[6]

Ever Yours
CHARLES DICKENS

[1] The circulation of the *Daily News* was falling during Feb and Mar, and both papers suffered from the falling off of railway advertising; one of the first "retrenchments" was the reduction of reporters' salaries from 7 guineas to 5 guineas.

[2] The *Morning Chronicle* was running at a loss for some time before 1848 when Easthope sold it (Fox Bourne, *English Newspapers*, II, 151–2).

[3] Possibly CD's salary: see *To* Forster, ?17–20 Apr 46, *fn.*

[4] "M. Michelet", unsigned, attacking the view that the wife is the husband's property and therefore must remain faithful.

[5] A paragraph on Lord Morpeth's elec-

tion (announced in the issue of Thurs 5 Feb) was included in a leader on the Ten Hours Bill ("diminished hours" being one of "many blessings, the road to which lies through Corn-Law repeal"); Morpeth was called "a statesman whose pure and lofty-mindedness has never been surpassed", and Yorkshire was congratulated on redeeming its "temporary apostacy".

[6] Probably the leader of 9 Feb on that night's debate, since it could have been written some days earlier, except for a reference to a meeting on Saturday which could have been inserted before it went to press.

To THOMAS HODGSKIN or J. H. POWELL,
[6 FEBRUARY 1846]

Mention in John Anderson Jr catalogue No. 1423; *MS* 1 p.; dated Devonshire Terrace, Friday—clearly 6 Feb: see *fn*. *Address:* since catalogue gives as to Hodgskin or Powell, almost certainly belonging with envelope (Dickens Exhibition, New Dudley Gallery, 1908): Immediate | Thomas Hodgskin Esquire, or J. H. Powell Esquire, | Daily News.

Enclosing a literary notice and a squib.[1]

To THE COUNTESS OF BLESSINGTON,
[9 FEBRUARY 1846]*

MS Benoliel Collection. *Date*: clearly 9 Feb after return from Rochester.

Devonshire Terrace | Monday Night

My Dear Lady Blessington.

I found the Jar (what a noble Jar it is!) of Ginger, awaiting me tonight on my return to town. I have been breathing fresh air on the top of Rochester Castle.[2] It is very kind of you to have remembered it. Thank you!

The Paragraph about Prince Albert is very curious and quite new to me—but I am afraid to insert it. You have no idea how many people would take offence at it, if it appeared in a New Paper.

The Paragraph about Prince Napoleon[3] was objected to (I meant to have told you this, the other day) by Crowe. He quite concurred in the spirit of it, but thought it unwise, with reference to our French Relations, to put it in. The subject of it coming distinctly within his department, I acquiesced.

Ever Believe me | Faithfully Yours

The Countess of Blessington   CHARLES DICKENS

---

[1] The "squib" (referred to in *To* Lord Nugent, ?12 Feb) must be the anti-Corn Law mock report, "Special Commission, Indictment of Robert Peel, John Russell, and John Tyrell . . . for the murder of Mrs. Food Monopoly Price", which appeared in the *Daily News*, Sat 7 Feb. This issue contained no literary notice; on Sat 14 Feb, there was no "squib", but a long and very favourable review of Thackeray's *Notes on a Journey from Cornhill to Cairo*, for which perhaps there was no room on 7 Feb.

[2] See *To* Forster, ?30 Jan. "To Rochester accordingly we had gone, he and Mrs. Dickens and her sister, with Maclise and Jerrold and myself; going over the old Castle, Watts's Charity, and Chatham fortifications on the Saturday, passing Sunday in Cobham church and Cobham

park; having our quarters both days at the Bull inn" (F, v, i, 387). Forster's memory was at fault in including Maclise: see *To* de la Rue, 16 Feb 46.

[3] Probably a comment on the French government's refusal to allow Louis Napoleon to visit his dying father in Florence, reported in the English papers on 29 Jan; on 12 Feb the *Morning Post* congratulated him on his honourable refusal to accept the government's terms and sue for his liberty. D'Orsay made great efforts to win over public opinion for him in the summer of 1846, when Forster inserted an article in the *Daily News* that D'Orsay said would give the Prince "great pleasure" (Madden, *Literary Life and Correspondence of the Countess of Blessington*, II, 418–19, 470).

To JOHN FORSTER, [9 FEBRUARY 1846]

Extract in F, v, i, 387. *Date:* "in the night of Monday, 9 February" according to Forster.

Written when he was tired to death and quite worn out *to say that he had just resigned his editorial functions.*[1]

To W. C. MACREADY, [?10 FEBRUARY 1846]*

MS Morgan Library. *Date:* Handwriting points to a date between Oct 45 and Apr 46; the only record of a call by Buckstone in Macready's *Diaries* at this period is Sat 14 Feb 46—therefore probably the previous Tues.

Devonshire Terrace | Tuesday Morning

My Dear Macready.

I have received the enclosed note from Buckstone—having reference to the note I wrote to him (and described to you)[2] in acknowledgment of his first communication.[3] I can't come to Clarence Terrace at the time he mentions—being busy—but I should like to know at your leisure what passed between you.

Always affectionately Yours

W. C. Macready Esquire

CD

---

[1] Forster adds: "I had not been unprepared", and at this point quotes the letter to him of 30 Jan, adding, "If long continuance with the paper was not likely, the earliest possible departure from it was desirable". Perhaps the final decision had been affected by something that occurred at the meeting arranged by *To* Bradbury & Evans, 6 Feb; but it is possible that they did not agree to the meeting and that CD stayed on at Rochester, as *To* Lady Blessington, ?9 Feb, suggests; in either case there was probably much discussion between CD and Forster over the week-end. Macready reports a call from Forster on the night of 9 Feb, "in very low spirits about *the Paper*, and said he 'had always felt as I did about it—it was precipitate; that no one could be a worse editor than Dickens,' etc! Alas!" On 12 Feb Forster told Macready that CD "had abdicated the editorship", that he had succeeded him as editor and looked forward to improving the paper. "He seemed elated with his position"; but Macready doubted his ability (*Diaries*, II, 321–2). The grounds for CD's dissatisfaction with Bradbury & Evans are suggested by *To* de la Rue, 16 Feb 46, and *To* Evans, 26 Feb 46. W. J. Fox in an undated letter (soon after 2 May 46) said, "Dickens broke down in the mechanical business", though he thought better of his "morale" as an editor than Forster's (R. Garnett, *Life of W. J. Fox*, p. 283).

[2] Possibly when they met on 6 Feb. CD might well act as intermediary, since he seems to have known Buckstone better than Macready, who at their only recorded previous meeting "thought him a coxcomb" (*Diaries*, I, 404).

[3] Buckstone called on Macready to ask for his "advocacy in his project of building a new theatre"; Macready says, "He promised me that women of the town should not be admitted *as such*, and I promised to give him any assistance in my power" (*Diaries*, II, 323). References in the *Theatrical Journal* this year, including a leading article on 6 June 46, show that the theatre was to be in Leicester Square, but that by Dec the plan had been abandoned.

To J. T. DANSON, [11 FEBRUARY 1846]

MS Lieut.-Col. J. H. Danson. *Date:* Accompanying envelope is postmarked 12
Feb 46 (Thurs). *Address:* J. T. Danson Esquire | 8 Shaftesbury Crescent | Eccleston
Square.

D.N. Office[1] | Wednesday Night.

My Dear Sir
    I should be glad to have your opinion of the "figure" part of the enclosed
letter.[2]

[CHARLES DICKENS]

To LORD NUGENT, [12 FEBRUARY 1846]*

MS Miss Elena Klasky. *Date:* the first Thursday after the insertion of the "squib"
on 7 Feb: see *To* Hodgskin or Powell, ?6 Feb and *fn*.

Devonshire Terrace | Thursday Morning

My dear Lord Nugent. If you will take potluck with me tomorrow at 6, I shall be
delighted to see you. Forgive me for this tardy answer to your note.
    I was delighted with the Squib—and let it off, instanter, (as you may have seen)
in the Daily News.

Ever Faithfully Yours
The Lord Nugent   CHARLES DICKENS

To THE COUNTESS OF BLESSINGTON, 12 FEBRUARY 1846

Mention in S. F. Henkels catalogue No. 1259; dated Devonshire Terrace, 12 Feb
46.[3]

To GEORGE CRUIKSHANK, 12 FEBRUARY 1846

MS New York Public Library.

Devonshire Terrace | Thursday Twelfth February | 1846

My Dear George. I am really ashamed to say, that Wills gave me your letter
punctually; but that in the hurry of many engagements I quite forgot it. I now
enclose a cheque in Miss White's favor, for Ten Pounds.[4]
    Will you dine here next Tuesday as ever comes, at Half Past Six? Answer this!
Ever Heartily Yours
CHARLES DICKENS

---

[1] If this letter and *To* Hazlitt, ?12 Feb
46, are correctly dated, CD continued to
attend the office in the week following his
resignation—which would be the natural
procedure, especially as Forster was to
succeed him.

[2] No enclosure survives; the signature
has been cut off.
[3] Almost certainly telling her that he had
resigned and that Forster was now editor.
[4] The payment appears in CD's account-
book (MS Messrs Coutts) on 12 Feb.

To WILLIAM GRANET, [?12 FEBRUARY 1846]

Mention in *To* de la Rue, 16 Feb 46. *Date:* perhaps including an invitation to dinner, and so on same date as *To* Cruikshank, 12 Feb.

To CHARLES MANBY,[1] 12 FEBRUARY 1846

Mention in Sotheran's catalogue, No. 822 (1931); *MS* 2 pp.; dated Devonshire Terrace, 12 Feb 46.

Directing that his scientific reports should be forwarded to Mr Forster at the Daily News.

To MR SHUM,[2] 12 FEBRUARY 1846*

MS Private.

1 Devonshire Terrace | York Gate Regents Park
Thursday Twelfth February | 1846.

Mr. Charles Dickens presents his compliments to Mr. Shum, and begs to express his regret at having been prevented, by absence from town, from attending the interesting Meeting[3] of last night.

To G. F. YOUNG,[4] 12 FEBRUARY 1846*

MS Mr Noel C. Peyrouton.

1 Devonshire Terrace | York Gate Regents Park.
Twelfth February 1846.

Dear Sir
I assure you I shall be very happy to confer with you at any time you may appoint, in your own neighbourhood, on the subject of your letter; and to have personal knowledge of the condition of that district. I could devote any Morning next week that may suit you, to this purpose. You write to me so freely, that I desire to respond in the very plainest and readiest spirit.

[1] Charles Manby (1804–84; *DNB*), Secretary to the Institute of Civil Engineers.
[2] Possibly Robert Shum, solicitor, of 3 King's Rd, Bedford Row.
[3] Not identified.
[4] George Frederick Young (1791–1870), MP for Tynemouth 1832–7; Chairman of Shipowners' Society and of New Zealand Co.; lived at 15 Church Row, Limehouse, where the "Colloquials", including Browning and Chris Dowson, Jr, used to meet— Frederick Dickens may have known him through his friendship with Dowson: see *To* Frederick Dickens, ?27 June 43; Vol. III, p. 516*n*. His correspondence with Lord Stanley was printed in the *Daily News*, 19 May 46.

I may mention that since the publication of my letter in the Daily News,[1] I have had an opportunity (I do not feel myself at liberty to explain it in detail) of turning the information I possess or can acquire, on the subject of Crime and Ignorance among the Poor, to the very best account; and that I have strong hope of striking a great blow with it within a few months.[2]

I leave the time of our appointment to you, if you please. And I take it for granted that you are friendly to the abandonment of all sectarian distinctions in Schools,[3] and the establishment in them of a common ground on which all kinds of christians may meet and be enlightened.[4]

Dear Sir | Faithfully Yours

George Frederick Young Esquire   CHARLES DICKENS

To WILLIAM HAZLITT, [?12 FEBRUARY 1846]

Text from N, I, 734. *Date:* The only extended notice of the French plays was on 12 Feb.

Thursday afternoon

My Dear Sir,

I saw the notice of the French Play this morning[5] and immediately perceived that the Readers had cut and maimed you. All I know about these gentlemen is, that there are plenty of them, and that they are well paid—unless I add of them that they are the very worst I ever had anything to do with in my life. I have laid in a chaldron or two of coals, and will haul *your* reader over them this evening.

I will communicate with you in reference to the other matter as soon as I have a minute's leisure.

My dear Sir, | Faithfully yours
[CHARLES DICKENS]

---

[1] "Crime and Education", on 4 Feb (reprinted in *Miscellaneous Papers*, pp. 17–21), in which CD emphasized the need for Ragged Schools "as a first step in the reformation" of the child offenders whom he had often seen in prisons, "enough to break the heart and hope of any man". His immediate occasion was a public lecture on Ragged Schools on 3 Feb by the Rev. Robert Ainslie, fully reported in the same issue. CD referred his readers to this report for facts about Ragged Schools, and urged them to visit such schools themselves; he described his own visit to the Field Lane Ragged School in Sep 43, rather more vividly than in his account written to Miss Coutts at the time (see Vol. III, pp. 562–4 and *ns*), and mentioned his fruitless

"endeavour to bring these Institutions under the notice of the Government".

[2] Probably his scheme for a Model Ragged School: see *To Kay-Shuttleworth, 28 Mar 46* and *fn*. As Chairman of the local Board of Guardians, Young would have been interested in the subject.

[3] CD thought highly of the Pauper School at Limehouse: see *To Miss Coutts, 26 May 46*.

[4] CD's one objection to the teaching in the Ragged Schools was its "not being sufficiently secular, and as presenting too many religious mysteries and difficulties" (*Daily News*, 4 Feb).

[5] *Marie, ou la Perle de Savoie*, at the St James's, in which Mme Albert made her last appearance (*Daily News*, 12 Feb).

To W. C. MACREADY, 15 FEBRUARY 1846*

MS Morgan Library.

Devonshire Terrace | Sunday Fifteenth February | 1846
My Dear Macready.

I want to see Jeffrey, and should very much like to run down to Edinburgh with you—remain there a couple of days—and then return solus. I wish you would tell me what your plans for starting, are,[1]—that I may revolve the feasibilities.

Did you see my Hymn for the Wiltshire Labourers, yesterday?[2] I dined at Lord John Russell's yesterday, and found it had made some impression.

Affecy. always
CD.

To EMILE DE LA RUE, 16 FEBRUARY 1846*

MS Berg Collection. *Address:* A Monsieur | M. Emile De la Rue | Messrs. De la Rue freres | Genoa | North Italy.

Devonshire Terrace, London | Sixteenth February 1846.
My Dear De la Rue.

Your business-like letter is perfectly plain and correct in all particulars. In the case of a Red Parcel, send straight to Paris if you think it best. But it is extremely probable that no Parcel at all may ever come to you. In the ordinary case, the correspondent sends his letters by Post; and nothing may happen to render an Express necessary. Still, I thought it best to take the precaution, as the Daily News *might* perhaps, through that means, make a hit. William[3] mentioned to me about your Subscription. Now, the plain matter of fact, is, that you will just button up that pocket of yours, and pay no Subscription at all. Whenever a Banking House (as is frequently the case in many parts of the World) renders such assistance as I have asked of you, the Newspaper is always sent free, as a compliment of course. The Name of the Agent in Paris is M. A. Fillonneau.[4] His residence Rue de Chaussée d' Antin—48 *bis*, I think; but I am not quite sure of the No. without previously sending to the office. I will tell Madame, when I write to her. Which will be soon, tell her, with my love.

---

[1] Macready left on 28 Feb.

[2] The lines, signed "Charles Dickens", appeared in the *Daily News* of 14 Feb (first collected in *The Plays and Poems of CD*, ed. R. H. Shepherd, 1885). They were inspired by a report in the *Daily News*, 13 Feb, of a meeting of agricultural labourers at Bramhill, Wilts, at which Lucy Simpkins, a poor woman with a young child, said "They say we be protected. If we be protected, we be starved". Sir John R. Robinson, then a youth on the *Wiltshire Independent*, sent the paragraph to the

Daily News (*Fifty Years of Fleet Street*, ed. Moy Thomas, 1904, pp. 18–19), but the account they inserted was said to be from the *Morning Chronicle* of 12 Feb.

[3] William Granet.

[4] André Guillaume Etienne Fillonneau, husband of Henry Austin's sister Amelia: see Vol. I, p. 52*n*. CD met them again in Paris in the winter of 1846–7 and gave Mme Filloneau the MS of *The Battle of Life* in exchange for that of a youthful composition, probably the Prologue to *Clari*, which she had preserved: see Vol. I, p. 18*n*.

William dines here tomorrow, with Mr. Petrie,[1] and your Yorkshire friends.[2] Tell Madame he was here the other day. He seems (not unnaturally) to avoid the subject of his Love.[3] Therefore, I do not feel it delicate or right to lead him to it. But I have written to him, earnestly, in the tone she suggests.

I am again a gentleman. I have handed over the Editing of the Paper (very laborious work indeed) to Forster; and am contemplating a New Book—most probably in Numbers. The Daily News is a great success—expences at first, however, most enormous of course. It is very much respected by the good men of both parties who are exceedingly anxious that it should succeed, by reason of its forbearance and sense of responsibility. But I am not quite trustful in, or quite satisfied with, some of the people concerned in its mechanical and business management, which is a very important part of such an undertaking. Therefore, I confine myself to writing, which is much more agreeable. I hope you have had a laugh at the 'Retreat at Albaro'. There is, to day, the first part of a Description of Genoa, which I suppose will not reach you, until after you have received This.[4]

The general impression here, is, that the Americans are Raving Mad. But it does not seem so probable today (a Packet arrived last night)[5] that they will force on a War,[6] as it has done for some weeks past. The Railroads are beginning to recover; and it is said that the really good schemes will come out very well indeed, after all. I hope so.

Maclise is taken with one of his fits of seclusion, and is never beheld by Mortal Eye. I believe he shaved last, on or about the fifteenth of January. We went down to Rochester (Kate, Georgy, Jerrold, and I) to spend my birthday; and when I asked him to come, he observed "that he didn't see the use of it". I believe he is painting very hard at a large Picture for the Academy Exhibition,[7] which has to be sent in, early in April; and that he works day and night. He has engaged himself to dine here, tomorrow—but I don't much expect him. He says he wishes he was a Wild Man. Which I tell him is unreasonable and discontented; he being already something so very near it.

What a Beast old Brown is! I am heartily glad I didn't give Thompson[8] a

---

[1] Possibly Samuel Petrie, of 46 Ebury St, who was chief clerk in the same department of the Treasury as Frederick Dickens.

[2] Unidentified.

[3] Miss Holskamp: see *To* de la Rue, 28 July 45.

[4] The fourth "Travelling Letter", "A Retreat at Albaro", had appeared 9 Feb; the fifth, "First Sketch of Genoa", appeared 16 Feb.

[5] The arrival of the *Hibernia* is noted in the *Daily News* of 16 Feb.

[6] The report in the *Daily News* of 16 Feb, and the first leader, on the Oregon dispute, suggest that the outlook was slightly more hopeful, though still uncertain; the leader-writer thought Calhoun's policy "perhaps more menacing to a settlement in our favour than even Mr. Polk's

precipitation". Two letters on the subject from Landor were published in the *Daily News*, 2 Feb and 5 Mar.

[7] *Ordeal by Touch*: see *To* de la Rue, 17 Apr 46 and *fn*.

[8] Christiana Thompson recorded that her husband was "disgusted with Mr. Brown's pompous vulgarity" when he called on him on 5 Jan. Christiana, however, though nervous of visiting the "bumptious consul" a few days later, "got on very agreeably"; in the "much dreaded consuless", she liked "the extreme candour and absence of etiquette". Brown "enquired into the tastes and pursuits" of Thompson, "and made other very personal interrogations finishing up by an apostrophe to Dickens which I am to transmit" (Christiana's journal, MS Mrs Sowerby).

letter to him. It is a brilliant thing that unconscious of his knowledge of me, he should have been impudent to Thompson. Which T describes to me very well. I mean, by the way, to write to Thompson as soon as I can find time. I constantly talk of coming back to Genoa for another Year; and I wish to Heaven I could so pluck myself up by the Roots again, as to let the house—pack up—buy another Carriage—and set off. But that, I fear, can't be just yet. When are we to expect you in London? You haven't fixed the day yet. Ever Heartily Yours my Dear De la Rue—

CHARLES DICKENS

To AMÉDÉE PICHOT, 16 FEBRUARY 1846*

MS Comtesse de Suzannet. *Address:* A Monsieur: | Monsr. Amédée Pichot | Revue Britannique | 1 Rue Grange Batelière | à Paris.

London. 1 Devonshire Terrace | Sixteenth February 1846.

Dear Sir

My connexion with The Daily News, does not extend to the Editing of that Paper in any of its Departments. But I have a very strong interest in its well-doing, and was active in projecting and establishing it.

The Foreign Staff[1] is such a very large one, that I believe there remains nothing to be done in that way. But I do not feel the less indebted to you for your kind and disinterested offer.

I shall be delighted to receive your Version of the Cricket,[2] through the hands of the Agent of the Daily News in Paris—M. Fillonneau, Rue de Chaussée d'Antin.

About the 'Mug of a bell'—In old times, Bells used to be christened, with great solemnity. When children are christened, it is a common custom in England for the Godfathers and Godmothers to give them Silver Mugs. Carrying out the idea of the Bells being christened, like children, I say, in the Chimes, that Henry the Eighth melted down their Mugs, because that king despoiled the churches of their Gold and Silver Wealth, and appropriated it to his own use.[3] Do you understand?

Faithfully Yours
CHARLES DICKENS

Monsieur Amédée Pichot

---

[1] Frederick Knight Hunt, in his account of the expenses of a daily paper in 1850 (clearly based on the *Daily News*), allows for correspondents in Paris, Madrid, Rome, Naples or Turin, Vienna, Berlin, and Lisbon, as well as a Paris reporter and an agent in Boulogne, and mentions the need of paid correspondents or agents in a dozen other places including Constantinople, New York, Bombay and China (*The Fourth Estate*, 1850, II, 196–206).

[2] "Le Grillon du Foyer", collected in Pichot's *Les Contes de Noel*, 1847.

[3] Pichot translated CD's explanation in a footnote (*Les Carillons*, Paris, 1847, p. 6*n*), adding a gloss on "mugs": "petits pots, gobelets, ou petites coupes".

To W. H. WILLS, 16 FEBRUARY 1846

MS Huntington Library.

Devonshire Terrace | Sixteenth February 1846

My Dear Mr. Wills

I miss you a great deal more than I miss the Paper.

May I ask you to reply to all strange letters, coming to the office addressed personally to me, that my connexion with the D.N. does not extend to the consideration or settlement of such matters, and that I have forwarded the letter to the Editor—dating, in all such cases, from *here*. I have sent this answer to all the enclosed documents that I have marked with a X.[1]

Among them, is an uncrossed Epistle from one Mrs. Dawson Wetherell,[2] referring to a first letter which I have *not* received. Do you know what it is about? If she want money, I do not like her style of correspondence at all, and would rather plead (as well I may) the immense number of similar appeals.

Always Believe me[3]

W. H. Wills Esquire   [CHARLES DICKENS]

To G. F. YOUNG, 16 FEBRUARY 1846*

MS Yale University Library. *Address:* George Frederick Young Esquire | Limehouse.

Devonshire Terrace | Sixteenth February 1846

Dear Sir.

I regret to say that I have dinner Engagements on both the days you mention. But—not to postpone the matter—I will call on you on Wednesday afternoon at about a Quarter before Three. It will be easy for me to return to town, in good time for my engagement.

Dear Sir | Faithfully Yours

George Frederick Young Esquire   CHARLES DICKENS

To W. H. WILLS, 17 FEBRUARY 1846*

MS Huntington Library.

Devonshire Terrace | Seventeenth February 1846

My Dear Mr. Wills

Many thanks for your kind note! I will not hesitate to trouble you one of these fine afternoons, when I find myself very "hard up" for assistance.

Always Faithfully Yours

W. H. Wills Esquire   CHARLES DICKENS

---

[1] Written very large.
[2] Unidentified.

[3] Strip cut away, removing signature.

To [?THE REV. W. J. FOX], [18 FEBRUARY 1846]

Mention in *To* Wills, 18 Feb.

To WILLIAM HOWITT,[1] 18 FEBRUARY 1846*

MS Jarndyce Books.

Devonshire Terrace | Eighteenth February 1846

My Dear Sir

As I am not the Editor of the Daily News, and am very rarely at the office, your letter was opened by a Confidential Secretary who attends there. I mention this, to account for my not immediately thanking you for your valuable communication, and expressing the pleasure the Authorities have in availing themselves of it.[2]

Believe me | Faithfully Yours

William Howitt Esquire.

CHARLES DICKENS

To CHARLES MANBY, 18 FEBRUARY 1846

Summary in N, I, 736 and Sotheran's catalogue No. 822 (1931); *MS* 2 pp.; dated Devonshire Terrace, 18 Feb 46.

As he is not the editor of the Daily News, *he cannot make engagements, but will take care the recommendation is not lost sight of.*

To W. H. WILLS, 18 FEBRUARY 1846

MS Huntington Library.

Devonshire Terrace | Eighteenth February 1846

My Dear Mr. Wills.

I have written to Howitt, and to Mr. Manby, and to Reynard the Fox.[3] I

---

[1] William Howitt (1792–1876; *DNB*), author; married Mary Botham 1821; both were prolific writers, separately and in collaboration, and William had established a reputation with *Rural Life of England*, 1836, and *Visits to Remarkable Places*, 1840. CD reviewed his *Boy's Country Book* in the *Examiner*, 7 Apr 39 (see Vol. I, p. 536, *hn*) but did not meet the Howitts until later—probably through Fox, Horne, or Southwood Smith, and certainly before their residence in Germany 1840–3. Their home at Clapton was the resort of many radical writers, and in 1846 both were contributing largely to the *People's Journal*, of which in

Apr they became co-editors and part-proprietors, with W. J. Linton and the publisher John Saunders. For the opening No., 3 Jan, Howitt wrote a 7-column article on CD, acclaiming him especially for his "championship of the weak and oppressed".

[2] Nothing appeared over Howitt's signature in the *Daily News*.

[3] Possibly W. J. Fox; he published no "pamphlet" under his own name at this time, but his *Lectures to the Working Classes* were being published in shilling parts. No review has been found in the *Daily News*.

think the pamphlet by the latter gentleman had better "be dealt with", favorably, "on the premises".

Do look at the enclosed from Mrs. Whats-her-name.[1] For a surprising audacity, it is remarkable even to me, who am positively bullied, and all but beaten, by these people. I wish you would do me the favor to write to her (in your own name and from your own address) stating that you answered her letter as you did, because if I were the wealthiest Nobleman in England I could not keep pace with one twentieth part of the demands upon me—and because you saw no internal evidence in her application to induce you to single it out for any especial notice. That the tone of this letter renders you exceedingly glad you did so; and that you decline, for me, holding any correspondence with her. Something to that effect, after what flourish your nature will.[2]

Faithfully Yours always
CD

W. H. Wills Esquire

To WILLIAM CULLENFORD, 19 FEBRUARY 1846

Extract in N, I, 736 from unidentified catalogue; dated Devonshire Terrace, 19 Feb 46. *Address* (envelope, MS Professor Harry Stone): William Cullenford Esq. | Stage Door | Theatre Royal Adelphi. PM 20 Feb 46.

The day and place of the proposed dinner will suit me perfectly well.

I have written a note to the Editor of the Daily News and begged him to mention the subject in a paragraph.[3]

To AUGUSTUS DICKENS, 20 FEBRUARY 1846*

MS Mrs Caroline Trollope.

Devonshire Terrace | Twentieth February 1846.

My Dear Augustus. I have not the slightest idea of the name of the man from whom that Post Office order for £1, came. He wrote to me, but his letter has been destroyed with a hundred others. All I remember, is, that he is a Catholic Priest at Stradbally[4] (wherever that may be)—and that he sent it to me for the Ragged Schools. If you will ever say so much to Mr. Lawrence,[5] Secretary's Office Post office, when you happen to be passing, I think you will find that there is not much difficulty in getting the money.

Affectionately Always
CHARLES DICKENS

Augustus Dickens Esquire

---

[1] Probably Mrs Dawson Wetherell.
[2] *Hamlet*, V, ii, 188.
[3] The *Daily News* did not mention the General Theatrical Fund.

[4] In Co. Waterford.
[5] Assistant Secretary at the General Post Office.

To THOMAS POWELL, 20 FEBRUARY 1846

Text from facsimile in Dawson's Book Shop, Los Angeles, catalogue No. 123 (1961).

Devonshire Terrace | Twentieth February 1846

My Dear Powell.

I sent your Epigrams, forthwith, to the working Editor of the D.N.[1] I fear, however, that they may be considered too personal for that Immacculate[2] Newspaper.

Faithfully Yours

Thomas Powell Esquire   CHARLES DICKENS

To F. M. EVANS, 24 FEBRUARY 1846

MS Dickens House.

Devonshire Terrace | Twenty Fourth February 1846

My Dear Evans.

I have seen Mr. Stanfield on the subject of Illustrations for the Travelling Letters;[3] and we purpose having about twelve—"drawn on Wood by George Stanfield, from designs by Clarkson Stanfield R.A." The first block to be ready a fortnight hence; the remainder to be furnished, two a week, until they are all done.

Mr. Stanfield wishes to know who are the best engravers on wood, of Landscape and architectural subjects, with small figures. If you will arrange with the best you can have, to have these blocks expected, and put in hand as they are supplied,—and will let me know that you have done so—the book will be fairly in progress.

He also wishes to know (and so do I) the *size* of the page. Upon this, I wish to see you, when you have considered the point. You will find me at home any morning between 11 and 1. That decided, we had best begin to[4]

To ARTHUR HILL,[5] 24 FEBRUARY 1846

MS Rosenbach Foundation.

Devonshire Terrace | Twenty Fourth February 1846

My Dear Sir

I am not a party to the Management of the Daily News (otherwise than as one

---

[1] No epigrams appeared in the *Daily News* up to the end of March. They may have resembled the verse squibs included in Powell's anonymous *Tales from Boccaccio*, 1846 (on "sleek Fusbos"—i.e. Forster, Wordsworth, Browning and others), which the *Athenæum* found "more curious than edifying" (21 Mar 46).

[2] Thus in MS.

[3] Further "Travelling Letters" appeared on 26 Feb, 2 Mar, and 11 Mar, making eight in all, representing five sections of

Pictures from Italy (less than half the book), and ending with "Piacenza to Bologna". The facts are mis-stated by most writers on CD: Kitton omits the eighth letter, and some suggest that the whole of *Pictures* appeared in the *Daily News*, Forster (F, v, i, 387) being ambiguous.

[4] These words are at the foot of the page; the rest of the letter is missing.

[5] Arthur Hill (1798–1885; *DNB*): see *To* Macready, 17 Aug 45, *fn*.

who has an interest in the paper)—and must therefore refer your letter and its enclosure,[1] to the Powers that be. But I will take care that it is promptly attended to; and that a communication be made to you on the subject, as soon as possible.

I was very sorry to lose the pleasure of coming to your interesting Party.—I am glad the Suffering Lady recovered—but not surprised; for what is Fame to a Polka!

Faithfully Yours

Arthur Hill Esquire   CHARLES DICKENS

To [J. H. STOCQUELER], 24 FEBRUARY 1846*

Text from transcript by Professor Edgar Johnson (MS Maurice Inman, Inc.).
Address: J. H. Stocqueler was editor of the *English Gentleman:* see *To* Stocqueler, ?1–4 Dec 45.

Devonshire Terrace | February 24, 1846

Dear Sir,

I am extremely sorry to hear that you have seceded from the English Gentleman;[2] because your management of that Paper, rendered the title no misnomer.

It does not surprise me that Young England[3] should be glad to get hold of anything in which it can exhibit itself. But it does surprise me very much, that anybody should give it the chance.

I have no connexion whatever, with the active management of the Daily News: having subsided (as I always intended) into my old, and much-better-loved pursuits. And I am sure that at this time, the Paper has no vacancy of any sort or kind; being, to say the truth, overcrowded. But I will make known to the authorities there, what you have made known to me; and I think if they should ever have the opportunity of availing themselves of your services, they would be really glad to do so.

Dear Sir, | Faithfully Yours

]⁴ Esquire   CHARLES DICKENS

P.S. I return your papers, in case you should have occasion for them.

To THE REV. JAMES WHITE,[5] 24 FEBRUARY 1846

Text from MDGH, I, 149.

1, Devonshire Terrace, York Gate, Regent's Park, | February 24th, 1846.

I cannot help telling you, my dear White, for I can think of no formal use of

---

[1] No reference to Bruce Castle school has been found in the *Daily News* of Feb or early Mar.

[2] Stocqueler had warmly welcomed the first three issues of the *Daily News*, in a leader of 24 Jan, saying that they corrected the "wild gossip" that was current; on 14 Feb he praised CD's article of 4 Feb, "Crime and Education" (see *To* Young, 12

Feb, *fn*) and said that several papers had passed it over in silence to avoid advertising a rival.

[3] Not known who succeeded Stocqueler; the *English Gentleman* came to an end on 12 Sep 46.

[4] Paper torn, removing name.

[5] The Rev. James White (1800–62; *DNB*), author. A Scot who had resigned

Mister to such a writer as you, that I have just now read your tragedy, "The Earl of Gowrie,"[1] with a delight which I should in vain endeavour to express to you. Considered with reference to its story, or its characters, or its noble poetry, I honestly regard it as a work of most remarkable genius. It has impressed me powerfully and enduringly. I am proud to have received it from your hand. And if I have to tell you what complete possession it has taken of me—that is, if I *could* tell you—I do believe you would be glad to know it.

Always faithfully yours

[CHARLES DICKENS]

To F. M. EVANS, 26 FEBRUARY 1846

Text from Jesse Quail, "CD and the 'Daily News'", *The Nineteenth Century and After*, LXXXVIII (1920), 632–42.

Devonshire Terrace | Thursday Twenty Sixth February 1846

My Dear Evans,

As you wish to know why I addressed myself to you in my letter of Tuesday last, I will tell you. You are at liberty, of course, to communicate to your partner as much or as little of my reason as you please.

I addressed you, because I am not in that state of feeling with reference to your partner, which would render a personal negociation with him agreeable to me. I consider that his interposition between me and almost every act of mine at the newspaper office, was as disrespectful to me as injurious to the enterprise. And I entertain so strong a sentiment on this point, that I have already informed my

---

his living on inheriting a considerable property from his wife's father, and lived at Bonchurch, Isle of Wight, where he wrote his series of historical plays on Scottish Kings. CD had met him, possibly for the first time, at Macready's on 5 Feb 46, when Macready read his play, *The King of the Commons*, "White reading the scenes of Laird Small", Thackeray, Fox, and Maddox of the Princess's Theatre also being present; Macready had been considering the play since Oct 45. CD told Macready next day "he was *disappointed* in it" but advised him "not to counsel White to withdraw it if Maddox accepted it"; Fox was also adverse, but Thackeray sent a note "sticking up" for it (Macready, *Diaries*, II, 321); Macready eventually produced it at the Princess's, 20 May 46. In his Preface to the play (published May 46) White said it had gained him "some friends of whom I may well be proud". His *John Savile of Haysted*, 1847, was dedicated to CD with his "highest admiration and affection".

[1] Published by Newby at the end of 1845; it was favourably reviewed in the *Athenæum*, 3 Jan 46 ("clever as an historical exposition, clever as a drama") and the *Edinburgh Review*, July 46 (CLXIX, 223–36). In his Preface to *The King of the Commons*, White says Procter had sent the MS of *The Earl of Gowrie* to Macready "with a very flattering judgment" (White was then "entirely unacquainted with both"); but no mention in Macready's diary. Phelps (at Sadler's Wells since 1844) showed interest in it, but White felt he could not connect himself with Sadler's Wells when Macready was putting on another of his plays (White *to* Forster, 2 Feb 46: W. May Phelps and J. Forbes-Robertson, *The Life and Work of Samuel Phelps*, 1886, p. 381). Phelps produced *Feudal Times* and *John Savile* in 1847 (see Vol. v), and finally, in 1852, *The Earl of Gowrie*, retitled *James VI, or the Earl of Gowrie's Plot*.

successor in the Editorship that I would, on no account, attend any meeting of
Proprietors at which he was likely to be present.

The two last instances in which he (without the slightest previous communication with me) took the course to which I so much object, may be enough to
mention here. Firstly, I ordered a gentleman to be sent down into the country to
attend an election of great importance[1]—in reference to which proceeding he
wrote a violent note to *Mr. Powell*(!) incorrect even in its facts. Secondly, a Mr.
Rourke[2]—I think that is his name—having been engaged by me for an essential
set of services and at a small salary; and having his engagement duly reported by
my father; was by his direction refused his first week's salary by Mr. Joyce,
whose courtesy and understanding of the matters over which he presides appear
to be upon a par[3]—and was compelled to apply to me. The position in which I
was placed in these cases was so galling and offensive to me, that I am as much
irritated by the recollection of them, as I was by their actual occurrence; and I
conceive I have a right to claim so much consideration as to hold your partner
bound in both these instances to have fulfilled my engagements without the least
enquiry, and then to have come to me and said anything in reference to them that
he desired to say.

These two examples are a part of a series of similar things—some of less, some
of equal importance—which offended me exceedingly and frequently, when I
was in the habit of attending the office. And to these I must add, with great pain,
that I have not always observed Mr. Bradbury's treatment of my father (than
whom there is not a more zealous, disinterested, or useful gentleman attached to
the paper)[4] to be very creditable to himself, or delicate towards me.

Finding greater difficulties and discouragements at first, than he anticipated,
but which anyone with a knowledge of newspapers could easily foresee, and
would steadily overcome, he seems to me to have become possessed of the idea
that everybody receiving a salary in return for his services, is his natural enemy,
and should be suspected and mistrusted accordingly. I have reason to believe
that this is not my own idea alone, and that it has its influence in the working of
the paper. Certainly if the point were ever referred to me, I should say that in the
worst times of Sir John Easthope and Mr. Duncan[5]—who were loudly complained
of among newspaper people, and are so still—I never saw anything approaching
Mr. Bradbury.

Of Mr. Bradbury as separated from the newspaper, I entertain my old high

[1] Presumably the West Riding by-
election of 4 Feb: see *To* Beard, ?1 Feb.
[2] "Bourke" in *To* Bradbury & Evans, 5
Mar.
[3] The accountant, recalled at the time
of his death in May 1865 as "rough—but
a good-hearted kind man" (MS Silver
Diary).
[4] Sir Joseph Crowe (*Reminiscences of
Thirty-five Years of my Life*, p.69) describes
John Dickens at the *Daily News* office:
"short, portly, obese, fond of a glass of
grog, full of fun, never given to much

locomotion, but sitting as chairman, and
looking carefully to the regular marking
and orderly despatch to the printers of the
numerous manuscripts thrown off at lightning speed by the men from the gallery";
see also *To* Beard, ?24 Jan 46, *fn*. His
death certificate (31 Mar 51) and the
announcement in the *Daily News* show
that he retained his post until his last illness.
[5] James Duncan, publisher and co-
proprietor of the *Morning Chronicle*.

opinion. I hold him, as separated from the newspaper, in my old regard. But I cannot separate him from it sufficiently, at this time, to affect a cordiality which (remembering the whole history of my connection with it) I do not feel.

If, as you intimate in your letter, you are determined to share the merit and assert the propriety of this line of proceeding, I can only say I am very sorry for it. But there must always remain in my mind this distinction between you,— that you come lagging in with your approval afterwards, and are not active in the spirit and the manner of such doings at the moment of their occurrence.

I do not find anything else in your letter which required an answer. I addressed myself to you, because I felt more pleasantly and kindly towards you, as having borne yourself in a kinder and more pleasant way generally, since this newspaper began.

Faithfully yours,
CHARLES DICKENS.

F. M. Evans Esquire.

To MISS WALEY,[1] 27 FEBRUARY 1846*

MS Free Library of Philadelphia.

Devonshire Terrace | Friday Twenty Seventh February | 1846.

Mr. Charles Dickens presents his compliments to Miss Waley, and begs to say that he has no doubt Miss Waley's benevolent offer will be very acceptable to the Managers of the Ragged Schools. Mr. Dickens scarcely knows, at this moment, to whom the parcel should be sent; but he is in communication with the teachers, and will be happy to take charge of it himself, if Miss Waley will have the kindness to entrust it to him.

To DR W. P. ALISON,[2] [27 FEBRUARY 1846]

Mention in *To* Macready, ?27 Feb 46. *Date:* one of the letters of introduction for Macready written 27 Feb 46.

To ANGUS FLETCHER,[3] [27 FEBRUARY 1846]

Mention in *To* Macready, ?27 Feb 46. *Date:* one of the letters of introduction for Macready written 27 Feb 46.

To LORD JEFFREY, [27 FEBRUARY 1846]

Mention in *To* Macready, ?27 Feb 46. *Date:* one of the letters of introduction for Macready written 27 Feb 46.

---

[1] Perhaps related to the Mr S. J. Waley of 22 Devonshire Place, who addressed the meeting of the Poor Man's Guardian Society on 8 Apr 46 at the Marylebone Literary and Scientific Institution.

[2] William Pulteney Alison, MD (1790–1859; *DNB*), Professor of the Institutes of Medicine, Edinburgh University since 1822: see Vol. II, p. 314*n*.

[3] Angus Fletcher of Dunans (1805–75), cousin of CD's friend of the same name: see Vol. II, p. 298*n*.

To LORD ROBERTSON, 27 FEBRUARY 1846*

MS Major A. Seafield Grant.

London. 1 Devonshire Terrace | York Gate Regents Park
Friday Twenty Seventh February | 1846

My Dear Lord Robertson

Mr. Macready—one of my dearest and most valued friends—has already an introduction to you from Lady Blessington; but I cannot deny myself the pleasure of adding mine, as it will be the greatest gratification to me to be at all instrumental in your becoming mutually acquainted.

You will be glad to hear that—the newspaper being now afloat—I take no further trouble with it than writing whatever appears there, with my name attached;[1] and that I am contemplating a new Story, with great ardour. Kate desires to be cordially remembered to you, and to all your house. In which request I earnestly join.

Being ever | In all Sincerity | Faithfully Yours

Lord Robertson   CHARLES DICKENS

P.S. When shall we take some more Gin Punch, and go to see the Puppets again ?[2]

To [JOHN WILSON], 27 FEBRUARY 1846*

MS Dickens House. *Address:* clearly to John Wilson as CD refers to J. T. Gordon as his son-in-law.

London. 1 Devonshire Terrace, | York Gate, Regents Park
Friday Twenty Seventh February | 1846

My Dear Sir

Three years and a half ago,[3] I had one of the greatest pleasures I have ever experienced, in becoming known to you. I want to communicate that pleasure to one who is in every way deserving of it, as I am sure you will say when you know him; and therefore I present to you in the person of Mr. Macready, one of my dearest and most cherished friends.

Mrs. Dickens sends her love to you, if you have not forgotten her. And though you have, she still sends it.

May I ask you to remember me, earnestly, to Mr Gordon[4] your Son in Law. I desire to live in his remembrance if he will allow me.[5]

[   ]
[CHARLES DICKENS]

---

[1] Since CD's resignation two "Travelling Letters" and the first letter on Capital Punishment had appeared over his name.

[2] The "Travelling Letter" of 26 Feb included the account of the puppet show.

[3] In fact in 1841.

[4] John Thomson Gordon (1813–65), advocate: see Vol. II, p. 314*n*.

[5] Ending and signature torn away.

To W. C. MACREADY, [27 FEBRUARY 1846]*

MS Morgan Library. *Date:* clearly the same date as *To* Robertson, 27 Feb, the Friday before Macready's arrival in Edinburgh on 2 Mar; confirmed by CD's reference to his second Capital Punishment letter. *Address:* W. C. Macready Esquire | Clarence Terrace.

Devonshire Terrace | Friday Night

My Dear Macready

I send you some Edinburgh letters. You would only be bored by an accumulation of them; and I have therefore confined them to the people we spoke of—only adding Dr. Alison—a most excellent and interesting man, who can shew you strange sights in the poor parts of the old Town—and Angus Fletcher of Dunans (not our Fletcher) who, if he be in Edinburgh, you will find a capital fellow to know.[1]

I have told Jeffrey that I hope to come down, before you leave.[2] I should like to do so, and return with you, or run with you on your way, whithersoever you go. When you know what your plans are, will you write to me, and let me know all about them?

Ever affectionately

W. C. Macready Esquire.   CD.

P.S. I hope to see my second Capital Punishment Letter, in print tomorrow.[3]

To JAMES WINSTON,[4] 28 FEBRUARY 1846

Mention in Sotheran's catalogue No. 59; *MS* (3rd pers.) 1 p.; dated Devonshire Terrace, 28 Feb 46.

Concerning his subscription to the Garrick Club.[5]

[1] Macready called on Lord Robertson Dr Alison, Fletcher of Dunans, Jeffrey and Professor John Wilson on 3 Mar (*Diaries*, II, 326).

[2] CD did not go to Edinburgh, but Jeffrey visited him in London shortly before 2 Apr, and told Cockburn he was "radiant with happiness & health & looking like an airy Cornet just vaulted out of a Cavalry Saddle, his *Boy* the fairest at all events & most dimply of all the F.J.s as yet on the list" (MS National Library of Scotland).

[3] In the *Daily News*, 28 Feb; the first had appeared on 23 Feb. Only the three March "Letters" were reprinted by F. G. Kitton in 1898 and in subsequent collections such as *Miscellaneous Papers*; that of 28 Feb was first reprinted by P. A. W. Collins in *The Law as Literature*, ed. Louis Blom-Cooper, 1961, and that of 23 Feb by K. Tillotson in the *Times Literary Supplement*, 12 Aug 1965. The opening "Letter" CD called "the first of two or three"; its occasion was the recent execution (13 Feb) of Bryan Seery in Ireland, and CD challenged both the reformative purpose of Capital Punishment and the justification of ever pronouncing an "irrevocable Doom". On 28 Feb, in describing the depraved excitement caused by public executions, he gave his own impression of the hanging of Courvoisier in 1840: see Vol. II, p. 86–7n. He also noted the tendency of juries to return verdicts of insanity—as in the recent case of Captain Johnstone, the subject of a leader in the *Daily News*, 6 Feb. For the series as a whole and its relation to the article planned for the *Edinburgh*, see *To* Napier, 28 July 45, *fn*.

[4] James Winston (?1773–1848), secretary of the Garrick Club: see Vol. I, p. 380n.

[5] CD's accounts show that he paid his subscription (£6.6.0) on 3 Mar.

To THE COUNTESS OF BLESSINGTON, 1 MARCH 1846*

MS Benoliel Collection.

Devonshire Terrace | Sunday First March 1846.

My Dear Lady Blessington

Do you or Count D'Orsay happen to have, in any unransacked corner, any letter I wrote you from Italy? I don't think it all[1] likely; but as drowning men catch at straws, I grasp at scraps of paper, to help myself on, in my travelling Recollections.

I have a vague remembrance of something I wrote to you about Bologna (I think) and Verona—and of something I wrote to Count D'Orsay about the models at Rome—both of which fragments I should like to recall more distinctly, if you could help me to a better remembrance of them.[2]

Always My Dear Lady Blessington | Faithfully Yours

The | Countess of Blessington.   CHARLES DICKENS

To THE COUNTESS OF BLESSINGTON, 2 MARCH 1846

MS Miss Winifred A. Myers.

Devonshire Terrace | Second March 1846.

My Dear Lady Blessington.

Many thanks for the letters! I will take the greatest care of them—though I blush to find how little they deserve it.

It vexes me very much, that I am going out on Friday and cannot help it. I have no strength of mind, I am afraid. I am always making engagements in which there is no prospect of satisfaction.

Vague thoughts of a new book are rife within me just now; and I go wandering about at night into the strangest places, according to my usual propensity at such a time—seeking rest, and finding none.[3] As an addition to my composure, I ran over a little dog in the Regents Park yesterday (killing him on the spot) and gave his little mistress—a girl of thirteen or fourteen—such exquisite distress as I never saw the like of.

I *must* have some talk with you about those American Singers.[4] They must

---

[1] Thus in MS, for "at all".

[2] CD was evidently now planning the later sections of *Pictures*. "Bologna" follows immediately after the last "Travelling Letter" published in the *Daily News* (11 Mar), but no letter describing it to Lady Blessington is known. For the letters he actually used in "Verona" and "Rome", see *To* Lady Blessington, 20 Nov 44, and *To* D'Orsay, 15 Mar 45.

[3] Like the unclean spirit: St Matthew, xii, 43, St Luke, xi, 24. Forster speaks of this as a "restless time" of "night-wanderings" when the characters of *Dombey and Son* "were growing in his mind" (F, v, i, 388).

[4] The Hutchinsons, a musical troupe of four of the children of Jesse and Mary Hutchinson—Judson, John, Jason and Abbey—were touring England in 1845-6 and reached London on 24 Jan 46. On 26 Jan they called on Catherine Dickens and Georgina and sang to them; CD was not at home, but invited them to dinner with Jerrold, Macready, Maclise, Rogers, Stanfield and others on 31 Jan, when they sang "The Bridge of Sighs" and "A Good Time Coming"; they often called at Devonshire Terrace afterwards (John W. Hutchinson, *The Story of the Hutchinsons*, Boston, 1896, I, 172–6; cf. Macready, *Diaries*, II, 321 and

never go back to their own country, without your having heard them sing Hood's Bridge of Sighs. My God how sorrowful and pitiful it is!

Best regards to Count D'Orsay and the young ladies.

Always My Dear Lady Blessington | Cordially Your friend
The | Countess of Blessington.   CHARLES DICKENS

To W. H. WILLS, 2 MARCH 1846

MS Huntington Library.

Devonshire Terrace | Monday Morning Second March | 1846
My Dear Mr. Wills.

I really don't know what to say, about the New Brunswicker. The idea *will* obtrude itself on my mind that he had no business to come here on such an expedition; and that it is a piece of the wild conceit for which his countrymen are so remarkable; and that I can hardly afford to be Steward to such adventurers. On the other hand, your description of him pleases me. Then that Purse which I never could keep shut in my life makes mouths at me: saying "See how empty I am!" Then I fill it; and it looks very rich indeed.

I think the best way is, to say, that if you think you can do him any *permanent* good with Five Pounds (that is, get him home again) I will give you the money. But I should be very much indisposed to give it him, merely to linger on here about town for a little time, and then be hard up again.

As to Employment, I do in my Soul believe that if I were Lord Chancellor of England, I should have been aground long ago, for the Patronage of a Messenger's place.

Say all that is[1] civil for me to the Proprietor of the Illustrated London News,[2] who really seems to be very liberal. "Other engagements" &c &c "prevent me from entertaining" &c &c. Faithfully Yours ever

CD   Over

W. H. Wills Esquire

Will you tell the Publisher to cause to be sent to Clarkson Stanfield Esquire R.A. 48 Mornington Place Hampstead Road, a complete set of the D.N. to this time —and to be regularly continued. He wishes to be a Subscriber.

People's Journal, 25 Apr 46). Their first London concert (attended by CD and his family) was on 10 Feb at the Hanover Square Rooms; Hogarth in the *Daily News*, 11 Feb, and other reports, specially mentioned "The Bridge of Sighs"—the poem, first published in *Hood's Magazine*, May 44, was set by the Hutchinsons. They were invited by Harriet Martineau to Gras-

mere and sang there in the open air on 18 June.

[1] MS reads "it".

[2] Herbert Ingram (1811–60; *DNB*), founder and proprietor from 1842; Mark Lemon was one of his advisers, and the paper was obviously sympathetic to CD and the causes he was interested in.

To WILLIAM LOCKE,[1] 2 MARCH 1846*

MS Mr Roger W. Barrett.

Private

1 Devonshire Terrace | Monday Evening | Second March 1846

Dear Sir.

I have an opportunity (I do not feel, just now, at liberty to explain it in detail) of using any facts I can collect in reference to the Ragged Schools, probably with solid and permanent advantage to those humane Institutions.[2] I have no intention, I may observe, of printing this information.

Any Statistics you can furnish me with, bearing on the schools in which you are more immediately interested, or on the subject generally,—or any statement you may feel inclined to make to me on these heads—I shall be happy to receive, and to use to the very utmost of my power.

If you should wish to see me when you have had leisure to think the matter over, I shall be glad to make an appointment with you for that purpose.

Dear Sir | Faithfully Yours

Mr. William Locke.   CHARLES DICKENS

To W. H. WILLS, 4 MARCH 1846

MS Huntington Library.

Devonshire Terrace | Fourth March 1846.

My Dear Mr. Wills.

I assure you I am very truly and unaffectedly sensible of your earnest friendli-ness—and in proof of my feeling its worth, I shall unhesitatingly trouble you sometimes, in the fullest reliance on your meaning what you say.

The letter from Nelson Square is a very manly and touching one. But I am more helpless in such a case as that, than in any other: having really fewer means of helping such a gentleman to employment, than I have of firing off the Guns in the Tower. Such appeals come to me here, in scores upon scores.

The letter from Little White Lion Street does not impress me favorably. It is not written in a simple or truthful manner—I am afraid. And Mr. Thomas Cooper is *not* a good reference. Moreover, I think it probable that the Writer may have deserted some pursuit for which he is qualified, for vague and less laborious strivings which he has no pretensions to make. However, I will certainly act on your impression of him, whatever it may be.

And if you could explain to the gentleman in Nelson Square, that I am not evading his request, but that I do not know of anything to which I can recommend him, it would be a great relief to me.

---

[1] William Locke, woollen-draper; active with S. R. Starey in the formation of the Ragged School Union; at its first meeting in July 44 they were appointed Hon. Secretaries and were responsible for drawing up the Union's rules. At a meeting of the Union on 20 Feb he had mentioned several visits to the schools by CD and other "distinguished individuals" (*Daily News*, 21 Feb).

[2] See *To* Kay-Shuttleworth, 28 Mar 46.

I trust the New Printer *is* a Tartar;[1] and I hope to God he will so proclaim and assert his Tartar breeding, as to excommunicate Bradbury[2] from the 'chapel'[3] over which he presides.[4]

Tell Powell (with my regards) that he needn't "deal with" the American Notices of the Cricket.[5] I never read one word of their abuse, and I should think it base to read their Praises. It is something to know that one is righted so soon; and knowing that, I can afford to know no more.

Ever Faithfully Yours

W. H. Wills Esquire.   CD.

To UNKNOWN CORRESPONDENT, 4 MARCH 1846*

MS Colonel Richard Gimbel.

Devonshire Terrace | Fourth March 1846.

Madam—for I take you to be a lady from your hand writing. But if you be of the sterner sex, attribute my mistake to my not being possessed of any instinct that leads me to address those correspondents of whom I have not a personal recollection, by their proper titles or even Sex, unless they give me some clue to those distinctions.

I beg to say, in reply to your favor, that I do not interfere with the current management of the Daily News, or the acceptance or rejection of articles that are offered for insertion in its columns. But as I am pretty sure that it would be quite out of the question with a Newspaper, to reprint an article from a Six Years' old Magazine, I will not (unless you desire it again) send your Manuscript to the Editor. I am not, however, the less obliged to you for your communication, or[6]

To THOMAS BEARD, 5 MARCH 1846

MS Dickens House. *Address:* Thomas Beard Esquire | "Morning Herald" Office | Shoe Lane Fleet Street.

Devonshire Terrace | Fifth March 1846 | Thursday

My Dear Beard.

Will you call here in the morning, on your way to the office, either tomorrow

---

[1] The name of Mr Jones's successor is not known: possibly the Mr Carter mentioned in an anecdote of 7 Sep 46 about Forster shouting to him (*The "Daily News" Jubilee*, p. 10).

[2] Name omitted from previously published versions.

[3] The meeting or association of journeymen in a printing-office.

[4] This was clearly a difficult period for the paper; Paxton wrote on 4 Mar: "I find them all in a Mess at the Daily News it must break down I do think" (MS Devonshire Collections).

[5] No American reviews are quoted in the *Daily News*.

[6] Second sheet cut off.

or Saturday as may be most convenient to you? I shall be at home and delighted to see you on either day.

Affecy. Always

Thomas Beard Esquire   CHARLES DICKENS

To MESSRS BRADBURY & EVANS, 5 MARCH 1846*

MS The Proprietors of *Punch*.

Devonshire Terrace | Fifth March 1846.

Dear Sirs.

I will make the calculation as soon as I can; but before I make it, I must have the letters already printed, set up (a specimen sheet at all events) in an average good page.[1] My casting-off must necessarily be imperfect, at the best; and before I can cast it off at all I must know what a column of the newspaper makes.

I have never expected the account to Christmas[2] before this time; and when I asked you for it, I stated my reason and attached no idea of its being late.[3] But I did expect that you would have paid in some money to Coutts's on account of the Newspaper;[4] and in that faith (without staying now, to enquire whether I should have known better) I have the satisfaction to find, tonight, that I have overdrawn my account.[5] Which, situated as I am with regard to Miss Coutts, I would not have willingly done for a Thousand Pounds.

I did expect too that someone on your behalf, you being otherwise engaged, would have taken such moderate pains with Oliver Twist as to have altered the advertisement and not let it stand, for a week, a ridiculous absurdity.[6] Further, I expected when Mr. Evans wrote to me about Mr. Bourke[7] that he would not be again refused his Salary. Which I understand he has been.

I am too sick at heart of such petty miseries, to trust myself to say now what kind of course I see beyond them. And the less I say tonight, the better.

Faithfully Yours

Messrs. Bradbury and Evans.   CHARLES DICKENS

---

[1] For *Pictures from Italy*: see *To* Bradbury & Evans, 11 Mar 46. "Travelling Letters" Nos I–VII had already appeared in the *Daily News* and No. VIII followed on 11 Mar.

[2] The half-year's statement ending 31 Dec 45 (not included in Bradbury & Evans's Accounts, MS V & A).

[3] CD's account-book (MS Messrs Coutts) shows £300.13.7 received from Bradbury & Evans 6 Mar. Most of this must represent profit on the December sales of the *Cricket*; later statements in Bradbury &

Evans's Accounts (MS V & A) show that the *Chimes* had not yet covered the expenses of its reprint of Jan 45.

[4] CD's salary was not paid until 29 Apr.

[5] Accounts confirm that this was so on 3 Mar 46.

[6] The advertisement of No. III of *Oliver Twist*, which was published 28 Feb, continued in the *Daily News* of 3 and 5 Mar in its earlier form: "will be published on the 28th inst." On 9 Mar it was altered to read "Now ready".

[7] See *To* Evans, 26 Feb 46.

To CLARKSON STANFIELD, 6 MARCH 1846†

MS Colonel Richard Gimbel.

Devonshire Terrace | Sixth March 1846.

My Dear Stanny. In reference to the Damage of the Candlesticks,[1] I beg to quote (from the Cricket on the Hearth, by the highly popular and deservedly so, Dick) this reply

"I'll damage you, if you enquire"[2]—

In reference to the Sanatorium, Sir, the arrangements are (generally speaking) Southwood Smith's, and therefore, I should think, Bad.[3] Southwood being born to Confuse Mankind.[4] But if you be afar off, I engage to Mutiny on the Spot.

Ever Yours,

My block reeving,
Main-brace splicing,
Lead heaving,
Ship conning,
Stun'-Sail bending,[5]
Deck swabbing,
Son of a Sea-Cook
Henry Bluff.[6]
H.M.S. "Timber"

To GIUSEPPE MAZZINI, 7 MARCH 1846

Extract in Anderson Galleries catalogue No. 4728 (1936); *MS* 1 p.; dated Devonshire Terrace, 7 Mar 46.

Miss Hogarth desires me to say that she would be ready to assist on a much more trying occasion than the trial of our friend Sigr. Scuroni.[7]

[1] No explanation; Field Stanfield told F. G. Kitton they were not a gift from CD to his father (*Dickens and his Illustrators,* p. 159).

[2] Said by John Peerybingle the Carrier to Caleb Plummer, in "Chirp the First", refusing to let him pay for the parcel.

a Not previously published.

[3] Written large.

[4] The Sanatorium committee gave a dinner to those responsible for the St James's Theatre performance of *Every Man in his Humour* on Sat 7 Mar. The *Critic,* 14 Mar, described it as "a sumptuous banquet . . . at the Clarendon Hotel" and named many of those present, among them John Dickens.

[5] Making fast the stern-sail.

[6] Written large. "Harry Bluff" is a song in Isaac Pocock's nautical melodrama *For England Ho!,* 1818; setting by Welsh, and long popular. The first lines are: "When

a boy Harry Bluff left his friends and his home | And his dear native land, o'er the ocean to roam".

[7] On 4 Mar Scurione was indicted at the Middlesex Sessions on the charge of obtaining £2 from CD under false pretences. Evidence was given by CD of the prisoner's delivery of the letter and pamphlet and of his reply enclosing £2, and by Mazzini of his refusal, a few days before the offence was committed, to give Scurione a letter of recommendation (see *To* Mazzini, ?late Jan 46 and *fn*). On being called to make his defence Scurione said he could not speak English well enough to be understood; but when no interpreter could be found, he claimed, in very good English, that the letter had been given to him by "Colonel Count Bertola" to whom he delivered the money. He was found guilty and sentenced to six months' imprisonment (*Daily News,* 5 Mar 46).

To UNKNOWN CORRESPONDENT, 7 MARCH 1846

Mention in John Anderson catalogue No. 1470; *MS* 1½ pp.; dated 7 Mar 46.

To H. G. ADAMS, 11 MARCH 1846

Text from N, I, 741.

1 Devonshire Terrace, | York Gate, Regents Park
Eleventh March 1846

Dear Sir,

I have no connexion whatever with the Editorship or current management of the Daily News; and have simply forwarded your verses[1] to the conductors of the Paper. I have not appended your suggestion in reference to the "Voices from the Crowd,"[2] because that title is, I conceive, the property of the gentleman who writes those pieces, and could not honorably be appropriated by anybody else.

Faithfully Yours
[CHARLES DICKENS]

To MESSRS BRADBURY & EVANS, 11 MARCH 1846*

MS The Proprietors of *Punch*.

Devonshire Terrace | Eleventh March 1846

Dear Sirs

As nearly as I can make the calculation, I should say there would be, in the book, 300 pages of the size you send. I allow five and a half to each column of the Paper, and take the total number of columns in round numbers at 60. My calculation is necessarily imperfect, but I think very close. Allowing for woodcuts, I should say the book would range from 300 to 330 pages as per specimen.[3]

Mr. Stanfield will want a lot of blocks sent him. He is ready to begin.

I think *you* had better see him about the number of Woodcuts and about the expence. I have told him so. I enclose a card of mine for you to write your names on, or his man may say he is out. His address is 48 Mornington Place Hampstead Road. I would not overdo the Illustration.

It is essential, I take it, that we should publish something in *May*,[4] and there-

---

[1] Nothing over Adams's signature has been found in the *Daily News*.

[2] The series title of Charles Mackay's verses which appeared irregularly in the *Daily News* from 21 Jan to 14 May 46 and were collected in a volume under the same title in June 46 (printed by Bradbury & Evans and published by Orr); it included the very popular "A Good Time Coming".

[3] *Pictures* in fact has 270 pages, but with only four illustrations; advertisements show that the size of the page appears to have

been changed from small octavo to foolscap octavo, some time after 25 Apr. Bradbury & Evans's accounts (MS V & A) include a charge "for alteration of size".

[4] Underlined five times. May publication was probably considered essential in order to be well ahead of the new novel in numbers (see *To* Bradbury & Evans, 16 Mar 46), which was advertised with *Pictures* on 18 Apr as "A NEW ENGLISH STORY ... now in preparation". CD no doubt also had financial reasons.

fore there should be brisk preparation both with the artist and the Engravers. You will use your own discretion, of course, as to the advertizing[1] of the book, but I think it would be well to put it out soon.

When you have seen Mr. Stanfield, there will be no difficulty in arranging the price. Would it not be well to have some good subject—Venice for Example —a woodcut on India Paper, in some fanciful way, for a Frontispiece?

Faithfully Yours

Messrs. Bradbury and Evans   CHARLES DICKENS

Will you begin to print, and send proofs to Mr. Stanfield and me?

To MESSRS CHAPMAN & HALL, 11 MARCH 1846

Extract in John Holt Schooling, "The Signatures of Charles Dickens", *Strand Magazine*, VII (1894), p. 85, dated 11 Mar 46.

Asking for accounts up to last Xmas . . . at the mysterious man's convenience.

To T. R. EELES,[2] 12 MARCH 1846*

MS Lesley College Library, Boston.

Devonshire Terrace | Twelfth March 1846

Dr. Mr. Eeles.

If you will have the goodness to call on me any morning between 11 and 1, I shall be glad to give you some directions about a little binding I want done.[3]

Faithfully Yours

Mr. Eeles.   CHARLES DICKENS

To CLARKSON STANFIELD, 12 MARCH 1846*

MS Brown University Library.

Devonshire Terrace | Twelfth March 1846

My Dear Stanny.

Of your decision (of course) I have not a word to say. You are the best judge whether your Creed recognizes and includes, with men of sense, such things as I

---

[1] *Pictures from Italy* was first advertised (in the *Daily News*, *Athenæum* and elsewhere) on 18 Apr, saying it would be published "early in May". Advertising was no doubt postponed when Stanfield gave up the illustrating: see *To* Stanfield, 12 Mar.

[2] Thomas Robert Eeles, bookbinder, 22 Cursitor St; responsible for CD's dummy books, and still binding for him in 1861.

[3] Perhaps the presentation copies for Frederick Salmon: see *To* Salmon, 28 Mar 46.

have shocked you by my mention of.[1] I am sorry to learn that it does—and think far worse of it than I did.

Ever Affectionately

CD

To EDWARD CHAPMAN, 13 MARCH 1846*

MS Princeton University Library.

Devonshire Terrace | Thirteenth March 1846

My Dear Sir

I have looked over the accounts to Christmas last,[2] and find them perfectly clear and intelligible.

There must be something of Animal Magnetism, I think, in our being mindful of the same subject at so nearly the same time.

Faithfully Yours

Edward Chapman Esquire.   CHARLES DICKENS

To MISS BURDETT COUTTS, 13 MARCH 1846

MS Morgan Library.

Devonshire Terrace | Thirteenth March 1846.

My dear Miss Coutts.

The "General Theatrical Fund" at whose dinner I am going to preside, have begged me to give the accompanying letter to you—in some remembrance, I presume, of my having represented you in the matter of your public subscription for the Elton Family.

You will not misunderstand me as having any lawless designs on your purse,

---

[1] Stanfield was received into the Catholic Church on 3 Oct 46. In what was so far printed in the "Travelling Letters" in the *Daily News*, which he had probably read as a whole only within the last week (see *To* Wills, 2 Mar), there was not much that need have shocked him, but he might have been alarmed by the warning footnote in the issue of 26 Feb, attached to the description of an altar with a picture (to "stimulate the charitable") of "a select party of souls frying": CD said he had no intention of disparaging the religious belief of the people, but "when any offshoot of it, strikes me as being ridiculous or offensive, I simply write down my own impression of that particular exhibition or practice, and desire to go no further. I very earnestly wish my readers to bear this in mind with a view to future letters". One such "letter" was

possibly No. VII (*Daily News*, 2 Mar) which has a brief and amusing account of the convent party on the occasion of a nun's final vows—omitted from the volume. The section on Rome, with its rather facetious account of Holy Week, was not yet written (see *To* Mme de la Rue, 17 Apr 46); but it is possible that Stanfield had lately seen a transcript of the original letters to Forster (see Preface, p. xv). CD claimed (*Pictures*, p. 3) that in his criticisms he had done "no more than many conscientious Catholics both abroad and at home"; at the other extreme, the *Dublin Review* found that "everything connected with the Catholic religion . . . is held up to ridicule" (Sep 46, XXXI, 190).

[2] CD's account-book (MS Messrs Coutts) shows a payment of £166 from Chapman & Hall on 14 Mar.

if I discharge my conscience of the statement that this Fund includes the Actors at Country and Minor Theatres, who cannot by any exertions, in the present and altered state of theatrical matters, qualify themselves for either of the other Funds —who are very poor, generally speaking—and have established this one with a patience and long foresight most remarkable to me.[1]

You will be pleased to hear that the eldest Miss Elton is Mistress of a large National School at Mitcham;[2] with a pretty house and garden, and everything happy about her, as she well deserves. Miss Wight (White, I think it should be) is quite recovered, and has obtained a situation as Companion to an old lady.

Always Dear Miss Coutts | Faithfully Yours

Miss Coutts. CHARLES DICKENS

To HENRY BIRT,[3] 16 MARCH 1846*

MS Miss Winifred A. Myers. *Address:* Henry Birt Esquire | 8 Bird Street | Oxford Street.

Devonshire Terrace | Sixteenth March 1846

Mr. Charles Dickens presents his compliments to Mr. Birt, and begs to say in reply to Mr. Birt's letter, that he has nothing whatever to do with the Editorship or current Management of the Daily News; and that the card of admission to the entertainment at Crosby Hall[4] should have been sent, in the ordinary course, to the Office of the Paper. Mr. Dickens has forwarded it to the gentleman who writes the Musical articles, but that gentleman exercises his own discretion on such subjects.

To MR BURKE,[5] 16 MARCH 1846*

MS Mr David Borowitz.

1 Devonshire Terrace | York Gate Regents Park.
Sixteenth March 1846.

Private

Mr. Charles Dickens presents his compliments to Mr. Burke, and begs to say, with thanks to Mr. Burke for his obliging letter, that he has always had it in contemplation to follow up the letters on Capital Punishment with a Letter on Secondary Punishments—in which he has taken some interest, and of which he

---

[1] This was the main point in CD's speech at the Anniversary Dinner of the Fund on 6 Apr (*Speeches*, ed. K. J. Fielding, pp. 73–7). He had become a trustee soon after the Fund was started in 1839: see Vol. III, p. 467 and *n*.

[2] Nothing is known about Esther's time at Mitcham; by Sep 54 she was married to a Mr Nash.

[3] Unidentified.

[4] A concert of "Gems of Scottish Song" at Crosby Hall on 17 Mar was advertised in the *Daily News* of 16 Mar, but was not reported.

[5] Unidentified.

has had some experience and observation for years past. But as the heading of such a letter, for the purposes of a Newspaper, is a different one, and as he objects on principle to the position that those who shew Capital Punishment to be ineffectual and demoralizing are at all bound to provide a substitute for it, he has not made any reference to this supplementary Article in his remarks on the Penalty of Death.

He is glad to assure Mr. Burke, however, that he has it already in preparation, and that he designs to complete and publish it—most probably within a week or so.[1]

To THE REV. HENRY COLMAN, 16 MARCH 1846

Mention in C. F. Libbie & Co. catalogue, May 1900; *MS* 1 p.; dated Devonshire Terrace, 16 Mar 46.

To CHARLES GILPIN,[2] 16 MARCH 1846

Text from N, 1, 742.

Devonshire Terrace | Sixteenth March 1846

Respected Friend,

I cannot positively *promise* to attend the meeting on the 29th April;[3] but I hope to do so, and if I can I certainly will. Make any arrangements that best suit thy friends. I will adapt my engagements to it, if possible.

Thine truly
[CHARLES DICKENS]

To MESSRS BRADBURY & EVANS, 16 MARCH 1846

MS Dickens House.

Devonshire Terrace. | Sixteenth March 1846. | Monday Night

Dear Sirs.

I was on the point of writing to you about Mr. Stanfield when I received your note. I had only known of his scruples[4] the day before.

---

[1] CD evidently found he had not time to write this letter; but he may instead have encouraged someone else to embody his ideas in an article on "Secondary Punishment" which appeared in the *Daily News* of 14 May 46. It considered how transportation might be improved and made reformative, on Maconochie's lines; the views are consistent with CD's, but it is not the kind of article he would have written himself, nor, except for a few sentences, at all like his style.

[2] Charles Gilpin (1815–74), bookseller, politician and philanthropist; born in Bristol of Quaker parents, nephew of Joseph Sturge of Birmingham, brother of

Henry Gilpin (see Vol. II, p. 74n); a liberal' follower of Bright and Cobden; spoke frequently at Exeter Hall and elsewhere on behalf of the Peace Society and other charitable and benevolent institutions; became director of various companies and later MP for Northampton.

[3] Of the Society for the Abolition of Capital Punishment, founded by Gilpin in 1846: see *To* Gilpin, 28 Apr 46. One of the pamphlets it published, by Frederic Rowton, was dedicated to CD "respectfully, and with permission . . . March 31st, 1846".

[4] N, 1, 741 reads "samples", in error.

I have thought it best to go to Colnaghi's, and ask if they could find me any clever young artist or Student who has been in Italy, and has brought home a Portfolio of such Sketches as I want. I did so on Saturday, and he assures me that he has little doubt of sending some such gentleman to me tomorrow. The book will require to be very carefully looked after, when it is once got under weigh, as it certainly must be published in May. I will leave all arrangements of detail with the artist to you, and will communicate with you again (I hope) tomorrow[1] or next day.

I want to know, when you have had time to think of it, how soon after June, you think we might, safely, and with real effect, begin a story in Monthly Numbers—so that it should not commence at a dead time of the year.[2]

[1] Colnaghi's (then at 14 Pall Mall East) evidently recommended the painter Samuel Palmer (1805–81; *DNB*); this was a difficult point in his career and he was supporting himself and his family mainly by teaching. He had recently spent some years in Italy and exhibited pictures of Italian scenes at the RA 1840-2 and at the Royal Society for Painters in Water Colours 1843-5. Ruskin in *Modern Painters*, I, vi, 2 (passage added in 3rd edn, 1846) praised his drawing of foliage—"I have never seen a stone-pine or a cypress drawn except by him". A letter from Palmer to an unknown correspondent (either his father-in-law, John Linnell, or his old friend, Edward Calvert), undated but probably 17 or 18 Mar 46, runs: "Mr. Dickens has applied to me to draw on wood vignettes of Italian subjects for a work he is about to publish (which it will be better not to mention till he advertises it) as he may not wish it known. As the time is very pressing he will (should he decide on seeing my sketches this afternoon) send the publishers to me to settle terms &c. If they ask me what I charge I shall not know what to ask. Mr. Dickens says that besides doing the drawings I shall have to oversee the blocks in their progress. [*Small drawing of a large house on a lake, with boat*] They will be about this size & like those in Rogers' *Italy*— | I should wish to do them cheaply but have not a notion about price. If you could give me a guess by return of post I should feel obliged & I will come over and speak to you about it as soon as possible but at present cannot leave —expecting Mr. Dickens at 4 o'clock & the publishers in the course of the day or tomorrow; the time when he will call is uncertain ... in great haste | The publishers are Bradbury & Evans" (MS Huntington). There was a slight delay, which caused Palmer great anxiety; but on ?19 Mar he had "a very polite note from the publisher" fixing a meeting on Friday or Saturday: "This has cheered me and quite revived poor Anny—I am as weak as a rat and a spectacle to the little boys in the street as I totter along—but have got home from Willesden without catching cold and if the dreadful day tomorrow can be got thro' hope for recovery" (Palmer *to* ?Linnell; MS Mr Raymond Lister). Palmer was paid £21 (Bradbury & Evans Accounts, V & A). Either from pressure of time, or difficulties of reproduction, the original plan for 12 illustrations was reduced; the four vignettes are: "The Street of the Tombs: Pompeii" on the title-page, "The Villa d'Este at Tivoli from the Cypress Avenue" at the beginning of the text, "The Colosseum of Rome" at the head of "Going through France" and an untitled vignette of a vineyard on the final page; an unused illustration of the Campagna survives as a pencil drawing with instructions to the engraver (Suzannet Collection, sold Sotheby's Nov 1971). Palmer was an accomplished etcher but not much accustomed to the medium of wood-engraving, and instructions to the engraver on the margin of the original drawing of the Villa d'Este and on the retouched proofs show his fastidiousness and the problems of reproducing his delicate drawing: the original drawing and the MS notes, then in the possession of A. H. Palmer, are reproduced by F. G. Kitton, *Dickens and his Illustrators*, plate IV and pp. 185-7; see also A. H. Palmer, *Life and Letters of Samuel Palmer*, 1892.

[2] Most of CD's serial novels started in March, April or May, and none in July, August or September; *Dombey* is the only one that starts in October.

Among the strange letters I receive every day, is the enclosed. I know nothing of the writer. If you should think it desirable to see the pamphlet and have some judgment on it, I will refer him to you. I have an idea that if it should prove to be well done, it might be worth so small a venture, and might make a noise just now, when some[1]

To E. F. SAVILLE,[2] 18 MARCH 1846

MS Boston Public Library.

1 Devonshire Terrace | York Gate Regents Park
Eighteenth March 1846

Sir.

I beg to assure you that I am not, in any way, connected with the editorship or current management of the Daily News; and that the letter of Judex,[3] though I approved of it ever so thoroughly, would have to be sent to the Editor of the Paper, at its office in Whitefriars.

But if you will allow me, as one who is very much interested in the subject,[4] to state my objections to it, I will do so. They are solely mine, and have no reference whatever to the paper; to which it can still be offered—except thus far. That I am sure it is enormously too long.

There can be no question of the intention with which it is written, and it is very well expressed. But such experience as I have of these matters, teaches me that nothing is got by defying the Public; and that they must be invited and coaxed into supporting such an institution. I do not think it wise to attack the other Funds, and I certainly think that to cast any reflections on those who support them, is to damage this project most decidedly. The writer scarcely seems to remember, too, that it has not, as yet, been plainly stated to the Public, and that they have had little opportunity of understanding its merits. If it had been elaborately explained and tried, and great appeals had been made in its favor, and all this had been unsuccessful, even then little more could be said, than is said in this letter.

Under these circumstances, and in these terms, I think it would prejudice the cause, wherever published. But this is merely my individual opinion, and I am (of course) as liable to be wrong as another.

I am Sir | Faithfully Yours

E. F. Saville Esquire.   CHARLES DICKENS

---

[1] These words come at the foot of the page; the rest of the letter is missing.

[2] Edmund Faucit Saville, stage name of Edmund Faucit (1811–57); son of John Saville Faucit, actor (known as Faucit Saville after separating from his wife, an actress), and brother of Helen Faucit (see Vol. III, p. 597*n*); began his stage career

1830 and came to London 1837, where he played in melodrama at the Surrey, Sadler's Wells, and Victoria Theatres.

[3] No letter with this signature appeared in the *Daily News*.

[4] Clearly related to the General Theatrical Fund; Saville was a member of the Committee.

To EDGAR ALLAN POE,[1] 19 MARCH 1846

MS Historical Society of Pennsylvania. *Address:* By Mail Steamer | Edgar. A. Poe Esquire | New York | U.S. of America.

1 Devonshire Terrace, London. | Nineteenth March 1846.

Dear Sir.

Although I have not received your Volume,[2] I avail myself of a leisure moment to thank you for the gift of it.

In reference to your proposal as regards the Daily News, I beg to assure you that I am not in any way connected with the Editorship or current Management of that Paper. I have an interest in it, and write such papers for it as I attach my name to. This is the whole amount of my connexion with the Journal.

Any such proposition as yours, therefore, must be addressed to the Editor. I do not know, for certain, how that gentleman might regard it; but I should say that he probably[3] has as many correspondents in America and elsewhere, as the Paper can afford space to.

I am Dear Sir | Faithfully Yours

Edgar. A. Poe Esquire   CHARLES DICKENS

To CAPTAIN ALEXANDER MACONOCHIE,[4] 21 MARCH 1846*

Text from typed copy in Dickens House.

Devonshire Terrace | Twenty First March 1846

Dear Sir

I dare say you know Mr. Chesterton (the Governor of the Middlesex House of Correction) by name. He is a very intelligent and humane gentleman, who has

[1] Edgar Allan Poe (1809–49; *DAB*): see Vol. III, p. 106*n*. Poe had been proprietor of the *Broadway Journal* in 1845, but it had just come to an end, and he was in difficulties.

[2] Probably *The Raven, and other Poems*, published in America Nov 45; dedicated to Elizabeth Barrett.

[3] "certainly" deleted.

[4] Captain Alexander Maconochie, RN (1787–1860), penal reformer; first secretary of the Royal Geographical Society, Professor of Geography at University College, London 1833–6; private secretary to Sir John Franklin, in Van Diemen's Land 1837–9; Governor of Norfolk Island 1840–4. He opposed the separate and silent systems in prison discipline and was a pioneer of the reformatory movement, but suffered much from opposition: his proposal to employ convicts in the building of Harbours of Refuge at Portland was rejected by the Home Office 23 Apr 46; a leader in defence of his system, and praising his "rare power of sympathy" and "subtle intellect", appeared in the *Daily News*, 28 Apr. Author of many pamphlets on the management of prisoners, and of *Crime and Punishment*, published July 46, his most important work. The "Marks system" by which he was chiefly known was simply a means to reform and rehabilitate prisoners through incentives (see P. A. W. Collins, *Dickens and Crime*, 1962, pp. 166–70, 335–6, and John Vincent Barry, *Alexander Maconochie of Norfolk Island*, 1958). A pamphlet of Maconochie's published in Hobart, Tasmania, 1839, was in the Gad's Hill library (with others by him) at CD's death, but it is not known when they first met; this letter suggests a recent acquaintance, perhaps through the Ragged School movement; Maconochie attended the meeting on 18 Mar (*Daily News*, 20 Mar).

great experience of Criminals, and whom I have frequently consulted in reference to their condition and improvement. It happened the other evening, when I met him somewhere at dinner, that he spoke with great interest of your system (which he had been studying in your explanation of it) and shewed that he quite understood and appreciated the principles on which it is founded. As he expressed, also, a desire to know you and to have an opportunity of conversing with you about it, I said I would endeavour to give him that opportunity.

Can you give me the pleasure of dining here next Saturday, this day week, at 6 o'Clock. In the meantime I shall be always at home between Eleven and One.

I think of publishing my letters, such as they are, on the Punishment of Death, in a Pamphlet,[1] with an additional chapter on Secondary Punishments. It would command more attention, and would be more important, in that form, I think, than in a Newspaper.

Faithfully Yours

Captain Maconochie   CHARLES DICKENS

To C. E. COTTERELL, 23 MARCH 1846*

MS Mitchell Library, Sydney.

Devonshire Terrace | Twenty Third March 1846

My Dear Sir

I have not seen any means whatever, as yet, (I regret to say) of doing anything with Le Gros' MSS.[2] But the opportunity of doing anything with them is as likely, I think, to present itself to me, as to anybody. And I would propose that you should leave them with me a little longer—unless you have any plan in reference to them—and allow me to write to you on the subject at Naples.

I am really shocked to find you still in London. I took it into my head, and was quite satisfied (though I should be puzzled to say why) that you had gone to Italy long ago.

You say 'in a day or two'. I hope that does not mean until after Saturday next, and that you will be able to dine here, that day, at 6. You would be interested, I think. I have two or three people coming, who are learned in Crime and Criminals (one of them the Governor of that Prison we saw, and whom I dare say you remember); and among them a late Governor of Norfolk Island, who is the inventor of a very remarkable system indeed, of Secondary Punishment: which I have no doubt will, in some modified form or other, become as the World grows better and more compassionate, very generally received. I hope you will be able to make this an Engagement between us.

Faithfully Yours always

C. E. Cotterell Esquire   CHARLES DICKENS

---

[1] No such pamphlet was published, but the intention seems to have persisted; Carlyle wrote to Forster on 22 Mar 48 (MS Forster Collection, V & A): "If you have a copy of Dickens's Pamphlet on Capital Punishments, send it by Espinasse, and I will read it". The pamphlet published by Dyson in Nov 1849 contained only the two letters to *The Times* on the Mannings' execution; J. C. Eckel (*First Editions of the Works of CD*, 1932, p. 179) and others following him have described it wrongly.

[2] Not traced.

To WILLIAM CULLENFORD, 23 MARCH 1846

Photograph, Dickens House.

Devonshire Terrace | Twenty Third March 1846

Dear Sir

The enclosed ⧺ (which is a curiosity) is from the renowned Mr. Toole; the most emphatic, vigorous, attentive, and stentorian toastmaster in the Queen's Dominions—I hope you will have him.

— Cullenford Esquire

Faithfully Yours

CHARLES DICKENS

To JAMES TOOLE,[1] 23 MARCH 1846*

MS Washington University Libraries.[2]

1 Devonshire Terrace | York Gate Regents Park
Twenty Third March 1846.

Dr. Mr. Toole.

If I had my will, I assure you there should never be a public dinner without you. You are the best and greatest of Toastmasters, and can never be too highly appreciated.

I have nothing to do with the arrangements for The General Theatrical Fund Dinner; but I have written to the Secretary, and told him that I hope he will not fail to secure me your assistance.[3]

Faithfully Yours

Mr. Toole.

CHARLES DICKENS

To THOMAS POWELL, 23 MARCH 1846*

MS Mr Thaddeus Crenshaw.

Devonshire Terrace | Monday Twenty Third March | 1846.

My Dear Powell.

I have thought of those subjects, but am at present taken (in a Newspaper point of view) lazy, and ill-conditioned.

I don't know what the most dangerous letters in the alphabet may be, unless they are U and I.

Faithfully Always

Thomas Powell Esquire

CD.

---

[1] James Toole, toastmaster of the East India Company; father of J. L. Toole, the comedian.

[2] CD wrote this letter twice, no doubt to ensure that Toole received it either at business or at home: MS New York Public Library (lacking the subscription, and with minor variants of punctuation and capitals) is addressed to "Mr. Toole | East India House".

[3] Reports show that Toole did act as toastmaster.

To AUGUSTUS TRACEY, 23 MARCH 1846*

MS University of Texas.

Devonshire Terrace | Monday Twenty Third March | 1846.
My Dear Tracey.

I have asked Captain Maconochie (late Governor of Norfolk Island, of whose system we were speaking at your house the other day) to dine here next Saturday at 6; and have asked Chesterton to meet him. If you tell me you are engaged, I shall attack you savagely in some public Journal, for having poured boiling water over that man's Thigh.

Ever Yours
CHARLES DICKENS

P.S. I shall head the article "Inhuman atrocity in Tothill Fields Prison.—Ferocious cruelty of the Governor."

To MISS ROSS,[1] [28 MARCH 1846]

Envelope only, MS Frederick T. Macartney. *Address:* Miss Ross | 4 Howard Street | Strand. PM 28 Mar 46.

To FREDERICK SALMON,[2] 28 MARCH 1846

Mention in Sotheby's catalogue, May 1899; dated 28 Mar 46.

Sending inscribed copies of Martin Chuzzlewit, A Christmas Carol, The Chimes *and* The Cricket on the Hearth.[3]

To DR JAMES KAY-SHUTTLEWORTH,[4] 28 MARCH 1846*

MS The Hon. Mrs Charles Leaf.

Devonshire Terrace | Twenty Eighth March 1846.
My Dear Sir

I regret to say that having some relatives bespoken to dinner tomorrow, I cannot have the pleasure of accepting your kind invitation.

---

[1] Thomasina Ross (1794–1875), author and translator: see Vol. III, p. 353 and *n*; in 1846 published translations in *Bentley's*, and of Count Saint-Marie's *Algeria in 1845*. As the elder sister, with whom CD had been in touch in 1842, the most likely recipient: a family tradition, however, associates the envelope with her sister Georgina (see Vol. I, p. 7*n*).

[2] Frederick Salmon (1796–1868), surgeon: see Vol. II, p. 404*n*.

[3] Inscribed "From his friend Charles Dickens", dated 28 Mar 46. The copies of the *Chimes* and the *Cricket* are in the Rosenbach Collection, the *Carol* was in the

catalogue of the Jerome Kern Collection, 1929, and *Chuzzlewit* was sold at Sotheby's, May 1899, with the letter from CD inserted.

[4] James Phillips Kay-Shuttleworth, MD (1804–77; *DNB*): see Vol. III, p. 557*n*. Founder of English system of popular education; had been an Assistant Poor Law Commissioner; established Battersea Training College 1839–40; his reports on the training of pauper children published 1841; first Secretary to the Committee of Council nominated to administer grants for popular education 1839–1849.

I made a similar foray *last* Sunday, and saw four Schools. I particularly desire to have an opportunity of discussing the subject with you.

There is no doubt that they are (almost of necessity so far) badly managed; and there is no doubt, I think, that the Union "take in" Schools, which are not, properly speaking, Ragged Schools at all.

Have you seen the School on Saffron Hill?—in West Street?[1] That *is* a Ragged School.

What I want to do, before moving legislatively in the matter, is, to try an experimental Normal Ragged School, on a system. It could be done, without reference to the Union, at a very small expence; and surely you and I could set one going, and ascertain, by facts and figures, and regular entries in books, what could be done in Three Months.[2] I am sure there would be no difficulty in getting Money by voluntary subscription for the purpose.

Then the boys would not be wearied to death, and driven away, by long Pulpit discourses, which it is out of the question that they can understand, and which it is equally out of the question to expect them to receive with interest and patience if they could. They might be amused, instructed, and in some sort reformed, with much greater hopefulness and visibility of effect. We should have some data to go upon, and something, of our own knowledge and within our own direction, to describe. And having that, and being enabled to describe favorably, I take it to be certain that such schools *must* become an Institution of the Country.

I am very strong upon this, because I fear that without some such step, the end will be greatly retarded.

Believe me always | Faithfully Yours

H.[3] Kay Shuttleworth Esquire   CHARLES DICKENS

To CLARKSON STANFIELD, 28 MARCH 1846*

MS Colonel Richard Gimbel.

Devonshire Terrace | Twenty Eighth March 1846

My Dear Stanny.

Let me congratulate you on Mrs. Stanfield's safety—if not on the new boy.[4] I suppose you are (like me) past all congratulations on that score.

---

[1] The Field Lane School at West St, Smithfield, visited by CD in Sep 43: see Vol. III, pp. 561–4, 574. Others were St Giles's in Streatham St, and Jurston St, New Cut, Lambeth. A further meeting had taken place at the Lambeth Ragged School 18 Mar, at which Kay-Shuttleworth was present; 300 children assembled and there were speeches by Lord Ashley, Benjamin Hawes and others (*Daily News*, 20 Mar 46).

[2] No such school was set up before CD went abroad, but it must have been the subject of the long letter to Lord John Russell "about the Ragged Schools" mentioned in *To* Forster, 28 June 46.

[3] Thus in MS.

[4] Edward Herbert Stanfield (1846–1931).

Although I am coming, anon, to see your pictures,[1] I write to say that I hope you mean to go to the General Theatrical Fund Dinner on Monday Week, where Mac will also dine. Let me know, that I may touch up the Committee to place you near me.

Being in the chair, I can guarantee you against a Speech, and will make it a point of honor to do so.

> Ever Heartily Yours
> Dick The Doomed.

To CHARLES COCHRANE,[2] 30 MARCH 1846

MS John Rylands Library.

Devonshire Terrace | Monday Morning | March Thirtieth 1846

My Dear Sir

I lose no time in expressing my regret that I cannot undertake to preside at the proposed Meeting, though I receive the Committee's request as one that does me much honor. Apart from my not knowing but that I may be summoned out of town at almost any hour after Monday next (which would be an insurmountable objection in itself) I have pledged myself to many Institutions to the effect that I have only leisure to occupy the chair at certain places I have named to them, but that *if*[3] I should increase my list of such engagements, I will certainly recognize their claim upon me. And my taking the chair at the Poor Man's Guardian Society[4] would involve me, consequently, in more engagements of that nature than I have time or money to discharge.

For these reasons I am obliged to decline. But if I should be in town when the Meeting is held, I shall be happy to move or second any Resolution that may not be bestowed upon a better advocate.

> Dear Sir | Faithfully Yours
Charles Cochrane Esquire.   CHARLES DICKENS

---

[1] Probably the four pictures Stanfield was sending to the RA, one of which was *Il Ponte Rotto, Rome*.

[2] Charles Cochrane (?1807–55), natural son of the Hon. Basil Cochrane. He travelled the country 1825–6, in Hungarian costume, singing to the guitar, and Mayhew's farce, *The Wandering Minstrel*, 1834, was based on his eccentricities. President of the National Philanthropic Institute, Leicester Square, 1842–50; founded Poor Man's Guardian Society 1846.

[3] Underlined twice.

[4] The object of the society was to "aid the poor in their application for parochial relief"; John Walter of *The Times* was President. Its first public meeting was held 8 Apr; the advertisement in the *Daily News* of 3 Apr named CD among the "noblemen and gentlemen who have promised their attendance", and in *The Times* advertisement he was in the list of Vice-presidents. At the meeting Cochrane explained his absence as due to "the pressure of other engagements". CD promised a subscription of 5 guineas (*The Times*, 16 Apr), which was paid 22 May (Account-book, MS Messrs Coutts).

To [J. G. GENT],[1] [?APRIL 1846]

Summary in the Ragged School Union Minute Book (MS Shaftesbury Society) of letter read at the Monthly Meeting of the Managing Committee of the Ragged School Union, 1 May 46. *Date:* letter clearly received soon after the previous monthly meeting on 3 Apr. *Address:* presumably addressed to Joseph George Gent: see *fn.*

Stating that he had subscriptions in his possession amounting to £4.2.0 to be devoted to Ragged Schools, which if not otherwise disposed of he would hand over to the Ragged School Union.[2]

To W. C. MACREADY, 4 APRIL 1846*

MS Morgan Library. *Address:* William Charles Macready Esq | 5 Clarence Terrace | Regents Park.

Bell Alley Coleman Street.[3] | 4th: April 1846.

Sir.

Yourself v Dickens.

We are requested by our Client Mr. Charles Dickens, to forward you the sum of half a crown, current money—the amount in wh. he considers himself to stand indebted to you.[4] We beg to add on our own behalf that we do so under protest, the transon being an illegal one.

We are | Sir | Your obedient Servants
Pitchcock, Swabber, Trillington, and Dawberry.

To | Mr. William Charles Macready.

To WILLIAM CULLENFORD, 5 APRIL 1846

Mention in Sotheby's catalogue, June 1911; *MS* 2 pp.; dated 5 Apr 46.

Concerning the Dinner in connection with the Theatrical Fund. He mentions that Stanfield is too ill to attend.

To COUNT D'ORSAY, 8 APRIL 1846*

MS Comte de Gramont.

Devonshire Terrace | Eighth April 1846

My Dear Count D'Orsay.

My private Opinion, is, that the Proprietors of the Daily News are Mad.

I have sent after Captain Taylor, and requested him, if he be in town, to

[1] Joseph George Gent (1811–94), one of the founders of the Ragged School Union; secretary 1849–50.

[2] The Ragged School Union Minutes for 3 Apr 46 record that Joseph George Gent had called at the *Daily News* offices for subscriptions left there for Ragged Schools, but was told that CD had the money; he was asked to get in touch with CD.

[3] Little Bell Alley, where most of the houses were occupied by small tradesmen. The letter is written in an attempt at a clerkly hand.

[4] Debt perhaps incurred on 1 Apr when Macready was at the Star and Garter, Richmond, with CD, Catherine and Georgina, Forster, Maclise and Stanfield: "a very merry—I suppose I must say *jolly* day—rather more tumultuous than I quite like" (Macready, *Diaries*, II, 333).

report himself to you immediately.[1] I am half ashamed to communicate with him; for I shall not be surprised if the Proprietors of the D. N. have been playing shabby tricks with him in his pursuit of his invention, as with most other people with whom they have had anything to do.

The letters I am taking religious care of. I will bring them back to my Lady, myself, as soon as I have done with them—in about a week or so.

Ever Affectionately Yours
CHARLES DICKENS

The Count D'Orsay.

To G. E. HERING,[2] 8 APRIL 1846

Mention in S. F. Henkels catalogue No. 1163; *MS* (3rd pers.); dated Devonshire Terrace, 8 Apr 46.

Apologizing for not being able to inspect his paintings.

To MISS BURDETT COUTTS, 9 APRIL 1846†

MS Morgan Library.

Devonshire Terrace. | Thursday Night | Ninth April 1846.

My Dear Miss Coutts.

I thank you for your kind note, which I received with great pleasure.

I shall be glad to tell you all about Charley and his forthcoming King's College Career, viva voce. And as I owe him a holiday, in consequence of his having conducted himself with brilliancy at School, I shall (unless you tell me you will not be there) bring him down pr. Railway, to make a Morning call on you at Brighton *next Monday Week.* *a*In the mean time I shall feel it necessary to get up some information about Locomotive Engines, or I shall be brought to a stand-still, and shall lose my position, before we get to Croydon, through not being able to answer questions.*a*

Believe me always | Faithfully Yours
CHARLES DICKENS

Miss Burdett Coutts.

To THOMAS BEARD, 11 APRIL 1846

MS Dickens House. *Address:* Thomas Beard Esquire | 42 Portman Place | Edgeware Road.

Devonshire Terrace | Saturday 11th. April 1846

My Dear Beard

Those dissenters ("may they be damned", as Maclise would say) demanded ten days more to consider, which will bring them to some time next week.

---

[1] Tayler's "Telephone" was a modification of an invention patented earlier for use on trains to facilitate communication between guard and engine-driver, a problem in which D'Orsay was also interested; he had proposed a rope running through rings at the side of the roof.

[2] George Edwards Hering (1805–79; *DNB*), landscape painter, especially of Italian scenery. A copy of his *Sketches on the Danube,* 1838, presented by Hering to Forster, given to CD by Forster 7 Feb 39, was in the Gad's Hill library at CD's death (*Catalogue of the Library of CD,* ed. J. H. Stonehouse, p. 57).

aa Mostly given in N, I, 743 from catalogue source; letter otherwise unpublished.

Forster attended the last meeting, which lasted *six hours*. Some of the dissenters, I believe, fell prostrate on the floor, and foamed at the mouth with exhaustion.[1]

Faithfully Ever

Thomas Beard Esquire. CHARLES DICKENS

To JAMES SHERMAN,[2] 11 APRIL 1846

Extract in J. A. Shavgordi Katalog 593; MS 1 p.; dated London, 11 Apr 46.

Mr. Charles Dickens presents his compliments to Mr. Sherman and begs to express his regret that he is prevented by other engagements from accepting the Invitation of the Officers and Stewards of the Asylum for Infant Orphans.[3]

To MISS BURDETT COUTTS, [13 APRIL 1846]*

MS Morgan Library. Date: clearly the Monday after 9 Apr: see To Miss Coutts, that day.

Devonshire Terrace | Monday Morning

My Dear Miss Coutts.

I write a hurried line—pending my hearing from you again—to say that if you should remain at Brighton this week, I can run down with Charley any morning except Friday and Saturday. I shall do so, if I find your second note propitious.[4]

Always Dear Miss Coutts | Faithfully Yours

Miss Burdett Coutts. CHARLES DICKENS

To COUNT D'ORSAY, 14 APRIL 1846*

MS Comte de Gramont.

Devonshire Terrace | Tuesday Fourteenth April | 1846

My Dear Count D'Orsay

Can you dine here, next Tuesday the Twenty First, at half past Six? Lord Robertson is going to dine with us—and Macready.

If you can, we have been thinking it will be as well to Christen the youngster

---

[1] Discussions about the future of the paper had been continuing for the past month, with a division of opinion among the "proprietors", who were now quite numerous (see *To* Mme de la Rue, 17 Apr). Paxton attended a meeting on 25 Mar, which was evidently indecisive; the "dissenters" then set up a sub-committee to inquire into the financial condition of the paper. On 30 Mar Forster wrote to Paxton to tell him that this "sub-committee of laymen" (presumably so-called because not concerned with the business management) were meeting Bradbury & Evans and himself at his chambers next day ("how I wish *you* were here!"); he thought this "inspiriting news". He named among them "Dr Campbell" as "the hard-headed Vulcan of

Dissent" (MS Devonshire Collections)—a joke, as this was clearly the Rev. John Campbell, D.D., Congregational minister at Moorfields, himself an editor of two periodicals and a fierce controversialist. CD's letter shows that their differences were not resolved by 11 Apr; see *To* Mitton, 20 Apr, *fn.*

[2] James Sherman, Secretary of the New Asylum for Infant Orphans.

[3] At Stamford Hill; for orphans under eight without distinction of religious connexion. The second Anniversary Dinner was held on 27 May; Lord Morpeth was in the Chair (*Daily News,* 7 Apr).

[4] Miss Coutts evidently preferred to see him in London the following week: see *To* Miss Coutts, 22 Apr.

on that day.[1] I protest, however, against your being summoned to the church part of the ceremony, because I can find you a Deputy, and save you the bore of coming out in the Morning.[2]

                                              Ever Affectionately
The Count D'Orsay.   CHARLES DICKENS

To W. C. MACREADY, 14 APRIL 1846*

MS Morgan Library. *Date:* Easter Sunday fell on 12 Apr in 1846.

                         Devonshire Terrace | Easter Tuesday Evening 1846.
My Dear Macready.

Lord Robertson stays (his custom always, in these holidays)[3] with Liston the Surgeon; and is to be found accordingly, at 5 Clifford Street Bond Street.

Wallie[4] appears to me to be everything that a Parent could desire. I foresee in this next generation the seeds of Seven League Boots—and in his wisdom concerning the two F's, of a prodigious pair.

Your Postscript is mean and drivelling. Was it for this, I settled this morning to christen the Babby on that Tuesday!!![5]

I am having engraved on a brass plate to be fixed up over the street door, and on another brass plate to be inlaid in the door steps, the following words (with a prospective reference) selected from that surprising combination of wit, wisdom, humour, fancy, and pleasantry, The Life and Adventures of Nicholas Nickleby

" 'We want no Babbies here,' said Mr. Kenwigs. 'Take 'em away to the Fondling!' "[6]

Let me recommend it to you and Mrs. Macready[7]—to whom my love. Is it true that you are to be examined before the House of Commons Committee on Population?

                                              Ever Heartily Yours
W. C. Macready Esquire.   CHARLES DICKENS

[1] Though Macready could not come (see next) the christening took place on 21 Apr. Tennyson (perhaps written to at the same time) was also at the dinner; Elizabeth Barrett heard of it from her brother, who had seen Tennyson 30 Apr—but knew only that he had been "meeting various celebrities"; by 7 May Browning had learnt more details: "And what, *what* do you suppose Tennyson's business to have been ...? He has been sponsor to Dickens' child *in company with Count D'Orsay*, and accordingly the *novus homo* glories in the prænomina, Alfred D'Orsay Tennyson Dickens! Ah, Charlie, if this don't prove to posterity that you might have been a Tennyson and were a D'Orsay—why excellent labour will have been lost! You observe, 'Alfred' is common to both the godfather and the—devil-father, as I take

the Count to be" (*Letters of Robert Browning and Elizabeth Barrett, 1845–1846*, II, 116, 135–6).

[2] CD's seemingly casual attitude to sponsorship did not escape Browning's criticism: "When you remember what the form of sponsorship is, to what it pledges you in the ritual of the Church of England—and *then* remember that Mr. Dickens is an enlightened Unitarian,—you will get a curious notion of the man, I fancy" (*ibid*).

[3] Cf. *Hamlet*, I, iv, 60.

[4] Walter Francis Sheil Macready, *b.* 27 June 40.

[5] Macready was evidently too busy to come (*Diaries*, II, 335–6).

[6] In Ch. 36, after the defection of Mr Lillyvick.

[7] Cecilia Benvenuta Macready was born 20 Aug 46.

To THOMAS MITTON, [?14 APRIL 1846]

MS Liverpool Public Libraries. *Date:* Handwriting (not completely consistent at that date) suggests Apr 46; there were grounds for expecting "News" that the paper could continue, on Wed 15 Apr: see *fn.*

Devonshire Terrace | Tuesday Night.

My Dear Mitton

I am afraid to make an engagement for tomorrow; for I think I may have in the afternoon, to hear Newspaper News.[1] But next day (Thursday) is likely, I imagine, to suit me very well. If you should not hear from me tomorrow before you leave business; will you understand that I will be with you on Thursday at $\frac{1}{2}$ past 4?

Faithfully Ever
CD.

To COUNT D'ORSAY, 16 APRIL 1846*

MS Comte de Gramont.

Devonshire Terrace | Sixteenth April 1846

My Dear Count D'Orsay.

Alfred D'Orsay Tennyson!

That shall be his name, or nothing. I never thought of Tennyson being Alfred too. Again I say

Alfred D'Orsay Tennyson!

Ever Yours
CHARLES DICKENS

To MADAME DE LA RUE, 17 APRIL 1846

MS Comtesse de Suzannet.

Devonshire Terrace.
Friday Seventeenth April 1846.

My Dearest Madame De la Rue.

I received your letter this morning, and immediately sit down to say that your patient was, beyond all question, mistaken, in regard to me. And to make this clearer to you, I will tell you what I have been delaying for, from day to day.

[1] Paxton was in London again, and Sarah, writing to him on Thurs 16 Apr, hoped that he was "by this time comparatively happy about the ill-fated Paper—if Mr William Allcard's scheme is carried out, & should prove a success he will deserve constellation!!!" (MS Devonshire Collections).

I am exceedingly unsettled in my plans. I think I told you some time ago—or I wrote it to De la Rue; I am not sure which—that I was not satisfied with the business Managers of the Newspaper.[1] In the course of a little more time, I saw so much reason to believe that they would be the Ruin of what might otherwise have been made a very fine property—and that their proceedings would so commit and involve me, who had no power either of getting rid of them or controulling them—that I straightway stopped my letters, and walked, bodily, out of the concern.[2] The result of this, has been a daily-widening division among all the halfhundred people connected with the Paper; and I am strongly inclined to believe that it will *stop* abruptly. Pending their disputes and differences among themselves, I cannot very well leave town. But if the Paper should go by the board, then I should be strongly disposed to do so, and to go abroad for another year. For I have engaged to produce a new story in twenty monthly parts, and I think I could write it more comfortably and easily, abroad, than at home. Now, I need not tell you that *I* want to go to Genoa! But Mrs. Dickens, who was never very well there, cannot be got to contemplate the Peschiere—though I have beset her in all kinds of ways.[3] Therefore, I think I should take a middle course, for the present[4] and, coming as near you as I could, pitch my tent somewhere on the Lake of Geneva—say at Lausanne, whence I should run over to Genoa immediately. Against my coming away at all, there is the consideration that I am (nominally, God knows) a Law Student, and have a certain number of 'terms to keep" before I can be called to the Bar; and it would be well for me to be called, as there are many little pickings to be got—pretty easily within my reach—which *can* only be bestowed on Barristers.[5] Again, there is the consideration that the good people of England seem to be fonder of their favorite (your humble servant and physician) now, than ever; and that it might be a pity to run away from them, when they are so very kind. On the other hand if these people *do* ruin the Paper, I shall be very much annoyed, and would rather not have to be questioned, and condoled with, and all sorts of things, in all kinds of society. Now, every day (to the exclusion of almost all other occupation) I have been discussing the pros and cons of all these questions, with Forster. Every day we have expected that the squabbling body of proprietors would decide on their course, and so enable me to decide on mine. Every day has brought with it a postponement to the next day. And all the time I have been in a condition of incessant restlessness, uneasiness, and uncertainty. From this I am not yet delivered. But I think this Week *must*[6] decide it; and the moment I resolve on my course, I will write to you again. Tell De la Rue, with my best regards, that I should have answered his letter,[7] but for the same reason, which rendered it impossible to write definitely.

[1] *To* de la Rue, 16 Feb 46, had told them of his resignation, but did not comment on the management.

[2] An inaccurate version; since CD's resignation, nine contributions with his name had appeared, the last on 16 Mar.

[3] CD's letter to Catherine of 5 Dec 53 (*Mr and Mrs CD*, ed. Walter Dexter, pp. 227–9), shows that she had been unhappy at Genoa about his obsession with the sufferings of Mme de la Rue.

[4] These three words added over caret.

[5] See Vol. I, p. 621*n*, and *To* Lord Morpeth, 20 June 46.

[6] Underlined twice.

[7] *To* de la Rue, 16 Feb 46, is endorsed "repondu le 17 mars".

Your magnetic case is a very extraordinary one, though nothing of that kind surprises me. I should like to see the lady very much, and to—no, not to try my hand upon her—to see you mesmerize her. Let us live in hope.

I shall publish, early next month, a little Volume called Pictures from Italy[1]— astonish the Consul by telling him the title, and give him my regards. An early Copy shall be got to you, by some means or other. You have been in my society these many days, for I have just finished Rome, and am now working back to Genoa.[2] The greater part of the descriptions were written in letters to Forster, but the putting of them together, and making additions to them, and touching them up, is rather a long job. I like them very much, and I think the Holy Week will make you laugh, and remind you of the reality.—My Diary of March the 19th. 1845 is lying open on my desk, and looking at it I see this entry "Madame D L R very ill in the night. Up 'till four." Good God how distinctly everything has been present to me as I have gone over all the ground again! And what a miserable Devil I seem, to be cooped up here, bothered by printers and stock jobbers, when there are bright Genoas (with bright patients in them!) and ruined Coliseums in the world.

I talk to all the Italian Boys who go about the streets with Organs and white mice, and give them mints of money per l'amore della bell'Italia.

Maclise has been painting a large picture for the Royal Academy Exhibition which opens in May. The subject is the Superstition of the Ordeal by Touch[3] —the old belief that if the Murderer touched the dead body of his Victim, it would bleed. It is very fine indeed, and buyers are fighting for it. He can have a Thousand Pounds for it, easily; but he says he "don't know"—and says nothing else. His last invention has been the abolition of straps to his trousers. We went down to Greenwich Fair last Monday, and walked about the[4]

To EDWARD BALDWIN, 18 APRIL 1846*

MS Goodspeed's Book Shop. *Date:* PM 18 Apr 46. *Address:* Edward Baldwin Esquire | Albion Hotel | Aldersgate Street.

Devonshire Terrace | Saturday Morning

My Dear Sir

I am truly sorry to be deprived of the gratification of dining with you today.[5]

---

[1] Published 18 May.

[2] In *Pictures*, CD does not "work back to Genoa" in any detail after the section on Rome, but concludes with "A Rapid Diorama" covering the actual travels of 6 Feb to 9 Apr 45, with only a few pages on the homeward journey which began 25 Mar. As he did not finish writing till 1 May, this reference must in fact have been to the whole "Diorama", unless there was a change of plan.

[3] Praised by Thackeray in his *Morning Chronicle* notice of 7 May 46 as "perhaps the best and greatest of the artist's works ... All the picture rolls and revolves round the little drop of blood in the centre" (*Contributions to the* Morning Chronicle, ed. G. N. Ray, pp. 145–6).

[4] Rest of letter missing.

[5] Baldwin gave an annual dinner for the literary staff of the *Herald* at the Albion, and on this occasion fifty staff presented him with a candelabra costing 380 guineas as a "testimonial"; the address was given by Beard with "taste, eloquence, and sincere feeling" (*Daily News*, 20 Apr 46).

For some weeks past, I have been, at intervals, a martyr to an affection of the nerves on one side of my face, originating in a cold. It has prevented me from going to all sorts of places, and makes me quite unfit, today, to join your party.

I regret this the more, because I sincerely wish you to believe that our intercourse hitherto has been most pleasant to me, and that I have an earnest desire to strengthen and improve it.

Believe me always | Faithfully Yours
CHARLES DICKENS

Edward Baldwin Esquire

To MISS MARION ELY, 19 APRIL 1846

Text from MDGH, I, 153.

Devonshire Terrace, Sunday, April 19th. 1846.

My Dear Miss Ely,

A mysterious emissary brought me a note in your always welcome handwriting at the Athenæum last night. I enquired of the servant in attendance whether the bearer of this letter was of my vast establishment. To which he replied "Yezzir." "Then," said I, "tell him not to wait."

Maclise was with me. It was then half-past seven. We had been walking, and were splashed to the eyes. We debated upon the possibility of getting to Russell Square in reasonable time—decided that it would be in the worst taste to appear when the performance[1] would be half over—and very reluctantly decided not to come. You may suppose how dirty and dismal we were when we went to the Thames Tunnel, of all places in the world, instead![2]

When I came home here at midnight I found another letter from you (I left off in this place to press it dutifully to my lips). Then my mind misgave me that *you* must have sent to the Athenæum. At the apparent rudeness of my reply, my face, as Hadji Baba says, was turned upside down[3] and fifty donkeys sat upon my father's grave[4]—or would have done so, but for his not being dead yet.

Therefore I send this humble explanation—protesting, however, which I do most solemnly, against being invited under such untoward circumstances; and claiming as your old friend and no less old admirer to be instantly invited to the next performance, if such a thing is ever contemplated.

Ever, my dear Miss Ely, | Faithfully yours
[CHARLES DICKENS]

---

[1] For theatricals at Talfourd's house, see Vol. III, p. 602*n*.

[2] A Fancy Fair was held in the tunnel, starting 23 Mar and visited that day by 12,994 people. The arches were illuminated and decorated.

[3] This quotation from James J. Morier, *Hajji Baba in England*, had appeared in *To* Forster, 15 Apr 42 (Vol. III, p. 196).

[4] Compare the similar quotation in *To* Beard, 8 Sep 42 (Vol. III, p. 321).

To MR EVILL,[1] 20 APRIL 1846*

MS Mitchell Library, Glasgow.

Devonshire Terrace | Monday 20th. April 1846

Mr. Charles Dickens presents his Compliments to Mr. Evill, and begs to say that he has not the least knowledge of the arrangements for the proposed Meeting.[2] He has no doubt that Mr. Gilpin of Bishopsgate Street[3] (whose exact address is appended to the advertisements) will be happy to entertain Mr. Evill's request.

To THOMAS MITTON, 20 APRIL 1846

MS University Library, Bergen.

Devonshire Terrace | Twentieth April 1846

My Dear Mitton

As They cannot make up their minds (They have been going to do so, every quarter of an hour since I saw you),[4] I have made up mine.—Abroad again!

Ever Yours

Thomas Mitton Esquire

CD

To JOHN FORSTER, [?17–20 APRIL 1846]

Extract in F, v, i, 388. *Date:* Forster introduces this extract with a reference to CD's connexion with the *Daily News* having ceased "in little more than four months from the day the paper started"; but May is impossible since CD's decision to go abroad was evidently taken between 17 and 20 Apr: see *To* Mme de la Rue, 17 Apr, and *To* Mitton, 20 Apr.

I don't think I *could* shut out the paper sufficiently, here, to write well.[5] No . . . I will write my book in Lausanne and in Genoa, and forget everything else if I

---

[1] Possibly William Evill (*b.* 1821), friend of Charles Kent, and a steward at CD's Farewell Dinner in 1867.

[2] On 29 Apr.

[3] See *To* Gilpin, 16 Mar.

[4] Long meetings continued in Whitefriars throughout the four days 22–25 Apr; Paxton found it "almost too much for human nature to bear" and by 24 Apr was "bewildered by three days' calculations" (i.e. about the expected effect of lowering the price of the paper). Dilke was present in the evening of 24 Apr, and on 25 Apr—when the final meeting lasted to 11 p.m.—Paxton was at last able to report that they had "at length settled all matters and the Paper *is to go on* entirely under the management of Dilk [*thus*] who appears most confident of success". By 28 Apr the "circular" was drafted (announcing the intention to lower the price from 5*d.* to 2½*d.*) and was

published as a leading article in the *Daily News* of 9 May—repeated on the front page from 11 May to 1 June, when the new price took effect. By 25 May large orders for the paper were "pouring in". (Paxton *to* Mrs Paxton, 24 and 25 Apr, 25 and 26 May; John Cottingham *to* Mrs Paxton, ?26 Apr; MS Devonshire Collections.) For the rise in circulation under Dilke's management, see *To* Chapman, 3 July and *fn.* According to McCarthy and Robinson, *The "Daily News" Jubilee*, p. 28, the proprietors gave Dilke and his son the option of taking up a fourth share in the paper. See also "Memoir" of Charles Wentworth Dilke in *Papers of a Critic*, 1875, I, 60ff.

[5] Forster probably wanted to dissuade him; he says that they had "much discussion", but that CD "was bent on again removing himself from London" (F, *ibid*).

can; and by living in Switzerland for the summer, and in Italy or France for the winter, I shall be saving money while I write.[1]

To WILLIAM PHILLIPS, 20 APRIL 1846

MS Dickens House.

1 Devonshire Terrace | Twentieth April 1846.

Dear Sir

I think of going abroad again for a twelvemonth, and once more letting my house during my absence. The halls and staircases have been repainted since we returned home, and the drawing-room very prettily decorated. Besides which, I should be quite willing, for a good tenant, to make any alteration that might be desired in the furnishing and arrangement of the top bedrooms.

Will you have the goodness to cause it to be entered in your books? It can be seen any day after Wednesday, between 2 and 4.

Faithfully Yours

William Phillips Esquire   CHARLES DICKENS

To THOMAS BEARD, 22 APRIL 1846

MS Dickens House. *Address:* Thomas Beard Esquire | 42 Portman Place | Edgeware Road.

Devonshire Terrace | Wednesday | Twenty Second April | 1846.

My Dear Beard.

I discovered, just in time, that Saturday Week is the day of the Royal Academy Dinner. I must substitute some other day. We will take counsel on Sunday.

Ever Cordially Yours

Thomas Beard Esquire   CD.

To MISS BURDETT COUTTS, 22 APRIL 1846

MS Morgan Library.

Devonshire Terrace
Wednesday Twenty Second April | 1846

My Dear Miss Coutts.

I call with Charley this morning to see you. But in case you should be out, or not yet returned, I write this to bring with me.

---

[1] His expenses would be lower; his resources, until the new novel began to appear, would consist of the rent from Devonshire Terrace, the proceeds of *Pictures from Italy*, and his salary for editing the *Daily News*. His accounts show that he received £1222.5.5 from Bradbury & Evans on 29 Apr (Account-book, MS Messrs Coutts); £500 of this was an advance (Bradbury & Evans *to* CD, 18 Feb 48, MS Bradbury & Evans's Accounts, V & A— this letter shows that the advance had not been repaid, owing to a misunderstanding); the remaining £722.5.5 presumably represents one-third of the agreed annual salary of £2000 plus extra payments for contributions after his resignation.

I saw Dr. Jelf some months ago; and then Dr. Major, into whose department of King's College Charley would fall. He seemed to think Charley rather young for the purpose (though he has some scholars not older) and suggested that it would certainly be better for him not to begin until the May term,[1] when the mornings would be lighter and finer for his daily Progresses down the Strand. Very much obliged to him for his consideration, I agreed to defer the business until May, and settled that shortly before that time I would see Dr. Major again. He knew Charley's present Master[2] by the bye—spoke highly of him—and said he couldn't be in better preparation.

Until within a fortnight or three weeks ago, I have retained the intention of entering Charley in May. But since then, I have conceived the idea of going to Switzerland for a year. Firstly, because I am most desirous to separate myself in a marked way from the Daily News (with which I have long since ceased to have any connexion, and in connecting myself with which at all, I have no doubt I made a mistake). Secondly, because I have a long book to write, which I could write better in retirement. Thirdly, because I want to get up some Mountain knowledge in all the four seasons of the year, for purposes of fiction.[3] Now I think that if I go to Lausanne or some such place, where there are English Clergymen who take pupils, and keep Charley in good training under such auspices, he will enter King's College at greater advantage and with a better prestige about him, than if he began as I originally designed. I have not said anything to Dr. Major or to Charley yet, as I wished to tell you what I had in my mind, first. But I have a very strong belief that I shall be all the better for acting on this resolution, and I should be glad if you thought with me that Charley would be none the worse.

Always Dear Miss Coutts | Faithfully Yours

Miss Burdett Coutts.   CHARLES DICKENS

To MR PRIESTLEY,[4] 22 APRIL 1846*

Text from typescript, Huntington Library.

1 Devonshire Terrace | York Gate, Regents Park.
Twenty Second April. 1846.

Mr Charles Dickens presents his compliments to Mr Priestley, and begs to decline the proposal with which he is favoured in Mr Priestley's letter of the 20th Instant.

---

[1] This began 1 May.
[2] Joseph Charles King.
[3] CD did not in fact use "Mountain knowledge" in his writings until the 1850s,

in "Lying Awake" (*Household Words*, 30 Oct 52) and *Little Dorrit*, Book II, Ch. 1; see also *To* Forster, ?6 Sep 46 and *fn*,
[4] Unidentified,

To H. P. SMITH, 22 APRIL 1846*

MS Miss Mabel Hodge.

Devonshire Terrace | Twenty Second April 1846

My Dear Smith

I have a long book to write—and, having settled my plan, think of going to Switzerland for a twelvemonth to write it peacefully, and get up some Mountain knowledge for another purpose at the same time.

In case any one should fall in your way who wants to hire a house (and take care of it) on reasonable terms—and who wants a house which is, though I say it who "didn't oughtn't"—as the Americans observe, in a very pretty condition—perhaps, in the words of the Poet Bunn,

You'll remember me[1] | Ever Yours
CHARLES DICKENS

My best remembrances to Mrs. Smith

To MR SYNGE,[2] 22 APRIL 1846*

MS Private.

1 Devonshire Terrace | York Gate Regents Park
Twenty Second April 1846.

Mr. Charles Dickens presents his compliments to Mr. Synge, and begs to say, in reply to Mr. Synge's letter, that he thinks Mrs. Quilp must have had good reasons for bearing witness to the attractive qualities of her husband. Mr. Dickens cannot speak quite confidently of any lady's reasons for anything, but he is inclined to believe that Mr. Quilp could have easily provided himself with another pretty wife, in the event of Mrs. Quilp's decease;[3] it being generally observable that men who are very hideous and disagreeable are successful in matrimonial ventures.

To W. H. WILLS, 22 APRIL 1846

MS Huntington Library.

Devonshire Terrace | Twenty Second April 1846.

My Dear Wills.

I meant to have written to you long ago, to tell you, in reference to the Theatrical Dinner, that I am sure you wrote the account in a spirit of regard for me: and that I care a great deal more for that, than for any number of columns of any number

---

[1] The refrain of a song in *The Bohemian Girl*, Act III, in which Bunn was recalling the refrain of Moore's "Go where glory waits thee", in *Irish Melodies*.

[2] Just possibly William Webb Follett Synge (1826–91), who later contributed to *Punch*.

[3] Cf. "If I was to die tomorrow, Quilp could marry anybody he pleased" (*Old Curiosity Shop*, Ch. 4).

of newspapers, and rate it much higher.[1] Do not think I say so the less heartily, because I say it after some delay.

Faithfully Yours
CHARLES DICKENS

W. H. Wills Esquire

To COUNT D'ORSAY, 24 APRIL 1846*

MS Comte de Gramont.

Devonshire Terrace | Twenty Fourth April 1846.

My Dear Count D'Orsay.

I send you, for trial, half a dozen of the wine I spoke of. I have plenty more, if you like it. It is called the Zeller Wine,[2] and is perfectly pure and genuine. I bought it out of an enormous cask under the Town Hall at Offenburg;[3] on the top of which Town Hall, there is an old, old Stork's nest, where the Storks, with their long legs, sit on a summer night, meditating or fly for a change to the neighbouring chimnies and sit there until it is too dark to see them. I have no doubt they improve the flavor of the wine, but I don't know how.

Ever Affectionately Yours
CHARLES DICKENS

The Count D'Orsay.

To SAMUEL PALMER, 27 APRIL 1846

Text from N, I, 748.

Devonshire Terrace | Twenty-Seventh April 1846

My Dear Sir,

The book I alluded to in my note, was a little pasteboard memorandum book with the few printed letters[4] pasted in it. I thought you took it away with you when you took Rogers.

I am afraid I cannot comfortably manage an S. What do you say to the word "on"?[5] Could you possibly do that?

Faithfully yours
[CHARLES DICKENS]

[1] The report of the Dinner in the *Daily News* of 7 Apr occupied about one-third of a column, and about half the space was devoted to CD's speech as chairman. Much longer reports appeared in the *Examiner* and other papers. CD also proposed the health of Benjamin Webster, to which, in Webster's absence, Jerrold replied, and of J. B. Buckstone, the Treasurer, with a humorous reference to his part in *Lend me Five Shillings* (*Speeches*, ed. K. J. Fielding, pp. 76–7).

[2] i.e. Zeller-Baden: a red wine, kept in the wood and bottled as required.

[3] On his way home from Genoa in June 45; Offenburg is 12 miles from Strasbourg. The proprietor of the chief inn was also a wine-merchant, famous for his Zeller wine (Murray, *Handbook for Travellers on the Continent*, 4th edn, 1843).

[4] Palmer did not illustrate any scenes from the letters already published.

[5] The original drawing of the Villa d'Este, the vignette now on p. 1, "The Reader's Passport" (see *To* Bradbury & Evans, 16 Mar 46, *fn*), includes two large initials "O N". But the published text begins with "If", and no large initial is included. The Villa must originally have been intended to stand at the beginning of "Going through France" (p. 5), where the first word is "On", with the text altered by CD from "It was the morning . . ." The "O" is in the form of a small wreath (not part of the vignette).

To MISS BURDETT COUTTS, 28 APRIL 1846*

MS Morgan Library.

Devonshire Terrace | Tuesday Twenty Eighth April
1846

My Dear Miss Coutts.

I will come to you between Twelve and One tomorrow, and shall be truly glad to see you again. Your Porter told me when I called with Charley, that you were unwell, which I was extremely sorry to hear.

The wisdom of what you say, in reference to the ordinary run of English Clergymen abroad, I strongly feel. But I think in a place like Lausanne, I might get Charley a very good year's teaching, and yet keep him under my own eye all the time. He is still such a little fellow that I should be pained to leave him at home.

Always Dear Miss Coutts | Faithfully Yours
CHARLES DICKENS

Miss Burdett Coutts

To CHARLES GILPIN, 28 APRIL 1846

Text from *Daily News*, 30 Apr 46.

April 28, 1846.

Esteemed Friend,

I am sorry that it will not be in my power to attend the meeting to-morrow night.[1] It is matter of regret to me, but I should regret it still more if I had ever given you an unconditional assurance that I should be there. You remember that I had some doubts of my ability to be present long ago? I need not say that I sympathise most heartily with the object of the meeting, or that the more I reflect upon the subject to which it is directed, the more I am convinced that the punishment of death must be, and will be before long abolished.

Thine faithfully,
CHARLES DICKENS

To Charles Gilpin.

To BENJAMIN WEBSTER, 28 APRIL 1846*

MS Mrs A. M. Stern.

1 Devonshire Terrace | Twenty Eighth April 1846

My Dear Sir

I am glad to receive your pleasant note, and am much obliged to you for the Private Box Card.[2] But I fear somebody must have been taking my name in

---

[1] W. J. Fox, who was on the platform, wrote to Eliza Flower: "Yes, it was very stupid both of Dickens and Jerrold not to be at Exeter Hall; but these literary people have no Public work in them after all" (R. Garnett, *Life of W. J. Fox*, p. 283).

[2] For Planché's *The Birds of Aristophanes* at the Haymarket.

vain, as I have not asked that favor. Not that I should have the least reluctance to ask it of *you*, or to avail myself of it now that it is here, but I am unfortunately engaged to dinner.[1] And fearing you might suppose me indifferent to your courtesy I write you these words of explanation.

Believe me | Faithfully Yours

Benjamin Webster Esquire   CHARLES DICKENS

To COUNT D'ORSAY, 1 MAY 1846*

MS Comte de Gramont.

Devonshire Terrace. | Friday May First 1846

My Dear Count D'Orsay.

I don't know how to thank you for the beautiful Pipe.[2] There shall come curling out of it, please Heaven, such affectionate thoughts and visions of you, as shall light up all Switzerland, and make my new book the pleasantest and friendliest of Volumes. I will sit down regularly after dinner, and puff away at it, until I see you through the smoke blending with everything that is delightful to my remembrance and soothing to my fancy. Whatever suggests itself to me at such times, I will give You the credit of; and Cornet Lightbody[3] himself was never so eloquent in anybody's praise as every little spiral thread from its bowl shall be to me in yours.

Ever affectionately | Your friend

The Count D'Orsay.   CHARLES DICKENS

To LORD DUDLEY COUTTS STUART, [?MAY 1846]

Envelope only, MS Knox College, Illinois. *Date:* Handwriting suggests 1846; possibly connected with the meeting of the Literary Association of the Friends of Poland on 4 May or the dinner on 16 May: see next. *Address:* The | Lord Dudley Stuart | Polish Literary Association | Sussex Chambers | Duke Street | St. James's.

To T. N. TALFOURD, 1 MAY 1846*

MS Free Library of Philadelphia.

Devonshire Terrace | First May 1846.

My Dear Talfourd.

A gentleman with two thirds of all the English consonants in his name, and none of the Vowels—Secretary to the Polish Association[4]—called on me this morning, and entreated me to use my influence with you to induce you to become

---

[1] At Lady Blessington's, where Forster, Macready, Quin, Landseer and Lord Robertson were among the guests (Macready, *Diaries*, II, 336).

[2] A cherrywood pipe, which D'Orsay sent on 30 Apr, saying "it is said that smoking inspires authors" (M. Lecomte, *Le Prince des Dandys*, p. 229).

[3] Lord Robertson, whom CD addresses as "Lightbody" in letter of 3 July 46.

[4] Charles Szulczewski (1814–84), Polish officer who came to London 1831; secretary to the Literary Association of the Friends of Poland from 1844 until his death.

a Steward for the dinner to be given to Lord Dudley Stuart (see enclosure) on the 16th. Instant, and further to induce you to attend the dinner.[1]

I told him how you avoided such things. But as he pressed me very hard; and as I have (as I believe you have) a real regard for Lord Dudley Stuart, I relented, and said I would write and tell you how anxious the Committee are to have you, and that I have yielded myself up, very willingly, because of my friendship for the man who is to be honored.[2]

Don't curse me!

Ever Yours Affectionately

Mr. Serjeant Talfourd.   CHARLES DICKENS

To W. C. MACREADY, [1 MAY 1846]*

MS Morgan Library. *Date:* endorsed by Macready "May 1"—the day before his visit to the Academy with CD in 1846; handwriting supports.

Devonshire Terrace | Friday Night

My Dear Macready

I shall be delighted to go to the Academy with you tomorrow.[3] I don't want to go too early, if I can help it, as I am finishing my little book. But let me know in the Morning at what time you will call for me; and I will be ready punctually. Your own time!—

Ever affectionately Yours

W. C. Macready   CHARLES DICKENS

To T. J. SERLE, 4 MAY 1846

MS Mr Peter Brandt.

Devonshire Terrace | Fourth May 1846.

My Dear Serle

I never go into the City; for it is long and long since I cut the Daily News, and never came again.

[1] Talfourd was not in the list of stewards, who included O'Connell, Milner Gibson, and Rogers; Lord Morpeth was in the chair. Lord Dudley Coutts Stuart was presented with a tapestry worked by the ladies of Poland.

[2] CD returned thanks for the Literary Association; according to the *Daily News* of 17 May, he said: "He could take to himself little credit for any service rendered to the cause of Poland, for he had not been as active a member of the association as he could have wished; but he ventured to reply to the toast, for no man could feel a profounder sympathy with the sufferings of Poland, and, he ventured to add, no one entertained a higher admiration for their noble guest, who was the chairman of the association". It is not known when CD joined the Literary Association; he was not present at the annual meeting on 4 May.

[3] They went to the exhibition and also attended the RA dinner, with Rogers and Landseer; Sir Martin Archer Shee was in the chair (*Daily News*, 4 May). At CD's suggestion he and Macready, Rogers, Landseer, Stanfield and Talfourd went on to the Lyceum to see General Tom Thumb, who was now acting in a drama specially written by Albert Smith, *Hop o' my Thumb* (Macready, *Diaries*, II, 326–7). An earlier letter from Catherine Dickens, probably to Willmott, had asked for a box for herself and her children (MS Royal Shakespeare Theatre).

I will come to you, or meet you at your own time here, any day this Week, of which you will give me notice. Mind, I can come to you with perfect ease, for I walk into all sorts of suburbs every day.[1]

I am going to Switzerland on the 1st. of June, and should like to arrange for leaving all this matter in good train.

Always Cordially Yours

T. J. Serle Esquire   CHARLES DICKENS

To MISS BURDETT COUTTS, 5 MAY 1846*

MS Morgan Library.

Devonshire Terrace | Fifth May 1846.

My Dear Miss Coutts.

I need not say that Charley will be delighted to come to you whenever you may find it most convenient.

I am making some enquiries in reference to the points you consulted me upon; and shall have, I hope, very reliable opinions to give you.

Do you think you could make it agreeable to yourself to let me accompany you one morning to Limehouse? I should particularly like you to see that Pauper School. I am sure it would please you, and it would give you a lively and a most encouraging picture of the Good you will do.[2]

Ever Believe me | Most Faithfully Yours

Miss Coutts.   CHARLES DICKENS

To OCTAVIAN BLEWITT, 7 MAY 1846

MS Royal Literary Fund.

Devonshire Terrace | Seventh May 1846

My Dear Sir

I regret to say that it will be quite out of my power to attend the Literary Fund Dinner. Otherwise I should have had great pleasure in returning thanks for the Novelists.[3]

Believe me | Faithfully Yours

Octavian Blewitt Esquire   CHARLES DICKENS

To FRANK STONE, 7 MAY 1846*

MS Benoliel Collection.

Devonshire Terrace | Seventh May 1846.

My Dear Stone.

I don't know our good friend Mr. Dillon's[4] address. Will you, like an Artistical Samaritan as you are, forward the enclosed letter to him? It is an

---

[1] Serle was living at Bayswater.

[2] See *To* Miss Coutts, 26 May 46.

[3] At the dinner on 13 May no speaker returned thanks for the novelists. Browning replied for the dramatists; he was very

anxious about his speech, and in fact spoke only two formal sentences of thanks.

[4] John Dillon was a member of the Elton Fund Committee.

application for his aid in disposing of the Boy Elton[1]—I felt as if nothing ought to come after "Boy", but "Jones"; the newspaper used to be so everlastingly coupling those two words.[2]

I saw Cuttriss the other night. He looked pale and worn. I think affectionate remembrances of the Shakspeare Club[3] are gnawing at his heart.

Faithfully Yours ever
CHARLES DICKENS

P.S. I am going to Switzerland. Can I do anything for you among the Milk-maids?[4]

To T. J. SERLE, 12 MAY 1846

MS Mr Peter Brandt.

Devonshire Terrace | Twelfth May 1846

My Dear Serle

I enclose you Mr. Dillon's letter. He is more than a man of his word, I do not doubt.

Faithfully Yours always

T. J. Serle Esquire. CHARLES DICKENS

To WILLIAM CULLENFORD, 13 MAY 1846

Mention in Sotheby's catalogue, Dec 1964; dated Devonshire Terrace, 13 May 46.

Thanking him for the resolution of the Directors of the General Theatrical Fund and saying that he will always be glad to assist it.[5]

To SAMUEL PALMER, 13 MAY 1846

MS Mr Bryan Palmer.

Devonshire Terrace. | Wednesday Thirteenth May | 1846

Dear Sir

I beg to assure you that I would, on no account, dream of allowing the book to go to Press, without the insertion of your name in the title page.[6] I placed it there, myself, two days ago.

---

[1] Edward S. Elton, the youngest of the children. He became an actor, making his first appearance at the Haymarket in 1851 (*Era Almanac*, 1869).

[2] In 1841: see Vol. II, p. 246 and *n*.

[3] The Club had come to an end in 1839: see Vol. I, p. 611*n*. Frank Stone had been secretary, and the meetings were held at Cuttriss's Piazza Coffee House.

[4] In reference to Stone's liking for sen-timental rural subjects—what Thackeray called his "rococo rustics" ("Picture Gossip", *Fraser's*, June 45; *Works*, 1908, II, 647).

[5] Besides speaking at the dinner, CD sent £5 on 11 Apr (Account-book, MS Messrs Coutts).

[6] The title-page of *Pictures from Italy* has "The Vignette Illustrations on Wood, by Samuel Palmer".

I have not seen the designs, but I have no doubt whatever (remembering your sketches) that they are very good.

Dear Sir | Faithfully Yours

Samuel Palmer Esquire CHARLES DICKENS

To W. C. MACREADY, 17 MAY 1846*

MS Morgan Library.

Devonshire Terrace | Seventeenth May 1846

My very dear Macready.

A Thousand thanks for your kindest of letters.[1] This next week, we are quite hopelessly engaged, but for one day in the week after, Kate shall come and joyfully arrange with Mrs. Macready tomorrow.[2]

I rely on your coming to Lausanne. We will take poles and guides, and go climbing up into the Mountains—provided that old age of yours, of which you are so intolerably boastful, will admit of your using those most staggering of legs that render you so impressive a spectacle of senility and decay.

Ever affectionately Yours

W. C. Macready Esquire CHARLES DICKENS

To MESSRS BRADBURY & EVANS, 18 MAY 1846

Mention in Sotheby's catalogue, July 1975; *MS* 1 p.; dated Devonshire Terrace, 18 May 46.

Asking them to send 12 copies of Pictures from Italy *in the course of the day.*

To MR JOYCE, 19 MAY 1846

MS Mr Lloyd E. Roscoe.

Devonshire Terrace | Nineteenth May 1846.

Sir

If you will have the goodness to send me half a dozen more of the Pictures, I will send out all my presentation copies,[3] myself.

Yours

Mr. Joyce. CHARLES DICKENS

---

[1] Macready had been "much distressed" on 22 Apr to hear of CD's plan to go to Switzerland (*Diaries*, II, 336).

[2] See *To* Macready, 21 May, *fn.*

[3] Bradbury & Evans's Accounts show that CD had 25 copies in all. Copies are known to have been sent to Lady Blessing-ton and Count D'Orsay (see next), and to William Chapman (see *To* Powell, 19 May), Douglas Jerrold (Yale University Library), Mitton (Widener Collection), Macready, Beard, Talfourd, Browning, and Mrs Costello.

To THE COUNTESS OF BLESSINGTON, 19 MAY 1846†

MS Benoliel Collection.

Devonshire Terrace | Nineteenth May 1846.

My Dear Lady Blessington.

*a*I will immediately take care that everything is settled in connexion with your engagement with the Daily News people[1]—and will come to you to report satisfactory progress.

I had not been unmindful of the subject, and would on no account have left Town without arranging it.*a*

If I had not a good reason for delaying to acknowledge the receipt of the book you so kindly sent me, I should be a most unworthy Dog. But I have been every day expecting to be able to send you the enclosed little Volume, and could get no copies until last night, in consequence of their running very fine against the subscription and demand.

May you like it!

I have been greatly entertained by the Femme de Chambre,[2] who paints Society from a Woman's eye (I think that the height of praise) and, sometimes, like a female Gil Blas. The Spirit of our two sweet friends Morgan[3] and Stepney,[4] shining through their Representative.[5] I would have identified the former, anywhere.

Count D'Orsay's copy of the "Pictures", with my cordial remembrance and regard.

Ever My Dear Lady Blessington | Faithfully Your friend
The | Countess of Blessington   CHARLES DICKENS

To G. W. FULCHER,[6] 19 MAY 1846*

MS Mr and Mrs Carl Bequist.

1 Devonshire Terrace, London. | Nineteenth May 1846.

Sir

I beg to thank you, very sincerely, for your obliging note and the presentation copy of your Poems. The latter has not yet reached me, but I have no doubt I shall receive it in due course.

I am Sir | Yours faithfully and obliged
G. W. Fulcher Esquire.   CHARLES DICKENS

[1] In May 46 she wrote to the managers stating that "it was not her intention to renew her engagement", and was paid £250 (R. R. Madden, *Literary Life and Correspondence of the Countess of Blessington*, I, 276).

aa Not previously published.

[2] Lady Blessington's *Memoirs of a Femme de Chambre*, 3 vols, published by Bentley 7 May.

[3] Sydney Owenson (?1783–1859; *DNB*),

Irish novelist, wife of Sir Thomas Morgan: see Vol. I, p. 489*n*.

[4] Catherine, Lady Stepney (d. 1845), novelist and contributor to the Annuals: see Vol. II, p. 292*n*.

[5] The "representative" of both ladies is Lady Caldersfoot (in III, Chs 11–16), a pretentious writer with a "thirst for celebrity".

[6] George Williams Fulcher (1795–1855; *DNB*), poet and miscellaneous writer,

To THOMAS MITTON, [?19 MAY 1846]*

MS Huntington Library. *Date: Pictures from Italy* was published 18 May: this letter probably the next day, the date inscribed by CD in Mitton's copy.

Devonshire Terrace | Tuesday

My Dear Mitton

House let to Sir James Duke[1] from 1st. of June. £300 for the first year. £250 for the Second, if he chooses to stop.

Subscription to the little book, between 4 and 5,000. Considered very large. Copies scarce.[2]

Faithfully Always
CD.

To WILLIAM PHILLIPS, 19 MAY 1846*

MS New York Public Library.

Devonshire Terrace | Nineteenth May 1846

Dear Sir

I forgot to say this morning that I do not take my lad John Thompson, abroad with me. He is an excellent footman who perfectly understands his business, and has been with me, eight years. If Sir James should want him, I can give him the very strongest recommendation. I would not lose him on my return, if I could help it, on any account.[3]

Faithfully Yours
William Phillips Esquire   CHARLES DICKENS

To THOMAS POWELL, 19 MAY 1846*

MS Brotherton Library, Leeds. *Address:* Thomas Powell Esquire | Messrs. Chapman | 2 Leadenhall Street.

Devonshire Terrace | Nineteenth May 1846.

My Dear Powell.

I am very much obliged to you for the trouble you have taken about my Box. Is there anything I can do for you in Switzerland—any apple or other fruit I can shoot off any friend's or relation's head—in return?

printer and bookseller of Market Hill, Sudbury; edited an annual, *The Sudbury Pocket-book*, from 1825, and selections in *Fulcher's Poetical Miscellany*, 1841, with contributions from Bernard Barton, the Howitts, and James Montgomery. His latest publication was *The Village Paupers*, 1845, which has an anti-Poor Law preface.

[1] Sir James Duke (1792–1873), MP for Boston 1837–49, and for the City of London 1849–65. His London address was 23 Botolph Lane. A signed copy of his pamphlet, *Sanatory Requirements of the City of London*, 1846, was in CD's library at his death.

[2] Bradbury & Evans's Accounts (V & A) show that 6000 were printed and 5251 bound; by 1 July 46 about 5000 had been sold. The "second edition" was published by 19 Sep; Bradbury & Evans's Accounts show that it was not a true 2nd edn, but a reissue with new title-pages.

[3] He remained in CD's employment: see Vol. II, p. 207n.

Roche (no 'La') *is* the Brave Courier.

I was sorry not to be able to comply with Mr. W. Chapman's[1] request. I had no Books[2] until last night.

Thomas Powell Esquire.

Faithfully Yours
CHARLES DICKENS

To FRANCIS VALCKENBERG,[3] 19 MAY 1846*

MS P. J. Valckenberg.

Devonshire Terrace | Nineteenth May 1846.

Dear Sir

I am on the eve of going abroad again—to Switzerland—and am not, therefore, laying in Wine just now. But I shall be very happy to see you, either on Thursday or Friday Morning between 11 and 1, if it should suit your convenience to call.

— Valckenberg Esquire

Faithfully Yours
CHARLES DICKENS

To WILLIAM PAGAN,[4] 20 MAY 1846*

MS Mr C. D. Pagan.

London. 1 Devonshire Terrace | York Gate Regents Park
Twentieth May 1846.

Sir.

I beg to thank you for your obliging note, and for the honor you have done me, in appending to your title page a quotation from one of my books.[5] I have not yet received the Volume you have kindly ordered to be sent to me, but I have no doubt it will arrive in due course.

William Pagan Esq

I am Sir | Yours faithfully and obliged
CHARLES DICKENS

[1] Doubtless a relation of Powell's employer Thomas Chapman, senior partner in John Chapman & Co., 2 Leadenhall St; possibly William Robert Chapman (1806–50), 4th son of Aaron Chapman, MP for Whitby, one of Thomas Chapman's partners. Their connexion with Thomas and William Chapman, merchants, of 36 Broad St (see *To* Powell, 2 Aug 45, *fn*), is not known, but they were almost certainly members of the same family.

[2] Copies of *Pictures from Italy*.

[3] Francis Valckenberg (1820–86); he and his brother Joseph were co-partners in the firm of Peter Joseph Valckenberg (their grandfather and founder of the firm), of Worms, growers and shippers of Liebfraumilch and other wines. The brothers often travelled in England, where they had many customers.

[4] William Pagan (1803–69), lawyer and manager of the British Linen Bank, Cupar, Fife; author of *Road Reform: a Plan for abolishing Turnpike Tolls*, Edinburgh, 1845.

[5] No quotation appears on the title-page of *Road Reform*; presumably a written inscription, with a quotation from Tony Weller in *Pickwick Papers*.

To W. C. MACREADY, 21 MAY 1846†

MS Morgan Library.

Devonshire Terrace | Twenty First May 1846

My Dear Macready

Maclise, Forster, and Stanfield (light jockey weights, the last-named!) have quartered themselves on my Phaeton today. I drive them down.[1]

*a*I never saw you more gallant and free, than in the gallant and free scenes last night.[2] It was perfectly captivating to behold you. However, it shall not interfere with my determination to address you as Old Parr in all future time.*a*

Ever affectionately
CD.

To THOMAS BEARD, [22 MAY 1846]

MS Dickens House. *Date:* PM 22 May 46. *Address:* Thomas Beard Esquire | 42 Portman Place | Edgeware Road.

Devonshire Terrace | Friday

My Dear Beard

We are so beset and worried by engagements[3] in this next last week before our departure, that we are most unwillingly obliged to declare off in respect of that Derby engagement.[4]

Ever Affectionately Yours
CD.

To THE COUNTESS OF BLESSINGTON, [?26 MAY 1846]*

MS Morgan Library. *Date:* 1846 on handwriting, and near 19 May when the same informal ending first appears; "take leave" suggests 26 May.

Devonshire Terrace | Tuesday Morning

My Dear Lady Blessington.

I grieve to say that I have not one leisure day between this time and my

[1] To dine with Talfourd at Richmond; Macready was also a guest, and Catherine and Georgina dined with Mrs Macready (*Diaries*, II, 338).

aa Wrongly given as P.S. to letter of 23 Nov 47 in MDGH, I, 183, MDGH 1893, p. 178, and N, II, 61.

[2] As King James V in James White's *The King of the Commons*, which opened on 20 May; he was greeted with "tremendous applause" and the author was called for (*Illustrated London News*, 21 May 46). Maclise wrote to Mrs Macready, with a spirited sketch of Macready in his part, saying "how fine he was last night" (MS New York Public Library, *n.d.*, but clearly this date; the sketch has been wrongly

described as of CD's Bobadil). Macready had been doubtful of his success, and noted that "Forster came into my room to speak of some *misses* in the play" (*Diaries*, II, 338). The *Athenæum* called it "a long and arduous part, requiring great energy and variety of temperament" but composed of "Macreadyisms— painfully so" (23 May). It had thirteen performances and was his last successful new part.

[3] Forster speaks of "many private dinners ... got up in those days of parting to give him friendliest farewell", and of Lord Melbourne's presence at one of them (F, v, i, 388).

[4] On 27 May.

departure. I am (for my sins) engaged to dinner every day; and get up every morning with an odious shadowing-forth of the evening that is to follow.

I begged Landor[1] to say to you, yesterday, that I would come to take leave of you on Friday at Two o'Clock. I shall be true to that purpose, unless you should tell me you are otherwise engaged.

The Burnham Beeches are charming. I know them well. I am ashamed to say of Gray's Church that I know the Elegy better than the place.

Here am I going away, and we have never been to Rosherville! I hope you won't go, now, until I come back—which is a modest aspiration. If I can possibly manage it, I think I shall run over early in December.

Always Dear Lady Blessington | Faithfully Your friend

The Countess of Blessington.   CHARLES DICKENS

To MISS BURDETT COUTTS, 26 MAY 1846

MS Morgan Library.

Devonshire Terrace | Twenty Sixth May 1846.

My Dear Miss Coutts.

I find those who are best acquainted with the subject and the class of persons to be addressed, decidedly in favor of the School and the Church[2] being *Free*. You may remember this to have been my impression at first, but I have not expressed any opinion of my own to those whom I have sounded on the subject.

In reference to the Asylum,[3] it seems to me very expedient that you should know, if possible, whether the Government would assist you to the extent of informing you from time to time into what distant parts of the World, women could be sent for marriage, with the greatest hope for their future families, and with the greatest service to the existing male population, whether expatriated from England or born there. If these poor women *could* be sent abroad with the distinct recognition and aid of the Government, it would be a service to the

---

[1] He was on a visit to Gore House till 3 June, while awaiting the publication of the volumes of *Imaginary Conversations*; on 31 May he dined at Forster's and met Macready (R. H. Super, *Walter Savage Landor*, New York, 1954, p. 361 and *n*.)

[2] The church of St Stephen, Westminster, which Miss Coutts built 1847–50 and endowed in memory of her father, and the associated school for poor children (*Letters from CD to Angela Burdett-Coutts*, ed. Edgar Johnson, 1955, p. 206*n*).

[3] The beginning of the plan for the "home for homeless women", Urania Cottage, established 1847, chiefly for reform-

ing prostitutes. Almost all the principles and policies outlined in this letter were adopted: for CD's "cheerful and hopeful" system of training, see the "Appeal to Fallen Women", written for distribution and sent to Miss Coutts, 28 Oct 47 (Vol. V, and P. A. W. Collins, *Dickens and Crime*, 1962, Ch. 4). Chesterton and Tracey became members of the committee and also Kay-Shuttleworth. CD's interest in "fallen women" is evident in "The Pawnbroker's Shop" (*Sketches by Boz*) and in *Oliver Twist*; but his practical plans are noticeably unsentimental.

effort. But I have (with reason) a doubt of all Governments in England considering such a question in the light, in which men undertaking that immense responsibility, are bound, before God, to consider it. And therefore I would suggest this appeal to you, merely as something which you owe to yourself and to the experiment; the failure of which, does not at all affect the immeasurable goodness and hopefulness of the project itself.

I do not think it would be necessary, in the first instance at all events, to build a house for the Asylum. There are many houses, either in London or in the immediate neighbourhood, that could be altered for the purpose. It would be necessary to limit the number of inmates, but I would make the reception of them as easy as possible to themselves. I would put it in the power of any Governor of a London Prison to send an unhappy creature of this kind (by her own choice of course) straight from his prison, when her term expired, to the Asylum. I would put it in the power of any penitent creature to knock at the door, and say For God's sake, take me in. But I would divide the interior into two portions; and into the first portion I would put all new-comers without exception, as a place of probation, whence they should pass, by their own good-conduct and self-denial alone, into what I may call the Society of the house. I do not know of any plan so well conceived, or so firmly grounded in a knowledge of human nature, or so judiciously addressed to it, for observance in this place, as what is called Captain Maconnochie's[1] Mark System, which I will try, very roughly and generally, to describe to you.

A woman or girl coming to the Asylum, it is explained to her that she has come there for *useful* repentance and reform, and because her past way of life has been dreadful in its nature and consequences, and full of affliction, misery, and despair *to herself*. Never mind Society while she is at that pass. Society has used her ill and turned away from her, and she cannot be expected to take much heed of its rights or wrongs. It is destructive to *herself*, and there is no hope in it, or in her, as long as she pursues it. It is explained to her that she is degraded and fallen, but not lost, having this shelter; and that the means of Return to Happiness are now about to be put into her own hands, and trusted to her own keeping. That with this view, she is, instead of being placed in this probationary class for a month, or two months, or three months, or any specified *time* whatever, required to earn there, a certain number of *Marks* (they are mere scratches in a book) so that she may make her probation a very short one, or a very long one, according to her own conduct. For so much work, she has so many Marks; for a day's good conduct, so many more. For every instance of ill-temper, disrespect, bad language, any outbreak of any sort or kind, so many— a very large number in proportion to her receipts—are deducted. A perfect Debtor and Creditor account is kept between her and the Superintendent, for every day; and the state of that account, it is in her own power and nobody else's, to adjust to her advantage. It is expressly pointed out to her, that before she can be considered qualified to return to any kind of society—even to the Society of the Asylum—she must give proofs of her power of self-restraint and her sincerity, and her determination to try to shew that she deserves the

---

[1] Thus in MS.

confidence it is proposed to place in her. Her pride, her emulation, her sense of shame, her heart, her reason, and her interest, are all appealed to at once, and if she pass through this trial, she *must* (I believe it to be in the eternal nature of things) rise somewhat in her own self-respect, and give the managers a power of appeal to her, in future, which nothing else could invest them with. I would carry a modification of this Mark System through the whole establishment; for it is its great philosophy and its chief excellence that it is not a mere form or course of training adapted to the life within the house, but is a preparation— which is a much higher consideration—for the right performance of duty out- side, and for the formation of habits of firmness and self-restraint. And the more these unfortunate persons were educated in their duty towards Heaven and Earth, and the more they were tried on this plan, the more they would feel that to dream of returning to Society, or of becoming Virtuous Wives, until they had earned a certain gross number of Marks required of everyone without the least exception, would be to prove that they were not worthy of restoration to the place they had lost. It is a part of this system, even to put at last, some temptation within their reach, as enabling them to go out, putting them in possession of some money, and the like; for it is clear that unless they are used to some temptation and used to resist it, within the walls, their capacity of resisting it without, cannot be considered as fairly tested.

What they would be taught in the house, would be grounded in religion, most unquestionably. It must be the basis of the whole system. But it is very essential in dealing with this class of persons to have a system of training established, which, while it is steady and firm, is cheerful and hopeful. Order, punctuality, cleanliness, the whole routine of household duties—as washing, mending, cooking—the establishment itself would supply the means of teaching practically, to every one. But then I would have it understood by all—I would have it written up in every room—that they were not going through a monotonous round of occupation and self-denial which began and ended there, but which began, or was resumed, under that roof, and would end, by God's blessing, in happy homes of their own.

I have said that I would put it in the power of Governors of Prisons to re- commend Inmates. I think this most important, because such gentlemen as Mr. Chesterton of the Middlesex House of Correction, and Lieutenant Tracey of Cold Bath Fields, Bridewell, (both of whom I know very well) are well acquainted with the good that is in the bottom of the hearts, of many of these poor creatures, and with the whole history of their past lives; and frequently have deplored to me the not having any such place as the proposed establishment, to which to send them—when they are set free from Prison. It is necessary to observe that very many of these unfortunate women are constantly in and out of the Prisons, for no other fault or crime than their original one of having fallen from virtue. Policemen can take them up, almost when they choose, for being of that class, and being in the streets; and the Magistrates commit them to Jail for short terms. When they come out, they can but return to their old occupation, and so come in again. It is well-known that many of them fee the Police to remain unmolested; and being too poor to pay the fee, or dissipating the money in some other way, are taken up again, forthwith. Very many of them are good, excellent, steady characters when under restraint—even without the advantage of systematic training, which they would have in this Institution—and are tender nurses to the sick, and are as kind and gentle as the best of women.

There is no doubt that many of them would go on well for some time, and would then be seized with a violent fit of the most extraordinary passion, apparently quite motiveless, and insist on going away. There seems to be something inherent in their course of life, which engenders and awakens a sudden restlessness and recklessness which may be long suppressed, but breaks out like Madness; and which all people who have had opportunities of observation in Penitentiaries and elsewhere, must have contemplated with astonishment and pity. I would have some rule to the effect that no request to be allowed to go away would be received for at least four and twenty hours, and that in the interval the person should be kindly reasoned with, if possible, and implored to consider well what she was doing. This sudden dashing down of all the building up of months upon months, is, to my thinking, so distinctly a Disease with the persons under consideration that I would pay particular attention to it, and treat it with particular gentleness and anxiety; *and I would not make one, or two, or three, or four, or six departures from the Establishment a binding reason against the re-admission of that person, being again penitent,* but would leave it to the Managers to decide upon the merits of the case: giving very great weight to general good conduct within the house.

I would begin with some comparatively small number—say thirty—and I would have it impressed upon them, from day to day, that the success of the experiment rested with them, and that on their conduct depended the rescue and salvation, of hundreds and thousands of women yet unborn. In what proportion this experiment would be successful, it is very difficult to predict; but I think that if the Establishment were founded on a well-considered system, and were well managed, one half of the Inmates would be reclaimed from the very beginning, and that after a time the proportion would be very much larger. I believe this estimate to be within very reasonable bounds.

The main question that arises, is, if the co-operation of the Government—beginning at that point when they are supposed to be reclaimed—cannot be secured, how are they to be provided for, permanently? Supposing the mark system and the training to be very successful, and gradually to acquire a great share of public confidence and respect, I think it not too sanguine to suppose that many good people would be glad to take them into situations. But the power of beginning life anew, in a world perfectly untried by them, would be so important in many cases, as an effectual detaching of them from old associates, and from the chances of recognition and challenge, that it is most desirable to be, somehow or other, attained.

I do not know whether you would be disposed to entrust me with any share in the supervision and direction of the Institution. But I need not say that I should enter on such a task with my whole heart and soul; and that in this respect, as in all others, I have but one sincere and zealous wish to assist you, by any humble means in my power, in carrying out your benevolent intentions.

And at all events it would be necessary for you to have, in the first instance, on paper, all the results of previous experience in this way, as regards scheme, plan, management, and expence.[1] These I think I could procure, and render plain, as quietly and satisfactorily as anyone. And I would suggest to you, this course of action.

That,—the School and Church proceeding—this Design remain in abeyance for the present. That when I go to Paris (whither I shall remove, please God, before Christmas) I examine every Institution of this sort existing there, and gather together all the information I possibly can. I believe more valuable knowledge is to be got there, on such a subject, than anywhere else; and this, combined with the results of our English experience, I would digest into the plainest and clearest form; so that you could see it, as if it were a Map. And in the meantime you would have these advantages.

1. That in the establishment of your school and Dispensary, you might find or make some Instruments that would be very important and useful in the working out of this scheme.

2. That there will then have been matured, and probably tried, certain partial schemes going a very little way on this same road, which are now on foot in the City of London, and the success or failure of which will be alike instructive.

3. That there is a very great probability of the whole Transportation system being shortly brought under the consideration of the Legislature; and it is particularly worthy of consideration that the various preliminary reports on the subject, (which I have lately been reading) recognize the question of sending out women to the different settlements, as one of very great importance.

I have that deep sense, dear Miss Coutts, of the value of your confidence in such a matter, and of the pure, exalted, and generous motives by which you are impelled, that I feel a most earnest anxiety that such an effort as you contemplate in behalf of your Sex, should have every advantage in the outset it can possibly receive, and should, if undertaken at all, be undertaken to the lasting honor of your name and Country. In this feeling, I make the suggestion I think best calculated to promote that end. Trust me, if you agree in it, I will not lose sight of the subject, or grow cold to it, or fail to bestow upon it my best exertions and reflection. But, if there be any other course you would prefer to take; and you will tell me so; I shall be as devoted to you in that as in this, and as much honored by being asked to render you the least assistance.

Ever Faithfully Yours
CD.

---

[1] By 1848, according to the *Quarterly Review* (June 1848), there were ten such institutions in London (including the Magdalen and Lock hospitals), but the total number of inmates was only 441, and many applicants anxious to be received had to be turned away. A fair proportion of those reclaimed eventually went into domestic service; no institution had any scheme for emigration. CD may have known Mrs Caroline Chisholm's pamphlet *Female Immigration*, 1842; in Oct 46 she returned from Australia to England and in Nov visited Lord Grey in the hope of getting government support for her scheme. CD met her in 1850.

To DOUGLAS JERROLD, 26 MAY 1846

MS Brotherton Library, Leeds.

Devonshire Terrace. | Tuesday Twenty Sixth May 1846.
My Dear Jerrold.

I send you herewith, some books belonging to you. A thousand thanks for the Hermit.[1] He took my fancy mightily, when I first saw him in the Illuminated; and I have stowed him away in the left-hand breast pocket of my travelling coat, that we may hold pleasant converse together on the Rhine. You see what confidence I have in him!

I wish you would seriously consider the expediency and feasibility of coming to Lausanne in the Summer or early Autumn. I must be at work myself during a certain part of every day almost, and you could do twice as much there as here. It is a wonderful place to see—and what sort of welcome you would find, I will say nothing about, for I have vanity enough to believe that you would be willing to feel yourself as much at home in my household as in any man's.

Do think it over. I could send you the minutest particular of the journey. It is nearly all Railroad and Steamboat, and the easiest in the world.

At Macready's on Thursday,[2] we shall meet, please God!

Always My Dear Jerrold | Cordially Yours
Douglas Jerrold Esquire   CHARLES DICKENS

To FRANCIS VALCKENBERG, 26 MAY 1846*

MS P. J. Valckenberg. *Address:* Fr. Valckenberg Esquire | 32 Craven Street | Strand.

Devonshire Terrace, | Tuesday Twenty Sixth May | 1846.
Dear Sir

I am much indebted to you for your obliging letter. Even though I should not have an opportunity of presenting your note of introduction on my way to Switzerland, I shall not be the less mindful of your kind attention, believe me. The next time you come to England, I shall hope to give you a more hospitable welcome.

Dear Sir | Faithfully Yours
Fr Valckenberg Esquire   CHARLES DICKENS

To MR HEATH,[3] 27 MAY 1846*

MS Mrs S. S. Clephan.

Devonshire Terrace | Wednesday Twenty Seventh May 1846.

Mr. Charles Dickens presents his compliments to Mr. Heath, and begs to thank him for his letter, and his obliging offer of the accompanying MS. In

---

[1] Jerrold's *Chronicles of Clovernook, with Some Account of the Hermit of Bellyfulle* appeared in the *Illuminated Magazine* 1843–4, and was published Apr 46; it was favourably noticed in the *Daily News*, 1 May 46.

[2] Not recorded in Macready's diary: but on Friday, 29 May, Macready says:

declining, with thanks, to accept the latter, Mr. Dickens begs to say that he does so without the least reference to its merits (of which he has no knowledge) but in pursuance of a rule he has always found it expedient to prescribe to himself.

To R. H. HORNE, 29 MAY 1846*

MS Free Library of Philadelphia.

Devonshire Terrace
Friday Night Twenty Ninth May | 1846

My Dear Horne.

I snatch a moment before going to bed after the busiest of days (I start tomorrow morning)[1] to say that I have had real pleasure in the receipt of your cordial note,[2] and that it is very pleasant to me.

With Mrs. Dickens' best regards, I am always My Dear Horne
Faithfully Your friend
R. H. Horne Esquire   CHARLES DICKENS

To JOHN FORSTER, [?7 JUNE 1846]

Extracts in F, v, ii, 390–1 and F, 1872–4, II, x, 196*n*. *Date:* clearly written during the journey, and probably from Strasbourg on Sunday 7 June.

Halting only at Ostend, Verviers, Coblenz, and Mannheim, they reached Strasbourg on the seventh of June. We have hardly seen a cloud in the sky since you and I parted at Ramsgate, and the heat has been extraordinary. *At Mayence there had come aboard their boat a German, who soon after accosted Mrs. Dickens on deck in excellent English:* "Your countryman Mr. Dickens is travelling this way just now, our papers say. Do you know him, or have you passed him anywhere?" *Explanations ensuing, it turned out by an odd chance that he had with him a letter of introduction to the brother of this gentleman;*[3] *who then spoke to him of the popularity of his books in Germany and of the many persons he had seen reading them in the steamboats as he came along. When CD remarked how great his own vexation was not to be able himself to speak a word of German,* "Oh dear! that needn't trouble you," *rejoined the other;* "for even in so small a town as ours, where we are mostly primitive people and have few travellers, I could make a party of at least forty people who understand and speak English as well as I do, and of at least as many more who could manage to read you in the original." *His town was*

"Dickens came in, and we shook hands once more" (*Diaries*. II, 339).

³ Unidentified.

¹ Forster's dates are therefore one day out; he says (F, v, i, 389) that the Dickenses dined with him on 30 May and left the following day.

² Horne had been in London 7–16 May

(*Letters of Robert Browning and Elizabeth Barrett, 1845–1846*, II, 135, 157).

³ The letter of introduction must have been to Joseph Valckenberg (1812–54), elder brother of Francis; CD met him on 6 June: see *To* Joseph Valckenberg, 25 June. Nothing is known of the third brother whom CD met on the steamer.

Worms,[1] a fine old place, though greatly shrunken and decayed in respect of its population; with a picturesque old cathedral standing on the brink of the Rhine, and some brave old churches shut up, and so hemmed in and overgrown with vineyards that they look as if they were turning into leaves and grapes.

On the same steamer were two travelling Englishmen who had got an immense barouche on board with them, and had no plan whatever of going anywhere in it. One of them wanted to have this barouche wheeled ashore at every little town and village they came to. The other was bent upon "seeing it out," *as he said—meaning, CD supposed, the river; though neither of them seemed to have the slightest interest in it.* The locomotive one would have gone ashore without the carriage, and would have been delighted to get rid of it; but they had a joint courier, and neither of them would part with *him* for a moment; so they went growling and grumbling on together, and seemed to have no satisfaction but in asking for impossible viands on board the boat, and having a grim delight in the steward's excuses.

To MM. LOMBARD, ODIER & CO., 13 JUNE 1846

Text from N, I, 756.

Rosemont, Lausanne | Juin 13 1846

Messieurs,

Je vous envois enclos, un document relatif à une grande caisse qui vous est consignée pour moi. Si vous me le pouvez envoyer ici, je serais bien obligé si vous le confiderez au porteur de cette lettre, M. Rodieu. S'il faut que j'envoie mon courier à votre bureau pour l'obtenir, je l'enverrai aussitôt que j'entendrai de vous qu'il est nécessaire.

Je serai bien aisé de payer, sur le champ, toutes les charges du transit &c, si vous aurez la bonté de m'envoyer un billet de la compte.

Recevez, Messieurs, l'assurance de ma considération.

J'ai l'honneur d'être, Messieurs,

Votre Serviteur
[CHARLES DICKENS]

To JOHN FORSTER, [?13 or 14 JUNE 1846]

Extracts in F, v, ii, 391–2. *Date:* CD arrived at Lausanne 11 June, and wrote as soon as his "two days" of "house-hunting" had been successful.

From Strasburg they went by rail on the 8th to Bâle, from which they started for Lausanne next day, in three coaches, two horses to each, taking three days for the journey. He described an uproar between the landlord of an inn on the road, and one of the voituriers who had libelled Boniface's establishment by complaining of the food.

---

[1] Formerly had 30,000 inhabitants, now only 8000: "grass growing . . . in the . . . streets, many houses untenanted and falling into ruin, and the whole city has a decayed and inanimate aspect" (Murray, *Handbook for Travellers on the Continent*, 1843).

After various defiances on both sides, the landlord said "Scélérat! Mécréant! Je vous boaxerai!" to which the voiturier replied, "Aha! Comment dites-vous? Voulez-vous boaxer? Eh? Voulez-vous? Ah! Boaxez-moi donc! Boaxez-moi!" —at the same time accompanying these retorts with gestures of violent significance which explained that this new verb-active was founded on the well-known English verb to boax, or box. If they used it once, they used it at least a hundred times, and goaded each other to madness with it always. *The travellers reached the Hotel Gibbon*[1] *at Lausanne on the evening of Thursday the 11th of June; having been tempted as they came along by a delightful glimpse of Neufchâtel.* On consideration however I thought it best to come on here, in case I should find, when I begin to write, that I want streets sometimes. In which case, Geneva (which I hope would answer the purpose) is only four and twenty miles away.

He at once began house-hunting, and had two days' hard work of it. He found the greater part of those let to the English like small villas in the Regent's Park, with verandahs, glass-doors opening on lawns, and alcoves overlooking the lake and mountains. One he was tempted by, higher up the hill, poised above the town like a ship on a high wave; *but the possible fury of its winter winds deterred him. Greater still was the temptation to him of "L'Elysée,"*[2] *more a mansion than a villa; with splendid grounds overlooking the lake, and in its corridors and staircases as well as furniture like an old-fashioned country house in England; which he could have got for twelve months for £160.* But when I came to consider its vastness, I was rather dismayed at the prospect of windy nights in the autumn, with nobody staying in the house to make it gay. *And so he again fell back upon the very first place he had seen, Rosemont, quite a doll's house; with two pretty little salons, a dining-room, hall, and kitchen, on the ground floor; and with just enough bedrooms upstairs to leave the family one to spare.* It is beautifully situated on the hill that rises from the lake, within ten minutes' walk of this hotel,[3] and furnished, though scantily as all here are, better than others except Elysée, on account of its having been built and fitted up (the little salons in the Parisian way) by the landlady and her husband for themselves. They live now in a smaller house like a porter's lodge, just within the gate. A portion of the grounds is farmed by a farmer, and *he* lives close by; so that, while it is secluded, it is not at all lonely. *The rent was to be ten pounds a month for half a year, with reduction to eight for the second half, if he should stay so long; and the rooms and furniture were to be described as soon as his own ingenious*

---

[1] The Hotel Gibbon, opened in 1839, and so called because on the same piece of property as "Le Grotto" where Gibbon finished his *History*; it commanded a fine view of the lake. Later illustrations show it as a large rectangular building. It was pulled down in 1920.

[2] The Hon. Richard Watson and his wife and family (see *To* Forster, 28 June, *fn*), who had arrived in Lausanne on 15 June, engaged L'Elysée next day at 2000 francs for six months, and took up residence on 18 June, finding "the quiet, and beauty of the place delightful" (Watson's Diary, MS

Commander Michael Saunders Watson; extracts published in L. C. Staples, "Sidelight on a Great Friendship", *D*, XLVII [1950], 16–21. The diary was then wrongly supposed to be Mrs Watson's).

[3] The house (pulled down in 1938) stood "in the midst of a then utterly unspoilt stretch of land, all meadows and fields and vineyards, extending all the way from the present *avenue de la Gare* to the . . . *quartier de Montchoisi*" (René Rapin, "Lausanne and some English Writers", *Etudes de Letters*, University of Lausanne, série II, II [1959], 104).

re-arrangements and improvements in the chairs and tables should be completed.
I shall merely observe at present therefore, that my little study is upstairs, and
looks out, from two French windows opening into a balcony, on the lake and
mountains; and that there are roses enough to smother the whole establishment
of the *Daily News* in. Likewise, there is a pavilion in the garden, which has but
two rooms in it; in one of which, I think you shall do your work when you come.
As to bowers for reading and smoking, there are as many scattered about the
grounds, as there are in Chalk-farm tea-gardens. But the Rosemont bowers are
really beautiful. Will you come to the bowers . . .?[1]

The country is delightful in the extreme—as leafy, green, and shady, as
England; full of deep glens, and branchy places (rather a Leigh Huntish expression), and bright with all sorts of flowers in profusion. It abounds in singing
birds besides—very pleasant after Italy; and the moonlight on the lake is noble.
Prodigious mountains rise up from its opposite shore (it is eight or nine miles
across, at this point), and the Simplon, the St. Gothard, Mont Blanc, and all the
Alpine wonders are piled there, in tremendous grandeur.[2] The cultivation is
uncommonly rich and profuse. There are all manner of walks, vineyards,
green lanes, cornfields, and pastures full of hay. The general neatness is as
remarkable as in England. There are no priests or monks in the streets, and
the people appear to be industrious and thriving. French (and very intelligible
and pleasant French) seems to be the universal language. I never saw so many
booksellers' shops crammed within the same space, as in the steep up-and-down
streets of Lausanne.

To DANIEL MACLISE, 14 JUNE 1846*

MS Comtesse de Suzannet. *Address:* Angleterre | Daniel Maclise Esquire. R.A. |
14 Russell Place | Fitzroy Square | London | England.

Hotel Gibbon, Lausanne Switzerland
Sunday Night Fourteenth June 1846.

My Dear Mac.

Notwithstanding the strange leaves you take of your friends, I think you will
be still glad to hear of and from them, when they are such friends as Self and
Co. Therefore I sit down to write you a short assurance of our safe arrival here
last Thursday in good health, and after a most extraordinarily hot journey—
borne, by the whole camp, with surpassing good humour and patience. We had
only one wet day, and that was among the Mountains—only one discomfort, and
that was the loss of a trifling portmanteau containing all the childrens'[3] clothes:
which has not yet come to hand.

We have taken a house, in all respects the opposite of our Italian Palazzo;
being a kind of beautiful bandbox. It stands in a most lovely situation on the
brink of the high slope that rises from the Lake, with the Alps piled up in

---

[1] Thomas Moore, *Irish Melodies.*
[2] The Simplon and St Gothard cannot
be seen from Lausanne, and Mont Blanc
was not visible from Rosemont.

[3] Thus in MS.

tremendous majesty before it. It is surrounded by a lawn, a vineyard, a garden, a corn-field, and some other agricultural trifles, of its own—and is, at present overwhelmed in a cluster of Roses. It is called Rosemont. So WHEN you write, address me at Rosemont, Lausanne. I feel like a landed proprietor, and think of writing a Pamphlet on the Free Trade question.

We move, tomorrow. In the meantime we are in this large hotel which is as ugly, I think, as anything can be made, in a situation of such extraordinary beauty. There are no Italian-Catholicity-Symptoms here, and no Monks or Friars in the streets. For which the people are all the more thriving and happy. We rode today some six or eight miles along the lake to see a little fête, in honor of the Republican Independence of this Canton.[1] It consisted of a dinner and ball in the open air; and between the dinner and the ball a good deal of speaking, in the "propogition" of toasts, from a tribune made of flags and flowers, where each Speaker mounted in succession with an immense silver Goblet in his hand. After each toast the artillery fired some Brass field pieces that are on the ground, and the soldier's band played some appropriate air. I wish you could have seen it. It was one of the prettiest sights I have ever seen. The women, in their immense straw hats and gay dresses looked like parti-colored Mushrooms (Brayvo Dick!)

As this letter is merely a trial of your remembrance of the person whose name is subscribed to it, I say no more at present: merely repeating that my address is, as above. All join in kind love to you. And I am ever My Dear Mac Your most affectionate friend CHARLES DICKENS

To FREDERICK DICKENS, [16 JUNE 1846]*

MS Huntington Library. *Date:* PM 16 June 46.[2] *Address:* Angleterre. | Frederick Dickens Esquire | Commissariat | Treasury | London | England.

My Dear Fred. We arrived at Lausanne last Thursday afternoon, safe and sound and in good health. We lived, until yesterday afternoon, at the hotel: not having been able to conclude arrangements for getting into this house (Rosemont) before. It is quite a bandbox, as most of the houses hereabouts, are—I think you might put it all into the great Sala of the Peschiere—but it stands in the midst of beautiful grounds, on the hill above the Lake, with the whole range of the Alps towering before it. Small as it is too, we can boast a couple of small spare rooms, in which we should be delighted to stow you away, with any travelling companion. The situation is lovely in the extreme; and the excessive greenness and shade of the Country give it a great advantage over Italy. Everything is very neatly kept too. There are no Priests or Monks to be seen; and the people seem to be very thriving and industrious. I never saw such a profusion of birds and flowers, in the richest parts of Devonshire.

[1] Probably at Morges, which is the right distance from Lausanne; the *Nouvelliste Vaudois* of 26 June 46 referred to "a patriotic fête" which had taken place several days previously, and mentioned earlier reports in the *Courier Suisse* and elsewhere which had unfairly hinted at socialist speeches in this "modeste et simple fête".

[2] Damage to the MS has removed the top of the first leaf; the address and date were probably on the missing piece of p. 1.

We pay £10 per month for the house, for the first 6 months, and £8 for the second six, supposing we should remain here. I am not sufficiently experienced yet, to say what market prices are, but I should think they were about the Genoa mark, and not so cheap as English people suppose. Some things are much cheaper than in Genoa, as, for instance, Piano hire. We have really a very good German Piano, for which we pay but ten francs (eight and fourpence) per month. House rent too is much cheaper. I could have got a very splendid house indeed (as large as the Peschiere) for £150 pr. year. But the largest houses are the cheapest, because they involve the necessity of a large establishment of servants. We have two pretty little drawing rooms here, opening into each other—a little dining room—a little study—a great balcony—a colonnade—an immense [   ]1 family live; and the Proprietress of [it is employed in]2 another little Villa just within the gate. It is not lonesome therefore, though secluded, and is within ten minutes walk of Lausanne—a mighty dull little [t]own. There are not many English people here; but there is an English Church, and there is an English Library. Geneva, a large city, is within four and twenty miles; and steamers on the Lake are always going there, and coming back.

If you should arrange to come, and are deterred by economical considerations, I dare say I could make all that easy with you, when you were once here; so, take that into your calculations. Agreeably to my promise, I give you, on the other side, full directions in reference to the Journey. As I promised the same to Augustus, shew it to him, or copy it for him.

There is a poor woman named Greenwood, who lodges in Blenheim Street Oxford Street, at a little Cobbler's. I have relieved her once, and know her case to be a good one. I wish you would go to her, and ask her how she is going on, and intimate that I left a Pound or Two with you for her benefit. She is very industrious, and has suffered a great deal. I must leave the details of relief to you, but I give you an order on Mitton (don't say to him what it is for) to the extent of £5, in case you should find, at any period during my absence, that a small sum, now and then, will do her real service. I need not, I know, recommend you to be careful in drawing and applying it.

Kate and Georgy and all the children unite with me in love to you, Anna,3 father, mother, Ka[te,]4 Letitia and Henry, [an]d all. Tell Henry I will write to him before long, *and that we think he and Letitia ought to take advantage of your paper of instructions, and come to see us here.* We had no intelligence of Alfred and his wife at Ostend5—as no doubt you know by this time.

Ever My Dear Fred | Affectionately Yours

CD.

1 Most of top line of p. 2, with space for 62–65 letters, is missing.

2 About 20 letters missing; traces of "employ" can be seen.

3 Anna Weller.

4 Unidentified.

5 Alfred Dickens married Helen Dobson of Strensall, near York, at St Andrew's, Holborn, on 16 May. A letter from Mrs CD to Phillips (MS Dickens House) on 14 May asked him not to send anyone to view the house on 16 May, "as one of Mr. Dickens's brothers is to be married from this house"; on 1 May she had written to Beard mentioning the date and reminding him of his "promise to breakfast with us on the occasion at 1 o'clock" (*Dickens to his Oldest Friend*, ed. W. Dexter, p. 273).

The best Hotel at Ostend, is the Hotel de la Cour Imperiale. From Ostend to Cologne, straight through, by Railway. Fare, 27 francs (extra charge for luggage, which is weighed). Time 15 hours. At Cologne, you sleep. Any hotel will serve your turn. The nearer the River, the better. Next day you pay your fare, and take your ticket, at the office of any of the Steam Packet Companies (the Cologne Company is the best, but they are all good) *through to Mannheim*. Fare, 22 francs. At the office, as well as everywhere else upon the Rhine, there is some one who can speak English. The boat will probably start at about 10 or half past 10 in the morning, and allow you to sleep at Coblentz that night: either going on next morning in the same boat, or in another boat belonging to the same company. The time from Cologne to Coblentz is about 8 hours. Any hotel at Coblentz, *except the Gia[nt.]*[1] They are all close to the River. From Coblentz to Mannheim is about [14] hours. Hotel at Mannheim, [the Hotel de] l'Europe. Very good, and close to the w[har]f. Sleep there. You will have dined on board: paying extra for your dinner. Next day, from Mannheim to Kehl, by Railway. Time about 6 hours. Fare, 1st. class, 14 francs. From Kehl to Strasburg (two or three miles) by Omnibus. The french custom house is on the road, where luggage is examined. (It is also examined on the Railroad between Ostend and Cologne. But all you have to do, is, to go into the room you are shewn; wait until you see your Portmanteau brought in; cry "halloa" at sight of it, open it, and afterwards lock it up again.) Hotel at Strasburg, the Hotel de la Ville de Paris, very good. You can sleep there, or go on to Bâle, also by Railway, by the next Train. Fare, 1st. class, 17 francs. Time, about 4 hours. Hotel at Bâle, the Hotel of the Three Kings, one of the very best on the Continent. At Bâle, there are the Mail, and at least two Diligences, starting, every day and evening, for Lausanne. Fare about 26 francs. Time, about 24 hours. I give the fares, and the times in all cases *about*. They are almost exactly stated. The account (excluding bed and board on the road) stands thus, from Ostend

	TIME Days	MONEY Francs
To Cologne	1	27
To Coblentz ⎱ To Mannheim ⎰	2	22
To Kehl & Strasburg, & then[ce to Bâ]le	1	31
Omnibuses from & to Railw[ay (addi]tional)		1
To Lausanne	1	26
	5	107 francs

I should say the Bed and board would not exceed 10 francs per day. And on the other hand, you must observe that I have charged the Railways as 1st. class, and that the 2nd. class carriages are cheaper, and most excellent. In returning, as the Boats then go *with* the stream, the Water-Journey is done in half the time.

---

[1] Wear down central fold of second leaf of MS has removed letters in several lines.

To DOUGLAS JERROLD, 16 JUNE 1846*

MS Mr Douglas Jerrold. *Address:* Angleterre | Douglas Jerrold Esquire | West Lodge | Putney Heath | *near* London | England.

Rosemont, Lausanne, Switzerland
Tuesday Sixteenth June 1846.

My Dear Jerrold.

We are established here, in a perfect doll's house which could be put, bodily, into the Hall of our Italian Palazzo. But it is in the most lovely and delicious situation imaginable, and there is a spare bedroom wherein we would make you as comfortable as need be. Bowers of roses for cigar-smoking, arbours for cool punch-drinking, mountain and Tyrolean countries close at hand, piled-up Alps before the windows, &c &c &c—

In the hope that you have not thought better (or worse) of your solemn promise and vow, to come here,[1] I proceed to give you elaborate and business-like directions for the Journey.

First and foremost, you cross to Ostend, either from Ramsgate or Dover. We took the former route, and found it a short passage. From Ostend to Cologne by Railway. Fare 27 francs (extra charge for luggage, which is weighed). Time 15 hours. At Cologne you sleep. Any hotel will serve your turn. The nearer the Rhine, the better. Next day, you pay your fare and take your ticket at the office of any of the Steam Packet Companies (the Cologne is the best, but they are all good) *through to Mannheim.* Fare 22 francs. The boat will probably start at about 10 or half past 10 in the Morning, and allow you to sleep at Coblentz that night: either going on next morning in the same boat, or in another belonging to the same company. The time from Cologne to Coblentz, is about 8 hours. Note, that the Beauties of the Rhine do not begin, until you are 2 hours and half, good, out of Cologne. Any hotel at Coblentz, *except the Giant.* They are all close to the river. From Coblentz to Mannheim is about 14 hours. You would probably start at 6 in the Morning, and arrive at about 8 in the evening: dining on board. Hotel at Mannheim, the Hotel de l'Europe, very good, and close to the wharf. Sleep there. Next day from Mannheim to Kehl by Railway. Time about 6 hours. Fare, 1st. class 14 francs. From Kehl to Strasbourg (two or three miles) by Omnibus. The French Custom House is on the road, where luggage is examined. Hotel at Strasbourg, the Hotel de la Ville de Paris, very good. You can sleep there, or go on to Bâle, also by Railway, by the next train. Fare, first class, 17 francs. Time, about 4 hours. Hotel at Bâle, the Hotel of the Three Kings. One of the very best on the Continent. At Bâle, there is the Mail, and there are at least two Diligences also, starting every day for Lausanne. Fare, about 26 francs. Time, about 24 hours. I give the fares and the times, in all cases,

---

[1] CD might suppose that Jerrold would have more time to take a holiday, since his engagement as a leader-writer on the *Daily News* had been terminated on 17 Apr, Forster having found him inefficient. In a letter to Forster of that date (MS Forster Collection, V & A), he admitted that on four occasions he had failed to supply copy in time. Cf. Walter Jerrold, *Douglas Jerrold*, II, 423f, and Richard Garnett, *Life of W. J. Fox*, p. 283.

about. They are almost exactly stated. The account (excluding bed and board on the road) stands thus, from Ostend.

	TIME	MONEY
	DAYS	francs
To Cologne	I	—— 27
To Coblentz	I⎫	—— 22
To Mannheim	I⎭	
To Kehl and Strasbourg, & thence to Bâle —	I	—— 31
Omnibus, additional		I
To Lausanne	I	—— 26
	5 days	107 francs

Returning; the Journey by the Rhine, being *with* the Stream, is performed in half the time. All along the Rhine, English is understood and spoken—French, everywhere.

I look forward to hearing from you that you have fixed a day for the Expedition. You shall work when you please (I am at work myself) and play when you please. And I need not say how truly delighted we should be to see you.

Mrs. Dickens and the little woman send their kind regards.

I am Ever My Dear Jerrold | Faithfully Your friend

Douglas Jerrold Esquire.   CHARLES DICKENS

To LORD MORPETH, 20 JUNE 1846*

MS Mr George Howard. *Address:* Private | Angleterre. | The | Viscount Morpeth | Grosvenor Place | LONDON.

Rosemont, Lausanne, Switzerland
Saturday June Twentieth 1846.

My Dear Lord Morpeth.

Let me premise in the very first line of this letter, that you are to read it at your convenience—and that if you be not at perfect leisure when you receive it, I beg you to fold it up again, until you have a few spare minutes to bestow on its perusal.

I wish to confide to you, a very earnest desire of mine, and to leave it entirely to your discretion and inclination, whether it shall remain a point in confidence between yourself and me, or whether you shall communicate it, at your own time, to anyone else.

I have an ambition for some public employment—some Commissionership, or Inspectorship, or the like, connected with any of those subjects in which I take a deep interest, and in respect of which the Public are generally disposed to treat me with confidence and regard. On any questions connected with the Education of the People, the elevation of their character, the improvement of their dwellings, their greater protection against disease and vice—or with the treatment of Criminals, or the administration of Prison Discipline, which I have long observed closely—I think I could do good service, and I am sure I should enter with my whole heart. I have hoped, for years, that I may become at last a

Police Magistrate,[1] and turn my social knowledge to good practical account from day to day; and I have the strongest hope that in any such position as I have glanced at, I could prove my fitness for improving the execution of that trust. It is not a very towering ambition perhaps; but never was a man's ambition so peculiarly associated with his constant sympathies—and, as I fancy, with his capabilities—as this of mine.[2]

Before I left London, political circumstances pointed so directly to a change in the Government, and the restoration, before long, of the Party with which you are proudly and honorably associated, that I more than once had the idea of speaking to some distinguished Member of it on this subject, and begging leave to mention the fact that I sought employment of this kind—and there an end. Had Lord Holland been living, I think I should have done so to him without hesitation. But, at one time thinking of you, and at another of Lord Lansdowne, and at another of Lord Normanby (from whom I have received great personal kindness)[3] I grew undecided and uneasy, and came away, at last, without doing anything.

Reverting to the question in this retirement, I have, somehow, accustomed myself to look at it, as it were from a distant time as well as a distant place. Fancying this letter a hundred years old, I cannot discern any reason why a Descendant of mine should come to the knowledge of it, with the least misgiving or reluctance. Therefore I think I may banish those feelings from my own mind, and boldly (though with an unaffected diffidence) state my object.

I feel that in doing so, I am as little open to the suspicion of sordid motives as any man, with such an object, can be. I entertain the wish, common to most Literary Men, of having some permanent dependance besides Literature. But I have no thought of abandoning that pursuit, which is a great happiness to me: and only seek this new avocation as its not unnatural offspring and companion. My writings, such as they are, are my credentials; and they have never been in greater favor at home and abroad, nor has my pen ever been more profitable to me, than at this time.

You may laughingly ask why I select you, after all, as the recipient of this letter? I will tell you the plain truth, without the slightest ornament. Though I have had the pleasure of your personal acquaintance—I had almost written, friendship—for but a short time, I am sure you have, naturally, a strong and kind inclination towards one in my position, which may be most implicitly confided in. In that assurance, I put my trust in you without reserve, and leave the substance of this letter to be remembered or forgotten by you, with a perfect reliance on your generous consideration.

I am ever | Dear Lord Morpeth
Yours faithfully and obliged
CHARLES DICKENS

The | Viscount Morpeth.

---

[1] See *To* Lord Brougham, 24 Sep 43: Vol. III, p. 570 and *n*.

[2] Forster heard later of this inquiry with "some surprise", and says the reply did not encourage CD to think of it further (F, v, i, 388).

[3] Probably on his visit to Mulgrave Castle in 1844: see *To* Mrs CD, 6 Apr 44 and *fn*. Forster refers to "many acts of sympathy and kindness" (F, v, vii, 445).

To JOHN FORSTER, [?22 JUNE 1846]

Extracts in F, v, ii, 392–3, 393–4, 392*n*, v, iii, 403*n*, v, ii, 394. *Date:* first, second and fifth extracts 22 June according to Forster; third extract from "another" letter than the first, but suggests early impressions, therefore probably same letter; fourth extract from letter "preceding" ?28 June.

Lausanne had its natural dulness increased by its streets going up and down hill abruptly and steeply, like the streets in a dream; and the consequent difficulty of getting about it. There are some suppressed churches in it, now used as packers' warehouses: with cranes and pulleys growing out of steeple-towers; little doors for lowering goods through, fitted into blocked-up oriel windows; and cart-horses stabled in crypts. These also help to give it a deserted and disused appearance. On the other hand, as it is a perfectly free place subject to no prohibitions or restrictions of any kind, there are all sorts of new French books and publications in it, and all sorts of fresh intelligence from the world beyond the Jura Mountains. It contains only one Roman Catholic church, which is mainly for the use of the Savoyards and Piedmontese who come trading over the Alps. As for the country, it cannot be praised too highly, or reported too beautiful. There are no great waterfalls, or walks through mountain-gorges, *close* at hand, as in some other parts of Switzerland; but there is a charming variety of enchanting scenery. There is the shore of the lake, where you may dip your feet, as you walk, in the deep blue water, if you choose. There are the hills to climb up, leading to the great heights above the town; or to stagger down, leading to the lake. There is every possible variety of deep green lanes, vineyard, cornfield, pasture-land, and wood. There are excellent country roads that might be in Kent or Devonshire: and, closing up every view and vista, is an eternally changing range of prodigious mountains—sometimes red, sometimes grey, sometimes purple, sometimes black; sometimes white with snow; sometimes close at hand; and sometimes very ghosts in the clouds and mist.

The view from each side of Rosemont was different in character, and from one there was visible the liveliest aspect of Lausanne itself, close at hand, and seeming to be always coming down the hill with its steeples and towers, not able to stop itself. From a fine long broad balcony on which the windows of my little study on the first floor (where I am now writing) open, the lake is seen to wonderful advantage,—losing itself by degrees in the solemn gorge of mountains leading to the Simplon pass. Under the balcony is a stone colonnade, on which the six French windows of the drawing-room open; and quantities of plants are clustered about the pillars and seats, very prettily. One of these drawing-rooms is furnished (like a French hotel) with red velvet, and the other with green; in both, plenty of mirrors and nice white muslin curtains; and for the larger one in cold weather there is a carpet, the floors being bare now, but inlaid in squares with different-coloured woods. *He went on to describe every other room, concluding* Walking out into the balcony as I write, I am suddenly reminded, by the sight of the Castle of Chillon[1]

---

[1] Not visible from Rosemont, as a correspondent pointed out to Forster (F, 1872–4, III, 519). He left the remark uncorrected in 1876; the mistake was presumably CD's. Several other castles were visible.

glittering in the sunlight on the lake, that I omitted to mention that object in my catalogue of the Rosemont beauties. Please to put it in, like George Robins,[1] in a line by itself.

There were regular evening walks of nine or ten miles, and he was thinking of his books. An odd shadowy undefined idea is at work within me, that I could connect a great battle-field somehow with my little Christmas story. Shapeless visions of the repose and peace pervading it in after-time; with the corn and grass growing over the slain, and people singing at the plough; are so perpetually floating before me, that I cannot but think there may turn out to be something good in them when I see them more plainly. . . . I want to get Four Numbers of the monthly book done here, and the Christmas book. If all goes well, and nothing changes, and I can accomplish this by the end of November, I shall run over to you in England for a few days with a light heart, and leave Roche to move the caravan to Paris in the meanwhile. It will be just the very point in the story when the life and crowd of that extraordinary place will come vividly to my assistance in writing.

The green woods and green shades about here, are more like Cobham in Kent, than anything we dream of at the foot of the Alpine passes.

There was an annual child's fête at the Signal[2] the other night: given by the town. It was beautiful to see perhaps a hundred couple of children dancing in an immense ring in a green wood. Our three eldest were among them, presided over by my landlord,[3] who was 18 years in the English Navy, and is the Sous Préfet of the town—a very good fellow indeed; quite an Englishman. Our landlady, nearly twice his age, used to keep the Inn (a famous one) at Zurich: and having made £50,000 bestowed it on a young husband. She might have done worse.

He ended with a promise to describe in his next letter the small colony of English.

To MISS BURDETT COUTTS, 25 JUNE 1846

MS Morgan Library. *Address:* Angleterre | Miss Burdett Coutts | Stratton Street | Piccadilly | London.

> Rosemont, Lausanne, Switzerland
> Twenty Fifth June 1846.

My Dear Miss Coutts.

The enclosed sheets of paper[4] are dated on the day on which—and at the place where—they were begun. When you have read and considered them, I shall hope to have the pleasure of receiving a letter from you.

---

[1] The well-known auctioneer.

[2] The Signal was situated on the north edge of the Bois de Sauvabellin, "a deep green wood, on the sides and summit of a very high hill overlooking the town and all the country round" (F, v, iii, 403). It was the usual place for popular festivals; Frederika Bremer describes a festival held on

2 July 1856 for family parties mostly of the artisan class. (*Two Years in Switzerland and Italy*, 1861, I, 34–5.)

[3] Jules Dor; he became Préfet in 1852, and retired in 1868.

[4] These are no longer with the letter. The postal charge shows that there cannot have been more than a few sheets—clearly,

This is an odd little house, which I think might be easily put into the great Sala of our old Genoese Palazzo—bodily. It stands in the midst of beautiful grounds, on the slope of the Hill going down to the Lake—and the blue waters thereof, and the whole range of Mountains, lie in front of the windows. Between it, and Ouchy, is a School, very famous in these parts, kept by a German gentleman; and in that School, Charley is imprisoned as a weekly Boarder.[1] As there are only three other English boys, I hope he will soon be a proficient in the French language. He went, last Monday. It was rather a trial for him, and indeed for all of us, that first departure from home in a strange place. But he went with a gallant heart; and when I saw him sitting at the Garden Gate last night as I walked by, though I had an idea that he was counting the hours until Saturday at noon, yet he looked happy, and very brown. His sisters have a little French Governess at home, who can't speak a word of English.

The heat as we came here, was more intense than any I have ever felt, and so it has been here, until the day before yesterday, when there was a violent thunder storm of some hours' duration, which I hope has cleared the air for good and all, as it is now quite cool and windy. I have a study, something larger than a Plate Warmer, opening into a Balcony and commanding a lovely view. I am contemplating terrific and tremendous industry—am mightily resolved to begin the book in Numbers without delay—and have already begun to look the little Christmas Volume in its small red face; though I hardly know it by sight yet.

As my handwriting always becomes very hideous under such circumstances (as I fear I need hardly mention to you, who have so much of it to read) I will only add that Mrs. Dickens unites with me in cordial remembrances to you, and that we desire to add our best regards to Mr. and Mrs. Brown. Ever Faithfully Yours—CHARLES DICKENS. I am much distressed by having no room for the flourish.

To JOHN FORSTER, 25 JUNE 1846

MS Comtesse de Suzannet. *Address:* Angleterre | John Forster Esquire | 58 Lincolns Inn Fields | London.

Rosemont, Lausanne. Twenty Fifth June 1846.

My Dear Forster.

Will you remember, in about a month or five weeks from the 21st. of this month, to have accounts from Bradbury and Evans and Chapman and Hall, and to adjust and settle them?[2]

from the reference in *To* Miss Coutts, 25 July, containing information about the Pentonville Society (and possibly other institutions) and presumably written during CD's journey or at the Hotel Gibbon.

[1] "The school, *La Villa*, stood on the site now occupied by no. 57, avenue d'Ouchy. It had been founded in 1840 by ... Theodore Devrient, born at Leipzig in 1808" (René Rapin, "Lausanne and some

English Writers", *Etudes de Lettres*, série II, II [1959], 104*n*).

[2] Forster followed his instructions in obtaining the accounts: Chapman & Hall wrote to him 25 July 46 enclosing the accounts to 30 June, "which we trust you will find correct and satisfactory. The balance we shall be happy to pay, immediately on receiving your instructions" (MS V & A). They show that £89.13.10

I am very anxious that you should put to Bradbury and Evans a doubt which is strongly present to my mind—and that is, whether it would not be better—whether it is not positively necessary as matters stand—for them to arrange with Chapman and Hall, for Chapman and Hall being the publishers of the new book in monthly numbers.[1] I have been so unwilling to awaken any new matters of difference between Bradbury and Evans and myself, and have been so sincerely anxious that the old ones should fade away and be forgotten along with the unfortunate, and unsettled, and irritating state of circumstances in which they were engendered—that I have not made any allusion to this desire of mine, before. But I have felt it very earnestly and constantly for some time, and never more so than when—at the very time of the publication of the Pictures from Italy, and when I was forcing myself to leave England, with the view of filling up the Pit in my literary life, made by that unhappy paper—their names were painted out from above the door in Fleet Street, and "Office of The Daily News" written up there, instead. So that when I was seeking, by the most decisive means to detach myself from that undertaking, my book was actually published at its office!

Pray explain to Bradbury and Evans that I do not make this, matter of complaint against them. I am most desirous that they should (as I now hope they will) recover their loss and turn the enterprize to good account. But the question whether it is proper that a book of mine should be published at a Newspaper office, is quite another thing; and that it is not advisable that it should be published at their place in Whitefriars, I take for granted.[2] Otherwise, they never would have started the house in Fleet Street, at all. Apart from this, I do not disguise from you, or them, that I question their having people about them, competent to the management of such a work; whereas we know that Chapman and Hall are used to it, and that the machinery is as familiar to them, as the ticking of their own watches.

I have a besetting anxiety on this subject, of quite an intense kind. There will be the beginning of the new book, and there will be the Christmas Book, close on each other's heels. There is all the preliminary announcement to be considered and arranged, and the board to be made quite clear and clean for the playing out of a very great stake; and I do not think—not because I will not, but because I cannot—that Bradbury and Evans's arrangements, so thoroughly unsettled, and so sweepingly changed by the Newspaper—are so capable of the undertaking

was due to CD (for works of which they owned a share of the copyright), and this sum was paid on 12 Aug (CD's Account-book, MS Messrs Coutts). Bradbury & Evans's accounts, also made up to 30 June, were presumably sent to Forster at about the same time; they show a balance due to CD of £629: see *To* Mitton, 30 Aug 46, *fn*. No adjustments were made; one might have expected the amount due from Chapman & Hall to be paid to Bradbury & Evans (see *To* Bradbury & Evans, 8 May 44).

[1] The change was not made; Forster must have advised against it, and rightly, in view of the Agreement of 1 June 44 and Bradbury & Evans's advertisements of the novel since 18 Apr 46.

[2] Because Whitefriars was the printing-office of the *Daily News*; in the *Athenæum's* first advertisement of *Pictures* and the "new English story", Bradbury & Evans's two addresses are given: "90, Fleet-street, and Whitefriars"; a week later (25 Apr) "and Whitefriars" is omitted; but Whitefriars alone is on the title-page.

as Chapman and Hall's. Pray, my dear Forster, take very grave counsel with Bradbury and Evans on this head, as soon as you conveniently can; and that they may not misunderstand the spirit in which I write, or consider me as being anything but good-humoured and friendly, read them as much of this letter, or all of it, as you please.

Ever affectionately Yours my Dear F.

John Forster Esquire.   CHARLES DICKENS

To JOSEPH VALCKENBERG, 25 JUNE 1846

MS Comtesse de Suzannet. *Address:* A Monsieur | Mons: Joseph Valckenberg | Worms | Sur le Rhine.

Rosemont, Lausanne, Switzerland
Twenty Fifth June 1846.

My Dear Sir.

I hasten to return you my best thanks for your very earnest and warm-hearted letter; and I assure you that if I can contrive to devote a day to Worms whenever I come down the Rhine, I shall certainly do so, and shall have great pleasure in becoming known to your family.

My movements depend so much on my industry here, and my industry depends so much on the humour I am in from day to day, that I cannot just now anticipate my movements with certainty. But whenever I strike my Swiss tent, I will write to you again. I think it is pretty sure that we shall remove to Paris before Christmas, and that I shall be running to London, towards the end of November.

It is impossible that I can be otherwise than pleased with the feeling in which your proposed remembrance of me, originates. And therefore all I have to say on the subject of the Liebfraumilch, is, that if it should come here, I will drink in it, the health of everybody, great and small, in that large family-house at Worms.

In the meantime, pray remember me to your home-circle—especially to your brother, and to that fair Wife of yours who did *not* come down to the Pier on the 6th of June. To whom Mrs. Dickens and her sister send their regards.

My small fellow-travellers arrived here in perfect health, and have grown so red in this farmhouse that they look as if they were in one perpetual Sunset.

Believe me, with regard | Faithfully Yours

Joseph Valckenberg Esquire.   CHARLES DICKENS

To LORD JOHN RUSSELL, [?15–26 JUNE 1846]

Mention in *To* Forster, ?28 June. *Date:* written at Rosemont, and completed before starting *Dombey* on 27 June.

About Ragged Schools.

To JOHN FORSTER, [?28 JUNE 1846]

Extracts in F, v, ii, 400, 394, iii, 402–3. *Date:* first extract 28 June according to Forster; second extract also 28 June, since the day before Haldimand's dinner (see *fn*); third extract probably same letter, since from one of "his first letters", but clearly well after the move to Rosemont.

I have not been idle since I have been here, though at first I was "kept out" of the big box[1] as you know. I had a good deal to write for Lord John about the Ragged schools. I set to work and did that. A good deal for Miss Coutts, in reference to her charitable projects. I set to work and did *that*. Half of the children's New Testament[2] to write, or pretty nearly. I set to work and did *that*. Next I cleared off the greater part of such correspondence as I had rashly pledged myself to; and then . . .

BEGAN DOMBEY!

I performed this feat yesterday—only wrote the first slip—but there it is, and it is a plunge straight over head and ears into the story. . . . Besides all this, I have really gone with great vigour at the French, where I find myself greatly assisted by the Italian; and am subject to two descriptions of mental fits in reference to the Christmas book: one, of the suddenest and wildest enthusiasm; one, of solitary and anxious consideration. . . . By the way, as I was unpacking the big box I took hold of a book, and said to "Them,"—"Now, whatever passage my thumb rests on, I shall take as having reference to my work." It was

[1] Forster mentions "the non-arrival of a box despatched from London before his own departure, containing not his proper writing materials only, but certain quaint little bronze figures that thus early stood upon his desk".

[2] Now generally known as "The Life of Our Lord"; written in the form of a letter to his children, in eleven chapters, and never intended for publication. In the last year of his life, when asked by Georgina to consider having it privately printed, CD reread the MS and took "a week or two to consider" before deciding against it (Georgina *to* Mrs Fields, 29 Sep 1870; MS Huntington, quoted in A. Adrian, *Georgina Hogarth and the Dickens Circle*, 1957, p. 161). The MS was among the private papers left to Georgina by CD and remained in family hands until 1939; it was published in 1934 with a foreword by Lady Dickens explaining that Sir Henry, CD's last surviving son (*d.* 1933), had stated in his will that this might be done after his death if the majority of the family agreed. Since 1964 the MS has been in the Free Library of Philadelphia; it is enclosed in a case bearing the monogram "MD" and an engraved plate "Written for his own Children by Charles Dickens 1849"—the date clearly a mistake on the part of Mamie, to whom Georgina gave it in Sep 1870. Both in CD's lifetime and later, a few copies were made: one by Mamie for Edward Bulwer Lytton Dickens before he left England in 1868 (Sotheby's catalogue, 22 July 1935), one by Georgina for Bessie Dickens in 1869, and one at some earlier but unknown date for Mark Lemon's children. This last was later given to Mrs Perugini and transcribed by B. W. Matz; it bore the correct date, 1846 (Winifred Matz, "My Copy of 'the Children's New Testament' ", *D*, xxx [1934], 89), which is also given by Gladys Storey, *Dickens and Daughter*, 1939, p. 78. Though Miss Storey says that CD wrote "part" in Paris in Nov, the present reference suggests that he completed it in June. The narrative begins with the Nativity and ends with the Conversion of St Paul and the persecution of the early Christians. Except at the beginning, there are few substantial omissions; St Luke is the main source, and CD's emphasis is not, as often stated, "Unitarian", but rather "Broad Church" (compare his admiration for Dr Arnold), and adapted to the understanding of young children.

TRISTRAM SHANDY, and opened at these words, "What a work it is likely to turn out! Let us begin it!"[1]
He still inclined strongly to the field of battle notion *for his Christmas book, but had not yet begun, wishing to have Forster's opinion.*

He mentioned Haldimand,[2] *who had a very fine seat just below Rosemont; his character and station had made him quite the little sovereign of the place.* He has founded and endowed all sorts of hospitals and institutions here, and he gives a dinner to-morrow to introduce our neighbours, whoever they are.[3]

The peasantry all about Lausanne were as pleasant a people as need be. He never passed on any of the roads, man, woman, or child without a salutation; and anything churlish or disagreeable he never noticed in them. It was unjust to call the Swiss the Americans of the Continent. They have not the sweetness and grace of the Italians, or the agreeable manners of the better specimens of French peasantry, but they are admirably educated (the schools of this canton are extraordinarily good, in every little village), and always prepared to give a civil and pleasant answer. There is no greater mistake. I was talking to my landlord about it the other day, and he said he could not conceive how it had ever arisen, but that when he returned from his eighteen years' service in the English Navy he shunned the people, and had no interest in them until they gradually forced their real

[1] Book VIII, Ch. 1.
[2] William Haldimand (1784–1862), philanthropist. Son of a merchant and brother of Mrs Jane Marcet; director of Bank of England 1809, and MP for Ipswich 1820–6; settled at Denantou, a country estate near Lausanne, in 1828. In 1843 founded, with the help of Mlle Elizabeth de Cerjat, the Asile des Aveugles in Lausanne, opened 1844; contributed £3000 to the construction of the English church at Lausanne; was noted for his hospitality to English and other travellers.
[3] The dinner was on 29 June. Those known to have been present (from Forster, and Watson's Diary) were the Watsons, the de Cerjats, and the Goffs, who, with Haldimand, constituted the circle of English residents who became CD's friends.

The Hon. Richard Watson (1800–52), youngest son of the 2nd Lord Sondes and Mary Elizabeth (*née* Milles); officer in the 10th Hussars 1817–30; MP for Canterbury, 1830–2, and supported the Reform Bill; succeeded to the Rockingham estates 1836 and married 1839. He built and supported a village school, restored the church, and made many additions to the Castle—which CD several times visited with his family (see next vol.), adopting some of its features for Chesney Wold in *Bleak House*, 1852–3.

Haldimand's dinner was the beginning of a warm friendship; Watson recorded his first impressions: "Met Boz, Mrs Dickens & her sister Miss Hogarth. Liked him altogether very much as well as his wife. He appears unaffected" (Diary, 29 June 46; MS Commander Michael Saunders Watson). At Watson's death CD called him "as thoroughly good and true a man as ever lived" (F, VI, vi, 533).

Lavinia Jane Watson (1816–88), daughter of Lord George Quin and Georgiana (*née* Spencer), and grand-daughter of the 1st Marquis of Headfort and of the 2nd Earl Spencer. Her three children, George (*b.* 1841), Edward Spencer (*b.* 1843), and Mary Georgiana (*b.* ?1845) were with them at Lausanne. She had resided there with her father in 1835–6, so had long known Haldimand and the de Cerjats. Surviving diaries, and CD's many letters to her, suggest a personality of great charm and intelligence, and a lover of the arts.

William Woodley Frederick de Cerjat (*d.* 1869), member of an old Vaudois family, and his wife Maria, daughter of Peter Holmes of Peterville, co. Tipperary.

George Goff (*d.* 1881), and his wife Elizabeth (married 1832), sister of Mrs de Cerjat.

character upon his observation. We have a cook and a coachman here, taken at hazard from the people of the town; and I never saw more obliging servants, or people who did their work so truly *with a will*. And in point of cleanliness, order, and punctuality to the moment, they are unrivalled.

To THOMAS CHAPMAN, 3 JULY 1846

MS Comtesse de Suzannet. *Address:* Angleterre | Thomas Chapman Esquire | 2 Leadenhall Street | London.

　　　　　　　　　　　　　　Rosemont, Lausanne. Friday Third July 1846

My Dear Sir

It was a very considerate and friendly act of you to time your communication on the most painful subject of the breach of confidence in your house,[1] as you did, and to make it to me yourself. Accept my thanks for this proof of your regard among many others: and with them the assurance of my friendship and esteem.

I have been perfectly horrified by the whole Story.[2] I could hardly name a man in London whom I should have thought less likely to stand so committed, than he. Not that I had any intimate knowledge of his pursuits, or any close acquaintance with himself or his usual mode of thinking and proceeding—but I had an idea of his great steadiness and reliability, and a conviction of his great respect and regard for you. God help him, I believe, even now, that he was sincere in the latter feeling, and was overcome and swept away by the tide of circumstances on which he had madly cast himself. The more I see and hear of such surprises, the more I echo that clause in Christ's prayer in which they are all shadowed forth,—and shrink from the prospect of temptation being presented to anybody dear to me, or to myself.

It has often awakened great wonder within me how all those publishing expences[3] (of the extent of which, I was able to form a pretty accurate idea) were defrayed. But whenever I have sounded Augustus on the subject; which I have done once or twice; he always hinted at a Rich Uncle, and some unknown share in some unknown business, which of course I could not gainsay. He told the tale as it was told to him, and had every reason to believe it. Indeed, I suppose you and your partners laboured under the like delusion?

---

[1] The discovery of Thomas Powell's defalcations, amounting to £10,000, and "effected both by forgery and peculation", according to a later letter from John Chapman (reproduced with other letters in CD's pamphlet, privately printed in Dec 49—denouncing Powell after he had escaped to New York and begun a new career of deception). See also Wilfred Partington, "Should a Biographer Tell?", *D*, XLIII (1947), 193–200, XLIV (1948), 14–23 and N, II, 181–2, 191, 193.

[2] After the discovery Powell attempted suicide with laudanum; Chapman dismissed but did not prosecute him, for the sake of his family.

[3] See Vol. III, p. 577*n*; his latest publication was *Tales from Boccaccio*, published by Bentley, Mar 46, revised as *Florentine Tales*, 1847; Powell presented a copy of the revised edn to Thomas and Mrs Chapman, 2 Jan 47, with an inscription "by the wretched and unhappy Author" (Stephen F. Fogle, "Leigh Hunt, Thomas Powell, and the *Florentine Tales*", *Keats-Shelley Journal*, XIV [1965], 79). A play, *Love's Rescue*, was produced at the Queen's Theatre, 14 Sep 46, but not published.

I should be very glad if you would tell me, when it is all done, whether you have any intelligence of him, or any knowledge of his destiny.[1] It is terrible to think of his wife and children.

Like you, I was greatly shocked by the death of Haydon,[2]—I thought the account of the Inquest one of the most affecting[3] pieces of fact I had ever read. But I quite agree with you, nevertheless, that all his life he had utterly mistaken his vocation. No amount of sympathy with him and sorrow for him in his manly pursuit of a wrong idea for so many years—until, by dint of his perseverance and courage it almost began to seem a right one—ought to prevent one from saying that he most unquestionably was a very bad painter, and that his pictures could not be expected to sell or to succeed. I went to that very exhibition at the Egyptian Hall of which he writes so touchingly in his Diary; and I assure you that when I saw his account of the Number of Visitors he had had, in one of the papers, my amazement was—not that they were so few, but that they were so many. There was one Picture—Nero entertaining himself with a Musical Performance, while Rome was burning—quite marvellous in its badness. It was difficult to look at it with a composed and decent face. There is no doubt, on the other hand, that in the Theory of his art, he was very clever, and in his general tone of thought a very superior man. And I must say that having written so well on Art,[4] and having suffered so much in a hopeless attempt to elevate it, I think he was (as his widow is) a very good subject for a Pension.

I little thought, once upon a time, that I should ever live to praise Peel. But

[1] Little is known of Powell until the end of 1848, when the Croydon magistrates issued a warrant for his arrest for further forgeries; he was then living at Burgh House, Banstead, seven miles from Croydon.

[2] Benjamin Robert Haydon (1788–1846; *DNB*), historical painter; had had much success in 1814–23, and was a friend of Keats, Leigh Hunt and Wordsworth; but was constantly involved in controversy (especially with the Academicians), alienated his patrons, and was several times imprisoned for debt. In 1835 his scheme for a Government School of Design was accepted; he had constantly advocated State patronage of art and hoped much from the Fine Arts Commission, but blamed them for not consulting him. He was deeply distressed by his failure in the cartoon competition in 1843, but, encouraged by the reception of his *Uriel and Satan* in the RA 1844, set to work on six large pictures to show how the House of Lords ought to be decorated. Two, *Aristides* and *Nero*, were ready in 1846, and, against advice, he opened his exhibition in a room at the Egyptian Hall, Piccadilly, on Easter Monday. Tom Thumb was simultaneously on show in the large room; in the first week Barnum (the dwarf's manager) took £600, Haydon £7.13.0. On 18 May Haydon closed his exhibition in despair, heavily in debt. This final sense of ridicule added to failure, many further demands for money, and the intensely hot weather of June, unbalanced a mind harassed by disappointment; on 22 June he put everything in order in his studio, wrote a number of farewell letters, and killed himself with a pistol and two razors, in front of his last unfinished picture (see Eric George, *The Life and Death of Benjamin Robert Haydon*, 2nd edn, 1967).

[3] The evidence of his last hours, his recent diary entries, and his daughter's description of finding his body, were particularly affecting. The verdict was that he killed himself while of unsound mind (*The Times*, 25 June).

[4] CD had no doubt read his *Lectures on Painting and Design*, 1844, 1846 (delivered 1835–46), and his many letters to the press; Haydon's views on fresco would particularly interest him.

d'Israeli and that Dunghill Lord[1] have so disgusted me, that I feel disposed to champion him—and should have done so, even if he hadn't shewn a striving artist, such delicate attention and compassion as he shewed to Haydon.[2] I suppose he is out of office by this time, and Lord John half in; though I don't see how they are to steer between Lord Grey and Lord Palmerston.[3] It must come in my opinion, as Cobden told them in the House, to a coalition between Peel and Lord John.[4] The first great question on which the Public become really excited—Education, perhaps,—or Church Reform, or, for anything we know just now, the Game Laws—is very likely to bring it about. There will then be a strong Government, and, as Governments go, a pretty good one.

I hear from Forster that the Daily News is doing wonders,[5] though he seems to me to be[6] uneasy there himself, and to feel the confinement and drudgery. It is very well done, I think—but I always suspect them on Railroad matters—and don't think they will ever bruise their foreheads by running, before the Public, against any bold idea. Well! I am very glad I have nothing to do with it, and have so far forgotten it now, that I have ceased to be sorry that I ever had a part in it.

Our house here would go bodily into the great Sala of our Italian House; but it is in a lovely situation, and in the midst of very pretty grounds. I have already settled down to work, and am glad of the repose and quiet. The new book in numbers, is begun; and the Christmas book is simmering over a slow fire. In

---

[1] Lord George Bentinck (1802–48), leader of the Protectionist faction in the Conservative party; on 8 June had made a violent personal attack on Peel—using, said Sidney Herbert, "language seldom heard in this House"—charging him with having hunted Canning to death in 1826. Peel rebutted the charge, but it was renewed by Disraeli on 19 June and Peel then made a defence described by Greville as "very triumphant, crushing George Bentinck and Disraeli, and received with something like enthusiasm by the House"; Russell and Lord Morpeth "spoke handsomely of Peel" and "nothing could be more miserable than the figure which the choice pair, George Bentinck and Disraeli, cut" (*Memoirs*, V, 408). Bentinck was frequently pilloried by *Punch*, once with a reference to "dunghills and gutters".

[2] Haydon wrote to Peel (who had previously assisted him) about his distresses and received £50, with a few lines of sympathy, on 17 June; the cheque was found untouched at his death, and one of his last letters on the morning of his suicide was a grateful note to Peel, hoping that his wife might be secure from want. She was granted a civil list pension of £50 a year,

and Peel and Lady Peel also subscribed generously to the fund set up by Talfourd for the family.

[3] For his difficulties, see *To* Nugent, 10 Dec 45, *fn*. In the event, Grey was Secretary for War and Colonies and Palmerston Foreign Secretary.

[4] The Government was defeated on 26 June on the Protection of Life (Ireland) Bill; during the debate Cobden said that he was voting against the Bill and not against Peel, unlike the Protectionists in Peel's own party who voted against the Bill to show no confidence in Peel; in Cobden's view the followers of Peel and Russell "had already fraternized, the battle between the chiefs must be abandoned, and a fusion must take place in that House" (*Annual Register*, 1846).

[5] As a result of lowering the price to $2\frac{1}{2}d$ on 1 June, the circulation, which had fallen to 4000 when Dilke took over, rose steadily throughout that month; on 3 July Paxton reported "Sale of the Daily News to-day about 19,500" (MS Devonshire Collections). The highest figure recorded was 22,000 ("Memoir", in C. W. Dilke, *Papers of a Critic*, I, 60).

[6] MS reads "to be to be".

such circumstances my handwriting usually becomes a very hideous and un-readable—as I am afraid you will have found out long before this place, if you ever reach it.

Mrs. Dickens begs me to say (with her and Miss Hogarth's love to Mrs. Chapman) that the house is large enough to leave us a spare bed; and that if you should make a summer trip in this direction, we should be delighted to welcome you. There is very little English society here, but what there is (two or three families) is agreeable and intelligent. As to the Swiss, they do me as much honor, and seem to be as interested in me, as if I were Swiss myself. I have a little Study, not unlike a large plate-warmer, which commands the whole Lake and range of mountains. There are beautiful and different views, on all the four sides of the house.

I have hardly left myself room to say that I am—but I want the less room, because it is[1] unnecessary—always My Dear Mr. Chapman Faithfully Your friend

CHARLES DICKENS

P.S. Everybody well, and the weather delicious.—Great thunder storms among the mountains.

To LORD ROBERTSON, 3 JULY 1846*

MS Yale University Library. *Address:* Angleterre | The Honorable | Lord Robertson | Edinburgh | Scotland.

Rosemont, Lausanne, Switzerland | Third July 1846.

My Dear Lightbody.

There was a gentleman in the prime of life—not stout, but inclining towards a goodly rotundity of person—who informed me, when you and I had the happiness of meeting at the house of our mutual friend Macready,[2] that he wished he might be something or othered if he didn't make an Autumnal excursion to this place, to see your humble servant who is most cordially and lovingly his friend. As he said this, "in a manner" which inspired me with confidence in the sincerity of his declaration, I shall feel obliged if you will have the kindness to sound him on the subject, and ask him whether he means to come; and if so, when; and if not, why not.

You can tell him if you please that although this house could easily be put into the large hall of my Italian Palazzo, it is large enough and elastic enough to hold him, and also that other man—whom the vile blows and buffets of the world have so incensed that he is reckless what he does to spite the world[3]—who swore at the same time that he would come, and sail upon the Lake. The heartiest of welcomes (and very little else) is ready for their reception.

I am hard at work; having already begun the new Story in numbers, and having the Christmas book on the top-bar, simmering gently over a slow fire. Surely there is no such place as London? I seem to have heard of it in my child-

---

[1] MS reads "us".
[2] On 7 May 46 (*Diaries*, II, 337).

[3] Clearly Macready. Cf. *Macbeth*, III, i, 109–11.

hood, but I am pretty sure it was a lie of the Nurse's. Mountains, valleys, lakes, vines, and green lanes, are all I believe in, in the way of locality.

Ramsgate to Ostend—Ostend (by Railroad) to Cologne. Cologne (by steamboat) to Mannheim. Mannheim (by Railroad) to Strasburg. Strasburg (by Railroad) to Bâle. Bâle (by Mail Coach, or any coach you like) to Lausanne. All along the road, through Belgium and Germany, the conversation is one perpetual Gaelic Sermon.[1] Everybody is nearest choaking, when most eloquent.

All perfectly well. Love from the Ladies. Ever Yours affectionately

CHARLES DICKENS

To JOHN FORSTER, [5 JULY 1846]

Extracts in F, v, iii, 404–5, 402 and *n*, v, ii, 394*n*, v, iii, 403–4, 413 and *n* (four extracts); F, 1872–4, II, xii, 236. *Date:* first three extracts 5 July according to Forster; fourth extract, describing the fête, in "the third week after his arrival"; fifth (about Haydon) at about the same time as *To* Chapman, 3 July; the next three "just at this time" and "the same letter" (as each other); final extract (about Mrs Lemon) probably same letter, since replaced in later edns by the extracts about Haydon and John Hunt (see *fn*).

He was feeling sometimes the want of streets in an extraordinary nervousness it would be hardly possible to describe, *that would come upon him after he had been writing all day.* I am writing slowly at first, of course, but I hope I shall have finished the first number in the course of a fortnight at farthest. I have done the first chapter, and begun another. I say nothing of the merits thus far, or of the idea beyond what is known to you; because I prefer that you should come as fresh as may be upon them. I shall certainly have a great surprise for people at the end of the fourth number;[2] and I think there is a new and peculiar sort of interest, involving the necessity of a little bit of delicate treatment[3] whereof I will expound my idea to you by and by. When I have done this number, I may take a run to Chamounix perhaps. . . . My thoughts have necessarily been called away from the Christmas book. The first *Dombey* done, I think I should fly off to that, whenever the idea presented itself vividly before me. I still cherish the Battle fancy, though it is nothing but a fancy as yet.

When it is very hot, it is hotter than in Italy.[4] The overhanging roofs of the houses, and the quantity of wood employed in their construction (where they use tile and brick in Italy), render them perfect forcing-houses. The walls and floors, hot to the hand all the night through, interfere with sleep; and thunder is almost always booming and rumbling among the mountains. *There was at first a plague of flies.* They cover everything eatable, fall into everything drinkable, stagger into the wet ink of newly-written words and make tracks on the writing paper,

[1] Macready recorded on 7 May that "Lord Robertson gave his after-dinner speeches, his Italian songs, and his Gaelic sermon with great effect".

[2] Paul's death was originally intended at that point.

[3] Ch. 16, "What the Waves were always saying", was probably already in his mind.

[4] The heat of this summer was abnormal, melting the snow and glaciers unusually early.

clog their legs in the lather on your chin while you are shaving in the morning, and drive you frantic at any time when there is daylight if you fall asleep.

The heat disabled him at the outset for all exertion until the lightning, thunder and rain arrived. He described the fruit as so abundant in the little farm, that the trees of the orchard in front of his house were bending beneath it; a field of wheat sloping down to the side window of his dining-room was already cut and carried; and the roses, which the hurricane of rain had swept away, were come back lovelier and in greater numbers than ever.

Setting off last night at six o'clock, in accordance with my usual custom, for a long walk, I was really quite floored when I got to the top of a long steep hill leading out of the town—the same by which we entered it. I believe the great heats, however, seldom last more than a week at a time; there are always very long twilights, and very delicious evenings; and now that there is moonlight, the nights are wonderful. The peacefulness and grandeur of the Mountains and the Lake are indescribable. There comes a rush of sweet smells with the morning air too, which is quite peculiar to the country.

He gave an account of a fête held at The Signal. There were various booths for eating and drinking, and the selling of trinkets and sweetmeats; and in one place there was a great circle cleared, in which the common people waltzed and polka'd, without cessation, to the music of a band. There was a great roundabout for children (oh my stars what a family were proprietors of it! A sunburnt father and mother, a humpbacked boy, a great poodle-dog possessed of all sorts of accomplishments, and a young murderer of seventeen who turned the machinery); and there were some games of chance and skill established under trees. It was very pretty. In some of the drinking booths there were parties of German peasants, twenty together perhaps, singing national drinking-songs, and making a most exhilarating and musical chorus by rattling their cups and glasses on the table and clinking them against each other, to a regular tune. You know it as a stage dodge, but the real thing is splendid. Farther down the hill, other peasants were rifle-shooting for prizes, at targets set on the other side of a deep ravine, from two to three hundred yards off. It was quite fearful to see the astonishing accuracy of their aim, and how, every time a rifle awakened the ten thousand echoes of the green glen, some men crouching behind a little wall immediately in front of the targets, sprung up with large numbers in their hands denoting where the ball had struck the bull's eye—and then in a moment disappeared again. Standing in a ring near these shooters was another party of Germans singing hunting-songs, in parts, most melodiously. And down in the distance was Lausanne, with all sorts of haunted-looking old towers rising up before the smooth water of the lake, and an evening sky all red, and gold, and bright green. When it closed in quite dark, all the booths were lighted up; and the twinkling of the lamps among the forest of trees was beautiful.

I am very sorry to hear of Haydon's death. If any subscription be proposed, put me down for five pounds.[1] *About John Hunt's death*: I quite shuddered at

[1] A meeting was held on 30 June at Talfourd's chambers, Lord Morpeth presiding, at which it was resolved that a public subscription should be opened to provide for Haydon's wife and daughter; a subscription list published 24 July included

John Hunt's[1] having applied to that generous duke.[2] It went against the grain with me, sorely, after the story of the two hundred pounds. I don't know what I should have done, if I had been Hunt.

I have been reading poor Hood's *Tylney Hall*:[3] the most extraordinary jumble of impossible extravagance, and especial cleverness, I ever saw. The man drawn to the life from the pirate-bookseller, is wonderfully good;[4] and his recommendation to a reduced gentleman from the university, to rise from nothing as he, the pirate, did, and go round to the churches and see whether there's an opening, and begin by being a beadle, is one of the finest things I ever read, in its way.[5]

I had a letter from Tagart the day before yesterday, with a curious little anecdote of the Duke of Wellington in it. They have had a small cottage at Walmer; and one day—the other day only—the old man met their little daughter Lucy, a child about Mamey's age, near the garden; and having kissed her, and asked her what was her name, and who and what her parents were, tied a small silver medal round her neck with a bit of pink ribbon, and asked the child to keep it in remembrance of him. There is something good, and aged, and odd in it. Is there not?

After turning Mrs. Lemon's portrait over, in my mind, I am convinced that there is not a grain of bad taste in the matter, and that there is a manly composure

CD's £5, and showed Forster, Dilke and Jerrold among the subscribers. The total raised over the next two months exceeded £2000.

[1] John Hunt (1812–46), Leigh Hunt's second son (known to CD as a contributor to *Bentley's* in 1837) had been constantly in difficulties; the Casebook of the Literary Fund described him, in about 1840, as "One of the most Persistent Begging Letter Writers in London", making use of his father's name when appealing for money (MS Royal Literary Fund). One of those who lent him money was the Duke of Devonshire, who had also assisted Leigh Hunt. Leigh Hunt learnt of this after John's death, and told Forster in a statement of his affairs when Forster was preparing an application for a pension: "With regard to poor unhappy — , who caused me such perpetual grief and alarm, what am I to say? I can only feel fright to think of the use he might have made of my name, and beg you to state what you know as strongly, and yet, somehow, as tenderly as you can" (Hunt *to* Forster, 11 Aug 46, Leigh Hunt, *Correspondence*, ed. Thornton Leigh Hunt, II, 89).

[2] Forster (F, v, iv, 413) tells, but misdates, the story of how Hunt asked the Duke for a loan for two years and repaid it on the last day, whereupon the Duke returned it, saying that "never before had

borrowed money come back to him" Contemporary letters show that the loan was made on 13 Jan 44 and the attempted repayment 12 Jan 46, when the Duke's diary mentions his visit to Hunt, "poor noble honorable man" (MS Devonshire Collections).

[3] *Tylney Hall*, 1834, Hood's only full-length novel, written in the hope (unfulfilled) of clearing his debts; its lively characters and comic episodes hardly redeemed a melodramatic and improbable plot.

[4] Timothy Twigg, the parvenu who sets up as a country landowner and provides, with his family, most of the incidental comedy, was supposed to be based on Thomas Tegg (1776–1845; *DNB*), the bookseller and abridger of popular works. He opposed Talfourd's Copyright Bill, and Hood, in letters to CD in 1842–3, referred to one of his piracies and joked about "the *Tegg*-rity of literary property" (*Letters*, ed. P. Morgan, pp. 509, 535). But Twigg is never presented as a "pirate bookseller", and it seems likely that Forster substituted these words for Tegg's name.

[5] Near the close of the novel (Vol. III, Ch. II) Twigg gives this advice to Tom: "that was my principle—commence humble. I once begun as a beadle, says you; but I leave off a bishop, with my share of church property".

and courage in the proceeding deserving of the utmost respect. If Lemon were one of your braggart honest men, he would set a taint of bad taste upon that action as upon everything else he might say or do; but being what he is, I admire him for it greatly, and hold it to be a proof of an exalted nature and a true heart. Your idea of him, is mine. I am sure he is an excellent fellow. We talk about not liking such and such a man because he doesn't look one in the face,—but how much we should esteem a man who looks the world in the face, composedly, and neither shirks it nor bullies it. Between ourselves, I say with shame and self-reproach that I am quite sure if Kate had been a Columbine her portrait would not be hanging, "in character," in Devonshire-terrace.[1]

To H. P. SMITH, 9 JULY 1846

MS Huntington Library.

Rosemont, Lausanne. | Ninth July 1846.

My Dear Smith.

I am quite ashamed to have forgotten your letter of Introduction to my Italianized Yorkshireman. Here it is, agreeably to your reminder conveyed to my brother Alfred. You will find him a good plain workaday bachelor, whose wine, cigars, brandy and water, and so forth, I punished cruelly when I was in those parts.

Our house here would go bodily into the Peschiere Sala, but it is very pretty, and splendidly situated. Don't you mean to pass this way? We are all well, thank God, and happy; and I am charged with more loves to Mrs. Smith and Co. (including my own) than this half sheet of paper will hold.

I have begun my new book and am up to the eyes in it—I suppose I ought rather to say, as it begins in the head, 'down to the toes'. You wouldn't entertain a proposal for ensuring imaginary lives, would you? If so, I would submit the life of—

[No.][2] The name shall not pass these lips, until the [Wa]lls of [the City[3] pro]claim it.

Ever Yours cordially

CD.

H. P. Smith Esquire

---

[1] In his "Corrections made in the Thirteenth Thousand of the Second Volume" (F, 1872–4, III, 520), Forster states that this passage has been removed from later issues, "the portrait which it referred to having been not that of the Lady mentioned, but of a relative bearing the same name". Mrs Lemon (*née* Romer) was formerly on the stage, as were several of her family; the "relative bearing the same name" was perhaps Ann Romer, her first cousin, who played Anne Page in CD's production of *Merry Wives* in 1848.

[2] A strip has been torn at the bottom of the sheet, removing a word of 2 or 3 letters; "No", the reading of N, I, 766, is a probable conjecture.

[3] A possible alternative to "the City" is "London".

To W. WALTON, 9 JULY 1846

MS Huntington Library.

Lausanne. Switzerland | Ninth July 1846.

My Dear Walton.

I beg to introduce to you, Mr. and Mrs. Smith—very particular friends of ours, for whom we have the greatest regard. I need say no more, I am sure, to recommend them to your kind offices. Mr. Smith is stimulated by my accounts of the Marble quarries and the Carrara Studii, to a wish to see those wonders; and I have told him that no one can shew them, half so satisfactorily and pleasantly as you.

Always Believe me | Faithfully Yours

W. Walton Esquire.   CHARLES DICKENS

To JOHN FORSTER, [?12 JULY 1846]

Extracts in F, v, iii, 405, 404, v, ii, 394–5 and *n*, 397–8, v, iii, 404*n*. *Date:* first extract "a week later" and second and last extracts "of a little later date" than 5 July according to Forster; third and fourth, clearly the next letter after the dinner on 6 July (see *fn*), and fifth, after his visit to the Blind Institution (on 8 July according to Forster).

He hoped to finish the first number by that day week or thereabouts, and should then run and look for his Christmas book in the glaciers at Chamounix. I think *Dombey* very strong—with great capacity in its leading idea; plenty of character that is likely to tell; and some rollicking facetiousness, to say nothing of pathos. I hope you will soon judge of it for yourself, however; and I know you will say what you think. I have been very constantly at work.

One of the farmer's people—a sister, I think—was married from here the other day. It is wonderful to see how naturally the smallest girls are interested in marriages. Katey and Mamey were as excited as if they were eighteen. The fondness of the Swiss for gunpowder on interesting occasions, is one of the drollest things. For three days before, the farmer himself, in the midst of his various agricultural duties, plunged out of a little door near my windows, about once in every hour, and fired off a rifle. I thought he was shooting rats who were spoiling the vines; but he was merely relieving his mind, it seemed, on the subject of the approaching nuptials. All night afterwards, he and a small circle of friends kept perpetually letting off guns under the casement of the bridal chamber. A Bride is always drest here, in black silk;[1] but this bride wore merino of that colour, observing to her mother when she bought it (the old lady is 82, and works on the farm), "You know, mother, I am sure to want mourning for you, soon; and the same gown will do."

He was invited to dinner by Mr. and Mrs. de Cerjat.[2] One of her brothers by the bye, now dead, had large property in Ireland—all Nenagh,[3] and the country

---

[1] A bride in "black silk dress, white wreath, and white veil" is mentioned in "A Swiss Wedding", *Monthly Packet*, May 1864, p. 426.

[2] CD dined with them on 6 July; other guests included the Watsons, "Haldimand, Mr Baird, &c" (Watson's Diary, MS Commander Michael Saunders Watson).

[3] In Co. Tipperary, and the scene of many acts of violence. Two Holmeses

about; and Cerjat told me, as we were talking about one thing and another, that when he went over there for some months to arrange the widow's affairs, he procured a copy of the curse which had been read at the altar by the parish priest of Nenagh, against any of the flock who didn't subscribe to the O'Connell tribute. *A difficulty occurred in his drive to Mr. Cerjat's dinner. He had set up, for use of his wife and children, an odd little one-horse-carriage, made to hold three people sideways, so that they should avoid the wind always blowing up or down the valley.* It can't be easily turned; and as you face to the side, all sorts of evolutions are necessary to bring you "broad-side to" before the door of the house where you are going. The country houses here are very like those upon the Thames between Richmond and Kingston (this, particularly), with grounds all round. At Mr. Cerjat's we were obliged to be carried, like the child's riddle, round the house and round the house, without touching the house; and we were presented in the most alarming manner, three of a row, first to all the people in the kitchen, then to the governess who was dressing in her bedroom, then to the drawing-room where the company were waiting for us, then to the dining-room where they were spreading the table, and finally to the hall where we were got out—scraping the windows of each apartment as we glared slowly into it.

He visited the Blind Institution and was particularly interested by two cases. The first was that of a young man of 18 born deaf and dumb, and stricken blind by an accident when he was about five years old.[1] The Director of the institution[2] is a young German, of great ability, and most uncommonly prepossessing appearance. He propounded to the scientific bodies of Geneva, a year ago (when this young man was under education in the asylum), the possibility of teaching him to speak—in other words, to play with his tongue upon his teeth and palate as if on an instrument, and connect particular performances with particular words conveyed to him in the finger-language. They unanimously agreed that it was quite impossible. The German set to work, and the young man now speaks very plainly and distinctly: without the least modulation, of course, but with comparatively little hesitation; expressing the words aloud as they are struck, so to speak, upon his hands; and showing the most intense and wonderful delight in doing it. This is commonly acquired, as you know, by the deaf and dumb who learn by sight; but it has never before been achieved in the case of a deaf, dumb, and blind subject. He is an extremely lively, intelligent, good-humoured fellow;

were in the Record Panel (of landowners for juries) of 1845: Basett Holmes of Kilmore House and John Gardiner Holmes of Lisduff (*Nenagh Guardian*, 1 May 45).

[1] Edouard Meystre (1826–99), blinded while playing with his twin brother and accidentally knocking down their father's loaded shotgun; the brother was killed. (René Rapin, "Lausanne and some English Writers", *Etudes de Lettres*, série II, II [1959], 107*n*, and William Warren Vernon, *Recollections of Seventy-two Years*, 1917, p. 48). Harriet Martineau gave his history in "Three Graces of Christian Science", *Household Words*, 20 May 54, and CD added a signed footnote about the cigars (see *To* Forster, ?24 Aug) and his later visit in Oct 53.

[2] Henri Hirzel (his name is added in 2nd edn), "an exceptionally brilliant man of thirty-one", was the first director; only one man before Hirzel, Dr Howe (see Vol. III, p. 317*n*), had succeeded in teaching a person blind, deaf and dumb to speak (René Rapin, *ibid*).

an excellent carpenter; a first-rate turner; and runs about the building with a certainty and confidence which none of the merely blind pupils acquire. He has a great many ideas, and an instinctive dread of death. He knows of God, as of Thought enthroned somewhere; and once told, on nature's prompting (the devil's of course), a lie. He was sitting at dinner, and the Director asked him whether he had had anything to drink; to which he instantly replied "No," in order that he might get some more, though he had been served in his turn. It was explained to him that this was a wrong thing, and wouldn't do, and that he was to be locked up in a room for it: which was done. Soon after this, he had a dream of being bitten in the shoulder by some strange animal. As it left a great impression on his mind, he told M. the Director that he had told another lie in the night. In proof of it he related his dream, and added, "it must be a lie you know, because there is no strange animal here, and I never was bitten." Being informed that this sort of lie was a harmless one, and was called a dream, he asked whether dead people ever dreamed while they were lying in the ground. He is one of the most curious and interesting studies possible.

When I was there, there had come in, that morning, a girl of ten years old, born deaf and dumb and blind, and so perfectly untaught that she has not learnt to have the least control even over the performance of the common natural functions. ... And yet she *laughs sometimes* (good God! conceive what at!)— and is dreadfully sensitive from head to foot, and very much alarmed, for some hours before the coming on of a thunderstorm. Mr. Haldimand has been long trying to induce her parents to send her to the asylum. At last they have consented; and when I saw her, some of the little blind girls were trying to make friends with her, and to lead her gently about. She was dressed in just a loose robe from the necessity of changing her frequently, but had been in a bath, and had had her nails cut (which were previously very long and dirty), and was not at all ill-looking—quite the reverse; with a remarkably good and pretty little mouth, but a low and undeveloped head of course. It was pointed out to me, as very singular, that the moment she is left alone, or freed from anybody's touch (which is the same thing to her), she instantly crouches down with her hands up to her ears, in exactly the position of a child before its birth; and so remains. I thought this such a strange coincidence with the utter want of advancement in her moral being, that it made a great impression on me; and conning it over and over, I began to think that this is surely the invariable action of savages too, and that I have seen it over and over again described in books of voyages and travels. Not having any of these with me, I turned to *Robinson Crusoe*; and I find De Foe says, describing the savages who came on the island after Will Atkins began to change for the better and commanded under the grave Spaniard for the common defence, "their posture was generally sitting upon the ground, with their knees up towards their mouth, and the head put between the two hands, leaning down upon the knees"[1]—exactly the same attitude!

Kate, Georgy, Mamey, Katey, Charley, Walley, Chickenstalker, and Sampson Brass, commend themselves unto your Honour's loving remembrance.

[1] In *The Further Adventures of Robinson Crusoe* (p. 114 of 1st edn, 1719).

To JOHN FORSTER, [18 JULY 1846]

Extracts in F, v, iii, 405, v, ii, 398, 395. *Date:* first extract 18 July according to Forster, and second extract in his "next week's letter" after 12 July; third extract, describing party of 16 July, is clearly same letter.

He had still eight slips to write to complete the fourth chapter of Dombey, *and for a week had put off Chamounix.* I think the general idea of *Dombey* is interesting and new, and has great material in it. But I don't like to discuss it with you till you have read number one, for fear I should spoil its effect. When done—about Wednesday or Thursday, please God—I will send it in two days' posts, seven letters each day.[1] If you have it set at once (I am afraid you couldn't read it, otherwise than in print) I know you will impress on B. & E. the necessity of the closest secrecy. The very name getting out, would be ruinous.[2] The points for illustration, and the enormous care required, make me excessively anxious. The man for Dombey, if Browne could see him, the class man to a T, is Sir A—— E——, of D——'s.[3] Great pains will be necessary with Miss Tox. The Toodle family should not be too much caricatured, because of Polly. I should like Browne to think of Susan Nipper, who will not be wanted in the first number. After the second number, they will all be nine or ten years older,[4] but this will not involve much change in the characters, except in the children and Miss Nipper. What a brilliant thing to be telling you all these names so familiarly, when you know nothing about 'em! I quite enjoy it. By the bye, I hope you may like the introduction of Solomon Gills. I think he lives in a good sort of house. ... One word more. What do you think, as a name for the Christmas book, of THE BATTLE OF LIFE? It is not a name I have conned at all, but has just occurred to me in connection with that foggy idea. If I can see my way, I think I will take it next, and clear it off. If you knew how it hangs about me, I am sure you would say so too. It would be an immense relief to have it done, and nothing standing in the way of *Dombey*.

I have not been to the Blind asylum again yet, but they tell me that the deaf and dumb and blind child's *face* is improving obviously, and that she takes great delight in the first effort made by the Director to connect himself with an occupation of her time. He gives her, every day, two smooth round pebbles to roll over and over between her two hands. She appears to have an idea that it is to

---

[1] According to Forster, CD sent the MS of all four chapters with his letter of 25–26 July.

[2] Because the title indicated a new departure— especially in its full form, *Dealings with the Firm of Dombey and Son, Wholesale, Retail, and for Exportation* (see J. Butt and K. Tillotson, *Dickens at Work*, 1957, pp. 91–2).

[3] Unidentified—and can have been only a matter of physical likeness. Forster repudiates the notion of any original for Mr Dombey, and his reference to the "amiable and excellent city-merchant whose name has been given" (F, VI, ii, 485) clearly points at Thomas Powell's absurd claim that he was based on "the merchant in whose office a relative of the novelist is clerk", i.e. Thomas Chapman (*Living Authors of England*, New York, 1849, pp. 158–9).

[4] CD changed his plan (see *To* Forster, 3 Oct 46): Paul is "nearly five" at the beginning of No. III, during which a year passes.

lead to something; distinctly recognizes the hand that gives them to her, as a friendly and protecting one; and sits for hours quite busy.

Describing a dinner-party of his own:[1] While we were sitting at dinner, one of the prettiest girls in Lausanne was drowned in the lake—in the most peaceful water, reflecting the steep mountains, and crimson with the setting sun. She was bathing in one of the nooks set apart for women, and seems somehow to have entangled her feet in the skirts of her dress. She was an accomplished swimmer, as many of the girls are here, and drifted, suddenly, out of only five feet water. Three or four friends who were with her, *ran away*, screaming. Our children's governess was on the lake in a boat with M. Verdeil (my prison-doctor)[2] and his family. They ran inshore immediately; the body was quickly got out; and M. Verdeil, with three or four other doctors, laboured for some hours to restore animation; but she only sighed once. After all that time, she was obliged to be borne, stiff and stark, to her father's house. She was his only child, and but 17 years old. He has been nearly dead since, and all Lausanne has been full of the story. I was down by the lake, near the place, last night; and a boatman *acted* to me the whole scene: depositing himself finally on a heap of stones, to represent the body.

To MISS BURDETT COUTTS, 25 JULY 1846

MS Morgan Library. *Address:* Angleterre | Miss Burdett Coutts | Stratton Street | Piccadilly | London.

Rosemont, Lausanne. Saturday Twenty Fifth July 1846.

My Dear Miss Coutts. I think I recollect to have seen a former appeal of that Pentonville Society,[3] and to have regarded it in exactly the same light as that in which you view this recent one. I certainly think that if it be well managed, it might form, *in part*, a model for your Institution, but I think it would be inexpedient for you to found yours, until you have a general knowledge of the management of many similar Institutions. Very little has yet been done in this respect; and if you could do no better than has been done already, I really doubt the expediency of founding an entirely new establishment in preference to assisting in the endowment of an existing one. I fear you would be disappointed in the result, and that you would spend your money to but little purpose.

Have you considered the practical difficulty of confining such an Institution to a single Parish? What would be the qualification (so to speak) for admission? Must the person have been born there, or must she have resided there, a certain

---

[1] On 16 July (not 15 July as Forster says). Watson's Diary entry runs: "Dined with the Dickenses and passed an evening such as one expects at the house of Boz. He was in extraordinary spirits, and was very amusing: Tricks, Charades, &c. 'The Brave' seems an excellent servant—his name is Roche—a Frenchman" (MS Commander Michael Saunders Watson).

[2] Auguste Verdeil (1795–1856), doctor and historian; governor of the prison and physician of the cantonal hospital at Lausanne. Published two accounts of the Lausanne Penitentiary in 1842.

[3] The London Female Penitentiary at Pentonville, established 1807; the 98 inmates did washing and took in needlework in order to qualify to support themselves respectably (Peter Cunningham, *Handbook of London*, 1849, p. 497).

time? If the latter, I fear the opposition of the Parish itself, and its perpetual hunting down of these unhappy objects lest they should be establishing themselves there, with some kind of faint view to the Asylum, would entail upon them a frightful persecution. If the former, I fear that some of the most pitiable, and truly distressing, and hopeful cases (those of young people coming from the Country, and sinking down into the vice of London) would be without any relief from you.

Your two objections to my sketch of a plan, I wish to offer half a dozen words upon.

1st. As to Marriage. I do not propose to put that before them as the immediate end and object to be gained, but assuredly to keep it in view as the possible consequence of a sincere, true, practical repentance, and an altered life. A kind of penitence is bred in our prisons and purgatories just now, which is a very pretty penitence inside the walls, but fades into nothing when it comes into contact with worldly realities. In the generality of cases, it is almost impossible to produce a penitence which shall stand the wear and tear of this rough world, without Hope—worldly hope—the hope of at one time or other recovering something like the lost station. I would make this Hope, however faint and afar off it might be, exactly the one that out of the Asylum and without its aid, seemed (and was) impossible of attainment.

2ndly. With regard to Temptation. I would simply ask you to consider whether we do not, all of us, in our stations, tempt our fellow creatures at every turn. Whether there is a merchant in London who does not hourly expose his servants to strong temptation. Whether a night or morning ever comes, when you do not tempt your butler with a hundred times the worth of his year's wages. Whether there are not, at the Banking House in the Strand, many young men whose lives are one exposure to, and resistance of, temptation. And whether it is not a Christian act to say to such unfortunate creatures as you purpose, by God's blessing, to reclaim "Test for yourselves the reality of your repentance and your power of resisting temptation, while you are *here*, and before you are in the World outside, to fall before it!"

Now about Punch. I have no influence whatever, with that Potentate save such as may lie in its being owned by my printers, and in my having a personal knowledge of some of its principal Contributors. You may guess how powerful my influence is, when I tell you that during my Stage Management, of the Amateur Play, I spoke to the gentleman most prominent among them,[1] about that very Duke[2]—more than once—and said that I believed him to be an excel-

---

[1] Douglas Jerrold.

[2] Probably the Duke of Richmond (1791–1860; *DNB*), a Protectionist, ally of Bentinck, and a notoriously dull speaker. Frequently mocked by *Punch* in 1845 as "the farmers' friend", and in the winter of 1845–6 for his speech of 8 Dec 45 denying the seriousness of the potato disease and suggesting that if the crop failed potatoes might be imported from Portugal; the most recent references were on 18 July (an anti-Game Law ballad dedicated to him) and 20 June (surprise at a speech of his being described by Lord Londonderry as "spicy"). A Governor of Pentonville, and possibly known to Miss Coutts and CD through his interest in prisons. The Duke of Norfolk, better known for his speech on the potato-famine at the meeting of 8 Dec 45 (in which he recommended labourers to use curry-powder to make soup), does not appear in *Punch* during June–July 46.

lent creature. That I had myself received the most remarkable courtesy from him, and that I knew that in his treatment of his Governess, and of others about him, he was a bright example to three fourths of the middle classes. The gentleman to whom I spoke, laughed about it, and said that there was no ill nature in their jokes at his expence, and that they merely jested at peculiarities of speech and manner that were generally notorious. After this conversation, or about the same time, however, the Duke happened to make a very unfortunate and apparently unfeeling, speech, about the diseased potatoes. This, Punch resented and took in great dudgeon. Between ourselves, I really hardly know how they could have done otherwise, for it was especially ill-timed and ill-chosen. But both on the occasions to which I have referred, and since, I have championed him strongly, in the same quarter. And, as I have already said, you may guess from this, how great my influence is. I thoroughly agree with you in all you say about him: but I never wrote, or stayed the writing, of a word in Punch, and am not in the least degree in his confidence or councils.

Mrs. Dickens, Charley, and his sisters, beg, with me, to be earnestly remembered in those two corners.

I am Ever | Dear Miss Coutts
Most Faithfully Yours
CHARLES DICKENS

Miss Burdett Coutts.

To JOHN FORSTER, [25–26 JULY 1846]

Extracts in F, VI, ii, 472–3, V, v, 422, V, ii, 398–9, 396, V, iii, 406 (2 extracts), V, ii, 400 and 400–1*n*, 396*n*, V, iii, 406, VI, ii, 473. *Date:* first four extracts 25 July according to Forster, and last three "the same letter" (the last two each described as "the close"); fifth and sixth extracts mention incidents which "preceded the trip to Chamounix" (28 July); seventh extract, about local society, undated, but likely to be same letter.

Sending the manuscript of the first four chapters: I will now go on to give you an outline of my immediate intentions in reference to *Dombey*. I design to show Mr. D with that one idea of the Son taking firmer and firmer possession of him, and swelling and bloating his pride to a prodigious extent. As the boy begins to grow up, I shall show him quite impatient for his getting on, and urging his masters to set him great tasks, and the like. But the natural affection of the boy will turn towards the despised sister; and I purpose showing her learning all sorts of things, of her own application and determination, to assist him in his lessons: and helping him always. When the boy is about ten years old (in the fourth number), he will be taken ill, and will die; and when he is ill, and when he is dying, I mean to make him turn always for refuge to the sister still, and keep the stern affection of the father at a distance. So Mr. Dombey—for all his greatness, and for all his devotion to the child—will find himself at arms' length from him even then; and will see that his love and confidence are all bestowed upon his sister, whom Mr. Dombey has used—and so has the boy himself too, for that matter—as a mere convenience and handle to him. The death of the boy is a death-blow, of course, to all the father's schemes and cherished hopes; and "Dombey and Son," as Miss Tox will say at the end of the number, "is a Daughter after all."[1] . . . From that time, I purpose changing his feeling of indifference and uneasiness towards his daughter into a positive hatred. For he will always remember how the boy had his arm round her neck when he was dying, and whispered to her, and would take things only from her hand, and never thought of him. . . . At the same time I shall change *her* feeling towards *him* for one of a greater desire to love him, and to be loved by him; engendered in her compassion for his loss, and her love for the dead boy whom, in his way, he loved so well too. So I mean to carry the story on, through all the branches and off-shoots and meanderings that come up; and through the decay and downfall of the house, and the bankruptcy of Dombey, and all the rest of it; when his only staff and treasure, and his unknown Good Genius always, will be this rejected daughter, who will come out better than any son at last, and whose love for him, when discovered and understood, will be his bitterest reproach. For the struggle with himself, which goes on in all such obstinate natures, will have ended then; and the sense of his injustice, which you may be sure has never quitted him, will have at last a gentler office than that of only making him more harshly unjust. . . . I rely very much on Susan Nipper grown up, and acting partly as Florence's maid, and partly as a kind of companion to her, for a strong character throughout the book. I also rely on the Toodles, and on Polly, who, like every-body else, will be found by Mr. Dombey to have gone over to his daughter and become attached to her. This is what cooks call "the stock of the soup." All kinds of things will be added to it, of course.

I have been thinking this last day or two that good Christmas characters might be grown out of the idea of a man imprisoned for ten or fifteen years: his im-prisonment being the gap between the people and circumstances of the first part and the altered people and circumstances of the second, and his own changed mind. Though I shall probably proceed with the Battle idea, I should like to know what you think of this one?[2]

Replying to Forster's comments on the blind child:[3] I do not think that there is reason for supposing that the savage attitude originates in the desire of warmth, because all naked savages inhabit hot climates; and their instinctive attitude, if it had reference to heat or cold, would probably be the coolest possible; like their delight in water, and swimming. I do not think there is any race of savage men, however low in grade, inhabiting cold climates, who do not kill beasts and wear their skins. The girl decidedly improves in face, and, if one can yet use the word as applied to her, in manner too. No communication by the speech of touch has yet been established with her, but the time has not been long enough.

---

[1] Ch. 16, the last of No. v, ends with " 'Dear me, dear me! To think,' said Miss Tox, bursting out afresh that night, as if her heart were broken, 'that Dombey and Son should be a Daughter after all!' " The sentence was dropped in the Library edn, 1858, and never restored (see K. Tillotson, "A Lost Sentence in *Dombey and Son*", *D*, xlvii [1951], 81–2, and *Dombey and Son* ed. Alan Horsman, 1974, pp. xxviii–ix).

[2] Forster comments that it was "after-wards used in a modified shape for the *Tale of Two Cities*" (F, v, v, 422); but first, surely, in *Little Dorrit*.

[3] i.e. on CD's description in his letter of ?12 July.

Some years ago, when they set about reforming the prison at Lausanne, they turned their attention, in a correspondence of republican feeling, to America; and taking the Philadelphian system for granted, adopted it. Terrible fits, new phases of mental affection, and horrible madness, among the prisoners, were very soon the result; and attained to such an alarming height, that M. Verdeil, in his public capacity, began to report against the system, and went on reporting and working against it until he formed a party who were determined not to have it, and caused it to be abolished—except in cases where the imprisonment does not exceed ten months in the whole. It is remarkable that in his notes of the different cases, there is *every effect* I mentioned as having observed myself at Philadelphia; even down to those contained in the description of the man who had been there thirteen years, and who *picked his hands* so much as he talked.[1] He has only recently, he says, read the *American Notes*; but he is so much struck by the perfect coincidence that he intends to republish some extracts from his own notes, side by side with these passages of mine translated into French. I went with him over the prison the other day. It is wonderfully well arranged for a continental jail, and in perfect order. The sentences however, or some of them, are very terrible. I saw one man sent there for murder under circumstances of mitigation—for 30 years. Upon the silent social system all the time! They weave, and plait straw, and make shoes, small articles of turnery and carpentry, and little common wooden clocks. But the sentences are too long for that monotonous and hopeless life; and, though they are well-fed and cared for, they generally break down utterly after two or three years. One delusion seems to become common to three-fourths of them after a certain time of imprisonment. Under the impression that there is something destructive put into their food "pour les guérir de crime" (says M. Verdeil), they refuse to eat![2]

Hallam[3] was visiting Haldimand. Heavens! how Hallam did talk yesterday! I don't think I ever saw him so tremendous. Very good-natured and pleasant, in his way, but Good Heavens! how he did talk. That famous day you and I remember was nothing to it. His son was with him, and his daughter (who has an impediment in her speech, as if nature were determined to balance that faculty in the family), and his niece, a pretty woman, the wife of a clergyman and a

---

[1] *American Notes*, Ch. 7; cf. Vol. III, p. 110 and *n*.

[2] Theodore Mügge (*Switzerland in 1847*, ed. Mrs Percy Sinnett, 1848, II, 202–19) gives an account of the prison system in Switzerland, from his visits in 1846: the silent system of Auburn was in operation at several, including Lausanne; others were unreformed, and Geneva followed the Pennsylvania system. "The director of the prison in Lausanne [was] decidedly opposed" to both systems; Mügge also describes the mental decline and despair of the prisoners.

[3] Henry Hallam (1777–1859; *DNB*), Whig historian; notorious for his contra-dictiousness in conversation—was said to have got up in the night to contradict the watchman about the hour and the weather. Watson, after meeting him on 25 July, noted that "a stranger would at first consider him a goodnatured bore of rough bad manners" (Watson's Diary, MS Commander Michael Saunders Watson). He had left London for Switzerland with his son Henry Fitzmaurice (1824–50) and his niece Jane Octavia Brookfield (*née* Elton; 1821–96) and returned in Sep. CD may have met him earlier at Holland House, where he was a frequent visitor; Hallam had signed his letter about copyright in July 42.

friend of Thackeray's. It strikes me that she must be "the little woman" he proposed to take us to drink tea with, once, in Golden-square. Don't you remember? His great favourite? She is quite a charming person anyhow.[1]

As Haldimand and Mrs. Marcet[2] and the Cerjats had devised a small mountain expedition for us for to-morrow,[3] I didn't like to allow Chamounix to stand in the way. So we go with them first, and start on our own account on Tuesday. We are extremely pleasant with these people.

He described his social circle in Lausanne as wonderfully friendly and hospitable. ... I do not think we could have fallen on better society. It is a small circle certainly, but quite large enough. The Watsons improve very much on acquaintance. Everybody is very well informed; and we are all as social and friendly as people can be, and very merry. We play whist with great dignity and gravity sometimes, interrupted only by the occasional facetiousness of the Inimitable.

I have been queer and had trembling legs for the last week. But it has been almost impossible to sleep at night. There is a breeze to-day and I hope another storm is coming up.... There is a theatre here; and whenever a troop of players pass through the town, they halt for a night and act. On the day of our tremendous dinner party of eight, there was an infant phenomenon; whom I should otherwise have seen.[4] Last night there was a Vaudeville company;[5] and Charley, Roche, and Anne went. The Brave reports the performances to have resembled Greenwich Fair. ... There are some Promenade Concerts in the open air[6] in progress now; but as they are just above one part of our garden we don't go: merely sitting outside the door instead, and hearing it all where we

---

[1] Brookfield wrote to his wife on 6 Aug 46: "Forster told me Dickens had met Hallam's party. Hallam in great force. And a lady of remarkable, etc. etc. He did not know her name, 'but,' said Forster, 'I have enlightened him on that point.' " (C. and F. Brookfield, *Mrs Brookfield and her Circle*, I, 188.) For Jane's friendship with Thackeray, see Gordon N. Ray, *Thackeray: the Age of Wisdom*, 1958, Ch. 3.

[2] Jane Marcet (1769–1858; *DNB*), writer for the young; only daughter of Francis Haldimand; married Alexander Marcet, MD, FRS (1770–1822; *DNB*), of Geneva and London. From 1806 to 1850 published numerous instructive dialogues and stories for children, widely used as text-books; her *Conversations on Political Economy*, 1816, were praised by Macaulay in 1825 and gave Harriet Martineau the idea of her *Illustrations*. Well known in literary and Whig social circles; lived in London with her daughter Lady Romilly, but often visited her brother's home in Lausanne. In 1846 she arrived there at the beginning of July.

[3] This part of the letter must have been written 26 July. Watson's Diary, 27 July, describes the outing as an "excursion by the Lac de Bret to Vevay ... Mr. Dickens most amusing at dinner &c and particularly at Ludlow's house" (i.e. the house which had belonged to Edmund Ludlow the regicide, who is buried in Vevey).

[4] "Mlle. Caroline Eramisque, surnommée La Petite Merveille, agée de 7 ans", appeared at the Théâtre de Lausanne on Thursday, 16 July, for one night only, in two comedies and two vaudevilles, along with the stock company under the resident director, M. Rousseau (*Nouvelliste Vaudois*, 14 July 46; the issue of 24 July regretted that the performance was poorly attended).

[5] Announced for Saturday, 25 July (apparently for one night only) in the *Nouvelliste Vaudois* of 21 July.

[6] Concerts in the Jardin de l'Arc began on 16 July. It was (and still is) the garden of a private archery club, L'Abbaye de l'Arc, standing above Rosemont and about half a mile to the west.

are. . . . Mont Blanc has been very plain lately. One heap of snow. A Frenchman got to the top, the other day.[1]

Two pieces of local news: My first news is that a crocodile is said to have escaped from the Zoological Gardens at Geneva, and to be now "zig-zag-zigging" about the lake. But I can't make out whether this is a great fact, or whether it is a pious fraud to prevent too much bathing and liability to accidents. The other piece of news is more serious. An English family whose name I don't know, consisting of a father, mother and daughter, arrived at the Hotel Gibbon here last Monday, and started off on some mountain expedition in one of the carriages of the country. It was a mere track, the road, and ought to have been travelled only by mules, but the Englishman persisted (as Englishmen do) in going on in the carriage; and in answer to all the representations of the driver that no carriage had ever gone up there, said he needn't be afraid he wasn't going to be paid for it, and so forth. Accordingly, the coachman got down and walked by the horses' heads. It was fiery hot; and, after much tugging and rearing, the horses began to back, and went down bodily, carriage and all, into a deep ravine. The mother was killed on the spot; and the father and daughter are lying at some house hard by, not expected to recover.[2]

He put an important question about Dombey and Son. About the boy,[3] who appears in the last chapter of the first number, I think it would be a good thing to disappoint all the expectations that chapter seems to raise of his happy connection with the story and the heroine, and to show him gradually and naturally trailing away, from that love of adventure and boyish light-heartedness, into negligence, idleness, dissipation, dishonesty, and ruin. To show, in short, that common, every-day, miserable declension of which we know so much in our ordinary life; to exhibit something of the philosophy of it, in great temptations and an easy nature; and to show how the good turns into bad, by degrees. If I kept some little notion of Florence always at the bottom of it, I think it might be made very powerful and very useful. What do you think? Do you think it may be done, without making people angry? I could bring out Solomon Gills and Captain Cuttle well, through such a history; and I descry, anyway, an opportunity for good scenes between Captain Cuttle and Miss Tox.[4] This question of the boy is very important. . . . Let me hear all you think about it. Hear! I wish I could.[5]

---

[1] The Comte de Bouillé, on 14 July with seven guides; the first ascent for two years (H. F. Montagnier, *A Bibliography of the Ascents of Mont Blanc from 1786–1853*, 1911).

[2] The accident to "Mr. and Mrs. Winter, of Bedford Row", on the way to the salt-mines above Bex, is described in similar terms by Baptist Noel, *Notes of a Tour in Switzerland*, 1848, p. 91; the death of Louisa Winter at Bex on 21 July was announced in *The Times* of 31 July 46.

[3] Walter Gay.

[4] No such scenes were written.

[5] "For reasons that need not be dwelt upon here, but in which Dickens ultimately acquiesced, Walter was reserved for a happier future" (F, VI, ii, 473): Forster may here be hinting at the danger of a parallel with Thomas Powell: see *To* Chapman, 3 July and *fn.*

To JOHN FORSTER, [2 AUGUST 1846]

Extracts in F, v, iii, 406–8, 408–9, VI, ii, 475. *Date:* first two extracts 2 Aug according to Forster; third extract probably same date since concerned with instructions
to Browne for cover and plates for No. 1 of *Dombey*.

I begin my letter to-night, but only begin, for we returned from Chamounix in
time for dinner just now, and are pretty considerably done up. We went by a
mountain pass not often crossed by ladies, called the Col de Balme, where your
imagination may picture Kate and Georgy on mules *for ten hours at a stretch*,
riding up and down the most frightful precipices.[1] We returned by the pass of
the Tête Noire, which Talfourd knows,[2] and which is of a different character,
but astonishingly fine too. Mont Blanc, and the Valley of Chamounix, and the
Mer de Glace, and all the wonders of that most wonderful place, are above and
beyond one's wildest expectations. I cannot imagine anything in nature more
stupendous or sublime. If I were to write about it now, I should quite rave—
such prodigious impressions are rampant within me... You may suppose that
the mule-travelling is pretty primitive. Each person takes a carpet-bag strapped
on the mule behind himself or herself: and that is all the baggage that can be
carried. A guide, a thorough-bred mountaineer, walks all the way, leading the
lady's mule; I say the lady's par excellence, in compliment to Kate; and all the
rest struggle on as they please. The cavalcade stops at a lone hut for an hour and
a half in the middle of the day, and lunches brilliantly on whatever it can get.
Going by that Col de Balme pass, you climb up and up and up for five hours and
more, and look—from a mere unguarded ledge of path on the side of the precipice
—into such awful valleys, that at last you are firm in the belief that you have
got above everything in the world, and that there can be nothing earthly overhead.
Just as you arrive at this conclusion, a different (and oh Heaven! what a free
and wonderful) air comes blowing on your face; you cross a ridge of snow; and
lying before you (wholly unseen till then), towering up into the distant sky, is the
vast range of Mont Blanc, with attendant mountains diminished by its majestic
side into mere dwarfs tapering up into innumerable rude Gothic pinnacles;
deserts of ice and snow; forests of firs on mountain sides, of no account at all in
the enormous scene; villages down in the hollow, that you can shut out with a
finger; waterfalls, avalanches, pyramids and towers of ice, torrents, bridges;
mountain upon mountain until the very sky is blocked away, and you must look
up, overhead, to see it. Good God, what a country Switzerland is, and what a
concentration of it is to be beheld from that one spot! And (think of this in
Whitefriars and in Lincoln's-inn!) at noon on the second day from here, the

---

[1] The night of Tuesday 28 July was
evidently spent at Martigny; the climb
through the Col de Balme was on 29 July,
and the two following days were spent at
Chamounix.

[2] The Tête Noire was the route taken by
Talfourd in 1841; he would have preferred
the Col de Balme, as it "presented one view
scarcely excelled in these regions", but was
persuaded by the guides to the easier climb,
a path "of quiet but exquisite beauty,
beside a bank towering up a grassy precipice to a range of trees" (*Vacation
Rambles and Thoughts*, 1845, 1, 109–11).
In 1843 he chose the Col de Balme, casting
a longing look on the "lovely pathway we
had before trodden", but found "ample
compensation" in the view from the top
(II, 207). In Sep 46 he took his children
over both passes.

first day being but half a one by the bye and full of uncommon beauty, you lie down on that ridge and see it all! . . . I think I must go back again (whether you come or not!) and see it again before the bad weather arrives. We have had sunlight, moonlight, a perfectly transparent atmosphere with not a cloud, and the grand plateau on the very summit of Mont Blanc so clear by day and night that it was difficult to believe in intervening chasms and precipices, and almost impossible to resist the idea that one might sally forth and climb up easily. I went into all sorts of places; armed with a great pole with a spike at the end of it, like a leaping-pole, and with pointed irons buckled on to my shoes; and am all but knocked up. I was very anxious to make the expedition to what is called "The Garden:"[1] a green spot covered with wild flowers, lying across the Mer de Glace, and among the most awful mountains: but I could find no Englishman at the hotels who was similarly disposed, and the Brave *wouldn't go*. No sir! He gave in point blank (having been horribly blown in a climbing excursion the day before), and couldn't stand it. He is too heavy for such work, unquestionably. In all other respects, I think he has exceeded himself on this journey: and if you could have seen him riding a very small mule, up a road exactly like the broken stairs of Rochester-castle; with a brandy bottle slung over his shoulder, a small pie in his hat, a roast fowl looking out of his pocket, and a mountain staff of six feet long carried cross-wise on the saddle before him; you'd have said so. He was (next to me) the admiration of Chamounix, but he utterly quenched me on the road.

On the road as they returned, the day before this letter was written, he was jingling slowly up the Tête Noire pass (his mule having thirty-seven bells on its head), riding at the moment quite alone, when an Englishman came bolting out of a little châlet in a most inaccessible and extraordinary place, and said with great glee "There has been an accident here sir!" I had been thinking of anything else you please; and, having no reason to suppose him an Englishman except his language, which went for nothing in the confusion, stammered out a reply in French and stared at him, in a very damp shirt and trowsers, as he stared at me in a similar costume. On his repeating the announcement, I began to have a glimmering of common sense; and so arrived at a knowledge of the fact that a German lady had been thrown from her mule and had broken her leg, at a short distance off, and had found her way in great pain to that cottage, where the Englishman, a Prussian, and a Frenchman, had presently come up; and the Frenchman, by extraordinary good fortune, was a surgeon! They were all from Chamounix, and the three latter were walking in company. It was quite charming to see how attentive they were. The lady was from Lausanne; where she had come from Frankfort to make excursions with her two boys, who are at the college here, during the vacation. She had no other attendants, and the boys were crying and very frightened. The Englishman was in the full glee of having just cut up one white dress, two chemises, and three pocket handkerchiefs, for bandages; the Frenchman had set the leg, skilfully; the Prussian had scoured a neighbouring wood for some men to carry her forward; and they were all at it, behind the hut,

---

[1] The expedition took another 2½ hours, and required a guide.

making a sort of hand-barrow on which to bear her. When it was constructed, she was strapped upon it; had her poor head covered over with a handkerchief, and was carried away; and we all went on in company: Kate and Georgy consoling and tending the sufferer, who was very cheerful, but had lost her husband only a year. *It was hoped that by means of relays of men at Martigny the poor lady might have been carried on some twenty miles in the cooler evening, to the head of the lake, and so have been got into the steamer; but she was too exhausted to be borne beyond the inn, and there she had to remain until joined by relatives from Frankfort.*

He expressed his anxiety about Browne's illustrations for Dombey, *with a nervous dread of caricature in the face of Mr. Dombey.* I do wish he could get a glimpse of A, for he is the very Dombey.[1]

To COUNT D'ORSAY, 5 AUGUST 1846*

MS Comte de Gramont.

Rosemont, Lausanne, Switzerland. Fifth August 1846.
My Dear Count D'Orsay.

Your Godson's Mama and Nurses, are, and have been ever since we left home, so desperately importunate to have a Report made to you—a true and ungarnished report of his unparalleled and never-sufficiently-to-be-wondered-at Goodness—that I must, for the sake of peace and quietness, begin my letter with it. So pray take notice that he is never known to cry; that he came through the long journey and great heat without the smallest remonstrance of any sort or kind; that he is perpetually laughing and good tempered; and that I see him at this moment lying in the Garden, in the shade, with two pink legs upreared in the air, and *the* bells and Coral forced into his mouth.

This place is on the hill between Lausanne and Ouchy—about midway between the two places. The house is small, but the grounds are extensive and very pretty; and it is certainly the most cheerful house here. The heat is, and has been, most intense; but I hope the weather will soon change, now that we have got into August. I should have written to you, long ago. But as soon as we were installed in these regions, I set to work on my new book, whereof I have done the first number and begun the second; and this has kept me constantly employed. I hope it will be liked; and I think there is a good idea in it. My leisure hours I devote to thinking of the Christmas Book, and I shall go to work on that, as soon as I have matured the idea which is afloat in my mind. We purpose leaving here about the end of November, and going to Paris, whence I shall hope to run over to London. I look forward to Paris with great interest and am very glad Lord

[1] Forster says that "as the glimpse of A was not to be had, it was resolved to send for selection by himself" a "sheetful" of "actual heads as well as fanciful ones" (F, VI, ii, 475). Forster reproduced this sheet of pencil-drawings in the *Life*; the original is in the Forster Collection. At the top of the page, Browne had made pencil notes of the leading features of Mr Dombey's appearance—all drawn from No. 1, and mostly from the description at the opening of Ch. 1. The arrows against five of the drawings probably indicate CD's preferences.

Normanby will be there,[1] as it will make all the difference between what is stately and what is agreeable.

We started off to Chamounix a week ago, and were delighted beyond all expression with the place. If I could have found any adventurous Englishman there, I would have made (I think) a start for the Summit of Mont Blanc, about which there was not one speck of vapour. But I couldn't find anybody disposed to join in such an expedition, so was forced to content myself by ingloriously climbing over the Mer de Glace and tumbling about, with a leaping pole, in one or two inaccessible places. What do you say to coming over and sharing in the enterprize? We have only to swear over the long pipe (I smoke it constantly) that we never will turn back without reaching the top—and the thing is done.

And talking of the long pipe, I am bound to say that the Brave Courier is a perfect Hookahbadahr (I think that's the way to spell it) and prepares it wonderfully. When he was at Cairo, he watched them getting up the Pipes, with a Courier's eye; and he does it quite in the Arabian Night manner.

At the Inn at Chamounix, there was a most splendid couple of travellers. An immense Frenchman and a very little Englishman, who had struck up an acquaintance at Geneva, and had agreed to make some mountain excursions together. The Englishman could speak no French, but the Frenchman could speak a little English; and the Englishman's patronage of him in consequence, was the most ridiculous thing I ever saw in my life. He had not the least idea that it was very good of the Frenchman to bother himself with the language, but seemed to think it was a laudable ambition in any poor fellow to plunge into the attempt (however hopeless) and that it deserved some condescencion;[2] and the way in which he set the Frenchman right—talking broken English to him, himself, as if the Frenchman were a child—and his look round the table at his countrymen, as much as to say "You hear this poor Devil? Excuse him! He means well"—was perfectly insupportable. I don't think I ever was so much tickled by anything; and being opposite to him, I was in a continual agony, for I could not help laughing. There was a pretty good Englishman on board of one of the Rhine boats, who *would* talk to a Prussian, in English, and persisted in making small jokes at which he expected the Prussian to laugh; and said of the Cutlets at dinner time "Very tough Sir, eh? A good deal of the old shoe in these chops Sir, eh?"—but the Englishman of Chamounix outshone him, very far.

There are only four English families here, but they are very agreeable people indeed, and we find Mr. Haldimand—of whom perhaps you know something—he has a beautiful house upon the lake—everything that is hospitable and friendly; I may say affectionate indeed. The Revolution is supposed to have frightened people and kept them away. However that may be, nearly every Country house is to let, and the Genius of Dulness seems to brood over the town. I find the common-people very polite and agreeable, though they seem to drink rather hard. At all the little fêtes and holidays they get drunk, but they are obliging and good-tempered to me always. As I am getting up my French with a view to Paris, I let it off upon the unfortunate Cottagers and people as I walk about in the

[1] He had been appointed British Ambassador by the new Government.

[2] Thus in MS.

evening, but I have never met with any churlish fellows among them, and I have plenty of such acquaintances on all the walks about here. There is going to be a great fête next Sunday, the anniversary of the declaration of the New Constitution, when the town is to be illuminated, and various illuminated boats are to be rowed about the Lake. My landlord (who is the Sous Prefect of the town) is immensely busy with the preparations and hints darkly at the probable magnificence.

So your friend Lord Auckland[1] is to be busy again, and Brougham is to be Captain Warner[2] to the new Government! What do you hear about the Daily News? Does it seem likely to succeed? Forster says the circulation is very great—more than 20,000, I think—but there he stops, and doesn't seem to know what to make of it beyond that. I take it for granted that Lady Blessington has concluded her engagement, without having any new reason of complaint, as Forster assured me, before I left town, that he would take the matter in his own hands, knowing my anxiety about it. Still I shall be very glad to hear that it is all over, and well over. Pray tell me when you write.

I find a burning disgust arising in my mind—a sort of morbid canker of the most frightful description—against Mister Hudson. His position seems to me to be such a monstrous one, and so illustrative of the breeches pocket side of the English character, that I can't bear it. There are some dogs who can't endure one particular note on the Piano. In like manner I feel disposed to throw up my head, and howl, whenever I hear Mr. Hudson mentioned. He is my rock ahead in life. If you can let me know anything bad of him,[3] pray do. It would be a great comfort. Something intensely mean and odious would be preferred, but anything bad, will be thankfully received.

Lord Morpeth, I find, is to make the Speech at Manchester,[4] this year. He reminds me of the Poles at Lord Dudley Stuart's dinner, just before I left. Good God! if you could have heard them, making inaudible and unintelligible speeches of the most hideous length, until past midnight! I never inclined so much towards the Emperor of Russia, as on that occasion. And Dudley Stuart himself (for whom I have a very strong regard) talking about celebrated Polish Women, and saying "but when I mention the hallowed name of Titchibowski—or of Lobski—or of Pastocrontiki—or of Sploshock—or of Screweyzlunskifi, that wife and mother"—and everybody professing to roar with enthusiasm at every

[1] First Lord of the Admiralty.

[2] Samuel Alfred Warner (*d.* 1853; *DNB*), commonly known as "Captain Warner", was an eccentric inventor whose project for a "long-range explosive" had been tested with unsatisfactory results in 1842 and 1844 and again in Dec 1846. Brougham was a constant source of embarrassment to Whig governments.

[3] The first signs of opposition to Hudson's methods appeared in July. At the Midland Railway Company's meeting on 25 July, his proposal that it should lease the Leeds and Bradford railway (he was chairman of

both) led to scenes of disorder among the shareholders. On the Eastern Counties railway—already notorious for its unpunctuality and excessive fares—a serious accident occurred on 18 July; at the inquest, the driver was blamed for reckless negligence, the jury adding "strong observations on the irregular management of the Company" (*Annual Register*). Hudson's defensive speech in Parliament drew unfavourable comment from *The Times* (3 Aug).

[4] At the Athenaeum Soirée. Morpeth referred in his speech to CD's presidency of the 1843 Soirée.

name, as if they knew all about it! There was a Lord (I forget his name) sat next me, who was so enthusiastic at one name, that I asked him afterwards, what association was connected with it; upon which he laughed and told me it was such a hard one that he felt sure the owner must have done something un-common: and had applauded accordingly.

I wish I had anything to tell you worth the trouble of wading through my letter; but as I have not, I fall back on the pleasant conviction that you will be glad to see my hand-writing, even to so little purpose as this. Give my love to Lady Blessington, and best remembrances to her fair nieces, and ever believe me, as I heartily am,

Your Affectionate friend
CHARLES DICKENS

The Count D'Orsay.

To JOHN FORSTER, [7 AUGUST 1846]

Extract in F, VI, ii, 473–4. *Date:* 7 Aug according to Forster; must have been sent independently of *To* Forster, ?9 Aug, since CD received his reply on 14 Aug.

I have received your letter to-day with the greatest delight, and am overjoyed to find that you think so well of the number.[1] I thought well of it myself, and that it was a great plunge into a story; but I did not know how far I might be stimulated by my paternal affection. . . . What should you say, for a notion of the illustrations, to "Miss Tox introduces the Party"? and "Mr. Dombey and family"? meaning Polly Toodle, the baby, Mr. Dombey, and little Florence: whom I think it would be well to have.[2] Walter, his uncle, and Captain Cuttle, might stand over. It is a great question with me, now, whether I had not better take this last chapter bodily out, and make it the last chapter of the second number; writing some other new one to close the first number. I think it would be impossible to take out six pages without great pangs.[3] Do you think such a proceeding as I suggest would weaken number one very much? I wish you would tell me, as soon as you can after receiving this, what your opinion is on the point. If you thought it would weaken the first number, beyond the counter-balancing advantage of strengthening the second, I would cut down somehow or other, and let it go. I shall be anxious to hear your opinion. In the mean-while I will go on with the second, which I have just begun. I have not been quite myself since we returned from Chamounix, owing to the great heat.

[1] Maclise, who was probably shown the proofs, wrote to Forster: "I think it very great—the old Nautical Instrument Seller novel—and most promising—I'm never up to his young girls—he is so very fond of the age of 'Nell' when they are most insipid—I hope he is not going to make another Slowboy, but I am only trying to say some-thing, and to find fault when there is none to find—*he is himself alone*" (undated letter; MS Forster Collection, V & A).

[2] "Miss Tox introduces 'the Party' " and "The Dombey Family" were decided upon.

[3] The proofs show that when set up the MS made 38 pages instead of 32. CD did eventually, with Forster's help, cut an equivalent amount after two changes of plan over Ch. 4: see *Dombey and Son*, ed. A. Horsman, pp. xvi–xix.

To JOHN FORSTER, [9 and 10 AUGUST 1846]

Extracts in F, VI, ii, 474; V, iv, 414; V, v, 424*n*, V, iii, 409–10 and *n*, 409; V, iii, 410.
Date: first extract "two days later" than 7 Aug according to Forster; second
extract "opening of the second week" in Aug; third extract "early in August" and
probably following second extract; fourth extract 9 Aug according to Forster; fifth
extract describes a visit between 2 and 9 Aug (see *fn*); final extract includes P.P.S.
dated 10 Aug.

I have begun a little chapter[1] to end the first number, and certainly think it
will be well to keep the ten pages of Wally and Co. entire for number two.[2]
But this is still subject to your opinion, which I am very anxious to know. I have
not been in writing cue all the week; but really the weather has rendered it next
to impossible to work.

He thought of turning to his Christmas book. It would be such a great relief to me
to get that small story out of the way.

What a storm that must have been in London![3] I wish we could get something
like it, here.... It is thundering while I write, but I fear it don't look black
enough for a clearance. The echoes in the mountains are of such a stupendous
sort, that a peal of thunder five or ten minutes long, is here the commonest of
circumstances.

*There was to be a prodigious fête that day in Lausanne, in honour of the anniversary
of the proclamation of the New Constitution*[4] beginning at sunrise with the firing
of great guns, and twice two thousand rounds of rifles by two thousand men;
proceeding at eleven o'clock with a great service, and some speechifying, in the
church; and ending to-night with a great ball in the public promenade, and a
general illumination of the town. *The authorities had invited him to a place of
honour in the ceremony; and though he did not go,* (having been up till three
o'clock in the morning, and being fast asleep at the appointed time), *the reply that
sent his thanks expressed also his sympathy. He had discovered in the* old *or* gentlemanly *party of the place* (including of course the sprinkling of English who are
always tory, hang 'em!) *so wonderfully sore a feeling about the revolution thus
celebrated, that to avoid the fête the majority had gone off by steamer the day before,
and those who remained were prophesying assaults on the unilluminated houses, and
other excesses.*[5] *He had no faith in such predictions.* The people are as perfectly

---

[1] The MS shows that what finally became
Ch. 7, introducing Miss Tox, was first
intended to begin No. II, and then to close
No. I.

[2] Ch. 4, ten MS pages, introduced Walter,
Sol Gills and Captain Cuttle.

[3] On Saturday, 1 Aug; a heavy thunderstorm with large hailstones ("stated
variously to be the size of hazel and wal-
nuts") raged for about two hours. The
damage to property was "estimated by
some to amount to £100,000" (*Examiner*,
8 Aug 46).

[4] Held at Monthenon, a terrace just
outside the town.

[5] Mügge, who visited Lausanne at this
time, refers to "the shameful calumnies
spread by the defeated party", and French
and German newspaper articles representing the festival as "a scene of the wildest
orgies of a mob-government"; he was
assured of the untruth of this by "several
impartial foreigners who had been present
... and were delighted with the cheerful,
yet serious and dignified, tone of the assembly" (*Switzerland in 1847*, II, 245).

good-tempered and quiet always, as people can be. I don't know what the last Government may have been, but they seem to me to do very well with this, and to be rationally and cheaply provided for. If you believed what the discontented assert, you wouldn't believe in one solitary man or woman with a grain of goodness or civility. I find nothing *but* civility; and I walk about in all sorts of out-of-the-way places, where they live rough lives enough, in solitary cottages.

Fanchette the cook, distracted by the forthcoming fête, madly refused to buy a duck yesterday as ordered by the Brave, and a battle of life ensued between those two powers. The Brave is of opinion that "datter woman have went mad." But she seems calm to-day; and I suppose won't poison the family.

He described a visit to Chillon.[1] The insupportable solitude and dreariness of the white walls and towers, the sluggish moat and drawbridge, and the lonely ramparts, I never saw the like of.[2] But there is a courtyard inside; surrounded by prisons, oubliettes, and old chambers of torture; so terrifically sad, that death itself is not more sorrowful. And oh! a wicked old Grand Duke's bedchamber upstairs in the tower, with a secret staircase down into the chapel where the bats were wheeling about; and Bonnivard's dungeon; and a horrible trap whence prisoners were cast out into the lake; and a stake all burnt and crackled up, that still stands in the torture-ante-chamber to the saloon of justice (!)— what tremendous places! Good God, the greatest mystery in all the earth, to me, is how or why the world was tolerated by its Creator through the good old times, and wasn't dashed to fragments.

P.S. 6 o'clock afternoon. The fête going on, in great force. Not one of "the old party" to be seen. I went down with one to the ground before dinner, and nothing would induce him to go within the barrier with me. Yet what they call a revolution was nothing but a change of government. Thirty-six thousand people, in this small canton, petitioned against the Jesuits—God knows with good reason. The Government chose to call them "a mob." So, to prove that they were not, they turned the Government out.[3] I honour them for it. They are a genuine people, these Swiss. There is better metal in them than in all the stars and stripes of all the fustian banners of the so-called, and falsely called, U-nited States. They are a thorn in the sides of European despots, and a good wholesome people to live near Jesuit-ridden Kings on the brighter side of the mountains.

P.P.S. August 10th. . . . The fête went off as quietly as I supposed it would; and they danced all night.

---

[1] "Between the second and the ninth of August", in F, 1872-4, II, xi, 230; altered to "Early in August", in 2nd edn.

[2] Talfourd in 1843 was not impressed by Chillon, which he simply disliked: "I saw a squalid building of white-washed brick-work, prodigal in unpicturesque angles, and surmounted by low pepper-box turrets, having the air of a provincial house of correction or a union workhouse" (*Vacation Rambles and Thoughts*, II, 107).

[3] The "revolution" of 14-15 Feb 45, headed by the chiefs of the Radical party, had effected the change of government without bloodshed or disturbance (Theodore Mügge, *Switzerland in 1847*, II, 221ff.).

To JOHN FORSTER, [13 and 14 AUGUST 1846]

Extracts in F, vi, ii, 474. *Date:* first extract "four days later" than letter of 9 Aug
according to Forster; second extract the next day.

I shall send you with this (on the chance of your being favourable to that
view of the subject) a small chapter[1] to close the first number, in lieu of the
Solomon Gills one. I have been hideously idle all the week, and have done
nothing but this trifling interloper; but hope to begin again on Monday—ding
dong. . . . The ink stand is to be cleaned out to-night, and refilled, preparatory
to execution. I trust I may shed a good deal of ink in the next fortnight.

I received yours to-day. A decided facer to me![2] I had been counting, alas!
with a miser's greed, upon the gained ten pages. . . . No matter. I have no
doubt you are right, and strength is everything. The addition of two lines to
each page, or something less,—coupled with the enclosed cuts,[3] will bring it all
to bear smoothly. In case more cutting is wanted, I must ask you to try your
hand. I shall agree to whatever you propose.

To MESSRS WRIGHT, SMITH & SHEPHERD,
15 AUGUST 1846*

MS Dickens House. *Address:* Messrs. Wright, Smith, and Shepherd | Solicitors |
15 Golden Square | London.

Rosemont, Lausanne, Switzerland.
Saturday Fifteenth August 1846.

Gentlemen.

I beg to acknowledge the receipt of your favor of the Tenth Instant.[4]

I retained the Editorship of the Daily News during so very short a period,
that I had ceased (to the best of my recollection) to be connected with it, when
Mr. Barrow wrote his first letter home from India.[5] Every business letter I
received from that gentleman I immediately despatched to the foreign department of the newspaper, as relating to matters with which I had no interest or
concern; and I have no such communications in my possession, either here, or
in England.

I am Gentlemen | Faithfully Your Servant

Messrs. Wright Smith and Shepherd.   CHARLES DICKENS

[1] The "new" Ch. 4 was evidently sent
off and set up, since the MS shows a mixture of proof and MS when CD was later
revising it to make it the closing chapter
(Ch. 7) of No. ii.

[2] Forster's opinion that the original Ch.
4 should remain in No. i meant heavy
cutting, and also that CD now had less in
hand for No. ii. For an important passage
which Forster thought "worth preserving
in a note", see F, vi, ii, 474n.

[3] CD's proof shows substantial cuts in
Chs 1–3, especially affecting the dialogue

and the descriptions of the Chicks, Miss
Tox, and Mr Toodle. The second proof of
Chs 1 and 2 has these cuts made, and
further cuts by Forster, including the detailed account of how Biler got his name
(see *Dombey and Son*, ed. A. Horsman, pp.
xvi–vii).

[4] Bradbury & Evans's solicitors were
presumably dealing with Barrow's claim
for payment for his letters to the *Daily
News.*

[5] See *To* Bradbury & Evans, ?14 Nov 45
and *fn.*

To MISS BURDETT COUTTS, 17 AUGUST 1846*

MS Morgan Library. *Address:* Angleterre | Miss Burdett Coutts | Stratton Street | Piccadilly | London.

Rosemont, Lausanne, Switzerland
Seventeenth August 1846.

My Dear Miss Coutts.

I will endeavour, in the course of this week, to comply with your request. I would do so at once, but that I am busy just now on my new book—with the printers behind me.

I would not write to you on so slight an occasion but that I am very anxious you should not suppose me to have intended to convey the least hint to *you* in the case I put, touching your clerks and servants.[1] I instanced you, as having everything about you on so great a scale, and as representing great wealth and a large establishment—but with no more reference, believe me, to your affairs as differing in the least from those of any other person similarly situated, or from mine as far as they go, than to those of the Great Mogul. As you had objected that we should leave temptation to the Almighty, I merely meant to ask you to consider whether we are not all (under His direction or permission) tempted by and through one another, in our common daily life, and whether that was not a reason for giving these unfortunates the means of testing their own power of resistance and their own practical repentance, within the Asylum.

The thick paper is an unspeakable comfort. The sensation of reading a long letter written on the impracticable paper specially intended for Foreign Service is (I should think) very like having to cut all one's teeth in a given time, without any Soothing Syrup.

Believe me dear Miss Coutts | Always Faithfully Yours
CHARLES DICKENS

To EMILE DE LA RUE, 17 AUGUST 1846*

MS Berg Collection.

Rosemont. | Monday August Seventeenth 1846.

My Dear De la Rue

I should have written to you today, though I had not heard from you yesterday. I gave you until now, to return from Chamounix (that glorious place!) where I thought you might make even a longer stay. Your note arrived in Lausanne in due course yesterday, but I did not get it until last night. The Thompsons were here[2] (they have taken a house hard by), and I did not send to the Post Office until late. Hence this delay in replying to it.

I want to know, before I propose a day for our meeting on board the Steamer, how long you are going to remain at that country house? Tell me. I have heard

---

[1] See *To* Miss Coutts, 25 July.
[2] They arrived at Lausanne 10 Aug, and after house-hunting took Clermont for eight months from 14 Aug; on 16 Aug Christiana recorded that they "dined at the Dickens" and "took a drive with Mrs D to the heights" (Diary, MS Mrs Sowerby).

from Talfourd that he is coming to dine with me, on his way to Italy, at some uncertain time that hangs over me like a Nightmare.[1] I have heard from my Illustrator in London, that he can't make out from my written description what I mean—and I am half afraid I may have to go to Bâle to meet him for a personal conference. I receive, every other day, pressing invitations from Printers to keep them hard at work, and I have divers delicate enquiries (unanswered) from Forster as to the time at which some remote hint of the nature of the Christmas Book may be expected to arrive in London. In short, I am set upon in all directions, and am not working with a very good will either.

So tell me how long you are going to remain in that country house, that I may look my plans in the face with that knowledge to help me.

Tell Madame De la Rue, with my love, that Mrs. Thompson disappoints me very much. She is a mere spoiled child, I think, and doesn't turn out half as well as I expected. Matrimony has improved him, and certainly has not improved her. She is to be confined here. I wish her well through it,—but upon my Soul, I feel as if her husband would have the worst, even of that.

Always My Dear De la Rue,

Faithfully Yours
CHARLES DICKENS

To JOHN FORSTER, [?15–17 AUGUST 1846]

Summary and extracts in F, v, iv, 415, 414, 416–17 (2 extracts), 414*n*, 415–16. *Date:* Forster makes the opening summary and final extract "his next letter" after the letter of 24 Aug, but Watson's Diary (see *fn*) shows that the "day's party" was on Mon 10 Aug; fourth extract refers to this party as "last Monday", and is in "the same letter" as third extract according to Forster; second extract describes a conversation with Watson on 11 Aug (see *fn*); fifth extract probably same letter, as Ainsworth's visit was "ten days before" 24 Aug according to Forster.

Describing a day's party of the Cerjats, Watsons, and Haldimands, among the neighbouring hills, which he had been unable to resist the temptation of joining. They went to a mountain-lake twelve miles off, had dinner at the public-house on the lake, and returned home by Vevay at which they rested for tea.[2]

He is a very intelligent agreeable fellow, the said Watson[3] by the bye; he sat for Northamptonshire[4] in the reform bill time, and is high sheriff of his county and all the rest of it; but has not the least nonsense about him, and is a thorough good liberal. He has a charming wife, who draws well, and is making a sketch of

---

[1] Talfourd left London on 20 Aug, but changed his plans and went to Italy by sea from Marseilles, visiting CD on his homeward journey (see *To* Talfourd, 25 Sep 46).

[2] "A party to the Lac de Brêt where we dined, and to Vevay. The Dickens, Haldimand, Ld. Vernon, Cerjats and Goffs" (Watson's Diary, 10 Aug, MS Commander Michael Saunders Watson).

[3] Watson appears to have organized the Vevey expedition, and his Diary records two other occasions during Aug when they entertained the Dickenses: "A party of ten to dinner. The Dickens, Haldimand, Cerjats and Goffs" (4 Aug); "Ld. G[*eorge Quin*], the Haldimands, Cerjats, and Taylours, & a small party in the evening. Boz in a state of great animation" (21 Aug).

[4] CD's error for Canterbury.

Rosemont[1] for us that shall be yours in Paris. He was giving me some good recollections of Lord Grey the other evening when we were playing at battledore[2] (old Lord Grey I mean), and of the constitutional impossibility he and Lord Lansdowne and the rest laboured under, of ever personally attaching a single young man, in all the excitement of that exciting time, to the leaders of the party. It was quite a delight to me, as I listened, to recall my own dislike of his style of speaking, *his fishy coldness, his uncongenial and unsympathetic politeness, and his insufferable though most gentlemanly artificiality.* The shape of his head (I see it now) was misery to me, and weighed down my youth.[3]

We have another English family here, one Sir Joseph and his lady, and ten children.[4] Sir Joseph, a large baronet something in the Graham style, with a little, loquacious, flat-faced, damaged-featured, *old young* wife. They are fond of society, and couldn't well have less. They delight in a view, and live in a close street at Ouchy, down among the drunken boatmen and the drays and omnibuses, where nothing whatever is to be seen but the locked wheels of carts scraping down the uneven, steep, stone pavement. The baronet plays double-dummy all day long, with an unhappy Swiss whom he has entrapped for that purpose; the baronet's lady pays visits; and the baronet's daughters play a Lausanne piano, which must be heard to be appreciated.

Another curious man is backwards and forwards here—a Lord Vernon, who is well-informed, a great Italian scholar deep in Dante,[5] and a very good-humoured gentleman, but who has fallen into the strange infatuation of attending every rifle-match that takes place in Switzerland, accompanied by two men who load rifles for him, one after another, which he has been frequently known to fire off, two a minute, for fourteen hours at a stretch, without once changing his position or leaving the ground. He wins all kinds of prizes;[6] gold watches, flags, teaspoons, teaboards, and so forth; and is constantly travelling about with them[7], from place

[1] Reproduced by permission of "its present possessor" in F, v, ii, facing p. 393. The whereabouts of the original is not known.

[2] "An evening alone with the Boz family. Played at Battledore & Shuttlecock with him" (Watson's Diary, 11 Aug).

aa F, 1872–4, II, vii, 238; omitted in later edns.

[3] Charles, 2nd Earl Grey (1764–1845; *DNB*), at the time when CD heard him, had "outlived the power of feeling or inspiring enthusiasm", and was "punctilious", "cold" and "timorous" (*DNB*). According to Charles Kent, CD's dislike dated from his reporting of the Edinburgh banquet of 15 Sep 34 ("CD as a Journalist", *Time*, v, [1881], 369).

[4] Sir Joseph Edward Leeds, 2nd Bart (1798–1862), of Croxton Park, near Cambridge; married Marian Stretton 1822, and had five sons and five daughters; was insol-

vent and imprisoned for debt in 1859. Mentioned once in Watson's Diary (15 July): "dined with Sir Joseph & Lady Leeds, & Daughters. The Ladies talked as much as Mrs. T."

[5] George John Warren Vernon, 5th Baron Vernon (1803–66; *DNB*), succeeded his father 1835 (wrongly identified in F, v, iv, 416*n*, although Forster included the correction in his list, F, 1872–4, III, 520); MP for Derby 1831–5. From 1839 lived mainly abroad, travelling and working on his edn of the *Inferno*, published 1858.

[6] Vernon's son mentions also a cow and a hive of honey (William Warren Vernon, *Recollections of Seventy-Two Years*, p. 14).

[7] It was customary to carry or wear such prizes, and Vernon's son describes his singular appearance on such occasions, with spoons and soup-ladle in his button-holes (*ibid*).

to place, in an extraordinary carriage, where you touch a spring and a chair flies out, touch another spring and a bed appears, touch another spring and a closet of pickles opens, touch another spring and disclose a pantry. While Lady Vernon[1] (said to be handsome and accomplished) is continually cutting across this or that Alpine pass in the night, to meet him on the road, for a minute or two, on one of his excursions; these being the only times at which she can catch him. The last time he saw her, was five or six months ago, when they met and supped together on the St. Gothard! It is a monomania with him, of course. He is a man of some note; seconded one of Lord Melbourne's addresses; and had forty thousand a year, now reduced to ten, but nursing and improving every day. He was with us last Monday, and comes back from some out-of-the-way place to join another small picnic next Friday. As I have said, he is the very soul of good nature and cheerfulness, but one can't help being melancholy to see a man wasting his life in such a singular delusion. Isn't it odd? He knows my books very well,[2] and seems interested in everything concerning them; being indeed accomplished in books generally, and attached to many elegant tastes.

He described a visit from Ainsworth[3] and his daughters on their way to Geneva. I breakfasted with him at the hotel Gibbon next morning and they dined here afterwards, and we walked about all day, talking of old days at Kensal-lodge.

Cerjat related anecdotes of Marryat.[4] It would seem, Mr. Cerjat tells me, that he was, when here, infinitely worse in his general style of conversation, than now—sermuchser, as Toodle says,[5] that Cerjat describes himself as having always been in unspeakable agony when he was at his table, lest he should forget himself (or remember himself, as I suggested) and break out before the ladies. There happened to be living here at that time a stately English baronet[6] and his

[1] Isabella Caroline, eldest daughter of Cuthbert Ellison, MP for Newcastle, married Vernon in 1824.

[2] Vernon's son remembered discovering the green-covered monthly Nos in his father's library in 1843–4: "The pictures were an untold delight" to him and his sister (*op. cit.*, p. 28).

[3] S. M. Ellis, *W. H. Ainsworth and his Friends*, II, 134, mentions Ainsworth's continental tour (with his daughters) as lasting from June to 12 Oct 46, but adds nothing to Forster's account of his meeting with CD.

[4] Not named by Forster, who describes him as "an excellent friend of ours, formerly resident at Lausanne . . . a distinguished writer", but his identity is clear. Marryat, with his wife and children, resided at L'Elysée for some months in 1836, and left his family there during his American visit (Florence Marryat, *Life and Letters of Captain Marryat*, I, 242ff.). A letter of 27 Nov 36 describes Lausanne society,

mentioning the bachelors' parties, one at "H—'s" (presumably Haldimand's)— "clever and sensible and hospitable . . . has taken a great fancy to Mrs. M.". He found Lausanne society "very pleasant and sociable—half English and half Swiss" (letter of 21 Feb 37 from London; I, 258).

[5] In a passage of dialogue with Mr Dombey which later had to be cut out from Ch. 2; Toodle is speaking of little Biler, his eldest son: " 'It ain't a common name. Sermuchser that when he was took to church, the gen'l'm'n said it wasn't a chris'en one, and he couldn't give it . . .' "

[6] Not mentioned in Marryat's letters of 1836—but one of his sons wrote to Forster after the publication of the *Life*, and Forster quoted him in his list of corrections (F, 1872–4, III, 520). He was present at "the outbreak good-naturedly exaggerated in Mr. Cerjat's account to Dickens", and said: "I well remember the dinner at Mr. Cerjat's alluded to in one of the letters from

wife, who had two *a*milksop*a* sons concerning whom they cherished the idea of accomplishing their education into manhood coexistently with such perfect purity and innocence, that they were hardly to know their own sex. Accordingly, they were sent to no school or college, but had masters of all sorts at home, and thus reached eighteen years or so, in what Falstaff calls a kind of male green-sickness.[1] At this crisis of their innocent existence, our ogre friend encountered these lambs at dinner, with their father, at Cerjat's house; and, as if possessed by a devil, launched out into such frightful and appalling impropriety—*a*ranging over every kind of forbidden topic and every species of forbidden word and every sort of scandalous anecdote*a*—that years of education in Newgate would have been as nothing compared with their experience of that one afternoon. After turning paler and paler, and more and more stoney, the baronet, with a half-suppressed cry, rose and fled. But the sons—intent on the ogre—remained behind instead of following *a*him; and are supposed to have been ruined from that hour.*a* Isn't that a good story? I can SEE our friend and his pupils now... Poor fellow! He seems to have [had][2] a hard time of it *a*with his wife. She had no interest whatever in her children; and was such a fury, that, being dressed to go out to dinner, she would sometimes, on no other provocation than a pin out of its place or some such thing, fall upon a little maid she had, beat her till she couldn't stand, then tumble into hysterics, and be carried to bed. He suffered martyrdom with her;*a* and seems to have been himself, in all good-natured easy-going ways, just what we know him now.

To FREDERICK DICKENS, [?MID AUGUST 1846]

Mention in *To* Fred Dickens, 9 Sep 46.

Enclosing a letter to John Dickens.

To JOHN DICKENS, [?MID AUGUST 1846]

Mention in *To* Fred Dickens, 9 Sep 46.

About Augustus, and his position in Mrs Smithson's house.

To EMILE DE LA RUE, 20 AUGUST 1846*

MS Berg Collection.

Rosemont. | Twentieth August 1846.

My Dear De la Rue.

I am afraid it would be impossible—or the next thing to it—for me to appoint

Lausanne in your Life of Dickens. It was not however our first acquaintance with the 'distinguished writer,' as he came with his family to stay at a Pension on the border of the Lake of Geneva where my father and his family were then living, and notwithstanding the gallant captain's 'habit'

the families subsequently became very intimate".

[1] 2 *Henry IV*, IV, iii, 92.

[2] Text reads "have".

aa F, 1872–4, II, xii, 241–2. Omitted in later edns; "with his wife" was altered to "in his home".

any day this week. Unless I hear from you to the contrary, I will meet you *at Vevay, next Wednesday.*[1] As it will be important for me, with a view to my next day's work, to return home that night (I don't care at what hour) I will repair to Vevay in one of the one-sided chars, whereof I have established a specimen on these premises. If I hear from you that you go to Vevay on the Tuesday, I will come over on Wednesday Morning to breakfast between 9 and 10. If I hear that you go on the Wednesday per boat, I will come over, in the aforesaid char, in time to meet you at the Landing-Place. Do you understand all this? *She* will, if you don't. I think the Vevay idea worthy of a Shakespeare, and look forward to a joyful day.

Tell me what you mean to do.

My troubles are not greater, thank God, than they usually are, when I am plunging neck and heels into a new Book. It is always an anxious and worrying time. Mais il faut manger.

We have said just nothing at all to the Thompsons, which seems to me to be the true way of cutting the Gordian Knot. My brother is under contract of holy matrimony to Mrs. T's sister! As they have nothing particular to live upon, I suppose it won't come off just yet.

To add to my other occupations, I hear with fear and trembling that Tennyson the Poet is at Chamounix and coming this way, in which event, I shall not only be taken from my work, but required to smoke pipes by the Score. Hallam the historian was here the other day—Ainsworth, the unintelligible novelist, a few days afterwards—a friend with the uncommon name of Smith, "looked in" for the whole day, yesterday—and Elliotson writes threats of coming next month! If anybody else threatens, I think I shall come to Genoa—murder Noli—and die in a good cause.

With my best Remembrances

Ever My Dear De la Rue | Heartily Yours
CHARLES DICKENS

P.S. I can't satisfacotrily account for my not having been born to a fine property.

To JOHN FORSTER, [24 and 25 AUGUST 1846]

Extracts in F, v, ii, 399; v, iv, 412, 412*n*, 414–15; v, v, 424*n*; v, iii, 411. *Date:* first four extracts 24 Aug according to Forster; fifth extract 25 Aug since referring to earthquake "yesterday week"; last extract dated by CD's receipt of Forster's reply to his letter of ?9–10 Aug.

The deaf, dumb, and blind girl is decidedly improved, and very much improved, in this short time. No communication is yet established with her, but that is not to be expected. They have got her out of that strange, crouching position; dressed her neatly; and accustomed her to have a pleasure in society. She laughs frequently, and also claps her hands and jumps; having, God knows how, some inward satisfaction. I never saw a more tremendous thing in its way, in my life, than when they stood her, t'other day, in the centre of a group of blind children who sang a chorus to the piano; and brought her hand, and kept it, in

---

[1] These four words underlined twice.

contact with the instrument. A shudder pervaded her whole being, her breath quickened, her colour deepened,—and I can compare it to nothing but returning animation in a person nearly dead. It was really awful to see how the sensation of the music fluttered and stirred the locked-up soul within her... The male subject is well and jolly as possible. He is very fond of smoking. I have arranged to supply him with cigars during our stay here; so he and I are in amazing sympathy. I don't know whether he thinks I grow them, or make them, or produce them by winking, or what. But it gives him a notion that the world in general belongs to me.

I am perfectly appalled by the hesitation and cowardice of the whigs. To bring in that arms bill, bear the brunt of the attack upon it, take out the obnoxious clauses, still retain the bill, and finally withdraw it[1], seems to me the meanest and most halting way of going to work that ever was taken. I cannot believe in them. Lord John must be helpless among them. They seem somehow or other never to know what cards they hold in their hands, and to play them out blindfold. The contrast with Peel (as he was last) is, I agree with you, certainly not favourable. I don't believe now they ever would have carried the repeal of the corn law, if they could. *The reluctance of public men of all parties to give the needful help to schemes of emigration,*[2] *he ascribed to a secret belief in* the gentle politico-economical principle that a surplus population must and ought to starve; *in which for himself he never could see anything but disaster for all who trusted to it.* I am convinced that its philosophers would sink any government, any cause, any doctrine, even the most righteous. There is a sense and humanity in the mass, in the long run, that will not bear them; and they will wreck their friends always, as they wrecked them in the working of the Poor-law bill. Not all the figures that Babbage's calculating machine could turn up in twenty generations, would stand in the long run against the general heart.

I hope you will follow up your idea about the defective state of the law in reference to women,[3] by some remarks on the inadequate punishment of that

[1] Russell had announced on 17 Aug that the Arms (Ireland) bill, to which there had been much opposition, was to be withdrawn.

[2] Successive governments had resisted demands for assisted emigration on a large scale, on the grounds that emigration figures were high enough (over a million to North America during the past twenty years and rising since 1845 as a result of the Irish famine) without Government intervention, and that those in need of free emigration and money grants were the very people who would not be willingly accepted in America or the colonies unless there were funds available to provide for their settlement. The Australian Land Sales Act of 1842 was intended to provide such funds, since the Colonial Land and Emigration Commissioners (set up in 1840) were empowered to apply money from sales of colonial land to the settlement of emigrants. But its passing was followed by the collapse of the land boom and the stock market in Australia, and although Stanley (Colonial Secretary in Peel's Government) sent out a few thousand agricultural workers, emigration was virtually stopped from 1842 because the Legislative Council of New South Wales made it conditional on an alternative method being found to pay for immigrants. Grey had not yet taken action to resolve these difficulties, but in Aug 47 he authorized the renewal of Government emigration and upwards of 8000 assisted immigrants arrived in Australia during 1848.

[3] Forster had evidently told CD about his idea for a leader on this subject to appear in the *Examiner* of 29 Aug. Under

ruffian flippantly called by the liners the Wholesale Matrimonial Speculator. My opinion is, that in any well-ordered state of society, and advanced spirit of social jurisprudence, he would have been flogged more than once (privately), and certainly sentenced to transportation for no less a term than the rest of his life. Surely the man who threw the woman out of window was no worse, if so bad.[1]

Not having your letter as usual, I sat down to write to you on speculation yesterday, but lapsed in my uncertainty into *Dombey*, and worked at it all day. It was, as it has been since last Tuesday morning, incessantly raining regular mountain rain. After dinner, at a little after seven o'clock, I was walking up and down under the little colonnade in the garden, racking my brain about *Dombeys* and *Battles of Lives*, when two travel-stained-looking men approached, of whom one, in a very limp and melancholy straw hat, ducked perpetually to me as he came up the walk. I couldn't make them out at all; and it wasn't till I got close up to them that I recognised [Tennyson] and (in the straw hat) [Moxon].[2] They had come from Geneva by the steamer, and taken a scrambling dinner on board. I gave them some fine Rhine wine, and cigars innumerable. [Tennyson] enjoyed himself and was quite at home. [Moxon] (an odd companion for a man of genius) was snobbish, but pleased and good-natured. [Tennyson] had a five pound note in his pocket which he had worn down by careless carrying about, to some two-thirds of its original size, and which was so ragged in its remains that when he took it out bits of it flew about the table. "Oh Lor you know—now really—like Goldsmith you know—or any of these great men!"

the heading "Killing No Murder" it noted the frequency of crimes against women and criticized juries for giving such offences "the encouragement of impunity positive or comparative", as in a recent case (18 Aug) when a verdict of manslaughter had been returned on a man who had beaten his wife to death.

[1] In June 46 Joseph Mortimer, the "Wholesale Matrimonial Speculator", had been sentenced to seven years' transportation for bigamously marrying three women, taking their property, and causing the death of one by his ill-treatment. The press shared CD's indignation that he had not been more severely punished, and made the same comparison of his sentence with that of transportation for life passed not long before on William Luff for throwing the woman he lived with out of the window, seriously injuring but not killing her. CD's suggestion that remarks on Mortimer's case should be included in a later article was not adopted by Forster in the *Examiner* or the *Daily News*; but the *Examiner* did return to the subject of crimes against women in an article of 12 Sep, in which the sentence of one month's imprisonment for

a policeman found guilty of ill-treating a pregnant woman was cited, with the comment, "At this rate women will soon be out of the law's protection".

[2] ("A." and "N." in F, v, iv, 415.) They had left England 2 Aug, travelling by the usual Rhine route, reached Bâle 7 Aug, and had already visited Lauterbrunnen and the Bernese Alps, which was the part of the tour that had impressed Tennyson ("mountains, great mountains, disappointed me. I couldn't take them in, I suppose, crags I could"). He described his visit to CD to Edward FitzGerald: "I called on Dickens at Lausanne who was very hospitable, and gave us biscuits (a rare luxury on the continent, not such as are sweet and soft, but hard and unsweet) and a flask of Liebfraumilch" (see *Alfred Lord Tennyson, a Memoir*, by his son, 1897, I, 230–4, and *Materials for a Life of A.T.*, privately printed, II, 308). According to Elizabeth Barrett, CD had asked him (when they met at the christening dinner on 21 Apr 46) to go with him to Switzerland; but Tennyson declined, fearing that they might "quarrel and part" (*Letters of Robert Browning and Elizabeth Barrett*, II, 116).

said [Moxon], with the very "snatches in his voice and burst of speaking" that reminded Leigh Hunt of Cloten.[1] . . . The clouds were lying, as they do in such weather here, on the earth, and our friends saw no more of Lake Leman than of Battersea. Nor had they, it might appear, seen more of the Mer de Glace, on their way here; their talk about it bearing much resemblance to that of the man who had been to Niagara and said it was nothing but water.

I forgot to tell you that yesterday week, at half-past 7 in the morning, we had a smart shock of an earthquake,[2] lasting, perhaps, a quarter of a minute. It awoke me in bed. The sensation was so curious and unlike any other, that I called out at the top of my voice I was sure it was an earthquake.

He commented on Forster's reply to his account of the anti-Jesuit celebration at Lausanne. I don't know whether I have mentioned before, that in the valley of the Simplon hard by here, where (at the bridge of St. Maurice, over the Rhone) this Protestant canton ends and a Catholic canton begins, you might separate two perfectly distinct and different conditions of humanity by drawing a line with your stick in the dust on the ground. On the Protestant side, neatness; cheerfulness; industry; education; continual aspiration, at least, after better things. On the Catholic side, dirt, disease, ignorance, squalor, and misery.[3] I have so constantly observed the like of this, since I first came abroad, that I have a sad misgiving that the religion of Ireland lies as deep at the root of all its sorrows, even as English misgovernment and Tory villainy.

To SAMUEL ROGERS, [27 AUGUST 1846]

MS Professor E. S. Pearson. *Date:* PM 27 Aug 46.

I can't let this go to you, although the man is waiting to carry it off to the post, without adding, for myself,[4] that I hope you won't forget us—and that when you are out on these airy walks at Broadstairs, I desire most to live in your memory. Let us promise and vow (God willing) to have tea there together, again, one windy night next Autumn, when you will go home to Ballard's afterwards, all aslant, against the gale, and when that dimmest of lamps at the corner will be winking and winking as if the spray inflamed its eye. The wind is blowing down the Lake now, driving fast shadows before it along the sides of the mountains; but it don't blow half as pleasantly, to my thinking, as over the North Foreland, or about that good old, tarry, salt, little pier. There's a Berne wom[an][5] in the garden,

[1] *Cymbeline*, IV, ii, 105–6.

[2] An earthquake on 17 Aug affected Italy, Switzerland and the South of France; three shocks were felt in the canton of Vaud (*Athenæum*, 29 Aug 46). Watson noted "a shock of an earthquake distinctly felt this morning at 8 o'clock" (Diary, MS Commander Michael Saunders Watson).

[3] CD is obviously recalling Murray's *Handbook for . . . Switzerland*, which notes the contrast between Vaud and the Valais, though without blaming the difference of

religion: "No one can cross the bridge of St. Maurice without being struck by the change in the condition of the inhabitants of the two cantons. The neatness and industry of the Vaudois . . . are exchanged within the space of a few hundred yards" for "filth and beggary . . . goitre, cretinism".

[4] The letter is a postscript to a letter from Catherine to Rogers, of which only the ending survives.

[5] Small tear at seal.

with a large stomacher and a gauzy cap, but she's nothing to Miss Crampton of the Terrace Baths. Wherever *I* am, I am always your affectionate friend, and shall always think it the best return in the world if you'll believe me so—though you *do* (in speaking to *her*) always call me
"Him".[1]

To JOSEPH VALCKENBERG, 27 AUGUST 1846

Extract in Maggs Bros catalogue No. 427 (1922); *MS* 1 p.; dated Rosemont, 27 Aug 46.

I hasten to tell you with many thanks that the wine has arrived safely and that its flavour is quite wonderful.

Heaven forgive me, but I feared some wicked German (if there be such a phenomenon) was drinking it on the road!

To JOHN FORSTER, [30 AUGUST 1846]

Extracts in F, v, v, 423; vi, ii, 476; v, iv, 414*n*, 417; v, v, 423, 422–3. *Date:* first two extracts 30 Aug according to Forster; third extract probably the same letter since about the Regatta "the other day" (25 Aug); fourth extract "his first September letter" according to Forster (but see *fn*); fifth extract "at the close" of the same letter as first extract according to Forster, and final extract ("a few weeks later" than 25 July) obviously follows on in same passage.

You can hardly imagine what infinite pains I take, or what extraordinary difficulty I find in getting on FAST. Invention, thank God, seems the easiest thing in the world; and I seem to have such a preposterous sense of the ridiculous, after this long rest, as to be constantly requiring to restrain myself from launching into extravagances in the height of my enjoyment. But the difficulty of going at what I call a rapid pace, is prodigious: it is almost an impossibility. I suppose this is partly the effect of two years' ease, and partly of the absence of streets and numbers of figures. I can't express how much I want these. It seems as if they supplied something to my brain, which it cannot bear, when busy, to lose. For a week or a fortnight I can write prodigiously in a retired place (as at Broadstairs), and a day in London sets me up again and starts me. But the toil and labour of writing, day after day, without that magic lantern, is IMMENSE!! I don't say this, at all in low spirits, for we are perfectly comfortable here, and I like the place very much indeed, and the people are even more friendly and fond of me than they were in Genoa. I only mention it as a curious fact, which I have never had an opportunity of finding out before. *My* figures seem disposed

---

[1] In an affectionate letter to Catherine of 20 Oct 46, recalling his own memories of Lausanne and J. P. Kemble, Rogers writes: "how much I value your friendship & how happy I should be if I was with you & *Him* & your dear Sister & among your dear Children by Lake-side" (Rogers called everybody's husband "He"; N, ii, 385); a postscript adds: "In writing to you I write to Him for in mercy I should spare him" (MS Morgan). Earlier letters show the warmth of his regard for Catherine, one of 17 Dec 43 saying "every hour brings me something to awaken my gratitude—my admiration!" (MS Morgan).

to stagnate without crowds about them. I wrote very little in Genoa (only the *Chimes*), and fancied myself conscious of some such influence there—but Lord! I had two miles of streets at least, lighted at night, to walk about in; and a great theatre to repair to, every night.

I shall gladly acquiesce in whatever more changes or omissions you propose. Browne seems to be getting on well.[1] . . . He will have a good subject in Paul's christening.[2] Mr. Chick is like D, if you'll mention that when you think of it. The little chapter of Miss Tox and the Major, which you alas! (but quite wisely) rejected from the first number, I have altered for the last of the second.[3] I have not quite finished the middle chapter[4] yet—having, I should say, three good days' work to do at it; but I hope it will be all a worthy successor to number one. I will send it as soon as finished.

We had a regatta at Ouchy[5] the other day, mainly supported by the contributions of the English handfull. It concluded with a rowing-match by women, which was very funny. I wish you could have seen Roche appear on the Lake, rowing, in an immense boat, Cook, Anne, two nurses, Katey, Mamey, Walley, Chickenstalker, and Baby; no boatmen or other degrading assistance; and all sorts of Swiss tubs splashing about them. . . . Senior[6] is coming here to-morrow, I believe, with his wife; and they talk of Brunel[7] and his wife[8] as on their way. We dine at Haldimand's to meet Senior—which solitary and most interesting piece of intelligence is all the news I know of. . . . Take care you don't back out of your Paris engagement; but that we really do have (please God) some happy

[1] Forster had presumably reported on Browne's progress with the cover, which CD had not yet seen; sketches for illustrations to No. 1 may have been sent any time after 17 Aug. One is reproduced in *Dombey and Son*, ed. A. Horsman, p. 865.

[2] Ch. 5, "Paul's Progress and Christening", was the first in No. 11; Browne's illustration was "The Christening Party".

[3] Ch. 7 (which had been proposed as Ch. 4), "A Bird's-eye glimpse of Miss Tox's dwelling-place": see *To* Forster, ?7 Aug and ?13 and 14 Aug 46, and *fns*.

[4] Ch. 6, "Paul's Second Deprivation".

[5] On 25 Aug; the club had been recently formed, and Cerjat had presented a "superbe pavillon". The regatta began at 2 p.m. and ended with a ladies' race. No English names appear in the report in the *Nouvelliste Vaudois*, 28 Aug.

[6] Nassau William Senior (1790–1864; *DNB*), economist; first Professor of Political Economy at Oxford 1825–30; Poor Law Commissioner 1833, and recently on Irish Poor Law Commission. Contributed to the *Quarterly* and (after 1840) to the *Edinburgh*, on literary as well as political topics; some of the articles in the former,

including his famous review of *Vanity Fair*, collected in *Essays on Fiction*, 1864. Married Mary Charlotte Mair 1821. CD is not mentioned by Senior's daughter in her account of their tour, although she does refer to Haldimand and "a delightful visit to the Marcets [*i.e. Mrs Marcet's son Frank and his wife*]" (W. C. M. Simpson, *Many Memories of Many People*, 1898, p. 39).

[7] Isambard Kingdom Brunel, FRS (1806–59; *DNB*), civil engineer; assisted his father Sir Marc Isambard Brunel with the Thames Tunnel, completed 1843; designed the *Great Western*, 1838, the *Great Britain*, 1845, and many railway works—he had personally escorted Lady Holland to Bowood when the new line was opened in 1841. Now at the height of his fame, he had recently advised on the building of railways in Sardinia; but had forebodings about the railway mania. He was an old friend of Babbage and may already have met CD: a letter of 1849 (N, II, 155) shows them on friendly terms.

[8] Mary, sister of John Calcott Horsley, RA; married 1836.

hours there. Kate, Georgy, Mamey, Katey, Charley, Walley, Chickenstalker, and Baby, send loves. . . . I am all anxiety and fever to know what we start *Dombey* with.[1]

There are two nice girls here, the Ladies Taylor,[2] daughters of Lord Headfort. Their mother was daughter (I think) of Sir John Stevenson, and Moore dedicated one part of the Irish Melodies to her.[3] They inherit the musical taste, and sing very well. A proposal is on foot for our all bundling off on Tuesday[4] (16 strong) to the top of the Great St. Bernard. But the weather seems to have broken, and the autumn rains to have set in; which I devoutly hope will break up the party. It would be a most serious hindrance to me, just now; but I have rashly promised. Do you know young Romilly?[5] He is coming over from Geneva when "the reading" comes off, and is a fine fellow I am told. There is not a bad little theatre here; and by way of an artificial crowd,[6] I should certainly have got it open with an amateur company, if we were not so few that the only thing we want is the audience.

He had pretty well matured the general idea of the Christmas book, and was burning to get to work on it. He thought it would be all the better, for a change, to have no fairies or spirits in it, but make it a simple domestic tale.

I shall begin the little story straightway,[7] but I have been dimly conceiving a very ghostly and wild idea, which I suppose I must now reserve for the *next* Christmas book.[8] *Nous verrons.* It will mature in the streets of Paris by night, as well as in London.

To THOMAS MITTON, 30 AUGUST 1846

MS Huntington Library. *Address:* Angleterre | Thomas Mitton Esquire |
23 Southampton Buildings | Chancery Lane | London.

Rosemont. Sunday Thirtieth August 1846.

My Dear Mitton. I received your letter yesterday, and send you a draft on Coutts's, agreeably to a form agreed upon between me and one of the Gentle-

[1] Not sales (unless sentence moved by Forster from a later letter), but subscriptions and advance orders. In later edns Forster altered "start" to "are starting".

[2] Mrs Watson's cousins, Lady Virginia and Lady Mary Taylour, daughters of Thomas, 2nd Marquis of Headfort, who married in 1822 Olivia (*d.* 1834), widow of Edward Dalton and daughter of Sir John Andrew Stevenson, the composer (?1760–1833; *DNB*).

[3] No. 10, the last number, dated May 1834, was dedicated to the Marchioness of Headfort, who "lent the aid of [her] beautiful voice . . . and exquisite feeling for music, to the happy circle who met, to sing them together, under [her] father's roof".

[4] 1 Sep; letter therefore written 30 Aug, not Sep as Forster says.

[5] Edward Romilly (1804–70), third son of Sir Samuel Romilly; MP for Ludlow 1837–66; married Sophia, youngest daughter of Mrs Marcet, 7 May 1830, at Berne. Not named in Watson's Diary as present at the reading on 12 Sep. Had been a steward at the dinner to Lord Dudley Coutts Stuart, 16 May 46.

[6] i.e. instead of crowds in streets.

[7] In fact he did not begin until Wed 9 Sep, five days after his return from the St Bernard: see *To* Forster, ?6 Sep.

[8] *The Haunted Man*, returned to in 1847, but not written till 1848.

men in the Inner Room there, to whom I spoke on the subject before I left England.

Bradbury and Evans's account for the half year is £1100 and odd, of which £500 was paid on account of the Pictures from Italy, before I left England, and the remainder is just now paid in.[1] They certainly keep a very active eye upon the expences and profits. You will know by the time you receive this, I dare say, the name of the new book.[2] I think it is an odd one, and therefore a good one. It struck B and E very much. The first No is considered very good indeed. So much so that Browne, who is generally the most indifferent fellow in the world, couldn't help writing me a long letter about it, and saying how pleased he was. I have taken immense pains, and think it strong. Some of it made me laugh so, that I couldn't see the paper as I was writing. The second is not behind it. Moses has taken one page of the wrapper, all through.[3]

Cramer's house never *did* business like any other house. And therefore I am not surprised at their sending in their bill too soon. I purchased the Piano at 12 months credit, because I found the allowance for ready money, so preposterously small. I bought it in *September*, & I am pretty sure towards the end of the month. But the note I have in my diary of the amount is £75. What is the rest of the bill? I know there are some other items, but I should like to know what they are. I will send you a draft for the whole, before the Month (of September) is out.[4] I do not recollect Brooks's small account,[5] nor can I call to mind what it can be for. I dare say, however, he is right. It may be paid, I have no doubt.

Unless B and E have taken charge of Kate's five letters (which is not likely, as all the proofs come by post) will you post 'em? Also Smale's,[6] which would seem to be an oddity. The best way of disposing of Mr. Van de Lieb[7] (whose MSS would bother me no less than you) would be to write him, if you will, a copy of the letter I have written on the other side—retaining his MSS in that never-opened tin box of mine, until he writes for them—if ever.

The Thompsons have taken a house here, for 8 months. She seems (between ourselves) to have a devil of a whimpering, pouting temper—but she is large in the family way, and that may have something to do with it. Charley is getting quite stout. Everybody else well and happy, and all uniting in kind regards.

---

[1] The statement of account which CD received from Bradbury & Evans for the half-year ending 30 June (MS V & A) showed that his share of profit on *Pictures* was £304.15.6, on the *Cricket* £294.6.5, *Oliver Twist* £81.7.2, the *Carol* £28.7.6; a deduction for his "share of deficiency of new edition of the *Chimes*" left a balance of £629. This agrees with CD's statement in the letter, but his own accounts show no payment from "Bradbury & Co" until 1 Oct (£729, which includes the £100 for *Dombey* No. 1). For the £500, see *To* Forster, ?17–20 Apr 46, *fn*.

[2] First advertised in *The Times, Morning Chronicle* and *Daily News* of 2 Sep: "On the 1st of October ... the First Number of DEALINGS WITH THE FIRM OF DOMBEY AND SON, Wholesale, Retail, and for Exportation".

[3] E. Moses & Son, tailors, of the Minories and Aldgate; their advertisements appeared on the back wrapper of each No.

[4] See *To* Mitton, 25 Sep 46.

[5] Probably paid by Mitton out of a £50 payment to him by CD on 31 Aug 46; unlikely to be the payment to a "Mr. Brooke" of £18.5.0 on 3 Apr 47 (Accountbook, MS Messrs Coutts).

[6] Perhaps Henry Lewis Smale: see Vol. III, p. 437 and *n*.

[7] Unidentified.

I regard your coming to Paris with me, as a solemn bargain, and can answer for your being greatly surprised, benefitted, and entertained. Nothing can be easier; and you never could hope to see it (*I* hope)[1] more pleasantly than with

Yours Ever

CD.

Address in English | date so and so Septembre 1846.

Monsieur.

Monsr. Charles Dickens, qui n'est pas a présent en Angleterre, ayant laissé á moi sa pleine confiance et l'autorite d'ouvrir ses lettres, je me trouve honoré de la votre.

J'aurai l'honneur, Monsieur de l'envoyer á mon ami qui va se rendre á Paris, Decembre prochain. En attendant, voulez-vous que je garde vos manuscrits? Ou voulez-vous que je les vous retourne?

Reçevez, Monsieur, l'assurance de ma consideration distinguée

Votre Serviteur trés fidele

Thomas Mitton

addressed outside
á Monsieur | Monsr. So and So

To ROBERT KEELEY, 31 AUGUST 1846†

MS Huntington Library.

Rosemont, Lausanne, Switzerland
Thirty First August 1846.

My Dear Sir

[a]I gave a promise to Willmott last year, that you should have my Christmas Book of *this* year, in time to dramatize and act, on the night of its publication, for another hundred pounds.[a] [2]

I have accidentally heard (I hope incorrectly) that you and Willmott have parted company.[3] But lest it should be so, and any confusion should arise on this subject in consequence, I think it well to tell you that I shall be perfectly willing to fulfil my engagement, if you please,—but that I hold you at perfect liberty to abandon it if *you* please, and shall be in no wise offended by your so doing.

I send this through my friend Mr. Forster who has full power from me to proceed in the matter, and is perfectly cognizant of all my arrangements.

I beg to be cordially remembered to Mrs. Keeley, and am

Very faithfully Yours

CHARLES DICKENS

Robert Keeley Esquire.

---

[1] "I" is underlined twice.

[aa] Given in N, 1, 785; letter otherwise unpublished.

[2] CD's account-book (MS Messrs Coutts) shows a payment of £100 from the Lyceum on 21 Nov 46.

[3] Willmott was joint proprietor with Strutt and Keeley at the Lyceum, 1844–5; it is not known whether he left in 1846, but a rumour that he had joined Mr Bunn is mentioned in the *Theatrical Journal*, 22 Aug 46.

To CHARLES LEVER, 31 AUGUST 1846

MS Widener Collection, Harvard. *Address:* A Monsieur: | Monsr. Charles Lever | Schloss Rieden | Breyenz[1] | Lac de Constance.

Lausanne. | Thirty First August 1846.

My Dear Lever.

I may write without the "Sir", though I *can't* come to Zurich. I can get so far, at all events.

Your second hospitable letter should have been answered long ago, but that I have been pondering all sorts of probabilities and possibilities. An excursion to Chamounix, however, and another to the Great St. Bernard—coupled with the invasions, past and to come, of people coming through here—have so encroached upon my time that I have now no choice but to put a grim face on all proposals of pleasure, and sit down, fiercely, at my desk.

Nevertheless, if, after Christmas and towards the Springtime, I should be anything like as free as I hope to be (by comparison with my approaching bondage) I shall still look forward to the pleasure of shaking hands with you bodily.[2]

In the meanwhile I must content myself with a more spiritual but not less hearty salutation.

Always Faithfully Yours
CHARLES DICKENS

—I forgot—New Work—Name, DOMBEY AND SON—Scene, English—Opening, in London.

To THE HON. RICHARD WATSON, 4 SEPTEMBER 1846*

MS Benoliel Collection.

Rosemont. | Friday Night September Fourth | 1846.

My Dear Mr. Watson

In the intervals of my tears, I write this, to send you in the Morning with Byron.—I have put a little piece of paper into the whereabout of the Prisoner of Chillon.

Grief and jolting[3] deprive me of the power of offering any remark, oral or written, on any subject whatever. I have merely strength of mind—and barely

---

[1] Thus in MS, for Bregenz (Brienz).

[2] Lever, living abroad for financial reasons since early 1845, had settled at Bregenz in May 46, and was there till Aug 47. On 15 Aug 46 he wrote that his "chateau continues full of company, with the visits of daily new arrivals"; he was then expecting "Charles Dickens and his wife". His "worthy publisher, Mr. Chapman, and wife" had stayed for three weeks (E. Downey, *Charles Lever. His Life in his Letters*, 1906, I, 211–12).

[3] On the St Bernard expedition: see next and *fns*. In returning, they spent the night of 3 Sep at Martigny and reached Lausanne at half-past three on Friday: "Boz very entertaining. He told me that he had written all his books *since* Pickwick for translation. He says all the French translations are horrible, but there is a very good Italian one of *Oliver Twist*" (Watson's Diary, 4 Sep, MS Commander Michael Saunders Watson).

strength of fingers—to offer my dismal regards to Mrs. Watson. Having done which, I return to the gorgeous red sofa, where I have been endeavouring, with my head very low, and my heels very high, to find some temporary consolation in the bosom of the newspapers.

Always believe me | Very faithfully Yours

The Hon. | Richard Watson.   CHARLES DICKENS

To JOHN FORSTER, [?6 SEPTEMBER 1846]

Extracts in F, v, iv, 418–20; v, v, 423–4*n*, 424; VI, ii, 476. *Date:* first extract 6 Sep according to Forster; second extract same letter, since No. II of *Dombey* reached Forster in second week of Sep; third extract, from the first letter after return from expedition on 4 Sep; fourth extract "a little later" than 30 Aug.

The weather obstinately clearing, we started off last Tuesday for the Great St. Bernard, returning here on Friday afternoon. The party consisted of eleven people and two servants—Haldimand, Mr. and Mrs. Cerjat and one daughter, Mr. and Mrs. Watson, two Ladies Taylor, Kate, Georgy, and I. We were wonderfully unanimous and cheerful; went away from here by the steamer; found at its destination a whole omnibus provided by the Brave (who went on in advance everywhere); rode therein to Bex; found two large carriages ready to take us to Martigny; slept there; and proceeded up the mountain on mules next day. Although the St. Bernard convent is, as I dare say you know, the highest inhabited spot but one in the world, the ascent is extremely gradual and uncommonly easy: really presenting no difficulties at all, until within the last league, when the ascent, lying through a place called the valley of desolation, is very awful and tremendous, and the road is rendered toilsome by scattered rocks and melting snow. The convent is a most extraordinary place, full of great vaulted passages, divided from each other with iron gratings; and presenting a series of the most astonishing little dormitories, where the windows are so small (on account of the cold and snow), that it is as much as one can do to get one's head out of them. Here we slept: supping, thirty strong, in a rambling room with a great wood-fire in it set apart for that purpose; with a grim monk, in a high black sugar-loaf hat with a great knob at the top of it, carving the dishes. At five o'clock in the morning the chapel bell rang in the dismallest way for matins: and I, lying in bed close to the chapel, and being awakened by the solemn organ and the chaunting, thought for a moment I had died in the night and passed into the unknown world.[1]

I wish to God you could see that place. A great hollow on the top of a range

---

[1] "Left Ouchy at $\frac{1}{4}$-past 11 & reached Martigny (Hotel de la Grande Maison) at $\frac{1}{4}$ before 7 Very good Inn" (Watson's Diary, 1 Sep; MS Commander Michael Saunders Watson; the entry also confirms the list of the party). "Left at 7 in Chars passing thro' Orsières to Lyddes where we mounted the mules of the Char and reached the convent about 7. The approach to which was very striking from its gloomy & desolate grandeur. Passed a disagreeable night, the bed broke down, &c" (2 Sep). The Hospice could accommodate 70 or 80 travellers; "the room appropriated to visitors is large and convenient"; the Clavandier or Bursar of the convent presided at dinner and supper (Murray, *Handbook for ... Switzerland*, 1843).

of dreadful mountains, fenced in by riven rocks of every shape and colour: and in the midst, a black lake, with phantom clouds perpetually stalking over it. Peaks, and points, and plains of eternal ice and snow, bounding the view, and shutting out the world on every side: the lake reflecting nothing: and no human figure in the scene. The air so fine, that it is difficult to breathe without feeling out of breath; and the cold so exquisitely thin and sharp that it is not to be described. Nothing of life or living interest in the picture, but the grey dull walls of the convent. No vegetation of any sort or kind. Nothing growing, nothing stirring. Everything iron-bound, and frozen up. Beside the convent, in a little outhouse with a grated iron door which you may unbolt for yourself, are the bodies of people found in the snow who have never been claimed and are withering away— not laid down, or stretched out, but standing up, in corners and against walls; some erect and horribly human, with distinct expressions on the faces; some sunk down on their knees; some dropping over on one side; some tumbled down altogether, and presenting a heap of skulls and fibrous dust. There is no other decay in that atmosphere; and there they remain during the short days and the long nights, the only human company out of doors, withering away by grains, and holding ghastly possession of the mountain where they died.[1]

It is the most distinct and individual place[2] I have seen, even in this transcendent country. But, for the Saint Bernard holy fathers and convent in themselves, I am sorry to say that they are a piece of as sheer humbug as we ever learnt to believe in, in our young days. Trashy French sentiment and the dogs (of which, by the bye, there are only three remaining) have done it all. They are a lazy set of fellows; not over fond of going out themselves; employing servants to clear the road (which has not been important or much used as a pass these hundred years); rich; and driving a good trade in Innkeeping: the convent being a common tavern in everything but the sign. No charge is made for their hospitality to be sure; but you are shown to a box in the chapel, where everybody puts in more than could, with any show of face, be charged for the entertainment; and from this the establishment derives a right good income. As to the self-sacrifice of living up there, they are obliged to go there young, it is true, to be inured to

---

[1] The bodies in the Morgue and the "bones of hundreds" in a walled enclosure were removed, according to Murray, a few years before 1843; either the clearance was incomplete, or a surprising number had since accumulated. Other travellers about this time refer to them; John W. Corson, an American doctor, explained the process of "dry decomposition" and mentioned the "blackened mummy-like faces" and "bones, the deposit of centuries" (*Loiterings in Europe*, New York, 1848, pp. 125–6).

[2] CD's recollections were still vivid nine years later when he described the pass and the Hospice, with many of the same details, in *Little Dorrit*, II, 1, including the "dead travellers", "silently assembled in a grated house, half-a-dozen paces removed"; "the

mother, storm-belated many winters ago, still standing in the corner with her baby at her breast; the man who had frozen with his arm raised to his mouth in fear or hunger, still pressing it with his dry lips after years and years". The "gloomy vaulted sleeping-rooms", the "parlour with a blazing fire", the dogs, reduced to three— one of whom accompanies a member of the order at a regular season of the year "to solicit aid for the convent"—all figure in the novel. In "Lying Awake", *Household Words*, 30 Oct 52 (collected in *Reprinted Pieces*), he also recalled, "the intensely cold convent with its ménagerie smell", the "breed of dogs fast dying out", and the "jolly young monks whom I mourn to know as humbugs".

the climate:[1] but it is an infinitely more exciting and various life than any other convent can offer; with constant change and company through the whole summer; with a hospital for invalids down in the valley, which affords another change; and with an annual begging-journey to Geneva and this place and all the places round for one brother or other, which affords farther change. The brother who carved at our supper could speak some English, and had just had *Pickwick* given him!—what a humbug he will think me when he tries to understand it! If I had had any other book of mine with me, I would have given it him, that I might have had some chance of being intelligible.

I hope to finish the second number to-morrow, and to send it off bodily by Tuesday's post. On Wednesday I purpose, please God, beginning the *Battle of Life*. I shall peg away at that, without turning aside to *Dombey* again; and *if* I can only do it within the month!

They had had wonderful weather, so clear that he could see from the Neuchatel road the outline of Mont Blanc, sixty miles off, as plainly as if he were standing close under it in the courtyard of the little inn at Chamounix; and, though it was raining again when he wrote, his nailed shoes *were by him and his* great waterproof cloak *in preparation for a* fourteen-mile walk *before dinner.*

Browne is certainly interesting himself, and taking pains. I think the cover[2] very good: perhaps with a little too much in it, but that is an ungrateful objection.[3]

To FREDERICK DICKENS, 9 SEPTEMBER 1846

MS Benoliel Collection.

Rosemont, Lausanne. | Wednesday Ninth September 1846.

My Dear Fred.

I want to point out to you what is a very great mistake, and error of judgment on your part.

I was very much surprised by Thompson's coming to me yesterday to ask if I had commissioned you to send him a copy of any part of my letter to Father, about Augustus.[4] Of course I said no: adding that beyond all question if I had

---

[1] "They are all young men, who enter upon this devoted service at 18, and few survive the time of their vow, 15 years; the severities of the winter, at this height, impair their health, and they are driven to retire to a lower and more genial clime, but often with broken constitutions and ruined health" (Murray, *op. cit.*).

[2] Bradbury & Evans's Accounts (MS V & A) have the entry "Paid Mr. Browne for Wrapper 8–8–0" on 5 Sep. Forster wrote to Browne, "I enclose you a cheque.—You charged too little for the design of the Cover. I took the liberty of changing the 5.5.0 into 8.8.0, and you will find the cheque thereto corresponding. | This liberty I am

sure you will excuse" (MS Yale University Library). The letter is undated, but must be near in date to 5 Sep; a postscript adds "Just received the plates".

[3] The cover foreshadows the course of the narrative more fully than in any earlier novel, but mainly in a general and allegorical way (see *Dombey and Son*, ed. A. Horsman, p. xviii). One or two incidents represented do not occur in the novel—e.g. Mr Dombey speaking in the House of Commons.

[4] Thompson had heard from Fred on 2 Sep (Christiana Thompson's Diary, MS Mrs Sowerby).

desired him to see it, I should have shewn it him myself. He replied he was quite sure of that—and expressed himself with some considerable earnestness on your having sent an extract to him, and furthermore shewn the letter to Mrs. Smithson.

Rely upon it this is a very great mistake, and places you in an exceedingly false position. Gentlemen don't do such things. You had no right whatever to transcribe any portion of that letter for Thompson's eye. When you mentioned to me, in a former letter, that you had shewn it to "a mutual friend", I was greatly surprised; but as most people place confidence in somebody or other, I imagined you might have shewn it, as a piece of confidence of your own: and though I was dissatisfied by the proceeding, I did not think myself justified in objecting to it when it was over. No person with any knowledge of becoming and delicate social usages would excuse you for sending the least word of it to Thompson. I hope you don't advise with Mr. Weller on such subjects. It is no disparagement to him to say that he makes enormous mistakes (as I had occasion to observe when he was at variance with Thompson), and is anything but a good leader. A letter entrusted to you, to deliver to some one else, is a sacred thing, and you have no kind of right over any syllable it contains. If I had empowered you to send any portion of it to Thompson, I should have considered that I adopted toward Thompson, in so doing, a very affronting and unpleasant course.

Therefore I could by no means defend you in it yesterday. About Augustus, and his absurd position in Mrs. Smithson's house, I spoke plainly, and evidently with effect. And I said that I presumed you had made this mistake, in some supposition that Mrs. Smithson had been beforehand with you, and related her version of the story to Thompson. Which he did not deny.

Rely upon this—the less you write in any such case as this quarrel, the better. You cannot be too careful in that. But to interfere with other people's writings, and other people's letters, is to slice at your own Nose with a sharp Razor.

I have been expecting to hear from you about your Lausanne plans, but I suppose these quarrels prevent the adjustment of anything. Will you tell Henry, with my love to him and Letitia that between my Xmas Book and Dombey, I am too much at my desk to be able to write letters, but that when we go to Paris, I shall hope to persuade them to come and stay some time with us.[1] I suppose it is now too late to expect them here. We think of leaving this, on the last day of November. We are all well, thank God, and happy. Kate and Georgy unite with me in loves to yourself and Anna.

Ever affectionately
CHARLES DICKENS

P.S. Charley, Mamey, Katey, Walley, Chickenstalker, and Sampson Brass (the baby) desire to be remembered.

---

[1] Austin left London 9 Dec 46 for Italy, Germany and Switzerland with Lieut. Waghorn to report on proposed lines of railway which might be available for the overland route.

To J. H. BARROW, 14 SEPTEMBER 1846

Mention in Sotheby's catalogue, June 1929; *MS* 2½ pp.; dated Rosemont, Lausanne, Switzerland, 14 Sep 46.

Concerning a dispute between Barrow and the Daily News *about his remuneration for a trip made to India.*

To MR B——, 16 SEPTEMBER 1846*

MS University of Texas.

1 Devonshire Terrace. | Sixteenth Sept 1846.

Mr. Charles Dickens presents his compliments to Mr. B   ,[1] and begs to say that his connexion with the Daily News does not extend to the acceptance or rejection of papers offered for publication in that Journal. He has however referred Mr. B.'s letter to the Editor who will no doubt reply to it without delay; and for himself he begs to thank Mr. B. for his obliging communication.

To JOHN FORSTER, [?20 SEPTEMBER 1846]

Extracts in F, v, v, 424, 425. *Date:* first extract eight days after the *Dombey* reading on 12 Sep, but wrongly called by Forster "three days" after ?6 Sep; second extract 20 Sep according to Forster.

The absence of any accessible streets continues to worry me, now that I have so much to do, in a most singular manner. It is quite a little mental phenomenon. I should not walk in them in the day time, if they were here, I dare say: but at night I want them beyond description. I don't seem able to get rid of my spectres unless I can lose them in crowds. However, as you say, there are streets in Paris, and good suggestive streets too: and trips to London will be nothing then. WHEN I have finished the Christmas book, I shall fly to Geneva for a day or two, before taking up with *Dombey* again. I like this place better and better; and never saw, I think, more agreeable people than our little circle is made up of. It is so little, that one is not "bothered" in the least; and their interest in the Inimitable seems to strengthen daily. I read them the first number[2] last night "was a" week, with unrelateable success; and old Mrs. Marcet, who is devilish 'cute, guessed directly (but I didn't tell her she was right) that little Paul would die. They were all so apprehensive that it was a great pleasure to read it;[3] and

---

[1] A cross has been pencilled against the "B". Probably the letter was sent to Wills as a model to be used in reply to anyone who submitted contributions.

[2] From the proofs: see F, v, iv, 417.

[3] "A Soiree at Mr. Dickens to hear him read the first number of his new work, 'Dombey and Son'. He reads remarkably well & we are all of opinion that the beginning of this work is more interesting than the Commencement of any of his other works. He has great expectations of it himself. He told me that he was at a Dissenters' School at Rochester though his Parents were not Dissenters. Mrs Marcet, Cerjats, Goffs, Lord Vernon, Sir T. Gage [*Sir Thomas Rokewode Gage, Bart, 1810–66, a friend of the Watsons*], Haldimand and a Mr and Mrs Thompson were present. The reading lasted about an hour and three-

I shall leave here, if all goes well, in a brilliant shower of sparks struck out of them by the promised reading of the Christmas book.

You remember your objection about the two stories. I made over light of it. I ought to have considered that I have never before really tried the opening of two together—having always had one pretty far ahead when I have been driving a pair of them. I know it all now. The apparent impossibility of getting each into its place, coupled with that craving for streets, so thoroughly put me off the track, that, up to Wednesday or Thursday last, I really contemplated, at times, the total abandonment of the Christmas book this year, and the limitation of my labours to *Dombey and Son!* I cancelled the beginning of a first scene[1]—which I have never done before—and, with a notion in my head, ran wildly about and about it, and could not get the idea into any natural socket. At length, thank Heaven, I nailed it all at once; and after going on comfortably up to yesterday, and working yesterday from half-past nine to six, I was last night in such a state of enthusiasm about it that I think I was an inch or two taller. I am a little cooler to-day, with a headache to boot; but I really begin to hope you will think it a pretty story, with some delicate notions in it agreeably presented, and with a good human Christmas groundwork.[2] I fancy I see a great domestic effect in the last part.

To THOMAS MITTON, 25 SEPTEMBER 1846*

MS Princeton University Library.

Rosemont, Lausanne. Twenty Fifth September 1846

My Dear Mitton. I enclose you a cheque, crossed, for the amount of Cramer's bill. At the same time, I cannot help thinking that the Piano Item requires explanation. I have got the price in my book £75, and I very seldom make mistakes—of that kind.[3]

As you may suppose, I am very busy. I never had to *begin* two stories together, before: and it is desperate work. There are no streets and crowds of people here,

quarters. The Career of Dombey, Son, and Daughter are settled, but I think none of the others" (Watson's Diary, 12 Sep; MS Commander Michael Saunders Watson). Christiana Thompson mentions the Taylours as also present: it was "a large assembly" and everyone was "very much delighted" (Diary, MS Mrs Sowerby).

[1] CD presumably means the point at which the action begins to develop, after the description of the battlefield and of the sisters' dance at the apple-picking in the orchard. In the manuscript (MS Morgan) these occupy the first two slips; the first substantial cancellation comes on the third slip (roughly corresponding with pp. 12–13

of 1st edn). It shows that CD first intended to make the transition from the battlefield-and-harvest theme by introducing at this point a "small man" (obviously Britain) acting as guide to two gentlemen, unnamed, who wish to see the site of the battle. Instead, CD decided to introduce the girls' father, Dr Jeddler, at once, and in the subsequent dialogue (pp. 13–16) no doubt he felt he had "nailed" the main idea.

[2] The ball at the end of Part II is in "the Christmas season".

[3] On 6 Oct CD's account-book (MS Messrs Coutts) shows a payment to Cramer & Co. of £88.13.0; perhaps in the interval Mitton made further inquiries.

to divert the attention. My head suffers. And that is very unusual, as you know, with me.

Everything depends upon my work; but if I can get Dombey No. 3 out of hand soon enough (I can't go to that, until I have done the Christmas Book) I shall leave here for Paris on the 10th. of November: otherwise I shall be on the road when I ought to be at my desk. I shall see my way pretty clearly (I hope) by about the 20th. or 25th. of October: and will let you know, of course, what my plans are finally.

Bradbury and Evans are in no very good odour with me just now, for other reasons,[1] but you quite mistake my allusion to their charges—being, as usual, on the doubtful side. I think *they keep the expences down*, decidedly, and know where and how to do so. The Pictures from Italy could not return any large sum: the price being so extremely low.[2] But that I knew before-hand. The Oliver subscription will be all profit.[3] The expences of the book are paid in the Nos.

We are all well and hearty. Its'[4] no use telling you any thing about Dombey. You will know all about the beginning of it, almost as soon as you know what is inside of this letter.[5]

Ever faithfully
CD.

Thomas Mitton Esquire.

To T. N. TALFOURD, 25 SEPTEMBER 1846*

MS Free Library of Philadelphia. *Address:* A Monsieur: | Monsr. Serjeant Talfourd. | Hotel de l'Union | Chamounix | En Suisse.

Rosemont, Lausanne. Twenty Fifth September 1846.

My Dear Talfourd.

Having received your letter today, with the greatest pleasure, I write a hasty note by return of Post, to say that I eschew all Scientific doings at Genoa (albeit they take place in my old house)[6] and remain a fixture here, until November. Therefore, "on Saturday the 3rd. of October, between 4 and 5 in the afternoon", we shall expect you here: and your wants being so moderate, in respect of beds, I am happy to say we shall be able to house you all. We are on the Ouchy Road, a very little way out of Lausanne.

I am horribly hard at work with my Christmas Book, which runs (rather inconveniently) in a Curricle just now, with "Dealings with the Firm of Dombey

---

[1] Possibly connected with the advertising of *Dombey*; references to "Boz" and "Phiz" ceased to appear from about 19 Sep.

[2] The price was six shillings. CD is commenting on the profits up to 30 June (see *To* Mitton, 30 Aug 46, *fn*); there was only a further £53.9.4 (including £17 from Tauchnitz) in the following six months.

[3] i.e. for the volume, published 26 Sep 46, a few days before the tenth and final monthly No. In Dec 46 he received £97.10.10, which included his half share of the profits on the sale of the volume as well as of the last three Nos (for the first seven, see *To* Mitton, 30 Aug 46, *fn*) and reprints of early Nos.

[4] Thus in MS.

[5] No. 1, for October, was published 30 Sep.

[6] The eighth annual Science Congress, 14–29 Sep; reported in the *Athenæum* ("Foreign Correspondence", 10, 17, 24 Oct), with references to dining in the Peschiere. Only a few English attended.

and Son"—for that's the name of the other; in the beginning whereof, I have pleased myself, and hope to please you. Your advent will be a most noble holiday for me; and please God we will take a glorious walk on the Sunday.

Mrs. Dickens and her sister join me in kindest regards. In case this letter should not reach you at Chamounix, I have dispatched a duplicate of it to the Poste Restante, Geneva.[1]

Ever Believe me | Most affectionately Yours

CHARLES DICKENS

To JOHN FORSTER, [26 SEPTEMBER 1846]

Extract in F, v, v, 426–7. *Date:* 26 Sep according to Forster.

I am going to write you a most startling piece of intelligence. I fear there may be NO CHRISTMAS BOOK! I would give the world to be on the spot to tell you this. Indeed I once thought of starting for London to-night. I have written nearly a third of it. It promises to be pretty; quite a new idea in the story, I hope; but to manage it without the supernatural agency[2] now impossible of introduction, and yet to move it naturally within the required space, or with any shorter limit than a *Vicar of Wakefield*, I find to be a difficulty so perplexing—the past *Dombey* work taken into account—that I am fearful of wearing myself out if I go on, and not being able to come back to the greater undertaking with the necessary freshness and spirit. If I had nothing but the Christmas book to do, I WOULD do it; but I get horrified and distressed beyond conception at the prospect of being jaded when I come back to the other, and making it a mere race against time. I have written the first part;[3] I know the end and upshot of the second;[4] and the whole of the third (there are only three in all). I know the purport of each character, and the plain idea that each is to work out; and I have the principal effects sketched on paper. It cannot end *quite* happily, but will end cheerfully and pleasantly. But my soul sinks before the commencement of the second part—the longest—and the introduction of the under-idea. (The main one already developed, with interest). I don't know how it is. I suppose it is the having been almost constantly at work in this quiet place; and the dread for the *Dombey*; and the not being able to get rid of it, in noise and bustle. The beginning two books together is also, no doubt, a fruitful source of the difficulty; for I am now sure I could not have invented the *Carol* at the commencement of the *Chuzzlewit*, or gone to a new book from the *Chimes*. But this is certain. I am sick, giddy, and capriciously despondent. I have bad nights; am full of disquietude

---

[1] Talfourd left Milan 24 Sep, spent 29–30 Sep in Chamounix, and 2 Oct at Vevey, presumably passing through Geneva.

[2] *The Battle of Life* is the only Christmas book without any supernatural "machinery"; perhaps before he worked out the story at all (see *To* Forster, ?30 Aug) CD thought of using the battlefield in this way. It is impossible to see how the present story would be assisted by "supernatural agency";

but as it stands the battlefield, which was the idea he began with, seems imperfectly connected with the rest. The MS shows some uncertainty (see *To* Forster, ?20 Sep, *fn*) and various attempts at the Doctor's speech on pp. 35–6.

[3] The first part introduces all the main characters except Michael Warden.

[4] Part II ends with the flight of Marion

and anxiety; and am constantly haunted by the idea that I am wasting the marrow of the larger book, and ought to be at rest. One letter that I wrote you before this, I have torn up. In that the Christmas book was wholly given up for this year: but I now resolve to make one effort more.[1] I will go to Geneva to-morrow, and try on Monday and Tuesday whether I can get on at all bravely, in the changed scene. If I cannot, I am convinced that I had best hold my hand at once; and not fritter my spirits and hope away, with that long book before me. You may suppose that the matter is very grave when I can so nearly abandon anything in which I am deeply interested, and fourteen or fifteen close MS pages[2] of which, that have made me laugh and cry, are lying in my desk. Writing this letter at all, I have a great misgiving that the letter I shall write you on Tuesday night will not make it better. Take it, for Heaven's sake, as an extremely serious thing, and not a fancy of the moment. Last Saturday after a very long day's work, and last Wednesday after finishing the first part, I was full of eager- ness and pleasure. At all other times since I began, I have been brooding and brooding over the idea that it was a wild thing to dream of, ever: and that I ought to be at rest for the *Dombey*.

To JOHN FORSTER, [30 SEPTEMBER and 1 OCTOBER 1846]

Extract in F, v, v, 427–8. *Date:* 30 Sep with postscript added 1 Oct according to Forster. *From* Geneva.

He was quite dismayed at first by the sight of gas in Geneva, and trembled at the noise in the streets, which was fully equal to the uproar of Richmond in Surrey. When I came here I had a bloodshot eye; and my head was so bad, with a pain across the brow, that I thought I must have got cupped. I have become a great deal better, however, and feel quite myself again to-day. . . . I still have not made up my mind as to what I CAN do with the Christmas book. I would give any money that it were possible to consult with you. I have begun the second part this morning, and have done a very fair morning's work at it, but I do not feel it *in hand* within the necessary space and divisions: and I have a great uneasiness in the prospect of falling behind hand with the other labour, which is so transcendently important. I feel quite sure that unless I (being in reasonably good state and spirits) like the Christmas book myself, I had better not go on with it; but had best keep my strength for *Dombey*, and keep my number in advance. On the other hand I am dreadfully averse to abandoning it, and am so torn between the two things that I know not what to do. It is impossible to express the wish I have that I could take counsel with you. Having begun the second part I will go on here, to-morrow and Friday (Saturday, the Talfourds come to us at Lausanne,

---

[1] With over two-thirds of the Christmas book still to write and a three days' stoppage since finishing the first part, and the neces- sity of writing the whole of No. III of *Dombey* before leaving Lausanne for Paris in six weeks' time (with further inevitable interruptions such as Talfourd's visit), CD

would have been pressed for time even if he had been more confident about the *Battle*.

[2] Part I occupies 14 pages of MS, with a few short passages for insertion on the backs of pages.

leaving on Monday morning), unless I see new reason to give it up in the mean-while. Let it stand thus—that my next Monday's letter shall finally decide the question. But if you have not already told Bradbury and Evans of my last letter I think it will now be best to do so. . . . This non-publication of a Christmas book, if it must be, I try to think light of with the greater story just begun, and with this *Battle of Life* story (of which I really think the leading idea is very pretty) lying by me, for future use. But I would like you to consider, in the event of my not going on, how best, by timely announcement, in November's or December's *Dombey*, I may seem to hold the ground prospectively.[1] . . . Heaven send me a good deliverance! If I don't do it, it will be the first time I ever abandoned anything I had once taken in hand; and I shall not have abandoned it until after a most desperate fight. I could do it, but for the *Dombey*, as easily as I did last year or the year before.[2] But I cannot help falling back on that continually: and this, combined with the peculiar difficulties of the story for a Christmas book,[3] and my being out of sorts, discourages me sadly. . . . Kate is here, and sends her love.

[P.S] Georgy has come over from Lausanne, and joins with Kate, &c. &c. My head remains greatly better. My eye is recovering its old hue of beautiful white, tinged with celestial blue. If I hadn't come here, I think I should have had some bad low fever. The sight of the rushing Rhone seemed to stir my blood again. I don't think I shall want to be cupped, this bout; but it looked, at one time, worse than I have confessed to you. If I have any return, I will have it done immediately.

To JOHN FORSTER, [3 OCTOBER 1846]

Extracts in F, v, v, 429–30; vi, ii, 477. *Date:* 3 Oct according to Forster.

In the breathless interval between our return from Geneva and the arrival of the Talfourds (expected in an hour or two), I cannot do better than write to you. For I think you will be well pleased if I anticipate my promise, and Monday, at the same time. I have been greatly better at Geneva, though I still am made uneasy by occasional giddiness and headache: attributable, I have not the least doubt, to the absence of streets. There is an idea here, too, that people are occasionally made despondent and sluggish in their spirits by this great mass of

[1] As was done in Sep 47, when he decided to postpone the *Haunted Man* until Christmas 1848, but not to announce this until Nov (F, VI, i, 466).

[2] The *Chimes* and the *Cricket* each occupied about a month of writing, but both were later in going to press than the *Battle*.

[3] Partly because of the limited length, and also, as Forster says, because "the serious parts were too much interwoven with the tale to render the subject altogether suitable to the old mirth-bringing season"; but CD attempts to justify it by emphasizing the "joy . . . at its close" and the character of Clemency (v, vi, 436). Two years later he still regretted that he had to "use the idea for so short a story" ("I was wretched when I sat down to the little book, to feel the great capacity there was in the idea, and the waste of it that the limits of the story hopelessly involved") and even thought he might "forge that bit of metal again" (*To* Lytton, 10 Apr and 4 Aug 48, N, II, 78; part quoted in F, v, vi, 437)—but he never did so.

still water, Lake Leman. At any rate I have been very uncomfortable: at any rate I am, I hope, greatly better: and (lastly) at any rate I hope and trust, *now*, the Christmas book will come in due course!! I have had three very good days' work at Geneva, and trust I may finish the second part (the third is the shortest) by this day week. Whenever I finish it, I will send you the first two together. I do not think they can begin to illustrate it, until the third arrives; for it is a single-minded story, as it were, and an artist should know the end: which I don't think very likely, unless he reads it.

He described the superhuman effort he was making to lodge his visitors in his doll's house. I didn't like the idea of turning them out at night. It is so dark in these lanes, and groves, when the moon's not bright.

He hoped that he would by great effort finish the Christmas book on the 20th; then he would fly to Geneva for a week to work a little at Dombey, *if he felt* pretty sound; *and in any case finish his third number by the 10th of November, and start for Paris that day* so that, instead of resting unprofitably here, I shall be using my interval of idleness to make the journey and get into a new house, and shall hope so to put a pinch of salt on the tail of the sliding number in advance.... I am horrified at the idea of getting the blues (and bloodshots) again.

On Forster's objections to parts of No. II:[1] Miss Tox's colony I will smash.[2] Walter's allusion to Carker (would you take it *all* out)? shall be dele'd. Of course, you understand the man? I turned that speech over in my mind; but I thought it natural that a boy should run on, with such a subject, under the circumstances: having the matter so presented to him.[3] ... I thought of the possibility of malice on christening points of faith, and put the drag on as I wrote.[4] Where would you make the insertion, and to what effect? *That* shall be done too. I want you to think the number sufficiently good stoutly to back up the first. It occurs to me—might not your doubt about the christening be a reason for not making the ceremony the subject of an illustration?[5] Just turn this over. Again: if I could do it (I shall have leisure to consider the possibility before I begin), do you think it would be advisable to make number three a kind of half-way house between Paul's infancy, and his being eight or nine years

[1] On receiving No. II (Chs 5–7) in the "second week of September" Forster evidently had it set up and made his suggestions for revision after seeing the proofs, which he sent to CD. The single surviving proof in the Forster Collection is marked with cuts and revisions in Forster's hand only, and is probably a duplicate of what he sent to the printer after hearing from CD. The No. was one page too long, but some of the cuts were obviously made for other reasons.

[2] The description of Miss Tox's little house in Princess's Place which opens Ch. 7 originally included the following sentence: "In any part of the house, visitors were usually cognizant of a prevailing mustiness; and in warm weather Miss Tox had been seen apparently writing in sundry chinks and crevices of the wainscot with the wrong end of a pen dipped in spirits of turpentine", i.e. to discourage bugs.

[3] A passage is deleted from the proof of Ch. 6 (after Walter and Florence see Mr Carker the Junior) in which Walter speculates about his strangeness, why he takes an interest in Walter and yet shuns him, and why he is never promoted though his younger brother is head manager; the substance of it appears instead in Ch. 13, in the dialogue between Walter and the Carkers.

[4] The MS does not show an increase of deletion and alteration in this passage.

[5] The christening party and not the ceremony was the subject of Browne's illustration.

old?—In that case I should probably not kill him until the fifth number. Do you think the people so likely to be pleased with Florence, and Walter, as to relish another number of them at their present age? Otherwise, Walter will be two or three and twenty, straightway. I wish you would think of this.[1] ... I am sure you are right about the christening. It shall be artfully and easily amended.[2] ... Eh?

To MISS BURDETT COUTTS, 5 OCTOBER 1846

MS Morgan Library. *Address:* Angleterre. | Miss Burdett Coutts | Stratton Street | Piccadilly | London.

Rosemont, Lausanne. | Fifth October 1846.

My Dear Miss Coutts.

I have made one or two attempts, in the midst of my other occupations to note down (as you asked me) the heads of what I had previously written to you. But I found it so difficult to collect them, while my attention was loaded with all sorts of imaginary baggage, and I was so afraid of bewildering you by putting down twenty after-ideas that I have not yet mentioned to you, and leaving out twenty I had mentioned—that I thought it best not to try any more—feeling assured that your kindness and consideration would attribute my silence, just now, to the right cause.

I will take care as soon as I am well set down in Paris (I hope to be there, by the middle of next month) to make some careful enquiries on the essential particular to which you call my attention—which I can also make, I think, without much difficulty, when I come to London. I shall have the greatest satisfaction at the same time in putting you in communication with two or three gentlemen who I am sure will be most valuable, willing, and suggestive advisers. The clergyman of that Westminster Prison[3] I think a very good man, and I k[now][4] he has great experience of these objects. [I] have no doubt whatever of the feasib[ility] of finding such inmates of the Asylum in the beginning, as would afford a most interesting and worthy trial of such a work.

The locality you suggest is a central and good one. But you would require to have a place attached, for exercise. Have you thought of that? The cultivation of little gardens, if they be no bigger than graves, is a great resource and a great

---

[1] Forster evidently agreed; in No. III Paul is "nearly five" in Ch. 8, and spends a year at Mrs Pipchin's with Florence; Walter visits Mr Dombey at Brighton to appeal for help for his uncle. The MS and proof show that Ch. 7 originally ended with a slightly different version of the paragraph that now begins Ch. 8 in No. III; the closing phrase was "until he woke—a Schoolboy!", obviously with the view of showing Paul at school in No. III, instead of, as now, in No. IV.

[2] CD probably added the two insertions

which appear in the proof in Forster's hand: between "the clergyman, in delivering" and "the closing exhortation", the parenthesis "(very unaffectedly and simply)" is added, and after this paragraph, the passage suggesting that Mr Dombey might have "thought of his own dignity a little less; and ... of the great origin and purpose of the ceremony ... a little more".

[3] The chaplain of the Tothill Fields Bridewell was the Rev. George Henry Hine.

[4] Letters missing through small tears in paper.

reward. It has always been found to be productive of good effects wherever it has been tried; and I earnestly hope you will be able to make it a part of your training.

When I know at what time I can come to London, I will write from Paris, and tell you beforehand. After that visit, I shall never be further away than Paris, and can constantly and frequently return, if I can be of service. I may mention that I saw in the Newspaper some weeks ago, an advertisement to the effect that a pamphlet descriptive of Captain Macconochie's[1] plan: *some modification* of which, I am so strongly inclined to recommend for adoption: is published, either by Hatchard or Ridgway in Piccadilly. I think the latter. It may be bought for two or three shillings.[2] It will certainly interest you if you will read it—I am sure of that—and we should then be able to talk it over on equal terms.

I am only half through my Christmas Book, for which I have a little notion that I should have been very glad indeed to have retained for a longer story, as it is necessarily very much contracted in its development in so small a space. I hear that the Dombey has been launched with great success. and was out of print on the first night.[3]

Mrs. Dickens sends her kind remembrances. Charley has won a Geneva watch by speaking French in three months. I rashly pledged myself to make that desperate present in the event of his succeeding—and as he *has* succeeded, I mean to go over to Geneva with him in great state, and endow him with his prize in as solemn a manner as I can possibly confer it. I think of enclosing it in a pathetic epistle. He sends his love, and says he means to distinguish himself at King's College.

Mr. and Mrs. Brown are well, I hope. I don't wish Mrs. Brown would be ill again, but I wish she would do something, which would lead to her suggesting another character to me,[4] as serviceable as Mrs. Gamp.

Ever believe me Dear Miss Coutts, Faithfully Yours

CHARLES DICKENS

To JOHN FORSTER, [10 OCTOBER 1846]

Extract in F, v, vi, 431. *Date:* "five days" after 5 Oct according to Forster; because of the urgency of sending MS, probably posted the day before next.

I send you in twelve letters, counting this as one, the first two parts (thirty-five slips)[5] of the Christmas book. I have two present anxieties respecting it. One to know that you have received it safely; and the second to know how it strikes you. Be sure you read the first and second parts together. . . . There seems to me to be interest in it, and a pretty idea; and it is unlike the others. . . . There will be some minor points for consideration: as, the necessity for some slight

---

[1] Thus in MS.

[2] Maconochie's *Crime and Punishment*, published in July 46 by Hatchard at 2*s* 6*d*.

[3] The first printing was 25,000.

[4] In 1849 some of Mrs Brown's charac-teristics were adopted for Rosa Dartle in *David Copperfield*: see M. Cardwell, "Rosa Dartle and Mrs Brown", D, LVI (1960), 29–33.

[5] i.e. MS pages.

alterations in one or two of the Doctor's speeches in the first part;[1] and whether it should be called "The Battle of Life. A Love Story"[2]—to express both a love story in the common acceptation of the phrase, and also a story of love; with one or two other things of that sort. We can moot these by and by. I made a tremendous day's work of it yesterday and was horribly excited—so I am going to rush out, as fast as I can: being a little used up, and sick. . . . But never say die! I have been to the glass to look at my eye. Pretty bright!

To JOHN FORSTER, [11 OCTOBER 1846]

Extracts in F, VI, ii, 477; V, v, 424–5; V, vi, 432–3, 430; V, v, 428–9; V, vi, 440. *Date:* first and third extracts 11 Oct according to Forster; second extract called by Forster "the very next letter" after a letter which he misdates (see *To* Forster, ?20 Sep), but more likely related to the second *Dombey* reading on 10 Oct; fourth extract probably same letter, since describes Talfourd's visit; fifth extract clearly soon after his return from Geneva; sixth, during period when most fully occupied with writing *Battle* and *Dombey*—i.e. before 17 Oct.

The *Dombey* success[3] is BRILLIANT! I had put before me thirty thousand as the limit of the most extreme success, saying that if we should reach that, I should be more than satisfied and more than happy; you will judge how happy I am![4] I read the second number here last night to the most prodigious and uproarious delight of the circle.[5] I never saw or heard people laugh so. You will allow me to observe that my reading of the Major has merit.

I was thinking the other day that in these days of lecturings and readings, a great deal of money might possibly be made (if it were not infra dig) by one's having Readings of one's own books. It would be an *odd* thing. I think it would take immensely. What do you say? Will you step to Dean-street, and see how Miss Kelly's engagement-book (it must be an immense volume!) stands? Or shall I take the St. James's?

You will know, long before you get this, all about the revolution at Geneva.[6] There were stories of plots against the Government when I was there, but I

---

[1] Only two slight alterations were made, in the speech on p. 36.

[2] This sub-title was used.

[3] Altered to "sale" in later edns. CD received the news the day after sending the MS of the *Battle* (F, v, vi, 431).

[4] Bradbury & Evans's Accounts (V & A) show that the first printing of No. I was 25,000, and that a reprint of 5000 was ready on 10 Oct. CD cannot therefore have been rejoicing at a sale of over 30,000 on 11 Oct, and *To* de Cerjat, 27 Nov shows that it was No. II that rose over 30,000. Forster had presumably forecast a still higher sale for No. I, as he might reasonably do (there were two further reprints, each of 2000, on 7 and 21 Nov, and the first printing of No. II was

30,000); but he was wrong in recalling that in mid-October he told CD that "the first number of *Dombey* had outstripped in sale the first of *Chuzzlewit*" (about 20,000) "by more than twelve thousand copies" (F, v, iv, 431).

[5] The Watsons were present, but left on Mon 12 Oct on a few weeks' tour of Italy (returning on 6 Nov). Mrs Watson in her travel diary noted that day, "Weather stormy & chilly, 'dead leaves falling sorrowfully' as Dickens said last Saturday" (MS Commander Michael Saunders Watson)—doubtless recalling the references to falling leaves in *Dombey*, Ch. 5.

[6] Briefly reported in *The Times* of 13 Oct, from the *Journal des Débats*. The revolt

didn't believe them; for all sorts of lies are always afloat against the radicals, and wherever there is a consul from a Catholic Power the most monstrous fictions are in perpetual circulation against them: as in this very place, where the Sardinian consul was gravely whispering the other day that a society called the Homicides had been formed, whereof the president of the council of state, the O'Connell of Switzerland and a clever fellow, was a member; who were sworn on skulls and cross-bones to exterminate men of property, and so forth. There was a great stir here, on the day of the fight in Geneva. We heard the guns (they shook this house) all day; and seven hundred men marched out of this town of Lausanne to go and help the radical party—arriving at Geneva just after it was all over. There is no doubt they had received secret help from here; for a powder barrel, found by some of the Genevese populace with "Canton de Vaud" painted on it, was carried on a pole about the streets as a standard, to show that they were sympathized with by friends outside. It was a poor mean fight enough, I am told by Lord Vernon,[1] who was present and who was with us last night. The Government was afraid; having no confidence whatever, I dare say, in its own soldiers; and the cannon were fired everywhere except at the opposite party, who (I mean the revolutionists) had barricaded a bridge with an omnibus only, and certainly in the beginning might have been turned with ease. The precision of the common men with the rifle was especially shown by a small party of *five*, who waited on the ramparts near one of the gates of the town, to turn a body of soldiery who were coming in to the Government assistance. They picked out every officer and struck him down instantly, the moment the party appeared; there were three or four of them; upon which the soldiers gravely turned round and walked off. I dare say there are not fifty men in this place who wouldn't click your card off a target a hundred and fifty yards away, at least. I have seen them, time after time, fire across a great ravine as wide as the ornamental ground in St. James's-park, and never miss the bull's-eye.

It is a horribly ungentlemanly thing to say here, though I *do* say it without the least reserve—but my sympathy is all with the radicals. I don't know any subject on which this indomitable people have so good a right to a strong feeling as Catholicity—if not as a religion, clearly as a means of social degradation. They know what it is. They live close to it. They have Italy beyond their mountains. They can compare the effect of the two systems at any time in their

---

broke out on 6 Oct; the Government capitulated on 8 Oct after some half-hearted resistance and very few casualties. The new President was James Fazy, head of the Radical party and editor of the *Revue de Genève*, "particularly dreaded by the aristocratic party, partly on account of his literary talents and of the influence with which his resolute character, his prepossessing countenance, and his eloquence inspired the people" (T. Mügge, *Switzerland in 1847*, II, Ch. 9). The leader in the *Daily News* of 13 Oct, sympathetic and taking the same line as CD, was perhaps

Forster's. The *Examiner*, 24 Oct, under its "Foreign News" quotes the *Revue de Genève* of 14 Oct, noting its "great moderation" and the small casualties. There is a "Postscript" mentioning the "latest accounts" showing that "Geneva was in a state of tranquillity".

[1] His letter to his son, quoted in W. W. Vernon, *Recollections of Seventy-five Years*, pp. 60–1, says he was "a spectator of the battle of October 7th", and refers to the wounded and to the killing of three animals "a horse—a dog—and a cat".

own valleys; and their dread of it, and their horror of the introduction of Catholic priests and emissaries into their towns, seems to me the most rational feeling in the world. Apart from this, you have no conception of the preposterous, insolent little aristocracy of Geneva: the most ridiculous caricature the fancy can suggest of what we know in England. I was talking to two famous gentlemen (very intelligent men) of that place, not long ago, who came over to invite me to a sort of reception there—which I declined.[1] Really their talk about "the people" and "the masses," and the necessity they would shortly be under of shooting a few of them as an example for the rest, was a kind of monstrosity one might have heard at Genoa. The audacious insolence and contempt of the people by their newspapers, too, is quite absurd. It is difficult to believe that men of sense can be such donkeys politically. It was precisely such a state of things that brought about the change here. There was a most respectful petition presented on the Jesuit question, signed by its tens of thousands of small farmers; the regular peasants of the canton, all splendidly taught in public schools, and intellectually as well as physically a most remarkable body of labouring men. This document is treated by the gentlemanly party with the most sublime contempt, and the signatures are said to be the signatures of "the rabble." Upon which, each man of the rabble shoulders his rifle, and walks in upon a given day agreed upon among them to Lausanne; and the gentlemanly party walk out without striking a blow.

The Talfourds stayed two days, and I think they were very happy. He was in his best aspect; the manner so well known to us, not the less loveable for being laughable; and if you could have seen him going round and round the coach that brought them, as a preliminary to paying the voiturier to whom he couldn't speak, in a currency he didn't understand, you never would have forgotten it.[2]

And now sir I will describe, modestly, tamely, literally, the visit to the small select circle which I promised[3] should make your hair stand on end. In our hotel were Lady A, and Lady B, mother and daughter,[4] who came to the Peschiere

---

[1] Not identified. Sir Charles Bunbury in his journal for 10 Sep 48, found "no bitterness of feeling" in the aristocratic party "except the De la Rives, who are violent Tories" (*Life, Letters and Journals of Sir Charles J. Bunbury, Bart.*, ed. F. J. Bunbury, 1894, I, 477).

[2] Talfourd describes at length his difficulties in 1842 with a *voiturier* whose patois he could not understand in *Vacation Rambles*, I, 244–5, and in 1843 he describes himself "stammering out wild English and an impotent attempt at French" at a drowsy porter, and finally resorting to "pantomimic action" (II, 120). Of the visit to CD he says "From Vevay, a *voiture* conveyed us to Lausanne, where our friend and the world's favourite, Mr. Charles Dickens, expected us to visit him . . . we were at home at the moment when we reached the hospitable roof of our friend". When they left, "the brave courier . . . procured a *voiture* for our conveyance through the delightful Munster Thal to Basle" (*Supplement to "Vacation Rambles"*, 1854, pp. 264–6).

[3] Obviously in the letter of 3 Oct. Forster makes it clear that the meeting took place at Geneva on 2 Oct.

[4] Lady Pellew and Lady Walpole (see *To* Forster, 24 May 45, *fn*). In F, 1872–4, Forster substituted these initials (although saying that the passage "could hardly now offend any one even if the names were given"), but in the 2nd edn referred to them as "a Mother and a Daughter" and so throughout the passage, except as noted below.

shortly before we left it, and who have a deep admiration for your humble servant the inimitable B. They are both very clever. Lady B, extremely well-informed in languages, living and dead; books, and gossip; very pretty; with two little children, and not yet five and twenty. Lady A, plump, fresh, and rosy; matronly, but full of spirits and good looks. Nothing would serve them but we *must* dine with them; and accordingly, on Friday at six, we went down to their room. I knew them to be rather odd. For instance, I have known Lady A, *full dressed*, walk alone through the streets of Genoa, the squalid Italian bye streets, to the Governor's soirée; and announce herself at the palace of state, by knocking at the door. I have also met Lady B, full dressed, without any cap or bonnet, walking a mile to the opera, with all sorts of jingling jewels about her, beside a sedan chair in which sat enthroned her mama. Consequently, I was not surprised at such little sparkles in the conversation (from the young lady) as "Oh God what a sermon we had here, last Sunday!" "And did you ever read such infernal trash as Mrs. Gore's?"[1]—and the like. Still, but for Kate and Georgy (who were decidedly in the way, as we agreed afterwards), I should have thought it all very funny; and, as it was, I threw the ball back again, was mighty free and easy, made some rather broad jokes, and was highly applauded. "You smoke, don't you?" said the young lady, in a pause of this kind of conversation. "Yes," I said, "I generally take a cigar after dinner when I am alone." "I'll give you a good 'un," said she, "when we go up-stairs." Well, sir, in due course we went up-stairs, and there we were joined by an American lady residing in the same hotel, who looked like what we call in old England "a reg'lar Bunter"[2]—fluffy face (rouged); considerable development of figure; one groggy eye; blue satin dress made low with short sleeves, and shoes of the same. Also a daughter; face likewise fluffy; figure likewise developed; dress likewise low, with short sleeves, and shoes of the same; and one eye not yet actually groggy, but going to be. American lady married at sixteen; daughter sixteen now, often mistaken for sisters, &c. &c. &c. When that was over, Lady B[3] brought out a cigar box, and gave me a cigar, made of negrohead she said, which would quell an elephant in six whiffs. The box was full of cigarettes—good large ones, made of pretty strong tobacco; I always smoke them here, and used to smoke them at Genoa, and I knew them well. When I lighted my cigar, Lady B lighted hers, at mine; leaned against the mantlepiece, in conversation with me; put out her stomach, folded her arms, and with her pretty face cocked up sideways and her cigarette smoking away like a Manchester cotton mill, laughed, and talked, and smoked, in the most gentlemanly manner I ever beheld. Lady A immediately lighted her cigar; American lady immediately lighted hers; and in five minutes the room was a cloud of smoke, with us four in the centre pulling away bravely, while American lady related stories of her "Hookah" up-stairs, and described different kinds of pipes. But even this was not all. For presently two Frenchmen came in, with whom, and the American lady, Lady B sat down to whist. The Frenchmen

---

[1] In 1846 she published *Peers and Parvenus*.

[2] A cant word for a woman who collects rags; hence any low, vulgar woman.

[3] "the younger of our entertainers" in 2nd edn.

smoked of course (they were really modest gentlemen, and seemed dismayed), and Lady B played for the next hour or two with a cigar continually in her mouth —never out of it. She certainly smoked six or eight. Lady A gave in soon—I think she only did it out of vanity. American lady had been smoking all the morning. I took no more; and Lady B and the Frenchmen had it all to themselves.

Conceive this in a great hotel, with not only their own servants, but half a dozen waiters coming constantly in and out! I showed no atom of surprise; but I never *was* so surprised, so ridiculously taken aback, in my life; for in all my experience of "ladies" of one kind and another, I never saw a woman—not a basket woman or a gipsy—smoke, before!

I will write to Landor as soon as I can possibly make time, but I really am so much at my desk perforce, and so full of work, whether I am there or elsewhere, between the Christmas book and *Dombey*, that it is the most difficult thing in the world for me to make up my mind to write a letter to anyone but you. I ought to have written to Macready.[1] I wish you would tell him, with my love, how I am situated in respect of pen, ink, and paper. One of the Lausanne papers, treating of free trade, has been very copious lately in its mention of LORD GOBDEN. Fact; and I think it a good name.

To EMILE DE LA RUE, 12 OCTOBER 1846

MS Berg Collection.

Rosemont, Lausanne | Monday Twelfth October 1846.

My Dear De la Rue

I have been at Geneva (left there immediately before the Revolution) and then found Serjeant Talfourd waiting for me here, whom I saw away to Bâsle. I am only just now in the receipt of your letter, and hasten to answer it, however briefly.

I think the best and plainest course will be for Madame to say nothing about us in her letter to Mrs. Thompson—taking everything for granted, and mentioning, as it were incidentally, that you are just then writing to me. It seems a course that will suit everything, and serve a whole world of chances.[2]

Dombey and Son is a most immense success. There is every present reason to suppose that it will beat all the other books. I am just going to sit down to the last part of the Christmas Volume. My work has been very severe of late.

I hope to be in Paris about the middle of next month; and from thence I will somehow send you my aforesaid books, please God. Give my best love to

---

[1] Forster's letter received on the 11th had probably mentioned that Macready was "well pleased with Dombey" (*To* Macready, 24 Oct 46).

[2] Perhaps CD wished to avoid any further talk about Fred and Anna Weller, especially as Mr Weller was visiting the Thompsons: see *To* Thompson, 16 Oct, *fn*.

Madame. I came back rather drearily from Vevay that night.[1] We had a happy day, and will have many more, please Heaven, somewhere or other.

In great haste | Ever Affectionately Yours

CD

Remember me to Brown.[2] I dined with Lady Walpole and Lady Pellew at Geneva the other day.

To C. R. LESLIE, 12 OCTOBER 1846

MS Mr Thomas L. Twidell. *Address:* C. R. Leslie Esquire R.A. | 12 Pineapple Place | Edgeware Road | London.

Rosemont, Lausanne, Switzerland | Twelfth October 1846.

My Dear Leslie—for call you 'Sir', who are closely related to Fielding, Smollet Sterne, Cervantes, Goldsmith, and others of that blood, I never will!

I am heartily obliged to you for your friendly letter in respect to the American publishers. I was previously aware that such an arrangement could be made. But on reviewing the whole system some three or four years ago, I came to the conclusion that it was so disgraceful and dishonest, that a man should not, for money, make himself a party to it. I therefore resolved that I never would treat with any Pirate whomsoever—would sell them no proof sheets, and so get by an evasion what the public honor of a country does not give me—and would leave my books to the general scramble.[4] I have never departed from that resolution since, otherwise I should have done so in favor of Mr. Carey's house[5] at Philadelphia, which is associated in my mind with some experience of their just and gentlemanly dealing.

I do not thank you the less for your kind remembrance.

Mrs. Dickens and her sister join me in cordial regards to Mrs. Leslie[6] and all your family. And I am ever, believe me,

Faithfully Your friend | And admirer

C. R. Leslie Esquire.   CHARLES DICKENS

To T. J. THOMPSON, [?MID-OCTOBER 1846]*

MS Mrs Sowerby. *Date:* Handwriting suggests 1846; and see *fn.*

My Dear Thompson

Behold the document! I have reserved the crick[7]—Heaven (and the Directors) forgive me for that same!

CD

[1] Probably 26 Aug: see *To* de la Rue, 20 Aug.

[2] Yeats Brown.

[3] Thus in MS.

[4] See Vol. III, pp. 404–5.

[5] Henry Carey was Leslie's brother-in-law: see Vol. III, p. 125*n.*

[6] Harriet (*née* Stone), married 1825.

[7] "Tom in bed half the day with his neck" (Christiana's Diary, 13 Oct 46; MS Mrs Sowerby). It seems possible that CD had been asked by Thompson to answer questions for a Life Assurance Company (the "document"), and referred jokingly to the usual question about the applicant's present state of health.

To T. J. THOMPSON, 16 OCTOBER 1846

Text from *A Dickens Friendship*, ed. W[ilfrid] M[eynell], privately printed, 1931, p. 55.

Rosemont, Sixteenth October, 1846

My dear Thompson,

I do not think—and I fear I have reason for that misgiving—that I shall be able to finish my little book until it is late, or going on for late, tomorrow night. I should be a Beast if, for any social purposes, I left it now until it was done; and I am therefore reluctantly obliged to propose that we dine together here on *Sunday*[1] instead of tomorrow, when we will broach some of the Rhine Wine to its success, and wreathe the bowl, etc. etc.

But what I particularly want you to do, is to lay violent hands on Mr. Weller,[2] and keep him until Sunday night at all events. If he goes away by the Mails, then he cannot go under more favourable circumstances. Firstly, because the Rhine Wine will give him an immensely improved taste for the Rhine water; and secondly because it will superinduce a disposition to sleep in the coach. We might further strengthen *that*, by walking in the day, which I should be delighted to do, if you're agreeable.

I make no apologies, for you know my strait.

Ever faithfully,
C.D.

To JOHN FORSTER, [18 OCTOBER 1846]

Extract in F, v, vi, 431. *Date:* 18 Oct according to Forster.

Sending the third and final part of The Battle of Life. I really do not know what this story is worth. I am so floored: wanting sleep, and never having had my head free from it for this month past. I think there are some places in this last part which I may bring better together in the proof, and where a touch or two may be of service; particularly in the scene between Craggs[3] and Michael Warden, where, as it stands, the interest seems anticipated.[4] But I shall have the benefit of your suggestions, and my own then cooler head, I hope; and I will be very careful with the proofs, and keep them by me as long as I can. . . . Mr. Britain must have another Christian name, then?[5] "Aunt Martha" is the Sally

---

[1] Christiana Thompson's diary confirms that they dined with the Dickenses on 18 Oct, "Dr. Elliotson of the party played at games—politics the clergy &c".

[2] Christiana's parents arrived on 11 Oct and Mr Weller called at the Dickenses' on 12 Oct. He did not leave for Paris until 20 Oct, and he and Thompson "took an immense walk" with CD before the dinner on 18 Oct (Christiana's Diary; MS Mrs Sowerby).

[3] Altered to "Snitchey" in MS.

[4] The dialogue between the lawyer and Warden (pp. 146–50) remained unchanged.

[5] Britain, generally "Britain" or "Mr. Britain" in the MS of Parts I and II where the published text has "Benjamin", had also been called "John", but in the first part of Part III "John", and sometimes "Mr. Britain", is generally deleted in favour of "Tim", and on p. 42 of the MS (p. 144 of 1st edn) settles down as "Tim". (He is twice addressed as "Tim" on p. 131 and once on p. 132; corrected in the Charles Dickens edn.) Forster may have objected to "John Britain" as recalling the real John Britton—and later, to Tim as the name of Tiny Tim.

of whom the Doctor speaks in the first part. Martha is a better name.[1] What do you think of the concluding paragraph? Would you leave it for happiness' sake? It is merely experimental.[2] . . . I am flying to Geneva to-morrow morning.

To JOHN FORSTER, [20 OCTOBER 1846]

Extracts in F, v, iii, 431–2; 433–4. *Date:* 20 Oct according to Forster. *From* Geneva.

We came here yesterday, and we shall probably remain until Katey's birthday, which is next Thursday week. I shall fall to work on number three of *Dombey* as soon as I can. At present I am the worse for wear, but nothing like as much so as I expected to be on Sunday last. I had not been able to sleep for some time, and had been hammering away, morning, noon, and night. A bottle of hock on Monday,[3] when Elliotson dined with us (he went away homeward yesterday morning), did me a world of good; the change comes in the very nick of time; and I feel in Dombeian spirits already. . . . But I have still rather a damaged head, aching a good deal occasionally, as it is doing now, though I have not been cupped—yet. . . . I dreamed all last week that the *Battle of Life* was a series of chambers impossible to be got to rights or got out of, through which I wandered drearily all night. On Saturday night I don't think I slept an hour. I was perpetually roaming through the story, and endeavouring to dove-tail the revolution here into the plot. The mental distress, quite horrible.

You never would suppose from the look of this town that there had been anything revolutionary going on. Over the window of my old bedroom there is a great hole made by a cannon-ball in the house-front; and two of the bridges are under repair. But these are small tokens which anything else might have brought about as well. The people are all at work. The little streets are rife with every sight and sound of industry; the place is as quiet by ten o'clock as Lincoln's-inn-fields; and the only outward and visible sign of public interest in political events is a little group at every street corner, reading a public announcement from the new Government of the forthcoming election of state-officers, in which the people are reminded of their importance as a republican institution, and desired to bear in mind their dignity in all their proceedings. Nothing very violent or bad could go on with a community so well educated as this. It is the best antidote to American experiences, conceivable. As to the nonsense "the gentlemanly interest" talk about, their opposition to property and so forth, there never was such mortal absurdity. One of the principal leaders[4] in the late movement has a stock of watches and jewellery here of immense value—and had, during the disturbance—perfectly unprotected. James Fahzey[5] has a rich house and a

[1] "Sally" in the MS of Part I (p. 36, 1st edn), "Martha" in Part III.
[2] The final paragraph hinting at the eventual marriage of Marion and Michael Warden was allowed to stand, with only slight verbal changes. It includes a reference to CD's own age: "Time . . . with whom I have the pleasure of a personal acquaintance of some five-and-thirty years' duration".
[3] Thus in text, for "Sunday".
[4] Among other leaders were Léonard Gentin, François Janin (vice-president), and Balthasar Decrey.
[5] CD's error for "Fazy"; corrected in later edns.

valuable collection of pictures; and, I will be bound to say, twice as much to lose as half the conservative declaimers put together. This house, the liberal one, is one of the most richly furnished and luxurious hotels on the Continent.[1] And if I were a Swiss with a hundred thousand pounds, I would be as steady against the Catholic cantons and the propagation of Jesuitism as any radical among 'em: believing the dissemination of Catholicity to be the most horrible means of political and social degradation left in the world. Which these people, thoroughly well educated, know perfectly. ... The boys of Geneva were very useful in bringing materials for the construction of the barricades on the bridges; and the enclosed song[2] may amuse you. They sing it to a tune that dates from the great French revolution—a very good one.

To THOMAS BEARD, 21 OCTOBER 1846

MS Comtesse de Suzannet. *Address:* Angleterre. Affranchie. | Thomas Beard Esquire | 42 Portman Place | Edgeware Road | London.

Geneva. October Twenty First 1846.

My Dear Beard. Having run over here for a day or two, to escape from a headache consequent upon the completion of the Christmas Book, I take up my pen (I employ that phrase as a new one) to report myself alive and hearty. Also to report everybody else alive and hearty. Also to report that I mean to strike my encampment at Lausanne about the tenth or fifteenth of next month, and go to Paris, where I shall take a house, and where, if you will make holiday, and come and unbend that bow which is kept strung in Shoe Lane, you shall have your old welcome and everything else you like. *This is a thing that must be done*, so turn it over in your mind before I run over to England in December.

Dombey is a prodigious success. Enthusiastic bulletins reach me daily. I hope you get yours as of old, and like it.

There are two men standing under the balcony of the hotel in which I am writing, who are really good specimens, and have amused me mightily. An immense Frenchman, with a face like a bright velvet pincushion—and a very little Englishman, whose head comes up to about the middle of the Frenchman's waistcoat. They are travelling together. I saw them at Mont Blanc, months ago. The Englishman can't speak a word of French, but the Frenchman can speak a very little English, with which he helps the Englishman out of abysses and ravines of difficulty. The Englishman instead of being obliged by this, condescends, good humouredly, to correct the Frenchman's pronunciation—patronizes him—would pat him on the head, if he could reach so high—and screeches at his mistakes.—There he is now, staggering over the stones in his

---

[1] The Hotel de l'Ecu (founded 1560), ranked by Murray with the Hotel des Bergues, had been rebuilt by A. B. Reverdin in 1841. Many notabilities stayed there.

[2] Forster continues "while he thus was sending me his Gamin de Genève . . ." No song of this name has been traced; but there is a song, "Le Gamin de Paris", words by Frédéric de Courcy, music by Charles Plantade [?1840]. Forster probably invented the name from his recollection of the Paris song.

little boots, and falling up against a watchmaker's window, in perfect convulsions of joy, because the beaming Giant, without whom he couldn't get a single necessary of life, has made some mistake in the English language! I never saw such a fellow. The last time I met them was at the other end of the Lake by Chillon, disembarking from the steamer. It is done in little boats: the water being shallow, close in shore: and in the confusion, the Giant had got into one boat, and the dwarf in another. A hairy sailor on board the steamer found the Dwarf's great coat on deck, and gave a great roar to him; upon which the Dwarf, standing up in the boat, cried out (in English) "Put it down. Keep it. I shall be back in an hour." The hairy sailor of course not understanding one word of this, roared again and shook the coat in the air. "Oh you damned fool!" said the dwarf (still in English) "Oh you precious jackass! Put it down, will you?" The Giant, perceiving from the other boat what was the matter, cried out to the hairy sailor what it was necessary for him to know, and then called out to the Dwarf, "I have tell him to cap it." I thought the dwarf would have died with delight. "Oh my God!" he said to himself, "you're a nice man! Tell him to cap it, have you? Yes yes. Ha ha ha!—Cap it, indeed! Oh Lord!"—and never left off chuckling 'till he landed.

I don't know what demon brought them under the window, but I was going to tell you that there are no signs of the late revolution here, except a few excoriated house-fronts, knocked about by cannon-balls—and that everything is as busy and peaceful as before. I was going to be rather luminous too about the Daily News[1]—whose advertisement list don't seem to me to be brilliant—and to say that I'm afraid Dilke is hardly the man for Baldwin. But as I haven't room, and as my main object after all was only to say how heartily I am your old friend wherever I am, I will spare you the rest. Kate and Georgy (and Toby: who goes to school at a German's at Lausanne) send their best regards to yourself and all your house. And I am Ever My Dear Beard

Most Cordially Yours
CHARLES DICKENS

P.S. Pray remember me, particularly, to Baldwin. I was sorry to see he had had domestic sorrow.[2]

To T. N. TALFOURD, 21 OCTOBER 1846

Text from N, i, 801–2.

Geneva | Wednesday, October Twenty-First 1846

My Dear Talfourd,

I am very glad to hear that you all arrived at home safely, and that Frank received the great coat which the Brave Courier sent in quest of him.

[1] The *Daily News* proprietors launched an evening paper, *The Express*, at twopence, on 1 Sep 46. For their other difficulties, see *To* Forster, 26 Oct.

[2] The *Morning Herald* of 23 Sep 46 reported the death on 20 Sep of "Georgiana Ann, daughter of Charles Baldwin Esq., of Sussex-square, Hyde Park", and granddaughter of Edward Baldwin, Beard's editor.

The appointment of the new Judge I had seen in the newspapers. I dare say I felt very much as you did, on the subject—indignant and disappointed at first, but very soon reconciled to the thing. I had had very little doubt in my own mind, I confess, that if the Solicitor General were not the Judge, you would be,—as everybody knows you had a first claim to that distinction at the hands of the present Government,—and therefore I had an uncomfortable feeling when I saw Vaughan Richards' name.[1]

But my sources of consolation are these.—In the first place I sincerely believe you are happier at the Bar, in your high position there, than you would be on the Bench. Hoisted up to that small elevation, you would be lifted out of the reach of a vast number of means of daily pleasure and variety in which you have as keen an interest as any man alive, and which, to one of your generous tastes and sympathies, are worth all the ermine that ever grew since the deluge. Secondly (and more selfishly) I feel that the world of letters and fancy cannot afford to lose you: and that, however you might remain with it, and be true to it, as I know you would, even if you were a Judge, you are more its property as you are, and can show your feeling for it in a thousand little ways which would then be closed to you. It is a part of your graceful and enviable position at present that no Government going, gone, or to come, could enlarge its circle of various usefulness; but it might easily contract it, and I do not like to think that my small corner of it might be cramped—for literature wants such men as you, sorely. That is the way I make the best of the business.

There has been a revolution here, since you were at Lausanne, and a few houses have been knocked about by cannon balls. With that exception everything is as it was, and in perfect peace and order. Snow has fallen on the hills about Lausanne: and their white tops are a great improvement to the beauty of the scene.

Kate and her sister ask me to send all sorts of remembrances and loves to Mrs. Talfourd and Mary (and to Miss Ely too) in which I join as heartily as an honest gentleman may. I am delighted by all the news I hear of Dombey of course, and am resting now, for a few days, after finishing the Christmas Book. Toby is coming over here on Friday, to be presented with a watch for his quick picking-up of French.

Ever believe me | My dear Talfourd | Most affectionately Yours
[CHARLES DICKENS]

---

[1] CD has confused Robert Vaughan Richards, QC, who had died in July, with Edward Vaughan Williams, recently appointed to the vacant judgeship of the Court of the Queen's Bench; the *Daily News* (2 Oct) approved of the appointment, but also remarked (13 Oct) that the claims of others, including Talfourd, were still unrecognized. The Solicitor-General was David Dundas (1799–1877; *DNB*), appointed 10 July; there had been a rumour in Sep that he would be "raised to the Bench", thus creating a vacancy, and according to the *Morning Herald* (quoted in the *Daily News*, 26 Sep), the "universal voice of the profession" favoured Talfourd's appointment as Solicitor-General.

To BERNHARD TAUCHNITZ,[1] 21 OCTOBER 1846

Extract in Kurt Otto, *Der Verlag Bernhard Tauchnitz, 1837–1912*, Leipzig, 1912.

Rosemont, Lausanne, October 21st, 1846.

In reference to the conditions on which I should be disposed to sanction your republication of my new book *Dealings with the Firm of Dombey and Son*, I am quite at a loss how to answer your question, as I really do not know what it would be fair and reasonable to require from you. But I have every reason to rely upon your honourable intentions; and if you will do me the favour to state your own proposal, I have little doubt that I shall be willing to assent to it.

To DOUGLAS JERROLD, 24 OCTOBER 1846

MS Comtesse de Suzannet. *Address:* Angleterre. Affranchie. | Douglas Jerrold Esquire | West Lodge | Putney Heath | *near* | London.

Geneva. Saturday October Twenty Fourth 1846.

My Dear Jerrold. This day week, I finished my little Christmas Book (writing, towards the close, the exact words of a passage in your affectionate letter, received this morning: to wit "after all, life has something serious in it"),[2] and ran over here, for a week's rest. I cannot tell you how much true gratification I have had in your most hearty letter.[3] Forster told me that the same spirit breathed through a notice of Dombey in your paper:[4] and I have been saying since to Kate and Georgina that there is no such good way of testing the worth of a literary friendship as by comparing its influence on one's mind, with any that literary animosity can produce. Mr. Warren will throw me into a violent fit of anger for the moment, it is true—but his acts and deeds pass into the death of all bad things next day, and rot out of my memory.[5] Whereas a generous sympathy like yours, is ever present to me, ever fresh and new to me: always stimulating, cheerful, and delightful. The pain of unjust malice is lost in an hour. The pleasure of a generous friendship is the steadiest joy in the world. What a glorious and comfortable thing that is to think of!

[1] See Vol. III, p. 579*n*.

[2] Doctor Jeddler, a few pages before the end, says "It's a serious world, with all its folly".

[3] Jerrold wrote after a "long silence", with congratulations on *Dombey* No. I, and much other news; he regretted that a visit was impossible (see Walter Jerrold, *Douglas Jerrold*, [1914], pp. 443–6).

[4] *Douglas Jerrold's Weekly Newspaper*, 3 Oct 46, pp. 272–3; the review ends with "satisfaction . . . that whilst our author will again delight his tens of thousands, he will disappoint the few, the petty, envious minority, who carp at the best and hardest won success".

[5] Jerrold's letter said "you have rebuked and for ever 'put down' the small things, half knave, half fool, that love to *make* the failure they 'feed on' ". CD's reference is probably to Warren's review of *American Notes* in *Blackwood's*, Dec 42 (see Vol. III, p.412*n*). There were further attacks (also by Warren) in "Things in General" in *Blackwood's*, Nov 46, countered by Jerrold in his *Weekly Newspaper* of 7 Nov; he attributed personal as well as political hostility to the writer.

No, I *don't* get the paper regularly.[1] To the best of my recollection I have not had more than three numbers—certainly not more than four. But I knew how busy you must be, and had no expectation of hearing from you, until I wrote from Paris (as I intended doing) and implored you to come and make merry with us there. I am truly pleased to receive your good account of that enterprize.[2] I feel all you say upon the subject of the literary man in his old age,[3] and know the incalculable benefit of such a resource. You can hardly fail to realize an independent property from such success; and I congratulate you upon it, with all my heart and soul. Two numbers of the Barber's Chair[4] have reached me. It is a capital idea, and capable of the best and readiest adaptation to things as they arise. The number that ought to have come with the letter I am acknowledging, is brilliantly replaced by—*The Spectator*!!![5] There is a printed slip inside, from the Post Office, saying that the envelopes of a great many newspapers, being badly put on, have come off that evening: and they hope the Paper they forward me, may prove to be the right one, but don't much expect it. Of all the papers going, they couldn't have picked me out a more unlikely one.

Anent the Comic History of England and similar comicalities (Snobs in general, included) I feel exactly as you do.[6] Their effect upon me is very disagreeable. Such joking is like the sorrow of an undertaker's mute, reversed—and is applied to serious things with the like propriety and force. I have not seen A'Beckett's book,[7] however. Did you see an allusion to "discontented" writers in an advertisement of Mr. Albert Smith's, fashioned like an act of Parliament? There was an impertinence in it that rather stirred my bile.[8] If it has not met your eye, I wish you'd look at it. It was about Christopher Tadpole—some fortnight ago.

---

[1] *Douglas Jerrold's Weekly Newspaper*; first number published 18 July 46; "combined with a succinct summary of the week's news, both parliamentary and general, outspoken comments on men and affairs" (W. Jerrold, *op. cit.*, p. 436); successful for the first nine months. F. G. Tomlins was sub-editor, and Thomas Cooper the Chartist, Angus Reach, Henry Chorley, and Eliza Meteyard were regular contributors. Jerrold said "'tis forwarded to you and I hope arrives".

[2] Jerrold's letter said the first number "went off 18,000" and "every week it is steadily advancing".

[3] "This newspaper . . . is hard to work; but it is *independence* . . . I have a feeling of dread—a something almost insane in its abhorrence of the condition of the old, worn-out literary man . . . flung upon literary funds while alive, with the hat to be sent round for his coffin and his widow".

[4] This weekly editorial feature in dialogue began in the third number and continued to Mar 47, when Jerrold was absent in Guernsey.

[5] R. S. Rintoul (see Vol. I, p. 130n) was still editor, but the paper, once radical, had been Peelite for some years; its recent reviews of CD had not been favourable.

[6] Jerrold had written, "Some men would, I believe, write the Comic Sermon on the Mount. Think of a Comic History of England; the drollery of Alfred; the fun of Sir Thomas More in the Tower; the farce of his daughter begging the dead head . . ." Gilbert A' Beckett's *Comic History of England* had been appearing in monthly parts since July, and Thackeray's *Snobs of England* in *Punch* since 28 Feb (continuing to 27 Feb 47). Jerrold said he "[did] not very cordially agree with [*Punch's*] new spirit . . . the world will get tired (at least I hope so) of this eternal guffaw".

[7] *The Quizziology of the British Drama*, recently published at the *Punch* Office.

[8] "An Act for the Establishment of a New Periodical Story called 'Christopher Tadpole' ", published by Bentley, appeared in the "Dombey and Son Advertiser", No. I. Its final clause was directed against the "ponderous attempt" of other writers to improve social conditions and persuade "contented" readers of their wrongs, in-

The Manchester Soirée[1] has not come off, I suppose? I saw, in Galignani, that you were going. I wish I were going with you.—I have often thought, believe me, of your domestic troubles, and more than once asked Forster about your daughter.[2] It is a sad story my dear Jerrold, God knows, but that which is a part of your regret, makes it lighter to her. As long as she can like him, she will feel it gently. Your boy at Baring's[3] does well, I hope? And the elder,[4] how does *he* go on! My father told me he had left the Daily News. How does *that* go on, I wonder! What B and He call the "adds", look shy, I fear. And Dilke is rather weighty, generally speaking.

Paris is good, both in the Spring and in the winter. So come, first, at Christmas, and let us have a few jolly holidays together, at what Mr. Rowland, of Hatton Garden, calls "that festive season of the year", when the human hair is peculiarly liable to come out of curl, unless &c.[5] I hope to reach there, bag and baggage, by the 20th. of next month. As soon as I am lodged, I will write to you. *Do* arrange to run over at Christmas time, and let us be as English and as merry as we can. Its nothing of a journey, and you shall write "o'mornings", as they say in Modern Elizabethan, as much as you like. Perhaps Forster (having finished with Madame Tussaud)[6] will come at the same time. I'll stir him up. By the bye, I have stirred up my French, and have come out rather strong.

The Newspapers seem to know as much about Switzerland as about the Esquimaux Country. I should like to shew you the people as they are here, or in the Canton de Vaud—their wonderful education[7]—splendid schools—comfortable homes—great intelligence—and noble independence of character. It

stead of providing harmless amusement; this was said to be a mere fashion, now "on the wane".

[1] At the Athenaeum on 22 Oct; the *Manchester Guardian* mentioned Jerrold's inability to attend; the *Weekly Newspaper* had a leader on the Manchester Athenaeum on 31 Oct.

[2] Jane Matilda, *b.* 1825, Jerrold's elder daughter; married Henry Mayhew in 1844. In Mar 46 Mayhew was finally dismissed from *Punch*; his wife, who was "deeply attached to him", had constantly to deal with his creditors (M. H. Spielmann, *The History of "Punch"*, 1895, p. 268). He applied for a certificate in bankruptcy, and in the Bankruptcy Court on 11 Feb 47 (*The Times*, 12 Feb) his balance sheet showed debts contracted between July 43 and July 46 amounting to £2018; in 1846 he had received £200 from *Punch*, various smaller sums from other publications, and £100 as part-proprietor of the *Era*. His own counsel said that he had perhaps been "too sanguine in his hopes, and somewhat irregular in his accounts"; early in 1846, he

had taken a large house called the Shrubbery in Parson's Green and some of his debts were for the furnishings. He claimed that *Punch* owed him £200, since they had not given him a year's notice, and that Mark Lemon owed him £200 on account of dramatic pieces written in collaboration. "This debt was denied". CD had probably heard of these claims from Jerrold.

[3] Douglas Edmund, *b.* 1828; the employment was evidently not a success, as in 1850 Jerrold told Forster he was "rather of the stuff for the bush than the clerk's desk" (W. Jerrold, *op. cit.*, p. 539); in the Treasury 1851, and went to Canada 1852.

[4] Blanchard Jerrold; he was on the *Daily News* again by 1855.

[5] A reference to such advertisements of Rowland's Macassar as: "Christmas Festivities.—The gaiety that reigns supreme at this festive season . . . induces both sexes to be more than usually desirous of shining in personal attraction" (*Britannia*, 23 Dec 43).

[6] See *To* Macready, 24 Oct.

[7] Mügge praises the schools of Vaud in

is the fashion among the English to decry them, because they are not servile. I can only say that if the first quarter of a century of the best general Education would rear such a peasantry in Devonshire as exists about here, or about Lausanne, ('bating their disposition towards drunkenness) it would do what I can hardly hope in my most sanguine moods it will effect in four times that period. The revolution here just now (which has my cordial sympathy) was conducted with the most gallant, true, and Christian spirit. The conquering party, moderate in the first transports of triumph—forbearing—and forgiving. I swear to you that some of the appeals to the Citizens of both parties, posted by the new Government (the people's) on the walls, and sticking there now, almost drew the tears into my eyes as I read them; they are so truly generous, and so exalted in their tone—so far above the miserable strife of politics, and so devoted to the General Happiness and Welfare.

Kate and Georgy send their best regards. The latter small person was making me weak with laughter only last night, by imitating Mrs. Bradbury, in a manner quite inconceivable. We often talk of you, and project Parisian entertainments. There are only a few English (some dozen or so) at Lausanne, but very agreeable and well-informed people. I have had great success again in Magnetism—this time with a male subject.[1] Elliotson, who has been with us for a week or so, holds my magnetic powers in great veneration; and I really think they are, by some conjunction of chances, strong.

Let them, or something else, hold you to me by the heart. Ever My Dear Jerrold—Affectionately Your friend   CD.

To W. C. MACREADY, 24 OCTOBER 1846†

MS Morgan Library. Address: Angleterre Affranchie. | W. C. Macready Esquire | 5 Clarence Terrace | Regents Park | London.

Geneva. Saturday October Twenty Fourth 1846.

My Dear Macready.

The welcome sight of your handwriting, moves me, (though I have nothing to say) to shew you mine. And if I could recollect the passage in Virginius, I would paraphrase it, and say "Does it seem to tremble boy? Is it a loving autograph? Does it beam with friendship and affection?"—all of which I say, as I write, with—oh Heaven!—such a splendid imitation of you—and finally give you one of those grasps and shakes with which I have seen you make the young Icilius stagger again.[2]

particular; under the law of 1833, education was compulsory from the age of seven to sixteen, and there were 725 schools and 31,857 pupils in the canton by 1845. Teachers were adequately paid and pensioned (*Switzerland in 1847*, II, 250ff.). Jerrold was already well informed on Swiss education, as shown in the leader in his *Weekly Newspaper* of 1 Aug: "in thirteen out of their twenty-two cantons, every child is at school between the ages of seven and fifteen".

[1] In *To* de la Rue, 24 Mar 47, CD says "I magnetized a man at Lausanne among unbelievers, and stretched him on the dining-room floor"; perhaps when he had Elliotson to dinner on 18 Oct.

[2] CD is recalling Sheridan Knowles's *Virginius*, 1820, I, ii: "Stop, Icilius! Thou seest that hand ... Is it weak in thy embrace?" CD and Catherine saw Macready's *Virginius* on 13 May 39: see Vol. I, p. 548.

Here I am, running away from a bad head ache, as Tristram Shandy ran away from Death,[1] and lodging for a week in the Hotel de l'Ecu de Geneve, wherein there is a large mirror shattered by a Cannon-Ball in the late Revolution. A revolution, whatever its merits, achieved by free spirits, nobly generous and moderate, even in the first transports of victory—elevated by a splendid popular Education—and bent on Freedom from all tyrants, whether their crowns be shaven or golden. The Newspapers may tell you what they please. I believe there is no country on earth but Switzerland, in which a violent change could have been effected in the Christian spirit shewn in this place, or in the same proud, independent, gallant style. Not one halfpennyworth of property was lost, stolen, or strayed. Not one atom of party malice survived the smoke of the last gun. Nothing is expressed in the Government Addresses to the Citizens, but a regard for the general happiness, and injunctions to forget all animosities—which they are practically obeying at every turn, though the late Government (of whose spirit I had some little previous knowledge) *did* load the guns with such material as should occasion gangrene in the wounds, and though the wounded *do* die, consequently, every day, in the hospital, of sores that in themselves were nothing.

You a mountaineer! *You* examine (I have seen you do it) the point of your young son's baton de Montagne before he went up into the snow![2] And *you* talk of coming to Lausanne in March! Why, Lord love your heart, William Tell, times are changed since you lived at Altorf. There is not a Mountain pass, open, until June. The snow is closing in on all the panorama already. I was at the Great St. Bernard two months ago, and it was bitter cold and frosty then. Do you think I would let you hazard your life by going up any pass worth seeing, in bleak March? Never shall it be said that Dickens sacrificed his friend upon the altar of his hospitality! Onward! To Paris! [Cue for Band. Dickens points off with truncheon 1st Entrance. P.S. Page delivers gauntlets, on one knee. Dickens puts 'em on, and gradually falls into a fit of musing. Mrs. Dickens lays her hand upon his shoulder. Business. Procession. Curtain.][3]

*a*I had a letter from Jerrold this morning, in which he tells me that Madame Tussaud[4] intends to do Forster next, as Kitely (in consequence of the success that has attended you as Coriolanus) and that he is to be put next Burke, in the Chamber of Horrors. Tell Mrs. Macready with my love. I know it will make her laugh.*a*

It is a great pleasure to me, my Dear Macready, to hear from yourself, as I had previously heard from Forster, that you are so well pleased with Dombey.

---

[1] Book VII, Chs 1–2.

[2] CD had probably first seen Macready in Knowles's *William Tell*, 1825, in 1838; in II, i, Tell is sending his son into the mountains and says "Shew me thy staff. Art sure | O' the point? I think 'tis loose. No—stay!" "The rough and hardy mountaineer" was one of Macready's most famous parts, and became "identified with the performer's voice, look, action, and manner; and not to see Macready in

William Tell would be like seeing *Hamlet* without Hamlet" (*Theatrical Journal*, 10 May 45).

[3] The brackets are CD's.

aa; bb; cc Not previously published.

[4] Macready (as Coriolanus) was one of the specially advertised additions to Madam Tussaud's exhibition in the summer of 46. Jerrold's joke is against Forster's imitation of Macready's Kitely, as well as his self-importance and appearance.

Which is evidently a great success, and a great hit, thank God! I felt that Mrs. Brown[1] was strong, but I was not at all afraid of giving as heavy a blow as I could to a piece of hot iron that lay ready at my hand. For that is my principle always—and I hope to come down with some heavier sledge-hammers than that.

I know the Lady Walpole[2] of whom you write. Smythe[3] left here, only yester-day. The story may arise only in her manner, which is extraordinarily free and careless. He was visiting her here, when I was here last—three weeks ago. I knew her in Italy. It is not her fault, if Scandal ever leaves her alone, for such a Braver of all conventionalities never wore petticoats. But I should be sorry to hear there was anything guilty in her conduct. She is very clever—really learned —very pretty—much neglected by her husband—and only four and twenty years of age.

*b*You may well be ashamed of your eight children—I don't wonder at your sometimes talking of flight to America. I have been very successful again, in the Animal Magnetic way, at Lausanne. A married English Lady there, was asking me the other night if I thought that influence might be exerted, in time, for lessening the pain which ladies suffer, who love their Lords. I implored her, for Heaven's sake, never to hint at the possibility of that operation being made more easy, or I didn't know what I myself,[4] but mainly some of my friends (I meant you and Mrs. Macready) might come to! And my opinion is—now—at twelve o'Clock—in the grave and sober light of noon—that you'll make that eight, eighteen, before you're done.

Well! Heaven preserve us from evil influences!*b* Kate and Georgy send their best loves to Mrs. and Miss Macready, and all your house. *c*And as to me, I'll forgive you anything—short of eight and twenty—and remain through all*c* your Most affectionate friend   CD.

To JOHN FORSTER, [26–29 OCTOBER 1846]

Extracts in F, v, vi, 434; vi, ii, 478; v, vi, 434–5, 436–7, 437, 435; v, v, 425. *Date:* first two extracts 26 Oct according to Forster; third extract, letter resumed "two days later"; fourth extract 28 Oct, and fifth and sixth extracts 29 Oct according to Forster; last extract probably same letter, as CD comments on Forster's reply to his letter of ?11 Oct, which he would find on return to Lausanne. *From* Geneva (26, 28 Oct) and Lausanne (29 Oct).

In reference to that *Daily News* revolution,[5] I have been walking and wandering

---

[1] She first appears in Ch. 6 (No. II, published 31 Oct); Macready had evidently been lent the proof to read.

[2] Name omitted in MDGH and later edns.

[3] Name omitted in MDGH and later edns. Probably George Smythe, later Viscount Strangford (1818–57; *DNB*); known to have been in Italy 1846; a Young Englander, and one of several claimants to be the "original" of Disraeli's Coningsby. Called on Charlotte Brontë at Haworth with the Ferrands and Lord John Manners in 1850; she found him "not so distin-guished-looking, shy and a little queer" (*The Brontes, their Lives, Friendships and Correspondence*, ed. J. Symington and T. J. Wise, 1932, III, 149).

[4] Sydney Smith Haldimand was born 18 Apr 47; CD had thought the pregnancy "a false alarm" in Aug 46 (*To* de la Rue, 24 Mar 47).

[5] Forster had sent him "news of a sudden change in Whitefriars". The *Daily News*

all day through a perfect Miss Burney's Vauxhall[1] of conjectural dark walks. Heaven send you enlighten me fully on Wednesday, or number three will suffer!

A week of perfect idleness has brought me round again—idleness so rusting and devouring, so complete and unbroken, that I am quite glad to write the heading of the first chapter of number three to-day. I shall be slow at first, I fear, in consequence of that change of the plan. But I allow myself nearly three weeks[2] for the number; designing, at present, to start for Paris on the 16th of November. Full particulars in future bills. Just going to bed. I think I can make a good effect, on the after story, of the feeling created by the additional number before Paul's death.

Beginning his journey back to Lausanne: I am in a great state of excitement on account of your intelligence, and desperately anxious to know all about it. I shall be put out to an unspeakable extent if I don't find your letter awaiting me. God knows there has been small comfort for either of us in the *D. N.*'s nine months.

I wonder whether you foresaw the end of the Christmas book! There are two or three places in which I can make it prettier, I think, by slight alterations. . . . I trust to Heaven you may like it. What an affecting story I could have made of it in one octavo volume. Oh to think of the printers transforming my kindly cynical old father into Doctor Taddler![3]

On returning to Rosemont: Do you think it worth while, in the illustrations, to throw the period back at all for the sake of anything good in the costume? The story may have happened at any time within a hundred years. Is it worth having coats and gowns of dear old Goldsmith's day? or thereabouts?[4] I really don't know what to say. The probability is, if it has not occurred to you or to the artists, that it is hardly worth considering; but I ease myself of it by throwing it out to you. It may be already too late, or you may see reason to think it best to "stick to the *last*" (I feel it necessary to italicize the joke), and abide by the ladies' and gentlemen's spring and winter fashions of this time. Whatever you think best, in this as in all other things, is best, I am sure. . . . I would go, in the illustrations, for "beauty" as much as possible; and I should like each part to have a general illustration to it at the beginning, shadowing out its drift and bearing:[5]

had not sufficient capital to compete with the Indian and other services of *The Times*, and on about 21 Oct their arrangement to share expenses with the *Herald* was ended. The proprietors accordingly passed a resolution authorizing Dilke to raise the price to 3*d*. Forster resisted this and on 22 Oct decided to resign; Fox (who thought the proprietors were "playing a very shabby trick upon the public") followed a few days later (Macready, *Diaries*, II, 347–8; R. Garnett, *Life of W. J. Fox*, p. 284). The change of price was announced on 28 Oct and attributed to the defection of the *Herald*.

[1] In *Evelina*.

[2] According to Forster (F, v, vi, 441), he finished on 9 Nov, some days earlier than he expected.

[3] Jeddler, in the *Battle of Life*; CD may by now have seen a proof of the first and second parts. "Jeddler", in CD's hand, often looks like "Taddler".

[4] Late 18th-century costume was used in the illustrations.

[5] Each part begins with an illustration which anticipates the action, but not by allegorical "shadowing"—unless the rider thrown from his horse in Doyle's illustration opening Part II is to be so understood.

much as Browne goes at that kind of thing on *Dombey* covers. I don't think I should fetter your discretion in the matter farther. The better it is illustrated, the better I shall be pleased of course.

I certainly am very glad of the result of the *Daily News* business, though my gladness is dashed with melancholy to think that you should have toiled there so long, to so little purpose. I escaped more easily. However, it is all past now.... As to the undoubted necessity of the course you took, I have not a grain of question in my mind.[1] That, being what you are, you had only one course to take and have taken it, I no more doubt than that the Old Bailey is not Westminster Abbey. In the utmost sum at which you value yourself, you were bound to leave; and now you *have* left, you will come to Paris, and there, and at home again, we'll have, please God, the old kind of evenings and the old life again, as it used to be before those daily nooses caught us by the legs and sometimes tripped us up. Make a vow (as I have done) never to go down that court with the little news-shop at the corner, any more,[2] and let us swear by Jack Straw as in the ancient times. ... I am beginning to get over my sorrow for your nights up aloft in Whitefriars, and to feel nothing but happiness in the contemplation of your enfranchisement. God bless you!

[1] Forster's long letter to Paxton on 9 Dec shows that the decision had not been easy, and demonstrates the cordiality of their personal relationship. After his resignation he had received from Paxton a "kind present", but delayed writing in the hope of seeing him; Paxton (who had been abroad) then wrote, and Forster immediately replied: "Your letter ... contains no expression of regret, or generous regard, that I do not most earnestly desire to reciprocate —with interest were it possible. | I had no anxiety so great in the late change as that *you* should thoroughly understand the motives which compelled me to it—and all the circumstances which (as I conceived) left me no alternative. These things are ill explained in letters—and most imperfectly in those which I presume you have seen. But I have hoped that our friends in Whitefriars, Messrs. Bradbury & Evans, would make all clear to you. | For the days to which you refer can never pass from my memory—and as long as I remember them, I must remember those qualities in your character which impressed me so much and made me resolve (if I could) to retain always your friendship and esteem. | It was a great sacrifice the step I took; and the most regretted of any of my life. You would smile if I told you the strange kind of *blank* my existence has since been. The reaction from what had become in some sort a part of me—seems to have left me without the least power of steadily encountering new duties. Yet—while I cannot help rejoicing in the success of which you tell me—I cannot regret to have acted as I did; or think I could do differently, were it to do again. | Let me feel at all events that nothing can intercept our mutual regard and friendly intercourse. It was no small consolation to me, throughout all the circumstances of the late change, that you were in no respect, even indirectly, mixed up with them. I have no association with you in this paper which I am not proud and happy to retain ... When [the] day arrives, of reward and compensation for all the trouble and trial you have undergone —it will not lessen my happiness in it, to have my name connected with the trial rather than with the triumph". He concluded by thanking Paxton for his invitation to Chatsworth, which he would have accepted at once but for his "promise to go early in January to Paris, to pass some little time with Mr Dickens" (MS Devonshire Collections).

[2] Pleydell St, Fleet St; Thomas Britton recalled the shop, "a tobacconists', with the *Daily News* exposed for sale ... kept by Mrs. Burton, formerly an actress" (*The "Daily News" Jubilee*, p. 11).

Continuing his joke about public readings: I don't think you have exercised your usual judgment in taking Covent–garden for me. I doubt it is too large for my purpose. However, I shall stand by whatever you propose to the proprietors.

To JOHN FORSTER, [31 OCTOBER 1846]

Extracts in F, v, vi, 437–8; vi, ii, 478. *Date:* first extract 31 Oct, and second "five . . . days" after 26 Oct according to Forster.

I only write to say that it is of no use my writing at length, until I have heard from you; and that I will wait until I shall have read your promised communication (as my father would call it) to-morrow. I have glanced over the proofs of the last part and really don't wonder, some of the most extravagant mistakes occurring in Clemency's account to Warden,[1] that the marriage of Grace and Alfred should seem rather unsatisfactory to you. Whatever is done about that must be done with the lightest hand, for the reader MUST take something for granted; but I think it next to impossible, without dreadful injury to the effect, to introduce a scene between Marion and Michael. The introduction must be in the scene between the sisters, and must be put, mainly, into the mouth of Grace.[2] Rely upon it there is no other way, in keeping with the spirit of the tale. With this amendment, and a touch here and there in the last part (I know exactly where they will come best), I think it may be pretty and affecting, and comfortable too. . . .

I am at work at *Dombey* with good speed, thank God.[3] All well here. Country stupendously beautiful. Mountains covered with snow. Rich crisp weather. *But he found the illustrations in No. II*[4] *so* dreadfully bad *that they made him* curl his legs up.

To JOHN FORSTER, [?OCTOBER–NOVEMBER 1846]

Extract in F, IV, iii, 322. *Date:* "from Switzerland" according to Forster; and probably after publication of *Dombey* No. I (see *fn*).

My feeling about the —— is the feeling common, I suppose, to three fourths of the reflecting part of the community in our happiest of all possible countries;

---

[1] *Battle*, p. 141; the MS is much congested with deletion and interlineation. The proofs do not survive, but the published text shows that hardly any corrections had been made.

[2] This was not done; but something of the desired effect was gained by the large addition to the scene between Alfred and Grace, p. 152 (from "He had not become a great man") to p. 156, none of which is in the MS.

[3] On No. III (Chs 8–10): see *To* Forster, ?26–29 Oct and 4 Nov. The MS suggests that, after some difficulty over the opening, it was written with ease.

[4] CD had proofs by 10 Oct; this might be an advance copy of No. II, published 31 Oct. Christiana Thompson "got the 2nd no of Dombey & Son" from CD on 29 Oct (Diary, MS Mrs Sowerby). The illustrations were "The Christening Party" and "Polly rescues the Charitable Grinder"; the figure of Florence is poorly drawn in the former, but there is no obvious fault in the latter, a spirited crowd scene, if perhaps with too much emphasis on the "wild confusion" described in the text.

and that is, that it is better to suffer a great wrong than to have recourse to the much greater wrong of the law.[1] I shall not easily forget the expense, and anxiety, and horrible injustice of the *Carol* case, wherein, in asserting the plainest right on earth, I was really treated as if I were the robber instead of the robbed. Upon the whole, I certainly would much rather NOT proceed. What do you think of sending in a grave protest against what has been done in this case, on account of the immense amount of piracy to which I am daily exposed, and because I have been already met in the Court of Chancery with the legal doctrine that silence under such wrongs barred my remedy: to which Talfourd's written opinion might be appended as proof that we stopped under no discouragement. It is useless to affect that I don't know I have a morbid susceptibility of exasperation, to which the meanness and badness of the law in such a matter would be stinging in the last degree. And I know of nothing that *could* come, even of a successful action, which would be worth the mental trouble and disturbance it would cost.

To JOHN FORSTER, [?OCTOBER–NOVEMBER 1846]

Extract in F, v, iv, 418. Date: Reference to snow suggests Oct–Nov.

There are two old ladies (English) living here who may serve me for a few lines of gossip—as I have intended they should, over and over again, but I have always forgotten it. There were originally four old ladies, sisters, but two of them have faded away in the course of eighteen years, and withered by the side of John Kemble[2] in the cemetery. They are very little, and very skinny; and each of them wears a row of false curls, like little rolling-pins, so low upon her brow, that there is no forehead; nothing above the eyebrows but a deep horizontal wrinkle, and then the curls. They live upon some small annuity. For thirteen years they have wanted very much to move to Italy, as the eldest old lady says the climate of this part of Switzerland doesn't agree with her, and preys upon her spirits; but they have never been able to go, because of the difficulty of moving "the books." This tremendous library belonged once upon a time to the father of these old ladies, and comprises about fifty volumes.[3] I have never been able to see what they are, because one of the old ladies always sits before them; but they look, outside

---

[1] Forster introduces this extract, which he places with his account of the *Carol* piracy, by saying that CD suffered a "repetition" of the same wrong "in so gross a form that proceedings were again advised by Talfourd and others". No early piracy of *Dombey* is known; it is just possible that CD had in mind "Pickwick Married" included in G. W. M. Reynolds's *Master Timothy's Bookcase*, first issued 1842, but again in 1846–7 in weekly penny Nos and monthly sixpenny parts, published by James Gilbert and advertised in *Dombey* No. 1 but not in later Nos.

[2] Rogers in his letter to Catherine of 20 Oct (see *To* Rogers, 27 Aug 46, *fn*) recalled

his visits to Kemble: "he lies very near you now in the Cemetery above the town"; Rogers had sat for "many an hour in his Garden over the Lake . . . by moonlight", with Kemble and his sister Mrs Siddons. Kemble was inclined to be jealous of Mont Blanc, and "could not endure the constant references" to it.

[3] The old ladies were the Miss Forbeses of *To* de Cerjat, 27 Nov 46. Mrs Watson, when staying in Lausanne in 1835 (before her marriage), met "les dames Forbes regular old maids"; later, "Miss Forbes brought me a Catalogue of their Library to choose out of" (MS Commander Michael Saunders Watson).

like very old backgammon-boards. The two deceased sisters died in the firm persuasion that this precious property could never be got over the Simplon without some gigantic effort to which the united family was unequal. The two remaining sisters live, and will die also, in the same belief. I met the eldest (evidently drooping) yesterday, and recommended her to try Genoa. She looked shrewdly at the snow that closes up the mountain prospect just now, and said that when the spring was quite set in, and the avalanches were down, and the passes well open, she would certainly try that place, if they could devise any plan, in the course of the winter, for moving "the books." The whole library will be sold by auction here, when they are both dead, for about a napoleon; and some young woman will carry it home in two journeys with a basket.

To T. J. THOMPSON, [3 NOVEMBER 1846]

MS Mrs Sowerby. *Date:* clearly Tues 3 Nov, the day of Elizabeth Thompson's birth.

Rosemont. | Tuesday Morning.

My Dear Thompson.

All kinds of hearty and cordial congratulations on the event.[1] We are all delighted that it is, at last, well over. There is an uncertainty attendant on Angelic Strangers (as Miss Tox says)[2] which it is a great relief to have so happily disposed of.

Ever Yours

T. J. Thompson Esquire.   CHARLES DICKENS

To JOHN FORSTER, [4 NOVEMBER 1846]

Extracts in F, v, vi, 438; VI, ii, 478; 479. *Date:* first and third extracts 4 Nov according to Forster; second extract "four days" after 31 Oct.

I shall hope to touch upon the Christmas book as soon as I get your opinion. I wouldn't do it without. I am delighted to hear of noble old Stanny.[3] Give my love to him, and tell him I think of turning Catholic. It strikes me (it may have struck you perhaps) that another good place for introducing a few lines of dialogue, is at the beginning of the scene between Grace and her husband, where he speaks about the messenger at the gate.[4]

---

[1] Elizabeth Southerden Thompson (1846 –1933; *DNB*) was born "at 13½ past two in the morning" of 3 Nov (Christiana Thompson's Diary, MS Mrs Sowerby). She became a well-known painter and married Sir William Francis Butler in 1877.

[2] Miss Tox's pincushion bears the device, "Welcome little Dombey"; "Welcome, Master Dombey" would have been more congenial to her feelings, "But the uncertainty attendant on angelic strangers, will, I hope, excuse what must otherwise appear an unwarrantable familiarity" (Ch. I).

[3] His agreement to supply three illustrations; they are "War" and "Peace" in Part I, and "The Nutmeg Grater" in Part III—"three morsels of English landscape which had a singular charm for Dickens" (F, v, vi, 439).

[4] See *To* Forster, ?31 Oct, *fn*; much more than "a few lines" were added.

Sending the first chapter[1] *of No. III:* The best subject for Browne will be at Mrs. Pipchin's; and if he liked to do a quiet odd thing, Paul, Mrs. Pipchin, and the Cat, by the fire, would be very good for the story. I earnestly hope he will think it worth a little extra care. The second subject,[2] in case he shouldn't take a second from that same chapter, I will shortly describe as soon as I have it clearly (to-morrow or next day), and send it to *you* by post.

I hope to finish the number by next Tuesday or Wednesday.[3] It is hard writing under these bird-of-passage circumstances, but I have no reason to complain, God knows, having come to no knot yet. . . . I hope you will like Mrs. Pipchin's establishment. It is from the life, and I was there—I don't suppose I was eight years old; but I remember it all as well, and certainly understood it as well, as I do now.[4] We should be devilish sharp in what we do to children. I thought of that passage in my small life, at Geneva. *a*Shall I leave you my life in MS. when I die?[5] There are some things in it that would touch you very much, and that might go on the same shelf with the first volume of Holcroft's.*a*[6]

---

[1] Ch. 8.

[2] "Captain Cuttle consoles his Friend" from Ch. 9.

[3] He was halfway through on 4 Nov, and finished on Mon 9 Nov, having written Chs 9 and 10 in five days, which Forster calls "marvellously rapid" (F, v, vi, 441).

[4] Writing of the period after Mrs Dickens and the younger children had joined John Dickens in the Marshalsea and CD was working at the blacking warehouse, he says: "I (small Cain that I was, except that I had never done harm to any one) was handed over as a lodger to a reduced old lady, long known to our family, in Little-college-street, Camden-town, who took children in to board, and had once done so at Brighton; and who, with a few alterations and embellishments, unconsciously began to sit for Mrs. Pipchin in *Dombey* when she took in me" (F, I, ii, 27, quoting CD's fragment of autobiography). Elsewhere, obviously drawing on the same fragment, Forster gives her name as Mrs Elizabeth Roylance, and "Mrs. Roylance" appears in the number plans for *Dombey*, No. II. According to F. G. Kitton (quoted by Ley, F, I, ii, 36*n*) the Rate-book of 1824 shows an "Elizabeth Raylace" living at No. 37 (rated at 1s), and the name Roylance "is still well known in the neighbourhood". The Dickenses are said to have lodged with her after leaving the Marshalsea in 1824. There is no evidence from as early a date as CD suggests in this letter, but in "New Year's Day" (*All the Year Round*, 1 Jan 59; *Miscellaneous Papers*, p. 652), recalling a period when he was

evidently about six years old, he gives the name Mrs Pipchin to the grim old lady who took him to the Soho Bazaar; and Charles Barrow is said to have taken refuge in her house at Brighton some time between 1810 and 1819: see W. J. Carlton, "Links with Dickens in the Isle of Man", *Journal of the Manx Museum*, VI (1958).

aa Printed in italics in F, 1872–4, II, xvi, 327, presumably because underlined by Forster.

[5] The dates given or implied by Forster for the writing of the autobiographical fragment seem to vary from 1845 to 1849, but are not necessarily inconsistent; the writing was probably spread over several years, the intention perhaps being formed early and the writing first seen by Forster "in its connected shape" on 20 Jan 49 (F, I, i, 11*n*; cf. VI, vi, 521). This implies that he had seen pieces of it earlier, often, no doubt, in letters; early memories appear in several of the letters from abroad. In *Dombey*, some of the Camden Town scenes as well as Mrs Pipchin may be partly "from the life".

[6] Thomas Holcroft (1745–1809; *DNB*) wrote the account of his early life which forms Book I of his *Memoirs*, completed by Hazlitt and published in 1816, shortly before his death. It carries the account to the end of his fifteenth year, includes some very early recollections, and emphasizes his sense of the change in his family's fortunes when he was only six; his father, a shoemaker and horse-dealer in Leicester Square, sold his horses and moved to the

To JOHN FORSTER, [7 NOVEMBER 1846]

Extracts in F, v, vi, 441; 438–9. *Date:* 7 Nov according to Forster.

He was in the agonies *of the last chapter of* Dombey *No. III.*

On the Battle of Life: Before I reply to your questions I wish to remark generally of the third part that all the passion that can be got into it, through my interpretation at all events, is there. I know that, by what it cost me; and I take it to be, as a question of art and interest, in the very nature of the story that it *should* move at a swift pace after the sisters are in each other's arms again.[1] Anything after that would drag like lead, and must. . . . Now for your questions. I don't think any little scene with Marion and anybody can prepare the way for the last paragraph of the tale: I don't think anything but a printer's line *can* go between it and Warden's speech.[2] A less period than ten years? Yes. I see no objection to six.[3] I have no doubt you are right. Any word from Alfred in his misery? Impossible: you might as well try to speak to somebody in an express train. The preparation for his change is in the first part, and he kneels down beside her in that return scene. He is left alone with her, as it were, in the world. I am quite confident it is wholly impossible for me to alter that.[4] . . . BUT (keep your eye on me) when Marion went away, she left a letter for Grace in which she charged her to encourage the love that Alfred would conceive for her, and FOREWARNED her that years would pass before they met again, &c. &c. This coming out in the scene between the sisters, and something like it being expressed in the opening of the little scene between Grace and her husband before the messenger at the gate, will make (I hope) a prodigious difference;[5] and I will try to put in something with Aunt Martha and the Doctor which shall carry the tale back more distinctly and unmistakeably to the battle-ground. I hope to make these alterations[6] next week, and to send the third part back to you before I leave here. If you think it can still be improved after that, say so to me in Paris and I will go at it again. I wouldn't have it limp, if it can fly. I say nothing to you of a great deal of this being already expressed in the sentiment of the beginning, because your delicate

country, and then was for five years a pedlar, travelling all over the country with his wife and child; these itinerant years contain details possibly recalled by CD in *Old Curiosity Shop.* Holcroft too was a precocious reader but with little education; at 12 he became a stable-boy, at 15 a shoemaker, and later a strolling player, beginning his literary career only in early middle age. CD admired his *Narrative* of the Gordon Riots (published under the pseudonym of "William Vincent") and made considerable use of it in *Barnaby Rudge.*

[1] p. 159; the story ends on p. 175. The MS shows that CD made certain additions in proof, but not of the kind Forster evidently wanted.

[2] In the 1st edn the final illustration of the two sisters (by Maclise) makes the

necessary break, the last paragraph standing by itself on the facing page.

[3] This is the period mentioned several times in Part III, including Warden's final speech; the MS had "ten" throughout.

[4] It was not altered.

[5] No addition was made to the scene between the sisters, but the addition at pp. 152–6 includes the account of the letter (pp. 154–5) as specified here. There is an added passage of dialogue between the Doctor and Aunt Martha (pp. 165–6).

[6] Dr Jeddler's speech (p. 167) was lengthened by the addition of a general reference to "a world on which the sun never rises, but it looks upon a thousand bloodless battles that are some set-off against the miseries and wickedness of Battle-Fields".

perception knows all that already. Observe for the artists. Grace will now only have *one child*—little Marion.[1]. . . . (*At night, on same day*) . . . You recollect that I asked you to read it all together, for I knew that I was working for that? But I have no doubt of *your* doubts, and will do what I have said. . . . I had thought of marking the time[2] in the little story, and will do so. . . . Think, once more, of the period between the second and third parts. I will do the same.

To WILLIAM HALDIMAND, [8 NOVEMBER 1846]*

MS Bibliothèque Cantonale et Universitaire, Lausanne. *Date:* clearly the Sunday before returning the proofs of *Battle:* see *To* Forster, ?13 Nov.

Rosemont. | Sunday Night

My Dear Haldimand.

Here you have (in an odiously loose and erratic form—"slips", these things which look like tailor's measures, are called technically) the two first parts of the most private and confidential of stories. I am going over the third, with a view to some little emendation. It will be ready for you, I hope, when you are ready for it.

You will recognize a word or two, and a sentiment or two, in the first part (I shouldn't wonder) which have a flavor of Lausanne and a certain dinner party there.

Ever Yours Cordially

William Haldimand Esquire.   CHARLES DICKENS

To M. DOR, 12 NOVEMBER 1846*

MS Bibliothèque Publique et Universitaire, Geneva. *Address:* À Monsieur: | Monsr. D'Or.

Rosemont. Thursday Morning | Twelfth November 1846.

Dear Sir

I am very glad to hear that you are so kind as to purpose going to the prison tomorrow. As I intend taking Mr. Thompson to the Blind Asylum[3] first, I will appoint half past One, if convenient to you, for meeting—say at the English Library.[4]

Faithfully Yours

à Monsieur | Monr. D'Or.[5]   CHARLES DICKENS

[1] The "daughter" referred to on p. 152 was "two . . . daughters" in the MS. She appears only in Doyle's illustration at the beginning of Part III. The artists had probably not yet begun; Leech was getting to work on 12 Nov and had not finished on 23 Nov. (Leech *to* Forster; MS Forster Collection, V & A).

[2] In the MS the period of the story is not specified; "about a hundred years ago" on p. 10 (sixth paragraph) was evidently added in proof: see *To* Forster, ?26–29 Oct.

[3] Forster says that before CD left Lau- sanne the blind, deaf and dumb youth he had seen on his first visit to the Asylum (see *To* Forster, ?12 July 46 and *fn*), "had been taught to say, 'Monsieur Dickens m'a donné les cigares,' and at their leavetaking his gratitude was expressed by incessant repetition of these words for a full half- hour" (F, v, ii, 399).

[4] Probably the "excellent *reading-room* (Cassino)" recommended in Murray's *Handbook*.

[5] Thus in MS.

To JOHN FORSTER, [13 NOVEMBER 1846]

Extracts in F, v, vi, 439, 441, 440–1. *Date:* first extract 13 Nov according to Forster; second extract from "his last letter but one"; third extract near the time of his departure, therefore probably same letter.

Returning the proofs of the Battle of Life: I hope you will think the third part (when you read it in type with these amendments) very much improved. I think it so[1]. If there should still be anything wanting, in your opinion, pray suggest it to me in Paris. I am bent on having it right, if I can. . . . If in going over the proofs you find the tendency to blank verse[2] (I *cannot* help it, when I am very much in earnest) too strong, knock out a word's brains here and there.

We have had some tremendous hurricanes at Lausanne. It is an extraordinary place now for wind, being peculiarly situated among mountains—between the Jura, and the Simplon, St. Gothard, St. Bernard, and Mont Blanc ranges; and at night you would swear (lying in bed) you were at sea. You cannot imagine wind blowing so, over earth. It is very fine to hear. The weather generally, however, has been excellent. There is snow on the tops of nearly all the hills, but none has fallen in the valley. On a bright day, it is quite hot between eleven and half past two. The nights and mornings are cold. For the last two or three days, it has been thick weather; and I can see no more of Mont Blanc from where I am writing now than if I were in Devonshire-terrace, though last week it bounded all the Lausanne walks. I would give a great deal that you could take a walk with me about Lausanne on a clear cold day. It is impossible to imagine anything more noble and beautiful than the scene; and the autumn colours in the foliage are more brilliant and vivid now than any description could convey to you. I took Elliotson, when he was with us, up to a ravine I had found out in the hills eight hundred or a thousand feet deep! Its steep sides dyed bright yellow, and deep red, by the changing leaves; a sounding torrent roaring down below; the lake of Geneva lying at its foot; one enormous mass and chaos of trees at its upper end; and mountain piled on mountain in the distance, up into the sky! He really was struck silent by its majesty and splendour.

He now, in a less romantic and more homely contemplation of the picture, *began to think of the advantages of Paris*. I have no doubt that constant change, too, is indispensable to me when I am at work: and at times something more than a doubt will force itself upon me whether there is not something in a Swiss valley that disagrees with me. Certainly, whenever I live in Switzerland again, it shall be on the hill-top. Something of the *goître* and *crétin* influence seems to settle on my spirits sometimes, on the lower ground. How sorry, ah yes! how sorry I shall be to leave the little society nevertheless. We have been thoroughly good-humoured and agreeable together, and I'll always give a hurrah for the Swiss and Switzerland.

---

[1] CD read the *Battle* to the Watsons when they dined with him on 12 Nov. "We are all inclined to think it the most poetical, and refined of all his works. He read it with wonderful charm, and spirit. Lavinia was quite overcome by it" (Watson's Diary; MS Commander Michael Saunders Watson).

[2] CD was perhaps more sensitive about this tendency since Horne's essay: see *To* C. Watson, 25 Apr 44, *fn.*

To T. J. THOMPSON, 13 NOVEMBER 1846*

MS Mrs Sowerby. *Address:* T. J. Thompson Esquire | Clermont.

Rosemont. | Friday Night 13th. Novr. 1846.

My Dear Thompson

I am very sorry to say that we are already engaged (to dine with Haldimand) on Sunday[1]—but if tomorrow would suit you equally well, we should be delighted.

It is so possible that your domestic arrangements might not be available (under the circumstances) for this substitution, that I shall not consider it "on", unless I hear from you to that effect.[2]

I can't write to night, I find. My hand will *not* make the letters.

Ever Faithfully | (With all kinds of remembrances)

T. J. Thompson Esquire.

CHARLES DICKENS

To JOHN FORSTER, [15 or 16 NOVEMBER 1846]

Extract in F, v, vi, 441–2. *Date:* after the final dinner at Haldimand's on 15 Nov: either late that night or early morning on day of departure.

He had said goodbye to his deaf, dumb, and blind friends, and was yet more terribly down in the mouth *at taking leave of his hearing, speaking, and seeing friends.* I shall see you soon, please God, and that sets all to rights. But I don't believe there are many dots on the map of the world where we shall have left such affectionate remembrances behind us, as in Lausanne. It was quite miserable this last night, when we left them at Haldimand's.[3]

To JOHN FORSTER, [21 NOVEMBER 1846]

Extracts in F, v, iii, 439; VI, ii, 479. *Date:* first extract 21 Nov according to Forster; second extract clearly same letter, as Forster says CD "wrote by return". *From* Paris.

Your Christmas book illustration-news makes me jump for joy.[4] I will write you at length to-morrow. I should like this dedication: This Christmas Book is

---

[1] The Watsons also dined there "to meet the Dickens who leave tomorrow to our great grief" (Watson's Diary, 15 Nov; MS Commander Michael Saunders Watson).

[2] "The Dickens came to dinner" (Christiana Thompson's Diary, 14 Nov; MS Mrs Sowerby).

[3] See *To* Thompson, 13 Nov, *fn*: Watson's diary entry continues: "It is impossible to describe the feelings of regard, & friendship with which he has inspired us. | He certainly is the most natural, unaffected distinguished man I ever met".

[4] The enlisting of Maclise as an illustrator, managed by Forster "as a glad surprise for him"; the publishers had previously engaged Leech and Doyle. Maclise was in fact not very co-operative; he seems to have resented not being asked by CD direct, and would "much prefer not engaging in the matter at all". Later, he was annoyed by the choice of engraver for the title and frontispiece, and finally was "mortified and humiliated" by the "little dirty scratches" of the final cuts and the work of the "demon printers" (Maclise *to* Forster, n.d., MS Forster Collection, V & A).

cordially inscribed To my English Friends in Switzerland.[1] Just those two lines, and nothing more. When I get the proofs again I think I may manage another word or two about the battle-field, with advantage. I am glad you like the alterations. I feel that they make it complete, and that it would have been incomplete without your suggestions.

About the proofs of No. III of Dombey: I have taken out about two pages and a half, and the rest I must ask you to take out with the assurance that you will satisfy me in whatever you do.[2] The sale, prodigious indeed![3] I am very thankful.

To JOHN FORSTER, [22 and 23 NOVEMBER 1846]

Extracts in F, VI, ii, 479; V, i, 384; V, vi, 442; V, vii, 443, 443*n*, 444. *Date:* first extract "Next day" after 21 Nov according to Forster; second extract 22 Nov in marginal note in F, 1872–4, II, ix, 187; third extract clearly in first long letter after arrival in Paris; remaining extracts 22 Nov according to Forster, with postscripts on "Monday" (23 Nov).

About Walter Gay: I see it will be best as you advise, to give that idea up; and indeed I don't feel it would be reasonable to carry it out now. I am far from sure it could be wholesomely done, after the interest he has acquired.[4] But when I have disposed of Paul (poor boy!) I will consider the subject farther.[5]

On another matter in Forster's letter he writes: OUR STRAW-HATTED FRIEND from Miss Kelly's![6] Oh my stars! To think of him, all that time—Macbeth in disguise; Richard the Third grown straight; Hamlet as he appeared on his sea-voyage to England. What an artful villain he must be, never to have made any sign of the melodrama that was in him! What a wicked-minded and remorseless Iago to have seen you doing Kitely night after night! raging to murder you and seize the part! Oh fancy Miss Kelly "getting him up" in Macbeth. Good Heaven! what a mass of absurdity must be shut up sometimes within the walls of that small theatre in Dean-street! FIREWORKS[7] will come out shortly, depend

[1] The exact words were used, but set out in four lines.

[2] Forster says (VI, ii, 479) that his first letter to CD in Paris told him he had over-written his No. by three pages; the proofs of No. III in the Forster Collection show 4 pp. of "overmatter", running to p. 100 instead of p. 96. CD made a number of short cuts in Chs 8 and 10 and also one long one in Ch. 10, a page of Mrs Chick and Miss Tox on the visit to Brighton. The general effect of the cutting was to reduce the incidental comedy; a reference of Walter's to Mr Carker the Junior in Ch. 10 was also removed, and a paragraph at the end about the Major at his club. Forster was able to avoid additional cuts: see *Dombey and Son,* ed. A. Horsman, p. xxvi.

[3] Forster had doubtless told CD of the

need for immediate further reprints of No. I and No. II (both dated 21 Nov in Bradbury & Evans's Accounts, MS V & A), bringing the total sales of No. I to 34,000 and of No. II to 32,000: see also *To* Forster, ?11 Oct 46, *fn.*

[4] Walter was sympathetically presented in Chs 9 and 10, and it would have been difficult to show him deteriorating as CD had originally intended: see *To* Forster, ?25 July.

[5] Forster says "The subject was never resumed".

[6] Bayntun Rolt: see *To* Thompson, 2 Dec 46 and *fn.*

[7] Described by Forster as "a solitary little girl, who flitted about so silently among our actors and actresses that she might have been deaf and dumb but for

upon it, in the dumb line; and will relate her history in profoundly unintelligible motions that will be translated into long and complicated descriptions by a grey-headed father, and a red-wigged countryman, his son. You remember the dumb dodge of relating an escape from captivity?[1] Clasping the left wrist with the right hand, and the right wrist with the left hand—alternately (to express chains) —and then going round and round the stage very fast, and coming hand over hand down an imaginary cord: at the end of which there is one stroke on the drum, and a kneeling to the chandelier? If Fireworks can't do that—and won't somewhere—I'm a Dutchman.

They travelled post to Paris in five days. We got through the journey charmingly, though not quite so quickly as we hoped. The children as good as usual, and even Skittles[2] jolly to the last. (That name has long superseded Sampson Brass, by the bye. I call him so, from something skittle-playing and public-housey in his countenance.) We have been up at five every morning, and on the road before seven. We were three carriages: a sort of wagon, with a cabriolet attached, for the luggage; a ramshackle villainous old swing upon wheels (hired at Geneva), for the children; and for ourselves, that travelling chariot which I was so kind as to bring here for sale.[3] It was very cold indeed crossing the Jura—nothing but fog and frost; but when we were out of Switzerland and across the French frontier, it became warmer, and continued so. We stopped at between six and seven each evening; had two rather queer inns, wild French country inns;[4] but the rest good. They were three hours and a half examining the luggage at the frontier custom-house[5]—atop of a mountain, in a hard and biting frost; where Anne and Roche had sharp work I assure you, and the latter insisted on volunteering the most astonishing and unnecessary lies about my books, for the mere pleasure of deceiving the officials. When we were out of the mountain country, we came at a good pace, but were a day late in getting to our hotel[6] here.

Residence in a hotel was not desirable with several tons of luggage, other tons of servants, and other tons of children, *and his first day in Paris did not close before he had offered for an* eligible mansion. *That same Saturday night he took a* colossal *walk about the city, of which the brilliancy and brightness almost frightened him; and*

---

sudden small shrieks and starts elicited by the wonders going on, which obtained for her the name of Fireworks" (F, v, i, 384).

[1] CD is recalling Fenella, the dumb girl of Portici, in *Masaniello*: the stage directions show the elaborateness of her miming; CD probably recalls Act I, "pointing to a window, she signs, that by tying together the sheets of the bed, she let herself safely down". The grey-headed father and red-wigged countryman are probably to be found in one of the numerous imitations.

[2] Alfred D'Orsay Tennyson Dickens, the baby.

[3] For Mr Goff: see *To* de Cerjat, 27 Nov 46.

[4] See *To* de Cerjat, 27 Nov.

[5] Between Verrières de Suisse and Verrières de France, on the road from Neuchâtel to Pontarlier. According to Murray's *Handbook for ... Switzerland*, 1843, the Custom-house regulations there were "more than usually rigorous". They crossed the frontier on 16 Nov.

[6] They reached the Hotel Brighton, Paris, on the evening of Friday 20 Nov.

among other things noticed rather a good book announced in a bookseller's window as *Les Mystères de Londres par Sir Trollopp.*[1] Do you know him?

The first man who took hold of me in the street, immediately outside this door, was Bruffum[2] in his check trousers, and without the proper number of buttons on his shirt, who was going away this morning, he told me, but coming back in two months, when we would go and dine—at some place known to him and fame. *On Sunday he took another long walk:* The dirty churches, and the clattering carts and waggons, and the open shops (I don't think I passed fifty shut up, in all my strollings in and out), and the work-a-day dresses and drudgeries, are not comfortable. Open theatres and so forth I am well used to, of course, by this time; but so much toil and sweat on what one would like to see, apart from religious observances, a sensible holiday, is painful.

As to the Review,[3] I strongly incline to the notion of a kind of *Spectator* (Addison's)—very cheap, and pretty frequent. We must have it thoroughly discussed. It would be a great thing to found something. If the mark between a sort of *Spectator*, and a different sort of *Athenæum*, could be well hit, my belief is that a deal might be done. But it should be something with a marked and distinctive and obvious difference, in its design, from any other existing periodical.

P.S. Monday afternoon. *Saying that a house was taken; that, unless the agreement should break off on any unforeseen fight between Roche and the agent,* a French Mrs. Gamp, *he was to be addressed at No.* 48, *Rue de Courcelles, Faubourg St. Honoré; and that he believed the premises were the* most ridiculous, extraordinary, unparalleled, and preposterous *in the whole world, something between a baby-house, a* shades,[4] *a haunted castle, and a mad kind of clock.* They belong to a Marquis Castellan, and you will be ready to die of laughing when you go over them.

P.S. *His lips should be sealed till Forster beheld for himself.* By Heaven it is not to be imagined by the mind of man!

P.S. One room is a tent. Another room is a grove. Another room is a scene at the Victoria. The upstairs rooms are like fanlights over street-doors. The nurseries—but no, no, no, no more!

To W. S. LANDOR, 22 NOVEMBER 1846

Text from MDGH, I, 157–9.

Paris, Sunday, November 22nd, 1846.

Young Man,

I will not go there if I can help it. I have not the least confidence in the value

---

[1] This must be a translation of *The Mysteries of London*, by G. W. M. Reynolds, E. L. Blanchard, and T. Miller, imitative of Sue's *Mystères de Paris*, and published as a penny weekly serial in 1846–8; the first series, completed 19 Sep 46, was published in two vols by the end of the month. The French publisher evidently associated it with Mrs Trollope, several of whose novels had been translated.

[2] Lord Brougham, whose plaid trousers were notorious; for his political interference while in Paris, see *To* de Cerjat, 27 Nov, *fn.*

[3] Forster calls this "another floating fancy for the weekly periodical which was still and always present to his mind".

[4] Wine vaults.

of your introduction to the Devil. I can't help thinking that it would be of better use "the other way, the other way," but I won't try it there either, at present, if I can help it. Your godson[1] says is that your duty? and he begs me to enclose a blush newly blushed for you.

As to writing, I have written to you twenty times and twenty more to that, if you only knew it. I have been writing a little Christmas book, besides, expressly for you. And if you don't like it, I shall go to the font of Marylebone Church as soon as I conveniently can and renounce you: I am not to be trifled with. I write from Paris. I am getting up some French steam. I intend to proceed upon the longing-for-a-lap-of-blood-at-last principle, and if you *do* offend me, look to it.

We are all well and happy, and they send loves to you by the bushel. We are in the agonies of house-hunting. The people are frightfully civil, and grotesquely extortionate. One man (with a house to let) told me yesterday that he loved the Duke of Wellington like a brother. The same gentleman wanted to hug me round the neck with one hand, and pick my pocket with the other.

Don't be hard upon the Swiss. They are a thorn in the sides of European despots, and a good wholesome people to live near Jesuit-ridden kings on the brighter side of the mountains. My hat shall ever be ready to be thrown up, and my glove ever ready to be thrown down for Switzerland. If you were the man I took you for, when I took you (as a godfather) for better and for worse, you would come to Paris and amaze the weak walls of the house I haven't found yet with that steady snore of yours, which I once heard piercing the door of your bedroom in Devonshire Terrace, reverberating along the bell-wire in the hall, so getting outside into the street, playing Eolian harps among the area railings, and going down the New Road like the blast of a trumpet.[2]

I forgive you your reviling of me: there's a shovelful of live coals for your head —does it burn? And am, with true affection—does it burn now?—

Ever yours,
[CHARLES DICKENS]

To [WILLIAM CULLENFORD], [?22–23 NOVEMBER 1846]

Extract from Argosy Book Stores catalogue No. 319; *MS* 1 p.; from Paris. *Date:* clearly 1846, since from Paris about General Theatrical Fund dinner, and presumably before deciding to return to London in Mar 47—a decision taken soon after hearing from his father on about 22 Nov: see *To* Forster, ?30 Nov. *Address:* Cullenford was the Fund's secretary.

He regretfully declines the invitation to preside at a dinner of the General Theatrical Fund,[3] *giving his reasons, and adding that* my interest in their Success and my desire to promote it by any means in my power, continues unabated.

---

[1] Walter Landor Dickens (1841–63): see Vol. II, p. 709 and *n*.

[2] Possibly in Dec 41 (see Vol. II, p. 431*n*); but more likely that Landor had stayed the night at Devonshire Terrace in Jan 46 when he was at the Twelfth Night party:

see *To* Webster, 6 Jan 46, *fn*. The sound is recalled in *Bleak House*, Ch. 9, where Esther is "awakened by Mr Boythorn's lusty snoring".

[3] On 29 Mar 47; CD was after all able to accept (see *To* Cullenford, 12 Dec 46).

To W. W. F. DE CERJAT, 27 NOVEMBER 1846†

MS Berg Collection. *Address:* William Cerjat Esquire | Belle Rive | pres de Lausanne | Canton de Vaud | La Suisse.

Paris. 48 Rue de Courcelles. St. Honoré.
Friday Twenty Seventh November 1846.

My Dear Cerjat. When we turned out of your view on that disconsolate Monday when you so kindly took horse and rode forth to say good by'e, we went on in a very dull and drowsy manner, I assure you. I could have borne a world of Punch in the rumble, and been none the better for it. There was an uncommonly cool Inn that night,[1] and quite a monstrous establishment at Auxonne the next night, full of flatulent passages and banging doors. The next night, we passed at Montbard, where there is one of the very best little Inns in all France. The next at Sens.[2] And so we got here. The roads were bad, but not very—for French roads. There was no deficiency of horses anywhere; and after Pontarlier, the weather was really not too cold for comfort. They weighed our plate at the Frontier custom House, spoon by spoon, and fork by fork, and we lingered about there, in a thick fog and a hard frost, for three long hours and a half, during which the officials committed all manner of absurdities, and got into all sorts of disputes with my Brave Courier. This was the only misery we encountered— except leaving Lausanne, and that was enough to last us, and *did* last us, all the way here. We are living on it now. I feel, myself, much as I should think the Murderer felt on that fair morning, when, with his grey-haired victim (those unconscious grey hairs, soon to be bedabbled with blood)[3] he went so far to- wards Heaven as the top of that mountain of St. Bernard, without one touch of remorse.[4] A weight is on my breast. The only difference between me and the Murderer is, that his weight was guilt, and mine is regret.

I haven't a word of news to send you. I shouldn't write at all, if I were not the vainest man in the world, impelled by a belief that you will be glad to hear from me, even though you hear no more than that I have nothing to say. Dombey is doing wonders. It went up, after the publication of the second number, over the thirty thousand. This is such a very large sale so early in the story, that I begin to think it will beat all the rest.[5] Keeley and his wife are making great prepara- tions for producing the Christmas story; and I have made them (as an old Stage- manager) carry out one or two expensive notions of mine about Scenery and so forth—in particular, a sudden change from the inside of the Doctor's house in the midst of the ball, to the orchard in the snow—which *ought* to tell very well.

---

[1] Probably at Pontarlier, ten hours' journey from Lausanne; there were three inns, the Poste ("very good"), the Croix Blanche, and the Lion d'Or. Les Rousses, also on the frontier, was "a hideous village ... in a cold, arid, upland country" (Murray, 1847 edn).

[2] Auxonne and Montbard had each a single inn, the Grand Cerf and the Point du Jour. In Sens they stopped at the Hotel de l'Ecu.

[3] Cf. *Richard III*, I, iv, 53–4.

[4] Probably a play de Cerjat and CD had seen at the little Lausanne theatre.

[5] CD must mean the three earlier monthly novels, not *Master Humphrey's Clock*; even so, his estimate is sanguine, for *Pickwick* and *Nickleby* had reached over 40,000.

But actors are so bad, in general, and the best are spread over so many theatres, that the "cast" is black despair and moody madness. There is no one to be got for Marion but a certain Miss May,[1] I am afraid—a pupil of Miss Kelly's who acted in the Private Theatricals I got up a year ago. Macready took her, afterwards, to play Virginia to his Virginius, but she made nothing of it, great as the chance was.[2] However, I have promised to show her what I mean, as near as I can— and if you will look into the English Opera House on the morning of the 17th 18th or 19th of next month, between the hours of 11 and 4, you will find me, in a very hot and dusty condition, playing all the parts of the piece, to the immense diversion of all the Actors, Actresses, Scene shifters, Carpenters, Musicians, chorus-people, tailors, dress-makers, scene painters, and general ragamuffins of the Theatre.

Moore, the poet, is very ill—I fear, dying. The last time I saw him was immediately before I left London, and I thought him sadly changed and tamed, but not much more so, than such a man might be under the heavy hand of Time. I believe he suffered severe grief, in the death of a son, some time ago.[3] The first man I met in Paris was Brougham,[4] who took hold of me as I was getting into a coach at the door of the hotel. He hadn't a button on his shirt (but I don't think he ever had), and you might have sewn[5] what boys call "mustard and cress" in the dust on his coat. I have not seen Lord Normanby yet, as we have only just got a house (the queerest house in Europe!) to lay our heads in—but there seems reason to fear that the growing dissensions between England and France, and the irritation of the French King, may lead to the withdrawal of the Minister on each side of the Channel.[6]

[1] Name omitted in MDGH.

[2] She had played Antoinette in *Comfortable Lodgings*, and early in Apr 46 joined the company at the Princess's where Macready was playing; on 29 Apr she appeared as Virginia in Knowles's *Virginius*: see *To Mrs CD*, 21–22 Dec 46.

[3] Moore had lost his eldest son and only surviving child, an officer of the French foreign legion in Algeria, in Mar; he lived till 1852 but with gradually decaying mental powers. He had been in London in May 46 for a few weeks, dining out frequently— but his letters and journal make no mention of the meeting with CD. There was a report of his serious illness in *Galignani's Messenger*, 15 Nov; the *Examiner* of 28 Nov denied the report, saying he was in good health.

[4] Name omitted in MDGH and later edns.

[5] Thus in MS.

[6] Palmerston had protested strongly to Guizot against the marriage in Oct 46 of the Queen of Spain's sister to the Duc de Montpensier, youngest son of Louis Philippe. Normanby's absence from the presentation of the *corps diplomatique* to the Duke and Duchess on 7 Nov had been the subject of much critical comment in the French press, and there was even an unfounded rumour that he was to be recalled (*The Times*, 11 Nov). Lord Brougham, who defended Louis Philippe and complained of Normanby's conduct, was referred to as "his faithful vassal, the Baron de Cannes" in the *Examiner* of 7 Nov, and made the subject of several of Leech's cartoons in *Punch*, including "Louis-Philippe Macaire instructing counsel [*Brougham*] for his defence in the English House of Lords" (28 Nov). Meanwhile Metternich had called a conference of the Northern Powers in Vienna at which Russia and Prussia agreed that the Republic of Cracow should be incorporated in the Austrian Empire, and on 16 Nov the Austrians put in a military governor. Guizot now found the quarrel over the Spanish Marriages an embarrassment; public opinion in France was strongly pro-Polish and demanded action, but when he proposed that Britain and France should send a joint protest at this breach of the

Have you cut down any more trees—played many more rubbers—propounded any more teazers to the players at the Game of Yes and No? How is the old horse, how is the grey mare, how is Crab[1] (to whom my respectful compliments) —Have you tried the Punch[2] yet—if yes, did it succeed—if no, why not? Is Mrs. Cerjat as happy and as well as I would have her—and all your house ditto ditto? Does Haldimand play Whist with any "science" yet? Ha ha ha! The idea of his saying *I* hadn't[3] any! And are those damask-cheeked Virgins, the 'Miss Forbes's'[4] still sleeping on dewey rose-leaves near the English church?

Remember me to all your house, and most of all to its other head, with all the regard and earnestness that a "Numble Individual" (as they always call it in the House of Commons) who once travelled with her in a car over a smooth Country, may charge you with. I have added two lines to the little Christmas Book that I hope both you and she may not dislike. Haldimand will tell you what they are. Kate and Georgy send their kindest loves—and Kate is "going" to write, "next week." Believe me always, my dear Cerjat, full of hearty and cordiall[5] recollections of this past Summer, and Autumn, and your part in my part of them—
Very faithfully Your Friend.
CHARLES DICKENS

P.S. Will you tell Mr. Goff from me that the Carriage did its duty admirably. It has been cleaned and put in perfect order, and is now at the Coachmakers. It shall be advertized next week. Not being sold in a fortnight or so, had it not better come here, where there is plenty of room for it, instead of standing where it would have rent to pay?

To WILLIAM HALDIMAND, 27 NOVEMBER 1846†

MS Bibliothèque Cantonale et Universitaire, Lausanne. *Address:* Affranchie. | William Haldimand Esquire | Denantou | pres de Lausanne | Canton de Vaud | La Suisse.

Paris. 48 Rue de Courcelles, St. Honoré.
Friday Twenty Seventh November 1846.

My Dear Haldimand. First, let me bestow upon you, through the Post, an accolade like that in which we indulged in descending from the Great Saint Bernard[6] on that memorable, bright, fresh morning when the lake behind the Monastery was brighter and crisper than any other party will see it until we go back there, and when I drowned the recollection of having been begrudged and denied more Bishop over-night, in the cold mountain streams that made the

Treaty of Vienna, Palmerston's answer was a copy of the note he had already sent to Metternich—a deliberate snub which Palmerston could safely indulge in, since he knew that there was in any case no possibility of effective joint action in defence of Poland.
[1] Unidentified.
[2] CD's recipe for making punch, given to Mrs Watson on 13 Nov (MS Rosenbach Foundation).
[3] "I" underlined three times.
[4] Name omitted in MDGH and later edns.
[5] Thus in MS.
a Not previously published.
[6] For the expedition, see *To* Forster, ?6 Sep 46 and *fns*.

road so pleasant. Secondly, let me report my small caravan safely arrived, and lodged in a most extraordinary house. Thirdly, let me release myself from the importunate messages of Mrs. Dickens and her sister by telling you that I never could write (unless I wrote a book for the purpose) half the remembrances and enquiries they are screaming out to me, every moment,—and therefore relinquish the idea in a mild despair.

I feel as if I had passed my life—or the best of it, in every sense—at Rosemont, and am strange and paralytic without Denantou, Belle Rive, and Elysée. Ages seem to have elapsed since we left Lausanne. I talk of it already, as of a recollection of old time. You are ethereal to my imagination. I play celestial whist with you, yes, and even exhibit "science", though you said (to the wife of my bosom) that I never did. I hear you trying to speak through what now appear to me to be the fogs and hoarsenesses of my infancy. The Brougham which you were perpetually getting in and out of, when we went to see the drunken man (for he *was* drunk; believe me, he was very drunk indeed) at that Lake public house, might have been a pumpkin once, and might now be a pumpkin again, for any air of work-a-day reality *I* can invest it with. A sort of pleasant sorrow seems to have settled over all our quiet Swiss life, and I don't believe a word of it.— Nevertheless ask Piron (is that the way to spell his name, or is there such a man?) to let that bed be sometimes turned, which I am to occupy next Spring. For I wouldn't let go of the belief and hope that I shall come back to see you all again, for more money than I could set forth in figures on this piece of paper.

And I wonder why it is, that I write on half a sheet! I have a wild and shadowy idea that Postage is precious, and ought not to be encouraged, but I have not the slightest conception why. I wish you would regard my Christmas Books, and Dombeys, and so forth, as letters to you: and when you find anything you particularly like, would take it as your own exclusive property. Then I should be entitled to an answer, and should always be an active and punctual correspondent. [a]Talking of which, reminds me to say that I have written to my printers, and told them to prefix to the Battle of life, a Dedication that is printed in illuminated capitals on my heart. It is only this

> *This Christmas Book is cordially inscribed*
> *To my English friends in Switzerland.*

I shall trouble you with a little parcel of three or four copies to distribute to those whose names will be found written in them, as soon as they can be made ready: and believe me there is no success or approval in the great world beyond the Jura, that will be more precious and delightful to me, than the hope that I shall be remembered of an evening in this coming winter time at one or two firesides I could mention, near the Lake of Geneva. It runs with a spring-tide that will always flow and never ebb, through my memory; and nothing less than the Waters of Lethe shall confuse the music of its running, until it loses itself in that great Sea for which all the currents of our life are desperately bent.[a1] There may be good parties to glorified St. Bernards beyond it—who knows!

Paris is just what you know it—as bright, and as wicked, and as wanton, as

[aa] Given in N, 1, 815; letter otherwise   [1] Cf. *Dombey*, Ch. 1.
unpublished.

ever. There is a great uproar afloat, about the Cracow business, and I hear this evening that the state of affairs with England is very feverish indeed, and that there is really solid foundation for the Newspaper Rumours.[1] If Lord Palmerston be not very careful, I am afraid he may split the Ministry before they meet the Parliament. He is a clever man, but I always doubt him, and feel afraid of his diplomacy.[2] It need be careful just now.

Try, by some friendly effort of imagination, to regard this as a letter—and whether you succeed or no, believe me, my dear Haldimand Affectionately Yours CHARLES DICKENS

William Haldimand Esquire.

To THE HON. RICHARD WATSON, 27 NOVEMBER 1846

MS Huntington Library. *Address:* Affranchie. | The Hon: Richard Watson | Elysée | pres de Lausanne | Canton de Vaud | La Suisse.

> Paris. 48 Rue de Courcelles. St. Honoré.
> Friday Twenty Seventh November 1846.

My Dear Watson. We were housed, only yesterday. I lose no time in dispatching this memorandum of our whereabout in order that you may not fail to write me a line before you come to Paris on your way towards England, letting me know on what day we are to expect you to dinner.

We arrived here, quite happily and well—I don't mean here, but at the Hotel Brighton in Paris—on Friday Evening between 6 and 7 o'Clock. The agonies of house-hunting were frightfully severe. It was one paroxysm for four mortal days. I am proud to express my belief that we are lodged, at last, in the most preposterous house in the world. The like of it cannot (and so far as my knowledge goes, does not), exist in any other part of the globe. The bedrooms are like opera boxes. The dressing-rooms, staircases, and passages, quite inexplicable. The dining room is a sort of cavern, painted (ceiling and all) to represent a Grove, with unaccountable bits of looking-glass sticking in among the branches of the trees. There is a gleam of reason in the drawing room. But it is approached, through a series of small chambers, like the joints in a telescope, which are hung with inscrutable drapery. The maddest man in Bedlam, having the materials given him, would be likely to devise such a suite, supposing his case to be hopeless and quite incurable.

Pray tell Mrs. Watson, with my best regards, that the dance of the two sisters in the little Christmas Book, is being done as an illustration by Maclise:[3] and that Stanfield is doing the Battle Ground, and the outside of the Nutmeg Grater

---

[1] CD was unduly influenced by what he read in the French press; feeling in England was less strong, as was noted in the *Examiner's* leader of 28 Nov.

[2] For CD's continued distrust of Palmerston (unjustified in this instance) see "The Thousand and One Humbugs", *Household Words*, 21 Apr 55, where he appears as the "Grand Vizier Parmastoon (or Twirling Weathercock)".

[3] The frontispiece; this was probably done by about 16 Nov, when Leech protested to Forster against having to follow Maclise's interpretation of the characters (MS Forster Collection).

Inn. Maclise is also drawing some smaller subjects[1] for the little Story, and they write me that they hope it will be very pretty, and that they think I shall like it. I shall have been in London before I see you, probably, and I hope the book itself will then be on its road to Lausanne to speak for itself, and to speak a word for me too. I have never left so many friendly and cheerful recollections[2] in any place: and to represent me in my absence its tone should be very eloquent and affectionate indeed.

Well! If I don't turn up again next summer, it shall not be my fault. In the meantime I shall often and often look that way with my mind's eye, and hear the sweet, clear, bell-like voice of Cheeseborough[3] with the ear of my imagination. In the event of there being any change—but it's not likely—in the appearance of his cravat behind—where it goes up into his head, I mean, and frets against his wig—I hope some one of my English friends will apprize me of it, for the love of the Great Saint Bernard.

I have not seen Lord Normanby yet. I have not seen anything, up to this time, but houses and lodgings. There seems to be immense excitement here on the subject of Cracow, however, and a perfectly stupendous sensation getting up. I saw the King,[4] the other day, coming into Paris. His carriage was surrounded by Guards on horseback; and he sat very far back in it, I thought, and drove at a great pace. It was strange to see the Prefet of Police on horseback, some hundred yards in advance, looking to the right and left as he rode, like a man who suspected every twig in every tree in the long Avenue.

The English relations look anything but promising, though I understand that the Count St. Aulaire is to remain in London, notwithstanding the newspaper alarms to the contrary. If there be anything like the sensation in England, about Cracow[5] that there is here, there will be a bitter resentment indeed. The democratic society of Paris have announced this morning, their intention of printing and circulating fifty thousand copies of an appeal[6] in its behalf, in every European language. It is a base business beyond question, and comes at an ill time.

Mrs. Dickens and her sister desire their best regards to be sent to you, and their best loves to Mrs. Watson. In which I join, as nearly as I may. Believe me, with great truth, Very Sincerely Yours.

CHARLES DICKENS

[a]Mrs. Dickens is going to write to Mrs. Watson, next week, she says.[a]

[1] Maclise's letters to Forster (MS Forster Collection) show that he first offered to do "a second subject" (not the illustrated title) and left the choice to Forster; eventually he did two, in addition to the frontispiece and title, and the choice fell on "The Secret Interview" and the final illustration of "The Sisters".

[2] MS reads "recollection".

[3] Name omitted in MDGH and later edns. The Rev. Isaac Cheesbrough, appointed as Minister of the French Protestant church at Ouchy in 1821, and to the English church when it first came into use in 1846 (G. E. Biber, *The English Church on the Continent*, 1845).

[4] Cf. *To* Forster, 30 Nov.

[5] Name omitted in MDGH.

[6] An address of the French democrats to the democrats of Europe (signed by the Abbé Lamennais and six others; an extract appeared in *The Times*, 30 Nov 46), urging them to unite in "unrelenting action" and ending "To-day the combat—to-morrow the triumph! Rise then!"

[aa] Omitted in MDGH, 1882, and later edns.

To SAXE BANNISTER,[1] 29 NOVEMBER 1846*

MS Dickens House.

48 Rue de Courcelles, Paris. | Twenty Ninth November 1846.

Mr. Charles Dickens presents his compliments to Mr. Saxe Bannister, and begs to thank him for his obliging letter, and for his pamphlet—only just now received, in consequence of Mr. Dickens having been absent from England, and residing in Switzerland for six months. Mr. Dickens hastens to assure Mr. Bannister that his connexion with the Daily News ceased very soon after the establishment of that Journal, and that he has no share whatever in that enterprize or its management.

To JOHN FORSTER [?30 NOVEMBER 1846]

Extracts in F, v, vii, 444, 444–5, 445 (two extracts), 446–7, 447*n*, v, vi, 440–1*n*. *Date:* first extract from the letter "following" 23 Nov, according to Forster—the natural time for him to describe the house more fully (but the reference to Henry Bulwer may come from a later letter: see *To* Thompson, 2 Dec); second extract 30 Nov according to Forster; third extract almost certainly same letter (cf. *To* Watson, 27 Nov), and fourth extract probably so; fifth and sixth extracts 30 Nov (or "same letter") according to Forster; final extract "end of November".

Never, till Forster saw it, should the house be described. I will merely observe that it is fifty yards[2] long, and eighteen feet high, and that the bedrooms are exactly like opera-boxes. It has its little courtyard and garden, and porter's house, and cordon to open the door, and so forth; and is a Paris mansion in little. There is a gleam of reason in the drawing-room. Being a gentleman's house, and not one furnished to let, it has some very curious things in it; some of the oddest things you ever beheld in your life; and an infinity of easy chairs and sofas. . . . Bad weather. It is snowing hard. There is not a door or window here—but that's nothing! there's not a door or window in all Paris—that shuts; not a chink in all the billions of trillions of chinks in the city that can be stopped to keep the wind out. And the cold!—but you shall judge for yourself; and also of this preposterous dining-room. The invention, sir, of Henry Bulwer,[3] who when he had executed it (he used to live here), got frightened at what he had done, as well he might, and went away. . . . The Brave called me aside on Saturday night, and showed me an improvement he had effected in the decorative way. "Which," he said, "will very much s'prize Mis'r Fors'er when he come." You are to be deluded into the belief that there is a perspective of chambers twenty miles in length, opening from the drawing-room.

He had not been two days in Paris when a letter from his father made him very anxious for the health of his eldest sister. I was going to the play (a melodrama in

[1] Saxe Bannister (1790–1877; *DNB*) wrote many pamphlets on colonial and miscellaneous subjects; the only one likely to have interested CD is *On Abolishing Transportation*, 1837.

[2] CD must mean feet.

[3] William Henry Lytton Bulwer (1801–72; *DNB*), diplomat, younger brother of Edward, had been in Paris as Secretary of the Embassy 1839–43, Chargé d'affaires 1839–40; since Nov 43 he had been Ambassador at Madrid.

eight acts, five hours long), but hadn't the heart to leave home after my father's letter, and sent Georgy and Kate by themselves. There seems to be no doubt whatever that Fanny is in a consumption.[1] *She had broken down in an attempt to sing at a party in Manchester; and subsequent examination by Sir Charles Bell's nephew,*[2] *who was present and took much interest in her, sadly revealed the cause.* He advised that neither she nor Burnett should be told the truth, and my father has not disclosed it. In worldly circumstances they are very comfortable, and they are very much respected.[3] They seem to be happy together, and Burnett has a great deal of teaching. You remember my fears about her when she was in London the time of Alfred's marriage,[4] and that I said she looked to me as if she were in a decline? Kate took her to Elliotson, who said that her lungs were certainly not affected then. And she cried for joy. Don't you think it would be better for her to be brought up, if possible, to see Elliotson again? I am deeply, deeply grieved about it. *Charles Sheridan*[5] *was dying of the same disease; and his chief, Lord Normanby, was* as informal and good-natured as ever, but not so gay as usual, and having an anxious haggard way with him, as if his responsibilities were more than he had bargained for.

A glimpse of the king impressed him unfavourably. There were two carriages. His was surrounded by horseguards. It went at a great pace, and he sat very far back in a corner of it, I promise you. It was strange to an Englishman to see the Prefet of Police riding on horseback some hundreds of yards in advance of the cortège, turning his head incessantly from side to side, like a figure in a Dutch clock, and scrutinizing everybody and everything, as if he suspected all the twigs in all the trees in the long avenue.

He saw almost everywhere signs of canker eating into the heart of the people themselves. It is a wicked and detestable place, though wonderfully attractive; and there can be no better summary of it, after all, than Hogarth's unmentionable phrase.[6]

He had got his papers into order and hoped to begin that day. But his Paris plans had been unsettled: he must, for family reasons, return to London in four months'

[1] She lived till 29 July 48: see next vol.

[2] This nephew of Sir Charles Bell (whom CD had met at the Edinburgh Dinner in 1841: see Vol. II, p. 309 and *n*) was Charles William Bell, MD, eldest son of Sir Charles's favourite brother George; he had been physician to the embassy to Persia in 1835; and later, physician to the Ardwick and Ancoats Dispensary; like his uncle, was interested in art.

[3] The Rev. James Griffin, minister of the Rusholme Road Congregational Chapel where the Burnetts led the choir, speaks highly of Fanny's character and calls her "a general favourite" (*Memories of the Past*, 1883, p. 200).

[4] 16 May 46; there is no reference to Fanny in CD's letters of that period.

[5] Charles Kinnaird Sheridan (?1817–47), youngest son of Thomas Sheridan and Caroline Sheridan the novelist, and brother of Caroline Norton; attaché to Lord Normanby. Macready had seen him as Charles Surface in an amateur production of *School for Scandal* on 20 Jan 45 (*Diaries*, II, 286–7). CD's letters to him of ?4 Dec and 29 Dec and the reference in *To* Thompson, 2 Dec, do not suggest illness. Sheridan died on 30 May 47 at the British Embassy.

[6] Hogarth was reported to have said that "French houses were gilt and b–sh–t" (article in *Biographia Britannica* on Sir James Thornhill, VI, part 2, Supplement 1766, p. 172). No doubt CD's letter quoted the actual words.

time—three months sooner than he had designed; and as his own house would not be free till July, would have to hire one from the end of March. In these circumstances I think I shall send Charley to King's-college after Christmas. I am sorry he should lose so much French, but don't you think to break another half-year's schooling would be a pity? Of my own will I would not send him to King's-college at all, but to Bruce Castle instead. I suppose, however, Miss Coutts is best. We will talk over all this when I come to London. *This would be in December; he suggested the middle of January for Forster's visit.* It will then be the height of the season, and a good time for testing the unaccountable French vanity which really does suppose there are no fogs here, but that they are all in London.

Mamey and Katey have come out in Parisian dresses, and look very fine. They are not proud,[1] and send their loves. Skittles is cutting teeth, and gets cross towards evening. Frankey is smaller than ever, and Walter very large. Charley in statu quo. Everything is enormously dear. Fuel, stupendously so. In airing the house, we burnt five pounds' worth of firewood in one week!! We mix it with coal now, as we used to do in Italy, and find the fires much warmer. To warm the house thoroughly, this singular habitation requires fires on the ground floor. We burn three.

I may tell you, now it is all over. I don't know whether it was the hot summer, or the anxiety of the two new books coupled with D.N. remembrances and reminders, but I was in that state in Switzerland, when my spirits sunk so, I felt myself in serious danger.[2] Yet I had little pain in my side; excepting that time at Genoa[3] I have hardly had any since poor Mary died,[4] when it came on so badly; and I walked my fifteen miles a day constantly, at a great pace.

To LORD JEFFREY, 30 NOVEMBER 1846†

MS Berg Collection. *Address:* Angleterre | The Hon: | Lord Jeffrey | Moray Place | Edinburgh | Scotland.

Paris. 48 Rue de Courcelles. | Thirtieth November 1846.

My very dear Lord Jeffrey. A word before the Post goes out!—*a*We have come from Switzerland, all well and happy, and purpose remaining here until the end of March. My friend Forster, who does all my business for me in England while I am away, and is my right hand and cool shrewd head too, will send you by post, probably in the course of this week, proofs of the Christmas Book. There is

---

[1] In *Nicholas Nickleby*, Ch. 16, when the Kenwigs's daughters are to be taught French by Nicholas, Mrs Kenwigs exhorts Morleena, "don't boast of it . . . don't say no more than 'We've got a private master comes to teach us at home, but we ain't proud, because ma says it's sinful' ".

[2] See *To* Forster, ?26 Sep and ?31 Oct;

the "reminders" were doubtless in Forster's letters to him throughout the autumn, not only at the time of the "revolution".

[3] See *To* Forster, ?31 Aug 44.

[4] 7 May 37; the letters of that summer do not mention this pain.

aa; bb Given in N, I, 817, from catalogue source; letter otherwise unpublished.

something in the idea, that I hope will please you. It will not be published until the 18th. of December.*ᵃ1*

I shall hope, when you have read it, to see your handwriting. Don't worry yourself to write much. Say "I am well and have not forgotten you", and that will be enough. Kate sends her love. *ᵇ*Your godson[2] thrives, and is a pretty fellow. Dombey is a *great* success. I have forgotten all about the newspaper, and don't believe I ever had anything to do with it,*ᵇ* or ever received a dissuasion from an affectionate friend "i' the North".[3]

God bless you! Our united regards to Mrs. Jeffrey. When shall I see Scotland again!

Ever Affectionately Yours
CHARLES DICKENS

To JOHN FORSTER, [?NOVEMBER–DECEMBER 1846]

Extract in F, VI, ii, 478. *Date:* on receiving *Dombey* No. III (probably an advance copy), published 30 Nov.

I am really *distressed* by the illustration of Mrs. Pipchin and Paul. It is so frightfully and wildly wide of the mark. Good Heaven! in the commonest and most literal construction of the text, it is all wrong. She is described as an old lady, and Paul's "miniature arm-chair" is mentioned more than once. He ought to be sitting in a little arm-chair down in a corner of the fireplace, staring up at her. I can't say what pain and vexation it is to be so utterly misrepresented.[4] I would cheerfully have given a hundred pounds to have kept this illustration out of the book. He never could have got that idea of Mrs. Pipchin if he had attended to the text. Indeed I think he does better without the text; for then the notion is made easy to him in short description, and he can't help taking it in.[5]

To T. J. THOMPSON, 2 DECEMBER 1846†

MS Mrs Sowerby. *Address:* A Monsieur | Monsr. T. J. Thompson | Clermont | Lausanne | Canton de Vaud | La Suisse.

48 Rue de Courcelles, St. Honoré, Paris.
Second December 1846.

My Dear Thompson. We got to Paris in due course, on the Friday Evening. We had a pleasant and prosperous journey, barring rather cold weather in

---

[1] The actual date was 19 Dec. Forster says that publication was delayed because Leech's illustrations were not ready (F, v, vi, 439).

[2] N misreads as "Gordon".

[3] Jeffrey's letter has not been traced.

[4] "Paul and Mrs. Pipchin", in Ch. 8. CD is hardly fair to Browne: the text does not actually say Paul is looking or staring *up* at her. His "little arm-chair by the fire", evidently visualized by CD as a low chair, but not further described, was taken by Browne, excusably, as a child's "high

chair"; it is in the scene with his father earlier in the chapter that "a miniature arm-chair" and "looking up" occur. Mrs Pipchin is sufficiently witch-like, and certainly not young, though not old enough to please CD and not "stooping" as in the initial description. The real trouble no doubt was that CD had a clear picture in his memory of Mrs Roylance.

[5] CD accordingly extracted and summarized part of his text in "short description" for the first illustration in No. IV (see *To* Browne, ?6 Dec).

Switzerland and on the borders thereof, and a slight detention of three hours and a half, at the frontier Custom House, atop of a mountain, in a hard frost and a dense fog. We came into this house last Thursday. It has a pretty drawing room, approached through four most extraordinary chambers. It is the most ridiculous and preposterous house in the world, I should think. It belongs to a Marquis Castellane, but was fitted up (so Paul-Pry Poole[1] said, who dined here yesterday) by Henry Bulwer[2] in a fit of temporary insanity, I have no doubt. The dining-room is mere midsummer madness, and is designed to represent a bosky grove.

At this present writing, snow is falling in the street, and the weather is very cold, but not so cold as it was yesterday. I dined with Lord Normanby on Sunday last. Everything seems to be queer and uncomfortable in the diplomatic way, and he is rather bothered and worried, to my thinking. I found young Sheridan (Mrs. Norton's brother) the attaché. I know him very well, and he is a good man for my sight-seeing purposes. There are to be no theatricals, unless the times should so adjust themselves as to admit of their being French, to which the Markis seems to incline, as a bit of conciliation, and a popular move.

Lumley, of Italian Opera notoriety, also dined here yesterday, and seems hugely afeared of the opposition opera at Covent Garden, who have already spirited away Grisi and Mario—which he pretends to consider a great comfort and relief.[3] I gave him some uncompromising information on the subject of his Pit, and told him that if [he d]idn't[4] conciliate the middle classes he might depend on being damaged—very de[cid]edly.[5] The danger of the Covent Garden enterprize seems to me to be that they are going [for] Ballet too; and I really don't think the house is large enough to repay the double expence.

[1] John Poole (1786–1872; *DNB*), dramatist and miscellaneous author; *Paul Pry*, 1825, was the best known of his many comedies and farces and often revived. CD chose his *Deaf as a Post* for the Montreal theatricals in 1842. His clever sketches in the *New Monthly*, 1826–34, collected in *Sketches and Recollections*, 1835, and his *Little Pedlington*, 1839, were also familiar to CD, some of the tales in *Sketches by Boz* and possibly the Crummles scenes in *Nickleby* showing their influence. Poole's last publication was *Christmas Festivities*, 1845; about that time his health broke down and by the summer of 1846 he was living in poverty in Paris. Some biographical sources mistakenly assert that he had been a Poor Brother of the Charterhouse but left, disliking their restrictions; but his name is not in the hospital's records and he can only have visited it to consider asking for a nomination, some time before CD succeeded in obtaining a Civil List pension for him in Dec 1850 (see N, II, 252–6, 375). For his application to the Literary Fund

in Jan 47, supported by Forster, Talfourd and CD (there said to have known him five or six years), and the theatricals for his benefit, see next vol.

[2] Name omitted in MDGH, 1882.

[3] Lumley in his *Reminiscences of the Opera*, 1864, pp. 152–8, describes the "secession of the *vieille garde*" in the 1846 season, headed by Costa, the conductor, and backed by Persiani, who provided the funds for the new company. He had recently been in Germany and had engaged Jenny Lind.

[4] A small tear has removed a few letters in three places.

[5] The other prices at Her Majesty's were so high that many of the "middle classes" were reduced to the pit, which consisted of "a dozen or eighteen benches" and "the disgusting conduct of the men who frequent it, the pushing, crushing, and hurtling of an English crowd, forbid the idea of any lady or even gentleman attempting to enter it" (letters in *Daily News*, 17 and 23 Sep 46).

Forster writes me that Mac has come out with tremendous vigor in the Xmas
Book, and took off his coat at it with a burst of such alarming energy that he has
done four Subjects! Stanfield has done three. Keeleys are making that "change"[1]
I was so hot upon at Lausanne, and seem ready to spend money with bold hearts,
but the cast (so far as I know it at present) would appear to be black despair
and moody madness. Mr. Leigh Murray[2] from the Princess's is to be the Alfred,
and Forster says there is a Mrs. Gordon[3] at Bolton's[4] *a*(that immeasurable
villain!)*a* who must be got for Grace. Oxberry,[5] I am horribly afraid, will do one
of the lawyers, and there seems to be nobody but Miss May[6] for Marion. I shall
run over and carry consternation into the establishment, as soon as I have done
the No. But I have not begun it yet—though I hope to do so tonight—having
been quite put out by chopping and changing about, and by a vile touch of
biliousness that makes my eyes feel as if they were yellow bullets. Dombey has
passed its 30,000 already. Do you remember a mysterious man in a straw hat—
low-crowned—and a Petersham coat, who was a sort of manager or amateur man
servant at Miss Kelly's? Mr. Bayntun Rolt, Sir—Came out, the other night, as
Macbeth, at the Royal Surrey Theatre.[7]

There's all my news for you! Let me know, in return, whether you have
fought a Duel yet, with your milingtary landlord, and whether Lausanne is still
that giddy whirl of dissipation it was wont to be. Also full particulars of your
fairer and better half, and of the baby; *b*respecting both of whom, Katherine
and Georgy are continually screaming out messages as I write. Commend me,

[1] The "transformation" in II, iv.

[2] See *To* Mrs CD, 19 Dec.

[3] Mrs Gordon had just begun to make a
name for herself as one of Bolton's company
at the Olympic; *The Times* of 19 Oct found
her "intelligent and accomplished . . . with
a great deal of feeling", and the *Examiner's*
review of *The Relapse* (31 Oct) praised the
"delicacy and spirit" of her Amanda. She
did not play Grace in the *Battle of Life*.

[4] George Bolton, actor and playwright.
In Apr 46 he took the Olympic Theatre for
a short season, opening with his own
comedy, *All about Love and Jealousy*; the
play was not a success and several notices
referred disparagingly to its "juvenile"
author, described by the *Theatrical Journal*,
18 Apr, as "a pale and somewhat thin
whiskerless young man". He returned to
the Olympic on 19 Oct for a longer season,
treated more seriously by the press; notices
gave him credit for his ambitious choice of
plays (especially a revival of *The Relapse*)
and lavish staging. His company was
generally agreed to be a strong one, although most were comparative newcomers
to the London stage; the weakest member
was Bolton himself, whom *Douglas Jerrold's
Weekly Newspaper*, 31 Oct, criticized for

making the theatre "a school for studying
the alphabet of his profession".

aa; bb Omitted in MDGH, 1882.

[5] William Henry Oxberry (1806–52;
DNB); well-known comic actor and writer
of farces and burlettas; had just joined the
Keeleys' company. Did not play in the
Battle; Snitchey was played by Drinkwater
Meadows and Craggs by Mr Turner. CD
doubtless feared that Oxberry would be too
broadly comic; he also had the reputation
of never knowing his lines on the first
night.

[6] See *To* Mrs CD, 22 Dec. Her name
and Oxberry's are omitted in MDGH,
1882.

[7] Mortimer Bayntun, an amateur who
called himself Bayntun Rolt, appeared five
times from 19 Nov as Macbeth at the
Surrey, and again in Dec at the Marylebone
Theatre; the *Era* (22 Nov) describes him as
over six feet tall, and says "his mode of
enunciation bore a marvellous affinity to a
person pelting out his syllables through a
pea-shooter" (which CD is evidently
imitating); his fight with Macduff was prolonged to great lengths and the audience
were in tears of laughter at his refusal to
die.

as lovingly as I may desire to be commended, to both of them, and give our united remembrances and regards to Mrs. Weller.*b* I will send a Christmas Book to Clermont, as soon as I get any copies. And so no more at present from Yours ever

CHARLES DICKENS

*c*P.S. Juvenile remembrances and blushes to Tom.*c1*

To CHARLES SHERIDAN, [?4 DECEMBER 1846]*

MS Princeton University Library. *Date:* Dec 46 rather than Jan 47, because of reference to Switzerland: 4 Dec the only possible Friday.

Rue de Courcelles | Friday

My Dear Sheridan

I find my man[2] must and will dine at the trois frères[3] today, as he goes away tomorrow. Two Sets of brothers running would be agin the Dombey, I'm afraid—frightful dissipation after Switzerland. Shall our lark stand over until Wednesday or Thursday in next week? Will that do for you? We shall meet, I dare say, in a day or two (why don't you come here?) and arrange.

Ever Faithfully

Charles Sheridan Esquire.
CD

To AUGUSTE-MARSEILLE BARTHÉLEMY,[4]
5 DECEMBER 1846*

MS Chas J. Sawyer.

48 Rue de Courcelles. | Samedi 5 Decembre 1846.

Monsieur:

Je m'empresse a repondre a votre billet. Croyez-moi, Monsieur, que vous vous tromper en supposant, un moment, que je suis insensible a l'honneur ou aux actes de politesse que vous m'avez rendu. Tout au contraire, Monsieur, je vous assure.

Mais il-y-a, Monsieur, deux semaines (dans tous les mois de l'an) quand je suis bien engagé dans ces poursuites litteraires aux quels vous aussi etes devoué, and avec quels vous pouvez bien sympathier. Ils arrivent, en generale, au commencement du mois, et alors je ne puis jamais rendre visite à personne— Dimanche excepté.

J'avais l'honneur de reçevoir votre carte avant-hier, et j'avais l'intention de me faire l'honneur de vous rendre visite et de vous donner cette explanation, demain.

---

cc Not previously published.

[1] Melville, Thompson's son, who had been staying with the Thompsons since 6 Sep.

[2] Unidentified.

[3] The Trois Frères Provençaux, in the Galerie Beaujolais of the Palais Royale.

[4] Auguste-Marseille Barthélemy (1796–1867), writer of political verse, translator and journalist; had recently returned to political writing with *Nouvelle Némésis*, 1844, a weekly anti-government pamphlet, and was publishing *Le Zodiaque*, a verse satire, in *Le Siècle*.

Permettez-moi d'esperer, Monsieur, que ce que j'ai dit est assez a un collabarateur,[1] et que vous le reçevrez, comme je l'ecris, de bonne foi et de bon coeur.

Reçevez, Monsieur, l'assurance de ma consideration distingue

CHARLES DICKENS

À Monsieur | Monsr. Barthèlemy

To JOHN FORSTER, [6 DECEMBER 1846]

Extracts in F, v, vii, 447–8, 446 (2 extracts); vi, ii, 479; v, vii, 445. *Date:* first and fourth extracts 6 Dec according to Forster; second and third extracts suggest that he had been in Paris for a week or more, and third deals with "politico-economical subjects" referred to in dated extract; fifth extract probably same letter since after "rather frequently" visiting the Morgue.

Cold intense. The water in the bedroom-jugs freezes into solid masses from top to bottom, bursts the jugs with reports like small cannon, and rolls out on the tables and wash-stands, hard as granite. I stick to the shower-bath, but have been most hopelessly out of sorts—writing sorts; that's all. Couldn't begin, in the strange place; took a violent dislike to my study, and came down into the drawing-room; couldn't find a corner that would answer my purpose; fell into a black contemplation of the waning month; sat six hours at a stretch, and wrote as many lines, &c. &c. &c. . . . Then, you know what arrangements are necessary with the chairs and tables; and then what correspondence had to be cleared off; and then how I tried to settle to my desk, and went about and about it, and dodged at it, like a bird at a lump of sugar. In short I have just begun; five printed pages[2] finished, I should say; and hope I shall be blessed with a better condition this next week, or I shall be behind-hand. I shall try to go at it—hard. I can't do more. . . . There is rather a good man lives in this street, and I have had a correspondence with him which is preserved for your inspection. His name is Barthélemy. He wears a prodigious Spanish cloak, a slouched hat, an immense beard, and long black hair. He called the other day, and left his card. Allow me

to enclose his card, which has originality and merit. Roche said I wasn't at home. Yesterday, he wrote me to say that he too was a "Littérateur"—that he had called, in compliment to my distinguished reputation—"qu'il n'avait pas

---

[1] Thus in MS.

[2] The first half of Ch. 11, "Paul's Introduction to a new Scene", i.e. Doctor Blimber's. The MS of this chapter is particularly congested with deletions and interlineations.

été reçu—qu'il n'était pas habitué à cette sorte de procédé—et qu'il pria Monsieur Dickens d'oublier son nom, sa mémoire, sa carte, et sa visite, et de considérer qu'elle n'avait pas été rendu!" Of course I wrote him a very polite reply immediately, telling him good-humouredly that he was quite mistaken, and that there were always two weeks in the beginning of every month when M. Dickens ne pouvait rendre visite à personne. He wrote back to say that he was more than satisfied; that it was his case too, at the end of every month; and that when busy himself, he not only can't receive or pay visits, but—"tombe, généralement, aussi, dans des humeurs noires qui approchent de l'anthropophagie!!!" I think that's pretty well.

The quays on the other side of the Seine were not safe after dark; nor were the best quarters of the city. I took Georgy out, the night before last, to show her the Palais Royal lighted up; and on the Boulevard, a street as bright as the brightest part of the Strand or Regent-street, we saw a man fall upon another, close before us, and try to tear the cloak off his back. It was in a little dark corner near the Porte St. Denis, which stands out in the middle of the street.[1] After a short struggle, the thief fled (there were thousands of people walking about), and was captured just on the other side of the road.

It is extraordinary what nonsense English people talk, write, and believe, about foreign countries. The Swiss (so much decried) will do anything for you, if you are frank and civil; they are attentive and punctual in all their dealings; and may be relied upon as steadily as the English. The Parisian workpeople and smaller shopkeepers are more like (and unlike) Americans than I could have supposed possible. To the American indifference and carelessness, they add a procrastination and want of the least heed about keeping a promise or being exact, which is certainly not surpassed in Naples. They have the American semi-sentimental independence too, and none of the American vigour or purpose. If they ever get free trade in France (as I suppose they will, one day), these parts of the population must, for years and years, be ruined. They couldn't get the means of existence, in competition with the English workmen. Their inferior manual dexterity, their lazy habits, perfect unreliability, and habitual insubordination, would ruin them in any such contest, instantly. They are fit for nothing but soldiering—and so far, I believe, the successors in the policy of your friend Napoleon have reason on their side. Eh bien, mon ami, quand vous venez à Paris, nous nous mettrons à quatre épingles, et nous verrons toutes les merveilles de la cité, et vous en jugerez. God bless me, I beg your pardon! It comes so natural.

Here am I, writing letters, and delivering opinions, politico-economical and otherwise, as if there were no undone number, and no undone Dick! Well. Così va il mondo (God bless me! Italian! I beg your pardon)—and one must keep one's spirits up, if possible, even under *Dombey* pressure. Paul, I shall slaughter at the end of number five. His school ought to be pretty good, but I

---

[1] A triumphal arch on the site of the Porte, at the entrance to the Rue du Faubourg St. Denis.

haven't been able to dash at it freely, yet. However, I have avoided unnecessary dialogue so far, to avoid overwriting;[1] and all I *have* written is point.

He went rather frequently to the Morgue,[2] until shocked by something so repulsive that he had not courage for a long time to go back. On that same occasion he had noticed the keeper smoking a short pipe at his little window and giving a bit of fresh turf to a linnet in a cage.

To H. K. BROWNE, [?6 DECEMBER 1846]

MS Comtesse de Suzannet. *Date:* Almost everything that CD tells Browne is included in the equivalent of "five printed pages" of Ch. 11 already written by 6 Dec.

1st Subject.

Paul (a year older) has left Mrs. Pipchin's, and gone to Dr. Blimber's establishment at Brighton. The Doctor only takes ten young gentlemen. Doctor Blimber's establishment is a great hothouse for the young mind, with a forcing apparatus always at work. Mental green peas are produced there, at Christmas, and intellectual asparagus all the year round. Every description of greek and latin vegetable is got off the driest twigs of boys, under the frostiest circumstances. Mrs. Blimber is proud of the boys not being like boys, and of their wearing collars and neck-kerchiefs. They have all blown before their time. The eldest boy in the school—Young Toots by name—with a swollen nose and an excessively large head—left off blowing suddenly one day, and people *do* say that the Doctor rather overdid it with him, and that when he began to have whiskers, he left off having brains. All the young gentlemen have great weights on their minds. They are haunted by verbs, noun-substantives, roots, and syntactic passages. Some abandoned hope half through the Latin Grammar, and others curse Virgil in the bitterness of their souls. Classical Literature in general is an immense collection of words to them. It's all words and grammar, and don't mean anything else.[3]

Subject. These young gentlemen out walking—very dismally and formally (observe; its a very expensive school) with this lettering

Doctor Blimber's young gentlemen as they appeared when enjoying themselves.[4]

---

[1] i.e. writing too many pages for the number. Though nearly half the first five pages of the chapter consist of dialogue, mainly between Mr Dombey and Mrs Pipchin, it is a necessary and economical way of introducing the plan of sending Paul to school.

[2] Unidentified bodies were exposed three days for public inspection; according to Galignani's *Guide*, about 300 were exposed annually. In "Lying Awake" (*Household Words*, 30 Oct 52) CD recalls the "ghastly beds, and the swollen saturated clothes hanging up, and the water dripping, drip-

ping all day long, upon that other swollen saturated something in the corner, like a heap of crushed over-ripe figs that I have seen in Italy". For a later visit with Maclise, see *To* Mrs CD, 28 July 50 (*Mr and Mrs CD*, ed. W. Dexter, pp. 140–1).

[3] This paragraph is a mixture of paraphrase and quotation from Ch. 11, except for the sentence "Some . . . souls", which is not in MS or printed text.

[4] CD is here looking ahead to Ch. 12, where the "walk before tea" is briefly described. The wording of the title for the plate is identical.

I think Doctor Blimber, a little removed from the rest, should bring up the rear, or lead the van, with Paul, who is much the youngest of the party. I extract the description of the Dr.[1]

"A portly gentleman in a suit of black, with strings at his knees, and stockings below them. He had a great bald head that shone tremendously, a deep voice, and a chin so very double that it was a wonder how he ever managed to shave into the creases. He had likewise a pair of little eyes that were always half shut up, and a mouth that was always half expanded into a grin, as if he had, that moment, posed a boy, and were waiting to convict him from his own lips. Insomuch that when the doctor put his right hand into the breast of his coat, and, with his other hand behind him, and a scarcely perceptible wag of his head, made the commonest observation to a nervous stranger, it was like a sentiment from the Sphynx, and settled his business."

Paul, as last described, but a twelvemonth older. No collars or neck-kerchief for him of course. I would make the next youngest boy, about three or four years older than he.[2]

To THOMAS FRASER, 8 DECEMBER 1846*

MS Yale University Library.

48 Rue de Courcelles | Tuesday December Eighth 1846.

Dear Fraser.

Last Sunday week, I went out to make some calls—taking with me a list of names and addresses. Among other places, I called at No. 9 Boulevart[3] des Capucines—or my coachman (I don't know him from Adam) stopped at a house which he swore was the veritable No. 9; and a shrill woman said nobody nearer your name than Fish-à lived there. After swearing which, she plunged into a little lodge and was seen no more.

When I got home, I looked high and low for your card, but couldn't find it. I concluded I had made some mistake in copying the address, and waited to tell you all this, until I should see you in the street or at the Theatre. Today I found it,—and with it, this identical address neatly printed in the corner!

As I may be obliged to leave Paris for a few days, on a visit, next week, and as I may not be able: being busy just now: to get out of doors at any Christian hour in the meantime—I write this note to explain an apparent but perfectly innocent delay on my part in returning the visit of an ancient Companion in arms. Though what mistake the Coachman and the woman contrived to make between them, Heaven knows.

Faithfully Yours
CHARLES DICKENS

T. Fraser Esquire.

---

[1] CD quotes from a passage already written for Ch. 11, with no change except the substitution of "great bald head that shone tremendously" for "bald head, highly polished".

[2] Browne followed his instructions, except for the number of the young gentle-men; the plate has 17. When CD saw the plate, he considered changing "ten" to "a limited number" in the proofs: see *Dombey and Son*, ed. A. Horsman, p. 142*n* and p. 867.

[3] Thus in MS.

To MM. FERRÈRE LAFFITTE, 10 DECEMBER 1846

Text from unidentified catalogue; *MS* 1 p.; dated Hotel Castellane, 48 Rue de Courcelles, 10 Dec 46.

M. Charles Dickens présente ses compliments à Messrs. Ferrère Laffitte, et sera très obligé s'ils auront la bonté de donner la valeur des billets de change circulaire enclos au porteur Louis Roche, son courier. M. Charles Dickens les a contresigné, et il a donné a Louis Roche sa lettre d'Indication.

M. Charles Dickens prie Messrs. Ferrère Laffitte d'accepter l'assurance de sa considération.

(Enclos cinq billets de change, chacun pour vingt livres sterling).[1]

To WILLIAM CULLENFORD, 12 DECEMBER 1846

Mention in Sotheby's catalogue, June 1911; *MS* 1 p.; dated Paris, 12 Dec 46.

He hopes to be able to return to London to preside at a dinner of the General Theatrical Fund.

To JOHN FORSTER, [?12 DECEMBER 1846]

Extracts in F, v, ii, 439–40; v, vii, 448*n*. *Date:* first extract not later than 12 Dec, for Forster to receive it before CD's arrival on 15 Dec (letters took two days), and hardly earlier, since "too late for remedy"; second extract doubtless in the last letter before the visit.

After seeing Leech's illustration: When I first saw it, it was with a horror and agony not to be expressed. Of course I need not tell *you*, my dear fellow, Warden has no business in the elopement scene. *He* was never there![2] In the first hot sweat of this surprise and novelty, I was going to implore the printing of that sheet to be stopped, and the figure taken out of the block. But when I thought of the pain this might give to our kind-hearted Leech; and that what is such a monstrous enormity to me, as never having entered my brain, may not so present itself to others,[3] I became more composed; though the fact is wonderful to me. No doubt a great number of copies will be printed by the time this reaches you, and therefore I shall take it for granted that it stands as it is. Leech otherwise is very good, and the illustrations altogether are by far the best that have been done for any of the Christmas books. You know how I build up temples in my mind that are not made with hands[4] (or expressed with pen and

---

[1] CD's account-book (MS Messrs Coutts) has the entry "Circular Notes £100.7.6" under 22 Dec.
[2] The illustration is towards the end of Part II, just before Alfred arrives to find Marion fled; all (including the reader) suspect that she has gone with Warden, but Part III reveals the truth. Leech did not illustrate Part III and presumably did

not read it. Forster says that Leech's mistake was not discovered "until too late for remedy, the publication having then been delayed for these drawings, to the utmost limit" (F, v, ii, 439).
[3] Forster says "Nobody made remark upon it " (F, *ibid*).
[4] Cf. Acts, xvii, 24.

ink, I am afraid), and how liable I am to be disappointed in these things. But I really am *not* disappointed in this case. Quietness and beauty are preserved throughout. Say everything to Mac and Stanny, more than everything! It is a delight to look at these little landscapes of the dear old boy. How gentle and elegant, and yet how manly and vigorous, they are! I have a perfect joy in them.

I shall bring the Brave, though I have no use for him. He'd die if I didn't.

To MRS CHARLES DICKENS, 19 DECEMBER 1846

MS British Museum. *Address:* À Madame | Madame Charles Dickens | 48 Rue de Courcelles | St. Honoré | Paris.

58 Lincoln's Inn Fields.[1] Saturday December Nineteenth 1846.

My dearest Kate. I really am bothered to death by this confounded *dramatization* of the Xmas Book.[2] They were in a state so horrible at Keeley's yesterday (as perhaps Forster told you when he wrote) that I was obliged to engage to read the book to them this morning. I have just finished. They all cried very much, and seemed honestly moved. It struck me that Mr. Leigh Murray, Miss Daly[3](!) and Vining[4] seemed to understand it best. Certainly Miss Daly knew best what she was about, yesterday—to my unbounded amazement. But she is too old for Grace, and not pretty enough. At 8 tonight, we have a Rehearsal with Scenery and band, and everything but dresses. I see no probability of escaping from it before 1 or 2 o'clock in the morning. And I was at the Theatre all day yesterday. Unless I had come to London, I do not think there would have been much hope of the Version being more than just tolerated—even that, doubtful. All the actors bad. All the business frightfully behind-hand. The very words of the book confused in the copying into the densest and most insufferable nonsense. I must exempt, however, from the general badness, both the Keeleys.[5] I hope they will be very good. I have never seen anything of its kind, better, than

---

[1] "He was in London eight days, from tne 15th to the 23rd of December, and among the occupations of his visit, besides launching his little story on the stage, was the settlement of a cheap edition of his writings, which began in the following year" (F, v, vii, 448). Business in connection with Fanny's illness (*To* Lady Blessington, 21 Dec), and probably the proofs of *Dombey* No. IV, also occupied him: they showed three pages of over-writing and had to be cut.

[2] Albert Smith's "authorized" version, made from the proof-sheets, was two weeks in advance of any rival version; three others followed on 4 Jan 47, all based on Smith's; three more later in Jan (Malcolm Morley, "*The Battle of Life* in the Theatre", *D*, xlviii [1952], 76–81). Smith's version alone was published.

[3] Ellen Daly, the stage-name of Mrs Phillips (?1813–90); started at the Adelphi, playing Smike in 1839; by this time a favourite performer in burletta, domestic drama, and burlesque; generally regarded as "decidedly pretty".

[4] Frederick Vining (?1790–1871; *DNB*), light comedian, still successfully playing young men's parts; at the Lyceum from the beginning of the Keeleys' management, playing Martin in *Martin Chuzzlewit* and Edward Plummer in the *Cricket*.

[5] Mrs Keeley's Clemency was regarded as the triumph of the piece (see *To* Mrs CD, 21 Dec); Keeley played Ben Britain; Warden was played by Vining, and Dr Jeddler by Frank Matthews; see also *To* Thompson, 2 Dec, *fn*.

the manner in which they played the little supper scene, between Clemency and Britain, yesterday. It was quite perfect, even to me.

The small manager,[1] Forster, Talfourd, Stanny, and Mac, dine with me at the Piazza to-day, before the Rehearsal. I have already one or two uncommonly good stories of Mac. I reserve them for narration. I have also a dreadful cold, which I would not reserve if I could help it. I can hardly hold up my hand, and fight through from hour to hour, but had serious thoughts just now, of walking off to bed.

Christmas Book published today—23,000 copies already gone!!![2] Browne's plates for the next Dombey, much better than usual.[3]

I have seen nobody yet, of course. But I sent Roche up to your mother[4] this morning, to say I am in town and will come shortly. The reading to the Lyceum people took place here. Forster provided 76 ham sandwiches (purchased in Holborn) of the largest size and newest bread; and when the shapes of the ladies were horribly deformed by the distention of these materials within them, his despatching the 42 uneaten sandwiches to the poor of the neighbourhood: with strict injunctions to Henry to find out very poor women and institute close enquiry into their life, conduct, and behaviour before leaving any sandwiches for them, was sublime.

There is a great thaw here today, and it is raining hard. I hope you have the advantage (if it be one: which I am not sure of) of a similar change in Paris. Of course I start again on Thursday. We are expecting (Roche & I) a letter from the Malle Poste people, to whom we have applied for places. The journey here was long and cold. 24 hours from Paris to Boulogne. Passage not very bad, and made in two hours.

I find I can't write at all, so I had best leave off. I am looking very impatiently for your letter on Monday Morning. I will write again on Monday or Tuesday. Give my best love to Georgy, and kisses to all the dear children. And believe me ever my love. Most affecy.   CD.

To MRS CHARLES DICKENS, 21 and 22 DECEMBER 1846

Text from MDGH, I, 166–7.

Piazza Coffee-House, Covent Garden,
Monday, Dec. 21st, 1846.

My Dearest Kate,

In a quiet interval of half an hour before going to dine at Macready's,[5] I sit down to write you a few words. But I shall reserve my letter for to-morrow's post, in order that you may hear what *I* hear of the "going" of the play to-night.

[1] Keeley.

[2] The first printing was 24,000; there was a reprint of 1500 on 26 Dec. The total sales in the accounts up to 31 Dec are 23,967; CD's three-quarter share of profits was £1281.15.4.

[3] "Doctor Blimber's Young Gentlemen as they appeared when enjoying themselves" and "Paul's Exercises".

[4] Mr and Mrs Hogarth were probably now in the lodgings in Albany Street where Charley was taken when he had scarlet fever in Feb 47.

[5] With nine other guests, including Forster, Elliotson, Lemon and Leech (*Diaries*, II, 351).

Think of my being there on Saturday, with a really frightful cold, and working harder than ever I did at the amateur plays, until two in the morning. There was no supper to be got, either here or anywhere else, after coming out; and I was as hungry and thirsty as need be. The scenery and dresses are very good indeed, and they have spent money on it *liberally*. The great change from the ball-room to the snowy night is most effective, and both the departure and the return will tell, I think, strongly on an audience.[1] I have made them very quick and excited in the passionate scenes, and so have infused some appearance of life into those parts of the play. But I can't make a Marion, and Miss [May] is awfully bad.[2] She is a mere nothing all through. I put Mr. Leigh Murray[3] into such a state, by making him tear about, that the perspiration ran streaming down his face. They have a great let. I believe every place in the house is taken. Roche is going.

Tuesday Morning.—The play went, as well as I can make out—I hoped to have had Stanny's report of it, but he is ill—with great effect. There was immense enthusiasm at its close, and great uproar and shouting for me.[4] Forster will go on Wednesday, and write you his account of it. I saw the Keeleys on the stage at eleven o'clock or so, and they were in prodigious spirits and delight.[5]

To MISS MARION ELY, [21 DECEMBER 1846]†

MS Library of Congress. *Date:* two days before CD's departure on 23 Dec; wrongly dated 2 Dec 44 in N, I, 648. *Address:* Miss Ely.

                                         Piazza Coffee House. | Monday Night.

My Dear Miss Ely.

^aComing home late—'home' I say naturally, but it is a ridiculous phrase

[1] Mr Phillips and Mr Hawthorn were responsible for the scenery, which was generally praised; the *Era* (27 Dec) described the "real large coach which comes along the road, and onto the stage", and the "clever scenic effect" in Act II in which "the company dance off . . . the ballroom sinks away . . . and we see the exterior of the old house . . . and the entire background of wintry landscape . . . This elaborate change, which worked admirably, was hailed with long and loud cheers".

[2] Name omitted in MDGH: see *To* Thompson, 2 Dec. Some criticisms referred to her nervousness and soft voice, but she was generally found "interesting", and Jerrold, in his *Weekly Newspaper*, praised her "intelligence and sensibility".

[3] Henry Leigh Murray (1820–70; *DNB*); acting in Edinburgh 1840–5, perhaps seen by CD in 1841; first appeared in London with Macready at the Princess's in Apr 45, in *The Hunchback*, and in 1846 played Malcolm Young in White's *The King of the Commons* and Icilius in *Virginius*. Later in the year he played in Shakespeare,

again with Macready, at the Royal Surrey; then at the Olympic with Bolton. Mrs Keeley described him as "the most perfec man I ever met . . . excessively handsome, with an elegant figure, graceful movements, and a most fascinating voice" (W. Goodman, *The Keeleys: on the Stage and at Home* 1895, p. 220).

[4] "There was a general call for Mr. Dickens but he was not in the house" (*Era*); Albert Smith was called with loud applause, and bouquets were thrown to Mrs Keeley (*Times*, 22 Dec). The play had a mixed reception from the critics, but all agreed on the brilliant performance of Mrs Keeley (the *Examiner* called her "as nearly as possible a facsimile of the writer's intention") which was regarded as one of her greatest triumphs.

[5] Text ends here; the letter, unlike others to Catherine, is not in MS BM, possibly because incomplete—by accident or design.

aa; bb Given in N, I, 648, from catalogue source; letter otherwise unpublished.

here—I found your kind note. For my sins, I am engaged tomorrow!—Hopelessly engaged to dine with Ainsworth.[a]

For my other sins (how many I must have committed!) I am going away next morning early. The sight of your handwriting is always so pleasant to me, that I have some consolation in putting your letter in my pocketbook, as a reminder of many old happy days—and braving the detestability[1] of the Packet and the Malle Poste on the strength of that talisman. But my main consolation is, that we are coming back in March, and that March is next to February, February to January, and January to December.

[b]If you can bear a Rehearsal,—God knows you must have a generous enthusiasm in such things. The first I ever saw, filled me with dismay; the second, with weariness.[b] But they have never disenchanted the Theatre to me, and when I saw you sitting in the Stalls the other night, I felt its captivation, under otherwise uncomfortable circumstances, more than ever.

The Loves I was to bring to Russell Square from Kate and Georgy!—Suppose them enclosed, with many more of mine, to all the house. And ever believe me

Most Cordially Yours
CHARLES DICKENS

My writing-desk is packed up already; and I have no envelope, pen, paper, ink, or sealing-wax.[2]

To THE COUNTESS OF BLESSINGTON, 22 DECEMBER 1846*

MS Benoliel Collection.

Piazza Coffee House
Tuesday Twenty Second December 1846.

My Dear Lady Blessington.

I came to you the other day to tell you how, much business, coupled with some family matters of a distressing nature, so beset me in my hurried visit that I could not avail myself of that kind offer you made me when we parted.[3] You were not at home. I was going to write to you yesterday, when I swore I would repeat my visit tomorrow morning, and Either strangle the man at the Gate, or force a way to your presence. This morning comes my servant to my bedside with an awful list of trains and steamboats, and obstinate tides, from which it seems that to be in time at Boulogne for the Malle Poste of Thursday, I must cross tomorrow (instead of next day as I had intended) and leave town at 8 o'Clock in the Morning. Everything is against me in my hurry and turmoil, and away I go again without having set eyes upon you!

But I am coming home for good, please God, in March: and if in the meantime you will think of me as having written you (in intention) scores of letters, you

---

[1] MS reads "destestability".
[2] The letter is written in ink, folded and sealed—the materials doubtless supplied by the Coffee House.

[3] On 29 May: see *To* Lady Blessington, 26 May 46.

will only do me justice. I should love to see your handwriting at No. 48 Rue de Courcelles, St. Honoré, Paris (Henry Bulwer's old house) and if you would give me my credentials to Eugene Sue,[1] I would rather have them from your hand than any other.

My love to Count D'Orsay, and the next thing to it to Miss Power and her sister.

Ever My Dear Lady Blessington | Most Heartily Yours
The Countess of Blessington.   CHARLES DICKENS

To FREDERICK DICKENS, [22 DECEMBER 1846]

MS Benoliel Collection. *Date:* PM 23 Dec 46 (Wednesday). *Address:* Frederick Dickens Esquire | Commissiariat | Treasury | Whitehall.

Piazza | Tuesday Night
My Dear Fred.

I had not received your note when I saw you tonight.

Mr. Weller had called here, I found when I returned, and left a memorandum on a card, saying he would call again, late. I was later than he, I have no doubt.

It is hardly necessary for me to say that you may depend he never gets any opinion on so delicate a subject from *me*, and that if he be disposed to play any tricks in this quarter, he will find that there are two parties to any such game.[2]

In the midst of packing and bustle | Ever affectionately
CD.

To THOMAS MITTON, [22 DECEMBER 1846]*

MS Yale University Library. *Date:* clearly same day as last. *Address:* Thomas Mitton Esquire | 23 Southampton Buildings.

Piazza | Tuesday
My Dear Mitton

I find, to my horror, that owing to the state of the tide in Boulogne Harbor, I must *leave town tomorrow morning at 8*, and I am driven to my wits' end to get my business done. I have only time to say, write to me when you have finally arranged with Alfred about coming to Paris. Sir James Duke will send you some money on account of his rent.

Ever Faithfully
CD.

To LORD JEFFREY, 27 DECEMBER 1846

Mention in Jeffrey *to* CD, 31 Jan 47, Lord Cockburn, *Life of Lord Jeffrey*, II, 406–8.

Answering Jeffrey's comments on Dombey, *and giving some account of his finances.*

[1] *To* Lady Blessington, 27 Jan 47 (see next vol.) shows that D'Orsay sent the introduction; Sue was not then in Paris, but some time during Forster's visit "we supped with ... Eugène Sue" (F, v, vi, 451).

[2] See *To* Fred Dickens, 28 Jan and 5 Feb 47 (N, II, 7, 11).

To JOHN FORSTER, 27 DECEMBER 1846

Text from MDGH, I, 167–9, and extract (*aa*) from F, VI, ii, 480–1 (wrongly dated "Christmas Day").

48, Rue de Courcelles, Paris,
Sunday Night, Dec. 27th, 1846

My Very Dear Forster,

Amen, amen. Many merry Christmases, many happy new years, unbroken friendship, great accumulation of cheerful recollections, affection on earth, and heaven at last, for all of us.

I enclose you a letter from Jeffrey,[1] which you may like to read. *Bring it back to me*[2] *when you come over.* I have told him all he wants to know.[3] Is it not a strange example of the hazards of writing in numbers that a man like him should form his notion of Dombey and Miss Tox on three months' knowledge? I have asked him the same question, and advised him to keep his eye on both of them as time rolls on. *ªI do not at heart, however, lay much real stress on his opinion, though one is naturally proud of awakening such sincere interest in the breast of an old man who has so long worn the blue and yellow. . . . He certainly did some service in his old criticisms, especially to Crabbe.[4] And though I don't think so highly of Crabbe as I once did (feeling a dreary want of fancy in his poems), I think he deserved the painstaking and conscientious tracking with which Jeffrey followed him.ª*

We had a cold journey here from Boulogne, but the roads were not very bad. The malle poste, however, now takes the trains at Amiens. We missed it by ten minutes, and had to wait three hours—from twelve o'clock until three, in which interval I drank brandy and water, and slept like a top. It is delightful travelling for its speed, that malle poste, and really for its comfort too. But on this occasion it was not remarkable for the last-named quality. The director of the post at Boulogne told me a lamentable story of his son at Paris being ill, and implored me to bring him on. The Brave doubted the representations altogether, but I

---

[1] Forster (F, VI, ii, 480*n*) quotes Jeffrey's letter of 14 Dec 46, which is not in Cockburn's *Life*. He praised the opening death scene, and Florence ("another Nelly"), Walter, and Susan Nipper, and continued: "Dombey is rather too hateful, and strikes me as a mitigated Jonas, without his brutal coarseness and ruffian ferocity. I am quite in the dark as to what you mean to make of Paul, but shall watch his development with interest. About Miss Tox, and her major, and the Chicks, perhaps I do not care enough. But you know I always grudge the exquisite painting you waste on such portraits. I love the Captain, tho', and his hook, as much as you can wish; and look forward to the future appearances of Carker Junior, with expectations which I know will not be disappointed".

[2] Text reads "to me back".

[3] Jeffrey's reply of 31 Jan 47 (Cockburn, *Life of Lord Jeffrey*, II, 406–8), shows that he had inquired about CD's financial returns on his novels; he found CD's statement "full and clear, if not every way satisfactory", but was "rather disappointed . . . at finding your *embankment* still so small", and gave him some further advice.

[4] Jeffrey wrote at length and with enthusiasm on all the volumes of new work published by Crabbe during his editorship of the *Edinburgh Review*, in 1808–19, and collected his reviews in *Contributions to the Edinburgh Review*, 1844, III, 3–101. In a note he says he has given "a larger space to Crabbe . . . than to any of his contemporary poets; not merely because I think more highly of him than of most of them, but also because I fancy that he has had less justice done him".

couldn't find it in my heart to say no; so we brought the director, bodkinwise, and being a large man, in a great number of greatcoats, he crushed us dismally until we got to the railroad. For two passengers (and it never carries more) it is capital. For three, excruciating.

Write to Poole[1] what you have said to me. You need write no more. He is full of vicious fancies and wrong suspicions, even of Hardwick,[2] and I would rather he heard it from you than from me, whom he is not likely to love much in his heart. I doubt it may be but a rusty instrument for want of use, the Pooleish[1] heart.

My most important present news is that I am going to take a jorum of hot rum and egg in bed immediately, and to cover myself up with all the blankets in the house. Love from all. I have a sensation in my head, as if it were "on edge". It is still very cold here, but the snow had disappeared on my return, both here and on the road, except within ten miles or so of Boulogne.

Ever affectionately

[CHARLES DICKENS]

To CHARLES SHERIDAN, 29 DECEMBER 1846

MS Brotherton Library, Leeds.

48 Rue de Courcelles | Tuesday Twenty Ninth December 1846

My Dear Sheridan

If your cold is better (I have had a beastly one, since I came back), I am your man, any afternoon this week except the day after to-morrow,[3] for stirring up the Parisian Lions. Supposing we sallied forth on some day when you had no dinner-engagement, we might perhaps send Charley home in the Bruffum, and dine tete a tete at the trois freres or the Cafe de Paris, or some such over-praised establishment?

Ever Yours faithfully

CHARLES DICKENS

The Wellington Statue seemed to me worse than Punch's wildest exaggeration of it.[4] I have more news of Wainewright the Murderer.[5]

[1] Name supplied from MDGH, 1882. Nothing is known of this particular trouble, but there is plenty of evidence of Poole's oddity and suspiciousness (see next vol.). Perhaps Forster, CD and Hardwick were already trying to get funds for him.

[2] John Hardwick (1791–1875), magistrate and brother of Philip, the well-known architect; probably the Hardwick who dined at Macready's on 21 Dec. In *To* Lord John Russell, 18 Dec 50 (N, II, 252–3), about a pension for Poole, CD says that he, Talfourd, Forster, and "Mr. Hardwick the Police Magistrate" are Poole's only English friends.

[3] On Thurs 31 Dec Watson, on his way home, dined with CD (Watson's Diary, MS Commander Michael Saunders Watson).

[4] Wyatt's controversial statue was raised on 29–30 Sep; *Punch* had a full-page illustration, "The Progress of the Wellington Statue", on 10 Oct, and many abusive comments appeared both before and after.

[5] Thomas Griffiths Wainewright: see Vol. I, p. 277n. Wainewright had been transported to Van Diemen's Land in 1837; his petition for ticket-of-leave in 1844 was rejected. He was still painting portraits (including one of Marguerite Power), and

To AMÉDÉE PICHOT, 30 DECEMBER 1846*

MS Universiteits-bibliotheek, Amsterdam. *Address:* À Monsieur: | Monsr. Amédée Pichot | Revue Britannique | 1 Rue Grange Bateliere | Paris.

48 Rue de Courcelles. | Wednesday Thirtieth December | 1846.

My Dear Sir

Allow me to thank you, very heartily, for your kind note, and the books with which it was accompanied. I glanced over some pages of the Christmas Stories before going to bed last night, and had great pleasure in seeing them so skilfully and *conscientiously* rendered into French.[1]

I am going to shut myself up as closely as I can (but I can never seal my doors hermetically) for about a fortnight. When that vigorous fit of writing shall be past and over, I shall hope to have an early opportunity of presenting you to Mrs. Dickens and my six live volumes now in private circulation.

Believe me | Dear Sir | Very faithfully Yours

Monsieur Amédée Pichot. CHARLES DICKENS

To JOHN FORSTER, [?31 DECEMBER 1846]

Extract in F, VI, ii, 481. *Date:* Forster calls this "six days later" than the letter which he dated Christmas Day but which is really 27 Dec. He then quotes a letter of "two days later", and "after three days more" an extract of which the third sentence begins "Friday morning" (i.e. 8 Jan), which would point to 2 Jan for the present letter. But difficult to see why CD should delay beginning No. v; *To* Pichot, 30 Dec suggests an immediate start, and Forster's visit was to begin as soon as the No. was finished, which at one point CD thought might be 13 Jan.

After sitting down to write No. V *of* Dombey, *he found himself* most abominably dull and stupid. I have only written a slip, but I hope to get to work in strong earnest to-morrow. It occurred to me on special reflection, that the first chapter should be[2] with Paul and Florence, and that it should leave a pleasant impression of the little fellow being happy, before the reader is called upon to see him die.

also teaching art. Watson's Diary (31 Dec) says that CD told him Wainewright's story, but does not mention anything that could rank as "more news"—unless it was that "his life is the foundation of Bulwer's new novel Lucretia", published 1 Dec. The news that he was recommended for a conditional pardon (*Hobart Town Gazette*, 17 Nov 46) could not yet have reached London or Paris.

[1] At this date the Christmas Books were the most popular of CD's works in France, and Pichot was the best-known and most successful of their translators. His versions had appeared in the *Revue Britannique* and in volume form (he had previously sent CD a copy of the *Cricket*: see *To* Pichot, 16

Feb 46), and in 1847 they were included in his collection, *Les Contes de Charles Dickens*, 1st and 2nd series. The number of French translations of CD's works rose sharply in 1847 (see F. Delattre, *Dickens et la France*, 1927, p. 45), but Anna Belloc remarked, in a letter of 18 Mar 47, that though he and his writings had been "welcomed in France, still I doubt the time of his popularity is come among us—he is too thoroughly English to be easily understood, appreciated and liked by foreigners in a translation, his faults will often come forward and eclipse the beauties" (MS Morgan).

[2] Perhaps Forster's error for "end".

I mean to have a genteel breaking-up at Doctor Blimber's therefore, for the Midsummer vacation; and to show him in a little quiet light (now dawning through the chinks of my mind), which I hope will create an agreeable impression.[1]

[1] The first and longest chapter in No. v, Ch. 14, "Paul grows more and more Old-fashioned, and goes Home for the Holidays", is mainly concerned with the breaking-up party and preparations for it, with very little about Paul and Florence. Two days later, according to Forster, CD sent a des-cription of the "first subject" ("Paul goes home for the holidays") which comes at the close of Ch. 14; but this was probably sent in anticipation of what he meant to write. The No. was finished on 15 Jan (not 14 Jan as Forster says).

APPENDICES

APPENDICES

A. AGREEMENTS WITH BRADBURY & EVANS, 1 JUNE 1844

MSS Mr H. C. Dickens.

On 1 June 44 CD executed several related Agreements with Bradbury & Evans, as anticipated in his letter of 8 May (p. 121). The chief of these, which apparently has not survived, is described by Forster:

> upon advance made to him of £2800, he assigned to them a fourth share in whatever he might write during the next ensuing eight years, to which the agreement was to be strictly limited ... no obligations were imposed as to what works should be written, if any, or the form of them.

There was also a provision that if a periodical were undertaken with CD "only partially editor or author" his share of copyright and profits should be two-thirds instead of three-fourths (F, IV, ii, 316). Bradbury & Evans's safeguard was CD's Life Assurance policy for £2000, expiring in June 1852. In his letter to them on 28 June 52 (N, II, 398) CD recalled having "effected two Britannia policies" for them in 1844; perhaps his other, smaller, Britannia policy was also deposited.

The first of the three Agreements given below is the dated copy retained by CD (without his signature); the other two are presumably drafts.

MEMORANDUM OF DEPOSIT OF LIFE ASSURANCE POLICY, 1 JUNE 1844

MEMORANDUM[1]—That the undersigned CHARLES DICKENS of Osnaburgh Terrace in the Parish of Saint Marylebone Esquire has this day deposited with the undersigned WILLIAM BRADBURY and FREDERICK MULLETT EVANS of Whitefriars in the City of London Printers and Publishers a certain Policy of Assurance effected on his own life in the Britannia Life Assurance Office for the sum of Two thousand pounds as a Security against the loss by them the said William Bradbury and Frederick Mullett Evans of Two thousand eight hundred pounds paid to him as the consideration for the purchase of a share in the Copyright of certain Works which may be hereafter composed by the said Charles Dickens And the said Charles Dickens hereby declares and directs that in case of his death prior to the twenty fourth day of June One thousand eight hundred and fifty two the monies due upon the said Policy shall be received by the said William Bradbury and Frederick Mullett Evans their executors or administrators and that their receipt alone shall be a good discharge to the Directors of the said Assurance Office or other persons paying the same and shall exonerate them from all responsibility as to the application thereof And it is hereby agreed between the said Charles Dickens and William Bradbury and Frederick Mullett Evans that in case the said Charles Dickens shall die previous to the said twenty fourth day of June One thousand eight hundred and fifty two and the monies due on the said Policy shall be received by the said William Bradbury and Frederick Mullett Evans their executors or administrators such monies shall be applied by them first in payment of any premiums of Assurance or other expences incurred

---

[1] Words and phrases given here in capitals represent either gothic lettering or small letters written bold.

for keeping up the said Policies then in discharge of the said sum of Two thousand eight hundred pounds or of so much thereof as after deducting the value of any Copyrights which shall subsequently to the date hereof have been absolutely assigned by the said Charles Dickens to the said William Bradbury and Frederick Mullett Evans and also the amount of any net profits received by them shall appear to be unpaid and the balance shall be paid over to the executors or administrators of the said Charles Dickens But in case the value of such Copyrights and the amount of the net profits received therefrom respectively together with any monies recoverable under the said Policy shall not be sufficient to repay the said sum of Two thousand eight hundred pounds without any Interest thereon then the balance of the said Two thousand eight hundred pounds shall remain and be a charge on the Estate of the said Charles Dickens AND it is lastly agreed that any differences which may arise between the said William Bradbury and Frederick Mullett Evans their executors or administrators and the executors or administrators of the said Charles Dickens as to the value of any Copyrights which may have been absolutely assigned to them as aforesaid and as to the amount of profits actually received by them in respect thereof shall be settled by reference in the usual manner And the said Charles Dickens further agrees to execute on request an assignment to the above effect at any time hereafter IN WITNESS whereof the said Charles Dickens hath hereto set his hand this first day of June One thousand eight hundred and forty four—

Witness   W. BRADBURY
   RICHD. WRIGHT.   F. M. EVANS

ASSIGNMENT OF MOIETY OF COPYRIGHT OF *OLIVER TWIST*, [1 JUNE 1844]

THIS INDENTURE made the [   ]¹ day of [   ] in the year of our Lord One thousand eight hundred and forty four BETWEEN CHARLES DICKENS of Osnaburgh Terrace in the parish of Saint Marylebone Esquire of the one part and WILLIAM BRADBURY and FREDERICK MULLETT EVANS of Whitefriars in the City of London Printers and Copartners of the other part WHEREAS the said Charles Dickens is possessed of or intitled to the Copyright of a certain Work called "Oliver Twist or ["] which is now published in three Volumes Octavo AND WHEREAS the said William Bradbury and Frederick Mullett Evans have agreed with the said Charles Dickens for the absolute purchase of a moiety or equal half part of and in the Copyright of the said Work Steelplates Stock and property belonging thereto subject to the covenants and agreements hereinafter contained for the sum of One thousand pounds NOW THIS INDEN-TURE WITNESSETH that in pursuance of the said agreement and in consideration of the said sum of One thousand pounds of lawful English money to him the said Charles Dickens in hand well and truly paid by the said William Bradbury and Frederick Mullett Evans at or before the sealing and delivery of these presents the receipt whereof the said Charles Dickens doth hereby acknowledge

¹ Empty square brackets indicate blank spaces in MS.

and from the same and every part thereof doth hereby acquit and discharge the said William Bradbury and Frederick Mullett Evans their executors and administrators He the said Charles Dickens DOTH by these presents bargain sell assign transfer and make over unto the said William Bradbury and Frederick Mullett Evans ALL that one equal half part or share of him the said Charles Dickens of and in the Copyright of and in the said Work Book or Composition called Oliver Twist or by whatsoever other name or names title or titles the said Work Book or Composition or any part or parts thereof are or is or has been or may be called known or distinguished And also the one equal half part or share of and in the Steel Plates stock and property belonging to the said Work Book or Composition and now consisting of twenty seven copies in Cloth and five hundred and eighty three copies in quires and of and in the gains and profits which may henceforth arise from the sale thereof and debts hereafter to become due to the said Charles Dickens William Bradbury and Frederick Mullett Evans on account thereof And all the estate right title interest property possession benefit claim and demand whatsoever both at Law and in Equity of him the said Charles Dickens in and to the said part share or interest profits and other the premises hereby assigned or intended so to be TO HAVE HOLD RECEIVE TAKE AND ENJOY the said one undivided moiety of and in the said Copyright Steel plates stock and all and singular other the premises hereby assigned or intended so to be with their and every of their appurtenances unto the said William Bradbury and Frederick Mullett Evans their executors administrators and assigns subject only to the covenants and agreements hereinafter contained AND the said Charles Dickens for himself his heirs executors and administrators doth hereby covenant and agree with the said William Bradbury and Frederick Mullett Evans their executors administrators and assigns in manner following (that is to say) that he the said Charles Dickens hath not at any time heretofore made done executed committed permitted or suffered any act deed matter or thing whatsoever whereby or by means whereof the said Work Book or Composition and other the premises or the part share or interest therein hereby assigned or intended so to be or any part thereof are is can shall or may be in anywise impeached charged incumbered or in anywise prejudicially affected but that he the said Charles Dickens now at the time of the sealing and delivery of these presents is the sole true and undoubted owner and proprietor of the Copyright of the said Work Book or Composition and other the premises hereinbefore assigned or intended so to be And that he the said Charles Dickens now hath in himself good rightfull power and lawful and absolute authority to bargain sell assign and set over the said moiety hereby assigned or intended so to be in manner hereinbefore mentioned AND ALSO that they the said William Bradbury and Frederick Mullett Evans their executors administrators and assigns shall and may at all times hereafter possess and enjoy the said half part or share hereby assigned or intended so to be and all profits and advantages arising from the same without any interruption claim or demand whatsoever of from or by him the said Charles Dickens his executors or administrators or any person or persons lawfully or equitably claiming or to claim by through under or in trust for him them or any of them And that free and clear and by the said Charles Dickens his executors or administrators freely clearly and absolutely exonerated discharged and indemnified of from and against all former and other bargains sales assignments right or equity of redemption or other rights interests charges and incumbrances claims or demands whatsoever AND MOREOVER that he the said Charles Dickens his executors or administrators and all and every other person and persons lawfully or equitably claiming or to claim by from under or in trust for him or them any right or interest in the premises hereby assigned or intended so to be or any part thereof will from time to time and at all times hereafter at the request costs and charges of the said William Bradbury and Frederick Mullett Evans or of one of them their or one of their executors administrators or assigns make do and execute or cause and procure to be made done and executed all such further and other acts deeds assignments and assurances whatsoever for the more effectually assigning assuring and confirming the premises hereby assigned and every or any part thereof unto the said William Bradbury and Frederick Mullett Evans their executors administrators and assigns in manner aforesaid and for the better enabling them to assert and protect the Copyright hereby assigned or intended so to be and also for the indemnifying of the said William Bradbury and Frederick Mullett Evans from any claims and demands on the part of the said Charles Dickens his executors or administrators in respect of the said premises hereby assigned as by the said William Bradbury and Frederick Mullett Evans or either of them their or either of their executors administrators and assigns or their any or either of their Counsel in the Law shall be lawfully and reasonably advised or required ALSO that he the said Charles Dickens his executors or administrators will not at any time hereafter sell or dispose of the remaining moiety of the said Copyright and premises hereby assigned or intended so to be or any part thereof until after he or they shall by writing under his or their hand or hands to be given to or left at the usual place of residence of the said William Bradbury and Frederick Mullett Evans or the survivor of them have offered the same to them or him at the lowest price at which the said Charles Dickens his executors or administrators shall be willing or shall propose to sell the same to any other person and such offer shall not within ten days from the delivering thereof have been accepted in writing AND the said William Bradbury and Frederick Mullett Evans for themselves jointly and severally and for their respective executors and administrators do hereby covenant and agree with the said Charles Dickens his executors administrators and assigns that they the said William Bradbury and Frederick Mullett Evans or either of them their or his executors or administrators will not at any time hereafter sell and dispose of the moiety of the said Copyright and premises hereby assigned or intended so to be or any part thereof until after they or he shall by writing under their or his hands or hand to be given to or left at the usual place of residence of the said Charles Dickens his executors or administrators have offered the same to him or them at the lowest price at which the said William Bradbury and Frederick Mullett Evans shall be willing or shall propose to sell the same to any other person and such offer shall not within ten days from the delivery thereof have been accepted in writing PROVIDED ALWAYS And it is hereby declared and agreed by and between the parties hereto That so long as the said Charles Dickens and the said William Bradbury and Frederick Mullett Evans or either of them shall remain jointly interested in the said Work

Book Composition and Premises hereby assigned or intended so to be the entire general management and superintendance of the publication thereof shall be undertaken and discharged by the said William Bradbury and Frederick Mullett Evans or the survivor of them and proper books of account shall be kept by them in which all receipts and payments in reference to the said Concern shall be entered and to which the said Charles Dickens his executors or administrators shall at all reasonable times have access and the said William Bradbury and Frederick Mullett Evans shall make up such half yearly accounts and render a copy thereof half yearly to the said Charles Dickens his executors or administrators   IN WITNESS whereof the said parties to these presents have hereunto set their hands and seals the day and year first above written

ASSIGNMENT OF ONE-QUARTER OF COPYRIGHT OF *A CHRISTMAS CAROL*, [1 JUNE 1844]

THIS INDENTURE made the [   ] day of [   ] in the year of our Lord One thousand eight hundred and forty four BETWEEN CHARLES DICKENS of Osnaburgh Terrace in the parish of Saint Marylebone Esquire of the one part and WILLIAM BRADBURY and FREDERICK MULLETT EVANS of Whitefriars in the City of London Printers and Copartners of the other part WHEREAS the said Charles Dickens is possessed of or intitled to the Copyright of a certain Work called a "Ghost Story being a Christmas Carol" which is now published in one Volume Quarto AND WHEREAS the said William Bradbury and Frederick Mullett Evans have agreed with the said Charles Dickens for the absolute purchase of one fourth part or share of him the said Charles Dickens of and in the Copyright of the said Work and the Steel Plates Wood Cuts Stock debts and property belonging thereto subject to the covenants and agreements hereinafter contained for the sum of Two hundred pounds NOW THIS INDENTURE WITNESSETH that in pursuance of the said agreement and in consideration of the said sum of Two hundred pounds of lawful English money to him the said Charles Dickens in hand well and truly paid by the said William Bradbury and Frederick Mullett Evans at or before the sealing and delivery of these presents the receipt whereof the said Charles Dickens doth hereby acknowledge and from the same and every part thereof doth hereby acquit and discharge the said William Bradbury and Frederick Mullett Evans their executors and administrators He the said Charles Dickens DOTH by these presents bargain sell assign transfer and make over unto the said William Bradbury and Frederick Mullett Evans ALL that one equal undivided fourth part or share of him the said Charles Dickens of and in the Copyright of and in the said Work Book or Composition called "A Ghost Story being a Christmas Carol" or by whatsoever other name or names title or titles the said Work Book or Composition or any part or parts thereof are or is or has been or may be called known or distinguished And also the one equal fourth part or share of and in the Steel Plates Woodcuts stock and property belonging to the said Work Book or Composition and which on the thirtieth day of April last consisted of two hundred and twenty seven copies in cloth and three hundred and thirty seven copies in Quires and of and in the gains and profits and the debts which as from the said thirtieth day of April last have arisen and become due to the said Charles Dickens from the sale thereof or which may hereafter arise and become due to the said Charles Dickens William Bradbury and Frederick Mullett Evans on account thereof And all the estate right title interest property possession benefit claim and demand whatsoever both at Law and in Equity of him the said Charles Dickens in and to the said part share or interest profits debts and other the premises hereby assigned or intended so to be To HAVE HOLD RECEIVE TAKE AND ENJOY the said one undivided equal fourth part of and in the said Copyright Steel Plates Woodcuts stock debts and all and singular other the premises hereby assigned or intended so to be with their and every of their appurtenances henceforth unto the said William Bradbury and Frederick Mullett Evans their executors administrators and assigns subject only to the covenants and agreements hereinafter contained And the said Charles Dickens for himself his heirs executors and administrators doth hereby covenant and agree with the said William Bradbury and Frederick Mullet Evans their executors administrators and assigns in manner following (that is to say) that he the said Charles Dickens hath not at any time heretofore made done executed committed permitted or suffered any act deed matter or thing whatsoever whereby or by means whereof the said Work Book or Composition and other the premises or the part share or interest therein hereby assigned or intended so to be or any part thereof are is can shall or may be impeached charged incumbered or in anywise prejudicially affected but that he the said Charles Dickens now at the time of the sealing and delivery of these presents is the sole true and undoubted Owner and Proprietor of the Copyright of the said Work Book or Composition and other the premises hereinbefore assigned or intended so to be And that he the said Charles Dickens now hath in himself good rightfull power and lawful and absolute authority to bargain sell assign and set over the said one fourth part or share hereby assigned or intended so to be in manner hereinbefore mentioned AND ALSO that they the said William Bradbury and Frederick Mullett Evans their executors administrators and assigns shall and may at all times hereafter possess and enjoy the said fourth part or share hereby assigned or intended so to be and all profits and advantages arising from the same without any interruption claim or demand whatsoever of from or by him the said Charles Dickens his executors or administrators or any person or persons lawfully or equitably claiming or to claim by through under or in trust for him them or any of them And that free and clear and by the said Charles Dickens his executors or administrators freely clearly and absolutely exonerated discharged and indemnified of from and against all former and other bargains sales assignments charges and incumbrances claims or demands whatsoever AND MOREOVER that he the said Charles Dickens his executors or administrators and all and every other person and persons lawfully or equitably claiming or to claim by from under or in trust for him or them any right or interest in the premises hereby assigned or intended so to be or any part thereof will from time to time and at all times hereafter at the request cost and charges of the said William Bradbury and Frederick Mullett Evans or of one of them their or one of their executors administrators or assigns make do and execute or cause and procure to be made done and executed all such further and other acts deeds assignments and assurances whatsoever for the more effectually assigning assuring and confirming the premises hereby assigned and every or any part thereof unto the said William Bradbury and Frederick Mullett Evans their executors administrators and assigns in manner aforesaid and for the better enabling them to assert and protect the Copyright hereby assigned or intended so to be and also for the indemnifying of the said William Bradbury and Frederick Mullett Evans from any claims and demands on the part of the said Charles Dickens his executors or administrators in respect of the said premises hereby assigned as by the said William Bradbury and Frederick Mullett Evans or either of them their or either of their executors administrators and assigns or their any or either of their Counsel in the Law shall be lawfully and reasonably advised or required ALSO that he the said Charles Dickens his executors or administrators will not at any time hereafter sell or dispose of the remaining three fourth parts or shares of and in the said Copyright and premises hereby assigned or intended so to be or any part thereof until after he or they shall by writing under his or their hand or hands to be given to or left at the usual place of residence of the said William Bradbury and Frederick Mullett Evans or the survivor of them have offered the same to them or him at the lowest price at which he the said Charles Dickens his executors or administrators shall be willing or shall propose to sell the same to any other person and such offer shall not within ten days from the delivery thereof have been accepted in writing AND the said William Bradbury and Frederick Mullett Evans for themselves jointly and severally and for their respective executors and administrators do hereby covenant and agree with the said Charles Dickens his executors administrators and assigns that they the said William Bradbury and Frederick Mullett Evans or either of them their or his executors or administrators will not at any time hereafter sell and dispose of the fourth part or share of and in the said Copyright and premises hereby assigned or intended so to be or any part thereof until after they or he shall by writing under their or his hands or hand to be given to or left at the usual place of residence of the said Charles Dickens his executors or administrators have offered the same to him or them at the lowest price at which the said William Bradbury and Frederick Mullet Evans shall be willing or shall propose to sell the same to any other person and such offer shall not within ten days from the delivery thereof have been accepted in writing PROVIDED ALWAYS And it is hereby declared and agreed by and between the parties hereto that so long as the said Charles Dickens and the said William Bradbury and Frederick Mullett Evans or either of them shall remain jointly interested in the said Work Book Composition and premises hereby assigned or intended so to be the entire general management and superintendence of the Publication thereof shall be undertaken and discharged by the said William Bradbury and Frederick Mullett Evans or the survivor of them and proper books of account shall be kept by them in which all receipts and payments in reference to the said Concern shall be entered and to which the said Charles Dickens his executors or administrators shall at all reasonable times have access and the said William Bradbury and Frederick Mullett Evans shall make up such half yearly accounts and render a copy thereof half yearly to the said Charles Dickens his executors or administrators IN WITNESS whereof the said parties to these Presents have hereunto set their hands and seals the day and year first above written.

B. MISCELLANEOUS

DICKENS'S AFFIDAVIT IN THE *CAROL* CASE, 9 JANUARY 1844

Text from E. T. Jaques, *CD in Chancery*, 1914, pp. 63–5.

In Chancery

Between CHARLES DICKENS, *Plaintiff*

and

RICHARD EGAN LEE and JOHN HADDOCK, *Defendants*

CHARLES DICKENS of Number 1 Devonshire Terrace York Gate Regents Park in the parish of Saint Marylebone in the county of Middlesex maketh oath and saith That he this deponent is the author of several books which have been printed and published and very extensively sold and whereby this deponent has derived great pecuniary profits And that before the month of December One thousand eight hundred and forty three this deponent invented composed and wrote an original tale or book entitled "A Christmas Carol in Prose being a Ghost Story of Christmas" and that the same is a work of invention and fancy And that the subject and incidents thereof and the characters and personages therein introduced and described are of this deponent's sole invention And this deponent was and is the author and sole proprietor of the said book And that the whole property of and in and the sole right of printing and publishing the same was and has at all times been and still is vested in this deponent And this deponent further saith that he this deponent has duly caused the said book and this deponent's proprietorship therein to be registered in the Book of Registry of the Stationers Company kept at the Hall of the said Company by the Officer appointed by the said Company in pursuance of and according to the directions in that behalf contained in the Act of Parliament of the fifth and sixth years of the reign of her present Majesty entitled "An Act to amend the law of Copyright" And that this Deponent caused his said Book to be printed And that on the nineteenth day of December One thousand eight hundred and forty three the same was published by Messieurs Chapman and Hall of the Strand in the County of Middlesex as the agents and publishers of this deponent and on this deponent's behalf And this deponent further saith that the Book produced to this deponent at the time of making this affidavit and marked with the letter "A" is a copy of the book or work so as aforesaid written and composed by this deponent and published as aforesaid And this deponent further saith that the said Book immediately upon its publication became extremely popular and that many copies thereof have been sold And that the same is still in course of publication and sale And this deponent further saith he has already made and received large profits thereby And that the same is of great value to this deponent as such sole owner and proprietor of the said book as aforesaid And that Richard Egan Lee and John Haddock who are the defendants in this suit have lately and without the permission or authority of this deponent made or procured to be made a colorable imitation of this the deponent's said book and they have printed and published a part of such imitation and they threaten and intend to continue to print and publish the same and hereafter to print and publish a continuation thereof until they shall have completed their imitation of this deponent's said book And that such part of the said defendants' said publication as has been already published has been entitled by the said defendants "A Christmas Ghost Story re-originated from the original by Charles Dickens Esquire, and analytically condensed expressly for this work" and purports to form the 16th number of a work called "Parley's Illuminated Library" which is published weekly And that such last mentioned number was first printed and published by the said defendants on the sixth day of January last And that upon the wrapper of the same number is a note or advertisement in the terms following that is to say "This week is commenced and will be continued until complete, 'A Christmas Ghost Story Re-originated from the original by Charles Dickens Esquire and analytically condensed expressly for this work' " And this Deponent further saith that the book or work now produced and shewn to this deponent marked with the letter "B" is to the best of this deponent's belief a copy of such book or work so published by the said defendants And this deponent further saith that the said number which has been so already printed and published as aforesaid contains a colorable imitation of about one half of this deponent's said book And that the said publication of the said defendants is a mere piracy of this deponent's said book and that the subject characters personages and incidents of the defendants' said publication are taken from and are the same as those contained in this deponent's said work except that the name of one of the personages in this deponent's said book called "Fezziwig" is in the said defendants' publication called "Fuzziwig" And that in many instances the language of the said defendants' said publication is the same with that of this deponent's said work And that although in many other instances the language of the defendants' said work has been altered yet that such alteration has been only colorable and has been used for the purpose of endeavouring to conceal the fact that the defendants' said work has been copied or imitated from this deponent's said book And this deponent further saith that he first became acquainted with the fact of the said defendants having so as aforesaid published and printed a portion of his said work on Saturday the sixth day of January instant about the hour of three of the clock in the afternoon of that day when one of the printed copies of the defendants' said publication was sent to this deponent by Messieurs Bradbury and Evans the printers of this deponent and his attention was thereby called to the defendants' said publication That this deponent thereupon carefully looked into the copy of the work so as aforesaid published by the said defendants and contrasted same with a copy of his this deponent's own production and on doing so found the defendants' said publication to contain in many parts thereof a colorable imitation of one half of this deponent's said book That thereupon this deponent on Monday the eighth day of January instant gave instructions to his solicitor Mr. Thomas Mitton of Southampton Buildings Chancery Lane to take the necessary steps on his this deponent's behalf for obtaining an injunction to restrain the defendants from continuing to print publish and sell any portion of this deponent's said work And this deponent further saith he firmly believes and is fully persuaded that it is the intention of the said defendants to print publish and sell the residue of this deponent's said work unless restrained by the Order and Injunction of this Honorable Court

Sworn at the Public Office Southampton
    Buildings Chancery Lane this 9th day of   CHARLES DICKENS
    January 1844 before me
      S. DUCKWORTH

SPEECH AT THE MANCHESTER ATHENAEUM, 24 OCTOBER 1845, COMPOSED BY DICKENS FOR FRANK STONE[1]

Text from *Manchester Guardian*, 25 Oct 45.

It would be presumptuous in him, after such eloquent addresses as they had listened to, to attempt to add anything in further illustration of the advantages of the institution, in a strictly literary point of view. Indeed, it was, perhaps, an act of great temerity for him to address the meeting at all, the rather that he was an artist, and that the appeals of artists to the public were usually made through a much different channel. But the kindly observations of the chairman, however undeserved, with respect to him (Mr. Stone), in connection with an art which had ever been allowed to possess a kindred, nay, sisterly relation, to the spirit of literature, emboldened him, very briefly, to give his impression of the Manchester Athenaeum with respect to its effects upon the fine arts generally, and upon their honour, study, and advantages in his native town of Manchester. The first sight of this overwhelming Manchester assemblage forcibly impressed him with the great and important change which had taken place in the town since he was a youthful seeker for such knowledge as must forward him in his onward course. Had such an institution as the Athenaeum, then existed, how many advantages would it have given him! He should have had the benefit of its library, the encouragement afforded by the association and fellowship of its members; and stimulating influence, arising from that association, of a better knowledge of the triumphs of others, and the inspiriting and ennobling assurance that at certain stated periods, assemblies such as this would meet together, to do honour to imaginative pursuits and their professors, and to encourage and promote a better understanding and appreciation of both arts and artists. As an artist he regarded his invitation to this meeting not merely as an honour personally to himself, but as an encouragement to all young students such as he had been. He inferred from that invitation, a sympathy on the part of the members of the Manchester Athenaeum for the fine arts, and although (as he was informed), there had not been hitherto instituted a public school of art, yet he ventured to hope that the time was fast approaching, when the graphic art would be placed within these walls, on a level with its sister arts, none of which were more calculated to instruct, improve, and soften the mind, and to stimulate it to a noble appreciation of all that was beautiful, good, and true. In his interest, and jealousy too, for the credit of his native town, he had sometimes looked with

---

[1] See *To* Talfourd, 22 Oct 45.

disappointment to the fact that it had hitherto been more tardy in the adoption of public means for the encouragement of the fine arts than other provincial towns. But, on reflection, he did not feel that this was so discouraging, for it was well known that it was more difficult to put a large machine in motion than a small one; but when the momentum was once given, the power was in proportion. He therefore hoped, that if this institution once undertook the promotion and encouragement of the fine arts, that the immediate benefits would be great, and that future progress would be at railway speed. He also wished to maintain, as one of the representatives of his own art, the immense importance of the sympathy of such an institution as this for all the peaceful pursuits which it encouraged and diffused. And he should promise that it would be rendered back to them again, so far as his own power lay, and in the power of his art, by attempting to illustrate the peaceful virtues of domestic life, which afforded themes as full of deep and absorbing interest, of sublime and heroic passion, when properly treated,—and as full of beauty he was sure when he looked around him,—themes that had always been as stimulating to him as all the high-flown histories that were ever written and that were seldom read.

CD'S MEMORANDA FOR A PROPOSED MEETING WITH THE STAFF ENGAGED FOR THE *DAILY NEWS*, 4 NOVEMBER 1845

MS Dickens House.[1]

To call the Gentlemen together, and state.[2]

That: they have been engaged on this projected Newspaper—in some instances, perhaps, with the inducement, beyond the Salary, of having reason to believe that I intended to connect myself with it. That before anything further is said, it must be understood that [*CD then wrote, and deleted* I had consented to write in the paper and to exercise *and then* I am myself no better off than they] the change of circumstances to which their attention is to be called, affects me no less than them, in so far as it immediately renders impossible the connexion I had been induced to promise by my friendship for, and business relation with, Bradbury and Evans. That I am, myself, most seriously and bitterly surprised by the Intelligence which is now to be communicated them, which[3] I have only learned this morning,[4] after great loss of time, the total alteration of my literary plans, and the most serious inconvenience and uneasiness.

That a very large Capital had been subscribed, and was still subscribing, for the conduct of this Journal. That a great failure has suddenly[5] occurred, seriously affecting many of the subscribing parties (of whom I was never one to the value

---

[1] Formerly in the possession of Mr W. L. Bradbury. Though CD probably at first wished to see the staff himself, in his anxiety to make his own position clear, he evidently gave the notes to Bradbury & Evans for their own guidance.

[2] Substituted for the original heading "To state.", probably when CD gave the memoranda to Bradbury & Evans.

[3] CD then wrote, and deleted, "has entailed upon me".

[4] See *To* Beard, 4 Nov 45.

[5] CD first wrote, and deleted, "in a moment".

of a farthing); and that to proceed with it, on the projected scale, at the projected time, is consequently impossible.

That the most important parties of all kinds retire therefore; and the design must be abandoned.

That, for the engagements made, the Proprietors desire to make a liberal and handsome compensation; and beg the Gentlemen to consider on what terms they will compound for them.

LEADING ARTICLE[1] IN "DUMMY NUMBER" OF THE *DAILY NEWS*, 19 JANUARY 1846

Text from "dummy number" in Office of the *Daily News* Ltd.

We cannot allow a trial at the Old Bailey, of which a full report appears in another part of our columns, to pass unnoticed. It is an extreme step, indeed, to enter a grave protest against the decision of a jury solemnly impanelled and chosen. But, in this instance, the duty of the journalist, and the common sense of the case, must be paramount to every other consideration.

A person named *Jones* (said to be of prepossessing and modest exterior) was indicted for that he wilfully and maliciously had occasioned the death of five bricklayers, seven carpenters, two furniture-warehouse porters, three painters, and a plasterer. He pleaded not guilty, and therefore took his trial.

It appeared from the evidence adduced on the part of the prosecution, that Jones had been suborned by certain other miscreants not in custody, to procure the completion, at any cost or sacrifice, of certain premises, in course of erection in Whitefriars, for purposes of the most despicable and atrocious nature. In pursuance of his horrible instructions, JONES (ever active in such matters) had waylaid the unfortunate men named in the indictment together with many others, and lured them to the performance of feats of bodily strength and supernatural muscular exertion; to which they fell an untimely sacrifice. It appeared that he had *watched* his victims, day and night—flouting, as it[2] with unparalled[2] barbarity over their agonies—and had, with unrelenting cruelty, contemplated them from the street, where he had frequentlp[2] been heard to say. "*It must be done. Some say no: but I say, yes; and I'll do it;* at the same time rubbing his hands, and testifying the liveliest satisfaction. On being asked, in the usual form, whether he desired to address any observations to the jury, in his defence, JONES distinctly admitted these facts; and added with an effrontery, for which there is perhaps no precedent at that bar, "that if it was proposed to him to do the same again, he'd do it."

In the teeth of this evidence; with these remarks of JONES, ringing as it were, in their ears, the Jury, without leaving the box, returned a verdict of JUSTIFIABLE HOMICIDE!

---

[1] This burlesque is the second of two leading articles. The first, a serious commentary on the execution of Tapping (24 Mar 45), has also been attributed to CD, but solely on account of its subject. The style is unlike his, and the account purports to be first hand; Fox or Jerrold (or both) was probably responsible.

[2] Thus in text.

Against this verdict we enter our solemn and indignant protest. On behalf of the bricklayers, carpenters, furniture-warehouse porters, painters, and plasterers of this great kingdom, we denounce it, as a piece of monstrous injustice and flagrant wrong. We claim for these humble, but useful members of society, the right we should claim for ourselves in a similar case X[1] supposing JONES to have left us any power of making our wants and wishes known. We denounce JONES. We require that the man should have his deserts. And we assure him, that if we were the Queen upon the throne, with power to punish and reward, he certainly should not remain long in his present situation.

[1] Thus in text.

C. INVENTORY OF CONTENTS OF
1 DEVONSHIRE TERRACE, MAY 1854

MS Mrs Katherine Parrish (formerly MS Major Philip Dickens).

The inventory was completed by 27 May 44 when the agreement with Mrs Sophia Onslow was signed. It is written in a common exercise book, on both sides of the page, partly by CD and partly by Catherine (*aa*). A few entries have subsequently been altered in pencil by another hand, possibly when the inventory was checked at the end of the tenancy; these alterations are not specified below. The entries are reproduced as written, without notes on inconsistent or irregular spelling. For the pictures in the furniture inventory, the names of artists have been added in square brackets where identification is possible.

For the books, the order presumably follows the arrangement of shelves and bookcases in the library. As is natural in such a list, few details are given; titles are shortened, and authors' names often omitted; and while many can be easily identified with the help of *Catalogue of the Library of CD*, ed. J. H. Stonehouse (indicated by *S*), over 100 works which are not included there have caused more difficulty, and a few have finally proved elusive. But the list is of considerable interest as showing the minimum size and range of CD's collection, well over 2000 volumes at the age of 32—minimum, because we have no evidence of how many books he took with him to Italy. Only a few are named in the letters (e.g. some volumes of Voltaire, and of Defoe, and, unexpectedly, Juvenal), but the total was probably substantial, and no inference can safely be drawn from the absence of any work from the inventory. There are also several groups of unspecified books, "sundry", "divers" or "various", and there are incomplete series, such as Bentley's Standard Novels and British Classics.

For CD's purchases at the sale of Thomas Hill's books in March 1841, see Vol. II, p. 229 and *n*. Many of his American books were probably included in Lea & Blanchard's "handsome Present" to him in 1842 (Vol. III, p. 250 and *n*).

*a*Entrance Hall.

Marble pattern floorcloth
3 mats. One rope—Two worsted
Four French polished Mahogany Hall chairs
  1   Do.   Do.   Writing Table
  1   Do.   Do.   Hat and Umbrella Stand
Stuffed bird in case.
Scagliola Piller*a* and Marble Bust
Ten Engravings in Gilt Frames—Flitch of Bacon. [Stothard]—Rent Day [Wilkie]—Proffered Kiss [unknown]—Canterbury Pilgrims [Stothard]—Reading the Will (proof) [Wilkie]—Battle of Trafalgar (proof) [?Stanfield]—Member of the Humane Society (proof) [Landseer]—Laying down the Law (proof) [Landseer]—Portrait of Macready (proof) in carved frame.
Two casts after Flaxman in Wainscoat frames—Night and Morning
Bronze Hall Lamp with two burners, line, and pullies

LIBRARY

Brussells Carpet to fit the room, and rug
Yellow silk damask curtains to two windows, two sets of white curtains, gilt cornice, fringe and trimmings complete
Spring Roller Blinds to Windows.

Steel fender and fire irons
Mirror in Mahogany frame
Two cut glass lustres—two bronze card racks—two glass vases for flowers
One french polished mahogany revolving study table, with drawers
One   Do.   Do.   Sofa table
Two small rosewood round pedestal tables with marble tops
One spring recumbent reading chair, with desk and candle sconce
One leathern covered easy chair—six old chairs (various)—one arm cane chair
Two waste paper baskets
One Mahogany What Not, and Writing Desk
Eleven plaster casts. One papier machie cast
One Mahogany Book stand—one rosewood letter box—one mahogany tray—one
metal vase for cards—Indian Dress—
Gilt Lamp with two burners, chain &c
Two proof Engravings in Gilt Frames. Tennyson and Carlyle.
Bookshelves fitted to room and windows. Books in a separate Inventory

DINING ROOM

Turkey carpet and rug—Imitation Oak oilcloth to fit the room
Crimson damask curtains to three Window-sweep, with gilt cornice, fringe, and
trimmings complete. Spring roller blinds to windows
Steel fender and fire irons—Two footstools
Gilt Lamp with Three Burners—Gilt Sideboard pedestal lamp with two burners
—Gilt Pedestal table lamp
French Polished Mahogany Sideboard, carved; with Mirror fitted
Crimson Damask Curtain & cornice fitted to recess
Three shelved french polished Mahogany Whatnot
Fire Screen—Rosewood Teapoy[1] (without Sugar basin)
Two old Pedestals for lights
Expanding French polished Mahogany Dining table with 5 leaves and painted
cover
Twelve french-polished Mahogany Chairs with green leather seats—one cane
armchair—one easy chair—one iron rocking chair
Gilt bracket & candelabra
Ten pictures in Gilt frames—A portrait—Girl at Waterfall by Maclise (with
Lamp and shade fitted)—Italian Picture of Fame[2]—2 Highland Sketches by
McIan—Little Landscape by [Thomas] Barker—Nell and old Woman—By
Mrs McIan—Kate Nickleby by Frith—Portrait of Mr. Dickens. By Maclise—
Dolly Varden By Frith—

DRESSING ROOM

Brussells Carpet to fit the room—And rug—Piece of floorcloth—one mat
Yellow silk damask curtains—two white Curtains—cornice & drapery complete—
2 muslin curtains to sash window—blind

---

[1] Originally, a three-legged table; later, any small ornamental table with fitted tea-equipment.

[2] Presented to CD in America; artist unknown—possibly Francis Alexander (see Vol. III, p. 90 and *n*).

Fender and fire irons
Stained Wood Tent bedstead, with chintz furniture, lined—Palliasse—Mattrass
—Feather bed—3 blankets & counterpane—Bolster & 2 pillows.
French polished Mahogany Wardrobe with pannells of fluted crimson silk, and
pier glass Mirror
One   Do.   Do.   dressing table, with drawers and leather top.
One rosewood Loo table, with painted cover.
One double Mahogany Washing Stand, with crockery complete.
Water bottle and glass—Large white jug and basin
Washing stand to turn over—with basin, cock, cistern, mirror, soap dish and
chamber—No other fittings.
Painted Towel horse.
Four Mahogany chairs, with leathern seats
Four Prints—one oil painting—one chalk drawing—two framed documents (one
with broken glass) two China Vases (broken)
Two little figures under glass shades (broken)—Plaster Bust of Basil Hall

STAIRCASE

Brussels Carpet and rods, the whole distance—two sets of covers for Stairs, & one
landing
Plaster cast[1]

FIRST LANDING

Painted Imitation Stained Glass Blind—Curtains & pole
Marble Slab on Rosewood Stand—Marble Bust of Landor
Two fancy cane bottomed chairs
One proof engraving after Raffael—One do. Dolly Varden—
One chalk Drawing—One oil portrait
Gilt bracket and Lamp

BEST BEDROOM

Brussels Carpet to fit the room. And rug. Piece of oilcloth. Mat
Four yellow lutestring silk curtains—2 sets of white curtains—pole & rings—
spring roller blinds to windows.
Fender and fire irons
Mirror in gilt frame—Stuffed bird in case—Pair of earthenware candlesticks.
French Polished Mahogany Four Post Bedstead, with Chintz *a*hangings lined.
Palliasse. Mattrass. featherbed, four blankets, two pillows, bolster and counter-
pane
Six french polished stained chairs with cane seats
Four old chairs (various)
French polished mahogany sofa, with horsehair squab (mended) and two pillows.
   Do.   Do.   expanding Mahogany table with two flaps and green cover—
gold embroidered (rather stained)
Deal toilette table, with two toilette petticoats, french polished. Mahogany
dressing glass, with Sconces.

---

   [1] Added in another hand.

Two occasional tables
French polished Mahogany double washing stand, with Marble top, and crockery complete. Bidet. Towel Horse.

    Do.   Do.   Chest of drawers

    Do.   Do.   large two winged wardrobe, cast in plaster on the top.

Drawing Room

Brussells carpet to fit the room. And rug
Two figured rich satin damask curtains, with chintz covers. two sets of white curtains, rich carved gilt cornice, fringe and trimmings to fit three window sweep.
Spring roller blinds to Windows
Bell ropes. Fender and fire irons. Bright bars to stove
Six French polished rosewood chairs covered with figured silk damask.

Two high backed praying chairs	Do.	Do.
Two couches, and pillows	Do.	Do.
Ottoman	Do.	Do.

Box Ottoman, worked.
Two small highed [*thus*] backed praying chairs—worked in embroidery. Rose pattern chintz covers for the whole.
Worked pedestal screen, and cover to match.
Three cane-bottomed fancy chairs
French polished rosewood sofa table, with painted cover

Two	Do.	Do.	card tables. Linings stained
Four	Do.	Do.	tables in nest

Green japanned table. Pair of screens to match. rosewood music stand.[a]
Large plate glass Chimney Mirror in gilt frame—
Small Do. Do. with marble slab & gilt brackets—Two pier do, with marble slabs—from floor to cornice
Pair of China Jars—Pair of Alabaster Vases with Glass Shades—stuffed American Birds, & glass shade
One pair candelabra with two burners each—China & gilt
One pair Vases enamelled on copper—one french clock (out of order) & glass shade
Five China Ornaments—and Marble Vase
Gilt Lamp & chain—three burners—Table lamp with China Stem.
Rosewood Cottage Piano by Cramer & Co.—pair of porcelain Candlesticks—and Music Stool
Six Water-Color Drawings. Sketch by Wilkie—two Sketches by Stanfield—Children, by Maclise—two drawings from the Old Curiosity Shop, by Cattermole.
[a]Green Wire Flower Stand, with Earthen Flower Pot (chipped)[a]

SECOND BEDROOM

Brussells Carpet to fit the room—Rug—Piece of floorcloth
Merino curtain, two white curtains, & cornice, Blind & two short Muslin Curtains
Fender and fire irons

French Polished Mahogany french bedstead & pole—Merino hangings—Palliasse. Two Mattrasses—Feather bed—bolster & 2 pillows. 4 blankets—& counterpane—Bell rope—Second counterpane

French polished Mahogany double Washing Stand, with crockery (imperfect) & painted cover.

  Do.   Do.   Dressing table & glass. 2 cut scent bottles

Boot Jack—Painted towel horse

Four french polished stained chairs with cane seats

French Polished Mahogany Chest of Drawers

Fixed Press, fitted to recess.

Seven Prints in frames

Ten miscellaneous Chimney Ornaments—Plaster Bust

SECOND LANDING

Fitted common carpet

Painted Deal table with green baize top

Old easy chair, with Convenience

Old Mahogany Press & letter rack

Bagatelle Board

DAY NURSERY

Kidderminster Carpet fitted to room—Holland Drugget—glazed chintz window curtains two roller blinds—

Nursery fender and fire irons

Eight chairs (damaged)—Nursing Chair

Painted chest of Drawers

Painted turn-up bedstead with Mattrass & feather bed & 3 blankets

Bolster & one pillow

Round table & cover

Coal scuttle & scoop

Two tea trays

NIGHT NURSERY

Kidderminster Carpet

Two green blinds—Nursery fender

Two Kettles

Two cribs, one with furniture, mattrass, & 4 blankets in all—& counterpane to one.

Painted French Bedstead with mattrass & featherbed. Bolster & pillows—3 blankets & counterpane

Another painted French Bedstead, with palliasse, mattrass, & bolster. Four blankets. One counterpane.

Painted Double Washing stand, with crockery imperfect.

Two baths, and two red pans.

Two stone water pitchers & tin can

Dutch clock (out of order)

Painted chest of Drawers
  Do.   Table
Two Towel horses—3 chairs—round table & cover

WOMEN'S BEDROOM

Two pieces of carpet—And rug
Green blind & two short curtains—Fender
Press fitted to recess
Large painted French Bedstead, with palliasse, mattrass, feather bed, bolster,
& two pillows—Three blankets and counterpane—Pole & chintz hangings
Painted deal table—Small mahogany dressing glass
Painted single Washing Stand—crockery imperfect
Two painted chairs, with cane seats

ATTIC

Two scissors bedsteads—One with pole & hangings—Two mattrasses—two
pillows—three blankets—one counterpane
Old table—Old Washing Stand—one chair—one piece of carpet—one fender

KITCHEN

Dressers. Shelves &c &c
Deal table—Four chairs—Meat screen—Dutch clock
 Kitchen Utensils in a separate Inventory)

STORE ROOM

Dresser—Deal table—two chairs—Screen with four flaps

BUTLER'S PANTRY

Bath—Board & tressels—Sandwich tray & fittings complete
Butler's tray & tressels—Bottle rack—Green curtain—roller Blind—
Press for Glass and China
Two chairs—Fender—Pair of Steps—Clothes Horse

CHINA

A blue dinner set containing:
  Ten dishes | One Soup tureen, stand, & cover | Four Vegetable Dishes &
  covers | Four Sauce tureens, dishes, & covers | 27 large plates | 12 small plates
  | 16 pie dishes | 11 soup plates | One Salad bowl with wooden spoon & fork |
  Two common blue dishes

A common green dinner-set, containing:
  Five dishes | One soup tureen, stand, & cover | One Hash Dish | Four
  Butter tureens | One Vegetable Dish | 24 large plates | 6 water plates

7 Earthenware Moulds | 3 Blue jugs | 2 Stone Do. | One brown Do. | 3 blue
halfpint Do.

Best Dinner Set, containing:
  One large dish | 1 less | 1 less | 2 less | 2 less | 2 less | 4 less | 1 large Well dish[1] | 20 other dishes | 54 dinner plates | 20 soup Do. | 40 small Do. | 2 Soup tureens & stands | 4 Sauce Do., 4 stands, & 3 covers | 1 Salad Bowl | 1 Fish Drain | 1 Pie Dish | 2 less | 4 dishes and covers | 1 Cheese Stand

Best Dessert Service, containing:
  18 plates | 8 dishes | 1 centre

Another Dessert Service, containing:
  1 centre | 7 dishes | 12 plates

Another Dessert Service (common green) containing:
  1 centre Dish | 4 other Dishes | 11 plates

Breakfast Service, containing:
  6 cups & saucers | 1 slop basin | 1 cream Jug | 6 egg cups | 4 dishes | 6 plates | Muffin Dish & cover

Blue Tea-Set, containing:
  10 teacups & saucers | 6 Coffee Do. | 1 Slop Basin | 1 Cream Jug | 2 dishes

Best Tea Set, containing:
  12 cups & saucers | 12 coffee Do. | 1 Slop Basin | 1 Cream Jug | 2 bread & butter plates | 12 small plates

2 Ice Pails | 2 Stone Jugs, with plated covers | 2 small do. | 2 Earthenware Moulds | 2 white basins | 6 pudding Do. | 2 small glazed blue basins | 7 Kitchen cups & saucers | Breadpan | Cheesepan & cover

GLASS

A cut Jug | Another cut Jug | 2 large ornamental water Goblets | 4 water bottles | 1 tumbler for Do. | 1 celery Glass | 12 glass dishes | 12 Wine glasses | 12 tumblers | 12 Sherry Glasses | 11 Engraved Cabinet Drinking Glasses | 1 Very large glass —Same pattern | 14 Champagne glasses. Oval shape | 14 long Do. | 12 ale glasses | 2 butter dishes, stands, & covers, with silver cows | 6 salts, cut glass | 12 Iceplates, cut & frosted | 14 finger glasses, cut & frosted | 2 small Glass dishes | 6 custard cups | 12 Hock Glasses | 1 Claret Jug | 11 liqueur glasses | 14 engraved claret glasses | 4 quart decanters & stoppers | 5 pint Do. Do. | Glass dish for Epergne | 1 Glass Basin | 1 Green glass Basin

MISCELLANEOUS

Two tea Urns | Two corkscrews | Japan Writing candlestick for two candles— With sliding shade | Eight Dinner Mats | Knives & forks | Do. do. small

KITCHEN UTENSILS

6 Iron Spoons | 24 patty pans | 2 tin moulds | 7 block tin dish covers | 6 common Do. | 2 large iron pots & covers | 1 Dutch Oven | 1 Fish Kettle | 4 large Iron Saucepans & covers | 6 small Do. | 1 Cheese Toaster | 3 Iron Stewpans | 1 Copper Do. | 2 tin saucepans | 1 Copper preserving pan | 2 copper coal scuttles |

---

[1] A meat dish with a receptacle at the end for gravy.

1 Warming Pan | 1 Coffee Pot | 1 Gridiron | 2 fryingpans | 1 steamer & cover | 1 Salamander[1] | 1 foot-warmer | 2 Brooms | 1 Iron Footman[2] | 2 knife trays | 2 plate baskets | 2 Metal Teapots | 6 Brass Candlesticks | 2 copper Moulds | 3 tin Do. | 1 Bread Grater | 1 Dripping Pan | Bottle Jack. Wheel. Chain. &c | 2 choppers | 1 Saw | 1 Egg Slice | 3 teakettles—one iron—one tin, one copper | 1 Shaving Pot | 1 Pewter Inkstand | 1 cullender | 1 Spice Box | 1 Flour Dredger | 2 Candleboxes | A toasting fork | Flour Jar & rolling pin | 4 rushlight Shades | Paste Board | A brass grog kettle | 1 Coal Shovel—Fender—Poker—& tongs | 5 Hair Sieves | 1 Coffee Pot | 2 Wooden Bowls | A Foot bath | A kitchen tray | 2 pails | A Water Cann | 2 flat irons & stand | 2 common lamps—one for bracket at the foot of the stairs | A pestle and mortar | Scales and Weights | A pepper box | 2 Cake tins | A coal scuttle | A fireguard | A Mustard pot | A Salt cellar | 2 housemaids' boxes—broom—& dustpan | 2 turks' heads[3] | 1 lemon Squeezer | 4 tartlet pans | 1 Fire Basket | 2 cannisters | 1 blackbeetle trap | 5 small teaplates | 3 rope mats | 5 Vegetable cutters | 1 Paste Brush | 2 Wine baskets | 4 kitchen teaspoons | 47 small preserving pots | 16 large Do. | 22 preserving bottles | 14 Stone Jars | 1 White Do. with cover | 1 funnel | 2 chopping Boards | A Mahogany Bed tray.

INVENTORY

OF THE BOOKS

	VOLUMES
White's Selborne	2
[*S*; Gilbert White, *Natural History of Selborne*, 1825]	
Buffon's Natural History	8
[*S*; 1797–1808]	
Mandeville's travels	1
[*S*; ed. J. O. Halliwell, 1839]	
Waterton's Essay on Natural History	1
[*S*; Charles Waterton, 1838]	
Holman's travels in Russia	2
[*S*; Lieut. James Holman, (the "blind traveller"), *Travels through Russia, Siberia, Poland . . .*, 1825]	
Beauties of England and Wales	26
[*S*; John Britton & others, 1801–]	
Gorton's Topographical Dictionary & Atlas	4
[*S*; John Gorton, 1833]	
Plays—Death of Marlowe &c	1
[*S*; R. H. Horne, 1839]	
Do. Blind Wife	1
[Thomas Powell, 1842]	
Do. Hunchback	1
[*S*; James Sheridan Knowles, 5th edn, 1832]	

[1] "A circular iron plate which is heated and placed over a pudding or other dish to brown it" (*OED*).

[2] A stand for a kettle before the fire.

[3] Round-headed brooms.

Deluge. A Poem	1
[Anon, 1821]	
Ion & Athenian Captive	1
[*S*; T. N. Talfourd, 1840]	
Do.	1
[T. N. Talfourd, 1844]	
Talfourd's Plays—Glencoe	1
[*S*; 2nd edn, 1840]	
Webster's Dramatic Works	4
[*S*; John Webster, ed. Rev. A. Dyce, 1830]	
Chatterton's Works[1]	3
[*S*; 1803]	
Spenser's Works by Todd	8
[*S*; 1805]	
Moores Do.	12
[*S*; Paris, Galignani, 1823–]	
Crabbe's Poems	8
[*S*; *Poetical Works* etc., 1834]	
Entertaining Knowledge—British Costume—Modern Egyptians —Egyptian Antiquities	5
[ed. Charles Knight, 1830–]	
Memoirs of Pepys	5
[*S*; ed. Lord Braybrooke, 1828]	
Evelyn	5
[ed. W. Bray, new edn, 1827]	
Wraxall's Historical Memoirs	7
[*S*; Sir N. W. Wraxall, *Historical Memoirs* and *Posthumous Memoirs*, 1836]	
Lady Mary Wortley Montagu's Works	3
[*S*; ed. Lord Wharncliffe, 1837]	
Memoirs of the Duchess D'Abrantes	2
[*S*; *Memoirs of Napoleon*, 1836]	
Paul de Kock's Novels	26
[*S*; 30 vols, Paris, 1835–40]	
Gibbon's Decline and Fall	8
[*S*; 1825]	
Thiers' French Revolution	5
[tr. F. Shoberl, 1838]	
Carlyle's Do.	3
[1837]	
Tracts on Scottish History	1
[? *Notices of Unprinted Documents illustrative of the History of Scotland*, Maitland Club, 1842]	

[1] The whole entry has been added in pencil by another hand.

VOLUMES

Langhorne's Plutarch	6
[*S*; Plutarch's *Lives,* translated by J. and W. Langhorne, 1819]	
Prescott's *Conquest of Mexico*	3
[*S*; 1843]	
Biographie Universelle	33
[*S*; 1811–]	
Do In parts, unbound	6
Hume & Smollett's England	13
[*S*; *History of England*, 1825]	
Life & Letters of Lady Russell	1
[i.e. Rachel Lady Russell; by Mary Barry, 1819]	
Napier's Peninsular War	5
[*S*; 3rd edn, 1835–40, 6 vols]	
Rollin's Ancient History	6
[*S*; 1828]	
Clavis Calendaria	2
[John Brady; ?1st edn, 1812]	
Charles O Malley	1
[Charles Lever, 1841]	
Byron's Works	6
[*S*; 1829]	
Southey's Cowper	15
[*S*; 1835]	
Campbell's Poems	1
[*S*; 1837]	
Dibdin's Sea Songs	1
[*S*; *Songs Naval and National*, 1841]	
Butler's Hudibras	1
[*S*; 1726]	
Foote's Works	3
[*S*; 1830]	
David Simple	2
[*S*; Sarah Fielding, 1772]	
Kentish Coronal	1
[H. G. Adams, 1841]	
Dodd's Reflections on Death	1
[1769]	
Do. Thoughts in Prison	1
[*S*; 1815]	
Ouseley's Poems	1
[T. J. Ouseley, ?1839]	
Another copy	1
Anatomy of Drunkenness	1
[Dr Robert Macnish, 1827]	
Domestic Verses by Delta	1
[*S*; D. M. Moir, 1843]	

VOLUMES

Iron Hand (translated)   1
  [cf. A. E. Scribe and De Leuven, *La Main de Fer*, 1841]
Jack the Giant Killer (burlesqued)   1
  [Percival Leigh, illustrated by Leech, 1843]
Flower Girl   1
  [Rhoda Maria Williams, *The Flower Girl and Other Poems*, 1843;
   CD's name is in list of subscribers]
Pickwick Papers   1
  [*S*; 1838]
Nicholas Nickleby   1
  [*S*; 1839]
Beaumont & Fletcher's Works   2
  [?1839 edn]
Cowper's Homer   4
  [*S*; *Iliad* and *Odyssey*, 1802]
Percy's Ancient Poetry   1
  [*S*; *Reliques of Ancient English Poetry*, 1839]
Milton's Paradise Lost   1
Life & Letters of Cicero   1
  [*S*; 1844]
Southey's Spain & Portugal   1
  [?1st edn, 1797]
Sketches by Boz   1
  [*S*; 1839]
Journal of the British Legion   1
  [*Journal of the Movements of the British Legion, By an Officer*
   (J. Richardson), 1836]
Pickwick Papers (another copy)   1
Oliver Twist   3
Francia's Reign of Terror   1
  [J. G. de Francia, 3rd vol. of *Letters on Paraguay*, 1839, *see below*]
Aeronautica by Monck Mason   1
  [Thomas Monck Mason, 1838]
Letters on Paraguay   2
  [John Parish and W. P. Robertson, *Letters on Paraguay*, 1838]
Lamb's Letters by Talfourd   2
  [*S*; 1837]
Carey on Wealth   1
  [Henry C. Carey, Vol. II of his *Principles of Political Economy*,
   1838]
Ainsworth's Magazine   1
  [probably Jan 1844]
Ovid's Mets   1
  [*Metamorphoses*]
Froissart's Chronicles   2
  [*S*; ed. Col. Johnes, 1839]

VOLUMES

Pictorial History of England 8
  [*S*; Charles Knight, 1838]
Decker's [*thus*] Gull's Hornbook 1
  [*S*; ed. G. F. Nott, 1812]
Lockhart's Spanish Ballads 1
  [*S*; 1823]
Encyclopaedia of Geography 3
  [*S*; Hugh Murray, Philadelphia, 1837]
Fox's Martyrs 1
  [*S*; *Actes and Monumentes*, 1838]
On the Penitentiary System of America 1
  [? William Crawford, 1834]
Stranger in America 1
  [Francis Lieber, Philadelphia, 1835]
Naaides [*thus*] 1
  [Isaac Lea, *Synopsis of the Family of Naiades*, Philadelphia, 1836]
Lee's Contributions to Geology 1
  [Isaac Lea, Philadelphia, 1833]
Rabelais by Urquhart 1
  [*S*; *Works*, trans. Sir Thomas Urquhart, ed. Theodore Martin, 1838]
Scotts Works   Novels 48 Vols (6 Wanting) 42
            Prose Works 28 Vols (1 Wanting) 27
            Poetry 12 Vols (3 Wanting) 9
  [*S*; Cadell & Davies edn, 1830–6]
            Life by Lockhart 7
  [*S*; 1837]
Tales of the Genii 2
  [James Ridley; edn of 1766 or later]
Persian Tales 2
  [Ambrose Phillips, 1709]
Arabian Nights 6
  [*S*; 1811]
Mackenzie's Works 8
  [*S*; Henry Mackenzie, 1808]
Shakespeare (Boswell's Malone) 21
  [*S*; 1821]
Bacon's Works by Montagu 16 Vols (3 wanting) 13
  [*S*; ed. Basil Montagu, 1825–34, 17 vols]
Dodsley's Old Plays 12
  [*S*; 1780]
Dryden's Plays 6
  [*S*; 1725]
Philip Van Artevelde 2
  [*S*; Sir Henry Taylor, 1834]

Congreve's Plays   3
  [*S*; 1753]
Otway's   Do.   3
  [*S*; 1768]
Annals of the Stage. By Collier   3
  [*S*; John Payne Collier, 1823]
Meredith. A Novel   2
  [Lady Blessington, 1843]
Biographia Britannica   7
  [*S*; 1747–66]
Malcolm's Anecdotes of London   2
  [*S*; J. P. Malcolm, 1808–11]
American Ornithology   4
  [Alexander Wilson; London, 3 vols, 1832; Boston, 1 vol., 1840]
Clarendon's History & Life   4
  [edn not identified]
Journies through England   2
  [*S*; *Journey through England*, 1722; attrib. to Defoe, but by John
  Macky]
Muse's Library   1
  [*S*; Mrs Elizabeth Cooper, 1741]
Carlyles Miscellanies   5
  [*S*; *Critical and Miscellaneous Essays*, 1840]
Defoe's Monsr. Mesnager   1
  [*S*; 1717]
Chartism. By Carlyle   1
  [1840]
Wilhelm Meister Do.   1
  [?1842]
Franklin's Works   3
  [*S*; Benjamin Franklin, 1806]
Strutt's Sports. By Hone   1
  [*S*; *Sports and Pastimes of the people of England*, ed. William
  Hone, 1838]
Every Day Book   4
  [*S*; William Hone, 1838]
Chronicles of London Bridge   1
  [*S*; Richard Thomson, 1827]
Pennant's London   1
  [*S*; Thomas Pennant, *Some Account of London*, 5th edn, 1813]
Burton's Anatomy of Melancholy   2
  [*S*; 1837]
Dance of Death   1
  [*S*; Francis Douce, 1833]
Hume's Essays   2
  [*S*; *Essays and Treatises*, 1825]

	VOLUMES
Pilgrim's Progress [*S*; ed. Southey, 1830]	1
Italy. A Poem [Samuel Rogers]	1
Waller's Poems [*S*; 6th edn, 1694]	1
Peter Pindar's Do. [*S*; Samuel Wolcott, 1788–9]	2
Dryden's Fables [*S*; 1713]	1
Puss in Boots (German Illustrns) [1844, with illustrations by Otto Spekter]	1
Chesterfield's Letters [1774 or later]	4
Annual Register (from commencement to 1827) [*S*; 1748–]	80
English Poets [*S*; ed. Alexander Chalmers, 1810]	21
Ben Jonson's Works [*S*; ed. Barry Cornwall, 1838]	1
Massinger & Ford's Works [*S*; ed. Hartley Coleridge, 1838]	1
Voltaire's Works in French 70 vols (2 wanting) [1785–9]	68
Standard Novels (Irregular)[1] [*Bentley's Standard Novels*, 1832– ; by May 1844, 93 vols published]	52
Wordsworth's Poems [*S*; 1836]	6
Milton's Do. [*S*; ed. Egerton Brydges, 1835]	6
Coleridge Do. [*S*; 1836]	3
Pope Do. [*S*; ed. G. Croly, 1835]	4
Curse of Kehama—Southey [*S*; 1818]	2
Thalaba Do. [*S*; 1814]	2
Joan of Arc Do. [*S*; 1817]	2
Tennyson's Poems [*S*; 1843]	2

[1] See Vol. I, p. 250 and *n*.

VOLUMES

Progresses of Queen Elizabeth	I
Do. King James	I
[*S*; John Nichol, 1823–8]	
Fabyan's Chronicles	I
[*S*; 1811]	
Stowe's Do.	I
[*S*; *Annales*, 1631–2]	
De Foe De Jure Divino	I
[*S*; 1706]	
Canova	2
[*S*; *Works in Sculpture*, 1824]	
Arnold's Chronicles	I
[*S*; Richard Arnold, ed. F. Douce, 1811]	
Dunlop's History of Fiction	3
[*S*; 1814]	
Richardson's Works	19[1]
[*S*; 19 vols, 1810]	
Sterne's Do.	
[*S*; 1815]	
Don Quixote	4
[*S*; 4 vols, 1820]	
Goldsmith's Works 4 (one wanting)	3
[?1792]	
Christmas Carol	I
[1843]	
Cakes and Ale	2
[Douglas Jerrold, 1842]	
Defoe (imperfect)	9
[1831 edn, vols IV–XII]	
Pursuit of Knowledge	2
[*S*; G. L. Craik, *Pursuit of Knowledge under Difficulties*, 1830,31]	
Fielding's Works By Murphy	10
[*S*; ed. A. Chalmers, with essay by Arthur Murphy, 1806]	
Smollett Do.	6
[*S*; 1820]	
Addison Do.	6
[?1811 edn]	
Johnson Do.	12
[?ed. A. Chalmers, 1806]	
Humphrey's Clock	2
[*Master Humphrey's Clock*, 1840–1]	
Swift's Works. By Scott 19 vols (1 wanting)	18
[*S*; 1824]	

[1] Altered in pencil to "16"—perhaps because CD later decided to take three vols with him.

	VOLUMES
Robinson Crusoe	2
[*S*; 1831]	
Curiosities of Literature (2 series)	6
[*S*; Isaac D'Israeli, 1823–4]	
Literary Character	1
[*S*; Isaac D'Israeli, 1818]	
Quarrels of Authors	3
[*S*; Isaac D'Israeli, 1814]	
Sources of Literary Pleasure	1
[*S*; *Essays on the Sources of the Pleasures received from Literary Compositions*, anon, but by Edward Mangin, 1809]	
Recreations of Christopher North	3
[*S*; John Wilson, 1842]	
State Trials	26
[*S*; 21 vols, 1809–14]	
Carleton's Memoirs	1
[?*The Memoires of Mary Carleton*, 1673]	
Nicholas Nickleby	1
[1839]	
Life in Mexico	1
[*S*; Mme Calderon de la Barca, 1843]	
Carlyle's Past & Present	1
[1843]	
Dreams & other poems by Mrs Norton	1
[1840]	
Encyclopaedia Britannica	20
Supplement	12
[*S*; 26 vols, 1810–24]	
American Archives	3
[*S*; 4th series, 1837–40]	
Swedenborg's Heaven & Hell	1
[?1st edn of translation by Thomas Hartley, 1778]	
Lysons' Environs of London	5
[*S*; 2nd edn, 1811]	
Marvell's Works	3
[*S*; 1776]	
Cooper's Novels & Tales	20
[*S*; 1841]	
Residence in Europe	2
[*Tales and Souvenirs of a Residence in Europe, by a Lady of Virginia*, Philadelphia, 1842]	
Boston Book	3
[An anthology; 1836 ed. Henry Tuckerman, 1837 ed. Benjamin Thatcher, 1841 ed. George Hillard]	

Mea Culpa   I
  [?*Le Mea Culpa de Napoleon Bonaparte*, Paris, 1814; "par N. L.
  P—", i.e. Noel-Laurent Pissot]
Poems of the Davidsons   2
  [Lucretia Maria Davidson and Margaret Miller Davidson, child-
  poets, USA]
Tecumseh   I
  [Poem by George H. Colton, New York, 1842]
Rambles & Reveries   I
  [H. T. Tuckerman, 1841]
Pocahontas   I
  [W. W. Waldron, *Pocahontas, and other Poems*, New York,
  1841; *or* Mrs Sigourney, same title, London and New York,
  1841]
Ladies' Wreath   I
  [Annual, New York]
Cooper's Poetical Remains   I
  [?*Poetical Remains of Miss Lucy Hooper*, ed. John Keese, New
  York, 1842]
Brainards Poems   I
  [John G. C. Brainard; Hartford, 1842]
Emerson's Essays   2
  [*S*; 1841]
The Token   I
  [?1842; Annual, ed. Samuel Goodrich, New York, 1828–42]
Memoirs of Tuckermann   I
  [?W. E. Channing's *Discourse on the Life and Character of Joseph
  Tuckermann*, 1841]
Poetical Literature of the West   I
  [*Selecti ons from the Poetical Literature of the West*, ed. William
  D. Gallagher, Cincinnati, 1841]
Thomas's Sketches   I
  [?E. S. Thomas, *Sketches of his own Life and Times*, Hartford,
  1840]
Lowell Offering   I
  [?1842]
Various American Guide Books   27
Poets of America   I
  [*S*; ed. John Keese, 1840–2, 2 vols; *or Poets and Poetry of
  America*, ed. R. W. Griswold, 1842]
Another copy   I
A Year in Spain   2
  [Alexander Slidell Mackenzie, 1831]
Earl Rupert   I
  [James Nack, *Earl Rupert and other Tales and Poems*, with a
  memoir by P. M. Wetmore, New York, 1839]

	VOLUMES
Journal of Miss Adams	1
[Abigail Adams, New York, 1841–2]	
Letters from the Old World	2
[Mrs Sarah Haight, New York, 1840]	
Notes on the Western States	1
[?*Remarks on the Western States of America*, 1839]	
North American Review	2 Nos
[?probably July 1842 and Jan 1843]	
Trial of McLeod	1
[Alexander MacLeod, 1841]	
Catalogue of Chinese Collection	1
[William B. Langdon's catalogue of Nathan Dunn's collection,	
exhibited at Hyde Park Corner; 18th edn, 1843]	
American Museum of Foreign Literature	15
[ed. Mathew Carey: see Vol. III, p. 250*n*]	
Geography of America	1
A New Home	1
["Mrs Mary Clavers", i.e. Caroline M. Kirkland, *A New Home*	
—*Who'll Follow? or, Glimpses of Western Life*, 1839]	
Zenobia	2
[William Ware, New York & London, 1838]	
Hyperion	2
[Longfellow, 1839]	
Society in America. Miss Martineau	2
[*S*; 3 vols, 1837–8]	
Diary in America Marryat	3
Do 2nd Series	3
[*S*; 1839]	
Retrospect of Western Travel. Miss Martineau	3
[*S*; 3 vols, 1837–8]	
Monaldi	1
[Washington Allston, 1841]	
Seaman's Manual	1
[R. H. Dana, 1841]	
Sundry Books	5
Encyclopaedia Americana	13
[ed. Francis Lieber and E. Wigglesworth, 1829–42: see Vol. III,	
p. 250*n*]	
Life of Jefferson	2
[?George Tucker, 1837]	
Naval History. United States	2
[?Fenimore Cooper, Philadelphia, 1839]	
Prize Essay	1
Irving's Columbus	1
[*S*; 1814]	

VOLUMES

Swallow Barn	1
[John Pendleton Kennedy, 1832]	
Hits at the times	1
[Unidentified]	
Trollope's American Manners	1
[*S*; 1832]	
Fairfield's Works	1
[Sumner Lincoln Fairfield, *Poems and Prose Writings*, Philadelphia, 1841, *or Poetical Works*, Philadelphia, 1842]	
Dunlap's Design	2
[?William Dunlap, *History of Arts and Designs in the United States*, New York, 1834]	
New York Historical Collections	1
[John W. Barber and Henry Howe, 1841]	
Catlin's American Notes	1
[George Catlin, *Letters and Notes on the ... North American Indians*, 2nd edn, 1842]	
Divers Books	14
Patchwork	3
[Basil Hall, 1841]	
Townsend's Mesmerism	1
[Chauncy Hare Townsend, *Facts in Mesmerism*, 1840]	
Sam Slick the Clockmaker	2
[Thomas Chandler Haliburton, 2 series, 1837–8]	
Voices of the Night—Ballads by same Author	2
[Longfellow; Cambridge, Mass., 1839 and 1841]	
Barnaby Rudge	1
[*S*; 1841]	
Various American copies of Mr. Dickens' Works	16
American Scenery	2
[Illustrations by W. H. Bartlett, 1840]	
Various Books	23
3 Copies of Oliver Twist	9
[i.e. 3–vol. edns of 1838–41]	
ᵃPic Nic Papers	1
[*S*; 1841]	
Hood's Comic Annual 1842	1
[*S*]	
Divers Books	9
Ditto	26
French Pickwick	1
[*S*; Paris, 1838]	
French Nickleby	2
[*S*; Paris, 1840]	
Celebrated Crimes in French	4
[*S*; Alexander Dumas, Brussels, 1841]	

VOLUMES

Memoirs of Grisquet 4
[Unidentified]
Schoolfellows 3
[Richard Johns, *The Schoolfellows, or, A By-way to Fame*, 1841]
Herberts 3
[*The Herberts*, by the author of *Elphinstone* (i.e. Alfred Butler),
1842]
The Fatalist 3
[Anon, 1839]
Wassail Bowl 3
[Albert Smith, 1843]
Tin trumpet 2
[*The Tin Trumpet, or, Heads and Tales*, 1836]
Hunt's Indicator & Companion 2
[1840]
The Neighbours 2
[Fredrika Bremer, trans. Mary Howitt, 1842]
Mirror of the Months 1
[P. G. Patmore, 1826]
Divers Books 25
Divers Books 62
British Poets 25
[*S*; Cooke's edn, 1806–]
Elegant Extracts—prose 5—verse 6—Epistles 6 17
[*S*; 1812]
The Family Library 61
[*S*; 60 vols, 1838–]
Latin Phrases 1
[*S*; W. Robertson, *Dictionary of Latin Phrases*, 1824]
Lexicon 1
French Dictionary 1
Walker's do 1
[*S*; *Walker's Pronouncing Dictionary*, ed. B. H. Smart, 1836]
Gradus 1
Latin Dictionary 1
Byron's Works 1
[*S*; 1837]
Pickwick Papers 2 copies 2
Irving's Works 2
[*S*; Philadelphia, 1840]
Lamb's Works 1
[1840]
Greek Tragic Theatre 5
[*S*; 1809]
Johnson's Plautus 5
[*S*; 1769–74, trans. Bonnell Thornton and others]

VOLUMES

Remains of Charles Pemberton	I
[*Life and Literary Remains of Charles Reece Pemberton*, ed. W. J. Fox, 1843]	
Petigrew's Medical Superstitions	I
[T. J. Pettigrew, 1844]	
Hood's Up the Rhine	I
[1840]	
Symms on Arts & Artisans	I
[J. C. Symms, 1839]	
Management of the Poor in Scotland	I
[W. P. Alison, *Observations on the Management of the Poor in Scotland*, 1840]	
Various Parliamentary reports	6
Life of Chalmers	I
[Unidentified—probably of George Chalmers]	
Philosophy of History	I
[Voltaire, ?trans H. W. Gandell, 1829]	
Memoir of Carpenter	I
[Lant Carpenter, by his Son, 1842]	
New Spirit of the Age	2
[R. H. Horne, 1843]	
Paul & Virginia (illustrated)	I
[Bernardin de St Pierre, Pictorial edn, 1839]	
Divers other Books & Pamphlets	
British Classics	17
[1803–10; complete, 24 vols]	
Statesmen of the Commonwealth	5
[*S*; John Forster, 1837–9]	
Essay on Formation of Opinion	I
[*S*; 3rd edn, 1837]	
Feltham's Resolves	I
[*S*; Owen Feltham, 1840 edn]	
Boswell's Johnson	10
[ed. J. W. Croker, revised T. Wright, 1835]	
Italian Novelists	4
[*S*; ed. Thomas Roscoe, 1825]	
German Novelists	4
[*S*; ditto]	
Schloss Hainfeld	I
[Basil Hall, 1836]	
Hogarth's Musical Drama	2
[George Hogarth, *Memoirs of the Musical Drama*, 1838]	
Lessing's Laocoon	I
[*S*; 1835]	

	VOLUMES
Decameron	1
[*S*; ed. E. Dubois, 1820]	
German Pickwick	5
[*S*; Leipzig, 1838]	
Do Sketches	1
[*S*; Leipzig, 1838]	
Philosophy of Sleep	1
[*S*; Dr Robert Macnish, 1840]	
Bachelor of Salamanca (in French)	2
[cf. play by A. E. Scribe and others, 1 vol, 1815]	
Charities of London	1
[S. Low and John Brownlow, *A Pocket Guide to the Charities of London*, 1836]	
Hogarths Musical History	
[1836]	
Talfourd's Speeches on Copyright	1
[*S*; 1840]	
Voyages of Columbus	1
[*S*; Washington Irving, Philadelphia, 2 vols, 1841]	
Ned Ward's London Spy	1
[*S*; 1753]	
Defoe's History of the Devil	1
[?1843 edn]	
German Pickwick (another copy)	5
-Do- Humphrey's Clock	5
-Do- Nickleby	6
-Do- Oliver Twist	3
-Do- Barnaby Rudge	2
[all *S*; Leipzig, 1838–41]	
Italian Oliver Twist	1
[*S*; Milan, 1840]	
Talfourd's Visit to the Alps	
[*S*; 1841]	
& divers other books	
Publications of the Shakespeare Society	17
[*S*; 1841–]	
Plays	3
Pamphlets	2
Book of the Church	2
[Southey; 1824 or 1825 edn]	
Howitt's Student Life in Germany	1
[1841]	
Bracebridge Hall	1
[Washington Irving, 1822]	
Divers Odd Books & Pamphlets[a]	

GARDEN

A rustic garden seat
Two Do. Stools
1   Do. little table
1   Do. stand for flowerpots

ADDENDUM

To T. J. SERLE, 12 FEBRUARY 1844

Text from Sotheby's catalogue, June 1976; MS 1 p.; dated Devonshire Terrace, 12 Feb. 44.

Not having received the promised exposition of the views of our illustrious friends,[1] I cannot answer the enclosed note. Which, to a man possessed of what the Americans (especially the Pennsylvanians)[2] call "a moral sense," is distressing.

[1] Presumably the other Elton trustees: see *To* Serle, 19 Jan 44.

[2] One of the claims made for the Separate System at the Eastern Penitentiary, Philadelphia, was that it encouraged the "moral sense" of prisoners.

INDEXES

INDEX OF CORRESPONDENTS

732

INDEX OF NAMES AND PLACES

Buildings, streets, districts etc are indexed under the town or city to which they belong, e.g. Blackheath under LONDON. If a separate entry is desirable, a cross-reference is given from the town to the separate entry, e.g. from LONDON: Chelsea to CHELSEA.

Married women are indexed under their married names, with cross-references when useful.

Books and writings are indexed under the name of the author. Writings of unknown authorship, and periodicals, are indexed by title. References to characters in Dickens's novels are listed as a sub-section under the title of the novel within the entry DICKENS, Charles: *Works*.

Sub-headings are arranged chronologically where events are concerned, and alphabetically in such cases as buildings listed under towns and cities, descriptive details etc.

Abbreviations and symbols
The letter D stands for the name Dickens, CD for Charles Dickens. The titles of Dickens's works are abbreviated as follows: *AN* for *American Notes*, *BR* for *Barnaby Rudge*, *Battle* for *Battle of Life*, *CC* for *Christmas Carol*, *Cricket* for *Cricket on the Hearth*; *DC* for *David Copperfield*, *Dombey* for *Dombey and Son*, *Dorrit* for *Little Dorrit*, *MC* for *Martin Chuzzlewit*, *MHC* for *Master Humphrey's Clock*, *NN* for *Nicholas Nickleby*, *OCS* for *Old Curiosity Shop*, *OT* for *Oliver Twist*, *PP* for *Pickwick Papers*, *Pictures* for *Pictures from Italy*, *SB* for *Sketches by Boz*, *SYC* for *Sketches of Young Couples*.

Those footnotes which contain the main particulars about a person are distinguished by an asterisk, e.g. 123n*.

The sign ~ is used to show that the reference which follows it is linked with the reference which precedes.

The names of Dickens's correspondents are printed in capitals.

F. T. D.